나의 **토익 목표 달성기**

KB084402

TEST 1을 풀고난 후, 점수에 따라 ~세요.

☐ [800점 이상] 2주 완성 학습 플랜	
☐ [600~795점] 3주 완성 학습 플랜	
☐ [595점 이하] 4주 완성 학습 플랜	

※ 일 단위의 상세 학습 플랜은 p.24~25에 있습니다.

각 TEST를 마친 후, 해당 TEST의 점수를 · 로 표시하여 자신의 점수 변화를 확인하세요.

Listening

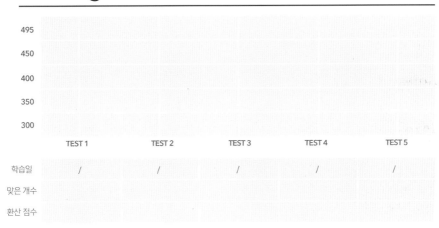

	TEST 1	TEST 2	TEST 3	TEST 4	TEST 5
학습일	/	/	/	/	
맞은 개수					
환산 점수					

Reading

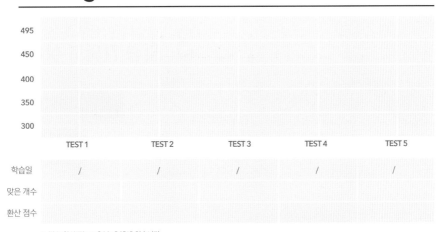

	TEST 1	TEST 2	TEST 3	TEST 4	TEST 5
학습일	/	/	/	/	/
맞은 개수					
환산 점수					

※ 점수 환산표는 p.244~245에 있습니다.

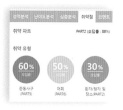

해커스 토익

토익

실전 LC+RC

모의고사 + 해설집

2

해커스 어학연구소

최신 토익 경향을
완벽하게 반영한 문제로
토익 목표 점수를 달성하세요.

토익 시험을 효과적으로 준비하려면
무엇보다도 최신 경향을 반영한 문제 풀이를 통해
'토익 실전 감각'을 길러야 합니다.

≪해커스 토익 실전 LC+RC 2≫는 2024년 상반기 출제 경향을 완벽 반영했습니다.
실제 시험과 가장 비슷한 문제들을 통해
여러분의 토익 목표 점수 달성에 확실한 해결책이 되기를 소망합니다.

'최신 토익 경향' 코너로
토익 트렌드 파악!

정확한 해석·해설로
정답과 오답의 근거 확실히 이해!

LC·RC 실전 모의고사 5회분으로
실전 감각 UP!

Contents

책의 특징 및 활용 방법   6

토익 소개   10

파트별 출제 유형 및 전략   12

수준별 맞춤 학습 플랜   24

정답   238

점수 환산표   244

Answer Sheet   247

📖 문제집 [본책]

TEST 1

LISTENING TEST   28
READING TEST   40

TEST 2

LISTENING TEST   70
READING TEST   82

TEST 3

LISTENING TEST   112
READING TEST   124

TEST 4

LISTENING TEST   154
READING TEST   166

TEST 5

LISTENING TEST   196
READING TEST   208

📖 해설집[책 속의 책]

TEST 1

LISTENING TEST 정답·스크립트·해석·해설   2
READING TEST 정답·해석·해설   27

TEST 2

LISTENING TEST 정답·스크립트·해석·해설   49
READING TEST 정답·해석·해설   74

TEST 3

LISTENING TEST 정답·스크립트·해석·해설   95
READING TEST 정답·해석·해설   120

TEST 4

LISTENING TEST 정답·스크립트·해석·해설   142
READING TEST 정답·해석·해설   167

TEST 5

LISTENING TEST 정답·스크립트·해석·해설   189
READING TEST 정답·해석·해설   214

 단어암기자료(HackersIngang.com)

 받아쓰기&쉐도잉 워크북(HackersIngang.com)

 온라인 실전모의고사(Hackers.co.kr)

책의 특징 및 활용 방법

01 최신 경향을 반영한 모의고사 5회분으로 실전 감각을 높이세요.

토익 실전 감각을 높이기 위해서는 최신 경향이 반영된 문제를 풀어보아야 합니다. ≪해커스 토익 실전 LC+RC 2≫는 2024년 상반기 출제 경향을 반영한 LC와 RC 실전 모의고사를 각 5회분씩 수록하여, 한 권의 교재로 토익 문제 풀이 연습을 끝낼 수 있도록 구성했습니다.

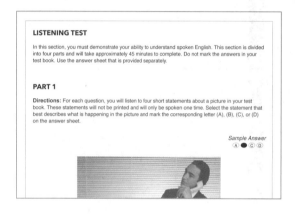

LISTENING TEST

최신 토익 시험의 출제 경향을 완벽하게 반영한 **LC 실전 모의고사 5회분**을 수록하였습니다. 실전과 가장 비슷한 문제들을 풀어보며 빠르게 실전 감각을 쌓을 수 있습니다.

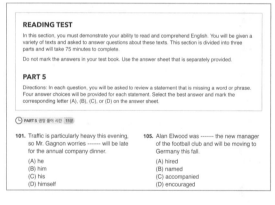

READING TEST

최신 토익 시험의 출제 경향을 완벽하게 반영한 **RC 실전 모의고사 5회분**을 수록하였습니다. 실전과 가장 비슷한 문제들을 풀어보며 빠르게 실전 감각을 쌓을 수 있습니다.

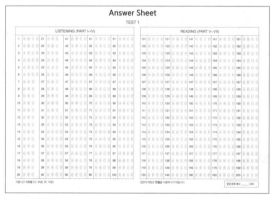

Answer Sheet

교재 뒤에 수록된 Answer Sheet를 활용하여, 답안지 마킹까지 실제 시험처럼 연습해 봄으로써 시간 관리 방법을 익히고, 실전 감각을 보다 극대화할 수 있습니다.

02 정확한 해석·해설로 정답과 오답의 근거를 확실히 파악하세요.

문제 풀이 후, 해석·해설을 확인하며 정답과 오답의 근거를 확실하게 정리하는 것이 중요합니다. ≪해커스 토익 실전 LC+RC 2≫는 모든 문제에 대한 정확한 해석과 해설을 수록하여, 틀린 문제의 원인을 파악하고 보완할 수 있도록 구성했습니다.

상세한 해석·해설

모든 문제에 대한 해석과 함께, 정답은 물론 오답의 이유까지 상세하게 설명한 해설을 통해 **틀린 문제의 원인을 파악하고 약점을 보완**할 수 있습니다.

최신 토익 경향

최신 토익 경향을 철저히 분석하여 출제 포인트와 함께 알아두면 좋을 빈출 표현들을 제공합니다. 이를 통해 **가장 최신 경향을 파악**하며 복습할 수 있습니다.

어휘

지문과 문제에서 사용된 **단어와 표현의 의미를 품사와 함께 수록**하여 문제를 복습할 때 사전을 찾는 불편을 덜 수 있습니다.

Paraphrasing

지문의 내용이 문제에서 패러프레이징된 경우, 이를 정리하여 한눈에 확인할 수 있도록 하였습니다.

책의 특징 및 활용 방법

03 다양한 부가 학습자료로 약점을 보완하세요.

문제 풀이 후, 자신의 약점이 무엇인지를 파악하고 다양한 학습자료를 이용하여 이를 보완하는 것이 중요합니다. ≪해커스 토익 실전 LC+RC 2≫는 자신의 약점을 보완하여 목표 점수에 좀 더 빠르게 도달할 수 있도록 다양한 부가 학습자료를 제공하고 있습니다.

인공지능 1:1 토익어플 '빅플'

교재의 문제를 풀고 답안을 입력하기만 하면, 인공지능 어플 '해커스토익 빅플'이 **자동 채점은 물론 성적분석표와 취약 유형 심층 분석까지 제공**합니다. 이를 통해, 자신이 가장 많이 틀리는 취약 유형이 무엇인지 확인하고, 관련 문제들을 추가로 학습하며 취약 유형을 집중 공략하여 약점을 보완할 수 있습니다.

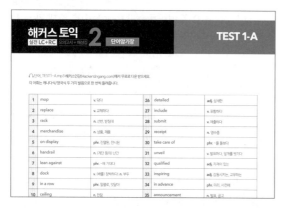

단어암기자료(PDF&MP3)

해커스인강(HackersIngang.com) 사이트에서 무료로 제공하는 **단어암기자료(PDF&MP3)**를 활용하여, 교재에 수록된 테스트의 중요 단어와 표현을 복습하고 암기할 수 있습니다.

받아쓰기&쉐도잉 워크북(PDF&MP3)

해커스인강(HackersIngang.com) 사이트에서 무료로 제공하는 **받아쓰기&쉐도잉 워크북(PDF&MP3)**을 활용하여, 교재에 수록된 핵심 문장을 복습하고 LC 점수를 향상할 수 있는 기본 실력을 갖출 수 있습니다.

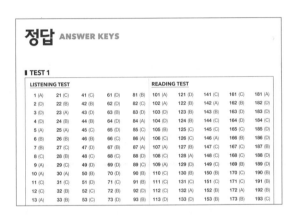

정답녹음 MP3

해커스인강(HackersIngang.com) 사이트에서 무료로 제공하는 **정답녹음 MP3**를 활용하여, 문제 풀이 후 보다 편리하게 채점할 수 있습니다.

무료 온라인 실전모의고사

해커스토익(Hackers.co.kr) 사이트에서 제공하는 온라인 **실전모의고사**를 추가로 풀어보며 실전 감각을 키울 수 있습니다.

방대한 무료 학습자료

해커스토익(Hackers.co.kr) 사이트에서 토익 적중 예상특강을 비롯한 **방대하고 유용한 토익 학습자료**를 무료로 이용할 수 있습니다.

토익 소개

토익이란 무엇인가?

TOEIC은 Test Of English for International Communication의 약자로 영어가 모국어가 아닌 사람들을 대상으로 언어 본래의 기능인 '커뮤니케이션' 능력에 중점을 두고 일상생활 또는 국제 업무 등에 필요한 실용영어 능력을 평가하는 시험입니다. 토익은 일상 생활 및 비즈니스 현장에서 필요로 하는 내용을 평가하기 위해 개발되었고 다음과 같은 실용적인 주제들을 주로 다룹니다.

- 협력 개발: 연구, 제품 개발
- 재무 회계: 대출, 투자, 세금 회계, 은행 업무
- 일반 업무: 계약, 협상, 마케팅, 판매
- 기술 영역: 전기, 공업 기술, 컴퓨터, 실험실
- 사무 영역: 회의, 서류 업무
- 물품 구입: 쇼핑, 물건 주문, 대금 지불

- 식사: 레스토랑, 회식, 만찬
- 문화: 극장, 스포츠, 피크닉
- 건강: 의료 보험, 병원 진료, 치과
- 제조: 생산 조립 라인, 공장 경영
- 직원: 채용, 은퇴, 급여, 진급, 고용 기회
- 주택: 부동산, 이사, 기업 부지

토익 파트별 구성

구성		내용	문항 수	시간	배점
LISTENING TEST	PART 1	사진 묘사	6문항(1번-6번)	45분	495점
	PART 2	질의응답	25문항(7번-31번)		
	PART 3	짧은 대화	39문항, 13지문(32번-70번)		
	PART 4	짧은 담화	30문항, 10지문(71번-100번)		
READING TEST	PART 5	단문 빈칸 채우기(문법/어휘)	30문항(101번-130번)	75분	495점
	PART 6	장문 빈칸 채우기(문법/어휘/문장 고르기)	16문항, 4지문(131번-146번)		
	PART 7	지문 읽고 문제 풀기(독해)	54문항, 15지문(147번-200번)		
		– 단일 지문(Single Passage)	– 29문항, 10지문(147번-175번)		
		– 이중 지문(Double Passages)	– 10문항, 2지문(176번-185번)		
		– 삼중 지문(Triple Passages)	– 15문항, 3지문(186번-200번)		
TOTAL	7 PARTs		200문항	120분	990점

토익, 접수부터 성적 확인까지

1. 토익 접수

접수 기간 확인		사진(jpg 형식) 준비		인터넷/애플리케이션 접수
· 접수 기간을 TOEIC위원회 인터넷 사이트(www.toeic.co.kr) 혹은 공식 애플리케이션에서 확인합니다.	→	· 접수 시, jpg 형식의 사진 파일이 필요하므로 미리 준비해둡니다.	→	· TOEIC위원회 홈페이지 또는 애플리케이션의 시험 접수 창에서 절차에 따라 정보를 입력합니다.

2. 토익 응시

준비물

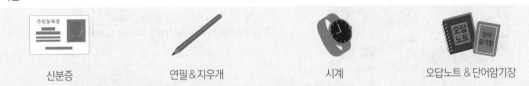

신분증   연필&지우개   시계   오답노트 & 단어암기장

* 시험 당일 신분증이 없으면 시험에 응시할 수 없으므로, 반드시 ETS에서 요구하는 신분증(주민등록증, 운전면허증, 공무원증 등)을 지참해야 합니다.
ETS에서 인정하는 신분증 종류는 TOEIC위원회 인터넷 사이트(www.toeic.co.kr)에서 확인 가능합니다.

시험 진행 순서

정기시험/추가시험 (오전)	추가시험 (오후)	진행 내용
AM 09:30 – 09:45	PM 2:30 – 2:45	답안지 작성 및 오리엔테이션
AM 09:45 – 09:50	PM 2:45 – 2:50	쉬는 시간
AM 09:50 – 10:10	PM 2:50 – 3:10	신분 확인 및 문제지 배부
AM 10:10 – 10:55	PM 3:10 – 3:55	듣기 평가(Listening Test)
AM 10:55 – 12:10	PM 3:55 – 5:10	독해 평가(Reading Test)

* 추가시험은 토요일 오전 또는 오후에 시행되므로 이 사항도 꼼꼼히 확인합니다.
* 당일 진행 순서에 대한 더 자세한 내용은 해커스토익(Hackers.co.kr) 사이트에서 확인할 수 있습니다.

3. 성적 확인

성적 발표일	시험일로부터 약 10일 이후 낮 12시 (성적 발표 기간은 회차마다 상이함)
성적 확인	TOEIC위원회 인터넷 사이트(www.toeic.co.kr) 혹은 공식 애플리케이션
성적표 수령 방법	우편 수령 또는 온라인 출력(시험 접수 시 선택 가능) *온라인 출력은 성적 발표 즉시 발급 가능하나, 우편 수령은 약 7일가량의 발송 기간이 소요될 수 있음

파트별 출제 유형 및 전략

PART 1 사진 묘사 (6문제)

■ PART 1은 주어진 4개의 보기 중에서 사진의 상황을 가장 잘 묘사한 보기를 선택하는 파트입니다.
■ 문제지에는 사진만 제시되고 음성에서는 4개의 보기를 들려줍니다.

문제 형태

[문제지]	[음성]
1. 	Number 1. Look at the picture marked number one in your test book. (A) A woman is serving a meal. (B) A woman is washing a bowl. (C) A woman is pouring some water. **(D) A woman is preparing some food.**

출제 경향 및 대비 전략

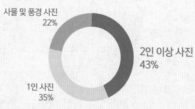

사물 및 풍경 사진
22%

2인 이상 사진
43%

1인 사진
35%

PART 1에서는 사람 중심 사진이 평균 4~5개로 가장 많이 출제됩니다. 사람 중심 사진에서는 2인 이상 사진이 3~4개로 가장 많이 출제되고, 1인 사진이 2~3개 정도 출제됩니다.

핵심 대비 전략

보기를 듣기 전에 사진 유형을 확인하고 관련 표현을 미리 연상합니다.
보기를 듣기 전에 사람의 유무 및 수에 따라 사진 유형을 확인하고, 사람의 동작/상태 또는 사물의 상태/위치와 관련된 표현들을 미리 연상하면 보기를 훨씬 명확하게 들을 수 있어 정답 선택이 쉬워집니다.

사람이 등장하는 사진에 사물을 묘사한 보기가 정답으로 출제될 수 있습니다.
사람이 등장하는 사진이지만, 사물을 묘사한 보기가 정답으로 출제되는 문제가 매회 평균 1문제씩 출제되니, 사진을 꼼꼼히 확인한 후 각 보기를 들어야 합니다.

PART 2 질의응답 (25문제)

- PART 2는 주어진 질문이나 진술에 가장 적절한 응답을 선택하는 파트입니다.
- 문제지에는 질문과 보기가 제시되지 않으며 음성에서는 질문과 3개의 보기를 들려줍니다.

문제 형태

[문제지]	[음성]
7. Mark your answer on your answer sheet.	Number 7. Where is the nearest park? **(A) There's one on Lincoln Avenue.** (B) No, I don't drive. (C) I'm nearly finished.

출제 경향 및 대비 전략

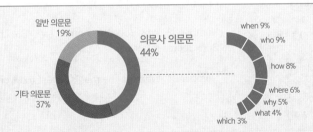

일반 의문문 19%
의문사 의문문 44%
기타 의문문 37%

when 9%
who 9%
how 8%
where 6%
why 5%
what 4%
which 3%

의문사 의문문이 평균 11~12개로 가장 많이 출제됩니다. 다음으로는 기타 의문문(평서문 및 선택/부가/제안·요청 의문문)이 평균 9~10개, 일반 의문문(조동사/Be동사/부정 의문문)이 평균 4~5개 출제됩니다.

핵심 대비 전략

질문의 첫 단어는 절대 놓치지 않고 듣습니다.
PART 2에서 평균 11~12문제 정도 출제되는 의문사 의문문은 첫 단어인 의문사만 들어도 대부분 정답을 선택할 수 있습니다. 단, 부가 의문문은 평서문 뒤에 덧붙여진 'isn't it'이나 'right', 선택 의문문은 질문 중간에 접속사 'or'를 듣고 그 유형을 파악해야 합니다.

질문에 간접적으로 응답하는 문제들이 최근 많이 출제되고 있습니다.
간접적인 응답에는 질문에 대해 되묻는 응답, Yes/No 대신 우회적으로 답하는 응답, 모르겠다는 의도의 모호한 응답이 포함되는데, 질문을 듣고 한 가지의 응답만 예상하기보다는 모든 보기들의 숨은 의도를 정확히 파악하여 가장 적절한 것을 정답으로 골라야 합니다.

파트별 출제 유형 및 전략

PART 3 짧은 대화 (총 13지문, 39문제)

- PART 3는 2~3명의 대화를 듣고 이와 관련된 3개의 문제의 정답을 선택하는 파트입니다.
- 문제지에는 하나의 질문과 4개의 보기로 구성된 39문제가 제시되고, 일부 문제는 시각 자료가 함께 제시됩니다. 음성으로는 하나의 대화와 이에 대한 3개의 문제의 질문을 각각 들려줍니다.

문제 형태

[문제지]

32. What did the woman do during lunchtime?

   (A) Spoke with a supervisor
   (B) Called an important client
   (C) Visited another company
   (D) Finished a report

33. Why does the woman say, "But I have to meet with a Sorel representative on Friday"?

   (A) To confirm an appointment
   (B) To explain a mistake
   (C) To express concern
   (D) To change a deadline

34. What do the men suggest the woman do?

   (A) Deal with a complaint
   (B) Work on another project
   (C) Review their proposals
   (D) Meet them after work

[음성]

Questions 32 through 34 refer to the following conversation with three speakers.

W: George, Jerry . . . I'm sorry I couldn't make it for lunch today. My boss wanted to talk with me about the advertising campaign for Sorel Incorporated. This is a big project, and I'm a little nervous about it.

M1: Don't worry. You're a hard worker. And our clients never complain about your work.

W: But I have to meet with a Sorel representative on Friday. I'm not sure if I'll be able to create a proposal in time.

M2: Why don't we all go to a café after work? We can help you come up with some ideas.

M1: Yeah. We're happy to help.

Number 32. What did the woman do during lunchtime?

Number 33. Why does the woman say, "But I have to meet with a Sorel representative on Friday"?

Number 34. What do the men suggest the woman do?

출제 경향 및 대비 전략

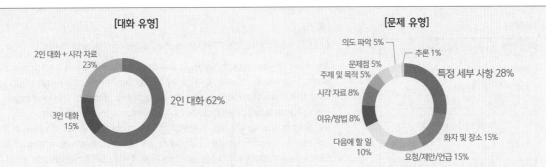

[대화 유형]

2인 대화 + 시각 자료
23%

2인 대화 62%

3인 대화
15%

[문제 유형]

의도 파악 5%
문제점 5%
주제 및 목적 5%
시각 자료 8%
이유/방법 8%
다음에 할 일
10%

추론 1%

특정 세부 사항 28%

화자 및 장소 15%

요청/제안/언급 15%

PART 3에서는 3인 대화가 매회 2개, 2인 대화가 매회 8개, 문제와 시각 자료를 함께 확인하면서 푸는 시각 자료 문제가 매회 3개 출제됩니다. 제시된 인용어구에 내포된 의도를 파악하는 의도 파악 문제는 매회 2개 출제됩니다.

핵심 대비 전략

대화를 듣기 전에 반드시 문제를 먼저 읽어야 합니다.
질문의 핵심 어구를 미리 읽으면 대화의 어느 부분을 중점적으로 들어야 할지 전략을 세울 수 있습니다. 시각 자료가 제시된 문제라면, 문제와 시각 자료를 함께 파악합니다. 의도 파악 문제라면, 제시된 인용어구를 먼저 확인하고 해당 인용어구가 사용될 수 있는 문맥을 미리 예측합니다.

대화를 들으면서 동시에 정답을 선택해야 합니다.
문제를 읽을 때 세워놓은 전략에 따라, 대화를 들으면서 3개 문제의 정답을 선택해야 합니다. 즉, 대화를 들려주는 음성이 끝날 때에는 3개 문제의 정답 선택도 완료되어 있어야 합니다.

대화의 초반은 반드시 들어야 합니다.
PART 3에서는 대화의 초반에 언급된 내용 중 80% 이상이 문제로 출제되며, 특히 주제 및 목적 문제나 화자 및 장소 문제처럼 전체 대화 관련 문제에 대한 정답의 단서는 대부분 대화의 초반에 언급됩니다. 대화 초반의 내용을 듣지 못하면 대화 후반에서 언급된 특정 표현을 사용한 오답을 정답으로 선택하는 오류를 범할 수 있으므로 주의해야 합니다.

3인이 등장하는 대화에 유의합니다.
3인 대화에서 같은 성별의 화자 2명은 다른 국적의 발음으로 구분되므로, 미국·영국·호주·캐나다식 발음을 듣고 화자를 구분하여 대화의 문맥을 정확하게 파악하는 연습을 합니다.

PART 4 짧은 담화 (총 10지문, 30문제)

- PART 4는 1명의 담화를 듣고 이와 관련된 3개의 문제의 정답을 선택하는 파트입니다.
- 문제지에는 하나의 질문과 4개의 보기로 구성된 30문제가 제시되고, 일부 문제는 시각 자료가 함께 제시됩니다.
  음성으로는 하나의 담화와 이에 대한 3개의 문제의 질문을 각각 들려줍니다.

문제 형태

[문제지]

Lunch Specials	
Item	Price
Panini Sandwich	$7
Spaghetti	$6
Dinner Specials	
Item	Price
Lasagna	$9
Grilled Chicken	$11

71. What did the speaker do yesterday?

    (A) Raised dish prices
    (B) Attended a staff gathering
    (C) Met with customers
    (D) Sent menu information

72. Look at the graphic. Which meal will come with a complimentary beverage?

    (A) Panini Sandwich
    (B) Spaghetti
    (C) Lasagna
    (D) Grilled Chicken

73. What will the speaker probably do next?

    (A) Arrange some tables
    (B) Stock some ingredients
    (C) Hand out a list
    (D) Print a coupon

[음성]

Questions 71 through 73 refer to the following talk and menu.

As many of you already know, our restaurant's menu will be updated soon. I sent everyone an e-mail with the details yesterday, but I'll go over the main changes quickly now. First, the prices of our dinner menu items have been reduced by 10 percent to attract more evening customers. Also, we will provide a complimentary coffee or soft drink with one of our lunch specials . . . uh, the cheaper one. Some new dishes will be offered as well. I will now pass around a list of these dishes and the ingredients they will contain. Please study it so you'll be able to answer diners' questions.

Number 71. What did the speaker do yesterday?

Number 72. Look at the graphic. Which meal will come with a complimentary beverage?

Number 73. What will the speaker probably do next?

출제 경향 및 대비 전략

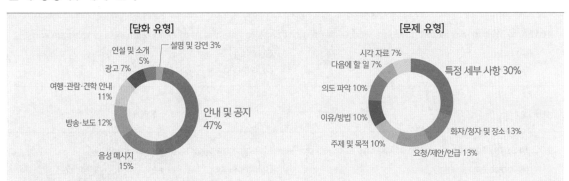

PART 4에서는 안내 및 공지와 음성 메시지가 매회 나오고 있습니다. 뉴스 보도나 팟캐스트 등의 방송·보도, 여행·관람·견학 안내, 광고 등의 담화도 자주 나오는 편입니다. 문제와 시각 자료를 함께 확인하면서 푸는 시각 자료 문제는 매회 2개 출제되고, 제시된 인용어구에 내포된 의도를 파악하는 의도 파악 문제는 매회 3개 출제됩니다.

핵심 대비 전략

담화를 듣기 전에 반드시 문제를 먼저 읽고, 시각 자료의 내용을 파악해야 합니다.
질문의 핵심 어구를 미리 읽으면 담화의 어느 부분을 중점적으로 들어야 할지 전략을 세울 수 있습니다. 시각 자료가 제시된 문제라면, 문제와 시각 자료를 함께 확인하면서 시각 자료의 종류와 내용을 파악합니다. 의도 파악 문제라면, 제시된 인용어구를 먼저 확인하고 해당 인용어구가 사용될 수 있는 문맥을 미리 예측합니다.

담화를 들으면서 동시에 정답을 선택해야 합니다.
문제를 읽을 때 세워놓은 전략에 따라, 담화를 들으면서 3개 문제의 정답을 선택해야 합니다. 즉, 담화를 들려주는 음성이 끝날 때에는 3개 문제의 정답 선택도 완료되어 있어야 합니다.

담화의 초반은 반드시 들어야 합니다.
PART 4에서는 담화의 초반에 언급된 내용 중 80% 이상이 문제로 출제되며, 특히 주제 및 목적 문제나 화자/청자 및 장소 문제처럼 전체 담화 관련 문제에 대한 정답의 단서는 대부분 담화의 초반에 언급됩니다. 담화 초반의 내용을 듣지 못할 경우, 더 이상 문제와 관련된 내용이 언급되지 않아 정답 선택이 어려워질 수 있으므로 주의해야 합니다.

PART 5 단문 빈칸 채우기 (30문제)

- PART 5는 한 문장의 빈칸에 알맞은 문법 사항이나 어휘를 4개의 보기 중에서 골라 채우는 파트입니다.
- PART 7 문제 풀이에 시간이 모자라지 않으려면 각 문제를 20~22초 내로, 총 30문제를 약 11분 내에 끝내야 합니다.

문제 형태

1. 문법

> **101.** Amy Wilson is a recent graduate who ------- a month ago to help the marketing team with graphic design.
>
> (A) hired (B) hiring
>
> **(C) was hired** (D) is hiring

2. 어휘

> **102.** In spite of the traffic delays, Mr. Cho showed up ------- for his coworker's retirement party.
>
> (A) gradually (B) intensely
>
> (C) considerably **(D) punctually**

출제 경향 및 대비 전략

Part 5에서는 문법 문제가 평균 20~21개, 어휘 문제가 평균 9~10개 출제됩니다. 문법 문제에서는 전치사, 접속사 문제가 매회 1~2개씩 꾸준히 출제됩니다. 어휘 문제에서는 문맥에 맞는 동사, 명사, 형용사, 부사 어휘를 고르는 문제가 매회 2~3개씩 골고루 나옵니다.

핵심 대비 전략

보기를 보고 문법 문제인지, 어휘 문제인지를 파악합니다.
보기가 어근은 같지만 형태가 다른 단어들로 구성되어 있다면 문법 문제, 같은 품사의 어휘들로 구성되어 있으면 어휘 문제입니다.

문제 유형에 따라 빈칸 주변이나 문장의 전체적인 구조 및 문맥을 통해 정답을 선택합니다.
문법 문제는 빈칸 주변이나 문장의 전체적인 구조를 통해 빈칸에 적합한 문법적 요소를 정답으로 선택합니다. 만약 구조만으로 풀 수 없는 경우, 문맥을 확인하여 정답을 선택합니다. 어휘 문제는 문맥에 가장 적합한 어휘를 정답으로 선택합니다.

PART 6 장문 빈칸 채우기 (총 4지문, 16문제)

- PART 6는 한 지문 내 4개의 빈칸에 알맞은 문법 사항이나 어휘, 또는 문장을 4개의 보기 중에서 골라 채우는 파트입니다.
- PART 7 문제 풀이에 시간이 모자라지 않으려면 각 문제를 25~30초 내로, 총 16문제를 약 8분 내에 끝내야 합니다.

문제 형태

Questions 131-134 refer to the following e-mail.

-------. As you know, you are in charge of driving our visitor from Fennel Corporation, Mr. Palmer. He will be
131.
here as scheduled from May 16 to 20. However, his arrival time from Dublin has been moved back four hours
because he ------- a quick stop in New York. This means you do not need to be at the airport until 2 P.M. on
132.
the 16th. Also, the factory tour ------- he was supposed to take on Monday morning has been canceled. He'll
133.
have a breakfast meeting with the plant manager instead at the Oberlin Hotel. Attached is a revised -------.
134.

131. (A) Regretfully, Mr. Palmer will no longer be needing our services.
(B) I'm writing to inform you of a few changes concerning our client.
(C) The following are some details about the new factory manager.
(D) Finally, I have received the new schedule for your flight to Dublin.

132. (A) will be made　**(B) is making**
(C) had made　(D) has been making

133. (A) this　(B) what
(C) when　**(D) that**

134. (A) itinerary　(B) estimate
(C) transcript　(D) inventory

출제 경향 및 대비 전략

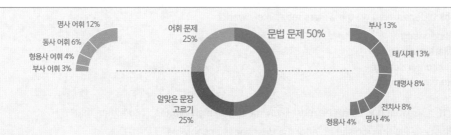

명사 어휘 12% / 동사 어휘 6% / 형용사 어휘 4% / 부사 어휘 3% / 어휘 문제 25% / 문법 문제 50% / 부사 13% / 태/시제 13% / 대명사 8% / 전치사 8% / 명사 4% / 형용사 4% / 알맞은 문장 고르기 25%

PART 6에서는 빈칸에 알맞은 문장을 고르는 문제가 매회 4개 출제됩니다. 문법 문제는 평균 7~8개, 어휘 문제는 평균 4~5개가 출제됩니다.

핵심 대비 전략

빈칸이 포함된 문장, 또는 앞뒤 문장이나 지문 전체의 문맥을 통해 정답을 선택합니다.
빈칸이 포함된 문장만으로 정답 선택이 어려울 경우, 앞뒤 문장이나 지문 전체의 문맥을 파악하여 가장 적합한 보기를 정답으로 선택해야 합니다.

파트별 출제 유형 및 전략

PART 7 지문 읽고 문제 풀기 (총 15지문, 54문제)

- PART 7은 제시된 지문과 관련된 질문들에 대해 4개의 보기 중에서 가장 적절한 답을 선택하는 파트입니다.
- 독해 지문은 단일 지문(Single Passage), 이중 지문(Double Passages), 삼중 지문(Triple Passages)으로 나뉘며, 단일 지문에서 29문제, 이중 지문에서 10문제, 삼중 지문에서 15문제가 출제됩니다.
- PART 7의 모든 문제를 제한 시간 내에 풀려면 한 문제를 약 1분 내에 풀어야 합니다.

문제 형태

1. 단일 지문(Single Passage)

Questions 149-150 refer to the following text-message chain.

Natasha Lee   4:08 P.M.
Robert, about the sponsorship packages for the Shoreland Music Festival, do you want to go for the Platinum package? It allows us to broadcast commercials during the event.

Robert Brown   4:09 P.M.
That would give us good exposure. Plus, we can put up company banners at the venue.

Natasha Lee   4:10 P.M.
That's right. So, should I go ahead and sign us up? The deadline is this Friday.

Robert Brown   4:10 P.M.
Well, we can't spend any more than $6,000 on this. How much is it?

Natasha Lee   4:12 P.M.
More than that. How about the Gold sponsorship package then? It costs $5,250, and festival announcers will mention our company over the loudspeakers throughout the day.

Robert Brown   4:13 P.M.
That sounds OK to me. Send me all the details once you're done.

---

149. In which department do the writers most likely work?

   (A) Accounting
   (B) Marketing
   (C) Customer service
   (D) Human resources

150. At 4:12 P.M., what does Ms. Lee most likely mean when she writes, "More than that"?

   (A) She believes that registering after the deadline is acceptable.
   (B) She acknowledges that a cost exceeds a budgeted amount.
   (C) She would like to receive some additional sponsorship benefits.
   (D) She doubts that $6,000 is their maximum spending allowance.

2. 이중 지문(Double Passages)

Questions 176-180 refer to the following e-mail and online form.

To	Joshua Ellis <j.ellis@jagmail.com>
From	Travis Whitman <t.whitman@mywebpress.com>
Date	November 1
Subject	Action Needed on Your Account

Dear Ms. Ellis,

Your MyWebPress account is due to renew in 10 days. You have the option to pay for another year at the rate of $29.99, or you may choose the three-year option at $79.99. We also offer a premium version of MyWebPress that enables many more features and design templates. One year of the higher level software costs $49.99 while the three-year package price is $129.99.

These special prices are only available if your renewal form is received by November 10.

Thank you,

Travis Whitman

MyWebPress Subscription Renewal Form   Date: November 8

Please fill out all information to process your renewal request and payment.

Account Name	Joshua Ellis	Account Number	83402839

Please choose your renewal option:

	One Year	Three Years
MyWebPress Standard	☐ $29.99	☐ $79.99
MyWebPress Premium	■ $49.99	☐ $129.99
Pre-made Forms Add-On	☐ $5.99	☐ $8.99
Graphic Design Add-On	☐ $12.99	☐ $18.99

Payment Information:

Credit Card Type	☐ Bankster	■ SureCredit	☐ YPay	Card Number	2934 4992 0041
Expiration Date	November 30			Security Code	557

176. What is indicated about Mr. Ellis?

(A) He is using a new credit card for payment.
(B) He failed to meet a deadline set by MyWebPress.
(C) He chose an upgraded version of his original plan.
(D) He added some security features to his package.

...

3. 삼중 지문(Triple Passages)

Questions 186-190 refer to the following Web page, form, and e-mail.

Laurel Art Center

Upcoming Events

Summer Sounds Fest
- Concert featuring local musicians
- June 5, from noon to 10 P.M.
- Tickets go on sale May 15

Spectacular Vistas
- Exhibit of watercolor paintings by local landscape artist Samantha Davey
- Opens 6 P.M., July 3, at the Campbell Gallery
- Refreshments provided by Gordon's Café

Exploring Wood
- Seminar conducted by Paula Sue
- Thursday July 6 from 10:00 P.M. to 4 P.M.
- $25 for eight classes (participants must bring safety glasses and a pair of work gloves)

Annual Craft Show
- Our biggest event of the year, featuring handicrafts made by talented local artists
- August 5, 10 A.M. to 4 P.M.
- Admission is $5 for adults and $2 for seniors
- Includes a buffet lunch from Kostas Mediterranean Kitchen

To join our mailing list, click here.

Laurel Art Center

Registration Form

Name	Ella Chung	Date	June 12
Telephone	555-3205	Address	108 Spruce Drive Hendersonville, TN 37075
E-mail	e.chung@mymail.net		
Event title	Exploring Wood		

Payment method

☐ Cash (Please pay two weeks in advance to reserve your slot)
■ Credit card: Liberty Bancard 2347-8624-5098-5728

To	Melissa Hamada <m.hamada@laurelart.org>
From	Hector Villa <h.villa@laurelart.org>
Subject	Catering
Date	June 21

Dear Melissa,

As we discussed yesterday afternoon, Kostas Mediterranean Kitchen had to back out of catering our August 5 event due to a scheduling conflict. However, I've received confirmation that Asian Flavors can take their place. Please update our Web site to reflect this change.

Hector Villa
Activities director, Laurel Art Center

186. What is suggested about Ms. Chung?

    (A) She is a member of the Laurel Art Center.
    (B) She will be attending an upcoming exhibit.
    (C) She is expected to bring gear to an activity.
    (D) She will be charged $5 for admission to an event.

187. Which event will Asian Flavors be catering?

    (A) Summer Sounds Fest
    (B) Spectacular Vistas
    (C) Exploring Wood
    (D) Annual Craft Show

...

출제 경향 및 대비 전략

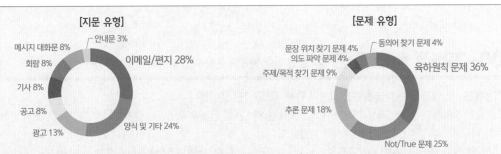

[지문 유형]

메시지 대화문 8% · 안내문 3%
회람 8%
기사 8%
공고 8%
광고 13%
이메일/편지 28%
양식 및 기타 24%

[문제 유형]

문장 위치 찾기 문제 4% · 동의어 찾기 문제 4%
의도 파악 문제 4%
주제/목적 찾기 문제 9%
추론 문제 18%
육하원칙 문제 36%
Not/True 문제 25%

PART 7의 단일 지문에서는 메시지 대화문이 매회 2개 출제되며, 이 지문에서 의도 파악 문제가 각 1문제씩 함께 출제됩니다. 이메일, 편지, 기사도 자주 출제되는 지문 유형입니다. 문장 위치 찾기 문제는 기사, 편지, 공고에서 자주 나오며, 추론 문제는 연계 문제로도 자주 출제됩니다.

핵심 대비 전략

지문의 종류나 글의 제목을 먼저 확인하여 지문의 개괄적인 내용을 추측해야 합니다.
지문 맨 위에 지문을 소개하는 문장을 통해 언급된 지문의 종류를 확인하거나 글의 제목을 읽어서 지문이 어떤 내용을 담고 있을지 추측하며 문제를 풀도록 합니다.

질문을 먼저 읽고, 질문의 핵심 어구와 관련된 정답의 단서를 지문에서 확인해야 합니다.
질문을 읽고 질문의 핵심 어구를 파악한 후, 핵심 어구와 관련된 내용이 언급된 부분을 지문에서 찾아 정답의 단서를 확인합니다. 이중 지문이나 삼중 지문과 같은 연계 지문의 경우, 처음 확인한 단서만으로 정답을 선택할 수 없으면 첫 번째 단서와 관련된 두 번째 단서를 다른 지문에서 찾아야 합니다.

정답의 단서를 그대로 언급했거나 바꾸어 표현한 보기를 정답으로 선택해야 합니다.
정답의 단서를 그대로 언급했거나 바꾸어 표현(Paraphrasing)한 보기를 정답으로 선택해야 합니다. 지문에 나오는 단어를 그대로 이용한 함정 보기가 항상 출제되므로, 지문의 내용과 질문의 의도를 정확하게 파악하여 정답을 고르는 것이 중요합니다.

수준별 맞춤 학습 플랜

TEST 1을 풀어본 뒤, 교재 뒤에 수록된 점수 환산표(p.244~245)에서 자신의 환산 점수를 확인하고 환산 점수에 맞는 학습 플랜을 선택하세요. 매일 박스에 체크하며 공부하고, 해설집과 다양한 부가 학습자료를 활용해 각 테스트를 꼼꼼하게 리뷰하세요.

800점 이상 학습 플랜 2주 동안 문제 풀이와 리뷰를 번갈아 하며 빠르게 실전 감각을 높이는 플랜

· 첫날에는 자신에게 맞는 학습 플랜을 고르기 위해, TEST 1을 풀어봅니다.
· 2주 동안 격일로 하루는 모의고사 1회분을 풀고, 다음 날 리뷰합니다.
· 각 테스트를 마친 후, 테스트 뒤에 수록된 Review 체크리스트를 활용하면 더욱 꼼꼼히 리뷰할 수 있습니다.

	1st Day	2nd Day	3rd Day	4th Day	5th Day
1st week	TEST 1 풀기 □	TEST 1 리뷰 □	TEST 2 풀기 □	TEST 2 리뷰 □	TEST 3 풀기 □
2nd week	TEST 3 리뷰 □	TEST 4 풀기 □	TEST 4 리뷰 □	TEST 5 풀기 □	TEST 5 리뷰 □

* 2주 완성의 경우 위의 표를 따르고, 1주 단기 완성을 원할 경우 위의 표에서 이틀 분량을 하루 동안 학습하세요.

600~795점 학습 플랜 3주 동안 심화 학습을 통해 약점을 완벽하게 보완하는 플랜

· 첫날에는 자신에게 맞는 학습 플랜을 고르기 위해, TEST 1을 풀어봅니다.
· 3주 동안 첫째 날에는 모의고사 1회분을 풀고, 둘째 날에는 틀린 문제 위주로 해설집과 함께 리뷰합니다. 셋째 날에는 각 테스트에 해당하는 부가 학습자료와 함께 심화 학습을 합니다.
· 각 테스트를 마친 후, 테스트 뒤에 수록된 Review 체크리스트를 활용하면 더욱 꼼꼼히 리뷰할 수 있습니다.

	1st Day	2nd Day	3rd Day	4th Day	5th Day
1st week	TEST 1 풀기 □	TEST 1 리뷰 □	TEST 1 심화 학습 □	TEST 2 풀기 □	TEST 2 리뷰 □
2nd week	TEST 2 심화 학습 □	TEST 3 풀기 □	TEST 3 리뷰 □	TEST 3 심화 학습 □	TEST 4 풀기 □
3rd week	TEST 4 리뷰 □	TEST 4 심화 학습 □	TEST 5 풀기 □	TEST 5 리뷰 □	TEST 5 심화 학습 □

595점 이하 학습 플랜 4주 동안 각 영역을 꼼꼼하게 리뷰하여 실력을 향상시키는 플랜

· 첫날에는 자신에게 맞는 학습 플랜을 고르기 위해, TEST 1을 풀어봅니다.
· 4주 동안 첫째 날에는 리스닝 모의고사 1회분을 풀고 둘째 날에 리뷰, 셋째 날에는 리딩 모의고사 1회분을 풀고 넷째 날에 리뷰
  합니다. 학습 플랜의 마지막 날에는 그간 공부한 내용을 총복습합니다.
· 각 테스트를 마친 후, 테스트 뒤에 수록된 Review 체크리스트를 활용하면 더욱 꼼꼼히 리뷰할 수 있습니다.

	1st Day	2nd Day	3rd Day	4th Day	5th Day
1st week	TEST 1 풀기 □	TEST 1 LC 리뷰 □	TEST 1 RC 리뷰 □	TEST 2 LC 풀기 □	TEST 2 LC 리뷰 □
2nd week	TEST 2 RC 풀기 □	TEST 2 RC 리뷰 □	TEST 3 LC 풀기 □	TEST 3 LC 리뷰 □	TEST 3 RC 풀기 □
3rd week	TEST 3 RC 리뷰 □	TEST 4 LC 풀기 □	TEST 4 LC 리뷰 □	TEST 4 RC 풀기 □	TEST 4 RC 리뷰 □
4th week	TEST 5 LC 풀기 □	TEST 5 LC 리뷰 □	TEST 5 RC 풀기 □	TEST 5 RC 리뷰 □	총복습 □

무료 토익 · 토스 · 오픽 · 지텔프 자료
Hackers.co.kr

TEST 1

LISTENING TEST

PART 1
PART 2
PART 3
PART 4

READING TEST

PART 5
PART 6
PART 7

Review 체크리스트

잠깐! 테스트 전 아래 사항을 꼭 확인하세요.

휴대전화의 전원을 끄셨나요? 예 □
Answer Sheet(p.247), 연필, 지우개, 시계를 준비하셨나요? 예 □
Listening MP3를 들을 준비가 되셨나요? 예 □

모든 준비가 완료되었으면 목표 점수를 떠올린 후 테스트를 시작합니다.
테스트를 마친 후, Review 체크리스트(p.68)를 보며 자신이 틀린 문제를 반드시 복습합니다.

※ TEST 1을 통해 본인의 실력을 평가해본 후, 본인에게 맞는 학습플랜(p.24~p.25)으로 본 교재를 효율적으로 학습해 보세요.

🎧 TEST 1.mp3
실전용·복습용 문제풀이 MP3 무료 다운로드 및 스트리밍 바로듣기 (HackersIngang.com)
* 실제 시험장의 소음까지 재현해 낸 고사장 소음/매미 버전 MP3, 영국식·호주식 발음 집중 MP3, 고속 버전 MP3까지 구매
  하면 실전에 더욱 완벽히 대비할 수 있습니다.

무료MP3 바로듣기

LISTENING TEST

In this section, you must demonstrate your ability to understand spoken English. This section is divided into four parts and will take approximately 45 minutes to complete. Do not mark the answers in your test book. Use the answer sheet that is provided separately.

PART 1

Directions: For each question, you will listen to four short statements about a picture in your test book. These statements will not be printed and will only be spoken one time. Select the statement that best describes what is happening in the picture and mark the corresponding letter (A), (B), (C), or (D) on the answer sheet.

Sample Answer

The statement that best describes the picture is (B), "The man is sitting at the desk." So, you should mark letter (B) on the answer sheet.

1.

2.

GO ON TO THE NEXT PAGE ➡

3.

4.

5.

6.

GO ON TO THE NEXT PAGE ➡

PART 2

Directions: For each question, you will listen to a statement or question followed by three possible responses spoken in English. They will not be printed and will only be spoken one time. Select the best response and mark the corresponding letter (A), (B), or (C) on your answer sheet.

7. Mark your answer on your answer sheet.

8. Mark your answer on your answer sheet.

9. Mark your answer on your answer sheet.

10. Mark your answer on your answer sheet.

11. Mark your answer on your answer sheet.

12. Mark your answer on your answer sheet.

13. Mark your answer on your answer sheet.

14. Mark your answer on your answer sheet.

15. Mark your answer on your answer sheet.

16. Mark your answer on your answer sheet.

17. Mark your answer on your answer sheet.

18. Mark your answer on your answer sheet.

19. Mark your answer on your answer sheet.

20. Mark your answer on your answer sheet.

21. Mark your answer on your answer sheet.

22. Mark your answer on your answer sheet.

23. Mark your answer on your answer sheet.

24. Mark your answer on your answer sheet.

25. Mark your answer on your answer sheet.

26. Mark your answer on your answer sheet.

27. Mark your answer on your answer sheet.

28. Mark your answer on your answer sheet.

29. Mark your answer on your answer sheet.

30. Mark your answer on your answer sheet.

31. Mark your answer on your answer sheet.

PART 3

Directions: In this part, you will listen to several conversations between two or more speakers. These conversations will not be printed and will only be spoken one time. For each conversation, you will be asked to answer three questions. Select the best response and mark the corresponding letter (A), (B), (C), or (D) on your answer sheet.

32. Who most likely are the speakers?
    (A) Cashiers
    (B) Bakers
    (C) Artists
    (D) Cleaners

33. Why does the woman apologize?
    (A) She arrived at her workplace late.
    (B) She forgot to perform a task.
    (C) She violated a company policy.
    (D) She bought the wrong item.

34. What does the man ask the woman to do?
    (A) Place an order
    (B) Check a schedule
    (C) Visit a store
    (D) Call a customer

35. What problem does the woman mention?
    (A) A store ran out of some paint.
    (B) A shipment has not been delivered.
    (C) A promotion is not going well.
    (D) A wall's appearance is unattractive.

36. Why do the speakers want to deal with an issue later?
    (A) A professional needs to be hired.
    (B) Some supplies are difficult to obtain.
    (C) Another task must be prioritized.
    (D) Some customers might be bothered.

37. What does the man suggest?
    (A) Covering an area with a poster
    (B) Extending business hours
    (C) Setting up some furniture
    (D) Cleaning out a basement

38. Where do the speakers most likely work?
    (A) At a software company
    (B) At a dental clinic
    (C) At a bank
    (D) At a restaurant

39. What is mentioned about the Easy Net Manage program?
    (A) It needs to be updated regularly.
    (B) It requires a monthly subscription.
    (C) It was only recently introduced.
    (D) It includes billing information.

40. What will the man do next?
    (A) Change a password
    (B) Check a Web site
    (C) Provide a link
    (D) Print out a manual

41. What did the woman recently do?
    (A) She moved into a new neighborhood.
    (B) She contacted a property owner.
    (C) She viewed an online posting.
    (D) She signed a lease agreement.

42. What does the man say about a townhouse?
    (A) It is undergoing renovation.
    (B) It is currently occupied.
    (C) It is highly affordable.
    (D) It is a two-bedroom unit.

43. Why does the woman say, "school doesn't start for two months"?
    (A) To explain the reason for a delay
    (B) To stress the urgency of a deadline
    (C) To change the date of an appointment
    (D) To indicate a willingness to wait

GO ON TO THE NEXT PAGE

44. What are the speakers surprised about?

(A) A business will close.
(B) A coworker will leave.
(C) A project will be canceled.
(D) A firm will be relocated.

45. What most likely is the woman's job?

(A) An accountant
(B) A lawyer
(C) An architect
(D) A salesperson

46. What does the man say he will do?

(A) Increase a budget
(B) Assign an employee
(C) Hire an applicant
(D) Postpone a deadline

---

47. What are the speakers mainly discussing?

(A) Expanding a company
(B) Updating a system
(C) Giving a presentation
(D) Revising a report

48. What is Brenda worried about?

(A) Changing a plan
(B) Canceling an event
(C) Meeting a deadline
(D) Making a mistake

49. What will the man most likely do next?

(A) Reschedule a meeting
(B) Reach out to a customer
(C) Submit an assignment
(D) Speak with an executive

---

50. What does the man find frustrating?

(A) An item was lost.
(B) A door cannot be opened.
(C) An employee is absent.
(D) An order has not arrived.

51. What did the woman do this morning?

(A) She replaced a door knob.
(B) She arranged a meeting.
(C) She organized a storage room.
(D) She requested a service.

52. What does the man ask the woman about?

(A) How to use a machine
(B) What time an office will open
(C) Where to find some paper
(D) When a printer will be fixed

---

53. Why is the woman calling?

(A) To find out the cost of repairs
(B) To ask about receiving a discount
(C) To inquire about selling a vehicle
(D) To arrange delivery of a purchase

54. What is the woman most likely planning to do?

(A) Move to a different country
(B) Apply for an open position
(C) Negotiate a business contract
(D) Send an international shipment

55. What does the man ask the woman to do?

(A) Visit a business
(B) Send an estimate
(C) Perform an inspection
(D) Confirm a schedule

---

56. Where does the conversation most likely take place?

(A) At a pharmacy
(B) At a supermarket
(C) At a hospital
(D) At a grocery store

57. Why is the woman unable to purchase Allenda?

(A) She misplaced her wallet.
(B) She went to the wrong branch.
(C) She needs a document.
(D) She forgot some information.

58. What does Alex suggest doing?

(A) Checking another branch
(B) Consulting an expert
(C) Following directions
(D) Ordering a product online

---

59. Why does the man plan on visiting a restaurant?

(A) To celebrate a special occasion
(B) To treat a staff member to lunch
(C) To conduct a meeting with clients
(D) To host a family gathering

60. What does the man mean when he says, "It's supposed to rain that day"?

(A) He prefers to be seated inside.
(B) He wants to change a reservation.
(C) He accepts a table recommendation.
(D) He needs a pickup service.

61. What does the woman say about the set lunch?

(A) It recently increased in price.
(B) It includes three separate courses.
(C) It is only served on specific days.
(D) It must be ordered in advance.

Elan Mascara $18.00	Herbals Foundation $24.00
New Matte Lipstick $12.95	Elan Powder Compact $21.50

62. Look at the graphic. How much will the woman pay?

(A) $18.00
(B) $24.00
(C) $12.95
(D) $21.50

63. How did the woman learn about the product?

(A) By using a mobile application
(B) By watching a TV program
(C) By talking with a friend
(D) By visiting a store branch

64. According to the man, what is a benefit of membership?

(A) Complimentary items
(B) Cash rewards
(C) Extended warranties
(D) Special discounts

GO ON TO THE NEXT PAGE

Belleville Expressway

Exit 8	Exit 9	Exit 10	Exit 11	Exit 12
⬆	⬆	⬆	⬆	⬆

Section A Section B Section C Section D

65. Who most likely are the speakers?

(A) Security guards
(B) Safety inspectors
(C) Tollbooth Operators
(D) Construction workers

66. Look at the graphic. Where will the speakers work?

(A) Section A
(B) Section B
(C) Section C
(D) Section D

67. What will the man most likely do next?

(A) Retrieve an item
(B) Submit a form
(C) Check a schedule
(D) Call an office

Weekly Art Classes

Monday	Tuesday	Wednesday	Thursday	Friday
Calligraphy	Sculpture	Photography	Painting	Origami

68. What problem are the speakers discussing?

(A) Booking cancellations
(B) Student performance
(C) Low enrollment
(D) High expenses

69. Look at the graphic. For which day's class will a discount be offered?

(A) Monday
(B) Tuesday
(C) Wednesday
(D) Thursday

70. What does the man want to confirm?

(A) A class is canceled.
(B) A payment is correct.
(C) A building is accessible.
(D) A sign is visible.

PART 4

Directions: In this part, you will listen to several short talks by a single speaker. These talks will not be printed and will only be spoken one time. For each talk, you will be asked to answer three questions. Select the best response and mark the corresponding letter (A), (B), (C), or (D) on your answer sheet.

71. Where is the announcement most likely being made?

(A) At a train station
(B) At a bus terminal
(C) At an airport
(D) At a ferry terminal

72. What has caused a delay?

(A) A traffic accident
(B) Bad weather
(C) A medical emergency
(D) Technical difficulties

73. According to the speaker, which item was found?

(A) A credit card
(B) A backpack
(C) A ticket
(D) A laptop

74. What kind of service is being advertised?

(A) Job training
(B) Language tutorials
(C) Fitness classes
(D) After-school tutoring

75. What is special about the business?

(A) It focuses on online courses.
(B) It has branches in many countries.
(C) It is staffed by volunteers.
(D) It offers services free of charge.

76. Why does the speaker encourage the listeners to visit a Web site?

(A) To participate in an assessment test
(B) To sign up for an online workshop
(C) To learn about available programs
(D) To get directions to an office location

77. What does the speaker imply when he says, "it is hosting a special event today"?

(A) An attraction is popular.
(B) An invitation is available.
(C) An area is inaccessible.
(D) A reservation is confirmed.

78. What is mentioned about the tour?

(A) It takes less than an hour to finish.
(B) It ends at the same place it starts.
(C) It involves stops at many stores.
(D) It requires long periods of walking.

79. What does the speaker ask the listeners to do?

(A) Stay in a seat
(B) Post a review
(C) Talk to a guide
(D) Make a payment

80. Who is Ms. Danton?

(A) A media representative
(B) A marketing director
(C) A government official
(D) A business owner

81. What does the speaker say Ms. Danton is good at?

(A) Planning events
(B) Analyzing data
(C) Dealing with disputes
(D) Increasing efficiency

82. What will the speaker discuss next?

(A) An investment plan
(B) A product release
(C) A company merger
(D) A government policy

GO ON TO THE NEXT PAGE

83. What is the class mainly about?

(A) Unique animals
(B) Science inventions
(C) Planets and stars
(D) Desert plants

84. What is being planned for next week?

(A) A field trip
(B) A review session
(C) A film showing
(D) A group presentation

85. What will the speaker do next?

(A) Hand out some documents
(B) Take some pictures
(C) Set up some equipment
(D) Move some furniture

---

86. Who most likely are the listeners?

(A) Instructors
(B) Gym members
(C) Sales representatives
(D) Technicians

87. What does the speaker imply when she says, "Everybody is busy these days"?

(A) Shorter sessions will be popular.
(B) More employees must be hired.
(C) Fewer people will be participating.
(D) New clients must be found.

88. What will the speaker probably do next?

(A) Introduce some clients
(B) Survey some customers
(C) Inspect a facility
(D) Give a demonstration

---

89. Why is Geneva Systems in the news?

(A) It developed a technology.
(B) It launched a new product.
(C) It lost a legal dispute.
(D) It replaced its CEO.

90. Who is Lawrence Khan?

(A) A corporate lawyer
(B) A company executive
(C) A business journalist
(D) A financial consultant

91. How can the listeners get more information about a story?

(A) By listening to a report
(B) By accessing a Web site
(C) By reading a publication
(D) By checking an e-mail

---

92. Why is the speaker calling?

(A) To offer assistance
(B) To arrange an appointment
(C) To make a complaint
(D) To request information

93. What does the speaker mean when she says, "I have a meeting soon"?

(A) She will not meet a deadline.
(B) She may not answer a call.
(C) A schedule may be changed.
(D) A process will take a long time.

94. What does the speaker say about tomorrow?

(A) A delivery will be made.
(B) An e-mail will be sent.
(C) An order will be confirmed.
(D) A business will be closed.

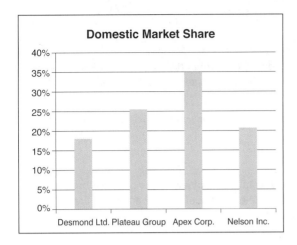

Domestic Market Share

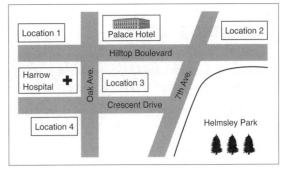

95. Look at the graphic. Which company does the speaker work for?

(A) Desmond Ltd.
(B) Plateau Group
(C) Apex Corp.
(D) Nelson Inc.

96. What is the speaker concerned about?

(A) Local trade restrictions
(B) Customer feedback
(C) International market share
(D) Shipping costs

97. What does the speaker suggest?

(A) Opening physical stores globally
(B) Increasing visibility on social media
(C) Improving some product designs
(D) Sponsoring some popular events

98. Where does the speaker most likely work?

(A) At a construction firm
(B) At an advertising agency
(C) At a real estate agency
(D) At a government office

99. What problem does the speaker mention?

(A) Costs have increased.
(B) A facility has shut down.
(C) A budget is inaccurate.
(D) Areas are overcrowded.

100. Look at the graphic. Which location might the listener be interested in seeing?

(A) Location 1
(B) Location 2
(C) Location 3
(D) Location 4

This is the end of the Listening test. Turn to PART 5 in your test book.

GO ON TO THE NEXT PAGE

READING TEST

In this section, you must demonstrate your ability to read and comprehend English. You will be given a variety of texts and asked to answer questions about these texts. This section is divided into three parts and will take 75 minutes to complete.

Do not mark the answers in your test book. Use the answer sheet that is separately provided.

PART 5

Directions: In each question, you will be asked to review a statement that is missing a word or phrase. Four answer choices will be provided for each statement. Select the best answer and mark the corresponding letter (A), (B), (C), or (D) on the answer sheet.

PART 5 권장 풀이 시간 11분

101. Traffic is particularly heavy this evening, so Mr. Gagnon worries ------- will be late for the annual company dinner.

(A) he
(B) him
(C) his
(D) himself

102. Nelson Media's CEO ------- that all employees are required to take part in the human resources seminar.

(A) announced
(B) being announced
(C) to announce
(D) was announced

103. Starworks Electronics plans to set up more assembly lines to meet the ------- demand for its medical devices.

(A) inspired
(B) rough
(C) convenient
(D) heightened

104. Evermart, America's largest ------- of consumer goods, is opening a logistics center in Mexico.

(A) retail
(B) retailed
(C) to retail
(D) retailer

105. Alan Elwood was ------- the new manager of the football club and will be moving to Germany this fall.

(A) hired
(B) named
(C) accompanied
(D) encouraged

106. The university's admission records ------- that the number of international students has declined over the past three years.

(A) having shown
(B) shows
(C) show
(D) is showing

107. Greenwood National Park is ------- visited in spite of its beautiful scenery.

(A) seldom
(B) almost
(C) earlier
(D) maybe

108. Fashueng Industries has published a corporate brochure ------- of its achievements.

(A) consistently
(B) consisted
(C) consisting
(D) consistent

109. A subway station has been proposed for Langford, the ------- populated neighborhood in the city.

(A) most densely
(B) denseness
(C) dense
(D) denser

110. The researchers are monitoring the ------- glacier movement in the Arctic to assess its impact on sea levels.

(A) activity
(B) actively
(C) active
(D) activates

111. RT Cosmetics' newest lipstick will be released within a month ------- there are no delays.

(A) rather than
(B) otherwise
(C) as long as
(D) resulting from

112. The executives from our Japanese partner company will be in town ------- for a few days before returning to Japan.

(A) quite
(B) ever
(C) only
(D) while

113. The factory manager decided to lease a ------- because there was not enough space in the storage area.

(A) tile
(B) party
(C) reward
(D) warehouse

114. Ms. Dench, ------- a team leader, strives to facilitate collaboration among team members.

(A) about
(B) by
(C) as
(D) of

115. The participants in the survey ------- the features of Neo Technology's photo-editing software from worst to best.

(A) opted
(B) ranked
(C) verified
(D) matched

116. The oldest bridge in the city will be closed for ------- four weeks while extensive repairs take place.

(A) approximate
(B) approximation
(C) approximated
(D) approximately

117. The ------- passed law prohibits hotels from providing single-use toiletries like small containers of shampoo.

(A) briefly
(B) recently
(C) generally
(D) extremely

118. The main ------- of the latest Connel smartphone model is the high-resolution camera.

(A) appeal
(B) appeals
(C) appealing
(D) appealed

119. Residents of the building adjacent ------- the construction site are complaining about noise and dust.

(A) to
(B) in
(C) on
(D) for

120. The tour guide informed the tourists that they were ------- through the day's itinerary.

(A) randomly
(B) indefinitely
(C) halfway
(D) elsewhere

GO ON TO THE NEXT PAGE

121. The company has rented a booth at the World Technology Fair to ------- its high-end line of products.

(A) perform
(B) accept
(C) collect
(D) showcase

122. Kelsey Haya, the CEO of Harvison Group, will not be at this year's conference, but a senior vice president ------- in her place.

(A) to attend
(B) may attend
(C) for attendance
(D) attending

123. The members of the global environmental group dedicate ------- to promoting the use of renewable energy.

(A) them
(B) themselves
(C) their own
(D) they

124. Visitors to the Philip Hospital may park ------- they see a green indicator on the third floor of the parking facility.

(A) whenever
(B) wherever
(C) whether
(D) instead of

125. City council heard various ------- from contractors interested in the transportation infrastructure project.

(A) lines
(B) agencies
(C) proposals
(D) capitals

126. ------- the potential for profit, MealFresh is going to allocate a significant portion of its budget to expanding into emerging markets.

(A) Except
(B) Though
(C) Given
(D) Provided that

127. Fort Frederick Museum's current exhibits will be transferred to a new ------- when renovations begin next week.

(A) locals
(B) location
(C) located
(D) locally

128. The marketing team has been analyzing the campaign's advertising performance ------- the last week of November.

(A) since
(B) then
(C) until
(D) still

129. The designer handbags sold on this Web site are as expensive as ------- sold at most major department stores.

(A) other
(B) whose
(C) one
(D) those

130. Adhere to the existing security ------- to guarantee that all sensitive data is protected from unauthorized access.

(A) durability
(B) protocol
(C) appearance
(D) settlement

PART 6

Directions: In this part, you will be asked to read four English texts. Each text is missing a word, phrase, or sentence. Select the answer choice that correctly completes the text and mark the corresponding letter (A), (B), (C), or (D) on the answer sheet.

🕐 **PART 6 권장 풀이 시간** 8분

Questions 131-134 refer to the following e-mail.

Date: August 17
To: Beatrice Xenakis <bxenakis@gomail.com>
From: Alfred Hendricks <ahendricks@moxtech.com>
Subject: Notice

Dear Ms. Xenakis,

I would like to inform you of Moxtech Electronics' decision to ------- a product recall. The
            131.
product is the Whirl-12 Miniature Fan, which you purchased last month. Unfortunately, this

model has a faulty motor. It may stop working and even catch fire ------- it is run on the
            132.
highest setting for a prolonged period of time. Results of tests on the appliance indicate the

motor is prone to overheating. -------, we advise you to stop using the Whirl-12 and call our
            133.
customer service center at your convenience. -------.
            134.

Thank you,

Alfred Hendricks, Customer Service Manager
Moxtech Electronics

131. (A) avoid
　　 (B) postpone
　　 (C) issue
　　 (D) monitor

132. (A) if
　　 (B) yet
　　 (C) whereas
　　 (D) also

133. (A) Furthermore
　　 (B) Instead
　　 (C) For example
　　 (D) Therefore

134. (A) The device is one of our most popular
　　　　 models.
　　 (B) You will be provided with instructions
　　　　 for getting a refund.
　　 (C) We are always interested in receiving
　　　　 customer feedback.
　　 (D) The initial interview will be conducted
　　　　 over the phone.

GO ON TO THE NEXT PAGE

Questions 135-138 refer to the following advertisement.

Get Fit with Cadenta!

Get in shape the smart way using our expertise and cutting-edge technology. For a limited time, first-time users will qualify for a 20 percent discount. It ------- to both Gold and Silver
135.
memberships. And if you start this month, one of our ------- professionals will help you
136.
design a custom fitness program for your personal needs.

------- this special offer, simply download the free Cadenta app onto your mobile phone and
137.
tap on the membership icon to get started. -------. Details about other membership benefits
138.
are available on our Web site.

---

135. (A) had applied
(B) will have applied
(C) applies
(D) has applied

136. (A) clumsy
(B) competent
(C) dominant
(D) recreational

137. (A) It is accessed
(B) By accessing
(C) Having accessed
(D) To access

138. (A) You will be reimbursed for the full amount of $39.
(B) Press play to follow along with the workout video.
(C) You should apply for a membership in person.
(D) It only takes a few minutes to sign up.

Questions 139-142 refer to the following press release.

FOR IMMEDIATE RELEASE

IRVINE (June 25)—Blackwell Publishing is pleased to announce its upcoming partnership

------- Cornerstone Books. The joint project will launch on July 1 and will involve the creation
139.

of a series of textbooks for students. -------.
140.

Chloe Samson, the CEO of Blackwell Publishing, first ------- this project five years ago.
141.

However, finding a suitable partner took much longer than anticipated. The wait has been

worth it, though. Cornerstone Books has a strong track record of producing ------- materials.
142.

Thus, Ms. Samson is confident about the success of this project for young learners.

Questions should be directed to Blackwell Publishing's PR manager, Jane Peters, at

j.peters@blackwell.com.

---

139. (A) for
(B) among
(C) with
(D) above

140. (A) We were greatly surprised by their
popularity.
(B) These books are intended for use in
public schools.
(C) Both companies are no longer offering
this service.
(D) There are several errors in the
publications.

141. (A) envisioning
(B) will envision
(C) envisioned
(D) to envision

142. (A) educational
(B) protective
(C) synthetic
(D) further

GO ON TO THE NEXT PAGE

Questions 143-146 refer to the following e-mail.

To: All customer service staff <customerservice@JBHotels.com>
From: Alaina Findley <a.findley@JBHotels.com>
Date: May 9
Subject: Inspections

Dear staff,

Please be aware that inspectors from the regional office will be visiting the hotel between

May 28 and June 2. In light of this, I would like you to familiarize yourself with our -------.
                                                                                        143.
These can be found in the employee handbook. Of particular concern is that some

procedures are being ignored when ------- regular guests check in. Please refrain from doing
                                      144.
this. -------.
       145.

Our previous inspection results were not ------- I expected. But if we all work together, I am
                                           146.
certain that we will do better this year.

Best,

Alaina Findley

---

143. (A) executives
(B) policies
(C) finances
(D) structures

144. (A) its
(B) their
(C) our
(D) her

145. (A) Many guests have asked to check out late tomorrow morning.
(B) That procedure will likely be changed in the near future.
(C) It will have a negative impact on our overall score.
(D) We will be making some changes to the check-in process.

146. (A) what
(B) whichever
(C) that
(D) whomever

PART 7

Directions: In this part, you will be asked to read several texts, such as advertisements, articles, instant messages, or examples of business correspondence. Each text is followed by several questions. Select the best answer and mark the corresponding letter (A), (B), (C), or (D) on your answer sheet.

PART 7 권장 풀이 시간 54분

Questions 147-148 refer to the following receipt.

Applegate Kitchen Supplies
The leading supplier of quality kitchen utensils and appliances!

Store Number: 03

Customer: Kent Harper

Store Location: 121 Parkway Drive, Seattle, WA

Date & Time of Sale: July 11, 4:32 P.M.

Item: Kellwood Espresso Maker (Model # 26152) **Quantity:** 1

Price:	$330.00
-20% Clearance Sale	$66.00
Total	$264.00
Cash Paid	$270.00
Change	$6.00

Thank you for visiting Applegate for your kitchen needs! If you want to learn new cooking techniques and recipes, we will be offering free cooking lessons starting next month. Each Saturday at 2 P.M., one of our talented instructors will teach you how to make delicious dishes from around the world. For details, visit www.applegate.com/learntocook.

---

147. What is indicated about Mr. Harper?

(A) He bought a gift card for his sister.
(B) He used a credit card for a payment.
(C) He made a purchase at a Seattle store.
(D) He returned an appliance for a refund.

148. What will likely happen in August?

(A) A Web site will be updated.
(B) A clearance sale will begin.
(C) A series of classes will be held.
(D) A special offer will end.

GO ON TO THE NEXT PAGE

Questions 149-150 refer to the following advertisement.

West Coast Cycle

We have proudly served San Francisco's cycling community for over a decade.

Don't miss the launch of our fourth shop! Stop by our Fillmore Street branch on May 15 to take part in the grand opening.

Event Details:
- One day only 50 percent flash sale on selected accessories
- 10 percent off preorders placed that day
- Hourly draws to win helmets, water bottles, and other prizes
- Snacks and barista coffees for everyone

For more information about the event, visit www.westcoastscycle.com.

149. What can be concluded about West Coast Cycle?

(A) It was established less than 10 years ago.
(B) It recently moved to a new location.
(C) It operates multiple store branches.
(D) It has parking spaces in front of the shop.

150. What is NOT listed as a feature of the event?

(A) Discounts will be offered on some products.
(B) Safety checks will be conducted for a small fee.
(C) Complimentary items will be given away.
(D) Refreshments will be available for attendees.

Questions 151-152 refer to the following e-mail.

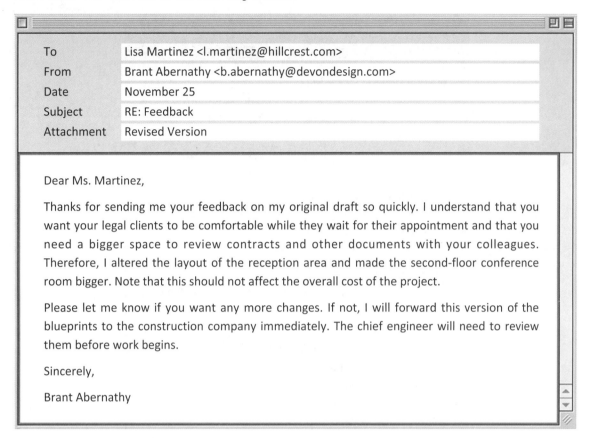

To	Lisa Martinez <l.martinez@hillcrest.com>
From	Brant Abernathy <b.abernathy@devondesign.com>
Date	November 25
Subject	RE: Feedback
Attachment	Revised Version

Dear Ms. Martinez,

Thanks for sending me your feedback on my original draft so quickly. I understand that you want your legal clients to be comfortable while they wait for their appointment and that you need a bigger space to review contracts and other documents with your colleagues. Therefore, I altered the layout of the reception area and made the second-floor conference room bigger. Note that this should not affect the overall cost of the project.

Please let me know if you want any more changes. If not, I will forward this version of the blueprints to the construction company immediately. The chief engineer will need to review them before work begins.

Sincerely,

Brant Abernathy

151. Who most likely is Ms. Martinez?

(A) A receptionist
(B) An architect
(C) A lawyer
(D) A doctor

152. What most likely is attached to the e-mail?

(A) A survey form
(B) A building plan
(C) A client list
(D) A logo design

GO ON TO THE NEXT PAGE

Questions 153-154 refer to the following text-message chain.

Beverly Willis [11:29 A.M.]
Hi, Noah. I'm at the entrance of our office, but my ID card doesn't seem to be working. The door won't open.

Noah Ruffalo [11:30 A.M.]
Really? Just call the security office to ask someone to let you in.

Beverly Willis [11:31 A.M.]
I already tried that, but no one is answering the phone. They are probably doing their regular inspections right now. Could I trouble you?

Noah Ruffalo [11:32 A.M.]
I'll be there in about 20 minutes. I have to make an important call to a client right now.

Beverly Willis [11:33 A.M.]
OK. I'll just wait here. Sorry to bother you.

Noah Ruffalo [11:34 A.M.]
You're in luck. Craig just left to get something from his car. He'll let you in on his way to the parking lot. Just hold on a minute.

Beverly Willis [11:35 A.M.]
That's great. Thanks.

153. At 11:31 A.M., what does Ms. Willis most likely mean when she writes, "Could I trouble you"?

(A) She needs help finding an ID card.
(B) She wants Mr. Ruffalo to open a door.
(C) She worries she will miss a phone call.
(D) She thinks Mr. Ruffalo should meet a client.

154. What is suggested about Craig?

(A) He is unable to enter an office building.
(B) He will contact one of the security guards.
(C) He cannot find an empty space for his vehicle.
(D) He is heading out to the parking lot.

Questions 155-157 refer to the following letter.

Mike Gallo
44 Pine Lane
Portland, OR, 97035

Dear Mr. Gallo,

We want to make sure that you haven't forgotten about your outstanding balance of $226.98 with Inland Cellular. — [1] —. As specified in the terms of the contract, you should have paid this within 10 business days of your cellphone service ending. Although it has been 30 days since your service was canceled, we have not received the final payment.

If this is an oversight on your part, we request that you take care of it immediately. — [2] —. Payment can be made through our new mobile app that became available last month or our Web site. You can also stop by any of our branch offices. — [3] —. If you wish to dispute this charge or are unable to pay it at this time due to financial problems, call us at 555-9383. Please note that a late fee of 15 percent will be applied to your balance on the first day of each month. — [4] —. Thank you.

Sincerely,

Beth Coyle
Inland Cellular Billing Team

155. What is the purpose of the letter?

(A) To explain a change in some contract terms
(B) To remind a customer about an overdue charge
(C) To offer to restore a previously canceled service
(D) To confirm that a final payment has been received

156. What happened last month?

(A) An application became accessible to the public.
(B) A branch office was temporarily closed down.
(C) A fee for late payments was increased.
(D) A billing date was changed for a customer.

157. In which of the positions marked [1], [2], [3] and [4] does the following sentence best belong?

"They are open from 10 A.M. to 8 P.M., Monday through Saturday."

(A) [1]
(B) [2]
(C) [3]
(D) [4]

GO ON TO THE NEXT PAGE

Questions 158-160 refer to the following article.

LOS ANGELES (April 15)—The city's first 3D-printed house went on the market today. Designed by Sandra Porter of Atlas Architecture, the 120-square-meter home is located in the heart of Belmont, a popular neighborhood for students.

The house was constructed using an innovative process that involves robotic arms applying layers of materials such as cement. These devices were programmed to follow the digital blueprints created by Porter during the design stage.

In a recent interview, Porter claimed that 3D-printing is the future of the construction industry and argued that it is a potential solution to the housing-shortage problem. "With this technology, a large number of affordable homes can be put up in a short period of time."

Porter also expressed her appreciation for Vernon Shaw, who took over Atlas Architecture just two months ago. "Mr. Shaw fully understands the advantages of 3D printing," she explained. "It was his enthusiastic support of the staff involved in this project that made it so successful."

158. Why was the article written?

(A) To congratulate an award recipient
(B) To provide an overview of a city's housing market
(C) To describe the use of new building method
(D) To explain the rising cost of local properties

159. The word "solution" in paragraph 3, line 4, is closest in meaning to

(A) mixture
(B) suggestion
(C) answer
(D) effect

160. What does Ms. Porter indicate about Atlas Architecture?

(A) It relocated to Los Angeles last year.
(B) It underwent a change in senior management recently.
(C) It announced a plan to hire additional staff members.
(D) It finalized some improvements to its design process.

Questions 161-163 refer to the following e-mail.

To: Hua Lin <h.lin@alloramed.com>
From: Wesley Harrison <w.harrison@selerant.com>
Date: June 24
Subject: RE: Partnership proposal

Dear Ms. Lin,

We appreciate that you considered Selerant as a partner to grow your business. However, after considering Alloramed's proposal, we have determined that it does not align with our strategic priorities at this time. At present, we are not seeking new ventures in the medical technology industry and are instead focused on advancing innovations in artificial intelligence, energy, and chip manufacturing. Furthermore, we are currently only pursuing partnerships with firms that are at an advanced stage of product development.

We do see the potential of your business idea and would like to recommend that you contact Boncorp Capital. Based in New York City, Boncorp Capital specializes in assisting start-ups in your industry. It can connect you to financial institutions with the resources you need to propel your business to the next stage.

Once again, thank you for your consideration, and we wish you all the best in your endeavors.

Sincerely,

Wesley Harrison
Senior Vice President, Selerant

161. Why does Mr. Harrison reject Ms. Lin's proposal?

(A) She was unable to meet a stated deadline.
(B) She did not provide some needed information.
(C) Her business does not fit with the company's goals.
(D) Her investment requirements are too large.

162. What is suggested about Alloramed?

(A) It is usually busy in June.
(B) It is in an early stage of development.
(C) It needs to hire a new chief executive.
(D) It is seeking assistance with repaying a loan.

163. According to the e-mail, what could be a benefit of working with Boncorp Capital?

(A) Acknowledgment from the global community
(B) Opportunities for cutting-edge research
(C) Support with creating management systems
(D) Connections to funding sources

GO ON TO THE NEXT PAGE

Emily Neal (1:20 P.M.)

Is everyone ready for the video conference with the representatives from Nova Electronics tomorrow? This company has the potential to be a major client. I want to make sure we are chosen to handle its marketing.

Luke Sawyer (1:21 P.M.)

I just finished making a few tweaks to the sample social media ad we plan to show. I changed the background color and made the company's logo a bit bigger.

Amanda Kim (1:23 P.M.)

What about the written content, Emily? Are there any revisions you'd like me to make? I will have some time later today to work on them.

Emily Neal (1:24 P.M.)

Not at all. You did a great job of highlighting the features of Nova Electronics' latest product, the Sound Wave Headphones.

Amanda Kim (1:25 P.M.)

That's good to hear. I was a little worried that I focused too much on how little they weigh and the protective case to carry them. You don't think we need some more material about the great sound quality or the sensitive microphone?

Emily Neal (1:27 P.M.)

We stressed that enough. The target market is people who need a wireless headset to wear while exercising or working outdoors. We want to make it clear how convenient they are to use.

Luke Sawyer (1:28 P.M.)

I agree. I think Nova Electronics is going to be impressed.

164. What can be concluded about the writers?

(A) They participated in a conference last week.
(B) They have missed the deadline of a project.
(C) They were recently hired by Nova Electronics.
(D) They are involved in the advertising field.

165. Who most likely is Mr. Sawyer?

(A) A computer technician
(B) A journalist
(C) A graphic designer
(D) A photographer

166. At 1:24 P.M., what does Ms. Neal mean when she writes, "Not at all"?

(A) She has not reviewed some content yet.
(B) She is satisfied with the current version.
(C) She cannot choose a feature to emphasize.
(D) She wants to promote a different product.

167. What is NOT true about the Sound Wave Headphones?

(A) They are made of lightweight material.
(B) They are sold with a carrying case.
(C) They do not come with a microphone.
(D) They do not require a cord to use.

Questions 168-171 refer to the following notice.

Secure Space—Long-Term Self-Storage

Thank you for booking a storage unit at Secure Space. All of our facilities feature a state-of-the-art security system and provide customers with round-the-clock access, 365 days a year. Please note the important information below:

Facility	Charges	Payment Method
Burlington Branch: 124 North Avenue, Burlington, VT, 02108	Unit Rental Fee: $225 ($75 per month for 3 months) Administrative Fee: $60 ($20 per month for 3 months) Tax: $25 Total: $310	Credit Card: XXXX-0505-03948 Outstanding Balance: $0

Customer Information	Unit Details
Name: Nelson Petrov Home Address: 234 Oak Street, Dallas, TX, 75001 Phone: 555-8273 E-mail: n.petrov@hotspot.com	Unit Size: 16 square meters Rental Period Start: April 1 at 3 P.M. Rental Period End: June 30 at 11 A.M. Additional Insurance Purchased: No

Notes:
- A $15 fee will be charged to replace each lost storage unit key.
- Customers must provide a detailed inventory of what will be stored before the rental period starts.
- Requests for a refund of a monthly fee must be made by visiting a branch in person.
- Go to www.securespace.com for a complete list of all facility regulations.

168. What is the purpose of the notice?

(A) To describe a method to improve security
(B) To explain a change to a rental policy
(C) To confirm a booking at a storage facility
(D) To introduce a regulation about insurance

169. What is suggested about Mr. Petrov?

(A) He can use the unit for a total of two months.
(B) He does not live in the city where the facility is located.
(C) He will be required to buy additional insurance.
(D) He has not paid the amount owed to Secure Space.

170. What will Mr. Petrov most likely submit to Secure Space?

(A) A deposit for a key
(B) A copy of an agreement
(C) A list of belongings
(D) An address for a delivery

171. How can customers request a refund?

(A) By calling a number
(B) By sending an e-mail
(C) By visiting a facility
(D) By accessing a Web site

GO ON TO THE NEXT PAGE

Devon Services

Devon Services is dedicated to preparing staff for the challenges of the future. — [1] —. We offer workshops on a wide range of topics, including leadership development, sales tactics, and business negotiations. These programs are designed to address both current market demands and emerging industry trends, ensuring your workforce remains competitive and prepared.

For more than 20 years, we have been the premier training facility in the Dallas area, and we have opened offices in Houston and Austin over the past three months. — [2] —. Our extensive client base spans diverse industries, ranging from financial services to healthcare. Whatever your employees do, we have the ability and knowledge to help them do it better. All of our instructors have advanced degrees in their respective fields. — [3] —.

On-site Workshops
- All manuals and other training materials will be provided in advance.
- Select from one of our popular workshop programs or collaborate with us to create a customized one that aligns with your specific goals.

Online Courses
- Enjoy convenient access to virtual classrooms, making it possible to learn from anywhere.
- All class materials (including recordings of lectures) are available for download after each session.

To arrange a preliminary discussion of your needs and how we can best fulfill them, call 555-3939. — [4] —. One of our coordinators will then travel to your place of business to meet with you. This should take 30 to 45 minutes at most, and there is absolutely no charge. We hope to hear from you soon!

172. What does Devon Services do?

(A) It provides corporate training events.
(B) It operates a mobile sales platform for retail outlets.
(C) It analyzes the financial performance of companies.
(D) It offers recruitment services for business owners.

173. What is mentioned about Devon Services?

(A) It plans to relocate to the Dallas area.
(B) It has recently expanded its operations.
(C) It requires an annual contract.
(D) It will simplify the consultation process.

174. What is true about the initial consultation?

(A) It can be arranged over the phone.
(B) It is held at the main office of Devon Services.
(C) It lasts for approximately two hours.
(D) It requires payment of a small fee.

175. In which of the positions marked [1], [2], [3] and [4] does the following sentence best belong?

"They also have a minimum of 10 years' relevant experience."

(A) [1]
(B) [2]
(C) [3]
(D) [4]

GO ON TO THE NEXT PAGE

Questions 176-180 refer to the following article and e-mail.

DUBAI (September 15)—Passengers flying into Dubai International Airport will soon have a new option to get downtown in a hurry! Palm Flight successfully completed the final safety tests on its unmanned air taxi system two months ago. The company, backed by the results of these tests, secured a short-term contract with the government. A three-month trial involving six Palm Flight air taxis will begin on October 1. If this trial is successful, regular operations will begin shortly afterward.

The drone aircraft, which can accommodate four passengers and their luggage, reduces the travel time from the airport to the city center from one hour to just 10 minutes. However, according to Palm Flight CEO Ahmed Habib, there are advantages that go beyond passenger convenience. "Our air taxis are fully electric and therefore do not generate any significant pollutants," he said at a press conference on Thursday. "Incorporating them into our transportation network will greatly improve the air quality of our city."

To	Ahmed Habib <a.habib@palmflight.com>
From	Lina Amin <l.amin@acesolutions.com>
Subject	Update
Date	February 25

Dear Mr. Habib,

I received your request for information about our progress in reviewing the air taxi project. My team is still analyzing the data we collected once the Palm Flight trial began on November 1. Given that this is the first time that drone aircraft have been used to transport passengers in our country, we do not want to rush the review process. I expect that our final analysis will be ready to submit to the Department of Transportation on March 3.

Please let me know if there is anything else I can assist you with.

Sincerely,

Lina Amin
Analyst
Ace Solutions

176. What is the purpose of the article?

(A) To announce the expansion of a public facility
(B) To clarify a safety procedure
(C) To provide an update on contract negotiations
(D) To introduce a new means of transportation

177. In the article, the word "backed" in paragraph 1, line 3, is closest in meaning to

(A) reversed
(B) supported
(C) organized
(D) represented

178. What did Mr. Habib discuss at a press conference?

(A) The risks of increased pollution
(B) The benefits of a technology
(C) The costs of a travel service
(D) The causes of poor air quality

179. What can be concluded about Palm Flight?

(A) It recently moved its headquarters to Dubai.
(B) It plans to hire someone to replace its current CEO.
(C) It delayed the start of a project by one month.
(D) It got government funds for a research project.

180. What will Ace Solutions do on March 3?

(A) Complete a final report
(B) Interview some passengers
(C) Test the safety of an aircraft
(D) Publish reviews of a service on its Web site

GO ON TO THE NEXT PAGE

Jarvis Gardening Center
We have everything your garden needs!

We are pleased to announce the opening of a third store on the corner of Park Road and Wilson Street. Make sure to stop by and check out our new location! Take advantage of the many special deals, including discounts, product samples, and bonus points for loyalty club members. And if you come to the store on Saturday, April 15, you can attend a free gardening class! See below for details.

Class	Time
Fruit Tree Pruning	9 A.M. to 10 A.M.
Natural Pest Control	11 A.M. to 12 P.M.
Organic Fertilizers	1 P.M. to 2 P.M.
Tropical Flowers	3 P.M. to 4 P.M.

To register online, go to www.jarvis.com/classes. Space is limited!

---

www.businessreviews.com

As an avid gardener, I was really interested in taking one the classes offered by the Jarvis Gardening Center on April 15. The class I attended was quite informative. We were introduced to flowers from several tropical countries. The instructor, Toma Mori, was very knowledgeable and even provided us each with a copy of his book. I had been considering buying it, so this was a nice surprise. My one issue with the class was that the instructor only gave partial explanations of some advanced gardening techniques. I had to search online for information afterward to completely understand them.

Posted by Laura Chen on April 17

181. What is indicated about Jarvis Gardening Center?

(A) It has more than one branch.
(B) It charges a fee to take part in its classes.
(C) It launched a new line of seed products.
(D) It moved to a different location.

182. According to the advertisement, what is NOT being offered to Jarvis Gardening Center customers?

(A) Price reductions
(B) Complimentary items
(C) Membership points
(D) Gift certificates

183. What time did the class that Ms. Chen attended begin?

(A) At 9 A.M.
(B) At 11 A.M.
(C) At 1 P.M.
(D) At 3 P.M.

184. What can be concluded about Mr. Mori?

(A) He has taught classes on many subjects.
(B) He resolved the issue with another instructor.
(C) He is the author of a published book.
(D) He sold some tools to his students.

185. What was Ms. Chen's problem with the class she attended?

(A) Instructors were not qualified.
(B) Questions were not answered.
(C) Materials were not clearly written.
(D) Methods were not fully explained.

GO ON TO THE NEXT PAGE

To: Sam Puller <s.puller@umail.com>
From: Grace Ewing <g.ewing@belluniversity.com>
Subject: Study Abroad Program
Date: May 28
Attachment: document list

Dear Mr. Puller,

Thank you for inquiring about Bell University's Study Abroad Program. You specified that you are interested in spending the fall semester at Central College in London. Fortunately, there is still space available at that institution. Let me briefly outline what you must do first if you would like to participate in the program. Along with your completed application form, you will need to submit several supplementary documents. I have attached a list of these documents. We accept copies of passports, but program applicants must provide the originals of the remaining documents. The deadline to submit everything is June 10.

In addition, you asked about living on-campus. Central College offers a variety of dormitory options at very reasonable rates. You can get more information at www.centralcollege.com/housing.

Sincerely,

Grace Ewing
Student Services, Bell University

Supplementary Document Checklist
Central College (London)

Document	Notes	√
Passport	It must be valid for a period of six months from date of departure.	
Health Records	Medical exam must have been performed within the past year.	
Letters of Reference	Provide two reference letters from your current or previous professors.	
Housing Request Form	A cheque for the advance deposit amount must be included with the request form (10% of accommodation fees for entire semester).	

Note that document requirements are subject to change depending on the regulations of the host university. In the event that this happens, all students affected by the new policy will receive a text message from the Student Services Office notifying them of the change.

To: Grace Ewing <g.ewing@belluniversity.com>
From: Sam Puller <s.puller@umail.com>
Subject: Re: Study Abroad Program
Date: June 9

Dear Ms. Ewing,

I reviewed the checklist and gathered the required documents. But as you probably know, I found out this morning that Central College now requires a four-page statement of purpose.

Given that I was informed about this at the last minute, I would like to request some additional time to prepare my application. I can have everything ready to drop off at your office by June 12, two days after the original cutoff date. I will begin working on the statement of purpose immediately.

Thank you,

Sam Puller

186. What is one purpose of the first e-mail?

(A) To point out a problem with an institution
(B) To confirm a choice of travel destination
(C) To reject an application for a program
(D) To explain an early stage of a process

187. What does Ms. Ewing say is required of program applicants?

(A) Contacting the foreign college directly
(B) Providing the originals of some documents
(C) Submitting an application through a Web site
(D) Visiting a university office on June 10

188. What can be concluded about Mr. Puller?

(A) He must renew his passport before departure.
(B) He will schedule a health checkup next month.
(C) He should provide three letters of reference.
(D) He will include a cheque with his application document.

189. What most likely happened on June 9?

(A) A dormitory reservation policy was changed.
(B) A notice about a job opening was posted online.
(C) An exchange program was canceled by an institution.
(D) A notification was sent to a group of students.

190. What does Mr. Puller request in his e-mail?

(A) A cost estimate
(B) A deadline extension
(C) An academic record
(D) An office address

GO ON TO THE NEXT PAGE

Questions 191-195 refer to the following e-mail, schedule, and online form.

To: Deborah Frank <d.frank@theusnewsstandard.com>
From: Kenan Marlow <kenan@miff.org>
Subject: RE: Media Accreditation
Date: April 22

Dear Ms. Frank,

Thank you for your interest in covering the 10th annual Memphis International Film Festival. The lineup this year is our most diverse yet, featuring the works of established and first-time filmmakers.

We are excited that you and three other reporters from your newspaper plan to attend the festival. To apply for media passes, please click here. The deadline to submit a request for accreditation is May 3, which is just two weeks away.

Your media pass will provide access to all film screenings and allow you to meet with directors and actors for interviews and photos. In addition, you will be able to attend our five gala premiere events. The media will have a special section on the red carpet.

Let me know if you have any further questions.

Sincerely,

Kenan Marlow
Media Supervisor
Memphis International Film Festival

Memphis International Film Festival Program
Gala Premiere Schedule

Date	Film	Description	Venue
May 20	*The Winds*	Renowned documentary filmmaker Adam Porter's examination of trends in politics	Vexor Cinema
May 21	*Anna and the Horse*	A new drama directed by Janice Tompkins	Vexor Cinema
May 23	*Secrets*	Hans Beyer's debut film and the winner of VIFF's Best New Film award	The Memphis Auditorium
May 24	*What Happened There*	Junko Takeshi's sequel to her critically acclaimed film *What Happens Now*	Vexor Cinema
May 25	*Shifts*	Director Tony Choi's work about a family moving to rural America	The Memphis Auditorium

Access to the premieres is limited to media representatives and individuals with special tickets. These events are not included in general festival passes.

https://www.miff.com/form

Memphis International Film Festival

Media Accreditation Form

Media Outlet	*The US News Standard*
Contact E-mail	d.frank@theusnewsstandard.com
Name of media representative	Deborah Frank
Additional media representatives	Hendrick Stevenson Pamela Consuelo (Photographer)
Media Pass Validity Period	May 20-May 24

SUBMIT

Please allow 24 hours for the form to be processed. You will receive a confirmation e-mail with a code. Visit the media tent at the festival to retrieve the physical media passes. Present identification for all representatives along with the code and confirmation e-mail.

191. In the e-mail, what is indicated about the Memphis International Film Festival?

(A) It will finalize its lineup at the end of April.
(B) It has been held multiple times in the past.
(C) It features only experienced filmmakers.
(D) It received funds from an international group.

192. What can be concluded about *The US News Standard*?

(A) It only covers events happening in America.
(B) It downsized a delegation to a festival.
(C) It no longer publishes a print edition.
(D) It merged with another media outlet.

193. According to the schedule, when will an award-winning film be shown?

(A) On May 20
(B) On May 21
(C) On May 23
(D) On May 25

194. What can be inferred about Ms. Frank?

(A) She will write about a festival in her own blog.
(B) She is a newspaper's only entertainment writer.
(C) She will miss the premiere of Mr. Choi's film.
(D) She has already seen Adam Porter's documentary.

195. What are media representatives asked to do at the media tent?

(A) Print some documents
(B) Pick up some passes
(C) E-mail some article drafts
(D) Apply for a photography permit

GO ON TO THE NEXT PAGE

Questions 196-200 refer to the following Web page, memo, and policy.

www.netsmartmag.com   *Net Smart Magazine*

| Home | Latest Issue | **Articles** | Subscribe | Help |

February 9—Software giant Optika Limited held its annual product showcase last week, during which it revealed its upcoming lineup of software programs to help companies boost the productivity of their remote workers:

- Group Hub simplifies project management, combining a highly functional scheduling system with tools to track progress toward specific goals.
- Hive Wire regularly backs up data to a secure cloud storage system so that important files are never lost.
- Team Space lets users communicate through video and makes it easy to record interactions for future reference.
- Whiteboard facilitates collaboration by creating a virtual whiteboard on which remote workers can view and revise shared files.

All of these applications will be released on February 12. Detailed reviews by our knowledgeable writers will be posted on that day.

Ryder Media
MEMO

To: All Employees
From: Jennifer Warnes, Human Resources Manager
Subject: Hybrid remote work system
Date: April 14

As was announced earlier, Ryder Media will be introducing a hybrid remote work system on May 1. To prepare for this, a number of teams were asked to experiment with various video conferencing applications to determine the best option. After extensive study, it has been decided to go with the application Optika Limited released in February. To ensure that everyone knows how to use it, a workshop has been arranged for April 20. An e-mail with more details about the workshop will be sent to everyone later today.

Hybrid Remote Work Policy

Eligibility

Ryder Media permits all employees to work remotely after completing their six-month probationary period. Junior employees may work from home two days per week, while team managers and department heads are limited to one day per week.

Requirements

Employees working remotely must be accessible and stay focused on their tasks during their scheduled work hours. Management retains the right to require employees to return to the office at any time if deemed necessary for a work-related task. A laptop with the necessary programs preinstalled will be provided to everyone working from home. It is the employee's responsibility to bring any technical issues to the attention of the IT team.

---

196. According to the Web page, what is true about Optika Limited?

(A) It released updates for its software programs.
(B) It announced that new products will be available soon.
(C) It rescheduled an annual marketing event.
(D) It collaborated with another company on a software project.

197. Which application will Ryder Media most likely use?

(A) Group Hub
(B) Hive Wire
(C) Team Space
(D) Whiteboard

198. What will readers of *Net Smart Magazine* be able to access on February 12?

(A) Expert evaluations of programs
(B) Trial versions of applications
(C) Videos recordings of a corporate event
(D) Biographies of technology writers

199. What is suggested about Ms. Warnes?

(A) She is responsible for scheduling hybrid work days.
(B) She will be unable to participate in a training session.
(C) She recently completed a mandatory probationary period.
(D) She is permitted to work from home one day each week.

200. According to the policy, what is NOT a requirement for remote workers?

(A) Being reachable during their shift
(B) Coming back to the office when needed
(C) Installing programs on a computer
(D) Reporting problems with a device

This is the end of the test. You may review Parts 5, 6, and 7 if you finish the test early.

점수 환산표 p.244 / 정답·해석·해설 [책 속의 책] p.2

▌다음 페이지에 있는 Review 체크리스트에 따라 틀린 문제를 다시 점검해보세요.

Review 체크리스트

TEST 1을 푼 다음, 아래 체크리스트에 따라 틀린 문제를 리뷰하고 박스에 완료 여부를 표시하세요.
만약 시험까지 얼마 남지 않았다면, 파란색으로 표시된 항목이라도 꼭 확인하세요.

☐ 틀린 문제의 경우, 다시 풀어봤다.

☐ 틀린 문제의 경우, 스크립트/해석을 확인하며 지문/문제의 내용을 정확하게 파악했다.

☐ 해설을 통해 각 문제의 정답과 오답의 근거가 무엇인지 정확하게 파악했다.

☐ PART 1과 PART 2에서 틀린 문제의 경우, 선택한 오답의 유형이 무엇이었는지 확인하고 같
   은 함정에 빠지지 않도록 정리해두었다.

☐ PART 3와 PART 4의 각 문제에서 사용된 패러프레이징을 확인했다.

☐ PART 5와 PART 6의 경우, 틀린 문제에서 사용된 문법 포인트 또는 정답 및 오답 어휘를 정
   리했다.

☐ PART 6의 알맞은 문장 고르기 문제의 경우, 지문 전체를 정확하게 해석하며 전체 글의 흐
   름과 빈칸 주변 문맥을 정확하게 파악하는 연습을 했다.

☐ PART 7에서 질문과 보기의 키워드를 찾아 표시하며 지문에서 정답의 근거가 되는 문장이
   나 구절을 찾아보고, 문제에서 사용된 패러프레이징을 확인했다.

☐ PART 1~PART 4는 받아쓰기 & 쉐도잉 워크북을 활용하여, TEST에 수록된 핵심 문장을 받
   아쓰고 따라 읽으며 복습했다.

☐ PART 1~PART 7은 단어암기자료를 활용하여, TEST에 수록된 핵심 어휘와 표현을 암기
   했다.

많은 양의 문제를 푸는 것도 중요하지만, 틀린 문제를 제대로 리뷰하는 것도 중요합니다.
틀린 문제를 한 번 더 꼼꼼히 리뷰한다면, 빠른 시간 내에 효과적으로 목표 점수를 달성할 수 있습니다.

TEST 2

LISTENING TEST

PART 1
PART 2
PART 3
PART 4

READING TEST

PART 5
PART 6
PART 7

Review 체크리스트

잠깐! 테스트 전 아래 사항을 꼭 확인하세요.

휴대전화의 전원을 끄셨나요? 예 □
Answer Sheet(p.249), 연필, 지우개, 시계를 준비하셨나요? 예 □
Listening MP3를 들을 준비가 되셨나요? 예 □

모든 준비가 완료되었으면 목표 점수를 떠올린 후 테스트를 시작합니다.
테스트를 마친 후, Review 체크리스트(p.110)를 보며 자신이 틀린 문제를 반드시 복습합니다.

🎧 TEST 2.mp3
실전용 · 복습용 문제풀이 MP3 무료 다운로드 및 스트리밍 바로듣기 (HackersIngang.com)
* 실제 시험장의 소음까지 재현해 낸 고사장 소음/매미 버전 MP3, 영국식 · 호주식 발음 집중 MP3, 고속 버전 MP3까지 구매
  하면 실전에 더욱 완벽히 대비할 수 있습니다.

무료MP3 바로듣기

LISTENING TEST

In this section, you must demonstrate your ability to understand spoken English. This section is divided into four parts and will take approximately 45 minutes to complete. Do not mark the answers in your test book. Use the answer sheet that is provided separately.

PART 1

Directions: For each question, you will listen to four short statements about a picture in your test book. These statements will not be printed and will only be spoken one time. Select the statement that best describes what is happening in the picture and mark the corresponding letter (A), (B), (C), or (D) on the answer sheet.

Sample Answer

The statement that best describes the picture is (B), "The man is sitting at the desk." So, you should mark letter (B) on the answer sheet.

1.

2.

GO ON TO THE NEXT PAGE →

3.

4.

5.

6.

GO ON TO THE NEXT PAGE

PART 2

Directions: For each question, you will listen to a statement or question followed by three possible responses spoken in English. They will not be printed and will only be spoken one time. Select the best response and mark the corresponding letter (A), (B), or (C) on your answer sheet.

7. Mark your answer on your answer sheet.

8. Mark your answer on your answer sheet.

9. Mark your answer on your answer sheet.

10. Mark your answer on your answer sheet.

11. Mark your answer on your answer sheet.

12. Mark your answer on your answer sheet.

13. Mark your answer on your answer sheet.

14. Mark your answer on your answer sheet.

15. Mark your answer on your answer sheet.

16. Mark your answer on your answer sheet.

17. Mark your answer on your answer sheet.

18. Mark your answer on your answer sheet.

19. Mark your answer on your answer sheet.

20. Mark your answer on your answer sheet.

21. Mark your answer on your answer sheet.

22. Mark your answer on your answer sheet.

23. Mark your answer on your answer sheet.

24. Mark your answer on your answer sheet.

25. Mark your answer on your answer sheet.

26. Mark your answer on your answer sheet.

27. Mark your answer on your answer sheet.

28. Mark your answer on your answer sheet.

29. Mark your answer on your answer sheet.

30. Mark your answer on your answer sheet.

31. Mark your answer on your answer sheet.

PART 3

Directions: In this part, you will listen to several conversations between two or more speakers. These conversations will not be printed and will only be spoken one time. For each conversation, you will be asked to answer three questions. Select the best response and mark the corresponding letter (A), (B), (C), or (D) on your answer sheet.

32. What is the woman preparing to do?

    (A) Return some merchandise
    (B) Purchase some furniture
    (C) Renew her apartment lease
    (D) Relocate to a new residence

33. What is the woman concerned about?

    (A) A rental fee was increased.
    (B) A chair was damaged.
    (C) A vehicle is too small.
    (D) A neighborhood is unfamiliar.

34. What does the man offer to do for the woman?

    (A) Transport some items
    (B) Call a moving service
    (C) Speak to a landlord
    (D) Decorate a new apartment

35. Where do the speakers most likely work?

    (A) At a catering company
    (B) At a factory
    (C) At a software firm
    (D) At a travel agency

36. What does the woman ask the man to do?

    (A) Call a shop
    (B) Order a meal
    (C) Find a phone
    (D) Make a list

37. What will the woman send by text message?

    (A) A Web site address
    (B) A product image
    (C) A sales receipt
    (D) A store location

38. Why is the man calling?

    (A) To request a discount
    (B) To inquire about a service
    (C) To ask about a price
    (D) To check on an order

39. Why does the woman offer the man free same-day service?

    (A) He operates a nearby business.
    (B) He referred several other clients.
    (C) He has become a regular customer.
    (D) He signed a long-term contract.

40. What does the man want the woman to do today?

    (A) Arrange a demonstration
    (B) Confirm an amount
    (C) Send a representative
    (D) Prepare an invoice

41. Who most likely is the woman?

    (A) An architect
    (B) A podcast host
    (C) An author
    (D) A travel agent

42. Why did the man travel to Spain?

    (A) To give a speech
    (B) To study at a college
    (C) To apply for a position
    (D) To accept an award

43. What will happen in September?

    (A) Interviews will be posted online.
    (B) Research will be finished.
    (C) A conference will be held.
    (D) A publication will be released.

GO ON TO THE NEXT PAGE

44. What is the conversation mainly about?

   (A) A business partnership
   (B) A marketing campaign
   (C) An overseas expansion
   (D) A performance evaluation

45. What is mentioned about some clothing items?

   (A) They come with free accessories.
   (B) They are highly durable.
   (C) They are very expensive.
   (D) They include natural materials.

46. Why has Tanya joined the meeting?

   (A) To discuss a sales strategy
   (B) To explain a legal document
   (C) To arrange a training workshop
   (D) To conduct a job interview

47. What are the speakers mainly discussing?

   (A) Finding a spot for a video shoot
   (B) Scheduling some time with an actor
   (C) Holding an event in a public park
   (D) Showing a film to an audience

48. What is the woman worried about?

   (A) Equipment for an activity is unavailable.
   (B) A location was not appropriate.
   (C) A musical event is not open to the public.
   (D) Approval for using a space is needed.

49. What does the man imply when he says, "I've done that before"?

   (A) He disapproves of a proposed plan.
   (B) He has been extremely busy lately.
   (C) He received assistance with a project.
   (D) He is willing to perform a task.

50. What event are the speakers preparing for?

   (A) A tax seminar
   (B) A grand opening
   (C) A company workshop
   (D) A product launch

51. Why would attendees use a QR code?

   (A) To receive instructions
   (B) To place an order
   (C) To access information
   (D) To make a reservation

52. What does the man say he will do today?

   (A) Proofread a document
   (B) E-mail some customers
   (C) Install a software update
   (D) Send out some invitations

53. What industry do the speakers most likely work in?

   (A) Publishing
   (B) Fashion
   (C) Tourism
   (D) Accounting

54. What have the men been asked to do?

   (A) Select a booth
   (B) Book a ticket
   (C) Hire a printer
   (D) Make a booklet

55. What will the woman do next?

   (A) Confirm a deadline
   (B) Review a list
   (C) Call a manager
   (D) Order a publication

56. Who most likely are the speakers?

(A) Accountants
(B) Interior designers
(C) Real estate agents
(D) Technicians

57. Why does the man say, "This is the second time he has hired us"?

(A) To verify some information
(B) To suggest an alternative
(C) To provide a reason
(D) To compliment staff

58. What topic will the speakers discuss next?

(A) A discount amount
(B) A business expansion
(C) A project start date
(D) A design proposal change

---

59. What event is most likely taking place?

(A) A facility tour
(B) A product test
(C) A job interview
(D) A sales presentation

60. Why is the man concerned?

(A) He will need to leave a session early.
(B) He forgot the answer to a question.
(C) He damaged an electronic device.
(D) He has never used a certain technology.

61. What does the man ask about?

(A) How long a session will be
(B) Whether instructions will be given
(C) What time an event will be held
(D) Which software will be installed

Sweet Life	**Issue #111**

Table of Contents

How to Host Your First Dinner Party	p. 6
Seven Days in Greece	p. 10
Healthy and Delicious Desserts	p. 18
A Barbecue Showdown in Texas	p. 20

62. Look at the graphic. Which article are the speakers discussing?

(A) How to Host Your First Dinner Party
(B) Seven Days in Greece
(C) Healthy and Delicious Desserts
(D) A Barbecue Showdown in Texas

63. What problem does the woman mention?

(A) A Web site is not loading.
(B) Some information is missing.
(C) A picture was not included.
(D) Some words are spelled incorrectly.

64. What does the woman suggest doing?

(A) Creating a new article
(B) Contacting a publisher
(C) Changing a page number
(D) Hiring an advertising firm

GO ON TO THE NEXT PAGE ▶

Linguana Language Center	
Course Schedule	
(Mondays and Wednesdays)	

Course	Time
German Level 1	9 A.M. – 10:30 A.M.
Spanish Level 2	12:30 P.M. – 2 P.M.
French Level 2	1 P.M. – 3 P.M.
Italian Level 1	4 P.M. – 5:30 P.M.

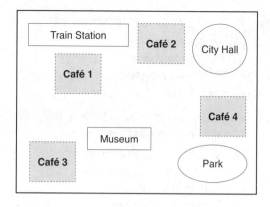

65. According to the man, what has Mr. Jennings decided to do?

(A) Hire an assistant
(B) Start a business
(C) Accept a position
(D) Request a raise

66. Look at the graphic. Which course does Mr. Jennings teach?

(A) German Level 1
(B) Spanish Level 2
(C) French Level 2
(D) Italian Level 1

67. What will the man most likely do next?

(A) Speak with a former colleague
(B) Publish a job advertisement
(C) Find new course material
(D) Look for some office equipment

68. What are the speakers discussing?

(A) A training session
(B) An updated menu
(C) A marketing event
(D) A branch opening

69. What does the man inquire about?

(A) Whether a task was completed
(B) When an activity will be over
(C) How some supplies were delivered
(D) Where an event will take place

70. Look at the graphic. Where do the speakers most likely work?

(A) Café 1
(B) Café 2
(C) Café 3
(D) Café 4

Directions: In this part, you will listen to several short talks by a single speaker. These talks will not be printed and will only be spoken one time. For each talk, you will be asked to answer three questions. Select the best response and mark the corresponding letter (A), (B), (C), or (D) on your answer sheet.

71. How will the tour group travel through the Verdant Grove Forest?

(A) On bicycles
(B) By bus
(C) By car
(D) On foot

72. What will the speaker teach the listeners about?

(A) Local architecture
(B) Rare plants
(C) An area's history
(D) Environmental issues

73. What are the listeners reminded to do?

(A) Check their belongings
(B) Bring their raincoats
(C) Wear their name tags
(D) Lock their hotel rooms

74. What is being advertised?

(A) A portable charger
(B) A smartwatch
(C) A dishwasher
(D) An exercise machine

75. What new feature does the speaker emphasize?

(A) It comes in a variety of colors.
(B) It stores a large amount of user data.
(C) It sends notifications to users.
(D) It has an advanced security system.

76. According to the speaker, what will buyers receive?

(A) A free accessory
(B) A limited-time discount
(C) A workout recommendation
(D) A software upgrade

77. What does the speaker's company manufacture?

(A) Eyeglasses
(B) Cosmetics
(C) Backpacks
(D) Tables

78. Why does the speaker say, "Unfortunately, we've had some problems with our ordering system"?

(A) To ask about an order
(B) To point out a solution
(C) To explain a procedure
(D) To apologize for a delay

79. What does the speaker offer the listener?

(A) A warranty extension
(B) A future discount
(C) A partial refund
(D) A free product

80. What is the broadcast mainly about?

(A) A blackout
(B) A labor strike
(C) An industrial accident
(D) A road closure

81. What type of event was canceled?

(A) An automobile race
(B) A football game
(C) A musical performance
(D) A fireworks exhibition

82. What will the listeners hear next?

(A) A weather forecast
(B) A brief advertisement
(C) A business report
(D) A traffic update

GO ON TO THE NEXT PAGE

83. Where is the announcement most likely being made?

(A) At a pharmacy
(B) At a supermarket
(C) At a furniture shop
(D) At an appliance store

84. What will happen in March?

(A) An establishment will celebrate an anniversary.
(B) A location will temporarily close for renovations.
(C) A sale event will be extended for one more week.
(D) A free sample will be given to each customer.

85. What does the speaker remind the listeners about?

(A) A regulation about on-site parking
(B) A policy on product returns
(C) A change in operating hours
(D) A process for providing feedback

86. Who most likely are the listeners?

(A) Software engineers
(B) Event organizers
(C) Accountants
(D) Lawyers

87. What did the speaker do last month?

(A) Agreed to a contract
(B) Signed up for a program
(C) Hired new staff members
(D) Attended a demonstration

88. What does the speaker imply when she says, "we may adopt it throughout the company"?

(A) The listeners' feedback is important.
(B) A team member's suggestion was useful.
(C) Some employees are ignoring a policy.
(D) A project needs additional volunteers.

89. Why is the speaker calling?

(A) To update a manager
(B) To order supplies for a store
(C) To request a rush job
(D) To address a payment problem

90. What does the speaker say about a company?

(A) It is concerned about a delayed shipment.
(B) It will send someone to check on arrangements.
(C) It will change the date of a grand opening.
(D) It plans to place additional orders.

91. What is the speaker willing to do?

(A) Pay for a larger option
(B) Retrieve an item
(C) Make some alterations
(D) Provide a store coupon

92. What problem does the speaker mention?

(A) A show will soon be canceled.
(B) A schedule was suddenly changed.
(C) A program is losing part of its audience.
(D) A presenter is planning to leave a show.

93. Who is Mike Cortez?

(A) A program director
(B) A journalism professor
(C) A television show host
(D) A script writer

94. What does the speaker mean when he says, "we have little time to waste"?

(A) A project is taking too long to complete.
(B) Some workers have not arrived at a meeting.
(C) An employee needs to work longer hours.
(D) A position needs to be filled quickly.

	Desserts	
Chocolate pudding		$3.99

Strawberry cheesecake		$4.99
Vanilla cupcake		$5.99
Carrot cake		$6.99

Option 1	Option 2	Option 3	Option 4
$40	$50	$80	$100
8 TB	10 TB	12 TB	14 TB

95. What is the announcement mainly about?

(A) A new product
(B) A baking class
(C) A promotional event
(D) A catering service

96. Look at the graphic. Which price has temporarily been changed?

(A) $3.99
(B) $4.99
(C) $5.99
(D) $6.99

97. What does the speaker recommend that the listeners do?

(A) Apply for a job
(B) Sign up for a program
(C) Taste some samples
(D) Try a new beverage

98. Where do the listeners most likely work?

(A) At a recruitment agency
(B) At an educational facility
(C) At a financial institution
(D) At a grocery store

99. Look at the graphic. Which option does the speaker recommend?

(A) Option 1
(B) Option 2
(C) Option 3
(D) Option 4

100. What task has Matilda been assigned?

(A) Testing features
(B) Installing upgrades
(C) Notifying applicants
(D) Distributing documents

This is the end of the Listening test. Turn to PART 5 in your test book.

GO ON TO THE NEXT PAGE

In this section, you must demonstrate your ability to read and comprehend English. You will be given a variety of texts and asked to answer questions about these texts. This section is divided into three parts and will take 75 minutes to complete.

Do not mark the answers in your test book. Use the answer sheet that is separately provided.

PART 5

Directions: In each question, you will be asked to review a statement that is missing a word or phrase. Four answer choices will be provided for each statement. Select the best answer and mark the corresponding letter (A), (B), (C), or (D) on the answer sheet.

🕐 **PART 5 권장 풀이 시간** 11분

101. The annual financial report of Natura Landscaping ------- shows the sources of all funds and how they were used.

(A) clear
(B) clearly
(C) to clear
(D) clearer

102. All apprentices in the construction industry should ------- themselves with safety regulations during their training period.

(A) anticipate
(B) familiarize
(C) identify
(D) compare

103. Nuffield Cutlery's booth at the Housewares Trade Show looked less ------- than those of the other participating companies.

(A) organize
(B) organizing
(C) organizes
(D) organized

104. Life Fit recently added a new feature to its mobile application, enabling users ------- their daily calorie intake.

(A) track
(B) tracking
(C) tracked
(D) to track

105. Currently, Ms. Demir ------- for her interview with Arc Stationery by studying the company's achievements.

(A) preparing
(B) is preparing
(C) was preparing
(D) who prepared

106. Mr. Daine has evaluated the performance of his workers fairly ------- provided feedback on how to improve.

(A) even though
(B) for example
(C) but
(D) as well as

107. Starting in July, Deep Blue Pool Cleaning Services will send billing ------- to its clients on a biweekly basis.

(A) states
(B) stated
(C) statement
(D) statements

108. Along with a valid passport, visitors to the country are required to ------- a visa that is appropriate for their purpose of travel.

(A) connect
(B) perform
(C) possess
(D) occupy

109. We planned to attend Ms. Iwata's retirement party, but -------, we were unable to make it due to a traffic jam.

(A) scarcely
(B) regretfully
(C) exceptionally
(D) deliberately

110. ------- a customer buys an upcycling product at EcoRevive, a $1 donation is made to the Environmental Conservation Foundation.

(A) So that
(B) Which
(C) Despite
(D) Whenever

111. Renowned chef Markus Lee discusses ------- culinary journey and experiences in a newly published book.

(A) he
(B) his
(C) him
(D) himself

112. Demand for suburban housing has ------- as people continue to look for larger living spaces outside of urban centers.

(A) drained
(B) earned
(C) soared
(D) reached

113. ------- personnel for the company is effectively handled by the human resources department.

(A) Recruit
(B) Recruiting
(C) Recruited
(D) Recruitment

114. The investors reacted ------- to the team's presentation but asked for more time to consider their options.

(A) mostly
(B) cautiously
(C) differently
(D) favorably

115. A ------- of research into market trends resulted in APS Fashion overestimating consumer interest in its products.

(A) lack
(B) cause
(C) consent
(D) risk

116. Please inform senior management by tomorrow ------- the contract negotiations have been successful.

(A) both
(B) either
(C) whether
(D) so

117. Pyle Flooring finished the carpet installation ahead of schedule ------- the deadline was tight.

(A) although
(B) in case
(C) above all
(D) regardless of

118. Images displayed online may not reflect the ------- condition of the goods being sold at Reyes Auction.

(A) close
(B) permanent
(C) exact
(D) gradual

119. Elena Patel will succeed in the position of data ------- given her years of experience as a research consultant.

(A) analyzed
(B) analyst
(C) analyzes
(D) analytical

120. As specified on Cobi Communication's Web site, customers may expect a ------- the same day they leave an inquiry.

(A) choice
(B) manuscript
(C) response
(D) degree

GO ON TO THE NEXT PAGE

121. Farmstead Grocers, known for its commitment to supporting local farmers, offers ------- priced vegetables.

(A) reasoned
(B) reasonable
(C) reasoning
(D) reasonably

122. According to the orientation schedule, the question-and-answer session with the new hires will end ------- 5 P.M.

(A) within
(B) until
(C) around
(D) except

123. Hughes Media announced that it is ------- creative copywriters to collaborate on a brand storytelling project.

(A) looking
(B) seeking
(C) concentrating
(D) conducting

124. The stress-management workshop teaches participants psychological techniques to remain ------- during high-pressure situations.

(A) calm
(B) calming
(C) calmly
(D) calmness

125. Vulcan Sportswear's sales revenues have risen ------- 13 percent since the company introduced its first line of sneakers.

(A) firmly
(B) shortly
(C) nearly
(D) adversely

126. Because ------- of the tickets for the train were nonrefundable, we couldn't change our travel plans.

(A) another
(B) everything
(C) those
(D) some

127. Visitors to the Nilsson Art Gallery have uniformly praised the artist's ability to paint landscapes in ------- detail.

(A) cluttered
(B) exquisite
(C) obedient
(D) sudden

128. The CEO of Sanford Industries requested employees' opinions ------- the proposed changes to the company's leave policies.

(A) beyond
(B) onto
(C) in
(D) about

129. First Track Entertainment's willingness to abandon ------- business strategies in favor of new approaches has made it a music industry leader.

(A) convene
(B) convention
(C) conventional
(D) conventionally

130. The management of Nex Engineering will make decisions on budget allocation ------- the shareholders' meeting.

(A) among
(B) like
(C) later
(D) following

PART 6

Directions: In this part, you will be asked to read four English texts. Each text is missing a word, phrase, or sentence. Select the answer choice that correctly completes the text and mark the corresponding letter (A), (B), (C), or (D) on the answer sheet.

🕐 **PART 6 권장 풀이 시간** **8분**

Questions 131-134 refer to the following e-mail.

To: Alejandra Morales <a.morales@ezmail.ca>
From: Marcus Clifford <m.clifford@clarendon.ca>
Date: 6 February
Subject: Re: Junior Chemist Position

Dear Ms. Morales,

Thank you for your application for the position of junior chemist. Your résumé was one of the

most impressive we have seen. -------, we would like to schedule you for an online test next
                                  131.
week. This exam is an important part of our hiring process. It allows us to ------- assess your
                                                                              132.
level of knowledge and suitability for the role in our laboratory. -------.
                                                                    133.

The test ------- about four hours. Therefore, make sure you have a block of free time in your
         134.
schedule on the day you choose.

Best Regards,

Marcus Clifford
Clarendon Laboratory

---

131. (A) Otherwise
(B) Rather
(C) Accordingly
(D) Meanwhile

132. (A) better
(B) likewise
(C) quite
(D) already

133. (A) Please e-mail the completed test form by 6 P.M.
(B) More than 50 people applied for the position.
(C) It is one of the most difficult aspects of the job.
(D) Let me know which day next week is best for you.

134. (A) takes
(B) took
(C) would have taken
(D) had taken

GO ON TO THE NEXT PAGE

Questions 135-138 refer to the following information.

Nuova Coffee Machine

The Nuova Coffee Machine brews the perfect pot of coffee every time! All you need to do is

follow these simple steps. First, put a paper filter in the basket and make sure it fits -------.

135.

Then, place one tablespoon of finely ground coffee in the filter for each cup of coffee you

intend to make. Finally, pour water into the machine and turn it on.

Please note the following ------- precautions. Never clean the machine while it is plugged in.

136.

-------. In addition, do not fill the machine ------- water past the maximum level which is

137. **138.**

marked by a red line.

---

135. (A) secure
(B) secures
(C) securely
(D) secured

136. (A) safety
(B) finance
(C) health
(D) environment

137. (A) This appliance is currently being offered at a discount.
(B) You may be exposed to the risk of electric shock.
(C) There are many types of coffee beans to choose from.
(D) Some people prefer iced coffee in the summer.

138. (A) from
(B) up
(C) with
(D) into

Scheduled Boiler Maintenance

It was previously announced that from May 10 to 15, the building will have ------- hot water
139.
outages due to boiler repairs. To minimize disruption, however, the daily schedule has been

altered. The maintenance work planned ------- between the hours of 7 A.M. and 11 A.M. will
140.
now take place between 1 P.M. and 5 P.M., when the fewest residents are at home.

The ------- from GDX Services have assured us that the work will be completed on schedule.
141.
If an unforeseen delay arises, you will be notified immediately. -------. Feel free to stop by the
142.
building management office if you have any questions.

---

139. (A) occasions
(B) occasional
(C) occasioned
(D) occasionally

140. (A) having conducted
(B) was conducted
(C) to be conducted
(D) had conducted

141. (A) plumbers
(B) pilots
(C) realtors
(D) lawyers

142. (A) The building manager will provide a
copy of your key.
(B) Other businesses specialize in lighting
installation.
(C) The repairs to your apartment will be
finished tomorrow.
(D) We appreciate your patience
throughout this process.

GO ON TO THE NEXT PAGE

Questions 143-146 refer to the following article.

Purple Line Drives Development

POTTERSVILLE (June 2)—The new Purple Line of the subway has ------- interest in many
                                                                              143.
communities outside Minneapolis, including the town of Pottersville. Express trains on the

Purple Line now make it possible to access downtown Minneapolis in 35 minutes. This

benefit, ------- tax incentives for new homeowners, has triggered the development of the
          144.
Pottersville area.

Over the last two years, more than 20,000 homes have been newly constructed in

Pottersville. Construction of a public high school and town library is also underway. -------,
                                                                                        145.
retailers have arrived, filling the new Hillcrest shopping center. -------.
                                                                    146.

---

143. (A) distracted
    (B) boosted
    (C) controlled
    (D) suspended

144. (A) ahead of
    (B) as for
    (C) along with
    (D) toward

145. (A) Until then
    (B) In contrast
    (C) Even so
    (D) In the meantime

146. (A) The housing shortage is unlikely to
       end soon.
    (B) The development has revitalized
       downtown Minneapolis.
    (C) The subway station will open in
       Pottersville next fall.
    (D) It is now a favored destination for
       residents.

PART 7

Directions: In this part, you will be asked to read several texts, such as advertisements, articles, instant messages, or examples of business correspondence. Each text is followed by several questions. Select the best answer and mark the corresponding letter (A), (B), (C), or (D) on your answer sheet.

PART 7 권장 풀이 시간 **54분**

Questions 147-148 refer to the following invitation.

All team leaders at Scanlon Marketing are invited to a special dinner!

The event will give you a chance to meet Miranda Jacobs, the award-winning graphic designer who will begin working with us next month.

Where: Cape Steakhouse (on the corner of Sixth Avenue and Balsam Street)
When: May 15 (from 6 P.M. to 10 P.M.)

Please note that the dinner will begin with some welcoming words from our CEO, so we ask that you do not arrive late. If you are planning on attending, please notify our receptionist, Neal Pringle, by noon on May 12.

We hope to see you there!

---

147. What is the purpose of the event?

(A) To introduce a new employee
(B) To promote a company's products
(C) To celebrate a worker's promotion
(D) To announce a special project

148. What will happen at the event?

(A) A design will be revealed.
(B) An award will be handed out.
(C) A speech will be made.
(D) A demonstration will be given.

GO ON TO THE NEXT PAGE

Questions 149-150 refer to the following e-mail.

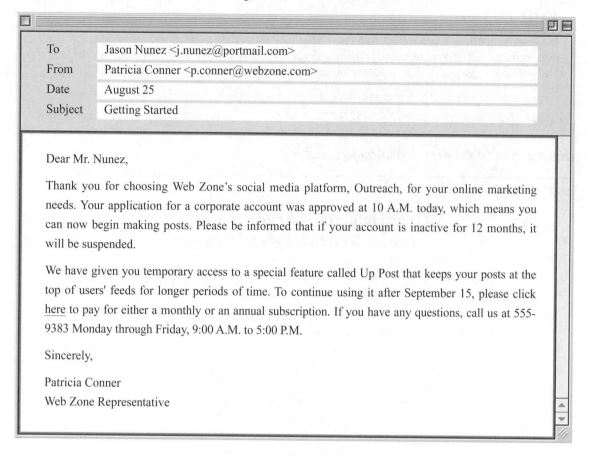

To	Jason Nunez <j.nunez@portmail.com>
From	Patricia Conner <p.conner@webzone.com>
Date	August 25
Subject	Getting Started

Dear Mr. Nunez,

Thank you for choosing Web Zone's social media platform, Outreach, for your online marketing needs. Your application for a corporate account was approved at 10 A.M. today, which means you can now begin making posts. Please be informed that if your account is inactive for 12 months, it will be suspended.

We have given you temporary access to a special feature called Up Post that keeps your posts at the top of users' feeds for longer periods of time. To continue using it after September 15, please click here to pay for either a monthly or an annual subscription. If you have any questions, call us at 555-9383 Monday through Friday, 9:00 A.M. to 5:00 P.M.

Sincerely,

Patricia Conner
Web Zone Representative

149. What happened on August 25?

(A) An account was activated.
(B) An online post was deleted.
(C) An application was rejected.
(D) A public event was announced.

150. What should Mr. Nunez do to retain access to Up Post?

(A) Call a representative
(B) Visit a service center
(C) Upgrade a subscription
(D) Make a payment

Ari Pearson (1:20 P.M.) Thank you for contacting the Westinghouse Appliances customer service center. How can I help you today?

Sarit Phan (1:21 P.M.) Hi. A technician is supposed to visit my home at 4 P.M. today to repair the dishwasher I purchased from one of your stores. But I have been called into work unexpectedly. Could I arrange another time?

Ari Pearson (1:23 P.M.) Of course, Mr. Phan. When do you have in mind?

Sarit Phan (1:24 P.M.) Well, I am free all day Friday. Maybe a repairperson could come to my home around noon?

Ari Pearson (1:25 P.M.) Friday is a national holiday. Is there another day that would work for you?

Sarit Phan (1:27 P.M.) Let me check my schedule for next week and get back to you.

Ari Pearson (1:27 P.M.) No problem. I will cancel your service request for this afternoon in the meantime.

[Send]

TEST 2

해커스 토익 실전 LC+RC 2

151. Why did Mr. Phan contact the customer service center?

(A) To request a refund for a recent purchase
(B) To confirm when a delivery will arrive
(C) To complain about a defective appliance
(D) To change a scheduled appointment

152. At 1:25 P.M., what does Ms. Pearson most likely mean when she writes, "Friday is a national holiday"?

(A) She hopes that Mr. Phan visits a store on another day.
(B) She realizes that a facility will change its hours of operation.
(C) She wants to notify Mr. Phan that a technician is unavailable.
(D) She needs to receive payment of an additional charge.

GO ON TO THE NEXT PAGE

MEMO

To: All Staff
From: Klaus Fischer, General Manager
Date: June 30
Subject: Summer Blowout Event

From July 20 to August 10, the Langford Department Store will be holding its first Summer Blowout Event. Customers will be able to save up to 40 percent on everything in the store. Because we will attract many more customers than we ordinarily do, we ask that employees avoid unnecessary absences. Of course, if you are ill or have an emergency situation, that is acceptable. However, please do not schedule your vacation until the sale is over.

In appreciation of your efforts, all employees will receive a bonus payment on September 1. The exact amount will be announced on August 25, once we have calculated the effect of the sale on the store's profits.

Thank you for all your hard work.

---

153. What is indicated about the Langford Department Store?

(A) It plans to hire temporary staff for an event.
(B) It stays open later on Fridays.
(C) It gives monthly bonuses to its employees.
(D) It will offer discounts on all of its products.

154. The word "ordinarily" in paragraph 1, line 3, is closest in meaning to

(A) typically
(B) distinctly
(C) ideally
(D) dully

155. When will the employees receive a financial reward?

(A) On July 20
(B) On August 10
(C) On August 25
(D) On September 1

NOTICE

As you know, our hair salon recently underwent its annual inspection by the Department of Health and Safety. Overall, the results were satisfactory. But a few issues came up that everyone working here must address.

To begin with, scissors, combs, and other tools that come into direct contact with our clients must be sanitized immediately once they have been used. And never reuse a gown—it must be put in the laundry as soon as the client takes it off. Furthermore, you need to make sure that the bathrooms are cleaned in the mornings and afternoons. I will set up a schedule so that this task is divided evenly among all of you. Finally, when sweeping the floor, check for hair that has fallen under the counters.

Thank you for your attention to these matters. Please let me know if you have any questions.

Amanda Thompson

156. Where would the notice most likely be found?

(A) At the entrance of a school
(B) At the dry cleaner's
(C) In the lobby of a hospital
(D) In an employee break room

157. When should tools be sanitized?

(A) At the start of each day
(B) In the afternoon
(C) Upon a client's request
(D) After each use

158. What is NOT mentioned as an issue that needs to be addressed?

(A) Washing gowns
(B) Cleaning bathrooms
(C) Wiping counters
(D) Sweeping floors

GO ON TO THE NEXT PAGE

Questions 159-160 refer to the following online post.

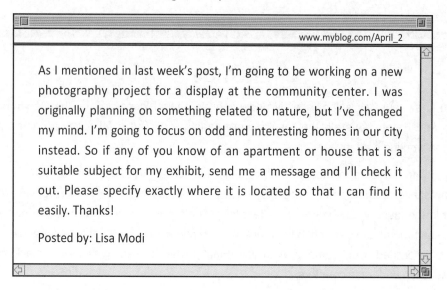

www.myblog.com/April_2

As I mentioned in last week's post, I'm going to be working on a new photography project for a display at the community center. I was originally planning on something related to nature, but I've changed my mind. I'm going to focus on odd and interesting homes in our city instead. So if any of you know of an apartment or house that is a suitable subject for my exhibit, send me a message and I'll check it out. Please specify exactly where it is located so that I can find it easily. Thanks!

Posted by: Lisa Modi

159. What is Ms. Modi's photography project about?

(A) Interesting vehicles
(B) Urban skylines
(C) Natural habitats
(D) Unusual residences

160. What does Ms. Modi request that people do?

(A) Submit an image of a structure
(B) Provide a specific location
(C) Contact the community center
(D) Read a message from an artist

Combining the excitement of ping-pong with a delightful dining experience, PingPong Plaza has implemented several policy changes to better serve our customers. — [1] —. We also have expanded our facility to accommodate more people. Please see the following changes:

- Ping-pong table rentals are now limited to two hours. — [2] —. However, there is no time constraint for events held in our new private rooms.
- Each table reservation requires a one-beverage minimum order per person, with an extensive selection of beverages available.
- Reservations can be conveniently made online at www.pingpongplaza.com. We no longer accept reservations over the phone.
- Visitors under 18 years old must be accompanied by an adult after 10 P.M. — [3] —. Valid identification may be requested for age verification.

We have rooms available for large parties. — [4] —. For inquiries regarding private events, please e-mail private@pingpongplaza.com.

161. What is being announced?

(A) A grand opening of a business
(B) Changes to a dining menu
(C) Updates to regulations
(D) An upcoming private event

162. What is true about PingPong Plaza?

(A) It will be shutting down for a week.
(B) It offers a special rate for large groups.
(C) It will now accept bookings over the phone.
(D) It has increased the size of a structure.

163. What is NOT mentioned as a change at PingPong Plaza?

(A) A time limit
(B) An order minimum
(C) An age restriction
(D) A dining menu

164. In which of the positions marked [1], [2], [3], and [4] does the following sentence best belong?

"These can accommodate groups of up to 16 people."

(A) [1]
(B) [2]
(C) [3]
(D) [4]

Questions 165-168 refer to the following text-message chain.

Mike Beale [11:10 A.M.]

Good morning, Ms. Arai. This is Mike Beale from the Broadview Auto Shop. When I was changing your car tires this morning, I noticed a problem that needs to be dealt with.

Keiko Arai [11:11 A.M.]

Do you mean the big dent in the fender? If so, I don't think that needs to be fixed right away. It looks bad, but it doesn't affect my driving.

Mike Beale [11:12 A.M.]

Actually, it's your rear brakes. As I inspected your tires, I saw that the brakes are really worn. I would recommend replacing them for your own safety. Given that you are a regular client here, I can do the work for only $200, including parts and labor.

Keiko Arai [11:16 A.M.]

Ok. I guess I don't really have a choice. Can I still pick up my car tomorrow afternoon?

Mike Beale [11:17 A.M.]

Unfortunately, no. It won't be until next Wednesday at the earliest that the work is completed.

Keiko Arai [11:18 A.M.]

Next Wednesday? Really?

Mike Beale [11:20 A.M.]

Yeah. I'll need to order the parts for your car model because I don't currently have any in stock.

Keiko Arai [11:21 A.M.]

Got it. I was hoping to drive to my hometown to visit my parents this weekend, but I guess I can put that off. Please text me when the work is complete.

---

165. Why did Mr. Beale contact Ms. Arai?

(A) To provide a reason for a cost increase
(B) To recommend a free service
(C) To discuss an unexpected problem
(D) To request some additional customer information

166. What is expected to cost $200?

(A) Inspecting a vehicle
(B) Repairing a fender
(C) Changing tires
(D) Replacing brakes

167. At 11:18 A.M., what does Ms. Arai imply when she writes, "Next Wednesday"?

(A) Mr. Beale requires more time than expected.
(B) An order should be confirmed quickly.
(C) A task will be completed ahead of schedule.
(D) Ms. Arai cannot visit a shop on that day.

168. What is suggested about Ms. Arai?

(A) She visited her hometown last weekend.
(B) She will request help from her parents.
(C) She has decided to postpone a trip.
(D) She intends to drive her car today.

Questions 169-171 refer to the following e-mail.

To: Emma Davies <e.davies@acefinancial.co.uk>
From: Carl Brenner <c.brenner@acefinancial.co.uk>
Date: 25 March
Subject: Evaluations

Hi Emma,

You were originally scheduled to submit the performance evaluations of your team members by 12 April, but I would like to get them by 2 April instead. I realise that you are very busy analysing the quarterly sales figures as well, so I apologise for asking this of you at the last minute. But, I have no other choice. Our CEO has requested that I oversee the opening of our new regional office in Shanghai, and I will be departing on 8 April. As I will be gone for a period of two months, I have to wrap up any projects I have here before I leave. Obviously, this includes reviewing the evaluations of your team members.

If the new schedule proves unworkable for you, phone me and I will have another team manager complete the analysis. The evaluations should be your priority over the next week.

Thanks,

Carl Brenner

169. What is the purpose of the e-mail?

(A) To determine the reason for a project delay
(B) To provide notice that a deadline has changed
(C) To suggest that a team include more members
(D) To inquire about the progress of new staff

170. What is indicated about Mr. Brenner?

(A) He has requested a transfer to another office.
(B) He is being considered for the CEO position.
(C) He conducted interviews of job applicants.
(D) He will work temporarily at a different branch.

171. Why would Ms. Davies most likely call Mr. Brenner?

(A) To arrange a meeting with a manager
(B) To discuss a previous evaluation
(C) To request that a task be reassigned
(D) To reschedule a training workshop

GO ON TO THE NEXT PAGE

Questions 172-175 refer to the following article.

SANTA MONICA (October 1)—In a surprise announcement, the Metro Art Gallery revealed that visitors will be able to view a collection of paintings by the famous abstract artist Philip Bernard from November 10 to 25. — [1] —. According to gallery director Marla Morris, she jumped at the sudden chance to work with such an esteemed figure in the art world. However, she was also quick to point out that the exhibit is the result of an unfortunate situation at another institution. — [2] —. "The Coleman Art Museum will be closed over the next several weeks while damage from a recent fire is repaired," she explained. "Mr. Bernard's works cannot be displayed there as originally planned, so his agent contacted us."

Despite the last-minute venue change, the gallery will offer complimentary guided tours twice daily to ensure visitors get the most from their experience. — [3] —. Tickets to enter the exhibit at the Metro Art Gallery have been priced at $25 and are available at www. metroart.com/admission. — [4] —. Admirers of Mr. Bernard should also note that the artist has for the first time given permission for prints of his paintings to be sold. "This is a unique opportunity that no art lover will want to pass up," said Ms. Morris. "I would urge anyone who visits our gallery during the exhibit to take advantage of it."

172. What is true about the Metro Art Gallery?

(A) It is operated by a well-known local artist.
(B) It has repaired some damage from a fire.
(C) It is co-hosting an event with another gallery.
(D) It will hold a special exhibit next month.

173. What is suggested about Mr. Bernard?

(A) He hopes to find a replacement for his current agent.
(B) He was required to find an alternative venue.
(C) He will display his art for the first time next month.
(D) He sold some paintings to the Metro Art Gallery.

174. What does Ms. Morris encourage visitors to do?

(A) Post reviews on a gallery Web site
(B) Take pictures of items on display
(C) Buy images of artworks
(D) Take a guided tour

175. In which of the positions marked [1], [2], [3], and [4] does the following sentence best belong?

"They are expected to sell out quickly due to the high level of interest in this artist's work."

(A) [1]
(B) [2]
(C) [3]
(D) [4]

GO ON TO THE NEXT PAGE

FOR IMMEDIATE RELEASE

CHICAGO (January 14)—WorkHere, a startup with co-working spaces throughout the country, will be launching its first branch in Chicago on February 17. Located in the Boxwood neighborhood, the facility will be the largest of its kind in the city.

Myra Sanders, who started WorkHere seven years ago in New York, is confident that there will be great demand for her company's services. "With the ongoing transition to the gig economy, more and more professionals in the Chicago area are working on a freelance basis," she explained.

The facility will feature all of the standard amenities of a co-working space, including Wi-Fi, comfortable workstations, meeting rooms, and printers. But Sanders wants her clients to see it as more than just a place to work. "We will include a game room, a gym, and even a lounge for the exclusive use of individuals with an annual WorkHere membership," she said. "We want people to interact with each other to expand their social and professional networks."

---

https://chicagobusinessreview.com

I was finding it hard to focus working from home as an independent software engineer, so I decided to try WorkHere. I am glad I did. The facility is very spacious, so I can always find a workstation that provides me with privacy. I also appreciate the stable, high-speed Internet connection and helpful staff. The facility includes a fitness center that I enjoy using after work. This has made me feel healthier and less stressed. My only complaint is the parking situation. There are no subway stations nearby, so I have to drive there. But the fees are really starting to add up. That being said, I highly recommend WorkHere to all of the freelancers out there.

Reviewed by Salman Rane on March 21

176. What is the purpose of the press release?

(A) To provide information about a branch opening

(B) To explain a decision to close a business

(C) To introduce a newly hired corporate executive

(D) To announce the formation of a new company

177. What is indicated about Ms. Sanders?

(A) She is a long-term Chicago resident.

(B) She currently works as a freelancer.

(C) She will move her firm to New York.

(D) She is the founder of a company.

178. In the press release, the word "expand" in paragraph 3, line 5, is closest in meaning to

(A) prolong

(B) broaden

(C) produce

(D) function

179. What is most likely true about Mr. Rane?

(A) He is an employee of a software company.

(B) He has used WorkHere in several cities.

(C) He purchased a one-year membership.

(D) He recently accepted a full-time position.

180. What did Mr. Rane suggest about the WorkHere facility in the review?

(A) It is easily accessible by public transit.

(B) It has issues with its Internet connection.

(C) It needs to add more workstations.

(D) It charges its users for parking.

GO ON TO THE NEXT PAGE

Questions 181-185 refer to the following e-mail and ticket.

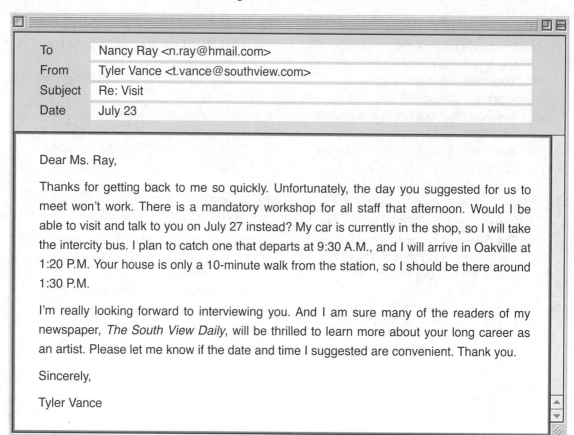

To: Nancy Ray <n.ray@hmail.com>
From: Tyler Vance <t.vance@southview.com>
Subject: Re: Visit
Date: July 23

Dear Ms. Ray,

Thanks for getting back to me so quickly. Unfortunately, the day you suggested for us to meet won't work. There is a mandatory workshop for all staff that afternoon. Would I be able to visit and talk to you on July 27 instead? My car is currently in the shop, so I will take the intercity bus. I plan to catch one that departs at 9:30 A.M., and I will arrive in Oakville at 1:20 P.M. Your house is only a 10-minute walk from the station, so I should be there around 1:30 P.M.

I'm really looking forward to interviewing you. And I am sure many of the readers of my newspaper, *The South View Daily*, will be thrilled to learn more about your long career as an artist. Please let me know if the date and time I suggested are convenient. Thank you.

Sincerely,

Tyler Vance

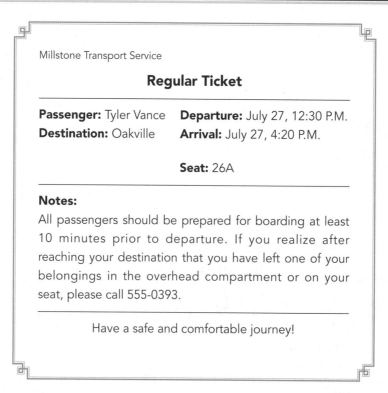

Millstone Transport Service

Regular Ticket

Passenger: Tyler Vance **Departure:** July 27, 12:30 P.M.
Destination: Oakville **Arrival:** July 27, 4:20 P.M.

Seat: 26A

Notes:
All passengers should be prepared for boarding at least 10 minutes prior to departure. If you realize after reaching your destination that you have left one of your belongings in the overhead compartment or on your seat, please call 555-0393.

Have a safe and comfortable journey!

181. What is the purpose of the e-mail?

(A) To decline an interview
(B) To arrange a meeting
(C) To organize an exhibit
(D) To make a reservation

182. According to the e-mail, why did Mr. Vance decide to take a bus?

(A) His vehicle is being repaired.
(B) He wants to avoid traffic congestion.
(C) He is unfamiliar with the route to a town.
(D) His company will reimburse his travel expenses.

183. What is suggested in the e-mail?

(A) Ms. Ray has just started her career as an artist.
(B) Mr. Vance works as a journalist for a publication.
(C) Ms. Ray attended a recent art show in Oakville.
(D) Mr. Vance will skip the management workshop.

184. What is most likely true about Mr. Vance?

(A) He took a taxi from the station to Ms. Ray's home.
(B) He changed his destination prior to departure.
(C) He paid an extra fee to select a specific seat.
(D) He left for Oakville later than planned.

185. Why would someone call the phone number on the ticket?

(A) To request a schedule update
(B) To ask for a seat upgrade
(C) To confirm an arrival time
(D) To report a forgotten item

해커스 토익 실전 LC+RC 2

GO ON TO THE NEXT PAGE

Sunnyside Hospitality Institute (SHI)—The Key to Success!

Whether you are hoping to open a small bed & breakfast or land a job with a major hotel chain, SHI can help you develop the knowledge and skills you need to succeed in the hospitality industry. We take great pride in the comprehensive training we provide through our state-of-the-art online platform. We also ensure that each class is led by a qualified professional who has spent at least 10 years working in a wide range of accommodation facilities. Below are just a few of our most recently added classes:

- **Facility Operations (SHI203)**
  Liza Gomez will teach you a systematic approach to prevent disruptions that negatively affect the guest experience.

- **Client Relations (SHI403)**
  Brian Chen will give you the communication tools necessary to ensure that interactions with guests always leave them with a positive impression.

- **Online Bookings (SHI345)**
  Beth Richard will show you how to use various applications to boost profits.

- **Tourism Trends (SHI137)**
  Kyle Morrison will walk you through the developments currently affecting the hospitality industry as well as projected ones.

For a complete list of courses and information about how to register, click **here**.

---

www.shi.com/studentforums/post_28373

SHI Online Forum for Students

Post Date & Time: Tuesday, October 5, 10:21 P.M.
Poster Name: Burzak Deniz
Topic: Study Group

If anyone is interested in forming a study group for the final exam in Ms. Richard's class, please leave a reply to this post. There is a lot of material to cover, and it would be easier to stay focused studying with others. We could meet in the library in the evenings. I would be available to start any time after October 8, the deadline for the case study. I still need to finish one section, which will take me a couple days because it involves reviewing and summarizing financial information.

Case Study Outline

Name: Burzak Deniz

Section 1 – Introduction to the Stanford Inn
Section 2 – Analysis of quarterly revenues and expenses for the past three years
Section 3 – Comparison of marketing strategies under current and previous management
Section 4 – Efforts to streamline the online reservation system and projected impact

186. What is suggested about SHI?

(A) It partners with a major hotel chain.
(B) It does not focus on a specific industry.
(C) It does not offer in-person classes.
(D) It arranges internships for students.

187. According to the advertisement, what is a requirement to teach at SHI?

(A) Familiarity with designing booking applications
(B) An advanced degree in the hospitality field
(C) A decade of relevant work experience
(D) Knowledge of online marketing techniques

188. Which course is Mr. Deniz currently taking?

(A) Facility Operations
(B) Client Relations
(C) Online Bookings
(D) Tourism Trends

189. What is most likely true about Mr. Deniz?

(A) He received a high mark on a final exam.
(B) He will submit an assignment on October 8.
(C) He has posted on the SHI forum previously.
(D) He made a request for a deadline extension.

190. Which section of the case study will Mr. Deniz most likely finish last?

(A) Section 1
(B) Section 2
(C) Section 3
(D) Section 4

GO ON TO THE NEXT PAGE

Plaza Amusement Park
Grand Opening

By Kevin Burton

SHEFFIELD (25 JUNE)—The Plaza Amusement Park opened its gates for the first time on 20 June. Located about seven kilometres from central Sheffield, it features a carousel, a Ferris wheel, and even a waterslide. But the longest lines by far are for the Screaming Eagle—the largest roller coaster in the region.

Mayor Anderson participated in the ribbon-cutting ceremony for the park, which cost just under £8 million to construct. "This establishment will draw thousands of tourists to our community each year," he said during his speech. "It is projected to lead to a 12 percent expansion of our economy."

And to show appreciation to the residents of Sheffield, the Plaza Amusement Park will be offering them a 20 percent discount each Thursday during the summer.

---

www.reviews.com/sheffield

Posted on 10 July by Mark Hasselt

Review of the Plaza Amusement Park (4/5 Stars)

I took my children to the Plaza Amusement Park. Overall, I was quite impressed. The 20 percent discount made the entire day affordable, and my children loved the rides. The only suggestion I have is to increase the number of first aid stations. When my son cut his hand, we had to walk quite a distance to get treatment. But the attendant, Abigail Walker, was incredibly helpful. After bandaging the cut, she gave me some good advice about how to prevent infection.

To: Yuen Lam <y.lam@plazapark.co.uk>
From: Dan Peters <d.peters@plazapark.co.uk>
Subject: Re: Feedback
Date: 15 July

Hi Yuen,

Thank you for forwarding me the link to Mr. Hasselt's review. I agree that this issue needs to be dealt with, and I want to let you know my plan. I have identified several additional sites throughout the park for first aid stations. And I will begin interviewing medical personnel with the intention of hiring 15 more attendants. The new stations will be fully operational by 1 September. I should also mention that on Wednesday I met with the attendant who treated Mr. Hasselt's son. I made sure she was aware that her efforts were appreciated and gave her a £100 gift card.

Best,

Dan Peters

191. What does the article mention about the Plaza Amusement Park?

(A) It is located in the center of Sheffield.
(B) It has been open for several days.
(C) It holds a special ceremony each week.
(D) It is larger than any other in the region.

192. According to the article, what is the most popular attraction at the Plaza Amusement Park?

(A) A carousel
(B) A Ferris wheel
(C) A waterslide
(D) A roller coaster

193. What can be concluded about Mr. Hasselt?

(A) He was treated for an injury.
(B) He was unable to find an open first aid station.
(C) He visited the amusement park on Thursday.
(D) He felt that the lines for many rides were too long.

194. What is the purpose of the e-mail?

(A) To request additional resources for a project
(B) To ask for feedback on a policy
(C) To explain a decision to increase a budget
(D) To outline how a problem is being addressed

195. Who did Mr. Peters meet with on Wednesday?

(A) Kevin Burton
(B) Mark Hasselt
(C) Abigail Walker
(D) Yuen Lam

GO ON TO THE NEXT PAGE

Norton's Wholesale Produce

Client: Micah Appel (Owner of Boardwalk Bistro)
Date: April 25
Account #: 4837376

Item	Quantity	Price
Carrots	60 kilograms	$125.00
Romaine Lettuce	40 kilograms	$110.00
Strawberries	25 kilograms	$180.00
Cucumbers	40 kilograms	$105.00

Subtotal: $520.00
Delivery: N/A
Discount (15%): $78.00

Total: $442.00

Clients that do not wish to take advantage of our delivery service must contact our warehouse in advance to arrange a pickup time.

Attention, All Clients

At Norton's Wholesale Produce, we take great pride in providing affordable, farm-fresh fruits and vegetables. Unfortunately, the soaring inflation rate makes it necessary for us to raise the prices of most food items by up to 10 percent. These changes will take effect on June 1. While we understand that this news is unwelcome, it is important to note that our decision is part of an industry-wide trend. Our goods will continue to be reasonably priced compared to those of our competitors. If you find the same product being sold for less by another wholesaler, simply contact our sales team at 555-0239 and we will match the price. Furthermore, clients will continue to receive a 15 percent discount whenever they refer us to another business that places an order.

To: Marcos Holt <m.holt@norton.com>
From: Grace Chung <g.chung@norton.com>
Subject: Request
Date: June 25

Hi Marcos,

Samantha Cove, the owner of Brighton Deli, called yesterday to inform me that Fremont Grocers is offering tomatoes for just $1.60 per kilogram. I told her that we would make the necessary adjustments to her invoice, but I'm getting worried. She is the fourth customer to call me about this price difference. I think we may have to find a less expensive source of tomatoes. Could you check with the farms that we get our produce from and find out if any are willing to lower their prices?

Thank you,

Grace Chung

---

196. What does the invoice indicate about Boardwalk Bistro?

(A) It made a purchase of produce twice in April.
(B) It changed a quantity prior to making payment.
(C) It picked up an order from a storage facility.
(D) It experienced a change in ownership recently.

197. What can be concluded about Mr. Appel?

(A) He forgot to contact a warehouse.
(B) He requested a partial refund.
(C) He switched to a new wholesaler.
(D) He recommended a company.

198. According to the notice, what does Norton's Wholesale Produce intend to do on June 1?

(A) Form a partnership with a competitor
(B) Increase the cost of some products
(C) Offer a discount to long-term clients
(D) Expand the selection of items for sale

199. Which department does Ms. Chung most likely belong to?

(A) Human Resources
(B) Sales
(C) Accounting
(D) Customer Service

200. What does Ms. Chung ask Mr. Holt to do?

(A) Eliminate some expenses
(B) Revise a billing document
(C) Meet with a customer
(D) Contact some suppliers

This is the end of the test. You may review Parts 5, 6, and 7 if you finish the test early.

⟋Review 체크리스트

TEST 2를 푼 다음, 아래 체크리스트에 따라 틀린 문제를 리뷰하고 박스에 완료 여부를 표시하세요.
만약 시험까지 얼마 남지 않았다면, 파란색으로 표시된 항목이라도 꼭 확인하세요.

☐ 틀린 문제의 경우, 다시 풀어봤다.

☐ 틀린 문제의 경우, 스크립트/해석을 확인하며 지문/문제의 내용을 정확하게 파악했다.

☐ 해설을 통해 각 문제의 정답과 오답의 근거가 무엇인지 정확하게 파악했다.

☐ PART 1과 PART 2에서 틀린 문제의 경우, 선택한 오답의 유형이 무엇이었는지 확인하고 같
  은 함정에 빠지지 않도록 정리해두었다.

☐ PART 3와 PART 4의 각 문제에서 사용된 패러프레이징을 확인했다.

☐ PART 5와 PART 6의 경우, 틀린 문제에서 사용된 문법 포인트 또는 정답 및 오답 어휘를 정
  리했다.

☐ PART 6의 알맞은 문장 고르기 문제의 경우, 지문 전체를 정확하게 해석하며 전체 글의 흐
  름과 빈칸 주변 문맥을 정확하게 파악하는 연습을 했다.

☐ PART 7에서 질문과 보기의 키워드를 찾아 표시하며 지문에서 정답의 근거가 되는 문장이
  나 구절을 찾아보고, 문제에서 사용된 패러프레이징을 확인했다.

☐ PART 1~PART 4는 받아쓰기 & 쉐도잉 워크북을 활용하여, TEST에 수록된 핵심 문장을 받
  아쓰고 따라 읽으며 복습했다.

☐ PART 1~PART 7은 단어암기자료를 활용하여, TEST에 수록된 핵심 어휘와 표현을 암기
  했다.

많은 양의 문제를 푸는 것도 중요하지만, 틀린 문제를 제대로 리뷰하는 것도 중요합니다.
틀린 문제를 한 번 더 꼼꼼히 리뷰한다면, 빠른 시간 내에 효과적으로 목표 점수를 달성할 수 있습니다.

TEST 3

LISTENING TEST

PART 1
PART 2
PART 3
PART 4

READING TEST

PART 5
PART 6
PART 7

Review 체크리스트

잠깐! 테스트 전 아래 사항을 꼭 확인하세요.

휴대전화의 전원을 끄셨나요? 예 □
Answer Sheet(p.251), 연필, 지우개, 시계를 준비하셨나요? 예 □
Listening MP3를 들을 준비가 되셨나요? 예 □

모든 준비가 완료되었으면 목표 점수를 떠올린 후 테스트를 시작합니다.
테스트를 마친 후, Review 체크리스트(p.152)를 보며 자신이 틀린 문제를 반드시 복습합니다.

🎧 TEST 3.mp3
실전용 · 복습용 문제풀이 MP3 무료 다운로드 및 스트리밍 바로듣기 (HackersIngang.com)
＊ 실제 시험장의 소음까지 재현해 낸 고사장 소음/매미 버전 MP3, 영국식 · 호주식 발음 집중 MP3, 고속 버전 MP3까지 구매
하면 실전에 더욱 완벽히 대비할 수 있습니다.

무료MP3 바로듣기

LISTENING TEST

In this section, you must demonstrate your ability to understand spoken English. This section is divided into four parts and will take approximately 45 minutes to complete. Do not mark the answers in your test book. Use the answer sheet that is provided separately.

PART 1

Directions: For each question, you will listen to four short statements about a picture in your test book. These statements will not be printed and will only be spoken one time. Select the statement that best describes what is happening in the picture and mark the corresponding letter (A), (B), (C), or (D) on the answer sheet.

Sample Answer
Ⓐ ● Ⓒ Ⓓ

The statement that best describes the picture is (B), "The man is sitting at the desk." So, you should mark letter (B) on the answer sheet.

1.

2.

GO ON TO THE NEXT PAGE

3.

4.

5.

6.

GO ON TO THE NEXT PAGE

PART 2

Directions: For each question, you will listen to a statement or question followed by three possible responses spoken in English. They will not be printed and will only be spoken one time. Select the best response and mark the corresponding letter (A), (B), or (C) on your answer sheet.

7. Mark your answer on your answer sheet.

8. Mark your answer on your answer sheet.

9. Mark your answer on your answer sheet.

10. Mark your answer on your answer sheet.

11. Mark your answer on your answer sheet.

12. Mark your answer on your answer sheet.

13. Mark your answer on your answer sheet.

14. Mark your answer on your answer sheet.

15. Mark your answer on your answer sheet.

16. Mark your answer on your answer sheet.

17. Mark your answer on your answer sheet.

18. Mark your answer on your answer sheet.

19. Mark your answer on your answer sheet.

20. Mark your answer on your answer sheet.

21. Mark your answer on your answer sheet.

22. Mark your answer on your answer sheet.

23. Mark your answer on your answer sheet.

24. Mark your answer on your answer sheet.

25. Mark your answer on your answer sheet.

26. Mark your answer on your answer sheet.

27. Mark your answer on your answer sheet.

28. Mark your answer on your answer sheet.

29. Mark your answer on your answer sheet.

30. Mark your answer on your answer sheet.

31. Mark your answer on your answer sheet.

PART 3

Directions: In this part, you will listen to several conversations between two or more speakers. These conversations will not be printed and will only be spoken one time. For each conversation, you will be asked to answer three questions. Select the best response and mark the corresponding letter (A), (B), (C), or (D) on your answer sheet.

32. What are the speakers preparing for?
    (A) A training session
    (B) A safety inspection
    (C) A building renovation
    (D) A sales presentation

33. What does the woman ask the man to do?
    (A) Replace an item
    (B) Print a document
    (C) Meet an official
    (D) Confirm a date

34. What will the woman write down for the man?
    (A) A company name
    (B) An office address
    (C) A phone number
    (D) A security code

35. Why was the man in Melbourne?
    (A) To have a vacation
    (B) To visit with a relative
    (C) To attend a corporate event
    (D) To study marine life

36. How did the woman learn about the resort?
    (A) By speaking with a travel agent
    (B) By reading a brochure
    (C) By viewing online pictures
    (D) By talking to a friend

37. What can be inferred about the resort?
    (A) It is no longer open for business.
    (B) It has locations around the world.
    (C) It is difficult to get a reservation at.
    (D) It is unsuitable for individual travelers.

38. Where most likely do the speakers work?
    (A) At a recruiting agency
    (B) At a retail outlet
    (C) At a legal firm
    (D) At a marketing company

39. What is Janet concerned about?
    (A) An applicant is unqualified.
    (B) A team is behind schedule.
    (C) A department is understaffed.
    (D) An area is too small.

40. What will the man most likely do next?
    (A) Conduct some interviews
    (B) Check some résumés
    (C) Look at some advertisements
    (D) Meet with some clients

41. What is the man planning to do?
    (A) Establish a business
    (B) Hire a receptionist
    (C) Meet with a consultant
    (D) Renovate a workplace

42. Why does the woman suggest that the man not purchase Hyman products?
    (A) They are difficult to install.
    (B) They have gotten bad reviews.
    (C) They have increased in price.
    (D) They are almost out of stock.

43. What does the woman offer to do?
    (A) Restock some shelves
    (B) Share a technique
    (C) Bring out some products
    (D) Provide a refund

GO ON TO THE NEXT PAGE

44. What problem does the woman mention?

(A) A presentation was canceled.
(B) A noise is distracting.
(C) A client is complaining.
(D) A schedule was changed.

45. What does the woman suggest?

(A) Calling a technician
(B) Changing a setting
(C) Replacing a device
(D) Checking a message

46. What will most likely happen next?

(A) A reservation will be made.
(B) A meeting will be held.
(C) An order will be placed.
(D) An office will be cleaned.

---

47. What is mentioned about the product launch?

(A) It is not open to the public.
(B) It will not include any presentations.
(C) It is going to be broadcast live.
(D) It will include an intermission.

48. Why is the woman at the event?

(A) To help with a product demonstration
(B) To write an article about a device
(C) To deliver an opening speech
(D) To answer media questions

49. What does the man say he will do next?

(A) Send text messages
(B) Distribute press passes
(C) Speak with a staff member
(D) Update an attendee list

50. Where does the conversation take place?

(A) At a tailor shop
(B) At a travel agency
(C) At a luggage store
(D) At a storage facility

51. What did the woman do yesterday?

(A) Renewed a membership
(B) Returned a purchase
(C) Booked a flight
(D) Joined a program

52. Why does the woman say, "I travel light"?

(A) To make a complaint
(B) To request a discount
(C) To reject a suggestion
(D) To recommend a brand

---

53. Who most likely are the speakers?

(A) Interior designers
(B) Real estate agents
(C) Construction workers
(D) Landscapers

54. What does Michael give the woman?

(A) Sales records
(B) An account number
(C) A floor plan
(D) Contact information

55. What does the woman plan to do this morning?

(A) Visit a dentist
(B) Call a client
(C) View a property
(D) Update a schedule

56. Who most likely is the man?

(A) An event organizer
(B) A photographer
(C) A food critic
(D) A reporter

57. What is mentioned about the event?

(A) It will be relocated to a different city.
(B) It will be held for the first time this year.
(C) It will allow attendees to try items for free.
(D) It will have participants from multiple countries.

58. What does the man recommend doing?

(A) Hiring additional employees
(B) Checking the event guidelines
(C) Making a decision quickly
(D) Decorating a festival booth

59. What are the speakers doing?

(A) Conducting some research
(B) Updating a Web site
(C) Repairing some equipment
(D) Preparing for a presentation

60. What problem does the man mention?

(A) He is late for a flight.
(B) A storage device is missing.
(C) Some e-mails were deleted.
(D) He misplaced some handouts.

61. Why does the woman say, "It's what's best for the environment"?

(A) To express support for an idea
(B) To propose a different plan
(C) To suggest delaying an activity
(D) To recommend another material

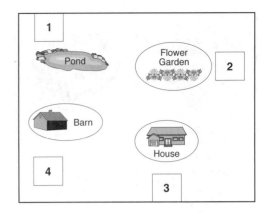

62. What did the woman do last month?

(A) Started a company
(B) Renovated a building
(C) Purchased a property
(D) Completed a project

63. Look at the graphic. Where does the woman want the guesthouse built?

(A) Location 1
(B) Location 2
(C) Location 3
(D) Location 4

64. What does the woman wonder about?

(A) When a construction project will end
(B) How long permits will take to get
(C) What the total cost of a building will be
(D) Who will submit a completed form

GO ON TO THE NEXT PAGE

| Option 1 | Option 2 |
| Option 3 | Option 4 |

Western Bank Account #3156-093809 Withdrawals	
June 5	$20
June 12	$8
June 16	$5
June 22	$15

65. What did the woman discuss with a manager?

(A) A deadline extension
(B) A team expansion
(C) A project cancellation
(D) A design change

66. What does the woman say will happen tomorrow?

(A) A game will be held.
(B) A shipment will arrive.
(C) A sample will be created.
(D) An owner will call.

67. Look at the graphic. Which logo does the man prefer?

(A) Option 1
(B) Option 2
(C) Option 3
(D) Option 4

68. What does the man ask the woman for?

(A) An identification card
(B) A phone number
(C) A transaction receipt
(D) An account password

69. Look at the graphic. Which amount does the woman inquire about?

(A) $20
(B) $8
(C) $5
(D) $15

70. What does the man offer to do?

(A) Refund a charge
(B) Cancel a service
(C) Open an account
(D) Explain an option

PART 4

Directions: In this part, you will listen to several short talks by a single speaker. These talks will not be printed and will only be spoken one time. For each talk, you will be asked to answer three questions. Select the best response and mark the corresponding letter (A), (B), (C), or (D) on your answer sheet.

71. What is the speaker mainly discussing?
    (A) Changes to a work schedule
    (B) Plans for a regular event
    (C) Results from a quarterly report
    (D) Topics for a future meeting

72. Who is Ms. Maxwell?
    (A) A technician
    (B) A salesperson
    (C) A receptionist
    (D) An accountant

73. What does the speaker ask the listeners to do?
    (A) Report a problem
    (B) Visit a venue
    (C) Address a complaint
    (D) Make a selection

74. Who is Nikki Lombard?
    (A) A painter
    (B) A musician
    (C) An author
    (D) An actress

75. What will happen momentarily?
    (A) A host will conduct an interview.
    (B) A band will perform some songs.
    (C) A sponsor will deliver a message.
    (D) A televised concert will begin.

76. According to the speaker, why should the listeners visit a Web site?
    (A) To place special requests
    (B) To give feedback on a show
    (C) To sign up for a giveaway
    (D) To learn more about a guest

77. What industry does the speaker most likely work in?
    (A) Aviation
    (B) Shipping
    (C) Hospitality
    (D) Medicine

78. What does the speaker say is a priority?
    (A) Organizing training sessions
    (B) Recruiting qualified workers
    (C) Promoting special offers
    (D) Increasing company profits

79. What benefit does the speaker mention?
    (A) Complimentary meals
    (B) Free transportation
    (C) Performance bonuses
    (D) Flexible schedules

80. What does the speaker's company sell?
    (A) Clothing
    (B) Utensils
    (C) Cosmetics
    (D) Bedding

81. What does the speaker mean when he says, "Your channel is quite popular"?
    (A) The listener will sign an exclusive contract.
    (B) The listener may require support.
    (C) The listener can increase sales.
    (D) The listener should change platforms.

82. What does the speaker ask the listener to provide?
    (A) A recording technique
    (B) A product preference
    (C) A development schedule
    (D) A compensation amount

GO ON TO THE NEXT PAGE

83. Where most likely is the speaker?

(A) At a bus stop
(B) At a train station
(C) At a ferry terminal
(D) At an airport

84. What does Mayor Fisher say about many residents of Newberg?

(A) They require cheaper transportation options.
(B) They tend to own more than one vehicle.
(C) They struggle to find affordable housing units.
(D) They have workplaces in another community.

85. According to the speaker, what is Wagner Transport planning to do in the future?

(A) Expand into more cities
(B) Hire additional employees
(C) Remove existing facilities
(D) Relocate to another country

86. Where do the listeners most likely work?

(A) At a bank
(B) At a restaurant
(C) At an electronics store
(D) At a catering company

87. What does the speaker reassure the listeners about?

(A) A device will be repaired soon.
(B) A payment will be accepted later.
(C) A schedule will be updated.
(D) A rule will be changed.

88. What does the speaker imply when she says, "There will be 30 instead of 10"?

(A) Additional employees are needed.
(B) A larger venue is recommended.
(C) Higher profits are expected.
(D) A significant delay is unavoidable.

89. What is the purpose of the talk?

(A) To postpone a planned company event
(B) To announce a power plant inspection
(C) To explain changes to an overtime policy
(D) To advise workers to be prepared

90. Why did the speaker's company send e-mails?

(A) An energy facility will be repaired.
(B) A project may be canceled.
(C) Power outages may occur.
(D) Fees will be increased.

91. What does the speaker want to know about in advance?

(A) Leave dates
(B) System changes
(C) Safety issues
(D) Project deadlines

92. What is the speaker discussing?

(A) A volunteer program
(B) A construction project
(C) A labor expense
(D) A transportation service

93. What does the speaker mean when she says, "But the client just chose another option"?

(A) A customer will be given a discount.
(B) A worker will present an alternative.
(C) A task will be completed on schedule.
(D) A budget will need to be increased.

94. According to the speaker, what will happen before noon?

(A) A product will be demonstrated.
(B) A contract will be negotiated.
(C) Supplies will be delivered.
(D) Clients will be notified.

Monday	☁
Tuesday	☀
Wednesday	☁
Thursday	☂

95. Where are the listeners?

(A) At a lake
(B) At a museum
(C) At a park
(D) At a school

96. Look at the graphic. What day is it today?

(A) Monday
(B) Tuesday
(C) Wednesday
(D) Thursday

97. What does the speaker say will happen in 30 minutes?

(A) The weather will change.
(B) A presentation will be given.
(C) The group will have a meal.
(D) A lecturer will give a talk.

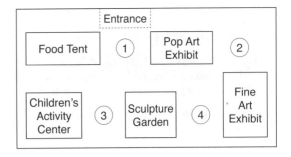

98. Look at the graphic. Where have additional booths been set up?

(A) Area 1
(B) Area 2
(C) Area 3
(D) Area 4

99. What does the speaker say about the artists?

(A) They requested additional spaces.
(B) They are all from Hollman City.
(C) They plan to take part in an art contest.
(D) They are members of an organization.

100. According to the speaker, what can be found on a mobile app?

(A) A venue map
(B) Artists' profiles
(C) A price list
(D) Food menus

This is the end of the Listening test. Turn to PART 5 in your test book.

GO ON TO THE NEXT PAGE

READING TEST

In this section, you must demonstrate your ability to read and comprehend English. You will be given a variety of texts and asked to answer questions about these texts. This section is divided into three parts and will take 75 minutes to complete.

Do not mark the answers in your test book. Use the answer sheet that is separately provided.

PART 5

Directions: In each question, you will be asked to review a statement that is missing a word or phrase. Four answer choices will be provided for each statement. Select the best answer and mark the corresponding letter (A), (B), (C), or (D) on the answer sheet.

🕐 **PART 5 권장 풀이 시간 11분**

101. Sonia Branson received the Science Communicator of the Year award for ------- television series on space.

(A) she
(B) hers
(C) her
(D) herself

102. Westport Financial charges reasonable transaction ------- for international bank transfers.

(A) fees
(B) volumes
(C) orders
(D) stocks

103. The project timeline was presented clearly ------- to keep all departments coordinated and on schedule.

(A) soon
(B) enough
(C) ever
(D) much

104. ------- route is taken from the Desmond Hotel to Atlanta International Airport, the travel time is approximately one hour.

(A) What
(B) Whichever
(C) However
(D) Another

105. The improved search function of Meter Market's Web site makes finding ------- items easier.

(A) suitability
(B) suitably
(C) suitable
(D) suitableness

106. As Systek's share of the laptop market has expanded ------- over the past year, the company is now enjoying record profits.

(A) tightly
(B) significantly
(C) responsibly
(D) thickly

107. Ms. Jensen believed her assistant was able to resolve her scheduling conflict in a ------- manner.

(A) satisfied
(B) satisfactory
(C) satisfaction
(D) satisfactorily

108. Oakville's local restaurants need to ------- with cleanliness standards and undergo annual inspections.

(A) associate
(B) discuss
(C) comply
(D) meet

109. In order to be considered for the open position, please contact the branch manager ------- by e-mail.

(A) direction
(B) directly
(C) directed
(D) directs

110. Canadian novelist Brad Wilkins published his first collection of short stories ------- the age of 26.

(A) in
(B) onto
(C) within
(D) at

111. Users will know the operating system has been installed ------- when a confirmation message pops up on the screen.

(A) closely
(B) curiously
(C) properly
(D) wishfully

112. To improve their report, the members of the marketing team added a few ------- showing their quarterly performance.

(A) visual
(B) visuals
(C) visually
(D) visualizes

113. Mr. Ingleby ran into a former university classmate at Nelson Station ------- he was waiting for his train to arrive.

(A) while
(B) during
(C) in order for
(D) since

114. After a week of orientation, the new employees have a ------- understanding of their duties.

(A) basic
(B) waived
(C) considerate
(D) chronic

115. Displays of popular brands are ------- placed throughout Winston Supermarket.

(A) strategy
(B) strategized
(C) strategically
(D) strategic

116. Security guards stand at the entrance to BioPharm's laboratory, where only ------- employees are allowed.

(A) concerned
(B) authorized
(C) vacant
(D) equal

117. The hike to the mountain was much more physically exhausting than the tour group members -------.

(A) anticipating
(B) had anticipated
(C) anticipate
(D) have anticipated

118. The shipment from Windhorn Tools is checked thoroughly by the warehouse staff ------- its arrival.

(A) behind
(B) across
(C) among
(D) upon

119. When selecting articles for ------- in the *Journal of Healthcare Systems*, the editorial staff verifies the credentials of the authors.

(A) inclusive
(B) inclusion
(C) includes
(D) included

120. NeoTek has developed a more durable case to maximize the ------- of its devices.

(A) reality
(B) probability
(C) authority
(D) longevity

GO ON TO THE NEXT PAGE

121. As a mentor, Dr. Bae strives to be helpful, -------, and patient in guiding his mentees through their career challenges.

(A) personal
(B) personable
(C) personally
(D) person

122. Mr. Delgado plans to renew his annual fitness club membership before it ------- in May.

(A) varies
(B) occurs
(C) expires
(D) neglects

123. After hastily ------- the lease agreement for her apartment, Ms. Kwon realized that the termination date was incorrect.

(A) to review
(B) review
(C) reviewers
(D) reviewing

124. A representative of Thumb Landscaping will visit us today ------- identify a location to plant a garden.

(A) on behalf of
(B) due to
(C) in order to
(D) as though

125. Glen Paper Products expects to increase its sales revenues ------- 14 percent over the next three years.

(A) by
(B) plus
(C) on
(D) with

126. Because Mr. Cromer made a ------- argument in favor of expanding overseas, the board of directors approved his plan.

(A) tentative
(B) narrow
(C) renewable
(D) convincing

127. Milestone Energy's ------- innovations have the potential to change the energy industry.

(A) engineered
(B) engineers
(C) be engineered
(D) engineering

128. Residents of Holmes Tower are urged to be aware of the emergency exits ------- there is a fire.

(A) in case
(B) as of
(C) without
(D) unless

129. The weekend flea market attracts dealers ------- in rare books and antique jewelry.

(A) specialize
(B) specializing
(C) specially
(D) specialists

130. Linia Beverage may not achieve ------- this quarter because of delays with the launch of its new product line.

(A) reaction
(B) profitability
(C) alignment
(D) effect

PART 6

Directions: In this part, you will be asked to read four English texts. Each text is missing a word, phrase, or sentence. Select the answer choice that correctly completes the text and mark the corresponding letter (A), (B), (C), or (D) on the answer sheet.

PART 6 권장 풀이 시간 8분

Questions 131-134 refer to the following letter.

24 November

Dear Ms. Ishioka,

Thank you for being a regular reader of *Science Explorers*. Your loyalty is invaluable. -------.
131.
We always strive to deliver informative and high-quality content that captivates and

educates readers like you.

To ensure continued access, it's time to renew your -------. By doing this now, you'll enjoy
132.
------- articles over the coming year. These will include in-depth analyses of scientific
133.
breakthroughs.

------- you have any questions, just reach out to customer service at 555-0389. You may also
134.
contact us through any of our online channels.

Sincerely,

Science Explorers

---

131. (A) There have been some delays with a recent shipment.
(B) The information on our Web site was corrected by our editor.
(C) We hope you've enjoyed every issue of the magazine.
(D) Your letter will be published in a future edition.

132. (A) method
(B) subscription
(C) license
(D) lease

133. (A) excluding
(B) exclusive
(C) exclusion
(D) exclusively

134. (A) Even
(B) Although
(C) Later
(D) Should

GO ON TO THE NEXT PAGE

Questions 135-138 refer to the following article.

KENOSHA (July 10)—Seaward Engineering announced that it will open its first overseas branch in Singapore. -------, CEO Lyra Bradshaw plans to travel to the country next week.
135.
She will be interviewing several local candidates for the position of regional manager. -------.
136.

Bradshaw anticipates that the new branch will begin operations on September 1. With a staff of 40 engineers and 100 support workers, it will help Seaward Engineering ------- in lucrative
137.
projects in the Asian market. Bradshaw ------- this an important opportunity for the company.
138.
"Our analysis has shown that the entire Asian region is poised for growth. We've chosen Singapore as our base of operations because it offers key advantages for firms in our industry."

135. (A) If so
(B) Alternatively
(C) Consequently
(D) Nevertheless

136. (A) The candidate outlined a winning strategy for investors.
(B) She is impressed with the applicant who was selected.
(C) A hiring decision will be made by the end of the month.
(D) Her promotion was confirmed by the CEO yesterday.

137. (A) participates
(B) participate
(C) will participate
(D) participated

138. (A) achieves
(B) remembers
(C) rejects
(D) considers

Questions 139-142 refer to the following notice.

In the upcoming month, every Pizza Duke franchise ------- a Culinart B70 wood-fired pizza
                                                      139.
oven. We had concerns about replacing the ovens that we have depended on for many

years. -------, we have tested the Culinart B70 at selected locations since March, and most
       140.
customers agree that it produces a better-tasting pizza. -------. It will allow us to serve
                                                          141.
delicious pizzas to more customers.

From this week, branches nationwide will be closed during installation. Customers are going

to be notified of the ------- closures through signs posted at each branch.
                       142.

139. (A) received
     (B) will receive
     (C) is received
     (D) receiving

140. (A) For instance
     (B) In addition
     (C) In particular
     (D) However

141. (A) A chef from Italy is designing the pizza
         menu.
     (B) Wood-fired ovens are not suitable for
         all kitchens.
     (C) Customers also appreciate the faster
         cooking time.
     (D) You can purchase one for less than
         $2,000.

142. (A) temporary
     (B) previous
     (C) frequent
     (D) suspicious

GO ON TO THE NEXT PAGE

Questions 143-146 refer to the following e-mail.

To: customerservice@blendsolutions.ca
From: c.yang@cindyscoffee.ca
Date: 21 March
Subject: Wrong order

I placed an order with your company last Saturday and received the shipment yesterday.

I was very impressed by the fast delivery of the products, which ------- in just two days.
143.

-------, it appears there may have been a mistake with my order. I ordered two blenders for
144.
making smoothies, but instead, I received two food processors, which cannot crush ice.

------- 1 April, I plan to offer fresh fruit smoothies at my café. Could you please confirm
145.
whether it's possible to correct my order by next week? -------.
146.

Thank you for your attention to this matter.

Best Regards,

Cindy Yang
Cindy's Coffee

---

143. (A) verified
(B) arrived
(C) examined
(D) responded

144. (A) Moreover
(B) Unfortunately
(C) In short
(D) After all

145. (A) Start
(B) Starter
(C) Starts
(D) Starting

146. (A) If you need more time, I will have to make other plans.
(B) Cindy's Coffee has been a part of the community for five years.
(C) First-time visitors can sample the beverage for free.
(D) Spring is the best time to visit though the area is crowded.

PART 7

Directions: In this part, you will be asked to read several texts, such as advertisements, articles, instant messages, or examples of business correspondence. Each text is followed by several questions. Select the best answer and mark the corresponding letter (A), (B), (C), or (D) on your answer sheet.

PART 7 권장 풀이 시간 **54분**

Questions 147-148 refer to the following text-message chain.

Mike Lee [11:15 A.M.]
Hi, Tanya. I have a quick question. Where did you put the new paper cups? The order I placed should have arrived during your shift at the coffee shop last night.

Tanya Lewis [11:16 A.M.]
I put everything away, but I didn't see any paper cups. There were just napkins and straws in the box.

Mike Lee [11:19 A.M.]
That's really strange. I'll contact our supplier now. Oh, one more thing. Denise wants to take tomorrow morning off because her parents are visiting. Would you be able to cover her shift?

Tanya Lewis [11:20 A.M.]
I have a doctor's appointment at 10. It's my annual medical checkup, and I don't want to put it off.

Mike Lee [11:21 A.M.]
Don't worry. I'll ask one of the other employees.

147. Where do the writers most likely work?

(A) At a factory
(B) At a café
(C) At a supermarket
(D) At a delivery company

148. At 11:20 A.M., what does Ms. Lewis most likely mean when she writes, "I have a doctor's appointment at 10"?

(A) She will submit a leave request.
(B) She did not check a schedule.
(C) She cannot fill in for a coworker.
(D) She has a serious medical condition.

GO ON TO THE NEXT PAGE

Questions 149-150 refer to the following schedule.

	Brittany Klancy
10 A.M.–11 A.M.	Interview David Hong for the tech support position
11 A.M.–12 P.M.	Check the references of all candidates
12 P.M.–1 P.M.	Team lunch at Whitewater Seafood Buffet (confirm reservation)
1 P.M.–2 P.M.	Meeting with Mr. Wallace (show the hardcopy version of the accounting software manual with his requested revisions)
2 P.M.–3 P.M.	Review the proposed department budget
3 P.M.–4 P.M.	HR presentation → Rescheduled to the same time on Thursday
4 P.M.–5 P.M.	Process any pending work orders
5 P.M.–6 P.M.	Finalize the report with recommendations for equipment upgrades

149. What can be inferred about Ms. Klancy?

(A) She authorized the purchase of new equipment.
(B) She will provide a reference for a former employee.
(C) She intends to request a larger budget for her department.
(D) She is involved in the process of hiring a technician.

150. What must Ms. Klancy bring to the event starting at 1 P.M.?

(A) A financial report from the accounting team
(B) A manual outlining new company policies
(C) An updated version of a software program
(D) An instructional booklet for an application

Washtab
Clean with Care

Doing laundry got you down? Save time by using Washtab, your go-to laundry service. What sets us apart is our user-friendly mobile app. It makes getting your laundry done a breeze!

Here's how our service works:
Use the app to schedule a time for us to pick up your laundry. You can also select which type of detergent should be used and indicate whether you want your clothes ironed. We will collect your laundry at your requested time and then return it within 24 hours.

New customers receive an exclusive 50 percent discount on their first order.

151. What is stated about Washtab?

(A) It operates out of multiple locations.
(B) It sells some merchandise on its app.
(C) It lets clients arrange a service online.
(D) It requires 48 hours' notice for large jobs.

152. What is indicated about the discount?

(A) It is only for new customers.
(B) It is offered once a week.
(C) It requires a minimum order.
(D) It must be used this month.

GO ON TO THE NEXT PAGE

Questions 153-154 refer to the following letter.

4 October

Riccardo Garcia
49 Trinity Square
Toronto, Canada M6E 3MS

Dear Mr. Garcia,

Congratulations! Your application for a Ventra Capital ProVenture credit card has been approved. Please find the card enclosed with this letter. Use the ProVenture card for all your corporate purchases, and enjoy the following benefits:

• Earn 3 percent cashback on transportation, accommodations, and related travel expenses.
• Take advantage of a flexible credit limit that can be raised or lowered to meet your business needs.
• Reach our 24/7 call centre for emergencies from anywhere in the world.
• Save 30 percent on movie tickets at select theatres.

To activate the card, go to www.ventracapital.co.ca or give us a call at (604) 555-3290.

Best,

Sandra Cho

Sandra Cho
Ventra Capital

---

153. What is NOT mentioned as a benefit of the ProVenture card?

(A) It offers financial rewards to business travelers.
(B) It has a credit limit that can be changed as needed.
(C) It provides access to international customer support.
(D) It has a low annual fee for the first two years.

154. Why would Mr. Garcia visit a Web page?

(A) To check his account balance
(B) To update his contact information
(C) To make a credit card ready for use
(D) To get a security code

SEATTLE (February 3)—The bustling neighborhood of Pioneer Square finally has its very own public library branch. Located at 75 Yesler Way, the library occupies an old print shop that was sold to the city back in the 1970s.

Preserving much of the original building's interior and exterior, the new library radiates a nostalgic charm. Along with this, it boasts modern amenities, including a computer room with scanners and printers. Beyond lending books to residents, the library will also serve as a learning center that offers classes on topics ranging from résumé-building to gardening.

Most of the funds for the building's renovation came from the municipal and state governments. The work was also partly financed by corporate donors.

The library will open its doors to the community with a celebration on February 10. The day-long event will feature a range of activities and will begin with some words by Seattle mayor Gregory Wilkins. For more information, visit www.seattlelibraries.com/pioneer_square.

155. What is the purpose of the article?

(A) To announce the opening of a facility
(B) To explain a change to a library regulation
(C) To request donations for a public institution
(D) To describe the history of a notable building

156. What is indicated about the renovation project?

(A) It took longer than anticipated to finish.
(B) It was partly supported by company donations.
(C) It required closing down a major road.
(D) It had to be approved by a community's residents.

157. What will happen on February 10?

(A) Community leaders will meet.
(B) An online service will be launched.
(C) A public official will give a speech.
(D) Class instructors will be selected.

GO ON TO THE NEXT PAGE

Questions 158-160 refer to the following e-mail.

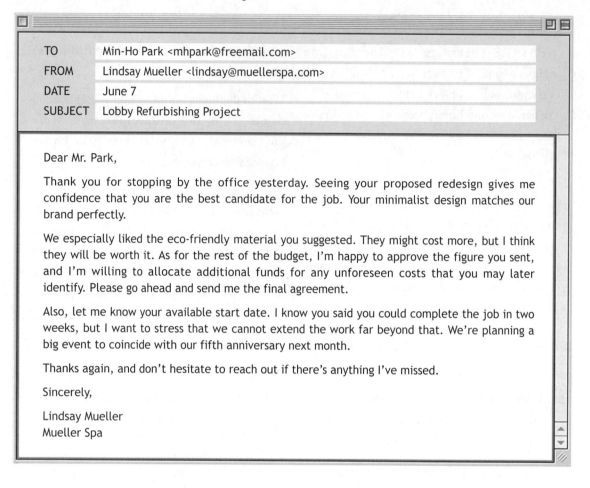

TO	Min-Ho Park <mhpark@freemail.com>
FROM	Lindsay Mueller <lindsay@muellerspa.com>
DATE	June 7
SUBJECT	Lobby Refurbishing Project

Dear Mr. Park,

Thank you for stopping by the office yesterday. Seeing your proposed redesign gives me confidence that you are the best candidate for the job. Your minimalist design matches our brand perfectly.

We especially liked the eco-friendly material you suggested. They might cost more, but I think they will be worth it. As for the rest of the budget, I'm happy to approve the figure you sent, and I'm willing to allocate additional funds for any unforeseen costs that you may later identify. Please go ahead and send me the final agreement.

Also, let me know your available start date. I know you said you could complete the job in two weeks, but I want to stress that we cannot extend the work far beyond that. We're planning a big event to coincide with our fifth anniversary next month.

Thanks again, and don't hesitate to reach out if there's anything I've missed.

Sincerely,

Lindsay Mueller
Mueller Spa

158. What did Mr. Park do on June 6?

(A) He visited a new spa facility.
(B) He presented a remodeling plan.
(C) He met with an interior decorator.
(D) He finalized a building blueprint.

159. What does Ms. Mueller mention about the budget?

(A) It includes the cost of hiring new employees.
(B) It matches that of another project.
(C) It has not been approved by her manager.
(D) It can be adjusted on Mr. Park's request.

160. What is true about Mueller Spa?

(A) It will offer a seasonal discount in two weeks.
(B) It is preparing to open a new branch.
(C) It is holding a celebration in July.
(D) It will change the look of its company logo.

Questions 161-164 refer to the following instructions.

A cover letter should be included whenever you submit your résumé for an open position. To write an effective one, there are a number of things that you must keep in mind. With regard to the basic elements, one of the most important is that the letter be no longer than a single page. — [1] —. You should also make sure that it is directed to a particular person-ideally, whoever is in charge of hiring. Do not rely on generic greetings such as "To Whom It May Concern" or "Dear Sir/Madam." And last but not least, proofread it carefully. Spelling and punctuation mistakes will make you look unprofessional.

In terms of the content, the first paragraph should explain how you heard about the position and why you are interested in it. — [2] —. The second should outline your hard skills and make reference to your work experience, qualifications, and so on that make you the ideal candidate. — [3] —. In the third paragraph, talk about your soft skills. For example, if you are an effective communicator who works well as a member of a team, you should mention it here. The final paragraph should briefly state your availability and how best to reach you with any follow-up questions or to arrange an interview. — [4] —.

161. For whom most likely are the instructions intended?

(A) Corporate executives
(B) Business owners
(C) College applicants
(D) Job seekers

162. What is NOT mentioned as a basic element of writing an effective letter?

(A) Keeping the length to one page
(B) Addressing it to a specific person
(C) Including an interesting greeting
(D) Checking it for any writing errors

163. What should be included in the last section of the letter?

(A) Educational achievements
(B) Personal interests
(C) Management experience
(D) Contact information

164. In which of the positions marked [1], [2], [3], and [4] does the following sentence best belong?

"Make sure to specify any certificates you have earned that are relevant."

(A) [1]
(B) [2]
(C) [3]
(D) [4]

GO ON TO THE NEXT PAGE

Questions 165-167 refer to the following information on a Web page.

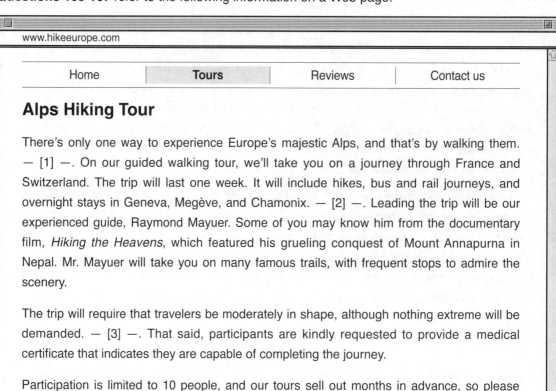

www.hikeeurope.com

| Home | **Tours** | Reviews | Contact us |

Alps Hiking Tour

There's only one way to experience Europe's majestic Alps, and that's by walking them. — [1] —. On our guided walking tour, we'll take you on a journey through France and Switzerland. The trip will last one week. It will include hikes, bus and rail journeys, and overnight stays in Geneva, Megève, and Chamonix. — [2] —. Leading the trip will be our experienced guide, Raymond Mayuer. Some of you may know him from the documentary film, *Hiking the Heavens*, which featured his grueling conquest of Mount Annapurna in Nepal. Mr. Mayuer will take you on many famous trails, with frequent stops to admire the scenery.

The trip will require that travelers be moderately in shape, although nothing extreme will be demanded. — [3] —. That said, participants are kindly requested to provide a medical certificate that indicates they are capable of completing the journey.

Participation is limited to 10 people, and our tours sell out months in advance, so please hurry. — [4] —. You can sign up <u>here</u>.

---

165. What is true about the Alps Hiking Tour?

(A) It will take place during the summer.
(B) It will pass through more than one country.
(C) It will last for over 10 days.
(D) It will be done entirely on foot.

166. What is suggested about Mr. Mayuer?

(A) He was recently hired by Hike Europe.
(B) He leads multiple tours a year.
(C) He authored a guide on hiking the Alps.
(D) He once appeared in a movie.

167. In which of the positions marked [1], [2], [3], and [4] does the following sentence best belong?

"We deliberately limit the difficulty of daily treks to accommodate all fitness levels."

(A) [1]
(B) [2]
(C) [3]
(D) [4]

Bedstay Introduces New Service

VANCOUVER (May 10)—Bedstay won't just let you stay in private residences, it will let you do as the locals do. Hoping to entice even more customers to its popular online rental platform, Bedstay recently announced the launch of a new service called Bedstay Encounters.

The service connects users with local hosts offering guided activities that cater to a range of interests, such as walking food tours of a city's marketplaces or yoga classes on a private beach. "The possibilities are endless," says Bedstay spokesperson Jerry Izumi, who adds that some "encounters" may even be customized to accommodate different group sizes and special requests.

Overall, the service offers users a new way to travel and connect with local communities while also allowing hosts to secure additional income. Currently, however, Bedstay Encounters is only being offered in eight countries across North America and Europe.

Still, the company has given assurances that it will gradually extend the service to all 120 countries that it operates in, noting that it receives thousands of inquiries daily from potential hosts. Bedstay, which recently reported record quarterly revenues, has grown to dominate the market for vacation rentals since it was established 15 years ago.

168. According to the article, what can Bedstay Encounters' users do?

(A) Extend rental periods at no charge
(B) Take part in activities with residents
(C) Get passes for popular attractions
(D) Enjoy exclusive deals on online transactions

169. The word "secure" in paragraph 3, line 2, is closest in meaning to

(A) protect
(B) obtain
(C) intensify
(D) consider

170. What is mentioned about Bedstay Encounters?

(A) It provides catering services for events.
(B) It has many followers on social media.
(C) It is currently not offered in Asia.
(D) It was originally conceived by Mr. Izumi.

171. What is a recent achievement of Bedstay?

(A) It opened additional branches.
(B) It merged with a travel company.
(C) It generated increased earnings.
(D) It received an industry award.

GO ON TO THE NEXT PAGE

Questions 172-175 refer to the following online chat discussion.

Tom Mercer (3:22 P.M.)		Hey, I wanted to remind everyone that the new model of the Proto ML55 sedan comes out tomorrow. We'll have several displayed in the front of the lot.
Gina Young (3:24 P.M.)		Yeah, I've seen the advertisements. The first model was popular, and I expect the new one to sell well too.
Tom Mercer (3:24 P.M.)		It has a lot of advantages over its predecessor. It's very fuel efficient, getting about 30 miles to the gallon. And it comes with a voice-controlled GPS navigation system. These will be major selling points.
Frank Chen (3:25 P.M.)		Right. And the advanced safety features like automatic braking and blind-spot monitoring are sure to appeal to customers. What do you think about putting up a sign that lists these benefits?
Tom Mercer (3:26 P.M.)		Agreed. We should also mention the free supplementary car insurance we're offering. That's something that distinguishes us from other dealerships.
Gina Young (3:27 P.M.)		Tom, do you want us to come in early to set up the new cars?
Tom Mercer (3:28 P.M.)		No. Greg will be doing that tomorrow morning. But it would be great if someone could post an announcement on our social media page about the cars.
Gina Young (3:29 P.M.)		I've posted on that page before. Give me a couple of hours, and I'll have something ready.

Send

172. Where do the writers most likely work?

(A) At a car dealership
(B) At an insurance company
(C) At a marketing firm
(D) At an auto manufacturer

173. What is indicated about the Proto ML55 sedan?

(A) It has been found to have a number of safety issues.
(B) It is being manufactured overseas.
(C) It is available in three different models.
(D) It has a voice-activated guidance system.

174. According to Mr. Mercer, what will Greg do tomorrow?

(A) He will make an announcement to the other staff.
(B) He will fuel some cars for the use of customers.
(C) He will put up some posters on a wall.
(D) He will arrange some vehicles at a place of business.

175. At 3:29 P.M., what does Ms. Young most likely mean when she writes, "I've posted on that page before"?

(A) She wants to learn more about a topic.
(B) She is willing to perform a task.
(C) She feels a decision is misguided.
(D) She needs to change her plan.

GO ON TO THE NEXT PAGE

Rochester Comedy Festival

Experience the laughter at the Rochester Comedy Festival on 20 and 21 February! Join us at the Davies Convention Centre for two days of comedy by talented comedians from around the country. Catch hilarious performances on four stages, featuring renowned stars like Jimmy Caryn, Crystal Miller, Ed Xion, and more! Tickets for full access on both days are only £50.

The festival is brought to you by the Variety Channel, the nation's most-watched entertainment channel for 20 years. Don't miss the chance to be part of the live filming of *Funny Talk*, the channel's hit reality show hosted by Kelly Asher! You could even see yourself on TV.

Visit www.rochestercomedyfest.co.uk for schedule details and ticket purchases. Get ready for a weekend of laughter at the Rochester Comedy Festival!

Rochester Comedy Festival: A Laughter-Packed Triumph!

ROCHESTER (23 February)—The Rochester Comedy Festival, held on 20 and 21 February, was an outstanding success, drawing more attendees than ever before. Sponsored by the Variety Channel, this laughter-filled event exceeded expectations. Local university student Victor Romero said, "The festival was amazing, and I saw a lot of comedians. I also got to attend an after-party, where I met the host of *Funny Talk*."

For those who missed the live event, catch the highlights on Sunday, 28 February, at 8 P.M. on the Variety Channel, or stream the same footage at www.varietychannel.com/rochestercomedyfest. The success of the Rochester Comedy Festival has left everyone eagerly anticipating next year's event.

176. What is stated about the Davies Convention Centre?

(A) It hosts all of a region's largest festivals.
(B) It has multiple performance areas.
(C) It exclusively sells tickets at its box office.
(D) It is only operational for part of the year.

177. What is mentioned about the Variety Channel?

(A) It is mostly known for its news broadcasts.
(B) It produces a show with a live audience.
(C) It recently won an award.
(D) It is preparing to launch a new televised comedy series.

178. In the article, the word "drawing" in paragraph 1, line 3, is closest in meaning to

(A) attracting
(B) controlling
(C) designing
(D) appointing

179. Who most likely did Mr. Romero meet at an after-party?

(A) Jimmy Caryn
(B) Crystal Miller
(C) Ed Xion
(D) Kelly Asher

180. What does the article suggest about the Rochester Comedy Festival?

(A) It will announce a new lineup of comedians.
(B) It will be held a second time later in the year.
(C) It will not be shown in full on television.
(D) It can be viewed online with a payment.

GO ON TO THE NEXT PAGE

Service Contract Agreement

This contract represents an agreement between Olga Stein(client) and John Garrison(owner of Acorn Design). Each party accepts the terms, and these cannot be changed unless both agree to do so.

Project location: 3515 Gallatin Pike, Nashville, TN 37216
Start/End date: September 18/September 25
Client's contact number: 555-2010
Brief project description: Bushes in the front yard to be removed and replaced by a flower garden, a stone walkway to be added from the driveway to the front door, and tree branches to be trimmed

Total cost: $5,400
Deposit paid: $1,350 (Date of Payment: September 5)
Remainder due: $4,050

Acorn Design will not be held responsible for delays caused by issues beyond its control, including inclement weather and traffic accidents. The client agrees to pay the remainder of the cost within two weeks (by October 9) of the completion date.

Signature of owner: _____
Signature of client: _____

To: John Garrison <john@acorndesign.com>
From: Olga Stein <o.stein444@newmail.com>
Subject: Contract
Date: September 12

Dear Mr. Garrison,

Thank you for sending over the contract. However, I noticed that the address stated is not correct. My house number is 3511, not 3515. Could the contract be revised and sent back to me? Please ensure that this does not delay the start of the project. It's important that I improve the appearance of the front yard soon. My real estate agent said these changes will make the property more attractive to prospective buyers. Once I receive the corrected contract, I will sign it and send it back to you. I plan to give you a check for my remaining balance on the final day of your scheduled work at my home.

Sincerely,

Olga Stein

181. What business is Mr. Garrison most likely in?

(A) Hardware
(B) Landscaping
(C) Interior design
(D) Banking

182. What is NOT listed in the contract?

(A) The due date for an outstanding balance
(B) The client's phone number
(C) The date of a deposit
(D) The penalty for late payment

183. What is one purpose of the e-mail?

(A) To request a correction to a document
(B) To suggest a price reduction
(C) To confirm receipt of a payment
(D) To provide notice of a schedule change

184. What is suggested about Ms. Stein?

(A) She intends to visit Mr. Garrison's office next week.
(B) She has used Acorn Design's services before.
(C) She has made the decision to sell her home.
(D) She is currently employed as a real estate agent.

185. When does Ms. Stein plan to pay the remaining balance?

(A) On September 12
(B) On September 18
(C) On September 25
(D) On October 9

GO ON TO THE NEXT PAGE

www.ezclean.com/packages

Home Cleaning Packages

Package 1 (Custom)
One of our experts will first visit your home to discuss your needs and provide a cost estimate. Then, our cleaners will arrive on your chosen date to perform the services you requested.

Package 2 (Basic)
One cleaner will visit your home on a weekly or monthly basis to vacuum, mop, and dust all rooms.

Package 3 (Moving Day)
Before you move into your new home, three cleaners will visit the empty residence to scrub and sanitize all surfaces.

Package 4 (Windows Only)
Two cleaners will wash the interior and exterior windows of your home.

Package 5 (Spring Cleaning)
Each room in your home will be thoroughly scrubbed by four cleaners, who will also shampoo the furniture and carpets as well as wash the windows.

To: Customer Service <customerservice@ezclean.com>
From: Vince Bauer <v.bauer@redmail.com>
Date: March 5
Subject: Cleaning

Hello,

I live in a 120-square-meter apartment on Riverside Drive in downtown Charlottesville, and I'm interested in scheduling a time to have it professionally cleaned. I will be out of town for the first two weeks of April, and I would like the work to be done then.

I read several reviews of your company on a Web site for local businesses, and all of them were excellent. So I feel confident that everything will be done to my satisfaction. However, I should mention that I have rather severe allergies. I would appreciate it if you could let me know which cleaning products you use in advance so I can determine if they will cause any issues for me. I couldn't find this information on your Web site.

Thank you,

Vince Bauer

To: Vince Bauer <v.bauer@redmail.com>
From: Yasmin Karim <customerservice@ezclean.com>
Date: March 7
Subject: Re: Cleaning
Attachment: Info

Dear Mr. Bauer,

Thank you for contacting EZ Clean. Please see the attachment for the information you requested. Hopefully, there won't be any problems.

We have staff available to clean your house on April 6. You will just need to tell me how to gain access to your apartment while you are away. I will also need to know which cleaning package you are interested in. Given that this is your first time with us, I would recommend the one that involves four cleaners. That way, you can be assured that your apartment will be spotless.

Sincerely,

Yasmin Karim
Customer Service

186. What is mentioned about Package 1?

(A) Its availability is limited to specific dates.
(B) It requires a preliminary consultation.
(C) It involves a minimum of three cleaners.
(D) Its cost is affected by a home's location.

187. What is the purpose of the first e-mail?

(A) To provide a reason for a schedule change
(B) To confirm the address of a residence
(C) To arrange an appointment for a service
(D) To complain about an unprofessional employee

188. What does Mr. Bauer mention about EZ Clean?

(A) It received positive feedback online.
(B) It recently changed its prices.
(C) Its advertisement was impressive.
(D) It has another location in Charlottesville.

189. What is most likely included in Ms. Karim's e-mail attachment?

(A) Locations of business branches
(B) Names of available employees
(C) Costs of special services
(D) Types of cleaning products

190. Which package does Ms. Karim recommend?

(A) Package 2
(B) Package 3
(C) Package 4
(D) Package 5

GO ON TO THE NEXT PAGE

SAN JOSE (May 2)—Event promoter Uptown Live recently announced that it will be relocating from San Jose to Philadelphia. According to CEO Margaret Harris, the decision was largely due to financial considerations. "Philadelphia's government is providing a package of tax breaks and similar incentives to lure entertainment companies to the city," Ms. Harris said. "It is simply too good of an opportunity to pass up."

The company has already secured office space next to the Central Main light-rail station. The move will take place in the last week of May, and the new office will begin operations on June 1. Ms. Harris assured music fans that the transition will not affect the company's lineup of concerts for June.

MEMO

To: All Uptown Live Staff
From: Margaret Harris
Date: June 1
Subject: June Concerts

I hope all of you are settling into our new office here in Baxter Tower. Don't forget to visit the building management office to request a parking pass if you plan on driving to work.

I want to remind everyone that we must not let the move interfere with the performances we are putting on this month. Our company's reputation is dependent on everything going smoothly. Make sure to tell me as early as possible about any complications so I can take action to minimize the impact on ticketholders. Here is the schedule for this month's concerts:

Date	Performer	Venue
June 12	Saskia Bernstein	Moreland Stadium
June 18	Beth Lord	Sawyer Concert Hall
June 26	Bobby Cabillo	Brentwood Auditorium
June 26	Andy Lee	Moon Plaza

To: Brian Keeper <b.keeper@uptownlive.com>
From: Nicole Kim <nicole@sdmail.com>
Subject: Re: Request
Date: June 7

Dear Mr. Keeper,

I have some unfortunate news. Flooding in our area has resulted in severe water damage to the lobby and auditorium of the Sawyer Concert Hall. As the repairs will take at least three weeks to complete, I'm afraid we will have to rebook the concert Uptown Live plans to hold here this month. Please let me know a date in August that works.

I realize that Uptown Live will have to issue refunds to individuals who are unwilling to exchange their tickets. Fortunately, our insurance policy covers this cost. Please contact our insurance agent, Carla Adams, for an explanation of how to claim compensation. Her number is 555-9283.

Thank you for understanding.

Nicole Kim
Venue Manager

---

191. Why did Uptown Live move to Philadelphia?

(A) To qualify for financial support
(B) To gain access to a larger customer base
(C) To take part in an investment opportunity
(D) To work on a government project

192. What is suggested about Baxter Tower?

(A) It includes a television studio.
(B) It is near a public transit facility.
(C) Its opening date was delayed.
(D) Its parking lot will be expanded.

193. What does the memo indicate about the performances?

(A) Some will be held on the same day.
(B) One will occur earlier than scheduled.
(C) The performers have the same nationality.
(D) They attracted more fans than expected.

194. Which performer's concert will most likely be rescheduled?

(A) Saskia Bernstein
(B) Beth Lord
(C) Bobby Cabillo
(D) Andy Lee

195. Why will Mr. Keeper contact Ms. Adams?

(A) To discuss the launch of a new business
(B) To purchase some insurance for an event
(C) To inquire about a reimbursement process
(D) To schedule repairs for a damaged venue

GO ON TO THE NEXT PAGE

Questions 196-200 refer to the following e-mail, questionnaire, and schedule.

To: Steve More <s.more@paxton.com>
From: Lucy Barton <l.barton@paxton.com>
Subject: Mystery Shoppers
Date: November 15

Hi Steve,

I wanted to follow up on our previous discussion about the need to ensure that all of our supermarket branches maintain a high standard of cleanliness and customer service. To address this, I have decided to implement a mystery shopper program. It will allow us to assess store conditions and staff performance from the perspective of a customer.

Given that we do not want store employees to recognize our mystery shoppers, I will use temp staff for this project. I had a meeting with Mike Coyle from Dale Recruitment Services last week, and he assures me that his company can meet our needs. All of the store assessments will be completed by December 11, and I will send you an update then.

Let me know if you have any questions.

Lucy Barton
Regional Manager, Paxton Supermarket

Mystery Shopper Questionnaire

Name: Alexa Miller

One form must be filled out for each store visited. Please e-mail the completed form to Lucy Barton with "Mystery Shopper" in the subject line.

Please answer the following questions objectively:

1. **Was the store well organized?** ☐ Yes ☑ No
   Comment: I entered the store in the morning right after it opened. A delivery must have just come in as there were boxes everywhere. Instead of placing all the boxes in the back room, the staff started unpacking merchandise on the sales floor.

2. **Was the store spotlessly clean?** ☑ Yes ☐ No
   Comment: Apart from the boxes, the store appeared clean. I checked if there was dust on the shelves, but I couldn't detect any.

3. **Did a store representative approach you in a friendly manner right away?** ☐ Yes ☑ No
   Comment: The staff was busy with the boxes and didn't acknowledge me.

4. **Did a store representative tell you about the current promotion?** ☐ Yes ☑ No
   Comment: No one talked to me about it.

Mystery Shopper Schedule for New York City Branches

Date	Time	Mystery Shopper	Location
December 9	10 A.M. – 12 P.M.	Alexa Miller	Soho
	1 P.M.– 3 P.M.	Dillon Kasich	Harlem
	3 P.M. – 5 P.M.	Alexa Miller	5th Avenue
	6 P.M. – 8 P.M.	Alexa Miller	Lexington
December 10	9 A.M. – 11:30 A.M.	Dillon Kasich	5th Avenue
	12 P.M. – 2 P.M.	Martin Chan	Lexington
	2 P.M. – 4 P.M.	Martin Chan	Harlem
	5 P.M. – 7 P.M.	Dillon Kasich	Soho

196. What is the purpose of the e-mail?

(A) To provide information about new store locations

(B) To describe a serious customer service problem

(C) To request permission to hire more workers

(D) To announce the implementation of a program

197. According to the e-mail, what did Ms. Barton do last week?

(A) She reviewed performance assessments.

(B) She conducted job applicant interviews.

(C) She met with a company representative.

(D) She visited a competing retail outlet.

198. Which location is the feedback in the questionnaire about?

(A) Soho

(B) Harlem

(C) 5th Avenue

(D) Lexington

199. What is indicated in the questionnaire?

(A) An employee provided great customer service.

(B) The shelves had not been cleaned properly.

(C) The sales floor was crowded with people.

(D) A promotion was not shared with customers.

200. What is probably true about Mr. Chan?

(A) He was asked to visit a store on December 9.

(B) He is not a permanent employee of a supermarket chain.

(C) He organized the schedules of other mystery shoppers.

(D) He is the general manager of a recruiting company.

This is the end of the test. You may review Parts 5, 6, and 7 if you finish the test early.

점수 환산표 p.244 / 정답·해석·해설 [책 속의 책] p.95

▌다음 페이지에 있는 Review 체크리스트에 따라 틀린 문제를 다시 점검해보세요.

/Review 체크리스트

TEST 3를 푼 다음, 아래 체크리스트에 따라 틀린 문제를 리뷰하고 박스에 완료 여부를 표시하세요.
만약 시험까지 얼마 남지 않았다면, 파란색으로 표시된 항목이라도 꼭 확인하세요.

☐ 틀린 문제의 경우, 다시 풀어봤다.

☐ 틀린 문제의 경우, 스크립트/해석을 확인하며 지문/문제의 내용을 정확하게 파악했다.

☐ 해설을 통해 각 문제의 정답과 오답의 근거가 무엇인지 정확하게 파악했다.

☐ PART 1과 PART 2에서 틀린 문제의 경우, 선택한 오답의 유형이 무엇이었는지 확인하고 같
   은 함정에 빠지지 않도록 정리해두었다.

☐ PART 3와 PART 4의 각 문제에서 사용된 패러프레이징을 확인했다.

☐ PART 5와 PART 6의 경우, 틀린 문제에서 사용된 문법 포인트 또는 정답 및 오답 어휘를 정
   리했다.

☐ PART 6의 알맞은 문장 고르기 문제의 경우, 지문 전체를 정확하게 해석하며 전체 글의 흐
   름과 빈칸 주변 문맥을 정확하게 파악하는 연습을 했다.

☐ PART 7에서 질문과 보기의 키워드를 찾아 표시하며 지문에서 정답의 근거가 되는 문장이
   나 구절을 찾아보고, 문제에서 사용된 패러프레이징을 확인했다.

☐ PART 1~PART 4는 받아쓰기 & 쉐도잉 워크북을 활용하여, TEST에 수록된 핵심 문장을 받
   아쓰고 따라 읽으며 복습했다.

☐ PART 1~PART 7은 단어암기자료를 활용하여, TEST에 수록된 핵심 어휘와 표현을 암기
   했다.

많은 양의 문제를 푸는 것도 중요하지만, 틀린 문제를 제대로 리뷰하는 것도 중요합니다.
틀린 문제를 한 번 더 꼼꼼히 리뷰한다면, 빠른 시간 내에 효과적으로 목표 점수를 달성할 수 있습니다.

TEST 4

LISTENING TEST

PART **1**
PART **2**
PART **3**
PART **4**

READING TEST

PART **5**
PART **6**
PART **7**

Review 체크리스트

잠깐! 테스트 전 아래 사항을 꼭 확인하세요.

휴대전화의 전원을 끄셨나요? 예 □
Answer Sheet(p.253), 연필, 지우개, 시계를 준비하셨나요? 예 □
Listening MP3를 들을 준비가 되셨나요? 예 □

모든 준비가 완료되었으면 목표 점수를 떠올린 후 테스트를 시작합니다.
테스트를 마친 후, Review 체크리스트(p.194)를 보며 자신이 틀린 문제를 반드시 복습합니다.

🎧 TEST 4.mp3
실전용·복습용 문제풀이 MP3 무료 다운로드 및 스트리밍 바로듣기 (HackersIngang.com)
* 실제 시험장의 소음까지 재현해 낸 고사장 소음/매미 버전 MP3, 영국식·호주식 발음 집중 MP3, 고속 버전 MP3까지 구매
  하면 실전에 더욱 완벽히 대비할 수 있습니다.

무료MP3 바로듣기

LISTENING TEST

In this section, you must demonstrate your ability to understand spoken English. This section is divided into four parts and will take approximately 45 minutes to complete. Do not mark the answers in your test book. Use the answer sheet that is provided separately.

PART 1

Directions: For each question, you will listen to four short statements about a picture in your test book. These statements will not be printed and will only be spoken one time. Select the statement that best describes what is happening in the picture and mark the corresponding letter (A), (B), (C), or (D) on the answer sheet.

Sample Answer

The statement that best describes the picture is (B), "The man is sitting at the desk." So, you should mark letter (B) on the answer sheet.

1.

2.

GO ON TO THE NEXT PAGE ➡

3.

4.

5.

6.

GO ON TO THE NEXT PAGE

PART 2

Directions: For each question, you will listen to a statement or question followed by three possible responses spoken in English. They will not be printed and will only be spoken one time. Select the best response and mark the corresponding letter (A), (B), or (C) on your answer sheet.

7. Mark your answer on your answer sheet.

8. Mark your answer on your answer sheet.

9. Mark your answer on your answer sheet.

10. Mark your answer on your answer sheet.

11. Mark your answer on your answer sheet.

12. Mark your answer on your answer sheet.

13. Mark your answer on your answer sheet.

14. Mark your answer on your answer sheet.

15. Mark your answer on your answer sheet.

16. Mark your answer on your answer sheet.

17. Mark your answer on your answer sheet.

18. Mark your answer on your answer sheet.

19. Mark your answer on your answer sheet.

20. Mark your answer on your answer sheet.

21. Mark your answer on your answer sheet.

22. Mark your answer on your answer sheet.

23. Mark your answer on your answer sheet.

24. Mark your answer on your answer sheet.

25. Mark your answer on your answer sheet.

26. Mark your answer on your answer sheet.

27. Mark your answer on your answer sheet.

28. Mark your answer on your answer sheet.

29. Mark your answer on your answer sheet.

30. Mark your answer on your answer sheet.

31. Mark your answer on your answer sheet.

PART 3

Directions: In this part, you will listen to several conversations between two or more speakers. These conversations will not be printed and will only be spoken one time. For each conversation, you will be asked to answer three questions. Select the best response and mark the corresponding letter (A), (B), (C), or (D) on your answer sheet.

32. What did the man recently do?

(A) He prepared a dessert.
(B) He attended a gathering.
(C) He watched a cooking program.
(D) He purchased an appliance.

33. What does the man ask the woman to do?

(A) Provide some utensils
(B) Host a dinner party
(C) Share some recipes
(D) Taste a new dish

34. What does the woman recommend?

(A) Ordering food from a Web site
(B) Uploading some videos
(C) Signing up for a cooking school
(D) Watching a cook online

35. Where most likely are the speakers?

(A) At a concert hall
(B) At a community center
(C) At a sports stadium
(D) At a movie theater

36. What is the woman concerned about?

(A) What time a venue will open
(B) Where a building is located
(C) How long parking is allowed
(D) Where a vehicle was left

37. Why does the man tell the woman to hurry?

(A) An event is about to start.
(B) Tickets are almost sold out.
(C) Seats cannot be reserved.
(D) A service will not be available.

38. Why is the woman visiting the store?

(A) To exchange a product
(B) To return an item
(C) To purchase a gift
(D) To redeem a voucher

39. What will be celebrated tonight?

(A) A graduation
(B) A birthday
(C) A wedding
(D) A promotion

40. What does the man suggest?

(A) Going to a different store
(B) Buying a gift card
(C) Using an online service
(D) Joining a membership program

41. Who most likely are the speakers?

(A) Safety inspectors
(B) Tour guides
(C) Interior designers
(D) Property investors

42. What did Kevin do yesterday?

(A) He bought some supplies.
(B) He printed some copies.
(C) He conducted a workshop.
(D) He delivered some items.

43. What will the woman most likely do next?

(A) Review a plan
(B) Attend a meeting
(C) Retrieve a document
(D) Contact a client

GO ON TO THE NEXT PAGE

44. What are the speakers mainly discussing?

(A) A worker's performance
(B) A product review
(C) A company regulation
(D) A customer's complaint

45. What does the woman praise about the company?

(A) It has an inviting atmosphere.
(B) It offers many vacation days.
(C) It has a flexible scheduling system.
(D) It provides generous salaries.

46. What does the woman apologize for?

(A) Making a mistake in a report
(B) Failing to meet a deadline
(C) Arriving late for work
(D) Breaking some equipment

47. Where most likely do the speakers work?

(A) At a supermarket
(B) At a restaurant
(C) At a medical clinic
(D) At a catering company

48. Why does the woman say, "I'm planning to interview applicants soon"?

(A) To offer reassurance
(B) To ask for information
(C) To admit to a mistake
(D) To indicate uncertainty

49. What does the woman offer to do for the man?

(A) Prepare training materials
(B) Give store credit
(C) Increase overall compensation
(D) Provide additional leave

50. What event is the man planning?

(A) A company retreat
(B) A press conference
(C) A service launch
(D) A staff meeting

51. What does the woman suggest?

(A) Contacting a manager
(B) Reviewing a feature list
(C) Testing a mobile device
(D) Attending a presentation

52. Why will Ms. Jameson be unavailable next week?

(A) She will inspect a production facility.
(B) She will write an analysis report.
(C) She will meet with a potential client.
(D) She will go on a business trip.

53. Why did the man request an inspection?

(A) He intends to sell his vehicle.
(B) He plans to go on a road trip.
(C) He hopes to pay less for insurance.
(D) He wants to avoid costly repairs.

54. What problem did Penny notice?

(A) Some tires are in poor condition.
(B) A service charge is too high.
(C) An engine part is damaged.
(D) Some components are out of stock.

55. What will the man do next?

(A) Make an appointment
(B) Talk to a relative
(C) Log in to a Web site
(D) Confirm a payment

56. What type of business does the man work at?

(A) A real estate agency
(B) An environmental organization
(C) An architecture firm
(D) A recycling center

57. According to the woman, what do many people find surprising about a product?

(A) Its price
(B) Its availability
(C) Its quality
(D) Its source

58. Why does the man say, "my clients prioritize sustainability"?

(A) To justify a decision
(B) To point out a problem
(C) To reject a proposal
(D) To offer some advice

59. Where does the woman most likely work?

(A) At a financial institution
(B) At a travel agency
(C) At a clothing store
(D) At a dining establishment

60. What problem does the man mention?

(A) He paid the incorrect amount.
(B) He damaged a personal item.
(C) He lost a transaction record.
(D) He missed a promotional event.

61. What will the woman most likely do next?

(A) Conduct a survey
(B) Check a price
(C) Request a discount
(D) Confirm a policy

Material	Price (per cubic foot)
Oak	$27
Pine	$22
Spruce	$18
Cedar	$34

62. What is the conversation mainly about?

(A) Building a fence
(B) Constructing a bridge
(C) Repairing a building
(D) Replacing a gate

63. According to the man, how has the company been advertising?

(A) By sending e-mails
(B) By putting up signs
(C) By handing out flyers
(D) By posting online

64. Look at the graphic. Which material does the woman prefer?

(A) Oak
(B) Pine
(C) Spruce
(D) Cedar

GO ON TO THE NEXT PAGE

Package	Price	Video on Demand
Basic	$25	
Standard	$40	
Premium	$55	V
Advanced	$65	V

65. Who recommended that the woman try Sky High Cable?

(A) A coworker
(B) A friend
(C) A neighbor
(D) A relative

66. Look at the graphic. Which package is most suitable for the woman?

(A) Basic
(B) Standard
(C) Premium
(D) Advanced

67. What does the man say he will do?

(A) Send a product brochure
(B) Authorize a transaction
(C) Describe a new feature
(D) Arrange an appointment

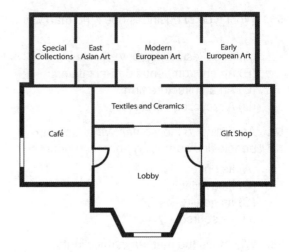

68. What does the woman mention about *Dutch Autumn*?

(A) It was purchased by another museum.
(B) It is Mr. Anderson's first painting.
(C) It was discussed in a publication.
(D) It is attracting many visitors.

69. According to the man, what will happen on May 21?

(A) A collection will be sold.
(B) An exhibit will be opened.
(C) An artist will receive an award.
(D) A museum will change its hours.

70. Look at the graphic. In which room are the works by Mr. Anderson located?

(A) East Asian Art
(B) Modern European Art
(C) Early European Art
(D) Textiles and Ceramics

Directions: In this part, you will listen to several short talks by a single speaker. These talks will not be printed and will only be spoken one time. For each talk, you will be asked to answer three questions. Select the best response and mark the corresponding letter (A), (B), (C), or (D) on your answer sheet.

71. What is the main purpose of the talk?

(A) To announce a company initiative
(B) To address recent client complaints
(C) To praise a team's performance
(D) To give reminders about an event

72. What does the speaker instruct the listeners to do?

(A) Arrive on time for appointments
(B) Double-check measurements
(C) Clean up after every job
(D) Perform a product test

73. What does the speaker say is important?

(A) Avoiding unnecessary delays
(B) Wearing proper safety gear
(C) Recalling information from training
(D) Providing good customer service

74. What is included in the price of the tour?

(A) A map of a building
(B) The viewing of a film
(C) The use of a device
(D) A copy of a guidebook

75. What does the speaker imply about Wildon Castle?

(A) It permits people to take photographs.
(B) It includes a booth that sells beverages.
(C) It offers ticket discounts to some visitors.
(D) It gets crowded at certain times of the day.

76. What are the listeners reminded to do?

(A) Browse a gift shop
(B) Return a rented item
(C) Leave an online review
(D) Avoid eating food

77. What is the purpose of the announcement?

(A) To explain why an event was canceled
(B) To give information about a race course
(C) To announce the finalists of a competition
(D) To provide notice of a schedule change

78. According to the speaker, what will happen on May 5?

(A) A thunderstorm will occur.
(B) A competition will be held.
(C) An awards ceremony will take place.
(D) Registration for an event will close.

79. What does the speaker imply when he says, "We have limited space near the water"?

(A) More space is needed for spectators.
(B) A different location will be chosen.
(C) An area is restricted to the public.
(D) Tickets may sell out soon.

80. What type of business does the speaker work for?

(A) A hotel chain
(B) An accounting firm
(C) A laundry service
(D) A delivery company

81. What problem does the speaker mention?

(A) An invoice was incorrect.
(B) A payment was not received.
(C) A shipment was missing.
(D) An e-mail was not answered.

82. What does the speaker say about tomorrow's service?

(A) It will take longer than usual.
(B) It will go on as planned.
(C) It needs to be rescheduled.
(D) It requires payment in advance.

GO ON TO THE NEXT PAGE

83. What industry does Ms. Beatty most likely work in?

(A) Agriculture
(B) Transportation
(C) Energy
(D) Robotics

84. What does the speaker mean when she says, "And 20 minutes scheduled"?

(A) An event has been added.
(B) Ms. Beatty is concerned about time.
(C) Ms. Beatty's speech was shortened.
(D) A plan has been changed.

85. What will happen at 2 P.M.?

(A) A video will be played.
(B) Refreshments will be served.
(C) Questions will be answered.
(D) A demonstration will be given.

---

86. What is the speaker mainly discussing?

(A) A potential customer
(B) An executive's promotion
(C) An equipment upgrade
(D) An advertising campaign

87. Where do the listeners most likely work?

(A) At a technical support center
(B) At a repair facility
(C) At a recruitment agency
(D) At a vehicle leasing company

88. What will Mr. Wallace check?

(A) A legal agreement
(B) A sales report
(C) A financial record
(D) A product description

---

89. What was the cause of the fire?

(A) Faulty equipment
(B) An unattended campfire
(C) Extreme weather
(D) A vehicle collision

90. Who is Mr. Hernandez?

(A) A company spokesperson
(B) A firefighter
(C) A city official
(D) A reporter

91. According to the report, what are residents of Holton Falls advised to do?

(A) Make a donation
(B) Read some guidelines
(C) Post some images
(D) Attend a class

---

92. What is mainly being discussed?

(A) Budget changes
(B) Training methods
(C) A company expansion
(D) A sales decline

93. What does the speaker's company produce?

(A) Furniture
(B) Software
(C) Luggage
(D) Footwear

94. Why does the speaker say, "You all have my e-mail address"?

(A) To remind the listeners how to get help with a project
(B) To tell the listeners to submit regular status updates
(C) To encourage the listeners to provide suggestions
(D) To ask the listeners to share contact information

Book Title	Checkout Date
Cross Channel: A Memoir	March 4
Early Modern Germany	March 6
Ancient Greek Philosophy	March 6
Black Forest: A Novel	March 8

95. Look at the graphic. Which book has the listener not yet returned?

(A) *Cross Channel: A Memoir*
(B) *Early Modern Germany*
(C) *Ancient Greek Philosophy*
(D) *Black Forest: A Novel*

96. What does the speaker mention about the library?

(A) It is closed one day a week.
(B) It increased overdue book fines.
(C) It has relocated its front desk.
(D) It will remove its drop-off box.

97. According to the speaker, what can library members do?

(A) Participate in free classes
(B) Watch popular movies
(C) Purchase used publications
(D) Access books in a digital format

Step 1 — Design Approval
Step 2 — Testing
Step 3 — Production
Step 4 — Product Launch

98. Which industry does the speaker work in?

(A) Electronics
(B) Housewares
(C) Fitness
(D) Clothing

99. Look at the graphic. Which step should be completed by June 15?

(A) Step 1
(B) Step 2
(C) Step 3
(D) Step 4

100. What does the speaker ask the listeners to do?

(A) Fill out some forms
(B) Recommend a service
(C) Assist some coworkers
(D) Reschedule a meeting

This is the end of the Listening test. Turn to PART 5 in your test book.

GO ON TO THE NEXT PAGE

READING TEST

In this section, you must demonstrate your ability to read and comprehend English. You will be given a variety of texts and asked to answer questions about these texts. This section is divided into three parts and will take 75 minutes to complete.

Do not mark the answers in your test book. Use the answer sheet that is separately provided.

PART 5

Directions: In each question, you will be asked to review a statement that is missing a word or phrase. Four answer choices will be provided for each statement. Select the best answer and mark the corresponding letter (A), (B), (C), or (D) on the answer sheet.

🕐 PART 5 권장 풀이 시간 **11분**

101. A political debate on the ------- of housing in the city will be broadcast on PBS on April 11.

(A) afford
(B) affording
(C) affordable
(D) affordability

102. The warranty for ------- machinery specifies that the owner can receive free inspections for five years.

(A) ours
(B) us
(C) our
(D) ourselves

103. The consumer trend report issued by Meicum Auto ------- that people are highly interested in electric cars.

(A) persuades
(B) discovers
(C) recommends
(D) suggests

104. The travel expense reimbursement requests should be submitted with receipts, ------- the accounting department will reject them.

(A) or
(B) by
(C) so
(D) but

105. The order that the purchasing team placed yesterday will be shipped ------- and will arrive within two days.

(A) prompt
(B) promptly
(C) prompted
(D) prompts

106. Please use the temporary ID card provided by human resources ------- you get the replacement.

(A) during
(B) until
(C) since
(D) also

107. A ------- of *Bizlast* magazine's most popular articles will be released as a limited-edition hardcover book.

(A) model
(B) type
(C) selection
(D) member

108. Asia Pacific Airlines is committed to ------- a convenient check-in experience and a high level of comfort on its flights.

(A) providers
(B) provide
(C) provision
(D) providing

109. Ms. Jahidmal has not ------- decided to accept the job offer she received from Pullman Chemical.

(A) once
(B) seldom
(C) yet
(D) shortly

110. The director explained that his movie was behind schedule because ------- weather had interfered with the filming of outdoor scenes.

(A) full
(B) severe
(C) precise
(D) scarce

111. Wrightvita Pharmacy's third branch is located ------- Greenwood Park.

(A) besides
(B) opposite
(C) into
(D) against

112. The software of the N350 smartphone will update automatically ------- the settings are changed to prevent it.

(A) unless
(B) now that
(C) almost
(D) whereas

113. Haskell Oil hired a senior accountant from Gold Accounting Ltd. ------- its corporate value.

(A) is evaluating
(B) will evaluate
(C) to evaluate
(D) evaluation

114. Noah Moskovitz is ------- of 12 people selected to participate in Verizon Group's summer internship program.

(A) both
(B) either
(C) one
(D) all

115. As rooms at the Coast Resort start at $500 per night, Mr. Hervey searched ------- for his vacation accommodations.

(A) anytime
(B) apart
(C) likewise
(D) elsewhere

116. The ------- made to customer invoices were a result of a pricing error discovered by the manager.

(A) roles
(B) setbacks
(C) clues
(D) adjustments

117. ------- sponsor of the St. Louis Pop Music Festival has its own designated stand for the duration of the event.

(A) Several
(B) Those
(C) Each
(D) Few

118. Radford Clinic is ------- for the security and integrity of its patients' medical records.

(A) eligible
(B) interactive
(C) accountable
(D) subject

119. The new system was introduced in order that the frequent issues occurring on the production line could be ------- addressed.

(A) effective
(B) effectively
(C) effected
(D) effects

120. Passengers bound for Howell Island should refrain ------- leaving the area as the ferry is boarding soon.

(A) past
(B) from
(C) upon
(D) onto

GO ON TO THE NEXT PAGE

121. The latest news about Picton's ------- of its main competitor was discussed on the *World Business* podcast today.

(A) acquire
(B) acquires
(C) acquired
(D) acquisition

122. The Evanston Public Library is now ------- with five self-checkout kiosks and a computer laboratory.

(A) presented
(B) equipped
(C) examined
(D) contained

123. Metlan's software is ------- the top three most widely used operating systems in the world, after Neusoft's and Adapta's.

(A) among
(B) prior to
(C) in between
(D) but for

124. Cyon Apparel will hold a press conference to address any ------- concerns about the company's financial health.

(A) deliberate
(B) accurate
(C) lingering
(D) versatile

125. For ------- coverage of unfair transactions, Kassandra Parker received a promotion at *The Chicago Slate* newspaper.

(A) except
(B) exceptional
(C) excepting
(D) exception

126. The rumor that ------- healthcare technologies were developed by MedPlus quickly spread throughout the stock market.

(A) promising
(B) to promise
(C) promised
(D) promise

127. ------- exciting is expected to be revealed in September by gaming start-up Void One, but no one knows what it is.

(A) Whatever
(B) Many
(C) Something
(D) Other

128. The furniture from Mados requires -------, but every product comes with the necessary tools.

(A) calculation
(B) assembly
(C) gravity
(D) inventory

129. All lawyers affiliated with Ross & Don Law ------- to continuously expand their knowledge of international law.

(A) encourage
(B) are encouraged
(C) encouraged
(D) have encouraged

130. Attracting talented applicants and retaining skilled workers are ------- challenging tasks for small business owners.

(A) often
(B) well
(C) far
(D) hard

PART 6

Directions: In this part, you will be asked to read four English texts. Each text is missing a word, phrase, or sentence. Select the answer choice that correctly completes the text and mark the corresponding letter (A), (B), (C), or (D) on the answer sheet.

🕐 **PART 6 권장 풀이 시간** **8분**

Questions 131-134 refer to the following notice.

NOTICE TO ALL FILM CREW MEMBERS

This weekend, we are shooting at Dolly Sods National Park. Shooting will start two hours ahead of schedule. That means you will have to be at the park entrance -------.
131.

When you arrive, look for the head of production. He will ------- you to your assigned place.
132.

We have little time to film our planned sequences, so all equipment must be set up and ready to go by 5 A.M. sharp. The director of photography ------- a rehearsal before the shoot.
133.

It would be wise for everyone to study the relevant portions of the script.

We've already arranged for a catering company to provide lunch. -------.
134.

---

131. (A) soon
(B) early
(C) briefly
(D) together

132. (A) allow
(B) direct
(C) mention
(D) resume

133. (A) was conducting
(B) conducted
(C) will conduct
(D) had to conduct

134. (A) We apologize for the inconvenience caused by the delay.
(B) There is a shortage of parking spaces near the entrance of the park.
(C) This is the most important sequence in the film.
(D) It will be served as soon as the morning shooting ends.

GO ON TO THE NEXT PAGE

Questions 135-138 refer to the following product description.

Slimline Computer Desk

Ferguson Furniture takes great pride in producing ------- home and office furniture. We have
                                                   135.

applied this approach to the design of the Slimline computer desk, which has a wide variety

of practical features.

What sets the Slimline computer desk apart is that it ------- to serve as either a standing or
                                              136.

sitting desk. -------. Regardless of ------- you use it, the ergonomic design will ensure that you
       137.   **138.**

never experience neck or back pain. It also includes a built-in power outlet with both

standard and USB sockets.

---

135. (A) seasonal
    (B) matching
    (C) functional
    (D) customizable

136. (A) was adjusting
    (B) by adjusting
    (C) has adjusted
    (D) can be adjusted

137. (A) We release a new line of furniture
        every spring and fall.
    (B) Refunds and exchanges are permitted
        within one week of purchase.
    (C) Just pull a lever to switch between the
        two modes.
    (D) You won't get a better deal from any
        of our competitors.

138. (A) how
    (B) which
    (C) whoever
    (D) whom

Blossom Haven: Your Floral Paradise Awaits

Visit our flower shop where your dreams come true! In Blossom Haven, you can discover a

stunning array of ------- flowers. Whether you're planning a special event or simply want to
139.

brighten someone's day, our florists are here to assist. -------.
140.

In celebration of our fourth anniversary, we have prepared a special gift for our valued

customers. For one week from April 1, all customers who ------- flowers at our store will
141.

receive a dried-flower frame made of marigold, lilac, and snapdragon.

-------, for the entire month of April, flower delivery is complimentary within Cumberland
142.

County. Visit www.blossomhaven.com to see photos of all our products.

---

139. (A) imported
(B) import
(C) importer
(D) importing

140. (A) There are various educational
institutions that train florists.
(B) Strict procedures should be followed
when exporting flowers.
(C) They are all professionals with over
three years of experience.
(D) Allow three to five days for delivery of
all flower orders.

141. (A) display
(B) purchase
(C) connect
(D) fold

142. (A) Instead
(B) If not
(C) After all
(D) Additionally

To: Hye-in Park <hipark@sabanbiz.com>
From: Leonard Smithers <l.smithers@mcclureconsulting.com>
Date: June 30
Subject: Follow-up

Dear Ms. Park,

We met at last week's seminar at the Millennium Center. As you'll recall, we talked about

rebranding your company and how McClure Consulting -------. My team and I have a
143.

proposal we'd like to present. We will be visiting your city July 12 ------- 16 for a trade
144.

convention. How about setting up a meeting around those dates?

We offer ------- services. The plan includes everything from positioning your brand
145.

competitively to eliciting customer loyalty and maintaining consistent messaging. Of course,

no plan will be complete without your feedback. -------. We look forward to your reply.
146.

Best Regards,

Leonard Smithers
Vice President, McClure Consulting

---

143. (A) that helps
(B) helped
(C) has helped
(D) could help

144. (A) along
(B) through
(C) beside
(D) toward

145. (A) arbitrary
(B) regional
(C) inflated
(D) comprehensive

146. (A) This is why we feel a detailed
discussion is necessary.
(B) Print ads are not as effective as they
once were.
(C) Customers responded positively to the
rebranding.
(D) Sales were up this quarter compared
to last year.

PART 7

Directions: In this part, you will be asked to read several texts, such as advertisements, articles, instant messages, or examples of business correspondence. Each text is followed by several questions. Select the best answer and mark the corresponding letter (A), (B), (C), or (D) on your answer sheet.

PART 7 권장 풀이 시간 **54분**

Questions 147-148 refer to the following product review.

Happy with My New Blender!

My old blender stopped working several weeks ago. As the warranty had expired, I decided to buy a new one. At first, I was considering the model my sister has. It's too expensive, though. Looking online didn't help because all the reviews seemed biased. But then a colleague suggested that I buy the Whirl Blade 234, and I'm glad I listened to him. I've been using it for a month now, and I'm very impressed. With five speed settings and a two-liter jug, I can use it to make everything from smoothies to soups. The only problem is that the base is quite bulky and takes up a lot of space on my counter. But this shortcoming is made up for by how quiet the blender is. I can't recommend it enough.

— Sofia Vega

---

147. Why did Ms. Vega select the Whirl Blade 234?

(A) It came with an extended warranty.
(B) It was the least costly option.
(C) It had many positive reviews online.
(D) It was recommended by a coworker.

148. What is one thing Ms. Vega does not like about the Whirl Blade 234?

(A) The limited number of speeds
(B) The low capacity of the jug
(C) The large size of the base
(D) The high level of noise

GO ON TO THE NEXT PAGE

Questions 149-150 refer to the following text-message chain.

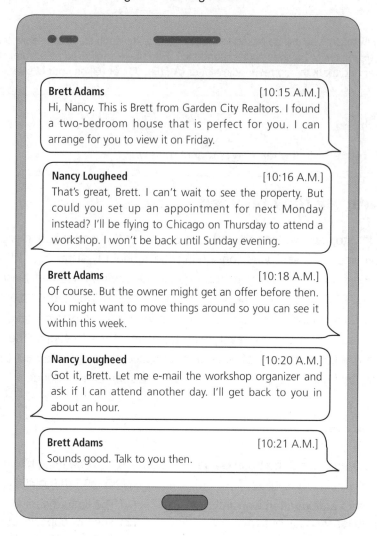

Brett Adams [10:15 A.M.]
Hi, Nancy. This is Brett from Garden City Realtors. I found a two-bedroom house that is perfect for you. I can arrange for you to view it on Friday.

Nancy Lougheed [10:16 A.M.]
That's great, Brett. I can't wait to see the property. But could you set up an appointment for next Monday instead? I'll be flying to Chicago on Thursday to attend a workshop. I won't be back until Sunday evening.

Brett Adams [10:18 A.M.]
Of course. But the owner might get an offer before then. You might want to move things around so you can see it within this week.

Nancy Lougheed [10:20 A.M.]
Got it, Brett. Let me e-mail the workshop organizer and ask if I can attend another day. I'll get back to you in about an hour.

Brett Adams [10:21 A.M.]
Sounds good. Talk to you then.

149. Why is Ms. Lougheed unavailable on Friday?

(A) She has a doctor's appointment.
(B) She has to inspect a property.
(C) She will meet a client for lunch.
(D) She plans to go on a business trip.

150. At 10:20 A.M., what does Ms. Lougheed mean when she writes, "Got it, Brett"?

(A) She intends to contact the owner.
(B) She is planning to move this week.
(C) She will try to follow his suggestion.
(D) She has already received his e-mail.

Questions 151-152 refer to the following e-mail.

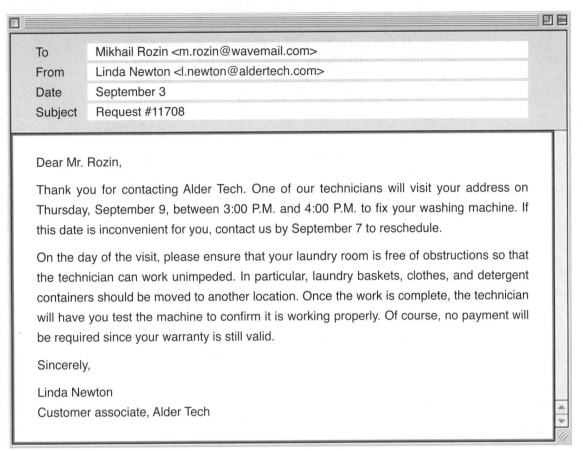

To	Mikhail Rozin <m.rozin@wavemail.com>
From	Linda Newton <l.newton@aldertech.com>
Date	September 3
Subject	Request #11708

Dear Mr. Rozin,

Thank you for contacting Alder Tech. One of our technicians will visit your address on Thursday, September 9, between 3:00 P.M. and 4:00 P.M. to fix your washing machine. If this date is inconvenient for you, contact us by September 7 to reschedule.

On the day of the visit, please ensure that your laundry room is free of obstructions so that the technician can work unimpeded. In particular, laundry baskets, clothes, and detergent containers should be moved to another location. Once the work is complete, the technician will have you test the machine to confirm it is working properly. Of course, no payment will be required since your warranty is still valid.

Sincerely,

Linda Newton
Customer associate, Alder Tech

151. What kind of service has Mr. Rozin most likely requested?

(A) A home renovation
(B) An appliance repair
(C) A safety inspection
(D) A device installation

152. What has Mr. Rozin been asked to do on Thursday?

(A) Confirm a payment was made
(B) Send his home address
(C) Remove items from an area
(D) Verify that a warranty is valid

GO ON TO THE NEXT PAGE

Questions 153-155 refer to the following article.

ALBANY (May 25)—Comfort Zone has released a new line of humidifiers that includes three models: the Fresh 370Z, the Mist 405E, and the Vapor 525X. The Fresh 370Z is the most expensive and the only one with Wi-Fi connectivity. Owners can turn it on and adjust its settings using their smartphones. In terms of capacity, the Vapor 525X has the smallest tank, holding only one liter of water. In contrast, the Mist 405E has a 2.2 liter tank, making it the largest of the three. One improvement that helps these three humidifiers stand out from previous models is their energy efficiency. They require very little electricity even when operating at their maximum levels.

Anyone in the market for a new humidifier should visit www.newproducts.com/comfortzone to look over early feedback from people who own one of these models. The humidifiers are available for purchase in all Comfort Zone stores and through the company's mobile application.

153. How is the Fresh 370Z different from the other models?

(A) It is possible to control through the Internet.
(B) It comes with a wide variety of accessories.
(C) It is able to turn on and off automatically.
(D) It is equipped with advanced safety settings.

154. What is an improvement shared by all three humidifiers?

(A) Simplified operation
(B) Increased durability
(C) Larger tank capacity
(D) Reduced power use

155. What does the article suggest that some people do?

(A) Complete an online customer survey
(B) Submit product feedback to a company
(C) Read customer reviews on a Web site
(D) Compare the prices of different models

Questions 156-158 refer to the following e-mail.

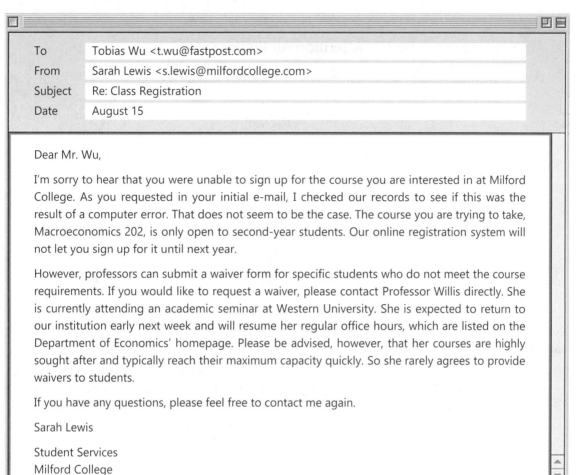

To	Tobias Wu <t.wu@fastpost.com>
From	Sarah Lewis <s.lewis@milfordcollege.com>
Subject	Re: Class Registration
Date	August 15

Dear Mr. Wu,

I'm sorry to hear that you were unable to sign up for the course you are interested in at Milford College. As you requested in your initial e-mail, I checked our records to see if this was the result of a computer error. That does not seem to be the case. The course you are trying to take, Macroeconomics 202, is only open to second-year students. Our online registration system will not let you sign up for it until next year.

However, professors can submit a waiver form for specific students who do not meet the course requirements. If you would like to request a waiver, please contact Professor Willis directly. She is currently attending an academic seminar at Western University. She is expected to return to our institution early next week and will resume her regular office hours, which are listed on the Department of Economics' homepage. Please be advised, however, that her courses are highly sought after and typically reach their maximum capacity quickly. So she rarely agrees to provide waivers to students.

If you have any questions, please feel free to contact me again.

Sarah Lewis

Student Services
Milford College

---

156. What is suggested about Tobias Wu?

(A) He missed the course registration deadline.
(B) He has taken Macroeconomics 202 previously.
(C) He is currently in his first year of college.
(D) He withdrew his tuition waiver request.

157. The word "meet" in paragraph 2, line 1, is closest in meaning to

(A) note
(B) fulfill
(C) encounter
(D) promise

158. What is NOT mentioned about Professor Willis?

(A) She is participating in a conference at another institution.
(B) She will go back to her usual work schedule next week.
(C) She teaches courses that attract many students.
(D) She has taught at Milford College for less than a year.

GO ON TO THE NEXT PAGE

Questions 159-160 refer to the following notice.

Attention All Visitors

We regret to announce that the special exhibit of ancient Roman and Greek artifacts has been postponed. Originally scheduled to run for the last two weeks of March, it will now begin on April 1 and end on April 12. The reason for the delay is an electrical problem in the hall where the items will be displayed. Our technicians will need to replace the wiring for all the light fixtures.

People who have purchased tickets for the exhibit but cannot visit during the new dates should contact our customer service department at (302) 555-0393 by March 15. Please note that refund requests will not be processed after this.

We apologize for any inconvenience and thank you for your understanding.

159. Where would the notice most likely be found?

(A) At a stadium
(B) At a museum
(C) At a theater
(D) At a train station

160. What is true about the tickets?

(A) They can be purchased at the venue.
(B) They are for an event occurring on March 15.
(C) They are sold at a discount to some people.
(D) They can be refunded over the phone.

Questions 161-163 refer to the following letter.

Dr. Lynn Butler
Gennexta Corporation
San Francisco, CA

June 12

Dear Dr. Butler,

I am writing on behalf of the Texas University Science Center, which is holding its annual conference from August 15 to 18. — [1] —. As one of this event's organizers, I am responsible for finding suitable guest speakers. I was hoping you would do us the honor of participating. — [2] —. Given that you are a senior researcher at Gennexta Corporation, your knowledge and expertise would be of great interest to attendees. — [3] —. In addition to covering your transportation expenses, we can offer you free accommodations. A dormitory is being renovated for the use of conference participants, and it will open on July 16. — [4] —. Someone from our office will be in touch with you by phone very soon.

Sincerely,

Vincent Ortiz
Texas University Science Center

TEST

4

해커스 토익 실전 LC+RC 2

161. What is the purpose of the letter?

(A) To welcome a new member to a group
(B) To announce changes to an upcoming event
(C) To extend an invitation to a speaker
(D) To confirm the details of a travel itinerary

162. What will happen in July?

(A) A science center will be opened.
(B) A renovation project will be finished.
(C) A research proposal will be submitted.
(D) A funding request will be approved.

163. In which of the positions marked [1], [2], [3], and [4] does the following sentence best belong?

"They would love to hear you talk about the projects you are currently working on."

(A) [1]
(B) [2]
(C) [3]
(D) [4]

GO ON TO THE NEXT PAGE

Questions 164-167 refer to the following information.

Webshow Subscription Plans

Effective February 1, Webshow will be implementing a new subscription model with three plans rather than the current two. We made this decision to reflect the responses to a nationwide survey we conducted last year. The message is clear—our subscribers feel that more options are needed to meet their streaming needs.

BASIC $10.99 per month	STANDARD $12.99 per month	PREMIUM $17.99 per month
• Includes advertisements • One supported device • Five downloads per month	• Includes advertisements • Two supported devices • All video in high-definition • Unlimited downloads	• No advertisements • Four supported devices • All video in high-definition • Unlimited downloads

To show our appreciation to our subscribers, we will be providing a three-month free trial of the Premium plan. For more information about this special offer, please visit www.webshow.com/upgrade. Please note that you will not be able to sign up for the free trial after February 8.

164. What is the purpose of the information?

(A) To clarify a company regulation
(B) To announce a corporate merger
(C) To explain an increase in a fee
(D) To describe a change to a service

165. What is stated about Webshow?

(A) It has redesigned its Web site.
(B) It gathered feedback from its customers.
(C) It recently expanded into other countries.
(D) It decided to stream additional content.

166. What is unique about the Premium plan?

(A) Marketing materials are not shown to viewers.
(B) Multiple devices can sign in to an account.
(C) High-definition videos are accessible.
(D) The number of downloads is not restricted.

167. What is mentioned about the special offer?

(A) It is designed to attract corporate clients.
(B) It requires a Premium plan subscription.
(C) It is only valid for a limited time period.
(D) It will first take effect on February 8.

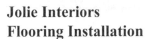

Jolie Interiors
Flooring Installation

Installing new flooring can dramatically change the look of a room and add value to your home or business. — [1] —. Therefore, we encourage you to request the guidance of the experts at Jolie Interiors.

Once you contact us, a consultant from our company will visit your space and take some measurements. During this visit, photographs will be taken of your space for documentation purposes and to ensure accurate planning of your project. The consultant will also show you a catalog of our products and help you decide which options are best. Our expert staff members have extensive experience in identifying the appropriate flooring for both residential and commercial properties. — [2] —. We carry a wide variety of materials to choose from.

After you have made your selections, you will be provided with a detailed invoice. — [3] —. A 50 percent deposit will be required prior to shipment of the materials from our warehouse. Barring unforeseen events, your order will arrive within two weeks, at which point the installation process will commence. — [4] —. This can take from two to five days depending on the size of the job. As an added convenience for our customers, we do not charge for the removal and disposal of old flooring.

168. What is the purpose of the brochure?

(A) To promote some new products
(B) To provide a process overview
(C) To announce a policy change
(D) To present some ordering options

169. What is mentioned about Jolie Interiors?

(A) It requires clients to take pictures.
(B) It specializes in renovating commercial properties.
(C) It sends employees to customers' residences.
(D) It publishes a catalog that can be accessed online.

170. What is indicated about the installation?

(A) It is done at no charge for large orders.
(B) It begins after full payment is received.
(C) It is performed by another company.
(D) It takes less than a week to finish.

171. In which of the positions marked [1], [2], [3], and [4] does the following sentence best belong?

"It will specify the cost of materials and labor, as well as any applicable taxes."

(A) [1]
(B) [2]
(C) [3]
(D) [4]

GO ON TO THE NEXT PAGE

Questions 172-175 refer to the following online chat discussion.

🔘 **Nicholas Yang**	(11:21 A.M.)	Hey team. We need to discuss the Medical Technology Conference in Tallinn next month. How are we looking?
Maya Kowalczyk	(11:22 A.M.)	We should be all set. I received the confirmation this morning for our flight and hotel bookings.
Emily Maxwell	(11:22 A.M.)	I'm still working on the demonstration of our company's latest software program, but it should be done soon.
🔘 **Nicholas Yang**	(11:23 A.M.)	Great! Maya, is our hotel near the conference center, or will we need to arrange transportation?
Maya Kowalczyk	(11:24 A.M.)	Unfortunately, all of the hotels near the center are booked. We'll have to take a taxi each day.
🔘 **Nicholas Yang**	(11:25 A.M.)	That could get expensive. But since none of us have ever been there, I guess we don't have any other choice.
Emily Maxwell	(11:26 A.M.)	Actually, why don't we download the Welcome to Tallinn mobile app? It's got a city guide, transit maps, and more. It may be possible to take a tram to the venue.
🔘 **Nicholas Yang**	(11:26 A.M.)	Thanks, Emily! I never thought of that. I'll bet there's lots of other useful information on the app as well.

172. Where do the writers most likely work?

(A) At a healthcare provider
(B) At a software development firm
(C) At a mobile phone company
(D) At an event-planning business

173. At 11:21 A.M., what does Mr. Yang most likely mean when he writes, "How are we looking"?

(A) He is uncertain about the possible uses of a technology.
(B) He is interested in the status of a service.
(C) He wants an update on preparations for an event.
(D) He requires more explanation about a company policy.

174. What can be concluded about the writers?

(A) They will be visiting Tallinn for the first time.
(B) They recently accepted jobs with a new firm.
(C) They are transferring to a branch in another country.
(D) They will receive free lodging during an event.

175. Why does Ms. Maxwell suggest downloading a mobile app?

(A) It allows users to book seats on a shuttle.
(B) It provides a conference schedule.
(C) It includes details about transportation options.
(D) It offers discounts on a variety of local services.

GO ON TO THE NEXT PAGE

Questions 176-180 refer to the following notice and e-mail.

Harbor Craft Market

Location: 321 Oakridge Drive

The Harbor Craft Market features unique, handmade products from many local shops. Open every weekend from 10 A.M. to 7 P.M., it is the perfect place to pick up something special for yourself or someone you care about.

Booth	Shop	Products
101	Scented Light	Candles with flower fragrances
102	Colors of the Sea	Unique necklaces made from beautiful sea glass
103	The Pottery Wheel	Distinctive ceramic dishes and vases
104	Best Friends	Friendship bracelets in a variety of styles
105	Cozy Corner	Padded quilts and blankets of all sizes

For more information, visit www.harbormarket.com. All inquiries should be directed to customerservice@harbormarket.com.

To: customerservice@harbormarket.com
From: Nina Reed <n.reed@zmail.com>
Date: May 24
Subject: Market

Hello,

I'm hoping you can help me. I would like to know how to get my money back for a purchase I made at the Harbor Craft Market last Saturday. I bought a large, decorative plate for my sister as a birthday present. It was just her style, so I was quite happy with it. But when I got home, I noticed a crack on the bottom. And I can't simply take it back to the booth where I bought it because the person I dealt with mentioned that it was the last day his shop would be participating in the market.

I would appreciate it if someone could contact me as soon as possible. The market is only two stops away from the subway station next to my apartment building, so I can drop by this weekend if necessary. Thank you.

Nina Reed

176. What is the similarity between Booth 102 and Booth 104?

(A) They sell jewelry pieces that are crafted by hand.
(B) They feature household items made of recycled glass.
(C) They offer customization services for an extra fee.
(D) They carry a selection of ocean-themed products.

177. At which booth did Ms. Reed probably make a purchase?

(A) Booth 101
(B) Booth 103
(C) Booth 104
(D) Booth 105

178. What is the purpose of the e-mail?

(A) To confirm a delivery has been made
(B) To inquire about a refund process
(C) To advertise some new blankets
(D) To find out how to exchange an item

179. In the e-mail, the word "just" in paragraph 1, line 3, is closest in meaning to

(A) simply
(B) minimally
(C) beyond
(D) exactly

180. What is indicated about Ms. Reed?

(A) She will contact the owner of a shop about a purchase.
(B) She visits local craft markets on a regular basis.
(C) She will move into a new apartment next month.
(D) She lives in an area near a public transit facility.

GO ON TO THE NEXT PAGE

Questions 181-185 refer to the following job posting and e-mail.

Blackstone Appliances is establishing a shipping center in the Knoxville area. It is expected to begin operations on August 14 and will serve as the company's primary distribution hub for the southeastern United States. To staff the center, we are currently accepting applications for the following positions:

Position	Requirements
Warehouse worker	• Good physical condition • One year of relevant experience
Administrative assistant	• Undergraduate degree (Business or related major) • One year of relevant experience
Security guard	• Security training certificate • Three years of relevant experience
Delivery truck driver	• Commercial driver's license • Two years of relevant experience

The successful applicants will receive a competitive salary and paid sick leave. They will also be able to take advantage of our on-site cafeteria at no charge during their shifts.

Click **here** to get an application, and then send the completed form to Denise Sawyer at humanresouces@blackstone.com. There is no need to include a résumé or cover letter. The deadline for all positions is July 1.

To: Denise Sawyer <humanresources@blackstone.com>
From: Dale Uchida <d.uchida@waymail.com>
Subject: Open Position
Date: June 27
Attachment: Application

Dear Ms. Sawyer,

I have attached my application for one of the positions advertised on your Web site. I should point out that while I have met the first listed requirement, I have only two years of experience rather than the specified three. However, I have an excellent reference from my previous employer, and I am confident that I will be able to handle any duties I am assigned at Blackstone.

Please contact me with any questions or concerns. I am in the process of moving to Johnson City, so I won't be available for an interview until July 4 at the earliest.

Sincerely,

Dale Uchida

181. What is true about Blackstone Appliances?

(A) It hired a new human resources manager.
(B) It moved its headquarters to Knoxville.
(C) It ships products for free within a region.
(D) It intends to open a new facility in August.

182. What position is Mr. Uchida most likely interested in?

(A) Warehouse worker
(B) Administrative assistant
(C) Security guard
(D) Delivery truck driver

183. According to the job posting, what will the successful candidates be able to do?

(A) Choose their work shifts each week
(B) Eat meals at work for free
(C) Get annual performance bonuses
(D) Take long vacations once a year

184. In the e-mail, the word "handle" in paragraph 1, line 4, is closest in meaning to

(A) permit
(B) reflect
(C) manage
(D) discover

185. What is indicated about Mr. Uchida?

(A) He missed a deadline to submit an application.
(B) He has worked for Blackstone before.
(C) He is relocating to a different city.
(D) He will reschedule a job interview for a later date.

GO ON TO THE NEXT PAGE

Questions 186-190 refer to the following Web page, advertisement, and review.

Customer: Brandon Chang

Wilson Office Supplies – Fresno Branch

About	Shop	**My Order**	Contact Us

Order Number: 08726
Date: September 14
Address: 121 Coleman Street, Fresno, CA 93650

Item	Quantity	Price	Total
Delta Color Printer Ink Cartridge	4	$22.00	$88.00
Brennan Letter-Size White Paper(500 sheets / pack)	2	$24.00	$48.00
Mainline Metal Stapler	1	$8.00	$8.00
Acme Standard Staples(3,000 staples / box)	5	$2.00	$10.00
		Subtotal	$154.00
		Tax	$12.00
		Total	$166.00

Pick up ○ Delivery ⊘

A fee of $10 will be added for deliveries within Fresno and $20 for deliveries to areas outside the city limits (waived for orders over $150).

Wilson Office Supplies

We have everything you need!

Visit any Wilson Office Supplies store to find the most popular brands at affordable prices. Each month, we offer new types of products at a discount. Here are the best deals for September:

➢ File folders (15% off)
➢ Pencils and ballpoint pens (10% off)
➢ Printer ink (20% off)
➢ Color paper (10% off)

For even greater savings, visit our new branch in Oakland. To celebrate its grand opening, everything at the store is 40 percent off!

Date: September 18
Rating: 4 stars ★★★★

After moving into my new apartment last weekend, I stopped by a nearby Wilson Office Supplies to buy some things for my home office. This is the chain's newest branch, so everything was very clean. I also appreciated how polite the staff members were. That being said, I wish the actual prices were displayed more prominently. I had a hard time figuring out how much some items cost. For example, the sticker on the Glide 230 Office Chair said $200. I assumed this was the sale price and the original price was over $300. But I was later told that $80 would be taken off the sticker price, meaning that I would only have to pay $120. It was pretty confusing.

— Zita Laurent

186. Why was a delivery fee not added to Mr. Chang's total?

(A) He lives within the city limits of Fresno.
(B) He chose to pick up his items from the store.
(C) He spent the required amount on an order.
(D) He intends to pay the delivery person directly.

187. What product did Mr. Chang purchase at a discount?

(A) Delta Color Printer Ink Cartridge
(B) Brennan Letter-Size White Paper
(C) Mainline Metal Stapler
(D) Acme Standard Staples

188. What will happen in October?

(A) Different items will be discounted.
(B) Additional stores will be opened.
(C) A new line of products will be launched.
(D) A popular brand will be discontinued.

189. What is suggested about Ms. Laurent?

(A) She decided to return one of her purchases.
(B) She will move into a new apartment soon.
(C) She shops regularly at Wilson Office Supplies.
(D) She is currently a resident of Oakland.

190. According to the review, what was Ms. Laurent not pleased with?

(A) Some employees were not well-mannered.
(B) Some office furniture was much too expensive.
(C) Some information was not clearly presented.
(D) Some products were very difficult to find.

GO ON TO THE NEXT PAGE

Lucia Cruz
34 Packerston Road
Victoria, BC, V8T 3R2

Dear Ms. Cruz,

Thank you for your past support of the Better Beginnings organization. With the assistance of generous donors like you, we have been able to offer school supplies and tutoring services to over 400 elementary school students from low-income families.

I would like to ask if you would be willing to make a donation for our latest program. The goal is to provide students from disadvantaged backgrounds with a tablet computer as well as Internet access. Any amount would help, but those who give $1,000 or more will be provided with a complimentary pass to our annual fundraising concert on May 15 as a gift.

I hope to hear from you soon.

Sincerely,

Kevin Yang
Funding Coordinator
Better Beginnings

To: Kevin Yang <k.yang@bb.com>
From: Beth Meyers <b.meyers@bb.com>
Subject: New Program
Date: April 10

Hi Kevin,

Congratulations on the successful fundraising campaign! The $3,000 donation from Ms. Cruz brings our total to $68,000. This greatly exceeds our original estimate, so I have made some adjustments to our plan. We will now be able to help 100 students rather than 75.

Redwood Communications will be providing one year of unlimited Internet access for only $180 per student. That is half the usual price. Company president Sara Martinez, who founded Redwood Communications less than a year ago, sees this program as a great marketing opportunity.

Regarding the devices, we can spend a maximum of $500 per tablet. I have contacted several electronics suppliers to find out our options. I will let you know when I have chosen a device.

Beth Myers, Program Manager
Better Beginnings

To: Beth Meyers <b.meyers@bb.com>
From: Amir Gupta <a.gupta@aspen.com>
Subject: Options
Date: April 21

Dear Ms. Myers,

I received your inquiry yesterday about a tablet computer for your new program. The Edge 340 is one of Aspen Electronics' best-selling models. It includes a 10-inch screen and 32 GB of storage. It also comes with a comprehensive one-year warranty. Best of all, we can offer you a 10 percent discount for such a large order, so you will only have to pay $600 per unit.

Please let me know if you have any questions about the tablet or the ordering process. I look forward to your response.

Sincerely,

Amir Gupta
Aspen Electronics

191. What is the purpose of the letter?

(A) To confirm the delivery of educational materials
(B) To make a request for a financial contribution
(C) To ask for assistance with student tutoring
(D) To explain the details of an online event

192. What did Ms. Cruz most likely receive?

(A) A school textbook
(B) A gift certificate
(C) A performance ticket
(D) A laptop computer

193. What is indicated about a program in the first e-mail?

(A) It was canceled due to a budget shortfall.
(B) It will provide work for a large number of student interns.
(C) It will involve more participants than originally planned.
(D) It was established by an instructor at a public school.

194. What is true about Redwood Communications?

(A) It has operated for less than a year.
(B) It is considering offering some free products.
(C) It limits student access to some online features.
(D) It launched a membership service.

195. Why most likely will Ms. Myers reject the Edge 340?

(A) The screen size is too small.
(B) The storage capacity is too low.
(C) The purchase cost is too high.
(D) The warranty period is too short.

GO ON TO THE NEXT PAGE

Questions 196-200 refer to the following Web page, e-mail, and notice.

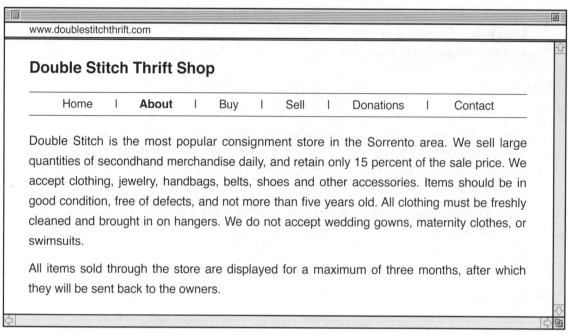

www.doublestitchthrift.com

Double Stitch Thrift Shop

Home | **About** | Buy | Sell | Donations | Contact

Double Stitch is the most popular consignment store in the Sorrento area. We sell large quantities of secondhand merchandise daily, and retain only 15 percent of the sale price. We accept clothing, jewelry, handbags, belts, shoes and other accessories. Items should be in good condition, free of defects, and not more than five years old. All clothing must be freshly cleaned and brought in on hangers. We do not accept wedding gowns, maternity clothes, or swimsuits.

All items sold through the store are displayed for a maximum of three months, after which they will be sent back to the owners.

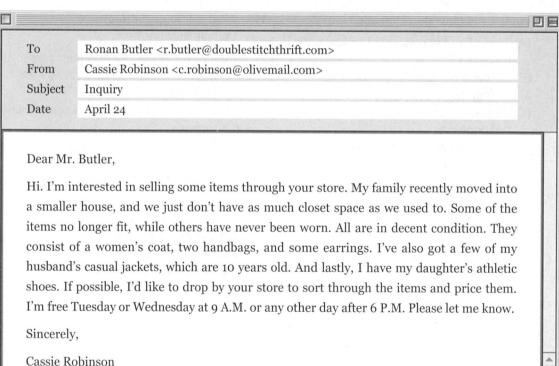

To	Ronan Butler <r.butler@doublestitchthrift.com>
To	
From	Cassie Robinson <c.robinson@olivemail.com>
Subject	Inquiry
Date	April 24

Dear Mr. Butler,

Hi. I'm interested in selling some items through your store. My family recently moved into a smaller house, and we just don't have as much closet space as we used to. Some of the items no longer fit, while others have never been worn. All are in decent condition. They consist of a women's coat, two handbags, and some earrings. I've also got a few of my husband's casual jackets, which are 10 years old. And lastly, I have my daughter's athletic shoes. If possible, I'd like to drop by your store to sort through the items and price them. I'm free Tuesday or Wednesday at 9 A.M. or any other day after 6 P.M. Please let me know.

Sincerely,

Cassie Robinson

Double Stitch Thrift Shop
Operating Hours

Monday	CLOSED
Tuesday	CLOSED
Wednesday	10 A.M. - 6 P.M.
Thursday	10 A.M. - 6 P.M.
Friday	9 A.M. - 7 P.M.
Saturday	1 P.M. - 5 P.M.
Sunday	1 P.M.- 5 P.M.

Exit Highway 55 at Airport Road. We are located across from the Haven Shopping Center. Ample paid parking is available nearby.

196. What is the purpose of the Web page?

(A) To announce some new items
(B) To explain a return process
(C) To outline some store policies
(D) To welcome new users

197. What is true about Double Stitch?

(A) It can perform minor repairs.
(B) It provides its own clothing hangers.
(C) It accepts mostly luxury merchandise.
(D) It returns unsold items after a few months.

198. What is indicated in the e-mail about Ms. Robinson?

(A) Her current home is less spacious than her previous one.
(B) She is searching for a property to purchase.
(C) Her family enjoys working out.
(D) She is employed in the fashion industry.

199. Which of Ms. Robinson's items will Double Stitch most likely reject?

(A) The women's coat
(B) The earrings
(C) The casual jackets
(D) The athletic shoes

200. On which day will Ms. Robinson bring her items?

(A) On Wednesday
(B) On Thursday
(C) On Friday
(D) On Saturday

This is the end of the test. You may review Parts 5, 6, and 7 if you finish the test early.

Review 체크리스트

TEST 4를 푼 다음, 아래 체크리스트에 따라 틀린 문제를 리뷰하고 박스에 완료 여부를 표시하세요.
만약 시험까지 얼마 남지 않았다면, 파란색으로 표시된 항목이라도 꼭 확인하세요.

☐ 틀린 문제의 경우, 다시 풀어봤다.

☐ 틀린 문제의 경우, 스크립트/해석을 확인하며 지문/문제의 내용을 정확하게 파악했다.

☐ 해설을 통해 각 문제의 정답과 오답의 근거가 무엇인지 정확하게 파악했다.

☐ PART 1과 PART 2에서 틀린 문제의 경우, 선택한 오답의 유형이 무엇이었는지 확인하고 같은 함정에 빠지지 않도록 정리해두었다.

☐ PART 3와 PART 4의 각 문제에서 사용된 패러프레이징을 확인했다.

☐ PART 5와 PART 6의 경우, 틀린 문제에서 사용된 문법 포인트 또는 정답 및 오답 어휘를 정리했다.

☐ PART 6의 알맞은 문장 고르기 문제의 경우, 지문 전체를 정확하게 해석하며 전체 글의 흐름과 빈칸 주변 문맥을 정확하게 파악하는 연습을 했다.

☐ PART 7에서 질문과 보기의 키워드를 찾아 표시하며 지문에서 정답의 근거가 되는 문장이나 구절을 찾아보고, 문제에서 사용된 패러프레이징을 확인했다.

☐ PART 1~PART 4는 받아쓰기 & 쉐도잉 워크북을 활용하여, TEST에 수록된 핵심 문장을 받아쓰고 따라 읽으며 복습했다.

☐ PART 1~PART 7은 단어암기자료를 활용하여, TEST에 수록된 핵심 어휘와 표현을 암기했다.

많은 양의 문제를 푸는 것도 중요하지만, 틀린 문제를 제대로 리뷰하는 것도 중요합니다.
틀린 문제를 한 번 더 꼼꼼히 리뷰한다면, 빠른 시간 내에 효과적으로 목표 점수를 달성할 수 있습니다.

TEST 5

LISTENING TEST

PART 1
PART 2
PART 3
PART 4

READING TEST

PART 5
PART 6
PART 7

Review 체크리스트

잠깐! 테스트 전 아래 사항을 꼭 확인하세요.

휴대전화의 전원을 끄셨나요? 예 □
Answer Sheet(p.255), 연필, 지우개, 시계를 준비하셨나요? 예 □
Listening MP3를 들을 준비가 되셨나요? 예 □

모든 준비가 완료되었으면 목표 점수를 떠올린 후 테스트를 시작합니다.
테스트를 마친 후, Review 체크리스트(p.236)를 보며 자신이 틀린 문제를 반드시 복습합니다.

🎧 TEST 5.mp3
실전용·복습용 문제풀이 MP3 무료 다운로드 및 스트리밍 바로듣기 (HackersIngang.com)
* 실제 시험장의 소음까지 재현해 낸 고사장 소음/매미 버전 MP3, 영국식·호주식 발음 집중 MP3, 고속 버전 MP3까지 구매
하면 실전에 더욱 완벽히 대비할 수 있습니다.

무료MP3 바로듣기

LISTENING TEST

In this section, you must demonstrate your ability to understand spoken English. This section is divided into four parts and will take approximately 45 minutes to complete. Do not mark the answers in your test book. Use the answer sheet that is provided separately.

PART 1

Directions: For each question, you will listen to four short statements about a picture in your test book. These statements will not be printed and will only be spoken one time. Select the statement that best describes what is happening in the picture and mark the corresponding letter (A), (B), (C), or (D) on the answer sheet.

Sample Answer

The statement that best describes the picture is (B), "The man is sitting at the desk." So, you should mark letter (B) on the answer sheet.

1.

2.

GO ON TO THE NEXT PAGE

3.

4.

5.

6.

GO ON TO THE NEXT PAGE ➡

PART 2

Directions: For each question, you will listen to a statement or question followed by three possible responses spoken in English. They will not be printed and will only be spoken one time. Select the best response and mark the corresponding letter (A), (B), or (C) on your answer sheet.

7. Mark your answer on your answer sheet.

8. Mark your answer on your answer sheet.

9. Mark your answer on your answer sheet.

10. Mark your answer on your answer sheet.

11. Mark your answer on your answer sheet.

12. Mark your answer on your answer sheet.

13. Mark your answer on your answer sheet.

14. Mark your answer on your answer sheet.

15. Mark your answer on your answer sheet.

16. Mark your answer on your answer sheet.

17. Mark your answer on your answer sheet.

18. Mark your answer on your answer sheet.

19. Mark your answer on your answer sheet.

20. Mark your answer on your answer sheet.

21. Mark your answer on your answer sheet.

22. Mark your answer on your answer sheet.

23. Mark your answer on your answer sheet.

24. Mark your answer on your answer sheet.

25. Mark your answer on your answer sheet.

26. Mark your answer on your answer sheet.

27. Mark your answer on your answer sheet.

28. Mark your answer on your answer sheet.

29. Mark your answer on your answer sheet.

30. Mark your answer on your answer sheet.

31. Mark your answer on your answer sheet.

PART 3

Directions: In this part, you will listen to several conversations between two or more speakers. These conversations will not be printed and will only be spoken one time. For each conversation, you will be asked to answer three questions. Select the best response and mark the corresponding letter (A), (B), (C), or (D) on your answer sheet.

32. What was recently announced?
    (A) A department restructuring
    (B) A business partnership
    (C) An overseas expansion
    (D) A team-building event

33. What does the man suggest?
    (A) Hiring an assistant
    (B) Applying for a position
    (C) Submitting a report
    (D) Making an announcement

34. What will the woman most likely do next?
    (A) Read through a guidebook
    (B) Visit a branch office
    (C) Speak with a colleague
    (D) Meet with a team

35. Who most likely is the man?
    (A) An event organizer
    (B) A real estate agent
    (C) A safety inspector
    (D) An interior designer

36. What is Cora concerned about?
    (A) The lack of parking spaces
    (B) The cost of renovations
    (C) The location of a building
    (D) The size of an area

37. What does the man say he will send to the women?
    (A) A legal agreement
    (B) A financial record
    (C) A business card
    (D) A marketing brochure

38. In what industry do the speakers most likely work?
    (A) Finance
    (B) Marketing
    (C) Health care
    (D) Film

39. What does the woman recommend that the man do?
    (A) Remove a photo
    (B) Buy a magazine
    (C) Take a picture
    (D) Cancel a project

40. What will probably happen tomorrow?
    (A) A representative will be called.
    (B) A presentation will be given.
    (C) A meeting will be rescheduled.
    (D) A payment will be processed.

41. What is the conversation mainly about?
    (A) Replacing an experienced worker
    (B) Addressing a client complaint
    (C) Attending a corporate event
    (D) Finding an appropriate venue

42. What did the manager specify as a priority?
    (A) A reasonable budget
    (B) A private space
    (C) A flexible schedule
    (D) A convenient location

43. What does the woman show the man?
    (A) A map
    (B) A menu
    (C) An image
    (D) An e-mail

GO ON TO THE NEXT PAGE

44. Why does the man call the woman?

(A) To ask her about a canceled order
(B) To confirm receipt of a package
(C) To notify her of a delivery delay
(D) To request payment for a product

45. What does the woman say she will do on Wednesday?

(A) Start a new job
(B) Return a damaged desk
(C) Remodel a home office
(D) Call a former employer

46. Why does the man plan to call a warehouse?

(A) He will arrange a search for a missing item.
(B) He will ask an employee to work overtime.
(C) He will verify a client's shipping address.
(D) He will inquire about a lost package.

47. Where does the conversation most likely take place?

(A) In a bookstore
(B) In a supermarket
(C) In a medical clinic
(D) In a car dealership

48. What type of event were staff members notified about?

(A) A fundraiser
(B) A grand opening
(C) A press conference
(D) A workshop

49. What will the woman most likely do next?

(A) Take a break
(B) Make a donation
(C) Talk to a coworker
(D) Set up a display

50. Why does the woman say, "The warranty may still be valid"?

(A) To offer a suggestion
(B) To request an explanation
(C) To ask for clarification
(D) To agree with a decision

51. What does the man ask the woman for?

(A) A manual
(B) A device
(C) A beverage
(D) A receipt

52. What will the woman tell some workers?

(A) A leave will be granted.
(B) A machine will be purchased.
(C) A center will be visited.
(D) A task will be delayed.

53. Where do the men most likely work?

(A) At a publishing company
(B) At an advertising agency
(C) At an art gallery
(D) At a photo studio

54. Why did the woman choose Mr. Amir?

(A) She viewed his work online.
(B) She was involved with him on a project.
(C) She was sent his portfolio by a company.
(D) She noticed him in an advertisement.

55. What does the woman ask about?

(A) Equipment features
(B) A clothing choice
(C) An account password
(D) Pricing options

56. Where most likely are the speakers?

(A) At a railway station
(B) At a bus stop
(C) At a ferry terminal
(D) At an airport

57. Why does the man say, "The limit is 18 kilograms"?

(A) To correct an assumption
(B) To apologize for a mistake
(C) To point out a change
(D) To provide a solution

58. What will the woman do next?

(A) Purchase some clothes
(B) Show an identification card
(C) Pay an additional fee
(D) Move some items

---

59. What did the Java Cup café chain announce?

(A) A loyalty club
(B) A product line
(C) A name change
(D) A price increase

60. What concern does the man express?

(A) A promotional event will end soon.
(B) A street will be blocked off.
(C) A restaurant will earn less money.
(D) A lunch special will be unpopular.

61. What does the woman suggest?

(A) Meeting with a consultant
(B) Offering regular discounts
(C) Opening another branch
(D) Changing some ingredients

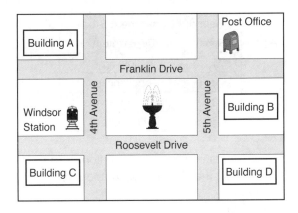

62. What problem does the woman mention?

(A) A technician will be late.
(B) A vehicle was damaged.
(C) A road is blocked.
(D) A facility will be closed.

63. Look at the graphic. Where will Ms. Sampson probably park?

(A) Building A
(B) Building B
(C) Building C
(D) Building D

64. What does the woman ask the man to do?

(A) Contact the owner of a garage
(B) Provide directions to an employee
(C) Request information from a client
(D) Purchase a parking pass

GO ON TO THE NEXT PAGE

Belmont Department Store	
Floor	Department
1	Clothing
2	Appliances
3	Sporting Goods
4	Furniture

Harvest Calendar

	June	July	August	September
Beets	√			
Pumpkins			√	
Cucumbers		√		
Potatoes				√

65. Look at the graphic. Which floor is the product the woman asked about on?

(A) Floor 1
(B) Floor 2
(C) Floor 3
(D) Floor 4

66. Why will the woman visit the store tomorrow?

(A) To exchange an earlier purchase
(B) To make use of a coupon
(C) To compare some models
(D) To purchase a gift certificate

67. What does the man assure the woman about?

(A) A membership card is valid.
(B) A package will be delivered today.
(C) A representative will return a call.
(D) A promotion is still available.

68. What does the man ask about?

(A) Storing fresh vegetables
(B) Attracting more customers
(C) Changing operating hours
(D) Hiring additional workers

69. Look at the graphic. Which is the busiest month at the market?

(A) June
(B) July
(C) August
(D) September

70. What does the man offer to do?

(A) Restock store shelves
(B) Contact a produce supplier
(C) Design marketing materials
(D) Make an online post

PART 4

Directions: In this part, you will listen to several short talks by a single speaker. These talks will not be printed and will only be spoken one time. For each talk, you will be asked to answer three questions. Select the best response and mark the corresponding letter (A), (B), (C), or (D) on your answer sheet.

71. Why is the speaker calling?
    (A) To notify the listener of a decision
    (B) To check that a unit is available
    (C) To ask the listener to consider an offer
    (D) To request to view an apartment

72. What is the speaker unsure about?
    (A) Where to send a contract
    (B) What to do in a neighborhood
    (C) Whether a facility is free to use
    (D) When a rental period will end

73. What does the speaker ask the listener to do?
    (A) Cancel an application
    (B) Process a deposit payment
    (C) Revise an agreement
    (D) Arrange an appointment

74. What will happen next Tuesday?
    (A) A store will close earlier than usual.
    (B) New items will be put on display.
    (C) Clothes will be offered at a discount.
    (D) A manager will inspect a workspace.

75. What does the speaker ask the listeners to do?
    (A) Work overtime on a weekly basis
    (B) Let him know about their availability
    (C) Place old clothing in a storage area
    (D) Clean the store after closing

76. According to the speaker, what will Mr. Parker provide?
    (A) Some safety gear
    (B) A registration form
    (C) A product list
    (D) Some cleaning supplies

77. What industry does the speaker work in?
    (A) Landscaping
    (B) Hospitality
    (C) Media
    (D) Shipping

78. What will the speaker give the listeners?
    (A) Instruction manuals
    (B) Application forms
    (C) Identification cards
    (D) Parking passes

79. What does the speaker mean when she says, "They will be easy to maintain"?
    (A) Local facilities are adequate.
    (B) She agrees with a choice.
    (C) She prefers another option.
    (D) Building materials are durable.

80. What does the speaker say is located near Tahoma Station?
    (A) A government office
    (B) A national museum
    (C) A sports facility
    (D) A public park

81. What is mentioned about Exit 3?
    (A) It is the main entrance.
    (B) It is near a taxi stand.
    (C) It is closed for repairs.
    (D) It is next to a large hotel.

82. According to the speaker, why will there be a delay?
    (A) A crew will be replaced.
    (B) A station will be cleaned.
    (C) A vehicle will be fueled.
    (D) A repair will be made.

GO ON TO THE NEXT PAGE

83. What type of event will happen in Harrison Park?

(A) A sports competition
(B) A musical performance
(C) A fireworks display
(D) An art exhibition

84. What does the speaker imply when he says, "The nearby streets are very narrow"?

(A) A proposal is acceptable.
(B) A plan is impractical.
(C) A location is unsuitable.
(D) A concern is legitimate.

85. What will the listeners hear next?

(A) An advertisement
(B) A traffic update
(C) A weather forecast
(D) An interview

---

86. What is being advertised?

(A) A housewares shop
(B) A clothing boutique
(C) An eyewear store
(D) A crafts market

87. What does the speaker say is special about the business?

(A) It creates custom products.
(B) It offers complimentary repairs.
(C) It uses natural materials.
(D) It provides a delivery service.

88. What does the speaker encourage the listeners to do?

(A) Sign up for a membership
(B) Participate in a raffle
(C) Place an online order
(D) Read some feedback

---

89. Who is the podcast intended for?

(A) Hotel owners
(B) Travelers
(C) Car enthusiasts
(D) Artists

90. What does the speaker say about the Coast Lodge?

(A) It has opened a second location.
(B) It may renovate its rooms soon.
(C) It can accommodate few guests.
(D) It provides guided tours to visitors.

91. What information will the speaker share?

(A) Event schedules
(B) Venue locations
(C) Business names
(D) Activity costs

---

92. What does the speaker's company most likely sell?

(A) Educational materials
(B) Cooking equipment
(C) Office supplies
(D) Sports gear

93. What does the speaker imply when she says, "And it's almost 10 already"?

(A) Some employees have arrived late.
(B) A store will close at its regular time.
(C) Some tasks must be done quickly.
(D) A deadline will likely be changed.

94. What will the listeners do next?

(A) Meet with an instructor
(B) Arrange some transportation
(C) Set up some furniture
(D) Give a demonstration

Scheduled Appointments		
		January 18
Time	Client	Employee
10:00 A.M.	Barbara Lloyd	Lydia Parker
11:30 A.M.	Steven Jeffrey	Maya Jimenez
2:15 P.M.	Simone Meyer	Connor Abramovich
6:00 P.M.	Kenichi Isaki	Dillon Smith

**Turner Lawn Mowers:
Percentage of Total Spending**

95. Look at the graphic. Which client will Brian most likely serve?

(A) Barbara Lloyd
(B) Steven Jeffrey
(C) Simone Meyer
(D) Kenichi Isaki

96. Who most likely are the listeners?

(A) Hair stylists
(B) Dentists
(C) Financial advisors
(D) Technicians

97. According to the speaker, what happened yesterday?

(A) An employee requested leave.
(B) A policy change was implemented.
(C) A project deadline was missed.
(D) A client made a complaint.

98. What is the purpose of the talk?

(A) To announce an increase to a budget
(B) To describe a measure to address a problem
(C) To criticize the implementation of a plan
(D) To praise the performance of a team

99. Look at the graphic. Which department does the speaker recommend cutting spending on?

(A) Manufacturing
(B) Marketing
(C) Sales
(D) Accounting

100. What will the speaker most likely do next?

(A) Distribute some documents
(B) Make some corrections
(C) Watch a group presentation
(D) Introduce a new speaker

This is the end of the Listening test. Turn to PART 5 in your test book.

GO ON TO THE NEXT PAGE

READING TEST

In this section, you must demonstrate your ability to read and comprehend English. You will be given a variety of texts and asked to answer questions about these texts. This section is divided into three parts and will take 75 minutes to complete.

Do not mark the answers in your test book. Use the answer sheet that is separately provided.

PART 5

Directions: In each question, you will be asked to review a statement that is missing a word or phrase. Four answer choices will be provided for each statement. Select the best answer and mark the corresponding letter (A), (B), (C), or (D) on the answer sheet.

PART 5 권장 풀이 시간 **11분**

101. The organizers ------- that the technology conference had a record-breaking attendance.

(A) reports
(B) reported
(C) reporter
(D) reporting

102. XinZu Eyewear is presenting its line of ------- that feature timeless frame styles.

(A) produce
(B) products
(C) production
(D) produced

103. If your contract is revised, go over it ------- to ensure you agree with the changes that have been made.

(A) careful
(B) carefulness
(C) carefully
(D) more careful

104. Renfrew Software has its managers participate in leadership seminars ------- to help them find ways to motivate their staff.

(A) artificially
(B) loosely
(C) overly
(D) periodically

105. Our keynote speaker this year delivered a speech ------- 20 minutes longer than the time allotted.

(A) last
(B) lasting
(C) lastly
(D) lasted

106. Alba Discount Mart has requested the ------- of all its workers at the opening of its new shopping center.

(A) reason
(B) companion
(C) presence
(D) method

107. Slansea Inc. had to pay a ------- fine for its failure to submit the required tax forms by the specified deadline.

(A) consider
(B) considerable
(C) consideration
(D) considering

108. ------- determinations by the board, management will be introducing some changes to the employee benefits package.

(A) Throughout
(B) Thereafter
(C) Meanwhile
(D) As a result of

109. The article published in *Business Weekly* ------- the various ways in which the new labor law will affect employers.

(A) transports
(B) covers
(C) distributes
(D) implements

110. The Wiltshire Convention Center ------- the region's most prestigious events for more than 10 years.

(A) was hosted
(B) has been hosting
(C) to be hosting
(D) which hosted

111. A shuttle service was launched in Boston with the ------- of providing tourists with easy access to the city's attractions.

(A) intention
(B) intend
(C) intended
(D) intends

112. All tenants are reminded to separate any recyclable materials ------- they dispose of their trash.

(A) when
(B) that
(C) besides
(D) which

113. The ------- position at Strachan Bookstore comes with many responsibilities, including recruitment.

(A) hesitant
(B) apparent
(C) supervisory
(D) obedient

114. Due to persistent technical problems, the venue manager was forced to ------- the concert to June 15.

(A) bother
(B) reschedule
(C) associate
(D) cancel

115. Dunbar Corporation is the chip ------- that Kayline Computers has selected to be its supplier for the next five years.

(A) manufacturer
(B) manufacture
(C) manufactures
(D) manufacturing

116. Upon hearing about the department head's resignation, Ms. Flint indicated ------- was interested in the position.

(A) she
(B) her
(C) hers
(D) herself

117. Both the paint supply store on Main Avenue and the one on Blackwell Street had ------- cans of white paint left.

(A) no
(B) every
(C) anyone
(D) another

118. ------- the increase in delivery fees, people continue to order food from mobile platforms.

(A) Rather than
(B) Even though
(C) Instead of
(D) Despite

119. Patients should notify the clinic ------- a day in advance if they expect to miss an appointment.

(A) evenly
(B) jointly
(C) at least
(D) too much

120. Because the mailing ------- was partially torn, the package could not be shipped to the recipient on schedule.

(A) program
(B) term
(C) sector
(D) label

해커스 토익 실전 LC+RC 2

GO ON TO THE NEXT PAGE

121. Applicants for the graphic designer position at Westwood Media are asked ------- their portfolios to the interview.

(A) have brought
(B) bringing
(C) will be bringing
(D) to bring

122. For quicker distribution of larger quantities of food, the ------- of volunteers to the Clover Soup Kitchen was inevitable.

(A) submission
(B) compliance
(C) addition
(D) formation

123. The earthquake was not powerful enough to produce any major ------- damage to buildings in the area.

(A) structuring
(B) structural
(C) structurally
(D) structures

124. Fox Laboratory has ------- urged scientists to examine their experimental data to make sure it is accurate.

(A) rigorous
(B) rigorousness
(C) rigorously
(D) more rigorous

125. Players of Dazzle Entertainment's popular online game have been ------- problems with downloading the latest update.

(A) passing
(B) experiencing
(C) relating
(D) establishing

126. Mr. Gresley created a comprehensive budget spreadsheet ------- expenses can be easily tracked.

(A) so that
(B) based on
(C) given that
(D) according to

127. Some cautious investors believe Beaumont Industries is too ------- in its plan to double its production capacity in two years.

(A) ambitious
(B) compliant
(C) reputable
(D) prevalent

128. Visitors to Nova Medical Supplies are allowed ------- as long as they have a valid guest pass.

(A) enter
(B) entry
(C) entering
(D) enters

129. City council member Ariak Miller is smart and efficient, but -------, she cares deeply about the welfare of vulnerable populations.

(A) in contrast
(B) until now
(C) to that end
(D) more importantly

130. Lyon Dairy signed a contract with a pest-control ------- to improve hygiene at its factory.

(A) identifier
(B) composer
(C) practitioner
(D) designer

PART 6

Directions: In this part, you will be asked to read four English texts. Each text is missing a word, phrase, or sentence. Select the answer choice that correctly completes the text and mark the corresponding letter (A), (B), (C), or (D) on the answer sheet.

🕐 **PART 6 권장 풀이 시간 8분**

Questions 131-134 refer to the following notice.

On August 5 at 2 P.M., the electricity on the third floor of our office will be shut down to let technicians conduct some electrical repairs. -------. Please save any files ------- you are
131.   **132.**
working on and turn off your computers before that time. An announcement ------- over the
133.
loudspeaker 15 minutes beforehand to remind you about this. We'll notify you later when you can turn your computers back on. We apologize for the -------. Should you have any
134.
questions, please direct them to your immediate supervisor.

131. (A) They assured us that the installation process was successful.
(B) The date the technicians will do the repairs has not been decided.
(C) The scheduling system sends real-time notifications.
(D) The work is expected to last for no more than 30 minutes.

132. (A) which
(B) among
(C) whose
(D) from

133. (A) to make
(B) will be made
(C) that was made
(D) had been made

134. (A) cancellation
(B) resistance
(C) inconvenience
(D) breakage

GO ON TO THE NEXT PAGE

Questions 135-138 refer to the following advertisement.

Choose an Internet Plan That's Just Right for You

With QuikLink, you'll get the fastest Internet speeds at the most affordable prices. Choose from five different home Internet plans ------- from Basic to Premium. -------. To learn more
135. **136.**
about our plans, ------- visit www.quicklink.com. Find the one that matches your needs, and
137.
then select the option to -------. The process is quick and easy, and you'll be signed up in no
138.
time. So what are you waiting for? Become a member of the QuikLink today!

---

135. (A) range
(B) ranging
(C) ranged
(D) ranges

136. (A) Both are suitable for residential or business clients.
(B) Each features a stable, high-speed connection.
(C) We've set up a program for the exclusive use of long-term members.
(D) They will be released by the end of the year.

137. (A) simply
(B) simple
(C) simplify
(D) simpler

138. (A) expand
(B) advance
(C) register
(D) search

Questions 139-142 refer to the following Web page information.

About the Eco-Trail Backpack

Chester Mountain Equipment recognizes that ------- who spends time in nature wants to
139.
protect it. In order to reduce waste, we ------- an eco-friendly backpack made from
140.
100 percent recycled materials. The fabric of the Eco-Trail Backpack is composed entirely of

plastic fibers from discarded beverage bottles. -------. The strength of these materials makes
141.
it possible to craft a very durable backpack. So owners will not need a ------- any time soon.
142.
The end result is a backpack that significantly reduces the environmental footprint of the

user.

---

139. (A) everyone
  (B) those
  (C) ourselves
  (D) others

140. (A) were creating
  (B) have created
  (C) will create
  (D) would be created

141. (A) This backpack can be easily stored in
    a small space.
  (B) The frame is made solely from
    recycled aluminum.
  (C) You will need to order this product in
    advance.
  (D) Several accessories are being sold
    separately.

142. (A) modification
  (B) confirmation
  (C) replacement
  (D) demonstration

GO ON TO THE NEXT PAGE

Questions 143-146 refer to the following instructions.

Thank you for purchasing the Welting G5B Electric Toothbrush. With its powerful rotating brush, this device will improve the ------- of your teeth as well as your oral health. Please
143.
follow these cleaning guidelines:

Approximately once a week, you should remove the brush head and run it under warm water. -------, use a damp cloth to wipe down the handle, making sure to get into the grooves
144.
or ridges. Never submerge the handle in water. -------. Finally, clean the charger with a mild
145.
disinfectant to prevent bacteria from forming on the toothbrush or charger. For your safety, please be ------- that you should unplug it before cleaning.
146.

143. (A) appear
(B) appearance
(C) appeared
(D) appearing

144. (A) In that case
(B) Similarly
(C) Next
(D) And yet

145. (A) Each component should be cleaned every day.
(B) It has been designed to be completely waterproof.
(C) There are electrical parts that may be damaged.
(D) The uneven surface makes it much easier to grip.

146. (A) advised
(B) affected
(C) evaluated
(D) provided

PART 7

Directions: In this part, you will be asked to read several texts, such as advertisements, articles, instant messages, or examples of business correspondence. Each text is followed by several questions. Select the best answer and mark the corresponding letter (A), (B), (C), or (D) on your answer sheet.

⏱ **PART 7 권장 풀이 시간** 54분

Questions 147-148 refer to the following job posting.

Server Position

The Broadview Diner is looking for a server to help create a memorable dining experience for guests. The successful applicant can choose between working days or evenings, but some weekend work will be necessary.

Previous experience as a restaurant server is preferred but not mandatory. However, we do require that applicants have completed the Food Server Certificate Program. In addition, they must demonstrate a capacity to perform multiple tasks simultaneously in a high-stress environment, as well as strong communication skills.

To apply for the position, send your résumé to Joshua Williams at j.williams@broadviewdiner.com.

---

147. What is indicated about the Broadview Diner?

(A) It is located in a rural region.
(B) It offers shift flexibility to staff.
(C) It stays open later on weekends.
(D) It is headed by an award-winning chef.

148. What is listed as a requirement for the position?

(A) Prior experience in a similar role
(B) Graduation from a culinary institute
(C) Ability to multitask under pressure
(D) Fluency in several languages

GO ON TO THE NEXT PAGE ➤

Questions 149-150 refer to the following information on a Web page.

www.riggsonproperties.com/listings

Commercial Space for Lease

If you are unhappy with the current location of your shop, consider renting this recently vacated commercial space in The Village Square in Sommerville. It has a clean, modern design and receives a substantial amount of foot traffic each day.

Details:
- 100 square meters
- A storage area with rear access
- Ample parking for employees and customers
- A one-year minimum contract, with favorable terms for longer contracts

Established 20 years ago, The Village Square is a beloved local landmark catering to large residential communities. It is situated close to the Rosedale Subway Station and many bus stops. For assistance, contact Riggson Properties at 517-555-0429 or click **here**.

149. For whom is the information intended?

(A) New home purchasers
(B) Job applicants
(C) Small business owners
(D) Residential tenants

150. What is true about The Village Square?

(A) It currently has several vacancies.
(B) It was only recently constructed.
(C) It includes a community center.
(D) It is accessible by public transportation.

Thank you for choosing Sanitaria for your cleaning needs. Complete the following chart. Indicate your satisfaction with each service by choosing a number from 1 to 5, with 5 being the highest level of satisfaction. Select N/A for any areas that do not apply.

Area	1	2	3	4	5	N/A
Bedroom					✓	
Living room				✓		
Dining room				✓		
Bathroom					✓	
Conference room						✓
Lobby						✓

Additional feedback: I appreciated that the workers arrived on schedule and completed the work very quickly. They also behaved in a professional and courteous manner. The only complaint I have is that it was very hard to book a time through your Web site. It kept freezing, and I was forced to sign in repeatedly.

Review by ___ Jared Louis

151. Where was the service most likely performed?

(A) In an office
(B) In a home
(C) In a convention center
(D) In a medical facility

152. What problem does Mr. Louis mention?

(A) A start time was pushed back unexpectedly.
(B) A cleaning took longer to complete than planned.
(C) A worker behaved in an unprofessional manner.
(D) An appointment was hard to schedule online.

GO ON TO THE NEXT PAGE

Questions 153-154 refer to the following text-message chain.

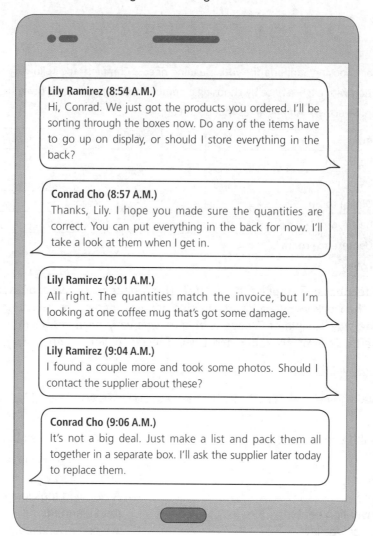

Lily Ramirez (8:54 A.M.)
Hi, Conrad. We just got the products you ordered. I'll be sorting through the boxes now. Do any of the items have to go up on display, or should I store everything in the back?

Conrad Cho (8:57 A.M.)
Thanks, Lily. I hope you made sure the quantities are correct. You can put everything in the back for now. I'll take a look at them when I get in.

Lily Ramirez (9:01 A.M.)
All right. The quantities match the invoice, but I'm looking at one coffee mug that's got some damage.

Lily Ramirez (9:04 A.M.)
I found a couple more and took some photos. Should I contact the supplier about these?

Conrad Cho (9:06 A.M.)
It's not a big deal. Just make a list and pack them all together in a separate box. I'll ask the supplier later today to replace them.

153. What does Ms. Ramirez ask about?

(A) Where to place items from an order
(B) What time a delivery will be made
(C) Whether a colleague is coming to work
(D) How to package the coffee mugs

154. At 9:06 A.M., what does Mr. Cho most likely mean when he writes, "It's not a big deal"?

(A) Ms. Ramirez will wait until he arrives.
(B) Ms. Ramirez can easily repair an item.
(C) Ms. Ramirez does not have to call a supplier.
(D) Ms. Ramirez will not attend a meeting.

Questions 155-157 refer to the following e-mail.

To	Nina Breyer <n.breyer@kbc_law.com>
From	Stefan Randolph <s.randolph@artkolekt.com>
Date	July 14
Subject	RE: Item #9199

Dear Ms. Breyer,

Thank you for your inquiry. — [1] —. I regret to inform you that item #9199 from our catalog, Adam Wynn's *Desert Landscape 1*, has been sold. As you know, he is quite a popular artist. That said, we do have other paintings to offer. — [2] —. One is a slightly smaller piece by Mr. Wynn. Another is from a newly discovered painter named Lena O'Lear. Both artworks have warm tones similar to the painting you wanted to buy, so they should match the colors of your new office. — [3] —. The painting by Ms. O'Lear will also be significantly cheaper.

You may click <u>here</u> to view the paintings online. — [4] —. Neither painting has been made available to the public yet, so access is currently restricted. As always, if there is anything else I can assist you with, do not hesitate to contact me.

Sincerely,

Stefan Randolph
Client Sales, Art Kolekt

155. What is probably true about Ms. O'Lear?

(A) She recently participated in an art exhibit.
(B) She studied art with Mr. Wynn.
(C) She sells her paintings in three different sizes.
(D) She is not as well-known as Mr. Wynn.

156. Why is Ms. Breyer buying a painting?

(A) To complete a personal collection
(B) To decorate a new office space
(C) To give as a gift to a friend
(D) To replace an artwork that was sold

157. In which of the positions marked [1], [2], [3], and [4] does the following sentence best belong?

"Please be ready to sign in with your registered username and password."

(A) [1]
(B) [2]
(C) [3]
(D) [4]

GO ON TO THE NEXT PAGE

Questions 158-160 refer to the following letter.

Kalina Winnicka
Winnicka Fashion
302 Coastal Drive
Los Angeles, CA, 90015

September 9

Dear Ms. Winnicka,

Our company is interested in an exclusive licensing deal to sell your clothing brands throughout South America. We believe such a venture has great potential for success. There is deep demand within the region for globally recognized fashion brands, particularly among your target demographic of consumers aged 12 to 16.

Decades of experience serving this market and an intimate knowledge of local conditions make our company uniquely positioned to meet this demand. In addition, our existing partnerships with retailers in the region will ensure that your clothes are made widely available.

A representative will be in touch with you soon to arrange a video conference call so that we can discuss our proposal in greater detail. I thank you in advance for your time and consideration.

Sincerely,

Andrew Kigame
President
Crosstown Fashion

---

158. What is suggested about Ms. Winnicka's company?

(A) It opened a factory in South America.
(B) It contacted Mr. Kigame about a partnership.
(C) It makes clothing for young consumers.
(D) It is seeking applicants for an open position.

159. The word "deep" in paragraph 1, line 2, is closest in meaning to

(A) immovable
(B) intense
(C) diverse
(D) decent

160. What is NOT mentioned as an advantage of working with Crosstown Fashion?

(A) Worldwide representation
(B) Extensive experience
(C) Local knowledge
(D) Regional partnerships

Royal Oak Publishing Ltd.

Royal Oak Publishing Ltd. takes pride in supporting new writers. We are therefore excited to include four works by first-time novelists in our summer collection. They will be available in bookstores across the country on 1 June, and we encourage you to check them out!

Complications by Pauline Mao
An exploration of the challenges faced by immigrants, this story follows Ms. Mao's childhood struggles to adapt to life in the United Kingdom. £11.99

Dark Reflection by Yolanda Wilcox
An intriguing historical novel about the murder of a nobleman that brings the world of 15th-century London to life for the reader. £10.99

A Path Forward by David Bach
Based on Mr. Bach's experience in the music business during the 1990s, this novel is about a young pop star trying to make it big. £12.99

Conflict Zone by Colin Sanders
Mr. Sanders draws on his 14 years in the military to create a thrilling World War II tale, complete with detailed maps and photographs of equipment from the period. £14.99

For more information about these books, visit www.royaloak.co.uk

161. What is the purpose of the advertisement?

(A) To publicize a company's special discounts
(B) To encourage participation in a summer program
(C) To promote the grand opening of a bookstore
(D) To announce the upcoming release of products

162. What is indicated about Mr. Bach?

(A) He relocated permanently to another country.
(B) He studied history as a university student.
(C) He worked in the entertainment industry.
(D) He served in the military for over a decade.

163. Which book includes various types of graphics?

(A) *Complications*
(B) *Dark Reflection*
(C) *A Path Forward*
(D) *Conflict Zone*

GO ON TO THE NEXT PAGE

The Gladstone Cultural Hub will be hosting a special showing of the documentary *The Depths Below*. — [1] —. It explores the Great Barrier Reef in Australia, focusing on the diverse organisms inhabiting this complex ecosystem and the many environmental risks they face. — [2] —. Selected as the winner in the Best New Documentary category by the National Arts Council last month, *The Depths Below* has been praised by critics for its stunning visuals and thought-provoking content.

The event will take place on April 5 from 6 P.M. to 9 P.M. The running time of the documentary is two hours, and it will be followed by a talk by the director, Peter Warren. — [3] —. Mr. Warren, who is also a renowned marine biologist, will discuss the challenges of making the documentary as well as what needs to be done to protect our oceans. Afterwards, he will respond to inquiries from audience members.

This documentary presentation is part of the Gladstone Cultural Hub's ongoing Environmental Awareness Series. Regular admission costs $23 and can be purchased online. — [4] —. Act now to avoid missing out on this amazing opportunity!

164. What is being announced?

(A) A play production
(B) An art exhibit
(C) A book signing
(D) A film screening

165. What is indicated about *The Depths Below*?

(A) It presents a description of a fictional situation.
(B) It is the recipient of a national award.
(C) It was released in theaters one month ago.
(D) It received widespread criticism from the public.

166. What will most likely happen during the final part of the event?

(A) New filming plans will be revealed.
(B) Participants will ask a director some questions.
(C) Donations will be requested for a charity.
(D) A handout will be distributed to the attendees.

167. In which of the positions marked [1], [2], [3], and [4] does the following sentence best belong?

"A portion of the ticket sales will go toward marine conservation efforts."

(A) [1]
(B) [2]
(C) [3]
(D) [4]

New Direction for the Indus Group

July 14—The Indus Group announced plans for a massive wind-solar power facility in the Gurjarat region of India. The site of the new hybrid plant has already been selected, and the groundbreaking ceremony is scheduled to take place on October 1. With a budget of over USD 40 million and a timeline of 18 months, the company is confident that there will be no problems during the building phase.

Indus Group CEO Alia Basu expressed her appreciation for the Indian government's assistance. "Without the various tax incentives and grants offered by the Ministry of Energy, the project would have never been considered," she said. "The plant will supply electricity to thousands of residents without producing pollution or contributing to climate change." This is Ms. Basu's first initiative since being moved up into the CEO position three months ago, and it represents her desire to make the Indus Group a major player in green technologies.

Despite the media hype surrounding the environmental benefits of the Indus Group's latest undertaking, there remains some opposition to it. Specifically, there are concerns that the hybrid power plant will not be profitable and will negatively affect the company's stock price. In response, the Indus Group plans to hold a special shareholders meeting next month. Additional financial and technical details about the project will be provided at that time.

168. What is expected to happen on October 1?

(A) The site of a power plant will finally be selected.
(B) An energy company will merge with a competitor.
(C) A construction project will officially commence.
(D) The operating budget of a facility will be approved.

169. What is suggested about the Ministry of Energy?

(A) It provided financial support to a company.
(B) It increased taxes on energy corporations.
(C) It strengthened regulations about pollution.
(D) It received complaints from many residents.

170. What is stated about Ms. Basu?

(A) She contributes funds to groups that fight climate change.
(B) She launched several initiatives involving the Indus Group.
(C) She was promoted to a senior management position recently.
(D) She has expressed uncertainty about using green technologies.

171. Why will the Indus Group hold a meeting next month?

(A) To provide information to journalists
(B) To introduce a new company executive
(C) To address the worries of investors
(D) To reveal a technical innovation

GO ON TO THE NEXT PAGE

Questions 172-175 refer to the following online chat discussion.

Carlos Ortega [10:20 A.M.]
Good morning, Nathan and Tara. I have something to share with you. Our CEO just informed me that the city of Brantford has chosen our company to design and build a new bridge over the Tyler River. The three of us will be taking the lead on this.

Nathan Boyle [10:22 A.M.]
Wow, that's going to be a major undertaking. I feel nervous but excited to be a part of it.

Tara Hong [10:23 A.M.]
Me too. Do you have any details about the budget for the project?

Carlos Ortega [10:24 A.M.]
It has been set at $6 million. I guess the Brantford city council organized a special event last year to collect funds from private and corporate donors. It was a great success.

Nathan Boyle [10:26 A.M.]
What about the bridge itself? What type will we be designing, and are there any special requirements that we need to be aware of?

Carlos Ortega [10:28 A.M.]
There's a strong preference for a suspension bridge similar to the one built in Greenville last year. But the catch is that the bridge over the Tyler River has to include a section that can be raised to allow ship traffic to pass underneath.

Tara Hong [10:30 A.M.]
Are you serious? That will be really complex. And it'll be expensive as well. I'm not sure we can pull it off without going over budget.

Nathan Boyle [10:32 A.M.]
I don't think it will be a problem, Carlos. I worked on a similar bridge project at my previous company. If you like, I can put together a presentation about the steps my team took to keep costs down. I could probably be ready by Wednesday afternoon.

Carlos Ortega [10:34 A.M.]
Thanks, Nathan. I'll contact our administrative assistant now and ensure that we can use the main conference room on that day.

Send

172. In what field do the writers most likely work?

(A) Recruitment
(B) Accounting
(C) Transportation
(D) Construction

173. What is mentioned about Brantford city council?

(A) It hired multiple companies.
(B) It purchased a new property.
(C) It held a fundraiser last year.
(D) It applied for a large loan.

174. At 10:30 A.M., what does Ms. Hong most likely mean when she writes, "Are you serious"?

(A) She is concerned about the feasibility of a project.
(B) She is grateful that a budget amount was increased.
(C) She is surprised by Mr. Ortega's rejection of an offer.
(D) She is eager to begin working on an assignment.

175. What will Mr. Ortega most likely do next?

(A) Prepare for a group presentation
(B) Make a reservation to use a facility
(C) Select a new member of a team
(D) Contact a building manager

GO ON TO THE NEXT PAGE

Wheelz Auto Rental
Customer Satisfaction Survey Summary (June)

Category	Customer Satisfaction Level	Change from Previous Month
Cleanliness of vehicles	93%	+8%
Variety of models	56%	-7%
Helpfulness of staff	78%	+10%
Affordability of rates	16%	-3%
Change in Overall Customer Satisfaction Level: +8%		

This analysis was conducted by Sandra Sharpe, Director of Marketing. Questions should be sent to s.sharpe@wzauto.com. Related reports can be accessed at www.wzauto.com/archives by authorized personnel.

MIAMI (September 12)—At a press conference yesterday afternoon, Wheelz Auto Rental laid out its plans to expand into eight more cities in Florida, Texas, and Kentucky. Adam Willis, who took over Sandra Sharpe's position this month following her decision to retire, told reporters that the expansion is necessary to protect the company's current share of the market and maintain profits. "We are under increased pressure from other car rental chains," he said. "If we are not moving forward, we are moving backward."

Willis also explained that the CEO of the company is directing the project personally to ensure that all of the new branches are fully operational by January 2. The company will start accepting job applications on November 15. "We don't anticipate any delays, and we look forward to making our car rental services available to even more people," Willis added in closing.

176. What is suggested in the report about Wheelz Auto Rental?

(A) It has made plans to offer more car models.
(B) Its vehicles are cleaned only rarely.
(C) Its fees are considered high by many clients.
(D) It saw an overall drop in customer satisfaction.

177. What is true about Mr. Willis?

(A) He produced a summary report in June.
(B) He has expressed his intention to retire.
(C) He will transfer to a branch in Florida.
(D) He works in the marketing department.

178. What is the purpose of the article?

(A) To analyze a recent market trend
(B) To introduce a new corporate executive
(C) To announce a company's relocation
(D) To describe a firm's expansion plans

179. In the article, the word "directing" in paragraph 2, line 1, is closest in meaning to

(A) leading
(B) covering
(C) sending
(D) restricting

180. According to the article, what will happen on November 15?

(A) A branch office will open.
(B) A project team will be formed.
(C) A business site will be selected.
(D) A hiring process will begin.

GO ON TO THE NEXT PAGE

Questions 181-185 refer to the following Web pages.

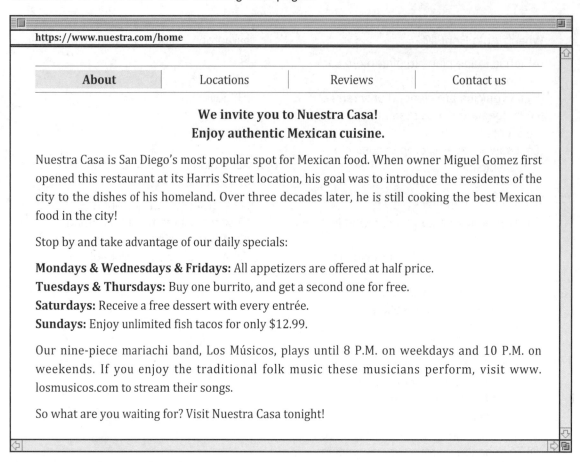

| About | Locations | Reviews | Contact us |

We invite you to Nuestra Casa!
Enjoy authentic Mexican cuisine.

Nuestra Casa is San Diego's most popular spot for Mexican food. When owner Miguel Gomez first opened this restaurant at its Harris Street location, his goal was to introduce the residents of the city to the dishes of his homeland. Over three decades later, he is still cooking the best Mexican food in the city!

Stop by and take advantage of our daily specials:

Mondays & Wednesdays & Fridays: All appetizers are offered at half price.
Tuesdays & Thursdays: Buy one burrito, and get a second one for free.
Saturdays: Receive a free dessert with every entrée.
Sundays: Enjoy unlimited fish tacos for only $12.99.

Our nine-piece mariachi band, Los Músicos, plays until 8 P.M. on weekdays and 10 P.M. on weekends. If you enjoy the traditional folk music these musicians perform, visit www.losmusicos.com to stream their songs.

So what are you waiting for? Visit Nuestra Casa tonight!

| About | Locations | **Reviews** | Contact us |

Having heard many positive things about this restaurant from coworkers and family members, I was excited to finally try it. A classmate from my university days was in town to meet a client, so I made a reservation for dinner there last Sunday. The daily special was reasonably priced and the ingredients were very fresh. I was also really impressed with the atmosphere. All of the staff members were friendly, and the decorations in the main dining area were bright and cheerful. The only issue I have with this restaurant is that the small parking lot was completely full when I arrived. I had to leave my car in a garage about three blocks away, which was inconvenient. Dealing with this issue would result in a better experience for customers.

Posted by Astrid Larsson, April 20

181. What is stated about Nuestra Casa?

(A) It features cuisine from several
countries.
(B) Its owner prepares food for customers.
(C) Its location has changed several
times.
(D) It is scheduled to reopen in April.

182. What is NOT true about Los Músicos?

(A) It includes a total of nine musicians.
(B) It performs until 8 P.M. on Saturdays.
(C) It plays a traditional style of folk music.
(D) It allows people to access its songs
online.

183. Who did Ms. Larsson have dinner with?

(A) A new coworker
(B) A family member
(C) A former classmate
(D) A business client

184. What is suggested about Ms. Larsson?

(A) She ordered a seafood dish for dinner.
(B) She thought the band was too loud.
(C) She has visited Nuestra Casa before.
(D) She changed the date of her
reservation.

185. According to the second Web page, how
can Nuestra Casa offer a better
experience for its customers?

(A) By reducing the prices of some dishes
(B) By providing staff with more training
(C) By redecorating the main dining area
(D) By securing additional parking spaces

GO ON TO THE NEXT PAGE

Questions 186-190 refer to the following e-mails and memo.

To: Neil Shannon <n.shannon@mexigo.com>
From: Rebecca Tan <r.tan@postouchsolutions.com>
Date: April 12
Subject: Agreed terms

Dear Mr. Shannon,

Thank you for meeting with us earlier. I am writing to summarize the terms of our agreement.

As agreed, POS Touch Solutions will install four self-ordering kiosks, one for each Mexigo restaurant in Woodbury. The initial installation charge will be $1,800 per unit. We will also provide free repairs of defective hardware and periodic software updates. Note that we do not anticipate a need for frequent repairs since our kiosks have a 99.9 percent uptime rate.

Other services that require a visit from a technician will be charged separately at a cost of $450 per visit, but we will only bill you $150 for technical issues that we can resolve remotely. Our technicians are available to service kiosks around the clock.

Please contact me if there are any errors. Otherwise, I will send the final contract before the end of the week.

Sincerely,

Rebecca Tan
Regional sales vice president, POS Touch Solutions

To: Rebecca Tan <r.tan@postouchsolutions.com>
From: Neil Shannon <n.shannon@mexigo.com>
Date: August 19
Subject: Equipment removal and reinstallation

Dear Ms. Tan,

I need to inform you that our restaurant on Goldfinch Street will be temporarily closing at the end of the month for renovations. We aim to move all equipment to our warehouse on Poplar Avenue by August 31. I'd therefore like to have the self-ordering kiosk removed before that date and reinstalled later.

At this time, I'm not sure when the renovations will be done. I can give you a firm answer by early next month. For now, please send a technician to the above location to carry out the removal.

Yours truly,

Neil Shannon
Regional operations manager, Mexigo Restaurant

MEMO

To: All Mexigo Staff (Goldfinch Branch)
From: Sarah Martinez, Branch Manager
Date: October 4
Subject: Quick update

I can confirm that the newly renovated location will be ready to open soon. As you may remember, people standing in line to order at the kiosk often blocked the main entrance. Therefore, we moved the kiosk next to the staff lounge and plan to put more tables in its place. We are just waiting on a shipment of new tabletops from our supplier before we reopen.

I'm sure many of you are eager to return after being reassigned to our other locations. To show appreciation for your patience and cooperation, the company has arranged for a picnic this Saturday at Hellman Park. I've already contacted the other branch managers about moving your shifts around to avoid any scheduling conflicts.

186. In the first e-mail, what is stated about POS Touch Solutions?

(A) It updates its software once a month.
(B) It provides some complimentary services.
(C) It plans to redesign its kiosks soon.
(D) It has its main office in Woodbury.

187. How much will Mexigo restaurant be charged by POS Touch Solutions in August?

(A) $0
(B) $150
(C) $450
(D) $1,800

188. When did Mr. Shannon most likely confirm an installation date with Ms. Tan?

(A) In August
(B) In September
(C) In October
(D) In November

189. What is suggested about the restaurant on Goldfinch Street?

(A) It will soon have more than one kiosk.
(B) It is the oldest of the four Woodbury locations.
(C) It is close to a warehouse on Poplar Avenue.
(D) It had an ordering area crowded with customers.

190. According to the memo, why did Ms. Martinez contact the other branch managers?

(A) To inquire about some hiring plans
(B) To invite them to an opening
(C) To reorganize some work hours
(D) To request assistance with a move

GO ON TO THE NEXT PAGE

Questions 191-195 refer to the following e-mails and invoice.

To	All Freelance Tour Guides
From	Brett Owen <b.owen@voyagertours.com>
Subject	Fees
Date	May 10

With the approach of tourist season, I want to provide an updated list of fees. It reflects the feedback we received from many of you last summer that the payments were insufficient. Hopefully, you are all satisfied with the changes.

Tour Type	Description	Fee
Individual Half-Day Tour	Provide one client with a tour of four city landmarks	$100
Individual Full-Day Tour	Provide one client with a tour of eight city landmarks	$175
Group Half-Day Tour	Provide up to six clients with a tour of four city landmarks	$140
Group Full-Day Tour	Provide up to six clients with a tour of eight city landmarks	$220
Surcharge	For longer-than-scheduled tours, an hourly rate will be applied to the extra time.	$25/hour

Make sure to reflect these updated fees in your billing invoices. Please note that our bookkeeper will be on leave in July, so you should e-mail the invoices directly to me during this period rather than to Mr. Parsons as you usually do.

Sincerely,

Brett Owen, Voyager Tours

Voyager Tours

Invoice #: 0112

Tour Guide: Madeline Terrence

E-Mail: m.terrence@speedmail.com

Date: June 29

Date	Details	Fee
June 11	Individual Half-Day Tour (A.M.)	$100
June 23	Group Full-Day Tour	$220
June 23	Surcharge	$25
	Total	$345

To: Madeline Terrence <m.terrence@speedmail.com>
From: Brett Owen <b.owen@voyagertours.com>
Subject: June Invoice
Date: July 4

Hi Madeline,

It looks like there is an error in your June invoice. You filled in for another tour guide, James Sand, when he became ill on June 15. However, the individual half-day tour you conducted that day is not included. Please send me the updated invoice as soon as possible. Once I receive it, I will transfer the payment to your account.

Also, I have been contacted by a travel agent that wishes to arrange a three-day group tour of the major tourist attractions in Southern California. Given that you always get positive reviews from clients, I think you would be perfect for this. Please call me at 555-0398 to discuss your fee.

Sincerely,

Brett Owen, Voyager Tours

191. What is the purpose of the first e-mail?

(A) To request that some tours be rescheduled
(B) To explain that additional guides will be hired
(C) To ask for feedback from staff
(D) To announce a payment change

192. Who most likely is Mr. Parsons?

(A) A salesperson
(B) A travel agent
(C) A tour guide
(D) An accountant

193. What can be concluded about Ms. Terrence?

(A) She had more tours in June than in other months.
(B) She led a tour that took longer than planned.
(C) She joined Voyager Tours a month ago.
(D) She made a request to change the date of a tour.

194. What amount has Ms. Terrence forgotten to bill Voyager Tours?

(A) $100
(B) $175
(C) $140
(D) $220

195. According to the second e-mail, why does Mr. Owen ask Ms. Terrence to call him?

(A) To confirm reimbursement of a travel expense
(B) To discuss reviews from customers
(C) To negotiate the price of a special service
(D) To get suggestions about popular tourist sites

GO ON TO THE NEXT PAGE

Skilled Builders Institute

www.skilledbuilders.au

Serving southeast Australia for over 40 years, Skilled Builders Institute produces graduates of a high calibre, offering hands-on instruction with a focus on developing usable skills. The following programs are open for enrolment:

Programs	Description
Certificate I	Learn basic skills in preparation for an apprenticeship
Certificate II	Learn the practical and theoretical aspects of the carpentry trade
Certificate III	Gain specialist skills in preparation for qualifying as a licensed plumber or electrician
Certificate IV	Obtain the skills and knowledge to manage construction projects or operate a construction business

Please inquire if you need financial assistance. Tuition subsidies are available through our partnership with the Australian government.

The Perth Standard

Skilled Builders Institute to Open Campus in Perth

by Ewan Reynolds

PERTH (18 November)—Skilled Builders Institute, a well-known training academy with campuses in Brisbane, Canberra, and Adelaide, is opening a fourth location in Perth. Students are already signing up for the first classes at this campus, which begin on 22 January.

At a press conference, Skilled Builders Institute CEO Leslie Mitchell said she expects to see a rise in enrolment as the country undergoes a construction boom. "My aim is for us to be the nation's leading supplier of trained personnel. Next year, I want to create more courses that cater to all of the building trades," she said.

Interested readers may contact info@skilledbuilders.au to learn more about course schedules, fees, and other details.

To: Skilled Builders <info@skilledbuilders.au>
From: Tony Ayoub <t.ayoub@peoplemail.com>
Subject: Urgent Inquiry
Date: 21 November

To Whom It May Concern,

My name is Tony Ayoub, and I am interested in taking a course at your new campus. I hope to take it at the next available date so that I can finish soon. There are many job opportunities in my area.

I want to take a course in preparation for a licensure exam. I was working as an electrician in my home country for many years before immigrating here to Australia.

I have a problem, however. Since I have been without work for several months, I am not sure that I can pay the tuition for a course. So I would like to apply for assistance. Could you tell me what the requirements are?

Thank you.

Tony Ayoub

196. What is indicated about Skilled Builders Institute in the brochure?

(A) It moved the start date of classes.
(B) It teaches students through practical training.
(C) It provides a job placement service for graduates.
(D) It allows students to participate in classes remotely.

197. According to the article, what does Ms. Mitchell want to do?

(A) Enter the construction business
(B) Introduce a larger variety of courses
(C) Accept more international students
(D) Provide courses for other industries

198. What is most likely true about Mr. Ayoub?

(A) He wants to start a course in January.
(B) He is preparing to move overseas.
(C) He applied for a government job.
(D) He started a new business in Perth.

199. Which course would best meet Mr. Ayoub's needs?

(A) Certificate I
(B) Certificate II
(C) Certificate III
(D) Certificate IV

200. What does Mr. Ayoub inquire about?

(A) Signing up on a Web site
(B) Taking some classes online
(C) Securing a tuition subsidy
(D) Finding a campus location

This is the end of the test. You may review Parts 5, 6, and 7 if you finish the test early.

⁄Review 체크리스트

TEST 5를 푼 다음, 아래 체크리스트에 따라 틀린 문제를 리뷰하고 박스에 완료 여부를 표시하세요.
만약 시험까지 얼마 남지 않았다면, 파란색으로 표시된 항목이라도 꼭 확인하세요.

☐ 틀린 문제의 경우, 다시 풀어봤다.

☐ 틀린 문제의 경우, 스크립트/해석을 확인하며 지문/문제의 내용을 정확하게 파악했다.

☐ 해설을 통해 각 문제의 정답과 오답의 근거가 무엇인지 정확하게 파악했다.

☐ PART 1과 PART 2에서 틀린 문제의 경우, 선택한 오답의 유형이 무엇이었는지 확인하고 같
  은 함정에 빠지지 않도록 정리해두었다.

☐ PART 3와 PART 4의 각 문제에서 사용된 패러프레이징을 확인했다.

☐ PART 5와 PART 6의 경우, 틀린 문제에서 사용된 문법 포인트 또는 정답 및 오답 어휘를 정
  리했다.

☐ PART 6의 알맞은 문장 고르기 문제의 경우, 지문 전체를 정확하게 해석하며 전체 글의 흐
  름과 빈칸 주변 문맥을 정확하게 파악하는 연습을 했다.

☐ PART 7에서 질문과 보기의 키워드를 찾아 표시하며 지문에서 정답의 근거가 되는 문장이
  나 구절을 찾아보고, 문제에서 사용된 패러프레이징을 확인했다.

☐ PART 1~PART 4는 받아쓰기 & 쉐도잉 워크북을 활용하여, TEST에 수록된 핵심 문장을 받
  아쓰고 따라 읽으며 복습했다.

☐ PART 1~PART 7은 단어암기자료를 활용하여, TEST에 수록된 핵심 어휘와 표현을 암기
  했다.

많은 양의 문제를 푸는 것도 중요하지만, 틀린 문제를 제대로 리뷰하는 것도 중요합니다.
틀린 문제를 한 번 더 꼼꼼히 리뷰한다면, 빠른 시간 내에 효과적으로 목표 점수를 달성할 수 있습니다.

해커스 토익 실전 LC+RC 2

정답
점수 환산표
ANSWER SHEET

정답 ANSWER KEYS

▌TEST 1

LISTENING TEST					READING TEST				
1 (A)	21 (C)	41 (C)	61 (D)	81 (B)	101 (A)	121 (D)	141 (C)	161 (C)	181 (A)
2 (D)	22 (B)	42 (B)	62 (D)	82 (C)	102 (A)	122 (B)	142 (A)	162 (B)	182 (D)
3 (D)	23 (A)	43 (D)	63 (B)	83 (D)	103 (D)	123 (B)	143 (B)	163 (D)	183 (D)
4 (D)	24 (B)	44 (B)	64 (D)	84 (A)	104 (D)	124 (B)	144 (C)	164 (D)	184 (C)
5 (A)	25 (A)	45 (C)	65 (D)	85 (C)	105 (B)	125 (C)	145 (C)	165 (C)	185 (D)
6 (B)	26 (B)	46 (B)	66 (C)	86 (A)	106 (C)	126 (C)	146 (A)	166 (B)	186 (D)
7 (B)	27 (C)	47 (D)	67 (B)	87 (A)	107 (A)	127 (B)	147 (C)	167 (C)	187 (B)
8 (C)	28 (B)	48 (C)	68 (C)	88 (D)	108 (C)	128 (A)	148 (C)	168 (C)	188 (D)
9 (A)	29 (C)	49 (D)	69 (D)	89 (C)	109 (A)	129 (D)	149 (C)	169 (B)	189 (D)
10 (A)	30 (A)	50 (B)	70 (D)	90 (B)	110 (C)	130 (B)	150 (B)	170 (C)	190 (B)
11 (C)	31 (C)	51 (D)	71 (C)	91 (B)	111 (C)	131 (C)	151 (C)	171 (C)	191 (B)
12 (C)	32 (B)	52 (C)	72 (B)	92 (D)	112 (C)	132 (A)	152 (B)	172 (A)	192 (B)
13 (A)	33 (B)	53 (C)	73 (D)	93 (B)	113 (D)	133 (D)	153 (B)	173 (B)	193 (C)
14 (A)	34 (A)	54 (A)	74 (A)	94 (D)	114 (C)	134 (B)	154 (D)	174 (A)	194 (C)
15 (C)	35 (D)	55 (A)	75 (D)	95 (B)	115 (B)	135 (C)	155 (B)	175 (C)	195 (B)
16 (B)	36 (D)	56 (A)	76 (C)	96 (C)	116 (D)	136 (B)	156 (A)	176 (D)	196 (B)
17 (A)	37 (A)	57 (C)	77 (C)	97 (B)	117 (B)	137 (D)	157 (C)	177 (B)	197 (C)
18 (A)	38 (B)	58 (C)	78 (B)	98 (C)	118 (A)	138 (D)	158 (C)	178 (B)	198 (A)
19 (C)	39 (D)	59 (C)	79 (A)	99 (A)	119 (A)	139 (C)	159 (C)	179 (C)	199 (D)
20 (A)	40 (C)	60 (A)	80 (B)	100 (B)	120 (C)	140 (B)	160 (B)	180 (A)	200 (C)

TEST 2

LISTENING TEST

1 (C)	21 (A)	41 (B)	61 (A)	81 (C)
2 (B)	22 (C)	42 (B)	62 (A)	82 (C)
3 (D)	23 (B)	43 (D)	63 (B)	83 (B)
4 (A)	24 (B)	44 (A)	64 (B)	84 (A)
5 (B)	25 (A)	45 (B)	65 (C)	85 (C)
6 (A)	26 (B)	46 (B)	66 (C)	86 (C)
7 (A)	27 (B)	47 (A)	67 (A)	87 (D)
8 (B)	28 (A)	48 (D)	68 (C)	88 (A)
9 (A)	29 (B)	49 (D)	69 (A)	89 (C)
10 (B)	30 (C)	50 (D)	70 (D)	90 (B)
11 (B)	31 (C)	51 (C)	71 (D)	91 (B)
12 (C)	32 (D)	52 (A)	72 (B)	92 (C)
13 (B)	33 (C)	53 (A)	73 (B)	93 (C)
14 (A)	34 (A)	54 (D)	74 (B)	94 (D)
15 (A)	35 (A)	55 (B)	75 (C)	95 (C)
16 (B)	36 (D)	56 (B)	76 (B)	96 (B)
17 (B)	37 (A)	57 (C)	77 (C)	97 (B)
18 (B)	38 (B)	58 (C)	78 (D)	98 (A)
19 (C)	39 (A)	59 (B)	79 (C)	99 (B)
20 (B)	40 (C)	60 (D)	80 (A)	100 (D)

READING TEST

101 (B)	121 (D)	141 (A)	161 (C)	181 (B)
102 (B)	122 (C)	142 (D)	162 (D)	182 (A)
103 (D)	123 (B)	143 (B)	163 (D)	183 (B)
104 (D)	124 (A)	144 (C)	164 (D)	184 (D)
105 (B)	125 (C)	145 (D)	165 (C)	185 (D)
106 (D)	126 (D)	146 (D)	166 (D)	186 (C)
107 (D)	127 (B)	147 (A)	167 (A)	187 (C)
108 (C)	128 (D)	148 (C)	168 (C)	188 (C)
109 (B)	129 (C)	149 (A)	169 (B)	189 (B)
110 (D)	130 (D)	150 (D)	170 (D)	190 (B)
111 (B)	131 (C)	151 (D)	171 (C)	191 (B)
112 (C)	132 (A)	152 (C)	172 (D)	192 (D)
113 (B)	133 (D)	153 (D)	173 (B)	193 (C)
114 (D)	134 (A)	154 (A)	174 (C)	194 (D)
115 (A)	135 (C)	155 (D)	175 (D)	195 (C)
116 (C)	136 (A)	156 (D)	176 (A)	196 (C)
117 (A)	137 (B)	157 (D)	177 (D)	197 (D)
118 (C)	138 (C)	158 (C)	178 (B)	198 (B)
119 (B)	139 (B)	159 (D)	179 (C)	199 (B)
120 (C)	140 (C)	160 (B)	180 (D)	200 (D)

정답 ANSWER KEYS

▌TEST 3

LISTENING TEST					READING TEST				
1 (C)	21 (A)	41 (D)	61 (A)	81 (C)	101 (C)	121 (B)	141 (C)	161 (D)	181 (B)
2 (C)	22 (B)	42 (B)	62 (C)	82 (D)	102 (A)	122 (C)	142 (A)	162 (C)	182 (D)
3 (D)	23 (B)	43 (C)	63 (A)	83 (B)	103 (B)	123 (D)	143 (B)	163 (D)	183 (A)
4 (B)	24 (C)	44 (B)	64 (B)	84 (D)	104 (B)	124 (C)	144 (B)	164 (C)	184 (C)
5 (D)	25 (A)	45 (B)	65 (A)	85 (A)	105 (C)	125 (A)	145 (D)	165 (B)	185 (C)
6 (C)	26 (B)	46 (C)	66 (B)	86 (B)	106 (B)	126 (D)	146 (A)	166 (D)	186 (B)
7 (B)	27 (C)	47 (A)	67 (C)	87 (A)	107 (B)	127 (D)	147 (B)	167 (C)	187 (C)
8 (B)	28 (C)	48 (B)	68 (A)	88 (A)	108 (C)	128 (A)	148 (C)	168 (B)	188 (A)
9 (B)	29 (A)	49 (C)	69 (C)	89 (D)	109 (B)	129 (B)	149 (D)	169 (B)	189 (D)
10 (A)	30 (A)	50 (C)	70 (B)	90 (C)	110 (D)	130 (B)	150 (D)	170 (C)	190 (D)
11 (C)	31 (C)	51 (D)	71 (B)	91 (A)	111 (C)	131 (C)	151 (C)	171 (C)	191 (A)
12 (B)	32 (B)	52 (C)	72 (C)	92 (B)	112 (B)	132 (B)	152 (A)	172 (A)	192 (B)
13 (A)	33 (A)	53 (B)	73 (D)	93 (C)	113 (A)	133 (B)	153 (D)	173 (D)	193 (A)
14 (B)	34 (D)	54 (D)	74 (B)	94 (C)	114 (A)	134 (D)	154 (C)	174 (D)	194 (B)
15 (C)	35 (A)	55 (A)	75 (A)	95 (C)	115 (C)	135 (C)	155 (A)	175 (B)	195 (C)
16 (B)	36 (C)	56 (A)	76 (C)	96 (B)	116 (B)	136 (C)	156 (B)	176 (B)	196 (D)
17 (C)	37 (C)	57 (D)	77 (C)	97 (C)	117 (B)	137 (B)	157 (C)	177 (B)	197 (C)
18 (B)	38 (C)	58 (C)	78 (B)	98 (D)	118 (D)	138 (D)	158 (B)	178 (A)	198 (A)
19 (B)	39 (D)	59 (D)	79 (A)	99 (B)	119 (B)	139 (B)	159 (D)	179 (D)	199 (D)
20 (B)	40 (C)	60 (B)	80 (D)	100 (C)	120 (D)	140 (D)	160 (C)	180 (C)	200 (B)

TEST 4

LISTENING TEST

1 (C)	21 (A)	41 (C)	61 (D)	81 (B)
2 (A)	22 (A)	42 (D)	62 (A)	82 (B)
3 (B)	23 (A)	43 (C)	63 (B)	83 (C)
4 (D)	24 (B)	44 (A)	64 (D)	84 (B)
5 (D)	25 (A)	45 (A)	65 (C)	85 (A)
6 (C)	26 (C)	46 (C)	66 (C)	86 (A)
7 (B)	27 (A)	47 (A)	67 (D)	87 (D)
8 (C)	28 (B)	48 (A)	68 (C)	88 (A)
9 (C)	29 (B)	49 (D)	69 (B)	89 (A)
10 (B)	30 (A)	50 (B)	70 (B)	90 (C)
11 (A)	31 (B)	51 (A)	71 (B)	91 (B)
12 (B)	32 (B)	52 (D)	72 (C)	92 (D)
13 (A)	33 (C)	53 (B)	73 (D)	93 (A)
14 (C)	34 (D)	54 (A)	74 (C)	94 (C)
15 (A)	35 (C)	55 (B)	75 (A)	95 (A)
16 (B)	36 (D)	56 (C)	76 (D)	96 (A)
17 (A)	37 (A)	57 (A)	77 (D)	97 (D)
18 (B)	38 (C)	58 (A)	78 (B)	98 (B)
19 (B)	39 (B)	59 (C)	79 (D)	99 (B)
20 (C)	40 (B)	60 (C)	80 (C)	100 (C)

READING TEST

101 (D)	121 (D)	141 (B)	161 (C)	181 (D)
102 (C)	122 (B)	142 (D)	162 (B)	182 (C)
103 (D)	123 (A)	143 (D)	163 (C)	183 (B)
104 (A)	124 (C)	144 (B)	164 (D)	184 (C)
105 (B)	125 (B)	145 (D)	165 (B)	185 (C)
106 (B)	126 (A)	146 (A)	166 (A)	186 (C)
107 (C)	127 (C)	147 (D)	167 (C)	187 (A)
108 (D)	128 (B)	148 (C)	168 (B)	188 (A)
109 (C)	129 (B)	149 (D)	169 (C)	189 (D)
110 (B)	130 (A)	150 (C)	170 (D)	190 (C)
111 (B)	131 (B)	151 (B)	171 (C)	191 (B)
112 (A)	132 (B)	152 (C)	172 (B)	192 (C)
113 (C)	133 (C)	153 (A)	173 (C)	193 (C)
114 (C)	134 (D)	154 (D)	174 (A)	194 (A)
115 (D)	135 (C)	155 (C)	175 (C)	195 (C)
116 (D)	136 (D)	156 (C)	176 (A)	196 (C)
117 (C)	137 (C)	157 (B)	177 (B)	197 (D)
118 (C)	138 (A)	158 (D)	178 (B)	198 (A)
119 (B)	139 (A)	159 (B)	179 (D)	199 (C)
120 (B)	140 (C)	160 (D)	180 (D)	200 (C)

정답 ANSWER KEYS

▌TEST 5

LISTENING TEST

1 (B)	21 (B)	41 (D)	61 (B)	81 (B)
2 (C)	22 (A)	42 (B)	62 (D)	82 (D)
3 (C)	23 (B)	43 (C)	63 (A)	83 (B)
4 (D)	24 (C)	44 (C)	64 (C)	84 (D)
5 (A)	25 (B)	45 (A)	65 (B)	85 (A)
6 (D)	26 (A)	46 (B)	66 (C)	86 (C)
7 (B)	27 (B)	47 (A)	67 (D)	87 (A)
8 (C)	28 (C)	48 (A)	68 (D)	88 (D)
9 (A)	29 (A)	49 (C)	69 (B)	89 (B)
10 (A)	30 (A)	50 (A)	70 (D)	90 (C)
11 (B)	31 (C)	51 (B)	71 (A)	91 (D)
12 (A)	32 (C)	52 (D)	72 (C)	92 (B)
13 (B)	33 (B)	53 (D)	73 (D)	93 (C)
14 (A)	34 (C)	54 (A)	74 (B)	94 (C)
15 (B)	35 (B)	55 (B)	75 (B)	95 (B)
16 (C)	36 (D)	56 (D)	76 (C)	96 (A)
17 (A)	37 (A)	57 (A)	77 (A)	97 (D)
18 (B)	38 (B)	58 (D)	78 (D)	98 (B)
19 (C)	39 (A)	59 (B)	79 (B)	99 (D)
20 (B)	40 (B)	60 (C)	80 (C)	100 (A)

READING TEST

101 (B)	121 (D)	141 (B)	161 (D)	181 (B)
102 (B)	122 (C)	142 (C)	162 (C)	182 (B)
103 (C)	123 (B)	143 (B)	163 (D)	183 (C)
104 (D)	124 (C)	144 (C)	164 (D)	184 (A)
105 (B)	125 (B)	145 (C)	165 (B)	185 (D)
106 (C)	126 (A)	146 (A)	166 (B)	186 (B)
107 (B)	127 (A)	147 (B)	167 (D)	187 (C)
108 (D)	128 (B)	148 (C)	168 (C)	188 (B)
109 (B)	129 (D)	149 (C)	169 (A)	189 (D)
110 (B)	130 (C)	150 (D)	170 (C)	190 (C)
111 (A)	131 (D)	151 (B)	171 (C)	191 (D)
112 (A)	132 (A)	152 (D)	172 (D)	192 (D)
113 (C)	133 (B)	153 (A)	173 (C)	193 (B)
114 (B)	134 (C)	154 (C)	174 (A)	194 (A)
115 (A)	135 (B)	155 (D)	175 (B)	195 (C)
116 (A)	136 (B)	156 (B)	176 (C)	196 (B)
117 (A)	137 (A)	157 (D)	177 (D)	197 (B)
118 (D)	138 (C)	158 (C)	178 (D)	198 (A)
119 (C)	139 (A)	159 (B)	179 (A)	199 (C)
120 (D)	140 (B)	160 (A)	180 (D)	200 (C)

무료 토익·토스·오픽·지텔프 자료
Hackers.co.kr

점수 환산표

※ 점수 환산표는 해커스토익 사이트 유저 데이터를 근거로 제작되었으며, 주기적으로 업데이트되고 있습니다. 해커스토익(Hackers.co.kr) 사이트에서 최신 경향을 반영하여 업데이트된 점수환산기를 이용하실 수 있습니다. (토익 > 토익게시판 > 토익점수환산기)

LISTENING

아래 점수 환산표로 자신의 토익 리스닝 점수를 예상해 봅니다.

정답수	예상 점수	정답수	예상 점수	정답수	예상 점수
100	495	66	305	32	135
99	495	65	300	31	130
98	495	64	295	30	125
97	495	63	290	29	120
96	490	62	285	28	115
95	485	61	280	27	110
94	480	60	275	26	105
93	475	59	270	25	100
92	470	58	265	24	95
91	465	57	260	23	90
90	460	56	255	22	85
89	455	55	250	21	80
88	450	54	245	20	75
87	445	53	240	19	70
86	435	52	235	18	65
85	430	51	230	17	60
84	425	50	225	16	55
83	415	49	220	15	50
82	410	48	215	14	45
81	400	47	210	13	40
80	395	46	205	12	35
79	390	45	200	11	30
78	385	44	195	10	25
77	375	43	190	9	20
76	370	42	185	8	15
75	365	41	180	7	10
74	355	40	175	6	5
73	350	39	170	5	5
72	340	38	165	4	5
71	335	37	160	3	5
70	330	36	155	2	5
69	325	35	150	1	5
68	315	34	145	0	5
67	310	33	140		

READING

아래 점수 환산표로 자신의 토익 리딩 점수를 예상해 봅니다.

정답수	예상 점수	정답수	예상 점수	정답수	예상 점수
100	495	66	305	32	125
99	495	65	300	31	120
98	495	64	295	30	115
97	485	63	290	29	110
96	480	62	280	28	105
95	475	61	275	27	100
94	470	60	270	26	95
93	465	59	265	25	90
92	460	58	260	24	85
91	450	57	255	23	80
90	445	56	250	22	75
89	440	55	245	21	70
88	435	54	240	20	70
87	430	53	235	19	65
86	420	52	230	18	60
85	415	51	220	17	60
84	410	50	215	16	55
83	405	49	210	15	50
82	400	48	205	14	45
81	390	47	200	13	40
80	385	46	195	12	35
79	380	45	190	11	30
78	375	44	185	10	30
77	370	43	180	9	25
76	360	42	175	8	20
75	355	41	170	7	20
74	350	40	165	6	15
73	345	39	160	5	15
72	340	38	155	4	10
71	335	37	150	3	5
70	330	36	145	2	5
69	320	35	140	1	5
68	315	34	135	0	5
67	310	33	130		

무료 토익 · 토스 · 오픽 · 지텔프 자료
Hackers.co.kr

Answer Sheet

TEST 1

LISTENING (PART I~IV)

#	A	B	C	D		#	A	B	C	D		#	A	B	C	D		#	A	B	C	D
1	Ⓐ	Ⓑ	Ⓒ	Ⓓ		21	Ⓐ	Ⓑ	Ⓒ	Ⓓ		41	Ⓐ	Ⓑ	Ⓒ	Ⓓ		81	Ⓐ	Ⓑ	Ⓒ	Ⓓ
2	Ⓐ	Ⓑ	Ⓒ	Ⓓ		22	Ⓐ	Ⓑ	Ⓒ	Ⓓ		42	Ⓐ	Ⓑ	Ⓒ	Ⓓ		82	Ⓐ	Ⓑ	Ⓒ	Ⓓ
3	Ⓐ	Ⓑ	Ⓒ	Ⓓ		23	Ⓐ	Ⓑ	Ⓒ	Ⓓ		43	Ⓐ	Ⓑ	Ⓒ	Ⓓ		83	Ⓐ	Ⓑ	Ⓒ	Ⓓ
4	Ⓐ	Ⓑ	Ⓒ	Ⓓ		24	Ⓐ	Ⓑ	Ⓒ	Ⓓ		44	Ⓐ	Ⓑ	Ⓒ	Ⓓ		84	Ⓐ	Ⓑ	Ⓒ	Ⓓ
5	Ⓐ	Ⓑ	Ⓒ	Ⓓ		25	Ⓐ	Ⓑ	Ⓒ	Ⓓ		45	Ⓐ	Ⓑ	Ⓒ	Ⓓ		85	Ⓐ	Ⓑ	Ⓒ	Ⓓ
6	Ⓐ	Ⓑ	Ⓒ	Ⓓ		26	Ⓐ	Ⓑ	Ⓒ	Ⓓ		46	Ⓐ	Ⓑ	Ⓒ	Ⓓ		86	Ⓐ	Ⓑ	Ⓒ	Ⓓ
7	Ⓐ	Ⓑ	Ⓒ	Ⓓ		27	Ⓐ	Ⓑ	Ⓒ			47	Ⓐ	Ⓑ	Ⓒ	Ⓓ		87	Ⓐ	Ⓑ	Ⓒ	Ⓓ
8	Ⓐ	Ⓑ	Ⓒ	Ⓓ		28	Ⓐ	Ⓑ	Ⓒ			48	Ⓐ	Ⓑ	Ⓒ	Ⓓ		88	Ⓐ	Ⓑ	Ⓒ	Ⓓ
9	Ⓐ	Ⓑ	Ⓒ			29	Ⓐ	Ⓑ	Ⓒ			49	Ⓐ	Ⓑ	Ⓒ	Ⓓ		89	Ⓐ	Ⓑ	Ⓒ	Ⓓ
10	Ⓐ	Ⓑ	Ⓒ			30	Ⓐ	Ⓑ	Ⓒ			50	Ⓐ	Ⓑ	Ⓒ	Ⓓ		90	Ⓐ	Ⓑ	Ⓒ	Ⓓ
11	Ⓐ	Ⓑ	Ⓒ			31	Ⓐ	Ⓑ	Ⓒ			51	Ⓐ	Ⓑ	Ⓒ	Ⓓ		91	Ⓐ	Ⓑ	Ⓒ	Ⓓ
12	Ⓐ	Ⓑ	Ⓒ			32	Ⓐ	Ⓑ	Ⓒ			52	Ⓐ	Ⓑ	Ⓒ	Ⓓ		92	Ⓐ	Ⓑ	Ⓒ	Ⓓ
13	Ⓐ	Ⓑ	Ⓒ			33	Ⓐ	Ⓑ	Ⓒ			53	Ⓐ	Ⓑ	Ⓒ	Ⓓ		93	Ⓐ	Ⓑ	Ⓒ	Ⓓ
14	Ⓐ	Ⓑ	Ⓒ			34	Ⓐ	Ⓑ	Ⓒ			54	Ⓐ	Ⓑ	Ⓒ	Ⓓ		94	Ⓐ	Ⓑ	Ⓒ	Ⓓ
15	Ⓐ	Ⓑ	Ⓒ			35	Ⓐ	Ⓑ	Ⓒ			55	Ⓐ	Ⓑ	Ⓒ	Ⓓ		95	Ⓐ	Ⓑ	Ⓒ	Ⓓ
16	Ⓐ	Ⓑ	Ⓒ			36	Ⓐ	Ⓑ	Ⓒ			56	Ⓐ	Ⓑ	Ⓒ	Ⓓ		96	Ⓐ	Ⓑ	Ⓒ	Ⓓ
17	Ⓐ	Ⓑ	Ⓒ			37	Ⓐ	Ⓑ	Ⓒ			57	Ⓐ	Ⓑ	Ⓒ	Ⓓ		97	Ⓐ	Ⓑ	Ⓒ	Ⓓ
18	Ⓐ	Ⓑ	Ⓒ			38	Ⓐ	Ⓑ	Ⓒ			58	Ⓐ	Ⓑ	Ⓒ	Ⓓ		98	Ⓐ	Ⓑ	Ⓒ	Ⓓ
19	Ⓐ	Ⓑ	Ⓒ			39	Ⓐ	Ⓑ	Ⓒ			59	Ⓐ	Ⓑ	Ⓒ	Ⓓ		99	Ⓐ	Ⓑ	Ⓒ	Ⓓ
20	Ⓐ	Ⓑ	Ⓒ			40	Ⓐ	Ⓑ	Ⓒ			60	Ⓐ	Ⓑ	Ⓒ	Ⓓ		100	Ⓐ	Ⓑ	Ⓒ	Ⓓ

시험시간: **120분** (LC 45분, RC 75분)

READING (PART V~VII)

#	A	B	C	D		#	A	B	C	D		#	A	B	C	D		#	A	B	C	D
101	Ⓐ	Ⓑ	Ⓒ	Ⓓ		121	Ⓐ	Ⓑ	Ⓒ	Ⓓ		141	Ⓐ	Ⓑ	Ⓒ	Ⓓ		161	Ⓐ	Ⓑ	Ⓒ	Ⓓ	181	Ⓐ	Ⓑ	Ⓒ	Ⓓ
102	Ⓐ	Ⓑ	Ⓒ	Ⓓ		122	Ⓐ	Ⓑ	Ⓒ	Ⓓ		142	Ⓐ	Ⓑ	Ⓒ	Ⓓ		162	Ⓐ	Ⓑ	Ⓒ	Ⓓ	182	Ⓐ	Ⓑ	Ⓒ	Ⓓ
103	Ⓐ	Ⓑ	Ⓒ	Ⓓ		123	Ⓐ	Ⓑ	Ⓒ	Ⓓ		143	Ⓐ	Ⓑ	Ⓒ	Ⓓ		163	Ⓐ	Ⓑ	Ⓒ	Ⓓ	183	Ⓐ	Ⓑ	Ⓒ	Ⓓ
104	Ⓐ	Ⓑ	Ⓒ	Ⓓ		124	Ⓐ	Ⓑ	Ⓒ	Ⓓ		144	Ⓐ	Ⓑ	Ⓒ	Ⓓ		164	Ⓐ	Ⓑ	Ⓒ	Ⓓ	184	Ⓐ	Ⓑ	Ⓒ	Ⓓ
105	Ⓐ	Ⓑ	Ⓒ	Ⓓ		125	Ⓐ	Ⓑ	Ⓒ	Ⓓ		145	Ⓐ	Ⓑ	Ⓒ	Ⓓ		165	Ⓐ	Ⓑ	Ⓒ	Ⓓ	185	Ⓐ	Ⓑ	Ⓒ	Ⓓ
106	Ⓐ	Ⓑ	Ⓒ	Ⓓ		126	Ⓐ	Ⓑ	Ⓒ	Ⓓ		146	Ⓐ	Ⓑ	Ⓒ	Ⓓ		166	Ⓐ	Ⓑ	Ⓒ	Ⓓ	186	Ⓐ	Ⓑ	Ⓒ	Ⓓ
107	Ⓐ	Ⓑ	Ⓒ	Ⓓ		127	Ⓐ	Ⓑ	Ⓒ	Ⓓ		147	Ⓐ	Ⓑ	Ⓒ	Ⓓ		167	Ⓐ	Ⓑ	Ⓒ	Ⓓ	187	Ⓐ	Ⓑ	Ⓒ	Ⓓ
108	Ⓐ	Ⓑ	Ⓒ	Ⓓ		128	Ⓐ	Ⓑ	Ⓒ	Ⓓ		148	Ⓐ	Ⓑ	Ⓒ	Ⓓ		168	Ⓐ	Ⓑ	Ⓒ	Ⓓ	188	Ⓐ	Ⓑ	Ⓒ	Ⓓ
109	Ⓐ	Ⓑ	Ⓒ	Ⓓ		129	Ⓐ	Ⓑ	Ⓒ	Ⓓ		149	Ⓐ	Ⓑ	Ⓒ	Ⓓ		169	Ⓐ	Ⓑ	Ⓒ	Ⓓ	189	Ⓐ	Ⓑ	Ⓒ	Ⓓ
110	Ⓐ	Ⓑ	Ⓒ	Ⓓ		130	Ⓐ	Ⓑ	Ⓒ	Ⓓ		150	Ⓐ	Ⓑ	Ⓒ	Ⓓ		170	Ⓐ	Ⓑ	Ⓒ	Ⓓ	190	Ⓐ	Ⓑ	Ⓒ	Ⓓ
111	Ⓐ	Ⓑ	Ⓒ	Ⓓ		131	Ⓐ	Ⓑ	Ⓒ	Ⓓ		151	Ⓐ	Ⓑ	Ⓒ	Ⓓ		171	Ⓐ	Ⓑ	Ⓒ	Ⓓ	191	Ⓐ	Ⓑ	Ⓒ	Ⓓ
112	Ⓐ	Ⓑ	Ⓒ	Ⓓ		132	Ⓐ	Ⓑ	Ⓒ	Ⓓ		152	Ⓐ	Ⓑ	Ⓒ	Ⓓ		172	Ⓐ	Ⓑ	Ⓒ	Ⓓ	192	Ⓐ	Ⓑ	Ⓒ	Ⓓ
113	Ⓐ	Ⓑ	Ⓒ	Ⓓ		133	Ⓐ	Ⓑ	Ⓒ	Ⓓ		153	Ⓐ	Ⓑ	Ⓒ	Ⓓ		173	Ⓐ	Ⓑ	Ⓒ	Ⓓ	193	Ⓐ	Ⓑ	Ⓒ	Ⓓ
114	Ⓐ	Ⓑ	Ⓒ	Ⓓ		134	Ⓐ	Ⓑ	Ⓒ	Ⓓ		154	Ⓐ	Ⓑ	Ⓒ	Ⓓ		174	Ⓐ	Ⓑ	Ⓒ	Ⓓ	194	Ⓐ	Ⓑ	Ⓒ	Ⓓ
115	Ⓐ	Ⓑ	Ⓒ	Ⓓ		135	Ⓐ	Ⓑ	Ⓒ	Ⓓ		155	Ⓐ	Ⓑ	Ⓒ	Ⓓ		175	Ⓐ	Ⓑ	Ⓒ	Ⓓ	195	Ⓐ	Ⓑ	Ⓒ	Ⓓ
116	Ⓐ	Ⓑ	Ⓒ	Ⓓ		136	Ⓐ	Ⓑ	Ⓒ	Ⓓ		156	Ⓐ	Ⓑ	Ⓒ	Ⓓ		176	Ⓐ	Ⓑ	Ⓒ	Ⓓ	196	Ⓐ	Ⓑ	Ⓒ	Ⓓ
117	Ⓐ	Ⓑ	Ⓒ	Ⓓ		137	Ⓐ	Ⓑ	Ⓒ	Ⓓ		157	Ⓐ	Ⓑ	Ⓒ	Ⓓ		177	Ⓐ	Ⓑ	Ⓒ	Ⓓ	197	Ⓐ	Ⓑ	Ⓒ	Ⓓ
118	Ⓐ	Ⓑ	Ⓒ	Ⓓ		138	Ⓐ	Ⓑ	Ⓒ	Ⓓ		158	Ⓐ	Ⓑ	Ⓒ	Ⓓ		178	Ⓐ	Ⓑ	Ⓒ	Ⓓ	198	Ⓐ	Ⓑ	Ⓒ	Ⓓ
119	Ⓐ	Ⓑ	Ⓒ	Ⓓ		139	Ⓐ	Ⓑ	Ⓒ	Ⓓ		159	Ⓐ	Ⓑ	Ⓒ	Ⓓ		179	Ⓐ	Ⓑ	Ⓒ	Ⓓ	199	Ⓐ	Ⓑ	Ⓒ	Ⓓ
120	Ⓐ	Ⓑ	Ⓒ	Ⓓ		140	Ⓐ	Ⓑ	Ⓒ	Ⓓ		160	Ⓐ	Ⓑ	Ⓒ	Ⓓ		180	Ⓐ	Ⓑ	Ⓒ	Ⓓ	200	Ⓐ	Ⓑ	Ⓒ	Ⓓ

답안지 마킹은 **연필**을 사용하시기 바랍니다.

맞은 문제개수: _____ / 200

절취선

무료 토익·토스·오픽·지텔프 자료
Hackers.co.kr

Answer Sheet

TEST 2

LISTENING (PART I~IV)

1	Ⓐ Ⓑ Ⓒ Ⓓ	21	Ⓐ Ⓑ Ⓒ Ⓓ	41	Ⓐ Ⓑ Ⓒ Ⓓ	61	Ⓐ Ⓑ Ⓒ Ⓓ	81	Ⓐ Ⓑ Ⓒ Ⓓ
2	Ⓐ Ⓑ Ⓒ Ⓓ	22	Ⓐ Ⓑ Ⓒ	42	Ⓐ Ⓑ Ⓒ Ⓓ	62	Ⓐ Ⓑ Ⓒ Ⓓ	82	Ⓐ Ⓑ Ⓒ Ⓓ
3	Ⓐ Ⓑ Ⓒ Ⓓ	23	Ⓐ Ⓑ Ⓒ	43	Ⓐ Ⓑ Ⓒ Ⓓ	63	Ⓐ Ⓑ Ⓒ Ⓓ	83	Ⓐ Ⓑ Ⓒ Ⓓ
4	Ⓐ Ⓑ Ⓒ Ⓓ	24	Ⓐ Ⓑ Ⓒ	44	Ⓐ Ⓑ Ⓒ Ⓓ	64	Ⓐ Ⓑ Ⓒ Ⓓ	84	Ⓐ Ⓑ Ⓒ Ⓓ
5	Ⓐ Ⓑ Ⓒ Ⓓ	25	Ⓐ Ⓑ Ⓒ	45	Ⓐ Ⓑ Ⓒ Ⓓ	65	Ⓐ Ⓑ Ⓒ Ⓓ	85	Ⓐ Ⓑ Ⓒ Ⓓ
6	Ⓐ Ⓑ Ⓒ Ⓓ	26	Ⓐ Ⓑ Ⓒ	46	Ⓐ Ⓑ Ⓒ Ⓓ	66	Ⓐ Ⓑ Ⓒ Ⓓ	86	Ⓐ Ⓑ Ⓒ Ⓓ
7	Ⓐ Ⓑ Ⓒ	27	Ⓐ Ⓑ Ⓒ	47	Ⓐ Ⓑ Ⓒ Ⓓ	67	Ⓐ Ⓑ Ⓒ Ⓓ	87	Ⓐ Ⓑ Ⓒ Ⓓ
8	Ⓐ Ⓑ Ⓒ	28	Ⓐ Ⓑ Ⓒ	48	Ⓐ Ⓑ Ⓒ Ⓓ	68	Ⓐ Ⓑ Ⓒ Ⓓ	88	Ⓐ Ⓑ Ⓒ Ⓓ
9	Ⓐ Ⓑ Ⓒ	29	Ⓐ Ⓑ Ⓒ	49	Ⓐ Ⓑ Ⓒ Ⓓ	69	Ⓐ Ⓑ Ⓒ Ⓓ	89	Ⓐ Ⓑ Ⓒ Ⓓ
10	Ⓐ Ⓑ Ⓒ	30	Ⓐ Ⓑ Ⓒ	50	Ⓐ Ⓑ Ⓒ Ⓓ	70	Ⓐ Ⓑ Ⓒ Ⓓ	90	Ⓐ Ⓑ Ⓒ Ⓓ
11	Ⓐ Ⓑ Ⓒ	31	Ⓐ Ⓑ Ⓒ	51	Ⓐ Ⓑ Ⓒ Ⓓ	71	Ⓐ Ⓑ Ⓒ Ⓓ	91	Ⓐ Ⓑ Ⓒ Ⓓ
12	Ⓐ Ⓑ Ⓒ	32	Ⓐ Ⓑ Ⓒ	52	Ⓐ Ⓑ Ⓒ Ⓓ	72	Ⓐ Ⓑ Ⓒ Ⓓ	92	Ⓐ Ⓑ Ⓒ Ⓓ
13	Ⓐ Ⓑ Ⓒ	33	Ⓐ Ⓑ Ⓒ	53	Ⓐ Ⓑ Ⓒ Ⓓ	73	Ⓐ Ⓑ Ⓒ Ⓓ	93	Ⓐ Ⓑ Ⓒ Ⓓ
14	Ⓐ Ⓑ Ⓒ	34	Ⓐ Ⓑ Ⓒ	54	Ⓐ Ⓑ Ⓒ Ⓓ	74	Ⓐ Ⓑ Ⓒ Ⓓ	94	Ⓐ Ⓑ Ⓒ Ⓓ
15	Ⓐ Ⓑ Ⓒ	35	Ⓐ Ⓑ Ⓒ	55	Ⓐ Ⓑ Ⓒ Ⓓ	75	Ⓐ Ⓑ Ⓒ Ⓓ	95	Ⓐ Ⓑ Ⓒ Ⓓ
16	Ⓐ Ⓑ Ⓒ	36	Ⓐ Ⓑ Ⓒ	56	Ⓐ Ⓑ Ⓒ Ⓓ	76	Ⓐ Ⓑ Ⓒ Ⓓ	96	Ⓐ Ⓑ Ⓒ Ⓓ
17	Ⓐ Ⓑ Ⓒ	37	Ⓐ Ⓑ Ⓒ	57	Ⓐ Ⓑ Ⓒ Ⓓ	77	Ⓐ Ⓑ Ⓒ Ⓓ	97	Ⓐ Ⓑ Ⓒ Ⓓ
18	Ⓐ Ⓑ Ⓒ	38	Ⓐ Ⓑ Ⓒ	58	Ⓐ Ⓑ Ⓒ Ⓓ	78	Ⓐ Ⓑ Ⓒ Ⓓ	98	Ⓐ Ⓑ Ⓒ Ⓓ
19	Ⓐ Ⓑ Ⓒ	39	Ⓐ Ⓑ Ⓒ	59	Ⓐ Ⓑ Ⓒ Ⓓ	79	Ⓐ Ⓑ Ⓒ Ⓓ	99	Ⓐ Ⓑ Ⓒ Ⓓ
20	Ⓐ Ⓑ Ⓒ	40	Ⓐ Ⓑ Ⓒ	60	Ⓐ Ⓑ Ⓒ Ⓓ	80	Ⓐ Ⓑ Ⓒ Ⓓ	100	Ⓐ Ⓑ Ⓒ Ⓓ

시험시간: **120분** (LC 45분, RC 75분)

READING (PART V~VII)

101	Ⓐ Ⓑ Ⓒ Ⓓ	121	Ⓐ Ⓑ Ⓒ Ⓓ	141	Ⓐ Ⓑ Ⓒ Ⓓ	161	Ⓐ Ⓑ Ⓒ Ⓓ	181	Ⓐ Ⓑ Ⓒ Ⓓ
102	Ⓐ Ⓑ Ⓒ Ⓓ	122	Ⓐ Ⓑ Ⓒ Ⓓ	142	Ⓐ Ⓑ Ⓒ Ⓓ	162	Ⓐ Ⓑ Ⓒ Ⓓ	182	Ⓐ Ⓑ Ⓒ Ⓓ
103	Ⓐ Ⓑ Ⓒ Ⓓ	123	Ⓐ Ⓑ Ⓒ Ⓓ	143	Ⓐ Ⓑ Ⓒ Ⓓ	163	Ⓐ Ⓑ Ⓒ Ⓓ	183	Ⓐ Ⓑ Ⓒ Ⓓ
104	Ⓐ Ⓑ Ⓒ Ⓓ	124	Ⓐ Ⓑ Ⓒ Ⓓ	144	Ⓐ Ⓑ Ⓒ Ⓓ	164	Ⓐ Ⓑ Ⓒ Ⓓ	184	Ⓐ Ⓑ Ⓒ Ⓓ
105	Ⓐ Ⓑ Ⓒ Ⓓ	125	Ⓐ Ⓑ Ⓒ Ⓓ	145	Ⓐ Ⓑ Ⓒ Ⓓ	165	Ⓐ Ⓑ Ⓒ Ⓓ	185	Ⓐ Ⓑ Ⓒ Ⓓ
106	Ⓐ Ⓑ Ⓒ Ⓓ	126	Ⓐ Ⓑ Ⓒ Ⓓ	146	Ⓐ Ⓑ Ⓒ Ⓓ	166	Ⓐ Ⓑ Ⓒ Ⓓ	186	Ⓐ Ⓑ Ⓒ Ⓓ
107	Ⓐ Ⓑ Ⓒ Ⓓ	127	Ⓐ Ⓑ Ⓒ Ⓓ	147	Ⓐ Ⓑ Ⓒ Ⓓ	167	Ⓐ Ⓑ Ⓒ Ⓓ	187	Ⓐ Ⓑ Ⓒ Ⓓ
108	Ⓐ Ⓑ Ⓒ Ⓓ	128	Ⓐ Ⓑ Ⓒ Ⓓ	148	Ⓐ Ⓑ Ⓒ Ⓓ	168	Ⓐ Ⓑ Ⓒ Ⓓ	188	Ⓐ Ⓑ Ⓒ Ⓓ
109	Ⓐ Ⓑ Ⓒ Ⓓ	129	Ⓐ Ⓑ Ⓒ Ⓓ	149	Ⓐ Ⓑ Ⓒ Ⓓ	169	Ⓐ Ⓑ Ⓒ Ⓓ	189	Ⓐ Ⓑ Ⓒ Ⓓ
110	Ⓐ Ⓑ Ⓒ Ⓓ	130	Ⓐ Ⓑ Ⓒ Ⓓ	150	Ⓐ Ⓑ Ⓒ Ⓓ	170	Ⓐ Ⓑ Ⓒ Ⓓ	190	Ⓐ Ⓑ Ⓒ Ⓓ
111	Ⓐ Ⓑ Ⓒ Ⓓ	131	Ⓐ Ⓑ Ⓒ Ⓓ	151	Ⓐ Ⓑ Ⓒ Ⓓ	171	Ⓐ Ⓑ Ⓒ Ⓓ	191	Ⓐ Ⓑ Ⓒ Ⓓ
112	Ⓐ Ⓑ Ⓒ Ⓓ	132	Ⓐ Ⓑ Ⓒ Ⓓ	152	Ⓐ Ⓑ Ⓒ Ⓓ	172	Ⓐ Ⓑ Ⓒ Ⓓ	192	Ⓐ Ⓑ Ⓒ Ⓓ
113	Ⓐ Ⓑ Ⓒ Ⓓ	133	Ⓐ Ⓑ Ⓒ Ⓓ	153	Ⓐ Ⓑ Ⓒ Ⓓ	173	Ⓐ Ⓑ Ⓒ Ⓓ	193	Ⓐ Ⓑ Ⓒ Ⓓ
114	Ⓐ Ⓑ Ⓒ Ⓓ	134	Ⓐ Ⓑ Ⓒ Ⓓ	154	Ⓐ Ⓑ Ⓒ Ⓓ	174	Ⓐ Ⓑ Ⓒ Ⓓ	194	Ⓐ Ⓑ Ⓒ Ⓓ
115	Ⓐ Ⓑ Ⓒ Ⓓ	135	Ⓐ Ⓑ Ⓒ Ⓓ	155	Ⓐ Ⓑ Ⓒ Ⓓ	175	Ⓐ Ⓑ Ⓒ Ⓓ	195	Ⓐ Ⓑ Ⓒ Ⓓ
116	Ⓐ Ⓑ Ⓒ Ⓓ	136	Ⓐ Ⓑ Ⓒ Ⓓ	156	Ⓐ Ⓑ Ⓒ Ⓓ	176	Ⓐ Ⓑ Ⓒ Ⓓ	196	Ⓐ Ⓑ Ⓒ Ⓓ
117	Ⓐ Ⓑ Ⓒ Ⓓ	137	Ⓐ Ⓑ Ⓒ Ⓓ	157	Ⓐ Ⓑ Ⓒ Ⓓ	177	Ⓐ Ⓑ Ⓒ Ⓓ	197	Ⓐ Ⓑ Ⓒ Ⓓ
118	Ⓐ Ⓑ Ⓒ Ⓓ	138	Ⓐ Ⓑ Ⓒ Ⓓ	158	Ⓐ Ⓑ Ⓒ Ⓓ	178	Ⓐ Ⓑ Ⓒ Ⓓ	198	Ⓐ Ⓑ Ⓒ Ⓓ
119	Ⓐ Ⓑ Ⓒ Ⓓ	139	Ⓐ Ⓑ Ⓒ Ⓓ	159	Ⓐ Ⓑ Ⓒ Ⓓ	179	Ⓐ Ⓑ Ⓒ Ⓓ	199	Ⓐ Ⓑ Ⓒ Ⓓ
120	Ⓐ Ⓑ Ⓒ Ⓓ	140	Ⓐ Ⓑ Ⓒ Ⓓ	160	Ⓐ Ⓑ Ⓒ Ⓓ	180	Ⓐ Ⓑ Ⓒ Ⓓ	200	Ⓐ Ⓑ Ⓒ Ⓓ

답안지 마킹은 **연필**을 사용하시기 바랍니다.

맞은 문제 개수: _____ / 200

자르는 선

무료 토익 · 토스 · 오픽 · 지텔프 자료
Hackers.co.kr

Answer Sheet

TEST 3

LISTENING (PART I~IV)

#	A B C D	#	A B C D	#	A B C D	#	A B C D	#	A B C D
1	Ⓐ Ⓑ Ⓒ Ⓓ	21	Ⓐ Ⓑ Ⓒ Ⓓ	41	Ⓐ Ⓑ Ⓒ Ⓓ	61	Ⓐ Ⓑ Ⓒ Ⓓ	81	Ⓐ Ⓑ Ⓒ Ⓓ
2	Ⓐ Ⓑ Ⓒ Ⓓ	22	Ⓐ Ⓑ Ⓒ Ⓓ	42	Ⓐ Ⓑ Ⓒ Ⓓ	62	Ⓐ Ⓑ Ⓒ Ⓓ	82	Ⓐ Ⓑ Ⓒ Ⓓ
3	Ⓐ Ⓑ Ⓒ Ⓓ	23	Ⓐ Ⓑ Ⓒ Ⓓ	43	Ⓐ Ⓑ Ⓒ Ⓓ	63	Ⓐ Ⓑ Ⓒ Ⓓ	83	Ⓐ Ⓑ Ⓒ Ⓓ
4	Ⓐ Ⓑ Ⓒ Ⓓ	24	Ⓐ Ⓑ Ⓒ Ⓓ	44	Ⓐ Ⓑ Ⓒ Ⓓ	64	Ⓐ Ⓑ Ⓒ Ⓓ	84	Ⓐ Ⓑ Ⓒ Ⓓ
5	Ⓐ Ⓑ Ⓒ Ⓓ	25	Ⓐ Ⓑ Ⓒ Ⓓ	45	Ⓐ Ⓑ Ⓒ Ⓓ	65	Ⓐ Ⓑ Ⓒ Ⓓ	85	Ⓐ Ⓑ Ⓒ Ⓓ
6	Ⓐ Ⓑ Ⓒ Ⓓ	26	Ⓐ Ⓑ Ⓒ Ⓓ	46	Ⓐ Ⓑ Ⓒ Ⓓ	66	Ⓐ Ⓑ Ⓒ Ⓓ	86	Ⓐ Ⓑ Ⓒ Ⓓ
7	Ⓐ Ⓑ Ⓒ	27	Ⓐ Ⓑ Ⓒ	47	Ⓐ Ⓑ Ⓒ Ⓓ	67	Ⓐ Ⓑ Ⓒ Ⓓ	87	Ⓐ Ⓑ Ⓒ Ⓓ
8	Ⓐ Ⓑ Ⓒ	28	Ⓐ Ⓑ Ⓒ	48	Ⓐ Ⓑ Ⓒ Ⓓ	68	Ⓐ Ⓑ Ⓒ Ⓓ	88	Ⓐ Ⓑ Ⓒ Ⓓ
9	Ⓐ Ⓑ Ⓒ	29	Ⓐ Ⓑ Ⓒ	49	Ⓐ Ⓑ Ⓒ Ⓓ	69	Ⓐ Ⓑ Ⓒ Ⓓ	89	Ⓐ Ⓑ Ⓒ Ⓓ
10	Ⓐ Ⓑ Ⓒ	30	Ⓐ Ⓑ Ⓒ	50	Ⓐ Ⓑ Ⓒ Ⓓ	70	Ⓐ Ⓑ Ⓒ Ⓓ	90	Ⓐ Ⓑ Ⓒ Ⓓ
11	Ⓐ Ⓑ Ⓒ	31	Ⓐ Ⓑ Ⓒ	51	Ⓐ Ⓑ Ⓒ Ⓓ	71	Ⓐ Ⓑ Ⓒ Ⓓ	91	Ⓐ Ⓑ Ⓒ Ⓓ
12	Ⓐ Ⓑ Ⓒ	32	Ⓐ Ⓑ Ⓒ	52	Ⓐ Ⓑ Ⓒ Ⓓ	72	Ⓐ Ⓑ Ⓒ Ⓓ	92	Ⓐ Ⓑ Ⓒ Ⓓ
13	Ⓐ Ⓑ Ⓒ	33	Ⓐ Ⓑ Ⓒ	53	Ⓐ Ⓑ Ⓒ Ⓓ	73	Ⓐ Ⓑ Ⓒ Ⓓ	93	Ⓐ Ⓑ Ⓒ Ⓓ
14	Ⓐ Ⓑ Ⓒ	34	Ⓐ Ⓑ Ⓒ	54	Ⓐ Ⓑ Ⓒ Ⓓ	74	Ⓐ Ⓑ Ⓒ Ⓓ	94	Ⓐ Ⓑ Ⓒ Ⓓ
15	Ⓐ Ⓑ Ⓒ	35	Ⓐ Ⓑ Ⓒ	55	Ⓐ Ⓑ Ⓒ Ⓓ	75	Ⓐ Ⓑ Ⓒ Ⓓ	95	Ⓐ Ⓑ Ⓒ Ⓓ
16	Ⓐ Ⓑ Ⓒ	36	Ⓐ Ⓑ Ⓒ	56	Ⓐ Ⓑ Ⓒ Ⓓ	76	Ⓐ Ⓑ Ⓒ Ⓓ	96	Ⓐ Ⓑ Ⓒ Ⓓ
17	Ⓐ Ⓑ Ⓒ	37	Ⓐ Ⓑ Ⓒ	57	Ⓐ Ⓑ Ⓒ Ⓓ	77	Ⓐ Ⓑ Ⓒ Ⓓ	97	Ⓐ Ⓑ Ⓒ Ⓓ
18	Ⓐ Ⓑ Ⓒ	38	Ⓐ Ⓑ Ⓒ	58	Ⓐ Ⓑ Ⓒ Ⓓ	78	Ⓐ Ⓑ Ⓒ Ⓓ	98	Ⓐ Ⓑ Ⓒ Ⓓ
19	Ⓐ Ⓑ Ⓒ	39	Ⓐ Ⓑ Ⓒ	59	Ⓐ Ⓑ Ⓒ Ⓓ	79	Ⓐ Ⓑ Ⓒ Ⓓ	99	Ⓐ Ⓑ Ⓒ Ⓓ
20	Ⓐ Ⓑ Ⓒ	40	Ⓐ Ⓑ Ⓒ	60	Ⓐ Ⓑ Ⓒ Ⓓ	80	Ⓐ Ⓑ Ⓒ Ⓓ	100	Ⓐ Ⓑ Ⓒ Ⓓ

시험시간: **120분** (LC 45분, RC 75분)

READING (PART V~VII)

#	A B C D	#	A B C D	#	A B C D	#	A B C D	#	A B C D
101	Ⓐ Ⓑ Ⓒ Ⓓ	121	Ⓐ Ⓑ Ⓒ Ⓓ	141	Ⓐ Ⓑ Ⓒ Ⓓ	161	Ⓐ Ⓑ Ⓒ Ⓓ	181	Ⓐ Ⓑ Ⓒ Ⓓ
102	Ⓐ Ⓑ Ⓒ Ⓓ	122	Ⓐ Ⓑ Ⓒ Ⓓ	142	Ⓐ Ⓑ Ⓒ Ⓓ	162	Ⓐ Ⓑ Ⓒ Ⓓ	182	Ⓐ Ⓑ Ⓒ Ⓓ
103	Ⓐ Ⓑ Ⓒ Ⓓ	123	Ⓐ Ⓑ Ⓒ Ⓓ	143	Ⓐ Ⓑ Ⓒ Ⓓ	163	Ⓐ Ⓑ Ⓒ Ⓓ	183	Ⓐ Ⓑ Ⓒ Ⓓ
104	Ⓐ Ⓑ Ⓒ Ⓓ	124	Ⓐ Ⓑ Ⓒ Ⓓ	144	Ⓐ Ⓑ Ⓒ Ⓓ	164	Ⓐ Ⓑ Ⓒ Ⓓ	184	Ⓐ Ⓑ Ⓒ Ⓓ
105	Ⓐ Ⓑ Ⓒ Ⓓ	125	Ⓐ Ⓑ Ⓒ Ⓓ	145	Ⓐ Ⓑ Ⓒ Ⓓ	165	Ⓐ Ⓑ Ⓒ Ⓓ	185	Ⓐ Ⓑ Ⓒ Ⓓ
106	Ⓐ Ⓑ Ⓒ Ⓓ	126	Ⓐ Ⓑ Ⓒ Ⓓ	146	Ⓐ Ⓑ Ⓒ Ⓓ	166	Ⓐ Ⓑ Ⓒ Ⓓ	186	Ⓐ Ⓑ Ⓒ Ⓓ
107	Ⓐ Ⓑ Ⓒ Ⓓ	127	Ⓐ Ⓑ Ⓒ Ⓓ	147	Ⓐ Ⓑ Ⓒ Ⓓ	167	Ⓐ Ⓑ Ⓒ Ⓓ	187	Ⓐ Ⓑ Ⓒ Ⓓ
108	Ⓐ Ⓑ Ⓒ Ⓓ	128	Ⓐ Ⓑ Ⓒ Ⓓ	148	Ⓐ Ⓑ Ⓒ Ⓓ	168	Ⓐ Ⓑ Ⓒ Ⓓ	188	Ⓐ Ⓑ Ⓒ Ⓓ
109	Ⓐ Ⓑ Ⓒ Ⓓ	129	Ⓐ Ⓑ Ⓒ Ⓓ	149	Ⓐ Ⓑ Ⓒ Ⓓ	169	Ⓐ Ⓑ Ⓒ Ⓓ	189	Ⓐ Ⓑ Ⓒ Ⓓ
110	Ⓐ Ⓑ Ⓒ Ⓓ	130	Ⓐ Ⓑ Ⓒ Ⓓ	150	Ⓐ Ⓑ Ⓒ Ⓓ	170	Ⓐ Ⓑ Ⓒ Ⓓ	190	Ⓐ Ⓑ Ⓒ Ⓓ
111	Ⓐ Ⓑ Ⓒ Ⓓ	131	Ⓐ Ⓑ Ⓒ Ⓓ	151	Ⓐ Ⓑ Ⓒ Ⓓ	171	Ⓐ Ⓑ Ⓒ Ⓓ	191	Ⓐ Ⓑ Ⓒ Ⓓ
112	Ⓐ Ⓑ Ⓒ Ⓓ	132	Ⓐ Ⓑ Ⓒ Ⓓ	152	Ⓐ Ⓑ Ⓒ Ⓓ	172	Ⓐ Ⓑ Ⓒ Ⓓ	192	Ⓐ Ⓑ Ⓒ Ⓓ
113	Ⓐ Ⓑ Ⓒ Ⓓ	133	Ⓐ Ⓑ Ⓒ Ⓓ	153	Ⓐ Ⓑ Ⓒ Ⓓ	173	Ⓐ Ⓑ Ⓒ Ⓓ	193	Ⓐ Ⓑ Ⓒ Ⓓ
114	Ⓐ Ⓑ Ⓒ Ⓓ	134	Ⓐ Ⓑ Ⓒ Ⓓ	154	Ⓐ Ⓑ Ⓒ Ⓓ	174	Ⓐ Ⓑ Ⓒ Ⓓ	194	Ⓐ Ⓑ Ⓒ Ⓓ
115	Ⓐ Ⓑ Ⓒ Ⓓ	135	Ⓐ Ⓑ Ⓒ Ⓓ	155	Ⓐ Ⓑ Ⓒ Ⓓ	175	Ⓐ Ⓑ Ⓒ Ⓓ	195	Ⓐ Ⓑ Ⓒ Ⓓ
116	Ⓐ Ⓑ Ⓒ Ⓓ	136	Ⓐ Ⓑ Ⓒ Ⓓ	156	Ⓐ Ⓑ Ⓒ Ⓓ	176	Ⓐ Ⓑ Ⓒ Ⓓ	196	Ⓐ Ⓑ Ⓒ Ⓓ
117	Ⓐ Ⓑ Ⓒ Ⓓ	137	Ⓐ Ⓑ Ⓒ Ⓓ	157	Ⓐ Ⓑ Ⓒ Ⓓ	177	Ⓐ Ⓑ Ⓒ Ⓓ	197	Ⓐ Ⓑ Ⓒ Ⓓ
118	Ⓐ Ⓑ Ⓒ Ⓓ	138	Ⓐ Ⓑ Ⓒ Ⓓ	158	Ⓐ Ⓑ Ⓒ Ⓓ	178	Ⓐ Ⓑ Ⓒ Ⓓ	198	Ⓐ Ⓑ Ⓒ Ⓓ
119	Ⓐ Ⓑ Ⓒ Ⓓ	139	Ⓐ Ⓑ Ⓒ Ⓓ	159	Ⓐ Ⓑ Ⓒ Ⓓ	179	Ⓐ Ⓑ Ⓒ Ⓓ	199	Ⓐ Ⓑ Ⓒ Ⓓ
120	Ⓐ Ⓑ Ⓒ Ⓓ	140	Ⓐ Ⓑ Ⓒ Ⓓ	160	Ⓐ Ⓑ Ⓒ Ⓓ	180	Ⓐ Ⓑ Ⓒ Ⓓ	200	Ⓐ Ⓑ Ⓒ Ⓓ

답안지 마킹은 **연필**을 사용하시기 바랍니다.

맞은 문제 개수: _____ / 200

무료 토익 · 토스 · 오픽 · 지텔프 자료
Hackers.co.kr

Answer Sheet

TEST 4

LISTENING (PART I~IV)

	A B C D		A B C D		A B C D		A B C D		A B C D
1	Ⓐ Ⓑ Ⓒ Ⓓ	21	Ⓐ Ⓑ Ⓒ Ⓓ	41	Ⓐ Ⓑ Ⓒ	61	Ⓐ Ⓑ Ⓒ Ⓓ	81	Ⓐ Ⓑ Ⓒ Ⓓ
2	Ⓐ Ⓑ Ⓒ Ⓓ	22	Ⓐ Ⓑ Ⓒ Ⓓ	42	Ⓐ Ⓑ Ⓒ	62	Ⓐ Ⓑ Ⓒ Ⓓ	82	Ⓐ Ⓑ Ⓒ Ⓓ
3	Ⓐ Ⓑ Ⓒ Ⓓ	23	Ⓐ Ⓑ Ⓒ Ⓓ	43	Ⓐ Ⓑ Ⓒ	63	Ⓐ Ⓑ Ⓒ Ⓓ	83	Ⓐ Ⓑ Ⓒ Ⓓ
4	Ⓐ Ⓑ Ⓒ Ⓓ	24	Ⓐ Ⓑ Ⓒ Ⓓ	44	Ⓐ Ⓑ Ⓒ	64	Ⓐ Ⓑ Ⓒ Ⓓ	84	Ⓐ Ⓑ Ⓒ Ⓓ
5	Ⓐ Ⓑ Ⓒ Ⓓ	25	Ⓐ Ⓑ Ⓒ Ⓓ	45	Ⓐ Ⓑ Ⓒ	65	Ⓐ Ⓑ Ⓒ Ⓓ	85	Ⓐ Ⓑ Ⓒ Ⓓ
6	Ⓐ Ⓑ Ⓒ Ⓓ	26	Ⓐ Ⓑ Ⓒ Ⓓ	46	Ⓐ Ⓑ Ⓒ	66	Ⓐ Ⓑ Ⓒ Ⓓ	86	Ⓐ Ⓑ Ⓒ Ⓓ
7	Ⓐ Ⓑ Ⓒ Ⓓ	27	Ⓐ Ⓑ Ⓒ	47	Ⓐ Ⓑ Ⓒ	67	Ⓐ Ⓑ Ⓒ Ⓓ	87	Ⓐ Ⓑ Ⓒ Ⓓ
8	Ⓐ Ⓑ Ⓒ Ⓓ	28	Ⓐ Ⓑ Ⓒ	48	Ⓐ Ⓑ Ⓒ	68	Ⓐ Ⓑ Ⓒ Ⓓ	88	Ⓐ Ⓑ Ⓒ Ⓓ
9	Ⓐ Ⓑ Ⓒ Ⓓ	29	Ⓐ Ⓑ Ⓒ	49	Ⓐ Ⓑ Ⓒ	69	Ⓐ Ⓑ Ⓒ Ⓓ	89	Ⓐ Ⓑ Ⓒ Ⓓ
10	Ⓐ Ⓑ Ⓒ Ⓓ	30	Ⓐ Ⓑ Ⓒ	50	Ⓐ Ⓑ Ⓒ	70	Ⓐ Ⓑ Ⓒ Ⓓ	90	Ⓐ Ⓑ Ⓒ Ⓓ
11	Ⓐ Ⓑ Ⓒ Ⓓ	31	Ⓐ Ⓑ Ⓒ	51	Ⓐ Ⓑ Ⓒ	71	Ⓐ Ⓑ Ⓒ Ⓓ	91	Ⓐ Ⓑ Ⓒ Ⓓ
12	Ⓐ Ⓑ Ⓒ Ⓓ	32	Ⓐ Ⓑ Ⓒ	52	Ⓐ Ⓑ Ⓒ	72	Ⓐ Ⓑ Ⓒ Ⓓ	92	Ⓐ Ⓑ Ⓒ Ⓓ
13	Ⓐ Ⓑ Ⓒ Ⓓ	33	Ⓐ Ⓑ Ⓒ	53	Ⓐ Ⓑ Ⓒ	73	Ⓐ Ⓑ Ⓒ Ⓓ	93	Ⓐ Ⓑ Ⓒ Ⓓ
14	Ⓐ Ⓑ Ⓒ Ⓓ	34	Ⓐ Ⓑ Ⓒ	54	Ⓐ Ⓑ Ⓒ	74	Ⓐ Ⓑ Ⓒ Ⓓ	94	Ⓐ Ⓑ Ⓒ Ⓓ
15	Ⓐ Ⓑ Ⓒ Ⓓ	35	Ⓐ Ⓑ Ⓒ	55	Ⓐ Ⓑ Ⓒ	75	Ⓐ Ⓑ Ⓒ Ⓓ	95	Ⓐ Ⓑ Ⓒ Ⓓ
16	Ⓐ Ⓑ Ⓒ Ⓓ	36	Ⓐ Ⓑ Ⓒ	56	Ⓐ Ⓑ Ⓒ	76	Ⓐ Ⓑ Ⓒ Ⓓ	96	Ⓐ Ⓑ Ⓒ Ⓓ
17	Ⓐ Ⓑ Ⓒ Ⓓ	37	Ⓐ Ⓑ Ⓒ	57	Ⓐ Ⓑ Ⓒ	77	Ⓐ Ⓑ Ⓒ Ⓓ	97	Ⓐ Ⓑ Ⓒ Ⓓ
18	Ⓐ Ⓑ Ⓒ Ⓓ	38	Ⓐ Ⓑ Ⓒ	58	Ⓐ Ⓑ Ⓒ	78	Ⓐ Ⓑ Ⓒ Ⓓ	98	Ⓐ Ⓑ Ⓒ Ⓓ
19	Ⓐ Ⓑ Ⓒ Ⓓ	39	Ⓐ Ⓑ Ⓒ	59	Ⓐ Ⓑ Ⓒ	79	Ⓐ Ⓑ Ⓒ Ⓓ	99	Ⓐ Ⓑ Ⓒ Ⓓ
20	Ⓐ Ⓑ Ⓒ Ⓓ	40	Ⓐ Ⓑ Ⓒ	60	Ⓐ Ⓑ Ⓒ	80	Ⓐ Ⓑ Ⓒ Ⓓ	100	Ⓐ Ⓑ Ⓒ Ⓓ

시험시간: **120분** (LC 45분, RC 75분)

READING (PART V~VII)

	A B C D		A B C D		A B C D		A B C D		A B C D
101	Ⓐ Ⓑ Ⓒ Ⓓ	121	Ⓐ Ⓑ Ⓒ Ⓓ	141	Ⓐ Ⓑ Ⓒ Ⓓ	161	Ⓐ Ⓑ Ⓒ Ⓓ	181	Ⓐ Ⓑ Ⓒ Ⓓ
102	Ⓐ Ⓑ Ⓒ Ⓓ	122	Ⓐ Ⓑ Ⓒ Ⓓ	142	Ⓐ Ⓑ Ⓒ Ⓓ	162	Ⓐ Ⓑ Ⓒ Ⓓ	182	Ⓐ Ⓑ Ⓒ Ⓓ
103	Ⓐ Ⓑ Ⓒ Ⓓ	123	Ⓐ Ⓑ Ⓒ Ⓓ	143	Ⓐ Ⓑ Ⓒ Ⓓ	163	Ⓐ Ⓑ Ⓒ Ⓓ	183	Ⓐ Ⓑ Ⓒ Ⓓ
104	Ⓐ Ⓑ Ⓒ Ⓓ	124	Ⓐ Ⓑ Ⓒ Ⓓ	144	Ⓐ Ⓑ Ⓒ Ⓓ	164	Ⓐ Ⓑ Ⓒ Ⓓ	184	Ⓐ Ⓑ Ⓒ Ⓓ
105	Ⓐ Ⓑ Ⓒ Ⓓ	125	Ⓐ Ⓑ Ⓒ Ⓓ	145	Ⓐ Ⓑ Ⓒ Ⓓ	165	Ⓐ Ⓑ Ⓒ Ⓓ	185	Ⓐ Ⓑ Ⓒ Ⓓ
106	Ⓐ Ⓑ Ⓒ Ⓓ	126	Ⓐ Ⓑ Ⓒ Ⓓ	146	Ⓐ Ⓑ Ⓒ Ⓓ	166	Ⓐ Ⓑ Ⓒ Ⓓ	186	Ⓐ Ⓑ Ⓒ Ⓓ
107	Ⓐ Ⓑ Ⓒ Ⓓ	127	Ⓐ Ⓑ Ⓒ Ⓓ	147	Ⓐ Ⓑ Ⓒ Ⓓ	167	Ⓐ Ⓑ Ⓒ Ⓓ	187	Ⓐ Ⓑ Ⓒ Ⓓ
108	Ⓐ Ⓑ Ⓒ Ⓓ	128	Ⓐ Ⓑ Ⓒ Ⓓ	148	Ⓐ Ⓑ Ⓒ Ⓓ	168	Ⓐ Ⓑ Ⓒ Ⓓ	188	Ⓐ Ⓑ Ⓒ Ⓓ
109	Ⓐ Ⓑ Ⓒ Ⓓ	129	Ⓐ Ⓑ Ⓒ Ⓓ	149	Ⓐ Ⓑ Ⓒ Ⓓ	169	Ⓐ Ⓑ Ⓒ Ⓓ	189	Ⓐ Ⓑ Ⓒ Ⓓ
110	Ⓐ Ⓑ Ⓒ Ⓓ	130	Ⓐ Ⓑ Ⓒ Ⓓ	150	Ⓐ Ⓑ Ⓒ Ⓓ	170	Ⓐ Ⓑ Ⓒ Ⓓ	190	Ⓐ Ⓑ Ⓒ Ⓓ
111	Ⓐ Ⓑ Ⓒ Ⓓ	131	Ⓐ Ⓑ Ⓒ Ⓓ	151	Ⓐ Ⓑ Ⓒ Ⓓ	171	Ⓐ Ⓑ Ⓒ Ⓓ	191	Ⓐ Ⓑ Ⓒ Ⓓ
112	Ⓐ Ⓑ Ⓒ Ⓓ	132	Ⓐ Ⓑ Ⓒ Ⓓ	152	Ⓐ Ⓑ Ⓒ Ⓓ	172	Ⓐ Ⓑ Ⓒ Ⓓ	192	Ⓐ Ⓑ Ⓒ Ⓓ
113	Ⓐ Ⓑ Ⓒ Ⓓ	133	Ⓐ Ⓑ Ⓒ Ⓓ	153	Ⓐ Ⓑ Ⓒ Ⓓ	173	Ⓐ Ⓑ Ⓒ Ⓓ	193	Ⓐ Ⓑ Ⓒ Ⓓ
114	Ⓐ Ⓑ Ⓒ Ⓓ	134	Ⓐ Ⓑ Ⓒ Ⓓ	154	Ⓐ Ⓑ Ⓒ Ⓓ	174	Ⓐ Ⓑ Ⓒ Ⓓ	194	Ⓐ Ⓑ Ⓒ Ⓓ
115	Ⓐ Ⓑ Ⓒ Ⓓ	135	Ⓐ Ⓑ Ⓒ Ⓓ	155	Ⓐ Ⓑ Ⓒ Ⓓ	175	Ⓐ Ⓑ Ⓒ Ⓓ	195	Ⓐ Ⓑ Ⓒ Ⓓ
116	Ⓐ Ⓑ Ⓒ Ⓓ	136	Ⓐ Ⓑ Ⓒ Ⓓ	156	Ⓐ Ⓑ Ⓒ Ⓓ	176	Ⓐ Ⓑ Ⓒ Ⓓ	196	Ⓐ Ⓑ Ⓒ Ⓓ
117	Ⓐ Ⓑ Ⓒ Ⓓ	137	Ⓐ Ⓑ Ⓒ Ⓓ	157	Ⓐ Ⓑ Ⓒ Ⓓ	177	Ⓐ Ⓑ Ⓒ Ⓓ	197	Ⓐ Ⓑ Ⓒ Ⓓ
118	Ⓐ Ⓑ Ⓒ Ⓓ	138	Ⓐ Ⓑ Ⓒ Ⓓ	158	Ⓐ Ⓑ Ⓒ Ⓓ	178	Ⓐ Ⓑ Ⓒ Ⓓ	198	Ⓐ Ⓑ Ⓒ Ⓓ
119	Ⓐ Ⓑ Ⓒ Ⓓ	139	Ⓐ Ⓑ Ⓒ Ⓓ	159	Ⓐ Ⓑ Ⓒ Ⓓ	179	Ⓐ Ⓑ Ⓒ Ⓓ	199	Ⓐ Ⓑ Ⓒ Ⓓ
120	Ⓐ Ⓑ Ⓒ Ⓓ	140	Ⓐ Ⓑ Ⓒ Ⓓ	160	Ⓐ Ⓑ Ⓒ Ⓓ	180	Ⓐ Ⓑ Ⓒ Ⓓ	200	Ⓐ Ⓑ Ⓒ Ⓓ

답안지 마킹은 **연필**을 사용하시기 바랍니다.

맞은 문제 개수: _____ / 200

자르는 선

무료 토익 · 토스 · 오픽 · 지텔프 자료
Hackers.co.kr

Answer Sheet

TEST 5

✂ 자르는 선

LISTENING (PART I~IV)

#					#					#					#				
1	Ⓐ Ⓑ Ⓒ Ⓓ		21	Ⓐ Ⓑ Ⓒ Ⓓ		41	Ⓐ Ⓑ Ⓒ Ⓓ		61	Ⓐ Ⓑ Ⓒ Ⓓ		81	Ⓐ Ⓑ Ⓒ Ⓓ
2	Ⓐ Ⓑ Ⓒ Ⓓ		22	Ⓐ Ⓑ Ⓒ Ⓓ		42	Ⓐ Ⓑ Ⓒ Ⓓ		62	Ⓐ Ⓑ Ⓒ Ⓓ		82	Ⓐ Ⓑ Ⓒ Ⓓ
3	Ⓐ Ⓑ Ⓒ Ⓓ		23	Ⓐ Ⓑ Ⓒ Ⓓ		43	Ⓐ Ⓑ Ⓒ Ⓓ		63	Ⓐ Ⓑ Ⓒ Ⓓ		83	Ⓐ Ⓑ Ⓒ Ⓓ
4	Ⓐ Ⓑ Ⓒ Ⓓ		24	Ⓐ Ⓑ Ⓒ Ⓓ		44	Ⓐ Ⓑ Ⓒ Ⓓ		64	Ⓐ Ⓑ Ⓒ Ⓓ		84	Ⓐ Ⓑ Ⓒ Ⓓ
5	Ⓐ Ⓑ Ⓒ Ⓓ		25	Ⓐ Ⓑ Ⓒ Ⓓ		45	Ⓐ Ⓑ Ⓒ Ⓓ		65	Ⓐ Ⓑ Ⓒ Ⓓ		85	Ⓐ Ⓑ Ⓒ Ⓓ
6	Ⓐ Ⓑ Ⓒ Ⓓ		26	Ⓐ Ⓑ Ⓒ Ⓓ		46	Ⓐ Ⓑ Ⓒ Ⓓ		66	Ⓐ Ⓑ Ⓒ Ⓓ		86	Ⓐ Ⓑ Ⓒ Ⓓ
7	Ⓐ Ⓑ Ⓒ		27	Ⓐ Ⓑ Ⓒ Ⓓ		47	Ⓐ Ⓑ Ⓒ Ⓓ		67	Ⓐ Ⓑ Ⓒ Ⓓ		87	Ⓐ Ⓑ Ⓒ Ⓓ
8	Ⓐ Ⓑ Ⓒ		28	Ⓐ Ⓑ Ⓒ Ⓓ		48	Ⓐ Ⓑ Ⓒ Ⓓ		68	Ⓐ Ⓑ Ⓒ Ⓓ		88	Ⓐ Ⓑ Ⓒ Ⓓ
9	Ⓐ Ⓑ Ⓒ		29	Ⓐ Ⓑ Ⓒ Ⓓ		49	Ⓐ Ⓑ Ⓒ Ⓓ		69	Ⓐ Ⓑ Ⓒ Ⓓ		89	Ⓐ Ⓑ Ⓒ Ⓓ
10	Ⓐ Ⓑ Ⓒ		30	Ⓐ Ⓑ Ⓒ Ⓓ		50	Ⓐ Ⓑ Ⓒ Ⓓ		70	Ⓐ Ⓑ Ⓒ Ⓓ		90	Ⓐ Ⓑ Ⓒ Ⓓ
11	Ⓐ Ⓑ Ⓒ		31	Ⓐ Ⓑ Ⓒ Ⓓ		51	Ⓐ Ⓑ Ⓒ Ⓓ		71	Ⓐ Ⓑ Ⓒ Ⓓ		91	Ⓐ Ⓑ Ⓒ Ⓓ
12	Ⓐ Ⓑ Ⓒ		32	Ⓐ Ⓑ Ⓒ Ⓓ		52	Ⓐ Ⓑ Ⓒ Ⓓ		72	Ⓐ Ⓑ Ⓒ Ⓓ		92	Ⓐ Ⓑ Ⓒ Ⓓ
13	Ⓐ Ⓑ Ⓒ		33	Ⓐ Ⓑ Ⓒ Ⓓ		53	Ⓐ Ⓑ Ⓒ Ⓓ		73	Ⓐ Ⓑ Ⓒ Ⓓ		93	Ⓐ Ⓑ Ⓒ Ⓓ
14	Ⓐ Ⓑ Ⓒ		34	Ⓐ Ⓑ Ⓒ Ⓓ		54	Ⓐ Ⓑ Ⓒ Ⓓ		74	Ⓐ Ⓑ Ⓒ Ⓓ		94	Ⓐ Ⓑ Ⓒ Ⓓ
15	Ⓐ Ⓑ Ⓒ		35	Ⓐ Ⓑ Ⓒ Ⓓ		55	Ⓐ Ⓑ Ⓒ Ⓓ		75	Ⓐ Ⓑ Ⓒ Ⓓ		95	Ⓐ Ⓑ Ⓒ Ⓓ
16	Ⓐ Ⓑ Ⓒ		36	Ⓐ Ⓑ Ⓒ Ⓓ		56	Ⓐ Ⓑ Ⓒ Ⓓ		76	Ⓐ Ⓑ Ⓒ Ⓓ		96	Ⓐ Ⓑ Ⓒ Ⓓ
17	Ⓐ Ⓑ Ⓒ		37	Ⓐ Ⓑ Ⓒ Ⓓ		57	Ⓐ Ⓑ Ⓒ Ⓓ		77	Ⓐ Ⓑ Ⓒ Ⓓ		97	Ⓐ Ⓑ Ⓒ Ⓓ
18	Ⓐ Ⓑ Ⓒ		38	Ⓐ Ⓑ Ⓒ Ⓓ		58	Ⓐ Ⓑ Ⓒ Ⓓ		78	Ⓐ Ⓑ Ⓒ Ⓓ		98	Ⓐ Ⓑ Ⓒ Ⓓ
19	Ⓐ Ⓑ Ⓒ		39	Ⓐ Ⓑ Ⓒ Ⓓ		59	Ⓐ Ⓑ Ⓒ Ⓓ		79	Ⓐ Ⓑ Ⓒ Ⓓ		99	Ⓐ Ⓑ Ⓒ Ⓓ
20	Ⓐ Ⓑ Ⓒ		40	Ⓐ Ⓑ Ⓒ Ⓓ		60	Ⓐ Ⓑ Ⓒ Ⓓ		80	Ⓐ Ⓑ Ⓒ Ⓓ		100	Ⓐ Ⓑ Ⓒ Ⓓ

시험시간: **120분** (LC 45분, RC 75분)

READING (PART V~VII)

#					#					#					#				
101	Ⓐ Ⓑ Ⓒ Ⓓ		121	Ⓐ Ⓑ Ⓒ Ⓓ		141	Ⓐ Ⓑ Ⓒ Ⓓ		161	Ⓐ Ⓑ Ⓒ Ⓓ		181	Ⓐ Ⓑ Ⓒ Ⓓ
102	Ⓐ Ⓑ Ⓒ Ⓓ		122	Ⓐ Ⓑ Ⓒ Ⓓ		142	Ⓐ Ⓑ Ⓒ Ⓓ		162	Ⓐ Ⓑ Ⓒ Ⓓ		182	Ⓐ Ⓑ Ⓒ Ⓓ
103	Ⓐ Ⓑ Ⓒ Ⓓ		123	Ⓐ Ⓑ Ⓒ Ⓓ		143	Ⓐ Ⓑ Ⓒ Ⓓ		163	Ⓐ Ⓑ Ⓒ Ⓓ		183	Ⓐ Ⓑ Ⓒ Ⓓ
104	Ⓐ Ⓑ Ⓒ Ⓓ		124	Ⓐ Ⓑ Ⓒ Ⓓ		144	Ⓐ Ⓑ Ⓒ Ⓓ		164	Ⓐ Ⓑ Ⓒ Ⓓ		184	Ⓐ Ⓑ Ⓒ Ⓓ
105	Ⓐ Ⓑ Ⓒ Ⓓ		125	Ⓐ Ⓑ Ⓒ Ⓓ		145	Ⓐ Ⓑ Ⓒ Ⓓ		165	Ⓐ Ⓑ Ⓒ Ⓓ		185	Ⓐ Ⓑ Ⓒ Ⓓ
106	Ⓐ Ⓑ Ⓒ Ⓓ		126	Ⓐ Ⓑ Ⓒ Ⓓ		146	Ⓐ Ⓑ Ⓒ Ⓓ		166	Ⓐ Ⓑ Ⓒ Ⓓ		186	Ⓐ Ⓑ Ⓒ Ⓓ
107	Ⓐ Ⓑ Ⓒ Ⓓ		127	Ⓐ Ⓑ Ⓒ Ⓓ		147	Ⓐ Ⓑ Ⓒ Ⓓ		167	Ⓐ Ⓑ Ⓒ Ⓓ		187	Ⓐ Ⓑ Ⓒ Ⓓ
108	Ⓐ Ⓑ Ⓒ Ⓓ		128	Ⓐ Ⓑ Ⓒ Ⓓ		148	Ⓐ Ⓑ Ⓒ Ⓓ		168	Ⓐ Ⓑ Ⓒ Ⓓ		188	Ⓐ Ⓑ Ⓒ Ⓓ
109	Ⓐ Ⓑ Ⓒ Ⓓ		129	Ⓐ Ⓑ Ⓒ Ⓓ		149	Ⓐ Ⓑ Ⓒ Ⓓ		169	Ⓐ Ⓑ Ⓒ Ⓓ		189	Ⓐ Ⓑ Ⓒ Ⓓ
110	Ⓐ Ⓑ Ⓒ Ⓓ		130	Ⓐ Ⓑ Ⓒ Ⓓ		150	Ⓐ Ⓑ Ⓒ Ⓓ		170	Ⓐ Ⓑ Ⓒ Ⓓ		190	Ⓐ Ⓑ Ⓒ Ⓓ
111	Ⓐ Ⓑ Ⓒ Ⓓ		131	Ⓐ Ⓑ Ⓒ Ⓓ		151	Ⓐ Ⓑ Ⓒ Ⓓ		171	Ⓐ Ⓑ Ⓒ Ⓓ		191	Ⓐ Ⓑ Ⓒ Ⓓ
112	Ⓐ Ⓑ Ⓒ Ⓓ		132	Ⓐ Ⓑ Ⓒ Ⓓ		152	Ⓐ Ⓑ Ⓒ Ⓓ		172	Ⓐ Ⓑ Ⓒ Ⓓ		192	Ⓐ Ⓑ Ⓒ Ⓓ
113	Ⓐ Ⓑ Ⓒ Ⓓ		133	Ⓐ Ⓑ Ⓒ Ⓓ		153	Ⓐ Ⓑ Ⓒ Ⓓ		173	Ⓐ Ⓑ Ⓒ Ⓓ		193	Ⓐ Ⓑ Ⓒ Ⓓ
114	Ⓐ Ⓑ Ⓒ Ⓓ		134	Ⓐ Ⓑ Ⓒ Ⓓ		154	Ⓐ Ⓑ Ⓒ Ⓓ		174	Ⓐ Ⓑ Ⓒ Ⓓ		194	Ⓐ Ⓑ Ⓒ Ⓓ
115	Ⓐ Ⓑ Ⓒ Ⓓ		135	Ⓐ Ⓑ Ⓒ Ⓓ		155	Ⓐ Ⓑ Ⓒ Ⓓ		175	Ⓐ Ⓑ Ⓒ Ⓓ		195	Ⓐ Ⓑ Ⓒ Ⓓ
116	Ⓐ Ⓑ Ⓒ Ⓓ		136	Ⓐ Ⓑ Ⓒ Ⓓ		156	Ⓐ Ⓑ Ⓒ Ⓓ		176	Ⓐ Ⓑ Ⓒ Ⓓ		196	Ⓐ Ⓑ Ⓒ Ⓓ
117	Ⓐ Ⓑ Ⓒ Ⓓ		137	Ⓐ Ⓑ Ⓒ Ⓓ		157	Ⓐ Ⓑ Ⓒ Ⓓ		177	Ⓐ Ⓑ Ⓒ Ⓓ		197	Ⓐ Ⓑ Ⓒ Ⓓ
118	Ⓐ Ⓑ Ⓒ Ⓓ		138	Ⓐ Ⓑ Ⓒ Ⓓ		158	Ⓐ Ⓑ Ⓒ Ⓓ		178	Ⓐ Ⓑ Ⓒ Ⓓ		198	Ⓐ Ⓑ Ⓒ Ⓓ
119	Ⓐ Ⓑ Ⓒ Ⓓ		139	Ⓐ Ⓑ Ⓒ Ⓓ		159	Ⓐ Ⓑ Ⓒ Ⓓ		179	Ⓐ Ⓑ Ⓒ Ⓓ		199	Ⓐ Ⓑ Ⓒ Ⓓ
120	Ⓐ Ⓑ Ⓒ Ⓓ		140	Ⓐ Ⓑ Ⓒ Ⓓ		160	Ⓐ Ⓑ Ⓒ Ⓓ		180	Ⓐ Ⓑ Ⓒ Ⓓ		200	Ⓐ Ⓑ Ⓒ Ⓓ

답안지 마킹은 **연필**을 사용하시기 바랍니다.

맞은 문제 개수: _____ / 200

무료 토익·토스·오픽·지텔프 자료
Hackers.co.kr

2024년 상반기 출제경향 완벽 반영

해커스 토익

실전 LC+RC
모의고사 + 해설집

2

초판 3쇄 발행 2025년 1월 20일

초판 1쇄 발행 2024년 7월 31일

지은이	해커스 어학연구소
펴낸곳	㈜해커스 어학연구소
펴낸이	해커스 어학연구소 출판팀

주소	서울특별시 서초구 강남대로61길 23 ㈜해커스 어학연구소
고객센터	02-537-5000
교재 관련 문의	publishing@hackers.com
동영상강의	HackersIngang.com

ISBN	978-89-6542-718-6 (13740)
Serial Number	01-03-01

외국어인강 1위, 해커스인강
HackersIngang.com

해커스인강

· 해커스 토익 스타강사의 **본 교재 인강**
· 단기 리스닝 점수 향상을 위한 **받아쓰기&쉐도잉 워크북**
· 들으면서 외우는 **단어암기장 및 단어암기 MP3**
· 빠르고 편리하게 채점하는 **정답녹음 MP3**

영어 전문 포털, 해커스토익
Hackers.co.kr

해커스 토익

· 최신 출제경향이 반영된 **온라인 실전모의고사**
· **매월 적중예상특강** 및 **실시간 토익시험 정답확인/해설강의**
· **매일 실전 LC/RC 문제** 및 **토익 기출보카 TEST, 정기토익 기출단어** 등 다양한 무료 학습 콘텐츠

헤럴드 선정 2018 대학생 선호브랜드 대상 '대학생이 선정한 외국어인강' 부문 1위

해커스 토익

실전 LC+RC

해설집 2

해커스 어학연구소

해커스 토익
실전 LC+RC 2

해설집

해커스 어학연구소

TEST 1

LISTENING TEST
p.28

1 (A)	21 (C)	41 (C)	61 (D)	81 (B)
2 (D)	22 (B)	42 (B)	62 (D)	82 (C)
3 (D)	23 (A)	43 (D)	63 (B)	83 (D)
4 (D)	24 (B)	44 (B)	64 (D)	84 (A)
5 (A)	25 (A)	45 (C)	65 (D)	85 (C)
6 (B)	26 (B)	46 (B)	66 (C)	86 (A)
7 (B)	27 (C)	47 (D)	67 (B)	87 (A)
8 (C)	28 (B)	48 (C)	68 (C)	88 (D)
9 (A)	29 (C)	49 (D)	69 (D)	89 (C)
10 (A)	30 (A)	50 (B)	70 (D)	90 (B)
11 (C)	31 (C)	51 (D)	71 (C)	91 (B)
12 (C)	32 (B)	52 (C)	72 (B)	92 (D)
13 (A)	33 (B)	53 (C)	73 (D)	93 (B)
14 (A)	34 (A)	54 (A)	74 (A)	94 (D)
15 (C)	35 (D)	55 (A)	75 (D)	95 (B)
16 (B)	36 (D)	56 (A)	76 (C)	96 (C)
17 (A)	37 (A)	57 (C)	77 (C)	97 (B)
18 (A)	38 (B)	58 (C)	78 (B)	98 (C)
19 (C)	39 (D)	59 (A)	79 (A)	99 (A)
20 (A)	40 (C)	60 (A)	80 (B)	100 (B)

READING TEST
p.40

101 (A)	121 (D)	141 (C)	161 (C)	181 (A)
102 (A)	122 (B)	142 (A)	162 (B)	182 (D)
103 (D)	123 (B)	143 (B)	163 (D)	183 (D)
104 (D)	124 (B)	144 (C)	164 (D)	184 (C)
105 (B)	125 (C)	145 (C)	165 (C)	185 (D)
106 (C)	126 (C)	146 (A)	166 (B)	186 (D)
107 (A)	127 (B)	147 (C)	167 (C)	187 (B)
108 (C)	128 (A)	148 (C)	168 (C)	188 (D)
109 (A)	129 (D)	149 (C)	169 (B)	189 (D)
110 (C)	130 (C)	150 (B)	170 (C)	190 (B)
111 (C)	131 (C)	151 (C)	171 (C)	191 (B)
112 (C)	132 (A)	152 (B)	172 (A)	192 (B)
113 (D)	133 (D)	153 (D)	173 (B)	193 (C)
114 (C)	134 (B)	154 (D)	174 (A)	194 (C)
115 (B)	135 (C)	155 (B)	175 (C)	195 (B)
116 (D)	136 (B)	156 (A)	176 (D)	196 (B)
117 (B)	137 (D)	157 (C)	177 (B)	197 (C)
118 (A)	138 (D)	158 (C)	178 (B)	198 (A)
119 (A)	139 (C)	159 (C)	179 (C)	199 (D)
120 (C)	140 (B)	160 (B)	180 (A)	200 (C)

PART 1

1 1인 사진
🔊 미국식

(A) He's mopping the floor of a hall.
(B) He's standing next to a bin.
(C) He's wiping a window with a cloth.
(D) He's replacing a warning sign.

mop v. 닦다 bin n. 쓰레기통 wipe v. 닦다 replace v. 교체하다
warning sign 경고 표지판

해석 (A) 그는 복도 바닥을 닦고 있다.
　　(B) 그는 쓰레기통 옆에 서 있다.
　　(C) 그는 천으로 창문을 닦고 있다.
　　(D) 그는 경고 표지판을 교체하고 있다.

해설 (A) [o] 남자가 복도 바닥을 닦고 있는 모습을 가장 잘 묘사한 정답이다.
　　(B) [x] 사진에서 쓰레기통(bin)을 확인할 수 없으므로 오답이다.
　　(C) [x] 남자가 바닥을 닦고 있는 상태인데, 창문(window)을 닦고 있다고 잘못 묘사한 오답이다. He's wiping(그는 닦고 있다)까지만 듣고 정답으로 선택하지 않도록 주의한다.
　　(D) [x] 사진에서 경고 표지판(warning sign)은 보이지만, 남자가 그것을 교체하고 있는(replacing) 모습은 아니므로 오답이다.

2 1인 사진
🔊 영국식

(A) She's shutting the door of a microwave.
(B) She's paying for some groceries.
(C) Some baskets have been placed on a rack.
(D) **Some merchandise is on display at a supermarket.**

shut v. (문 등을) 닫다 microwave n. 전자레인지
groceries n. 식료품(류) rack n. 선반, 받침대
merchandise n. 상품, 제품 on display 진열된, 전시된

해석 (A) 그녀는 전자레인지 문을 닫고 있다.
　　(B) 그녀는 몇몇 식료품의 값을 지불하고 있다.
　　(C) 몇몇 바구니들이 선반 위에 놓여 있다.
　　(D) **몇몇 상품이 슈퍼마켓에 진열되어 있다.**

해설 (A) [x] 사진에서 전자레인지(microwave)를 확인할 수 없으므로 오답이다. 사진에 있는 냉장고의 문(door)을 사용하여 혼동을 주었다.
　　(B) [x] paying(값을 지불하고 있다)은 여자의 동작과 무관하므로 오답이다. 사진의 장소인 슈퍼마켓과 관련된 groceries(식료품)를 사용하여 혼동을 주었다.
　　(C) [x] 사진에 바구니는 보이지만 여러 개가 아닌 한 개이고, 선반 위에 놓여 있는(have been placed on a rack) 모습도 아니므로 오답이다.

(D) [o] 상품이 슈퍼마켓에 진열되어 있는 모습을 가장 잘 묘사한 정답이다.

최신토익경향

최근 Part 1에서는 문장 뒤에 전치사구를 덧붙여 사진을 상세히 묘사하는 보기가 자주 출제되고 있다. 빈출 전치사구를 함께 알아두자.

- **near** a fenced area 울타리가 있는 지역 근처에
- **behind** the counter 카운터 뒤에
- **on** the ground 바닥에
- **at** an outdoor café 야외 카페에

3 2인 이상 사진 🎧 캐나다식

(A) One of the men is holding a handrail.
(B) One of the people is wearing a backpack.
(C) One of the women is going up the staircase.
(D) One of the people is using a laptop computer.

handrail n. (계단 등의) 난간   staircase n. 계단
laptop computer 노트북 컴퓨터

해석 (A) 남자들 중 한 명이 난간을 잡고 있다.
(B) 사람들 중 한 명이 배낭을 메고 있다.
(C) 여자들 중 한 명이 계단을 오르고 있다.
(D) 사람들 중 한 명이 노트북 컴퓨터를 사용하고 있다.

해설 (A) [×] 사진에 난간을 잡고 있는(holding a handrail) 남자가 없으므로 오답이다.
(B) [×] 사진에 배낭을 메고 있는(wearing a backpack) 사람이 없으므로 오답이다. 사진에 있는 배낭(backpack)을 사용하여 혼동을 주었다.
(C) [×] 사진에 계단을 오르고 있는(going up the staircase) 여자가 없으므로 오답이다. 사진에 있는 계단(staircase)을 사용하여 혼동을 주었다.
(D) [o] 사람들 중 한 명이 노트북 컴퓨터를 사용하고 있는 모습을 가장 잘 묘사한 정답이다.

4 1인 사진 🎧 호주식

(A) Some containers have fallen onto the ground.
(B) There is a ladder leaning against a railing.
(C) Some tools have been left near a doorway.
(D) There is a cart near some shelves.

container n. 용기   ground n. 바닥, 땅   ladder n. 사다리
lean against ~에 기대다   railing n. 난간   doorway n. 출입구

해석 (A) 몇몇 용기들이 바닥에 떨어져 있다.
(B) 난간에 기대어져 있는 사다리가 있다.
(C) 몇몇 도구들이 출입구 근처에 놓여 있다.
(D) 몇몇 선반들 근처에 카트가 있다.

해설 (A) [×] 용기들(containers)이 바닥에 떨어져 있는 것이 아니라, 카트에 실려 있으므로 오답이다.
(B) [×] 사진에서 사다리(ladder)를 확인할 수 없으므로 오답이다.
(C) [×] 사진에서 출입구(doorway)를 확인할 수 없으므로 오답이다.
(D) [o] 선반들 근처에 카트가 있는 모습을 가장 잘 묘사한 정답이다.

5 사물 및 풍경 사진 🎧 영국식

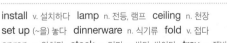

(A) Some boats are docked in a row.
(B) A flag has been raised on a pole.
(C) A boat is passing under a bridge.
(D) Some equipment is being lowered into the water.

dock v. (배를) 정박하다; n. 부두   in a row 일렬로, 잇달아   flag n. 깃발
raise v. 높이 게양하다, 올리다   pole n. 기둥, 막대기
equipment n. 장비

해석 **(A) 몇몇 배들이 일렬로 정박되어 있다.**
(B) 깃발이 기둥 위에 높이 게양되어 있다.
(C) 배가 다리 밑을 지나가고 있다.
(D) 몇몇 장비가 물속으로 내려지고 있다.

해설 (A) [o] 여러 대의 배가 일렬로 정박되어 있는 모습을 가장 잘 묘사한 정답이다.
(B) [×] 사진에서 깃발(flag)을 확인할 수 없으므로 오답이다. 사진에 있는 기둥(pole)을 사용하여 혼동을 주었다.
(C) [×] 사진에서 배(boat)는 보이지만 다리 밑을 지나가고 있는(passing under a bridge) 모습은 아니므로 오답이다.
(D) [×] 사진에서 물속으로 내려지고 있는(being lowered into the water) 장비를 확인할 수 없으므로 오답이다. 사진에 있는 장비(equipment)를 사용하여 혼동을 주었다.

최신토익경향

매회 1~2문제 정도 출제되는 사물 및 풍경 사진에는 해변이나 강, 호수 등의 풍경이 자주 등장한다. 해변·강·호수 등을 묘사하는 풍경 사진에 나올 수 있는 단어들을 함께 알아두자.

- **dock** (배를) 정박하다; 부두
- **row** 배를 젓다
- **float** (물에) 뜨다
- **sail** 항해하다
- **paddle** (노를) 젓다; 노
- **flow** 흐르다
- **on the shore** 물가에
- **along the beach** 해변을 따라

6 2인 이상 사진 🎧 호주식

(A) The men are installing lamps on the ceiling.
(B) One of the men is setting up dinnerware on a table.
(C) The men are folding aprons in the kitchen.
(D) One of the men is carrying a stack of dishes on a tray.

install v. 설치하다   lamp n. 전등, 램프   ceiling n. 천장
set up (~을) 놓다   dinnerware n. 식기류   fold v. 접다
apron n. 앞치마   stack n. 더미; v. 쌓다, 쌓이다   tray n. 쟁반

해석 (A) 남자들이 천장에 전등을 설치하고 있다.
　　(B) 남자들 중 한 명이 탁자에 식기류를 놓고 있다.
　　(C) 남자들이 주방에서 앞치마를 접고 있다.
　　(D) 남자들 중 한 명이 쟁반에 접시 더미를 나르고 있다.

해설 (A) [×] installing(설치하고 있다)은 남자들의 동작과 무관하므로 오
　　　답이다. 사진에 있는 전등(lamps)을 사용하여 혼동을 주었다.
　　(B) [○] 남자들 중 한 명이 탁자에 식기류를 놓고 있는 모습을 가장 잘
　　　묘사한 정답이다.
　　(C) [×] folding aprons(앞치마를 접고 있다)는 남자들의 동작과 무
　　　관하므로 오답이다. 사진에 있는 앞치마(aprons)를 사용하여
　　　혼동을 주었다.
　　(D) [×] 사진에 접시 더미를 나르고 있는(carrying) 남자가 없으므로
　　　오답이다. 사진에 있는 접시(dishes)와 쟁반(tray)을 사용하
　　　여 혼동을 주었다.

최신토익경향

Part 1에서 동사 set은 여러 형태의 숙어 표현들로 출제되는 경우가 많다.
set과 관련된 숙어 표현들을 함께 알아두자.

- **set up** some refreshments 다과를 준비하다
- **set out** some items 물품들을 진열하다
- **set down** the bag 가방을 내려놓다
- **set aside** the chairs 의자들을 한쪽으로 치우다

PART 2

7 Where 의문문
　　　　　　　　　　　　　　　3해 캐나다식 → 미국식

Excuse me. Where can I find the model number of this hair dryer?
(A) The recently launched model.
(B) On the back of the device.
(C) No, I'm fine with your plan.

launch v. 출시하다, 출간하다　device n. 기기

해석 실례합니다. 이 헤어드라이어의 모델 번호는 어디에서 찾을 수 있나
　　　요?
　　(A) 최근에 출시된 모델이요.
　　(B) 기기 뒷면에서요.
　　(C) 아뇨, 저는 당신의 계획에 찬성해요.

해설 (A) [×] 질문의 model을 반복 사용하여 혼동을 준 오답이다.
　　(B) [○] 기기 뒷면이라는 말로, 모델 번호가 있는 위치를 언급했으므
　　　로 정답이다.
　　(C) [×] 의문사 의문문에 No로 응답했으므로 오답이다. find - fine
　　　의 유사 발음 어휘를 사용하여 혼동을 주었다.

8 Who 의문문
　　　　　　　　　　　　　　　3해 호주식 → 영국식

Who left the door open?
(A) The lid is open.
(B) With wood material.
(C) Oh, I forgot to close it.
　　　　　　　　　　　　　　　　　　　　　○

lid n. 뚜껑　wood material 목재　forget v. 깜빡하다, 잊다

해석 누가 문을 열어 둔 건가요?
　　(A) 뚜껑이 열려 있어요.
　　(B) 목재로요.
　　(C) 아, 제가 닫는 것을 깜빡했어요.

해설 (A) [×] 질문의 open을 반복 사용하여 혼동을 준 오답이다.
　　(B) [×] 질문의 door(문)에서 연상할 수 있는 wood material(목재)을
　　　사용하여 혼동을 준 오답이다.
　　(C) [○] 자신이 닫는 것을 깜빡했다는 말로, 문을 열어 둔 사람을 언급
　　　했으므로 정답이다.

9 평서문
　　　　　　　　　　　　　　　3해 영국식 → 캐나다식

Our whole team is attending the concert tonight.
(A) I didn't get the memo.
(B) That was a great performance.
(C) The marketing team.

해석 우리 팀 전체가 오늘 밤 콘서트에 갈 거예요.
　　(A) 저는 회람을 받지 못했어요.
　　(B) 그건 훌륭한 공연이었어요.
　　(C) 마케팅팀이요.

해설 (A) [○] 자신은 회람을 받지 못했다며, 오늘 밤 콘서트에 가는지 몰랐
　　　다는 의견을 제시했으므로 정답이다.
　　(B) [×] 질문의 concert(콘서트)와 관련 있는 performance(공연)를
　　　사용하여 혼동을 준 오답이다.
　　(C) [×] 질문의 team을 반복 사용하여 혼동을 준 오답이다.

최신토익경향

평균 3~5문제 출제되는 평서문은 객관적 사실을 전달하거나 의견을 제시
하는 등 다양한 의도를 전달할 수 있기 때문에 전형적인 응답이 정해져 있
지 않아 고난도 문제이다. 따라서 질문과 답변의 의도를 정확하게 파악하
는 것이 중요하다. 객관적인 사실을 언급하는 평서문에 올 수 있는 다양한
응답 패턴을 알아두자.

Formal dress is required for tomorrow's event.
내일 행사를 위해서는 격식을 갖춘 복장이 필요해요.
<답변 1> I'll be sure to wear a suit.
　　　　　꼭 정장을 입을게요.
<답변 2> It's actually been canceled.
　　　　　그것은 사실 취소됐어요.
*<답변 1> 내일 행사에 격식을 갖춘 복장이 필요하다는 객관적인 사실을 전
　　　　　달하는 평서문에 꼭 정장을 입겠다는 추가 정보를 전달한 응답
　<답변 2> 내일 행사에 격식을 갖춘 복장이 필요하다는 객관적인 사실을 전달
　　　　　하는 평서문에 내일 행사가 취소됐다는 추가 정보를 전달한 응답

10 What 의문문
　　　　　　　　　　　　　　　3해 미국식 → 캐나다식

What are you getting Bonnie for her retirement party?
(A) A flower bouquet.
(B) I'm glad you liked the party.
(C) No. I'm busy today.

retirement adj. 은퇴의, 퇴직자를 위한; n. 은퇴, 퇴직
flower bouquet 꽃다발

해석 Bonnie의 은퇴 파티에서 그녀에게 무엇을 줄 건가요?
 (A) 꽃다발이요.
 (B) 당신이 그 파티를 좋아해 줘서 기뻐요.
 (C) 아니요. 저는 오늘 바빠요.

해설 (A) [○] 꽃다발이라며, Bonnie의 은퇴 파티에서 그녀에게 줄 것을 언급했으므로 정답이다.
 (B) [×] 질문의 party를 반복 사용하여 혼동을 준 오답이다.
 (C) [×] 의문사 의문문에 No로 응답했고, Bonnie에게 무엇을 줄 것인지를 물었는데, 이와 관련이 없는 오늘 바쁘다는 내용으로 응답했으므로 오답이다.

11 Where 의문문
③3 호주식 → 영국식

Where did you put the magazines I ordered?
(A) Yes. They will arrive tomorrow.
(B) What is the shipping fee?
(C) I left them on the desk in your office.

magazine n. 잡지 arrive v. 도착하다 shipping fee 운송료

해석 제가 주문했던 잡지들을 어디에 두셨나요?
 (A) 네. 그것들은 내일 도착할 거예요.
 (B) 운송료가 얼마인가요?
 (C) 당신의 사무실 책상 위에 두었어요.

해설 (A) [×] 의문사 의문문에 Yes로 응답했으므로 오답이다. 질문의 ordered(주문했다)에서 연상할 수 있는 arrive(도착하다)를 사용하여 혼동을 주었다.
 (B) [×] 질문의 ordered(주문했다)와 관련 있는 shipping fee(운송료)를 사용하여 혼동을 준 오답이다.
 (C) [○] 사무실 책상 위에 두었다는 말로, 잡지들을 둔 장소를 언급했으므로 정답이다.

12 부정 의문문
③3 캐나다식 → 호주식

Shouldn't we tell the client we're going to be late?
(A) The feedback was mostly positive.
(B) It was a productive meeting.
(C) I can't seem to find his number.

client n. 고객, 의뢰인 feedback n. 의견, 피드백
positive adj. 긍정적인 productive adj. 생산적인

해석 우리가 늦을 거라고 고객에게 말해야 하지 않나요?
 (A) 의견은 대게 긍정적이었어요.
 (B) 그건 생산적인 회의였어요.
 (C) 그의 번호를 찾을 수 없는 것 같아요.

해설 (A) [×] 질문의 client(고객)에서 연상할 수 있는 feedback(의견)을 사용하여 혼동을 준 오답이다.
 (B) [×] 질문의 client(고객)와 관련 있는 meeting(회의)을 사용하여 혼동을 준 오답이다.
 (C) [○] 그의 번호를 찾을 수 없다는 말로, 고객에게 늦을 거라고 말을 해야 하는데 할 수 없음을 간접적으로 전달했으므로 정답이다.

13 Which 의문문
③3 호주식 → 영국식

Which of the documents do you want me to copy?
(A) Both of them, please.
(B) This is a newly released book.
(C) Mr. Han wrote that.

document n. 문서, 서류 copy v. 복사하다; n. (책·신문 등의) 한 부

해석 어떤 문서를 복사해 드릴까요?
 (A) 둘 다 부탁드려요.
 (B) 이건 새로 출간된 책이에요.
 (C) Mr. Han이 그것을 썼어요.

해설 (A) [○] 둘 다 부탁한다는 말로, 복사하길 원하는 문서를 언급했으므로 정답이다.
 (B) [×] 질문의 copy(복사하다)를 '한 부'라는 의미의 명사로 생각했을 때, 이와 관련 있는 book(책)을 사용하여 혼동을 준 오답이다.
 (C) [×] 질문의 documents(문서)와 관련 있는 wrote(썼다)를 사용하여 혼동을 준 오답이다.

14 제안 의문문
③3 미국식 → 호주식

Would you like me to revise the estimate right now?
(A) It just needs to be done this afternoon.
(B) Thanks for paying the bill.
(C) Did it take long to change?

revise v. 수정하다, 변경하다 estimate n. 견적(서)
pay a bill 청구서를 지불하다

해석 지금 바로 견적서를 수정할까요?
 (A) 오늘 오후에만 완료되면 돼요.
 (B) 청구서를 지불해 주셔서 감사해요.
 (C) 변경하는 데 시간이 오래 걸렸나요?

해설 (A) [○] 오늘 오후에만 완료되면 된다는 말로, 지금 바로 견적서를 수정하겠다는 제안을 간접적으로 거절했으므로 정답이다.
 (B) [×] 질문의 estimate(견적서)와 관련 있는 bill(청구서)을 사용하여 혼동을 준 오답이다.
 (C) [×] 질문의 revise(수정하다)와 관련 있는 change(변경하다)를 사용하여 혼동을 준 오답이다.

15 평서문
③3 호주식 → 영국식

Ms. Walker wants the logo design to be finished today.
(A) No, in research and development.
(B) Effective time management.
(C) We'll be working overtime, then.

research and development 연구 개발 effective adj. 효과적인
overtime n. 초과 근무, 야근

해석 Ms. Walker는 로고 디자인이 오늘 마무리되기를 원해요.
 (A) 아니요, 연구 개발에서요.
 (B) 효과적인 시간 관리요.
 (C) 그럼, 우리는 초과 근무를 해야 하겠군요.

해설 (A) [x] 질문의 design(디자인)에서 연상할 수 있는 development (개발)를 사용하여 혼동을 준 오답이다.
(B) [x] 질문의 today(오늘)와 관련 있는 time(시간)을 사용하여 혼동을 준 오답이다.
(C) [o] 그럼 초과 근무를 해야 하겠다는 말로, Ms. Walker가 로고 디자인이 오늘 마무리되기를 원한다는 문제점에 대한 해결책을 제시했으므로 정답이다.

16 Why 의문문

영국식 → 미국식

Why wasn't Ms. Peterson at the press conference?
(A) A media representative.
(B) Because she is in the hospital.
(C) No. You must attend it.

press conference 기자 회견 representative n. 대표

해석 Ms. Peterson은 왜 기자 회견에 오지 않은 건가요?
(A) 대중 매체 대표요.
(B) 그녀는 병원에 있기 때문이에요.
(C) 아니요. 당신은 거기에 참석해야 해요.

해설 (A) [x] 질문의 press conference(기자 회견)와 관련 있는 media (대중 매체)를 사용하여 혼동을 준 오답이다.
(B) [o] 그녀가 병원에 있기 때문이라며, Ms. Peterson이 기자 회견에 오지 않은 이유를 언급했으므로 정답이다.
(C) [x] 의문사 의문문에 No로 응답했고, Ms. Peterson이 기자 회견에 오지 않은 이유를 물었는데, 이와 관련 없는 상대방이 거기에 참석해야만 한다는 내용으로 응답했으므로 오답이다.

17 Who 의문문

영국식 → 캐나다식

Who will analyze the customer survey results?
(A) Ms. Lee asked Mr. Hong to handle that.
(B) Many customers participated in it.
(C) Your analysis was very detailed.

analyze v. 분석하다 survey n. (설문) 조사
result n. 결과; v. 결과로서 생기다 handle v. 처리하다, 다루다
participate v. 참여하다 detailed adj. 상세한

해석 고객 설문 조사 결과는 누가 분석할 건가요?
(A) Ms. Lee가 Mr. Hong에게 그걸 처리해 달라고 부탁했어요.
(B) 많은 고객이 참여했어요.
(C) 당신의 분석은 매우 상세했어요.

해설 (A) [o] Ms. Lee가 Mr. Hong에게 그것을 처리해 달라고 부탁했다며, 고객 설문 조사 결과를 분석할 사람을 언급했으므로 정답이다.
(B) [x] 질문의 customer를 customers로 반복 사용하여 혼동을 준 오답이다.
(C) [x] analyze - analysis의 유사 발음 어휘를 사용하여 혼동을 준 오답이다.

18 Be동사 의문문

미국식 → 캐나다식

Are you planning to include more charts in the report?
(A) I just submitted it to my manager.
(B) Do you want a cart?
(C) A number of grammar errors.

include v. 포함하다 chart n. 도표 submit v. 제출하다
a number of 많은

해석 보고서에 더 많은 도표를 포함할 계획인가요?
(A) 저는 그것을 막 관리자에게 제출했어요.
(B) 카트를 원하시나요?
(C) 많은 문법 오류들이요.

해설 (A) [o] 그것을 막 관리자에게 제출했다는 말로, 보고서에 더 많은 도표를 포함할 계획이 아님을 간접적으로 전달했으므로 정답이다.
(B) [x] charts - cart의 유사 발음 어휘를 사용하여 혼동을 준 오답이다.
(C) [x] 질문의 report(보고서)에서 연상할 수 있는 errors(오류들)를 사용하여 혼동을 준 오답이다.

19 선택 의문문

영국식 → 호주식

Will you be eating here, or is this to go?
(A) Give me a receipt.
(B) Here's the menu.
(C) Put it in a bag, please.

receipt n. 영수증

해석 여기에서 드실 건가요, 아니면 가지고 가실 건가요?
(A) 영수증을 주세요.
(B) 여기 메뉴판이요.
(C) 봉투에 넣어 주세요.

해설 (A) [x] 질문의 be eating here(여기에서 먹다)에서 연상할 수 있는 receipt(영수증)를 사용하여 혼동을 준 오답이다.
(B) [x] 질문의 be eating here(여기에서 먹다)와 관련 있는 menu (메뉴판)를 사용하여 혼동을 준 오답이다.
(C) [o] 봉투에 넣어달라는 말로, 가지고 가는 것을 간접적으로 선택했으므로 정답이다.

20 How 의문문

호주식 → 영국식

How far is it to the department store?
(A) Just a couple of blocks.
(B) In the menswear section.
(C) Once a week, usually.

department store 백화점 section n. 구역

해석 백화점까지 거리가 얼마나 되나요?
(A) 몇 블록만 가면 돼요.
(B) 남성복 구역 안에요.
(C) 보통 일주일에 한 번이요.

해설 (A) [o] 몇 블록만 가면 된다는 말로, 백화점이 멀지 않은 곳에 있다고
응답했으므로 정답이다.
(B) [x] 질문의 department store(백화점)와 관련 있는 menswear
section(남성복 구역)을 사용하여 혼동을 준 오답이다.
(C) [x] 백화점까지 거리가 얼마나 되는지를 물었는데 빈도로 응답했
으므로 오답이다. 빈도를 묻는 How often 의문문 문제가 아
님을 주의한다.

21 요청 의문문　　　　　🎧 미국식 → 캐나다식

Could you take care of my cat during my business trip?
(A) Check your suitcase.
(B) A flight to Tokyo.
(C) That won't be a problem.

take care of ~을 돌보다　business trip 출장　suitcase n. 여행 가방

해설 출장 기간 동안 저희 고양이를 돌봐주실 수 있나요?
(A) 여행 가방을 확인하세요.
(B) 도쿄행 비행기요.
(C) 문제없을 거예요.

해설 (A) [x] 질문의 business trip(출장)에서 연상할 수 있는 suitcase
(여행 가방)를 사용하여 혼동을 준 오답이다.
(B) [x] 질문의 business trip(출장)에서 연상할 수 있는 flight(비행
기)를 사용하여 혼동을 준 오답이다.
(C) [o] 문제없을 것이라는 말로, 출장 기간 동안 고양이를 돌봐달라
는 요청을 수락한 정답이다.

22 선택 의문문　　　　　🎧 캐나다식 → 영국식

Should we walk to the theater or go by car?
(A) Our seats are in the front row.
(B) Driving would be faster.
(C) Buy our tickets online.

row n. 줄, 열

해설 우리는 극장까지 걸어가야 하나요, 아니면 차로 가야 하나요?
(A) 우리 좌석은 맨 앞줄에 있어요.
(B) 운전하는 것이 더 빠를 거예요.
(C) 온라인으로 표를 구입하세요.

해설 (A) [x] 질문의 theater(극장)와 관련 있는 seats(좌석)를 사용하여
혼동을 준 오답이다.
(B) [o] 운전하는 것이 더 빠를 것이라며, 차로 가는 것을 선택했으므
로 정답이다.
(C) [x] 질문의 theater(극장)와 관련 있는 tickets(표)를 사용하여 혼
동을 준 오답이다.

23 부가 의문문　　　　　🎧 영국식 → 캐나다식

The products at the education expo were amazing, weren't
they?
(A) They were better than last year's.
(B) The product will be unveiled soon.

(C) It will begin tomorrow.

expo n. 박람회, 전람회　amazing adj. 놀라운
unveil v. 발표하다, 덮개를 벗기다

해설 교육 박람회의 제품들은 놀라웠어요, 그렇지 않나요?
(A) 작년 것들보다 더 좋았어요.
(B) 그 제품은 곧 발표될 거예요.
(C) 그것은 내일 시작될 거예요.

해설 (A) [o] 작년 것들보다 더 좋았다는 말로, 교육 박람회의 제품들이 놀
라웠다는 말에 간접적으로 동의했으므로 정답이다.
(B) [x] 질문의 products를 product로 반복 사용하여 혼동을 준 오
답이다.
(C) [x] 교육 박람회의 제품들이 놀랍지 않았는지를 물었는데, 이와
관련이 없는 그것이 내일 시작될 것이라는 내용으로 응답했
으므로 오답이다. 질문의 education expo(교육 박람회)를
나타낼 수 있는 It을 사용하여 혼동을 주었다.

24 부정 의문문　　　　　🎧 미국식 → 영국식

Wouldn't you rather be the keynote speaker?
(A) Probably on Johnson Avenue.
(B) Maksim is more qualified.
(C) Well, the speech was inspiring.

keynote speaker 기조연설자　qualified adj. 자격이 있는
inspiring adj. 감동시키는, 고무하는

해석 기조연설자인 편이 낫지 않나요?
(A) 아마 Johnson가에서요.
(B) Maksim이 더 자격이 있어요.
(C) 음, 그 연설은 감동적이었어요.

해설 (A) [x] 기조연설자인 편이 낫지 않는지를 물었는데, 이와 관련이 없
는 Johnson가에서라고 응답했으므로 오답이다.
(B) [o] Maksim이 더 자격이 있다는 말로, 기조 연설자인 편이 낫지
않음을 간접적으로 전달했으므로 정답이다.
(C) [x] 지문의 keynote speaker(기조연설자)와 관련 있는
speech(연설)를 사용하여 혼동을 준 오답이다.

25 조동사 의문문　　　　　🎧 호주식 → 미국식

Should we add more parking spaces to this building?
(A) No. I think there are enough already.
(B) It's got four-wheel drive.
(C) I don't need a ride.

four-wheel drive 사륜 자동차　ride n. 태우고 감, 태움; v. 타다

해석 이 건물에 주차 공간을 더 늘려야 하나요?
(A) 아니요. 이미 충분한 것 같아요.
(B) 이건 사륜 자동차예요.
(C) 태워줄 필요 없어요.

해설 (A) [o] No로 건물에 주차 공간을 늘릴 필요가 없음을 전달한 후, 이
미 충분한 것 같다는 부연 설명을 했으므로 정답이다.
(B) [x] 질문의 parking spaces(주차 공간)에서 연상할 수 있는 자동

차와 관련된 four-wheel drive(사륜 자동차)를 사용하여 혼동을 준 오답이다.

(C) [×] 질문의 parking spaces(주차 공간)에서 연상할 수 있는 자동차와 관련된 ride(태우고 감)를 사용하여 혼동을 준 오답이다.

26 부가 의문문

🔊 캐나다식 → 미국식

We should get more chairs for the presentation, shouldn't we?
(A) More than two weeks.
(B) All of the staff will be attending.
(C) No. The presenter hasn't arrived.

presentation n. 발표

해석 발표를 위해 의자를 좀 더 가져와야 해요, 그렇지 않나요?
(A) 2주 넘게요.
(B) 모든 직원이 참석할 거예요.
(C) 아니요. 발표자가 도착하지 않았어요.

해설 (A) [×] 질문의 more를 반복 사용하여 혼동을 준 오답이다.
(B) [○] 모든 직원이 참석할 것이라는 말로, 의자를 좀 더 가져와야 한다고 간접적으로 전달했으므로 정답이다.
(C) [×] presentation - presenter의 유사 발음 어휘를 사용하여 혼동을 준 오답이다.

최신토익경향

매회 2문제 정도 출제되는 부가 의문문은 평서문에 그 내용을 확인하는 꼬리말 의문문이 붙어 있는 의문문으로, Yes/No로 답변할 수 있다. 최근에는 질문과 관련이 없어 보이는 예측하기 어려운 응답들이 자주 출제되고 있으므로 예문과 함께 실전에 대비하자.

The new director's ideas are really great, aren't they?
새로운 관리자의 아이디어가 매우 좋아요, 그렇지 않나요?
<답변> Well, he used to work at Western Electronics.
음, 그는 Western Electronics사에서 일했었어요.
* 새로운 관리자의 아이디어가 매우 좋다는 생각에 관한 의견을 묻는 부가 의문문에 대해, 그가 Western Electronics사에서 일했었다며 새로운 관리자의 아이디어가 좋은 이유를 전달한 응답

27 평서문

🔊 미국식 → 캐나다식

I haven't heard anything about the project being canceled.
(A) The projector in the meeting room.
(B) Cancel at least one week in advance.
(C) An announcement was made today.

projector n. 영사기   in advance 미리, 사전에
announcement n. 발표, 공고

해석 저는 그 프로젝트가 취소되는 것에 대해 들은 게 없어요.
(A) 회의실에 있는 영사기요.
(B) 최소 일주일 전에 미리 취소하세요.
(C) 오늘 발표가 있었어요.

해설 (A) [×] project - projector의 유사 발음 어휘를 사용하여 혼동을 준 오답이다.
(B) [×] 질문의 canceled를 Cancel로 반복 사용하여 혼동을 준 오

답이다.
(C) [○] 오늘 발표가 있었다는 말로, 프로젝트가 취소되는 것에 대해 상대방이 듣지 못한 원인을 언급했으므로 정답이다.

28 How 의문문

🔊 호주식 → 미국식

How do I get a company ID?
(A) For security purposes.
(B) Didn't the HR manager explain?
(C) I don't like my picture.

security adj. 보안의; n. 보안

해석 사원증은 어떻게 받는 건가요?
(A) 보안 목적으로요.
(B) 인사부장이 설명하지 않았나요?
(C) 저는 제 사진이 마음에 들지 않아요.

해설 (A) [×] 질문의 company ID(사원증)에서 연상할 수 있는 회사 출입과 관련된 security purposes(보안 목적)를 사용하여 혼동을 준 오답이다.
(B) [○] 인사부장이 설명하지 않았는지를 되물어, 사원증을 받는 방법을 모른다는 것을 간접적으로 전달했으므로 정답이다.
(C) [×] 질문의 company ID(사원증)에서 연상할 수 있는 picture(사진)를 사용하여 혼동을 준 오답이다.

최신토익경향

의문사(Who, Where, When, What, Which, Why, How)로 시작하는 의문사 의문문은 출제 빈도가 가장 높다. 특히, 최근에는 의문사 의문문에 다시 의문문으로 되물어 답하는 응답이 정답으로 출제되고 있으니, 예문과 함께 의문사 의문문에 되묻는 답변을 살펴보자.

When do I have to water this plant?
이 식물에 언제 물을 줘야 하나요?
<답변> What species is it?
어떤 종이죠?
* 식물에 물을 언제 줘야 하는지를 묻는 의문사 의문문에 어떤 식물 종인지를 되물어 추가 정보를 요구하는 응답

29 조동사 의문문

🔊 미국식 → 호주식

Have you already interviewed all the applicants?
(A) Because I haven't applied yet.
(B) By submitting my résumé.
(C) I was too busy preparing for the conference.

interview v. 면접을 보다, 면담하다; n. 면접
applicant n. 지원자, 신청자   apply v. 지원하다, 신청하다
résumé n. 이력서   conference n. 회의, 학회

해석 모든 지원자들을 이미 면접 보셨나요?
(A) 저는 아직 지원하지 않았기 때문이에요.
(B) 저의 이력서를 제출함으로써요.
(C) 회의 준비로 너무 바빴어요.

해설 (A) [×] applicants - applied의 유사 발음 어휘를 사용하여 혼동을 준 오답이다.
(B) [×] 질문의 applicants(지원자들)와 관련 있는 résumé(이력서)

를 사용하여 혼동을 준 오답이다.

(C) [○] 회의 준비로 너무 바빴다는 말로, 모든 지원자들을 아직 면접 보지 못했다고 간접적으로 전달했으므로 정답이다.

30 평서문

영국식 → 캐나다식

We should make a reservation for the team lunch now.
(A) I need to complete my report first.
(B) I booked a flight for my trip.
(C) The daily lunch special.

make a reservation 예약하다 complete v. 완성하다, 완료하다
book v. 예약하다

해석 우리는 지금 팀 점심을 예약해야 해요.
(A) 저는 보고서를 먼저 완성해야 해요.
(B) 제 여행을 위해 항공편을 예약해 두었어요.
(C) 일일 점심 특선이요.

해설 (A) [○] 보고서를 먼저 완성해야 한다는 말로, 팀 점심을 예약하자는 제안을 간접적으로 거절했으므로 정답이다.
(B) [×] 질문의 make a reservation(예약하다)과 관련 있는 booked(예약했다)를 사용하여 혼동을 준 오답이다.
(C) [×] 질문의 lunch를 반복 사용하여 혼동을 준 오답이다.

31 When 의문문

호주식 → 미국식

When will the new software be installed?
(A) There is no cost for the installation.
(B) About new techniques.
(C) You will be notified by message.

installation n. 설치 notify v. 통보하다, 알리다

해석 새로운 소프트웨어는 언제 설치되나요?
(A) 설치 비용은 없어요.
(B) 새로운 기술에 대해서요.
(C) 당신은 메시지로 통보받을 거예요.

해설 (A) [×] installed - installation의 유사 발음 어휘를 사용하여 혼동을 준 오답이다.
(B) [×] 질문의 new를 반복 사용하고, software(소프트웨어)와 관련 있는 techniques(기술)를 사용하여 혼동을 준 오답이다.
(C) [○] 메시지로 통보받을 것이라는 말로, 새로운 소프트웨어가 언제 설치될지 모른다는 것을 간접적으로 전달했으므로 정답이다.

PART 3

[32-34]

미국식 → 호주식

Questions 32-34 refer to the following conversation.

W: ³²**We need to bake more of these chocolate pastries every morning.** They're really popular with our customers.
M: Absolutely. But we're almost out of chocolate. ³³**You said you were going to order some last week.**

W: ³³**Oh, I'm sorry. It just slipped my mind.** I was kind of busy setting up our new display cases.
M: That's OK. We've got enough for today. ³⁴**Could you order some this afternoon?**
W: I won't forget.

popular adj. 인기 있는 be out of ~이 떨어지다
slip one's mind 깜빡 잊다, 잊어 버리다 set up ~을 설치하다
display case 진열장

해석
32-34번은 다음 대화에 관한 문제입니다.

여: ³²우리는 매일 아침 이 초콜릿 페이스트리를 더 많이 구워야 해요. 그것들은 우리 고객들에게 매우 인기 있어요.
남: 물론이죠. 하지만 초콜릿이 거의 다 떨어졌어요. ³³당신이 지난주에 주문할 거라고 말했었어요.
여: ³³아, 미안해요. 제가 깜빡 잊었네요. 새로운 진열장을 설치하느라 좀 바빴어요.
남: 괜찮아요. 오늘 분량은 충분해요. ³⁴오늘 오후에 그것을 좀 주문해 주시겠어요?
여: 잊지 않을게요.

32 화자 문제

해석 화자들은 누구인 것 같은가?
(A) 계산원들
(B) 제빵사들
(C) 예술가들
(D) 청소부들

해설 대화에서 신분 및 직업과 관련된 표현을 놓치지 않고 듣는다. 여자가 "We need to bake more of these chocolate pastries every morning."이라며 매일 아침 초콜릿 페이스트리를 더 많이 구워야 한다고 한 후, 초콜릿 페이스트리를 위한 재료가 다 떨어졌다는 내용으로 대화가 이어지고 있다. 이를 통해 화자들이 제빵사들이라는 것을 알 수 있다. 따라서 (B)가 정답이다.

어휘 cashier n. 계산원, 점원 baker n. 제빵사

33 이유 문제

해석 여자는 왜 사과하는가?
(A) 직장에 늦게 도착했다.
(B) 작업을 수행하는 것을 잊었다.
(C) 회사 정책을 위반했다.
(D) 잘못된 물건을 샀다.

해설 질문의 핵심 어구(apologize)와 관련된 내용을 주의 깊게 듣는다. 남자가 "You said you were going to order some last week."이라며 여자가 지난주에 주문할 거라고 말했었다고 하자, 여자가 "Oh, I'm sorry. It just slipped my mind."라며 미안하다고 한 후, 깜빡 잊었다고 하였다. 따라서 (B)가 정답이다.

어휘 workplace n. 직장 violate v. 위반하다, 어기다

Paraphrasing

slipped ~ mind 깜빡 잊었다 → forgot 잊었다

34 요청 문제

해석 남자는 여자에게 무엇을 하라고 요청하는가?
(A) 주문을 한다.
(B) 일정을 확인한다.
(C) 가게를 방문한다.
(D) 손님에게 전화한다.

해설 남자의 말에서 요청과 관련된 표현이 포함된 문장을 주의 깊게 듣는다. 남자가 여자에게 "Could you order some this afternoon?" 이라며 오늘 오후에 주문을 좀 해달라고 하였다. 따라서 (A)가 정답이다.

어휘 place an order 주문하다   schedule n. 일정

[35-37]

📻 영국식 → 캐나다식

Questions 35-37 refer to the following conversation.

W: Good morning, Dan. 35**Have you seen this wall? It looks terrible with some of the paint coming off.** Do you think we could repaint it?

M: We still have some paint in the basement. I could touch it up now before the shop opens.

W: Hmm . . . 36**The smell might be too strong for our customers. Maybe you should do that after closing tonight, instead.**

M: Right. 37**Let's put a poster over that part of the wall in the meantime.**

come off (붙어 있던 것이) 떨어지다   repaint v. 다시 칠하다
basement n. 지하실   touch up ~을 손보다, 고치다
in the meantime 그동안에

해석

35-37번은 다음 대화에 관한 문제입니다.

여: 좋은 아침이에요, Dan. 35이 벽 봤어요? 일부 페인트가 떨어져서 끔찍해 보여요. 다시 칠할 수 있을까요?

남: 아직 지하실에 페인트가 조금 있어요. 제가 지금 영업 시작 전에 손볼 수 있어요.

여: 흠... 36냄새가 손님들에게 너무 강할 수도 있어요. 대신, 오늘 밤 문을 닫은 후에 당신이 그걸 하는 게 좋겠어요.

남: 네. 37그동안에 벽의 저 부분에 포스터를 붙입시다.

35 문제점 문제

해석 여자는 무슨 문제를 언급하는가?
(A) 가게에 페인트가 다 떨어졌다.
(B) 배송품이 배달되지 않았다.
(C) 홍보가 잘 진행되지 않고 있다.
(D) 벽의 외관이 보기 좋지 않다.

해설 여자의 말에서 부정적인 표현이 언급된 주변을 주의 깊게 듣는다. 여자가 "Have you seen this wall? It looks terrible with some of the paint coming off."라며 벽의 일부 페인트가 떨어져 끔찍해 보인다고 하였다. 따라서 (D)가 정답이다.

어휘 run out of ~이 떨어지다, ~이 없어지다   shipment n. 배송품, 수송
promotion n. 홍보, 승진   appearance n. 외관

unattractive adj. 보기 좋지 않은, 매력적이지 않은

Paraphrasing

looks terrible 끔찍해 보이다 → is unattractive 보기 좋지 않다

36 이유 문제

해석 화자들은 왜 나중에 문제를 처리하기를 원하는가?
(A) 전문가가 고용되어야 한다.
(B) 몇몇 물품이 구하기 어렵다.
(C) 다른 작업이 우선시되어야 한다.
(D) 몇몇 손님들이 불편해할 수 있다.

해설 질문의 핵심 어구(deal with an issue later)와 관련된 내용을 주의 깊게 듣는다. 여자가 "The smell might be too strong for our customers. Maybe you should do that after closing tonight, instead."라며 냄새가 손님들에게 너무 강할 수 있기 때문에 오늘 밤 문을 닫은 후에 페인트를 다시 칠하는 것이 좋을 것 같다고 하였다. 따라서 (D)가 정답이다.

어휘 professional n. 전문가   obtain v. 구하다, 얻다
prioritize v. 우선시하다

37 제안 문제

해석 남자는 무엇을 제안하는가?
(A) 포스터로 한 부분을 가리기
(B) 영업시간을 연장하기
(C) 가구를 설치하기
(D) 지하실을 청소하기

해설 남자의 말에서 제안과 관련된 표현이 언급된 다음을 주의 깊게 듣는다. 남자가 "Let's put a poster over that part of the wall in the meantime."이라며 벽의 저 부분, 즉 페인트가 떨어진 부분에 포스터를 붙이자고 하였다. 따라서 (A)가 정답이다.

어휘 cover v. 가리다, 씌우다   extend v. 연장하다
business hour 영업시간

[38-40]

📻 호주식 → 미국식

Questions 38-40 refer to the following conversation.

M: 38**Do you understand the system we use to make dental appointments for patients?**

W: Yes, I think I've got it. Thanks for explaining it to me. But what's this program called Easy Net Manage? I've never heard of it.

M: We use it to manage our patients' information. 39**It shows their complete dental records, billing details, and more.**

W: OK. You can see everything in one place. Will I need to create an account?

M: Yes. All staff members must have one. It lets us keep track of any edits made to a patient's information. 40**I'll send a link for the sign-up page.**

dental adj. 치과의   appointment n. 예약   patient n. 환자
manage v. 관리하다   complete adj. 전체의, 완전한

해석

38-40번은 다음 대화에 관한 문제입니다.

남: ³⁸당신은 우리가 환자들을 위해 치과 예약을 할 때 사용하는 시스템을 이해하셨나요?

여: 네, 이해한 것 같아요. 설명해 주셔서 감사해요. 하지만 Easy Net Manage라고 불리는 이 프로그램은 무엇인가요? 한 번도 들어본 적이 없어요.

남: 우리는 환자의 정보를 관리하는 데 그것을 사용합니다. ³⁹그것은 그들의 전체 치과 기록, 청구 내역 등을 보여줘요.

여: 네, 한 곳에서 모든 것을 볼 수 있군요. 제가 계정을 만들어야 하나요?

남: 네, 모든 직원이 가지고 있어야 해요. 그것은 우리가 환자의 정보에 대한 수정 사항을 기록하게 해줘요. ⁴⁰제가 가입 페이지의 링크를 보내드릴게요.

38 화자 문제

해석 화자들이 어디에서 일하는 것 같은가?
(A) 소프트웨어 회사에서
(B) 치과에서
(C) 은행에서
(D) 식당에서

해설 대화에서 신분 및 직업과 관련된 표현을 놓치지 않고 듣는다. 남자가 여자에게 "Do you understand the system we use to make dental appointments for patients?"라며 환자들을 위해 치과 예약을 할 때 사용하는 시스템에 대해 이해했는지 물은 후, 환자의 정보를 관리하는 데 사용하는 프로그램에 관해 설명하고 있다. 이를 통해 화자들이 치과에서 일하고 있음을 알 수 있다. 따라서 (B)가 정답이다.

39 언급 문제

해석 Easy Net Manage 프로그램에 대해 무엇이 언급되는가?
(A) 정기적으로 업데이트되어야 한다.
(B) 월간 구독이 필요하다.
(C) 최근에서야 도입되었다.
(D) 청구 정보가 포함되어 있다.

해설 질문의 핵심 어구(Easy Net manage program)와 관련된 내용을 주의 깊게 듣는다. 남자가 "It shows their[patients'] complete dental records, billing details, and more."라며 Easy Net Manage 프로그램은 환자들의 전체 치과 기록, 청구 내역 등을 보여준다고 하였다. 따라서 (D)가 정답이다.

어휘 regularly adv. 정기적으로 subscription n. 구독

40 다음에 할 일 문제

해석 남자는 다음에 무엇을 할 것인가?
(A) 비밀번호를 변경한다.
(B) 웹사이트를 확인한다.
(C) 링크를 제공한다.
(D) 설명서를 출력한다.

해설 대화의 마지막 부분을 주의 깊게 듣는다. 남자가 "I'll send a link for the sign-up page."라며 가입 페이지의 링크를 보내주겠다고 한 것을 통해 남자가 다음에 여자에게 링크를 제공할 것임을 알 수 있다. 따라서 (C)가 정답이다.

어휘 print out 출력하다 manual n. 설명서

Paraphrasing

send 보내다 → Provide 제공하다

[41-43]

🎧 미국식 → 호주식

Questions 41-43 refer to the following conversation.

W: Hi. ⁴¹**I recently saw a listing on your Web site for a three-bedroom townhouse in the Edgewood neighborhood.** My husband and I are interested in it because our daughter's new school is in that area. Is it still available?

M: Yes. ⁴²**But the owner just notified me that the current tenant will not be moving out until August 31, which is about six weeks from now.**

W: I see. Is there any chance it will become available sooner?

M: Unfortunately, no. ⁴³**Can you wait that long?**

W: Well, school doesn't start for two months. ⁴³**Please arrange a time for us to view it.**

townhouse n. 연립 주택(한 건물 안에서 여러 가구가 각각 주거 생활을 할 수 있도록 지은 공동 주택) neighborhood n. 지역, 인근
tenant n. 세입자 move out 이사를 나가다
unfortunately adv. 유감스럽게도 arrange v. 정하다, 마련하다

해석

41-43번은 다음 대화에 관한 문제입니다.

여: 안녕하세요. ⁴¹최근 귀하의 웹사이트에서 Edgewood 지역에 있는 침실 세 개짜리 연립 주택 매물을 보았습니다. 제 남편과 저는 딸의 새 학교가 그 지역에 있어서 관심이 있어요. 아직 구입 가능한가요?

남: 네. ⁴²하지만 현재 세입자가 지금부터 약 6주 후인 8월 31일이 되어서야 이사를 나갈 것이라고 집주인이 방금 알려주셨어요.

여: 알겠습니다. 더 빨리 입주할 수 있을 가능성이 있나요?

남: 유감스럽게도, 없습니다. ⁴³그렇게 오래 기다리실 수 있나요?

여: 음, 학교는 두 달 후에 시작해요. ⁴³우리가 그곳을 둘러볼 수 있도록 시간을 정해주세요.

41 특정 세부 사항 문제

해석 여자는 최근에 무엇을 했는가?
(A) 새 지역으로 이사 왔다.
(B) 집주인에게 연락했다.
(C) 온라인 게시물을 보았다.
(D) 임대차 계약서에 서명했다.

해설 질문의 핵심 어구(recently)가 언급된 주변을 주의 깊게 듣는다. 여자가 "I recently saw a listing on your Web site for a three-bedroom townhouse in the Edgewood neighborhood."라며 최근 웹사이트에서 Edgewood 지역에 있

는 침실 세 개짜리 연립 주택 매물을 봤다고 하였다. 따라서 (C)가 정답이다.

어휘 property owner 집주인 posting n. 게시물
lease agreement 임대차 계약(서)

42 언급 문제

해석 남자는 연립 주택에 대해 무엇을 말하는가?
(A) 개조 중이다.
(B) 현재 사람이 살고 있다.
(C) 매우 저렴하다.
(D) 침실이 두 개인 세대이다.

해설 남자의 말에서 질문의 핵심 어구(townhouse)와 관련된 내용을 주의 깊게 듣는다. 남자가 "But the owner just notified me that the current tenant will not be moving out until August 31, which is about six weeks from now."라며 현재 세입자가 지금부터 약 6주 후인 8월 31일이 되어서야 이사를 나갈 것이라고 집주인이 방금 알려주었다고 하였다. 따라서 (B)가 정답이다.

어휘 undergo v. 진행하다, ~을 겪다 renovation n. 개조, 보수
occupy v. (사람이) 살다, 거주하다
affordable adj. 저렴한, (가격 등이) 알맞은

43 의도 파악 문제

해석 여자는 왜 "학교는 두 달 후에 시작해요"라고 말하는가?
(A) 지연에 대한 이유를 설명하기 위해
(B) 기한의 긴급성을 강조하기 위해
(C) 약속 날짜를 변경하기 위해
(D) 기다릴 의향이 있음을 나타내기 위해

해설 질문의 인용어구(school doesn't start for two months)가 언급된 주변을 주의 깊게 듣는다. 남자가 "Can you wait that long?"이라며 그렇게 오래 기다릴 수 있는지를 묻자, 여자가 "Please arrange a time for us to view it."이라며 그곳을 둘러볼 수 있는 시간을 정해달라고 한 것을 통해 여자가 기다릴 의향이 있음을 나타내고 있다는 것을 알 수 있다. 따라서 (D)가 정답이다.

어휘 stress v. 강조하다 urgency n. 긴급성 indicate v. 나타내다
willingness n. 의향, 의지

[44-46]

3n 영국식 → 캐나다식

Questions 44-46 refer to the following conversation.

W: **⁴⁴I can't believe Carlos is quitting the firm at the end of March.** He seemed really happy here.

M: **⁴⁴I'm shocked too.** I heard he is going to pursue a business opportunity.

W: I hope everything goes well for him, but **⁴⁵this may cause issues with the floor plan for the new law office I'm working on. He's been helping me design the lobby and reception areas.**

M: He won't have time for that now. But don't worry. **⁴⁶I'll put one of the senior architects on the project with you.**

quit v. 그만두다 pursue v. 모색하다, 추구하다

opportunity n. 기회 floor plan (건물의) 평면도
senior adj. 상급의, 상위의 architect n. 건축가

해석
44-46번은 다음 대화에 관한 문제입니다.

여: ⁴⁴Carlos가 3월 말에 회사를 그만둔다니 믿을 수가 없어요. 그는 여기서 정말 행복해 보였어요.

남: ⁴⁴저도 충격을 받았어요. 저는 그가 사업 기회를 모색할 거라고 들었어요.

여: 그를 위해 모든 일이 잘되기를 바라지만, ⁴⁵이것 때문에 제가 작업 중인 새 법률 사무소의 평면도에 문제가 생길 수도 있어요. 그는 제가 로비와 접수 구역을 설계하는 것을 도와왔어요.

남: 그는 지금 그럴 시간이 없을 거예요. 하지만 걱정하지 마세요. ⁴⁶제가 상급 건축가 중 한 명을 당신의 프로젝트에 투입할게요.

44 특정 세부 사항 문제

해석 화자들은 무엇에 대해 놀랐는가?
(A) 사업체가 문을 닫을 것이다.
(B) 동료가 그만둘 것이다.
(C) 프로젝트가 취소될 것이다.
(D) 회사가 이전할 것이다.

해설 질문의 핵심 어구(surprised)와 관련된 내용을 주의 깊게 듣는다. 여자가 "I can't believe Carlos is quitting the firm at the end of March."라며 Carlos가 3월 말에 회사를 그만둔다는 것을 믿을 수 없다고 하자, 남자가 "I'm shocked too."라며 자신도 충격을 받았다고 하였다. 따라서 (B)가 정답이다.

어휘 coworker n. 동료 relocate v. 이전하다

Paraphrasing

is quitting 그만둘 것이다 → will leave 그만둘 것이다

45 화자 문제

해석 여자의 직업은 무엇인 것 같은가?
(A) 회계사
(B) 변호사
(C) 건축가
(D) 영업 사원

해설 대화에서 신분 및 직업과 관련된 표현을 놓치지 않고 듣는다. 여자가 "this may cause issues with the floor plan for the new law office I'm working on. He's been helping me design the lobby and reception areas."라며 Carlos가 그만두는 것 때문에 자신이 작업 중인 새 법률 사무소의 평면도에 문제가 생길 수도 있다고 한 후, Carlos가 로비와 접수 구역을 설계하는 것을 도와왔다고 한 것을 통해 여자가 건축가임을 알 수 있다. 따라서 (C)가 정답이다.

어휘 accountant n. 회계사 lawyer n. 변호사
salesperson n. 영업 사원

46 다음에 할 일 문제

해석 남자는 무엇을 할 것이라고 말하는가?
(A) 예산을 늘린다.

(B) 직원을 배치한다.
(C) 지원자를 채용한다.
(D) 마감일을 연기한다.

해설 대화의 마지막 부분을 주의 깊게 듣는다. 남자가 "I'll put one of the senior architects on the project with you."라며 상급 건축가 중 한 명을 여자의 프로젝트에 투입할 것이라고 하였다. 따라서 (B)가 정답이다.

어휘 **budget** n. 예산 **assign** v. (사람을) 배치하다
postpone v. 연기하다

[47-49] 　　　　　　　　　　　 3인 캐나다식 → 미국식 → 영국식

Questions 47-49 refer to the following conversation with three speakers.

M: **⁴⁷I read through the current version of our company's annual report, and I think we need to make the wording of some sections clearer.**

W1: Yeah. Especially the part about our expansion plan. It's a little hard to follow. **⁴⁸What do you think, Brenda?**

W2: I agree. The introduction requires some work as well. **⁴⁸I'm a little concerned about whether we can do this in time, though.** We're supposed to send the final draft to our CEO for review by Friday.

M: Actually, **⁴⁹I have a meeting with her in about 15 minutes. I'll explain the situation and see if we can get a few more days.**

---

current adj. 현재의 **annual** adj. 연간의, 연례의
wording n. 단어 선택 **expansion** n. 확장 **follow** v. 이해하다
introduction n. 서론 **in time** 늦지 않게, 시간 맞춰 **final draft** 최종안
review n. 검토; v. 검토하다

해석

47-49번은 다음 세 명의 대화에 관한 문제입니다.

남: ⁴⁷제가 현재 버전의 우리 회사 연간 보고서를 읽어봤는데, 몇몇 부분의 단어 선택을 좀 더 명확하게 해야 할 것 같아요.

여1: 네. 특히 확장 계획에 관한 부분이요. 이해하기가 좀 어려워요. ⁴⁸어떻게 생각하세요, Brenda?

여2: 동의해요. 서론도 약간의 작업이 필요하겠어요. ⁴⁸하지만 우리가 이것을 늦지 않게 할 수 있을지 조금 걱정돼요. 우리는 금요일까지 검토를 위해 대표이사님께 최종안을 보내야 해요.

남: 사실, ⁴⁹저는 15분 정도 후에 그녀와 회의가 있어요. 제가 상황을 설명하고 며칠 더 시간을 벌 수 있을지 알아볼게요.

47 주제 문제

해석 화자들은 주로 무엇에 대해 이야기하고 있는가?
(A) 회사를 확장하는 것
(B) 시스템을 업데이트하는 것
(C) 발표를 하는 것
(D) 보고서를 수정하는 것

해설 대화의 주제를 묻는 문제이므로, 대화의 초반을 반드시 듣는다. 남자가 "I read through the current version of our company's annual report, and I think we need to make the wording of

some sections clearer."라며 현재 버전의 연간 보고서를 읽어봤는데 몇몇 부분의 단어 선택을 좀 더 명확하게 해야 할 것 같다고 한후, 보고서 수정에 대한 내용으로 대화가 이어지고 있다. 따라서 (D)가 정답이다.

어휘 **expand** v. 확장하다 **presentation** n. 발표

48 문제점 문제

해석 Brenda는 무엇에 대해 걱정하는가?
(A) 계획을 바꾸는 것
(B) 행사를 취소하는 것
(C) 마감일을 맞추는 것
(D) 실수를 하는 것

해설 Brenda의 말에서 부정적인 표현이 언급된 주변을 주의 깊게 듣는다. 여자1이 "What do you think, Brenda?"라며 Brenda에게 어떻게 생각하는지 묻자, 여자2[Brenda]가 "I'm a little concerned about whether we can do this in time, though."라며 보고서를 수정하는 것을 늦지 않게 할 수 있을지 조금 걱정된다고 하였다. 따라서 (C)가 정답이다.

Paraphrasing

do ~ in time ~을 늦지 않게 하다 → Meeting a deadline 마감일을 맞추는 것

49 다음에 할 일 문제

해석 남자는 다음에 무엇을 할 것 같은가?
(A) 회의 일정을 변경한다.
(B) 고객에게 연락을 취한다.
(C) 과제를 제출한다.
(D) 경영진과 대화한다.

해설 대화의 마지막 부분을 주의 깊게 듣는다. 남자가 "I have a meeting with her[CEO] in about 15 minutes. I'll explain the situation and see if we can get a few more days."라며 15분 정도 후에 대표이사와 회의가 있다고 한 후, 상황을 설명하고 며칠 더 시간을 벌 수 있을지 알아보겠다고 한 것을 통해 남자가 경영진과 대화할 것임을 알 수 있다. 따라서 (D)가 정답이다.

어휘 **reschedule** v. 일정을 변경하다 **reach out** 연락을 취하다
assignment n. 과제, 임무 **executive** n. 경영진, 임원

[50-52] 　　　　　　　　　　　 2인 호주식 → 미국식

Questions 50-52 refer to the following conversation.

M: Lindsey, **⁵⁰I can't get into the storeroom. It's really frustrating. I've tried my key several times, but the door won't open.**

W: Oh, your key isn't the problem. The door lock is broken. **⁵¹I contacted a locksmith this morning and asked him to replace the lock.** He should be arriving any moment now.

M: Thanks. **⁵²By the way, I need paper for the printer. Do you know where I could get some?**

W: I have some right here. Take as much as you want. I'll ○

---

hand out copies of the new door key tomorrow morning.

storeroom n. 창고, 저장실 frustrating adj. 답답한, 불만스러운
locksmith n. 자물쇠 수리인 hand out 나눠주다, 배포하다

해석

50-52번은 다음 대화에 관한 문제입니다.

남: Lindsey, ⁵⁰저는 창고에 들어갈 수 없어요. 정말 답답하네요. 제 열쇠로 여러 번 시도했지만, 문이 열리지 않아요.

여: 아, 당신의 열쇠는 문제가 아니에요. 문 잠금장치가 고장 났어요. ⁵¹제가 오늘 아침에 자물쇠 수리인에게 연락해서 자물쇠를 교체해달라고 요청했어요. 그가 이제 곧 도착할 거예요.

남: 감사해요. ⁵²그건 그렇고, 프린터에 종이가 필요해요. 어디에서 구할 수 있는지 아세요?

여: 여기 조금 있어요. 원하는 만큼 가져가세요. 제가 내일 아침에 문의 새 열쇠 복사본을 나눠드릴게요.

50 특정 세부 사항 문제

해석 남자는 무엇이 답답하다고 생각하는가?
(A) 물건이 분실되었다.
(B) 문을 열 수 없다.
(C) 직원이 결근했다.
(D) 주문품이 도착하지 않았다.

해설 질문의 핵심 어구(frustrating)가 언급된 주변을 주의 깊게 듣는다. 남자가 "I can't get into the storeroom. It's really frustrating. I've tried my key several times, but the door won't open." 이라며 창고에 들어갈 수 없어서 정말 답답하다고 한 후, 열쇠로 여러 번 시도했지만 문이 열리지 않는다고 하였다. 따라서 (B)가 정답이다.

51 특정 세부 사항 문제

해석 여자는 오늘 아침에 무엇을 했는가?
(A) 문 손잡이를 교체했다.
(B) 회의를 주선했다.
(C) 창고를 정리했다.
(D) 정비를 요청했다.

해설 질문의 핵심 어구(this morning)가 언급된 주변을 주의 깊게 듣는다. 여자가 "I contacted a locksmith this morning and asked him to replace the lock."이라며 오늘 아침에 자물쇠 수리인에게 연락해서 자물쇠를 교체해달라고 요청했다고 하였다. 따라서 (D)가 정답이다.

어휘 knob n. 손잡이 organize v. 정리하다 request v. 요청하다

52 특정 세부 사항 문제

해석 남자는 여자에게 무엇에 대해 물어보는가?
(A) 기계를 어떻게 사용하는지
(B) 사무실이 몇 시에 문을 여는지
(C) 종이를 어디에서 찾을 수 있는지
(D) 프린터가 언제 수리될 것인지

해설 대화에서 남자의 말을 주의 깊게 듣는다. 남자가 여자에게 "By the way, I need paper for the printer. Do you know where I could get some?"이라며 프린터에 종이가 필요한데 어디에서 구할 수 있는지 물었다. 따라서 (C)가 정답이다.

[53-55]

3캐 캐나다식 → 미국식

Questions 53-55 refer to the following conversation.

M: Thank you for calling Denton Used Cars. This is Mark Denton. What can I do for you today?

W: Hi. ⁵³**I was wondering if you would be interested in purchasing my car.**

M: Possibly. I just need to know the model of your car and how old it is.

W: Of course. It's a Cetna TR80 sedan. I bought it new three years ago. ⁵⁴**But I just signed a contract with a company overseas, so I won't need it anymore.**

M: I see. I am definitely interested. ⁵⁵**Could you bring it here this afternoon?** I'll inspect it and then give you an estimate.

W: OK. I can be there in about half an hour.

wonder v. 궁금하다 possibly adv. 어쩌면, 아마도
sign a contract 계약을 맺다 overseas adj. 해외에 있는
definitely adv. 분명히, 확실히 inspect v. 검사하다
estimate n. 견적서, 추정치

해석

53-55번은 다음 대화에 관한 문제입니다.

남: Denton 중고차에 전화해 주셔서 감사합니다. Mark Denton입니다. 오늘 무엇을 도와드릴까요?

여: 안녕하세요. ⁵³혹시 제 차를 구입하는 것에 관심이 있으신지 궁금합니다.

남: 어쩌면요. 고객님 차의 모델과 그것이 얼마나 오래되었는지 알고 싶어요.

여: 물론이죠. Cetna TR80 세단이에요. 3년 전에 새로 샀어요. ⁵⁴하지만 저는 막 해외에 있는 회사와 계약을 맺어서, 그것이 더 이상 필요하지 않을 거예요.

남: 그렇군요. 저는 분명 관심이 있어요. ⁵⁵오늘 오후에 여기로 가져다주실 수 있나요? 제가 검사해 보고 견적서를 드릴게요.

여: 네. 30분 정도면 갈 수 있어요.

53 목적 문제

해석 여자는 왜 전화를 하고 있는가?
(A) 수리 비용을 알아보기 위해
(B) 할인을 받는 것에 대해 묻기 위해
(C) 차량을 판매하는 것에 대해 문의하기 위해
(D) 구매품의 배송을 준비하기 위해

해설 전화의 목적을 묻는 문제이므로, 대화의 초반을 반드시 듣는다. 여자가 "I was wondering if you would be interested in purchasing my car."라며 자신의 차를 구입하는 것에 관심이 있는지 궁금하다고 한 것을 통해 여자가 차량을 판매하는 것에 대해 문의하기 위해 전화하고 있음을 알 수 있다. 따라서 (C)가 정답이다.

어휘 repair n. 수리; v. 수리하다 inquire v. 문의하다
delivery n. 배송, 배달

54 특정 세부 사항 문제

해석 여자는 무엇을 하려고 계획하고 있는 것 같은가?

(A) 다른 나라로 이주한다.
(B) 공석에 지원한다.
(C) 사업 계약을 협상한다.
(D) 국제 배송물을 보낸다.

해설 질문의 핵심 어구(planning to do)와 관련된 내용을 주의 깊게 듣는다. 여자가 "But I just signed a contract with a company overseas, so I won't need it[car] anymore."라며 자신이 막 해외에 있는 회사와 계약을 맺어서 차가 더 이상 필요하지 않을 것이라고 한 것을 통해 여자가 다른 나라로 이주할 계획임을 알 수 있다. 따라서 (A)가 정답이다.

어휘 open position 공석 negotiate v. 협상하다

55 요청 문제

해석 남자는 여자에게 무엇을 하라고 요청하는가?

(A) 사업체를 방문한다.
(B) 견적서를 보낸다.
(C) 검사를 수행한다.
(D) 일정을 확인한다.

해설 남자의 말에서 요청과 관련된 표현이 언급된 다음을 주의 깊게 듣는다. 남자가 여자에게 "Could you bring it here[Denton Used Cars] this afternoon?"이라며 오늘 오후에 차를 Denton 중고차에 가져다줄 수 있는지 물었다. 따라서 (A)가 정답이다.

어휘 inspection n. 검사, 검토 confirm v. 확인하다, 확정하다

[56-58]

🔊 영국식 → 캐나다식 → 호주식

Questions 56-58 refer to the following conversation with three speakers.

W: Excuse me. ⁵⁶**I'm looking for an allergy medicine called Allenda. I couldn't find it on your shelves.**

M1: Oh, ⁵⁷**that's because you need a prescription to buy it.**

W: I see. ⁵⁷**I don't have one.** Is there something similar you could recommend?

M1: Hold on. ⁵⁸**Hey, Alex. Do we have any medicine like Allenda that doesn't require a prescription?**

M2: Claraffin. It's effective and safe. ⁵⁸**Just follow the instructions, and don't take more than four tablets in a day.**

W: I'll be sure to do that. Thank you!

look for ~을 찾다 allergy n. 알레르기 shelf n. 진열대, 선반
prescription n. 처방전 effective adj. 효과적인 tablet n. 알약

해석

56-58번은 다음 세 명의 대화에 관한 문제입니다.

여: 실례합니다. ⁵⁶Allenda라는 알레르기 약을 찾고 있어요. 진열대에서 찾을 수가 없네요.

남1: 아, ⁵⁷그건 처방전이 있어야 살 수 있기 때문이에요.

여: 그렇군요. ⁵⁷저는 처방전이 없어요. 추천해 주실 수 있는 비슷한 것이 있나요?

남1: 잠깐만요. ⁵⁸저기, Alex. 처방전이 필요 없는 Allenda 같은 약이 있나요?

남2: Claraffin이요. 효과적이면서 안전해요. ⁵⁸지침을 따르시고, 하루에 네 알 넘게 복용하지 마세요.

여: 꼭 그렇게 할게요. 감사합니다!

56 장소 문제

해석 대화는 어디에서 일어나고 있는 것 같은가?

(A) 약국에서
(B) 슈퍼마켓에서
(C) 병원에서
(D) 식료품점에서

해설 대화에서 장소와 관련된 표현을 놓치지 않고 듣는다. 여자가 "I'm looking for an allergy medicine called Allenda. I couldn't find it on your shelves."라며 Allenda라는 알레르기 약을 찾고 있는데 진열대에서 찾을 수 없다고 하였다. 이를 통해 약국에서 대화가 일어나고 있음을 알 수 있다. 따라서 (A)가 정답이다.

어휘 pharmacy n. 약국 grocery store 식료품점

57 이유 문제

해석 여자는 왜 Allenda를 구매할 수 없는가?

(A) 지갑을 잃어버렸다.
(B) 다른 지점으로 갔다.
(C) 서류가 필요하다.
(D) 일부 정보를 잊어버렸다.

해설 질문의 핵심 어구(unable to purchase Allenda)와 관련된 내용을 주의 깊게 듣는다. 남자1이 "that's because you need a prescription to buy it[Allenda]"이라며 처방전이 있어야 Allenda를 살 수 있다고 하자, 여자가 "I don't have one."이라며 자신은 처방전이 없다고 하였다. 따라서 (C)가 정답이다.

Paraphrasing

a prescription 처방전 → a document 서류

58 제안 문제

해석 Alex는 무엇을 하라고 제안하는가?

(A) 다른 지점 확인하기
(B) 전문가와 상의하기
(C) 지시에 따르기
(D) 온라인으로 제품 주문하기

해설 Alex의 말에서 제안과 관련된 표현이 언급된 내용을 주의 깊게 듣는다. 남자1이 "Hey, Alex. Do we have any medicine like Allenda ~?"라며 Alex에게 Allenda 같은 약이 있는지 묻자, 남자2[Alex]가 "Just follow the instructions, and don't take more than four tablets in a day."라며 지침을 따르고 하루에 네 알 넘게 복용하지 말라고 하였다. 따라서 (C)가 정답이다.

어휘 branch n. 지점 consult v. 상의하다, 상담하다 expert n. 전문가

Paraphrasing

the instructions 지침 → directions 지시

[59-61]

🎧 캐나다식 → 영국식

Questions 59-61 refer to the following conversation.

M: ⁵⁹Sumi, could you book a table at Alfredo's Restaurant for Thursday at noon? It's for a client meeting.

W: Sure. How many people is it for?

M: There'll be six of us.

W: Thanks. And ⁶⁰would you like a table on the patio?

M: It's supposed to rain that day. ⁶⁰The main dining room would be better.

W: Got it. Just one more thing. ⁶¹The restaurant's Web site shows that it has a set lunch. It's only 18 dollars per person, but the restaurant will need to know beforehand how many people in your party will be ordering it.

M: I'd rather let our clients order what they like.

patio n. 테라스, 베란다 dining room 다이닝 룸(식당, 방)
beforehand adv. 사전에, 미리

해석

59-61번은 다음 대화에 관한 문제입니다.

남: ⁵⁹Sumi, 목요일 정오에 Alfredo 식당에 테이블을 예약해 주실 수 있나요? 고객 회의를 위해서요.

여: 물론이죠. 몇 명을 위한 자리인가요?

남: 여섯 명일 거예요.

여: 감사해요. 그리고 ⁶⁰테라스에 있는 테이블을 원하시나요?

남: 그날 비가 온다고 하네요. ⁶⁰메인 다이닝 룸이 더 좋겠어요.

여: 알았어요. 한 가지만 더요. ⁶¹식당 웹사이트에 점심 세트가 있다고 나와 있어요. 1인당 18달러인데, 식당에서는 일행 중 몇 명이 그걸 주문할 건지 사전에 알아야 할 거예요.

남: 저는 고객들이 원하는 것을 주문하게 하고 싶어요.

59 이유 문제

해석 남자는 왜 식당을 방문할 계획인가?
(A) 특별한 행사를 축하하기 위해
(B) 직원에게 점심을 대접하기 위해
(C) **고객들과의 회의를 진행하기 위해**
(D) 가족 모임을 주최하기 위해

해설 질문의 핵심 어구(visiting a restaurant)와 관련된 내용을 주의 깊게 듣는다. 남자가 여자에게 "Sumi, could you book a table at Alfredo's Restaurant for Thursday at noon? It's for a client meeting."이라며 목요일 정오에 고객 회의를 위해 Alfredo 식당에 테이블을 예약해 달라고 하였다. 따라서 (C)가 정답이다.

어휘 celebrate v. 축하하다 occasion n. 행사
treat v. 대접하다, 한턱내다 conduct v. 진행하다
gathering n. 모임

60 의도 파악 문제

해석 남자는 "그날 비가 온다고 하네요"라고 말할 때 무엇을 의도하는가?
(A) 실내에 앉는 것을 선호한다.
(B) 예약을 변경하길 원한다.
(C) 테이블 추천을 받아들인다.
(D) 픽업 서비스가 필요하다.

해설 질문의 인용어구(It's supposed to rain that day)가 언급된 주변을 주의 깊게 듣는다. 여자가 "would you like a table on the patio?"라며 테라스에 있는 테이블을 원하는지 묻자, 남자가 "The main dining room would be better."라며 메인 다이닝 룸이 더 좋겠다고 하였으므로 남자가 실내에 앉는 것을 선호함을 알 수 있다. 따라서 (A)가 정답이다.

어휘 recommendation n. 추천

61 언급 문제

해석 여자는 점심 세트에 대해 무엇을 말하는가?
(A) 최근에 가격이 올랐다.
(B) 별개의 세 가지 코스를 포함한다.
(C) 특정 요일에만 제공된다.
(D) **미리 주문되어야 한다.**

해설 여자의 말에서 질문의 핵심 어구(set lunch)가 언급된 주변을 주의 깊게 듣는다. 여자가 "The restaurant's Web site shows that it has a set lunch. ~ the restaurant will need to know beforehand how many people in your party will be ordering it."이라며 식당 웹사이트에 점심 세트가 있다고 나와 있다고 한 후, 식당에서는 일행 중 몇 명이 그걸 주문할 건지 사전에 알아야 할 거라고 하였다. 따라서 (D)가 정답이다.

어휘 separate adj. 별개의, 서로 다른 in advance 미리

Paraphrasing

beforehand 사전에 → in advance 미리

[62-64]

🎧 미국식 → 호주식

Questions 62-64 refer to the following conversation and product display.

W: Good morning. ⁶²I'm here to purchase an Elan Powder Compact. The one with organic ingredients. ⁶³It was mentioned in a television show I watched last night.

M: You're in luck. We only have a few of those left in stock. It's a very popular product.

W: Great. I also heard that you have a loyalty program.

M: That's right. ⁶⁴You should consider getting a membership while you're here because we'll be offering all of our products at reduced prices to members next week. I can sign you up now if you give me your full name and phone number.

organic adj. 유기농의 ingredient n. 성분, 재료
have ~ in stock 재고가 있다
loyalty program 회원 프로그램, 고객 보상 프로그램
reduced adj. 할인된, 줄인 sign up 가입하다

해석

62-64번은 다음 대화와 제품 진열에 관한 문제입니다.

여: 좋은 아침이에요. ⁶²저는 Elan 파우더 콤팩트를 구매하려고 왔어요. 유기농 성분이 함유된 거요. ⁶³어젯밤에 본 텔레비전 쇼에서 언급됐어요.

남: 운이 좋으시네요. 재고가 몇 개 남지 않았거든요. 아주 인기 있는 제품이에요.

여: 좋아요. 회원 프로그램도 있다고 들었어요.

남: 맞아요. ⁶⁴다음 주에 회원들에게 모든 제품을 할인된 가격에 제공할 예정이니 여기 계시는 동안 멤버십에 가입하는 것을 고려해 보세요. 이름과 전화번호를 알려주시면 지금 바로 가입해 드릴 수 있어요.

Elan 마스카라
18.00달러

허브 파운데이션
24.00달러

신상 매트 립스틱
12.95달러

Elan 파우더 콤팩트
⁶²21.50달러

62 시각 자료 문제

해석 시각 자료를 보아라. 여자는 얼마를 지불할 것인가?
(A) 18.00달러
(B) 24.00달러
(C) 12.95달러
(D) 21.50달러

해설 제시된 제품 진열의 정보를 확인한 후 질문의 핵심 어구(pay)와 관련된 내용을 주의 깊게 듣는다. 여자가 "I'm here to purchase an Elan Powder Compact."라며 Elan 파우더 콤팩트를 구매하려고 왔다고 하였으므로 여자가 지불할 금액은 21.50달러임을 제품 진열에서 알 수 있다. 따라서 (D)가 정답이다.

63 방법 문제

해석 여자는 어떻게 제품에 대해 알게 되었는가?
(A) 모바일 애플리케이션을 이용함으로써
(B) TV 프로그램을 봄으로써
(C) 친구와 이야기를 나눔으로써
(D) 분점을 방문함으로써

해설 여자의 말에서 질문의 핵심 어구(learn about the product)와 관련된 내용을 주의 깊게 듣는다. 여자가 "It[Elan Powder Compact] was mentioned in a television show I watched last night."라며 Elan 파우더 콤팩트가 어젯밤에 본 텔레비전 쇼에서 언급됐다고 하였다. 따라서 (B)가 정답이다.

어휘 store branch 분점

Paraphrasing

a television show 텔레비전 쇼 → a TV program TV 프로그램

64 특정 세부 사항 문제

해석 남자에 따르면, 멤버십의 혜택은 무엇인가?
(A) 무료 제품
(B) 현금 보상
(C) 연장된 보증
(D) 특별 할인

해설 질문의 핵심 어구(membership)가 언급된 주변을 주의 깊게 듣는다. 남자가 여자에게 "You should consider getting a membership ~ because we'll be offering all of our products at reduced prices to members next week."이라며 다음 주에 회원들에게 모든 제품을 할인된 가격에 제공할 예정이니 멤버십에 가입하는 것을 고려해 보라고 하였다. 따라서 (D)가 정답이다.

어휘 complimentary adj. 무료의   warranty n. (품질 등의) 보증

[65-67]

🎧 호주식 → 영국식

Questions 65-67 refer to the following conversation and map.

> M: ⁶⁵Tanya, is anyone using this safety helmet? Mine is broken, and I'll need to wear one at the work site.
>
> W: No. That's an extra one. Feel free to use it.
>
> M: Great. ⁶⁶By the way, do you know which part of the expressway we'll be building the overpass on today?
>
> W: ⁶⁶The section between Exit 10 and Exit 11. It'll take us about 15 minutes to drive there. And we need to be at the construction site by 8 A.M.
>
> M: Perfect. ⁶⁷That gives me enough time to drop off this leave request form at the administration office. I'll do that now. Just give me a few minutes.

work site 작업 현장   extra adj. 여분의   expressway n. 고속도로
overpass n. 고가 도로   construction site 공사 현장, 건축 부지
drop off ~을 내다, 제출하다   administration office 행정실

해석

65-67번은 다음 대화와 지도에 관한 문제입니다.

남: ⁶⁵Tanya, 혹시 누가 이 안전모를 사용하나요? 제 안전모가 망가졌는데, 작업 현장에서 착용할 것이 필요해요.

여: 아니요. 그건 여분의 것이에요. 편하게 사용하세요.

남: 잘됐네요. ⁶⁶그나저나, 오늘 우리가 고속도로의 어느 부분에 고가 도로를 지을지 아시나요?

여: ⁶⁶10번 출구와 11번 출구 사이의 구간이요. 운전해서 가는 데 15분 정도 걸릴 거예요. 그리고 우리는 오전 8시까지 공사 현장에 도착해야 해요.

남: 완벽해요. ⁶⁷그럼 이 휴가 신청서를 행정실에 낼 시간은 충분하겠네요. 지금 그렇게 할게요. 몇 분만 시간을 주세요.

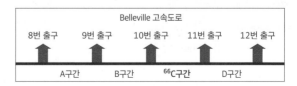

Belleville 고속도로

| 8번 출구 | 9번 출구 | 10번 출구 | 11번 출구 | 12번 출구 |
| A구간 | B구간 | ⁶⁶C구간 | D구간 |

65 화자 문제

해석 화자들은 누구인 것 같은가?

(A) 보안 요원들
(B) 안전 점검원들
(C) 도로 요금소 직원들
(D) 건설 근로자들

해설　대화에서 신분 및 직업과 관련된 표현을 놓치지 않고 듣는다. 남자가 여자에게 "Tanya, is anyone using this safety helmet? Mine is broken, and I'll need to wear one at the work site."라며 누가 이 안전모를 사용하는지 물으며, 자신의 것이 망가져 작업 현장에서 착용할 것이 필요하다고 한 후, 오늘 있을 고가 도로 건설 작업에 대한 내용으로 대화가 이어지고 있다. 이를 통해 화자들이 건설 현장에서 일하는 건설 근로자들이라는 것을 알 수 있다. 따라서 (D)가 정답이다.

어휘　security guard 보안 요원　inspector n. 점검원
　　　tollbooth n. 도로 요금소

66 시각 자료 문제

해설　시각 자료를 보아라. 화자들은 어디에서 일할 것인가?
(A) A구간
(B) B구간
(C) C구간
(D) D구간

해설　제시된 지도의 정보를 확인한 후 질문의 핵심 어구(work)와 관련된 내용을 주의 깊게 듣는다. 남자가 "By the way, do you know which part of the expressway we'll be building the overpass on today?"라며 오늘 고속도로의 어느 부분에 고가 도로를 지을지 알고 있는지 묻자, 여자가 "The section between Exit 10 and Exit 11."이라며 10번 출구와 11번 출구 사이의 구간이라고 하였으므로 화자들이 C구간에서 일할 것임을 지도에서 알 수 있다. 따라서 (C)가 정답이다.

67 다음에 할 일 문제

해설　남자는 다음에 무엇을 할 것 같은가?
(A) 물품을 회수한다.
(B) 양식을 제출한다.
(C) 일정을 확인한다.
(D) 사무실에 전화한다.

해설　대화의 마지막 부분을 주의 깊게 듣는다. 남자가 "That gives me enough time to drop off this leave request form at the administration office. I'll do that now."라며 휴가 신청서를 행정실에 낼 시간이 충분하겠다고 한 후, 지금 그렇게 하겠다고 한 것을 통해 남자가 양식을 제출할 것임을 알 수 있다. 따라서 (B)가 정답이다.

어휘　retrieve v. 회수하다, 검색하다

Paraphrasing

drop off ~을 내다 → Submit 제출하다

[68-70]　　　🎧 영국식 → 캐나다식

Questions 68-70 refer to the following conversation and schedule.

> W: **68I'm a little concerned, Devon. The number of students enrolled in one of our weekly art classes is really low.** Do you think we should just cancel it?
> M: No. **69Lots of people are interested in painting. Maybe we need to run a promotion.** Providing free snacks might bring in more students.
> W: I think we need to do something bigger. **69What about reducing the cost of that class by 10 percent?**
> M: Good idea. **70We should also make sure that the sign outside our building with information about the class is easy to see. I'll go check that now.**

enroll v. 등록하다　cancel v. 취소하다　promotion n. 홍보 (활동)
reduce v. (가격 등을) 낮추다, 줄이다　cost n. 비용
sign n. 표지판, 표시　origami n. 종이접기

해석
68-70번은 다음 대화와 일정표에 관한 문제입니다.

여: 68저는 조금 걱정이에요, Devon. 우리의 주간 예술 수업 중 하나에 등록한 학생 수가 정말 적어요. 그것을 그냥 취소해야 한다고 생각하시나요?

남: 아니요. 69많은 사람들이 그리기에 관심이 있어요. 우리가 홍보를 진행해야 할 것 같아요. 무료 간식을 제공하는 것은 더 많은 학생을 유치할 수도 있어요.

여: 더 큰 무언가를 해야 할 것 같아요. 69그 수업의 비용을 10퍼센트 낮추는 건 어떨까요?

남: 좋은 생각이에요. 70우리는 또한 건물 밖에 수업에 대한 정보가 담긴 표지판이 잘 보이도록 해야 해요. 제가 지금 그것을 확인하러 가볼게요.

주간 예술 수업				
월요일	화요일	수요일	69목요일	금요일
캘리그라피	조소	사진술	그리기	종이접기

68 문제점 문제

해석　화자들은 무슨 문제에 대해 이야기하고 있는가?
(A) 예약 취소
(B) 학생 성적
(C) 낮은 등록자 수
(D) 높은 비용

해설　대화에서 부정적인 표현이 언급된 주변을 주의 깊게 듣는다. 여자가 "I'm a little concerned, Devon. The number of students enrolled in one of our weekly art classes is really low."라며 주간 예술 수업 중 하나에 등록한 학생 수가 정말 적어서 조금 걱정이라고 하였다. 따라서 (C)가 정답이다.

어휘　cancellation n. 취소　performance n. 성적, 성과
　　　enrollment n. 등록자 수　expense n. 비용

69 시각 자료 문제

해석 시각 자료를 보라. 어떤 날의 수업에 할인이 제공될 것인가?

(A) 월요일
(B) 화요일
(C) 수요일
(D) 목요일

해설 제시된 일정표의 정보를 확인한 후 질문의 핵심 어구(discount)와 관련된 내용을 주의 깊게 듣는다. 남자가 "Lots of people are interested in painting. Maybe we need to run a promotion."이라며 많은 사람들이 그리기에 관심이 있다고 한 후, 홍보를 진행해야 할 것 같다고 하자, 여자가 "What about reducing the cost of that class by 10 percent?"라며 그 수업의 비용을 10퍼센트 낮추자고 제안하였으므로 할인이 제공될 수업이 있는 날은 목요일임을 일정표에서 알 수 있다. 따라서 (D)가 정답이다.

Paraphrasing

> a discount 할인 → reducing the cost 비용을 낮추는 것

70 특정 세부 사항 문제

해석 남자는 무엇을 확인하고 싶어 하는가?

(A) 수업이 취소되었다.
(B) 지불금이 정확하다.
(C) 건물에 접근할 수 있다.
(D) 표지판이 눈에 띈다.

해설 질문의 핵심 어구(want to confirm)와 관련된 내용을 주의 깊게 듣는다. 남자가 "We should also make sure that the sign ~ is easy to see. I'll go check that now."라며 표지판이 잘 보이도록 해야 한다고 한 후, 지금 그것을 확인하러 가보겠다고 하였다. 따라서 (D)가 정답이다.

어휘 payment n. 지불금, 대금 accessible adj. 접근 가능한 visible adj. 눈에 띄는, (눈에) 보이는

Paraphrasing

> confirm 확인하다 → check 확인하다
> is easy to see 잘 보이다 → is visible 눈에 띄다

PART 4

[71-73]

🎧 캐나다식

Questions 71-73 refer to the following announcement.

Attention, passengers. **71This is an important notice about a flight delay. 72Due to adverse weather conditions in Georgia, Sierra Air Flight 118 to Atlanta will be arriving at 10 A.M., about one hour later than scheduled.** We apologize for any inconvenience this may cause. **73And a laptop has been found at Gate 4.** It is currently being stored in our lost-and-found office. If you believe the item ⊙

is yours, please proceed there to claim it. Thank you for your attention.

> adverse adj. 안 좋은, 불리한 weather condition 기상 조건
> schedule v. 예정하다 inconvenience n. 불편 store v. 보관하다
> lost-and-found office 분실물 보관소 proceed v. 이동하다, 진행하다
> claim v. 받다, 얻다

해석
71-73번은 다음 공지에 관한 문제입니다.

주목해 주세요, 승객 여러분. 71이것은 비행기 지연에 대한 중요한 공지입니다. 72조지아주의 안 좋은 기상 조건으로 인해, 애틀랜타행 Sierra 항공사 118 항공편이 예정된 것보다 1시간 정도 늦은 오전 10시에 도착할 것입니다. 이것이 초래할 모든 불편에 대해 사과드립니다. 73그리고 4번 탑승구에서 노트북이 발견되었습니다. 그것은 현재 저희 분실물 보관소에 보관 중입니다. 그 물건이 귀하의 것이라고 생각되시면, 그것을 받기 위해 그곳으로 이동하십시오. 관심을 가져 주셔서 감사합니다.

71 장소 문제

해석 공지는 어디에서 이뤄지고 있는 것 같은가?

(A) 기차역에서
(B) 버스 터미널에서
(C) 공항에서
(D) 여객선 터미널에서

해설 지문에서 장소와 관련된 표현을 놓치지 않고 듣는다. "This is an important notice about a flight delay."라며 비행기 지연에 대한 중요한 공지가 있다고 한 것을 통해 공지가 이루어지고 있는 장소가 공항임을 알 수 있다. 따라서 (C)가 정답이다.

어휘 ferry n. 여객선, 나룻배

72 특정 세부 사항 문제

해석 무엇이 지연을 초래했는가?

(A) 교통사고
(B) 안 좋은 날씨
(C) 응급 의료 상황
(D) 기술적 어려움

해설 질문의 핵심 어구(delay)와 관련된 내용을 주의 깊게 듣는다. "Due to adverse weather conditions in Georgia, Sierra Air Flight 118 to Atlanta will be arriving at 10 A.M., about one hour later than scheduled."라며 조지아주의 안 좋은 기상 조건으로 인해 애틀랜타행 Sierra 항공사 118 항공편이 예정된 것보다 1시간 정도 늦은 오전 10시에 도착할 것이라고 하였다. 따라서 (B)가 정답이다.

어휘 medical adj. 의료의 emergency n. 응급 상황 technical adj. 기술적인

Paraphrasing

> adverse 안 좋은 → Bad 안 좋은

73 특정 세부 사항 문제

해석 화자에 따르면, 어떤 물건이 발견되었는가?
(A) 신용카드
(B) 배낭
(C) 표
(D) 노트북

해설 지문의 핵심 어구(found)가 언급된 주변을 주의 깊게 듣는다. "And a laptop has been found at Gate 4."라며 4번 탑승구에서 노트북이 발견되었다고 하였다. 따라서 (D)가 정답이다.

[74-76]

영국식

Questions 74-76 refer to the following advertisement.

Are you a recent graduate seeking employment? **74Boost your career prospects by signing up for a training program with Skill Up Canada.** Get hands-on experience in your chosen field and develop useful skills for employment. Our professional programs offer nationally recognized qualifications. **75Unlike similar programs, ours are entirely funded by the government, so you won't have to pay any fees. 76Visit our Web site to find out which programs are available in your area.**

employment n. 일자리, 취업 boost v. 높이다, 활성화하다
career prospect 직업 전망 hands-on adj. 실무의, 실제의
experience n. 경험 professional adj. 전문적인
nationally adv. 국가적으로 recognize v. 인정하다, 공인하다
qualification n. 자격 entirely adv. 전적으로
fund v. 자금을 지원하다

해석

74-76번은 다음 광고에 관한 문제입니다.

당신은 일자리를 찾고 있는 최근 졸업자인가요? **74Skill Up Canada사의 연수 프로그램에 등록함으로써 당신의 직업 전망을 높이세요.** 당신이 선택한 분야에서 실무 경험을 쌓고 취업에 유용한 기술들을 개발하세요. 저희 전문 프로그램들은 국가적으로 인정되는 자격을 제공합니다. **75유사 프로그램들과 달리, 정부로부터 전적으로 자금을 지원받으므로, 당신은 비용을 낼 필요가 없습니다. 76당신의 지역에서 어떤 프로그램이 이용 가능한지 알아보기 위해 저희 웹사이트를 방문하십시오.**

74 주제 문제

해석 어떤 종류의 서비스가 광고되고 있는가?
(A) 직무 연수
(B) 언어 지도서
(C) 운동 수업
(D) 방과 후 개인지도

해설 광고의 주제를 묻는 문제이므로, 지문의 초반을 반드시 듣는다. "Boost your career prospects by signing up for a training program with Skill Up Canada."라며 Skill Up Canada사의 연수 프로그램에 등록하여 직업 전망을 높이라고 한 것을 통해 직무 연수 서비스가 광고되고 있음을 알 수 있다. 따라서 (A)가 정답이다.

어휘 tutorial n. 지도서 after-school adj. 방과 후의

75 특정 세부 사항 문제

해석 업체에 대해 어떤 점이 특별한가?
(A) 온라인 강좌에 중점을 둔다.
(B) 많은 국가에 지사가 있다.
(C) 직원이 자원봉사자들로 구성된다.
(D) 서비스를 무료로 제공한다.

해설 질문의 핵심 어구(special about the business)와 관련된 내용을 주의 깊게 듣는다. "Unlike similar programs, ~ you won't have to pay any fees."라며 유사 프로그램들과 달리, 비용을 낼 필요가 없다고 하였다. 따라서 (D)가 정답이다.

어휘 staff v. ~에 직원을 두다
volunteer n. 자원봉사자; v. 자원봉사로 하다
free of charge 무료로

76 이유 문제

해석 화자는 왜 청자들에게 웹사이트를 방문하도록 권장하는가?
(A) 평가 시험에 참여하기 위해
(B) 온라인 워크숍에 등록하기 위해
(C) 이용 가능한 프로그램에 대해 알아보기 위해
(D) 사무실 위치로 가는 길을 알기 위해

해설 질문의 핵심 어구(visit a Web site)가 언급된 주변을 주의 깊게 듣는다. "Visit our Web site to find out which programs are available in your area."라며 청자들의 지역에서 어떤 프로그램이 이용 가능한지 알아보기 위해 웹사이트를 방문하라고 하였다. 따라서 (C)가 정답이다.

어휘 encourage v. 권장하다, 장려하다
participate in ~에 참여하다, 참석하다
assessment test 평가 시험 location n. 위치, 장소

[77-79]

호주식

Questions 77-79 refer to the following talk.

Welcome to the Boston Bus Tour. My name is Adam Harper, and I'll be your guide as we explore the city. I should point out that **77we usually stop by the Public Garden**, but, well . . . it is hosting a special event today. **77There will be lots of other things to see, though. 78And you can check out the gift shop once we return here at the end of the tour.** You will be able to buy some wonderful souvenirs. OK . . . We are about to begin. **79Please make sure to remain seated while the bus is moving.**

explore v. 답사하다, 탐험하다 point out 알려 주다, 지적하다
stop by ~에 들르다 host v. 주최하다 check out 확인하다
souvenir n. 기념품

해석

77-79번은 다음 담화에 관한 문제입니다.

보스턴 버스 투어에 오신 것을 환영합니다. 제 이름은 Adam Harper이고, 우리가 도시를 답사하는 동안 제가 여러분의 가이드가 될 것입니다. **77우리는 보통 퍼블릭 가든에 들르지만, 음... 오늘은 그곳이 특별한 행사를 주최한다는 것을 알려드려야겠네요. 77하지만 다른 볼거리가 많을 것입니다. 78그리고 투**

어 마지막에 우리가 여기로 돌아오면 선물 가게를 확인하실 수 있습니다. 여러분은 멋진 기념품을 살 수 있을 거예요. 좋아요... 이제 곧 시작해요. **79버스가 이동하는 동안 자리에 계속 앉아 계시기 바랍니다.**

77 의도 파악 문제

해석 화자는 "오늘은 그곳이 특별한 행사를 주최한다"라고 말할 때 무엇을 의도하는가?
(A) 명소가 인기 있다.
(B) 초대가 가능하다.
(C) 구역에 접근할 수 없다.
(D) 예약이 확정되었다.

해설 질문의 인용어구(it is hosting a special event today)가 언급된 주변을 주의 깊게 듣는다. "We usually stop by the Public Garden"이라며 보통 퍼블릭 가든에 들른다고 한 후, "There will be lots of other things to see, though."라며 하지만 다른 볼거리가 많을 것이라고 한 것을 통해 오늘은 퍼블릭 가든에 접근할 수 없음을 알 수 있다. 따라서 (C)가 정답이다.

어휘 attraction n. 명소 invitation n. 초대(장)
inaccessible adj. 접근할 수 없는

78 언급 문제

해석 투어에 대해 무엇이 언급되는가?
(A) 마치는데 한 시간이 채 안 걸린다.
(B) 시작하는 곳과 같은 곳에서 끝난다.
(C) 많은 상점에 들르는 것을 포함한다.
(D) 오랜 시간 걷는 것이 필요하다.

해설 질문의 핵심 어구(tour)가 언급된 주변을 주의 깊게 듣는다. "And you can check out the gift shop once we return here at the end of the tour."라며 투어 마지막에 여기로 돌아오면 선물 가게를 확인할 수 있다고 하였다. 따라서 (B)가 정답이다.

79 요청 문제

해석 화자는 청자들에게 무엇을 하라고 요청하는가?
(A) 자리에 앉아 있는다.
(B) 후기를 게시한다.
(C) 가이드에게 이야기한다.
(D) 대금을 지불한다.

해설 지문의 중후반에서 요청과 관련된 표현이 포함된 문장을 주의 깊게 듣는다. "Please make sure to remain seated while the bus is moving."이라며 버스가 이동하는 동안 자리에 계속 앉아 있으라고 하였다. 따라서 (A)가 정답이다.

어휘 post v. 게시하다 payment n. 대금, 지불

Paraphrasing

remain seated 자리에 계속 앉아 있다 → Stay in a seat 자리에 앉아 있다

[80-82]

Questions 80-82 refer to the following podcast.

Thanks for listening to today's episode of the *Business Insider* podcast. I will be joined by **80Nina Danton, the head of marketing at Cortez Beverages. 81She is well-known for her skill at examining sales records to identify and predict consumer trends with regard to sports drinks.** But before I interview her, **82I would like to first talk a bit about BDS Insurance's decision to join with its main competitor, Cullman Limited, to form a new company.** Assuming this plan receives government approval, it may create many new opportunities for investors.

well-known adj. 유명한, 잘 알려진 sales records 판매 기록
identify v. 파악하다, 확인하다 predict v. 예측하다
with regard to ~과 관련된 decision n. 결정
join v. 합병하다 competitor n. 경쟁사 form v. 설립하다, 형성하다
assuming conj. ~라고 가정하고, 가령 ~라면 approval n. 승인
opportunity n. 기회 investor n. 투자자

해석
80-82번은 다음 팟캐스트에 관한 문제입니다.
Business Insider 팟캐스트의 오늘의 에피소드를 들어주셔서 감사합니다. 80Cortez Beverages사의 마케팅부장인 Nina Danton도 저와 함께 할 예정입니다. 81그녀는 스포츠음료와 관련된 소비자 동향을 파악하고 예측하기 위해 판매 기록을 조사하는 능력으로 유명합니다. 하지만 그녀를 인터뷰하기 전에, 82저는 먼저 주요 경쟁사인 Cullman Limited사와 합병하여 새로운 회사를 설립하기로 한 BDS Insurance사의 결정에 대해 이야기하고 싶습니다. 이 계획이 정부의 승인을 받는다고 가정하면, 그것은 투자자들에게 많은 새로운 기회를 만들어 줄 수도 있습니다.

80 특정 세부 사항 문제

해석 Ms. Danton은 누구인가?
(A) 언론사 직원
(B) 마케팅 책임자
(C) 정부 관계자
(D) 사업체 소유주

해설 질문 대상(Ms. Danton)의 신분 및 직업과 관련된 표현을 놓치지 않고 듣는다. "Nina Danton, the head of marketing at Cortez Beverages"라며 Nina Danton이 Cortez Beverages사의 마케팅부장이라고 하였다. 따라서 (B)가 정답이다.

어휘 representative n. 직원, 대표(자) director n. 책임자, 감독
government official 정부 관계자

Paraphrasing

the head of marketing 마케팅부장 → A marketing director
마케팅 책임자

81 특정 세부 사항 문제

해석 화자는 Ms. Danton이 무엇을 잘한다고 말하는가?
(A) 행사를 기획하는 것
(B) 데이터를 분석하는 것

(C) 분쟁을 처리하는 것
(D) 효율성을 높이는 것

해설 질문의 핵심 어구(Ms. Danton is good at)와 관련된 내용을 주의 깊게 듣는다. "She is well-known for her skill at examining sales records to identify and predict consumer trends with regard to sports drinks."라며 스포츠음료와 관련된 소비자 동향을 파악하고 예측하기 위해 판매 기록을 조사하는 능력으로 유명하다고 하였다. 따라서 (B)가 정답이다.

어휘 analyze v. 분석하다 deal with (문제·과제 등을) 처리하다
dispute n. 분쟁, 논쟁 efficiency n. 효율성

Paraphrasing

examining sales records 판매 기록을 조사하는 것 → Analyzing data 데이터를 분석하는 것

82 특정 세부 사항 문제

해석 화자는 다음에 무엇에 대해 논의할 것인가?
(A) 투자 계획
(B) 제품 출시
(C) 회사 합병
(D) 정부 정책

해설 질문의 핵심 어구(discuss next)와 관련된 내용을 주의 깊게 듣는다. "I would like to first talk a bit about BDS Insurance's decision to join with its main competitor, Cullman Limited, to form a new company"라며 먼저 주요 경쟁사인 Cullman Limited사와 합병하여 새로운 회사를 설립하기로 한 BDS Insurance사의 결정에 대해 이야기하고 싶다고 하였다. 따라서 (C)가 정답이다.

어휘 release n. 출시, 공개 merger n. 합병

[83-85]

3ᴹ 미국식

Questions 83-85 refer to the following talk.

83In today's class, we are going to talk about the unique plants that can be found in deserts around the world. 84Everyone will get a chance to see some examples of these plants during our trip to the local botanical gardens next week. For now, I have some pictures to show you. 85I will need a moment to get the projector ready, so in the meantime, I'd like you to please look over the handout I distributed earlier.

unique adj. 독특한 desert n. 사막 example n. 예, 본보기
local adj. 지역의, 현지의 botanical garden 식물원
projector n. 영사기 in the meantime 그동안에
look over ~을 살펴보다, 대충 훑어보다
distribute v. 나누어 주다, 배부하다

해석
83-85번은 다음 담화에 관한 문제입니다.

83오늘 수업에서, 우리는 전 세계 사막에서 볼 수 있는 독특한 식물들에 관해 이야기할 것입니다. 84다음 주 지역 식물원으로의 견학 동안 모두가 이 식물들의 몇 가지 예를 볼 수 있는 기회를 얻게 될 것입니다. 지금, 제가 보여

드릴 사진이 몇 장 있습니다. 85제가 영사기를 준비하는 데 잠시 시간이 필요할 것이므로, 그동안에, 여러분께서는 아까 나눠드린 유인물을 살펴봐 주시기 바랍니다.

83 주제 문제

해석 수업은 주로 무엇에 대한 것인가?
(A) 독특한 동물들
(B) 과학 발명품들
(C) 행성들과 별들
(D) 사막 식물들

해설 수업의 주제를 묻는 문제이므로, 지문의 초반을 반드시 듣는다. "In today's class, we are going to talk about the unique plants that can be found in deserts around the world."라며 오늘 수업에서 전 세계 사막에서 볼 수 있는 독특한 식물들에 관해 이야기할 것이라고 하였다. 따라서 (D)가 정답이다.

어휘 invention n. 발명품, 발명 planet n. 행성

84 특정 세부 사항 문제

해석 다음 주에 무엇이 계획되고 있는가?
(A) 현장 학습
(B) 복습 시간
(C) 영화 상영
(D) 그룹 발표

해설 질문의 핵심 어구(next week)가 언급된 주변의 내용을 주의 깊게 듣는다. "Everyone will get a chance to see some examples of these plants during our trip to the local botanical gardens next week."이라며 다음 주 지역 식물원으로의 견학 동안 모두가 이 식물들의 몇 가지 예를 볼 수 있는 기회를 얻게 될 것이라고 하였다. 따라서 (A)가 정답이다.

어휘 field trip 현장 학습 review n. 복습 session n. 시간, 기간

85 다음에 할 일 문제

해석 화자는 다음에 무엇을 할 것인가?
(A) 서류를 나눠준다.
(B) 사진을 찍는다.
(C) 장비를 설치한다.
(D) 가구를 옮긴다.

해설 지문의 마지막 부분을 주의 깊게 듣는다. "I will need a moment to get the projector ready"라며 영사기를 준비하는 데 잠시 시간이 필요할 것이라고 하였다. 따라서 (C)가 정답이다.

어휘 set up ~을 설치하다, 준비하다 equipment n. 장비

Paraphrasing

get the projector ready 영사기를 준비하다 → Set up some equipment 장비를 설치하다

[86-88]

3ⁿ 영국식

Questions 86-88 refer to the following talk.

Welcome, everyone. Today, **⁸⁶I'll be showing you how to teach our new Pilates class.** **⁸⁷It's only half as long as our regular class**, and we will begin holding it at our studio next week. You may be wondering why we are introducing this type of class. Everybody is busy these days. **⁸⁷Our clients just don't have time for a full-length class.** **⁸⁸Anyway, let me show you the routine, and you can follow along.** Any suggestions for improvement are welcome. I want you to feel confident while teaching. **⁸⁸Now, I will walk you through the first part of the class.**

regular adj. 정규의, 정기적인 routine n. 루틴(정해진 일련의 동작)
suggestion n. 제안, 제의 improvement n. 개선, 향상
confident adj. 자신감 있는, 대담한
walk A through A에게 ~을 차근차근 보여주다

해석

86-88번은 다음 담화에 관한 문제입니다.

환영합니다, 여러분. 오늘, ⁸⁶제가 여러분께 우리의 새 필라테스 수업을 가르치는 방법을 보여드리겠습니다. ⁸⁷그것은 정규 수업의 절반밖에 안 되는 길이이고, 다음 주부터 우리 스튜디오에서 진행하기 시작할 거예요. 여러분은 우리가 왜 이런 종류의 수업을 도입할 것인지 궁금하실지도 모르겠네요. 요즘은 모두가 바쁘잖아요. ⁸⁷우리 고객들은 정규 수업을 들을 시간이 없어요. ⁸⁸어쨌든, 제가 루틴을 보여드릴 테니, 여러분은 따라 하시면 됩니다. 개선을 위한 모든 제안은 환영합니다. 저는 여러분이 가르치면서 자신감을 가지시면 좋겠습니다. ⁸⁸자, 제가 수업의 첫 번째 부분부터 차근차근 보여드리겠습니다.

86 청자 문제

해석 청자들은 누구인 것 같은가?
(A) 강사들
(B) 체육관 회원들
(C) 영업 사원들
(D) 기술자들

해설 지문에서 신분 및 직업과 관련된 표현을 놓치지 않고 듣는다. "I'll be showing you how to teach our new Pilates class"라며 새 필라테스 수업을 가르치는 방법을 보여주겠다고 한 것을 통해 청자들이 필라테스 강사들임을 알 수 있다. 따라서 (A)가 정답이다.

87 의도 파악 문제

해석 화자는 "요즘은 모두가 바쁘잖아요"라고 말할 때 무엇을 의도하는가?
(A) 더 짧은 수업이 인기 있을 것이다.
(B) 더 많은 직원이 고용되어야 한다.
(C) 더 적은 수의 사람들이 참여할 것이다.
(D) 새로운 고객들을 찾아야 한다.

해설 질문의 인용어구(Everybody is busy these days)가 언급된 주변을 주의 깊게 듣는다. "It[new Pilates class]'s only half as long as our regular class"라며 새 필라테스 수업이 정규 수업의 절반밖에 안 되는 길이라고 한 후, "Our clients just don't have time for a full-length class."라며 고객들이 정규 수업을 들을 시간이 없

다고 한 것을 통해 더 짧은 수업이 인기 있을 것임을 알 수 있다. 따라서 (A)가 정답이다.

88 다음에 할 일 문제

해석 화자는 다음에 무엇을 할 것 같은가?
(A) 몇몇 고객들을 소개한다.
(B) 몇몇 고객들을 대상으로 설문 조사한다.
(C) 시설을 점검한다.
(D) 시범을 보여준다.

해설 지문의 마지막 부분을 주의 깊게 듣는다. "Anyway, let me show you the routine, and you can follow along.", "Now, I will walk you through the first part of the class."라며 자신이 루틴을 보여주면 청자들이 따라 하면 된다고 한 후, 수업의 첫 번째 부분부터 차근차근 보여주겠다고 한 것을 통해 시범을 보여줄 것임을 알 수 있다. 따라서 (D)가 정답이다.

어휘 survey v. (많은 사람들을 대상으로 설문) 조사하다; n. (설문) 조사
demonstration n. 시범 (설명)

Paraphrasing

walk ~ through ~을 차근차근 보여주다 → Give a demonstration
시범을 보여주다

[89-91]

3ⁿ 캐나다식

Questions 89-91 refer to the following news report.

⁸⁹In today's business news, Geneva Systems has lost a lawsuit brought against it by Bantam Technologies. The case involved a software application that the two companies developed together six years ago. According to **⁹⁰Bantam Technologies CEO Lawrence Khan**, the project was canceled, and both companies agreed not to use the software. However, Geneva Systems later installed it on its digital watches. As a result, Geneva Systems must now pay Bantam Technologies over 10 million dollars in compensation. **⁹¹For more information about this story, visit the KBC News Web site.**

lawsuit n. 소송, 고소 case n. (소송) 사건
involve v. 관련이 있다, 수반하다 develop v. 개발하다
install v. 설치하다 compensation n. 보상

해석

89-91번은 다음 뉴스 보도에 관한 문제입니다.

⁸⁹오늘의 경제 뉴스에서, Geneva Systems사가 Bantam Technologies사에 의해 제기된 소송에서 패소했습니다. 이 소송 사건은 6년 전 두 회사가 함께 개발한 소프트웨어 애플리케이션과 관련된 것입니다. ⁹⁰Bantam Technologies사의 대표이사인 Lawrence Khan에 따르면, 해당 프로젝트는 취소되었고, 두 회사는 그 소프트웨어를 사용하지 않기로 합의했습니다. 그러나, Geneva Systems사는 그러고 나서 디지털시계에 이 소프트웨어를 설치했습니다. 그 결과, Geneva Systems사는 이제 Bantam Technologies사에 천만 달러가 넘는 보상금을 지급해야 합니다. ⁹¹이 보도에 대한 더 많은 정보를 원하시면, KBC 뉴스 웹사이트를 방문하세요.

89 이유 문제

해석 Geneva Systems사가 뉴스에 나온 이유는 무엇인가?
(A) 기술을 개발했다.
(B) 신제품을 출시했다.
(C) 법적 분쟁에서 패소했다.
(D) 대표이사를 교체했다.

해설 질문의 핵심 어구(Geneva Systems in the news)와 관련된 내용을 주의 깊게 듣는다. "In today's business news, Geneva Systems has lost a lawsuit brought against it by Bantam Technologies."라며 오늘의 경제 뉴스에서 Geneva Systems사가 Bantam Technologies사에 의해 제기된 소송에서 패소했다고 하였다. 따라서 (C)가 정답이다.

어휘 legal dispute 법적 분쟁

Paraphrasing

a lawsuit 소송 → a legal dispute 법적 분쟁

90 특정 세부 사항 문제

해석 Lawrence Khan은 누구인가?
(A) 기업 변호사
(B) 회사 임원
(C) 경제부 기자
(D) 재정 자문가

해설 질문 대상(Lawrence Khan)의 신분 및 직업과 관련된 표현을 놓치지 않고 듣는다. "Bantam Technologies CEO Lawrence Khan"이라며 Lawrence Khan이 Bantam Technologies사의 대표이사라고 하였다. 따라서 (B)가 정답이다.

어휘 corporate adj. 기업의   consultant n. 자문가, 상담가

Paraphrasing

CEO 대표이사 → A company executive 회사 임원

91 방법 문제

해석 청자들은 어떻게 보도에 대한 더 많은 정보를 얻을 수 있는가?
(A) 보도를 들음으로써
(B) 웹사이트에 접속함으로써
(C) 출판물을 읽음으로써
(D) 이메일을 확인함으로써

해설 질문의 핵심 어구(more information about a story)가 언급된 주변을 주의 깊게 듣는다. "For more information about this story, visit the KBC News Web site."라며 이 보도에 대한 더 많은 정보를 원하면 KBC 뉴스 웹사이트를 방문하라고 하였다. 따라서 (B)가 정답이다.

어휘 publication n. 출판물

Paraphrasing

visit ~ Web site 웹사이트를 방문하다 → accessing a Web site 웹사이트에 접속함

[92-94]

Questions 92-94 refer to the following telephone message.

Good morning. This is Myra Gomez from Office Land. When you ordered the Westport desk yesterday, you forgot to include your street number in the delivery address. **92/93Could you call me back and let me know the street number?** My number is 555-9283. I have a meeting soon, **93but please just leave a message.** To receive your shipment today, make sure to call before 2 P.M. **94We won't be open tomorrow because of the national holiday, so no deliveries will be made then.** Thanks.

address n. 주소   leave v. 남기다, 떠나다   shipment n. 배송품
national holiday 공휴일

해석

92-94번은 다음 전화 메시지에 관한 문제입니다.

좋은 아침입니다. Office Land사의 Myra Gomez입니다. 귀하께서 어제 Westport 책상을 주문하셨을 때, 배송 주소에 거리 번호를 포함하는 것을 잊으셨습니다. **92/93다시 저에게 전화를 주셔서 거리 번호를 알려주시겠어요?** 제 번호는 555-9283입니다. 저는 곧 회의가 있어요, **93하지만 그냥 메시지를 남겨주세요.** 귀하의 배송품을 오늘 받기 위해서는, 오후 2시 전에 반드시 전화를 주셔야 합니다. **94내일은 공휴일이라 저희가 영업을 하지 않으므로, 그때는 배송이 되지 않을 것입니다.** 감사합니다.

92 목적 문제

해석 화자는 왜 전화를 하고 있는가?
(A) 도움을 제공하기 위해
(B) 약속을 잡기 위해
(C) 불만을 제기하기 위해
(D) 정보를 요청하기 위해

해설 전화의 목적을 묻는 문제이므로, 지문의 초반을 반드시 듣는다. "Could you call me back and let me know the street number?"라며 다시 자신에게 전화를 하여 거리 번호를 알려줄 수 있는지 묻고 있다. 따라서 (D)가 정답이다.

어휘 assistance n. 도움, 지원   complaint n. 불만, 항의

93 의도 파악 문제

해석 화자는 "저는 곧 회의가 있어요"라고 말할 때 무엇을 의도하는가?
(A) 그녀가 기한을 지키지 못할 것이다.
(B) 그녀가 전화를 받지 않을 수도 있다.
(C) 일정이 변경될 수 있다.
(D) 절차가 오랜 시간이 걸릴 것이다.

해설 질문의 인용어구(I have a meeting soon)가 언급된 주변을 주의 깊게 듣는다. "Could you call me back and let me know the street number?"라며 다시 자신에게 전화를 하여 거리 번호를 알려줄 수 있는지 물은 후, "but please just leave a message."라며 그냥 메시지를 남겨달라고 한 것을 통해 그녀가 전화를 받지 않을 수도 있음을 알 수 있다. 따라서 (B)가 정답이다.

어휘 process n. 절차, 과정

94 언급 문제

해석 화자는 내일에 대해 무엇을 말하는가?
(A) 배송이 될 것이다.
(B) 이메일이 발송될 것이다.
(C) 주문이 확정될 것이다.
(D) 사업체가 문을 닫을 것이다.

해설 질문의 핵심 어구(tomorrow)가 언급된 주변을 주의 깊게 듣는다. "We won't be open tomorrow because of the national holiday, so no deliveries will be made then."이라며 내일이 공휴일이라 영업을 하지 않으므로 배송이 되지 않을 것이라고 하였다. 따라서 (D)가 정답이다.

Paraphrasing

won't be open 영업을 하지 않을 것이다 → will be closed 문을 닫을 것이다

[95-97]

🎧 미국식

Questions 95-97 refer to the following excerpt from a meeting and graph.

Good news, everyone. We have increased our share of the national toothpaste market, and **⁹⁵our company now ranks second overall domestically**. If we keep up our marketing efforts while continuing to do product research, I think we can gradually increase our market share without lowering our prices. **⁹⁶Looking at international markets, however, the picture is less optimistic. In both Germany and China, we have lost ground to local competitors.** I don't think traditional advertising will be enough in those countries. **⁹⁷We should try to make our brand stand out on social media instead.**

share n. 점유율 rank v. (순위를) 차지하다
domestically adv. 국내에서 continue v. 계속하다
gradually adv. 점진적으로 market share 시장 점유율
lower v. 낮추다 international adj. 국제적인 picture n. 상황
optimistic adj. 낙관적인 lose ground to ~에 밀리다, 패배하다
traditional adj. 전통적인 stand out 돋보이다, 눈에 띄다

해석

95-97번은 다음 회의 발췌록과 그래프에 관한 문제입니다.

좋은 소식입니다, 여러분. 우리는 국내 치약 시장에서의 점유율을 높였고, **⁹⁵우리 회사는 현재 국내에서 전체 2위를 차지하고 있습니다.** 우리가 제품 연구를 계속하면서 마케팅 노력을 지속한다면, 우리의 가격을 낮추지 않고도 점진적으로 시장 점유율을 높일 수 있다고 생각합니다. **⁹⁶하지만, 국제 시장을 살펴보면, 상황은 덜 낙관적입니다. 독일과 중국 모두에서, 우리는 현지 경쟁사들에 밀렸습니다.** 저는 그 나라들에서는 전통적인 광고만으로는 충분하지 않을 것이라고 생각합니다. **⁹⁷대신 우리는 소셜 미디어에서 우리 브랜드를 돋보이게 하기 위해 노력해야 합니다.**

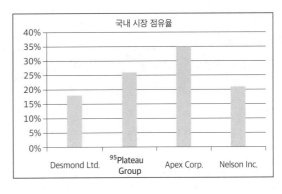

국내 시장 점유율

(그래프: Desmond Ltd. 약 18%, ⁹⁵Plateau Group 약 26%, Apex Corp. 약 35%, Nelson Inc. 약 21%)

95 시각 자료 문제

해석 시각 자료를 보아라. 화자는 어느 회사에서 근무하는가?
(A) Desmond Ltd.
(B) Plateau Group
(C) Apex Corp.
(D) Nelson Inc.

해설 제시된 그래프의 정보를 확인한 후 질문의 핵심 어구(speaker work for)와 관련된 내용을 주의 깊게 듣는다. "our company now ranks second overall domestically"라며 화자의 회사가 현재 국내에서 전체 2위를 차지하고 있다고 하였으므로, 화자가 근무하는 회사가 Plateau Group임을 그래프에서 알 수 있다. 따라서 (B)가 정답이다.

96 특정 세부 사항 문제

해석 화자는 무엇에 대해 걱정하는가?
(A) 현지 무역 제한
(B) 고객 의견
(C) 국제 시장 점유율
(D) 배송 비용

해설 질문의 핵심 어구(concerned about)와 관련된 내용을 주의 깊게 듣는다. "Looking at international markets, however, the picture is less optimistic. In both Germany and China, we have lost ground to local competitors."라며 국제 시장에서는 상황이 덜 낙관적이라고 한 후, 독일과 중국 모두에서 현지 경쟁사들에 밀렸다고 하였다. 따라서 (C)가 정답이다.

어휘 trade n. 무역, 거래 restriction n. 제한

97 제안 문제

해석 화자는 무엇을 제안하는가?
(A) 세계적으로 실제 매장들 열기
(B) 소셜 미디어에서 가시성 높이기
(C) 몇몇 제품 디자인 개선하기
(D) 인기 있는 행사들 후원하기

해설 지문의 중후반에서 제안과 관련된 표현이 언급된 다음을 주의 깊게 듣는다. "We should try to make our brand stand out on social media instead."라며 대신 소셜 미디어에서 브랜드를 돋보이게 하기 위해 노력해야 한다고 하였다. 따라서 (B)가 정답이다.

어휘 physical adj. 실제의, 물질의 visibility n. 가시성, 눈에 보이는 정도

sponsor v. 후원하다, 주관하다

[98-100]

🔊 호주식

Questions 98-100 refer to the following telephone message and map.

Hi. **⁹⁸This is Gary Morton from A-Plus Property.** I looked into the neighborhood that you inquired about in your e-mail. **⁹⁹Unfortunately, a new convention center being built nearby has caused home prices there to skyrocket, placing them out of your budget.** **¹⁰⁰You may want to consider other areas.** For your convenience, I've prepared a list of alternatives. **¹⁰⁰There is one in particular you may like at the intersection of 7th Avenue and Hilltop Boulevard.** It's in a lively district with plenty of restaurants and cafés. I'd be happy to show it to you this afternoon if you're available. Please let me know.

look into ~을 주의 깊게 살펴보다 inquire v. 문의하다
skyrocket v. 급등하다 convenience n. 편의 alternative n. 대안
in particular 특히, 특별히 intersection n. 교차 지점, 교차로
boulevard n. 대로, 도로 lively adj. 활기찬 district n. 지역, 구역
plenty of 많은, 충분한

해석
98-100번은 다음 전화 메시지와 지도에 관한 문제입니다.

안녕하세요. ⁹⁸A-Plus 부동산의 Gary Morton입니다. 저는 귀하께서 이메일에서 문의하신 동네를 주의 깊게 살펴봤습니다. ⁹⁹유감스럽게도, 근처에 건설 중인 새로운 컨벤션 센터로 인해 그곳의 집값이 급등하였고, 이는 귀하의 예산을 벗어나게 했습니다. ¹⁰⁰다른 지역들을 고려해 보시는 게 좋겠습니다. 귀하의 편의를 위해, 제가 대안 목록을 준비했습니다. ¹⁰⁰7번가와 Hilltop 대로의 교차 지점에 귀하께서 특히 마음에 들어 할 만한 것이 있습니다. 그것은 식당과 카페가 많은 활기찬 지역에 있습니다. 오늘 오후에 시간이 되시면 제가 기꺼이 보여드리겠습니다. 제게 알려주세요.

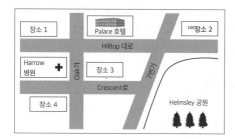

98 화자 문제

해석 화자는 어디에서 일하는 것 같은가?
(A) 건설 회사에서
(B) 광고 대행사에서
(C) 부동산 중개소에서
(D) 관공서에서

해설 지문에서 신분 및 직업과 관련된 표현을 놓치지 않고 듣는다. "This is Gary Morton from A-Plus Property."라며 화자가 자신을 A-Plus 부동산의 Gary Morton이라고 소개한 후, 청자가 관심 있어 할 만한 매물에 대해 알려주는 내용으로 지문이 이어지고 있다. 이를 통해 화자가 부동산 중개소에서 일한다는 것을 알 수 있다. 따라서 (C)가 정답이다.

어휘 firm n. 회사 agency n. 대행사, 대리점

99 특정 세부 사항 문제

해석 화자는 무슨 문제를 언급하는가?
(A) 비용이 증가했다.
(B) 시설이 문을 닫았다.
(C) 예산이 부정확하다.
(D) 지역이 너무 붐빈다.

해설 질문의 핵심 어구(problem)와 관련된 내용을 주의 깊게 듣는다. "Unfortunately, a new convention center being built nearby has caused home prices there to skyrocket, placing them out of your budget."이라며 근처에 건설 중인 새로운 컨벤션 센터로 인해 그곳의 집값이 급등하였고, 이는 예산을 벗어나게 했다고 하였다. 따라서 (A)가 정답이다.

어휘 shut down 문을 닫다 inaccurate adj. 부정확한
overcrowded adj. 너무 붐비는

100 시각 자료 문제

해석 시각 자료를 보아라. 청자는 어느 지역을 둘러보는 것에 관심이 있을 수 있는가?
(A) 장소 1
(B) 장소 2
(C) 장소 3
(D) 장소 4

해설 제시된 지도의 정보를 확인한 후 질문의 핵심 어구(interested in seeing)와 관련된 내용을 주의 깊게 듣는다. "You may want to consider other areas."라며 다른 지역들을 고려해 보는 게 좋겠다고 한 후, "There is one in particular you may like at the intersection of 7th Avenue and Hilltop Boulevard."라며 7번가와 Hilltop 대로의 교차 지점에 특히 마음에 들어 할 만한 것이 있다고 하였으므로 청자가 둘러보는 것에 관심이 있을 수도 있는 지역은 장소 2임을 지도에서 알 수 있다. 따라서 (B)가 정답이다.

PART 5

101 격에 맞는 인칭대명사 채우기

해설 이 문장은 동사(worries)의 목적어 역할을 하는 명사절의 명사절 접속사 that이 생략된 문장이다. 명사절에 동사(will be)만 있고 주어가 없으므로 주어 역할을 할 수 있는 주격 인칭대명사 (A)와 소유대명사 (C)가 정답의 후보이다. '그가 연례 회사 만찬에 늦을까 봐 걱정하다'라는 의미가 되어야 하므로 주격 인칭대명사 (A) he가 정답이다. 소유대명사 (C)를 쓸 경우 '그의 것이 연례 회사 만찬에 늦을까 봐 걱정하다'라는 어색한 의미를 만들기 때문에 답이 될 수 없다. 목적격 인칭대명사 (B)와 재귀대명사 (D)는 주어 자리에 올 수 없다. 참고로, (C) his는 소유격 인칭대명사로 쓰일 경우, 뒤에 명사가 와야 되는 것을 알아둔다.

해석 오늘 저녁은 교통이 특히나 혼잡해서, Mr. Gagnon은 그가 연례 회사 만찬에 늦을까 봐 걱정한다.

어휘 traffic n. 교통(량), 차량들 particularly adv. 특히나, 특별하게

102 태에 맞는 동사 채우기

해설 이 문장은 주어(Nelson Media's CEO)만 있고 동사가 없으므로 동사 (A)와 (D)가 정답의 후보이다. 주어(Nelson Media's CEO)와 동사(announce)가 'Nelson 언론사의 CEO가 발표하다'라는 능동의 의미를 가지므로 능동태 동사 (A) announced가 정답이다.

해석 Nelson 언론사의 CEO는 모든 직원들이 인적 자원 세미나에 참여하도록 요구된다고 발표했다.

어휘 take part in ~에 참여하다

103 형용사 어휘 고르기

해설 '높아진 수요를 충족하기 위해 더 많은 조립 라인을 설치할 계획이다'라는 문맥이므로 형용사 (D) heightened(높아진)가 정답이다. (A) inspired는 '감명받은', (B) rough는 '개략적인, 거친', (C) convenient는 '편리한'이라는 의미이다.

해석 Starworks 전자제품사는 의료 기기에 대한 높아진 수요를 충족하기 위해 더 많은 조립 라인을 설치할 계획이다.

어휘 set up ~을 설치하다 assembly line 조립 라인 demand n. 수요

104 의미 구별하여 명사 채우기

해설 빈칸은 최상급 표현(America's largest)의 수식을 받는 명사 자리이고, '미국의 가장 큰 소매업체'라는 의미가 되어야 하므로 명사 (D) retailer(소매업체)가 정답이다. (A) retail(소매)을 쓰면 '미국의 가장 큰 소매'라는 어색한 의미를 만들기 때문에 답이 될 수 없다. 동사 또는 과거분사 (B)와 to 부정사 (C)는 형용사의 수식을 받는 명사 자리에 올 수 없다.

해석 미국의 가장 큰 소비재 소매업체인 Evermart는 멕시코에 물류 센터를 열 것이다.

어휘 consumer goods 소비재 logistics center 물류 센터

105 동사 어휘 고르기

해설 'Alan Elwood는 새로운 감독으로 임명되다'라는 문맥이므로 동사 name(임명하다)의 p.p.형 (B) named가 정답이다. 참고로, 이 문장은 목적어와 목적격 보어를 취하는 5형식 동사 name(임명하다, 명명하다)이 수동태로 쓰이면서 목적어(Alan Elwood)가 주어 자리에 오고 목적격 보어(the new manager of the football club)가 동사 뒤에 남은 형태임을 알아둔다. (A)의 hire(고용하다)도 해석상 그럴듯해 보이지만, 3형식 동사로 쓰이는 hire는 수동태로 쓰일 경우 뒤에 목적어를 취할 수 없다. (C)의 accompany는 '동반하다', (D)의 encourage는 '격려하다, 권장하다'라는 의미이다.

해석 Alan Elwood는 축구 클럽의 새로운 감독으로 임명되었고 올가을에 독일로 전근 갈 것이다.

어휘 manager n. 감독, 관리자

106 주어와 수일치하는 동사 채우기

해설 문장에 동사가 없으므로 동사 (B), (C), (D)가 정답의 후보이다. 주어(The university's admission records)가 복수이므로 복수 동사 (C) show가 정답이다. (A)는 동명사 또는 현재분사의 완료형으로 동사 자리에 올 수 없다.

해석 그 대학교의 입학 기록들은 국제 학생 수가 지난 3년 동안 감소해 왔다는 것을 보여준다.

어휘 admission n. 입학, 입장 decline v. 감소하다, 줄어들다

107 빈도 부사 채우기

해설 '아름다운 풍경에도 불구하고 거의 방문되지 않다'라는 의미가 되어야 하므로 (A) seldom(거의 ~않는)이 정답이다. (B) almost(거의), (C) earlier(더 일찍), (D) maybe(아마, 어쩌면)를 쓸 경우 어색한 문맥이 된다.

해석 Greenwood 국립 공원은 그곳의 아름다운 풍경에도 불구하고 거의 방문되지 않는다.

어휘 scenery n. 풍경, 경치

108 현재분사와 과거분사 구별하여 채우기

해설 이 문장은 주어(Fashueng Industries), 동사(has published), 목

적어(a corporate brochure)를 갖춘 완전한 절이므로, ____ of its achievements는 수식어 거품으로 보아야 한다. 이 수식어 거품은 빈칸 앞의 명사(a corporate brochure)를 꾸미고 있으므로 수식어 거품을 이끌면서 명사를 뒤에서 수식할 수 있는 과거분사 (B)와 현재분사 (C)가 정답의 후보이다. 수식 받는 명사(a corporate brochure)와 분사가 '기업 책자는 자사의 성과로 이루어지다'라는 의미의 능동 관계이므로 동사 consist(이루어지다)의 현재분사 (C) consisting이 정답이다. 과거분사 (B)를 쓸 경우 해석상 그럴듯해 보이지만, 동사 consist는 자동사이므로 과거분사로 쓸 수 없다. 부사 (A)와 형용사 (D)는 수식어 거품을 이끌 수 없다. 참고로, consist of(~으로 이루어지다)를 관용구로 알아둔다.

해석 Fashueng 산업사는 자사의 성과로 이루어져 있는 기업 책자를 발간했다.

어휘 brochure n. 책자, 설명서 achievement n. 성과, 업적

109 최상급 표현 채우기

해설 빈칸 뒤의 분사(populated)를 꾸밀 수 있는 것은 부사이므로 부사 densely(밀집하여, 빽빽이)의 최상급 표현인 (A) most densely가 정답이다. 명사 (B), 형용사 (C), 형용사의 비교급 (D)는 부사 자리에 올 수 없다.

해석 지하철역이 그 도시에서 가장 많은 인구가 밀집된 지역인 랭퍼드에 제안되었다.

어휘 propose v. 제안하다 populated adj. 많은 인구가 밀집된 neighborhood n. 지역, 인근 dense adj. 밀집한, 빽빽한

110 형용사 자리 채우기

해설 빈칸 앞에 정관사(the), 빈칸 뒤에 명사(glacier movement)가 있으므로 명사를 꾸미는 형용사 (C) active(활동 중인)가 정답이다. 명사 (A) activity(활동)는 glacier movement와 복합 명사를 이루지 못하며, 부사 (B)와 동사 (D)는 명사를 꾸밀 수 없다.

해석 연구원들은 북극의 빙하가 해수면에 미치는 영향력을 평가하기 위해 북극의 활동 중인 빙하의 움직임을 관찰하고 있다.

어휘 monitor v. 관찰하다, 감시하다 glacier n. 빙하 assess v. 평가하다, 가늠하다 sea level 해수면 actively adv. 적극적으로 activate v. 활성화시키다, 작동시키다

111 부사절 접속사 채우기

해설 이 문장은 필수성분(RT Cosmetics' newest lipstick ~ within a month)을 갖춘 완전한 절이므로 ____ there are no delays는 수식어 거품으로 보아야 한다. 이 수식어 거품은 동사(are)가 있는 거품절이므로, 거품절을 이끌 수 있는 부사절 접속사 (C) as long as(~하는 한)가 정답이다. (A) rather than(~보다는)과 (D) resulting from(~으로 인한)은 절이 아닌 구 앞에 온다. 부사 (B) otherwise(그렇지 않으면)는 거품절을 이끌 수 없다.

해석 RT 화장품사의 최신 립스틱은 지연이 없는 한 한 달 이내에 공개될 것이다.

어휘 release v. 공개하다, 발표하다 within prep. ~ 이내에 delay n. 지연, 지체

112 강조 부사 채우기

해설 빈칸 뒤의 전치사구(for a few days)를 꾸며줄 수 있는 부사 (A), (B), (C)가 정답의 후보이다. '오직 며칠 동안만 시내에 있다'라는 의미가 되어야 하므로 강조를 나타내는 부사 (C) only(오직 ~만)가 정답이다. (A) quite(꽤, 상당히)은 주로 형용사 또는 'a/an + 명사'를 앞에서 강조할 때 쓰고, (B) ever(지금까지)는 주로 부정문 또는 비교급/최상급의 의미를 강조할 때 쓴다. 부사절 접속사 또는 명사 (D) while(~하는 동안; 잠깐)은 부사 자리에 올 수 없다.

해석 일본 파트너 회사의 임원진들은 일본으로 돌아가기 전에 오직 며칠 동안만 시내에 있을 것이다.

어휘 executive n. 임원진, 경영진 return v. 돌아가다

113 명사 어휘 고르기

해설 '보관 구역에 충분한 공간이 없었기 때문에 창고를 임대하다'라는 문맥이므로 (D) warehouse(창고)가 정답이다. (A) tile은 '타일, 기와', (B) party는 '파티, 정당', (C) reward는 '보상'이라는 의미이다.

해석 공장 관리자는 보관 구역에 충분한 공간이 없었기 때문에 창고를 임대하기로 결정했다.

어휘 lease v. 임대하다, 대여하다 storage n. 보관, 저장

114 전치사 채우기

해설 '팀장으로서 애쓰다'라는 의미가 되어야 하므로 자격 또는 신분을 나타내는 (C)의 as(~로서)가 정답이다. (A) about은 '~에 관하여', (B) by는 '~에 의해, ~까지', (D) of는 '~의, ~에 관하여'라는 의미이다.

해석 팀장으로서 Ms. Dench는 팀 구성원들 사이의 협력을 촉진하기 위해 애쓴다.

어휘 strive v. 애쓰다, 분투하다 facilitate v. 촉진하다, 용이하게 하다 collaboration n. 협력

115 동사 어휘 고르기

해설 '설문조사 참가자들이 소프트웨어의 기능을 최악부터 최고까지 등급을 매기다'라는 문맥이므로 rank(등급을 매기다)의 과거형 (B) ranked가 정답이다. (A)의 opt(선택하다)도 해석상 그럴듯해 보이지만 주로 opt for의 형태로 쓰이므로 답이 될 수 없다. (C)의 verify는 '확인하다', (D)의 match는 '일치하다'라는 의미이다.

해석 설문조사 참가자들은 Neo 기술사의 사진 편집 소프트웨어의 기능을 최악부터 최고까지 등급을 매겼다.

어휘 participant n. 참가자 feature n. 기능, 특징

116 부사 자리 채우기

해설 형용사 역할을 하는 수 표현(four)을 꾸밀 수 있는 것은 부사이므로 부사 (D) approximately(약, 대략)가 정답이다. 형용사 또는 동사 (A), 명사 (B), 동사 또는 과거분사 (C)는 형용사를 꾸밀 수 없다. 참고로, 빈칸이 꾸미는 것은 명사(weeks)가 아닌 형용사(four)이므로, '숫자+명사' 앞에는 형용사가 아닌 부사가 온다는 것을 알아둔다.

해석 그 도시에서 가장 오래된 다리는 대규모 수리가 진행되는 동안 약 4주간 폐쇄될 것이다.

여휘 extensive adj. 대규모의, 광범위한 repair n. 수리, 보수
take place 진행되다, 일어나다
approximate adj. 근사치인; v. 근사치를 내다, 비슷하다

117 부사 어휘 고르기

해설 '최근에 통과된 법이 일회용 세면도구 제공을 금지하다'라는 문맥이므로 (B) recently(최근에)가 정답이다. (A) briefly는 '잠시, 간단히', (C) generally는 '일반적으로', (D) extremely는 '극도로'라는 의미이다.

해석 최근에 통과된 법은 호텔들이 작은 용기에 담긴 샴푸 같은 일회용 세면도구들을 제공하는 것을 금지한다.

여휘 law n. 법, 법률 prohibit v. 금지하다 single-use adj. 일회용의
toiletries n. 세면도구

118 명사 자리 채우기

해설 빈칸 앞의 형용사(main)의 꾸밈을 받을 수 있는 것은 명사이므로 명사 (A) appeal(매력)이 정답이다. 동명사 또는 현재분사 (C)는 동명사로 쓰일 경우 형용사의 꾸밈을 받을 수 없고, 현재분사로 쓰일 경우 명사 자리에 올 수 없다. 참고로, appeal은 '매력'이라는 의미의 명사로 쓰일 때는 불가산 명사로 쓰이고, 동사로 쓰일 경우 appeal to의 형태로 쓰여 '~의 흥미를 끌다'라는 의미를 갖는다는 것도 알아둔다.

해석 Connel 스마트폰 신형 모델의 주된 매력은 고해상도 카메라이다.

여휘 main adj. 주된, 중요한 high-resolution adj. 고해상도의
appeal n. 매력; v. 관심을 끌다

119 전치사 채우기

해설 형용사 adjacent는 전치사 to와 함께 쓰여 '~에 인접한'의 의미를 나타내므로 (A) to가 정답이다.

해석 그 건설 현장에 인접한 건물의 주민들은 소음과 먼지에 대해 불평하고 있다.

여휘 resident n. 주민, 거주자 construction site 건설 현장
dust n. 먼지

최신토익경향

전치사 문제는 매회 평균 4~5문제로 꾸준히 출제되고 있다. 동사, 형용사, 명사와 함께 짝을 이루는 전치사가 자주 출제되므로 주요 표현을 알아두자.

- belong to ~의 소유이다
- prepare for ~을 준비하다
- collaborate on ~을 협력하다
- familiar with ~에 익숙한
- under one's leadership ~의 지도하에
- responsible/accountable for ~에 책임이 있는
- adjacent to ~에 인접한
- at the age of ~의 나이에
- access to ~에의 접근/출입

120 부사 어휘 고르기

해설 '일정의 절반쯤 지나다'라는 문맥이므로 (C) halfway(절반쯤)가 정답이다. (A) randomly는 '무작위로', (B) indefinitely는 '무기한으로', (D) elsewhere는 '다른 곳에서'라는 의미이다. 참고로, halfway through(절반 정도, 도중에)를 관용구로 외워둔다.

해석 그 여행 가이드는 관광객들에게 하루 일정의 절반쯤 지났다고 알려주었다.

여휘 inform v. 알리다 itinerary n. 일정(표), 여행 일정

121 동사 어휘 고르기

해설 '자사의 고성능 제품들을 선보이기 위해 부스를 빌리다'라는 문맥이므로 (D) showcase(선보이다)가 정답이다. (A) perform은 '수행하다', (B) accept는 '인정하다, 수락하다', (C) collect는 '수집하다'라는 의미이다.

해석 그 회사는 자사의 고성능 제품들을 선보이기 위해 세계 기술 박람회에서 부스 하나를 빌렸다.

여휘 rent v. 빌리다, 임차하다 booth n. 부스
high-end adj. 고성능의, 최고급의

122 동사 자리 채우기

해설 등위접속사 but(그러나) 뒤에 주어(a senior vice president)만 있고 동사가 없으므로 동사 자리에 들어갈 수 있는 (B) may attend (참석할 수도 있다)가 정답이다. to 부정사구 (A), 전치사구 (C), 명사 또는 현재분사 (D)는 동사 자리에 올 수 없다.

해석 Harvison Group의 CEO인 Kelsey Haya는 올해의 학회에는 참석하지 않을 예정이지만, 그녀 대신에 수석 부사장이 참석할 수도 있다.

여휘 senior vice president 수석 부사장, 상무 in one's place ~ 대신에

123 재귀대명사 채우기

해설 동사(dedicate)의 목적어 자리에 올 수 있는 목적격 인칭대명사 (A), 재귀대명사 (B), 소유대명사 역할을 하는 (C)가 정답의 후보이다. '환경 단체의 구성원들이 재생 가능한 에너지 사용을 장려하는 데 전념하다'라는 의미가 되어야 하므로 동사 dedicate와 함께 쓰여 '~에 전념하다'라는 의미의 어구 dedicate oneself to를 만드는 재귀대명사 (B) themselves가 정답이다.

해석 그 세계적인 환경 단체의 구성원들은 재생 가능한 에너지 사용을 장려하는 데 전념한다.

여휘 environmental adj. 환경의 promote v. 장려하다, 촉진하다
renewable adj. 재생 가능한

최신토익경향

인칭대명사를 고르는 문제는 매회 2~3문제씩 꾸준히 출제되는데, 특히 최근에는 목적어 자리에 재귀대명사를 고르는 문제들이 자주 출제되고 있다. 재귀대명사를 목적어로 취하는 표현을 알아두자.

- dedicate oneself to ~에 전념하다
- commit oneself to ~에 전념하다
- familiarize oneself with ~에 익숙하게 하다
- pride oneself on ~에 자부심을 갖다
- surround oneself with ~에 둘러싸이다

124 부사절 접속사 채우기

해설 이 문장은 필수성분(Visitors ~ may park)을 갖춘 완전한 절이므로 ____ ~ parking facility는 수식어 거품으로 보아야 한다. 이 수식

어 거품은 동사(see)가 있는 거품절이므로, 거품절을 이끌 수 있는 부사절 접속사 (A), (B), (C)가 정답의 후보이다. '초록 표시가 보이는 어디에나 주차하다'라는 의미가 되어야 하므로 복합관계부사 (B) wherever(~한 어디에나)가 정답이다. (A) whenever와 (C) whether는 각각 '초록 표시가 보이는 언제나/보이든 (아니든) 주차하다'라는 어색한 의미를 만들기 때문에 답이 될 수 없다. 전치사 (D) instead of(~ 대신에)는 거품절을 이끌 수 없다.

해석 Philip 병원의 방문객들은 주차 시설 3층의 초록 표시가 보이는 어디에나 주차해도 된다.

어휘 indicator n. 표시, 지표 facility n. 시설

125 명사 어휘 고르기

해설 '교통 기반 시설 프로젝트에 관심이 있는 도급업자들로부터 다양한 제안들을 듣다'라는 문맥이므로 proposal(제안)의 복수형 (C) proposals가 정답이다. (A)의 line은 '(노래의) 가사, (생산) 라인', (B)의 agency는 '대리점, 대행사', (D)의 capital은 '자본금'이라는 의미이다.

해석 시 의회는 교통 기반 시설 프로젝트에 관심이 있는 도급업자들로부터 다양한 제안들을 들었다.

어휘 various adj. 다양한 contractor n. 도급업자, 계약자
infrastructure n. (사회) 기반 시설

126 전치사 채우기

해설 이 문장은 필수성분(MealFresh is going to allocate ~ into emerging markets)을 갖춘 완전한 절이므로 ____ ~ for profit은 수식어 거품으로 보아야 한다. 이 수식어 거품은 동사가 없는 거품구이므로, 거품구를 이끌 수 있는 전치사 (A)와 (C)가 정답의 후보이다. '수익에 대한 잠재력을 고려하여 예산을 배정하다'라는 의미가 되어야 하므로 (C) Given(~을 고려하여)이 정답이다. (A) Except은 '~을 제외하고'라는 의미이고, 부사절 접속사 (B) Though(비록 ~이지만)와 (D) Provided that(~을 고려할 때)은 거품구가 아닌 거품절을 이끈다.

해석 수익에 대한 잠재력을 고려하여, MealFresh사는 신흥 시장으로 확장하는 데에 상당한 부분의 예산을 배정할 것이다.

어휘 potential n. 잠재력, 가능성 profit n. 수익, 이익
allocate v. 배정하다 significant adj. 상당한, 중요한
portion n. 부분 emerging market 신흥 시장

최신토익경향

최근 분사 형태의 전치사가 자주 출제되고 있으므로 형태만 보고 형용사로 혼동하지 않도록 아래의 전치사 표현을 알아두자.

- given ~을 고려하여
- following ~ 이후에
- regarding/concerning ~에 관하여
- including ~을 포함하여
- pertaining to ~에 관계된
- depending on ~에 따라

127 사람명사 추상명사 구별하여 채우기

해설 형용사(new)의 꾸밈을 받을 수 있는 것은 명사이므로 명사 (A)와 (B)가 정답의 후보이다. '전시품들은 새로운 장소로 옮겨질 것이다'라는 의미가 되어야 하므로 추상명사 (B) location(장소, 위치)이 정답이다. 사람명사 (A) locals(주민들)를 쓰면 '전시품들은 새로운 주민들에게

옮겨질 것이다'라는 어색한 의미를 만들기 때문에 답이 될 수 없다. 동사 또는 과거분사 (C)와 부사 (D)는 명사 자리에 올 수 없다.

해석 Fort Frederick 박물관의 현재 전시품들은 다음 주에 보수 공사가 시작될 때 새로운 장소로 옮겨질 것이다.

어휘 exhibit n. 전시품; v. 전시하다 transfer v. 옮기다, 이동하다
renovation n. 보수 (공사) local n. 주민, 현지인; adj. 지역의, 현지의

128 전치사 채우기

해설 이 문장은 필수성분(The marketing team ~ advertising performance)을 갖춘 완전한 절이므로 ____ ~ of November는 수식어 거품으로 보아야 한다. 이 수식어 거품은 동사가 없는 거품구이므로, 거품구를 이끌 수 있는 전치사 (A)와 (C)가 정답의 후보이다. '11월 마지막 주 이후로 광고 성과를 분석해 오고 있다'라는 의미가 되어야 하므로 현재완료진행형(has been analyzing)과 함께 쓰이는 (A) since(~ 이후로)가 정답이다. (C) until은 '~까지'라는 의미로 특정 시점까지 완료된 동작을 나타내므로 현재완료진행형과 어울리지 않으며, 부사 (B) then(그다음에, 그때)과 (D) still(여전히, 그런데도)은 수식어 거품구를 이끌 수 없다.

해석 그 마케팅팀은 11월 마지막 주 이후로 그 캠페인의 광고 성과를 분석해 오고 있다.

어휘 analyze v. 분석하다 advertising n. 광고 performance n. 성과

129 지시대명사 those 채우기

해설 빈칸은 과거분사구(sold ~ stores)의 꾸밈을 받는 명사 자리이므로 부정대명사 (C)와 지시대명사 (D)가 정답의 후보이다. '대부분의 주요 백화점에서 판매되는 가방들만큼 비싸다'라는 의미가 되어야 하므로 앞에 나온 복수 명사(handbags)를 대신하는 지시대명사 (D) those가 정답이다. (C) one은 단수 명사인 불특정한 대상을 가리킬 때 사용하므로 답이 될 수 없다. (A) other는 이미 언급한 것 이외의 몇몇을 가리키는 형용사로 쓰이며, 대명사로 사용될 경우에는 others나 the other(s)의 형태로 쓰여 각각 '(이미 언급한 것 이외의) 다른 것들', '나머지 전부'를 의미한다. 소유격 관계대명사 (B) whose는 앞에 선행사인 명사가 나와야 한다.

해석 이 웹사이트에서 판매되는 디자이너 가방들은 대부분의 주요 백화점에서 판매되는 것들만큼 비싸다.

어휘 sell v. 판매하다, 팔다 major adj. 주요한, 중대한

130 명사 관련 어구 완성하기

해설 '무단 접근으로부터 보호받는 것을 보장하기 위해 현재 사용되는 보안 규약을 준수하다'라는 문맥에서 빈칸 앞의 명사 security와 함께 쓰여 '보안 규약'이라는 의미의 어구를 이루는 (B) protocol(규약)이 정답이다. (A) durability는 '내구성', (C) appearance는 '모습, 출현', (D) settlement는 '합의, 해결'이라는 의미이다.

해석 모든 민감한 자료들이 무단 접근으로부터 보호받는 것을 보장하기 위해 현재 사용되는 보안 규약을 준수하세요.

어휘 adhere to ~을 준수하다 existing adj. 현재 사용되는, 기존의
guarantee v. 보장하다, 품질 보증을 하다
unauthorized adj. 무단의, 승인되지 않은 access n. 접근, 접속

PART 6

131-134번은 다음 이메일에 관한 문제입니다.

날짜: 8월 17일
수신: Beatrice Xenakis <bxenakis@gomail.com>
발신: Alfred Hendricks <ahendricks@moxtech.com>
제목: 알림

Ms. Xenakis께,

¹³¹저는 귀하에게 제품 회수를 공표하고자 하는 Moxtech 전자제품사의 결정을 알려드리려 합니다. 그 제품은 Whirl-12 소형 선풍기로, 이는 귀하께서 지난달에 구매하신 것입니다. 유감스럽게도, 이 모델은 결함이 있는 모터가 탑재되어 있습니다. ¹³²그것은 만약 가장 높은 설정으로 장기간 작동되면 작동을 멈출 수 있으며 심지어 불이 날 수도 있습니다. 기기에 대한 실험 결과는 그 모터가 과열에 취약하다는 것을 보여줍니다. ¹³³따라서, 저희는 귀하께서 Whirl-12를 사용하는 것을 중단하시고 편하신 때에 당사의 고객 서비스 센터로 전화주시기를 권고합니다. ¹³⁴귀하께서는 환불을 받기 위한 설명을 제공받으실 것입니다.

감사합니다,

Alfred Hendricks 드림, 고객 서비스 담당자
Moxtech 전자제품사

inform v. 알리다 decision n. 결정 recall n. 회수
miniature adj. 소형의 fan n. 선풍기 purchase v. 구매하다, 구입하다
faulty adj. 결함이 있는, 잘못된 prolonged adj. 장기의, 오래 계속되는
appliance n. (가정용) 기기, 가전제품 indicate v. 보여주다, 나타내다
be prone to ~에 취약하다 overheating n. 과열

131 동사 어휘 고르기 전체 문맥 파악

해설 '저는 귀하에게 제품 회수를 _____ 하고자 하는 결정을 알려드리려 합니다'라는 문맥이므로 (B), (C), (D)가 정답의 후보이다. 빈칸이 있는 문장만으로는 정답을 고를 수 없으므로 주변 문맥이나 전체 문맥을 파악한다. 뒤에서 선풍기에 결함이 있다고 했고, Whirl-12를 사용하는 것을 중단하고 당사의 고객 서비스 센터로 전화해달라고 했으므로 제품 회수를 공표하고자 함을 알 수 있다. 따라서 동사 (C) issue(공표하다)가 정답이다. (B) postpone은 '연기하다', (D) monitor는 '추적 관찰하다, 감시하다'라는 의미로 전체 문맥상 적절하지 않다.

어휘 avoid v. 방지하다, 피하다

132 부사절 접속사 채우기

해설 이 문장은 필수성분(It may ~ catch fire)을 갖춘 완전한 절이므로 _____ ~ period of time은 수식어 거품으로 보아야 한다. 이 수식어 거품은 동사(is run)가 있는 거품절이므로, 거품절을 이끌 수 있는 부사절 접속사 (A)와 (C)가 정답의 후보이다. '만약 가장 높은 설정으로 장기간 작동되면 불이 날 수도 있다'라는 의미가 되어야 하므로 조건을 나타내는 부사절 접속사 (A) if(만약 ~라면)가 정답이다. (C) whereas(~한 반면에)를 쓰면 '가장 높은 설정으로 장기간 작동된 반면에 불이 날 수도 있다'라는 어색한 문맥을 만든다. 부사 (B)와 (D)는 거품절을 이끌 수 없다.

어휘 yet adv. 아직

133 접속부사 채우기 주변 문맥 파악

해설 빈칸이 콤마와 함께 문장의 맨 앞에 온 접속부사 자리이므로, 앞 문장과 빈칸이 있는 문장의 의미 관계를 파악하여 정답을 선택한다. 앞 문장에서 기기에 대한 실험 결과는 해당 모터가 과열에 취약하다는 것을 보여준다고 했고, 빈칸이 있는 문장에서는 Whirl-12 사용을 중단하고 당사의 고객 서비스 센터로 전화할 것을 권고한다고 했으므로, 원인에 대한 결과를 나타낼 때 사용되는 (D) Therefore(따라서, 그러므로)가 정답이다.

어휘 furthermore adv. 더욱이, 뿐만 아니라 instead adv. 대신에

134 알맞은 문장 고르기

해설 (A) 그 기기는 당사의 가장 인기 있는 모델 중 하나입니다.
(B) 귀하께서는 환불을 받기 위한 설명을 제공받으실 것입니다.
(C) 저희는 항상 고객들의 의견을 받는 것에 관심이 있습니다.
(D) 첫 면접은 전화로 수행될 것입니다.

해설 앞 문장 'we advise you to stop using the Whirl-12 and call our customer service center at your convenience'에서 Whirl-12 사용을 중단하고 고객 서비스 센터로 전화할 것을 권고한다고 했으므로 빈칸에는 환불을 받기 위한 설명을 제공받을 거라는 고객 서비스 관련 내용이 들어가야 함을 알 수 있다. 따라서 (B)가 정답이다.

어휘 instruction n. 설명, 지시 initial adj. 처음의, 최초의
interview n. 면접 conduct v. 수행하다, (활동을) 하다

135-138번은 다음 광고에 관한 문제입니다.

Cadenta와 함께 건강해지세요!

저희의 전문 지식과 최첨단 기술을 활용하여 현명한 방법으로 좋은 몸 상태를 유지하세요. 한정된 기간 동안, 최초 이용자들은 20퍼센트 할인을 받을 자격을 얻을 것입니다. ¹³⁵그것은 골드 회원권과 실버 회원권 둘 다에 적용됩니다. ¹³⁶그리고 만약 이번 달에 시작하신다면, 저희의 유능한 전문가들 중 한 명이 귀하의 개인적인 요구에 맞춰 맞춤형 건강 프로그램을 설계할 수 있도록 도울 것입니다.

¹³⁷이 특별한 제안을 이용하기 위해서, 단지 귀하의 휴대폰에 무료 Cadenta 앱을 다운로드하고 시작을 위해 회원권 아이콘을 누르기만 하면 됩니다. ¹³⁸가입하는 데 몇 분밖에 걸리지 않습니다. 다른 회원권 혜택에 관한 세부사항은 저희의 웹사이트에서 확인하실 수 있습니다.

expertise n. 전문 지식 cutting-edge adj. 최첨단의
qualify for ~의 자격을 얻다 professional n. 전문가
design v. 설계하다, 고안하다 personal adj. 개인적인, 개인의
tap v. (가볍게) 누르다, 두드리다 benefit n. 혜택, 이익
available adj. 확인할 수 있는, 이용 가능한

135 올바른 시제의 동사 채우기 주변 문맥 파악

해설 '20퍼센트 할인은 골드 회원권과 실버 회원권 둘 다에 적용된다'라는 문맥인데, 이 경우 빈칸이 있는 문장만으로는 올바른 시제의 동사를 고를 수 없으므로 주변 문맥이나 전체 문맥을 파악하여 정답을 고른다. 앞부분에서 '최초 이용자들은 20퍼센트 할인을 받을 자격이 주어질 것이다(first-time users will qualify for a 20 percent discount)'라고 했고, 할인이 적용되는 대상은 일반적인 사실이므로 현재 시제 (C) applies가 정답이다. 참고로, (B)는 미래완료 시제(will have p.p.)로 미래의 특정 시점 이전에 발생한 동작이 미래의 그 시점에 완료될 것임을 나타낸다.

어휘 apply to ~에 적용되다

136 형용사 어휘 고르기

해설 '유능한 전문가들 중 한 명이 맞춤형 건강 프로그램을 설계할 수 있도록 도울 것이다'라는 문맥이므로 (B) competent(유능한)가 정답이다. (A) clumsy는 '서투른, 어설픈', (C) dominant는 '우세한, 지배적인', (D) recreational은 '오락의, 레크리에이션의'라는 의미이다.

137 to 부정사 채우기

해설 이 문장은 주어가 없는 명령문(simply download ~ get started)이므로, ___ this special offer는 수식어 거품으로 보아야 한다. 이 수식어 거품은 동사가 없는 거품구이므로, 거품구를 이끌 수 있는 전치사구 (B), 분사구 (C), to 부정사구 (D)가 정답의 후보이다. '특별한 제안을 이용하기 위해서 앱을 다운로드하다'라는 의미가 되어야 하므로 목적을 나타내는 to 부정사구 (D) To access가 정답이다. (B) By accessing(이용함으로써)과 (C) Having accessed(이용한 후에)를 쓸 경우 어색한 문맥을 만들기 때문에 답이 될 수 없다.

어휘 access v. 이용하다, 접근하다; n. 접근(권), 입장

138 알맞은 문장 고르기

해석 (A) 39달러에 해당하는 총금액을 배상받으실 것입니다.
(B) 운동 영상을 따라 하시려면 재생 버튼을 누르십시오.
(C) 귀하는 직접 회원권을 신청해야 합니다.
(D) 가입하는 데 몇 분밖에 걸리지 않습니다.

해설 앞 문장 'simply download the free Cadenta app onto your mobile phone and tap on the membership icon to get started'에서 단지 휴대폰에 무료 Cadenta 앱을 다운로드하고 시작을 위해 회원권 아이콘을 누르기만 하면 된다고 했으므로, 빈칸에는 회원 가입과 관련된 내용이 들어가야 함을 알 수 있다. 따라서 (D)가 정답이다.

어휘 reimburse v. 배상하다, 변제하다   press v. 누르다
workout n. 운동   in person 직접   sign up 가입하다, 등록하다

139-142번은 다음 보도 자료에 관한 문제입니다.

즉각 보도용

어바인 (6월 25일) - ¹³⁹Blackwell 출판사는 Cornerstone Books와의 다가오는 파트너십을 발표하게 되어 기쁘다. 이 공동 프로젝트는 7월 1일에 시작될 예정이며 학생들을 위한 일련의 교과서 제작을 포함할 것이다. ¹⁴⁰이 책들은 공립 학교에서의 사용을 위한 것이다.

¹⁴¹Blackwell 출판사의 CEO인 Chloe Samson은 5년 전에 이 프로젝트를 처음 구상했다. 하지만, 적절한 동업자를 찾는 것이 예상했던 것보다 훨씬 오래 걸렸다. 그렇지만, 이 기다림은 그만한 가치가 있었다. ¹⁴²Cornerstone Books는 교육 자료를 제작하는 데 있어 견고한 실적을 가지고 있다. 그래서, Ms. Samson은 어린 학습자들을 대상으로 ◦

하는 이 프로젝트의 성공에 대해 확신하고 있다.

질문은 Blackwell 출판사의 홍보 담당자인 Jane Peters에게 j.peters@blackwell.com으로 보내져야 한다.

upcoming adj. 다가오는, 곧 있을   joint adj. 공동의, 합동의
launch v. 시작하다   involve v. 포함하다   creation n. 제작, 창작
a series of 일련의   textbook n. 교과서   suitable adj. 적절한, 적합한
anticipate v. 예상하다, 기대하다   track record 실적
material n. 자료, 재료   confident adj. 확신하는   direct v. 보내다

139 전치사 채우기

해설 'Blackwell 출판사는 Cornerstone Books와의 파트너십을 발표하다'라는 의미가 되어야 하므로 (C) with(~와)가 정답이다. (A) for는 '~을 위한'이란 의미로 목적이나 대상을, (B) among은 '~ 사이에, ~ 중에'라는 의미로 보통 셋 이상의 사람이나 사물 사이를, (D) above는 '~ 위에, ~ 이상'이라는 의미이다.

140 알맞은 문장 고르기

해석 (A) 우리는 그것들의 인기에 크게 놀랐다.
(B) 이 책들은 공립 학교에서의 사용을 위한 것이다.
(C) 두 회사 모두 더 이상 이 서비스를 제공하지 않을 것이다.
(D) 그 출판물에는 여러 오류들이 있다.

해설 앞 문장 'The joint project will launch on July 1 and will involve the creation of a series of textbooks for students.'에서 합동 프로젝트는 학생들을 위한 일련의 교과서 제작을 포함할 것이라고 했으므로, 빈칸에는 합동 프로젝트로 제작되는 교과서들에 관한 내용이 들어가야 함을 알 수 있다. 따라서 (B)가 정답이다.

어휘 popularity n. 인기   offer v. 제공하다   publication n. 출판(물)

141 시간 표현과 일치하는 시제의 동사 채우기

해설 빈칸이 있는 문장에 주어(Chloe Samson, the CEO of Blackwell Publishing)만 있고 동사가 없으므로 동사 (B)와 (C)가 정답의 후보이다. 빈칸 뒤에 과거를 나타내는 시간 표현(five years ago)이 있으므로 과거 시제 (C) envisioned가 정답이다. 동명사 또는 현재분사 (A), to 부정사 (D)는 동사 자리에 올 수 없다.

어휘 envision v. 구상하다

142 형용사 어휘 고르기 주변 문맥 파악

해설 'Cornerstone Books는 ___ 자료 제작에 있어 견고한 실적을 가지다'라는 문맥이므로 (A), (C), (D)가 정답의 후보이다. 빈칸이 있는 문장만으로 정답을 고를 수 없으므로 주변 문맥이나 전체 문맥을 파악한다. 뒤 문장에서 'Ms. Samson은 어린 학습자들을 대상으로 한 이 프로젝트의 성공에 대해 확신하고 있다(Ms. Samson is confident about the success of this project for young learners)'라고 했으므로 Cornerstone Books가 교육 자료 제작에 있어 견고한 실적을 가지고 있다는 문맥이 되어야 한다. 따라서 (A) educational (교육의)이 정답이다.

어휘 protective adj. 보호하는   synthetic adj. 인조의, 합성의
further adj. 추가의

143-146번은 다음 이메일에 관한 문제입니다.

수신: 고객 서비스 전 직원 <customerservice@JBHotels.com>
발신: Alaina Findley <a.findley@JBHotels.com>
날짜: 5월 9일
제목: 점검

직원들께,

지사의 점검원들이 5월 28일과 6월 2일 사이에 호텔을 방문할 예정이라는 점을 알고 계시기 바랍니다. ¹⁴³이를 고려하여, 저는 여러분들이 자사의 회사 방침에 대해 숙지하고 있길 바랍니다. 이것들은 직원 안내서에서 찾아볼 수 있습니다. ¹⁴⁴특히 염려되는 부분은 우리의 정기적인 고객들이 체크인을 할 때 일부 절차들이 무시되고 있다는 것입니다. 이러한 일을 하는 것은 지양하기 바랍니다. ¹⁴⁵그것은 우리의 종합적인 점수에 부정적인 영향을 끼칠 것입니다.

¹⁴⁶우리의 이전 점검 결과는 제가 예상했던 것과 달랐습니다. 하지만 만약 우리가 함께 노력한다면, 올해에는 더 나을 것이라고 확신합니다.

Alaina Findley 드림

---

inspector n. 점검원, 감독관 regional adj. 지역의, 지방의
in light of ~을 고려하여
familiarize oneself with ~에 대해 숙지하다, 익숙해지다
handbook n. 안내서, 편람 procedure n. 절차
ignore v. 무시하다 regular adj. 정기적인
refrain from ~을 지양하다, ~을 삼가다 previous adj. 이전의

143 명사 어휘 고르기 전체 문맥 파악

해설 '자사의 회사 ____에 대해 숙지하고 있길 바라다'라는 문맥이므로 모든 보기가 정답의 후보이다. 빈칸이 있는 문장만으로 정답을 고를 수 없으므로 주변 문맥이나 전체 문맥을 파악한다. 뒤 문장에서 '이것들은 직원 안내서에서 찾아볼 수 있다(These can be found in the employee handbook).'라고 했고, 뒷부분에서 '특히 염려되는 부분은 정기적인 고객들이 체크인할 때 일부 절차들이 무시되는 것이다(Of particular concern is that some procedures are being ignored ~ guests check in).'라고 했으므로, 빈칸에는 직원 안내서에서 찾아볼 수 있는 회사 방침을 숙지하기를 바란다는 문맥이 되어야 한다. 따라서 (B) policies(방침)가 정답이다.

어휘 executive n. 임원, 대표 finance n. 재정, 금융
structure n. 구조

144 인칭대명사 채우기 전체 문맥 파악

해설 '특히 염려되는 부분은 ____ 정기적인 고객들이 체크인할 때 일부 절차들이 무시되고 있다는 것이다'라는 문맥이므로 모든 보기가 정답의 후보이다. 빈칸이 있는 문장만으로 정답을 고를 수 없으므로 주변 문맥이나 전체 문맥을 파악한다. 이메일의 수신자가 'All customer service staff(고객 서비스 전 직원)'이고 지문의 뒷부분에서 '만약 우리가 함께 노력한다면, 올해에는 더 나을 것이라고 확신한다(if we all work together, I am certain that we will do better this year)'라고 했으므로 우리의 정기적인 고객임을 알 수 있다. 따라서 (C) our(우리의)가 정답이다.

145 알맞은 문장 고르기

해석 (A) 많은 고객들이 내일 아침 늦게 체크아웃할 것을 요청했습니다.
(B) 그 절차는 가까운 시일 내에 변경될 가능성이 있습니다.
(C) 그것은 우리의 종합적인 점수에 부정적인 영향을 끼칠 것입니다.
(D) 우리는 체크인 절차에 몇 가지 변화를 줄 것입니다.

해설 앞 문장 'Please refrain from doing this.'에서 절차를 무시하는 것은 지양해 달라고 요청하고 있으므로, 빈칸에는 절차를 무시하는 것이 초래할 수 있는 부정적인 결과에 대한 내용이 들어가야 함을 알 수 있다. 따라서 (C)가 정답이다.

어휘 procedure n. 절차 overall adj. 종합적인, 전체의

146 명사절 접속사 채우기

해설 빈칸이 포함된 절(____ I expected)이 동사(were)의 보어 역할을 하고 있으므로 문장 내에서 보어로 쓰일 수 있는 명사절을 이끄는 명사절 접속사인 모든 보기가 정답의 후보이다. '이전 점검 결과는 예상했던 것과 다르다'라는 의미가 되어야 하고 빈칸이 포함된 절에 동사(expect)의 목적어가 없으므로, 그 자체가 명사절의 목적어 역할을 하여 뒤에 불완전한 절이 오는 의문대명사 (A) what이 정답이다. 명사절 접속사 (C) that(~라는 것)은 뒤에 완전한 절이 오고, 복합관계대명사 또는 복합관계형용사 (B) whichever(어느 것이든)와 복합관계대명사 (D) whomever(누구든)는 문맥상 어울리지 않으므로 답이 될 수 없다.

PART 7

147-148번은 다음 영수증에 관한 문제입니다.

Applegate 주방용품
질 좋은 주방 도구와 가전제품의 선도적인 공급업체!

상점 번호: 03¹⁴⁷⁻⁽ᶜ⁾상점 위치: 121번지 Parkway로, 시애틀, 워싱턴주
고객: Kent Harper   날짜&판매 시간: ¹⁴⁸7월 11일, 오후 4시 32분

제품: Kellwood 에스프레소 메이커   수량: 1   가격: 330달러
(모델 번호 26152)

-20퍼센트 점포 정리 세일	66달러
합계	264달러
¹⁴⁷⁻⁽ᴮ⁾**현금 지불**	270달러
잔돈	6달러

당신의 주방에 필요한 것을 위해 Applegate를 방문해 주셔서 감사합니다! 만약 당신이 새로운 요리 기술과 요리법을 배우고 싶다면, ¹⁴⁸다음 달부터 무료 요리 수업을 제공할 것입니다. 매주 토요일 오후 2시에, 저희의 재능 있는 강사들 중 한 명이 당신에게 전 세계의 맛있는 요리를 만드는 방법을 가르쳐 줄 것입니다. 세부 사항을 위해서는, www.applegate.com/learntocook을 방문하세요.

---

kitchen supplies 주방용품 quality adj. 질 좋은, 양질의
utensil n. 도구, 기구 appliance n. 가전제품, 기기
talented adj. 재능 있는 instructor n. 강사

147 Not/True 문제

해석 Mr. Harper에 대해 명시된 것은?
(A) 누나를 위해 상품권을 샀다.
(B) 결제에 신용카드를 사용했다.
(C) 시애틀 매장에서 물건을 구매했다.
(D) 환불을 위해 가전제품을 반품했다.

해설 지문의 'Store Location: 121 Parkway Drive, Seattle, WA'에서 Mr. Harper가 물건을 구매한 상점이 시애틀에 있는 것을 알 수 있으므로 (C)가 정답이다. (B)는 'Cash Paid'에서 현금 결제를 했으므로 지문의 내용과 일치하지 않는다. (A)와 (D)는 지문에 언급되지 않은 내용이다.

어휘 payment n. 결제, 지불 make a purchase 물건을 구매하다

148 추론 문제

해석 8월에 무슨 일이 일어날 것 같은가?
(A) 웹사이트가 업데이트될 것이다.
(B) 점포 정리 세일이 시작될 것이다.
(C) 일련의 수업이 열릴 것이다.
(D) 특가 판매가 끝날 것이다.

해설 지문의 'we will be offering free cooking lessons starting next month'에서 다음 달부터 무료 요리 수업을 제공할 것이라고 했고, 영수증의 날짜가 7월이므로, 다음 달인 8월에 수업이 열린다는 사실을 추론할 수 있다. 따라서 (C)가 정답이다.

어휘 a series of 일련의

Paraphrasing

lessons 수업 → classes 수업

149-150번은 다음 광고에 관한 문제입니다.

West Coast 자전거
저희는 10년 넘게 샌프란시스코의 자전거 타기 커뮤니티에 자랑스럽게 서비스를 제공해왔습니다.

¹⁴⁹저희의 네 번째 매장 개점을 놓치지 마세요! 개점식에 참여하기 위해 5월 15일에 Fillmore가 지점에 들르세요.

행사 세부 사항:
- ¹⁵⁰⁻⁽ᴬ⁾선별된 부대용품들에 대해 하루만 50퍼센트 반짝세일
- 당일에 하는 선주문 10퍼센트 할인
- ¹⁵⁰⁻⁽ᶜ⁾헬멧, 물병 및 기타 상품을 획득하기 위한 매시간 추첨
- ¹⁵⁰⁻⁽ᴰ⁾모두를 위한 간식과 바리스타의 커피

행사에 대한 더 많은 정보를 얻으시려면, www.westcoastscycle.com을 방문하세요.

proudly adv. 자랑스럽게 decade n. 10년 launch n. 개점, 시작
take part in ~에 참여하다 flash sale 반짝세일 preorder n. 선주문
draw n. 추첨 win v. 획득하다, 따다

---

149 추론 문제

해석 West Coast 자전거에 대해 결론지을 수 있는 것은?

(A) 설립된 지 10년이 되지 않았다.
(B) 최근에 새로운 위치로 옮겼다.
(C) 여러 지점을 운영하고 있다.
(D) 매장 앞에 주차 공간이 있다.

해설 지문의 'Don't miss the launch of our fourth shop!'에서 네 번째 매장의 개점을 놓치지 말라고 했으므로, 다른 매장이 세 개 더 있다는 사실을 추론할 수 있다. 따라서 (C)가 정답이다.

어휘 establish v. 설립하다 operate v. 운영하다

150 Not/True 문제

해석 행사의 특징으로 나열되지 않은 것은?
(A) 몇몇 제품에 대한 할인이 제공될 것이다.
(B) 적은 수수료로 안전 점검이 수행될 것이다.
(C) 무료 물품들이 나누어질 것이다.
(D) 참석자들에게 다과가 제공될 것이다.

해설 (A)는 'One day only 50 percent flash sale on selected accessories'에서 선별된 부대용품들에 대해 50퍼센트 반짝세일을 한다고 했으므로 지문의 내용과 일치한다. (B)는 지문에 언급되지 않은 내용이다. 따라서 (B)가 정답이다. (C)는 'Hourly draws to win helmets, water bottles, and other prizes'에서 헬멧, 물병 및 기타 상품을 획득하기 위한 추첨이 진행된다고 했으므로 지문의 내용과 일치한다. (D)는 'Snacks and barista coffees for everyone'에서 모두를 위한 간식과 커피가 제공된다고 했으므로 지문의 내용과 일치한다.

어휘 feature n. 특징 complimentary adj. 무료의
refreshment n. 간식, 다과 attendee n. 참석자

Paraphrasing

50 percent flash sale on selected accessories 선별된 부대용품들에 대해 50퍼센트 반짝세일 → Discounts will be offered on some products 몇몇 제품에 대한 할인이 제공될 것이다

Snacks and barista coffees 간식과 바리스타의 커피 → Refreshments 다과

151-152번은 다음 이메일에 관한 문제입니다.

수신: Lisa Martinez <l.martinez@hillcrest.com>
발신: Brant Abernathy <b.abernathy@devondesign.com>
날짜: 11월 25일
제목: 회신: 피드백
¹⁵²첨부 파일: 수정된 버전

Ms. Martinez께,

제 원본 초안에 대한 피드백을 정말 빨리 보내주셔서 감사합니다. ¹⁵¹저는 당신이 당신의 법률 고객들이 약속을 기다리는 동안 편안하기를 원하며, 당신의 동료와 계약서 및 다른 문서들을 검토할 수 있는 더 큰 공간이 필요하다는 것을 이해합니다. 그래서, ¹⁵²저는 접수 공간의 배치를 바꾸고 2층 회의실을 더 크게 만들었습니다. 이것이 프로젝트의 전체 비용에 영향을 미치지는 않을 것이라는 점을 알아두세요.

더 변경하고 싶은 사항이 있으시면 제게 알려주세요. 그렇지 않으

면, ¹⁵²건설사에 바로 이 버전의 청사진을 전달할 것입니다. 작업이 시작되기 전에 수석 엔지니어가 그것들을 검토해야 할 것입니다.

Brant Abernathy 드림

draft n. 초안 legal adj. 법률의 comfortable adj. 편안한
appointment n. 약속 contract n. 계약서 colleague n. 동료
alter v. 바꾸다, 변경하다 layout n. 배치 reception n. 접수
conference room 회의실 affect v. 영향을 미치다
overall adj. 전체의, 전반적인 forward v. 전달하다, 보내다
blueprint n. 청사진 construction n. 건설

151 추론 문제

해석 Ms. Martinez는 누구인 것 같은가?
(A) 접수 담당자
(B) 건축가
(C) 변호사
(D) 의사

해설 지문의 'I understand that you[Ms. Martinez] want your legal clients to be comfortable while they wait for their appointment and that you need a bigger space to review contracts ~.'에서 Ms. Martinez가 그녀의 법률 고객이 약속을 기다리는 동안 편안하기를 원하고 동료와 계약서 및 다른 문서들을 검토할 수 있는 더 큰 공간이 필요하다는 것을 이해한다고 했으므로 Ms. Martinez가 변호사임을 추론할 수 있다. 따라서 (C)가 정답이다.

어휘 receptionist n. 접수 담당자 architect n. 건축가

152 추론 문제

해석 이메일에 무엇이 첨부된 것 같은가?
(A) 조사 양식
(B) 건축 설계도
(C) 고객 목록
(D) 로고 디자인

해설 지문의 'Attachment'의 'Revised Version'에서 첨부 파일이 수정된 버전이고, 'I altered the layout of the reception area and made the second-floor conference room bigger'에서 접수 공간의 배치를 바꾸고 2층 회의실을 더 크게 만들었다고 한 후, 'I will forward this version of the blueprints to the construction company immediately'에서 건설사에 이 버전의 청사진을 전달할 것이라고 했으므로 첨부된 파일이 건축 설계도의 수정된 버전임을 추론할 수 있다. 따라서 (B)가 정답이다.

어휘 survey n. (설문) 조사

Paraphrasing

blueprints 청사진 → A building plan 건축 설계도

153-154번은 다음 문자 메시지 대화문에 관한 문제입니다.

Beverly Willis [오전 11시 29분]
안녕하세요, Noah. 제가 지금 사무실 입구에 있는데, 저의 사원증이 작동하지 않는 것 같아요. 문이 안 열리네요.

Noah Ruffalo [오전 11시 30분]
정말요? ¹⁵³누군가 당신을 들여보낼 수 있도록 그냥 경비실에 전화하세요.

Beverly Willis [오전 11시 31분]
¹⁵³이미 시도해 봤는데, 아무도 전화를 받지 않아요. 아마 그들은 지금 정기 점검을 하고 있을 거예요. 당신을 귀찮게 해도 될까요?

Noah Ruffalo [오전 11시 32분]
저는 약 20분 후에 거기에 도착할 거예요. 저는 지금 당장 고객에게 중요한 전화를 해야 해요.

Beverly Willis [오전 11시 33분]
알겠어요. 그냥 여기서 기다릴게요. 귀찮게 해서 죄송해요.

Noah Ruffalo [오전 11시 34분]
당신은 운이 좋네요. ¹⁵⁴Craig가 그의 차에서 뭔가를 가져오려고 방금 나갔어요. 주차장으로 가는 길에 당신을 들여보내 줄 거예요. 잠시만 기다려 주세요.

Beverly Willis [오전 11시 35분]
잘됐네요. 감사해요.

let ~ in ~를 들여보내다 inspection n. 점검, 검사
trouble v. 실례하다, 귀찮게 하다 bother v. 귀찮게 하다

153 의도 파악 문제

해석 오전 11시 31분에, Ms. Willis가 "Could I trouble you"라고 썼을 때, 그녀가 의도한 것 같은 것은?
(A) 사원증을 찾는 데 도움이 필요하다.
(B) Mr. Ruffalo가 문을 열어주기를 바란다.
(C) 전화를 놓칠까 봐 걱정한다.
(D) Mr. Ruffalo가 고객을 만나야 한다고 생각한다.

해설 지문의 'Just call the security office to ask someone to let you in.'에서 Noah Ruffalo가 Ms. Willis에게 누군가 그녀를 들여보낼 수 있도록 경비실에 전화하라고 하자, 'I already tried that, but no one is answering the phone. They are probably doing their regular inspections right now.'에서 Ms. Willis가 이미 시도해 봤는데 아무도 전화를 받지 않는다고 한 뒤 'Could I trouble you?'(당신을 귀찮게 해도 될까요)라고 한 것을 통해, Mr. Ruffalo가 문을 열어주기를 바란다는 것을 알 수 있다. 따라서 (B)가 정답이다.

154 추론 문제

해석 Craig에 대해 암시되는 것은?
(A) 사무실 건물에 들어갈 수 없다.
(B) 경비원들 중 한 명에게 연락할 것이다.
(C) 차를 댈 비어있는 공간을 찾을 수 없다.
(D) 주차장으로 향하고 있다.

해설 지문의 'Craig just left to get something from his car. He'll let you in on his way to the parking lot.'에서 Craig가 차에서 뭔가를 가져오려고 방금 나갔고 주차장으로 가는 길에 Ms. Willis를 들여보내 줄 거라고 했으므로 Craig가 주차장으로 향하고 있다는 것을 추론할 수 있다. 따라서 (D)가 정답이다.

어휘 empty adj. 비어있는 vehicle n. 차량

155-157번은 다음 편지에 관한 문제입니다.

Mike Gallo
44번지 Pine로
포틀랜드, 오리건주, 97035

Mr. Gallo께,

¹⁵⁵Inland Cellular와의 미결제액 226.98달러에 대해 귀하께서 잊지 않으셨기를 확실히 하고 싶습니다. ― [1] ―. 계약 조건에 명시된 바와 같이, 귀하는 휴대폰 서비스 종료 후 영업일 기준 10일 이내에 이를 지불하셨어야 했습니다. 귀하의 서비스가 취소된 지 30일이 지났지만, 저희는 최종 대금을 받지 못했습니다.

만약 이것이 귀하 측의 실수라면, 저희는 귀하께서 그것을 즉시 처리할 것을 요청합니다. ― [2] ―. ¹⁵⁶지불은 지난달부터 이용 가능해진 저희의 새로운 모바일 앱 또는 저희 웹사이트를 통해 하실 수 있습니다. ¹⁵⁷귀하는 또한 저희 지점들 중 어느 곳이든 들르셔도 됩니다. ― [3] ―. 만약 귀하께서 이 요금에 이의를 제기하고 싶으시거나 재정적인 문제로 인해 현재 지불할 수 없다면, 555-9383으로 저희에게 전화주십시오. 매달 첫날에 귀하의 잔액에 15퍼센트의 연체료가 적용될 것이라는 점을 알아두십시오. ― [4] ―. 감사합니다.

Beth Coyle 드림
Inland Cellular 청구서 발송팀

outstanding balance 미결제액 specify v. 명시하다
terms n. 조건 contract n. 계약 business day 영업일
payment n. 대금, 지불 oversight n. 실수 stop by ~에 들르다
dispute v. 이의를 제기하다, 논쟁하다 unable adj. ~할 수 없는
balance n. 잔액, 잔고 billing n. 청구서 발송

155 목적 찾기 문제

해석 편지의 목적은 무엇인가?
(A) 몇몇 계약 조건의 변경을 설명하기 위해
(B) 연체된 요금에 대해 고객에게 상기시키기 위해
(C) 이전에 취소된 서비스를 되돌리는 것을 제안하기 위해
(D) 최종 대금이 수령됐음을 확인하기 위해

해설 지문의 'We want to make sure that you haven't forgotten about your outstanding balance of $226.98 with Inland Cellular.'에서 Inland Cellular와의 미결제액 226.98달러에 대해 고객이 잊지 않았기를 확실히 하고 싶다고 했으므로 (B)가 정답이다.

어휘 remind v. 상기시키다 overdue adj. 연체된, 지불 기한이 지난
restore v. 되돌리다, 복구하다 confirm v. 확인하다

Paraphrasing

outstanding balance 미결제액 → an overdue charge 연체된 요금

156 육하원칙 문제

해석 지난달에 무슨 일이 있었는가?
(A) 애플리케이션이 대중에게 이용 가능하게 되었다.
(B) 지점이 잠정적으로 폐쇄되었다.
(C) 연체료가 인상되었다.
(D) 고객을 위해 청구 날짜가 변경되었다.

해설 지문의 'Payment can be made through our new mobile app that became available last month or our Web site.'에서 지불은 지난달부터 이용 가능해진 새로운 모바일 앱 또는 웹사이트를 통해 할 수 있다고 했으므로 (A)가 정답이다.

어휘 accessible adj. 이용 가능한 temporarily adv. 잠정적으로
increase v. 인상하다, 늘어나다

157 문장 위치 찾기 문제

해석 [1], [2], [3], [4]로 표시된 위치 중, 다음 문장이 들어갈 곳으로 가장 적절한 것은?

"그것들은 월요일부터 토요일, 오전 10시부터 오후 8시까지 영업합니다."

(A) [1]
(B) [2]
(C) [3]
(D) [4]

해설 주어진 문장은 매장 영업과 관련된 내용 주변에 나올 것임을 예상할 수 있다. [3]의 앞 문장인 'You can also stop by any of our branch offices.'에서 지점들 중 어느 곳이든 들러도 된다고 했으므로, [3]에 주어진 문장이 들어가면 지점들 중 어느 곳이든 들러도 되는데, 그것들은 월요일부터 토요일, 오전 10시부터 오후 8시까지 영업한다는 자연스러운 문맥이 된다는 것을 알 수 있다. 따라서 (C)가 정답이다.

158-160번은 다음 기사에 관한 문제입니다.

로스앤젤레스 (4월 15일)―¹⁵⁸도시의 3D 프린터로 인쇄된 첫 번째 집이 오늘 시장에 나왔다. Atlas 건축사의 Sandra Porter가 설계한 120제곱미터 크기의 이 집은 학생들에게 인기 있는 지역인 벨몬트의 중심부에 위치해 있다.

¹⁵⁸이 집은 시멘트와 같은 재료를 여러 겹 바르는 로봇 팔을 포함하는 혁신적인 과정을 사용하여 건설되었다. 이 장치들은 설계 단계 동안 Porter가 만들어 낸 디지털 청사진을 따르도록 프로그래밍되었다.

최근의 인터뷰에서, Porter는 3D 프린팅이 건설 산업의 미래라고 주장했고 그것이 ¹⁵⁹주택 부족 문제에 대한 잠재적인 해결책이라고 주장했다. "이 기술로, 알맞은 가격대의 수많은 집들이 단기간에 지어질 수 있습니다."

^{160-(B)}Porter는 또한 불과 두 달 전에 Atlas 건축사를 인수한 Vernon Shaw에게 감사를 표했다. "Mr. Shaw는 3D 프린팅의 장점들을 완전히 이해하고 있습니다,"라고 그녀가 설명했다. "이 프로젝트를 매우 성공적으로 만든 것은 바로 이 프로젝트에 관련된 직원들에 대한 그의 열렬한 지지였습니다."

neighborhood n. 지역, 근처 innovative adj. 혁신적인
involve v. 포함하다 material n. 재료 device n. 장치, 기구
claim v. 주장하다 potential adj. 잠재적인
housing-shortage 주택 부족 put up (건물 등을) 짓다, 세우다
appreciation n. 감사 advantage n. 장점, 이점
enthusiastic adj. 열렬한

158 목적 찾기 문제

해석 기사는 왜 쓰여졌는가?
(A) 수상자를 축하하기 위해
(B) 도시의 주택 시장에 대한 개요를 제공하기 위해
(C) 새로운 건축 방법의 이용을 설명하기 위해
(D) 지역 부동산의 상승하는 비용을 설명하기 위해

해설 지문의 'The city's first 3D-printed house went on the market today.'에서 3D 프린터로 인쇄된 첫 번째 집이 오늘 시장에 나왔다고 했고, 'The house was constructed using an innovative process that involves robotic arms applying layers of materials such as cement.'에서 그 집은 시멘트와 같은 재료를 여러 겹 바르는 로봇 팔을 포함하는 혁신적인 과정을 사용하여 건설되었다고 한 후, 건설 산업에서 3D 프린팅 이용이 주는 이점 등을 설명하고 있으므로 (C)가 정답이다.

어휘 award recipient 수상자 overview n. 개요
describe v. 설명하다 method n. 방법 property n. 부동산, 재산

159 동의어 찾기 문제

해석 3문단 네 번째 줄의 단어 "solution"은 의미상 -와 가장 가깝다.
(A) 혼합물
(B) 제안
(C) 해결책
(D) 효과

해설 solution을 포함한 구절 'solution to the housing-shortage problem'에서 solution은 '해결책'이라는 뜻으로 사용되었다. 따라서 (C)가 정답이다.

160 Not/True 문제

해석 Ms. Porter가 Atlas 건축사에 대해 명시하는 것은?
(A) 작년에 로스앤젤레스로 이전했다.
(B) 최근 고위 경영진이 변경되었다.
(C) 추가 직원들을 채용할 계획을 발표했다.
(D) 디자인 과정에 대한 몇몇 개선 작업을 완료했다.

해설 지문의 'Porter also expressed her appreciation for Vernon Shaw, who took over Atlas Architecture just two months ago.'에서 Porter는 두 달 전에 Atlas 건축사를 인수한 Vernon Shaw에게 감사를 표했다고 했으므로 최근에 Atlas 건축사의 고위 경영진이 변경되었다는 것을 알 수 있다. 따라서 (B)가 정답이다. (A), (C), (D)는 지문에 명시되지 않은 내용이다.

어휘 relocate to ~로 이전하다 undergo v. 겪다, 경험하다
additional adj. 추가의 finalize v. 완료하다

161-163번은 다음 이메일에 관한 문제입니다.

수신: Hua Lin <h.lin@alloramed.com>
발신: Wesley Harrison <w.harrison@selerant.com>
날짜: 6월 24일
제목: 회신: 제휴 제안

Ms. Lin께,

Selerant사를 귀하의 사업을 성장시킬 동업자로 생각해 주셔서 감사합니다. 하지만, Alloramed사의 제안을 고려해 본 결과, [161]현재로서는 당사의 전략적 우선순위와 맞지 않다고 판단했습니다. 현재, 당사는 의료 기술 산업에서 새로운 벤처 기업을 찾고 있는 것이 아니라 대신 인공지능, 에너지, 그리고 칩 제조의 혁신을 추진하는 데 주력하고 있습니다. 게다가, [162]당사는 현재 제품 개발의 진보된 단계에 있는 기업들과만 제휴를 추구하고 있습니다.

당사는 귀하의 사업 아이디어의 잠재력을 잘 알고 있으며, 귀하께서 Boncorp 캐피털사에 연락하는 것을 추천하고 싶습니다. 뉴욕시에 기반을 둔 Boncorp 캐피털사는 귀하의 산업에 속한 신생기업들을 지원하는 것을 전문으로 합니다. [163]그곳은 귀하의 사업을 다음 단계로 나아가게 하는 데 필요한 자원을 갖춘 금융 기관과 연결해 드릴 수 있습니다.

다시 한번, 고려해 주셔서 감사드리며, 귀하의 모든 노력에 행운이 깃들기를 기원합니다.

Wesley Harrison 드림
수석 부사장, Selerant사

proposal n. 제안 consider v. 생각하다, 고려하다
determine v. 판단하다 align v. 맞추다, 제휴하다
strategic adj. 전략적인 priority n. 우선순위
advance v. 추진하다, 진행시키다 artificial intelligence 인공지능
manufacturing n. 제조 pursue v. 추구하다
advanced adj. 진보된, 상급의 development n. 개발, 발달
specialize v. 전문으로 하다 assist v. 지원하다 start-up n. 신생기업
resource n. 자원, 자금 propel v. 나아가게 하다 endeavor n. 노력

161 육하원칙 문제

해석 Mr. Harrison은 왜 Ms. Lin의 제안을 거절하는가?
(A) 그녀는 정해진 마감기한을 맞추지 못했다.
(B) 그녀는 몇몇 필요한 정보를 제공하지 않았다.
(C) 그녀의 사업은 회사의 목표와 맞지 않는다.
(D) 그녀의 투자 요구 사항이 너무 많다.

해설 지문의 'we have determined that it does not align with our strategic priorities at this time'이라며 Selerant사의 전략적 우선순위와 맞지 않다고 했고, 이어서 'At present, we are not seeking new ventures in the medical technology industry and are instead focused on advancing innovations in ~.'에서 현재 Mr. Harrison의 회사는 의료 기술 산업에서 새로운 벤처 기업을 찾고 있는 것이 아니라 인공지능, 에너지, 그리고 칩 제조의 혁신을 추진하는 데 주력하고 있다고 했으므로 (C)가 정답이다.

어휘 reject v. 거절하다, 거부하다 stated adj. 정해진, 규정된
investment n. 투자 requirement n. 요구 사항, 필요조건

162 추론 문제

해석 Alloramed사에 대해 암시되는 것은?
(A) 6월에 대개 바쁘다.
(B) 개발 초기 단계에 있다.
(C) 새로운 최고 경영자를 고용해야 한다.
(D) 대출 상환에 대한 도움을 구하고 있다.

해설 지문의 'we[Selerant] are currently only pursuing

partnerships with firms that are at an advanced stage of product development'에서 Selerant사는 제품 개발의 진보된 단계에 있는 기업들과만 제휴를 추구하고 있을 뿐이라고 하며 Alloramed사의 제안을 거절하고 있으므로 Alloramed사는 개발 초기 단계에 있다는 것을 추론할 수 있다. 따라서 (B)가 정답이다.

어휘 **chief executive** 최고 경영자 **assistance** n. 도움
repay v. 상환하다, 갚다 **loan** n. 대출

163 육하원칙 문제

해석 이메일에 따르면, Boncorp 캐피털사와 함께 일하는 것의 이익은 무엇일 수 있는가?
(A) 전 세계의 지역사회로부터의 인정
(B) 최첨단 연구를 위한 기회
(C) 관리 시스템 구축에 대한 지원
(D) 자금 출처와의 연결

해설 지문의 'It[Boncorp Capital] can connect you to financial institutions with the resources you need to propel your business to the next stage.'에서 Boncorp 캐피털사가 사업을 다음 단계로 나아가게 하는 데 필요한 자원을 갖춘 금융 기관과 연결해 줄 수 있다고 했으므로 (D)가 정답이다.

어휘 **acknowledgment** n. 인정, 승인 **cutting-edge** adj. 최첨단의

Paraphrasing

financial institutions with the resources 자원을 갖춘 금융 기관 → funding sources 자금 출처

164-167번은 다음 문자 메시지 대화문에 관한 문제입니다.

Emily Neal (오후 1시 20분)
내일 Nova 전자회사 담당자들과 화상회의를 할 준비가 다 되었나요? ¹⁶⁴이 회사는 주요 고객이 될 가능성이 있어요. 저는 우리가 그 회사의 마케팅을 담당할 수 있게 선정되도록 확실히 하고 싶어요.

Luke Sawyer (오후 1시 21분)
¹⁶⁵저는 우리가 보여주려고 계획한 샘플 소셜 미디어 광고를 약간 수정하는 것을 지금 막 끝냈어요. 배경색을 변경했고 회사 로고를 조금 더 크게 만들었습니다.

Amanda Kim (오후 1시 23분)
¹⁶⁶작성된 내용은 어떤가요, Emily? 제가 수정했으면 하는 내용이 있나요? 제가 오늘 늦게 그것을 작업할 시간이 좀 있을 거예요.

Emily Neal (오후 1시 24분)
전혀 없어요. ¹⁶⁶Nova 전자회사의 최신 제품인 음파 헤드폰의 특징을 정말 잘 강조하셨어요.

Amanda Kim (오후 1시 25분)
다행이네요. ¹⁶⁷⁻⁽ᴬ⁾무게가 얼마나 적게 나가는지 그리고 ¹⁶⁷⁻⁽ᴮ⁾그것을 가지고 다닐 보호용 케이스에 신경을 너무 많이 써서 조금 걱정이 됐어요. 뛰어난 음질이나 ¹⁶⁷⁻⁽ᶜ⁾감도가 좋은 마이크에 대한 자료는 더 필요 없을까요?

Emily Neal (오후 1시 27분)
우리는 그것을 충분히 강조했어요. 타깃 시장은 운동하거나 야외에서 일하는 동안 쓸 ¹⁶⁷⁻⁽ᴰ⁾무선 헤드셋이 필요한 사람들이에요. 우리는

그것들이 사용하기에 얼마나 편리한지 분명히 하고 싶어요.

Luke Sawyer (오후 1시 28분)
동의해요. Nova 전자회사가 감명받을 것 같아요.

representative n. 담당자, 대표자 **potential** n. 가능성, 잠재력
tweak n. (약간의) 수정, 변경 **highlight** v. 강조하다
sound wave 음파 **weigh** v. 무게가 나가다
protective adj. 보호용의, 보호하는 **sensitive** adj. 감도가 좋은, 민감한
stress v. 강조하다 **wireless** adj. 무선의 **convenient** adj. 편리한
impressed adj. 감명받은

164 추론 문제

해석 작성자들에 대해 결론지을 수 있는 것은?
(A) 지난주에 학회에 참여했다.
(B) 프로젝트 마감일을 놓쳤다.
(C) 최근 Nova 전자회사에 고용되었다.
(D) 광고 분야에 종사하고 있다.

해설 지문의 'This company[Nova Electronics] has the potential to be a major client. I want to make sure we are chosen to handle its marketing.'에서 Emily Neal이 Nova 전자회사는 주요 고객이 될 가능성이 있어서 우리가 이 회사의 마케팅을 담당하고 싶다고 한 후, 회의에서 보여줄 샘플 광고에 대한 내용으로 메시지가 이어지고 있으므로 메시지 작성자들이 광고 분야에 종사하고 있음을 추론할 수 있다. 따라서 (D)가 정답이다.

어휘 **field** n. 분야

165 추론 문제

해석 Mr. Sawyer는 누구일 것 같은가?
(A) 컴퓨터 기술자
(B) 기자
(C) 그래픽 디자이너
(D) 사진작가

해설 지문의 'I just finished making a few tweaks to the sample social media ad we plan to show. I changed the background color and made the company's logo a bit bigger.'에서 Mr. Sawyer가 샘플 소셜 미디어 광고를 약간 수정했다며, 배경색을 변경했고 회사 로고를 조금 더 크게 만들었다고 했으므로 Mr. Sawyer는 그래픽 디자이너임을 추론할 수 있다. 따라서 (C)가 정답이다.

어휘 **technician** n. 기술자

166 의도 파악 문제

해석 오후 1시 24분에, Ms. Neal이 "Not at all"이라고 썼을 때 무엇을 의도하는가?
(A) 일부 내용을 아직 검토하지 않았다.
(B) 현재 버전에 만족한다.
(C) 강조할 특징을 선택할 수 없다.
(D) 다른 제품을 홍보하고 싶어 한다.

해설 지문의 'What about the written content, Emily? Are there any revisions you'd like me to make?'에서 Ms. Kim이 작

성된 내용에서 수정했으면 하는 것이 있는지 묻자, Ms. Neal이 'Not at all'(전혀 없어요)이라고 한 후, 'You did a great job of highlighting the features of Nova Electronics' latest product, the Sound Wave Headphones.'에서 Nova 전자회사의 최신 제품인 음파 헤드폰의 특징을 잘 강조했다고 한 것을 통해, 현재 버전에 만족한다는 것을 알 수 있다. 따라서 (B)가 정답이다.

어휘 satisfy v. 만족시키다 current adj. 현재의
emphasize v. 강조하다 promote v. 홍보하다

167 Not/True 문제

해석 음파 헤드폰에 대해 사실이 아닌 것은?
(A) 가벼운 재료로 만들어진다.
(B) 가지고 다닐 케이스와 함께 판매된다.
(C) 마이크가 달려 있지 않다.
(D) 사용하기 위해 코드가 필요하지 않다.

해설 (A)는 'how little they weigh'에서 무게가 적게 나간다고 했으므로 지문의 내용과 일치한다. (B)는 'the protective case to carry them'에서 가지고 다닐 보호용 케이스가 있다고 했으므로 지문의 내용과 일치한다. (C)는 'sensitive microphone'에서 감도가 좋은 마이크를 제공한다고 했으므로 지문의 내용과 일치하지 않는다. 따라서 (C)가 정답이다. (D)는 'a wireless headset'에서 무선 헤드셋을 제공한다고 했으므로 지문의 내용과 일치한다.

어휘 lightweight adj. 가벼운 come with ~이 딸려 있다

Paraphrasing

> how little they weigh 얼마나 무게가 적게 나가는지 → lightweight 가벼운
>
> wireless 무선의 → do not require a cord to use 사용하기 위해 코드가 필요하지 않다

168-171번은 다음 공고에 관한 문제입니다.

Secure Space — 장기 셀프 보관소

[168]Secure Space에 보관 칸을 예약해 주셔서 감사합니다. 저희의 모든 시설은 최첨단 보안 시스템을 갖추고 있으며 고객에게 365일 24시간 이용 서비스를 제공합니다. [168]아래의 중요한 정보에 주목해 주십시오:

시설	요금	지불 방법
[169]벌링턴 지점: 124번지 North가, 벌링턴, 버몬트주 02108	공간 임대료: 225달러 (3개월 동안 월 75달러) 관리비: 60달러 (3개월 동안 월 20달러) 세금: 25달러 총액: 310달러	신용카드: XXXX-0505-03948 미결제액: 0달러

고객 정보	공간 세부 사항
이름: Nelson Petrov [169]집 주소: 234번지, Oak가, 댈러스, 텍사스주, 75001 전화번호: 555-8273 이메일: n.petrov@hotspot.com	공간 크기: 16평방미터 임대 기간 시작: 4월 1일 오후 3시 임대 기간 종료: 6월 30일 오전 11시 추가 구매 보험: 없음

비고:
• 분실된 각 보관 칸 열쇠를 교체하는 데 15달러의 수수료가 부과될 것입니다.
• [170]고객들은 임대 기간이 시작하기 전에 보관될 물건에 대한 상세한 물품 목록을 제공해야 합니다.
• [171]월 사용료에 대한 환불 요청은 지점에 직접 방문해서 하셔야 합니다.
• 모든 시설 규정의 완전한 목록을 위해서는 www.securespace.com을 방문하십시오.

long-term adj. 장기적인 storage n. 보관(소), 저장
state-of-the-art adj. 최첨단의, 최신식의
round-the-clock adj. 24시간 연속의
administrative adj. 관리의, 행정의
outstanding balance 미결제액, 체납액 insurance n. 보험
inventory n. 물품 목록, 재고 store v. 보관하다 in person 직접
regulation n. 규정

168 목적 찾기 문제

해석 공지의 목적은 무엇인가?
(A) 보안을 개선하는 방법을 설명하기 위해
(B) 대여 정책의 변경을 설명하기 위해
(C) 보관 시설 예약을 확인하기 위해
(D) 보험에 대한 규정을 소개하기 위해

해설 지문의 'Thank you for booking a storage unit at Secure Space.'에서 Secure Space에 보관 칸을 예약해 주셔서 감사하다고 했고, 예약 정보들을 표로 보여주며 확인하라고 했으므로 (C)가 정답이다.

어휘 method n. 방법 introduce v. 소개하다

169 추론 문제

해석 Mr. Petrov에 대해 암시되는 것은?
(A) 총 두 달 동안 공간을 사용할 수 있다.
(B) 그 시설이 위치한 도시에 살지 않는다.
(C) 추가 보험에 가입해야 할 것이다.
(D) Secure Space에 지불해야 할 금액을 지불하지 않았다.

해설 지문의 'Burlington Branch: 124 North Avenue, Burlington, VT, 02108'과 'Home Address: 234 Oak Street, Dallas TX, 75001'에서 보관 시설은 벌링턴에 있다고 했고, Mr. Petrov의 집은 텍사스주의 댈러스에 있다고 했으므로 Mr. Petrov가 그 시설과 같은 도시에 살지 않는다는 것을 추론할 수 있다. 따라서 (B)가 정답이다.

어휘 owe v. 지불할 의무가 있다

170 추론 문제

해석 Mr. Petrov는 Secure Space에 무엇을 제출할 것 같은가?
(A) 열쇠에 대한 보증금
(B) 계약서 사본
(C) 소지품 목록
(D) 배송 주소

해설 지문의 'Customers must provide a detailed inventory of

what will be stored before the rental period starts.'에서 고객은 임대 기간이 시작하기 전에 보관될 물건에 대한 상세한 물품 목록을 제공해야 한다고 했으므로 Mr. Petrov가 소지품 목록을 제출할 것이라는 것을 추론할 수 있다. 따라서 (C)가 정답이다.

어휘 deposit n. 보증금 agreement n. 계약서, 계약
belongings n. 소지품, 소유물

171 육하원칙 문제

해석 고객들은 어떻게 환불을 요청할 수 있는가?
(A) 번호로 전화함으로써
(B) 이메일을 보냄으로써
(C) 시설을 방문함으로써
(D) 웹사이트에 접속함으로써

해설 지문의 'Requests for a refund of a monthly fee must be made by visiting a branch in person.'에서 월 사용료에 대한 환불 요청은 지점에 직접 방문해서 해야 한다고 했으므로 (C)가 정답이다.

172-175번은 다음 광고에 관한 문제입니다.

Devon 서비스사

Devon 서비스사는 직원들이 미래의 도전에 대비하는 것에 전념합니다. — [1] —. 172저희는 리더십 개발, 영업 전략 및 비즈니스 협상을 포함한 광범위한 주제에 대한 워크숍을 제공합니다. 이 프로그램들은 현 시장의 수요와 새로운 업계 트렌드를 모두 충족하도록 고안되어 귀사의 직원들이 확실히 경쟁력을 갖추고 준비된 상태를 유지할 수 있도록 합니다.

20년 이상, 댈러스 지역에서 최고의 교육 시설이었으며, 173-(B)지난 3개월 동안 휴스턴과 오스틴에 사무실을 열었습니다. — [2] —. 당사의 폭넓은 고객층은 금융 서비스에서 보건 의료에 이르기까지 다양한 업계를 포괄하고 있습니다. 귀사의 직원들이 무엇을 하든, 저희는 그들이 더 잘할 수 있게 도울 능력과 지식이 있습니다. 175저희의 모든 강사들은 각자의 분야에서 고급 학위를 가지고 있습니다. — [3] —.

현장 워크숍
• 모든 매뉴얼 및 기타 교육 자료는 사전에 제공될 것입니다.
• 인기 있는 워크숍 프로그램들 중 하나를 선택하거나 당사와 협력하여 귀사의 특정 목표에 맞춰 조정한 맞춤형 워크숍을 만드십시오.

온라인 과정
• 가상의 강의실에 편리하게 접속하여 어디서나 학습할 수 있습니다.
• 모든 수업 자료(강의 녹화 포함)를 매 수업 후 다운로드할 수 있습니다.

174-(A)귀하의 요구 사항과 그것들을 가장 잘 충족시킬 수 있는 방법에 대한 사전 논의 일정을 잡기 위해서는 555-3939로 전화하세요. — [4] —. 174-(B)그러면 저희 책임자들 중 한 명이 귀하를 뵙기 위해 귀하의 사업장을 방문할 것입니다. 174-(C)이것은 최대 30분에서 45분이 소요될 것이며, 174-(D)비용은 전혀 없습니다. 곧 소식을 들을 수 있기를 바랍니다!

---

challenge n. 도전 tactic n. 전략, 전술 negotiation n. 협상
premier adj. 최고의 diverse adj. 다양한 industry n. 업계, 산업
healthcare n. 보건 의료 knowledge n. 지식
respective adj. 각자의 on-site adj. 현장의 virtual adj. 가상의
fulfill v. 충족시키다 coordinator n. 책임자 absolutely adv. 전혀

172 육하원칙 문제

해석 Devon 서비스사는 무슨 일을 하는가?
(A) 기업 교육 행사를 제공한다.
(B) 소매점을 위한 모바일 판매 플랫폼을 운영한다.
(C) 기업들의 재무 실적을 분석한다.
(D) 사업주를 위한 채용 서비스를 제공한다.

해설 지문의 'We offer workshops on a wide range of topics, including leadership development, sales tactics, and business negotiations.'에서 Devon 서비스사가 리더십 개발, 영업 전략 및 비즈니스 협상을 포함한 광범위한 주제에 대한 워크숍을 제공한다고 했으므로 (A)가 정답이다.

어휘 corporate adj. 기업의 operate v. 운영하다
recruitment n. 채용

Paraphrasing

workshops 워크숍 → corporate training events 기업 교육 행사

173 Not/True 문제

해석 Devon 서비스사에 대해 언급된 것은?
(A) 댈러스 지역으로 이전할 계획이다.
(B) 최근에 사업을 확장했다.
(C) 연간 계약서를 요구한다.
(D) 상담 절차를 간소화할 것이다.

해설 지문의 'we have opened offices in Houston and Austin over the past three months'에서 지난 3개월 동안 휴스턴과 오스틴에 사무실을 열었다고 했으므로 (B)가 정답이다.

어휘 expand v. 확장하다, 확대하다 operation n. 사업, 영업
simplify v. 간소화하다

174 Not/True 문제

해석 첫 상담에 대해 사실인 것은?
(A) 전화로 준비될 수 있다.
(B) Devon 서비스사의 본사에서 일어난다.
(C) 약 2시간 동안 지속된다.
(D) 약간의 수수료를 지불해야 한다.

해설 (A)는 'To arrange a preliminary discussion ~, call 555-3939.'에서 사전 논의 일정을 잡기 위해서는 555-3939로 전화하라고 했으므로 지문의 내용과 일치한다. 따라서 (A)가 정답이다. (B)는 'One of our coordinators will then travel to your place of business'에서 책임자들 중 한 명이 귀하의 사업장으로 갈 것이라고 했으므로 지문의 내용과 일치하지 않는다. (C)는 'This should take 30 to 45 minutes at most'에서 이것은 최대 30분에서 45분이 소요될 것이라고 했으므로 지문의 내용과 일치하지 않는다. (D)는 'there is absolutely no charge'에서 비용은 전혀 없다고 했으므로 지문의 내용과 일치하지 않는다.

어휘 arrange v. 준비하다, 주선하다, 예정을 세우다 last for 지속하다
fee n. 수수료

175 문장 위치 찾기 문제

해석 [1], [2], [3], [4]로 표시된 위치 중, 다음 문장이 들어갈 곳으로 가장 적절한 것은?

"그들은 또한 최소 10년 이상의 관련 경험이 있습니다."

(A) [1]
(B) [2]
(C) [3]
(D) [4]

해설 주어진 문장은 경력과 관련된 내용 주변에 나올 것임을 예상할 수 있다. [3]의 앞 문장인 'All of our instructors have advanced degrees in their respective fields.'에서 모든 강사들은 각자의 분야에서 고급 학위를 가지고 있다고 했으므로, [3]에 주어진 문장이 들어가면 모든 강사들이 각자의 분야에서 고급 학위를 가지고 있고 최소 10년 이상의 관련 경험이 있다는 자연스러운 문맥이 된다는 것을 알 수 있다. 따라서 (C)가 정답이다.

어휘 minimum n. 최소   relevant adj. 관련 있는

176-180번은 다음 기사와 이메일에 관한 문제입니다.

두바이 (9월 15일) — ¹⁷⁶두바이 국제 공항으로 비행기를 타고 들어오는 승객들은 시내에 서둘러 도착할 수 있는 새로운 선택권을 곧 갖게 될 것이다! Palm 항공사는 두 달 전 자사의 무인 항공 택시 시스템에 대한 최종 안전 테스트를 성공적으로 마쳤다. ¹⁷⁷이 테스트 결과에 지지를 받아, 회사는 정부와의 단기 계약을 얻어 냈다. ¹⁷⁹Palm 항공사의 항공 택시 여섯 대가 참여하는 3개월간의 시운전이 10월 1일에 시작될 것이다. 만약 이 시운전이 성공적이면, 그 후에 곧 정기적인 운영이 시작될 것이다.

네 명의 승객과 그들의 짐을 수용할 수 있는 그 드론 항공기는 공항에서 도심까지의 이동 시간을 1시간에서 단 10분으로 줄인다. 그러나, Palm 항공사의 CEO Ahmed Habib에 따르면, 승객의 편의를 넘어서는 장점들이 있다. ¹⁷⁸"저희 항공 택시는 완전히 전기로 움직이고 그렇기 때문에 그 어떠한 주목할 만한 오염 물질도 발생시키지 않습니다"라고 목요일 기자회견에서 말했다. "그것들을 저희의 교통망에 포함하는 것은 도시의 공기 질을 크게 향상시킬 것입니다."

in a hurry 서둘러   successfully adv. 성공적으로
unmanned adj. 무인의   secure v. (특히 힘들게) 얻어 내다, 획득하다
contract n. 계약   government n. 정부   trial n. 시운전, 시험
aircraft n. 항공기   accommodate v. 수용하다
convenience n. 편의   electric adj. 전기로 움직이는
generate v. 발생시키다   significant adj. 주목할 만한, 중대한
pollutant n. 오염 물질   press conference 기자회견
incorporate v. 포함하다   transportation n. 교통

수신: Ahmed Habib<a.habib@palmflight.com>
발신: Lina Amin<l.amin@acesolutions.com>
제목: 최신 정보
날짜: 2월 25일

Mr. Habib께,

항공 택시 프로젝트의 검토 진행 상황에 대한 귀하의 정보 요청을 받았습니다. ¹⁷⁹저희 팀은 11월 1일에 Palm 항공사의 시운전이 시작 ○

되었을 때 수집한 데이터를 아직 분석 중입니다. 우리나라에서 드론 항공기가 승객을 운송하는 데 사용된 것은 이번이 처음이기 때문에, 검토 과정을 서두르고 싶지 않습니다. ¹⁸⁰저희의 최종 분석은 3월 3일에 교통부에 제출할 준비가 될 것으로 예상합니다.

제가 더 도와드릴 일이 있으면 알려주세요.

Lina Amin 드림
분석가
Ace Solutions사

---

analyze v. 분석하다   collect v. 수집하다   rush v. 서두르다
analysis n. 분석   analyst n. 분석가

176 목적 찾기 문제

해석 기사의 목적은 무엇인가?
(A) 공공시설 확장을 발표하기 위해
(B) 안전 절차를 명확하게 하기 위해
(C) 계약 협상에 대한 최신 정보를 제공하기 위해
(D) 새로운 교통수단을 소개하기 위해

해설 기사의 'Passengers flying into Dubai International Airport will soon have a new option to get downtown in a hurry!'에서 두바이 국제 공항으로 비행기를 타고 들어오는 승객들은 시내에 서둘러 도착할 수 있는 새로운 선택권을 곧 갖게 될 것이라고 했고 기사에서 드론 항공기의 도입 일정과 장점에 대해 다루고 있으므로 (D)가 정답이다.

어휘 expansion n. 확장, 확대   public facility 공공시설
clarify v. 명확하게 하다   procedure n. 절차   means n. 수단, 방법

177 동의어 찾기 문제

해석 기사에서, 1문단 세 번째 줄의 단어 "backed"는 의미상 -와 가장 가깝다.
(A) 거꾸로 된
(B) 지원받는
(C) 조직화된
(D) 대변되는

해설 backed를 포함한 구절 'The company, backed by the results of these tests, secured a short-term contract with the government.'에서 backed는 '지지를 받는'이라는 뜻으로 사용되었다. 따라서 (B)가 정답이다.

178 육하원칙 문제

해석 Mr. Habib이 기자회견에서 논의한 것은 무엇인가?
(A) 증가한 오염의 위험성
(B) 기술의 이점
(C) 여행 서비스 비용
(D) 좋지 못한 공기 질의 원인

해설 기사의 '"Our air taxis are fully electric and therefore do not generate any significant pollutants," ~. "Incorporating them into our transportation network will greatly improve the air quality of our city."'에서 Ahmed Habib은 기자회견에서 항공 택시는 완전히 전기로 움직이고 그렇기 때문에 주목할 만한

오염 물질을 발생시키지 않고, 그것들을 교통망에 포함하면 도시의 공기 질이 크게 향상될 것이라고 말했다고 했으므로 (B)가 정답이다.

어휘 **risk** n. 위험성 **pollution** n. 오염 **benefit** n. 이점

179 추론 문제 연계

해석 Palm 항공사에 대해 결론지을 수 있는 것은?
(A) 최근에 본사를 두바이로 옮겼다.
(B) 현 최고 경영자를 대신할 누군가를 채용할 계획이다.
(C) 프로젝트 시작을 한 달 연기했다.
(D) 연구 프로젝트를 위해 정부 자금을 받았다.

해설 질문의 핵심 어구인 Palm Flight이 언급된 이메일을 먼저 확인한다.
단서 1 이메일의 'My team[Ace Solutions] is still analyzing the data we collected once the Palm Flight trial began on November 1.'에서 Ace Solutions사에서 11월 1일에 Palm 항공사의 시운전이 시작되었을 때 수집한 데이터를 아직 분석 중이라고 했다. 그런데 Palm 항공사의 시운전이 언제 시작되었는지에 대해 제시되지 않았으므로 기사에서 관련 내용을 확인한다.
단서 2 기사의 'A three-month trial involving six Palm Flight air taxis will begin on October 1.'에서 Palm 항공사의 항공 택시 여섯 대가 참여하는 3개월간의 시운전이 10월 1일에 시작될 것이었다는 것을 알 수 있다.
두 단서를 종합할 때, Palm 항공사가 시운전을 한 달 늦게 시작한 것을 추론할 수 있다. 따라서 (C)가 정답이다.

어휘 **replace** v. 바꾸다, 교체하다 **delay** v. 연기하다, 미루다
fund n. 자금 **research** n. 연구

180 추론 문제

해석 3월 3일에 Ace Solutions사는 무엇을 할 것인가?
(A) 최종 보고서를 완료한다.
(B) 몇몇 승객들을 인터뷰한다.
(C) 항공기의 안전성을 테스트한다.
(D) 자사 웹사이트에 서비스 후기를 게시한다.

해설 이메일의 'I expect that our final analysis will be ready to submit to the Department of Transportation on March 3.'에서 최종 분석은 3월 3일에 교통부에 제출할 준비가 될 것으로 예상한다고 했으므로 최종 보고서를 완료할 것임을 추론할 수 있다. 따라서 (A)가 정답이다.

어휘 **publish** v. 발표하다, 출간하다

Paraphrasing

be ready to submit 제출할 준비가 되다 → complete 완료하다

181-185번은 다음 광고와 후기에 관한 문제입니다.

Jarvis 원예 센터
당신의 정원에 필요한 모든 것이 있습니다!

[181]저희는 Park로와 Wilson가 모퉁이에 세 번째 매장의 개업을 알리게 되어 기쁩니다. 꼭 들르셔서 저희의 새로운 매장을 확인하세요! [182-(A)]할인, [182-(B)]제품 샘플, [182-(C)]로열티 클럽 회원들을 위한 보너스 포인트를 포함한 많은 특별한 혜택들을 이용하세요. 그리고 4월 ↻

15일 토요일에 매장으로 오시면, 무료 원예 수업에 참석하실 수 있습니다! 자세한 내용은 아래를 참조하십시오.

수업	시간
과일나무 가지치기	오전 9시에서 오전 10시
천연 해충 방제	오전 11시에서 오후 12시
유기질 비료	오후 1시에서 오후 2시
[183]열대 꽃	[183]오후 3시에서 오후 4시

온라인으로 등록하시려면, www.jarvis.com/classes로 가세요. 자리는 한정되어 있습니다!

gardening n. 원예, 정원 가꾸기 **take advantage of** ~을 이용하다 **prune** v. 가지치기하다 **pest** n. 해충 **organic fertilizer** 유기질 비료 **register** v. 등록하다

열렬한 원예사로서, 4월 15일에 Jarvis 원예 센터에서 제공되는 수업들 중 하나를 듣는 것에 진심으로 관심이 있었습니다. [183]제가 참석한 수업은 꽤 유익했습니다. 저희는 여러 열대 국가의 꽃들을 접하게 되었습니다. [184]강사인 Toma Mori는 지식이 매우 풍부했고 심지어 저희에게 그의 책을 한 권씩 주기도 했습니다. 제가 그것을 구매하려고 했었기 때문에, 이는 뜻밖의 기쁜 일이었습니다. [185]그 수업에 대한 한 가지 문제는 그 강사가 몇몇 고급 원예 기술들에 대해 부분적인 설명만 제공했다는 점입니다. 저는 그것들을 완전히 이해하기 위해 나중에 온라인으로 정보를 검색해야 했습니다.

4월 17일에 Laura Chen 작성

avid adj. 열렬한, 열심인 **informative** adj. 유익한 **introduce** v. 접하게 하다, 소개하다 **instructor** n. 강사 **knowledgeable** adj. 지식이 풍부한, 박식한 **issue** n. 문제, 안건 **partial** adj. 부분적인 **explanation** n. 설명 **afterward** adv. 나중에 **completely** adv. 완전히

181 추론 문제

해석 Jarvis 원예 센터에 대해 암시되는 것은?
(A) 한 개가 넘는 지점이 있다.
(B) 수업에 참여하기 위한 비용을 부과한다.
(C) 씨앗 제품의 새로운 라인을 출시했다.
(D) 다른 위치로 이전했다.

해설 광고의 'We[The Jarvis Gardening Center] are pleased to announce the opening of a third store ~.'에서 Jarvis 원예 센터는 세 번째 매장의 개업을 알리게 되어 기쁘다고 했으므로 Jarvis 원예 센터가 한 개가 넘는 지점이 있다는 것을 추론할 수 있다. 따라서 (A)가 정답이다.

어휘 **seed** n. 씨앗

182 Not/True 문제

해석 광고에 따르면, Jarvis 원예 센터 고객들에게 제공되지 않는 것은?
(A) 가격 할인
(B) 무료 물품
(C) 멤버십 포인트
(D) 상품권

해설 (A)는 광고의 'discounts'에서 할인을 제공한다고 했으므로 지문의 내용과 일치한다. (B)는 'product samples'에서 제품 샘플을 제공한다고 했으므로 지문의 내용과 일치한다. (C)는 'bonus points for loyalty club members'에서 로열티 클럽 회원들을 위한 보너스 포인트를 제공한다고 했으므로 지문의 내용과 일치한다. (D)는 지문에 언급되지 않은 내용이다. 따라서 (D)가 정답이다.

어휘 reduction n. 할인, 인하 complimentary adj. 무료의
gift certificate 상품권

Paraphrasing

discounts 할인 → Price reductions 가격 할인

product samples 제품 샘플 → Complimentary items 무료 물품

bonus points for loyalty club members 로열티 클럽 회원들을 위한 보너스 포인트 → Membership points 멤버십 포인트

183 육하원칙 문제 연계

해석 Ms. Chen이 참석했던 수업은 몇 시에 시작하는가?
(A) 오전 9시에
(B) 오전 11시에
(C) 오후 1시에
(D) 오후 3시에

해설 Ms. Chen이 작성한 후기를 먼저 확인한다.
단서 1 후기의 'The class I[Ms. Chen] attended was quite informative. We were introduced to flowers from several tropical countries.'에서 Ms. Chen이 참석한 수업은 꽤 유익했고, 여러 열대 국가의 꽃들을 접하게 되었다고 했다. 그런데 열대 꽃 수업이 몇 시에 시작했는지 제시되지 않았으므로 광고에서 관련 내용을 확인한다.
단서 2 광고의 'Tropical Flowers'와 '3 P.M. to 4 P.M.'에서 열대 꽃 수업이 오후 3시에 시작했다는 것을 확인할 수 있다.
두 단서를 종합할 때, Ms. Chen이 참석한 열대 꽃 수업이 3시에 시작했다는 것을 알 수 있다. 따라서 (D)가 정답이다.

184 추론 문제

해석 Mr. Mori에 대해 결론지을 수 있는 것은?
(A) 많은 주제에 대해 수업을 했다.
(B) 다른 강사와의 문제를 해결했다.
(C) 출판된 책의 저자이다.
(D) 학생들에게 몇몇 도구들을 팔았다.

해설 Mr. Mori가 언급된 후기에서 관련 내용을 확인한다. 후기의 'The instructor, Toma Mori, was very knowledgeable and even provided us each with a copy of his book.'에서 강사인 Toma Mori는 지식이 매우 풍부했고 그의 책을 한 권씩 줬다고 했으므로 Mr. Mori가 출판된 책의 저자라는 것을 추론할 수 있다. 따라서 (C)가 정답이다.

어휘 subject n. 주제 resolve v. 해결하다

185 육하원칙 문제

해석 Ms. Chen이 참석했던 수업에 대한 그녀의 문제는 무엇인가?
(A) 강사들이 자격을 갖추고 있지 않았다.

(B) 질문이 답변되지 않았다.
(C) 자료가 명확하게 작성되지 않았다.
(D) 방법이 충분히 설명되지 않았다.

해설 Ms. Chen이 작성한 후기의 'My[Ms. Chen's] one issue with the class was that the instructor only gave partial explanations of some advanced gardening techniques.'에서 그 수업에 대한 한 가지 문제는 강사가 몇몇 고급 원예 기술들에 대해 부분적인 설명만 제공했다는 점이라고 했으므로 방법이 충분히 설명되지 않았던 점이 문제라는 것을 알 수 있다. 따라서 (D)가 정답이다.

어휘 material n. 자료, 재료 fully adv. 충분히, 완전히

Paraphrasing

techniques 기술들 → Methods 방법

only gave partial explanations 부분적인 설명만 제공했다
→ were not fully explained 충분히 설명되지 않았다

186-190번은 다음 두 이메일과 체크리스트에 관한 문제입니다.

수신: Sam Puller <s.puller@umail.com>
발신: Grace Ewing <g.ewing@belluniversity.com>
제목: 유학 프로그램
날짜: 5월 28일
첨부 파일: 서류 목록

Mr. Puller께,

Bell 대학교의 유학 프로그램에 대해 문의해 주셔서 감사합니다. 런던에 있는 Central 대학에서 가을 학기를 보내는 것에 관심이 있다고 명시하셨습니다. 다행히도, 그 기관에는 아직 자리가 남아 있습니다. [186]프로그램에 참여하고 싶으시다면 당신이 먼저 해야 할 일이 무엇인지 간단히 설명해 드리겠습니다. 작성이 완료된 지원서와 함께, 몇 가지 추가 서류를 제출하셔야 할 것입니다. 제가 이 서류들의 목록을 첨부했습니다. [187]저희는 여권의 사본은 받지만, 프로그램 지원자들은 나머지 서류의 원본을 제공해야 합니다. 모든 것을 제출하는 마감일은 6월 10일입니다.

[188]또한, 캠퍼스 내에서 사는 것에 대해 문의하셨습니다. Central 대학은 매우 합리적인 가격으로 다양한 기숙사 선택권을 제공합니다. www.centralcollege.com/housing에서 더 많은 정보를 얻으실 수 있습니다.

Grace Ewing 드림
학생처, Bell 대학교

abroad adv. 해외에 inquire v. 문의하다 specify v. 명시하다
semester n. 학기 institution n. 기관 briefly adv. 간단히
participate in ~에 참여하다 application form 지원서, 신청서
supplementary adj. 추가의, 보충의 original n. 원본
dormitory n. 기숙사 reasonable adj. 합리적인

추가 서류 체크리스트
Central 대학 (런던)

서류	비고	√
여권	출발일로부터 6개월 동안 유효해야 합니다.	

건강 기록	지난 1년 이내에 건강검진을 받았어야 합니다.	
추천서	현재 또는 이전 교수로부터의 두 개의 추천서를 제공하세요.	
188기숙사 신청서	**188**신청서에는 선입금에 대한 수표(학기 전체 숙박 요금의 10퍼센트)가 포함되어야 합니다.	

189서류 필요조건은 주관 대학교의 규정에 따라 변경될 수 있음을 유의하십시오. 이런 일이 발생하는 경우, 새 정책에 영향을 받는 모든 학생들은 학생처 사무실로부터 변경 내용을 알리는 문자 메시지를 받을 것입니다.

valid adj. 유효한 departure n. 출발 a letter of reference 추천서
cheque n. 수표 deposit n. 보증금 subject to ~될 수 있는

수신: Grace Ewing <g.ewing@belluniversity.com>
발신: Sam Puller <s.puller@umail.com>
제목: 회신: 유학 프로그램
날짜: **189**6월 9일

Ms. Ewing께,

체크리스트를 검토했고 필요한 서류를 모았습니다. 그런데 아마 아시다시피, **189**Central 대학이 이제 4페이지 분량의 학업 계획서를 요구한다는 것을 오늘 아침에 알게 되었습니다.

마지막 순간에 이것에 대해 통지받았기 때문에, **190**지원서를 준비하는 데 시간을 좀 더 요청하고 싶습니다. 원래의 마감일로부터 이틀 후인 6월 12일까지 모든 것을 사무실에 갖다 줄 수 있게 준비할 수 있습니다. 저는 바로 학업 계획서 작업을 시작하겠습니다.

감사합니다,

Sam Puller 드림

gather v. 모으다 statement of purpose 학업 계획서
at the last minute 마지막 순간에, 임박해서 drop off 갖다 주다
cutoff date 마감일

186 목적 찾기 문제

해석 첫 번째 이메일의 한 가지 목적은 무엇인가?
(A) 기관의 문제점을 지적하기 위해
(B) 여행지 선택을 확인하기 위해
(C) 프로그램 신청을 거절하기 위해
(D) 진행 과정의 초기 단계를 설명하기 위해

해설 첫 번째 이메일의 'Let me briefly outline what you must do first if you would like to participate in the program.'에서 프로그램에 참여하고 싶으면 먼저 해야 할 일이 무엇인지 간단히 설명해주겠다고 했으므로 (D)가 정답이다.

어휘 point out ~을 지적하다 travel destination 여행지

187 육하원칙 문제

해석 Ms. Ewing은 프로그램 지원자들에게 무엇이 요구된다고 말하는가?
(A) 외국 대학에 직접 연락하는 것
(B) 몇몇 서류의 원본을 제공하는 것
(C) 웹사이트를 통해 지원서를 제출하는 것
(D) 6월 10일에 대학교 사무실에 방문하는 것

해설 첫 번째 이메일의 'We accept copies of passports, but program applicants must provide the originals of the remaining documents.'에서 여권은 사본을 받지만, 프로그램 지원자들은 나머지 서류들의 원본을 제공해야 한다고 했으므로 (B)가 정답이다.

어휘 directly adv. 직접

188 추론 문제 연계

해석 Mr. Puller에 대해 결론지을 수 있는 것은?
(A) 출발 전에 여권을 갱신해야 한다.
(B) 다음 달에 건강검진 일정을 잡을 것이다.
(C) 세 개의 추천서를 제공해야 한다.
(D) 신청 서류에 수표를 포함할 것이다.

해설 Mr. Puller에게 보낸 첫 번째 이메일을 먼저 확인한다.
단서 1 첫 번째 이메일의 'In addition, you[Mr. Puller] asked about living on-campus. Central College offers a variety of dormitory options at very reasonable rates.'에서 Mr. Puller가 캠퍼스 내에서 사는 것에 대해 문의했다는 것을 알 수 있다. 그런데 어떻게 기숙사를 이용할 수 있는지 제시되지 않았으므로 체크리스트에서 관련 내용을 확인한다.
단서 2 체크리스트의 'Housing Request Form', 'A cheque for the advance deposit amount must be included with the request form (10% of accommodation fees for entire semester).'에서 기숙사 신청서에는 선 입금 금액에 대한 수표가 포함되어야 한다는 것을 알 수 있다.
두 단서를 종합할 때, Mr. Puller는 기숙사 신청 서류에 선입금으로 수표를 포함할 것임을 추론할 수 있다. 따라서 (D)가 정답이다.

어휘 renew v. 갱신하다

Paraphrasing

request form 신청서 → application document 신청 서류

189 추론 문제 연계

해석 6월 9일에 무슨 일이 일어났을 것 같은가?
(A) 기숙사 예약 정책이 변경되었다.
(B) 온라인에 구인 공고가 게시되었다.
(C) 한 기관에 의해 교환학생 프로그램이 취소되었다.
(D) 한 그룹의 학생들에게 통지가 보내졌다.

해설 질문의 핵심 어구인 June 9에 작성된 두 번째 이메일을 먼저 확인한다.
단서 1 두 번째 이메일의 'I found out this morning that Central College now requires a four-page statement of purpose'에서 Central 대학이 이제 4페이지 분량의 학업 계획서를 요구한다는 것을 오늘 아침에 알게 되었다고 했다. 그런데 어떻게 알게 되었는지에 대해 제시되지 않았으므로 체크리스트에서 관련 내용을 확인한다.
단서 2 체크리스트의 'Note that document requirements are subject to change depending on the regulations of the host university. In the event that this happens, all students affected by the new policy will receive a text message

from the Student Services Office notifying them of the change.'에서 서류 필요조건은 주관 대학교의 규정에 따라 변경될 수 있으며 이런 일이 발생하는 경우, 새 정책에 영향을 받는 모든 학생들은 학생처 사무실로부터 변경 내용을 알리는 문자 메시지를 받게 될 것이라는 것을 알 수 있다.

두 단서를 종합할 때, 6월 9일에 학생들에게 문자 메시지로 서류 변경 사항에 대한 통지가 보내졌음을 추론할 수 있다. 따라서 (D)가 정답이다.

어휘 exchange program 교환학생 프로그램

190 육하원칙 문제

해석 Mr. Puller는 그의 이메일에서 무엇을 요청하는가?
(A) 견적서
(B) 마감일 연장
(C) 성적표
(D) 사무실 주소

해설 두 번째 이메일의 'I would like to request some additional time to prepare my application. I can have everything ready to drop off at your office by June 12, two days after the original cutoff date.'에서 지원서를 준비하는 데 시간을 좀 더 요청하고 싶으며, 원래의 마감일로부터 이틀 후인 6월 12일까지 모든 것을 사무실에 갖다 줄 수 있게 준비할 수 있다고 했으므로, Mr. Puller가 마감일 연장을 요청하는 것을 알 수 있다. 따라서 (B)가 정답이다.

어휘 cost estimate 견적서 extension n. (기간의) 연장
academic record 성적표

191-195번은 다음 이메일, 일정표, 온라인 양식에 관한 문제입니다.

수신: Deborah Frank <d.frank@theusnewsstandard.com>
발신: Kenan Marlow <kenan@miff.org>
제목: 회신: 미디어 인증
날짜: 4월 22일

Ms. Frank께,

¹⁹¹제10회 연례 멤피스 국제 영화제를 취재하는 데 관심을 가져 주셔서 감사합니다. 올해 라인업은 역대 가장 다양하며, 저명한 영화 제작자들과 신인 영화 제작자들의 작품들을 특별히 포함합니다.

¹⁹²귀하와 소속 신문사의 다른 세 명의 기자분이 축제에 참석할 계획이라니 기대됩니다. 미디어 패스권을 신청하시려면, 여기를 클릭하십시오. 인증 요청서 제출 마감일은 5월 3일로, 2주밖에 남지 않았습니다.

귀하의 미디어 패스권은 모든 영화 상영에 대한 입장권을 제공하고 인터뷰와 사진을 위해 감독과 배우들을 만날 수 있게 해줄 것입니다. 게다가, 귀하는 5개의 특별한 영화 시사회 행사에 참석할 수 있을 것입니다. 미디어 측은 레드 카펫에서 특별 구역을 가질 것입니다.

더 궁금한 점이 있으시면 알려주세요.

Kenan Marlow 드림
미디어 관리자
멤피스 국제 영화제

accreditation n. 인증 diverse adj. 다양한
established adj. 저명한, 인정받는 filmmaker n. 영화 제작자
submit v. 제출하다 gala adj. 특별 개최의
premiere n. 영화 시사회, (연극의) 초연 section n. 구역

멤피스 국제 영화제 프로그램
특별한 영화 시사회 일정표

날짜	영화	설명	장소
5월 20일	The Winds	저명한 다큐멘터리 영화 제작자 Adam Porter의 정치 동향 분석	Vexor 영화관
5월 21일	Anna and the Horse	Janice Tompkins에 의해 연출된 새로운 드라마	Vexor 영화관
¹⁹³5월 23일	¹⁹³Secrets	¹⁹³Hans Beyer의 데뷔작이자 VIFF의 최우수 신작 영화상 수상작	멤피스 강당
5월 24일	What Happened There	비평가들의 극찬을 받은 Junko Takeshi의 영화 What Happens Now의 속편	Vexor 영화관
¹⁹⁴5월 25일	¹⁹⁴Shifts	¹⁹⁴미국 시골로 이주하는 가족을 다룬 Tony Choi 감독의 작품	멤피스 강당

시사회 입장은 미디어 대표자들 및 특별 티켓을 소지한 개인으로 제한됩니다. 이 행사들은 일반 축제 패스권에는 포함되어 있지 않습니다.

renowned adj. 저명한, 유명한 examination n. 분석, 검토
politics n. 정치 auditorium n. 강당 sequel n. 속편
critically acclaimed 비평가들의 극찬을 받은 rural adj. 시골의

멤피스 국제 영화제
미디어 인증 양식

언론사	The US News Standard
연락 이메일	d.frank@theusnewsstandard.com
¹⁹²미디어 대표자의 이름	¹⁹²Deborah Frank
¹⁹²추가 미디어 대표자	¹⁹²Hendrick Stevenson Pamela Consuelo(사진작가)
¹⁹⁴미디어 패스권 유효기간	¹⁹⁴5월 20일-5월 24일

제출하기

서류가 처리될 때까지 24시간 동안 기다려 주십시오. 귀하는 코드가 포함된 확인 이메일을 받게 될 것입니다. ¹⁹⁵축제에서 미디어 텐트를 방문하여 실물 미디어 패스권을 찾으십시오. 코드와 확인 이메일과 함께 모든 대표자의 신분증을 제시하십시오.

process v. 처리하다 confirmation n. 확인, 확증
retrieve v. 찾다, 회수하다 identification n. 신분증

191 추론 문제

해석 이메일에서, 멤피스 국제 영화제에 대해 암시되는 것은?
(A) 4월 말에 라인업이 완성될 것이다.
(B) 과거에 여러 번 개최된 적이 있다.
(C) 경험 있는 영화 제작자만 참석한다.

(D) 국제단체로부터 자금을 받았다.

해설 이메일의 'the 10th annual Memphis International Film Festival'에서 제10회 연례 멤피스 국제 영화제라고 했으므로 멤피스 국제 영화제가 과거에 여러 번 개최된 적이 있다는 것을 추론할 수 있다. 따라서 (B)가 정답이다.

어휘 finalize v. 완성하다 multiple adj. 여럿의, 다양한

192 추론 문제 연계

해석 The US News Standard에 대해 결론지을 수 있는 것은?
(A) 미국에서 개최하는 행사들만 다룬다.
(B) 축제의 대표단 규모를 줄였다.
(C) 더 이상 인쇄판을 발행하지 않는다.
(D) 다른 언론사와 합병했다.

해설 The US News Standard가 언급된 온라인 양식을 먼저 확인한다.
단서 1 온라인 양식 내 표의 'Name of media representative: Deborah Frank', 'Additional media representatives: Hendrick Stevenson, Pamela Consuelo (Photographer)'에서 The US News Standard의 축제에 참가할 대표단이 총 세 명인 것을 확인한다. 그런데, 대표단 규모에 대한 정보는 제시되지 않았으므로 The US News Standard의 대표단 중 한 명인 Deborah Frank에게 보낸 이메일에서 관련 정보를 확인한다.
단서 2 이메일의 'We are excited that you[Ms. Frank] and three other reporters from your newspaper plan to attend the festival.'에서 Ms. Frank와 소속 신문사의 다른 세 명의 기자들이 참석할 예정이었다는 것을 알 수 있다.
두 단서를 종합할 때, The US News Standard에서 축제에 총 네 명의 대표자가 참석할 예정이었으나 세 명으로 대표단 규모를 줄였음을 추론할 수 있다. 따라서 (B)가 정답이다.

어휘 downsize v. 줄이다, 축소하다 delegation n. 대표단, 사절단
publish v. 발행하다, 출판하다 merge v. 합병하다

193 육하원칙 문제

해석 일정표에 따르면, 수상작은 언제 상영될 것인가?
(A) 5월 20일에
(B) 5월 21일에
(C) 5월 23일에
(D) 5월 25일에

해설 일정표의 'May 23', 'Secrets: 'Hans Beyer's debut film and the winner of VIFF's Best New Film award'에서 Hans Beyer의 데뷔작이자 VIFF의 최우수 신작 영화상 수상작인 Secrets가 5월 23일에 상영될 것임을 알 수 있다. 따라서 (C)가 정답이다.

어휘 award-winning adj. 수상작의, 상을 받은

Paraphrasing

the winner of VIFF's Best New Film award VIFF의 최우수 신작 영화상 수상작 → an award-winning film 수상작

194 추론 문제 연계

해석 Ms. Frank에 대해 추론될 수 있는 것은?

(A) 자신의 블로그에 축제에 대한 글을 쓸 것이다.
(B) 신문사의 유일한 엔터테인먼트 기자이다.
(C) Mr. Choi의 영화 시사회를 놓칠 것이다.
(D) Adam Porter의 다큐멘터리를 이미 본 적이 있다.

해설 Ms. Frank가 작성한 온라인 양식을 먼저 확인한다.
단서 1 온라인 양식의 'Media Pass Validity Period: May 20-May 24'에서 Ms. Frank의 미디어 패스 유효기간이 5월 20일부터 24일까지라는 것을 알 수 있다. 그런데 그녀가 참석할 영화 시사회에 대한 정보는 제시되지 않았으므로 영화 시사회 일정을 다룬 일정표에서 관련 정보를 확인한다.
단서 2 일정표의 'May 25', 'Shifts', 'Director Tony Choi's work about a family moving to rural America'에서 5월 25일에 Tony Choi 감독의 작품 Shifts가 상영된다는 것을 알 수 있다.
두 단서를 종합할 때, 5월 24일에 미디어 패스가 종료되는 Ms. Frank는 5월 25일에 상영되는 Mr. Choi의 영화 시사회를 놓칠 것임을 추론할 수 있다. 따라서 (C)가 정답이다.

어휘 miss v. 놓치다

195 육하원칙 문제

해석 미디어 대표자들은 미디어 텐트에서 무엇을 할 것이 요구되는가?
(A) 몇몇 문서를 인쇄한다.
(B) 몇몇 패스권을 수령한다.
(C) 몇몇 기사의 초안을 이메일로 보낸다.
(D) 사진 촬영 허가를 신청한다.

해설 온라인 양식의 'Visit the media tent at the festival to retrieve the physical media passes.'에서 축제에서 미디어 텐트를 방문하여 실물 미디어 패스권을 찾으라고 했으므로, 미디어 대표자들이 미디어 텐트에서 몇몇 패스권을 수령할 것임을 알 수 있다. 따라서 (B)가 정답이다.

어휘 document n. 문서, 서류 draft n. 초안, 원고 permit n. 허가

Paraphrasing

retrieve 찾다 → pick up 수령하다

196-200번은 다음 웹페이지, 회람, 정책에 관한 문제입니다.

Net Smart Magazine

홈	최신 호	**기사**	구독	도움

2월 9일—196-(B)소프트웨어 대기업인 Optika Limited사는 지난주 연례 제품 공개 행사를 개최하였고, 행사 동안 기업들이 원격 근무자들의 생산성을 북돋는 것을 도울 곧 나올 소프트웨어 프로그램 라인업을 공개했다:

- Group Hub는 고도로 기능적인 일정 관리 시스템과 특정 목표에 대한 진행 상황을 추적하는 도구를 결합하여 프로젝트 관리를 간소화한다.
- Hive Wire는 정기적으로 데이터를 안전한 클라우드 스토리지 시스템에 백업하여 중요한 파일이 절대 손실되지 않도록 한다.
- 197Team Space는 사용자들이 비디오를 통해 소통하고 나중에 참조할 수 있도록 소통 내용을 쉽게 녹화할 수 있게 해준다.

- **Whiteboard**는 원격 근무자들이 공유된 파일을 보고 수정할 수 있는 가상의 화이트보드를 만들어 협업을 용이하게 한다.

¹⁹⁸이 모든 애플리케이션은 2월 12일에 출시될 예정이다. 박식한 자사의 작가들이 작성한 자세한 후기가 그날 게시될 것이다.

showcase n. 공개 행사 reveal v. 공개하다, 밝히다
boost v. 북돋우다 productivity n. 생산성 remote adj. 원격의, 외진
combine v. 결합하다 highly adv. 고도로, 매우 track v. 추적하다
secure adj. 안전한, 확실한 interaction n. 소통 내용, 상호 작용
reference n. 참조, 언급 facilitate v. 용이하게 하다
collaboration n. 협업, 협력 virtual adj. 가상의
revise v. 수정하다, 변경하다 knowledgeable adj. 박식한, 많이 아는

Ryder 언론사
회람

수신: 전 직원
발신: ¹⁹⁹Jennifer Warnes, 인사부장
제목: 하이브리드 원격 근무 시스템
날짜: 4월 14일

앞서 발표한 바와 같이 Ryder 언론사는 5월 1일에 하이브리드 원격 근무 시스템을 도입할 예정입니다. 이를 준비하기 위해, ¹⁹⁷최적의 선택안을 결정하도록 여러 팀에 다양한 화상 회의 애플리케이션을 실험해 보는 것을 요청했습니다. 폭넓은 조사 끝에, Optika Limited사가 2월에 출시한 애플리케이션을 선택하기로 결정했습니다. 모든 분들이 사용법을 확실히 알 수 있도록, 4월 20일에 워크숍을 마련했습니다. 워크숍에 대한 더 많은 세부 사항들이 담긴 이메일이 오늘 중으로 모든 분들께 발송될 것입니다.

experiment with ~을 실험해 보다 determine v. 결정하다, 알아내다
extensive adj. 폭넓은, 광범위한 go with ~을 선택하다

하이브리드 원격 근무 정책

자격 요건
Ryder 언론사는 모든 직원이 6개월의 수습 기간을 마친 후 원격으로 근무할 수 있도록 허용합니다. 신입 직원들은 일주일에 2일 재택 근무가 가능하며, ¹⁹⁹팀 매니저들과 부서장들은 일주일에 1일로 제한됩니다.

요구 사항
^{200-(A)}원격으로 근무하는 직원들은 그들의 예정된 근무 시간 동안 접근이 가능해야 하며 업무에 집중해야 합니다. ^{200-(B)}경영진은 일과 관련된 업무에 필요하다고 판단되는 경우 언제든지 직원에게 사무실에 복귀하도록 요구할 권한을 가지고 있습니다. ^{200-(C)}필요한 프로그램이 사전 설치된 노트북이 재택근무하는 모든 직원들에게 제공될 것입니다. ^{200-(D)}어떠한 기술적인 문제라도 IT 팀에게 알리는 것은 해당 직원의 책임입니다.

eligibility n. 자격 요건 probationary period 수습 기간
be limited to ~에 제한되다 accessible adj. 접근이 가능한
retain v. 가지다, 보유하다 deem v. (~로) 판단하다, 생각하다
preinstall v. 사전에 설치하다 responsibility n. 책임, 책무
bring ~ to the attention ~을 알리다

---

196 Not/True 문제

해석 웹페이지에 따르면, Optika Limited에 대해 사실인 것은?
(A) 소프트웨어 프로그램의 업데이트를 공개했다.
(B) 곧 새로운 제품을 출시할 것이라고 발표했다.
(C) 연례 마케팅 행사의 일정을 변경했다.
(D) 다른 회사와 소프트웨어 프로젝트를 공동으로 진행했다.

해설 웹페이지의 'Software giant Optika Limited held its annual product showcase last week, during which it revealed its upcoming lineup of software programs'에서 소프트웨어 대기업인 Optika Limited사가 지난주 연례 제품 공개 행사를 개최하였고, 곧 나올 소프트웨어 프로그램 라인업을 공개했다고 했으므로 (B)가 지문의 내용과 일치한다. 따라서 (B)가 정답이다. (A), (C), (D)는 지문에 언급되지 않은 내용이다.

어휘 release v. 공개하다, 발표하다

Paraphrasing

its upcoming lineup of software programs 곧 나올 소프트웨어 프로그램 라인업 → new products ~ available soon 곧 출시할 새로운 제품

197 추론 문제 연계

해석 Ryder 언론사는 어떤 애플리케이션을 사용할 것 같은가?
(A) Group Hub
(B) Hive Wire
(C) Team Space
(D) Whiteboard

해설 질문의 핵심 어구인 Ryder 언론사의 회람을 먼저 확인한다.
단서 1 회람의 'a number of teams were asked to experiment with various video conferencing applications to determine the best option. After extensive study, it has been decided to go with the application Optika Limited released in February.'에서 최적의 선택안을 결정하도록 여러 팀에 다양한 화상 회의 애플리케이션을 실험해 보는 것을 요청했고, 폭넓은 조사 끝에 Optika Limited사가 2월에 출시한 애플리케이션을 선택하기로 결정했다고 하였다. 그런데 화상 회의 애플리케이션이 어떤 것인지에 대해 제시되지 않았으므로 웹페이지에서 관련 내용을 확인한다.
단서 2 웹페이지의 'Team Space lets users communicate through video and makes it easy to record interactions for future reference'에서 Team Space는 사용자들이 비디오를 통해 소통하고 나중에 참조할 수 있도록 소통 내용을 쉽게 녹화할 수 있게 해준다고 하였다.
두 단서를 종합할 때, Ryder 언론사는 Team Space를 사용할 것임을 추론할 수 있다. 따라서 (C)가 정답이다.

198 육하원칙 문제

해석 *Net Smart Magazine*의 독자들은 2월 12일에 무엇을 이용할 수 있는가?
(A) 프로그램에 대한 전문적인 평가
(B) 애플리케이션 체험판

(C) 기업 행사 녹화 영상

(D) 과학 기술 작가들의 전기

해설 웹페이지의 'All of these applications will be released on February 12. Detailed reviews by our knowledgeable writers will be posted on that day.'에서 이 모든 애플리케이션은 2월 12일에 출시될 예정이고, 박식한 자사의 작가들이 작성한 자세한 후기가 그날 게시될 것이라고 했으므로 (A)가 정답이다.

어휘 **expert** adj. 전문적인, 전문가의 **evaluation** n. 평가
trial version 체험판 **corporate** adj. 기업의
biography n. 전기, 자서전

Paraphrasing

> reviews by our knowledgeable writers 박식한 작가들의 후기 → Expert evaluations 전문적인 평가

199 추론 문제 연계

해석 Ms. Warnes에 대해 암시되는 것은?

(A) 원격 근무일의 일정을 세우는 데 책임이 있다.

(B) 교육 세션에 참여할 수 없을 것이다.

(C) 최근 의무 수습 기간을 마쳤다.

(D) 매주 하루 재택근무를 하도록 허용된다.

해설 질문의 핵심 어구인 Ms. Warnes가 작성한 회람을 먼저 확인한다.
단서 1 회람의 'Jennifer Warnes, Human Resources Manager'에서 Ms. Warnes가 인사부장임을 확인할 수 있다. 그런데 Ms. Warnes의 근무에 대해 제시되지 않았으므로 정책에서 관련 내용을 확인한다.
단서 2 정책의 'team managers and department heads are limited to one day per week'에서 팀 매니저들과 부서장들은 일주일에 1일 재택 근무하는 것으로 제한된다는 것을 확인할 수 있다. 두 단서를 종합할 때, 인사부장인 Ms. Warnes는 매주 하루 재택근무를 할 수 있다는 것을 추론할 수 있다. 따라서 (D)가 정답이다.

어휘 **mandatory** adj. 의무의

200 Not/True 문제

해석 정책에 따르면, 재택근무자들에 대한 요구 사항이 아닌 것은?

(A) 근무 시간 동안 연락이 가능할 것

(B) 필요할 때 사무로 복귀할 것

(C) 컴퓨터에 프로그램들을 설치할 것

(D) 기기의 문제들을 보고할 것

해설 정책의 'A laptop with the necessary programs preinstalled will be provided to everyone working from home.'에서 필요한 프로그램이 사전 설치된 노트북이 재택근무하는 모든 직원들에게 제공될 것이라고 했으므로 (C)는 요구 사항이 아니다. 따라서 (C)가 정답이다. (A)는 'Employees working remotely must be accessible ~ during their scheduled work hours'에서 원격으로 근무하는 직원들은 자신의 예정된 근무 시간 동안 접근이 가능해야 한다고 했으므로 요구 사항이 맞다. (B)는 'Management retains the right to require employees to return to the office at any time if deemed necessary for a work-related task.'에서 경영진은 일과 관련된 업무에 필요하다고 판단되는 경우 언제든

지 직원에게 사무실 복귀를 요구할 권한을 가지고 있다고 했으므로 요구 사항이 맞다. (D)는 'It is the employee's responsibility to bring any technical issues to the attention of the IT team.'에서 어떠한 기술적인 문제라도 IT 팀에게 알리는 것은 해당 직원의 책임이라고 했으므로 요구 사항이 맞다.

어휘 **reachable** adj. 연락이 가능한 **install** v. 설치하다

Paraphrasing

> accessible 접근이 가능한 → reachable 연락이 가능한
> scheduled work hours 예정된 근무 시간 → shift 근무 시간
> bring ~ issues to the attention 문제를 알리다 → Reporting problems 문제를 보고하는 것

TEST 2

LISTENING TEST

p.70

1 (C)	21 (A)	41 (B)	61 (A)	81 (C)
2 (B)	22 (C)	42 (B)	62 (A)	82 (C)
3 (D)	23 (B)	43 (D)	63 (B)	83 (B)
4 (A)	24 (B)	44 (A)	64 (B)	84 (A)
5 (B)	25 (A)	45 (B)	65 (C)	85 (C)
6 (A)	26 (B)	46 (B)	66 (C)	86 (C)
7 (A)	27 (B)	47 (A)	67 (A)	87 (D)
8 (B)	28 (A)	48 (D)	68 (C)	88 (A)
9 (A)	29 (D)	49 (D)	69 (A)	89 (C)
10 (B)	30 (C)	50 (D)	70 (A)	90 (B)
11 (B)	31 (C)	51 (C)	71 (D)	91 (B)
12 (C)	32 (D)	52 (A)	72 (B)	92 (C)
13 (B)	33 (C)	53 (A)	73 (B)	93 (C)
14 (A)	34 (A)	54 (D)	74 (B)	94 (D)
15 (B)	35 (A)	55 (B)	75 (C)	95 (C)
16 (B)	36 (D)	56 (B)	76 (B)	96 (B)
17 (B)	37 (A)	57 (C)	77 (C)	97 (B)
18 (B)	38 (B)	58 (C)	78 (D)	98 (A)
19 (C)	39 (A)	59 (B)	79 (C)	99 (B)
20 (B)	40 (C)	60 (D)	80 (A)	100 (D)

READING TEST

p.82

101 (B)	121 (D)	141 (A)	161 (C)	181 (B)
102 (B)	122 (C)	142 (D)	162 (D)	182 (A)
103 (D)	123 (B)	143 (B)	163 (D)	183 (B)
104 (D)	124 (A)	144 (C)	164 (C)	184 (D)
105 (B)	125 (C)	145 (D)	165 (C)	185 (D)
106 (D)	126 (D)	146 (D)	166 (C)	186 (C)
107 (D)	127 (B)	147 (A)	167 (A)	187 (C)
108 (C)	128 (D)	148 (C)	168 (C)	188 (C)
109 (B)	129 (C)	149 (A)	169 (B)	189 (B)
110 (D)	130 (D)	150 (D)	170 (D)	190 (B)
111 (B)	131 (C)	151 (D)	171 (C)	191 (B)
112 (C)	132 (A)	152 (C)	172 (D)	192 (D)
113 (B)	133 (D)	153 (D)	173 (B)	193 (C)
114 (D)	134 (A)	154 (A)	174 (C)	194 (D)
115 (A)	135 (C)	155 (D)	175 (C)	195 (C)
116 (C)	136 (A)	156 (D)	176 (A)	196 (C)
117 (A)	137 (B)	157 (D)	177 (D)	197 (D)
118 (C)	138 (C)	158 (C)	178 (B)	198 (B)
119 (B)	139 (B)	159 (B)	179 (B)	199 (B)
120 (C)	140 (C)	160 (B)	180 (D)	200 (D)

PART 1

1 2인 이상 사진

3別 호주식

(A) They're climbing over a rock.
(B) They're gathering under some trees.
(C) They're looking in the same direction.
(D) They're putting their hats into a backpack.

climb over ~을 (타고) 넘다 gather v. (사람들이) 모이다
direction n. 방향, 지시 backpack n. 배낭, 등짐

해석 (A) 그들은 바위를 넘고 있다.
(B) 그들은 나무 아래에 모여 있다.
(C) 그들은 같은 방향을 바라보고 있다.
(D) 그들은 그들의 모자를 배낭에 넣고 있다.

해설 (A) [x] climbing over(넘고 있다)는 사람들의 동작과 무관하므로 오답이다. 사진에 있는 바위(rock)를 사용하여 혼동을 주었다.
(B) [x] 사진에 나무(trees)가 없으므로 오답이다. They're gathering(그들은 모여 있다)까지만 듣고 정답으로 선택하지 않도록 주의한다.
(C) [o] 두 사람이 같은 방향을 바라보고 있는 모습을 가장 잘 묘사한 정답이다.
(D) [x] putting their hats into a backpack(그들의 모자를 배낭에 넣고 있다)은 사람들의 동작과 무관하므로 오답이다. 사진에 있는 모자(hats)와 배낭(backpack)을 사용하여 혼동을 주었다.

2 1인 사진

3別 캐나다식

(A) The man is taking off his gloves.
(B) The man is lifting a suitcase from a pile.
(C) The man is boarding an airplane.
(D) The man is measuring the height of a piece of luggage.

take off ~을 벗다, 이륙하다 lift v. 들어 올리다 suitcase n. 여행 가방
pile n. 더미, 쌓아 놓은 것 board v. 탑승하다, 승선하다
measure v. 재다, 측정하다 luggage n. 수하물

해석 (A) 남자가 장갑을 벗고 있다.
(B) 남자가 더미에서 여행 가방을 들어 올리고 있다.
(C) 남자가 비행기에 탑승하고 있다.
(D) 남자가 수하물 한 개의 높이를 재고 있다.

해설 (A) [x] taking off his gloves(장갑을 벗고 있다)는 남자의 동작과 무관하므로 오답이다.
(B) [o] 남자가 여행 가방을 들어 올리고 있는 모습을 가장 잘 묘사한 정답이다.

(C) [×] boarding an airplane(비행기에 탑승하고 있다)은 남자의 동작과 무관하므로 오답이다. 사진에 있는 비행기(airplane)를 사용하여 혼동을 주었다.

(D) [×] measuring the height(높이를 재고 있다)는 남자의 동작과 무관하므로 오답이다. 사진에 있는 수하물(luggage)을 사용하여 혼동을 주었다.

최신토익경향

최근 Part 1에서는 사람의 동작이 모호하여 다양한 방식으로 묘사될 수 있는 사진이 자주 출제되고 있다. 예를 들어, 사진 속 남자가 쓰레기통을 들어 올리고 있는지 바닥에 놓고 있는지 명확하지 않은 경우, 정답 보기로 다음과 같은 것들이 나올 수 있으니, 동작을 묘사할 때 사용되는 여러 표현들을 잘 알아두자.

• He's **lifting** a bin **from** the floor.
  그는 쓰레기통을 바닥에서 들어 올리고 있다.

• He's **putting** a bin **on** the floor.
  그는 쓰레기통을 바닥에 놓고 있다.

3 2인 이상 사진

[3㎞] 미국식

(A) Some people are attaching notices to a bulletin board.
(B) One of the men is pointing at an entrance.
(C) Some people are standing in line to pay for books.
(D) One of the men is browsing through a book.

---

attach v. 붙이다, 첨부하다 **bulletin board** 게시판
point at ~을 가리키다 entrance n. 입구 **stand in line** 일렬로 서다
browse through ~을 훑어보다

해석 (A) 몇몇 사람들이 게시판에 공고문을 붙이고 있다.
(B) 남자들 중 한 명이 입구를 가리키고 있다.
(C) 몇몇 사람들이 책값을 지불하기 위해 일렬로 서 있다.
(D) 남자들 중 한 명이 책을 훑어보고 있다.

해설 (A) [×] 사진에 게시판(bulletin board)이 없고, attaching notices(공고문을 붙이고 있다)는 사람들의 동작과 무관하므로 오답이다.
(B) [×] 사진에 입구(entrance)가 없으므로 오답이다.
(C) [×] standing in line to pay for books(책값을 지불하기 위해 일렬로 서 있다)는 사람들의 동작과 무관하므로 오답이다. Some people are standing(몇몇 사람들이 서 있다)까지만 듣고 정답으로 선택하지 않도록 주의한다.
(D) [○] 남자들 중 한 명이 책을 훑어보고 있는 모습을 가장 잘 묘사한 정답이다.

최신토익경향

최근 Part 1에서는 '훑어보다'라는 의미의 동사 browse가 자주 출제되고 있다. 이외에도 '보다'라는 뜻의 빈출 표현으로는 look at(~을 보다)과 examine(살펴보다) 등이 있으니 함께 알아두자.

• **browse through** some magazines 잡지들을 훑어보다
• **look at** a camera 카메라를 보다
• **examine** some items 몇몇 물건들을 살펴보다

4 2인 이상 사진

[3㎞] 호주식

(A) The women are facing each other.
(B) One of the women is cleaning her glasses.
(C) One of the women is dusting a monitor on a desk.
(D) The women are looking down at some documents.

---

face v. 마주보다, 직면하다 **each other** 서로
dust v. 먼지를 털다; n. 먼지 **look down** ~을 내려다보다
document n. 서류, 문서

해석 **(A) 여자들이 서로 마주 보고 있다.**
(B) 여자들 중 한 명이 안경을 닦고 있다.
(C) 여자들 중 한 명이 책상에 있는 모니터의 먼지를 털고 있다.
(D) 여자들이 몇몇 서류들을 내려다보고 있다.

해설 (A) [○] 여자들이 서로 마주 보고 있는 모습을 가장 잘 묘사한 정답이다.
(B) [×] 사진에 안경을 닦고 있는(cleaning her glasses) 여자가 없으므로 오답이다. 사진에 있는 안경(glasses)을 사용하여 혼동을 주었다.
(C) [×] 사진에 먼지를 털고 있는(dusting) 여자가 없으므로 오답이다. 사진에 있는 모니터(monitor)와 책상(desk)을 사용하여 혼동을 주었다.
(D) [×] looking down(내려다보다)은 여자들의 동작과 무관하므로 오답이다. 사진에 있는 서류들(documents)을 사용하여 혼동을 주었다.

5 사물 및 풍경 사진

[3㎞] 영국식

(A) A rug has been rolled up on the floor.
(B) A television is mounted on the wall.
(C) Some plants are arranged on a patio.
(D) Some bottles have been lined up on a shelf.

---

roll up 둥글게 말다 **be mounted on** ~에 고정되어 있다, 설치되어 있다
patio n. 테라스, 베란다 **line up** ~을 일렬로 세우다
shelf n. 선반, 책꽂이

해석 (A) 깔개가 바닥에 둥글게 말려 있다.
(B) 텔레비전이 벽에 고정되어 있다.
(C) 몇몇 식물들이 테라스에 배치되어 있다.
(D) 몇몇 병들이 선반 위에 일렬로 세워져 있다.

해설 (A) [×] 사진에서 깔개는 보이지만, 둥글게 말려 있는(has been rolled up) 모습은 아니므로 오답이다.
(B) [○] 텔레비전이 벽에 고정되어 있는 모습을 가장 잘 묘사한 정답이다.
(C) [×] 사진의 장소가 테라스(patio)가 아니므로 오답이다. Some plants are arranged(몇몇 식물들이 배치되어 있다)까지만 듣고 정답으로 선택하지 않도록 주의한다.
(D) [×] 사진에서 선반 위에 일렬로 세워져 있는 병들(bottles)이 없으므로 오답이다. 사진에 있는 선반(shelf)을 사용하여 혼동을 주었다.

사물이 고정되어 있거나 설치되어 있는 모습을 묘사할 때 정답으로 자주 출제되는 표현을 함께 알아두자.

- be mounted on ~에 고정되어 있다
- be installed on/in ~에 설치되어 있다
- be attached to ~에 붙어 있다

6 사물 및 풍경 사진　　　　🔊 미국식

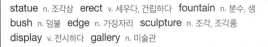

(A) **A statue has been erected on the ground.**
(B) There's a fountain in front of some bushes.
(C) Some flowers have been planted at the edge of a garden.
(D) Some sculptures are being displayed in a gallery.

statue n. 조각상　erect v. 세우다, 건립하다　fountain n. 분수, 샘
bush n. 덤불　edge n. 가장자리　sculpture n. 조각, 조각품
display v. 전시하다　gallery n. 미술관

해석　(A) 조각상이 땅 위에 세워져 있다.
(B) 분수가 몇몇 덤불들 앞에 있다.
(C) 몇몇 꽃들이 정원 가장자리에 심겨 있다.
(D) 몇몇 조각들이 미술관 안에 전시되어 있다.

해설　(A) [o] 조각상이 땅 위에 세워져 있는 모습을 가장 잘 묘사한 정답이다.
(B) [×] 사진에 분수(fountain)가 없으므로 오답이다. 사진에 있는 덤불들(bushes)을 사용하여 혼동을 주었다.
(C) [×] 사진에 꽃들(flowers)이 없으므로 오답이다.
(D) [×] 사진의 장소가 미술관(gallery) 내부가 아니므로 오답이다. Some sculptures are being displayed(몇몇 조각들이 전시되어 있다)까지만 듣고 정답으로 선택하지 않도록 주의한다.

PART 2

7 선택 의문문　　　　🔊 캐나다식 → 미국식

Should I ask Paul or Hee-su to participate in the trade show?
(A) **I'd speak to Paul.**
(B) It was a fair trade.
(C) The show was interesting.

trade show 무역 박람회　fair adj. 공정한, 공평한

해석　무역 박람회에 참석해 달라고 Paul에게 요청해야 할까요, 아니면 Hee-su에게 요청해야 할까요?
(A) 저라면 Paul에게 이야기하겠어요.
(B) 공정한 거래였어요.
(C) 박람회는 흥미로웠어요.

해설　(A) [o] 자신이라면 Paul에게 이야기하겠다는 말로, 무역 박람회에 참석해 달라고 Paul에게 요청하는 것을 선택한 정답이다.

(B) [×] 질문의 trade를 반복 사용하여 혼동을 준 오답이다.
(C) [×] 질문의 show를 반복 사용하여 혼동을 준 오답이다.

8 Be동사 의문문　　　　🔊 영국식 → 호주식

Are you coming on the company outing today?
(A) A can of soda, please.
(B) **Of course. I can't wait to go.**
(C) Actually, I'm looking forward to working with him.

outing n. 야유회, 여행　soda n. 탄산음료
look forward to ~을 기대하다

해석　오늘 회사 야유회에 오시나요?
(A) 탄산음료 한 캔 주세요.
(B) 물론이죠. 얼른 가고 싶네요.
(C) 사실, 저는 그와 함께 일하기를 기대하고 있어요.

해설　(A) [×] 질문의 outing(야유회)에서 연상할 수 있는 다과와 관련된 soda(탄산음료)를 사용하여 혼동을 준 오답이다.
(B) [o] Of course로 회사 야유회에 갈 것임을 전달한 후, 얼른 가고 싶다고 의견을 전달했으므로 정답이다.
(C) [×] 질문의 company(회사)와 관련 있는 working(일하기)을 사용하여 혼동을 준 오답이다.

9 Where 의문문　　　　🔊 캐나다식 → 영국식

Where should the visitors park in this building?
(A) **In Section B on Basement Level 1.**
(B) Yes, you can let me off right here.
(C) It's nice to take a walk in the park.

park v. 주차하다; n. 공원　basement n. 지하(층)
let ~ off ~를 (차 등에서) 내리게 하다　take a walk 산책하다

해석　방문객들은 이 건물에서 어디에 주차해야 하나요?
(A) 지하 1층의 B구역에요.
(B) 네, 바로 여기에 내려주세요.
(C) 공원에서 산책하기 좋네요.

해설　(A) [o] 지하 1층의 B구역이라는 말로, 방문객들이 건물 내 주차해야 하는 위치를 전달했으므로 정답이다.
(B) [×] 의문사 의문문에 Yes로 응답했으므로 오답이다. park(주차하다)에서 연상할 수 있는 차량과 관련된 let ~ off(~를 (차 등에서) 내리게 하다)를 사용하여 혼동을 주었다.
(C) [×] 질문의 park(주차하다)를 '공원'이라는 의미의 명사 park로 반복 사용하여 혼동을 준 오답이다.

10 Why 의문문　　　　🔊 미국식 → 캐나다식

Why did you decide to become a tour guide?
(A) Have the guidelines changed?
(B) **I enjoy helping others experience new places.**
(C) On a business trip to Argentina.

guideline n. 지침, 가이드라인　business trip 출장

해석 당신은 왜 여행 가이드가 되기로 결심했나요?

(A) 지침이 변경되었나요?

(B) 저는 다른 사람들이 새로운 장소를 경험하도록 돕는 것을 즐겨요.

(C) 아르헨티나로의 출장에서요.

해설 (A) [×] guide - guidelines의 유사 발음 어휘를 사용하여 혼동을 준 오답이다.

(B) [○] 다른 사람들이 새로운 장소를 경험하도록 돕는 것을 즐긴다는 말로, 여행 가이드가 되기로 결심한 이유를 언급했으므로 정답이다.

(C) [×] 질문의 tour(여행)와 관련 있는 business trip(출장)을 사용하여 혼동을 준 오답이다.

11 What 의문문

🔊 호주식 → 영국식

What time does the gallery close today?

(A) I can show you around the gallery.

(B) At 5 P.M. on weekdays.

(C) Put it in the closet.

on weekdays 평일에   closet n. 벽장

해석 미술관은 오늘 몇 시에 문을 닫나요?

(A) 제가 당신에게 미술관을 안내해 드릴게요.

(B) 평일에는 오후 5시에요.

(C) 그것을 벽장 안에 넣으세요.

해설 (A) [×] 질문의 gallery를 반복 사용하여 혼동을 준 오답이다.

(B) [○] 평일에는 오후 5시라며, 미술관이 오늘 문을 닫는 시간을 언급했으므로 정답이다.

(C) [×] close - closet의 유사 발음 어휘를 사용하여 혼동을 준 오답이다.

12 제안 의문문

🔊 캐나다식 → 호주식

Why don't we replace the air conditioner in the office?

(A) By adjusting the temperature.

(B) Yes. They are waiting in my office.

(C) We're already over budget.

adjust v. 조절하다, 조정하다   temperature n. 온도   budget n. 예산

해석 사무실에 있는 에어컨을 교체하는 게 어때요?

(A) 온도를 조절함으로써요.

(B) 네. 그들은 제 사무실에서 기다리고 있어요.

(C) 우리는 이미 예산을 초과했어요.

해설 (A) [×] 질문의 air conditioner(에어컨)와 관련 있는 temperature(온도)를 사용하여 혼동을 준 오답이다.

(B) [×] 질문의 office를 반복 사용하여 혼동을 준 오답이다.

(C) [○] 이미 예산을 초과했다는 말로, 사무실에 있는 에어컨을 교체하자는 제안을 간접적으로 거절한 정답이다.

최신토익 경향

상대방에게 무엇을 할 것을 제안하는 제안 의문문은 매회 평균 2문제 출제되며 "That sounds great.", "I'd love to." 등의 답변으로 제안에 직접적으로 수락하는 답변이 나오기도 한다. 하지만 최근에는 간접적으로 제안

을 수락하거나 거절하는 응답들이 출제되고 있으므로 예문과 함께 그 표현을 미리 학습해 두자.

Why don't we take a walk through the park?

공원에서 산책하는 거 어때요?

<수락> I'll go grab my jacket.

가서 제 재킷을 가져올게요.

<거절> There will be rain with strong winds.

강풍을 동반한 비가 내릴 거예요.

*<수락> 재킷을 가져올 것이라며 공원 산책을 하자는 제안을 수락한 응답

<거절> 강풍을 동반한 비가 내릴 것이라며 공원 산책을 하자는 제안을 거절한 응답

13 선택 의문문

🔊 영국식 → 호주식

Have you finished the revenue report, or is there more to do?

(A) OK, that's fine with me.

(B) I'm almost done.

(C) About 3,000 dollars a month.

revenue n. 수익, 수입   almost adv. 거의

해석 수익 보고서 작성을 마쳤나요, 아니면 할 일이 더 있나요?

(A) 알겠어요, 저는 괜찮아요.

(B) 거의 다 끝났어요.

(C) 한 달에 대략 3,000달러요.

해설 (A) [×] 수익 보고서 작성을 마쳤는지를 물었는데, 이와 관련이 없는 자신은 괜찮다는 말로 응답했으므로 오답이다.

(B) [○] 거의 다 끝냈다는 말로, 할 일이 더 있음을 간접적으로 선택했으므로 정답이다.

(C) [×] 질문의 revenue(수익)와 관련 있는 3,000 dollars(3,000달러)를 사용하여 혼동을 준 오답이다.

14 How 의문문

🔊 미국식 → 캐나다식

How can I order some sandwiches for the seminar?

(A) The deli across the street delivers.

(B) No, I didn't go this time.

(C) Because it's out of order again.

deli n. 조제 식품 판매점   deliver v. 배달하다   out of order 고장이 난

해석 세미나를 위해 샌드위치를 주문하려면 어떻게 해야 하나요?

(A) 길 건너편에 있는 조제 식품 판매점에서 배달해 줘요.

(B) 아뇨, 저는 이번에 가지 않았어요.

(C) 또 고장이 났기 때문이에요.

해설 (A) [○] 길 건너편에 있는 조제 식품 판매점에서 배달해 준다는 말로, 샌드위치를 주문하는 방법을 전달했으므로 정답이다.

(B) [×] 의문사 의문문에 No로 응답했으므로 오답이다. seminar(세미나)에서 연상할 수 있는 go(가다)를 사용하여 혼동을 주었다.

(C) [×] 질문의 order(주문하다)를 '고장이 난'이라는 의미의 out of order로 반복 사용하여 혼동을 준 오답이다.

15 평서문

I need to change my doctor's appointment to next week.
(A) We can fit you in on Wednesday at 11.
(B) That's what my doctor recommended.
(C) To get my prescription.

---

appointment n. 예약, 약속 fit v. 맞추다, 맞다
recommend v. 추천하다, 권고하다 prescription n. 처방전

해석 저는 의사 선생님과의 예약을 다음 주로 변경해야 해요.
(A) 수요일 11시로 맞춰드릴 수 있어요.
(B) 그것은 의사 선생님이 추천했던 거예요.
(C) 저의 처방전을 받기 위해서요.

해설 (A) [○] 수요일 11시로 맞춰줄 수 있다는 말로, 예약을 다음 주로 변경해야 한다는 요청을 수락한 정답이다.
(B) [×] 질문의 doctor를 반복 사용하여 혼동을 준 오답이다.
(C) [×] 질문의 doctor(의사)와 관련 있는 prescription(처방전)을 사용하여 혼동을 준 오답이다.

16 부정 의문문

Don't you have the rental contract with you?
(A) I've already paid my rent.
(B) Yes. It's in my bag.
(C) My name and contact information.

---

rental contract 임대 계약서 rent n. 임차료, 집세

해석 당신이 그 임대 계약서를 가지고 있지 않나요?
(A) 저는 이미 임차료를 지불했어요.
(B) 네. 제 가방 안에 있어요.
(C) 제 이름과 연락처 정보요.

해설 (A) [×] rental - rent의 유사 발음 어휘를 사용하여 혼동을 준 오답이다.
(B) [○] Yes로 자신이 임대 계약서를 가지고 있음을 전달한 후, 가방 안에 있다는 부연 설명을 했으므로 정답이다.
(C) [×] contract - contact의 유사 발음 어휘를 사용하여 혼동을 준 오답이다.

17 What 의문문

What's the price of dry cleaning an evening gown?
(A) Because it's too expensive.
(B) Between 10 and 20 dollars.
(C) The red dress fits you well.

---

price n. 가격 evening gown 이브닝 가운(야회복, 예복)
expensive adj. 비싼 fit v. 어울리다, 꼭 맞다

해석 이브닝 가운의 드라이클리닝 비용은 얼마인가요?
(A) 그게 너무 비싸기 때문이에요.
(B) 10달러에서 20달러 사이요.
(C) 빨간 드레스가 당신에게 잘 어울려요.

해설 (A) [×] 질문의 price(비용)와 관련 있는 expensive(비싼)를 사용하

여 혼동을 준 오답이다.
(B) [○] 10달러에서 20달러 사이라며, 이브닝 가운의 드라이클리닝 비용을 언급했으므로 정답이다.
(C) [×] evening gown(이브닝 가운)에서 연상할 수 있는 의상과 관련된 dress(드레스)를 사용하여 혼동을 준 오답이다.

최신토익경향

가격을 묻는 의문문에 구체적인 금액을 언급하여 응답하는 경우도 있지만, 최근에는 between, from A to B 등의 전치사를 이용하여 금액의 범위를 언급하는 응답들이 출제되고 있다. 가격을 묻는 의문문에 대한 답변으로 금액의 범위가 언급될 경우, 오답으로 혼동하기 쉬우므로 주의하자.

How much would it cost to repair these pants?
이 바지를 수선하는 데 얼마나 들까요?
<답변 1> Between 10 and 20 dollars.
　　　　 10달러에서 20달러 사이요.
<답변 2> From 10 to 20 dollars.
　　　　 10달러에서 20달러 정도요.

18 When 의문문

When is the next meeting of the department heads?
(A) In Room 105, actually.
(B) Let me check the schedule.
(C) Three hours long.

---

schedule n. 일정표

해석 다음 부서장 회의는 언제인가요?
(A) 실은, 105호에서요.
(B) 제가 일정표를 확인할게요.
(C) 세 시간 길이요.

해설 (A) [×] 질문의 meeting(회의)과 관련 있는 Room 105(105호)를 사용하여 혼동을 준 오답이다. 질문의 When을 Where로 혼동하여 이를 정답으로 선택하지 않도록 주의한다.
(B) [○] 일정표를 확인하겠다는 말로, 다음 부서장 회의가 언제인지 모른다는 것을 간접적으로 전달했으므로 정답이다.
(C) [×] 다음 부서장 회의가 언제인지를 물었는데, 기간으로 응답했으므로 오답이다.

19 Why 의문문

Why are there so many people lined up outside that bakery?
(A) Should we buy a cake for Sarah's birthday?
(B) He has decided to become a baker.
(C) Because it was featured on a TV show.

---

baker n. 제빵사
feature v. 출연하다, (신문·잡지·텔레비전에서) 특집으로 다루다

해석 저 빵집 밖에 왜 이렇게 많은 사람들이 줄을 서 있나요?
(A) Sarah의 생일을 위해 케이크를 사야 할까요?
(B) 그는 제빵사가 되기로 마음먹었어요.
(C) TV 쇼에 출연했기 때문이에요.

해설 (A) [×] 질문의 bakery(빵집)와 관련 있는 cake(케이크)를 사용하여 혼동을 준 오답이다.

(B) [×] bakery - baker의 유사 발음 어휘를 사용하여 혼동을 준 오답이다.

(C) [o] TV 쇼에 출연했기 때문이라는 말로, 빵집 밖에 많은 사람들이 줄을 서 있는 원인을 언급했으므로 정답이다.

20 부가 의문문
호주식 → 영국식

There's a break after this session, right?
(A) She is the guest speaker.
(B) Yes. For 10 minutes.
(C) No, I just ate breakfast.

session n. 회의, 시간 guest speaker 초청 연사

해석 이번 회의 이후에 휴식 시간이 있어요, 그렇죠?
(A) 그녀는 초청 연사예요.
(B) 네. 10분 동안이요.
(C) 아뇨, 저는 방금 아침을 먹었어요.

해설 (A) [×] 질문의 session(회의)과 관련 있는 guest speaker(초청 연사)를 사용하여 혼동을 준 오답이다.
(B) [o] Yes로 휴식 시간이 있음을 전달한 후, 휴식 시간이 10분 동안이라는 부연 설명을 했으므로 정답이다.
(C) [×] break - breakfast의 유사 발음 어휘를 사용하여 혼동을 준 오답이다.

21 Who 의문문
미국식 → 캐나다식

Who drafted the project proposal?
(A) Koji did, I think.
(B) They changed the project deadline.
(C) Five pages in total.

draft v. 초안을 작성하다; n. 초안 proposal n. 제안서, 제안
deadline n. 마감일, 마감 시간

해석 누가 이 프로젝트 제안서의 초안을 작성했나요?
(A) Koji가 했던 것 같아요.
(B) 그들이 프로젝트 마감일을 변경했어요.
(C) 총 다섯 페이지요.

해설 (A) [o] Koji가 했던 것 같다며, 프로젝트 제안서의 초안을 작성한 사람을 언급했으므로 정답이다.
(B) [×] 질문의 project를 반복 사용하여 혼동을 준 오답이다.
(C) [×] 질문의 proposal(제안서)과 관련 있는 pages(페이지)를 사용하여 혼동을 준 오답이다.

22 Where 의문문
영국식 → 호주식

Where is a good store to buy some camping gear?
(A) Come back tomorrow to buy them.
(B) We're still waiting for a delivery.
(C) I mostly shop online.

camping gear 캠핑 장비 delivery n. 배송, 배달

해석 캠핑 장비를 구매할 만한 좋은 가게가 어디에 있나요?

(A) 그것들을 구매하려면 내일 다시 오세요.
(B) 우리는 여전히 배송을 기다리고 있어요.
(C) 저는 주로 온라인으로 사요.

해설 (A) [×] 질문의 buy를 반복 사용하여 혼동을 준 오답이다.
(B) [×] 질문의 buy(구매하다)와 관련 있는 delivery(배송)를 사용하여 혼동을 준 오답이다.
(C) [o] 자신은 주로 온라인으로 산다는 말로, 캠핑 장비를 구매하기 좋은 곳을 간접적으로 전달했으므로 정답이다.

23 평서문
캐나다식 → 미국식

I cleaned up the spilled coffee on our break room floor.
(A) Your desk is really clean.
(B) I really appreciate that.
(C) Which café did you go to?

spill v. 엎지르다, 쏟다 break room 휴게실
appreciate v. 고마워하다

해석 제가 우리 휴게실 바닥에 엎질러진 커피를 치웠어요.
(A) 당신의 책상이 정말 깨끗하네요.
(B) 정말 고마워요.
(C) 어느 카페에 가셨나요?

해설 (A) [×] 질문의 cleaned(치웠다)를 '깨끗한'이라는 의미의 형용사 clean으로 반복 사용하여 혼동을 준 오답이다.
(B) [o] 정말 고맙다는 말로, 휴게실 바닥에 엎질러진 커피를 치운 것에 대해 고마움을 표현했으므로 정답이다.
(C) [×] coffee - café의 유사 발음 어휘를 사용하여 혼동을 준 오답이다.

24 요청 의문문
미국식 → 영국식

Can you cater a party of more than 200 people?
(A) Yes, in the kitchen cabinet.
(B) I have a large enough staff.
(C) The caterer was talented.

cater v. 음식을 조달하다 caterer n. 음식 공급 업체
talented adj. 유능한, 재능이 있는

해석 200명이 넘는 파티에 음식을 조달해 주실 수 있나요?
(A) 네, 주방 캐비닛 안에요.
(B) 저는 충분히 많은 직원을 데리고 있어요.
(C) 그 음식 공급 업체는 유능했어요.

해설 (A) [×] 질문의 cater(음식을 조달하다)에서 연상할 수 있는 kitchen(주방)을 사용하여 혼동을 준 오답이다.
(B) [o] 충분히 많은 직원을 데리고 있다는 말로, 200명이 넘는 파티에 음식을 조달해달라는 요청을 간접적으로 수락한 정답이다.
(C) [×] cater - caterer의 유사 발음 어휘를 사용하여 혼동을 준 오답이다.

25 부정 의문문
미국식 → 호주식

Isn't the technician supposed to be here by now?
(A) He called to reschedule.

(B) Some amazing technical advances.

(C) A well-known IT company.

technician n. 기술자, 기사 reschedule v. 일정을 변경하다
advance n. 발전, 진전

해석 지금쯤 기술자가 여기 와있어야 하는 것이 아닌가요?
(A) 그가 일정을 변경하려고 전화했어요.
(B) 몇 가지 놀라운 기술 발전이요.
(C) 유명한 정보통신 회사요.

해설 (A) [○] 그가 일정을 변경하려고 전화했다는 말로, 기술자가 여기 와
있어야 하는 일정이 변경되었다는 것을 간접적으로 전달했으
므로 정답이다.
(B) [×] technician - technical의 유사 발음 어휘를 사용하여 혼동
을 준 오답이다.
(C) [×] 질문의 technician(기술자)과 관련 있는 IT company(정보
통신 회사)를 사용하여 혼동을 준 오답이다.

26 Where 의문문
[3]) 캐나다식 → 미국식

Where can I pick up my identification badge?
(A) By tomorrow evening.
(B) At the security desk on the first floor.
(C) They come in two colors.

identification badge 신분 확인 명찰 security adj. 보안의, 안전의
desk n. 창구, 책상

해석 저의 신분 확인 명찰을 어디에서 받을 수 있나요?
(A) 내일 저녁까지요.
(B) 1층 보안 창구에서요.
(C) 그것들은 두 가지 색상으로 나와요.

해설 (A) [×] 신분 확인 명찰을 어디에서 받을 수 있는지 물었는데, 기한으
로 응답했으므로 오답이다.
(B) [○] 1층 보안 창구라며, 신분 확인 명찰을 받을 수 있는 장소를 언
급했으므로 정답이다.
(C) [×] 질문의 badge(명찰)에서 연상할 수 있는 colors(색상)를 사
용하여 혼동을 준 오답이다.

27 조동사 의문문
[3]) 미국식 → 캐나다식

Do you think we have enough fabric to make another dress?
(A) From a renowned fashion school.
(B) Ms. Walker is bringing some more.
(C) It's very durable.

fabric n. 천, 직물 bring v. 가지고 오다, 가져다주다
durable adj. 내구성이 있는, 오래가는

해석 우리가 또 다른 드레스를 만들 정도로 충분한 천을 가지고 있다고 생
각하시나요?
(A) 명성 있는 패션 학교로부터요.
(B) Ms. Walker가 조금 더 가지고 올 거예요.
(C) 그것은 매우 내구성이 있어요.

해설 (A) [×] 질문의 dress(드레스)에서 연상할 수 있는 패션과 관련된
fashion school(패션 학교)을 사용하여 혼동을 준 오답이다.
(B) [○] Ms. Walker가 조금 더 가지고 올 것이라는 말로, 또 다른 드
레스를 만들 정도로 충분한 천을 가지고 있지 않다는 것을 간
접적으로 전달했으므로 정답이다.
(C) [×] 질문의 fabric(천)을 나타낼 수 있는 It을 사용하고, fabric(천)
에서 연상할 수 있는 durable(내구성 있는)을 사용하여 혼동
을 준 오답이다.

28 부정 의문문
[3]) 호주식 → 미국식

Isn't Mr. Wang going to help us prepare for the annual
conference?
(A) No. He'll be too busy this week.
(B) A marketing campaign.
(C) It was repaired yesterday.

prepare v. 준비하다, 대비하다 annual adj. 연례의, 매년의
conference n. 회의, 회담 repair v. 수리하다

해석 Mr. Wang이 우리가 연례 회의를 준비하는 것을 도와줄 예정이 아닌
가요?
(A) 아니요. 그는 이번 주에 너무 바쁠 거예요.
(B) 광고 캠페인이요.
(C) 그것은 어제 수리되었어요.

해설 (A) [○] No로 Mr. Wang이 연례 회의를 준비하는 것을 도와주지 않
을 것이라고 전달한 후, 그가 이번 주에 너무 바쁠 것이라는 부
연 설명을 했으므로 정답이다.
(B) [×] 질문의 conference(회의)에서 연상할 수 있는 회의 주제와
관련된 marketing campaign(광고 캠페인)을 사용하여 혼
동을 준 오답이다.
(C) [×] prepare - repaired의 유사 발음 어휘를 사용하여 혼동을
준 오답이다.

29 평서문
[3]) 호주식 → 캐나다식

Security cameras should be installed in our building.
(A) I took the pictures on my phone.
(B) Let's get an estimate on the cost.
(C) By following the directions.

install v. 설치하다, 설비하다 estimate n. 견적(서)
direction n. 방향, 지시

해석 보안 카메라들이 우리 건물 내부에 설치되어야 해요.
(A) 제가 그 사진들을 제 휴대전화로 찍었어요.
(B) 비용에 대한 견적을 받아봐요.
(C) 지시를 따름으로써요.

해설 (A) [×] 질문의 cameras(카메라들)와 관련 있는 pictures(사진들)를
사용하여 혼동을 준 오답이다.
(B) [○] 비용에 대한 견적을 받아보자는 말로, 보안 카메라들이 건물
내부에 설치되어야 한다는 의견에 동의했으므로 정답이다.
(C) [×] 질문의 install(설치하다)에서 연상할 수 있는 directions(지
시, 사용법)를 사용하여 혼동을 준 오답이다.

30 선택 의문문

🔊 영국식 → 캐나다식

Will our booth be in the middle or by the entrance of the venue?
(A) There's a long line of people.
(B) That was a good demonstration.
(C) Matthew did the booking.

booth n. 부스, 전시장 demonstration n. 시연, 전시
booking n. 예약

해석 우리 부스가 행사장 중앙에 있을 건가요, 아니면 입구 근처에 있을 건가요?
(A) 긴 줄을 선 사람들이 있어요.
(B) 그것은 훌륭한 시연이었어요.
(C) Matthew가 예약했어요.

해설 (A) [×] 질문의 venue(행사장)와 관련 있는 long line(긴 줄)을 사용하여 혼동을 준 오답이다.
(B) [×] 질문의 booth(부스)와 관련 있는 demonstration(시연)을 사용하여 혼동을 준 오답이다.
(C) [○] Matthew가 예약했다는 말로, 부스의 위치를 모른다는 것을 간접적으로 전달했으므로 정답이다.

최신토익경향

질문에 대한 간접적인 응답으로, Yes/No를 의도하는 답변이 정답으로 출제되기도 하지만, 최근에는 모르겠다는 의도를 나타내는 응답이 매회 평균 1~2문제 정도 출제되고 있다. 특히, 모르겠다는 응답은 다양하게 나올 수 있으므로 아래 예문과 같이 최근에 자주 나오고 있는 응답을 기억해 두자.

Is the office dress code going to go into effect this week, or next month?
사무실 복장 규정은 이번 주에 시행될 건가요, 아니면 다음 달에 시행될 건가요?

<답변 1> We're going to discuss that at the morning meeting tomorrow.
내일 아침 회의에서 그것에 관해 논의할 거예요.

<답변 2> I think Pete will know.
제 생각에는 Pete가 알 것 같아요.

<답변 3> I haven't heard anything about that.
저는 그것에 대해 들어 본 적이 없어요.

31 Who 의문문

🔊 호주식 → 미국식

Who is available to edit the article?
(A) An employee manual.
(B) Is she a reporter for the newspaper?
(C) I think Xian is free this morning.

edit v. 편집하다 manual n. 안내서, 설명서 reporter n. 기자

해석 누가 그 기사를 편집할 수 있나요?
(A) 직원 안내서요.
(B) 그녀가 그 신문사의 기자인가요?
(C) Xian이 오늘 아침에 한가한 것 같아요.

해설 (A) [×] 질문의 edit(편집하다)에서 연상할 수 있는 서류와 관련된 manual(안내서)을 사용하여 혼동을 준 오답이다.
(B) [×] 질문의 article(기사)과 관련 있는 newspaper(신문사)를 사

용하여 혼동을 준 오답이다.
(C) [○] Xian이 오늘 아침에 한가한 것 같다며, 기사를 편집할 수 있는 사람을 간접적으로 언급했으므로 정답이다.

PART 3

[32-34]

Questions 32-34 refer to the following conversation.

🔊 미국식 → 캐나다식

W: **³²I'm getting ready to move my things into my new apartment.** But I don't want to bring this couch and those chairs with me.
M: Have you considered giving them to a local charity?
W: That sounds great. **³³But I'm not sure I'll be able to transport them. My van isn't big enough to hold them.**
M: **³⁴I actually have a large truck. If you like, I can take them to the charity.**

couch n. 소파, 긴 의자 consider v. 고려하다 charity n. 자선 단체
transport v. 옮기다, 운송하다

해석
32-34번은 다음 대화에 관한 문제입니다.
여: ³²저는 새 아파트로 제 물건들을 옮길 준비를 하고 있어요. 그런데 저는 이 소파와 저 의자들을 가지고 가고 싶지 않아요.
남: 지역 자선 단체에 그것들을 기부하는 걸 고려해 봤어요?
여: 좋은 생각이네요. ³³하지만 제가 그것들을 옮길 수 있을지 모르겠어요. 제 승합차는 그것들을 실을 수 있을 정도로 충분히 크지 않거든요.
남: ³⁴사실 제가 큰 트럭을 가지고 있어요. 당신이 괜찮다면, 제가 그것들을 자선 단체로 가지고 갈게요.

32 특정 세부 사항 문제

해석 여자는 무엇을 할 준비를 하고 있는가?
(A) 상품을 반품한다.
(B) 가구를 구입한다.
(C) 아파트 임대 계약을 갱신한다.
(D) 새로운 거주지로 이사한다.

해설 질문의 핵심 어구(preparing to do)와 관련된 내용을 주의 깊게 듣는다. 여자가 "I'm getting ready to move my things into my new apartment."라며 새 아파트로 물건들을 옮길 준비를 하고 있다고 하였다. 따라서 (D)가 정답이다.

어휘 return v. 반품하다, 반납하다 purchase v. 구입하다, 사다
renew v. 갱신하다, 재개하다 lease n. 임대 계약
relocate to ~로 이주하다 residence n. 거주지, 주택

Paraphrasing

is ~ preparing to ~할 준비를 하고 있다 → 'm getting ready to ~할 준비를 하고 있다

33 문제점 문제

해석 여자는 무엇에 대해 걱정하는가?

(A) 임대료가 올랐다.
(B) 의자가 손상되었다.
(C) 차량이 너무 작다.
(D) 지역이 낯설다.

해설 여자의 말에서 부정적인 표현이 언급된 다음을 주의 깊게 듣는다. 여자가 "But I'm not sure I'll be able to transport them. My van isn't big enough to hold them."이라며 자신이 물건들을 옮길 수 있을지 모르겠다고 한 후, 자신의 승합차가 그것들을 실을 수 있을 정도로 충분히 크지 않다고 하였다. 따라서 (C)가 정답이다.

어휘 rental fee 임대료, 사용료 damage v. 손상하다
vehicle n. 차량, 탈것 neighborhood n. 지역, 이웃
unfamiliar adj. 낯선

Paraphrasing

> van 승합차 → A vehicle 차량
> isn't big enough 충분히 크지 않다 → is too small 너무 작다

34 제안 문제

해석 남자는 여자를 위해 무엇을 해주겠다고 제안하는가?
(A) 몇몇 물건들을 옮긴다.
(B) 이사 서비스에 전화한다.
(C) 임대주에게 이야기한다.
(D) 새로운 아파트를 꾸민다.

해설 남자의 말에서 여자를 위해 해주겠다고 언급한 내용을 주의 깊게 듣는다. 남자가 여자에게 "I actually have a large truck. If you like, I can take them to the charity."라며 큰 트럭을 가지고 있다고 한 후, 괜찮다면 그것들을 자선 단체로 가지고 가겠다고 하였다. 따라서 (A)가 정답이다.

어휘 landlord n. 임대주, 건물 소유주 decorate v. 꾸미다, 장식하다

[35-37] 3ㅔ(b) 영국식 → 호주식
Questions 35-37 refer to the following conversation.

W: ³⁵We still need some things for the dinner party we will be supplying food for tomorrow. ³⁶Can you write them down and then buy them at the store on Fourth Street?
M: Just a moment . . . I'll use my phone.
W: OK. We need disposable paper plates, plastic cutlery, and white placemats. There will be 75 guests, but maybe get 100 of each to be safe.
M: Got it. Maybe I will be able to get a discount for making a bulk purchase.
W: Oh, that reminds me . . . ³⁷There is a coupon you can download for 10 percent off. I'll text you the link now.

---

write down 적다, 써내려 가다
disposable adj. 일회용의, 처분이 가능한 cutlery n. 식기류
placemat n. 식기용 깔개 bulk purchase 대량 구매
remind v. 생각나게 하다, 상기시키다 text v. 문자로 보내다; n. 글, 문서

해석
35-37번은 다음 대화에 관한 문제입니다.

여: ³⁵우리가 내일 음식을 제공할 예정인 저녁 파티에 아직 필요한 것들이 있어요. ³⁶받아 적어주시고 4번가에 있는 상점에서 그것들을 구입해주실 수 있나요?
남: 잠시만요... 제 휴대전화를 이용할게요.
여: 네. 우리는 일회용 종이 접시, 플라스틱 식기류, 흰색 식기용 깔개가 필요해요. 75명의 손님이 있을 건데, 안전하게 각각 100개씩 준비해 주세요.
남: 알겠습니다. 아마 대량 구매하면 할인을 받을 수 있을 거예요.
여: 아, 그러고 보니 생각났네요... ³⁷다운로드할 수 있는 10퍼센트 할인 쿠폰이 있어요. 제가 지금 링크를 문자로 보내드릴게요.

35 화자 문제

해석 화자들은 어디에서 일하는 것 같은가?
(A) 음식 공급 업체에서
(B) 공장에서
(C) 소프트웨어 회사에서
(D) 여행사에서

해설 대화에서 신분 및 직업과 관련된 표현을 놓치지 않고 듣는다. 여자가 "We still need some things for the dinner party we will be supplying food for tomorrow."라며 내일 음식을 제공할 예정인 저녁 파티에 아직 필요한 것들이 있다고 한 것을 통해 화자들이 음식 공급 업체에서 일한다는 것을 알 수 있다. 따라서 (A)가 정답이다.

어휘 firm n. 회사 agency n. 회사, 기관, 단체

36 요청 문제

해석 여자는 남자에게 무엇을 하라고 요청하는가?
(A) 상점에 전화한다.
(B) 음식을 주문한다.
(C) 휴대전화를 찾는다.
(D) 목록을 작성한다.

해설 여자의 말에서 요청과 관련된 표현이 언급된 다음을 주의 깊게 듣는다. 여자가 남자에게 "Can you write them[some things] down and then buy them at the store on Fourth Street?"라며 필요한 것들을 받아 적고 4번가에 있는 상점에서 구입해달라고 하였다. 따라서 (D)가 정답이다.

Paraphrasing

> write ~ down 받아 적다 → Make a list 목록을 작성하다

37 특정 세부 사항 문제

해석 여자는 문자 메시지로 무엇을 보낼 것인가?
(A) 웹사이트 주소
(B) 제품 이미지
(C) 판매 영수증
(D) 매장 위치

해설 질문의 핵심 어구(send by text message)와 관련된 내용을 주의 깊게 듣는다. 여자가 "There is a coupon you can download for 10 percent off. I'll text you the link now."라며 다운로드할 수 있는 10퍼센트 할인 쿠폰이 있는데, 지금 링크를 문자로 보내겠다고 하였다. 따라서 (A)가 정답이다.

어휘 **product** n. 제품 **receipt** n. 영수증

Paraphrasing

the link 링크 → A Web site address 웹사이트 주소

[38-40]

🎧 호주식 → 미국식

Questions 38-40 refer to the following conversation.

M: Hello. ³⁸**I'm calling to ask about your commercial laundry service. I just opened a small hotel in the area, and I'll need the bedding and towels washed regularly.** It's the Fairfax Lodge on the corner of Walker Avenue and Baker Street.

W: Oh, ³⁹**that's not far from here at all. In that case, we can provide you with same-day service at no additional charge.**

M: That sounds great. ⁴⁰**Could you arrange for someone from your business to drop by my hotel today to discuss everything?**

W: Of course. My assistant manager will be there right after lunch.

commercial adj. 상업용의, 이윤을 낳는 **laundry** n. 세탁
bedding n. 침구 **regularly** adv. 정기적으로 **additional** adj. 추가의
charge n. 요금; v. (요금을) 청구하다 **arrange** v. 준비하다, 마련하다
assistant manager 부팀장

해석

38-40번은 다음 대화에 관한 문제입니다.

남: 안녕하세요. ³⁸상업용 세탁 서비스에 관해 문의하기 위해 전화드려요. 제가 작은 호텔을 이 지역에 막 열었는데, 침구와 수건이 정기적으로 세탁돼야 해요. Walker가와 Baker가의 모퉁이에 있는 Fairfax Lodge입니다.

여: 아, ³⁹여기서 전혀 멀지 않네요. 그렇다면, 저희가 추가 요금 없이 당일 서비스를 제공해 드릴 수 있습니다.

남: 좋아요. ⁴⁰오늘 업체에서 누군가가 제 호텔에 들러 모든 것을 논의하도록 준비해 주실 수 있나요?

여: 물론이죠. 저희 부팀장이 점심 직후 그곳으로 갈 거예요.

38 목적 문제

해석 남자는 왜 전화를 하고 있는가?
(A) 할인을 요청하기 위해
(B) 서비스에 대해 문의하기 위해
(C) 가격에 대해 문의하기 위해
(D) 주문을 확인하기 위해

해설 전화의 목적을 묻는 문제이므로, 대화의 초반을 반드시 듣는다. 남자가 "I'm calling to ask about your commercial laundry service. I just opened a small hotel in the area, and I'll need the bedding and towels washed regularly."라며 상업용 세탁 서비스에 관해 문의하기 위해 전화한다고 한 후, 작은 호텔을 이 지역에 막 열었는데 침구와 수건이 정기적으로 세탁돼야 한다고 한 것을 통해 서비스에 대해 문의하기 위해 전화하고 있음을 알 수 있다. 따라서 (B)가 정답이다.

어휘 **request** v. 요청하다; n. 요청 **inquire** v. 문의하다
order n. 주문; v. 주문하다

39 이유 문제

해석 여자는 왜 남자에게 무료 당일 서비스를 제공하는가?
(A) 근처에서 사업체를 운영한다.
(B) 다른 여러 고객을 추천했다.
(C) 단골손님이 되었다.
(D) 장기 계약을 체결했다.

해설 질문의 핵심 어구(free same-day service)와 관련된 내용을 주의 깊게 듣는다. 여자가 "that[Fairfax Lodge]'s not far from here at all. In that case, we can provide you with same-day service at no additional charge."라며 남자의 호텔인 Fairfax Lodge가 전혀 멀지 않으므로 추가 요금 없이 당일 서비스를 제공해 줄 수 있다고 하였다. 따라서 (A)가 정답이다.

어휘 **operate** v. 운영하다, 가동하다
refer v. (사람을) 보내다, 참조하게 하다 **regular customer** 단골손님

Paraphrasing

free 무료의 → at no additional charge 추가 요금 없이

40 특정 세부 사항 문제

해석 남자는 오늘 여자가 무엇을 하기를 원하는가?
(A) 시연을 준비한다.
(B) 금액을 확인한다.
(C) 직원을 보낸다.
(D) 청구서를 준비한다.

해설 질문의 핵심 어구(today)가 언급된 주변을 주의 깊게 듣는다. 남자가 "Could you arrange for someone from your business to drop by my hotel today to discuss everything?"이라며 오늘 업체에서 누군가가 호텔에 들러 모든 것을 논의하도록 준비해 달라고 요청하였다. 따라서 (C)가 정답이다.

어휘 **confirm** v. 확인하다, 확정하다 **representative** n. 직원, 대표
invoice n. 청구서

[41-43]

🎧 영국식 → 캐나다식

Questions 41-43 refer to the following conversation.

W: ⁴¹**Welcome to my architecture podcast.** Today, I'll be interviewing Jake Miller, who designed the Terrace Art Gallery. Could you tell us about this building, Mr. Miller?

M: Sure. One of my goals was to create an open space with lots of natural light. So the ceilings are very high, and the exterior walls have many windows.

W: That's interesting. Were you influenced by another structure?

M: Yes. ⁴²**I traveled to Spain to attend Madrid University when I was younger.** While there, I visited a famous cathedral. I was really impressed with how spacious and full of sunlight it was.

W: Sounds wonderful. And ⁴³**I heard you're writing a book about future architectural trends.**

M: Right. ⁴³**It'll be available for purchase on September 1.**

architecture n. 건축학, 건축 양식 **ceiling** n. 천장 ◯

exterior adj. 외부의, 겉의; n. 외부, 겉모습
influence v. 영향을 미치다; n. 영향(력) structure n. 건축물, 구조
cathedral n. 대성당 spacious adj. 넓은 architectural adj. 건축의

해석
41-43번은 다음 대화에 관한 문제입니다.
여: ⁴¹저희 건축학 팟캐스트에 오신 것을 환영합니다. 오늘, Jake Miller를 인터뷰할 것인데, Terrace 미술관을 설계하신 분입니다. 이 건물에 대해 말씀해 주시겠어요, Mr. Miller?
남: 물론이죠. 제 목표 중 하나는 자연광이 많이 들어오는 열린 공간을 만드는 것이었어요. 그래서 천장이 매우 높고, 외벽에는 많은 창문이 있습니다.
여: 흥미롭네요. 다른 건축물의 영향을 받으셨나요?
남: 네. ⁴²저는 어렸을 때 마드리드 대학교에 다니기 위해 스페인에 갔어요. 그곳에 있으면서, 유명한 대성당을 방문했어요. 그곳이 얼마나 넓고 햇빛이 가득 들어오는지에 매우 감명받았습니다.
여: 멋지네요. 그리고 ⁴³미래 건축 동향에 관한 책을 집필 중이라고 들었어요.
남: 맞아요. ⁴³9월 1일에 구매가 가능할 거예요.

41 화자 문제

해석 여자는 누구인 것 같은가?
(A) 건축가
(B) 팟캐스트 진행자
(C) 작가
(D) 여행사 직원

해설 대화에서 신분 및 직업과 관련된 표현을 놓치지 않고 듣는다. 여자가 "Welcome to my architecture podcast."라며 자신의 건축학 팟캐스트에 온 것을 환영한다고 한 것을 통해 여자가 팟캐스트 진행자임을 알 수 있다. 따라서 (B)가 정답이다.

42 이유 문제

해석 남자는 왜 스페인에 갔는가?
(A) 연설을 하기 위해
(B) 대학에서 공부하기 위해
(C) 일자리에 지원하기 위해
(D) 상을 받기 위해

해설 질문의 핵심 어구(travel to Spain)가 언급된 주변을 주의 깊게 듣는다. 남자가 "I traveled to Spain to attend Madrid University when I was younger."라며 어렸을 때 마드리드 대학교에 다니기 위해 스페인에 갔다고 하였다. 따라서 (B)가 정답이다.

어휘 speech n. 연설 apply for ~에 지원하다
position n. (일)자리, 지위 accept v. 받다, 받아들이다

Paraphrasing

attend ~ University 대학교에 다니다 → study at a college 대학에서 공부하다

43 다음에 할 일 문제

해석 9월에 무슨 일이 일어날 것인가?
(A) 인터뷰가 온라인에 게시될 것이다.
(B) 연구가 종료될 것이다.

(C) 학회가 열릴 것이다.
(D) 출판물이 발간될 것이다.

해설 질문의 핵심 어구(September)가 언급된 주변을 주의 깊게 듣는다. 여자가 "I heard you're writing a book about future architectural trends"라며 미래 건축 동향에 관한 책을 집필 중이라고 들었다고 하자, 남자가 "It'll be available for purchase on September 1."라며 그것은 9월 1일에 구매가 가능할 것이라고 한 것을 통해 9월에 출판물이 발간될 것임을 알 수 있다. 따라서 (D)가 정답이다.

어휘 post v. 게시하다, 발송하다 publication n. 출판물, 간행물
release v. 발간하다, 공개하다; n. 출시, 공개

Paraphrasing

a book 책 → A publication 출판물
be available for purchase 구매가 가능하다 → be released 발간되다

[44-46] 🎧 미국식 → 호주식 → 영국식

Questions 44-46 refer to the following conversation with three speakers.

W1: Mr. Nolan. **⁴⁴I just want to say how thrilled we are at Western Department Store about this collaboration with your company.** Your tracksuits are sure to be popular with our customers.
M: I'm glad to hear it. **⁴⁵We made sure that they are not only stylish and reasonably priced but also highly resistant to damage.**
W1: We will make sure to mention that in the marketing materials. Oh, good . . . **⁴⁶Our lawyer Tanya has arrived with the contract.**
W2: Hi. **⁴⁶I'm going to go over each section of this agreement with you,** Mr. Nolan. OK, let's begin . . .

thrilled adj. 기쁜, 신나는 collaboration n. 협업, 공동 작업
tracksuit n. 운동복 reasonably adv. 합리적으로, 상당히
resistant to ~에 강한, 저항하는 material n. 자료, 재료
go over ~을 검토하다, 살펴보다 agreement n. 합의(서), 동의

해석
44-46번은 다음 세 명의 대화에 관한 문제입니다
여1: Mr. Nolan. ⁴⁴저희 Western 백화점이 귀사와의 이번 협업에 대해 얼마나 기뻐하고 있는지 말씀드리고 싶어요. 당신의 운동복들은 저희 고객들에게 확실히 인기가 있을 거예요.
남: 다행이네요. ⁴⁵저희는 그것들이 유행에 따르면서도 합리적으로 가격이 매겨질 뿐만 아니라 손상에도 매우 강할 수 있도록 확실하게 했어요.
여1: 마케팅 자료에도 그 점을 언급하도록 하겠습니다. 아, 좋아요... ⁴⁶저희 변호사인 Tanya가 계약서를 가지고 왔네요.
여2: 안녕하세요. ⁴⁶당신과 이 합의서의 각 조항을 검토하려고 합니다, Mr. Nolan. 그럼, 시작하죠...

44 주제 문제

해석 대화는 주로 무엇에 대한 것인가?

(A) 사업 협력
(B) 광고 캠페인
(C) 해외 진출
(D) 성과 평가

해설 대화의 주제를 묻는 문제이므로, 대화의 초반을 반드시 듣는다. 여자1이 "I just want to say how thrilled we are at Western Department Store about this collaboration with your company."라며 Western 백화점이 남자의 회사와의 이번 협업에 대해 얼마나 기뻐하고 있는지 말하고 싶다고 한 후, 협업에 대한 구체적인 내용으로 대화가 이어지고 있다. 따라서 (A)가 정답이다.

어휘 expansion n. 진출, 확장 performance n. 성과, 공연
evaluation n. 평가

Paraphrasing

collaboration with ~ company 회사와의 협업 → A business partnership 사업 협력

45 언급 문제

해석 몇몇 의류 제품에 대해 무엇이 언급되는가?
(A) 무료 액세서리가 딸려 있다.
(B) 내구성이 매우 뛰어나다.
(C) 매우 비싸다.
(D) 천연 소재를 포함한다.

해설 질문의 핵심 어구(clothing items)와 관련된 내용을 주의 깊게 듣는다. 남자가 "We made sure that they[tracksuits] are not only stylish and reasonably priced but also highly resistant to damage."라며 운동복들이 유행에 따르면서도 합리적으로 가격이 매겨질 뿐만 아니라 손상에도 매우 강할 수 있도록 확실하게 했다고 하였다. 따라서 (B)가 정답이다.

어휘 durable adj. 내구성이 뛰어난, 견고한

Paraphrasing

resistant to damage 손상에 강한 → durable 내구성이 뛰어난

46 이유 문제

해석 Tanya는 왜 회의에 참여했는가?
(A) 영업 전략을 논의하기 위해
(B) 법률 문서를 설명하기 위해
(C) 교육 워크숍을 준비하기 위해
(D) 면접을 진행하기 위해

해설 질문의 핵심 어구(Tanya)가 언급된 주변을 주의 깊게 듣는다. 여자1이 "Our lawyer Tanya has arrived with the contract."라며 변호사인 Tanya가 계약서를 가지고 왔다고 하자, 여자2[Tanya]가 "I'm going to go over each section of this agreement with you"라며 남자와 합의서의 각 조항을 검토하려고 한다고 하였다. 따라서 (B)가 정답이다.

어휘 strategy n. 전략 legal adj. 법률의
conduct v. 진행하다, 실행하다

Paraphrasing

go over ~ agreement 합의서를 검토하다 → explain a legal document 법률 문서를 설명하다

[47-49]
3째 미국식 → 캐나다식

Questions 47-49 refer to the following conversation.

W: **⁴⁷Albert, we still need to choose a location for our shoot next week.** Where would be a good place to film the last scene of the music video?
M: What about Grayson Park?
W: That's perfect. **⁴⁸Um, but there's an issue . . . We have to get permission before we film in a public area.**
M: I've done that before. **⁴⁹I'll drop by city hall to submit the request form.**

location n. 장소, 위치 shoot n. 촬영 film v. 촬영하다; n. 영화
scene n. 장면, 상황 issue n. 문제, 주제 permission n. 허가, 승인
city hall 시청, 시 당국 submit v. 제출하다 request form 신청서

해석
47-49번은 다음 대화에 관한 문제입니다.

여: ⁴⁷Albert, 우리는 여전히 다음 주 촬영을 위한 장소를 선정해야 해요. 뮤직비디오의 마지막 장면을 촬영하기 위한 좋은 장소가 어디일까요?
남: Grayson 공원은 어때요?
여: 아주 좋아요. ⁴⁸음, 그렇지만 문제가 하나 있어요... 우리는 공공장소에서 촬영하기 전에 허가를 받아야 해요.
남: 제가 전에 그것을 해봤어요. ⁴⁹신청서를 제출하러 시청에 잠깐 들를게요.

47 주제 문제

해석 화자들이 주로 논의하고 있는 것은 무엇인가?
(A) 영상 촬영을 위한 장소 찾기
(B) 배우와 시간 약속 잡기
(C) 공원에서 행사 개최하기
(D) 관객에게 영화 상영하기

해설 대화의 주제를 묻는 문제이므로, 대화의 초반을 반드시 듣는다. 여자가 "Albert, we still need to choose a location for our shoot next week."이라며 다음 주 촬영을 위한 장소를 선정해야 한다고 한 후, 영상 촬영을 위한 장소를 찾는 것에 대한 내용으로 대화가 이어지고 있다. 따라서 (A)가 정답이다.

어휘 spot n. 장소, 점 hold v. 개최하다 audience n. 관객, 청중

Paraphrasing

choose a location 장소를 선정하다 → Finding a spot 장소 찾기

48 문제점 문제

해석 여자는 무엇에 대해 걱정하는가?
(A) 활동을 위한 장비가 이용 불가하다.
(B) 위치가 적절하지 않았다.
(C) 음악 행사가 일반 사람들에게 공개되지 않는다.
(D) 공간을 사용하기 위한 승인이 필요하다.

해설 여자의 말에서 부정적인 표현이 언급된 주변을 주의 깊게 듣는다. 여자가 "Um, but there's an issue . . . We have to get permission before we film in a public area."라며 문제가 하나 있다고 한 후, 공공장소에서 촬영하기 전에 허가를 받아야 한다고 하였다. 따라서 (D)가 정답이다.

어휘 appropriate adj. 적절한 public n. 일반 사람들, 대중
approval n. 승인, 인정

Paraphrasing

> have to get permission 허가를 받아야 한다 → Approval ~ is needed 승인이 필요하다

49 의도 파악 문제

해석 남자는 "제가 전에 그것을 해봤어요"라고 말할 때 무엇을 의도하는가?
(A) 제안된 계획에 반대한다.
(B) 최근에 매우 바빴다.
(C) 프로젝트에 대한 도움을 받았다.
(D) 기꺼이 일을 수행할 의향이 있다.

해설 질문의 인용어구(I've done that before)가 언급된 주변을 주의 깊게 듣는다. 남자가 "I'll drop by city hall to submit the request form."이라며 신청서를 제출하러 시청에 잠깐 들르겠다고 한 것을 통해 남자가 기꺼이 일을 수행할 의향이 있음을 알 수 있다. 따라서 (D)가 정답이다.

어휘 proposed adj. 제안된 extremely adv. 매우, 극심하게
be willing to 기꺼이 ~하다

[50-52]　　　　　　　　🎧 영국식 → 캐나다식

Questions 50-52 refer to the following conversation.

> W: **50How are the preparations for the release of our latest lawnmower going?**
> M: **50No issues so far.** The venue is booked, and I've sent invitations to media representatives.
> W: Great. What is there left to do?
> M: Well, I'm preparing the pamphlet about the product. I'm considering an electronic version rather than a physical one. What do you think?
> W: That'd be more cost-effective. **51We could send it to attendees in advance and also put up QR codes at the venue to download the file.**
> M: OK. **52I'm going to go through the pamphlet this afternoon to check for any errors.**
>
> preparation n. 준비 release n. 출시, 개봉; v. 발표하다, 공개하다
> lawnmower n. 잔디 깎는 기계 invitation n. 초대(장), 초청(장)
> representative n. 대표자, 대리인 electronic adj. 전자의
> physical adj. 물질의, 신체의 attendee n. 참석자
> in advance 미리, 사전에

해석
50-52번은 다음 대화에 관한 문제입니다.
여: 50저희의 최신 잔디 깎는 기계 출시 준비는 어떻게 진행되고 있나요?
남: 50지금까지 문제는 없습니다. 장소는 예약이 완료되었고, 미디어 관계자

들에게 초대장을 보냈어요.
여: 좋아요. 이제 남은 일은 무엇인가요?
남: 음, 제품에 관한 팸플릿을 준비 중이에요. 실물 버전보다는 전자 버전을 고려하고 있습니다. 어떻게 생각하시나요?
여: 그게 더 비용 효율적일 것 같네요. 51참석자들에게 미리 그것을 전송하고 행사장에 QR 코드를 붙여 그 파일을 다운로드할 수 있도록 해도 되겠어요.
남: 알겠습니다. 52오늘 오후에 팸플릿을 검토하여 오류가 있는지 확인할게요.

50 특정 세부 사항 문제

해석 화자들은 어떤 행사를 준비하고 있는가?
(A) 세무 세미나
(B) 개업식
(C) 회사 워크숍
(D) 제품 출시

해설 질문의 핵심 어구(preparing)와 관련된 내용을 주의 깊게 듣는다. 여자가 "How are the preparations for the release of our latest lawnmower going?"이라며 최신 잔디 깎는 기계 출시 준비는 어떻게 진행되고 있는지 묻자, 남자가 "No issues so far."라며 지금까지 문제가 없다고 하였다. 따라서 (D)가 정답이다.

어휘 tax n. 세금, 조세 launch n. 출시, 개시; v. 출시하다, 시작하다

Paraphrasing

> the release 출시 → launch 출시

51 이유 문제

해석 참석자들은 왜 QR 코드를 사용할 것인가?
(A) 지시 사항을 받기 위해
(B) 주문을 하기 위해
(C) 정보를 이용하기 위해
(D) 예약을 하기 위해

해설 질문의 핵심 어구(QR code)가 언급된 주변을 주의 깊게 듣는다. 여자가 "We could send it to attendees in advance and also put up QR codes at the venue to download the file."이라며 참석자들에게 미리 그것, 즉 전자 버전의 팸플릿을 전송하고 행사장에 QR 코드를 붙여 그 파일을 다운로드할 수 있도록 해도 되겠다고 하였다. 따라서 (C)가 정답이다.

어휘 instruction n. 지시 사항, 설명
access v. 이용하다, 접속하다; n. 입장, 접근 reservation n. 예약

52 다음에 할 일 문제

해석 남자는 오늘 무엇을 할 것이라고 말하는가?
(A) 문서 교정을 본다.
(B) 몇몇 고객들에게 이메일을 보낸다.
(C) 소프트웨어 업데이트를 설치한다.
(D) 몇몇 초대장을 보낸다.

해설 질문의 핵심 어구(today)와 관련된 내용을 주의 깊게 듣는다. 남자가 "I'm going to go through the pamphlet this afternoon to check for any errors."라며 오늘 오후에 팸플릿을 검토하여 오류가 있는지 확인할 것이라고 하였다. 따라서 (A)가 정답이다.

어휘 proofread v. 교정을 보다 install v. 설치하다

Paraphrasing

go through ~ to check for any errors 검토하여 오류가 있는지
확인하다 → Proofread 교정을 보다

the pamphlet 팸플릿 → a document 문서

[53-55]

🎧 미국식 → 캐나다식 → 호주식

Questions 53-55 refer to the following conversation with three speakers.

W: David, Brett . . . ⁵³**You'll both be attending the National Book Fair in Seattle, right?**

M1: Yeah. ⁵⁴**Our manager also asked us to create a promotional brochure to hand out to the people who visit our company's booth at the event.**

M2: That's right. And ⁵⁴**we need to have it ready for the printer by Monday,** so the deadline is a little tight. Maybe you could help us?

W: Of course. What do you want me to do?

M1: Well, ⁵⁵**we have this list of about 30 book descriptions and author biographies. But we need to get it down to 15.**

W: ⁵⁵**I'll go through it right now and then give you my recommendations.**

promotional adj. 홍보용의 brochure n. 책자
hand out 나눠주다, 배포하다 printer n. 인쇄소, 인쇄업자
deadline n. 마감 기한 tight adj. 촉박한
description n. 설명, 서술 biography n. 약력, 전기
recommendation n. 추천(서), 권고

해석
53-55번은 다음 세 명의 대화에 관한 문제입니다.

여: David, Brett... ⁵³두 분 다 시애틀에서 열리는 국내 도서전에 참석할 거죠, 그렇죠?

남1: 네. ⁵⁴관리자가 행사에서 우리 회사 부스를 방문하는 사람들에게 나눠줄 홍보용 책자를 만들어 달라고도 부탁했어요.

남2: 맞아요. 그리고 ⁵⁴월요일까지 그걸 인쇄소에 넘길 수 있도록 해야 해서, 마감 기한이 조금 촉박해요. 혹시 저희 좀 도와주실 수 있을까요?

여: 물론이죠. 제가 무엇을 하면 될까요?

남1: 음, ⁵⁵약 30권 정도의 도서 설명과 저자 약력에 관한 목록이 여기 있습니다. 하지만 15권으로 줄여야 해요.

여: ⁵⁵지금 바로 그것을 살펴본 다음에 제 추천 목록을 드릴게요.

53 화자 문제

해석 화자들은 어떤 산업에서 일하는 것 같은가?
(A) 출판
(B) 패션
(C) 관광
(D) 회계

해설 대화에서 신분 및 직업과 관련된 표현을 놓치지 않고 듣는다. 여자가 "You'll both be attending the National Book Fair in Seattle, right?"라며 남자들에게 둘 다 시애틀에서 열리는 국내 도서전에 참석할 것인지 물은 후, 국내 도서전에서 배포할 홍보용 책자를 제작하는 것에 대한 내용으로 대화가 이어지고 있다. 이를 통해 화자들이 출판 산업에서 일한다는 것을 알 수 있다. 따라서 (A)가 정답이다.

54 요청 문제

해석 남자들은 무엇을 하도록 요청받았는가?
(A) 부스를 선택한다.
(B) 표를 예매한다.
(C) 인쇄소를 고용한다.
(D) 책자를 만든다.

해설 남자들의 말에서 요청과 관련된 표현이 언급된 다음을 주의 깊게 듣는다. 남자1이 "Our manager also asked us to create a promotional brochure to hand out to the people who visit our company's booth at the event."라며 관리자가 행사에서 회사 부스를 방문하는 사람들에게 나눠줄 홍보용 책자를 만들어 달라고 부탁했다고 하자, 남자2가 "we need to have it ready for the printer by Monday"라며 월요일까지 그것을 인쇄소에 넘길 수 있도록 해야 된다고 하였다. 따라서 (D)가 정답이다.

어휘 select v. 선택하다 booklet n. (소)책자

Paraphrasing

create a ~ brochure 책자를 만들다 → Make a booklet 책자를
만들다

55 다음에 할 일 문제

해석 여자는 다음에 무엇을 할 것인가?
(A) 마감 기한을 확정한다.
(B) 목록을 검토한다.
(C) 관리자에게 전화한다.
(D) 출판물을 주문한다.

해설 대화의 마지막 부분을 주의 깊게 듣는다. 남자1이 "we have this list of about 30 book descriptions and author biographies. But we need to get it down to 15."이라며 약 30권 정도의 도서 설명과 저자 약력에 관한 목록이 있는데 15권으로 줄여야 한다고 하자, 여자가 "I'll go through it right now and then give you my recommendations."라며 지금 바로 그것을 살펴본 다음에 추천 목록을 주겠다고 하였다. 따라서 (B)가 정답이다.

Paraphrasing

go through 살펴보다 → Review 검토하다

[56-58]

🎧 호주식 → 미국식

Questions 56-58 refer to the following conversation.

M: Sally, could you follow up with Mr. Porter today? ⁵⁶**He is waiting for an estimate of the cost to redesign his kitchen.**

🔊

W: I'm still working on the quote. It won't be ready until the end of the day.

M: That's fine. **57Don't forget to offer him a discount. This is the second time he has hired us.** **57I'm hoping this will encourage him to give us other projects in the future.**

W: I'll do that. But **58he will probably also want to know which day we will be ready to begin the work. Let's take a few minutes now to figure that out.**

---

follow up with 후속 조치하다 estimate n. 견적(서)
redesign v. 다시 디자인하다 quote n. 견적 figure out ~을 알아내다

해석

56-58번은 다음 대화에 관한 문제입니다.

남: Sally, 오늘 Mr. Porter에게 후속 조치를 해주시겠어요? 56그가 자신의 주방을 다시 디자인하는 비용에 대한 견적을 기다리고 있어요.

여: 저는 아직 견적을 내는 중이에요. 오늘이 끝날 무렵이 되어서야 준비가 될 거예요.

남: 괜찮아요. 57그에게 할인을 제공하는 것을 잊지 마세요. 이번이 그가 우리를 고용한 두 번째예요. 57저는 이번 기회로 그가 앞으로도 다른 프로젝트를 우리에게 맡기기를 바라고 있어요.

여: 그렇게 하겠습니다. 그런데 58그는 아마 우리가 작업을 시작할 준비가 되는 날이 언제일지도 알고 싶어 할 거예요. 지금 몇 분 정도 그것을 알아보도록 해요.

56 화자 문제

해석 화자들은 누구인 것 같은가?
(A) 회계사들
(B) 인테리어 디자이너들
(C) 부동산 중개인들
(D) 기술자들

해설 지문에서 신분 및 직업과 관련된 표현을 놓치지 않고 듣는다. 남자가 "He[Mr. Porter] is waiting for an estimate of the cost to redesign his kitchen."이라며 고객인 Mr. Porter가 자신의 주방을 다시 디자인하는 비용에 대한 견적을 기다리고 있다고 한 것을 통해 화자들이 인테리어 디자이너들임을 알 수 있다. 따라서 (B)가 정답이다.

어휘 real estate 부동산

57 의도 파악 문제

해석 남자는 왜 "이번이 그가 우리를 고용한 두 번째예요"라고 말하는가?
(A) 몇몇 정보를 확인하기 위해
(B) 대안을 제안하기 위해
(C) 이유를 전하기 위해
(D) 직원을 칭찬하기 위해

해설 질문의 인용어구(This is the second time he has hired us)가 언급된 주변을 주의 깊게 듣는다. 남자가 "Don't forget to offer him[Mr. Porter] a discount."라며 Mr. Porter에게 할인을 제공하는 것을 잊지 말라고 한 후, "I'm hoping this will encourage him to give us other projects in the future."라며 이번 기회로 그가 앞으로도 다른 프로젝트를 자신들에게 맡기기를 바라고 있다고

한 것을 통해 할인을 제공하려는 이유를 전하기 위함임을 알 수 있다. 따라서 (C)가 정답이다.

어휘 verify v. 확인하다, 입증하다 alternative n. 대안 compliment v. 칭찬하다

58 특정 세부 사항 문제

해석 화자들은 다음에 어떤 주제를 논의할 것인가?
(A) 할인 금액
(B) 사업 확장
(C) 프로젝트 시작일
(D) 디자인 제안 변경

해설 질문의 핵심 어구(discuss next)와 관련된 내용을 주의 깊게 듣는다. 여자가 "he[Mr. Porter] will probably also want to know which day we will be ready to begin the work. Let's take a few minutes now to figure that out."이라며 Mr. Porter가 아마 자신들이 작업을 시작할 준비가 되는 날이 언제일지도 알고 싶어 할 거라며, 지금 몇 분 정도 그것을 알아보자고 하였다. 따라서 (C)가 정답이다.

Paraphrasing

which day ~ will be ready to begin the work 작업을 시작할 준비가 되는 날이 언제일지 → A project start date 프로젝트 시작일

[59-61]

미국식 → 캐나다식

Questions 59-61 refer to the following conversation.

W: **59Thank you for volunteering to try out a product for Pace Incorporated.** As you may already know, we are one of the country's largest suppliers of VR headsets.

M: **60Actually, I'm a little worried. I don't have any experience using VR devices.**

W: That's fine. Our target market is made up of first-time users of the technology.

M: That's good to hear. **61How long will it take to complete the trial?**

W: It shouldn't take more than half an hour.

---

volunteer v. 자원하다, 자원봉사로 하다; n. 자원봉사자
supplier n. 제품 제조업자, 공급 회사 target market 표적 시장
be made up of ~으로 구성되다 complete v. 완료하다
trial n. 시용, 실험

해석

59-61번은 다음 대화에 관한 문제입니다.

여: 59Pace사의 제품을 시용해보는 것에 자원해 주셔서 감사합니다. 이미 아시다시피, 저희는 국내 최대 규모의 VR 헤드셋 제품 제조업자 중 하나입니다.

남: 60사실, 저는 조금 걱정이 돼요. 제가 VR 기기를 사용해 본 경험이 없거든요.

여: 그건 괜찮아요. 저희의 표적 시장이 이 기술의 첫 사용자들로 구성되어 있어요.

남: 다행이네요. 61시용을 완료하는 데 얼마나 걸릴까요?

여: 30분 넘게 걸리지는 않을 거예요.

59 특정 세부 사항 문제

해석 무슨 행사가 열리고 있는 것 같은가?
(A) 시설 견학
(B) 제품 시험
(C) 취업 면접
(D) 제품 소개

해설 질문의 핵심 어구(event)와 관련된 내용을 주의 깊게 듣는다. 여자가 "Thank you for volunteering to try out a product for Pace Incorporated."라며 Pace사의 제품을 시용해보는 것에 자원해 주어 고맙다고 하였다. 따라서 (B)가 정답이다.

Paraphrasing

try out a product 제품을 시용해보다 → A product test 제품 시험

60 이유 문제

해석 남자는 왜 걱정하는가?
(A) 활동을 일찍 떠나야 할 것이다.
(B) 질문에 대한 답을 잊었다.
(C) 전자 기기를 파손했다.
(D) 특정 기술을 사용해 본 적이 없다.

해설 질문의 핵심 어구(concerned)와 관련된 내용을 주의 깊게 듣는다. 남자가 "Actually, I'm a little worried. I don't have any experience using VR devices."라며 사실 조금 걱정이 된다고 한 후, VR 기기를 사용해 본 경험이 없다고 하였다. 따라서 (D)가 정답이다.

어휘 damage v. 파손하다, 손상시키다; n. 손상 device n. 기기, 장치

Paraphrasing

is ~ concerned 걱정하다 → 'm a little worried 조금 걱정이 되다

61 특정 세부 사항 문제

해석 남자는 무엇에 대해 물어보는가?
(A) 특정 활동 시간이 얼마나 걸릴지
(B) 설명이 주어질지
(C) 몇 시에 행사가 열릴지
(D) 어떤 소프트웨어가 설치될 것인지

해설 대화에서 남자의 말을 주의 깊게 듣는다. 남자가 "How long will it take to complete the trial?"이라며 시용을 완료하는 데 얼마나 걸릴지 물었다. 따라서 (A)가 정답이다.

어휘 instruction n. 설명, 지시

Paraphrasing

the trial 시용 → a session 특정 활동 시간

[62-64]

🎧 영국식 → 호주식

Questions 62-64 refer to the following conversation and table of contents.

W: The latest issue of *Sweet Life* magazine is out. ⁶²It includes the article we worked on for three weeks! ○

M: Wow. And ⁶²it's on Page 6, near the front of the magazine.

W: ⁶³Something's not right, though. I just noticed that the extra details we decided to add to the last page of the article were not included in the published version.

M: What should we do?

W: ⁶⁴We can call the publisher to see if the details can be added to the online version of the magazine.

---

magazine n. 잡지 include v. 포함하다 article n. 기사
detail n. 세부 사항 healthy adj. 건강한
showdown n. 대결, 마지막 결전

해석
62-64번은 다음 대화와 목차에 관한 문제입니다.

여: *Sweet Life* 잡지의 최신 호가 나왔어요. ⁶²그건 우리가 3주 동안 작업했던 기사를 포함하고 있어요!

남: 와. 그리고 ⁶²그건 잡지의 초반부인 6페이지에 실렸네요.

여: ⁶³그런데 뭔가 이상해요. 기사의 마지막 페이지에 덧붙이기로 했던 추가적인 세부 사항이 출판된 버전에는 포함되지 않은 걸 방금 발견했어요.

남: 우리가 무엇을 해야 할까요?

여: ⁶⁴출판사에 전화해서 세부 사항이 그 잡지의 온라인 버전에 추가될 수 있는지 확인해 봐요.

Sweet Life	111호
목차	
⁶²첫 만찬을 주최하는 방법	6페이지
그리스에서의 7일	10페이지
건강하고 맛있는 디저트	18페이지
텍사스에서의 바비큐 대결	20페이지

62 시각 자료 문제

해석 시각 자료를 보아라. 화자들이 논의하고 있는 기사는 무엇인가?
(A) 첫 만찬을 주최하는 방법
(B) 그리스에서의 7일
(C) 건강하고 맛있는 디저트
(D) 텍사스에서의 바비큐 대결

해설 제시된 목차의 정보를 확인한 후 질문의 핵심 어구(article)가 언급된 주변을 주의 깊게 듣는다. 여자가 "It[latest issue of ~ magazine] includes the article we worked on for three weeks!"라며 잡지의 최신 호가 화자들이 3주 동안 작업했던 기사를 포함하고 있다고 하자, 남자가 "it's on Page 6, near the front of the magazine"이라며 그것이 잡지의 초반부인 6페이지 실렸다고 하였으므로 화자들이 논의하고 있는 기사는 첫 만찬을 주최하는 방법임을 목차에서 알 수 있다. 따라서 (A)가 정답이다.

63 문제점 문제

해석 여자는 무슨 문제를 언급하는가?
(A) 웹사이트가 로딩되지 않는다.
(B) 일부 정보가 누락됐다.
(C) 사진이 포함되지 않았다.
(D) 몇몇 단어들의 철자가 부정확하게 쓰였다.

해설 여자의 말에서 부정적인 표현이 언급된 주변을 주의 깊게 듣는다. 여자가 "Something's not right, though. I just noticed that the extra details we decided to add to the last page of the article were not included in the published version."이라며 뭔가 이상하다고 한 후, 기사의 마지막 페이지에 덧붙이기로 했던 추가적인 세부 사항이 출판된 버전에는 포함되지 않은 걸 방금 발견했다고 하였다. 따라서 (B)가 정답이다.

어휘 load v. (데이터 등이) 로딩되다 spell v. 철자를 쓰다
incorrectly adv. 부정확하게

Paraphrasing

> not included 포함되지 않은 → missing 누락된

64 제안 문제

해석 여자는 무엇을 하라고 제안하는가?
(A) 새로운 기사 작성하기
(B) 출판사에 연락하기
(C) 페이지 번호 바꾸기
(D) 광고 회사 고용하기

해설 여자의 말에서 제안과 관련된 표현이 언급된 다음을 주의 깊게 듣는다. 여자가 "We can call the publisher to see if the details can be added to the online version of the magazine."이라며 출판사에 전화해서 세부 사항이 그 잡지의 온라인 버전에 추가될 수 있는지 확인해 보자고 하였다. 따라서 (B)가 정답이다.

어휘 hire v. 고용하다 advertising firm 광고 회사

Paraphrasing

> call 전화하다 → Contacting 연락하기

[65-67]

3ᵐ 캐나다식 → 영국식

Questions 65-67 refer to the following conversation and schedule.

> M: Have you heard? **65Byron Jennings turned in his resignation letter. He was offered a job at a translation firm and decided to take it.**
>
> W: Yes, I just heard. **66We have to find someone by the end of the month to take over Mr. Jennings's 1 P.M. class.** Hmm . . . **67How about Sylvia Osborn? She taught here before, and she recently called asking about teaching opportunities.**
>
> M: Good idea. **67I'll talk to her now to see if she is available.**
>
> turn in 제출하다 resignation letter 사직서 translation n. 번역
> take over 인계받다 opportunity n. 기회

해석

65-67번은 다음 대화와 일정표에 관한 문제입니다.

남: 그거 들었어요? 65Byron Jennings가 사직서를 제출했어요. 그가 번역 회사에서 일자리를 제안받고 수락하기로 했어요.

여: 네, 저도 방금 들었어요. 66저희는 이번 달 말까지 Mr. Jennings의 오후 1시 수업을 인계받을 사람을 찾아야 해요. 흠... 67Sylvia Osborn은 어때

요? 그녀는 전에 이곳에서 가르쳤고, 최근에 강의 기회에 대해 문의하러 전화하기도 했어요.

남: 좋은 생각이에요. 67제가 지금 그녀와 이야기해서 시간이 되는지 확인해 볼게요.

Linguana 어학 센터 수업 일정 (월요일과 수요일)	
수업	시간
독일어 레벨 1	오전 9시- 오전 10시 30분
스페인어 레벨 2	오후 12시 30분 - 오후 2시
66프랑스어 레벨 2	오후 1시 - 오후 3시
이탈리아어 레벨 1	오후 4시 - 오후 5시 30분

65 특정 세부 사항 문제

해석 남자에 따르면, Mr. Jennings는 무엇을 하기로 결정했는가?
(A) 조수를 고용한다.
(B) 사업을 시작한다.
(C) 일자리를 수락한다.
(D) 임금 인상을 요청한다.

해설 질문의 핵심 어구(Mr. Jennigs decided)가 언급된 주변을 주의 깊게 듣는다. 남자가 "Byron Jennings turned in his resignation letter. He was offered a job at a translation firm and decided to take it."이라며 Byron Jennings가 사직서를 제출했다고 한 후, 그가 번역 회사에서 일자리를 제안받고 수락하기로 했다고 하였다. 따라서 (C)가 정답이다.

어휘 assistant n. 조수 raise n. 임금 인상; v. 올리다

Paraphrasing

> take 수락하다 → Accept 수락하다
> a job 일자리 → a position 일자리

66 시각 자료 문제

해석 시각 자료를 보아라. Mr. Jennings는 어느 수업을 가르치는가?
(A) 독일어 레벨 1
(B) 스페인어 레벨 2
(C) 프랑스어 레벨 2
(D) 이탈리아어 레벨 1

해설 제시된 일정표의 정보를 확인한 후 질문의 핵심 어구(Mr. Jennings teach)와 관련된 내용을 주의 깊게 듣는다. 여자가 "We have to find someone by the end of the month to take over Mr. Jennings's 1 P.M. class."라며 이번 달 말까지 Mr. Jennings의 오후 1시 수업을 인계받을 사람을 찾아야 한다고 하였으므로 Mr. Jennings가 가르치는 수업이 프랑스어 레벨 2임을 일정표에서 알 수 있다. 따라서 (C)가 정답이다.

67 다음에 할 일 문제

해석 남자는 다음에 무엇을 할 것 같은가?
(A) 이전 동료와 이야기한다.

(B) 구직 광고를 게재한다.
(C) 새로운 수업 자료를 찾아본다.
(D) 몇몇 사무용 장비를 찾아본다.

해설 대화의 마지막 부분을 주의 깊게 듣는다. 여자가 "How about Sylvia Osborn? She taught here before, and she recently called asking about teaching opportunities."라며 Sylvia Osborn이 전에 이곳에서 가르쳤고 최근에 강의 기회에 대해 문의하러 전화하기도 했다고 하자, 남자가 "I'll talk to her now to see if she is available."이라며 지금 그녀와 이야기해서 시간이 되는지 확인해 보겠다고 한 것을 통해 남자가 이전 동료인 Sylvia Osborn과 이야기할 것임을 알 수 있다. 따라서 (A)가 정답이다.

어휘 colleague n. 동료   material n. 자료, 재료
look for ~을 찾다, 구하다

[68-70]   🔊 영국식 → 캐나다식
Questions 68-70 refer to the following conversation and map.

W: Steven, could you assist me? ⁶⁸**We need to prepare more samples for our café's promotion.** All we need to do is pour the beverages into the sample cups and put lids on them.
M: Sure. I can help with that.
W: Great! Please handle the Peppermint Lime.
M: Oh, ⁶⁹**did you put the stickers on the lids?** Our manager wants to make sure potential customers see our café's logo when they try the samples.
W: I did. ⁷⁰**Once we're done, we're going to offer them to people going into the park next to our café.** Please hurry.

assist v. 돕다, 도움이 되다   prepare v. 준비하다
promotion n. 판촉 (행사), 판촉 활동   pour v. 붓다
beverage n. 음료   lid n. 뚜껑   handle v. 처리하다, 다루다
potential adj. 잠재적인

해석
68-70번은 다음 대화와 지도에 관한 문제입니다.

여: Steven, 저를 도와주실 수 있나요? ⁶⁸**우리는 카페 판촉 행사를 위한 견본을 더 많이 준비해야 해요.** 견본용 컵들에 음료를 붓고 그것들에 뚜껑을 덮기만 하면 돼요.
남: 물론이죠. 제가 도와드릴 수 있어요.
여: 좋아요! 페퍼민트 라임을 처리해 주세요.
남: 아, ⁶⁹**뚜껑에 스티커를 붙이셨나요?** 관리자가 잠재 고객들이 견본을 맛볼 때 카페 로고를 볼 수 있도록 확실히 하기를 원해요.
여: 했어요. ⁷⁰**우리가 다 끝내면, 우리 카페 옆 공원으로 들어가는 사람들에게 그것들을 나눠줄 거예요.** 서둘러 주세요.

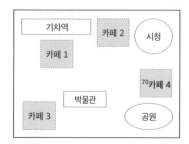

68 주제 문제

해석 화자들은 무엇에 대해 이야기하고 있는가?
(A) 강습회
(B) 업데이트된 메뉴
(C) 마케팅 행사
(D) 지점 개설

해설 대화의 주제를 묻는 문제이므로, 대화의 초반을 반드시 듣는다. 여자가 "We need to prepare more samples for our café's promotion."이라며 카페 판촉 행사를 위한 견본을 더 많이 준비해야 한다고 한 후, 카페 판촉 행사로 음료를 사람들에게 나눠주는 것에 대한 내용으로 대화가 이어지고 있다. 따라서 (C)가 정답이다.

어휘 branch n. 지점

Paraphrasing

promotion 판촉 행사 → A marketing event 마케팅 행사

69 특정 세부 사항 문제

해석 남자는 무엇에 대해 문의하는가?
(A) 작업이 완료되었는지
(B) 활동이 언제 종료될 것인지
(C) 몇몇 용품들이 어떻게 배송되었는지
(D) 행사가 어디에서 열릴 것인지

해설 대화에서 남자의 말을 주의 깊게 듣는다. 남자가 "did you put the stickers on the lids?"라며 뚜껑에 스티커를 붙였는지 물었다. 따라서 (A)가 정답이다.

어휘 activity n. 활동   deliver v. 배송하다, 배달하다

70 시각 자료 문제

해석 시각 자료를 보아라. 화자들이 어디에서 일하는 것 같은가?
(A) 카페 1
(B) 카페 2
(C) 카페 3
(D) 카페 4

해설 제시된 지도의 정보를 확인한 후 질문의 핵심 어구(speakers ~ work)와 관련된 내용을 주의 깊게 듣는다. 여자가 "Once we're done, we're going to offer them[samples] to people going into the park next to our café."라며 다 끝내면 자신들의 카페 옆 공원으로 들어가는 사람들에게 견본을 나눠줄 것이라고 하였으므로 화자들이 일하는 곳은 카페 4임을 지도에서 알 수 있다. 따라서 (D)가 정답이다.

PART 4

[71-73]   🔊 호주식
Questions 71-73 refer to the following tour information.

Welcome to the Verdant Grove Forest Tour. ⁷¹**Today, we'll be hiking through the woods to explore the forest ecosystem.** ⁷²As we go, you will encounter a wide array of unique plants that thrive in this environment. I will provide you with insights into some of the rare species we will be seeing. ⁷³It seems likely that we'll get a rain shower on our way, so don't forget to take your raincoats! Anything you don't want to carry can be left here on the tour bus. We will start our journey in 10 minutes.

---

hike v. 도보 여행을 하다; n. 도보 여행 explore v. 탐험하다
ecosystem n. 생태계 encounter v. 접하다, 마주하다
a wide array of 다수의 thrive v. 번성하다, 잘 자라다
environment n. 환경 insight n. 식견, 통찰력, 이해
rare adj. 진귀한, 드문 species n. (생물)종 rain shower 소나기
journey n. 여정, 여행

해석

71-73번은 다음 관광 안내에 관한 문제입니다.

Verdant Grove 숲 투어에 오신 것을 환영합니다. ⁷¹오늘, 우리는 삼림 생태계를 탐험하기 위해 숲속으로 도보 여행을 할 것입니다. ⁷²가면서, 여러분은 이 환경에서 번성하는 다수의 독특한 식물들을 접하게 될 것입니다. 저는 여러분에게 우리가 보게 될 몇몇 진귀한 종들에 대한 식견을 제공할 것입니다. ⁷³도중에 소나기가 올 것 같으니, 우비를 가져가는 것을 잊지 마세요! 휴대하고 싶지 않은 것은 여기 투어 버스에 두고 가셔도 됩니다. 10분 후에 여정을 시작할게요.

71 방법 문제

해석 투어 그룹은 Verdant Grove 숲을 어떻게 이동할 것인가?
(A) 자전거로
(B) 버스로
(C) 자동차로
(D) 도보로

해설 질문의 핵심 어구(travel through the Verdant Grove Forest)와 관련된 내용을 주의 깊게 듣는다. "Today, we'll be hiking through the woods to explore the forest ecosystem."이라며 오늘 삼림 생태계를 탐험하기 위해 숲속으로 도보 여행을 할 것이라고 하였다. 따라서 (D)가 정답이다.

72 특정 세부 사항 문제

해석 화자는 청자들에게 무엇에 대해 알려줄 것인가?
(A) 현지 건축
(B) 진귀한 식물
(C) 지역의 역사
(D) 환경 문제

해설 질문의 핵심 어구(teach)와 관련된 내용을 주의 깊게 듣는다. "As we go, you will encounter a wide array of unique plants ~. I will provide you with insights into some of the rare species we will be seeing."이라며 가면서 다수의 독특한 식물들을 접하게 될 것인데, 보게 될 몇몇 진귀한 종들에 대한 식견을 제공할 것이라고 하였다. 따라서 (B)가 정답이다.

어휘 environmental adj. 환경의

73 특정 세부 사항 문제

해석 청자들에게 무엇을 하라고 상기시키는가?

(A) 소지품을 확인한다.
(B) 우비를 가져간다.
(C) 이름표를 착용한다.
(D) 호텔 객실의 문을 잠근다.

해설 질문의 핵심 어구(reminded)와 관련된 내용을 주의 깊게 듣는다. "It seems likely that we'll get a rain shower on our way, so don't forget to take your raincoats!"라며 도중에 소나기가 올 것 같으니, 우비를 가져가는 것을 잊지 말라고 하였다. 따라서 (B)가 정답이다.

어휘 belongings n. 소지품 lock v. (문을) 잠그다; n. 잠금장치

Paraphrasing

> take 가져가다 → Bring 가져가다

[74-76]

3) 영국식

Questions 74-76 refer to the following advertisement.

⁷⁴**Experience a smarter way to monitor your health and fitness. Prion's new Trackband Watch 5 is designed to be integrated into your daily life.** It has a user-friendly interface and advanced features like auto-start and auto-pause. So you can easily and accurately record your workout progress. ⁷⁵**A notable difference from the previous model is that it can send health alerts to users.** For example, if your heart rate increases suddenly, it will notify you. Visit any Prion store to buy one. ⁷⁶**Customers who purchase this model will receive a 10 percent discount for this month only.**

---

monitor v. 추적 관찰하다, 감독하다 integrate v. 통합시키다
user-friendly adj. 사용하기 쉬운
interface n. 인터페이스(사용자가 기기를 쉽게 동작시키기 위해 도움을 주는 시스템) advanced adj. 고급의, 선진의
feature n. 기능, 특징; v. 특징을 이루다 accurately adv. 정확하게
notable adj. 눈에 띄는, 중요한 alert n. 경고 메시지; v. 경보를 발하다
heart rate 심박수 suddenly adv. 갑자기, 급작스럽게
notify v. 알리다, 통지하다

해석

74-76번은 다음 광고에 관한 문제입니다.

⁷⁴당신의 건강과 체력을 추적 관찰할 수 있는 더 현명한 방식을 경험해 보세요. Prion의 새로운 Trackband 워치 5는 여러분들의 일상생활에 통합되도록 설계되었습니다. 사용하기 쉬운 인터페이스와 자동 시작 및 자동 일시 중지 같은 고급 기능을 갖추고 있습니다. 따라서 운동 진행 상황을 쉽고 정확하게 기록할 수 있습니다. ⁷⁵이전 모델과의 눈에 띄는 차이점은 사용자들에게 건강 경고 메시지를 보낼 수 있다는 점입니다. 예를 들어 심박수가 갑자기 증가하면, 그것을 당신에게 알려줍니다. Prion 매장을 방문하여 구매하세요. ⁷⁶이 모델을 구매하시는 고객분들은 이번 달에만 10퍼센트의 할인을 받게 되실 것입니다.

74 주제 문제

해석 무엇이 광고되고 있는가?
(A) 휴대용 충전기
(B) 스마트워치
(C) 식기 세척기

(D) 운동 기구

해설 광고의 주제를 묻는 문제이므로, 지문의 초반을 반드시 듣는다. "Experience a smarter way to monitor your health and fitness. Prion's new Trackband Watch 5 is designed to be integrated into your daily life."라며 건강과 체력을 추적 관찰할 수 있는 더 현명한 방식을 경험해 보라고 한 후, Prion의 새로운 Trackband 워치 5는 일상생활에 통합되도록 설계되었다고 하였다. 따라서 (B)가 정답이다.

어휘 portable adj. 휴대용의, 들고 다닐 수 있는 charger n. 충전기
dishwasher n. 식기 세척기

75 특정 세부 사항 문제

해석 화자는 어떤 새로운 특징을 강조하는가?
(A) 다양한 색상으로 출시된다.
(B) 방대한 양의 사용자 정보를 저장한다.
(C) 사용자들에게 알림을 보낸다.
(D) 고급 보안 시스템을 가지고 있다.

해설 질문의 핵심 어구(new feature)와 관련된 내용을 주의 깊게 듣는다. "A notable difference from the previous model is that it can send health alerts to users."라며 이전 모델과의 눈에 띄는 차이점은 사용자들에게 건강 경고 메시지를 보낼 수 있다는 점이라고 하였다. 따라서 (C)가 정답이다.

어휘 a variety of 다양한, 여러 가지의 notification n. 알림, 통지

Paraphrasing

alerts 경고 메시지 → notifications 알림

76 특정 세부 사항 문제

해석 화자에 따르면, 구매자들은 무엇을 받을 것인가?
(A) 무료 액세서리
(B) 기간 한정 할인
(C) 운동 추천
(D) 소프트웨어 업그레이드

해설 질문의 핵심 어구(buyers receive)와 관련된 내용을 주의 깊게 듣는다. "Customers who purchase this model will receive a 10 percent discount for this month only."라며 이 모델을 구매하는 고객들은 이번 달에만 10퍼센트의 할인을 받게 될 것이라고 하였다. 따라서 (B)가 정답이다.

어휘 accessory n. 액세서리, 장신구 recommendation n. 추천, 권고

Paraphrasing

for this month only 이번 달에만 → limited-time 기간 한정의

[77-79]

Questions 77-79 refer to the following telephone message.

Good morning, Ms. Parker. This is William Harris calling from Outward Incorporated. We received your e-mail regarding **77the backpack you purchased on our Web site. 78You stated that it still hasn't arrived yet, even though** you placed the order two weeks ago. Unfortunately, we've had some problems with our ordering system. I called our shipping manager, and he said that your order will be sent out before the end of the day and will arrive by Friday. To make up for your inconvenience, **79we will return 50 dollars of your original 200-dollar purchase amount.** This will be charged back to your credit card. Please let me know if you have any questions.

regarding prep. ~에 관하여 state v. 말하다, 진술하다
make up for ~을 보상하다, 변상하다
inconvenience n. 불편, 불편하게 하는 것 return v. 돌려주다, 반납하다
original adj. 원래의, 처음의 charge v. 청구하다

해석
77-79번은 다음 전화 메시지에 관한 문제입니다.

안녕하세요, Ms. Parker. 저는 Outward사의 William Harris입니다. 77저희 웹사이트에서 구매하셨던 배낭에 관한 귀하의 이메일을 받았습니다. 782주 전에 주문하셨음에도 불구하고 그것이 아직 도착하지 않았다고 말씀하셨는데요. 유감스럽게도, 주문 시스템에 몇 가지 문제가 있었습니다. 저희 배송 담당자에게 전화해 보니, 귀하의 주문품은 오늘 중으로 발송되어 금요일까지 도착할 것이라고 합니다. 불편에 대해 보상하기 위해, 79원래 구매 금액인 200달러 중 50달러를 돌려드리겠습니다. 이것은 회원님의 신용카드로 다시 청구될 것입니다. 궁금한 점이 있으시면 언제든지 알려주세요.

77 특정 세부 사항 문제

해석 화자의 회사는 무엇을 제조하는가?
(A) 안경
(B) 화장품
(C) 배낭
(D) 탁자

해설 질문의 핵심 어구(company manufacture)와 관련된 내용을 주의 깊게 듣는다. "the backpack you purchased on our Web site"라며 청자가 화자의 웹사이트에서 구매했던 배낭이라고 한 것을 통해 화자의 회사가 배낭을 제조한다는 것을 알 수 있다. 따라서 (C)가 정답이다.

어휘 manufacture v. 제조하다, 생산하다; n. 제조, 생산

78 의도 파악 문제

해석 화자는 왜 "유감스럽게도, 주문 시스템에 몇 가지 문제가 있었습니다"라고 말하는가?
(A) 주문에 대해 문의하기 위해
(B) 해결책을 언급하기 위해
(C) 절차를 설명하기 위해
(D) 지연에 대해 사과하기 위해

해설 질문의 인용어구(Unfortunately, we've had some problems with our ordering system)가 언급된 주변을 주의 깊게 듣는다. "You stated that it[backpack] still hasn't arrived yet, even though you placed the order two weeks ago."라며 청자가 2주 전에 배낭을 주문했음에도 불구하고 그것이 아직 도착하지 않았다고 말했다고 한 것을 통해 지연에 대해 사과하기 위함임을 알 수 있다. 따라서 (D)가 정답이다.

어휘 **point out** 언급하다, 지적하다 **solution** n. 해결책, 해법
apologize v. 사과하다

79 특정 세부 사항 문제

해석 화자는 청자에게 무엇을 제공하는가?
(A) 보증 연장
(B) 향후 할인
(C) 부분 환불
(D) 무료 제품

해설 질문의 핵심 어구(offer)와 관련된 내용을 주의 깊게 듣는다. "we will return 50 dollars of your original 200-dollar purchase amount"라며 원래 구매 금액인 200달러 중 50달러를 돌려주겠다고 하였다. 따라서 (C)가 정답이다.

어휘 **warranty** n. (품질 등의) 보증 **partial** adj. 부분적인, 불완전한

Paraphrasing

return 돌려주다 → refund 환불

[80-82]
[3] 미국식

Questions 80-82 refer to the following broadcast.

Good morning, Houston. **80Yesterday afternoon, the entire city experienced a power outage for several hours.** According to Governor Michaels, this was caused by winter weather affecting the state electrical grid. Technicians took action quickly, but the outage still disabled traffic signals before the early evening rush hour. Furthermore, **81it caused a band performance to be canceled at Longhorn Stadium.** While power has now been restored, the weather is expected to worsen, so everyone is advised to take precautions. **82Up next, we have Jennifer Oliver with the business news.**

entire adj. 전체의, 온 power outage 정전, 단전
governor n. 주지사, 운영 위원 affect v. 영향을 미치다, 발생하다
electrical grid 전력망 take action 조치하다, 결정하다
disable v. (기계를) 고장 나게 하다 traffic signals (교통) 신호등
restore v. 복구하다, 회복시키다 advise v. 권고하다, 조언하다
precaution n. 예방 조치, 예방책

해석

80-82번은 다음 방송에 관한 문제입니다.

좋은 아침입니다, 휴스턴 시민 여러분. **80어제 오후에, 도시 전체가 몇 시간 동안 정전을 겪었습니다.** Michaels 주지사에 따르면, 이것은 주 전력망에 영향을 미친 겨울 날씨에 의한 것이었습니다. 기술자들이 신속하게 조치했지만, 정전은 초저녁 교통 혼잡 시간대 전까지 계속해서 신호등을 고장 나게 했습니다. 게다가, **81그것은 Longhorn 경기장에서의 밴드 공연이 취소되게 하였습니다.** 전력은 이제 복구가 되었지만, 날씨가 더 악화할 것으로 예상되므로, 모두 예방 조치하도록 권고됩니다. **82다음으로, Jennifer Oliver의 비즈니스 뉴스입니다.**

80 주제 문제

해석 방송은 주로 무엇에 대한 것인가?
(A) 정전

(B) 노동쟁의
(C) 산업 재해
(D) 도로 폐쇄

해설 방송의 주제를 묻는 문제이므로, 지문의 초반을 반드시 듣는다. "Yesterday afternoon, the entire city experienced a power outage for several hours."라며 어제 오후에 도시 전체가 몇 시간 동안 정전을 겪었다고 한 후, 정전의 원인과 정전이 끼친 영향에 대한 내용으로 지문이 이어지고 있다. 따라서 (A)가 정답이다.

어휘 **blackout** n. 정전 **strike** n. 쟁의, 파업
industrial adj. 산업의, 공업 시설이 많은 **closure** n. 폐쇄, 종료

Paraphrasing

a power outage 정전 → A blackout 정전

81 특정 세부 사항 문제

해석 어떤 종류의 행사가 취소되었는가?
(A) 자동차 경주
(B) 축구 경기
(C) 음악 공연
(D) 불꽃놀이

해설 질문의 핵심 어구(canceled)가 언급된 주변을 주의 깊게 듣는다. "it[power outage] caused a band performance to be canceled at Longhorn Stadium."이라며 정전은 Longhorn 경기장에서의 밴드 공연이 취소되게 했다고 하였다. 따라서 (C)가 정답이다.

어휘 **automobile race** 자동차 경주 **fireworks exhibition** 불꽃놀이

Paraphrasing

a band performance 밴드 공연 → A musical performance 음악 공연

82 특정 세부 사항 문제

해석 청자들은 다음에 무엇을 들을 것인가?
(A) 일기 예보
(B) 짧은 광고
(C) 비즈니스 보도
(D) 교통 정보

해설 지문의 핵심 어구(hear next)와 관련된 내용을 주의 깊게 듣는다. "Up next, we have Jennifer Oliver with the business news."라며 다음은 Jennifer Oliver의 비즈니스 뉴스라고 하였다. 따라서 (C)가 정답이다.

어휘 **weather forecast** 일기 예보 **brief** adj. 짧은, 간단한

[83-85]
[3] 캐나다식

Questions 83-85 refer to the following announcement.

Attention, Robertson's shoppers. **83We would like to inform you that we are having a special sale on household cleaners, laundry detergents, and bath products until 8 P.M. today.** And that's not all. Members of our rewards ○

program will earn double the points for every dollar they spend on grocery purchases. **⁸⁴This is our way of thanking you as we celebrate our 50th year in business this March. And lastly, ⁸⁵be reminded that we will be closing early during the upcoming holiday weekend.** Make sure to get here before 7 P.M. on Saturday and Sunday if you need to do some last-minute shopping.

inform v. 알리다, 알아내다 household adj. 가정용의; n. 가정
detergent n. 세제 rewards program 보상 프로그램
earn v. 얻다, 벌다 celebrate v. 기념하다, 축하하다
remind v. 생각나게 하다, 상기시키다 upcoming adj. 곧 있을
make sure 반드시 ~하도록 하다
last-minute adj. 막바지의, 마지막 순간의

해석

83-85번은 다음 공지에 관한 문제입니다.

주목해 주세요, Robertson 쇼핑객 여러분. ⁸³저희는 오늘 오후 8시까지 가정용 세정제, 세탁 세제, 욕실용품에 대한 특별 할인을 진행하고 있다는 점을 알려드리고자 합니다. 그리고 그뿐만이 아닙니다. 보상 프로그램 회원들은 식료품 구매 시 지출한 1달러당 두 배의 포인트를 얻게 될 것입니다. ⁸⁴이것은 올해 3월에 영업 50주년을 기념하여 여러분께 감사를 표하는 방법입니다. 그리고 마지막으로, ⁸⁵곧 있을 연휴 주말 동안에는 일찍 문을 닫을 것임을 기억해 주시기를 바랍니다. 막바지 쇼핑을 해야 한다면 반드시 토요일과 일요일 오후 7시 전에 여기에 오셔야 합니다.

83 장소 문제

해석 공지는 어디에서 이뤄지고 있는 것 같은가?
(A) 약국에서
(B) 슈퍼마켓에서
(C) 가구 상점에서
(D) 가전제품 상점에서

해설 공지가 이루어지는 장소를 묻는 문제이므로, 장소와 관련된 표현을 놓치지 않고 듣는다. "We would like to inform you that we are having a special sale on household cleaners, laundry detergents, and bath products until 8 P.M. today."라며 오늘 오후 8시까지 가정용 세정제, 세탁 세제, 욕실용품에 대한 특별 할인을 진행하고 있다는 점을 알리고자 한다는 것을 통해 공지가 이루어지고 있는 장소가 슈퍼마켓임을 알 수 있다. 따라서 (B)가 정답이다.

어휘 pharmacy n. 약국, 조제실

84 다음에 할 일 문제

해석 3월에 무슨 일이 일어날 것인가?
(A) 상점이 기념일을 축하할 것이다.
(B) 장소가 보수를 위해 일시적으로 문을 닫을 것이다.
(C) 할인 행사가 일주일 더 연장될 것이다.
(D) 무료 견본품이 각 고객에게 주어질 것이다.

해설 질문의 핵심 어구(March)가 언급된 주변을 주의 깊게 듣는다. "This is our way of thanking you as we celebrate our 50th year in business this March."라며 이것, 즉 특별 할인과 포인트 적립 행사가 올해 3월에 영업 50주년을 기념하여 청자들에게 감사를 표하

는 방법이라고 하였으므로 3월에 영업 50주년을 기념할 것임을 알 수 있다. 따라서 (A)가 정답이다.

어휘 establishment n. 상점, 시설 anniversary n. 기념일, 주년
temporarily adv. 일시적으로 renovation n. 보수, 개조
extend v. 연장하다

Paraphrasing

50th year in business 영업 50주년 → an anniversary 기념일

85 특정 세부 사항 문제

해석 화자는 청자들에게 무엇에 대해 상기시키는가?
(A) 현장 주차에 관한 규정
(B) 제품 환불에 관한 정책
(C) 영업시간의 변경
(D) 의견 제시를 위한 절차

해설 질문의 핵심 어구(remind)가 언급된 주변을 주의 깊게 듣는다. "be reminded that we will be closing early during the upcoming holiday weekend"라며 곧 있을 연휴 주말 동안에는 일찍 문을 닫을 것임을 기억해달라고 하였다. 따라서 (C)가 정답이다.

어휘 regulation n. 규정, 규제 on-site adj. 현장의, 현지의
operating hours 영업시간·

[86-88]

📄 영국식

Questions 86-88 refer to the following excerpt from a meeting.

> Next Tuesday, you will begin testing new accounting software. Hopefully, **⁸⁶it will let you process your clients' tax returns and other financial documents more easily. ⁸⁷During the demonstration I witnessed last month, the software seemed fast and capable.** I'm optimistic it will lead to an overall increase in productivity here. But **⁸⁸to be sure, we will test it for two weeks. Then, your evaluations will be reviewed thoroughly. Based on these,** we may adopt it throughout the company.

accounting n. 회계 hopefully adv. 바라건대, 희망을 품고
tax return 소득 신고서 financial adj. 재무의, 재정의
witness v. 관찰하다, 목격하다 capable adj. 성능이 뛰어난
optimistic adj. 낙관하는, 낙관적인 overall adj. 전반적인, 전체의
productivity n. 생산성 evaluation n. 평가
thoroughly adv. 철저히, 완전히 adopt v. 채택하다

해석

86-88번은 다음 회의 발췌록에 관한 문제입니다.

다음 주 화요일에, 여러분은 새로운 회계 소프트웨어를 시험하기 시작할 것입니다. 바라건대, ⁸⁶그것은 여러분이 고객의 소득 신고서 및 기타 재무 서류들을 더 쉽게 처리하도록 해줄 거예요. ⁸⁷지난달에 제가 관찰했던 시연 동안, 그 소프트웨어는 빠르고 성능이 뛰어난 것 같았습니다. 저는 그것이 이곳의 전반적인 생산성 향상으로 이어질 것이라고 낙관합니다. 하지만 ⁸⁸확실히 하기 위해서, 우리는 2주 동안 그것을 시험해 볼 거예요. 그러고 나서, 여러분의 평가가 철저히 검토될 것입니다. 그것들에 따라, 우리는 그것을 회사 전체에 채택할 수도 있습니다.

86 청자 문제

해석 청자들은 누구인 것 같은가?

(A) 소프트웨어 기술자들
(B) 행사 주최자들
(C) 회계사들
(D) 변호사들

해설 지문에서 신분 및 직업과 관련된 표현을 놓치지 않고 듣는다. "it[new accounting software] will let you process your clients' tax returns and other financial documents more easily"라며 새로운 회계 소프트웨어는 청자들이 고객의 소득 신고서 및 기타 재무 서류들을 더 쉽게 처리하도록 해줄 것이라고 한 것을 통해 청자들이 회계사들임을 알 수 있다. 따라서 (C)가 정답이다.

87 특정 세부 사항 문제

해석 화자는 지난달에 무엇을 했는가?

(A) 계약에 합의했다.
(B) 프로그램에 등록했다.
(C) 새로운 직원들을 고용했다.
(D) 시연에 참석했다.

해설 질문의 핵심 어구(last month)가 언급된 주변을 주의 깊게 듣는다. "During the demonstration I witnessed last month, the software seemed fast and capable."이라며 지난달에 관찰했던 시연 동안, 그 소프트웨어가 빠르고 성능이 뛰어난 것 같았다고 하였다. 따라서 (D)가 정답이다.

어휘 sign up for ~에 등록하다

88 의도 파악 문제

해석 화자는 "우리는 그것을 회사 전체에 채택할 수도 있습니다"라고 말할 때 무엇을 의도하는가?

(A) 청자들의 의견이 중요하다.
(B) 팀 구성원의 제안이 유용했다.
(C) 몇몇 직원들이 정책을 무시하고 있다.
(D) 프로젝트는 추가적인 지원자들을 필요로 한다.

해설 질문의 인용어구(we may adopt it throughout the company)가 언급된 주변을 주의 깊게 듣는다. "to be sure, we will test it[new accounting software] for two weeks. Then, your evaluations will be reviewed thoroughly."라며 확실히 하기 위해서 2주 정도 새로운 회계 소프트웨어를 시험해 볼 것이고, 그러고 나서 청자들의 평가가 철저히 검토될 것이라고 한 후, "Based on these, we may adopt it throughout the company."라며 청자들의 평가에 따라, 그것을 회사 전체에 채택할 수도 있다고 한 것을 통해 청자들의 의견이 중요함을 알 수 있다. 따라서 (A)가 정답이다.

어휘 useful adj. 유용한, 쓸모 있는 ignore v. 무시하다, 못 본 척하다

[89-91] ³📻 미국식

Questions 89-91 refer to the following telephone message.

This is Eve Morgan from Chicken Stop. I'm calling about the banner we ordered for our grand opening at Northland Mall next week. ⁸⁹**I know you said it would be ready** ○

by Thursday, but I need to get it by Monday instead. I can pay extra if necessary. This is very important. ⁹⁰**Headquarters is sending a manager to assess all our preparations.** He will also check if the banner matches company specifications. Could you call me back? ⁹¹**I can pick up the banner as soon as it's ready.**

banner n. 현수막, 플래카드
pay extra 추가 요금을 내다, 별도로 돈을 치르다
headquarters n. 본사, 본부 assess v. 평가하다
preparation n. 준비 (사항) match v. 일치하다, 어울리다
specification n. 규격, 설명서

해석
89-91번은 다음 전화 메시지에 관한 문제입니다.

저는 Chicken Stop의 Eve Morgan입니다. 다음 주 Northland 쇼핑몰에서의 개업식을 위해 저희가 주문했던 현수막에 관해 전화드려요. ⁸⁹그것이 목요일까지 준비될 거라고 말씀해 주신 것은 알지만, 그 대신 월요일까지 그것을 받아야 해요. 필요하다면 추가 요금을 낼 수 있습니다. 이것은 매우 중요한 일이에요. ⁹⁰본사에서 저희의 모든 준비 사항을 평가하기 위해 관리자를 보낼 겁니다. 그가 현수막이 회사 규격과 일치하는지도 확인할 거예요. 저에게 다시 전화 주시겠어요? ⁹¹저는 현수막이 준비되는 대로 그것을 찾으러 갈 수 있습니다.

89 목적 문제

해석 화자는 왜 전화하고 있는가?

(A) 관리자에게 최신 정보를 알려주기 위해
(B) 매장을 위한 물품들을 주문하기 위해
(C) 급한 업무를 요청하기 위해
(D) 지불 문제를 해결하기 위해

해설 전화의 목적을 묻는 문제이므로, 지문의 초반을 반드시 듣는다. "I know you said it[banner] would be ready by Thursday, but I need to get it by Monday instead."라며 현수막이 목요일까지 준비될 것이라고 말해준 것은 알지만 그 대신 월요일까지 그것을 받아야 한다고 한 것을 통해 화자가 급한 업무를 요청하기 위해 전화하고 있음을 알 수 있다. 따라서 (C)가 정답이다.

어휘 rush adj. 급한, 바쁜 address v. 해결하다, 연설하다
payment n. 지불(금), 지급

90 언급 문제

해석 화자는 회사에 대해 무엇을 말하는가?

(A) 지연된 발송에 대해 걱정한다.
(B) 준비에 관해 확인하기 위해 누군가를 보낼 것이다.
(C) 개업식의 날짜를 변경할 것이다.
(D) 추가 주문을 할 계획이다.

해설 질문의 핵심 어구(company)와 관련된 내용을 주의 깊게 듣는다. "Headquarters is sending a manager to assess all our preparations."라며 본사에서 모든 준비 사항을 평가하기 위해 관리자를 보낼 것이라고 하였다. 따라서 (B)가 정답이다.

어휘 shipment n. 발송, 수송 arrangement n. 준비

Paraphrasing

> assess ~ preparations 준비 사항을 평가하다 → check on arrangements 준비에 관해 확인하다

91 특정 세부 사항 문제

해석 화자는 무엇을 할 의향이 있는가?
(A) 더 큰 옵션의 대금을 지급한다.
(B) 물건을 가져온다.
(C) 몇 가지 수정을 한다.
(D) 매장 쿠폰을 제공한다.

해설 질문의 핵심 어구(willing to do)와 관련된 내용을 주의 깊게 듣는다. "I can pick up the banner as soon as it's ready."라며 현수막이 준비되는 대로 찾으러 갈 수 있다고 하였다. 따라서 (B)가 정답이다.

어휘 retrieve v. 가져오다, 되찾다 alteration n. 수정, 변경 사항

Paraphrasing

> pick up 찾으러 가다 → Retrieve 가져오다
>
> the banner 현수막 → an item 물건

[92-94]

3ᵈ 캐나다식

Questions 92-94 refer to the following talk.

> As everyone on this team knows, **⁹²our television program,** *Live with Mike,* **is in trouble. The weekly ratings indicate we are losing younger viewers, and we are now ranked below our competitors in the same time slot.** ⁹³**Mike Cortez does an excellent job of presenting entertainment news and interviewing guests**, but he cannot seem to connect with younger audiences. I've decided that we will add a co-host to the program who is closer to our viewers' average age. However, we have little time to waste. ⁹⁴**The co-host needs to start next month, so I'd like you to make a list of potential candidates we can contact. We'll begin interviews as soon as possible.**

> be in trouble 곤란한 상황에 놓이다, 곤경에 빠지다
> rating n. 시청률, 순위 indicate v. 보여주다, 나타내다
> rank v. 순위에 위치하다, 평가하다; n. 지위 competitor n. 경쟁 상대
> time slot 시간대 connect with 가까워지다, 친해지다
> audience n. 청중, 관객 average adj. 평균의, 일반적인
> waste v. 낭비하다; n. 낭비 candidate n. 후보자

해석

92-94번은 다음 담화에 관한 문제입니다.

모든 팀원분이 아시다시피, ⁹²우리 텔레비전 프로그램인 *Live with Mike*가 곤란한 상황에 놓여있습니다. 주간 시청률은 젊은 시청자들을 잃고 있다는 것을 보여주고, 현재 우리는 동시간대의 경쟁 상대들보다 아래 순위에 있습니다. ⁹³Mike Cortez는 연예 뉴스를 발표하고 게스트들을 인터뷰하는 것을 훌륭히 해내지만, 젊은 청중들과 가까워지지는 못한 것처럼 보입니다. 저는 시청자들의 평균 연령대에 더 가까운 공동 진행자를 프로그램에 추가하기로 했습니다. 하지만, 우리는 낭비할 시간이 거의 없어요. ⁹⁴공동 진행자는 다음 달부터 시작해야 해서, 저는 우리가 연락해 볼 만한 가능성 있는 후보자들의 명단을 여러분들이 작성해 주셨으면 합니다. 가능한 한 빨리 면접을 시작할 거예요.

92 특정 세부 사항 문제

해석 화자는 무슨 문제를 언급하는가?
(A) 프로그램이 곧 취소될 것이다.
(B) 일정이 갑자기 변경되었다.
(C) 프로그램이 청중의 일부를 잃고 있다.
(D) 진행자가 프로그램을 떠날 계획이다.

해설 질문의 핵심 어구(problem)와 관련된 내용을 주의 깊게 듣는다. "our television program, *Live with Mike*, is in trouble. The weekly ratings indicate we are losing younger viewers, and we are now ranked below our competitors in the same time slot."이라며 텔레비전 프로그램인 *Live with Mike*가 곤란한 상황에 놓여있다고 한 후, 주간 시청률이 젊은 시청자들을 잃고 있다는 것을 보여주고, 현재 동시간대의 경쟁 상대들보다 아래 순위에 있다고 하였다. 따라서 (C)가 정답이다.

어휘 show n. 프로그램, 쇼 presenter n. 진행자, 발표자

Paraphrasing

> younger viewers 젊은 시청자들 → part of ~ audience 청중의 일부

93 특정 세부 사항 문제

해석 Mike Cortez는 누구인가?
(A) 프로그램 감독
(B) 언론학 교수
(C) 텔레비전 프로그램 진행자
(D) 대본 작가

해설 질문의 대상(Mike Cortez)의 신분 및 직업과 관련된 표현을 놓치지 않고 듣는다. "Mike Cortez does an excellent job of presenting entertainment news and interviewing guests"라며 Mike Cortez가 연예 뉴스를 발표하고 게스트들을 인터뷰하는 것을 훌륭히 해낸다고 하였다. 따라서 (C)가 정답이다.

어휘 director n. 감독, 관리자 journalism n. 언론(학) professor n. 교수 script writer 대본 작가, 시나리오 작가

94 의도 파악 문제

해석 화자는 "우리는 낭비할 시간이 거의 없어요"라고 말할 때 무엇을 의도하는가?
(A) 프로젝트가 완료되는 데 너무 오래 걸리고 있다.
(B) 몇몇 작업자들이 회의에 도착하지 않았다.
(C) 직원이 더 오랜 시간 업무를 해야 한다.
(D) 자리가 신속하게 채워져야 한다.

해설 질문의 인용어구(we have little time to waste)가 언급된 주변을 주의 깊게 듣는다. "The co-host needs to start next month, so I'd like you to make a list of potential candidates we can contact. We'll begin interviews as soon as possible."이라며 공동 진행자는 다음 달부터 시작해야 하므로 연락해 볼 만한 가능성 있는 후보자들의 명단을 작성해 주었으면 하고, 가능한 한 빨리 면접을 시작할 것이라고 한 것을 통해 공동 진행자 자리가 신속하게 채워져야 함을 알 수 있다. 따라서 (D)가 정답이다.

[95-97]

Questions 95-97 refer to the following announcement and menu.

🎧 영국식

> Good afternoon, all Wilson's Bakery customers. ⁹⁵**We are having a special promotion this month on desserts.** ⁹⁶**Our best-selling strawberry cheesecake is only $2.99.** You won't find a better deal anywhere! In addition, purchase your favorite beverage and get a free refill. ⁹⁷**Members of our Wilson's Bakery Rewards Program also get 10 percent off on beverages every day. So if you have not signed up yet, you should definitely do that today!** Feel free to ask one of our employees for more information.
>
> ---
>
> promotion n. 판촉 활동, 승진 deal n. 거래 beverage n. 음료
> sign up 가입하다, 등록하다 definitely adv. 반드시, 확실하게

해석

95-97번은 다음 공지와 메뉴에 관한 문제입니다.

안녕하세요, Wilson 빵집 손님 여러분. ⁹⁵저희는 이번 달에 디저트를 대상으로 특별 판촉 활동을 진행하고 있습니다. ⁹⁶저희의 가장 잘 팔리는 딸기 치즈케이크가 단돈 2.99달러입니다. 어디에서도 더 좋은 거래는 못 찾을 겁니다! 또한, 가장 좋아하는 음료를 구매하시고 무료 리필을 받으세요. ⁹⁷저희 Wilson 빵집의 보상 프로그램 회원들은 음료에 대해 매일 10퍼센트 할인도 받습니다. 그러니 만약 아직 가입하지 않으셨다면, 반드시 오늘 가입하세요! 더 많은 정보를 원하시면 저희 직원 중 한 명에게 편하게 문의해 주세요.

디저트	
초콜릿 푸딩	3.99달러
딸기 치즈케이크	⁹⁶4.99달러
바닐라 컵케이크	5.99달러
당근 케이크	6.99달러

95 주제 문제

해석 공지는 주로 무엇에 대한 것인가?

(A) 신제품
(B) 제빵 수업
(C) 판촉 행사
(D) 출장연회 서비스

해설 공지의 주제를 묻는 문제이므로, 지문의 초반을 반드시 듣는다. "We are having a special promotion this month on desserts."라며 이번 달에 디저트를 대상으로 특별 판촉 활동을 진행하고 있다고 한 후, 특별 판촉 활동에 대한 구체적인 내용으로 지문이 이어지고 있다. 따라서 (C)가 정답이다.

어휘 promotional adj. 판촉의, 홍보의
catering service 출장연회 서비스

96 시각 자료 문제

해석 시각 자료를 보아라. 어느 가격이 일시적으로 변경되었는가?

(A) 3.99달러
(B) 4.99달러
(C) 5.99달러
(D) 6.99달러

해설 제시된 메뉴의 정보를 확인한 후 질문의 핵심 어구(price ~ changed)와 관련된 내용을 주의 깊게 듣는다. "Our best-selling strawberry cheesecake is only $2.99."라며 가장 잘 팔리는 딸기 치즈케이크가 단돈 2.99달러라고 하였으므로 딸기 치즈케이크의 원래 가격인 4.99달러가 일시적으로 2.99달러로 변경됐음을 메뉴에서 알 수 있다. 따라서 (B)가 정답이다.

97 제안 문제

해석 화자는 청자들에게 무엇을 하라고 제안하는가?

(A) 일자리에 지원한다.
(B) 프로그램에 가입한다.
(C) 몇몇 견본품을 시식한다.
(D) 새로운 음료를 시도해 본다.

해설 지문의 중후반에서 제안과 관련된 표현이 포함된 문장을 주의 깊게 듣는다. "Members of our Wilson's Bakery Rewards Program also get 10 percent off on beverages every day. So if you have not signed up yet, you should definitely do that today!"라며 Wilson 빵집의 보상 프로그램 회원들은 음료에 대해 매일 10퍼센트 할인도 받는다고 한 후, 만약 아직 가입하지 않았다면 반드시 오늘 가입하라고 하였다. 따라서 (B)가 정답이다.

어휘 apply for ~에 지원하다, 신청하다 taste v. 시식하다, 맛보다

[98-100]

🎧 호주식

Questions 98-100 refer to the following excerpt from a meeting and table.

> ⁹⁸**We now require all job applicants to submit a video introduction for us to share with potential employers.** Unfortunately, we are almost at the limit of our data storage capacity. But I think I may have found a solution. There are several companies that provide online storage services that are both secure and convenient to use. The one I am looking at offers four affordable options. To begin, ⁹⁹**I recommend that we go for the 50-dollar one.** That will more than meet our needs right now. But if necessary, we can upgrade to the 80-dollar option in the future. ¹⁰⁰**Matilda, could you hand out these brochures to everyone?** They include an overview of the service's many features.
>
> ---
>
> introduction n. 소개 storage n. 저장, 보관
> capacity n. 용량, 수용력, 능력 secure adj. 안전한, 확실한
> look at ~에 대해 고려하다, 살펴보다
> affordable adj. 저렴한, 감당할 수 있는 go for ~을 택하다
> hand out 나눠주다 brochure n. 책자, 설명서
> overview n. 개요, 개관

98-100번은 다음 회의 발췌록과 표에 관한 문제입니다.

98현재 모든 입사 지원자는 우리가 잠재적 고용주들과 공유할 수 있도록 영상 소개를 제출해야 합니다. 유감스럽게도, 우리는 데이터 저장 용량이 거의 한계에 다다랐습니다. 하지만 해결책을 찾은 것 같습니다. 안전하고 사용하기 편리한 온라인 저장 서비스를 제공하는 여러 회사가 있어요. 제가 고려하고 있는 업체는 네 가지의 저렴한 옵션들을 제공합니다. 우선, **9950달러짜리를 택할 것을 제안합니다.** 이 정도면 지금 당장 우리가 필요한 것 이상을 충족시켜 줄 거예요. 하지만 필요하다면, 나중에 80달러 옵션으로 업그레이드할 수도 있습니다. **100Matilda, 이 책자를 모두에게 나눠 주시겠어요?** 그것들은 해당 서비스의 다양한 기능에 대한 개요를 포함하고 있어요.

옵션 1	99옵션 2	옵션 3	옵션 4
40달러	50달러	80달러	100달러
8테라바이트	10테라바이트	12테라바이트	14테라바이트

98 청자 문제

해석 청자들은 어디에서 일하는 것 같은가?
(A) 채용 정보 회사에서
(B) 교육 시설에서
(C) 금융 기관에서
(D) 식료품점에서

해설 지문에서 신분 및 직업과 관련된 표현을 놓치지 않고 듣는다. "We now require all job applicants to submit a video introduction for us to share with potential employers."라며 현재 모든 입사 지원자는 자신들의 회사가 잠재적 고용주들과 공유할 수 있도록 영상 소개를 제출해야 한다고 한 것을 통해 청자들이 채용 정보 회사에서 일한다는 것을 알 수 있다. 따라서 (A)가 정답이다.

어휘 recruitment agency 채용 정보 회사

99 시각 자료 문제

해석 시각 자료를 보아라. 화자는 어느 옵션을 추천하는가?
(A) 옵션 1
(B) 옵션 2
(C) 옵션 3
(D) 옵션 4

해설 제시된 표의 정보를 확인한 후 질문의 핵심 어구(recommend)가 언급된 주변을 주의 깊게 듣는다. "I recommend that we go for the 50-dollar one"이라며 50달러짜리를 택할 것을 제안한다고 했으므로 화자가 추천하는 옵션은 옵션 2임을 표에서 알 수 있다. 따라서 (B)가 정답이다.

100 특정 세부 사항 문제

해석 Matilda에게 어떤 업무가 배정되었는가?
(A) 기능 테스트하기
(B) 업그레이드 설치하기
(C) 지원자들에게 알리기
(D) 문서 나눠 주기

해설 질문의 핵심 어구(Matilda)가 언급된 주변을 주의 깊게 듣는다. "Matilda, could you hand out these brochures to everyone?"이라며 Matilda에게 책자를 모두에게 나눠 주라고 요청하였다. 따라서 (D)가 정답이다.

Paraphrasing

> hand out 나눠 주다 → Distributing 나눠 주기
>
> brochures 책자 → documents 문서

PART 5

101 부사 자리 채우기

해설 동사(shows)를 꾸미기 위해서는 부사가 와야 하므로 부사 (B) clearly가 정답이다. 형용사 또는 동사 (A), to 부정사 (C), 형용사의 비교급 (D)는 동사를 꾸밀 수 없다.

해석 Natura 조경사의 연간 재무 보고서는 모든 자금의 출처와 그것들이 어떻게 사용되었는지를 명확히 보여준다.

어휘 report n. 보고서 source n. 출처, 원천 fund n. 자금
clear adj. 분명한; v. 명백하게 하다

102 동사 관련 어구 완성하기

해설 '모든 견습생들은 교육 기간 동안 안전 규정에 익숙해져야 한다'라는 문맥이므로 빈칸 뒤의 전치사 with와 함께 '~에 익숙해지다'라는 의미의 어구를 이루는 (B) familiarize(익숙하게 하다)가 정답이다. (familiarize oneself with: ~에 익숙해지다) (A) anticipate은 '예상하다', (C) identify는 '확인하다, 알아보게 하다', (D) compare는 '비교하다'라는 의미이다. compare도 전치사 with와 함께 'compare oneself with'의 형태로 쓰일 수 있지만 문맥상 적절하지 않으므로 답이 될 수 없다.

해석 건설업계의 모든 견습생들은 그들의 교육 기간 동안 안전 규정에 익숙해져야 한다.

어휘 apprentice n. 견습생, 수습생 industry n. 업, 산업
regulation n. 규정 period n. 기간

103 현재분사와 과거분사 구별하여 채우기

해설 2형식 동사 look은 주격 보어를 가지는 동사이고, 빈칸이 동사(looked) 뒤에 왔으므로 주격 보어 자리에 올 수 있는 현재분사 (B)와 과거분사 (D)가 정답의 후보이다. '부스가 정리가 덜 되어 보였다'라는 의미가 되어야 하므로 과거분사 (D) organized(정리된)가 정답이다. 타동사(organize)의 현재분사는 뒤에 목적어를 가져야 하는데, 빈칸 뒤에 목적어가 없으므로 현재분사 (B)는 답이 될 수 없다.

해석 가정용품 박람회에서 Nuffield 식기류사의 부스는 다른 참가 업체들의 부스들에 비해 정리가 덜 되어 보였다.

어휘 cutlery n. 식기류 housewares n. 가정용품
organize v. 정리하다

104 to 부정사를 취하는 동사

해설 빈칸 앞의 현재분사 enabling은 동사(enable)의 성질을 유지하는데, 동사 enable(~할 수 있게 하다)은 목적격 보어로 to 부정사를 취하므로, to 부정사 (D) to track이 정답이다.

해석 Life Fit은 최근 모바일 애플리케이션에 새로운 기능을 추가하여 사용자들이 그들의 일일 칼로리 섭취량을 추적할 수 있게 했다.

어휘 feature n. 기능, 특징 enable v. ~을 할 수 있게 하다, 가능하게 하다 intake n. 섭취(량)

최신토익경향

to 부정사 문제는 매회 1문제씩 꾸준히 출제되고 있다. 특히, 빈칸 앞에 쓰인 동사를 보고 to 부정사를 고르는 1초컷 문제들이 자주 나오므로 to 부정사를 취하는 동사를 알아두자.

<목적격 보어로 to 부정사를 취하는 동사>
• enable + 목적어 + to 부정사 ~하는 것을 가능하게 하다
• allow + 목적어 + to 부정사 ~하는 것을 허가하다
• permit + 목적어 + to 부정사 ~하는 것을 허가하다
• help + (목적어) + (to) 부정사 ~하는 것을 돕다
<목적어로 to 부정사를 취하는 동사>
• plan + to 부정사 ~할 계획이다
• aim + to 부정사 ~하는 것을 목표로 하다
• expect + to 부정사 ~할 것을 기대하다, 예상하다

105 시간 표현과 일치하는 시제의 동사 채우기

해설 현재를 나타내는 시간 표현(Currently)이 있으므로 현재 시점에 진행되고 있는 일을 나타낼 때 사용되는 현재진행 시제 (B) is preparing이 정답이다.

해석 현재, Ms. Demir는 그 회사의 업적들을 검토하며 Arc 문구사와의 면접을 준비하고 있다.

어휘 stationery n. 문구류 achievement n. 업적, 성취한 것

106 상관접속사 채우기

해설 동사 has evaluated와 동사(has) provided를 대등하게 연결할 수 있는 (C)와 (D)가 정답의 후보이다. '개선 방법에 대한 피드백을 제공했을 뿐만 아니라 공정하게 평가했다'라는 문맥이므로 B as well as A의 형태로 쓰여 'A뿐만 아니라 B도'라는 의미를 나타내는 상관접속사 (D) as well as가 정답이다. 등위접속사 (C) but(하지만)은 문맥상 어색하므로 답이 될 수 없다. 부사절 접속사 (A)는 뒤에 주어와 동사가 와야 하는데 빈칸 뒤에 주어가 없으므로 답이 될 수 없다. 접속부사 (B)는 뒤에 세미콜론(;)과 함께 절이 와야 한다.

해석 Mr. Daine은 개선 방법에 대한 피드백을 제공했을 뿐만 아니라 그의 직원들의 성과를 공정하게 평가했다.

어휘 evaluate v. 평가하다 performance n. 성과 fairly adv. 공정하게

107 명사 자리 채우기

해설 빈칸은 동사(will send)의 목적어 자리이므로 빈칸 앞 명사 billing과 함께 복합 명사를 이루는 명사 (C)와 (D)가 정답의 후보이다. 명사 statement는 가산 명사이고 빈칸 앞에 부정관사 a(n)이 없으므로 복수 명사 (D) statements가 정답이다. (billing statement: 청구

내역서) 동사 또는 명사 (A)는 명사일 경우 보통 나라나 자치구를 의미하므로 billing과 함께 쓰일 수 없다. (B)를 빈칸 앞의 명사(billing)를 수식하는 과거분사로 본다 해도, 분사가 목적어나 전치사구를 동반하지 않고 단독으로 쓰일 경우 명사 앞에 와야 하므로 답이 될 수 없다.

해석 7월부터, Deep Blue 수영장 청소 서비스는 당사 고객들에게 청구 내역서를 격주로 발송할 것이다.

어휘 biweekly adj. 격주의 state v. 명시하다, 서술하다; n. 상태, 나라

최신토익경향

'명사 + 명사' 형태의 복합 명사 문제는 자주 출제되지는 않지만 모르고 있을 경우 오답을 고르기 쉽다. 최근 출제됐던 복합 명사를 하나의 단어로 알아두자.

• board meeting 이사회 회의
• travel arrangement 출장 준비
• safety protocol 안전 규칙
• distribution center 유통 센터
• employee productivity 직원 생산성
• sales figures 판매 수치
• price reduction 가격 인하
• price increase 가격 인상
• product line 제품 라인, 제품군

108 동사 어휘 고르기

해설 '그 나라를 방문하는 관광객은 적합한 비자를 가지고 있을 것이 요구된다'라는 문맥이므로 (C) possess(가지다)가 정답이다. (D) occupy는 '차지하다'라는 의미로 시간이나 공간 앞에 쓰이므로 답이 될 수 없다. (A) connect는 '연결하다, 관련시키다', (B) perform은 '수행하다, 이행하다'라는 의미이다.

해석 유효한 여권과 함께, 그 나라를 방문하는 관광객들은 그들의 여행 목적에 적합한 비자를 가지고 있을 것이 요구된다.

어휘 valid adj. 유효한, 타당한 appropriate adj. 적합한, 적절한

109 부사 어휘 고르기

해설 '은퇴 파티에 참석할 계획이었지만, 유감스럽게도 교통 정체 때문에 참석할 수 없었다'라는 문맥이므로 (B) regretfully(유감스럽게도)가 정답이다. (A) scarcely는 '겨우, 간신히', (C) exceptionally는 '특별히, 예외적으로', (D) deliberately는 '고의로, 의도적으로'라는 의미이다.

해석 우리는 Ms. Iwata의 은퇴 파티에 참석할 계획이었지만, 유감스럽게도 교통 정체 때문에 참석할 수 없었다.

어휘 retirement n. 은퇴 make it 가다, 참석하다

110 부사절 접속사 채우기

해설 이 문장은 필수성분(a $1 donation is made)을 갖춘 완전한 절이므로 ____ a customer buys an upcycling product at EcoRevive는 수식어 거품으로 보아야 한다. 이 수식어 거품은 동사(buys)가 있는 거품절이므로, 거품절을 이끌 수 있는 부사절 접속사 (A)와 (D)가 정답의 후보이다. '제품을 구매할 때마다, 기부된다'라는

의미가 되어야 하므로 (D) Whenever(~할 때마다)가 정답이다. (A) So that은 '~하기 위해서'라는 의미로 목적을 나타낸다.

해석 고객이 EcoRevive에서 업사이클링 제품을 구매할 때마다, 환경보호 재단에 1달러가 기부된다.

어휘 donation n. 기부, 기증

111 격에 맞는 인칭대명사 채우기

해설 명사구(culinary journey and experiences) 앞에서 형용사처럼 쓰일 수 있는 인칭대명사는 소유격이므로 (B) his가 정답이다.

해석 유명한 요리사 Markus Lee는 새로 출간된 책에서 그의 요리 여정과 경험을 공유한다.

어휘 renowned adj. 유명한, 저명한 culinary adj. 요리의
publish v. 출간하다, 공표하다

112 동사 어휘 고르기

해설 '사람들이 도심 바깥쪽에 있는 더 큰 주거 공간을 계속해서 찾음에 따라 교외 주택에 대한 수요가 급증했다'라는 문맥이므로 soar(급증하다)의 p.p.형 (C) soared가 정답이다. (A)의 drain은 '소모시키다', (B)의 earn은 '얻다', (D)의 reach는 '도달하다'라는 의미이다.

해석 사람들이 도심 바깥쪽에 있는 더 큰 주거 공간을 계속해서 찾음에 따라 교외 주택에 대한 수요가 급증했다.

어휘 demand n. 수요 suburban adj. 교외의
look for ~을 찾다, 구하다

113 동명사 채우기

해설 문장에서 be동사(is) 앞에 위치한 ____ ~ for the company는 주어이다. 주어 자리에 올 수 있으면서 뒤에 목적어(personnel)를 가질 수 있는 것은 동명사이므로 (B) Recruiting이 정답이다. 명사 (D)를 명사 personnel과 함께 복합 명사 Recruitment personnel(채용 담당 직원들)을 이룬다고 본다 해도 personnel은 집합 명사로 복수 취급하므로 단수 동사(is)가 아닌 복수 동사(are)가 와야 한다. 동사 (A)와 (C)는 주어 자리에 올 수 없다.

해석 회사를 위한 직원들을 채용하는 것은 인사 부서에 의해 효과적으로 처리된다.

어휘 personnel n. 직원들, 인원 effectively adv. 효과적으로

114 부사 어휘 고르기

해설 '투자자들은 발표에 호의적으로 반응했지만 선택할 수 있는 것들을 고려할 시간을 더 달라고 요청했다'라는 문맥이므로 (D) favorably(호의적으로)가 정답이다. (A) mostly는 '대부분, 주로', (B) cautiously는 '신중하게, 조심스럽게', (C) differently는 '다르게'라는 의미이다.

해석 투자자들은 그 팀의 발표에 호의적으로 반응했지만 그들이 선택할 수 있는 것들을 고려할 시간을 더 달라고 요청했다.

어휘 investor n. 투자자 react v. 반응하다

115 명사 관련 어구 완성하기

해설 '부족한 조사는 제품에 대한 소비자들의 관심을 과대평가하는 결과를 낳았다'라는 문맥에서 빈칸 앞의 부정관사(a)와 뒤의 전치사(of)와 함께 쓰여 '부족한'이라는 의미의 어구를 이루는 (A) lack이 정답이다. (a lack of: 부족한, 결여된) (B) cause는 '원인', (C) consent는 '동의', (D) risk는 '위험'이라는 의미이다.

해석 시장 동향에 대한 부족한 조사는 APS 패션사가 당사의 제품에 대한 소비자들의 관심을 과대평가하는 결과를 낳았다.

어휘 overestimate v. 과대평가하다

최신토익경향

최근 Part 5에서 빈칸 주변의 단어와 어구를 이루는 명사를 고르는 문제가 자주 출제되고 있다. 최근 출제됐던 명사 관련 어구를 의미와 함께 알아두자.

- a lack of 부족한, 결여된
- a series of 일련의
- a variety of 다양한
- a range of 다양한
- a selection of 엄선된, 다양한
- in recognition of ~을 인정하여

116 명사절 접속사 채우기

해설 빈칸은 타동사(inform)의 직접 목적어 역할을 하는 명사절(the contract negotiations ~ successful)을 이끄는 명사절 접속사 자리이므로 명사절 접속사 (C) whether(~인지)가 정답이다. 형용사 또는 대명사 (A) both(둘 다의; 둘 다)와 (B) either(어느 한쪽의; 어느 한쪽), 부사 또는 등위접속사 (D) so(그렇게; 그래서)는 명사절을 이끌 수 없다. 참고로, 이 문장에서 타동사 inform이 2개의 목적어, 즉 간접 목적어(senior management)와 직접 목적어(whether the contract negotiations ~ successful)를 갖는 4형식 동사로 쓰였음을 알아둔다.

해석 계약 협상이 성공적이었는지를 내일까지 고위 경영진에게 알려주세요.

어휘 inform v. 알리다 negotiation n. 계약

117 부사절 접속사 채우기

해설 이 문장은 필수성분(Pyle Flooring finished ~ ahead of schedule)을 갖춘 완전한 절이므로 ____ ~ was tight은 수식어 거품으로 보아야 한다. 이 수식어 거품은 동사(was)가 있는 거품절이므로, 거품절을 이끌 수 있는 부사절 접속사 (A)와 (B)가 정답의 후보이다. '비록 마감 기한이 빠듯했지만 예정보다 일찍 카펫 설치를 마쳤다'라는 의미가 되어야 하므로 (A) although(비록 ~이지만)가 정답이다. (B) in case는 '~에 대비하여'라는 의미이므로 이 문맥에 어울리지 않는다. 접속부사 (C)와 전치사 (D)는 절과 절을 연결할 수 없으므로 답이 될 수 없다.

해석 비록 마감 기한이 빠듯했지만 Pyle 바닥재사는 예정보다 일찍 카펫 설치를 마쳤다.

어휘 installation n. 설치, 장치 tight adj. 빠듯한, 빡빡한

118 형용사 어휘 고르기

해설 '온라인상에 보여지는 이미지는 상품들의 정확한 상태를 반영하지 않을 수도 있다'라는 문맥이므로 (C) exact(정확한)가 정답이다. (A) close는 '가까운', (B) permanent는 '영구적인', (D) gradual은 '점진적인'이라는 의미이다.

해석 온라인상에 보여지는 이미지는 Reyes 경매에서 판매되고 있는 상품들의 정확한 상태를 반영하지 않을 수도 있다.

어휘 display v. 보여주다, 전시하다 reflect v. 반영하다

119 명사 자리 채우기

해설 빈칸은 전치사(of)의 목적어 자리이므로 빈칸 앞 명사 data와 함께 복합 명사 data analyst를 이루는 명사 (B) analyst가 정답이다. 동사 또는 과거분사 (A)를 빈칸 앞의 명사(data)를 수식하는 과거분사로 본다 해도, 분사가 목적어나 전치사구를 동반하지 않고 단독으로 쓰일 경우 명사 앞에 와야 하므로 답이 될 수 없다. 동사 (C)와 형용사 (D)는 명사 자리에 올 수 없다.

해석 Elena Patel은 연구 고문으로서의 다년간의 경험을 고려해 볼 때 데이터 분석가 직위를 승계할 예정이다.

어휘 succeed v. 승계하다, (자리·지위 등의) 뒤를 잇다
consultant n. 고문, 상담가 analyze v. 분석하다
analyst n. 분석가

120 명사 어휘 고르기

해설 '고객들은 문의를 남긴 당일에 답변을 기대하다'라는 문맥이므로 (C) response(답변)가 정답이다. (A) choice는 '선택', (B) manuscript는 '원고, 사본', (D) degree는 '정도, 학위'라는 의미이다.

해석 Cobi 커뮤니케이션사의 웹사이트에 명시된 바와 같이, 고객들은 문의를 남긴 당일에 답변을 기대할 수 있다.

어휘 specify v. 명시하다 inquiry n. 문의

121 부사 자리 채우기

해설 형용사(priced)를 꾸미기 위해서는 부사가 와야 하므로 부사 (D) reasonably(합리적으로)가 정답이다. 동사 또는 과거분사 (A), 형용사 (B), 명사 또는 현재분사 (C)는 형용사를 꾸밀 수 없다.

해석 지역 농가를 지원하는 데 전념하는 것으로 유명한 Farmstead 식료품 잡화점은 합리적으로 가격이 책정된 채소를 제공한다.

어휘 commitment n. 전념 support v. 지원하다, 지지하다

122 전치사 채우기

해설 '오후 5시쯤'이라는 의미가 되어야 하므로 (C) around(~쯤, 대략)가 정답이다. (A) within(~이내에)도 의미상 그럴듯해 보이지만, within은 기간과 함께 사용되는 전치사이므로 뒤에 기간을 나타내는 4 hours, 2 days와 같은 표현이 와야 하므로 답이 될 수 없다. (B) until(까지)은 상황이나 상태가 지속될 때 쓰이므로 답이 될 수 없다. (D) except는 '~ 외에는'이라는 의미이다.

해석 오리엔테이션 일정에 따르면, 신규 채용자들과 갖는 질의응답 시간은 오후 5시쯤 끝날 것이다.

123 동사 어휘 고르기

해설 'Hughes 미디어사는 광고 문안 작성자를 찾고 있다'라는 문맥이므로 be동사(is)와 함께 현재 진행형을 완성하는 seek(찾다)의 현재분사 (B) seeking이 정답이다. (A)의 look은 '보다'라는 의미로 뒤에 목적어가 오려면 전치사와 함께 써야 하고, '~을 찾다'라는 의미로 쓰려면 전치사 for와 함께 look for(~을 찾다)의 형태로 써야 한다. (C)의 concentrate은 '집중하다', (D)의 conduct는 '(특정한 활동을) 하다'라는 의미이다.

해석 Hughes 미디어사는 브랜드 스토리텔링 프로젝트에 공동으로 일할 창의적인 광고 문안 작성자를 찾고 있다고 알렸다.

어휘 copywriter n. 광고 문안 작성자, 카피라이터
collaborate v. 공동으로 일하다, 협력하다

124 형용사 자리 채우기

해설 빈칸은 2형식 동사 remain(~한 상태로 유지하다)의 주격 보어 자리이므로 형용사 (A), 현재분사 (B), 명사 (D)가 정답의 후보이다. '침착한 상태로 유지하기 위한 심리적 기법'이라는 의미가 되어야 하므로 형용사 (A) calm(침착한)이 정답이다. 현재분사 (B) calming(진정시키는)을 쓸 경우 '진정시키는 상태로 유지하기 위한 심리적 기법'이라는 어색한 문맥이 되고, 명사 (D) calmness(침착, 평온)를 쓸 경우 '침착으로 유지하기 위한 심리적 기법'이라는 어색한 문맥이 되므로 답이 될 수 없다. 부사 (C)는 주격 보어 자리에 올 수 없다.

해석 스트레스 관리 워크숍에서는 참가자들에게 강압적인 상황에서 침착한 상태로 유지하기 위한 심리적 기법을 가르친다.

어휘 psychological adj. 심리적인, 정신적인 technique n. 기법, 기술

125 부사 어휘 고르기

해설 '판매 수익이 거의 13퍼센트 증가하다'라는 문맥이므로 (C) nearly(거의)가 정답이다. (A) firmly는 '확고하게', (B) shortly는 '곧', (D) adversely는 '불리하게'라는 의미이다.

해석 Vulcan 스포츠 의류사의 판매 수익은 당사의 첫 번째 운동화 라인을 출시한 이후 거의 13퍼센트 증가했다.

어휘 revenue n. 수익, 수입 rise v. 증가하다

126 부정대명사 채우기

해설 빈칸은 부사절의 주어 자리로 명사가 와야 하므로 대명사인 모든 보기가 정답의 후보이다. '몇몇 기차 티켓은 환불이 불가능했기 때문에 여행 계획을 바꿀 수 없었다'라는 의미가 되어야 하므로 부정대명사 (D) some(몇몇)이 정답이다. 부정대명사 (A) another(또 다른 하나)는 이미 언급된 것 이외 또 다른 하나를 의미하므로 답이 될 수 없다. 대명사 (B) everything은 단수 취급하므로 복수 동사 were의 주어 자리에 올 수 없다. 지시대명사 (C) those는 '그것들'이라는 의미로 앞에 언급된 복수 명사를 대신할 때 쓰거나 '~한 사람들'이라는 의미로 쓰이므로 답이 될 수 없다.

해석 몇몇 기차 티켓은 환불이 불가능했기 때문에, 우리는 우리의 여행 계획을 바꿀 수 없었다.

어휘 **nonrefundable** adj. 환불이 불가능한

127 형용사 어휘 고르기

해설 '미술관 방문객들은 풍경을 극상의 정교함으로 표현해 내는 그 예술가의 능력에 찬사를 보냈다'라는 문맥이므로 (B) exquisite(극상의)이 정답이다. (A) cluttered는 '어수선한', (C) obedient는 '순종하는, 고분고분한', (D) sudden은 '갑작스러운'이라는 의미이다.

해석 Nilsson 미술관 방문객들은 풍경을 극상의 정교함으로 표현해 내는 그 예술가의 능력에 한결같이 찬사를 보냈다.

어휘 **uniformly** adv. 한결같이, 균등하게 **praise** v. 찬사를 보내다

128 전치사 채우기

해설 '휴가 방침 변경안에 대한 직원들의 의견'이라는 의미가 되어야 하므로 (D) about(~에 대한)이 정답이다. (A) beyond는 '~ 너머', (B) onto는 '~ 위쪽으로', (C) in은 '~ 안에'라는 의미이다.

해석 Sanford 산업사의 CEO는 제안된 휴가 방침 변경안에 대한 직원들의 의견을 요청했다.

어휘 **request** v. 요청하다 **opinion** n. 의견 **leave policy** 휴가 방침

129 형용사 자리 채우기

해설 빈칸 뒤의 명사구(business strategies)를 꾸밀 수 있는 것은 형용사이므로 (C) conventional(기존의, 관습적인)이 정답이다. 동사 (A), 부사 (D)는 명사를 꾸밀 수 없다. 명사 (B)는 business strategies와 복합 명사를 이루지 않으므로 답이 될 수 없다.

해석 First Track 엔터테인먼트사가 기존의 비즈니스 전략을 버리고 새로운 접근 방식을 기꺼이 택한 것은 당사를 음악 업계의 선두 주자로 만들었다.

어휘 **willingness** n. 기꺼이 하는 마음 **abandon** v. 버리다
approach n. 접근 방식, 접근법 **convene** v. 모이다, 소집하다
convention n. 관습, 협약

130 전치사 채우기

해설 '주주총회 후에 예산 분배에 대한 결정을 내릴 것이다'라는 의미가 되어야 하므로 (D) following(~후에)이 정답이다. (A) among은 '~중에서', (B) like는 '~와 같이'라는 의미로 문맥상 어색해지므로 답이 될 수 없다. (C) later(더 늦게; 나중에)는 형용사 또는 부사의 비교급이므로 전치사 자리에 올 수 없다.

해석 Nex 엔지니어링사의 경영진은 주주총회 후에 예산 분배에 대한 결정을 내릴 것이다.

어휘 **budget** n. 예산, 경비 **allocation** n. 분배, 할당

최신토익경향

전치사 관련 문제는 매회 평균 4~5문제로 꾸준히 출제되고 있다. 최근, 이전에 출제되지 않아 익숙하지 않은 전치사들이 자주 출제되고 있으니 의미와 함께 알아두자.

• **regardless of** ~와는 상관없이
• **on account of** ~ 때문에, ~으로
• **along with** ~에 덧붙여, ~와 마찬가지로

• **in the event of** (만일) ~의 경우에
• **prior to** ~에 앞서, ~ 전에
• **in light of** ~을 고려하여
• **if not for** ~가 없었다면, ~가 아니었다면

PART 6

131-134번은 다음 이메일에 관한 문제입니다.

수신: Alejandra Morales <a.morales@ezmail.ca>
발신: Marcus Clifford <m.clifford@clarendon.ca>
날짜: 2월 6일
제목: 회신: 신입 화학 연구직

Ms. Morales께,

신입 화학 연구직에 지원해 주셔서 감사합니다. 귀하의 이력서는 저희가 본 것 중 가장 인상 깊은 것 중 하나였습니다. **131**따라서, 다음 주에 귀하의 온라인 시험 일정을 잡고자 합니다. 이 시험은 저희의 채용 과정의 중요한 부분입니다. **132**그것은 귀하의 지식수준과 저희 실험실에서 맡을 일에 대한 적합성을 저희가 더 잘 평가할 수 있게 합니다. **133**귀하께 다음 주 중 가장 편한 요일을 제게 알려주십시오.

134시험은 약 4시간이 소요됩니다. 그러므로, 귀하가 선택하신 당일 일정에 여유 시간을 반드시 확보해 주십시오.

Marcus Clifford 드림
Clarendon 실험실

junior adj. 신입의, 초급의 **chemist** n. 화학 연구원, 화학자
application n. 지원; 적용 **résumé** n. 이력서
impressive adj. 인상 깊은, 감명 깊은 **assess** v. 평가하다
suitability n. 적합성, 어울림 **role** n. 역할

131 접속부사 채우기 주변 문맥 파악

해설 빈칸이 콤마와 함께 문장의 맨 앞에 온 접속부사 자리이므로, 앞 문장과 빈칸이 있는 문장의 의미 관계를 파악하여 정답을 선택한다. 앞 문장에서 이력서가 Clarendon 실험실에서 받아 본 것 중 가장 인상 깊은 것 중 하나였다고 했고, 빈칸이 있는 문장에서는 다음 주에 온라인 시험 일정을 잡고자 한다고 했으므로, 앞에서 말한 내용에 따른 결과를 언급할 때 사용되는 (C) Accordingly(따라서)가 정답이다.

어휘 **otherwise** adv. 그렇지 않으면 **rather** adv. 오히려
meanwhile adv. 한편, 그동안에

132 부사 어휘 고르기 주변 문맥 파악

해설 '그것은 귀하의 지식수준과 저희 실험실에서 맡을 일에 대한 적합성을 저희가 ____ 평가할 수 있게 합니다'라는 문맥이므로 (A)와 (B)가 정답의 후보이다. 빈칸이 있는 문장만으로 정답을 고를 수 없으므로 주변 문맥이나 전체 문맥을 파악한다. 앞 문장에서 '시험이 채용 과정의 중요한 부분이다(This exam is an important part of our hiring process).'라고 했으므로 지원자를 더 잘 평가하게 한다는 문맥이 되는 것이 자연스럽다. 따라서 (A) better(더 잘)가 정답이다.

어휘 **likewise** adv. 마찬가지로 **quite** adv. 꽤, 상당히 **already** adv. 이미

133 알맞은 문장 고르기

해석 (A) 작성된 시험 양식을 오후 6시까지 이메일로 보내주십시오.
(B) 50명이 넘는 사람들이 그 직책에 지원했습니다.
(C) 그것이 그 직무의 가장 어려운 측면 중 하나입니다.
(D) 귀하께 다음 주 중 가장 편한 요일을 제게 알려주십시오.

해설 뒤 문장 'Therefore, make sure you have a block of free time in your schedule on the day you choose.'에서 선택한 당일 일정에 여유 시간을 반드시 확보해 달라고 했으므로, 빈칸에는 시험 일정과 관련된 내용이 들어가야 함을 알 수 있다. 따라서 (D)가 정답이다.

어휘 apply v. 지원하다, 신청하다 aspect n. 측면, 양상

134 올바른 시제의 동사 채우기

해설 문장에 동사가 없으므로 모든 보기가 정답의 후보이다. 시험은 약 4시간이 소요된다는 일반적인 사실 또는 규칙을 언급하는 문맥이므로 현재 시제 (A) takes가 정답이다.

135-138번은 다음 정보에 관한 문제입니다.

Nuova 커피 머신

Nuova 커피 머신은 매번 완벽한 커피 한 주전자를 끓여냅니다! 여러분은 다음의 간단한 단계들을 따르기만 하면 됩니다. 먼저, ¹³⁵종이 필터를 바스켓에 넣고 단단히 끼워졌는지 확인하세요. 그런 다음, 여러분이 만들려는 커피 한 잔당 곱게 간 커피 한 큰 술을 필터에 넣습니다. 마지막으로, 머신에 물을 붓고 전원을 켜세요.
¹³⁶다음의 안전 예방책에 유의하세요. 전원이 연결된 상태에서는 절대로 머신을 청소하지 마세요. ¹³⁷감전 위험에 노출될 수 있습니다. ¹³⁸또한, 머신에 물을 빨간색 선으로 표시된 최대치를 넘어서 채우지 마세요.

brew v. 끓이다 fit v. 끼우다, 맞다, 적합하다
tablespoon n. 큰 술, 큰 스푼 finely adv. 곱게, 미세하게
grind v. 갈다, 빻다 intend to ~하려고 하다 pour v. 붓다, 따르다
precaution n. 예방책, 예방 조치 plug in 전원을 연결하다
past prep. 넘어서, 지나서

---

135 부사 자리 채우기

해설 빈칸 앞의 동사(fits)를 꾸밀 수 있는 것은 부사이므로 부사 (C) securely(단단히, 확실히)가 정답이다. 동사 또는 형용사 (A), 동사 (B)와 (D)는 동사를 꾸밀 수 없다.

어휘 secure v. 단단히 고정하다, 안전하게 하다; adj. 안전한

136 명사 관련 어구 완성하기 | 주변 문맥 파악

해설 '다음의 _____ 예방책에 유의하세요'라는 문맥이므로 (A)와 (C)가 정답의 후보이다. 빈칸이 있는 문장만으로 정답을 고를 수 없으므로 주변 문맥이나 전체 문맥을 파악한다. 뒤 문장에서 '전원이 연결된 상태에서는 절대로 머신을 청소하지 마세요(Never clean the machine while it is plugged in).'라고 했으므로 안전 예방책에 유의하라는 것임을 알 수 있다. 따라서 (A) safety(안전)가 정답이다. (C) health(건강)도 명사 precautions와 함께 쓰여 '건강 대비책(health

---

precautions)'이라는 의미의 복합 명사를 만들 수 있지만, 지문이 의료와 관련된 내용이 아니므로 이 문맥에는 어울리지 않는다.

137 알맞은 문장 고르기

해석 (A) 이 기기는 현재 할인된 가격으로 제공되고 있습니다.
(B) 감전 위험에 노출될 수 있습니다.
(C) 선택할 수 있는 커피 원두의 종류는 많습니다.
(D) 몇몇 사람들은 여름철에 아이스 커피를 선호합니다.

해설 앞 문장 'Never clean the machine while it is plugged in.'에서 전원이 연결된 상태에서는 절대로 머신을 청소하지 말라고 했으므로, 빈칸에는 주의를 준 이유와 관련된 내용이 들어가야 함을 알 수 있다. 따라서 (B)가 정답이다.

어휘 appliance n. (가정용) 기기, 기구 expose v. 노출시키다
electric shock 감전

138 전치사 채우기

해설 '머신에 물을 채우다'라는 의미가 되어야 하므로 빈칸 앞의 동사 fill과 함께 'A에 B를 채우다'라는 의미의 어구 fill A with B를 만드는 전치사 (C) with가 정답이다. (B)의 up도 fill과 함께 쓰일 수 있지만, fill up(~을 가득 채우다)의 형태로 쓰이므로 답이 될 수 없다. (A) from은 '~로부터', (D) into는 '~ 안으로'라는 의미이다.

139-142번은 다음 공고에 관한 문제입니다.

예정된 보일러 정비

¹³⁹5월 10일부터 15일까지 보일러 보수로 인해 건물에 간헐적인 온수 공급 중단이 있을 예정이라고 이전에 공지되었습니다. 그러나, 지장을 최소화하기 위해 일일 일정이 변경되었습니다. ¹⁴⁰오전 7시부터 오전 11시 사이에 실시될 예정되었던 보수 작업은 이제 가장 적은 주민들이 집에 있는 시간인 오후 1시부터 오후 5시 사이에 이루어질 것입니다.

¹⁴¹GDX 서비스사의 배관공들은 작업이 일정대로 완료될 것이라고 장담했습니다. 예기치 못한 지연이 발생할 경우 여러분은 즉시 통보받을 것입니다. ¹⁴²이 과정 동안의 여러분의 인내심에 감사드립니다. 문의가 있으시면 언제든지 건물 관리 사무실에 들러 주세요.

maintenance n. 정비, 보수 previously adv. 이전에
outage n. 공급 중단, 정전 disruption n. 지장, 혼란 alter v. 변경하다
take place 이루어지다, 발생하다 resident n. 주민, 거주자
assure v. 장담하다, 확언하다 unforeseen adj. 예기치 못한, 뜻밖의
notify v. 통보하다, 알리다 immediately adv. 즉시
stop by ~에 들르다, 방문하다

---

139 형용사 자리 채우기

해설 명사(hot water outages)를 꾸밀 수 있는 것은 형용사이므로 형용사 (B) occasional(간헐적인, 이따금씩의)이 정답이다. 빈칸이 목적어(hot water outages)를 취하는 동사 자리라고 하더라도 '건물이 간헐적인 온수 공급 중단을 야기한 것이 될 것이다'라는 어색한 문맥을 만들기 때문에 동사 occasion(~을 야기하다)의 p.p.형 (C) occasioned는 답이 될 수 없다.

어휘 occasion n. 경우, 시기; v. ~을 야기하다
　　occasionally adv. 가끔, 때때로

140 to 부정사 채우기

해설 이 문장은 주어(The maintenance work)와 동사(will ~ take place)를 갖춘 완전한 절이므로, planned ____ ~ 11 A.M.은 앞에 나온 주어(The maintenance work)를 수식하는 거품구로 보아야 한다. 빈칸 앞에 to 부정사와 함께 쓰이는 동사 plan의 p.p.형 planned가 있으므로 to 부정사 (C) to be conducted가 정답이다. 동사 (B)와 (D)는 수식어 거품이 될 수 없다.

어휘 conduct v. 실시하다, 수행하다

141 명사 어휘 고르기 전체 문맥 파악

해설 지문의 전체 문맥상 보일러를 수리할 수 있는 직업이 들어가야 하므로 plumber(배관공)의 복수형 (A) plumbers가 정답이다. (B)의 pilot은 '조종사, 비행사', (C)의 realtor는 '부동산업자', (D)의 lawyer는 '변호사'라는 의미이다.

142 알맞은 문장 고르기

해석 (A) 건물 관리자가 열쇠 사본을 제공할 것입니다.
　　(B) 다른 사업체들은 조명 설치를 전문으로 합니다.
　　(C) 여러분의 아파트에 대한 수리는 내일 끝날 것입니다.
　　(D) 이 과정 동안의 여러분의 인내심에 감사드립니다.

해설 앞부분에서 보일러 보수로 인해 간헐적인 온수 공급 중단이 있을 예정이라고 했고, 앞 문장 'If an unforeseen delay arises, ~ immediately.'에서 예기치 못한 지연이 발생할 경우를 언급하고 있으므로 빈칸에는 이 모든 과정 동안의 여러분의 인내심에 감사한다는 내용이 들어가야 함을 알 수 있다. 따라서 (D)가 정답이다.

어휘 specialize in ~을 전문으로 하다　appreciate v. 감사하다

143-146번은 다음 기사에 관한 문제입니다.

> 보라 노선이 발전을 주도한다
>
> 포터스빌 (6월 2일)-¹⁴³**새로운 보라 지하철 노선은 포터스빌 마을을 포함하여 미니애폴리스 외곽의 많은 지역 사회에 대한 관심을 북돋았다.** 보라 노선의 급행열차는 이제 미니애폴리스 도심부까지 35분 만에 접근할 수 있게 해준다. ¹⁴⁴**이러한 이점은 신규 주택 소유주에 대한 세금 우대 조치와 함께, 포터스빌 지역의 발전을 일으켰다.**
>
> 지난 2년에 걸쳐, 포터스빌에 2만 채가 넘는 주택이 새로 건설되었다. 공립 고등학교와 마을 도서관 건설도 진행 중이다. ¹⁴⁵**그 사이에, 소매업체들이 들어섰고, 새로운 Hillcrest 쇼핑센터를 채우고 있다.** ¹⁴⁶**이제 이곳은 주민들이 선호하는 목적지이다.**
>
> line n. 노선　benefit n. 이점, 혜택　incentive n. 우대 조치, 동기
> trigger v. 일으키다, 촉발시키다　underway adj. 진행 중인
> retailer n. 소매업체, 소매상인

143 동사 어휘 고르기 주변 문맥 파악

해설 '미니애폴리스 외곽의 많은 지역 사회에 대한 관심을 ____ 했다'라는 문맥이므로 모든 보기가 정답의 후보이다. 빈칸이 있는 문장만

으로 정답을 고를 수 없으므로 주변 문맥이나 전체 문맥을 파악한다. 뒤 문장에서 '보라 노선의 급행열차는 이제 미니애폴리스 도심부까지 35분 만에 접근할 수 있게 해주고, 이 이점은 포터스빌 지역의 발전을 일으켰다(Express trains on the Purple Line now make it possible to access downtown Minneapolis in 35 minutes. This benefit ~ has triggered the development of the Pottersville area).'라고 했으므로 새로운 지하철 노선은 포터스빌의 마을을 포함하여 미니애폴리스 외곽의 많은 지역 사회에 대한 관심을 북돋웠다는 것임을 알 수 있다. 따라서 boost(북돋다)의 과거형 (B) boosted가 정답이다.

어휘 distract v. (주의를) 딴 데로 돌리다
　　control v. 제어하다, 제한하다　suspend v. 중단하다

144 전치사 채우기

해설 '이러한 이점은 신규 주택 소유주에 대한 세금 우대 조치와 함께 발전을 일으키다'라는 의미가 되어야 하므로, 전치사 (C) along with(~와 함께)가 정답이다. (A) ahead of는 '~에 앞서', (B) as for는 '~에 관하여', (D) toward는 '~ 쪽으로'라는 의미이다.

145 접속부사 채우기 주변 문맥 파악

해설 빈칸이 콤마와 함께 문장의 맨 앞에 온 접속부사 자리이므로, 앞 문장과 빈칸이 있는 문장의 의미 관계를 파악하여 정답을 선택한다. 앞 문장에서 지난 2년에 걸쳐, 포터스빌에 2만 채가 넘는 주택이 건설되었으며, 고등학교와 마을 도서관 건설도 진행 중이라고 했고, 빈칸이 있는 문장에서는 소매업체들이 들어서면서 새로운 쇼핑센터를 채우고 있다고 했으므로, 동시에 일어나고 있는 일을 제시할 때 사용되는 (D) In the meantime(그 사이에, 그동안에)이 정답이다.

어휘 until then 그때까지　in contrast 그에 반하여, 반대로
　　even so 그렇기는 하지만

146 알맞은 문장 고르기

해석 (A) 주택 부족 현상이 곧 끝날 것 같지 않다.
　　(B) 그 발전은 미니애폴리스 도심부에 활기를 불어넣었다.
　　(C) 내년 가을에 포터스빌에 그 지하철역이 개통될 것이다.
　　(D) 이제 이곳은 주민들이 선호하는 목적지이다.

해설 앞 문장 'retailers have arrived, filling the new Hillcrest shopping center'에서 소매업체들이 들어서면서 새로운 Hillcrest 쇼핑센터를 채우고 있다고 했으므로, 빈칸에는 이 장소에 대해 부연 설명하는 내용이 들어가야 함을 알 수 있다. 따라서 (D)가 정답이다.

어휘 shortage n. 부족, 결핍　revitalize v. 활기를 불어넣다
　　favored adj. 선호하는, 호감을 얻고 있는
　　resident n. 주민, 거주자

## PART 7

147-148번은 다음 초대장에 관한 문제입니다.

> Scanlon 마케팅사의 모든 팀장들은 특별한 저녁 식사에 초대됩니다!
>
> ¹⁴⁷행사는 다음 달부터 우리와 함께 근무를 시작할 예정인 수상 경력이 있는 그래픽 디자이너, Miranda Jacobs를 만날 수 있는 기회를 제공할 것입니다.
>
> 장소: Cape 스테이크하우스(6번가와 Balsam가의 모퉁이)
> 언제: 5월 15일 (오후 6시~오후 10시)
>
> ¹⁴⁸저녁 식사는 회사 최고 경영자의 환영 연설로 시작될 것이므로, 늦게 도착하지 않으시기를 부탁드립니다. 참석할 예정이면, 5월 12일 정오까지 접수 담당자인 Neal Pringle에게 알려주시기를 바랍니다.
>
> 그곳에서 만나 뵙기를 바랍니다!
>
> award-winning adj. 상을 받은 welcoming adj. 환영의, 맞이하는
> notify v. 알리다 receptionist n. 접수 담당자

147 목적 찾기 문제

해석 행사의 목적은 무엇인가?
(A) 신입사원을 소개하기 위해
(B) 회사의 제품을 홍보하기 위해
(C) 근로자의 승진을 축하하기 위해
(D) 특별한 프로젝트를 발표하기 위해

해설 지문의 'The event will give you a chance to meet Miranda Jacobs, the award-winning graphic designer who will begin working with us next month.'에서 행사는 다음 달부터 근무를 시작할 예정인 그래픽 디자이너 Miranda Jacobs를 만날 수 있는 기회를 제공할 것이라고 했으므로 (A)가 정답이다.

어휘 promote v. 홍보하다 promotion n. 승진

148 육하원칙 문제

해석 행사에서는 무슨 일이 일어날 것인가?
(A) 디자인이 공개될 것이다.
(B) 상이 주어질 것이다.
(C) 연설이 있을 것이다.
(D) 시연이 진행될 것이다.

해설 지문의 'Please note that the dinner will begin with some welcoming words from our CEO, so we ask that you do not arrive late.'에서 저녁 식사는 회사 최고 경영자의 환영 연설로 시작될 것이라고 했으므로 (C)가 정답이다.

어휘 reveal v. 공개하다, 밝히다 hand out ~을 주다, 분배하다

Paraphrasing

> welcoming words 환영 연설 → speech 연설

149-150번은 다음 이메일에 관한 문제입니다.

> 수신: Jason Nunez <j.nunez@portmail.com>
> 발신: Patricia Conner <p.conner@webzone.com>

> 날짜: ¹⁴⁹8월 25일
> 제목: 시작하기
>
> Mr. Nunez께,
>
> 귀하의 온라인 마케팅에 필요한 것들을 위해 Web Zone의 소셜 미디어 플랫폼인 Outreach를 선택해 주셔서 감사합니다. ¹⁴⁹귀하의 법인 계정 신청이 오늘 오전 10시에 승인되었으며, 이는 귀하가 이제 게시물 올리는 것을 시작할 수 있음을 의미합니다. 귀하의 계정이 12개월 동안 비활성화되어 있으면, 계정이 일시 정지될 것임을 유의하세요.
>
> 게시물을 사용자들의 피드 상단에 더 오랫동안 유지해 주는 Up Post라는 특별한 기능을 임시로 이용하실 수 있는 권한을 부여해 드렸습니다. ¹⁵⁰9월 15일 이후에도 그것을 계속 이용하시려면, 여기를 클릭하여 월간 또는 연간 구독료를 지불하시길 바랍니다. 질문이 있으시면, 월요일부터 금요일, 오전 9시부터 오후 5시까지 555-9383으로 저희에게 전화하시길 바랍니다.
>
> Patricia Conner 드림
> Web Zone 담당자
>
> application n. 신청 corporate adj. 법인의, 기업의
> account n. 계정, 계좌 approve v. 승인하다
> inactive adj. 비활성의, 활동하지 않는
> suspend v. 일시 정지하다, 유예하다 temporary adj. 임시의, 일시적인
> annual adj. 연간의 subscription n. 구독료, 구독

149 육하원칙 문제

해석 8월 25일에 무슨 일이 일어났는가?
(A) 계정이 활성화되었다.
(B) 온라인 게시물이 삭제되었다.
(C) 신청이 거부되었다.
(D) 공개 행사가 발표되었다.

해설 지문의 'Date: August 25'와 'Your application for a corporate account was approved at 10 A.M. today, which means you can now begin making posts.'에서 기업 계정 신청이 오늘 즉, 8월 25일 오전 10시에 승인되었으며, 이제 게시물 올리는 것을 시작할 수 있다고 했으므로 (A)가 정답이다.

어휘 activate v. 활성화시키다 reject v. 거부하다

150 육하원칙 문제

해석 Mr. Nunez가 Up Post를 계속 이용하려면 무엇을 해야 하는가?
(A) 담당자에게 전화한다.
(B) 서비스 센터를 방문한다.
(C) 구독을 업그레이드한다.
(D) 결제를 한다.

해설 지문의 'To continue using it after September 15, please click here to pay for either a monthly or an annual subscription.'에서 9월 15일 이후에도 계속 이용하려면, 월간 또는 연간 구독료를 지불하라고 했으므로 (D)가 정답이다.

어휘 retain v. 계속하다, 유지하다

Paraphrasing

> pay 지불하다, (돈을) 내다 → make a payment 결제를 하다

Ari Pearson (오후 1시 20분)
Westinghouse 가전제품 고객 서비스 센터에 연락해 주셔서 감사합니다. 오늘 무엇을 도와드릴까요?

Sarit Phan (오후 1시 21분)
안녕하세요. ¹⁵¹귀사의 매장 중 한 곳에서 구매한 식기세척기를 수리하기 위해 기술자가 오늘 오후 4시에 저희 집에 방문하기로 되어 있어요. 그런데 제가 갑자기 회사의 호출을 받았어요. 다른 시간으로 잡을 수 있을까요?

Ari Pearson (오후 1시 23분)
물론이죠, Mr. Phan. 언제로 생각하고 계시나요?

Sarit Phan (오후 1시 24분)
¹⁵²음, 저는 금요일 하루 종일 시간이 있어요. 혹시 정오쯤에 수리공이 저희 집에 올 수 있을까요?

Ari Pearson (오후 1시 25분)
금요일은 국경일입니다. ¹⁵²되시는 다른 날이 있을까요?

Sarit Phan (오후 1시 27분)
다음 주에 제 일정을 확인하고 나중에 다시 연락드리겠습니다.

Ari Pearson (오후 1시 27분)
문제없어요. 그동안 저는 오늘 오후의 서비스 요청을 취소하겠습니다.

unexpectedly adv. 갑자기, 뜻밖에
have in mind 생각하다, 염두에 두다 repairperson n. 수리공
noon n. 정오 national holiday 국경일
work v. 되다, (조건·상황에) 맞다 in the meantime 그동안

151 목적 찾기 문제

해석 Mr. Phan은 왜 고객 서비스 센터에 연락했는가?
(A) 최근 구매에 대한 환불을 요청하기 위해
(B) 배송품이 언제 도착할지 확인하기 위해
(C) 결함이 있는 기기에 대해 불평하기 위해
(D) 예정된 약속을 변경하기 위해

해설 지문의 'A technician is supposed to visit my home at 4 P.M. today to repair the dishwasher I purchased from one of your stores. But I have been called into work unexpectedly. Could I arrange another time?'에서 매장에서 구매한 식기세척기를 수리하기 위해 기술자가 오늘 오후 4시에 자신의 집에 방문하기로 되어 있었는데 갑자기 회사의 호출을 받게 되었다며 다른 시간으로 잡을 수 있는지 물었으므로 (D)가 정답이다.

어휘 refund n. 환불 defective adj. 결함이 있는

152 의도 파악 문제

해석 오후 1시 25분에, Ms. Pearson이 "Friday is a national holiday"라고 썼을 때, 그녀가 의도한 것은?
(A) Mr. Phan이 다른 날에 매장을 방문하기를 바란다.
(B) 시설의 운영 시간이 변경될 것이라는 것을 안다.
(C) 기술자와 만날 수 없다는 것을 Mr. Phan에게 알리고 싶어 한다.
(D) 추가 요금에 대한 지불을 받아야 한다.

해설 지문의 'Well, I am free all day Friday. Maybe a repairperson

could come to my home around noon?'에서 Mr. Phan이 금요일 하루 종일 시간이 있다며 정오쯤에 수리공이 집에 올 수 있을지 묻자, Ms. Pearson이 'Friday is a national holiday'(금요일은 국경일입니다)라고 한 후, 'Is there another day that would work for you?'에서 다른 날이 되는지 묻는 것을 통해, 기술자와 만날 수 없을 것임을 알리려는 것을 알 수 있다. 따라서 (C)가 정답이다.

어휘 realize v. 알다, 깨닫다 operation n. 운영
unavailable adj. 만날 수 없는

회람

수신: 전 직원
발신: Klaus Fischer, 총지배인
날짜: 6월 30일
주제: Summer Blowout 행사

7월 20일부터 8월 10일까지, Langford 백화점은 첫 번째 Summer Blowout 행사를 개최할 것입니다. ¹⁵³⁻⁽ᴰ⁾고객들은 매장의 모든 것에 대해 최대 40퍼센트까지 할인받을 수 있을 것입니다. ¹⁵⁴보통 때 그랬던 것보다 더 많은 고객을 유치할 예정이므로 직원 여러분들은 불필요한 부재를 자제해 주시기 바랍니다. 물론, 아프거나 위급한 경우가 있다면, 그것은 용인됩니다. 하지만, 세일이 끝나고 나서 휴가 일정을 잡으시길 바랍니다. ¹⁵⁵여러분의 노고에 대한 감사의 표시로, 모든 직원은 9월 1일에 보너스 급여를 받을 것입니다. 판매량이 매장의 수익에 미치는 결과를 산정하자마자, 정확한 금액은 8월 25일에 발표될 것입니다.

여러분들의 노고에 감사드립니다.

hold v. 개최하다 avoid v. 자제하다, 피하다
unnecessary adj. 불필요한 absence n. 부재, 결석
emergency n. 위급한 경우 acceptable adj. 용인되는, 받아들여지는
appreciation n. 감사 exact adj. 정확한
calculate v. 산정하다, 계산하다 profit n. 수익, 이익

153 Not/True 문제

해석 Langford 백화점에 대해 명시된 것은?
(A) 행사를 위해 임시 직원을 채용할 계획이다.
(B) 금요일은 늦게까지 영업한다.
(C) 직원들에게 매월 보너스를 준다.
(D) 모든 제품에 대해 할인을 제공할 것이다.

해설 지문의 'Customers will be able to save up to 40 percent on everything in the store.'에서 매장의 모든 제품을 최대 40퍼센트까지 할인받을 수 있다고 했으므로 (D)는 지문의 내용과 일치한다. 따라서 (D)가 정답이다.

어휘 temporary adj. 임시의 monthly adj. 매월의

Paraphrasing

save up to 40 percent on everything 모든 것에 대해 최대 40퍼센트까지 할인받다 → offer discounts on all of its products 모든 제품에 대해 할인을 제공하다

154 동의어 찾기 문제

해석 1문단 세 번째 줄의 단어 "ordinarily"는 의미상 ~와 가장 가깝다.

(A) 보통
(B) 뚜렷하게
(C) 이상적으로
(D) 지루하게

해설 ordinarily를 포함한 구절 'Because we will attract many more customers than we ordinarily do'에서 ordinarily는 '보통 때'라는 뜻으로 사용되었다. 따라서 (A)가 정답이다.

155 육하원칙 문제

해석 직원들은 언제 금전적 보상을 받을 것인가?

(A) 7월 20일에
(B) 8월 10일에
(C) 8월 25일에
(D) 9월 1일에

해설 지문의 'In appreciation of your efforts, all employees will receive a bonus payment on September 1.'에서 노고에 대한 감사의 표시로, 모든 직원은 9월 1일에 보너스 급여를 받을 것이라고 했으므로 (D)가 정답이다.

어휘 financial adj. 금전적인 reward n. 보상

Paraphrasing

bonus payment 보너스 급여 → financial reward 금전적 보상

156-158번은 다음 공고에 관한 문제입니다.

공고

아시다시피, ¹⁵⁶우리 미용실은 최근에 보건안전부의 연례 점검을 받았습니다. 전반적으로, 결과는 만족스러웠습니다. 그러나 ¹⁵⁶여기에서 일하는 모든 직원들이 반드시 처리해야 할 몇 가지 사항들이 발생하였습니다.

첫째로, ¹⁵⁷가위, 빗, 그리고 저희 고객들과 직접 접촉하는 다른 도구들은 일단 한 번 사용되고 나면 즉시 살균되어야 합니다. 그리고 ¹⁵⁸⁻⁽ᴬ⁾가운은 절대 재사용하면 안 됩니다—고객이 그것을 벗자마자 세탁실에 넣어야 합니다. 게다가, ¹⁵⁸⁻⁽ᴮ⁾오전과 오후에 화장실이 청소되어 있는지 확인해야 합니다. 저는 이 일이 여러분 모두에게 공평하게 나누어지도록 일정을 잡을 것입니다. 마지막으로, ¹⁵⁸⁻⁽ᴰ⁾바닥을 쓸 때, 카운터 아래에 떨어진 머리카락을 확인하십시오.

이 문제에 관심을 가져 주셔서 감사합니다. 질문이 있으시면 제게 알려주시기 바랍니다.

Amanda Thompson

annual adj. 연례의, 매년의 inspection n. 점검
satisfactory adj. 만족스러운 come up 발생하다, 생기다
address v. 처리하다 come into contact with ~과 접촉하다
sanitize v. 살균하다 evenly adv. 공평하게, 균등하게
sweep v. 쓸다, 청소하다 fall v. 떨어지다 attention n. 관심, 주목

156 추론 문제

해석 공지는 어디에서 발견될 것 같은가?

(A) 학교의 입구에서
(B) 드라이클리닝 전문점에서
(C) 병원 로비에서
(D) 직원 휴게실에서

해설 지문의 'our hair salon ~'에서 이곳이 미용실임을 알 수 있고, 'But a few issues came up that everyone working here must address.'에서 직원들에게 처리해야 할 사항들이 발생하였다고 알리고 있으므로 미용실의 직원 휴게실에 걸린 공지일 것임을 추론할 수 있다. 따라서 (D)가 정답이다.

어휘 break room 휴게실

157 육하원칙 문제

해석 도구들은 언제 소독되어야 하는가?

(A) 매일 하루를 시작할 때
(B) 오후에
(C) 고객의 요청 시에
(D) 매번 사용 후에

해설 지문의 'To begin with, scissors, combs, and other tools that come into direct contact with our clients must be sanitized immediately once they have been used.'에서 가위, 빗, 고객들과 직접 접촉하는 다른 도구들은 일단 한 번 사용되고 나면 즉시 살균되어야 한다고 했으므로 (D)가 정답이다.

어휘 upon request 요청 시

158 Not/True 문제

해석 처리되어야 할 문제점으로 언급되지 않은 것은?

(A) 가운 세탁하기
(B) 화장실 청소하기
(C) 카운터 닦기
(D) 바닥 쓸기

해설 지문의 'never reuse a gown—it must be put in the laundry as soon as the client takes it off'에서 가운을 절대 재사용해서는 안 되고, 고객이 그것을 벗자마자 세탁실에 넣어야 한다고 했으므로 (A)는 지문의 내용과 일치한다. 'you need to make sure that the bathrooms are cleaned in the mornings and afternoons'에서 오전과 오후에 화장실이 청소되어 있는지 확인해야 한다고 했으므로 (B)는 지문의 내용과 일치한다. 'when sweeping the floor, check for hair that has fallen under the counters'에서 바닥을 쓸 때, 카운터 아래에 떨어진 머리카락을 확인하라고 했으므로 (D)는 지문의 내용과 일치한다. (C)는 지문에 언급되지 않은 내용이다. 따라서 (C)가 정답이다.

159-160번은 다음 온라인 게시물에 관한 문제입니다.

지난주 게시물에서 언급했듯이, 저는 커뮤니티 센터 전시를 위한 새로운 사진 프로젝트를 진행하려고 합니다. 저는 원래 자연과 관련된 것을 계획하고 있었지만, 마음을 바꾸었습니다. ¹⁵⁹저는 대신에 저희 도시에 있는 특이하고 흥미로운 집들에 초점을 맞출 것입니다. 그러니○

제 전시에 적합한 주제인 아파트나 집을 아시는 분이 계신다면, 메시지를 보내주시면 확인해 보겠습니다. ¹⁶⁰제가 쉽게 찾을 수 있게 그것이 어디에 위치해 있는지 정확하게 명시해 주시기 바랍니다. 감사합니다!

게시글 작성자: Lisa Modi

display n. 전시, 진열 related to ~과 관련된 odd adj. 특이한, 이상한
suitable adj. 적합한 exhibit n. 전시회 specify v. 명시하다

159 육하원칙 문제

해석 Ms. Modi의 사진 프로젝트는 무엇에 대한 것인가?

(A) 흥미로운 차량
(B) 도시의 스카이라인
(C) 자연 서식지
(D) 특이한 거주지

해설 지문의 'I'm going to focus on odd and interesting homes in our city instead.'에서 도시에 있는 특이하고 흥미로운 집들에 초점을 맞출 것이라고 했으므로 (D)가 정답이다.

어휘 urban adj. 도시의 habitat n. 서식지 residence n. 거주지, 주택

Paraphrasing

odd and interesting 특이하고 흥미로운 → unusual 특이한, 흔치 않은
homes 집 → residences 거주지

160 육하원칙 문제

해석 Ms. Modi는 사람들에게 무엇을 하기를 요청하는가?

(A) 구조물의 이미지를 제출한다.
(B) 구체적인 위치를 제공한다.
(C) 커뮤니티 센터에 연락한다.
(D) 작가에게 온 메시지를 읽는다.

해설 지문의 'Please specify exactly where it is located so that I can find it easily.'에서 자신이 쉽게 찾을 수 있게 어디에 위치해 있는지 정확하게 명시해 달라고 했으므로 (B)가 정답이다.

어휘 structure n. 구조물, 건축물 specific adj. 구체적인, 특정한

161-164번은 다음 공고에 관한 문제입니다.

탁구의 즐거움과 기분 좋은 식사 경험을 결합한 ¹⁶¹PingPong 플라자는 저희 고객님들께 더 나은 서비스를 제공하기 위해 몇 가지 정책 변경을 시행했습니다. — [1] —. ¹⁶²⁻⁽ᴰ⁾저희는 또한 더 많은 사람들을 수용하기 위해 저희의 시설을 확장했습니다. 다음 변경 사항들을 참고하세요:

- ¹⁶³⁻⁽ᴬ⁾탁구대 대여는 이제 2시간으로 제한됩니다. — [2] —. 하지만, 새로 생긴 개인실에서 열리는 행사에는 시간제한이 없습니다.
- ¹⁶³⁻⁽ᴮ⁾각 테이블 예약은 1인당 1개의 음료 최소 주문이 필요하며, 다양한 음료를 이용할 수 있습니다.
- 예약은 www.pingpongplaza.com에서 편리하게 온라인으로 할 수 있습니다. ¹⁶²⁻⁽ᶜ⁾전화로는 더 이상 예약을 받지 않습니다.
- ¹⁶³⁻⁽ᶜ⁾18세 미만 방문객은 오후 10시 이후 성인과 동반해야 합니다. — [3] —. 나이 확인을 위해 유효한 신분증이 요구될 수 있습니다.

¹⁶⁴저희는 큰 단체를 위한 방이 있습니다. — [4] —. 개인 행사에 관한 문의는 private@pingpongplaza.com으로 이메일을 보내 주세요.

combine v. 결합하다 excitement n. 즐거움, 흥분
delightful adj. 기쁨을 주는 dining n. 식사 implement v. 시행하다
policy n. 정책 expand v. 확장하다 accommodate v. 수용하다
constraint n. 제한 reservation n. 예약 beverage n. 음료
conveniently adv. 편리하게 accompany v. 동반하다, 동행하다
valid adj. 유효한 identification n. 신분증 verification n. 확인

161 주제 찾기 문제

해석 공지되고 있는 것은 무엇인가?

(A) 한 사업체의 개장
(B) 식사 메뉴에 대한 변경
(C) 규정의 업데이트 사항
(D) 곧 있을 개인 행사

해설 지문의 'PingPong Plaza has implemented several policy changes to better serve our customers'에서 PingPong 플라자는 더 나은 서비스를 제공하기 위해 몇 가지 정책 변경을 시행했다고 한 후, 변경된 규정에 대해 설명하고 있으므로 (C)가 정답이다.

어휘 regulation n. 규정

Paraphrasing

policy changes 정책 변화 → Updates to regulations 규정의 업데이트 사항

162 Not/True 문제

해석 PingPong Plaza에 대해 사실인 것은?

(A) 일주일 동안 문을 닫을 것이다.
(B) 대규모 그룹을 위한 특별 할인 요금을 제공한다.
(C) 이제 전화로 예약을 받을 것이다.
(D) 건물의 규모를 늘렸다.

해설 지문의 'We also have expanded our facility to accommodate more people'에서 더 많은 사람들을 수용할 수 있도록 시설을 확장했다고 했으므로 (D)는 지문의 내용과 일치한다. 따라서 (D)가 정답이다. (A)와 (B)는 지문에 언급되지 않은 내용이다. (C)는 'We no longer accept reservations over the phone.'에서 전화로는 더 이상 예약을 받지 않는다고 했으므로 지문의 내용과 일치하지 않는다.

어휘 shut down 문을 닫다, 정지시키다 special rate 특별 할인 요금

Paraphrasing

have expanded ~ facility 시설을 확장했다 → has increased the size of a structure 건물의 규모를 늘렸다

163 Not/True 문제

해석 PingPong Plaza에서의 변화로 언급되지 않은 것은?

(A) 시간제한
(B) 최소 주문
(C) 연령 제한
(D) 식사 메뉴

해설 (A)는 지문의 'Ping-pong table rentals are now limited to two hours.'에서 탁구대 대여는 이제 2시간으로 제한된다고 했으므로 지문에 언급된 내용이다. (B)는 'Each table reservation requires a one-beverage minimum order per person'에서 각 테이블 예약은 1인당 1개의 음료 최소 주문을 포함한다고 했으므로 지문에 언급된 내용이다. (C)는 'Visitors under 18 years old must be accompanied by an adult after 10 P.M.'에서 18세 미만 방문객은 오후 10시 이후 성인과 동반해야 한다고 했으므로 지문에 언급된 내용이다. (D)는 지문에 언급되지 않은 내용이다. 따라서 (D)가 정답이다.

어휘 restriction n. 제한

164 문장 위치 찾기 문제

해석 [1], [2], [3], [4]로 표시된 위치 중, 다음 문장이 들어갈 곳으로 가장 적절한 것은?

"이것들은 최대 16명으로 이루어진 그룹을 수용할 수 있습니다."

(A) [1]
(B) [2]
(C) [3]
(D) [4]

해설 주어진 문장은 최대 16명으로 이루어진 그룹을 수용할 수 있는 것과 관련된 내용이 나오는 부분에 들어가야 함을 예상할 수 있다. [4]의 앞 문장인 'We have rooms available for large parties.'에서 큰 단체를 위한 방이 있다고 했으므로, [4]에 주어진 문장이 들어가면 큰 단체를 위한 방이 있고, 이 방들이 최대 16명까지의 그룹을 수용할 수 있다는 자연스러운 문맥이 된다는 것을 알 수 있다. 따라서 (D)가 정답이다.

165-168번은 다음 문자 메시지 대화문에 관한 문제입니다.

Mike Beale [오전 11시 10분]
안녕하세요, Ms. Arai. Broadview 자동차 정비소의 Mike Beale입니다. **165오늘 아침에 당신의 자동차 타이어를 교체하던 중에, 처리되어야 하는 문제를 발견했어요.**

Keiko Arai [오전 11시 11분]
펜더 안에 크게 움푹 들어간 부분을 말씀하시는 건가요? 그렇다면, 당장 고칠 필요는 없을 것 같네요. 보기에는 좋지 않지만, 운전에는 영향을 주지 않아요.

Mike Beale [오전 11시 12분]
사실, 뒤쪽 브레이크입니다. 제가 타이어를 점검하면서, 브레이크가 정말 닳아 있는 것을 봤어요. **166당신의 안전을 위해 교체하는 것을 추천해요. 이곳의 단골 고객이신 점을 고려해서, 부품 및 인건비를 포함하여 200달러만 받고 작업을 해드릴 수 있어요.**

Keiko Arai [오전 11시 16분]
알겠습니다. 어쩔 수 없죠. 여전히 내일 오후에 차를 찾으러 갈 수 있을까요?

Mike Beale [오전 11시 17분]
안타깝게도 안 됩니다. **167작업이 끝나는 가장 빠른 날이 다음 주 수요일이 될 거예요.**

Keiko Arai [오전 11시 18분]
다음 주 수요일이요? 정말인가요? ○

Mike Beale [오전 11시 20분]
167네. 현재 재고가 없기 때문에 당신의 자동차 모델에 필요한 부품을 주문해야 할 거예요.

Keiko Arai [오전 11시 21분]
알겠습니다. **168이번 주말에 부모님을 뵈러 차를 운전해서 고향에 가고 싶었는데, 미뤄도 될 것 같아요.** 작업이 완료되면 문자 주세요.

dent n. 움푹 들어간 부분 fender n. (자동차의) 펜더, 바퀴 덮개
fix v. 고치다, 수리하다 rear adj. 뒤쪽의 inspect v. 점검하다
worn adj. 닳은, 해진 in stock 재고가 있는
put ~ off ~을 미루다, 연기하다

165 목적 찾기 문제

해석 Mr. Beale은 왜 Ms. Arai에게 연락했는가?
(A) 비용 인상에 대한 이유를 제공하기 위해
(B) 무료 서비스를 추천하기 위해
(C) 예상치 못한 문제를 논의하기 위해
(D) 일부 추가적인 고객 정보를 요청하기 위해

해설 지문의 'When I was changing your car tires this morning, I noticed a problem that needs to be dealt with.'에서 오늘 아침에 자동차 타이어를 교체하던 중에, 처리되어야 하는 문제를 발견했다고 했으므로 (C)가 정답이다.

어휘 unexpected adj. 예상치 못한

166 육하원칙 문제

해석 200달러의 비용이 들 것으로 예상되는 것은?
(A) 차량을 점검하는 것
(B) 펜더를 수리하는 것
(C) 타이어를 교체하는 것
(D) 브레이크를 교체하는 것

해설 지문의 'I would recommend replacing them for your own safety. Given that you are a regular client here, I can do the work for only $200, including parts and labor.'에서 뒤쪽 브레이크를 교체하는 것을 추천한다고 하면서, 단골 고객인 점을 고려해 부품 및 인건비를 포함하여 200달러만 받고 작업을 해줄 수 있다고 했으므로 (D)가 정답이다.

어휘 replace v. 교체하다

167 의도 파악 문제

해석 오전 11시 18분에, Ms. Arai가 "Next Wednesday"라고 썼을 때, 그녀가 의도한 것은?
(A) Mr. Beale은 예상했던 것보다 더 많은 시간을 필요로 한다.
(B) 주문이 빨리 확인돼야 한다.
(C) 작업이 예정보다 빨리 완료될 것이다.
(D) Ms. Arai는 그날 가게를 방문할 수 없다.

해설 지문의 'It won't be until next Wednesday at the earliest that the work is completed.'에서 Mr. Beale이 작업이 끝나는 가장 빠른 날이 다음 주 수요일이 될 것이라고 하자, Ms. Arai가 'Next Wednesday?'(다음 주 수요일이요?)라고 되물었다. 이에 대해 Mr. Beale이 'Yeah. I'll need to order the parts for your car model because I don't currently have any in stock.'에서 현재 재고가 없기 때문에 자동차 모델에 필요한 부품을 주문해야 할 거라고 한 것을 통해, Mr. Beale이 예상했던 것보다 더 많은 시간을 필요로 한다는 것을 알 수 있다. 따라서 (A)가 정답이다.

어휘 expect v. 예상하다   ahead of ~보다 빨리

168 추론 문제

해석 Ms. Arai에 대해 암시되는 것은?
(A) 지난 주말에 고향을 방문했다.
(B) 부모님께 도움을 요청할 것이다.
(C) 여행을 연기하기로 결정했다.
(D) 오늘 그녀의 차를 운전할 예정이다.

해설 지문의 'I was hoping to drive to my hometown to visit my parents this weekend, but I guess I can put that off.'에서 이번 주말에 부모님을 뵈러 차를 운전해서 고향에 가고 싶었는데, 미뤄도 될 것 같다고 했으므로 여행을 연기하기로 결정했다는 것을 추론할 수 있다. 따라서 (C)가 정답이다.

어휘 postpone v. 연기하다   intend v. 예정하다, ~할 작정이다

Paraphrasing

put ~ off 미루다, 연기하다 → postpone 연기하다

169-171번은 다음 이메일에 관한 문제입니다.

수신: Emma Davies <e.davies@acefinancial.co.uk>
발신: Carl Brenner <c.brenner@acefinancial.co.uk>
날짜: 3월 25일
제목: 평가

안녕하세요 Emma,

¹⁶⁹당신은 원래 4월 12일까지 팀원들의 성과 평가를 제출하기로 되어 있었지만, 저는 대신 4월 2일까지 받고 싶습니다. 당신이 또한 분기별 매출 수치를 분석하느라 매우 바쁘다는 것을 알고 있으므로, 임박해서 이런 부탁을 한 것에 대해 사과드립니다. 하지만, 저는 다른 선택권이 없습니다. ¹⁷⁰우리의 최고 경영자는 저에게 상하이에 새로운 지역 사무소를 여는 것을 감독해 달라고 요청했고, 저는 4월 8일에 떠날 것입니다. 제가 두 달 동안 떠나있을 것이므로, 떠나기 전에 여기에 있는 모든 프로젝트를 끝내야 합니다. 물론, 이것은 당신의 팀원들에 대한 평가를 검토하는 것을 포함합니다.

¹⁷¹새로운 일정이 실행 불가능한 것으로 판단되면, 저에게 전화를 주시고 제가 다른 팀장님께 분석을 완료하게 할 것입니다. 다음 주 동안에는 평가가 당신의 우선 사항이 되어야 할 것입니다.

감사합니다.

Carl Brenner 드림

evaluation n. 평가   figure n. 수치
at the last minute 임박해서, 마지막 순간에   oversee v. 감독하다
regional adj. 지역의   depart v. 출발하다   wrap up 끝내다
unworkable adj. 실행 불가능한   priority n. 우선 사항

169 목적 찾기 문제

해석 이메일의 목적은 무엇인가?
(A) 프로젝트 지연의 이유를 알아내기 위해
(B) 마감일이 변경되었다는 것을 통지하기 위해
(C) 팀에 더 많은 구성원을 포함할 것을 제안하기 위해
(D) 신규 직원의 진척 상황에 대해 문의하기 위해

해설 지문의 'You were originally scheduled to submit the performance evaluations of your team members by 12 April, but I would like to get them by 2 April instead.'에서 원래 4월 12일까지 팀원들의 성과 평가를 제출하기로 되어있었지만, 대신 4월 2일까지 받고 싶다며 마감일이 변경되었다는 것을 알리고 있으므로 (B)가 정답이다.

어휘 determine v. 알아내다, 밝히다   inquire v. 문의하다

170 추론 문제

해석 Mr. Brenner에 대해 암시되는 것은?
(A) 다른 사무실로의 전근을 요청했다.
(B) 최고 경영자직에 고려되고 있다.
(C) 입사 지원자들의 면접을 진행했다.
(D) 다른 지점에서 일시적으로 일할 것이다.

해설 지문의 'Our CEO has requested that I[Mr. Brenner] oversee the opening of our new regional office in Shanghai, and I will be departing on 8 April. As I will be gone for a period of two months, ~'에서 최고 경영자가 Mr. Brenner에게 상하이에 새로운 지역 사무소를 여는 것을 감독해 달라고 요청했고 두 달 동안 떠나있을 것이라고 했으므로 다른 지점에서 일시적으로 일할 것임을 추론할 수 있다. 따라서 (D)가 정답이다.

어휘 transfer n. 전근, 이동   temporarily adv. 일시적으로

Paraphrasing

for a period of two months 두 달 동안 → temporarily 일시적으로
new regional office in Shanghai 상하이에 있는 새로운 지역 사무소 → a different branch 다른 지점

171 추론 문제

해석 Ms. Davies는 왜 Mr. Brenner에게 전화할 것 같은가?
(A) 관리자와의 회의를 주선하기 위해
(B) 이전 평가에 대해 논의하기 위해
(C) 업무가 다시 할당되도록 요청하기 위해
(D) 교육 워크숍 일정을 변경하기 위해

해설 지문의 'If the new schedule proves unworkable for you, phone me and I will have another team manager complete the analysis.'에서 새로운 일정이 실행 불가능할 것 같아 자신에게 전화를 주면 다른 팀장이 분석을 완료하게 할 것이라고 했으므로 Ms. Davies는 업무가 다시 할당되도록 요청하기 위해 Mr. Brenner에게 전화할 것이라는 것을 추론할 수 있다. 따라서 (C)가 정답이다.

어휘 reassign v. 다시 할당하다   reschedule v. 일정을 변경하다

172-175번은 다음 기사에 관한 문제입니다.

산타 모니카 172-(D)(10월 1일) — 깜짝 발표에서, Metro 미술관은 방문객들이 11월 10일부터 25일까지 유명한 추상화 예술가 Philip Bernard의 그림 소장품을 볼 수 있을 것이라고 밝혔다. — [1] —. 미술관 책임자 Marla Morris에 따르면, 그녀는 예술계에서 그렇게 존경받는 인물과 함께 일할 수 있는 172-(D)뜻밖의 기회에 기꺼이 응했다. 하지만, 그녀는 또한 이 전시회가 다른 기관의 유감스러운 상황의 결과임을 재빨리 지적했다. — [2] —. "Coleman 미술관은 최근 화재의 피해가 복구되는 동안 앞으로 몇 주 동안 문을 닫을 것입니다,"라고 그녀가 설명했다. ¹⁷³Mr. Bernard의 작품은 원래 계획대로 그곳에 전시될 수 없어서, 그의 에이전트가 저희에게 연락했습니다."

막판의 장소 변경에도 불구하고, 그 미술관은 방문객들이 확실히 최대한의 경험을 가져갈 수 있도록 매일 두 차례의 무료 가이드 투어를 제공할 것이다. — [3] —. ¹⁷⁵Metro 미술관의 전시회 입장권은 25달러로 책정되었으며 www.metroart.com/admission에서 구입할 수 있다. — [4] —. ¹⁷⁴Mr. Bernard의 팬들은 이 예술가가 처음으로 자신의 그림의 인쇄본이 판매되는 것에 대해 허락했다는 사실에도 주목해야 한다. "이것은 어떤 예술 애호가도 놓치고 싶어 하지 않을 특별한 기회입니다,"라고 Ms. Morris가 말했다. "¹⁷⁴전시회 동안 저희 미술관을 방문하는 누구나 이 기회를 이용하라고 권하고 싶습니다."

abstract n. 추상화 jump at ~에 기꺼이 응하다, ~을 받아들이다
sudden adj. 뜻밖의, 갑작스러운 esteemed adj. 존경받는
figure n. 인물 point out ~을 지적하다
unfortunate adj. 유감스러운, 불행한 institution n. 기관
admirer n. 팬 note v. 주목하다 print n. 인쇄본
opportunity n. 기회 pass up (기회를) 놓치다
urge v. 권하다, 촉구하다 take advantage of ~을 이용하다

172 Not/True 문제

해석 Metro 미술관에 대해 사실인 것은?
(A) 유명한 지역 예술가에 의해 운영된다.
(B) 화재로 인한 일부 손상을 복구했다.
(C) 다른 갤러리와 행사를 공동 주최하고 있다.
(D) 다음 달에 특별한 전시를 개최할 것이다.

해설 지문의 '(October 1)—In a surprise announcement, the Metro Art Gallery revealed that visitors will be able to view a collection of paintings by the famous abstract artist Philip Bernard from November 10 to 25.'에서 10월 1일 자 기사에 따르면, Metro 미술관은 방문객들이 11월 10일부터 25일까지 유명한 추상화 예술가 Philip Bernard의 그림 소장품을 볼 수 있을 것이라고 밝혔다고 했고 '~ jumped at the sudden chance'를 통해 이 전시가 예정에 없던 특별한 것임을 알 수 있으므로 (D)는 지문의 내용과 일치한다. 따라서 (D)가 정답이다.

어휘 well-known adj. 유명한, 잘 알려진

173 추론 문제

해석 Mr. Bernard에 대해 암시되는 것은?
(A) 그의 현재의 에이전트를 대신할 사람을 찾고 싶어 한다.
(B) 대체 가능한 장소를 찾을 것을 요구받았다.
(C) 다음 달에 처음으로 자신의 작품을 전시할 것이다.
(D) Metro 미술관에 몇 점의 그림을 팔았다.

해설 지문의 'Mr. Bernard's works cannot be displayed there as originally planned, so his agent contacted us[Metro Art Gallery].'에서 Mr. Bernard의 작품은 원래 계획대로 그곳에 전시될 수 없어서, 그의 에이전트가 Metro 미술관에 연락했다고 했으므로 Mr. Bernard가 전시를 할 다른 장소를 찾도록 요구받았을 것임을 추론할 수 있다. 따라서 (B)가 정답이다.

어휘 replacement n. 대신할 사람 alternative adj. 대체 가능한
venue n. 장소

174 육하원칙 문제

해석 Ms. Morris는 방문객들에게 무엇을 하도록 권장하는가?
(A) 미술관 웹사이트에 후기를 올린다.
(B) 전시된 물품의 사진을 찍는다.
(C) 미술품의 이미지를 구입한다.
(D) 가이드 투어를 한다.

해설 지문의 'Admirers of Mr. Bernard should also note that the artist has for the first time given permission for prints of his paintings to be sold.', 'I would urge anyone who visits our gallery during the exhibit to take advantage of it.'에서 Mr. Bernard의 팬들은 이 예술가가 처음으로 자신의 그림의 인쇄본이 판매되는 것에 대해 허락했다는 사실에도 주목해야 한다며, 전시회 동안 미술관을 방문하는 누구나 이 기회를 이용하라고 권하고 싶다고 했으므로 (C)가 정답이다.

어휘 on display 전시된, 진열된 artwork n. 미술품

Paraphrasing

paintings 그림 → artwork 미술품

175 문장 위치 찾기 문제

해석 [1], [2], [3], [4]로 표시된 위치 중, 다음 문장이 들어갈 곳으로 가장 적절한 것은?

"이 예술가의 작품에 대한 높은 관심으로 인해 그것들은 빠르게 매진될 것으로 예상된다."

(A) [1]
(B) [2]
(C) [3]
(D) [4]

해설 주어진 문장은 매진될 것으로 예상되는 것과 관련된 내용이 나오는 부분에 들어가야 함을 예상할 수 있다. [4]의 앞 문장인 'Tickets to enter the exhibit ~ at $25 and are available at www.metroart.com/admission.'에서 전시회 입장권은 25달러이며 www.metroart.com/admission에서 구입할 수 있다고 했으므로, [4]에 주어진 문장이 들어가면 전시회 입장권은 웹사이트에서 구매할 수 있으며, 예술가의 작품에 대한 관심이 높아 티켓이 빠르게 매진될 것으로 예상된다는 자연스러운 문맥이 된다는 것을 알 수 있다. 따라서 (D)가 정답이다.

어휘 be expected to ~할 것으로 예상되다 sell out 매진되다, 다 팔리다

176-180번은 다음 보도 자료와 후기에 관한 문제입니다.

즉각 보도용

시카고 (1월 14일)-176전국에 공동 작업 공간을 갖춘 스타트업인 WorkHere가 2월 17일에 시카고에 첫 지점을 개점할 것이다. Boxwood 지역에 위치한 이 시설은 도시 내에서 해당 분야의 가장 큰 시설이 될 것이다.

1777년 전 뉴욕에서 WorkHere를 시작한 Myra Sanders는 그녀의 회사 서비스에 대한 큰 수요가 있을 것이라고 확신한다. 178"긱 이코노미로의 계속되는 전환과 함께, 시카고 지역의 점점 더 많은 전문가들이 프리랜서로 일하고 있습니다."라고 그녀는 설명했다.

이 시설은 와이파이, 편안한 작업 공간, 회의실, 프린터 등을 포함한 공동 작업 공간의 모든 표준 편의시설을 특별히 포함할 것이다. 하지만 Sanders는 고객들이 이곳을 단순히 일하는 장소 이상의 것으로 보기를 원한다. 179"저희는 WorkHere 연간 회원권을 가진 개인들이 독점적으로 사용할 수 있는 오락실, 체육관, 심지어 라운지까지 포함할 것입니다,"라고 그녀가 말했다. "저희는 사람들이 사회적이고 전문적인 네트워크를 확장하기 위해 서로 교류하기를 원합니다."

confident adj. 확신하는 ongoing adj. 계속되는
gig economy 긱 이코노미(일자리에 계약직이나 프리랜서 등을 주로 채용하는 현상) professional n. 전문가 amenity n. 편의시설
workstation n. 작업 공간, 일하는 자리 exclusive adj. 독점적인
individual n. 개인 annual adj. 연간의, 매년의
interact v. 교류하다, 상호 작용하다

저는 독립적인 소프트웨어 엔지니어로서 재택근무하는 것에 집중하기가 어려웠기 때문에, WorkHere를 이용해 보기로 결심했습니다. 제가 그랬다는 것이 기쁩니다. 그 시설은 매우 넓어서, 항상 사생활을 보호하는 공동 작업 공간을 찾을 수 있습니다. 또한 안정적이고, 초고속 인터넷 연결과 도움을 주는 직원들에게 감사드립니다. 179시설은 제가 퇴근 후에 애용하는 피트니스센터를 포함하고 있습니다. 이로 인해 더 건강해지는 것을 느꼈고 스트레스를 덜 받게 되었습니다. 180저의 유일한 불만은 주차 상황입니다. 근처에 지하철역이 없어서, 운전해서 그곳에 가야 합니다. 그런데 주차 요금이 정말이지 계속 늘어나기 시작했습니다. 그렇기는 하지만, 모든 프리랜서들에게 WorkHere를 매우 추천합니다.

3월 21일에 Salman Rane이 후기를 작성

independent adj. 독립적인 spacious adj. 넓은
stable adj. 안정적인 complaint n. 불만, 불평
add up 계속 늘어나다 that being said 그렇기는 하지만

176 목적 찾기 문제

해석 보도 자료의 목적은 무엇인가?
(A) 지점 개점에 대한 정보를 제공하기 위해
(B) 사업체를 폐업하는 결정을 설명하기 위해
(C) 신규 채용된 기업체 간부를 소개하기 위해
(D) 새로운 회사의 설립을 발표하기 위해

해설 보도 자료의 'WorkHere, a startup with co-working spaces throughout the country, will be launching its first branch in Chicago on February 17.'에서 전국에 공동 작업 공간을 갖춘 스타트업인 WorkHere가 2월 17일에 시카고에 첫 지점을 개점할

것이라고 했으므로 (A)가 정답이다.

어휘 formation n. 설립, 형성

177 Not/True 문제

해석 Ms. Sanders에 대해 명시된 것은?
(A) 시카고의 장기 거주자이다.
(B) 현재 프리랜서로 일하고 있다.
(C) 그녀의 회사를 뉴욕으로 옮길 것이다.
(D) 회사의 설립자이다.

해설 보도 자료의 'Myra Sanders, who started WorkHere seven years ago in New York'에서 7년 전 뉴욕에서 WorkHere를 시작한 Myra Sanders라고 했으므로 Ms. Sanders가 회사의 설립자라는 것을 알 수 있다. 따라서 (D)가 정답이다.

어휘 long-term adj. 장기적인 resident n. 거주자 firm n. 회사
founder n. 설립자

178 동의어 찾기 문제

해석 보도 자료에서, 3문단 다섯 번째 줄의 단어 "expand"는 의미상 -와 가장 가깝다.
(A) 연장하다
(B) 확장하다
(C) 생산하다
(D) 기능하다

해설 expand를 포함한 구절 'We want people to interact with each other to expand their social and professional networks.'에서 expand는 '확장하다'라는 뜻으로 사용되었다. 따라서 (B)가 정답이다.

179 추론 문제 연계

해석 Mr. Rane에 대해 사실일 것 같은 것은?
(A) 소프트웨어 회사의 직원이다.
(B) 여러 도시에서 WorkHere를 이용해 왔다.
(C) 1년짜리 회원권을 구입했다.
(D) 최근에 정규직 일자리를 수락했다.

해설 Mr. Rane이 작성한 후기를 먼저 확인한다.
단서 1 후기의 'The facility includes a fitness center that I enjoy using after work.'에서 시설은 퇴근 후 애용하는 피트니스센터도 포함하고 있다고 했다.
단서 2 보도 자료의 'We will include a game room, a gym, and even a lounge for the exclusive use of individuals with an annual WorkHere membership'에서 WorkHere 연간 회원권을 가진 개인들은 독점적으로 사용할 수 있는 오락실, 체육관, 심지어 라운지까지 이용할 수 있다는 것을 알 수 있다.
두 단서를 종합할 때, Mr. Rane은 1년짜리 회원권을 구입했음을 알 수 있다. 따라서 (C)가 정답이다.

어휘 accept v. 수락하다 position n. 일자리, 직위

Paraphrasing

annual 연간의 → one-year 1년의

---

180 추론 문제

해석   Mr. Rane이 후기에서 WorkHere 시설에 대해 암시하는 것은?
(A) 대중교통으로 쉽게 접근이 가능하다.
(B) 인터넷 연결에 문제가 있다.
(C) 작업 공간을 더 추가해야 한다.
(D) 이용자들에게 주차비를 청구한다.

해설   후기의 'My only complaint is the parking situation. There are no subway stations nearby, so I have to drive there. But the fees are really starting to add up.'에서 유일한 불만은 주차 상황이며, 근처에 지하철역이 없어서 운전해서 그곳에 가야 하는데 주차 요금이 정말이지 계속 늘어나기 시작했다고 했으므로 WorkHere가 이용자들에게 주차비를 청구한다는 것을 추론할 수 있다. 따라서 (D)가 정답이다.

어휘   accessible adj. 접근이 가능한   public transit 대중교통
add v. 추가하다   charge v. 청구하다

181-185번은 다음 이메일과 티켓에 관한 문제입니다.

수신: Nancy Ray <n.ray@hmail.com>
발신: Tyler Vance <t.vance@southview.com>
제목: 회신: 방문
날짜: 7월 23일

Ms. Ray께,

저에게 빠르게 답장해 주셔서 감사합니다. [181]안타깝게도, 저희가 만나기로 제안하신 날은 안 될 것 같습니다. 그날 오후에 모든 직원들을 대상으로 의무적인 워크숍이 있습니다. [181]대신 7월 27일에 방문해서 이야기를 나눌 수 있을까요? [182]제 차가 현재 수리점에 있어서 시외버스를 탈 예정입니다. [184]오전 9시 30분에 출발하는 버스를 탈 계획이며, 오후 1시 20분에 오크빌에 도착할 것입니다. 당신의 집은 역에서 도보로 10분 거리에 있어서, 저는 오후 1시 30분쯤 거기에 도착할 것 같습니다.

[183]저는 당신을 인터뷰하는 것을 정말로 고대하고 있습니다. 그리고 저희 신문인 The South View Daily 독자들 중 많은 분들이 예술가로서 당신의 오래된 경력에 대해 알게 되어 아주 기뻐할 것이라고 확신합니다. 제가 제안한 날짜와 시간이 편하신지 알려주세요. 감사합니다.

Tyler Vance 드림

mandatory adj. 의무의   intercity bus 시외버스   depart v. 출발하다
thrilled adj. 아주 기쁜, 황홀해하는

Millstone 운송 서비스
정기권

승객: Tyler Vance   [184]출발: 7월 27일 오후 12시 30분
목적지: 오크빌   [184]도착: 7월 27일 오후 4시 20분

좌석: 26A

안내:
모든 승객들은 적어도 출발 10분 전에 탑승 준비가 되어 있어야 합니다. [185]목적지에 도착하신 후 소지품들 중 하나를 머리 위 칸이나 좌석에 두고 왔다는 것을 알게 되시면 555-0393으로 전화하십시오.

안전하고 편안한 여정 되세요!   ○

---

passenger n. 승객   destination n. 목적지   belongings n. 소지품
overhead adj. 머리 위의   compartment n. 칸, 객실

181 목적 찾기 문제

해석   이메일의 목적은 무엇인가?
(A) 인터뷰를 거절하기 위해
(B) 만남을 주선하기 위해
(C) 전시회를 준비하기 위해
(D) 예약하기 위해

해설   이메일의 'Unfortunately, the day you suggested for us to meet won't work.', 'Would I be able to visit and talk to you on July 27 instead?'에서 만나자고 제안한 날은 안 될 것 같다며, 대신 7월 27일에 방문해서 이야기를 나눌 수 있을지 묻고 있으므로 (B)가 정답이다.

어휘   decline v. 거절하다   arrange v. 주선하다
organize v. 준비하다, 조직하다   make a reservation 예약하다

182 육하원칙 문제

해석   이메일에 따르면, 왜 Mr. Vance는 버스를 타기로 결정했는가?
(A) 그의 차가 수리 중이다.
(B) 교통 혼잡을 피하고 싶어 한다.
(C) 마을로 가는 경로를 잘 모른다.
(D) 회사에서 여행 경비를 상환해 줄 것이다.

해설   이메일의 'My car is currently in the shop, so I will take the intercity bus'에서 Mr. Vance가 그의 차가 수리점에 있어서 시외버스를 탈 예정이라고 했으므로 (A)가 정답이다.

어휘   congestion n. 혼잡   unfamiliar with ~을 잘 모르는
reimburse v. 상환해 주다, 배상하다

Paraphrasing

car is ~ in the shop 차가 수리점에 있다 → vehicle is being repaired 차가 수리 중이다

183 추론 문제

해석   이메일에서 암시되는 것은?
(A) Ms. Ray는 이제 막 예술가로서 일을 시작했다.
(B) Mr. Vance는 출판물의 기자로 일한다.
(C) Ms. Ray는 최근 오크빌에서 미술 전시회에 참석했다.
(D) Mr. Vance는 관리 워크숍을 빠질 것이다.

해설   이메일의 'I[Mr. Vance]'m really looking forward to interviewing you[Ms. Ray]. And I am sure many of the readers of my newspaper, The South View Daily, will be thrilled to learn more about your long career as an artist.'에서 Mr. Vance는 Ms. Ray를 인터뷰하는 것을 정말로 고대하고 있고, 자신의 신문 The South View Daily 독자들 중 많은 사람들이 예술가로서 Ms. Ray의 오래된 경력에 대해 알게 되어 아주 기뻐할 것이라고 확신한다고 했으므로 Mr. Vance가 기자로 일하고 있다는 것을 추론할 수 있다. 따라서 (B)가 정답이다.

어휘   journalist n. 기자   publication n. 출판물, 간행물   skip v. 빠지다

Paraphrasing

newspaper 신문 → publication 출판물

184 추론 문제 연계

해석 Mr. Vance에 대해 사실일 것 같은 것은?
(A) 역에서 Ms. Ray의 집까지 택시를 타고 갔다.
(B) 출발 전에 목적지를 바꿨다.
(C) 특정 좌석을 선택하기 위해 추가 요금을 지불했다.
(D) 계획했던 것보다 늦게 오크빌로 떠났다.

해설 Mr. Vance가 작성한 이메일을 먼저 확인한다.
단서 1 이메일의 'I[Mr. Vance] plan to catch one that departs at 9:30 A.M., and I will arrive in Oakville at 1:20 P.M.'에서 오전 9시 30분에 출발하는 차를 탈 계획이며, 오후 1시 20분에 오크빌에 도착할 것이라고 했다.
단서 2 티켓의 'Departure: July 27, 12:30 P.M.'과 'Arrival: July 27, 4:20 P.M.'에서 7월 27일 오후 12시 30분에 출발하고, 오후 4시 20분에 도착했다는 것을 알 수 있다.
두 단서를 종합할 때, Mr. Vance가 계획보다 늦게 오크빌로 출발했음을 추론할 수 있다. 따라서 (D)가 정답이다.

어휘 prior to ~ 전에 specific adj. 특정한 leave for ~로 떠나다

185 육하원칙 문제

해석 누군가는 왜 티켓에 있는 전화번호로 전화하겠는가?
(A) 일정 업데이트를 요청하기 위해
(B) 좌석 업그레이드를 요청하기 위해
(C) 도착 시간을 확인하기 위해
(D) 잃어버린 물품을 알리기 위해

해설 티켓의 'If you realize after reaching your destination that you have left one of your belongings in the overhead compartment or on your seat, please call 555-0393.'에서 목적지에 도착한 후 소지품들 중 하나를 머리 위 칸이나 좌석에 두고 왔다는 것을 알게 되면 555-0393으로 전화하라고 했으므로, 누군가가 잃어버린 물품을 알리기 위해 티켓에 있는 전화번호로 전화할 것임을 알 수 있다. 따라서 (D)가 정답이다.

어휘 ask for ~을 요청하다 report v. 알리다, 전하다

186-190번은 다음 광고, 온라인 포럼 게시물, 개요에 관한 문제입니다.

Sunnyside Hospitality Institute (SHI) —성공을 위한 열쇠!

소규모 민박집을 개업하든 주요 호텔 체인점에 직장을 구하기를 희망하는 경우이든, SHI는 여러분이 접객 사업에서 성공하는 데 필요한 지식과 기술을 개발하는 데 도움을 줄 수 있습니다. **186저희는 최첨단 온라인 플랫폼을 통해 제공하는 포괄적인 교육에 큰 자부심을 갖습니다.** **187또한 각 수업이 다양한 숙박 시설에서 최소 10년 이상 근무한 자격을 갖춘 전문가에 의해 지도되는 것을 보장합니다.** 아래는 가장 최근에 추가된 수업 중 몇 가지입니다:

• 시설 운영 (SHI203)
  Liza Gomez는 고객 경험에 부정적으로 영향을 미치는 방해 요소를 방지하기 위한 체계적인 접근법을 가르칠 것입니다. ↻

• 고객 관계 (SHI403)
  Brian Chen은 고객과의 상호 작용이 항상 긍정적인 인상을 남긴다는 것을 확실하게 하는 데 필요한 소통 도구를 제시할 것입니다.

• **188온라인 예약 (SHI345)**
  Beth Richard는 수익을 증대시키기 위해 다양한 애플리케이션을 이용하는 방법을 보여드릴 것입니다.

• 관광 동향 (SHI137)
  Kyle Morrison은 현재 서비스업에 영향을 미치고 있는 개발들과 예상되는 개발에 대해 안내할 것입니다.

수업의 전체 목록과 등록 방법에 대한 정보를 보시려면 여기를 클릭하십시오.

bed and breakfast 민박집(아침 식사를 제공하는 숙박 시설)
land a job 직장을 구하다 hospitality industry 접객 사업, 서비스업
comprehensive adj. 포괄적인 ensure v. 보장하다, 확실하게 하다
qualified adj. 자격을 갖춘 accommodation facility 숙박 시설
systematic adj. 체계적인 approach n. 접근법
interaction n. 상호 작용 impression n. 인상
boost v. 증대시키다 projected adj. 예상되는

학생들을 위한 SHI 온라인 포럼

게시 날짜 & 시간: 10월 5일 화요일, 오후 10시 21분
게시자 이름: Burzak Deniz
주제: 스터디 그룹

188Ms. Richard의 수업에서 기말고사를 대비한 스터디 그룹을 구성하는 것에 관심이 있는 분이 있다면, 이 게시물에 답장을 남겨주세요. 다룰 자료도 많고, 다른 사람들과 함께 공부에 집중하는 것이 더 쉬울 것입니다. 우리는 저녁마다 도서관에서 만날 수 있습니다. **189사례 연구 마감일인 10월 8일 이후에는 아무 때나 시작할 수 있을 것 같습니다.** **190저는 아직 한 영역을 끝내야 하는데, 금융 정보를 검토하고 요약해야 하기 때문에 며칠 더 걸릴 것입니다.**

material n. 자료 case study 사례 연구 summarize v. 요약하다

사례 연구 개요

이름: Burzak Deniz

영역 1 - Stanford 호텔 소개
190영역 2 - 지난 3년간의 분기별 수익 및 비용 분석
영역 3 - 현재 및 이전 경영 하에서의 마케팅 전략 비교
영역 4 - 온라인 예약 시스템 간소화를 위한 노력 및 예상되는 영향

inn n. (작은) 호텔, 여관 analysis n. 분석 quarterly adj. 분기별의
revenue n. 수익 expense n. 비용 comparison n. 비교
effort n. 노력 streamline v. 간소화하다, 능률화하다

186 추론 문제

해석 SHI에 대해 암시되는 것은?
(A) 주요 호텔 체인과 제휴하고 있다.
(B) 특정 산업에 초점을 맞추지 않는다.
(C) 대면 수업은 제공하지 않는다.
(D) 학생들을 위한 인턴십을 마련한다.

해설 광고의 'We[SHI] take great pride in the comprehensive

training we provide through our state-of-the-art online platform.'에서 SHI가 최첨단 온라인 플랫폼을 통해 제공하는 포괄적인 교육에 큰 자부심을 느낀다고 했으므로 SHI가 대면 수업을 제공하지 않는다는 것을 추론할 수 있다. 따라서 (C)가 정답이다.

어휘 partner with ~와 제휴하다 in-person adj. 대면의

187 육하원칙 문제

해석 광고에 따르면, SHI에서 가르치기 위한 필요조건은 무엇인가?
(A) 예약 애플리케이션 설계에 대한 숙지
(B) 접객 분야에서의 고급 학위
(C) 10년간의 관련 업무 경험
(D) 온라인 마케팅 기법에 대한 지식

해설 광고의 'We also ensure that each class is led by a qualified professional who has spent at least 10 years working in a wide range of accommodation facilities.'에서 각 수업이 다양한 숙박 시설에서 최소 10년 이상 근무한 자격을 갖춘 전문가에 의해 지도되는 것을 보장한다고 했으므로, SHI에서 가르치기 위한 필요조건이 10년간의 관련 업무 경험임을 알 수 있다. 따라서 (C)가 정답이다.

어휘 requirement n. 필요조건, 요건 familiarity n. 숙지, 친숙함
field n. 분야 decade n. 10년 relevant adj. 관련된

Paraphrasing

10 years 10년 → decade 10년

188 육하원칙 연계

해석 Mr. Deniz는 현재 어떤 과정을 수강하고 있는가?
(A) 시설 운영
(B) 고객 관계
(C) 온라인 예약
(D) 관광 동향

해설 Mr. Deniz가 작성한 온라인 포럼 게시물을 먼저 확인한다.
단서 1 온라인 포럼 게시물의 'If anyone is interested in forming a study group for the final exam in Ms. Richard's class, please leave a reply to this post.'에서 Mr. Deniz가 Ms. Richard의 수업에서 기말고사를 대비하는 스터디 그룹을 구성하는 것에 관심이 있는 분이 있다면, 이 게시물에 답장을 남겨달라고 했다. 그런데 Ms. Richard의 수업이 어떤 것인지 제시되지 않았으므로 광고에서 관련 내용을 확인한다.
단서 2 광고의 'Online Bookings (SHI345)', 'Beth Richard will show you how to use various applications to boost profits.'에서 Ms. Richard가 수익 증대를 위한 애플리케이션 이용법을 다루는 온라인 예약 과정을 가르치는 것을 확인할 수 있다.
두 단서를 종합할 때, Mr. Deniz는 Ms. Richard가 가르치는 온라인 예약을 현재 수강하고 있음을 알 수 있다. 따라서 (C)가 정답이다.

189 추론 문제

해석 Mr. Deniz에 대해 사실일 것 같은 것은?
(A) 기말고사에서 높은 점수를 받았다.
(B) 10월 8일에 과제를 제출할 것이다.

(C) 이전에 SHI 포럼에 글을 게시한 적이 있다.
(D) 마감일 연장을 요청했다.

해설 온라인 포럼 게시물의 'I would be available to start any time after October 8, the deadline for the case study.'에서 사례 연구 마감일인 10월 8일 이후에는 아무 때나 시작할 수 있을 것 같다고 했으므로 Mr. Deniz가 10월 8일에 과제를 제출할 것임을 추론할 수 있다. 따라서 (B)가 정답이다.

어휘 mark n. 점수, 표시 assignment n. 과제 extension n. 연장

190 추론 문제 연계

해석 Mr. Deniz가 마지막에 끝낼 것 같은 사례 연구는 어떤 영역인가?
(A) 영역 1
(B) 영역 2
(C) 영역 3
(D) 영역 4

해설 Mr. Deniz가 작성한 온라인 포럼 게시물을 먼저 확인한다.
단서 1 온라인 포럼 게시물의 'I still need to finish one section, which will take me a couple days because it involves reviewing and summarizing financial information.'에서 아직 한 영역을 끝내야 하는데, 금융 정보를 검토하고 요약해야 하기 때문에 며칠 더 걸릴 것이라고 했다. 그런데 금융 정보를 검토하고 요약해야 하는 것이 어떤 영역인지에 대해 제시되지 않았으므로 개요에서 관련 내용을 확인한다.
단서 2 개요의 'Section 2 — Analysis of quarterly revenues and expenses for the past three years'에서 영역 2가 지난 3년간의 분기별 수익 및 비용 분석이라는 것을 알 수 있다.
두 단서를 종합할 때, Mr. Deniz가 마지막에 끝낼 것 같은 사례 연구는 영역 2임을 추론할 수 있다. 따라서 (B)가 정답이다.

191-195번은 다음 기사, 후기, 이메일에 관한 문제입니다.

Plaza 놀이공원 개장
Kevin Burton 작성

셰필드 191-(B)(6월 25일)—Plaza 놀이공원이 6월 20일에 처음으로 문을 열었다. 191-(A)셰필드의 중심부에서 약 7킬로미터 떨어진 곳에 위치한 그곳은 회전목마, 관람차, 그리고 심지어 워터슬라이드까지 특별히 포함한다. 192하지만 지금까지 가장 긴 줄은 그 지역에서 가장 큰 롤러코스터인 Screaming Eagle을 위한 것이다.

Anderson 시장은 건설하는 데 800만 파운드가 조금 안 들었던 그 놀이공원의 리본 커팅식에 참석했다. "이 시설은 매년 수천 명의 관광객들을 우리 지역 사회로 끌어모을 것입니다,"라고 그는 연설 중에 말했다. "우리 경제의 12퍼센트 성장으로 이어질 것으로 예상됩니다."

193그리고 셰필드 주민들에게 감사를 표하기 위해, Plaza 놀이공원은 여름 동안 매주 목요일에 그들에게 20퍼센트 할인을 제공할 것이다.

amusement park 놀이공원 carousel n. 회전목마
by far 지금까지 construct v. 건설하다
establishment n. 시설, 기관 draw v. 끌어모으다
project v. 예상하다 expansion n. 성장, 확장 resident n. 주민

7월 10일 Mark Hasselt에 의해 게시됨

Plaza 놀이공원 후기 (별 4/5개)

저는 제 아이들을 데리고 Plaza 놀이공원에 갔습니다. 대체로, 저는 꽤 감명받았습니다. ¹⁹³20퍼센트 할인 덕분에 하루 종일 저렴했고, 아이들은 놀이 기구를 매우 좋아했습니다. 제가 제안할 유일한 점은 응급 처치 시설을 늘리는 것입니다. 제 아들이 손을 베었을 때, 치료를 받기 위해 꽤 먼 거리를 걸어야 했습니다. ¹⁹⁵하지만 안내원인 Abigail Walker가 매우 도움이 되었습니다. 상처 부위에 붕대를 감은 후, 그녀는 저에게 감염을 예방하는 방법에 대해 좋은 조언을 해줬습니다.

ride n. 놀이 기구, 탈 것 first aid 응급 처치 distance n. 거리
treatment n. 치료, 대우 attendant n. 안내원
incredibly adv. 매우, 믿을 수 없을 정도로 prevent v. 예방하다, 막다
infection n. 감염

수신: Yuen Lam <y.lam@plazapark.co.uk>
발신: Dan Peters <d.peters@plazapark.co.uk>
제목: 회신: 피드백
날짜: 7월 15일

안녕하세요 Yuen,

¹⁹⁴Mr. Hasselt의 후기 링크를 저에게 전달해 주셔서 감사합니다. 저는 이 문제가 해결되어야 한다는 데 동의하고, 제 계획을 알려드리고자 합니다. 저는 공원 곳곳에 응급 처치 시설을 위한 장소 몇 곳을 추가로 발견했습니다. 그리고 15명의 안내원들을 더 고용할 의도로 의료 인력 면접을 시작할 예정입니다. 새로운 시설들은 9월 1일까지 완전히 사용 가능해질 것입니다. ¹⁹⁵수요일에 Mr. Hasselt의 아들을 치료해 준 안내원을 만났다는 것도 추가로 언급해야겠습니다. 저는 그녀가 자신의 노력을 인정받았다는 사실을 인지하도록 확실히 해주었고, 그녀에게 100파운드짜리 상품권을 제공했습니다.

Dan Peters 드림

forward v. 전달하다 deal with ~을 해결하다, 처리하다
identify v. 발견하다, 확인하다 additional adj. 추가의 site n. 장소
medical personnel 의료 인력 with the intention of ~할 의도로
fully adv. 완전히 operational adj. 사용 가능한, 운영상의

191 Not/True 문제

해석 기사가 Plaza 놀이공원에 대해 언급하는 것은?
(A) 셰필드의 중심부에 위치해 있다.
(B) 며칠 동안 영업을 해왔다.
(C) 매주 특별한 기념식을 개최한다.
(D) 그 지역에서 다른 어떤 것보다 더 크다.

해설 기사의 '(25 JUNE)—The Plaza Amusement Park opened its gates for the first time on 20 June.'에서 기사가 작성된 날짜가 6월 25일이고, Plaza 놀이공원이 6월 20일 처음으로 문을 열었다고 했으므로 (B)가 정답이다. (A)는 'Located about seven kilometres from central Sheffield'에서 셰필드의 중심부에서 약 7킬로미터 떨어진 곳에 위치해 있다고 했으므로 지문의 내용과 일치하지 않는다. (C)와 (D)는 지문에 언급되지 않은 내용이다.

어휘 hold v. 개최하다

192 육하원칙 문제

해석 기사에 따르면, Plaza 놀이공원에서 가장 인기 있는 즐길 거리는 무엇인가?
(A) 회전목마
(B) 관람차
(C) 워터슬라이드
(D) 롤러코스터

해설 기사의 'But the longest lines by far are for the Screaming Eagle—the largest roller coaster in the region.'에서 지금까지 가장 긴 줄은 그 지역에서 가장 큰 롤러코스터인 Screaming Eagle을 위한 것이라고 했으므로, Plaza 놀이공원에서 가장 인기 있는 즐길 거리는 롤러코스터임을 알 수 있다. 따라서 (D)가 정답이다.

어휘 attraction n. 즐길 거리

193 추론 문제 연계

해석 Mr. Hasselt에 대해 결론지을 수 있는 것은?
(A) 부상으로 치료를 받았다.
(B) 문을 연 응급 처치 시설을 찾을 수 없었다.
(C) 목요일에 놀이공원을 방문했다.
(D) 많은 놀이 기구들의 줄이 너무 길다고 느꼈다.

해설 질문의 핵심 어구인 Mr. Hasselt가 작성한 후기를 먼저 확인한다.
[단서 1] 후기의 'The 20 percent discount made the entire day affordable'에서 20퍼센트 할인 덕분에 하루 종일 저렴했다고 했다.
[단서 2] 기사의 'And to show appreciation to the residents of Sheffield, the Plaza Amusement Park will be offering them a 20 percent discount each Thursday during the summer.'에서 Sheffield 주민들에게 감사를 표하기 위해, Plaza 놀이공원은 여름 동안 매주 목요일에 주민들에게 20퍼센트 할인을 제공할 것이라고 했다.
두 단서를 종합할 때, Mr. Hasselt가 목요일에 놀이공원을 방문했음을 추론할 수 있다. 따라서 (C)가 정답이다.

어휘 injury n. 부상

194 목적 찾기 문제

해석 이메일의 목적은 무엇인가?
(A) 프로젝트에 대한 추가 자원을 요청하기 위해
(B) 정책에 대한 의견을 요청하기 위해
(C) 예산을 늘리기 위한 결정을 설명하기 위해
(D) 문제가 어떻게 해결되고 있는지 개요를 서술하기 위해

해설 이메일의 'Thank you for forwarding me the link to Mr. Hasselt's review. I agree that this issue needs to be dealt with, and I want to let you know my plan.'에서 Mr. Hasselt의 후기 링크를 전달해 주어서 고맙다고 하고, 이 문제가 해결되어야 한다는 데 동의하며, 자신의 계획을 알려주고자 한다고 했으므로 (D)가 정답이다.

어휘 resource n. 자원 budget n. 예산 outline v. 개요를 서술하다
address v. 해결하다, 처리하다

Paraphrasing

issue 문제 → problem 문제

be dealt with 해결되다 → is being addressed 해결되고 있다

195 육하원칙 문제 연계

해석 Mr. Peters는 수요일에 누구를 만났는가?
(A) Kevin Burton
(B) Mark Hasselt
(C) Abigail Walker
(D) Yuen Lam

해설 Mr. Peters가 작성한 이메일을 먼저 확인한다.

단서 1 이메일의 'I[Mr. Peters] should also mention that on Wednesday I met with the attendant who treated Mr. Hasselt's son.'에서 Mr. Peters가 수요일에 Mr. Hasselt의 아들을 치료해 준 안내원을 만났다고 했다. 그런데 Mr. Hasselt의 아들을 치료해 준 안내원이 누구인지 제시되지 않았으므로 후기에서 관련 내용을 확인한다.

단서 2 후기의 'When my son cut his hand, we had to walk quite a distance to get treatment. But the attendant, Abigail Walker, was incredibly helpful.'에서 아들이 손을 베었을 때, 치료를 받기 위해 먼 거리를 걸어야 했지만, 안내원인 Abigail Walker가 매우 도움이 되었다고 했으므로, Mr. Hasselt의 아들을 치료해 준 안내원이 Abigail Walker임을 확인할 수 있다.

두 단서를 종합할 때, Mr. Peters는 수요일에 Abigail Walker를 만났음을 알 수 있다. 따라서 (C)가 정답이다.

196-200번은 다음 송장, 공고, 이메일에 관한 문제입니다.

Norton's 도매 농산물 업체

고객: Micah Appel (Boardwalk Bistro의 소유주)

날짜: 4월 25일

고객 번호: 4837376

품목	수량	가격
당근	60킬로그램	125.00달러
로메인 상추	40킬로그램	110.00달러
딸기	25킬로그램	180.00달러
오이	40킬로그램	105.00달러

소계: 520.00달러
[196]배송: 해당 없음
[197]할인(15%): 78.00달러
합계: 442달러

[196]배송 서비스를 이용하지 않으려는 고객은 미리 창고에 연락하여 픽업 시간을 정해야 합니다.

---

produce n. 농산물, 생산품 owner n. 소유주, 주인
account n. 고객, 거래처 quantity n. 수량, 양
subtotal n. 소계, 부분 합계 warehouse n. 창고 in advance 미리

모든 고객분들께 안내 드립니다.

Norton's 도매 농산물 업체에서, 저희는 저렴한 가격의 농장 직송 ◯

과일과 채소를 제공하는 것에 큰 자부심을 느낍니다. [198]안타깝게도, 치솟는 물가 상승률로 저희는 대부분의 식품 가격을 최대 10퍼센트까지 인상해야 합니다. 이러한 변화는 6월 1일에 시행될 것입니다. 이 소식이 반갑지 않다는 것을 이해하지만, 저희의 결정이 업계 전반 추세의 일환이라는 점에 주목하는 것이 중요합니다. 저희 상품들은 경쟁업체의 상품들과 비교하여 합리적인 가격으로 계속 유지될 것입니다. [199]만약 같은 상품이 다른 도매업자에 의해 더 싸게 팔리는 것을 발견하시면, 555-0239로 저희 영업팀에 연락해 주시면 저희가 가격을 맞출 것입니다. [197]게다가, 주문하는 다른 사업체에 고객님들이 저희를 언급할 때마다 계속해서 15퍼센트 할인을 받을 것입니다.

farm-fresh adj. 농장 직송의 soaring adj. 치솟는
take effect 시행되다 unwelcome adj. 반갑지 않은
reasonably adv. 합리적으로 competitor n. 경쟁업체, 경쟁사
wholesaler n. 도매업자 refer v. 언급하다, 가리켜 말하다

수신: Marcos Holt <m.holt@norton.com>
발신: Grace Chung <g.chung@norton.com>
제목: 요청 사항
날짜: 6월 25일

안녕하세요 Marcos,

[199]Brighton Deli의 사장인 Samantha Cove가 어제 Fremont 식료품 잡화점이 킬로그램당 단 1.60달러에 토마토를 제공하고 있다고 알려주기 위해 전화했습니다. 그녀에게 송장에 필요한 조정을 하겠다고 말했지만, 저는 걱정됩니다. 그녀는 이 가격 차이에 대해 저에게 전화를 건 네 번째 고객입니다. [200]저는 우리가 더 저렴한 토마토 공급원을 찾아야 할 수도 있다고 생각합니다. 우리가 농산물을 공급받는 농장들에 확인하고 가격을 낮출 의향이 있는 곳이 있는지 알아봐 주시겠어요?

감사합니다,

Grace Pearson 드림

inform v. 알리다 adjustment n. 조정 difference n. 차이
expensive adj. 비싼 willing to ~할 의향이 있는

196 Not/True 문제

해석 송장이 Boardwalk Bistro에 대해 명시하는 것은?
(A) 4월에 두 번 농산물을 구매했다.
(B) 결제하기 전에 수량을 변경했다.
(C) 보관 시설에서 주문품을 픽업했다.
(D) 최근에 소유권의 변화를 겪었다.

해설 송장의 'Delivery: N/A'와 'Clients that do not wish to take advantage of our delivery service must contact our warehouse in advance to arrange a pickup time.'에서 Boardwalk Bistro가 배송 서비스를 이용하지 않았고, 배송 서비스를 이용하지 않으려는 고객은 미리 창고에 연락하여 픽업 시간을 정해야 한다고 했으므로 Boardwalk Bistro가 보관 시설에서 주문품을 픽업했다는 것을 알 수 있다. 따라서 (C)가 정답이다.

어휘 prior to ~ 전에 storage n. 보관 ownership n. 소유권

Paraphrasing

warehouse 창고 → storage facility 보관 시설

197 추론 문제 연계

해석 Mr. Appel에 대해 결론지을 수 있는 것은?
(A) 창고에 연락할 것을 잊어버렸다.
(B) 부분 환불을 요청했다.
(C) 새로운 도매업체로 바꾸었다.
(D) 회사를 추천했다.

해설 질문의 핵심 어구인 Mr. Appel에게 보내진 송장을 먼저 확인한다.
단서 1 송장의 'Discount (15%): $78.00'에서 Mr. Appel이 15퍼센트인 78달러를 할인받은 것을 확인할 수 있다.
단서 2 공고의 'Furthermore, clients will continue to receive a 15 percent discount whenever they refer us to another business that places an order.'에서 Norton's 도매 농산물 업체를 주문하는 다른 사업체에 언급할 때마다 고객은 계속해서 15퍼센트 할인을 받을 것이라고 했다.
두 단서를 종합할 때, Mr. Appel이 회사(Norton's 도매 농산물 업체)를 다른 사업체에 추천했음을 추론할 수 있다. 따라서 (D)가 정답이다.

어휘 partial adj. 부분의

198 육하원칙 문제

해석 공고에 따르면, 6월 1일에 Norton's 도매 농산물 업체가 하려는 것은 무엇인가?
(A) 경쟁업체와 제휴한다.
(B) 일부 상품의 가격을 인상한다.
(C) 장기 고객에게 할인을 제공한다.
(D) 판매 품목에 대한 선택의 폭을 확대한다.

해설 공고의 'Unfortunately, the soaring inflation rate makes it necessary for us to raise the prices of most food items by up to 10 percent. These changes will take effect on June 1.'에서 치솟는 물가 상승률로 대부분의 식품 가격을 최대 10퍼센트까지 인상해야 하며, 이러한 변화는 6월 1일에 시행될 것이라고 했으므로, 6월 1일에 일부 상품의 가격을 인상할 것임을 알 수 있다. 따라서 (B)가 정답이다.

어휘 form a partnership 제휴하다

Paraphrasing

raise the prices 가격을 인상하다 → increase the cost 가격을 인상하다

199 추론 문제 연계

해석 Ms. Chung은 어느 부서에 속할 것 같은가?
(A) 인사
(B) 영업
(C) 회계
(D) 고객 서비스

해설 Ms. Chung이 어느 부서에 속할 것 같은지를 묻고 있으므로 Ms. Chung이 작성한 이메일을 먼저 확인한다.
단서 1 이메일의 'Samantha Cove, the owner of Brighton Deli, called yesterday to inform me ~'에서 Brighton Deli의 사장인 Samantha Cove가 어제 Ms. Chung에게 전화했다는 것을 알 수 있다. 그런데 Samantha Cove가 어떤 부서로 전화했는지 제시되지 않았으므로 공고에서 관련 내용을 확인한다.
단서 2 공고의 'If you find the same product being sold for less by another wholesaler, simply contact our sales team at 555-0239 and we will match the price.'에서 만약 같은 상품이 다른 도매업자에 의해 더 싸게 팔리는 것을 발견하면, 555-0239로 영업팀에 연락하라고 했다.
두 단서를 종합할 때, Ms. Chung이 영업 부서에 속할 것임을 추론할 수 있다. 따라서 (B)가 정답이다.

200 육하원칙 문제

해석 Ms. Chung은 Mr. Holt에게 무엇을 하라고 요청하는가?
(A) 일부 비용을 뺀다.
(B) 청구 문서를 수정한다.
(C) 고객과 만난다.
(D) 몇몇 공급업체에 연락한다.

해설 이메일의 'I[Ms. Chung] think we may have to find a less expensive source of tomatoes. Could you[Mr. Holt] check with the farms that we get our produce from and find out if any are willing to lower their prices?'에서 Ms. Chung은 더 저렴한 토마토 공급원을 찾아야 할 수도 있다고 생각한다며, 농산물을 공급받는 농장들에 확인하고 가격을 낮출 의향이 있는 곳이 있는지 알아봐 달라고 했으므로, Ms. Chung은 Mr. Holt에게 몇몇 공급업체에 연락해 달라고 요청하는 것을 알 수 있다. 따라서 (D)가 정답이다.

어휘 eliminate v. 빼다, 없애다   billing n. 청구

TEST 3

LISTENING TEST

p.112

1 (C)	21 (A)	41 (D)	61 (A)	81 (C)
2 (C)	22 (B)	42 (B)	62 (C)	82 (D)
3 (D)	23 (B)	43 (C)	63 (A)	83 (B)
4 (B)	24 (C)	44 (B)	64 (B)	84 (D)
5 (D)	25 (A)	45 (B)	65 (A)	85 (A)
6 (C)	26 (B)	46 (C)	66 (B)	86 (B)
7 (B)	27 (C)	47 (A)	67 (C)	87 (A)
8 (B)	28 (C)	48 (B)	68 (A)	88 (A)
9 (B)	29 (A)	49 (C)	69 (C)	89 (D)
10 (A)	30 (A)	50 (C)	70 (B)	90 (C)
11 (C)	31 (C)	51 (D)	71 (B)	91 (A)
12 (B)	32 (B)	52 (C)	72 (C)	92 (B)
13 (A)	33 (A)	53 (B)	73 (D)	93 (C)
14 (B)	34 (D)	54 (D)	74 (B)	94 (C)
15 (C)	35 (A)	55 (A)	75 (A)	95 (C)
16 (B)	36 (C)	56 (A)	76 (C)	96 (B)
17 (C)	37 (D)	57 (D)	77 (C)	97 (C)
18 (B)	38 (C)	58 (C)	78 (B)	98 (D)
19 (B)	39 (D)	59 (B)	79 (A)	99 (B)
20 (B)	40 (C)	60 (B)	80 (D)	100 (C)

READING TEST

p.124

101 (C)	121 (B)	141 (C)	161 (D)	181 (B)
102 (A)	122 (C)	142 (A)	162 (C)	182 (D)
103 (B)	123 (D)	143 (B)	163 (D)	183 (A)
104 (B)	124 (C)	144 (B)	164 (C)	184 (C)
105 (C)	125 (A)	145 (D)	165 (B)	185 (C)
106 (B)	126 (D)	146 (A)	166 (D)	186 (B)
107 (B)	127 (D)	147 (B)	167 (C)	187 (C)
108 (C)	128 (A)	148 (C)	168 (B)	188 (A)
109 (B)	129 (B)	149 (B)	169 (B)	189 (D)
110 (D)	130 (B)	150 (D)	170 (C)	190 (D)
111 (C)	131 (C)	151 (C)	171 (C)	191 (A)
112 (B)	132 (B)	152 (A)	172 (A)	192 (B)
113 (A)	133 (B)	153 (D)	173 (D)	193 (A)
114 (A)	134 (D)	154 (C)	174 (D)	194 (B)
115 (C)	135 (C)	155 (A)	175 (B)	195 (C)
116 (B)	136 (C)	156 (B)	176 (B)	196 (D)
117 (B)	137 (D)	157 (C)	177 (B)	197 (C)
118 (D)	138 (D)	158 (B)	178 (A)	198 (A)
119 (B)	139 (D)	159 (D)	179 (D)	199 (D)
120 (D)	140 (D)	160 (C)	180 (C)	200 (B)

PART 1

1 1인 사진

[3제] 캐나다식

(A) The man is inflating a bicycle tire.
(B) The man is putting on a sweater.
(C) The man is biking on a street.
(D) The man is exiting a tunnel.

inflate v. 공기를 넣다, 부풀리다   bike v. 자전거를 타다; n. 자전거
exit v. 빠져나가다, 떠나다

해석 (A) 남자가 자전거 바퀴에 공기를 넣고 있다.
(B) 남자가 스웨터를 입고 있다.
(C) 남자가 길에서 자전거를 타고 있다.
(D) 남자가 터널을 빠져나가고 있다.

해설 (A) [×] inflating(공기를 넣고 있다)은 남자의 동작과 무관하므로 오답
이다. 사진에 있는 자전거 바퀴(bicycle tire)를 사용하여 혼
동을 주었다.
(B) [×] putting on(입고 있다)은 남자의 동작과 무관하므로 오답이
다. 옷·모자·구두 등을 이미 입은 상태를 나타내는 wearing
과 입고 있는 중이라는 동작을 나타내는 putting on을 혼동
하지 않도록 주의한다.
(C) [○] 남자가 길에서 자전거를 타고 있는 모습을 가장 잘 묘사한 정
답이다.
(D) [×] 사진에 터널(tunnel)이 없으므로 오답이다.

2 2인 이상 사진

[3제] 호주식

(A) One of the workers is reaching for an electrical wire.
(B) There are some step stools in a corner.
(C) Boxes have been stacked on shelves.
(D) One of the workers is hanging up a safety vest.

reach v. 손을 뻗다   electrical wire 전선   step stool 계단식 의자
stack v. 쌓다   hang up ~을 걸다   safety vest 안전 조끼

해석 (A) 작업자들 중 한 명이 전선으로 손을 뻗고 있다.
(B) 몇몇 계단식 의자들이 구석에 있다.
(C) 박스들이 선반에 쌓여 있다.
(D) 작업자들 중 한 명이 안전 조끼를 걸고 있다.

해설 (A) [×] 사진에 손을 뻗고 있는(reaching for) 작업자가 없으므로 오
답이다. 사진에 있는 전선(electrical wire)을 사용하여 혼동
을 주었다.
(B) [×] 사진에 계단식 의자들(step stools)이 없으므로 오답이다.
(C) [○] 박스들이 선반에 쌓여 있는 모습을 가장 잘 묘사한 정답이다.
(D) [×] 사진에 걸고 있는(hanging up) 작업자가 없으므로 오답이

다. 사진에 있는 안전 조끼(safety vest)를 사용하여 혼동을 주었다.

3 사물 및 풍경 사진 🔊 미국식

(A) A vehicle is stopped at a traffic signal.
(B) A line is being painted on a sidewalk.
(C) Some bushes are being trimmed in a garden.
(D) Several cars are parked along a walkway.

traffic signal 교통신호 sidewalk n. 보도 bush n. 덤불
trim v. 다듬다, 손질하다 walkway n. 보도, 통로

해석 (A) 한 차량이 교통신호에 멈춰 있다.
(B) 선이 보도에 그려지고 있다.
(C) 정원에서 몇몇 덤불들이 다듬어지고 있다.
(D) 여러 대의 자동차가 보도를 따라 주차되어 있다.

해설 (A) [×] 사진에 교통신호(traffic signal)가 없으므로 오답이다. 사진에 있는 차량(vehicle)을 사용하여 혼동을 주었다.
(B) [×] 사진에서 선은 보이지만, 그려지고 있는(being painted) 모습은 아니므로 오답이다.
(C) [×] 사진에서 덤불들은 보이지만, 다듬어지고 있는(being trimmed) 모습은 아니므로 오답이다.
(D) [○] 여러 대의 자동차가 보도를 따라 주차되어 있는 모습을 가장 잘 묘사한 정답이다.

4 1인 사진 🔊 영국식

(A) He's taking a container out of his backpack.
(B) He's pulling a handcart down the road.
(C) He's twisting the cap off a bottle.
(D) He's loading some items onto a van.

container n. 용기, 통 handcart n. 손수레

twist ~ off ~을 비틀어 열다 load v. 싣다 van n. 승합차

해석 (A) 그는 배낭에서 용기를 꺼내고 있다.
(B) 그는 길을 따라 손수레를 끌고 있다.
(C) 그는 병뚜껑을 비틀어 열고 있다.
(D) 그는 몇몇 물건들을 승합차에 싣고 있다.

해설 (A) [×] taking a container out of his backpack(배낭에서 용기를 꺼내고 있다)은 남자의 동작과 무관하므로 오답이다. 사진에 있는 용기(container)와 배낭(backpack)을 사용하여 혼동을 주었다.
(B) [○] 남자가 길을 따라 손수레를 끌고 있는 모습을 가장 잘 묘사한 정답이다.
(C) [×] twisting the cap off a bottle(병뚜껑을 비틀어 열고 있다)은 남자의 동작과 무관하므로 오답이다.
(D) [×] loading some items(몇몇 물건들을 싣고 있다)는 남자의 동작과 무관하므로 오답이다. 사진에 있는 승합차(van)를 사용하여 혼동을 주었다.

5 사물 및 풍경 사진 🔊 호주식

(A) A chair is propped against a wall.
(B) The sunlight is being blocked by some curtains.
(C) Some cabinets are facing a window.
(D) A laptop has been left open on a desk.

prop against ~에 기대어 놓다, 받쳐 놓다 sunlight n. 햇빛
block v. 차단하다, 막다 face v. ~을 향하다, 마주보다

해석 (A) 의자가 벽에 기대어 놓여 있다.
(B) 몇몇 커튼으로 인해 햇빛이 차단되고 있다.
(C) 몇몇 캐비닛들이 창문을 향하고 있다.
(D) 노트북이 책상 위에 열린 채로 있다.

해설 (A) [×] 사진에서 의자는 보이지만, 벽에 기대어 놓여 있는(is propped against a wall) 모습은 아니므로 오답이다.
(B) [×] 사진에 커튼(curtains)이 없으므로 오답이다.
(C) [×] 사진에 캐비닛들(cabinets)이 없으므로 오답이다. 사진에 있는 창문(window)을 사용하여 혼동을 주었다.
(D) [○] 노트북이 책상 위에 열린 채로 있는 모습을 가장 잘 묘사한 정답이다.

6 1인 사진 🔊 미국식

(A) The man is brushing snow from the top of some stairs.
(B) A shovel is leaning against the side of a fence.
(C) Snow is being cleared away from the ground.
(D) The man is spreading sand on an icy road.

brush v. 털어내다 stairs n. 계단
shovel n. 삽; v. 삽으로 퍼내다, 삽질하다 lean against ~에 기대다
fence n. 울타리 clear away 치우다, 정돈하다
spread v. 뿌리다, (얇게 펴서) 바르다 icy road 빙판길

해석 (A) 남자가 계단 꼭대기에서 눈을 털어내고 있다.
(B) 삽이 울타리의 옆면에 기대어 있다.
(C) 눈이 땅바닥에서 치워지고 있다.
(D) 남자가 빙판길에 모래를 뿌리고 있다.

해설 (A) [×] 남자가 계단 꼭대기에 있지 않으므로 오답이다. 사진에 있는 눈(snow)과 계단(stairs)을 사용하여 혼동을 주었다.
(B) [×] 사진에 울타리(fence)가 없으므로 오답이다. 사진에 있는 삽 (shovel)을 사용하여 혼동을 주었다.
(C) [○] 눈이 땅바닥에서 치워지고 있는 모습을 가장 잘 묘사한 정답 이다.
(D) [×] spreading sand(모래를 뿌리고 있다)는 남자의 동작과 무관 하므로 오답이다.

최신토익경향

최근 Part 1에서는 눈이 쌓여 있는 풍경 사진이 종종 출제되고 있다. 눈을 배경으로 하는 사진에 정답으로 자주 출제되는 표현들을 함께 알아두자.

· The man **is shoveling snow**.
  남자가 삽으로 눈을 퍼내고 있다.
· Some outdoor furniture **is covered in snow**.
  몇몇 야외의 가구들이 눈으로 덮여 있다.
· She is **clearing snow from** a path.
  그녀는 길에서 눈을 치우고 있다.

PART 2

7 조동사 의문문

[3m] 미국식 → 호주식

Should we take a taxi to our meeting tomorrow morning?
(A) He arrived at 8:30 A.M.
(B) Yes. That will save time.
(C) Tax season is our busy period.

tax season 납세 기간

해석 저희는 내일 아침 회의에 택시를 타고 가야 하나요?
(A) 그는 오전 8시 30분에 도착했어요.
(B) 네. 그게 시간을 절약할 거예요.
(C) 납세 기간은 저희의 가장 바쁜 시기예요.

해설 (A) [×] 질문의 morning(아침)과 관련 있는 8:30 A.M.(오전 8시 30분)을 사용하여 혼동을 준 오답이다.
(B) [○] Yes로 택시를 타고 가야 한다고 전달한 후, 그것이 시간을 절 약할 것이라는 부연 설명을 했으므로 정답이다.
(C) [×] taxi - Tax의 유사 발음 어휘를 사용하여 혼동을 준 오답이다.

8 Who 의문문

[3m] 캐나다식 → 미국식

Who told you to set up a display case near the main entrance?
(A) To set up my desk.
(B) The store manager.
(C) Some special offers.

display case 진열장 entrance n. 출입구, 문 offer n. (단기간의) 할인

해석 누가 출입구 근처에 진열장을 설치하라고 했나요?
(A) 제 책상을 설치하기 위해서요.
(B) 매장 관리자요.
(C) 일부 특별 할인이요.

해설 (A) [×] 질문의 set up을 반복 사용하여 혼동을 준 오답이다.
(B) [○] 매장 관리자라며, 출입구 근처에 진열장을 설치하라고 한 사 람을 언급했으므로 정답이다.
(C) [×] 질문의 display case(진열장)에서 연상할 수 있는 제품과 관 련된 offers(할인)를 사용하여 혼동을 준 오답이다.

9 Why 의문문

[3m] 미국식 → 캐나다식

Why weren't you at Mr. Hwang's retirement party yesterday?
(A) No, it didn't work out for me.
(B) Because I had a doctor's appointment.
(C) Sometime yesterday.

retirement party 은퇴 파티 doctor's appointment 진료 예약

해석 어제 왜 Mr. Hwang의 은퇴 파티에 오지 않으셨나요?
(A) 아뇨, 그것은 저에게 잘 맞지 않았어요.
(B) 진료 예약이 있었기 때문이에요.
(C) 어제 어느 때쯤이었어요.

해설 (A) [×] 의문사 의문문에 No로 응답했으므로 오답이다.
(B) [○] 진료 예약이 있었기 때문이라는 말로, 어제 은퇴 파티에 오지 않은 이유를 언급했으므로 정답이다.
(C) [×] 질문의 yesterday를 반복 사용하여 혼동을 준 오답이다.

10 Be동사 의문문

[3m] 미국식 → 호주식

Are you going to the premiere of the movie *Shadow of Serendipity*?
(A) I have to work, unfortunately.
(B) Mostly local actors.
(C) Didn't you download that music?

premiere n. (연극·영화의) 첫날, (특별) 개봉 local adj. 지역의

해석 영화 *Shadow of Serendipity*의 첫 상연에 가실 건가요?
(A) 유감스럽게도, 전 일을 해야 해요.
(B) 대부분 지역 배우들이에요.
(C) 그 노래를 내려받지 않았나요?

해설 (A) [○] 유감스럽게도 일을 해야 한다는 말로, 첫 상연에 가지 못할 것 이라는 것을 간접적으로 전달했으므로 정답이다.
(B) [×] 질문의 movie(영화)와 관련 있는 actors(배우들)를 사용하여 혼동을 준 오답이다.
(C) [×] 질문의 movie(영화)에서 연상할 수 있는 download(내려받 다)를 사용하여 혼동을 준 오답이다.

최신토익경향

Be동사 의문문에 대한 응답으로 최근에는 Yes/No가 생략된 고난도의 문 제가 자주 출제되고 있다. 아래의 예문을 통해 고난도 문제에 대비하자.

Are you going to attend the meeting tomorrow?
당신은 내일 회의에 참석하시나요?

<긍정> I have some issues to discuss.
　　저는 논의할 안건들이 좀 있어요.
<부정> I have to do a building inspection.
　　저는 건물 점검을 해야 해요.
*<긍정> 논의할 안건들이 있다며 내일 회의에 참석할 것이라는 응답
　<부정> 건물 점검을 해야 한다며 내일 회의에 참석하지 않을 것이라는 응답

11 제안 의문문
호주식 → 미국식

Why don't we discuss our travel plans together?
(A) An updated manual.
(B) Three hours of traveling time.
(C) Sure, sounds good to me.

discuss v. 상의하다, 논의하다　manual n. 설명서

해석　우리의 여행 계획에 대해 함께 상의해 보는 게 어때요?
(A) 최신 설명서요.
(B) 세 시간의 이동 시간이요.
(C) 물론이죠, 전 좋아요.

해설　(A) [×] 여행 계획에 대해 함께 상의해 보는 게 어떤지 물었는데, 이와 관련이 없는 최신 설명서라는 말로 응답했으므로 오답이다.
(B) [×] 질문의 travel을 traveling으로 반복 사용하여 혼동을 준 오답이다.
(C) [○] Sure로 여행 계획에 대해 함께 상의해 보자는 제안을 수락한 정답이다.

12 Who 의문문
영국식 → 캐나다식

Who else is working on the project?
(A) Thanks, it is very helpful.
(B) Here is the list of team members.
(C) The projector is in the auditorium.

helpful adj. 도움이 되는　projector n. 영사기
auditorium n. 강당, 객석

해석　그 프로젝트에 참여하고 있는 사람은 또 누구인가요?
(A) 고마워요, 그것은 매우 도움이 돼요.
(B) 여기 팀원 목록이 있어요.
(C) 영사기는 강당에 있어요.

해설　(A) [×] 프로젝트에 참여하고 있는 사람이 또 누구인지를 물었는데, 이와 관련이 없는 고맙다는 말로 응답했으므로 오답이다.
(B) [○] 여기 팀원 목록이 있다는 말로, 자신은 그 프로젝트에 참여하고 있는 사람이 누구인지 모른다는 것을 간접적으로 전달했으므로 정답이다.
(C) [×] project - projector의 유사 발음 어휘를 사용하여 혼동을 준 오답이다.

13 평서문
미국식 → 영국식

You should upgrade to the latest computer model to improve your work efficiency.
(A) I've been thinking about it.

(B) Just a résumé is needed.
(C) Our online reviews.

efficiency n. 능률, 효율성　résumé n. 이력서　review n. 평가

해석　당신은 업무 능률을 향상시키기 위해 최신 컴퓨터 모델로 업그레이드해야 해요.
(A) 그것에 관해 생각해 보고 있었어요.
(B) 이력서만 필요해요.
(C) 우리의 온라인 평가요.

해설　(A) [○] 그것에 관해 생각해 보고 있었다는 말로, 최신 컴퓨터 모델로 업그레이드해야 한다는 의견에 동의했으므로 정답이다.
(B) [×] 질문의 work(업무)에서 연상할 수 있는 취업과 관련된 résumé(이력서)를 사용하여 혼동을 준 오답이다.
(C) [×] 질문의 computer(컴퓨터)와 관련 있는 online(온라인)을 사용하여 혼동을 준 오답이다.

14 When 의문문
호주식 → 영국식

When are we moving into our new office space?
(A) It's very spacious.
(B) Next month, at the latest.
(C) On the 14th floor.

office space 사무실 공간　spacious adj. 널찍한
at the latest 늦어도

해석　우리는 언제 새로운 사무실 공간으로 이동하나요?
(A) 그곳은 매우 널찍해요.
(B) 늦어도 다음 달에요.
(C) 14층에서요.

해설　(A) [×] space - spacious의 유사 발음 어휘를 사용하여 혼동을 준 오답이다.
(B) [○] 늦어도 다음 달이라는 말로, 새로운 사무실 공간으로 이동하는 시점을 전달했으므로 정답이다.
(C) [×] 새로운 사무실 공간으로 언제 이동하는지를 물었는데 장소로 응답했으므로 오답이다. 질문의 When을 Where로 혼동하여 이를 정답으로 선택하지 않도록 주의한다.

15 부가 의문문
미국식 → 호주식

Our flight to Rome is scheduled for 9 A.M., right?
(A) I prefer an aisle seat.
(B) A one-way ticket.
(C) The storm may cause a delay.

flight n. 항공편, 비행기　be scheduled for ~으로 예정되어 있다
aisle seat 통로 쪽 좌석　one-way adj. 편도의, 일방통행의
storm n. 폭풍

해석　우리의 로마행 항공편이 오전 9시로 예정되어 있어요, 그렇죠?
(A) 저는 통로 쪽 좌석을 선호해요.
(B) 편도 항공권이요.
(C) 폭풍이 지연을 야기할 수도 있어요.

해설　(A) [×] 질문의 flight(항공편)와 관련 있는 aisle seat(통로 쪽 좌석)을

사용하여 혼동을 준 오답이다.

(B) [×] 질문의 flight(항공편)와 관련 있는 one-way ticket(편도 항공권)을 사용하여 혼동을 준 오답이다.

(C) [○] 폭풍이 지연을 야기할 수도 있다며, 로마행 항공편의 예정된 시간에 변동이 있을 수도 있다는 것을 간접적으로 전달했으므로 정답이다.

16 Which 의문문
🎧 호주식 → 영국식

Which file is the most up-to-date?
(A) Because there were some errors.
(B) The one I e-mailed you.
(C) Yes, I put it in the filing cabinet.

up-to-date adj. 최신의, 최근의 error n. 오류
filing cabinet 서류 캐비닛

해석 어떤 파일이 가장 최신인가요?
(A) 몇 가지 오류가 있었기 때문이에요.
(B) 제가 이메일로 보냈던 것이요.
(C) 네, 제가 그것을 서류 캐비닛에 넣어두었어요.

해설 (A) [×] 질문의 file(파일)에서 연상할 수 있는 errors(오류)를 사용하여 혼동을 준 오답이다.
(B) [○] 이메일로 보냈던 것이라는 말로, 가장 최신 파일이 어떤 것인지 전달했으므로 정답이다.
(C) [×] 의문사 의문문에 Yes로 응답했으므로 오답이다. 질문의 file을 filing으로 반복 사용하여 혼동을 주었다.

17 How 의문문
🎧 캐나다식 → 미국식

How many candles are sold at the Westport branch monthly?
(A) The new product line.
(B) To address a quality issue.
(C) Around 1,000.

branch n. 지점 product line 제품군
address v. (문제 등을) 해결하다, 다루다

해석 Westport 지점에서 매월 몇 개의 양초가 판매되나요?
(A) 새로운 제품군이요.
(B) 품질 문제를 해결하기 위해서요.
(C) 약 1,000개요.

해설 (A) [×] 질문의 candles(양초)와 관련 있는 product line(제품군)을 사용하여 혼동을 준 오답이다.
(B) [×] 질문의 candles(양초)에서 연상할 수 있는 제품과 관련된 quality issue(품질 문제)를 사용하여 혼동을 준 오답이다.
(C) [○] 약 1,000개라며, 매월 판매되는 양초의 수를 언급했으므로 정답이다.

18 부정 의문문
🎧 영국식 → 캐나다식

Wasn't Hikaru supposed to join us for lunch today?
(A) Just half the order.
(B) He had an unexpected meeting.   ○

(C) A free buffet lunch.

be supposed to ~할 예정이다, ~하기로 되어 있다
join v. 함께 하다, 합류하다 unexpected adj. 예상치 못한

해석 Hikaru가 오늘 점심에 우리와 함께 할 예정이지 않았나요?
(A) 주문의 절반만요.
(B) 그는 예상치 못한 회의가 있었어요.
(C) 무료 뷔페식 점심이요.

해설 (A) [×] 질문의 lunch(점심)에서 연상할 수 있는 order(주문)를 사용하여 혼동을 준 오답이다.
(B) [○] 그는 예상치 못한 회의가 있었다는 말로, Hikaru가 오늘 점심에 함께할 예정이었으나, 못 오게 되었음을 간접적으로 전달했으므로 정답이다.
(C) [×] 질문의 lunch를 반복 사용하여 혼동을 준 오답이다.

19 How 의문문
🎧 캐나다식 → 미국식

How often do you clean your swimming pool?
(A) Because I try to swim every day.
(B) We haven't used it this year.
(C) A local cleaning company.

clean v. 청소하다 swimming pool 수영장 try to ~하려고 노력하다

해석 당신은 수영장을 얼마나 자주 청소하나요?
(A) 제가 매일 수영하려고 노력하기 때문이에요.
(B) 우리는 올해 그걸 사용하지 않았어요.
(C) 지역 청소 업체요.

해설 (A) [×] 질문의 swimming pool(수영장)과 관련 있는 swim(수영하다)을 사용하여 혼동을 준 오답이다.
(B) [○] 올해 그것을 사용하지 않았다는 말로, 수영장을 사용하지 않아서 청소를 하지 않는다는 간접적인 응답을 했으므로 정답이다.
(C) [×] 질문의 clean을 cleaning으로 반복 사용하여 혼동을 준 오답이다.

최신토익 경향

최근 how 의문문에 대해 예측하기 어려운 응답이 출제되고 있다. 보기를 주의 깊게 들으면서 의도를 정확히 파악하는 연습을 하자.

How long does it take to go to the market?
시장까지 가는 데 얼마나 걸리나요?
<답변 1> It is already closed.
　　　　이미 닫혔어요.
<답변 2> Let me give you a ride.
　　　　제가 태워드릴게요.
*<답변 1> 이미 시장이 닫혔다는 말로, 시장을 가지 않는 것이 좋겠다는 응답
　<답변 2> 자신이 차로 태워주겠다는 말로, 시장까지 거리가 꽤 있다는 응답

20 평서문
🎧 영국식 → 호주식

These shipments need to be sorted by the end of today.
(A) No, it wasn't in storage.
(B) I can help you if you want.   ○

(C) I sorted through my files.

> shipment n. 배송품, 수송   sort v. 분류하다, 구분하다
> storage n. 창고
> sort through (찾거나 정리하기 위해) ~을 자세히 살펴보다

해석   이 배송품들은 오늘 안으로 분류되어야 해요.
  (A) 아뇨, 그것은 창고에 없었어요.
  (B) 원하시면 제가 도와드릴 수 있어요.
  (C) 저는 제 파일을 자세히 살펴봤어요.

해설   (A) [×] 질문의 shipments(배송품들)에서 연상할 수 있는 storage
    (창고)를 사용하여 혼동을 준 오답이다.
  (B) [○] 원한다면 자신이 도와줄 수 있다는 말로, 배송품들이 오늘 안
    으로 분류되어야 하는 문제점에 대한 해결책을 제시했으므로
    정답이다.
  (C) [×] 질문의 sorted를 반복 사용하여 혼동을 준 오답이다.

21 When 의문문
🎧 호주식 → 영국식

> When will the order of office supplies arrive?
> **(A) By Friday afternoon, hopefully.**
> (B) Mainly pens and paper.
> (C) In the supply closet.

> office supplies 사무용품   hopefully adv. 바라건대, 희망을 갖고
> supply closet 비품 보관함

해석   사무용품 주문품이 언제 도착할까요?
  (A) 바라건대, 금요일 오후까지요.
  (B) 대개 펜과 종이예요.
  (C) 비품 보관함 안에요.

해설   (A) [○] 금요일 오후라며, 사무용품 주문품이 도착할 시점을 전달했으
    므로 정답이다.
  (B) [×] 질문의 office supplies(사무용품)와 관련 있는 pens and
    paper(펜과 종이)를 사용하여 혼동을 준 오답이다.
  (C) [×] 질문의 supplies를 supply로 반복 사용하여 혼동을 준 오답
    이다.

22 부정 의문문
🎧 캐나다식 → 미국식

> Shouldn't we call a plumber to fix the leaking pipe in the
> bathroom?
> (A) The bathroom is just down the hall.
> **(B) Someone will be here this afternoon.**
> (C) The broken door handle.

> plumber n. 배관공   leak v. (지붕·배·수조·파이프가) 새다

해석   화장실에 있는 새는 배관을 고치려면 배관공을 불러야 하지 않나요?
  (A) 화장실은 복도를 쭉 따라가면 있어요.
  (B) 누군가가 오늘 오후에 올 거예요.
  (C) 고장 난 문고리요.

해설   (A) [×] 질문의 bathroom을 반복 사용하여 혼동을 준 오답이다.
  (B) [○] 누군가가 오늘 오후에 올 것이라는 말로, 배관공을 부를 필요
    가 없음을 간접적으로 전달했으므로 정답이다.

(C) [×] 질문의 leaking(새는)과 관련 있는 broken(고장 난)을 사용하
    여 혼동을 준 오답이다.

23 Where 의문문
🎧 영국식 → 캐나다식

> Where is the application form for the management class?
> (A) There are too many internship applicants.
> **(B) On our Web site.**
> (C) The former department manager.

> application form 신청서, 지원서   management n. 경영, 관리
> applicant n. 지원자   former adj. 이전의, 전의

해석   경영 수업 신청서는 어디에 있나요?
  (A) 인턴십 지원자가 너무 많아요.
  (B) 우리 웹사이트에요.
  (C) 이전 부서장이요.

해설   (A) [×] application - applicants의 유사 발음 어휘를 사용하여 혼
    동을 준 오답이다.
  (B) [○] 웹사이트에 있다며, 경영 수업 신청서가 있는 장소를 언급했
    으므로 정답이다.
  (C) [×] management - manager의 유사 발음 어휘를 사용하여 혼
    동을 준 오답이다.

24 요청 의문문
🎧 캐나다식 → 영국식

> Could you send me a copy of the workshop agenda?
> (A) Sure, let me replace the coffee filter.
> (B) Thirty people attended.
> **(C) I'm on my way to an appointment now.**

> copy n. 복사본   agenda n. 안건, 의제   replace v. 교체하다
> on one's way ~하는 중에

해석   워크숍 안건의 복사본을 제게 보내주실 수 있나요?
  (A) 물론이죠, 제가 커피 필터를 교체할게요.
  (B) 30명이 참석했어요.
  (C) 저는 지금 약속에 가는 중이에요.

해설   (A) [×] copy - coffee의 유사 발음 어휘를 사용하여 혼동을 준 오답
    이다. Sure까지만 듣고 정답으로 고르지 않도록 주의한다.
  (B) [×] 질문의 workshop(워크숍)에서 연상할 수 있는 참석과 관련
    된 attended(참석했다)를 사용하여 혼동을 준 오답이다.
  (C) [○] 지금 약속에 가는 중이라는 말로, 워크숍 안건의 복사본을 보
    내달라는 요청을 간접적으로 거절한 정답이다.

25 When 의문문
🎧 호주식 → 캐나다식

> When will the human resources department confirm the
> recruitment plan?
> **(A) The deadline is in two weeks.**
> (B) In the lobby.
> (C) With the hiring committee.

> human resources 인사 부서   confirm v. 확정하다
> recruitment n. 채용   deadline n. 마감일   ○

hiring committee 고용 위원회

해석 인사 부서가 언제 채용 계획을 확정할까요?
(A) 마감일은 2주 후예요.
(B) 로비에서요.
(C) 고용 위원회와 함께요.

해설 (A) [○] 마감일이 2주 후라는 말로, 인사 부서가 채용 계획을 확정할
시점을 전달했으므로 정답이다.
(B) [×] 인사 부서가 언제 채용 계획을 확정할지를 물었는데, 이와 관
련이 없는 로비에서라는 내용으로 응답했으므로 오답이다.
(C) [×] 질문의 recruitment(채용)와 관련 있는 hiring committee
(고용 위원회)를 사용하여 혼동을 준 오답이다.

26 평서문
3 영국식 → 호주식

I still haven't received the editor's revisions to the article on
the housing crisis.
(A) Thanks for editing the report I wrote.
(B) There are a lot of projects underway.
(C) I plan to sell my house later this year.

editor n. 편집자, 편집장 revision n. 교정본, 수정 사항 crisis n. 위기
edit v. 수정하다, 편집하다 underway adj. 진행 중인

해석 주택 위기에 관한 기사에 대한 편집자의 교정본을 아직 받지 못했어요.
(A) 제가 작성한 보고서를 수정해 주셔서 감사해요.
(B) 진행 중인 프로젝트가 많아요.
(C) 저는 올해 말에 집을 팔 계획이에요.

해설 (A) [×] editor's - editing의 유사 발음 어휘를 사용하여 혼동을 준
오답이다.
(B) [○] 진행 중인 프로젝트가 많다는 말로, 편집자로부터의 교정본이
늦어지는 원인에 대해 언급했으므로 정답이다.
(C) [×] housing - house의 유사 발음 어휘를 사용하여 혼동을 준
오답이다.

27 Where 의문문
3 캐나다식 → 영국식

Where did those flowers come from?
(A) It usually blooms in spring.
(B) Would you like to come with me?
(C) Someone delivered them this morning.

bloom v. 꽃이 피다 deliver v. 배달하다, 배송하다

해석 그 꽃들은 어디에서 온 건가요?
(A) 그것은 보통 봄에 꽃이 피어요.
(B) 저와 함께 가시겠어요?
(C) 누군가 오늘 아침에 그것들을 배달했어요.

해설 (A) [×] 질문의 flowers(꽃들)와 관련 있는 blooms(꽃이 피다)를 사
용하여 혼동을 준 오답이다.
(B) [×] 질문의 come을 반복 사용하여 혼동을 준 오답이다.
(C) [○] 누군가 오늘 아침에 그것들을 배달했다는 말로, 꽃들이 어디
에서 온 것인지 모른다는 것을 간접적으로 전달했으므로 정
답이다.

28 선택 의문문
3 미국식 → 호주식

Should our fabric samples be sent by regular or express
mail?
(A) Let's take the express train.
(B) The post office on Maple Street.
(C) They need to arrive tomorrow.

fabric n. 원단 express adj. 특급의, 급행의

해석 원단 견본이 일반 우편으로 보내져야 하나요, 아니면 특급 우편으로
보내져야 하나요?
(A) 급행열차를 탑시다.
(B) Maple가에 있는 우체국이요.
(C) 그것들은 내일 도착해야 해요.

해설 (A) [×] 질문의 express를 반복 사용하여 혼동을 준 오답이다.
(B) [×] 질문의 mail(우편)과 관련 있는 post office(우체국)를 사용
하여 혼동을 준 오답이다.
(C) [○] 그것들이 내일 도착해야 한다는 말로, 특급 우편으로 보내져
야 함을 간접적으로 선택했으므로 정답이다.

최신토익경향

선택 의문문에 대한 응답으로 선택 사항을 직접적으로 고를 수도 있지만, 간
접적으로 고르는 응답도 자주 출제되고 있다. 간접적으로 선택 사항을 고르
는 경우, 고난도로 출제될 수 있으므로 아래 예문을 통해 미리 학습해 두자.

Do you want to come eat with us, or did you pack your lunch?
저희와 함께 식사하러 가실 건가요, 아니면 도시락을 싸 오셨나요?
<답변 1> I'll find a restaurant.
제가 식당을 찾을게요.
<답변 2> It's in the refrigerator.
냉장고에 있어요.
*<답변 1> 자신이 식당을 찾겠다는 말로, 함께 식사하러 가는 것을 간접적으
로 선택한 응답
<답변 2> 도시락이 냉장고에 있다는 말로, 도시락을 먹는 것을 간접적으로
선택한 응답

29 How 의문문
3 캐나다식 → 영국식

How can I get reimbursed for my travel expenses?
(A) By submitting your receipts.
(B) We charge more for color printing.
(C) It's more expensive than I thought.

reimburse v. 상환하다, 갚다 expense n. 경비, 비용
submit v. 제출하다 receipt n. 영수증 charge v. (비용을) 청구하다

해석 제 출장 경비를 어떻게 상환받을 수 있나요?
(A) 영수증을 제출해서요.
(B) 우리는 컬러 인쇄에 더 큰 비용을 청구해요.
(C) 그건 제가 생각했던 것보다 비싸요.

해설 (A) [○] 영수증을 제출해서라는 말로, 출장 경비를 상환받는 방법을
전달했으므로 정답이다.
(B) [×] 질문의 expenses(경비)와 관련 있는 charge(청구하다)를 사
용하여 혼동을 준 오답이다.
(C) [×] expenses - expensive의 유사 발음 어휘를 사용하여 혼동
을 준 오답이다.

30 Who 의문문

③ 호주식 → 영국식

Who is going to notify the employees about the policy?
(A) Could you do that for me?
(B) That policy is very unpopular.
(C) Some political news.

notify v. 공지하다, 알리다 policy n. 정책 political adj. 정치적인

해석 그 정책에 관해 누가 직원들에게 공지할 건가요?
(A) 저 대신 그것을 해 주실 수 있나요?
(B) 그 정책은 아주 인기가 없어요.
(C) 몇몇 정치적인 뉴스요.

해설 (A) [○] 그것을 대신해 줄 수 있는지 되물어, 상대방에게 정책에 관해 공지해 달라고 요청한 정답이다.
(B) [×] 질문의 policy를 반복 사용하여 혼동을 준 오답이다.
(C) [×] policy - political의 유사 발음 어휘를 사용하여 혼동을 준 오답이다.

31 평서문

③ 미국식 → 캐나다식

Mr. Pavlova in the accounting department has gotten a promotion.
(A) A late departure.
(B) To find a suitable investment opportunity.
(C) He deserves it, in my opinion.

accounting n. 회계 promotion n. 승진, 판촉 departure n. 출발
suitable adj. 적절한, 알맞은 investment n. 투자
deserve v. ~할 자격이 있다

해석 회계 부서의 Mr. Pavlova가 승진했어요.
(A) 늦은 출발이요.
(B) 적절한 투자 기회를 찾기 위해서요.
(C) 제 생각에, 그는 그럴 자격이 있어요.

해설 (A) [×] department - departure의 유사 발음 어휘를 사용하여 혼동을 준 오답이다.
(B) [×] 질문의 accounting(회계)에서 연상할 수 있는 기업의 재무 상태와 관련된 investment(투자)를 사용하여 혼동을 준 오답이다.
(C) [○] 그는 그럴 자격이 있다는 말로, Mr. Pavlova가 승진한 것에 대한 의견을 전달했으므로 정답이다.

PART 3

[32-34]

③ 미국식 → 호주식

Questions 32-34 refer to the following conversation.

W: Hi, Lorenzo. ³²**Thanks for checking that all of the smoke detectors and fire alarms in our building are working. I don't want any problems when the inspector visits tomorrow.**
M: Of course. Is there anything else you need?
W: Actually, there is. The emergency exit map on the third◉

---

floor is faded. ³³**Could you take it down and put up a new one?**
M: Sure. Where do we keep the extra ones?
W: They are in the storage room. ³⁴**But it is secured with an electronic lock. Let me write down the numbers you must enter to open it.**

smoke detector 연기 감지기 fire alarm 화재경보기
inspector n. 검사관, 조사관 emergency exit 비상구
faded adj. (색이) 바랜, 시든 secure v. 잠가 두다, 보안 장치를 하다
electronic lock 전자자물쇠 enter v. 입력하다

해석
32-34번은 다음 대화에 관한 문제입니다.

여: 안녕하세요, Lorenzo. ³²우리 건물의 모든 연기 감지기 및 화재경보기가 작동하는지 확인해 주셔서 감사합니다. 내일 검사관이 방문할 때 아무 문제가 없으면 좋겠어요.
남: 물론이죠. 더 해야 할 일이 있을까요?
여: 사실, 있어요. 3층에 있는 비상구 지도의 색이 바랬어요. ³³그걸 떼어내고 새로운 것을 붙여주실 수 있나요?
남: 물론이죠. 여분의 것을 어디에 두나요?
여: 창고에 있어요. ³⁴하지만 그곳은 전자자물쇠로 잠겨 있어요. 열기 위해 입력해야 하는 숫자들을 적어드릴게요.

32 특정 세부 사항 문제

해석 화자들은 무엇을 준비하고 있는가?
(A) 연수 과정
(B) 안전 점검
(C) 건물 보수
(D) 제품 소개

해설 질문의 핵심 어구(preparing for)와 관련된 내용을 주의 깊게 듣는다. 여자가 "Thanks for checking that all of the smoke detectors and fire alarms in our building are working. I don't want any problems when the inspector visits tomorrow."라며 건물의 모든 연기 감지기 및 화재경보기가 작동하는지 확인해 주어서 고맙다고 한 후, 내일 검사관이 방문할 때 아무 문제가 없으면 좋겠다고 하였다. 따라서 (B)가 정답이다.

어휘 inspection n. 점검, 조사 renovation n. 보수, 개조
sales presentation 제품 소개

33 요청 문제

해석 여자는 남자에게 무엇을 하라고 요청하는가?
(A) 물품을 교체한다.
(B) 문서를 인쇄한다.
(C) 관리자를 만난다.
(D) 날짜를 확인한다.

해설 여자의 말에서 요청과 관련된 표현이 언급된 다음을 주의 깊게 듣는다. 여자가 남자에게 "Could you take it[emergency exit map] down and put up a new one?"이라며 비상구 지도를 떼어내고 새로운 것을 붙여줄 수 있는지를 물었다. 따라서 (A)가 정답이다.

어휘 replace v. 교체하다, 바꾸다 document n. 문서, 서류

official n. 관리자, 공무원   confirm v. 확인하다, 확정하다

Paraphrasing

> take ~ down and put up a new one ~을 떼어내고 새로운 것을 붙이다 → Replace 교체하다

34 특정 세부 사항 문제

해석 여자는 남자를 위해 무엇을 적어줄 것인가?
(A) 회사 이름
(B) 사무실 주소
(C) 전화번호
(D) 보안 코드

해설 질문의 핵심 어구(write down)가 언급된 주변을 주의 깊게 듣는다. 여자가 "But it[storage room] is secured with an electronic lock. Let me write down the numbers you must enter to open it."이라며 창고는 전자자물쇠로 잠겨 있다고 한 후, 그것을 열기 위해 입력해야 하는 숫자들을 적어주겠다고 하였다. 따라서 (D)가 정답이다.

어휘 address n. 주소   security code 보안 코드

Paraphrasing

> the numbers 숫자들 → code 코드

[35-37]

3 영국식 → 캐나다식

Questions 35-37 refer to the following conversation.

W: ³⁵**How was your trip to Melbourne? Did you have a good holiday?**

M: It was great. The highlight was staying at the Coral Reef Resort. My room was underwater!

W: Oh, ³⁶**I've heard of that hotel. There were some incredible pictures of marine life near the hotel on a travel blog I follow.**

M: Yes, I had fun. ³⁷**But I had to wait a long time for a room to be available. In fact, I had to book almost a year in advance.**

---

holiday n. 휴가   highlight n. 가장 흥미로운 부분, 하이라이트
underwater adj. 물속에 있는   incredible adj. 멋진, 엄청난
marine life 해양 생물   available adj. 이용 가능한, 얻을 수 있는
book v. 예약하다   in advance 미리, 전부터

해석

35-37번은 다음 대화에 관한 문제입니다.

여: ³⁵멜버른 여행은 어땠나요? 즐거운 휴가를 보내셨나요?

남: 아주 좋았어요. 가장 흥미로운 부분은 Coral Reef 리조트에 머문 것이었어요. 제 객실이 물속에 있었어요!

여: 아, ³⁶그 호텔에 대해 들어본 적이 있어요. 제가 팔로우하는 여행 블로그에 호텔 근처의 멋진 해양 생물 사진들이 있었어요.

남: 네, 재미있었어요. ³⁷하지만 객실이 이용 가능해질 때까지 한참을 기다려야 했어요. 사실, 거의 1년 전에 미리 예약해야 했어요.

35 이유 문제

해석 남자는 왜 멜버른에 있었는가?
(A) 휴가를 보내기 위해
(B) 친척을 방문하기 위해
(C) 회사 행사에 참석하기 위해
(D) 해양 생물을 연구하기 위해

해설 질문의 핵심 어구(Melbourne)가 언급된 주변을 주의 깊게 듣는다. 여자가 남자에게 "How was your trip to Melbourne? Did you have a good holiday?"라며 멜버른 여행이 어땠는지 물은 후, 즐거운 휴가를 보냈는지 물었다. 따라서 (A)가 정답이다.

어휘 relative n. 친척   corporate adj. 회사의, 법인의

Paraphrasing

> holiday 휴가 → a vacation 휴가

36 방법 문제

해석 여자는 리조트에 대해 어떻게 알게 되었는가?
(A) 여행사 직원과 이야기함으로써
(B) 책자를 읽음으로써
(C) 온라인 사진을 봄으로써
(D) 친구와 이야기함으로써

해설 질문의 핵심 어구(learn about the resort)와 관련된 내용을 주의 깊게 듣는다. 여자가 "I've heard of that hotel. There were some incredible pictures of marine life near the hotel on a travel blog I follow."라며 그 호텔에 대해 들어본 적이 있다고 한 후, 자신이 팔로우하는 여행 블로그에 호텔 근처의 멋진 해양 생물 사진들이 있었다고 하였다. 따라서 (C)가 정답이다.

어휘 travel agent 여행사 직원   view v. 보다

Paraphrasing

> on a ~ blog 블로그에 → online 온라인의

37 추론 문제

해석 리조트에 대해 추론될 수 있는 것은?
(A) 더 이상 영업을 하지 않는다.
(B) 전 세계에 지점이 있다.
(C) 예약하기가 어렵다.
(D) 개인 여행객들에게는 적합하지 않다.

해설 질문의 핵심 어구(resort)와 관련된 내용을 주의 깊게 듣는다. 남자가 "But I had to wait a long time for a room to be available. In fact, I had to book almost a year in advance."라며 객실이 이용 가능해질 때까지 한참을 기다려야 했다고 한 후, 거의 1년 전에 미리 예약했다고 한 것을 통해 리조트는 예약하기가 어렵다는 것을 알 수 있다. 따라서 (C)가 정답이다.

어휘 location n. 지점, 장소   reservation n. 예약
unsuitable adj. 적합하지 않은   individual adj. 개인의, 개인적인

🎧 캐나다식 → 미국식 → 영국식

Questions 38-40 refer to the following conversation with three speakers.

M: **38So we're all agreed on which applicants to hire for the legal assistant positions?**

W1: Yeah. I think these six candidates are really promising. **39What about you, Janet?**

W2: I agree. **39I'm worried that we won't have enough room for them, though.** Our office is pretty crowded already.

M: Maybe we should relocate to a bigger one.

W1: But we don't have much time. Do you think we can find a suitable place in such a short period?

M: **40I'll check some online property ads now.**

applicant n. 지원자 candidate n. 후보자, 지원자
promising adj. 유망한, 촉망되는 relocate v. 이전하다, 이사하다
suitable adj. 적합한 period n. 기간 property n. 부동산, 재산

해석
38-40번은 다음 세 명의 대화에 관한 문제입니다.

남: **38그럼 우리가 법률 보조원 자리에 어떤 지원자들을 채용할지 모두 동의한 건가요?**

여1: 네. 이 여섯 명의 후보자들이 정말 유망하다고 생각해요. **39당신은 어때요, Janet?**

여2: 저도 동의해요. **39하지만 그들을 위한 자리가 충분하지 않을까 봐 걱정이에요.** 우리 사무실은 이미 꽤 붐비고 있어요.

남: 우리는 더 넓은 곳으로 이전해야 할 것 같아요.

여1: 하지만 시간이 많지 않아요. 그렇게 짧은 기간에 적합한 장소를 찾을 수 있을까요?

남: **40지금 온라인 부동산 광고를 좀 확인해 볼게요.**

38 화자 문제

해석 화자들은 어디에서 일하는 것 같은가?
(A) 채용 기관에서
(B) 소매점에서
(C) 법률 회사에서
(D) 마케팅 회사에서

해설 대화에서 신분 및 직업과 관련된 표현을 놓치지 않고 듣는다. 남자가 "So we're all agreed on which applicants to hire for the legal assistant positions?"라며 법률 보조원 자리에 어떤 지원자들을 채용할지 모두 동의하는지 묻는 것을 통해 화자들이 법률 회사에서 일한다는 것을 알 수 있다. 따라서 (C)가 정답이다.

어휘 recruit v. 채용하다 retail adj. 소매의

39 문제점 문제

해석 Janet은 무엇에 대해 걱정하는가?
(A) 지원자가 부적격하다.
(B) 팀은 일정보다 늦어지고 있다.
(C) 부서는 인력이 부족하다.
(D) 공간이 너무 작다.

해설 Janet의 말에서 부정적인 표현이 언급된 주변을 주의 깊게 듣는다. 여자1이 "What about you, Janet?"이라며 Janet에게 의견을 묻자, 여자2[Janet]가 "I'm worried that we won't have enough room for them, though."라며 신입 직원들을 위한 자리가 충분하지 않을까 봐 걱정된다고 하였다. 따라서 (D)가 정답이다.

어휘 unqualified adj. 부적격한, 자격이 없는
behind schedule 일정보다 늦은
understaffed adj. 인력이 부족한, 인원이 부족한

40 다음에 할 일 문제

해석 남자는 다음에 무엇을 할 것 같은가?
(A) 면접을 진행한다.
(B) 이력서를 확인한다.
(C) 광고를 본다.
(D) 고객들을 만난다.

해설 대화의 마지막 부분을 주의 깊게 듣는다. 남자가 "I'll check some online property ads now."라며 지금 온라인 부동산 광고를 좀 확인해 보겠다고 한 것을 통해 남자가 광고를 볼 것임을 알 수 있다. 따라서 (C)가 정답이다.

어휘 conduct v. (특정한 활동을) 진행하다, 수행하다 résumé n. 이력서

Paraphrasing
check some ~ ads 광고를 확인하다 → Look at some advertisements 광고를 보다

🎧 호주식 → 영국식

Questions 41-43 refer to the following conversation.

M: Excuse me. **41I'm planning to remodel my consulting firm's office**, and I was thinking of this green wallpaper. Would it match well with a brown sofa?

W: **42That's a Hyman brand wallpaper, right? I would avoid that brand. We have received negative feedback from people who purchased that company's products.** Our manager is even considering not carrying them anymore.

M: Then, could you recommend some alternatives?

W: Actually, we just got some new stock. **43Why don't I get a few rolls for you to look at?**

M: That would be great.

wallpaper n. 벽지 match v. 어울리다 negative adj. 부정적인
carry v. (가게에서 품목을) 취급하다 recommend v. 추천하다
alternative n. 대안 stock n. 재고(품) roll n. 두루마리, 롤

해석
41-43번은 다음 대화에 관한 문제입니다.

남: 실례합니다. **41저의 자문 회사 사무실을 개조할 계획인데, 이 녹색 벽지를 생각하고 있어요. 이것이 갈색 소파와 잘 어울릴까요?**

여: **42그거 Hyman 브랜드 벽지네요, 맞죠? 저는 그 브랜드를 피할 거예요. 저희는 그 회사의 제품을 구매한 사람들로부터 부정적인 의견을 받았습니다.** 저희 관리자는 그것들을 더 이상 취급하지 않는 것도 고려하고 있어요.

남: 그렇다면, 대안을 추천해 주시겠어요?

여: 사실, 새로운 재고품이 막 들어왔습니다. ⁴³제가 두루마리 몇 개를 가져와서 보여드리면 어떨까요?

남: 그럼 좋겠네요.

41 특정 세부 사항 문제

해석 남자는 무엇을 하려고 계획하고 있는가?
(A) 사업체를 설립한다.
(B) 접수원을 고용한다.
(C) 상담가를 만난다.
(D) 일터를 개조한다.

해설 질문의 핵심 어구(planning)가 언급된 주변을 주의 깊게 듣는다. 남자가 "I'm planning to remodel my consulting firm's office"라며 자신의 자문 회사 사무실을 개조할 계획이라고 하였다. 따라서 (D)가 정답이다.

어휘 establish v. 설립하다   receptionist n. 접수원

Paraphrasing

remodel 개조하다 → Renovate 개조하다
office 사무실 → a workplace 일터

42 이유 문제

해석 여자는 왜 남자에게 Hyman 제품들을 구매하지 말 것을 제안하는가?
(A) 설치하기가 어렵다.
(B) 안 좋은 후기를 받았다.
(C) 가격을 인상했다.
(D) 재고가 거의 없다.

해설 질문의 핵심 어구(not purchase Hyman products)와 관련된 내용을 주의 깊게 듣는다. 여자가 "That's a Hyman brand wallpaper, right? I would avoid that brand. We have received negative feedback from people who purchased that company's products."라며 자신은 Hyman 브랜드를 피할 것이라고 한 후, 그 회사의 제품을 구매한 사람들로부터 부정적인 의견을 받았다고 하였다. 따라서 (B)가 정답이다.

어휘 install v. 설치하다   out of stock 재고가 거의 없는

Paraphrasing

negative feedback 부정적인 의견 → bad reviews 안 좋은 후기

43 제안 문제

해석 여자는 무엇을 해주겠다고 제안하는가?
(A) 선반에 물건을 다시 채운다.
(B) 기술을 공유한다.
(C) 일부 제품을 가져온다.
(D) 환불을 해준다.

해설 여자의 말에서 남자를 위해 해주겠다고 언급한 내용을 주의 깊게 듣는다. 여자가 "Why don't I get a few rolls for you to look at?"이라며 두루마리 몇 개를 가져와서 보여주겠다고 하였다. 따라서 (C)가 정답이다.

어휘 restock v. 다시 채우다

[44-46]

Questions 44-46 refer to the following conversation.   3에 미국식 → 캐나다식

W: Sam, ⁴⁴**your phone keeps beeping. It's preventing me from focusing on my work**, and I have a very important presentation at 3 P.M.

M: I'm sorry. It's the new messenger app that we're supposed to use for communications with clients. It isn't working properly. I'm waiting for someone in the IT department to check what's wrong.

W: ⁴⁵**Maybe you could just put the app in silent mode for now.**

M: Of course. Oh, by the way . . . ⁴⁶**Some of us in the office are getting pizza delivered for lunch, and I was just about to call the restaurant. Would you like some?**

W: ⁴⁶**That would be great.**

---

beep v. 신호음이 울리다, 삐 소리가 나다   focus on ~에 집중하다
presentation n. 발표   properly adv. 제대로, 적절히
silent adj. 무음의, 소리 없는   for now 우선은

해석
44-46번은 다음 대화에 관한 문제입니다.

여: Sam, ⁴⁴당신의 휴대전화에서 계속 신호음이 울려요. 그것 때문에 제가 업무에 집중할 수 없는데, 전 오후 3시에 아주 중요한 발표가 있어요.

남: 미안해요. 우리가 고객들과의 커뮤니케이션을 위해 사용하기로 한 새로운 메신저 앱이에요. 제대로 작동하지 않네요. IT 부서의 누군가가 무엇이 문제인지 확인해 주기를 기다리는 중이에요.

여: ⁴⁵우선은 앱을 그냥 무음 모드로 설정하면 될 거예요.

남: 물론이죠. 아, 그런데... ⁴⁶사무실에 있는 몇몇 사람들이 점심으로 피자를 배달시킬 예정이라, 전 방금 식당에 전화하려던 참이었어요. 좀 드실래요?

여: ⁴⁶좋아요.

44 문제점 문제

해석 여자는 무슨 문제를 언급하는가?
(A) 발표가 취소되었다.
(B) 소음이 집중을 방해하고 있다.
(C) 고객이 불만을 제기하고 있다.
(D) 일정이 변경되었다.

해설 여자의 말에서 부정적인 표현이 언급된 주변을 주의 깊게 듣는다. 여자가 "your phone keeps beeping"이라며 남자의 휴대전화에서 계속 신호음이 울린다고 한 후, "It's preventing me from focusing on my work"라며 그것 때문에 업무에 집중할 수 없다고 하였다. 따라서 (B)가 정답이다.

어휘 distracting adj. 집중을 방해하는

45 제안 문제

해석 여자는 무엇을 제안하는가?
(A) 기술자를 부르기
(B) 설정 변경하기
(C) 기기를 교체하기
(D) 메시지를 확인하기

TEST 3   PART 3   **105**

해설 여자의 말에서 제안과 관련된 표현이 언급된 다음을 주의 깊게 듣는다. 여자가 남자에게 "Maybe you could just put the app in silent mode for now."라며 우선은 앱을 그냥 무음 모드로 설정하면 될 거라고 하였다. 따라서 (B)가 정답이다.

어휘 technician n. 기술자 setting n. 설정, 환경 replace v. 교체하다
device n. 기기

46 다음에 할 일 문제

해석 다음에 무슨 일이 일어날 것 같은가?
(A) 예약이 이루어질 것이다.
(B) 회의가 열릴 것이다.
(C) 주문이 될 것이다.
(D) 사무실이 청소될 것이다.

해설 대화의 마지막 부분을 주의 깊게 듣는다. 남자가 "Some of us ~ are getting pizza delivered for lunch, and I was just about to call the restaurant. Would you like some?"이라며 몇몇 사람들이 점심으로 피자를 배달시킬 예정이라 방금 식당에 전화하려던 참이었는데 좀 먹을지 묻자, 여자가 "That would be great."라며 좋다고 한 것을 통해 다음에 주문이 될 것임을 알 수 있다. 따라서 (C)가 정답이다.

어휘 reservation n. 예약

[47-49]

🔊 미국식 → 호주식

Questions 47-49 refer to the following conversation.

> W: Hi. My name is Michelle Peters. **⁴⁷I'm here for the product launch of the Silver Plate Tablet.**
> M: Do you work for Silver Tech Corporation? **⁴⁷Attendance is limited to employees and representatives of the press.**
> W: Actually, **⁴⁸I am a member of the press. I'm working on a story about the tablet for *Tech Weekly*.** Here's my press pass.
> M: You aren't on our list for some reason. **⁴⁹Hold on while I talk to someone from the public relations team.**
>
> launch n. 출시 attendance n. 참석 representative n. 대표자
> press n. 기자단, 언론 press pass 기자증
> for some reason 무슨 이유에서인지, 어떤 이유로
> public relations 홍보

해석
47-49번은 다음 대화에 관한 문제입니다.

여: 안녕하세요. 제 이름은 Michelle Peters예요. ⁴⁷저는 Silver Plate 태블릿 제품 출시를 위해 여기에 왔어요.
남: Silver Tech사에서 일하시나요? ⁴⁷참석은 직원들과 기자단 대표자들로 제한돼요.
여: 사실, ⁴⁸저는 기자단의 일원이에요. *Tech Weekly*에 실릴 태블릿에 대한 기사를 작성하고 있어요. 여기 제 기자증이요.
남: 무슨 이유에서인지 명단에 없네요. ⁴⁹제가 홍보팀의 누군가와 얘기하는 동안 잠시만 기다려주세요.

47 언급 문제

해석 제품 출시에 대해 무엇이 언급되는가?
(A) 대중에게 공개되지 않는다.
(B) 발표를 포함하지 않을 것이다.
(C) 생방송으로 진행될 것이다.
(D) 중간 휴식 시간을 포함할 것이다.

해설 질문의 핵심 어구(product launch)가 언급된 주변을 주의 깊게 듣는다. 여자가 "I'm here for the product launch of the Silver Plate Tablet."이라며 Silver Plate 태블릿 제품 출시를 위해 여기에 왔다고 하자, 남자가 "Attendance is limited to employees and representatives of the press."라며 참석은 직원들과 기자단 대표자들로 제한된다고 하였다. 따라서 (A)가 정답이다.

어휘 broadcast live 생방송하다, 생중계하다
intermission n. 중간 휴식 시간

48 이유 문제

해석 여자는 왜 행사에 있는가?
(A) 제품 시연을 돕기 위해
(B) 기기에 대한 기사를 작성하기 위해
(C) 개회사를 하기 위해
(D) 매체 질문에 답변하기 위해

해설 질문의 핵심 어구(event)와 관련된 내용을 주의 깊게 듣는다. 여자가 "I am a member of the press. I'm working on a story about the tablet for *Tech Weekly*."라며 자신이 기자단의 일원이고, *Tech Weekly*에 실릴 태블릿에 대한 기사를 작성하고 있다고 하였다. 따라서 (B)가 정답이다.

어휘 opening speech 개회사

Paraphrasing

> a story about the tablet 태블릿에 대한 기사 → an article about a device 기기에 대한 기사

49 다음에 할 일 문제

해석 남자는 다음에 무엇을 할 것이라고 말하는가?
(A) 문자 메시지를 보낸다.
(B) 기자증을 배부한다.
(C) 직원과 이야기한다.
(D) 참석자 명단을 업데이트한다.

해설 대화의 마지막 부분을 주의 깊게 듣는다. 남자가 "Hold on while I talk to someone from the public relations team."이라며 자신이 홍보팀의 누군가와 얘기하는 동안 잠시만 기다려 달라고 하였다. 따라서 (C)가 정답이다.

어휘 distribute v. 배부하다, 배포하다 attendee n. 참석자

[50-52]

🔊 호주식 → 영국식

Questions 50-52 refer to the following conversation.

> M: ⁵⁰Thank you for visiting Brentwood Bags. Can I help you find anything?
> ○

W: ⁵⁰**I need a new suitcase.** I'd prefer one with a hard case.

M: OK. Do you have a particular brand in mind?

W: Actually, I have this digital coupon for 10 percent off all Benson models. ⁵¹**I got it when I signed up for a loyalty club membership through your Web site yesterday.**

M: ⁵²**Well, what about this one? It has a large capacity.**

W: I travel light. ⁵²**Can I see that smaller one over there?**

---

particular adj. 특정한, 특별한　sign up for ~에 가입하다, 등록하다
capacity n. 용량, 수용력

해석

50-52번은 다음 대화에 관한 문제입니다.

남: ⁵⁰Brentwood Bags를 방문해 주셔서 감사합니다. 찾는 것을 도와드릴까요?

여: ⁵⁰저는 새 여행 가방이 필요해요. 하드케이스인 것을 선호하고요.

남: 네. 염두에 두고 있는 특정 브랜드가 있으신가요?

여: 사실, Benson의 모든 모델을 10퍼센트 할인받을 수 있는 디지털 쿠폰이 있어요. ⁵¹어제 웹사이트를 통해 고객 클럽 멤버십에 가입할 때 받았어요.

남: ⁵²음, 이건 어떠세요? 용량이 커요.

여: 저는 여행을 가볍게 다녀요. ⁵²저기 있는 더 작은 것을 볼 수 있을까요?

50 장소 문제

해석　대화는 어디에서 일어나는가?
(A) 양복점에서
(B) 여행사에서
(C) 여행 가방 가게에서
(D) 보관 시설에서

해설　대화에서 장소와 관련된 표현을 놓치지 않고 듣는다. 남자가 "Thank you for visiting Brentwood Bags. Can I help you find anything?"이라며 Brentwood Bags를 방문해 주어서 고맙다고 한 후, 무엇을 찾는지 묻자, 여자가 "I need a new suitcase."라며 새 여행 가방이 필요하다고 한 것을 통해 여행 가방 가게에서 대화가 일어나고 있음을 알 수 있다. 따라서 (C)가 정답이다.

어휘　tailor shop 양복점　luggage n. 여행 가방, 수하물　facility n. 시설

Paraphrasing

suitcase 여행 가방 → luggage 여행 가방

51 특정 세부 사항 문제

해석　여자는 어제 무엇을 했는가?
(A) 멤버십을 갱신했다.
(B) 구입품을 반품했다.
(C) 항공편을 예약했다.
(D) 프로그램에 가입했다.

해설　질문의 핵심 어구(yesterday)가 언급된 주변을 주의 깊게 듣는다. 여자가 "I got it[digital coupon] when I signed up for a loyalty club membership through your Web site yesterday."라며 어제 웹사이트를 통해 고객 클럽 멤버십에 가입할 때 디지털 쿠폰을 받았다고 하였다. 따라서 (D)가 정답이다.

어휘　purchase n. 구입(품); v. 구입하다　join v. 가입하다

Paraphrasing

signed up for a loyalty club membership 고객 클럽 멤버십에 가입했다 → Joined a program 프로그램에 가입했다

52 의도 파악 문제

해석　여자는 왜 "저는 여행을 가볍게 다녀요"라고 말하는가?
(A) 불만을 제기하기 위해
(B) 할인을 요청하기 위해
(C) 제안을 거절하기 위해
(D) 브랜드를 추천하기 위해

해설　질문의 인용어구(I travel light)가 언급된 주변을 주의 깊게 듣는다. 남자가 "Well, what about this one? It has a large capacity."라며 용량이 큰 가방을 추천하자, 여자가 "Can I see that smaller one over there?"라며 더 작은 가방을 보여달라고 한 것을 통해 여자가 용량이 큰 가방을 권하는 남자의 제안을 거절하고 있음을 알 수 있다. 따라서 (C)가 정답이다.

어휘　complaint n. 불만, 불평　reject v. 거절하다, 거부하다
suggestion n. 제안, 제의

[53-55]　🎧 영국식 → 캐나다식 → 호주식

Questions 53-55 refer to the following conversation with three speakers.

W: ⁵³**One of my clients is inquiring about houses in Greenfield. Do either of you know of any properties for sale in that area?**

M1: There's a two-bedroom place on Baker Street.

W: Hmm . . . She wants at least three bedrooms. ⁵⁴**What about you, Michael?**

M2: Actually, ⁵⁴**I spoke to someone yesterday about selling their home in Greenfield**. It sounds like what you need. ⁵⁴**Here is the name and phone number.**

W: Oh, great. I'll arrange a time to view it when I get back to the office after lunch. ⁵⁵**I have a dental appointment at 10 A.M.**

---

inquire v. 문의하다　property n. 부동산, 재산　at least 최소한, 적어도
arrange v. 마련하다, 정리하다　dental adj. 치과의, 치아의

해석

53-55번은 다음 세 명의 대화에 관한 문제입니다.

여: ⁵³제 고객 중 한 분이 Greenfield에 있는 주택에 대해 문의하고 있어요. 두 분 중 그 지역에 매물로 나온 부동산을 알고 계신 분이 있나요?

남1: Baker가에 침실 두 개짜리 집이 있어요.

여: 흠... 그녀는 최소 침실 세 개를 원해요. ⁵⁴당신은 어때요, Michael?

남2: 사실, ⁵⁴어제 어떤 사람과 Greenfield에 있는 집을 파는 것에 대해 이야기를 나눴어요. 당신이 필요로 하는 것 같네요. ⁵⁴여기 이름과 전화번호예요.

여: 아, 잘됐네요. 점심 먹고 사무실로 돌아와서 볼 수 있는 시간을 마련할 거예요. ⁵⁵전 오전 10시에 치과 예약이 있어요.

53 화자 문제

해석 화자들은 누구인 것 같은가?
(A) 인테리어 디자이너들
(B) 부동산 중개인들
(C) 건설 노동자들
(D) 조경사들

해설 신분 및 직업과 관련된 표현을 놓치지 않고 듣는다. 여자가 "One of my clients is inquiring about houses in Greenfield. Do either of you know of any properties for sale in that area?" 라며 자신의 고객 중 한 명이 Greenfield에 있는 주택에 대해 문의한 다고 한 후, 두 남자에게 그 지역에 매물로 나온 부동산을 알고 있는 지 묻는 것을 통해 화자들이 부동산 중개인들임을 알 수 있다. 따라서 (B)가 정답이다.

어휘 real estate 부동산, 부동산 중개업 construction n. 건설, 공사
landscaper n. 조경사, 정원사

54 특정 세부 사항 문제

해석 Michael은 여자에게 무엇을 주는가?
(A) 판매 기록
(B) 계좌 번호
(C) 평면도
(D) 연락처 정보

해설 Michael의 말에서 질문의 핵심 어구(give)와 관련된 내용을 주의 깊 게 듣는다. 여자가 "What about you, Michael?"이라며 Michael 에게 의견을 묻자, 남자2[Michael]가 "I spoke to someone yesterday about selling their home in Greenfield", "Here is the name and phone number."라며 어제 어떤 사람과 Greenfield에 있는 집을 파는 것에 대해 이야기를 나눴다며, 그 사람 의 이름과 전화번호를 주었다. 따라서 (D)가 정답이다.

어휘 record n. 기록, 이력 floor plan 평면도

Paraphrasing

the name and phone number 이름과 전화번호 → Contact information 연락처 정보

55 특정 세부 사항 문제

해석 여자는 오늘 아침에 무엇을 할 계획인가?
(A) 치과를 방문한다.
(B) 고객에게 전화한다.
(C) 부동산을 본다.
(D) 일정을 업데이트한다.

해설 질문의 핵심 어구(this morning)와 관련된 내용을 주의 깊게 듣는 다. 여자가 "I have a dental appointment at 10 A.M."이라며 오 전 10시에 치과 예약이 있다고 하였다. 따라서 (A)가 정답이다.

어휘 dentist n. 치과, 치과 의사

Paraphrasing

have a dental appointment 치과 예약이 있다 → Visit a dentist 치과를 방문하다

[56-58]

Questions 56-58 refer to the following conversation.

M: Hello, Ms. Sanders. My name is Brad Mendez, and **56I'm organizing the Toronto International Food Festival.** I was hoping that you would participate this year.

W: Hello, Mr. Mendez. Can you give me more details?

M: Of course. The festival allows city residents to try cuisines from around the world. **57This year, chefs from more than 20 countries will participate.** I think the Jamaican dishes you create would be a great addition.

W: I'll need to check if I can get enough staff to help out, though.

M: I understand. **58But you should decide soon.** There are a limited number of booths available.

organize v. 조직하다, 주최하다 international adj. 국제의, 국제적인
participate v. 참여하다, 참가하다 detail n. 자세한 내용, 세부 사항
resident n. 거주자, 주민 cuisine n. 요리 addition n. 보탬, 추가
help out 도움을 주다

해석
56-58번은 다음 대화에 관한 문제입니다.

남: 안녕하세요, Ms. Sanders. 제 이름은 Brad Mendez이고, **56저는 토론 토 국제 음식 축제를 조직하고 있어요.** 당신이 올해에 참여해 주시면 좋 겠어요.

여: 안녕하세요, Mr. Mendez. 더 자세한 내용을 알려주실 수 있나요?

남: 물론이죠. 이 축제는 도시 거주자들이 전 세계의 요리를 맛볼 수 있게 해 요. **57올해, 20개가 넘는 나라에서 온 요리사들이 참여할 거예요.** 당신이 만드는 자메이카 요리가 큰 보탬이 될 거라고 생각해요.

여: 하지만 도움을 줄 수 있는 충분한 직원이 있을지 확인해 봐야 해요.

남: 알겠어요. **58그런데 곧 결정하셔야 해요.** 이용 가능한 부스 수가 한정되 어 있어요.

56 화자 문제

해석 남자는 누구인 것 같은가?
(A) 행사 조직자
(B) 사진작가
(C) 음식 평론가
(D) 기자

해설 대화에서 신분 및 직업과 관련된 표현을 놓치지 않고 듣는다. 남자가 "I'm organizing the Toronto International Food Festival"이 라며 자신이 토론토 국제 음식 축제를 조직하고 있다고 한 것을 통해 남자가 행사 조직자임을 알 수 있다. 따라서 (A)가 정답이다.

어휘 critic n. 평론가, 비평가

57 언급 문제

해석 행사에 대해 무엇이 언급되는가?
(A) 다른 도시로 이전할 것이다.
(B) 올해 처음 개최될 것이다.
(C) 참석자들이 무료로 제품을 체험해 보게 할 것이다.
(D) 여러 나라에서 온 참가자들이 있을 것이다.

해설 질문의 핵심 어구(event)와 관련된 내용을 주의 깊게 듣는다. 남자가 "This year, chefs from more than 20 countries will participate."라며 올해 20개가 넘는 나라에서 온 요리사들이 참여할 것이라고 하였다. 따라서 (D)가 정답이다.

어휘 relocate v. 이전하다, 이동하다   hold v. 개최하다, 열다

Paraphrasing

> more than 20 countries 20개가 넘는 나라 → multiple countries
> 여러 나라

58 제안 문제

해석 남자는 무엇을 하라고 제안하는가?
(A) 추가 직원 고용하기
(B) 행사 지침 확인하기
(C) 신속하게 결정하기
(D) 축제 부스 꾸미기

해설 남자의 말에서 제안과 관련된 표현이 언급된 내용을 주의 깊게 듣는다. 남자가 "But you should decide soon."이라며 곧 결정해야 한다고 하였다. 따라서 (C)가 정답이다.

어휘 guideline n. 지침, 가이드라인   decorate v. 꾸미다

Paraphrasing

> decide soon 곧 결정하다 → Making a decision quickly 신속하게
> 결정하기

[59-61]

3인 미국식 → 캐나다식

Questions 59-61 refer to the following conversation.

W: ⁵⁹**Everything is set up for your presentation, Mr. Jones. You just need to plug your USB drive into the computer.**

M: ⁶⁰**Unfortunately, the airline lost my bag with my memory stick in it.**

W: Oh, do you have another copy of your file?

M: Yes. I have a backup copy in my e-mail. I can just download it onto the computer.

W: Sure. ⁶¹**Will you need to print any handouts?**

M: ⁶¹**No. I'd rather not waste paper. I have the files posted on my Web site for people to access as needed.**

W: It's what's best for the environment.

set up ~을 준비하다, 설치하다   plug v. ~을 꽂다   airline n. 항공사
backup n. 백업 (파일), 예비   handout n. 유인물, 인쇄물
waste v. 낭비하다   access v. 접근하다   environment n. 환경

해석
59-61번은 다음 대화에 관한 문제입니다.
여: ⁵⁹발표를 위한 모든 것이 준비되었어요, Mr. Jones. USB 드라이브를 컴퓨터에 꽂기만 하면 돼요.
남: ⁶⁰유감스럽게도, 항공사에서 제 메모리 스틱이 든 가방을 잃어버렸어요.
여: 아, 파일의 다른 복사본이 있나요?
남: 네. 제 이메일에 백업 복사본이 있어요. 컴퓨터에 다운로드만 하면 돼요.
여: 좋아요. ⁶¹유인물을 인쇄해야 하나요?

남: ⁶¹아니요. 종이를 낭비하고 싶지 않아요. 사람들이 필요에 따라 접근할 수 있도록 제 웹사이트에 파일을 게시해 두었어요.
여: 그게 환경에 최선이죠.

59 주제 문제

해석 화자들은 무엇을 하고 있는가?
(A) 연구 수행하기
(B) 웹사이트 업데이트하기
(C) 몇몇 장비 수리하기
(D) 발표 준비하기

해설 대화의 주제를 묻는 문제이므로, 대화의 초반을 반드시 듣는다. 여자가 "Everything is set up for your presentation, ~. You just need to plug your USB drive into the computer."라며 발표를 위한 모든 것이 준비되었고, USB 드라이브를 컴퓨터에 꽂기만 하면 된다고 한 것을 통해, 화자들이 발표를 준비하고 있음을 알 수 있다. 따라서 (D)가 정답이다.

어휘 conduct v. (특정한 활동을) 수행하다   equipment n. 장비, 용품

60 문제점 문제

해석 남자는 무슨 문제를 언급하는가?
(A) 비행시간에 늦었다.
(B) 저장 장치가 분실되었다.
(C) 몇몇 이메일이 삭제되었다.
(D) 몇몇 유인물을 잘못 두었다.

해설 남자의 말에서 부정적인 표현이 언급된 주변을 주의 깊게 듣는다. 남자가 "Unfortunately, the airline lost my bag with my memory stick in it."이라며 항공사에서 자신의 메모리 스틱이 든 가방을 잃어버렸다고 하였다. 따라서 (B)가 정답이다.

어휘 misplace v. ~을 잘못 두다

Paraphrasing

> memory stick 메모리 스틱 → A storage device 저장 장치

61 의도 파악 문제

해석 여자는 왜 "그게 환경에 최선이죠"라고 말하는가?
(A) 의견에 대한 지지를 표현하기 위해
(B) 다른 계획을 제안하기 위해
(C) 활동을 연기하는 것을 제안하기 위해
(D) 다른 재료를 추천하기 위해

해설 질문의 인용어구(It's what's best for the environment)가 언급된 주변을 주의 깊게 듣는다. 여자가 "Will you need to print any handouts?"라며 유인물을 인쇄해야 하는지 묻자, 남자가 "No. I'd rather not waste paper. I have the files posted on my Web site for people to access as needed."라며 종이를 낭비하고 싶지 않다고 한 후, 사람들이 필요에 따라 접근할 수 있도록 웹사이트에 파일을 게시해 두었다고 한 것을 통해 여자가 종이를 낭비하고 싶지 않다는 남자의 의견에 대한 지지를 표현하고 있음을 알 수 있다. 따라서 (A)가 정답이다.

어휘 express v. 표현하다, 나타내다   support n. 지지; v. 지지하다

propose v. 제안하다 material n. 재료, 자료

[62-64]

🎧 호주식 → 미국식

Questions 62-64 refer to the following conversation and map.

M: Good morning. I'm from Randolph Construction, and I'm here about the guesthouse you would like built on your property.

W: Great. After ⁶²**I bought this farm last month**, I decided to add a place for friends and family members to stay.

M: I see. ⁶³**Do you want it near the garden?**

W: Actually, ⁶³**I want my guests to enjoy the beautiful view of the pond from the guesthouse.**

M: All right. You'll need to apply for the necessary government permits before we can begin the work.

W: ⁶⁴**Will the permits take long to get?**

M: They should be issued in about a week. I'll e-mail you the request form for the permits.

---

construction n. 건설, 건축 property n. 소유지, 부동산, 재산
pond n. 연못 apply v. 신청하다 necessary adj. 필요한, 필수적인
permit n. 허가 issue v. 발급하다 request form 신청서

해석
62-64번은 다음 대화와 지도에 관한 문제입니다.

남: 좋은 아침입니다. 저는 Randolph 건설에서 나왔는데, 고객님께서 소유지에 지으시려는 게스트 하우스 일로 왔습니다.

여: 좋아요. ⁶²지난달에 이 농장을 매입한 후, 친구들과 가족들이 머물 수 있는 공간을 추가하기로 결정했어요.

남: 그렇군요. ⁶³정원 근처를 원하시나요?

여: 사실, ⁶³전 손님들이 게스트 하우스에서 연못의 아름다운 경치를 즐기면 좋겠어요.

남: 알겠어요. 작업을 시작하기 전에 고객님께서 필요한 정부 허가를 신청하셔야 해요.

여: ⁶⁴허가를 받는 데 시간이 오래 걸릴까요?

남: 일주일 정도면 허가가 발급될 거예요. 제가 허가 신청서를 이메일로 보내드릴게요.

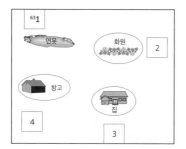

62 특정 세부 사항 문제

해석 여자는 지난달에 무엇을 했는가?
(A) 사업을 시작했다.
(B) 건물을 개조했다.
(C) 부동산을 매입했다.
(D) 프로젝트를 완료했다.

해설 질문의 핵심 어구(last month)가 언급된 주변을 주의 깊게 듣는다. 여자가 "I bought this farm last month"라며 지난달에 농장을 매입했다고 하였다. 따라서 (C)가 정답이다.

어휘 complete v. 완료하다, 작성하다

Paraphrasing

bought ~ farm 농장을 매입했다 → Purchased a property 부동산을 매입했다

63 시각 자료 문제

해석 시각 자료를 보아라. 여자는 게스트 하우스를 어디에 짓기를 원하는가?
(A) 위치 1
(B) 위치 2
(C) 위치 3
(D) 위치 4

해설 제시된 지도의 정보를 확인한 후 질문의 핵심 어구(guesthouse built)와 관련된 내용을 주의 깊게 듣는다. 남자가 "Do you want it[guesthouse] near the garden?"이라며 게스트 하우스가 정원 근처이길 원하는지 묻자, 여자가 "I want my guests to enjoy the beautiful view of the pond from the guesthouse"라며 손님들이 게스트 하우스에서 연못의 아름다운 경치를 즐기면 좋겠다고 하였으므로, 여자가 게스트 하우스를 짓기를 원하는 곳은 위치 1임을 지도에서 알 수 있다. 따라서 (A)가 정답이다.

64 특정 세부 사항 문제

해석 여자는 무엇에 대해 궁금해하는가?
(A) 건설 프로젝트가 언제 끝날지
(B) 허가를 받는 데 얼마나 걸릴지
(C) 건물의 총 가격은 얼마일지
(D) 작성된 양식을 누가 제출할지

해설 대화에서 여자의 말을 주의 깊게 듣는다. 여자가 "Will the permits take long to get?"이라며 허가를 받는 데 시간이 오래 걸릴지 물었다. 따라서 (B)가 정답이다.

[65-67]

🎧 영국식 → 호주식

Questions 65-67 refer to the following conversation and logo designs.

W: ⁶⁵**I just had a meeting with our manager. I asked him for another week to finish the project for the Hartford Tigers soccer team, and he agreed.**

M: Did you tell him that the client requested more time to consider the team logo options we provided?

W: Yes. He thinks that seeing the sample uniforms with the logos will help the team owner decide. ⁶⁶**They'll be delivered to our office by 2 P.M. tomorrow.**

M: I'll ask the team owner to stop by and look at them. ⁶⁷**Hopefully, he will choose the logo with the stars. That's clearly the best one.**

---

team owner 구단주 deliver v. 배송하다, 배달하다
stop by ~에 잠시 들르다 clearly adv. 분명히, 확실히

해석

65-67번은 다음 대화와 로고 디자인에 관한 문제입니다.

여: ⁶⁵방금 관리자와 회의를 했어요. 제가 Hartford Tigers 축구팀 프로젝트를 완료하기 위해 일주일 더 달라고 요청했고, 그가 승낙했어요.

남: 고객이 우리가 제공한 팀 로고 옵션을 고려할 시간을 더 요청했다고 그에게 말씀하셨나요?

여: 네. 그는 로고가 있는 견본 유니폼들을 보면 구단주가 결정하는 데 도움이 될 거라고 생각해요. ⁶⁶그것들은 내일 오후 2시까지 우리 사무실로 배송될 거예요.

남: 제가 구단주에게 잠시 들러서 그것들을 보라고 요청할게요. ⁶⁷바라건대, 그가 별 모양이 있는 로고를 선택하면 좋겠네요. 분명 그게 가장 좋아요.

옵션 1   옵션 2
⁶⁷옵션 3   옵션 4

65 특정 세부 사항 문제

해석   여자는 관리자와 무엇을 논의했는가?
(A) 마감일 연장
(B) 팀 확대
(C) 프로젝트 취소
(D) 디자인 변경

해설   질문의 핵심 어구(manager)가 언급된 주변을 주의 깊게 듣는다. 여자가 "I just had a meeting with our manager. I asked him for another week to finish the project ~, and he agreed."라며 방금 관리자와 회의를 했다고 한 후, 프로젝트를 완료하기 위해 일주일 더 달라고 요청했고, 그가 승낙했다고 하였다. 따라서 (A)가 정답이다.

어휘   deadline n. 마감일   extension n. 연장   expansion n. 확대, 확장   cancellation n. 취소

66 다음에 할 일 문제

해석   여자는 내일 무슨 일이 일어날 것이라고 말하는가?
(A) 경기가 개최될 것이다.
(B) 배송품이 도착할 것이다.
(C) 견본품이 만들어질 것이다.
(D) 구단주가 전화할 것이다.

해설   여자의 말에서 질문의 핵심 어구(tomorrow)가 언급된 주변을 주의 깊게 듣는다. 여자가 "They[sample uniforms]'ll be delivered to our office by 2 P.M. tomorrow."라며 견본 유니폼들이 내일 오후 2시까지 사무실로 배송될 것이라고 한 것을 통해 내일 배송품이 도착할 것임을 알 수 있다. 따라서 (B)가 정답이다.

어휘   shipment n. 배송품, 수송품

Paraphrasing

be delivered 배송되다 → arrive 도착하다

67 시각 자료 문제

해석   시각 자료를 보아라. 남자는 어떤 로고를 선호하는가?
(A) 옵션 1
(B) 옵션 2
(C) 옵션 3
(D) 옵션 4

해설   제시된 로고 디자인의 정보를 확인한 후 질문의 핵심 어구(logo ~ prefer)와 관련된 내용을 주의 깊게 듣는다. 남자가 "Hopefully, he[team owner] will choose the logo with the stars. That's clearly the best one."이라며 구단주가 별 모양이 있는 로고를 선택하길 바란다고 한 후, 분명 그게 가장 좋다고 하였으므로, 남자가 선호하는 로고는 옵션 3임을 로고 디자인에서 알 수 있다. 따라서 (C)가 정답이다.

[68-70]   🔊 캐나다식 → 미국식

Questions 68-70 refer to the following conversation and bank record.

M: Welcome to Western Bank. How can I help you today?

W: ⁶⁹**There's an account transaction that I don't recognize. I was hoping you could explain what it is.** My account number is 3156-093809.

M: Of course. ⁶⁸**I'll just need to see a piece of photo ID.**

W: Here you go. Um, ⁶⁹**it's the withdrawal on June 16**.

M: Oh, that's a monthly service charge. You must've signed up to receive hard copies of your monthly statements. ⁷⁰**But I can cancel that option for you.**

W: Please do that. Thanks.

transaction n. 거래, 처리   recognize v. 알다, 인식하다
account number 계좌 번호   withdrawal n. 인출, 출금
monthly adj. 매월의   charge n. 요금, 청구 금액   hard copy 출력물
statement n. 명세서

해석

68-70번은 다음 대화와 은행 기록에 관한 문제입니다.

남: Western 은행에 오신 것을 환영합니다. 무엇을 도와드릴까요?

여: ⁶⁹제가 알지 못하는 계좌 거래가 있어요. 그게 무엇인지 설명해 주셨으면 해요. 제 계좌 번호는 3156-093809예요.

남: 물론이죠. ⁶⁸사진이 있는 신분증 한 개를 보여주세요.

여: 여기 있어요. 음, ⁶⁹6월 16일에 인출된 것이요.

남: 아, 월 서비스 요금이네요. 월별 명세서의 출력물을 받도록 신청하셨을 거예요. ⁷⁰하지만 그 옵션을 취소해 드릴 수 있어요.

여: 그렇게 해 주세요. 감사합니다.

68 요청 문제

해석 남자는 여자에게 무엇을 요청하는가?
(A) 신분증
(B) 전화번호
(C) 거래 영수증
(D) 계좌 비밀번호

해설 남자의 말에서 요청과 관련된 표현이 언급된 다음을 주의 깊게 듣는다. 남자가 여자에게 "I'll just need to see a piece of photo ID."라며 사진이 있는 신분증 한 개를 보여달라고 하였다. 따라서 (A)가 정답이다.

어휘 identification card 신분증

69 시각 자료 문제

해석 시각 자료를 보아라. 여자는 어느 금액에 대해 문의하는가?
(A) 20달러
(B) 8달러
(C) 5달러
(D) 15달러

해설 제시된 은행 기록의 정보를 확인한 후 질문의 핵심 어구(amount ~ inquire about)와 관련된 내용을 주의 깊게 듣는다. 여자가 "There's an account transaction that I don't recognize. I was hoping you could explain what it is."라며 자신이 알지 못하는 계좌 거래가 있는데 그게 무엇인지 설명해 주었으면 한다고 한 후, "it's the withdrawal on June 16"라며 6월 16일에 인출된 것이라고 하였으므로, 여자가 문의하는 금액은 5달러임을 은행 기록에서 알 수 있다. 따라서 (C)가 정답이다.

70 제안 문제

해석 남자는 무엇을 해주겠다고 제안하는가?
(A) 요금을 환불한다.
(B) 서비스를 취소한다.
(C) 계좌를 개설한다.
(D) 옵션을 설명한다.

해설 남자의 말에서 여자를 위해 해주겠다고 언급한 내용을 주의 깊게 듣는다. 남자가 "But I can cancel that option for you."라며 그 옵션, 즉 월별 명세서의 출력물을 받는 옵션을 취소해 줄 수 있다고 하였다. 따라서 (B)가 정답이다.

어휘 refund v. 환불하다

PART 4

[71-73] 호주식

Questions 71-73 refer to the following excerpt from a meeting.

Before you go back to your desks, I'd just like to remind everyone that ⁷¹**next Friday is the last day of the quarter. That means it's time for our usual departmental luncheon.** Instead of going out to eat, however, we're going to have the meal right here in the office. ⁷²**Our receptionist, Lisa Maxwell**, will handle ordering the food for everyone. After we leave here, she's going to e-mail you links to the menus of several restaurants. ⁷³**Please let her know your preference by Wednesday.** We will order from the one that the most people choose. Have a good weekend.

remind v. 상기시키다, 생각나게 하다 **quarter** n. 분기, 4분의 1
departmental adj. 부서의 **luncheon** n. 오찬, 점심 식사
receptionist n. 접수 담당자, 접수원 **handle** v. 처리하다, 다루다
preference n. 선호되는 것, 선호

해석

71-73번은 다음 회의 발췌록에 관한 문제입니다.

책상으로 돌아가시기 전에, 저는 모두에게 ⁷¹다음 주 금요일이 이번 분기의 마지막 날이라는 것을 상기시켜 드리고 싶습니다. ⁷¹그것은 통상적인 부서 오찬을 할 시기가 되었다는 것을 의미합니다. 하지만, 밖에 나가서 식사를 하는 대신, 우리는 바로 이곳 사무실 안에서 식사를 할 것입니다. ⁷²접수 담당자인 Lisa Maxwell이 모두를 위해 음식을 주문하는 일을 처리할 것입니다. 우리가 여기에서 나간 후에, 그녀가 몇몇 식당 메뉴의 링크를 이메일로 보낼 것입니다. ⁷³수요일까지 선호되는 것을 그녀에게 알려주세요. 우리는 가장 많은 사람들이 선택한 곳에서 주문할 것입니다. 좋은 주말 되세요.

71 주제 문제

해석 화자는 주로 무엇에 대해 이야기하고 있는가?
(A) 작업 일정의 변경
(B) 정기 행사에 대한 계획
(C) 분기별 보고서의 결과
(D) 향후 회의를 위한 주제

해설 회의의 주제를 묻는 문제이므로, 지문의 초반을 반드시 듣는다. "next Friday is the last day of the quarter. That means it's time for our usual departmental luncheon."이라며 다음 주 금요일이 이번 분기의 마지막 날이며, 그것은 통상적인 부서 오찬을 할 시기가 되었다는 것을 의미한다고 한 후, 오찬이 이뤄지는 장소와 메뉴에 대한 내용으로 지문이 이어지고 있다. 따라서 (B)가 정답이다.

Paraphrasing

usual departmental luncheon 통상적인 부서 오찬 → a regular event 정기 행사

72 특정 세부 사항 문제

해석 Ms. Maxwell은 누구인가?
(A) 기술자
(B) 판매원

(C) 접수 담당자

(D) 회계사

해설 질문 대상(Ms. Maxwell)의 신분 및 직업과 관련된 표현을 놓치지 않고 듣는다. "Our receptionist, Lisa Maxwell"이라며 Lisa Maxwell이 접수 담당자라고 하였다. 따라서 (C)가 정답이다.

어휘 salesperson n. 판매원   accountant n. 회계사

73 요청 문제

해석 화자는 청자들에게 무엇을 하라고 요청하는가?

(A) 문제를 보고한다.

(B) 장소를 방문한다.

(C) 불만을 처리한다.

(D) 선택을 한다.

해설 지문의 중후반에서 요청과 관련된 표현이 포함된 문장을 주의 깊게 듣는다. "Please let her[Lisa Maxwell] know your preference by Wednesday."라며 수요일까지 선호되는 것을 Lisa Maxwell에게 알려달라고 하였다. 따라서 (D)가 정답이다.

어휘 venue n. 장소   selection n. 선택

[74-76]

🎧 캐나다식

Questions 74-76 refer to the following broadcast.

Good evening, and welcome to another edition of *The Roadshow*. I'm your host, Rob Cassidy. On tonight's program, [74]**we are joined in the studio by Nikki Lombard, who is here to promote her latest album, *Sideways*.** [75]**In a moment, we'll speak to the singer herself about the inspiration for her album.** But first, I'd like to remind listeners that we still have tickets to next month's Austin Folk Fest. [76]**Register now on our Web site for a chance to win tickets every hour.**

edition n. 시리즈, 호, 판   host n. 진행자, 주인
promote v. 홍보하다, 승진시키다   in a moment 곧, 바로
inspiration n. 영감, 영감을 주는 것
remind v. 다시 한번 알려 주다, 상기시키다
register v. 등록하다, 신고하다

해석

74-76번은 다음 방송에 관한 문제입니다.

안녕하세요, 그리고 The Roadshow의 또 다른 시리즈에 오신 것을 환영합니다. 저는 진행자, Rob Cassidy입니다. 오늘 밤 프로그램에서는, [74]Nikki Lombard와 스튜디오에서 함께할 것인데, 그녀는 최신 앨범인 Sideways를 홍보하기 위해 옵니다. [75]곧, 앨범의 영감에 대해 가수와 직접 이야기해 볼 텐데요. 하지만 먼저, 청취자 여러분들께 다음 달에 열리는 Austin Folk 축제 표가 아직 남아있다는 사실을 다시 한번 알려드리고자 합니다. [76]매시간 표를 받을 수 있는 기회를 위해 지금 저희 웹사이트에서 등록하세요.

74 특정 세부 사항 문제

해석 Nikki Lombard는 누구인가?

(A) 화가

(B) 음악가

(C) 작가

(D) 배우

해설 질문 대상(Nikki Lombard)의 신분 및 직업과 관련된 표현을 놓치지 않고 듣는다. "we are joined in the studio by Nikki Lombard, who is here to promote her latest album, *Sideways*"라며 Nikki Lombard와 함께할 것인데, 그녀는 최신 앨범인 *Sideways*를 홍보하기 위해 온다고 하였다. 따라서 (B)가 정답이다.

75 다음에 할 일 문제

해석 곧 무슨 일이 일어날 것인가?

(A) 진행자가 인터뷰를 할 것이다.

(B) 밴드가 몇 곡을 연주할 것이다.

(C) 광고주가 메시지를 전달할 것이다.

(D) 텔레비전으로 방송되는 콘서트가 시작될 것이다.

해설 질문의 핵심 어구(momentarily)와 관련된 내용을 주의 깊게 듣는다. "In a moment, we'll speak to the singer herself about the inspiration for her album."이라며 곧 앨범의 영감에 대해 가수와 직접 이야기할 것이라고 하였다. 따라서 (A)가 정답이다.

어휘 momentarily adv. 곧, 금방
sponsor n. 광고주, 후원자; v. 후원하다, 주최하다
televise v. 텔레비전으로 방송하다

Paraphrasing

momentarily 곧 → In a moment 곧

76 이유 문제

해석 화자에 따르면, 청자들은 왜 웹사이트를 방문해야 하는가?

(A) 특별한 요청을 하기 위해

(B) 방송에 대한 의견을 제공하기 위해

(C) 경품을 신청하기 위해

(D) 게스트에 대해 더 알아보기 위해

해설 질문의 핵심 어구(Web site)가 언급된 주변을 주의 깊게 듣는다. "Register now on our Web site for a chance to win tickets every hour."라며 매시간 표를 받을 수 있는 기회를 위해 지금 웹사이트에서 등록하라고 하였다. 따라서 (C)가 정답이다.

어휘 feedback n. 의견   giveaway n. 경품, 증정품

[77-79]

🎧 미국식

Questions 77-79 refer to the following excerpt from a meeting.

The summer peak season starts in less than a month, so we're going to be busy. [77]**Unfortunately, we still don't have enough room attendants, parking valets, and night clerks.** We've had to compete for staff with other accommodation facilities. This has proven to be a challenge despite the many advertisements we've placed. [78]**Our priority is hiring applicants with the necessary skills and experience,** and we would like your help with this. If you know people who are suitable for one of our open positions, please encourage them to submit an application. [79]**Make sure to mention that we offer free lunch and dinner every day.** Thanks everyone!

peak season 성수기 attendant n. 종업원, 안내원
valet n. 주차요원 compete v. 경쟁하다
accommodation n. 숙박, 거처 challenge n. 난제, 문제
priority n. 최우선 과제, 우선순위 open position 공석

해석

77-79번은 다음 회의 발췌록에 관한 문제입니다.

여름 성수기가 시작되기까지 한 달도 채 남지 않아서, 우리는 바쁠 예정입니다. ⁷⁷유감스럽게도, 우리는 여전히 충분한 객실 종업원, 주차요원, 야간 접수계 직원이 없습니다. 우리는 직원을 두고 다른 숙박 시설들과 경쟁해야 했습니다. 우리가 많은 광고를 게재했음에도 불구하고 이는 난제로 드러났습니다. ⁷⁸우리의 최우선 과제는 필요한 기술과 경험을 갖춘 지원자들을 고용하는 것이며, 이것에 여러분들의 도움을 받고자 합니다. 우리의 공석 중 하나에 적합한 사람을 알고 계신다면, 그들에게 지원서를 제출하도록 권유해 주시기 바랍니다. ⁷⁹우리가 매일 무료 점심 및 저녁 식사를 제공한다는 점도 꼭 언급해 주세요. 감사합니다 여러분!

77 화자 문제

해석 화자는 어떤 분야에서 일하는 것 같은가?
(A) 항공
(B) 해운
(C) 접객
(D) 의약

해설 지문에서 신분 및 직업과 관련된 표현을 놓치지 않고 듣는다. "Unfortunately, we still don't have enough room attendants, parking valets, and night clerks."라며 유감스럽게도 여전히 충분한 객실 종업원, 주차요원, 야간 접수계 직원이 없다고 한 것을 통해, 화자가 접객 분야에서 일하고 있음을 알 수 있다. 따라서 (C)가 정답이다.

어휘 aviation n. 항공, 항공기 산업 hospitality n. 접객, 환대
medicine n. 의약, 약제

78 특정 세부 사항 문제

해석 화자는 무엇이 최우선 과제라고 말하는가?
(A) 교육 과정 구성하기
(B) 자격을 갖춘 직원들 채용하기
(C) 특가 할인 홍보하기
(D) 회사 이익 늘리기

해설 질문의 핵심 어구(priority)가 언급된 주변을 주의 깊게 듣는다. "Our priority is hiring applicants with the necessary skills and experience"라며 최우선 과제는 필요한 기술과 경험을 갖춘 지원자들을 고용하는 것이라고 하였다. 따라서 (B)가 정답이다.

어휘 organize v. 구성하다, 조직하다 recruit v. 채용하다, 모집하다

Paraphrasing

hiring applicants with the necessary skills and experience 필요한 기술과 경험을 갖춘 지원자들을 고용하는 것 → Recruiting qualified workers 자격을 갖춘 직원들 채용하기

79 특정 세부 사항 문제

해석 화자는 어떤 혜택을 언급하는가?
(A) 무료 식사
(B) 무료 교통수단
(C) 성과 상여금
(D) 유동적인 일정

해설 질문의 핵심 어구(benefit)와 관련된 내용을 주의 깊게 듣는다. "Make sure to mention that we offer free lunch and dinner every day."라며 매일 무료 점심 및 저녁 식사를 제공한다는 점도 꼭 언급해 달라고 하였다. 따라서 (A)가 정답이다.

어휘 complimentary adj. 무료의
performance bonus 성과 상여금, 성과급
flexible adj. 유동적인, 유연한

Paraphrasing

free lunch and dinner 무료 점심 및 저녁 식사 → Complimentary meals 무료 식사

[80-82] 호주식

Questions 80-82 refer to the following telephone message.

Hello, Ms. Chen. My name is David Wilkes, and I represent Deep Sleep. ⁸⁰I recently came across your videos recommending our Softy Pillow on the GroupView social media platform. ^{80/81}I'm interested in having you promote our new line of bed sheets. Your channel is quite popular. ⁸¹I feel that it could lead to a significant growth in revenue for us. If this interests you, please call me back at 555-0938. ⁸²I'll need to know how much you would expect in payment for each video you develop for us, so please prepare this information before contacting me. I look forward to hearing back from you.

represent v. 대표하다, 대리하다 recommend v. 추천하다, 권고하다
interest v. 관심을 끌다 bed sheet 홑이불 significant adj. 상당한
revenue n. 수익, 수입 payment n. 보수, 지불

해석

80-82번은 다음 전화 메시지에 관한 문제입니다.

안녕하세요, Ms. Chen. 제 이름은 David Wilkes이고, Deep Sleep을 대표하고 있습니다. ⁸⁰저는 최근에 GroupView 소셜 미디어 플랫폼에서 저희의 Softy Pillow를 추천하는 귀하의 영상들을 보게 되었습니다. ^{80/81}저는 귀하가 저희의 새로운 홑이불 제품군을 홍보해 주는 것에 관심이 있습니다. 귀하의 채널은 상당히 인기가 있습니다. ⁸¹저는 이것이 저희의 상당한 수익 성장으로 이어질 수 있다고 생각합니다. 만약 이것이 귀하의 관심을 끈다면, 555-0938로 저에게 다시 전화해 주세요. ⁸²저는 귀하께서 저희를 위해 제작하는 각각의 영상에 대한 보수로 얼마를 기대하고 계시는지 알아야 하므로, 저에게 연락하기 전에 이 정보를 준비해 주세요. 회신을 기다리겠습니다.

80 특정 세부 사항 문제

해석 화자의 회사가 판매하는 것은 무엇인가?
(A) 의류
(B) 가정용품

(C) 화장품

(D) 침구

해설 질문의 핵심 어구(company sell)와 관련된 내용을 주의 깊게 듣는다. "I recently came across your videos recommending our Softy Pillow on the GroupView social media platform."이라며 최근에 GroupView 소셜 미디어 플랫폼에서 자신들의 Softy Pillow를 추천하는 영상들을 보게 되었다고 한 후, "I'm interested in having you promote our new line of bed sheets."라며 청자가 자신들의 새로운 홑이불 제품군을 홍보해 주는 것에 관심이 있다고 하였다. 따라서 (D)가 정답이다.

어휘 utensil n. 가정용품, 용구 cosmetics n. 화장품
bedding n. 침구, 이부자리

81 의도 파악 문제

해석 화자는 "귀하의 채널은 상당히 인기가 있습니다"라고 말할 때 무엇을 의도하는가?

(A) 청자는 독점 계약을 맺을 것이다.

(B) 청자는 지원을 필요로 할 수도 있다.

(C) 청자는 매출을 늘릴 수 있다.

(D) 청자는 플랫폼을 변경해야 한다.

해설 질문의 인용어구(Your channel is quite popular)가 언급된 주변을 주의 깊게 듣는다. "I'm interested in having you promote our new line of bed sheets."라며 청자가 자신들의 새로운 홑이불 제품군을 홍보해 주는 것에 관심이 있다고 한 후, "I feel that it could lead to a significant growth in revenue for us."라며 이것이 상당한 수익 성장으로 이어질 수 있다고 생각한다고 한 것을 통해 청자가 매출을 늘릴 수 있음을 알 수 있다. 따라서 (C)가 정답이다.

어휘 exclusive adj. 독점적인, 전용의

Paraphrasing

lead to a significant growth in revenue 상당한 수익 성장으로 이어지다 → increase sales 매출을 늘리다

82 요청 문제

해석 화자는 청자에게 무엇을 제공해 달라고 요청하는가?

(A) 녹화 기법

(B) 제품 선호도

(C) 개발 일정

(D) 보수 금액

해설 지문의 중후반에서 요청과 관련된 표현이 포함된 문장을 주의 깊게 듣는다. "I'll need to know how much you would expect in payment for each video you develop for us, so please prepare this information ~."이라며 제작하는 각각의 영상에 대한 보수로 얼마를 기대하고 있는지 알아야 하므로, 이 정보를 준비해 달라고 하였다. 따라서 (D)가 정답이다.

어휘 recording n. 녹화, 기록 compensation n. 보수, 보상

Paraphrasing

payment 보수 → compensation 보수

Questions 83-85 refer to the following news report.

> [83]I'm reporting live from Westgate Station, where Wagner Transport held an event to celebrate the addition of a new railway line connecting Newberg to the city of Bern. [84]Newberg Mayor Hans Fisher explained that many residents of the town work in Bern. Therefore, having an environmentally friendly alternative to commuting by car is important. [85]During the event, a representative of Wagner Transport outlined its plans for the future. The company has already reached an agreement with the national government to extend its rail network. [85]It will provide service to six additional urban centers over the coming year. This is Jenna Thompson for HBC News.

celebrate v. 기념하다, 축하하다 railway n. 철도 resident n. 거주민
environmentally friendly 환경친화적인 alternative n. 대안
commute v. 통근하다 outline v. 윤곽을 드러내다
agreement n. 합의 national adj. 국가의
network n. (운하·철도·전선·혈관 등의) 망 urban center 도심지

해석
83-85번은 다음 뉴스 보도에 관한 문제입니다.

[83]저는 Westgate역에서 생방송으로 보도하고 있는데, 이곳은 Wagner Transport사가 Newberg와 Bern시를 연결하는 새로운 철도 노선의 추가를 기념하는 행사를 개최한 곳입니다. [84]Newberg의 시장 Hans Fisher는 그 도시의 많은 거주민이 Bern에서 일을 한다고 설명했습니다. 그러므로, 자동차로 통근하는 것에 대한 환경친화적인 대안을 갖는 것이 중요합니다. [85]행사 중에, Wagner Transport사의 대표는 미래를 위한 계획의 윤곽을 드러냈습니다. 그 회사는 이미 중앙 정부와 철도망을 확장하기 위한 합의에 이르렀습니다. [85]그곳은 내년에 여섯 개의 추가 도심지에 서비스를 제공할 것입니다. 저는 HBC 뉴스의 Jenna Thompson입니다.

83 장소 문제

해석 화자는 어디에 있는 것 같은가?

(A) 버스 정류장에

(B) 기차역에

(C) 페리 터미널에

(D) 공항에

해설 지문에서 장소와 관련된 표현을 놓치지 않고 듣는다. "I'm reporting live from Westgate Station, where Wagner Transport held an event to celebrate the addition of a new railway line"이라며 Wagner Transport사가 새로운 철도 노선의 추가를 기념하는 행사를 개최한 곳인 Westgate역에서 생방송으로 보도하고 있다고 한 것을 통해 화자가 기차역에 있음을 알 수 있다. 따라서 (B)가 정답이다.

어휘 terminal n. 터미널, 종점, 기점

84 언급 문제

해석 Fisher 시장은 많은 Newberg 거주민에 대해 무엇을 말하는가?

(A) 더 저렴한 교통수단 선택지를 필요로 한다.

(B) 차량을 한 대보다 많이 소유한 경향이 있다.

(C) 저렴한 주택을 찾는 데 어려움을 겪는다.

(D) 다른 지역 사회에 직장을 가지고 있다.

해설 질문의 핵심 어구(many residents of Newberg)와 관련된 내용을 주의 깊게 듣는다. "Newberg Mayor Hans Fisher explained that many residents of the town work in Bern."이라며 Newberg의 시장 Hans Fisher가 그 도시의 많은 거주민이 Bern에서 일을 한다고 설명했다고 하였다. 따라서 (D)가 정답이다.

어휘 struggle v. 어려움을 겪다, 분투하다

Paraphrasing

work 일하다 → have workplaces 직장을 가지고 있다

85 특정 세부 사항 문제

해석 화자에 따르면, Wagner Transport사가 미래에 하기로 계획하고 있는 것은 무엇인가?
(A) 더 많은 도시로 확장한다.
(B) 추가 직원들을 고용한다.
(C) 기존 시설들을 없앤다.
(D) 다른 국가로 이전한다.

해설 질문의 핵심 어구(future)가 언급된 주변을 주의 깊게 듣는다. "During the event, a representative of Wagner Transport outlined its plans for the future."라며 행사 중에 Wagner Transport사의 대표가 미래를 위한 계획의 윤곽을 드러냈다고 한 후, "It will provide service to six additional urban centers over the coming year."라며 내년에 여섯 개의 추가 도심지에 서비스를 제공할 것이라고 하였다. 따라서 (A)가 정답이다.

어휘 existing adj. 기존의, 존재하는   relocate v. 이전하다, 옮기다

Paraphrasing

provide service to six additional urban centers 여섯 개의 추가 도심지에 서비스를 제공하다 → Expand into more cities 더 많은 도시로 확장하다

[86-88]

Questions 86-88 refer to the following announcement. 〔3〕 영국식

Attention, everyone. There is something you all need to be aware of before the lunch hour begins. Due to technical issues with the card reader, we will not be able to process any electronic payments for the time being. **86Please notify our diners that we can only take cash for now. 87I realize this may be stressful for you, but don't worry . . . Our card reader will be fixed in a few hours.** Lastly, we have a private function tonight for the Lieberman Corporation. **88But I was just notified that the number of guests has changed.** There will be 30 instead of 10. **88If you're available to help out tonight, let me know as soon as possible.**

technical adj. 기술적인, 기술의   process v. 처리하다, 가공하다
electronic adj. 전자의   payment n. 결제, 지불
notify v. 알리다, 통보하다   private adj. 사적인, 개인적인
function n. 행사, 기능

해석
86-88번은 다음 공지에 관한 문제입니다.

주목해 주세요, 여러분. 점심시간이 시작되기 전에 여러분 모두가 알아야 할 것이 있습니다. 카드 판독기에 기술적인 문제가 있어, 우리는 당분간 전자 결제를 처리할 수 없을 것입니다. 86식사하시는 손님들께 우리가 지금은 현금만 받을 수 있다고 알려주시기 바랍니다. 87이것이 여러분에게 스트레스를 일으킬 수 있다는 것을 알고 있지만, 걱정하지 마세요... 우리의 카드 판독기는 몇 시간 내로 수리될 것입니다. 마지막으로, 우리는 오늘 밤 Lieberman사를 위한 사적인 행사가 있습니다. 88하지만 저는 손님들의 인원수가 변경되었다고 지금 막 통보를 받았습니다. 10명이 아니라 30명이 있을 것입니다. 88오늘 밤에 도움을 주는 것이 가능하다면, 가능한 한 빨리 저에게 알려주세요.

86 청자 문제

해석 청자들은 어디에서 일하는 것 같은가?
(A) 은행에서
(B) 식당에서
(C) 전자 기기 가게에서
(D) 음식 공급 업체에서

해설 지문에서 신분 및 직업과 관련된 표현을 놓치지 않고 듣는다. "Please notify our diners that we can only take cash for now."라며 식사하는 손님들에게 지금은 현금만 받을 수 있다고 알려 주라고 한 것을 통해 청자들이 식당에서 일하고 있음을 알 수 있다. 따라서 (B)가 정답이다.

어휘 catering n. 음식 공급

87 특정 세부 사항 문제

해석 화자는 무엇에 대해 청자들을 안심시키는가?
(A) 기기가 곧 수리될 것이다.
(B) 결제가 이후에 승인될 것이다.
(C) 일정이 업데이트될 것이다.
(D) 규칙이 변경될 것이다.

해설 질문의 핵심 어구(reassure)와 관련된 내용을 주의 깊게 듣는다. "I realize this may be stressful for you, but don't worry . . . Our card reader will be fixed in a few hours."라며 카드 판독기가 고장 난 상황이 스트레스를 일으킬 수 있다는 것을 알고 있지만 걱정하지 말라고 한 후, 카드 판독기가 몇 시간 내로 수리될 것이라고 하였다. 따라서 (A)가 정답이다.

Paraphrasing

card reader will be fixed in a few hours 카드 판독기가 몇 시간 내로 수리될 것이다 → A device will be repaired soon 기기가 곧 수리될 것이다

88 의도 파악 문제

해석 화자가 "10명이 아니라 30명이 있을 것입니다"라고 말할 때 무엇을 의도하는가?
(A) 추가 직원들이 필요하다.
(B) 더 큰 장소가 추천된다.
(C) 더 높은 수익이 예상된다.
(D) 상당한 지연이 불가피하다.

해설 질문의 인용어구(There will be 30 instead of 10)가 언급된 주변을 주의 깊게 듣는다. "But I was just notified that the number of guests has changed."라며 손님들의 인원수가 변경되었다고 지금 막 통보를 받았다고 한 후, "If you're available to help out tonight, let me know as soon as possible."이라며 오늘 밤에 도움을 주는 것이 가능하다면 가능한 한 빨리 자신에게 알려 달라고 한 것을 통해 추가 직원들이 필요함을 알 수 있다. 따라서 (A)가 정답이다.

어휘 venue n. 장소 profit n. 수익, 이윤
unavoidable adj. 불가피한, 어쩔 수 없는

[89-91]

3째 캐나다식

Questions 89-91 refer to the following talk.

> **89I gathered everyone here today to make sure you are ready for the upcoming heat wave.** It will increase demand for electricity, which will put pressure on our power plant. **90We sent e-mails to our customers yesterday warning about the possibility of power failures.** However, we must do everything we can to avoid this. So we need to ensure that we have sufficient staff on-site to deal with any system failures. **91If you are going to miss work over the next week, please inform me of the days you will be absent.**

gather v. 모으다, 모이다 heat wave 폭염 demand n. 수요
pressure n. 부담, 압력 power plant 발전소 possibility n. 가능성
power failure 정전 ensure v. 확실히 하다, 보장하다
sufficient adj. 충분한 deal with 대처하다, 다루다
absent adj. 결근한, 결석한

해석

89-91번은 다음 담화에 관한 문제입니다.

89저는 다가오는 폭염에 대한 준비를 확실히 하기 위해 오늘 모두를 이곳에 모셨습니다. 그것은 전력 수요를 증가시킬 것이고, 이는 우리 발전소에 부담을 줄 것입니다. 90우리는 어제 우리 고객들에게 정전 가능성에 대해 경고하는 이메일을 발송했습니다. 하지만, 우리는 이것을 방지하기 위해 할 수 있는 모든 것을 해야만 합니다. 그래서 모든 시스템 장애에 대처할 수 있도록 현장에 충분한 직원이 있는 것을 확실히 해야 합니다. 91다음 주에 일을 쉬고자 한다면, 결근할 날짜를 저에게 알려주시기 바랍니다.

89 목적 문제

해석 담화의 목적은 무엇인가?
(A) 계획된 기업 행사를 미루기 위해
(B) 발전소 점검을 알리기 위해
(C) 초과 근무 정책의 변경을 설명하기 위해
(D) 직원들에게 대비하도록 권고하기 위해

해설 담화의 목적을 묻는 문제이므로, 지문의 초반을 반드시 듣는다. "I gathered everyone here today to make sure you are ready for the upcoming heat wave."라며 다가오는 폭염에 대한 준비를 확실히 하기 위해 오늘 모두를 모이게 했다고 한 후, 직원들에게 폭염으로 인한 정전에 대비하도록 권고하는 내용으로 지문이 이어지고 있다. 따라서 (D)가 정답이다.

어휘 postpone v. 미루다, 연기하다 inspection n. 점검, 사찰
overtime adj. 초과 근무의; n. 초과 근무

Paraphrasing

> are ready for ~에 대한 준비를 하다 → be prepared 대비하다

90 이유 문제

해석 화자의 회사는 왜 이메일을 보냈는가?
(A) 에너지 시설이 수리될 것이다.
(B) 프로젝트가 취소될 수도 있다.
(C) 정전이 일어날 수도 있다.
(D) 요금이 오를 것이다.

해설 질문의 핵심 어구(e-mails)가 언급된 주변을 주의 깊게 듣는다. "We sent e-mails to our customers yesterday warning about the possibility of power failures."라며 어제 고객들에게 정전 가능성에 대해 경고하는 이메일을 발송했다고 하였다. 따라서 (C)가 정답이다.

Paraphrasing

> power failures 정전 → Power outages 정전

91 특정 세부 사항 문제

해설 화자는 사전에 무엇에 대해 알기를 바라는가?
(A) 휴가 날짜
(B) 제도 변경
(C) 안전 문제
(D) 프로젝트 마감일

해설 질문의 핵심 어구(want to know about in advance)와 관련된 내용을 주의 깊게 듣는다. "If you are going to miss work over the next week, please inform me of the days you will be absent."라며 다음 주에 일을 쉬고자 한다면 결근할 날짜를 알려 달라고 하였다. 따라서 (A)가 정답이다.

[92-94]

3째 미국식

Questions 92-94 refer to the following talk.

> Good morning, everyone. I was informed that the floor tiles we ordered are out of stock. They won't be available for over a week. **92/93This could have caused a delay with our current renovation project. But the client just chose another option. 93They are available at a building supply store just over an hour's drive from here.** So I'll need two volunteers to help me pick up the materials while the rest of you proceed to the job site. **94We'll bring the tiles over before noon.**

inform v. 연락하다, 알리다 out of stock 품절된, 재고가 없는
supply n. 자재, 보급품 volunteer n. 자원자 material n. 자재, 재료
proceed v. 이동하다 site n. 현장, 장소

해석

92-94번은 다음 담화에 관한 문제입니다.

좋은 아침입니다, 여러분. 저는 우리가 주문했던 바닥 타일이 품절되었다는 연락을 받았습니다. 그것들은 일주일 넘게 이용할 수 없을 것입니다. 92/93이는 현재의 보수 프로젝트를 지연되게 할 수 있었습니다. 하지만 고객님이 방

금 다른 선택지를 고르셨습니다. ⁹³그것들은 여기에서 차로 한 시간 조금 넘는 거리에 있는 건축 자재 상점에서 구할 수 있습니다. 그래서 저는 나머지 분들이 작업 현장으로 이동하는 동안 자재 수령을 도울 두 명의 자원자가 필요합니다. ⁹⁴우리는 정오 전까지 타일들을 가져올 겁니다.

92 주제 문제

해석 화자는 무엇에 대해 이야기하고 있는가?
(A) 자원봉사 프로그램
(B) 건설 프로젝트
(C) 인건비
(D) 교통 서비스

해설 담화의 주제를 묻는 문제이므로, 지문의 초반을 반드시 듣는다. "This could have caused a delay with our current renovation project."라며 바닥 타일이 품절된 것이 현재의 보수 프로젝트를 지연되게 할 수 있었다고 한 후, 보수 프로젝트에 필요한 자재를 구하는 내용으로 지문이 이어지고 있다. 따라서 (B)가 정답이다.

어휘 labor expense 인건비

Paraphrasing

renovation project 보수 프로젝트 → A construction project 건설 프로젝트

93 의도 파악 문제

해석 화자는 "하지만 고객님이 방금 다른 선택지를 고르셨습니다"라고 말할 때 무엇을 의도하는가?
(A) 고객은 할인을 받게 될 것이다.
(B) 작업자가 대안을 제시할 것이다.
(C) 일이 일정대로 완수될 것이다.
(D) 예산이 늘어날 필요가 있을 것이다.

해설 질문의 인용어구(But the client just chose another option)가 언급된 주변을 주의 깊게 듣는다. "This could have caused a delay with our current renovation project."라며 바닥 타일이 품절된 것이 현재의 보수 프로젝트를 지연되게 할 수 있었다고 한 후, "They are available at a building supply store just over an hour's drive from here."라며 고객이 고른 다른 선택지는 차로 한 시간 조금 넘는 거리에 있는 건축 자재 상점에서 구할 수 있다고 한 것을 통해 고객이 바닥 타일에 대해 다른 선택지를 골랐으므로 일이 일정대로 완수될 것임을 알 수 있다. 따라서 (C)가 정답이다.

어휘 present v. 제시하다, 주다 alternative n. 대안 budget n. 예산

94 다음에 할 일 문제

해석 화자에 따르면, 정오 전에 무슨 일이 일어날 것인가?
(A) 제품이 시연될 것이다.
(B) 계약이 협상될 것이다.
(C) 자재들이 전달될 것이다.
(D) 고객들이 통지를 받을 것이다.

해설 질문의 핵심 어구(before noon)가 언급된 주변을 주의 깊게 듣는다. "We'll bring the tiles over before noon."이라며 정오 전까지 타일들을 가져올 것이라고 하였다. 따라서 (C)가 정답이다.

어휘 demonstrate v. 시연하다 contract n. 계약
negotiate v. 협상하다, 교섭하다

Paraphrasing

the tiles 타일들 → Supplies 자재들

[95-97]   🎧 영국식

Questions 95-97 refer to the following tour information and weather forecast.

⁹⁵**We will begin today's tour here in the Groveland Nursery, where gardeners employed by the city grow all of the plants and flowers that you see throughout this park.** It was first built over a hundred years ago. ⁹⁶**We're very fortunate to be having this weather. The bright sunlight brings out all of the wonderful colors.** Once we exit the nursery, we will go to a spot with a view of the beautiful Jefferson Lake. ⁹⁷**We will have a picnic lunch there in about 30 minutes.**

nursery n. 양묘장, 양식장 gardener n. 정원사
employ v. 고용하다, 채용하다 fortunate adj. 운이 좋은, 다행한
bright adj. 밝은 bring out (빛깔·성질을) 드러나게 하다
spot n. 장소, 곳

해석
95-97번은 다음 여행 정보와 일기 예보에 관한 문제입니다.

⁹⁵우리는 오늘의 투어를 이곳 Groveland 양묘장에서 시작할 것인데, 이곳은 시에 고용되어 있는 정원사들이 이 공원 곳곳에서 볼 수 있는 모든 나무와 꽃을 기르고 있는 곳이에요. 이곳은 100년도 더 전에 처음 지어졌습니다. ⁹⁶이런 날씨를 맞이하게 되다니 우리는 참 운이 좋네요. 밝은 햇살이 모든 아름다운 색들을 드러나게 하고 있습니다. 양묘장을 나서면, 우리는 아름다운 Jefferson 호수가 보이는 장소로 갈 거예요. ⁹⁷우리는 대략 30분 후에 그곳에서 소풍 도시락을 먹을 것입니다.

월요일	☁
⁹⁶화요일	☀
수요일	☁
목요일	☔

95 장소 문제

해석 청자들은 어디에 있는가?
(A) 호수에
(B) 박물관에
(C) 공원에
(D) 학교에

해설 지문에서 장소와 관련된 표현을 놓치지 않고 듣는다. "We will

begin today's tour here in the Groveland Nursery, where gardeners employed by the city grow all of the plants and flowers that you see throughout this park."라며 오늘의 투어를 Groveland 양묘장에서 시작할 것인데, 이곳은 시에 고용되어 있는 정원사들이 이 공원 곳곳에서 볼 수 있는 모든 나무와 꽃을 기르고 있는 곳이라고 한 것을 통해 청자들이 공원에 있음을 알 수 있다. 따라서 (C)가 정답이다.

96 시각 자료 문제

해석 시각 자료를 보아라. 오늘은 무슨 요일인가?
(A) 월요일
(B) 화요일
(C) 수요일
(D) 목요일

해설 제시된 일기 예보의 정보를 확인한 후, 질문의 핵심 어구(today)와 관련된 내용을 주의 깊게 듣는다. "We're very fortunate to be having this weather. The bright sunlight brings out all of the wonderful colors."라며 이런 날씨를 맞이하게 되어 운이 좋다고 한 후, 밝은 햇살이 모든 아름다운 색들을 드러나게 하고 있다고 하였으므로 오늘이 화요일임을 일기 예보에서 알 수 있다. 따라서 (B)가 정답이다.

97 다음에 할 일 문제

해석 화자는 30분 후에 무슨 일이 일어날 것이라고 말하는가?
(A) 날씨가 바뀔 것이다.
(B) 발표가 있을 것이다.
(C) 무리가 식사를 할 것이다.
(D) 강사가 강연을 할 것이다.

해설 질문의 핵심 어구(in 30 minutes)가 언급된 주변을 주의 깊게 듣는다. "We will have a picnic lunch there in about 30 minutes."라며 대략 30분 후에 소풍 도시락을 먹을 것이라고 하였다. 따라서 (C)가 정답이다.

어휘 meal n. 식사 give a talk 강연하다

Paraphrasing

have a picnic lunch 소풍 도시락을 먹다 → have a meal 식사를 하다

[98-100]   캐나다식

Questions 98-100 refer to the following talk and map.

I have a few announcements to make. First, the Hollman Art Fair has added more spaces for food vendors this year. **98To supplement the food tent, additional booths have been set up between the sculpture garden and the fine art exhibit.** Second, the event has attracted a lot more interest than we expected. **99Over 300 artists, all from Hollman City, will be showcasing their work at the fair**, and more than 2,000 visitors are expected to stop by during the three-day period from July 24 to 26. **100To help visitors attending the fair, we developed a mobile app. It features a list of artworks by participating artists and their prices.**

---

vendor n. 노점, 행상인   supplement v. 추가하다, 보충하다
sculpture n. 조각   exhibit n. 전시(물)   attract v. 끌다, 끌어모으다
showcase v. 전시하다, 소개하다   feature v. 특별히 포함하다

해석
98-100번은 다음 담화와 지도에 관한 문제입니다.

저는 몇 가지 공지할 것이 있습니다. 첫째, Hollman 미술 박람회는 올해 음식 노점을 위한 더 많은 공간을 추가했습니다. 98음식 천막을 추가하기 위해, 추가 부스가 조각 공원과 순수 미술 전시 사이에 설치되었습니다. 둘째, 행사는 우리가 예상했던 것보다 더 많은 관심을 끌었습니다. 99모두가 Hollman 시 출신인 300명이 넘는 예술가들이 박람회에서 그들의 작품을 전시할 것이고, 7월 24일부터 26일까지 3일 동안 2,000명이 넘는 방문객들이 들를 것으로 예상됩니다. 100박람회에 참석하는 방문객들을 돕기 위해, 우리는 모바일 앱을 개발했습니다. 그것은 참가하는 예술가의 미술 작품들과 그것들의 가격 목록을 특별히 포함합니다.

98 시각 자료 문제

해석 시각 자료를 보아라. 추가 부스는 어디에 설치되었는가?
(A) 구역 1
(B) 구역 2
(C) 구역 3
(D) 구역 4

해설 제시된 지도의 정보를 확인한 후 질문의 핵심 어구(additional booths ~ set up)가 언급된 주변을 주의 깊게 듣는다. "To supplement the food tent, additional booths have been set up between the sculpture garden and the fine art exhibit."라며 음식 천막을 추가하기 위해 추가 부스가 조각 공원과 순수 미술 전시 사이에 설치되었다고 하였으므로, 추가 부스가 설치된 곳은 구역 4임을 지도에서 알 수 있다. 따라서 (D)가 정답이다.

99 언급 문제

해석 화자는 예술가들에 대해 무엇을 말하는가?
(A) 추가 공간을 요구했다.
(B) 모두 Hollman 시 출신이다.
(C) 미술 대회에 참가할 계획이다.
(D) 한 조직의 회원들이다.

해설 질문의 핵심 어구(artists)가 언급된 주변을 주의 깊게 듣는다. "Over 300 artists, all from Hollman City, will be showcasing their work at the fair"라며 모두가 Hollman 시 출신인 300명이 넘는 예술가들이 박람회에서 그들의 작품을 전시할 것이라고 하였다. 따라서 (B)가 정답이다.

어휘 take part in ~에 참가하다   organization n. 조직

100 특정 세부 사항 문제

해석 화자에 따르면, 모바일 앱에서 무엇을 찾을 수 있는가?
(A) 장소의 지도
(B) 예술가의 프로필
(C) 가격 목록
(D) 음식 메뉴

해설 질문의 핵심 어구(mobile app)가 언급된 주변을 주의 깊게 듣는다. "To help visitors attending the fair, we developed a mobile app. It features a list of artworks by participating artists and their prices."라며 박람회에 참석하는 방문객들을 돕기 위해 모바일 앱을 개발했다고 한 후, 그것이 참가하는 예술가의 미술 작품들과 그것들의 가격 목록을 특별히 포함한다고 하였다. 따라서 (C)가 정답이다.

PART 5

101 격에 맞는 인칭대명사 채우기

해설 명사(television series) 앞에서 형용사처럼 쓰일 수 있는 인칭대명사는 소유격이므로 (C) her가 정답이다.

해석 Sonia Branson은 우주에 관한 그녀의 텔레비전 시리즈로 올해의 과학 커뮤니케이터 상을 받았다.

어휘 receive v. 받다, 받아들이다

102 명사 관련 어구 완성하기

해설 '이체에 합리적인 거래 수수료를 청구한다'라는 문맥에서 빈칸 앞의 명사(transaction)와 함께 쓰여 '거래 수수료'라는 의미의 어구를 이루는 (A) fees가 정답이다. (B)의 volume은 '양, 부피', (C)의 order는 '주문, 명령', (D)의 stock은 '재고, 주식'이라는 의미이다.

해석 Westport 금융사는 국가 간의 은행 송금에 합리적인 거래 수수료를 청구한다.

어휘 charge v. 청구하다, 부과하다
reasonable adj. 합리적인, 너무 비싸지 않은 transaction n. 거래
transfer n. 송금, 이체

103 부사 어휘 고르기

해설 '프로젝트 타임라인은 충분히 명확하게 제시되었다'라는 문맥이므로 (B) enough(충분히)가 정답이다. (A) soon은 '곧', (C) ever는 '이전에, 언제나', (D) much는 '매우, 많이'라는 의미이다. 참고로, enough는 뒤에 to 부정사와 함께 '~할 정도로 충분히'라는 의미의 표현으로 쓰인다.

해석 프로젝트 타임라인은 모든 부서를 조직화하고 일정에 맞게 유지하도록 충분히 명확하게 제시되었다.

어휘 present v. 제시하다 clearly adv. 명확하게
coordinate v. 조직화하다

104 부사절 접속사 채우기

해설 이 문장은 필수성분(the travel time is ~ one hour)을 갖춘 완전한 절이므로 ____ route is taken ~ to Atlanta International Airport는 수식어 거품으로 보아야 한다. 이 수식어 거품은 동사(is taken)가 있는 거품절이므로 거품절을 이끌면서, 빈칸 뒤의 명사(route)를 꾸며주는 형용사 역할을 할 수 있는 것이 들어가야 한다. '어느 경로를 선택하든 간에'라는 의미가 되어야 하므로 복합관계형용사 (B) Whichever(어느 것이든 간에)가 정답이다. (A) What(무슨)은 의문형용사로 쓰일 경우, 뒤에 명사를 꾸밀 수 있지만, 거품절을 이끌 수 없다. (C) However(아무리 ~하더라도)는 복합관계부사로 쓰일 경우, 거품절을 이끌 수 있지만, 뒤에 형용사 또는 부사를 꾸미기 때문에 답이 될 수 없다. 대명사 또는 형용사 (D) Another(다른 사람; 다른 하나의)는 거품절을 이끌 수 없다.

해석 Desmond 호텔에서 애틀랜타 국제공항까지 어느 경로를 이용하든 간에 이동 시간은 대략 1시간이다.

어휘 route n. 경로, 길 approximately adv. 대략

105 형용사 자리 채우기

해설 빈칸 뒤의 명사(items)를 꾸며 줄 수 있는 것은 형용사이므로 형용사 (C) suitable(적합한)이 정답이다. 명사 (A)와 (D), 부사 (B)는 명사를 꾸밀 수 없다.

해석 Meter 마켓의 웹사이트의 개선된 검색 기능은 적합한 물품들을 찾는 것을 더 쉽게 만든다.

어휘 function n. 기능 suitability n. 적합, 적당

106 부사 어휘 고르기

해설 '시장 점유율이 상당히 확대되면서 기록적인 수익을 누리고 있다'라는 문맥이므로 (B) significantly(상당히)가 정답이다. (A) tightly는 '빽빽이, 단단히', (C) responsibly는 '책임감 있게', (D) thickly는 '두껍게'라는 의미이다.

해석 Systek의 노트북 시장 점유율이 지난 한 해 동안 상당히 확대되면서, 그 회사는 현재 기록적인 수익을 누리고 있다.

어휘 share n. 점유율, 몫, 지분 record profit 기록적인 수익

107 형용사 자리 채우기

해설 빈칸 뒤의 명사(manner)를 꾸며 줄 수 있는 과거분사 (A)와 형용사 (B)가 정답의 후보이다. '만족스러운 방식으로'라는 의미가 되어야 하므로 형용사 (B) satisfactory(만족스러운)가 정답이다. 과거분사 (A) satisfied는 '만족하는'이라는 의미로 사람의 감정을 나타낼 때 쓰인다. 명사 (C)와 부사 (D)는 명사를 꾸밀 수 없다.

해석 Ms. Jensen은 그녀의 겹치는 일정을 그녀의 비서가 만족스러운 방식으로 해결할 수 있다고 믿었다.

어휘 assistant n. 비서, 보조원 resolve v. 해결하다
scheduling conflict 겹치는 일정

108 동사 관련 어구 완성하기

해설 '청결 기준을 준수해야 하고 연례 점검을 받아야 한다'라는 문맥에서

빈칸 뒤의 with와 함께 쓰여 '~을 준수하다'라는 의미의 어구를 이루는 동사 (C) comply가 정답이다. (D) meet은 '충족시키다'라는 의미로 문맥상 가능할 것 같지만 '충족시키다, 지키다'의 의미로 쓰일 경우에는 전치사 with와 함께 쓰일 수 없으므로 답이 될 수 없다. (A) associate은 '어울리다, 관련시키다', (B) discuss는 '논의하다'라는 의미이다.

해석 오크빌의 현지 식당들은 청결 기준을 준수해야 하고 연례 점검을 받아야 한다.

어휘 cleanliness n. 청결   standard n. 기준, 표준
undergo v. 받다, 겪다   inspection n. 점검, 검사

최신토익경향

최근 Part 5에서 오답률이 높은 문제는 보통 어휘 문제로 출제된다. 특히, 빈칸 뒤의 전치사와 함께 어구를 이루는 동사를 고르는 문제가 꾸준히 출제되고 있으므로 '동사 + 전치사' 표현을 알아두자.

- familiarize with ~에 익숙해지다
- serve as ~로서의 역할을 하다
- lead to ~을 야기하다
- subscribe to ~을 정기 구독하다
- coincide with ~과 일치하다
- qualify for ~의 자격을 얻다
- contribute to ~에 기여하다
- relocate from A to B A에서 B로 이전하다

109 부사 자리 채우기

해설 동사(contact)를 꾸미기 위해서는 부사가 와야 하므로 부사 (B) directly(직접)가 정답이다. 명사 (A), 동사 또는 과거분사 (C), 동사 (D)는 동사를 꾸밀 수 없다.

해석 그 공석에 고려되기 위해서, 지사 관리자에게 직접 이메일로 연락하세요.

어휘 open position 공석   branch n. 지사, 분점
direct v. 향하다; adj. 직접적인

110 전치사 채우기

해설 '26세의 나이에'라는 의미가 되어야 하므로 (D) at(~에)이 정답이다. (A) in은 '~에, ~ 안에', (B) onto는 '~ 쪽으로', (C) within은 '~ 이내에'라는 의미이다. (A) in과 (C) within은 특정 나이 앞에는 쓰이지 않으므로 답이 될 수 없다. 참고로, at the age of는 '~의 나이에'라는 의미의 관용 표현이다.

해석 캐나다의 소설가 Brad Wilkins는 26세의 나이에 그의 첫 단편 소설집을 출간했다.

어휘 novelist n. 소설가   short story 단편 소설

111 부사 어휘 고르기

해설 '확인 메시지가 나타나면 운영 체제가 제대로 설치되었음을 알게 될 것이다'라는 문맥이므로 (C) properly(제대로, 알맞게)가 정답이다. (A) closely는 '면밀하게, 가까이', (B) curiously는 '호기심을 갖고', (D) wishfully는 '간절히 바라며'라는 의미이다.

해석 화면에 확인 메시지가 나타나면 사용자들은 운영 체제가 제대로 설치

되었음을 알게 될 것이다.

어휘 install v. 설치하다   confirmation n. 확인, 확정
pop up (불쑥) 나타나다

112 명사 자리 채우기

해설 빈칸 앞의 수량 형용사(a few)와 빈칸 뒤의 분사구(showing ~ performance)의 꾸밈을 받을 수 있는 것은 명사이므로 명사 (B) visuals(시각 자료)가 정답이다. 명사 또는 형용사 (A)를 명사로 본다 해도, 수량 표현 a few는 복수 명사 앞에 올 수 있으므로 답이 될 수 없다. 부사 (C)와 동사 (D)는 명사 자리에 올 수 없다.

해석 그들의 보고서를 개선하기 위해, 마케팅 팀의 팀원들은 그들의 분기별 성과를 보여주는 약간의 시각 자료들을 추가했다.

어휘 quarterly adj. 분기별의   visual adj. 시각의; n. 시각 자료
visualize v. 상상하다

113 부사절 접속사 채우기

해설 이 문장은 필수성분(Mr. Ingleby ~ at Nelson Station)을 갖춘 완전한 절이므로 _____ ~ to arrive는 수식어 거품으로 보아야 한다. 이 수식어 거품은 동사(was waiting)가 있는 거품절이므로, 거품절을 이끌 수 있는 부사절 접속사 (A)와 (D)가 정답의 후보이다. '기차가 도착하는 것을 기다리는 동안 예전 대학 동기와 우연히 만났다'라는 의미가 되어야 하므로 (A) while(~하는 동안)이 정답이다. (D) since는 '~한 이래로, ~하기 때문에'라는 의미로 어색한 문맥을 만든다. 전치사 (B) during(~ 동안)과 (C) in order for(~을 위해서)는 절과 절을 연결할 수 없으므로 답이 될 수 없다.

해석 Mr. Ingleby는 그의 기차가 도착하기를 기다리는 동안 Nelson 역에서 이전 대학 동기와 우연히 만났다.

어휘 run into ~와 우연히 만나다

최신토익경향

시간을 나타내는 부사절 접속사 문제는 매회 1~2문제씩 꾸준히 출제되고 있다. 특히, while(~하는 동안)과 until(~하기까지)이 자주 출제되는데, 전치사 during(~동안)이 보기에 자주 함께 출제되므로 혼동하지 않도록 주의해야 한다.

114 형용사 어휘 고르기

해설 '일주일의 오리엔테이션 후에, 업무에 대한 기본적인 이해를 갖게 된다'라는 문맥이므로 (A) basic(기본적인)이 정답이다. (B) waived는 '포기한, 철회한', (C) considerate는 '사려 깊은', (D) chronic은 '만성적인'이라는 의미이다.

해석 일주일의 오리엔테이션 후에, 신입 사원들은 자신의 업무에 대한 기본적인 이해를 갖게 된다.

어휘 understanding n. 이해, 지식   duty n. 업무, 직무

115 부사 자리 채우기

해설 동사(are placed)를 꾸밀 수 있는 것은 부사이므로 부사 (C) strategically(전략적으로)가 정답이다. 명사 (A), 동사 또는 과거분사 (B), 형용사 (D)는 동사를 꾸밀 수 없다.

해석 Winston 슈퍼마켓 곳곳에는 인기 있는 브랜드들의 배치가 전략적으로 되어 있다.

어휘 display n. 배치, 전시 strategy n. 전략
strategize v. 전략을 짜다, 면밀히 계획하다 strategic adj. 전략적인

116 형용사 어휘 고르기

해설 '그곳에는 승인을 받은 직원들만 출입이 가능하다'라는 문맥이므로 (B) authorized(승인을 받은)가 정답이다. (A) concerned는 '우려하는', (C) vacant는 '비어 있는', (D) equal은 '동등한, 평등한'이라는 의미이다.

해석 BioPharm 실험실 입구에는 경비원들이 서 있는데, 그곳에는 승인을 받은 직원들만 출입이 가능하다.

어휘 security guard 경비원 entrance n. 입구 laboratory n. 실험실

117 올바른 시제의 동사 채우기

해설 종속절(than ~ ____)에 주어(the tour group members)만 있고 동사가 없으므로 동사 (B), (C), (D)가 정답의 후보이다. 주절(The hike ~ exhausting)의 동사(was)의 시제가 과거이므로 종속절에는 과거 시제 또는 과거 완료 시제가 와야 하는데, 보기에 과거 시제가 없으므로 과거완료 시제 (B) had anticipated가 정답이다. 현재 시제 (C)는 주로 반복적인 행동이나 습관을 나타내고 현재완료 시제 (D)는 과거에 발생한 일이 현재까지 영향을 미치거나 방금 완료된 것을 표현할 때 사용된다. 동명사 또는 현재분사 (A)는 동사 자리에 올 수 없다.

해석 그 산으로의 등산은 투어 그룹의 구성원들이 예상했던 것보다 신체적으로 훨씬 더 힘들었다.

어휘 physically adv. 신체적으로 exhausting adj. 힘든

118 전치사 채우기

해설 '배송품은 도착 즉시 창고 직원에 의해 철저히 검사된다'라는 의미가 되어야 하므로 (D) upon(~하는 즉시)이 정답이다. (A) behind는 '~ 뒤에', (B) across는 '~을 가로질러', (C) among은 '~ 사이에'라는 의미이다.

해석 Windhorn 도구사로부터의 배송품은 도착 즉시 창고 직원에 의해 철저히 검사된다.

어휘 thoroughly adv. 철저히 warehouse n. 창고

119 명사 자리 채우기

해설 전치사(for)와 전치사(in) 사이에 올 수 있는 것은 명사이므로 명사 (B) inclusion(포함)이 정답이다. 형용사 (A), 동사 (C)와 (D)는 명사 자리에 올 수 없다.

해석 의료 제도 학술지에 포함하기 위한 논문을 선정할 때, 편집진은 저자의 자격을 확인한다.

어휘 article n. 논문, 기사, 글 editorial adj. 편집의
verify v. 확인하다, 입증하다 credentials n. 자격
inclusive adj. 모든 것을 포함한

120 명사 어휘 고르기

해설 '기기의 수명을 극대화하기 위해 더 내구성이 있는 케이스를 개발했다'라는 문맥이므로 (D) longevity(수명)가 정답이다. (A) reality는 '현실', (B) probability는 '가능성, 확률', (C) authority는 '권한, 권력'이라는 의미이다.

해석 NeoTek은 기기의 수명을 극대화하기 위해 더 내구성이 있는 케이스를 개발했다.

어휘 durable adj. 내구성이 있는 maximize v. 극대화하다

121 형용사 자리 채우기

해설 빈칸 앞뒤로 형용사(helpful)와 형용사(patient)가 A, B, and C의 구조로 연결되어 있으므로 빈칸에도 형용사가 들어가야 한다. 따라서 형용사인 (A)와 (B)가 정답의 후보이다. '도움이 되고, 상냥하고, 인내심을 가지고 지도하다'라는 의미가 되어야 하므로 형용사 (B) personable(상냥한, 호감 가는)이 정답이다. (A) personal(개인적인)을 쓸 경우 '개인적이고, 인내심을 가지고 지도하다'라는 어색한 문맥이 된다. 부사 (C)와 명사 (D)는 명사를 꾸밀 수 없다.

해석 멘토로서 Dr. Bae는 멘티들의 경력상 도전에서 그들을 지도함에 있어서 도움이 되고, 상냥하고, 인내심을 가지기 위해 노력한다.

어휘 strive to ~하기 위해 노력하다 patient adj. 인내심 있는
challenge n. 도전

최신토익경향

형용사 관련 문제는 매회 2~3문제씩 꾸준히 출제되고 있다. 특히, 형용사 자리 문제에서 비슷하게 생긴 형용사의 의미를 구별하는 문제는 오답률이 높은 편이므로 의미를 정확히 알아두자.

- ideal 이상적인 — idealistic 이상주의적인
- considerable 상당한, 중요한 — considerate 사려 깊은
- comparable 비슷한, 비교할 만한 — comparative 비교의
- informed 정통한, 알고 있는, 정보에 입각한 — informative 유익한

122 동사 어휘 고르기

해설 '5월에 회원권이 만료되기 전에 갱신할 계획이다'라는 문맥이므로 동사 expire(만료되다)의 단수형 (C) expires가 정답이다. (A)의 vary는 '다르다, 달라지다', (B)의 occur는 '발생하다', (D)의 neglect는 '무시하다, 소홀히 하다'라는 의미이다.

해석 Mr. Delgado는 5월에 그의 연간 피트니스 클럽의 회원권이 만료되기 전에 그것을 갱신할 계획이다.

어휘 renew v. 갱신하다

123 분사구문 채우기

해설 빈칸은 부사절 접속사(After)가 이끄는 부사절로 주어가 생략된 분사구문을 완성하는 분사 자리이므로 현재분사 (D) reviewing이 정답이다. After를 전치사로 보고 빈칸을 명사 자리라고 본다 해도 명사는 뒤에 목적어(the lease agreement)를 취하지 못하므로 명사 (B)와 (C)는 답이 될 수 없다.

해석 그녀의 아파트 임대 계약서를 성급하게 검토한 후에, Ms. Kwon은 만기 날짜가 잘못되었다는 것을 알게 되었다.

124 to 부정사의 in order to 채우기

해설 이 문장은 필수성분(A representative ~ us today)을 갖춘 완전한 절이므로 ____ identify ~ a garden은 수식어 거품으로 보아야 한다. 빈칸 뒤의 동사(identify)를 이끌면서 '정원을 갖출 장소를 찾기 위해'라는 목적을 나타내는 (C) in order to가 정답이다. 전치사 (A)와 (B)는 명사 앞에 와야 하고, 부사절 접속사 (D)는 주어와 동사로 이루어진 거품절을 이끈다.

해석 Thumb 조경사의 담당자가 정원을 갖출 장소를 찾기 위해 오늘 방문할 것이다.

어휘 representative n. 담당자, 대표 identify v. 찾다, 확인하다

125 전치사 채우기

해설 '14퍼센트 정도'라는 의미가 되어야 하므로 양이나 정도를 나타내는 (A) by(~ 정도, ~ 만큼)가 정답이다. (B) plus는 '~에 더하여', (C) on은 '~ 위에', (D) with는 '~과 함께'라는 의미이다.

해석 Glen 종이 제품사는 향후 3년 동안 당사의 판매 매출이 14퍼센트 정도 증가할 것으로 예상한다.

어휘 revenue n. 수익, 수입

126 형용사 어휘 고르기

해설 '설득력 있는 주장을 했기 때문에, 이사회는 계획을 승인했다'라는 문맥이므로 (D) convincing(설득력 있는)이 정답이다. (A) tentative는 '잠정적인, 임시의', (B) narrow는 '편협한, 좁은', (C) renewable은 '재생 가능한'이라는 의미이다.

해석 Mr. Cromer가 해외 진출을 지지하는 설득력 있는 주장을 했기 때문에, 이사회는 그의 계획을 승인했다.

어휘 argument n. 주장, 논거 in favor of ~을 지지하는, ~에 찬성하는 expand v. 확장하다, 넓히다 board of directors 이사회 approve v. 승인하다, 찬성하다

127 다른 명사를 수식하는 명사 채우기

해설 빈칸은 소유격(Milestone Energy's)의 꾸밈을 받는 명사 자리이므로 명사 (B)와 (D)가 정답의 후보이다. '공학 기술 혁신은 산업을 변화시킬 잠재력을 가지고 있다'라는 의미가 되어야 하므로 명사 innovations와 함께 복합 명사를 만드는 명사 (D) engineering(공학 기술)이 정답이다. 과거분사 (A)를 빈칸에 넣으면 '제작된 혁신'이라는 어색한 의미가 된다. 명사 (B)를 써서 engineers innovations를 복합 명사로 본다 해도, 복합 명사를 복수형으로 만들 때는 뒤의 명사에 -(e)s를 붙여야 하므로 답이 될 수 없다.

해석 Milestone 에너지사의 공학 기술 혁신은 에너지 산업을 변화시킬 잠재력을 가지고 있다.

어휘 innovation n. 혁신 potential n. 잠재력, 가능성

128 부사절 접속사 채우기

해설 이 문장은 필수성분(Residents ~ exits)을 갖춘 완전한 절이므로 ____ there is a fire는 수식어 거품으로 보아야 한다. 이 수식어 거품은 동사(is)가 있는 거품절이므로, 거품절을 이끌 수 있는 부사절 접속사 (A)와 (D)가 정답의 후보이다. '화재가 날 경우에 대비해서 비상구를 알고 있다'라는 의미가 되어야 하므로 (A) in case(~할 경우에 대비해서)가 정답이다. (D) unless는 '만약 ~이 아니라면'이라는 의미이므로 이 문맥에 어울리지 않는다. 전치사 (B) as of(~부터)와 (C) without(~ 없이)은 거품절을 이끌 수 없다.

해석 Holmes 타워의 거주자들은 화재가 날 경우에 대비해서 비상구를 알고 있을 것이 권고된다.

어휘 resident n. 거주자 urge v. 권고하다 be aware of ~을 알다

129 형용사 자리 채우기

해설 이 문장은 필수성분(The weekend flea market ~ dealers)을 갖춘 완전한 절이고 ____ in rare books and antique jewelry는 빈칸 앞의 명사(dealers)를 꾸미고 있으므로 형용사 역할을 하는 현재분사 (B) specializing이 정답이다.

해석 주말 벼룩시장은 희귀 서적과 골동품 장신구를 전문적으로 다루는 상인들을 끌어들인다.

어휘 flea market 벼룩시장 attract v. 끌어들이다, 주의를 끌다 dealer n. 상인 rare adj. 희귀한, 드문

130 명사 어휘 고르기

해설 '신제품 라인의 출시 지연으로 인해 수익을 달성하지 못할 수도 있다'라는 문맥이므로 (B) profitability(수익, 이윤율)가 정답이다. (A) reaction은 '반응', (C) alignment는 '(일렬) 정렬', (D) effect는 '영향, 효과'라는 의미이다.

해석 Linia 음료사는 신제품 라인의 출시 지연으로 인해 이번 분기에 수익을 달성하지 못할 수도 있다.

어휘 achieve v. 달성하다, 이루다 quarter n. 분기, 4분의 1 delay n. 지연 launch n. 출시

PART 6

131-134번은 다음 편지에 관한 문제입니다.

> 11월 24일
>
> Ms. Ishioka께,
>
> *Science Explorers*의 정기 독자가 되어 주셔서 감사합니다. 귀하의 지지는 매우 값집니다. **131잡지의 모든 호를 재미있게 읽으셨기를 바랍니다.** 저희는 귀하와 같은 독자들의 마음을 사로잡아 교육시키는 유익하고 수준 높은 내용을 제공하기 위해 항상 노력하고 있습니다.
>
> **132계속 이용하실 수 있도록, 귀하의 구독을 갱신할 때입니다. 133지금 이렇게 하시면,** 내년에 독점 기사들을 즐겨 볼 수 있습니다. 이것들은 과학적 혁신에 대한 심층 분석이 포함될 것입니다.
>
> **134문의 사항이 있다면, 고객 서비스 센터 555-0389로 연락해 주 ○

세요. 온라인 채널을 통해서도 저희에게 연락하실 수 있습니다.

Science Explorers 드림

loyalty n. 지지, 충성(심)	invaluable adj. 매우 값진, 귀중한
informative adj. 유익한	captivate v. 마음을 사로잡다
renew v. 갱신하다	in-depth adj. 심층적인
breakthrough n. 혁신, 큰 발전	

131 알맞은 문장 고르기

해석 (A) 최근 배송이 일부 지연되었습니다.
(B) 저희 웹사이트의 그 정보는 저희 편집자에 의해 수정되었습니다.
(C) 잡지의 모든 호를 재미있게 읽으셨기를 바랍니다.
(D) 귀하의 편지는 다음 판에 실릴 예정입니다.

해설 빈칸에 들어갈 알맞은 문장을 고르는 문제이므로 주변 문맥 또는 전체 문맥을 파악한다. 앞 문장 'Your loyalty is invaluable.'에서 독자로서 귀하의 지지는 매우 값지다고 했고, 뒤 문장 'We always strive to deliver informative and high-quality content that captivates and educates readers like you.'에서 귀하와 같은 독자들의 마음을 사로잡아 교육시키는 유익하고 수준 높은 내용을 제공하기 위해 노력하고 있다고 했으므로, 빈칸에는 잡지를 구독한 독자와 관련된 내용이 들어가야 함을 알 수 있다. 따라서 (C)가 정답이다.

어휘 shipment n. 배송 correct v. 바로잡다, 정정하다; adj. 정확한

132 명사 어휘 고르기 전체 문맥 파악

해설 '계속 이용할 수 있도록, 귀하의 ___을 갱신할 때가 되다'라는 문맥이므로 (B), (C), (D)가 정답의 후보이다. 빈칸이 있는 문장만으로 정답을 고를 수 없으므로 주변 문맥이나 전체 문맥을 파악한다. 앞부분에서 '정기 독자가 되어 주셔서 감사하다(Thank you for being a regular reader of ~)'라고 했고, 빈칸 뒤에서는 이렇게 하면 내년에 기사를 즐길 수 있다고 했으므로 계속 이용하기 위해서 구독을 갱신해야 함을 알 수 있다. 따라서 (B) subscription(구독)이 정답이다.

어휘 method n. 방법 license n. 면허증; v. (공적으로) 허가하다
lease n. 임대차 계약; v. 임대하다

133 형용사 자리 채우기

해설 빈칸 뒤의 명사(articles)를 꾸밀 수 있는 것은 형용사이므로 형용사 역할을 할 수 있는 현재분사 (A)와 형용사 (B)가 정답의 후보이다. '독점 기사들'이라는 의미가 되어야 하므로 형용사 (B) exclusive(독점의)가 정답이다. 현재분사 (A)를 쓰면 '배제하는 기사들'이라는 어색한 문맥이 된다. 명사 (C)는 article과 복합 명사를 이룰 수 없고, 부사 (D)는 명사를 꾸밀 수 없다.

어휘 exclusion n. 제외, 차단 exclusively adv. 전적으로

134 if 없는 가정법

해설 이 문장은 필수성분(just reach out ~ at 555-0389)을 갖춘 완전한 절이므로 ___ you have ~ questions는 수식어 거품으로 보아야 한다. 이 수식어 거품은 동사(have)가 있는 거품절이므로, 거품절을 이끌 수 있는 부사절 접속사 (B)와 if가 생략된 가정법에 쓰여 도치를 이루는 조동사 (D)가 정답의 후보이다. '문의 사항이 있다면, 고객

서비스 센터 555-0389로 연락해 주세요.'라는 의미가 되어야 하므로 (D) Should가 정답이다. (B) Although는 '비록 ~이지만'이라는 의미로 양보를 나타낸다. 부사 (A) Even(심지어 ~조차)과 (C) Later(나중에)은 수식어 거품을 이끌 수 없다. 참고로, 가정법 미래 문장에서 If가 생략되는 경우, 'Should + 주어 + 동사원형, 주어 + will(can, may, should) + 동사원형'의 형태를 만든다.

135-138번은 다음 기사에 관한 문제입니다.

케노샤(7월 10일)-Seaward 엔지니어링사는 싱가포르에 첫 해외 지사를 개업할 것이라고 발표했다. [135]따라서, CEO인 Lyra Bradshaw가 다음 주에 그 나라로 출장을 갈 계획이다. 그녀는 지사장직을 맡을 현지 후보자 몇 명을 면접할 예정이다. [136]이달 말까지 채용 결정이 내려질 것이다.

Bradshaw는 새 지사가 9월 1일에 운영을 시작할 것으로 예상하고 있다. [137]40명의 엔지니어와 100명의 지원 인력으로 구성될 그곳은 Seaward 엔지니어링사가 아시아 시장에서 수익성 높은 사업에 참여하도록 도울 것이다. [138]Bradshaw는 이를 회사에 중요한 기회로 여긴다. "우리의 분석에 따르면 아시아 지역 전체가 성장할 준비가 되어 있습니다. 그곳이 우리 업계 기업들에게 주요 이점을 제공하기 때문에 싱가포르를 사업 거점으로 선택했습니다."

overseas adj. 해외의; adv. 해외로	regional adj. 지역의
anticipate v. 예상하다, 기대하다	
lucrative adj. 수익성 높은, 이윤이 되는	entire adj. 전체의
poise v. 준비를 하다 base n. 거점, 근거지 operation n. 사업, 영업	
key adj. 주요한, 핵심적인	

135 접속부사 채우기 주변 문맥 파악

해설 빈칸이 콤마와 함께 문장의 맨 앞에 온 접속부사 자리이므로, 앞 문장과 빈칸이 있는 문장의 의미 관계를 파악하여 정답을 선택한다. 앞 문장에서 Seaward 엔지니어링사는 싱가포르에 첫 해외 지사를 개업할 것이라고 발표했다고 했고, 빈칸이 있는 문장에서는 CEO가 다음 주에 그 나라로 출장을 갈 계획이라고 했으므로, 앞 문장의 결과를 나타낼 때 사용되는 (C) Consequently(따라서)가 정답이다.

어휘 if so 만일 그렇다면 alternatively adv. 그 대신에
nevertheless adv. 그럼에도 불구하고

136 알맞은 문장 고르기

해석 (A) 그 후보자는 투자자들을 위한 승리 전략을 간략히 설명했다.
(B) 그녀는 선발된 지원자에게 감명을 받았다.
(C) 이달 말까지 채용 결정이 내려질 것이다.
(D) 그녀의 승진은 어제 CEO에 의해 확정되었다.

해설 앞 문장 'She will be interviewing several local candidates for the position of regional manager.'에서 그녀는 지사장직을 맡을 현지 후보자 몇 명을 면접할 예정이라고 했으므로, 빈칸에는 채용 일정과 관련된 내용이 들어가야 함을 알 수 있다. 따라서 (C)가 정답이다.

어휘 outline v. 간략히 설명하다, 개요를 말하다 investor n. 투자자
impressed adj. 감명을 받은 applicant n. 지원자, 신청자

137 원형 부정사 채우기

해설 빈칸이 포함된 문장의 동사 help는 5형식 동사로 목적어와 목적격 보어를 가지는데, 동사(help) 뒤에 목적어(Seaward Engineering)가 있으므로 빈칸은 목적격 보어 자리이다. help는 목적격 보어로 원형 부정사 또는 to 부정사를 가지므로 원형 부정사 (B) participate가 정답이다.

어휘 participate v. 참여하다

138 동사 어휘 고르기

해설 '회사에 중요한 기회로 여기다'라는 문맥이므로 동사 consider(여기다)의 3인칭 단수형 (D) considers가 정답이다. (B)의 remember는 '기억하다'라는 뜻으로 해석상 그럴듯해 보이지만, remember는 뒤에 목적어와 목적격 보어를 쓸 수 없으므로 답이 될 수 없다. (A)의 achieve는 '성취하다', (C)의 reject는 '거절하다'라는 의미이다. 참고로, 동사 consider는 'consider A B(A를 B로 여기다)'의 형태로 쓰인다.

139-142번은 다음 공고에 관한 문제입니다.

---

[139]다음 달에 모든 Pizza Duke 체인점에 장작불로 요리하는 피자 오븐인 Culinart B70을 들일 예정입니다. 저희는 수년 동안 의지해 왔던 오븐을 교체하는 것에 대해 우려했습니다. [140]하지만, 선정된 지점들에서 3월부터 Culinart B70을 시험해 왔고, 대부분의 고객들이 그것이 더 맛있는 피자를 만들어낸다는 데 동의합니다. [141]고객들은 또한 더 빨라진 조리 시간을 높이 평가합니다. 그것은 저희가 더 많은 고객분들께 맛있는 피자를 제공할 수 있게 해 줄 것입니다.

이번 주부터, 전국에 있는 지점들은 설치 기간 동안 문을 닫을 것입니다. [142]고객들은 각 지점에 게시된 안내문을 통해 일시적 휴업에 대해 공지받을 예정입니다.

replace v. 교체하다, 대신하다 depend v. 의지하다, 의존하다
selected adj. 선정된, 엄선한 serve v. 제공하다, 역할을 하다
nationwide adj. 전국적인 installation n. 설치
notify v. 통지하다, 알리다 closure n. 휴업, 폐쇄

---

139 시간 표현과 일치하는 시제의 동사 채우기

해설 문장에 동사가 없으므로 동사 (A), (B), (C)가 정답의 후보이다. 빈칸이 있는 문장에 미래 시간 표현(In the upcoming month)이 있으므로 미래 시제 (B) will receive가 정답이다.

어휘 receive v. (물건을) 안에 들이다, 받다

140 접속부사 채우기 주변 문맥 파악

해설 빈칸이 콤마와 함께 문장의 맨 앞에 온 접속부사 자리이므로, 앞 문장과 빈칸이 있는 문장의 의미 관계를 파악하여 정답을 선택한다. 앞 문장에서 수년 동안 의지해 왔던 오븐을 교체하는 것을 우려했다고 했고, 빈칸이 있는 문장에서는 선정된 매장들에서 Culinart B70을 시험해 보았는데, 대부분의 고객들이 더 맛있는 피자를 만들어낸다는 데 동의한다고 했으므로, 앞의 내용과 상반되는 내용을 언급할 때 사용되는 (D) However(하지만)가 정답이다.

어휘 for instance 예를 들어 in addition 게다가
in particular 특히

141 알맞은 문장 고르기

해석 (A) 한 이탈리아 출신 요리사가 피자 메뉴를 구상 중입니다.
(B) 장작불로 요리하는 오븐이 모든 주방에 적합한 것은 아닙니다.
(C) 고객들은 또한 더 빨라진 조리 시간을 높이 평가합니다.
(D) 여러분들은 2,000달러 미만으로 하나를 구매할 수 있습니다.

해설 앞 문장 'most customers agree that it produces a better-tasting pizza'에서 대부분의 고객들은 새로운 오븐이 더 맛있는 피자를 만들어낸다는 데 동의했고, 뒤 문장 'It will allow us to serve delicious pizzas to more customers.'에서 더 많은 고객들에게 맛있는 피자를 제공할 수 있게 해 줄 것이라고 했으므로, 빈칸에는 새 오븐이 좋은 이유와 관련된 내용이 들어가야 함을 알 수 있다. 따라서 (C)가 정답이다.

어휘 chef n. 요리사, 주방장 design v. 구상하다, 계획하다
suitable adj. 적합한, 적절한

142 형용사 어휘 고르기 주변 문맥 파악

해설 '각 지점에 게시된 안내문을 통해 ____ 휴업에 대해 공지 받을 것이다'라는 문맥이므로 (A)와 (C)가 정답의 후보이다. 빈칸이 있는 문장만으로 정답을 고를 수 없으므로 주변 문맥이나 전체 문맥을 파악한다. 앞 문장에서 '전국에 있는 지점들은 설치 기간 동안 문을 닫을 것이다(branches nationwide will be closed during installation)'라고 했으므로 임시 휴업에 대해 공지 받을 것임을 알 수 있다. 따라서 (A) temporary(임시의)가 정답이다. (B) previous는 '이전의', (C) frequent는 '빈번한, 잦은', (D) suspicious는 '의심스러운'이라는 의미이다.

143-146번은 다음 이메일에 관한 문제입니다.

수신: customerservice@blendsolutions.ca
발신: c.yang@cindyscoffee.ca
날짜: 3월 21일
제목: 잘못된 주문

저는 지난주 토요일에 귀사에 물품을 주문했고 어제 그 배송품을 받았습니다. [143]단 이틀 만에 도착한 제품의 빠른 배송에 매우 감동했습니다.

[144]유감스럽게도, 제 주문에 실수가 있었던 것 같습니다. 저는 스무디를 만들기 위해 두 대의 믹서기를 주문했는데, 그 대신 얼음을 분쇄하지 못하는 두 대의 만능 조리 기구를 받았습니다.

[145]4월 1일부터, 저는 제 카페에서 신선한 과일 스무디를 제공할 계획입니다. 다음 주까지 제 주문을 바로잡을 수 있는지 확인해 주시겠습니까? [146]시간이 더 필요하시다면, 저는 다른 계획을 세워야 할 것입니다.

이 문제에 관심을 가져 주셔서 감사합니다.

Cindy Yang 드림
Cindy's Coffee

shipment n. 배송(품) delivery n. 배달, 전달 appear v. ~인 것 같다
food processor 만능 조리 기구(식재료를 자르고 섞을 때 쓰는 기구) ○

---

crush v. 분쇄하다, 밀어 넣다 confirm v. 확인하다, 확정하다
attention n. 관심, 주의 matter n. 문제, 사안

143 동사 어휘 고르기

해설 '단 이틀 만에 도착한 빠른 배송에 감동했다'라는 문맥이므로 arrive (도착하다)의 과거형 (B) arrived가 정답이다. (A)의 verify는 '확인 하다', (C)의 examine은 '확인하다', (D)의 respond는 '응답하다' 라는 의미이다.

144 접속부사 채우기 주변 문맥 파악

해설 빈칸이 콤마와 함께 문장의 맨 앞에 온 접속부사 자리이므로, 앞 문장 과 빈칸이 있는 문장의 의미 관계를 파악하여 정답을 선택한다. 앞 문 장에서 지난주 토요일에 주문했던 상품의 빠른 배송에 감동했다고 했 고, 빈칸이 있는 문장에서 주문에 실수가 있었던 것 같다고 했으므로, 앞에서 말한 상황과 다르게 안 좋은 내용을 언급할 때 사용되는 (B) Unfortunately (유감스럽게도)가 정답이다.

어휘 moreover adv. 게다가 in short 요컨대, 즉
after all 결국에는, 어쨌든

145 분사구문 채우기

해설 이 문장은 필수성분(I plan to offer ~ smoothies)을 갖춘 완전한 절이므로, ____ 1 April은 수식어 거품으로 보아야 한다. 보기 중 수 식어 거품이 될 수 있는 것은 현재분사이므로 (D) Starting이 정답이 다. 명사 (B), 동사 (A)와 (C)는 수식어 거품을 이끌 수 없다. 참고로, Starting은 분사형 전치사로 보통 시점 앞에 쓰여 '~부터'라는 의미 를 나타낸다는 것을 알아둔다.

146 알맞은 문장 고르기

해석 (A) 시간이 더 필요하시다면, 저는 다른 계획을 세워야 할 것입니다.
(B) Cindy's Coffee는 5년 동안 이 지역 사회의 일원이었습니다.
(C) 첫 방문객들은 음료를 무료로 시음할 수 있습니다.
(D) 봄에 그 지역이 붐비기는 하지만 방문하기 가장 좋은 시기입니다.

해설 빈칸에 들어갈 알맞은 문장을 고르는 문제이므로 주변 문맥 또 는 전체 문맥을 파악한다. 앞 문장 'I plan to offer fresh fruit smoothies at my café. Could you please confirm whether it's possible to correct my order by next week?'에서 신선한 과일 스무디를 제공할 계획인데, 다음 주까지 주문을 바로잡을 수 있 는지 확인해 달라고 했으므로 빈칸에는 잘못된 주문을 바로잡는 것과 관련된 내용이 들어가야 함을 알 수 있다. 따라서 (A)가 정답이다.

어휘 sample v. 시음(시식)하다 beverage n. 음료

PART 7

147-148번은 다음 문자 메시지 대화문에 관한 문제입니다.

Mike Lee	[오전 11시 15분]

안녕하세요, Tanya. 빠르게 질문 하나 할게요. 새로운 종이컵들을 어디 에 두셨나요? ¹⁴⁷제가 한 주문이 어젯밤 당신의 교대 근무 시간

중에 커피숍에 도착했어야 해요.

Tanya Lewis	[오전 11시 16분]

제가 모두 치웠는데, 종이컵은 하나도 보지 못했어요. 상자 안에는 냅 킨과 빨대만 있었어요.

Mike Lee	[오전 11시 19분]

정말 이상하네요. 지금 공급업체에 연락해 볼게요. 아, 한 가지만 더요. ¹⁴⁸Denise가 부모님이 방문하셔서 내일 아침 근무에 휴가를 내길 원 해요. 그녀의 교대 근무 시간을 맡아줄 수 있나요?

Tanya Lewis	[오전 11시 20분]

저는 10시에 진료 예약이 있어요. ¹⁴⁸매년 하는 건강검진인데, 미루 고 싶지 않아요.

Mike Lee	[오전 11시 21분]

걱정하지 마세요. 다른 직원 중 한 명에게 물어볼게요.

place v. (주문을) 넣다 shift n. 교대 근무 시간
put ~ away ~을 치우다 supplier n. 공급업체
take ~ off ~에 휴가를 내다 annual adj. 매년의, 연례의 put off 미루다

147 추론 문제

해석 글쓴이들은 어디에서 일할 것 같은가?
(A) 공장에서
(B) 카페에서
(C) 슈퍼마켓에서
(D) 택배회사에서

해설 지문의 'The order I placed should have arrived during your shift at the coffee shop last night.'에서 자신이 주문한 것이 어 젯밤 당신의 교대 근무 시간 중에 커피숍에 도착했어야 한다고 했으 므로 글쓴이들이 카페에서 일한다는 것을 추론할 수 있다. 따라서 (B) 가 정답이다.

어휘 delivery company 택배회사

148 의도 파악 문제

해석 오전 11시 20분에, Ms. Lewis가 "I have a doctor's appointment at 10"이라고 썼을 때, 그녀가 의도한 것 같은 것은?
(A) 휴가 요청서를 제출할 것이다.
(B) 일정을 확인하지 않았다.
(C) 동료를 대신할 수 없다.
(D) 심한 질병을 앓고 있다.

해설 지문의 'Denise wants to take tomorrow morning off because her parents are visiting. Would you be able to cover her shift?'에서 Mr. Lee가 Denise가 내일 아침 휴가를 내 기를 원하니 근무 시간을 대신 맡아줄 수 있는지 묻자, Ms. Lewis가 'I have a doctor's appointment at 10'(저는 10시에 진료 예약이 있어요)이라고 한 후, 'It's my annual medical checkup, and I don't want to put it off.'에서 매년 하는 건강검진인데 미루고 싶 지 않다고 한 것을 통해, Ms. Lewis가 동료인 Denise 대신 일할 수 없음을 의도했다는 것을 알 수 있다. 따라서 (C)가 정답이다.

어휘 leave request 휴가 요청서 fill in for ~를 대신하다
medical condition 질병

149-150번은 다음 일정표에 관한 문제입니다.

	Brittany Klancy
오전 10시-오전 11시	¹⁴⁹기술 지원 직책에 대해 David Hong 면접하기
오전 11시-오후 12시	¹⁴⁹모든 지원자들의 추천서 확인하기
오후 12시-오후 1시	Whitewater 해산물 뷔페에서 팀 점심 식사(예약 확인하기)
¹⁵⁰오후 1시-오후 2시	¹⁵⁰Mr. Wallace와의 회의(그가 요청한 수정 사항이 담긴 회계 소프트웨어 매뉴얼의 하드카피 버전 보여주기)
오후 2시-오후 3시	제안된 부서 예산 검토하기
오후 3시-오후 4시	인사 프레젠테이션 → 목요일 같은 시간으로 일정 변경됨
오후 4시-오후 5시	보류 중인 업무 지시 처리하기
오후 5시-오후 6시	장비 업그레이드에 대한 권장 사항이 포함된 보고서 마무리하기

reference n. 추천서, 참조 candidate n. 지원자
hardcopy n. 하드카피, 인쇄물 pending adj. 보류 중인
finalize v. 마무리하다, 완료하다

149 추론 문제

해석 Ms. Klancy에 대해 추론될 수 있는 것은?
(A) 새로운 장비의 구매를 승인했다.
(B) 이전 직원에게 추천서를 제공할 것이다.
(C) 그녀의 부서에 더 많은 예산을 요청하려고 한다.
(D) 기술자를 채용하는 과정에 관여하고 있다.

해설 지문의 'Interview David Hong for the tech support position', 'Check the references of all candidates'에서 기술 지원 직책에 대한 David Hong 면접을 보고, 모든 지원자들의 추천서를 확인한다고 했으므로 Ms. Klancy가 기술자를 채용하는 과정에 관여하고 있다는 사실을 추론할 수 있다. 따라서 (D)가 정답이다.

어휘 authorize v. 승인하다, 권한을 주다 former adj. 이전의
be involved in ~에 관여하다

150 육하원칙 문제

해석 오후 1시에 시작되는 행사에 Ms. Klancy는 무엇을 가져와야 하는가?
(A) 회계 팀의 재무 보고서
(B) 새로운 회사 정책을 요약한 매뉴얼
(C) 소프트웨어 프로그램의 업데이트된 버전
(D) 애플리케이션에 대한 지침서

해설 지문의 오후 1시-오후 2시 일정에서 'Meeting with Mr. Wallace (show the hardcopy version of the accounting software manual with his requested revisions)'에서 오후 1시부터 오후 2시까지 Mr. Wallace와의 회의가 있고, 그가 요청한 수정 사항이 담긴 회계 소프트웨어 매뉴얼의 하드카피 버전을 보여준다고 했으므로 애플리케이션에 대한 지침서를 가져와야 되는 것을 알 수 있다. 따라서 (D)가 정답이다.

어휘 outline v. 요약하다 instructional adj. 지침의, 교육용의

Paraphrasing

hardcopy version of ~ manual 매뉴얼의 하드카피 버전
→ instructional booklet 지침서
software 소프트웨어 → application 애플리케이션

151-152번은 다음 광고에 관한 문제입니다.

Washtab
세심하게 세탁합니다.

빨래로 지치셨나요? 당신의 믿을 만한 세탁 서비스인 Washtab을 이용하여 시간을 절약하세요. 저희가 차별화되는 점은 사용자 친화적인 모바일 앱입니다. 그것은 당신이 세탁을 하는 것을 쉬운 일로 만듭니다.

저희의 서비스 이용 방법은 다음과 같습니다:
¹⁵¹앱을 사용하여 저희가 당신의 세탁물을 수거할 시간을 예약하세요. 당신은 또한 사용되어야 할 세제의 종류를 선택하고 당신의 옷이 다리미질 되기를 원하는지 여부를 표시할 수도 있습니다. 저희는 당신이 요청한 시간에 세탁물을 수거하고 나서 24시간 이내에 돌려드릴 것입니다.

¹⁵²신규 고객은 첫 주문에 대해 50퍼센트 전용 할인을 받게 됩니다.

laundry n. 세탁 get ~ down ~을 지치게 하다 go-to adj. 믿을 만한
breeze n. 쉬운 일 detergent n. 세제 iron v. 다리미질 하다
exclusive adj. 전용의, 독점적인

151 Not/True 문제

해석 Washtab에 대해 언급된 것은?
(A) 여러 지점에서 운영한다.
(B) 앱에서 몇몇 상품을 판매한다.
(C) 고객이 온라인으로 서비스를 예약하게 한다.
(D) 대규모 작업은 48시간 사전 통지가 필요하다.

해설 지문의 'Use the app to schedule a time for us to pick up your laundry.'에서 앱을 사용하여 당신의 세탁물을 수거할 시간을 예약하라고 했으므로 (C)가 정답이다. (A), (B), (D)는 지문에 언급되지 않은 내용이다.

어휘 operate v. 운영하다 merchandise n. 상품

Paraphrasing

schedule a time 시간을 예약하다 → arrange a service 서비스를 예약하다
Use the app 앱을 사용하다 → online 온라인으로

152 Not/True 문제

해석 할인에 대해 명시된 것은?
(A) 오로지 신규 고객들을 위한 것이다.
(B) 일주일에 한 번 제공된다.
(C) 최소 주문량이 요구된다.
(D) 이번 달에 사용되어야 한다.

해설 지문의 'New customers receive an exclusive 50 percent discount on their first order.'에서 신규 고객은 첫 주문에 대해 50퍼센트 전용 할인을 받는다고 했으므로 (A)는 지문의 내용과 일치한다. 따라서 (A)가 정답이다. (B), (C), (D)는 지문에 언급되지 않은 내용이다.

Paraphrasing

exclusive 전용의, 독점적인 → only for 오로지 ~를 위한

153-154번은 다음 편지에 관한 문제입니다.

10월 4일

Riccardo Garcia
49번지 Trinity 광장
토론토, 캐나다 M6E 3MS

Mr. Garcia께,

축하합니다! 귀하의 Ventra Capital사 ProVenture 신용카드 신청이 승인되었습니다. 이 편지에 동봉된 카드를 확인하십시오. ProVenture 카드를 모든 법인 구매에 사용하시고 다음 혜택을 누리십시오:

- 153-(A)교통, 숙박, 그리고 출장 관련 비용에 대해 3퍼센트를 현금으로 돌려받으십시오.
- 153-(B)당신의 사업상 필요에 따라 높이거나 낮출 수 있는 유연한 신용 한도를 활용하세요.
- 153-(C)비상시에는 전 세계 어디에서나 연중무휴인 저희의 콜센터에 연락하십시오.
- 엄선된 극장에서 영화표의 30퍼센트를 절약하세요.

154카드를 활성화하시려면 www.ventracapital.co.ca를 방문하시거나 (604) 555-3290으로 저희에게 전화주십시오.

Sandra Cho 드림
Ventra Capital사

application n. 신청 approve v. 승인하다 enclosed adj. 동봉된
corporate adj. 법인의, 기업의 purchase n. 구매 benefit n. 혜택
transportation n. 교통 accommodation n. 숙박
expense n. 비용 raise v. 높이다, 올리다 lower v. 낮추다
select adj. 엄선된 activate v. 활성화하다

153 Not/True 문제

해석 ProVenture 카드의 혜택으로 언급되지 않은 것은?
(A) 출장객들에게 금전상의 보상을 제공한다.
(B) 필요에 따라 변경될 수 있는 신용 한도를 가지고 있다.
(C) 국제적인 고객 지원 서비스를 이용할 수 있다.
(D) 첫 2년간은 수수료가 낮다.

해설 (A)는 'Earn 3 percent cashback on transportation, accommodations, and related travel expenses.'에서 교통, 숙박, 사업 관련 비용에 대해 3퍼센트를 현금으로 돌려준다고 했으므로 지문의 내용과 일치한다. (B)는 'Take advantage of a flexible credit limit that can be raised or lowered to meet your business needs.'에서 신용 한도가 조정될 수 있다고 했다. (C)는 'Reach our 24/7 call centre for emergencies from anywhere in the world.'에서 전 세계 어디에서나 연중무휴인 콜

센터에 연락할 수 있다고 했다. (D)의 수수료 관련 내용은 지문에 언급되지 않았으므로 (D)가 정답이다.

어휘 reward n. 보상 low adj. 낮은

Paraphrasing

flexible 유연한 → can be changed 변경될 수 있는

154 육하원칙 문제

해석 Mr. Garcia는 왜 웹페이지를 방문할 것인가?
(A) 계좌 잔고를 확인하기 위해
(B) 연락처를 업데이트하기 위해
(C) 신용카드를 사용할 수 있게 준비하기 위해
(D) 보안 코드를 받기 위해

해설 지문의 'To activate the card, go to www.ventracapital. co.ca or give us a call at (604) 555-3290.'에서 카드를 활성화하려면 www.ventracapital.co.ca를 방문하거나 전화하라고 했으므로 (C)가 정답이다.

어휘 account n. 계좌 balance n. 잔고 security n. 보안

Paraphrasing

activate 활성화하다 → make ~ ready for use 사용할 수 있게 준비하다

155-157번은 다음 기사에 관한 문제입니다.

시애틀 (2월 3일) — 155북적거리는 Pioneer 광장 인근에 마침내 자체 공공 도서관 지점이 생긴다. Yesler로 75번지에 위치한 그 도서관은 1970년대에 시에 매각되었던 오래된 인쇄소 자리를 차지하고 있다.

원래 건물의 내부와 외부의 많은 부분을 보존하고 있는 그 신규 도서관은 향수를 불러일으키는 매력을 발산한다. 이와 더불어, 그것은 스캐너와 프린터가 있는 컴퓨터실을 포함하여 현대적인 편의 시설을 자랑한다. 주민들에게 책을 빌려주는 것 외에도, 그 도서관은 이력서 작성부터 정원 가꾸기까지 다양한 주제의 강좌를 제공하는 학습 센터로서의 역할도 할 것이다.

건물 개조를 위한 대부분의 자금은 시와 주 정부로부터 왔다. 156그 작업은 또한 기업 기부자들에 의해서도 부분적으로 자금이 조달되었다.

도서관은 1572월 10일에 축하 행사와 함께 지역사회에 문을 열 것이다. 157그 하루 동안의 행사는 다양한 활동을 포함할 것이고 시애틀의 시장인 Gregory Wilkins의 말로 시작할 것이다. 더 많은 정보를 위해서는, www.seattlelibraries.com/pioneer_square를 방문하면 된다.

bustling adj. 북적거리는 neighborhood n. 인근, 근처
occupy v. 차지하다, 점거하다 preserve v. 보존하다
exterior adj. 외부의 radiate v. 발산하다, 내뿜다
nostalgic adj. 향수를 불러일으키는 charm n. 매력
boast v. 자랑하다 amenity n. 편의 시설
serve as ~로서의 역할을 하다 fund n. 자금
partly adv. 부분적으로, 일부 finance v. 자금을 조달하다
donor n. 기부자, 증정자 feature v. 특별히 포함하다

155 목적 찾기 문제

해석 기사의 목적은 무엇인가?

(A) 한 시설의 개장을 발표하기 위해

(B) 도서관 규정의 변경을 설명하기 위해

(C) 공공 기관을 위한 기부를 요청하기 위해

(D) 주목할 만한 건물의 역사를 설명하기 위해

해설 지문의 'The bustling neighborhood of Pioneer Square finally has its very own public library branch.'에서 Pioneer 광장에 마침내 공공 도서관이 생길 것이라고 알리면서 기사를 시작하고 있고 기사 전반에서 도서관의 시설 설명과 자금이 어떻게 조달되었는지 등을 설명하고 마지막에 다시 한번 개장 날짜를 알리고 있으므로 (A)가 정답이다.

어휘 notable adj. 주목할 만한

Paraphrasing

library 도서관 → facility 시설

156 Not/True 문제

해석 개조 프로젝트에 대해 명시된 것은?

(A) 완료하는 데 예상보다 더 오래 걸렸다.

(B) 회사 기부금으로 일부 지원되었다.

(C) 주요 도로를 폐쇄해야 했다.

(D) 지역 사회 주민들에 의해 승인을 받아야 했다.

해설 지문의 'The work[building's renovation] was also partly financed by corporate donors.'에서 그 작업은 또한 기업 기부자들에 의해서도 부분적으로 자금이 조달되었다고 했으므로 (B)는 지문의 내용과 일치한다. 따라서 (B)가 정답이다.

어휘 anticipate v. 예상하다 donation n. 기부금

Paraphrasing

corporate donors 기업 기부자들 → company donations 회사 기부금

157 육하원칙 문제

해석 2월 10일에 무슨 일이 일어날 것인가?

(A) 지역 사회 리더들이 만날 것이다.

(B) 온라인 서비스가 출범될 것이다.

(C) 공무원이 연설을 할 것이다.

(D) 수업 강사들이 선정될 것이다.

해설 지문의 '~ with a celebration on February 10. The day-long event will feature a range of activities and will begin with some words by Seattle mayor Gregory Wilkins.'에서 도서관은 2월 10일에 문을 열 것이며, 그날 행사에서 시애틀의 시장이 몇 마디 말을 할 것이라고 했다. 따라서 (C)가 정답이다.

어휘 select v. 선정하다

Paraphrasing

mayor 시장 → public official 공무원

158-160번은 다음 이메일에 관한 문제입니다.

수신: Min-Ho Park <mhpark@freemail.com>

발신: Lindsay Mueller <lindsay@muellerspa.com>

158/160-(C)날짜: 6월 7일

158제목: 로비 재단장 프로젝트

Mr. Park께,

158어제 사무실에 들러 주셔서 감사합니다. 당신이 제안한 신규 디자인을 보면 당신이 그 일에 가장 적합한 후보라는 확신이 듭니다. 당신의 미니멀리즘 디자인은 저희 브랜드와 완벽하게 어울립니다.

저희는 특히 당신이 제안한 친환경 재료가 좋았습니다. 비용이 더 들 수도 있지만, 그만한 가치가 있을 것이라고 생각합니다. 159나머지 예산에 관해서는, 보내주신 액수를 기꺼이 승인하며, 나중에 예상치 못한 비용이 발생할 경우 추가 자금을 배정할 의향이 있습니다. 진행하시고 최종 계약서를 보내 주십시오.

또한, 당신이 가능한 시작 날짜를 알려주십시오. 2주 안에 작업을 완료할 수 있다고 하신 건 알지만, 그 이상으로 작업을 연장할 수 없다는 점을 강조하고 싶습니다. 160-(C)저희는 다음 달에 저희의 5주년과 동시에 일어날 큰 행사를 계획하고 있습니다.

다시 한번 감사드리며, 제가 놓친 것이 있으면 주저하지 마시고 연락 주십시오.

Lindsay Mueller 드림

Mueller 스파

refurbish v. 재단장하다, 새로 꾸미다 stop by ~에 들르다

propose v. 제안하다 confidence n. 확신, 자신

match v. 어울리다, 일치하다 eco-friendly adj. 친환경적인

material n. 재료 worth adj. ~할 가치가 있는 approve v. 승인하다

figure n. 액수, 가격 allocate v. 할당하다

unforeseen adj. 예상치 못한 identify v. 확인하다

agreement n. 계약서, 계약

coincide with ~과 동시에 일어나다, ~과 일치하다

hesitate v. 주저하다, 망설이다

158 육하원칙 문제

해석 Mr. Park은 6월 6일에 무엇을 했는가?

(A) 새로운 스파 시설을 방문했다.

(B) 리모델링 계획을 제시했다.

(C) 실내 장식가와 만났다.

(D) 건물 청사진을 마무리 지었다.

해설 지문의 'Date: June 7'을 통해 이메일을 쓴 날짜가 6월 7일임을 알 수 있고, 제목의 'Subject: Lobby Refurbishing Project'와 첫 번째 문장인 'Thank you for stopping by the office yesterday. Seeing your proposed redesign'을 통해 Mr. Park이 6월 6일에 사무실에 들러 로비 재단장 프로젝트에 대한 신규 디자인을 제안한 것을 알 수 있으므로 (B)가 정답이다.

어휘 present v. 제시하다 blueprint n. 청사진, 계획

Paraphrasing

refurbishing 재단장 → remodeling 리모델링

159 Not/True 문제

해석 Ms. Mueller가 예산에 대해 언급하는 것은?
(A) 신입사원 채용 비용을 포함한다.
(B) 다른 프로젝트의 예산과 일치한다.
(C) 관리자의 승인을 받지 못했다.
(D) Mr. Park의 요청에 따라 조정될 수 있다.

해설 지문의 'As for the rest of the budget, I'm happy to approve the figure you sent, and I'm willing to allocate additional funds for any unforeseen costs that you may later identify.'에서 나머지 예산에 관해서는 Mr. Park이 보낸 액수를 기꺼이 승인하며, 나중에 예상치 못한 비용이 발생할 경우 추가 자금을 배정할 의향이 있다고 했으므로 (D)가 정답이다.

어휘 adjust v. 조정하다

160 Not/True 문제

해석 Mueller 스파에 대해 사실인 것은?
(A) 2주 후에 계절 할인을 제공할 것이다.
(B) 새로운 지점을 개점하는 것을 준비하고 있다.
(C) 7월에 기념행사를 열 것이다.
(D) 회사 로고의 모양을 바꿀 것이다.

해설 지문의 'We're planning a big event to coincide with our fifth anniversary next month.'에서 다음 달에 스파의 5주년과 동시에 일어날 큰 행사를 계획하고 있다고 했는데 이메일을 쓴 시점이 6월이므로 다음 달인 7월에 행사가 열릴 것임을 알 수 있다. 따라서 (C)가 정답이다.

어휘 branch n. 지점 celebration n. 기념행사

Paraphrasing

> a big event to coincide with our fifth anniversary 5주년과 동시에 일어날 큰 행사 → celebration 기념행사

161-164번은 다음 설명에 관한 문제입니다.

[161]당신이 공석에 이력서를 제출할 때마다 자기소개서가 포함되어야 합니다. 효과적인 자기소개서를 작성하려면, 염두에 두어야 할 몇 가지 사항이 있습니다. 기본적인 요소와 관련하여, 가장 중요한 것 중 하나는 [162-(A)]자기소개서가 한 페이지보다 길지 않아야 한다는 것입니다. — [1] —. 당신은 또한 [162-(B)]그것이 특정인에게 보내져야 한다는 점을 확실히 해야 합니다—이상적으로 이는 채용을 담당하는 담당자입니다. "관계자분께" 또는 "담당자분께"와 같은 포괄적인 인사말에 의존하지 마십시오. 마지막이지만 여전히 중요한 것으로, [162-(D)]그것을 주의 깊게 교정보십시오. 철자와 구두점 실수는 당신을 전문가답지 않아 보이게 만들 것입니다.

내용 면에서, 첫 번째 단락은 당신이 해당 직책에 대해 어떻게 듣게 되었으며, 왜 그것에 관심이 있는지를 설명해야 합니다. — [2] —. [164]두 번째 단락은 당신이 가진 하드 스킬에 대해 개요를 서술하고 여러분을 이상적인 지원자로 만드는 업무 경험, 자격 등을 언급해야 합니다. — [3] —. 세 번째 단락에서는, 당신의 소프트 스킬에 대해 이야기하세요. 예를 들어, 당신이 팀의 구성원으로서 일을 잘하는 유능한 커뮤니케이터라면, 여기서 그것을 언급해야 합니다. [163]마지막 ○

단락은 후속 질문을 하거나 면접을 잡기 위해 당신이 언제 시간이 가능한지와 당신에게 연락할 수 있는 가장 좋은 방법을 간단히 명시해야 합니다. — [4] —.

submit v. 제출하다 open position 공석 element n. 요소
direct v. ~로 보내다, 향하다 ideally adv. 이상적으로
in charge of ~을 담당하는 generic adj. 포괄적인, 총칭의
greeting n. 인사말, 인사 proofread v. 교정보다
punctuation n. 구두점 unprofessional adj. 전문가답지 않은
outline v. 개요를 서술하다 hard skill 하드 스킬(직무 기술)
make reference to ~을 언급하다, 참조하다 qualification n. 자격
soft skill 소프트 스킬(대인관계 기술) effective adj. 유능한

161 추론 문제

해석 설명은 누구를 대상으로 하는 것 같은가?
(A) 기업 임원
(B) 사업주
(C) 대학 지원자
(D) 구직자

해설 지문의 'A cover letter should be included whenever you submit your résumé for an open position.'에서 당신이 공석에 이력서를 제출할 때마다 자기소개서가 포함되어야 한다고 했으므로 구직자를 대상으로 한다는 것을 추론할 수 있다. 따라서 (D)가 정답이다.

어휘 executive n. 임원 applicant n. 지원자

162 Not/True 문제

해석 효과적인 자기소개서를 쓰는 것의 기본 요소로 언급되지 않은 것은?
(A) 길이를 한 페이지로 유지하는 것
(B) 특정한 사람에게 보내는 것
(C) 흥미로운 인사말을 포함하는 것
(D) 어떠한 오류라도 확인하는 것

해설 (A)는 'the letter be no longer than a single page'에서 자기소개서가 한 페이지보다 길지 않아야 한다고 했으므로 지문의 내용과 일치한다. (B)는 'it is directed to a particular person'에서 특정인에게 보내져야 한다고 했으므로 지문의 내용과 일치한다. (C)는 지문에 언급되지 않은 내용이다. 따라서 (C)가 정답이다. (D)는 '~ proofread it[cover letter] carefully. Spelling and punctuation mistakes will make you look unprofessional.'에서 자기소개서를 주의 깊게 교정보라고 하면서, 철자와 구두점 실수는 전문가답지 않아 보이게 만들 것이라고 했으므로 지문의 내용과 일치한다.

어휘 length n. 길이

Paraphrasing

> be no longer than a single page 한 페이지보다 길지 않아야 한다
> → keeping the length to one page 길이를 한 페이지로 유지하는 것
> direct 보내다 → address 보내다
> particular 특정한 → specific 특정한

163 육하원칙 문제

해석 자기소개서의 마지막 부분에 무엇이 포함되어야 하는가?
(A) 교육적 성과
(B) 개인적인 관심사
(C) 관리 경험
(D) 연락처

해설 지문의 'The final paragraph should briefly state your availability and how best to reach you with any follow-up questions or to arrange an interview.'에서 마지막 단락은 후속 질문을 하거나 면접을 잡기 위해 당신이 언제 시간이 가능한지와 당신에게 연락할 수 있는 가장 좋은 방법을 간단히 명시해야 한다고 했으므로 (D)가 정답이다.

어휘 achievement n. 성취, 달성 interest n. 관심사, 취미

Paraphrasing

how best to reach you 당신에게 연락할 수 있는 가장 좋은 방법
→ contact information 연락처

164 문장 위치 찾기 문제

해석 [1], [2], [3], [4]로 표시된 위치 중, 다음 문장이 들어갈 곳으로 가장 적절한 것은?

"당신이 받은 모든 관련된 자격증을 반드시 명시하십시오."

(A) [1]
(B) [2]
(C) [3]
(D) [4]

해설 주어진 문장은 자격증과 관련된 내용이 나오는 부분에 들어가야 함을 알 수 있다. [3]의 앞 문장인 'The second should outline your hard skills and make reference to your work experience, qualifications, and so on that make you the ideal candidate.'에서 두 번째 단락은 당신이 가진 하드 스킬에 대해 개요를 서술하고 업무 경험, 자격 등을 언급해야 한다고 했으므로, [3]에 주어진 문장이 들어가면 자신의 능력을 보여주기 위해 보유한 자격증을 명시하라는 자연스러운 문맥이 된다는 것을 알 수 있다. 따라서 (C)가 정답이다.

어휘 specify v. 명시하다 certificate n. 자격증, 증명서
earn v. 받다, 얻다 relevant adj. 관련된

165-167번은 다음 웹페이지의 정보에 관한 문제입니다.

홈	**투어**	후기	연락처

알프스 도보 여행

유럽의 장엄한 알프스산맥을 경험하는 유일한 방법은 그곳을 걷는 것입니다. ― [1] ―. 165-(B)저희의 가이드가 안내하는 도보 여행에서는, 여러분을 프랑스와 스위스를 거치는 여행으로 데려갈 것입니다. 165-(C)그 여행은 일주일 동안 지속될 것입니다. 165-(D)도보, 버스와 철도 여행, 그리고 제네바, 메제브, 그리고 샤모니에서의 1박을 포함할 것입니다. ― [2] ―. 166그 여행은 저희의 경험 많은 가이드인 Raymond Mayuer가 이끌 것입니다. 여러분 중 몇 분은 그의 네팔 안나푸르나 산의 험난한 정복기를 다루었던 다큐멘터리 영화 Hiking the

*Heavens*를 통해 그를 알고 있을지도 모릅니다. Mr. Mayuer는 많은 유명한 산길로 여러분을 데리고 갈 것이고, 경치를 감탄하며 바라보기 위해 자주 멈출 것입니다.

167과격한 것은 아무것도 요구되지 않을 것이지만, 이 여행은 여행자들에게 체력을 적당히 관리하는 것을 요구할 것입니다. ― [3] ―. 그렇긴 하지만, 참가자들은 그들이 여행을 마칠 수 있다는 것을 보여주는 진단서를 기꺼이 제공하도록 요구됩니다.

참가는 10명으로 제한되어 있고, 저희의 투어는 몇 달 전부터 매진되니, 서둘러 주세요. ― [4] ―. 여기에서 신청하실 수 있습니다.

majestic adj. 장엄한, 위풍당당한 journey n. 여행
overnight stay 1박 grueling adj. 대단히 힘든 conquest n. 정복
admire v. 감탄하며 바라보다 scenery n. 경치
moderately adv. 적당히 extreme adj. 과격한
demand v. 요구하다 participant n. 참가자
kindly adv. 기꺼이, 친절하게 medical certificate 진단서
indicate v. 보여주다 be capable of ~할 수 있는 sell out 매진되다

165 Not/True 문제

해석 알프스 도보 여행에 대해 사실인 것은?
(A) 여름 동안 진행될 것이다.
(B) 하나 이상의 나라를 지나갈 것이다.
(C) 10일 이상 지속될 것이다.
(D) 전적으로 도보로 이루어질 것이다.

해설 지문의 'On our guided walking tour, we'll take you on a journey through France and Switzerland.'에서 프랑스와 스위스를 거치는 여행이라고 했으므로 (B)는 지문의 내용과 일치한다. 따라서 (B)가 정답이다. (C)는 'The trip will last one week.'에서 여행이 일주일 동안 지속될 것이라고 했으므로 지문의 내용과 일치하지 않는다. (D)는 'It will include hikes, bus and rail journeys'에서 도보, 버스와 철도 여행을 포함할 것이라고 했으므로 지문의 내용과 일치하지 않는다. (A)는 지문에 언급되지 않은 내용이다.

어휘 entirely adv. 전적으로, 완전히 on foot 도보로, 걸어서

166 추론 문제

해석 Mr. Mayuer에 대해 암시되는 것은?
(A) 최근 Hike Europe에 고용되었다.
(B) 1년에 여러 투어를 이끈다.
(C) 알프스 도보 여행에 관한 안내서를 저술했다.
(D) 예전에 영화에 출연했었다.

해설 지문의 'Leading the trip will be our experienced guide, Raymond Mayuer. Some of you may know him from the documentary film, *Hiking the Heavens*, which featured his grueling conquest of Mount Annapurna in Nepal.'에서 그의 안나푸르나 산의 험난한 정복기를 다룬 다큐멘터리 영화 *Hiking the Heavens*를 통해 가이드인 Raymond Mayuer를 알고 있을지도 모른다고 했으므로 Mr. Mayuer가 영화에 출연한 적이 있다는 것을 추론할 수 있다. 따라서 (D)가 정답이다.

어휘 multiple adj. 여럿의, 다양한 author v. 저술하다, 쓰다
appear v. 출연하다, 나타나다

해석 [1], [2], [3], [4]로 표시된 위치 중, 다음 문장이 들어갈 곳으로 가장 적절한 것은?

"저희는 모든 체력 수준을 수용하기 위해 일일 트레킹의 난이도를 의도적으로 제한합니다."

(A) [1]

(B) [2]

(C) [3]

(D) [4]

해설 주어진 문장은 여행에 요구되는 체력 수준과 관련된 내용이 나오는 부분에 들어가야 함을 알 수 있다. [3]의 앞 문장인 'The trip will require that travelers be moderately in shape, although nothing extreme will be demanded.'에서 과격한 것이 요구되지 않을 것이지만, 여행자들에게 체력을 적당히 관리하는 것을 요구할 것이라고 했으므로, [3]에 주어진 문장이 들어가면 체력을 적당히 관리하는 것을 요구할 것이고, 모든 체력 수준을 수용하기 위해 일일 트레킹의 난이도를 의도적으로 조절할 것이라는 자연스러운 문맥이 된다는 것을 알 수 있다. 따라서 (C)가 정답이다.

어휘 deliberately adj. 의도적으로   trek n. 트레킹
accommodate v. 수용하다

168-171번은 다음 기사에 관한 문제입니다.

Bedstay가 새로운 서비스를 도입한다

밴쿠버 (5월 10일)—Bedstay는 여러분이 개인 주택에 머물게 해 줄 뿐만 아니라, 현지인처럼 생활하게 해줄 것이다. 훨씬 더 많은 고객들을 인기 있는 온라인 임대 플랫폼으로 유인하기를 바라며, Bedstay는 최근 Bedstay Encounters라는 새로운 서비스의 출시를 발표했다. **168그 서비스는 사용자들을 도시의 시장을 걷는 음식 투어나 개인 해변에서의 요가 수업과 같이 다양한 관심사를 만족시키는 가이드가 딸린 활동을 제공하는 현지 호스트들과 연결한다.** "가능성은 무한합니다," 라고 Bedstay의 대변인 Jerry Izumi가 말하면서 일부 "만남"은 심지어 다양한 그룹의 크기와 특별한 요구 사항들을 수용하도록 사용자의 요구에 맞춰질 수도 있다고 덧붙였다.

169전반적으로, 그 서비스는 사용자들이 여행하고 지역 사회와 연결될 수 있는 새로운 방법을 제공하는 동시에 호스트들이 추가 수입을 확보할 수 있게 한다. 170-(C)그러나, 현재 Bedstay Encounters는 북미와 유럽 전역의 8개국에서만 제공되고 있다.

그럼에도 불구하고, 회사는 잠재적인 호스트들로부터 매일 수천 개의 문의를 받는다고 언급하면서, 자사가 운영하는 모든 120개국에 서비스를 점진적으로 확장할 것이라고 장담했다. **171최근에 기록적인 분기별 수익을 보고했던** Bedstay는 15년 전 설립된 이래로 공유 숙박 시장을 장악할 정도로 성장했다.

private adj. 개인의   entice v. 유인하다, 유혹하다   encounter n. 만남
cater v. (요구를) 만족시키다, 음식을 공급하다   marketplace n. 시장
endless adj. 무한한   spokesperson n. 대변인
additional adj. 추가의, 부가의   income n. 수입, 소득
assurance n. 장담, 확언   note v. 언급하다   potential adj. 잠재적인
record adj. 기록적인; n. 기록   quarterly adj. 분기별의
dominate v. 장악하다, 지배하다   vacation rental 공유 숙박

해석 기사에 따르면, Bedstay Encounters의 사용자들은 무엇을 할 수 있는가?

(A) 비용을 들이지 않고 임대 기간을 연장한다.

(B) 주민들과 함께하는 활동에 참여한다.

(C) 인기 있는 명소의 이용권을 얻는다.

(D) 온라인 거래에 대해 독점 할인 혜택을 즐긴다.

해설 지문의 'The service connects users with local hosts offering guided activities that cater to a range of interests, such as walking food tours of a city's marketplaces or yoga classes on a private beach.'에서 그 서비스는 사용자들을 도시의 시장을 걷는 음식 투어나 개인 해변에서의 요가 수업과 같이 다양한 관심사를 만족시키는 가이드가 딸린 활동을 제공하는 현지 호스트들과 연결한다고 했으므로 (B)가 정답이다.

어휘 extend v. 연장하다, 늘리다   take part in ~에 참여하다
attraction n. 명소   transaction n. 거래

Paraphrasing

local hosts 현지 호스트들 → residents 주민들

해석 3문단 두 번째 줄의 단어 "secure"는 의미상 -와 가장 가깝다.

(A) 보호하다

(B) 얻다

(C) 강화하다

(D) 고려하다

해설 secure를 포함한 구절 'Overall, the service offers users a new way to travel and connect with local communities while also allowing hosts to secure additional income.'에서 secure는 '확보하다'라는 뜻으로 사용되었다. 따라서 (B)가 정답이다.

해석 Bedstay Encounters에 대해 언급된 것은?

(A) 행사를 위한 출장 요리 서비스를 제공한다.

(B) 소셜 미디어에 많은 팔로워들을 보유하고 있다.

(C) 현재 아시아에서는 제공되지 않는다.

(D) 원래 Mr. Izumi가 생각해 낸 것이다.

해설 지문의 'Currently, however, Bedstay Encounters is only being offered in eight countries across North America and Europe.'에서 현재 Bedstay Encounters는 북미와 유럽 전역의 8개국에서만 제공되고 있다고 했으므로 (C)는 지문의 내용과 일치한다. 따라서 (C)가 정답이다. (A), (B), (D)는 지문에 언급되지 않은 내용이다.

어휘 originally adv. 원래   conceive v. 생각해 내다

해석 Bedstay의 최근 성과는 무엇인가?

(A) 추가 지점들을 열었다.

(B) 여행사와 합병했다.

(C) 증가한 수익을 발생시켰다.

(D) 업계에서 상을 받았다.

해설   지문의 'Bedstay, which recently reported record quarterly revenues'에서 Bedstay가 최근에 기록적인 분기별 수익을 보고했다고 했으므로 (C)가 정답이다.

어휘   merge v. 합병하다, 합치다   generate v. 발생시키다
      earnings n. 수익, 이익

Paraphrasing

> revenue 수익 → earnings 수익

172-175번은 다음 온라인 채팅 대화문에 관한 문제입니다.

> **Tom Mercer (오후 3시 22분)**
> 172여러분, 저는 내일 Proto ML55 세단의 새로운 모델이 나온다는 것을 모두에게 상기시키고 싶었어요. 우리는 부지 앞쪽에 여러 대를 전시해 놓을 거예요.
>
> **Gina Young (오후 3시 24분)**
> 네, 광고 봤어요. 첫 번째 모델이 인기 있었고, 새 모델도 잘 팔릴 것으로 기대해요.
>
> **Tom Mercer (오후 3시 24분)**
> 이전 모델보다 많은 장점이 있어요. 갤런당 약 30마일을 주행할 수 있어 연료 효율이 매우 높아요. 173-(D)그리고 음성으로 제어되는 GPS 내비게이션 시스템이 딸려 있어요. 이것들은 상품의 주요 강조점이 될 거예요.
>
> **Frank Chen (오후 3시 25분)**
> 맞아요. 그리고 자동 브레이크나 사각지대 모니터링 같은 고급 안전 기능도 고객들의 관심을 끌 것으로 보입니다. 이 혜택들을 나열한 팻말을 세우는 것에 대해 어떻게 생각하세요?
>
> **Tom Mercer (오후 3시 26분)**
> 동의해요. 저희가 제공하는 무료 추가 자동차 보험도 언급해야 합니다. 172그것이 우리를 다른 대리점들과 구별 짓는 것이에요.
>
> **Gina Young (오후 3시 27분)**
> 174Tom, 새 차들을 설치하기 위해 저희가 일찍 출근하길 원하시나요?
>
> **Tom Mercer (오후 3시 28분)**
> 아니요. 174Greg가 내일 아침에 그것을 할 거예요. 175하지만 누군가가 우리의 소셜 미디어 페이지에 차에 대한 공지를 게시해 주시면 좋을 거예요.
>
> **Gina Young (오후 3시 29분)**
> 제가 전에 그 페이지에 포스팅을 해 본 적이 있어요. 175두어 시간만 주시면, 제가 무언가를 준비할게요.

advantage n. 장점 predecessor n. 이전 모델, 전임자
fuel efficient 연료 효율이 높은, 저연비의
selling point (판매 때의) 상품의 강조점 advanced adj. 고급의
automatic adj. 자동의 appeal v. 관심을 끌다
supplementary adj. 추가의 insurance n. 보험
distinguish v. 구별 짓다 dealership n. 대리점

---

172 추론 문제

해설   작성자들은 어디에서 일하는 것 같은가?

    (A) 자동차 대리점에서

    (B) 보험 회사에서

    (C) 마케팅 회사에서

    (D) 자동차 제조 회사에서

해설   지문의 'Hey, I wanted to remind everyone that the new model of the Proto ML55 sedan comes out tomorrow. We'll have several displayed in the front of the lot.'에서 내일 Proto ML55 세단의 새로운 모델이 나온다는 것을 상기시키면서 부지 앞쪽에 여러 대를 전시할 것이라고 했고 'That's something that distinguishes us from other dealerships.'에서 우리를 다른 대리점들과 구별 짓는 것이라고 했으므로 메시지 작성자들이 자동차 대리점에서 일한다는 것을 추론할 수 있다. 따라서 (A)가 정답이다.

어휘   manufacturer n. 제조 회사

---

173 Not/True 문제

해설   Proto ML55 세단에 대해 명시된 것은?

    (A) 여러 가지 안전 문제가 있는 것으로 밝혀졌다.

    (B) 해외에서 제조되고 있다.

    (C) 세 가지 다른 모델이 있다.

    (D) 음성으로 활성화되는 안내 시스템이 있다.

해설   지문의 'And it comes with a voice-controlled GPS navigation system.'에서 Mr. Mercer가 음성으로 제어할 수 있는 GPS 내비게이션 시스템이 딸려 있다고 했으므로 (D)는 지문의 내용과 일치한다. 따라서 (D)가 정답이다.

어휘   overseas adv. 해외에서 guidance n. 안내

Paraphrasing

> a voice-controlled GPS navigation system 음성으로 제어되는 GPS 내비게이션 시스템 → a voice-activated guidance system 음성으로 활성화되는 안내 시스템

---

174 육하원칙 문제

해설   Mr. Mercer에 따르면, Greg는 내일 무엇을 할 것인가?

    (A) 다른 직원들에게 발표를 할 것이다.

    (B) 고객들의 사용을 위해서 몇몇 차량을 주유할 것이다.

    (C) 벽에 몇 개의 포스터를 붙일 것이다.

    (D) 사업장에 몇 대의 차량을 배치할 것이다.

해설   지문의 'Do you want us to come in early to set up the new cars?'에서 Ms. Young이 새 차들을 설치하기 위해 자신들이 일찍 출근하길 원하는지 묻자, Mr. Mercer가 'Greg will be doing that tomorrow morning.'에서 Greg가 내일 아침에 그것을 할 거라고 했으므로 (D)가 정답이다.

어휘   fuel v. 주유하다, 연료를 공급하다 arrange v. 배치하다, 준비하다

Paraphrasing

> set up the new cars 새 차들을 설치하다 → arrange some vehicles 몇 대의 차량을 배치하다

175 의도 파악 문제

해석 오후 3시 29분에, Ms. Young이 "I've posted on that page before"라고 썼을 때, 그녀가 의도한 것 같은 것은?
(A) 주제에 대해 더 자세히 알고 싶어 한다.
(B) 작업을 수행할 의향이 있다.
(C) 결정이 잘못 판단된 것이라고 생각한다.
(D) 그녀의 계획을 변경해야 한다.

해설 지문의 'But it would be great if someone could post an announcement on our social media page about the cars.'에서 Mr. Mercer가 누군가가 소셜 미디어 페이지에 차에 대한 공지를 게시해 주면 좋을 거라고 하자, Ms. Young이 'I've posted on that page before'(제가 전에 그 페이지에 포스팅을 해 본 적이 있어요)라고 한 후, 'Give me a couple of hours, and I'll have something ready.'에서 두어 시간만 주면 자신이 무언가를 준비하겠다고 한 것을 통해, Ms. Young이 소셜 미디어 페이지에 공지를 올리는 업무를 수행할 의향이 있음을 알 수 있다. 따라서 (B)가 정답이다.

어휘 perform v. 수행하다 decision n. 결정
misguide v. 잘못 판단하다

176-180번은 다음 광고와 기사에 관한 문제입니다.

> ### 로체스터 코미디 축제
>
> 2월 20일과 21일에 열리는 로체스터 코미디 축제에서 웃음을 경험하세요! Davies 컨벤션 센터에서 전국의 재능 있는 코미디언들에 의한 이틀간의 코미디에 참여해 보세요. Jimmy Caryn, Crystal Miller, Ed Xion 등과 같은 유명한 스타들이 출연하는 176-(B)**4개의 무대에서 펼쳐지는 재미있는 공연을 만나보세요!** 이틀 모두 입장할 수 있는 티켓은 단 50파운드입니다.
>
> 177-(B)**축제는 20년 동안 나라에서 가장 많이 시청된 엔터테인먼트 채널인 Variety 채널에 의해 여러분께 제공됩니다.** 179Kelly Asher에 의해 진행되는 177-(B)**그 채널의 인기 리얼리티 쇼인 Funny Talk의 라이브 촬영에 참여할 수 있는 기회를 놓치지 마세요!** 여러분은 심지어 TV에서 여러분의 모습을 볼 수 있습니다.
>
> 일정 세부 사항들과 티켓 구매를 위해서는 www.rochestercomedyfest.co.uk를 방문하세요. 로체스터 코미디 축제에서 주말 동안 웃음꽃을 피울 준비를 하세요!
>
> laughter n. 웃음 talented adj. 재능 있는
> hilarious adj. 재미있는, 아주 우스운 renowned adj. 유명한
> host v. 진행하다

> ### 로체스터 코미디 축제: 웃음 가득한 승리!
>
> 로체스터 (2월 23일) - 2월 20일과 21일에 열린 로체스터 코미디 축제는 178그 어느 때보다 많은 참석자들을 끌어모으며 뛰어난 성공을 거두었다. Variety 채널의 후원을 받은 이 웃음 가득한 행사는 기대를 넘어섰다. 지역 대학생인 Victor Romero는 "그 축제는 놀라웠고, 많은 코미디언들을 보았습니다. 179저는 또한 뒤풀이 파티에 참석하게 되었고, 거기서 Funny Talk의 진행자를 만났습니다."라고 말했다.
>
> 라이브 이벤트를 놓친 사람들은 1802월 28일 일요일 오후 8시에 Variety 채널에서 하이라이트를 시청하거나 www.varietychannel.◑

com/rochestercomedyfest에서 같은 장면을 스트리밍하면 된다. 로체스터 코미디 축제의 성공은 모든 사람들이 내년 행사를 간절히 고대하게 만들었다.

triumph n. 승리 outstanding adj. 뛰어난, 두드러진
attendee n. 참석자 exceed v. 넘어서다, 초과하다
expectation n. 기대, 예상
highlight n. 하이라이트(가장 흥미 있는 부분) footage n. 장면, 화면
eagerly adv. 간절히 anticipate v. 고대하다, 예상하다

---

176 Not/True 문제

해석 Davies 컨벤션 센터에 대해 언급된 것은?
(A) 지역의 가장 큰 축제들을 모두 개최한다.
(B) 여러 공연 구역들이 있다.
(C) 매표소에서 티켓을 독점적으로 판매한다.
(D) 1년 중 일부 동안만 운영된다.

해설 광고의 'Catch hilarious performances on four stages'에서 4개의 무대에서 펼쳐지는 재미있는 공연을 만나보라고 했으므로 (B)는 지문의 내용과 일치한다. 따라서 (B)가 정답이다. (A), (C), (D)는 지문에 언급되지 않은 내용이다.

어휘 region n. 지역 exclusively adv. 독점적으로
operational adj. 운영상의, 사용할 수 있는

Paraphrasing

> four stages 4개의 무대 → multiple performance areas 여러 공연 구역들

---

177 Not/True 문제

해석 Variety 채널에 대해 언급된 것은?
(A) 주로 뉴스 방송으로 알려져 있다.
(B) 라이브 시청자와 함께하는 쇼를 제작한다.
(C) 최근에 상을 받았다.
(D) TV로 방영되는 새로운 코미디 시리즈를 출시할 준비를 하고 있다.

해설 광고의 'The festival is brought to you by the Variety Channel'에서 축제가 Variety 채널에 의해 제공된다고 한 후, 'Don't miss the chance to be part of the live filming of Funny Talk, the channel's hit reality show ~'에서 그 채널의 인기 리얼리티 쇼인 Funny Talk의 라이브 촬영에 참여할 수 있는 기회를 놓치지 말라고 했으므로 Variety 채널이 라이브 시청자와 함께하는 쇼를 제작한다는 것을 알 수 있다. 따라서 (B)가 정답이다. (A), (C), (D)는 지문에 언급되지 않은 내용이다.

어휘 broadcast n. 방송 televised adj. TV로 방영되는

---

178 동의어 찾기 문제

해석 기사에서, 1문단 세 번째 줄의 단어 "drawing"은 의미상 -와 가장 가깝다.
(A) 끌어들이는
(B) 통제하는
(C) 고안하는
(D) 임명하는

해설 drawing을 포함한 구절 '~ an outstanding success, drawing more attendees than ever before'에서 drawing은 '끌어모으는'이라는 뜻으로 사용되었다. 따라서 (A)가 정답이다.

어휘 appoint v. 임명하다

179 추론 문제 연계

해석 Mr. Romero는 뒤풀이 파티에서 누구와 만났을 것 같은가?
(A) Jimmy Caryn
(B) Crystal Miller
(C) Ed Xion
(D) Kelly Asher

해설 질문의 핵심 어구인 Mr. Romero가 언급된 기사를 먼저 확인한다.
단서 1 기사의 'I[Mr. Romero] also got to attend an after-party, where I met the host of *Funny Talk*'에서 Mr. Romero가 뒤풀이 파티에 참석하게 되었고, 거기서 *Funny Talk*의 진행자를 만났다고 했다. 그런데 *Funny Talk*의 진행자가 누구인지에 대해 제시되지 않았으므로 광고에서 관련 내용을 확인한다.
단서 2 광고의 '*Funny Talk*, the channel's hit reality show hosted by Kelly Asher'에서 *Funny Talk*가 Kelly Asher에 의해 진행되는 리얼리티 쇼임을 확인한다.
두 단서를 종합할 때, Mr. Romero는 뒤풀이 파티에서 *Funny Talk*의 진행자인 Kelly Asher와 만났음을 알 수 있다. 따라서 (D)가 정답이다.

180 추론 문제

해석 기사가 로체스터 코미디 축제에 대해 암시하는 것은?
(A) 새로운 코미디언 라인업을 발표할 것이다.
(B) 올해 말에 두 번째로 열릴 것이다.
(C) 텔레비전에서는 전부 보여주지 않을 것이다.
(D) 결제를 하면 온라인으로 볼 수 있다.

해설 기사의 'catch the highlights on Sunday, 28 February, at 8 P.M. on the Variety Channel'에서 2월 28일 일요일 오후 8시에 Variety 채널에서 하이라이트를 시청하라고 했으므로 Rochester 코미디 축제가 텔레비전에서는 전부를 보여주지 않을 것임을 추론할 수 있다. 따라서 (C)가 정답이다.

어휘 in full 전부

181-185번은 다음 계약서와 이메일에 관한 문제입니다.

서비스 계약 협약

181이 계약은 Olga Stein(고객)과 John Garrison(Acorn 디자인사의 소유주) 간의 협약을 나타낸다. 각 당사자는 조건들을 수락하며, 양쪽이 동의하지 않는 한 이 조건들은 변경될 수 없다.

프로젝트 장소: 3515번지 갤러틴 파이크, 내슈빌, 테네시주 37216
시작일: 9월 18일/185종료일: 9월 25일
182-(B)고객 연락처: 555-2010
181간략한 프로젝트 설명: 앞마당 덤불 제거 후 꽃밭으로 교체, 진입로에서 정문까지 돌길 추가, 그리고 나뭇가지 다듬기

총비용: 5,400달러
182-(C)지불된 보증금: 1,350달러 (지불일: 9월 5일)

남은 금액: 4,050달러

Acorn 디자인사는 기상악화와 교통사고를 포함한 통제 불능의 문제로 인한 지연에 대해서는 책임을 지지 않는다. 182-(A)고객은 완료일로부터 2주 이내(10월 9일까지)에 나머지 비용을 지불하는 데 동의한다.

소유주 서명: _____
고객 서명: _____

---

agreement n. 협약, 계약 **represent** v. 나타내다, 대표하다
term n. 조건, 용어 **bush** n. 덤불 **driveway** n. 진입로
branch n. 나뭇가지 **trim** v. 다듬다 **deposit** n. 보증금, 착수금
remainder n. 나머지 **be held responsible for** ~에 책임을 지다
inclement adj. 좋지 못한, 궂은 **completion** n. 완료

수신: John Garrison <john@acorndesign.com>
발신: Olga Stein <o.stein444@newmail.com>
제목: 계약서
날짜: 9월 12일

Mr. Garrison께,

계약서를 보내 주셔서 감사합니다. 183그러나, 명시된 주소가 정확하지 않은 것을 알아차렸습니다. 저의 집 번지는 3515가 아니라 3511입니다. 계약서를 수정하여 저에게 다시 보내주실 수 있나요? 이것이 프로젝트 시작을 지연시키지 않게 해주세요. 제가 곧 앞마당의 외관을 개선하는 것이 중요합니다. 184제 부동산 중개인은 이러한 변경 사항이 장래의 구매자들에게 부동산을 더 매력적으로 만들 것이라고 말했습니다. 수정된 계약서를 받으면, 제가 서명하여 다시 보내 드리겠습니다. 185저희 집에서 예정된 작업의 마지막 날에 남은 잔액을 수표로 드릴 계획입니다.

Olga Stein 드림

---

house number 집 번지 **revise** v. 수정하다, 변경하다
appearance n. 외관, 겉모습 **real estate agent** 부동산 중개인
property n. 부동산, 소유지 **prospective** adj. 장래의, 미래의
check n. 수표

---

181 추론 문제

해석 Mr. Garrison은 어떤 사업에 있을 것 같은가?
(A) 철물
(B) 조경
(C) 인테리어 디자인
(D) 은행

해설 계약서의 'This contract represents an agreement between Olga Stein(client) and John Garrison(owner of Acorn Design).'에서 Mr. Garrison이 디자인사의 소유주임을 알 수 있고, 'Brief project description: Bushes in the front yard to be removed and replaced by a flower garden, a stone walkway to be added from the driveway to the front door, and tree branches to be trimmed'에서 프로젝트가 앞마당 덤불 제거 후 꽃밭으로 교체, 진입로에서 정문까지 돌길 추가, 그리고 나뭇가지를 다듬는 것이라고 했으므로 Mr. Garrison이 조경 사업에 종사하고 있을 것임을 추론할 수 있다. 따라서 (B)가 정답이다.

어휘 hardware n. 철물, 장비 landscaping n. 조경

182 Not/True 문제

해석 계약서에 명시되지 않은 것은?
(A) 미결제액 지급일
(B) 고객의 전화번호
(C) 보증금 날짜
(D) 연체에 대한 위약금

해설 (A)는 계약서의 'The client agrees to pay the remainder of the cost within two weeks (by October 9) of the completion date.'에서 고객은 완료일로부터 2주 이내(10월 9일까지)에 나머지 비용을 지불하는 데 동의한다고 했으므로 지문에 명시되어 있다. (B)는 'Client's contact number: 555-2010'에서 연락처가 제시되어 있으므로 지문에 명시되어 있다. (C)는 'Deposit Paid: $1,350 (Date of Payment: September 5)'에서 지불된 보증금이 1,350 달러이고 9월 5일에 지불되었다고 했으므로 지문에 명시되어 있다. (D)는 지문에 언급되지 않은 내용이다. 따라서 (D)가 정답이다.

어휘 due date 지급일, 만기일 outstanding balance 미결제액
penalty n. 위약금, 벌금

Paraphrasing

remainder of the cost 나머지 비용 → outstanding balance 미결제액

contact number 연락처 → phone number 전화번호

183 목적 찾기 문제

해석 이메일의 목적은 무엇인가?
(A) 문서에 수정을 요청하기 위해
(B) 가격 인하를 제안하기 위해
(C) 지불을 받았음을 확인하기 위해
(D) 일정 변경에 대한 통지를 하기 위해

해설 이메일의 'However, I noticed that the address stated is not correct. My house number is 3511, not 3515. Could the contract be revised and sent back to me?'에서 계약서에 명시된 주소가 정확하지 않은 것을 확인했고 집 번지가 3515가 아니라 3511이라고 하면서 계약서를 수정하여 다시 보내줄 수 있는지 묻고 있으므로 (A)가 정답이다.

어휘 correction n. 수정, 정정 reduction n. 인하
receipt n. 받음, 수령

Paraphrasing

contract 계약서 → document 문서

184 추론 문제

해석 Ms. Stein에 대해 암시되는 것은?
(A) 다음 주에 Mr. Garrison의 사무실을 방문하려고 한다.
(B) 전에 Acorn 디자인사의 서비스를 이용한 적이 있다.
(C) 그녀의 집을 팔기로 결정했다.
(D) 현재 부동산 중개인으로 고용되어 있다.

해설 이메일의 'My real estate agent said these changes will make the property more attractive to prospective buyers.'에서 부동산 중개인이 이러한 변경 사항이 장래의 구매자들에게 부동

산을 더 매력적으로 만들 것이라고 말했다고 했으므로 Ms. Stein이 자신의 집을 팔기로 결정했다는 것을 추론할 수 있다. 따라서 (C)가 정답이다.

185 육하원칙 문제 연계

해석 Ms. Stein은 언제 남은 잔액을 지불할 계획인가?
(A) 9월 12일에
(B) 9월 18일에
(C) 9월 25일에
(D) 10월 9일에

해설 Ms. Stein이 언제 남은 잔액을 지불할 계획인지를 묻고 있으므로 Ms. Stein이 작성한 이메일을 먼저 확인한다.
[단서 1] 이메일의 'I[Ms. Stein] plan to give you a check for my remaining balance on the final day of your scheduled work at my home'에서 Ms. Stein의 집에서 예정된 작업의 마지막 날에 남은 잔액을 수표로 줄 계획이라고 했다. 그런데 작업의 마지막 날이 언제인지 제시되지 않았으므로 계약서에서 관련 내용을 확인한다.
[단서 2] 계약서의 'End date: September 25'에서 종료일이 9월 25일이라는 것을 확인할 수 있다.
두 단서를 종합할 때, Ms. Stein은 자신의 집에서 예정된 작업의 종료일인 9월 25일에 남은 잔액을 지불할 계획임을 알 수 있다. 따라서 (C)가 정답이다.

186-190번은 다음 웹페이지와 두 이메일에 관한 문제입니다.

집 청소 패키지

패키지 1 (고객 맞춤)
[186]저희의 전문가들 중 한 명이 당신이 필요한 사항을 논의하고 비용 견적을 제공하기 위해 먼저 당신의 집을 방문할 것입니다. 그런 다음, 당신이 선택한 날짜에 저희의 청소부들이 방문하여 요청하신 서비스를 수행할 것입니다.

패키지 2 (기본)
매주 또는 매월 한 명의 청소부가 집을 방문하여 모든 방을 진공청소기로 청소하고, 걸레질하며, 먼지를 제거할 것입니다.

패키지 3 (이사 당일)
새집으로 이사하기 전에, 세 명의 청소부들이 빈집을 방문하여 모든 표면을 문지르고 살균할 것입니다.

패키지 4 (창문만)
두 명의 청소부들이 집의 실내와 실외 창문을 닦을 것입니다.

패키지 5 (봄맞이 청소)
[190]네 명의 청소부들이 집안의 각 방을 철저히 청소하고, 또한 창문을 닦아줄 뿐만 아니라, 가구와 카펫도 세제로 닦아낼 것입니다.

expert n. 전문가 cost estimate 비용 견적 dust v. 먼지를 제거하다
residence n. 거주지, 주택 sanitize v. 살균하다 surface n. 표면
thoroughly adv. 철저히 shampoo v. (세제로) 닦다, 청소하다

수신: Customer Service <customerservice@ezclean.com>
발신: Vince Bauer <v.bauer@redmail.com>
날짜: 3월 5일

제목: 청소

안녕하세요,

저는 샬로츠빌 시내 Riverside로에 있는 120평방미터 아파트에 살고 있는데, **187집이 전문적으로 청소될 수 있는 시간을 예약하고 싶습니다.** 제가 4월 첫 2주 동안 도시를 떠나 있을 예정이고, 그때 작업이 되면 좋겠습니다.

188-(A)지역 기업용 웹사이트에서 귀사에 대한 여러 후기들을 읽었고, 모두 훌륭한 내용이었습니다. 그래서, 모든 것이 만족스럽게 처리될 것이라고 확신합니다. 하지만, 제가 꽤 심한 알레르기가 있다는 점을 말씀드리고 싶습니다. 저에게 어떠한 문제라도 야기할지 알아내기 위해 **189어떤 청소 제품들을 사용하시는지 미리 알려주시면 감사하겠습니다.** 웹사이트에서 이 정보를 찾을 수 없었습니다.

감사합니다.

Vince Bauer

out of town 도시를 떠나서, 외부에 나가 있는 rather adv. 꽤, 상당히
severe adj. 심한 determine v. 알아내다, 밝히다

수신: Vince Bauer <v.bauer@redmail.com>
발신: Yasmin Karim <customerservice@ezclean.com>
날짜: 3월 7일
제목: 회신: 청소
189첨부 파일: 정보

Mr. Bauer께,

EZ Clean에 연락해 주셔서 감사합니다. **189요청하신 정보는 첨부파일을 확인해 주시기 바랍니다.** 부디 아무 문제 없으시길 바랍니다.

4월 6일에 당신의 집을 청소할 수 있는 직원들이 있습니다. 당신이 집을 비우는 동안 아파트에 들어갈 수 있는 방법을 알려주시기만 하면 됩니다. 또한 관심 있으신 청소 패키지를 알고 싶습니다. 저희와 함께 하는 것이 처음이라는 점을 고려하여, **190네 명의 청소부가 포함된 패키지를 추천해 드립니다.** 그렇게 하면, 당신의 아파트에 티끌 하나 없을 것이라고 확신할 수 있습니다.

Yasmin Karim 드림
고객 서비스

attachment n. 첨부 파일 gain access to ~에 들어가다, ~로 접근하다
given that ~을 고려하여 involve v. 포함하다 assure v. 확신시키다
spotless adj. 티끌 하나 없는

186 Not/True 문제

해석 패키지 1에 대해 언급된 것은?
(A) 이용 가능 여부는 특정 날짜로 한정되어 있다.
(B) 사전 상담이 요구된다.
(C) 최소 세 명의 청소부들을 포함한다.
(D) 비용은 집의 위치의 영향을 받는다.

해설 웹페이지의 Package 1을 보면 'One of our experts will first visit your home to discuss your needs and provide a cost estimate.'에서 전문가들 중 한 명이 필요한 사항을 논의하고 비용 견적을 제공하기 위해 먼저 고객의 집을 방문할 것이라고 했으므로 (B)가 정답이다.

어휘 specific adj. 특정한, 구체적인 preliminary adj. 사전의, 예비의
a minimum of 최소한의 affect v. 영향을 주다

Paraphrasing

> first visit your home to discuss your needs 필요한 사항을 논의하기 위해 먼저 당신의 집을 방문하다
> → preliminary consultation 사전 상담

187 목적 찾기 문제

해석 첫 번째 이메일의 목적은 무엇인가?
(A) 일정 변경에 대한 이유를 제공하기 위해
(B) 거주지의 주소를 확인하기 위해
(C) 서비스 예약을 잡기 위해
(D) 전문적이지 못한 직원에 대해 불만을 제기하기 위해

해설 첫 번째 이메일의 'I'm interested in scheduling a time to have it professionally cleaned'에서 집이 전문적으로 청소될 수 있는 시간을 예약하고 싶다고 했으므로 (C)가 정답이다.

어휘 arrange v. (일정을) 잡다 unprofessional adj. 전문적이지 못한

Paraphrasing

> scheduling a time 시간 일정을 잡는 것
> → arrange an appointment 예약을 잡다

188 Not/True 문제

해석 Mr. Bauer가 EZ Clean에 대해 언급하는 것은?
(A) 온라인에서 긍정적인 의견을 받았다.
(B) 최근에 가격을 변경했다.
(C) 광고가 인상적이었다.
(D) 샬로츠빌에 다른 지점이 있다.

해설 이메일의 'I[Mr. Bauer] read several reviews of your company on a Web site for local businesses, and all of them were excellent.'에서 지역 기업용 웹사이트에서 EZ Clean에 대한 여러 후기들을 읽었고, 모두 훌륭한 내용이었다고 했으므로 (A)는 지문의 내용과 일치한다. 따라서 (A)가 정답이다.

어휘 impressive adj. 인상적인 location n. 지점, 위치

Paraphrasing

> reviews ~ all of them were excellent 후기들 모두 훌륭한 내용이었다 → positive feedback 긍정적인 의견
> on a Web site 웹사이트에서 → online 온라인에서

189 추론 문제 연계

해석 Ms. Karim의 이메일 첨부 파일에 무엇이 포함되어 있을 것 같은가?
(A) 사업체 지점들의 위치
(B) 근무 가능한 직원들의 이름
(C) 특별한 서비스의 비용
(D) 청소 제품의 종류

해설 Ms. Karim의 이메일에 첨부된 파일에 포함된 것을 묻고 있으므로 Ms. Karim이 작성한 이메일을 먼저 확인한다.
단서 1 두 번째 이메일의 'Please see the attachment for the

information you requested.'에서 Mr. Bauer가 요청한 정보를 첨부파일에서 확인하라고 했다. 그런데 Mr. Bauer가 무슨 정보를 요청했는지에 대해 알 수 없으므로 Mr. Bauer가 보낸 이메일에서 관련 내용을 확인한다.

[단서 2] 첫 번째 이메일의 'I would appreciate it if you could let me know which cleaning products you use in advance'에서 EZ Clean에서 사용하는 청소 제품들이 어떤 것들인지 알려달라고 했음을 알 수 있다.

두 단서를 종합할 때, Ms. Karim의 이메일 첨부 파일에 청소 제품들의 종류에 대한 정보가 포함되어 있음을 추론할 수 있다. 따라서 (D)가 정답이다.

어휘 **business** n. 사업(체) **type** n. 종류, 유형

190 육하원칙 문제 연계

해석 Ms. Karim은 어떤 패키지를 추천하는가?
(A) 패키지 2
(B) 패키지 3
(C) 패키지 4
(D) 패키지 5

해설 Ms. Karim이 추천하는 패키지를 묻고 있으므로 Ms. Karim이 작성한 이메일을 먼저 확인한다.

[단서 1] 두 번째 이메일의 'I would recommend the one that involves four cleaners'에서 네 명의 청소부들이 포함된 패키지를 추천한다고 했다. 그런데 이 패키지가 어떤 것인지 알 수 없으므로 패키지에 대한 설명이 제시되어 있는 웹페이지를 확인한다.

[단서 2] 웹페이지의 Package 5를 보면 'Each room in your home will be thoroughly scrubbed by four cleaners'에서 네 명의 청소부들이 집 안의 각 방을 청소할 것이라고 했다.

두 단서를 종합할 때, Ms. Karim은 패키지 5를 추천함을 알 수 있다. 따라서 (D)가 정답이다.

191-195번은 다음 기사, 회람, 이메일에 관한 문제입니다.

새너제이 (5월 2일) — 행사 기획사 Uptown Live는 최근 새너제이에서 필라델피아로 이전할 것이라고 발표했다. [191]최고 경영자 Margaret Harris에 따르면, 그 결정은 주로 재정적인 고려 때문이었다. "필라델피아 정부는 엔터테인먼트 회사들을 도시로 유인하기 위해 일련의 세금 우대 조치 및 비슷한 장려책들을 제공하고 있습니다," 라고 Ms. Harris가 말했다. "그것은 놓치기에는 그저 너무 좋은 기회입니다."

[192]회사는 이미 Central Main 경전철 역 옆에 사무실 공간을 확보했다. 이사는 5월 마지막 주에 진행될 것이며, 새 사무실은 6월 1일에 운영을 시작할 것이다. Ms. Harris는 음악 팬들에게 이 변화가 6월 회사의 콘서트 라인업에 영향을 미치지 않을 것이라고 확신시켰다.

promoter n. 기획사 **relocate** v. 이전하다 **government** n. 정부
tax break 세금 우대 조치 **incentive** n. 장려책, 우대책
lure v. 유인하다, 유혹하다 **pass up** 놓치다, 거절하다
secure v. 확보하다 **transition** n. 변화

회람

수신: 모든 Uptown Live 직원

발신: Margaret Harris
날짜: 6월 1일
제목: 6월 콘서트

[192]저는 여러분 모두가 이곳 Baxter 타워에 있는 우리의 새 사무실에 자리 잡으시길 바랍니다. 차로 출근하실 계획이라면 건물 관리 사무실에 방문하여 주차권을 요청하는 것을 잊지 마세요.

저는 이 이동이 이번 달에 있을 공연들에 지장을 줘서는 안 된다는 것을 모두에게 상기시키고 싶습니다. 우리 회사의 평판은 모든 것이 순조롭게 진행되는 것에 달려 있습니다. 티켓 소지자들에게 미치는 영향을 최소화하기 위해 제가 조치를 취할 수 있도록 어떠한 문제에 대해서라도 가능한 한 빨리 말씀해 주세요. 이번 달 콘서트 일정은 여기 있습니다:

날짜	공연자	장소
6월 12일	Saskia Bernstein	Moreland 경기장
6월 18일	[194]Beth Lord	[194]Sawyer 콘서트홀
[193]6월 26일	Bobby Cabillo	Brentwood 강당
[193]6월 26일	Andy Lee	Moon 광장

settle into 자리 잡다 **interfere** v. 지장을 주다, 방해하다
reputation n. 평판, 명성 **dependent on** ~에 달려 있는
complication n. 문제 **take action** 조치를 취하다
minimize v. 최소화하다 **impact** n. 영향 **auditorium** n. 강당

수신: Brian Keeper <b.keeper@uptownlive.com>
발신: Nicole Kim <nicole@sdmail.com>
제목: 회신: 요청
날짜: [194]6월 7일

Mr. Keeper께,

유감스러운 소식이 있습니다. [194]우리 지역에 발생한 홍수가 Sawyer 콘서트홀 로비와 객석이 심하게 물에 잠기는 피해를 야기했습니다. 수리가 완료되는 데 최소 3주가 소요될 것이므로, Uptown Live가 이번 달에 이곳에서 개최하기로 계획한 콘서트를 다시 예약해야 할 것 같습니다. 8월 중 가능한 날짜를 제게 알려주세요.

저는 Uptown Live가 티켓을 교환하고 싶어 하지 않는 사람들에게 환불해 주어야 할 것을 알고 있습니다. 다행히, 저희 보험 정책이 이 비용을 보장합니다. [195]보상을 청구하는 방법에 대한 설명은 저희의 보험 설계사인 Carla Adams에게 문의하세요. 그녀의 번호는 555-9283입니다.

양해해 주셔서 감사합니다.

Nicole Kim
장소 관리자

issue a refund 환불해 주다 **individual** n. 사람, 개인
unwilling adj. ~하고 싶어 하지 않는 **insurance** n. 보험
cover v. 보장하다 **claim compensation** 보상을 청구하다

191 육하원칙 문제

해석 Uptown Live는 왜 필라델피아로 이전했는가?
(A) 재정 지원의 자격을 얻기 위해
(B) 더 폭넓은 고객층에 접근하기 위해
(C) 투자 기회에 참여하기 위해

(D) 정부 프로젝트를 수행하기 위해

해설 기사의 'According to CEO Margaret Harris, the decision was largely due to financial considerations. "Philadelphia's government is providing a package of tax breaks and similar incentives to lure entertainment companies to the city," Ms. Harris said.'에서 최고 경영자 Margaret Harris에 따르면 이전 결정은 주로 재정적인 고려 때문이었고, 필라델피아 정부가 엔터테인먼트 회사들을 도시로 유인하기 위해 일련의 세금 우대 조치 및 비슷한 장려책들을 제공하고 있다고 했으므로, Uptown Live가 재정 지원의 자격을 얻기 위해 필라델피아로 이전했음을 알 수 있다. 따라서 (A)가 정답이다.

어휘 qualify for ~의 자격을 얻다 gain access to ~에 접근하다
take part in ~에 참여하다 investment n. 투자

Paraphrasing

> a package of tax breaks and similar incentives 세금 우대 조치 및 비슷한 장려책 → financial support 재정 지원

192 추론 문제 연계

해석 Baxter 타워에 대해 암시되는 것은?
(A) 텔레비전 스튜디오를 포함한다.
(B) 대중교통 시설 근처에 있다.
(C) 오픈 날짜가 지연되었다.
(D) 주차장이 확장될 것이다.

해설 질문의 핵심 어구인 Baxter Tower가 언급된 회람을 먼저 확인한다.
단서 1 회람의 'I hope all of you are settling into our new office here in Baxter Tower.'에서 여러분 모두가 이곳 Baxter 타워에 있는 새 사무실에 자리 잡길 바란다고 했다.
단서 2 기사의 'The company has already secured office space next to the Central Main light-rail station.'에서 회사가 Central Main 경전철 역 옆에 사무실 공간을 확보했다는 것을 알 수 있다.
두 단서를 종합할 때, 새 사무실이 있는 Baxter 타워는 대중교통 시설 근처에 있음을 추론할 수 있다. 따라서 (B)가 정답이다.

어휘 public transit 대중교통 delay v. 지연시키다, 연기하다
expand v. 확장시키다

Paraphrasing

> next to the ~ light-rail station 경전철 역 옆에 → near a public transit facility 대중교통 시설 근처에

193 Not/True 문제

해석 회람이 공연에 대해 명시하는 것은?
(A) 일부는 같은 날에 개최될 것이다.
(B) 하나는 예정보다 일찍 일어날 것이다.
(C) 공연자들은 같은 국적을 가지고 있다.
(D) 예상보다 많은 팬들을 끌어모았다.

해설 회람의 공연 일정표에서 6월 26일에 공연 두 개가 있다고 명시했으므로 공연 일부가 같은 날에 개최될 것이라는 것을 알 수 있다. 따라서 (A)가 정답이다.

어휘 nationality n. 국적

194 추론 문제 연계

해석 어떤 공연자의 콘서트가 일정이 변경될 것 같은가?
(A) Saskia Bernstein
(B) Beth Lord
(C) Bobby Cabillo
(D) Andy Lee

해설 어떤 공연자의 콘서트가 일정이 변경될 것 같은지를 묻고 있으므로 관련된 내용이 언급된 이메일을 먼저 확인한다.
단서 1 이메일의 'Flooding in our area has resulted in severe water damage to the lobby and auditorium of the Sawyer Concert Hall. ~ I'm afraid we will have to rebook the concert Uptown Live plans to hold here this month.'에서 홍수로 인해 Sawyer 콘서트홀 로비와 객석이 심하게 물에 잠겨서 Uptown Live가 이번 달에 여기서 개최하기로 계획한 콘서트를 다시 예약해야 할 것 같다고 했다. 그런데 Sawyer 콘서트홀에서 개최하기로 계획한 콘서트의 공연자가 누구인지 제시되지 않았으므로 회람에서 관련 내용을 확인한다.
단서 2 회람에서 Sawyer 콘서트홀에서 개최하기로 계획한 콘서트의 공연자가 Beth Lord임을 확인할 수 있다.
두 단서를 종합할 때, Beth Lord의 콘서트가 일정이 변경될 것임을 추론할 수 있다. 따라서 (B)가 정답이다.

195 육하원칙 문제

해석 Mr. Keeper는 왜 Ms. Adams에게 연락할 것인가?
(A) 새로운 사업의 시작을 논의하기 위해
(B) 행사를 위한 몇몇 보험에 가입하기 위해
(C) 배상 절차에 대해 문의하기 위해
(D) 피해를 입은 장소에 대한 수리 일정을 잡기 위해

해설 이메일의 'Please contact our insurance agent, Carla Adams, for an explanation of how to claim compensation.'에서 보상을 청구하는 방법에 대한 설명은 보험 설계사인 Carla Adams에게 문의하라고 했으므로, Mr. Keeper가 배상 절차에 대해 문의하기 위해 Ms. Adams에게 연락할 것임을 알 수 있다. 따라서 (C)가 정답이다.

어휘 reimbursement n. 배상, 상환

Paraphrasing

> compensation 보상 → reimbursement 배상

196-200번은 다음 이메일, 설문지, 일정표에 관한 문제입니다.

> 수신: Steve More <s.more@paxton.com>
> 발신: Lucy Barton <l.barton@paxton.com>
> 제목: 미스터리 쇼퍼
> 날짜: 11월 15일
>
> 안녕하세요 Steve,
>
> 저는 모든 슈퍼마켓 지점들이 높은 수준의 청결과 고객 서비스를 유지하도록 보장해야 할 필요성에 대한 우리의 이전 논의에 대한 후속 ↻

해커스 토익 실전 LC+RC 2

조치를 하고 싶었습니다. ¹⁹⁶이것을 처리하기 위해, 저는 미스터리 쇼퍼 프로그램을 시행하기로 결정했습니다. 그것은 우리가 고객의 관점에서 매장 상태와 직원의 업무 능력을 평가하게 해 줄 것입니다.

매장 직원들이 미스터리 쇼퍼들을 알아보지 않길 바란다는 점을 고려하여, ²⁰⁰이 프로젝트를 위해 임시 직원들을 고용할 것입니다. ¹⁹⁷저는 지난주에 Dale 채용 서비스사의 Mike Coyle과 회의를 했고, 그는 그의 회사가 우리의 요구를 충족시킬 수 있다고 확신합니다. 모든 매장 평가는 12월 11일까지 완료될 것이고, 그때 업데이트 정보를 보내드리겠습니다.

궁금한 점이 있으시면 알려주세요.

Lucy Barton
지역 관리자, Paxton 슈퍼마켓

cleanliness n. 청결 address v. 해결하다 implement v. 시행하다
mystery shopper 미스터리 쇼퍼(고객으로 가장하여 상점의 서비스 등을
조사하는 사람) assess v. 평가하다 condition n. 상태
performance n. 업무 능력, 성과 perspective n. 관점
recognize v. 알아보다 temp staff 임시 직원
assure v. 확신하다 assessment n. 평가 regional adj. 지역의

미스터리 쇼퍼 설문지

¹⁹⁸이름: Alexa Miller

방문하는 각 매장마다 한 장의 양식이 작성되어야 합니다. 작성한 양식을 제목란에 "미스터리 쇼퍼"를 넣어 Lucy Barton에게 이메일로 보내주세요.

다음 질문에 객관적으로 답변해 주시기 바랍니다:

1. 매장이 잘 정리되어 있었나요? □ Yes ☑ No
   의견: ¹⁹⁸오픈한 직후 아침에 매장에 들어갔습니다. 곳곳에 상자가 있는 것으로 보아 틀림없이 배달이 막 들어온 모양이었습니다. 모든 상자들을 안쪽 방에 두는 대신, 직원들은 매장에서 상품들을 꺼내기 시작했습니다.

2. 매장은 흠잡을 데 없이 깨끗했나요? ☑ Yes □ No
   의견: 상자들을 제외하고는, 매장이 깨끗해 보였습니다. 선반에 먼지가 있는지 확인했지만, 하나도 발견하지 못했습니다.

3. 매장 판매원이 친절한 태도로 바로 다가왔나요? □ Yes ☑ No
   의견: 직원들은 상자 때문에 바빴고 저를 알은척하지 않았습니다.

4. ¹⁹⁹매장 판매원이 현재 진행 중인 판촉 행사에 대해 말해 주었나요? □ Yes ☑ No
   ¹⁹⁹의견: 아무도 저에게 그것에 대해 이야기하지 않았습니다.

questionnaire n. 설문지 objectively adv. 객관적으로
organize v. 정리하다, 준비하다 back room 안쪽 방
unpack v. 꺼내다, 풀다 merchandise n. 상품, 물품
sales floor 매장 spotlessly adv. 흠잡을 데 없는, 티끌 하나 없는
apart from ~을 제외하고 shelf n. 선반 detect v. 발견하다
acknowledge v. 알은척하다 promotion n. 판촉 행사

뉴욕시 지점 미스터리 쇼퍼 일정표

날짜	시간	²⁰⁰미스터리 쇼퍼	지점
12월 9일	¹⁹⁸오전 10시 - 오후 12시	¹⁹⁸Alexa Miller	¹⁹⁸소호
	오후 1시 - 오후 3시	Dillon Kasich	할렘
	오후 3시 - 오후 5시	Alexa Miller	5번가
	오후 6시 - 오후 8시	Alexa Miller	렉싱턴
12월 10일	오전 9시 - 오전 11시 30분	Dillon Kasich	5번가
	오후 12시 - 오후 2시	²⁰⁰Martin Chan	렉싱턴
	오후 2시 - 오후 4시	²⁰⁰Martin Chan	할렘
	오후 5시 - 오후 7시	Dillon Kasich	소호

---

196 목적 찾기 문제

해석 이메일의 목적은 무엇인가?
(A) 새 매장 위치에 대한 정보를 제공하기 위해
(B) 심각한 고객 서비스 문제를 설명하기 위해
(C) 직원을 더 채용할 수 있도록 허가를 요청하기 위해
(D) 프로그램의 실행을 알리기 위해

해설 이메일의 'To address this, I have decided to implement a mystery shopper program.'에서 미스터리 쇼퍼 프로그램을 시행하기로 결정했다고 했으므로 (D)가 정답이다.

어휘 describe v. 설명하다, 묘사하다 permission n. 허가
implementation n. 실행, 이행

197 육하원칙 문제

해석 이메일에 따르면, Ms. Barton은 지난주에 무엇을 했는가?
(A) 업무 능력 평가를 검토했다.
(B) 구직자 면접을 실시했다.
(C) 회사 담당자와 만났다.
(D) 경쟁 소매점을 방문했다.

해설 이메일의 'I[Ms. Barton] had a meeting with Mike Coyle from Dale Recruitment Services last week'에서 Ms. Barton이 지난주에 Dale 채용 서비스사의 Mike Coyle과 회의를 했다고 했으므로, Ms. Barton이 지난주에 회사 담당자와 만났다는 것을 알 수 있다. 따라서 (C)가 정답이다.

어휘 conduct v. 실시하다 job applicant 구직자 retail outlet 소매점

198 육하원칙 문제 연계

해석 설문지에 있는 의견은 어떤 지점에 대한 것인가?
(A) 소호
(B) 할렘
(C) 5번가
(D) 렉싱턴

해설 설문지는 어떤 지점에 대한 의견인지를 물었으므로 설문지를 먼저 확인한다.
단서 1 설문지의 'I[Alexa Miller] entered the store in the morning right after it opened.'에서 Alexa Miller가 오픈 직후 아침에 매장에 들어갔다고 했다. 그런데 매장 방문 시간이 제시되지 않았으므로 일정표에서 관련 내용을 확인한다.
단서 2 일정표에서 Alexa Miller가 방문한 시간대 중 오전 시간은

'10 A.M. – 12 P.M.'의 'Soho' 매장임을 확인할 수 있다.

두 단서를 종합할 때, 설문지에 있는 의견이 소호 지점에 대한 것임을 알 수 있다. 따라서 (A)가 정답이다.

199 Not/True 문제

해석 설문지에 명시된 것은?
(A) 한 직원이 훌륭한 고객 서비스를 제공했다.
(B) 선반이 제대로 청소되지 않았었다.
(C) 매장이 사람들로 붐볐다.
(D) 판촉 행사가 고객과 공유되지 않았다.

해설 설문지의 4번 질문인 'Did a store representative tell you about the current promotion?'에 대해 No에 체크되어 있고 'Comment: No one talked to me about it.'에서 아무도 그것에 대해 이야기하지 않았다고 했으므로 (D)가 정답이다.

어휘 properly adv. 제대로, 적절히　be crowded with ~로 붐비다

200 추론 문제 연계

해석 Mr. Chan에 대해 사실일 것 같은 것은?
(A) 12월 9일에 매장을 방문하라는 요청을 받았다.
(B) 슈퍼마켓 체인점의 정규직 사원이 아니다.
(C) 다른 미스터리 쇼퍼들의 일정을 정리했다.
(D) 채용 회사의 총지배인이다.

해설 Mr. Chan이 언급된 일정표를 먼저 확인한다.
　단서 1　일정표의 'Mystery Shopper', 'Martin Chan'에서 Mr. Chan이 미스터리 쇼퍼임을 알 수 있다. 그런데 미스터리 쇼퍼에 대한 내용은 제시되지 않았으므로 이메일에서 관련 내용을 확인한다.
　단서 2　이메일의 'I will use temp staff for this project.'에서 이 프로젝트를 위해 임시 직원들을 고용할 것이라고 했다.
두 단서를 종합할 때, Mr. Chan은 슈퍼마켓의 미스터리 쇼퍼 프로젝트를 위해 고용된 임시 직원으로 정규직 사원이 아닌 것을 추론할 수 있다. 따라서 (B)가 정답이다.

어휘 permanent adj. 정규직의, 영구적인

Paraphrasing

temp staff 임시 직원들 → not ~ permanent employee 정규직이 아닌

TEST 4

1 (C)	21 (A)	41 (C)	61 (D)	81 (B)
2 (A)	22 (A)	42 (D)	62 (A)	82 (B)
3 (B)	23 (A)	43 (C)	63 (B)	83 (C)
4 (D)	24 (B)	44 (A)	64 (D)	84 (B)
5 (D)	25 (A)	45 (A)	65 (C)	85 (A)
6 (C)	26 (C)	46 (C)	66 (C)	86 (A)
7 (B)	27 (A)	47 (A)	67 (D)	87 (D)
8 (C)	28 (B)	48 (A)	68 (C)	88 (A)
9 (C)	29 (B)	49 (D)	69 (B)	89 (A)
10 (B)	30 (A)	50 (B)	70 (B)	90 (C)
11 (A)	31 (B)	51 (A)	71 (B)	91 (A)
12 (B)	32 (B)	52 (D)	72 (C)	92 (D)
13 (A)	33 (C)	53 (B)	73 (D)	93 (A)
14 (C)	34 (D)	54 (A)	74 (C)	94 (C)
15 (A)	35 (C)	55 (B)	75 (A)	95 (A)
16 (B)	36 (C)	56 (C)	76 (D)	96 (A)
17 (A)	37 (A)	57 (A)	77 (D)	97 (D)
18 (B)	38 (C)	58 (A)	78 (B)	98 (B)
19 (B)	39 (C)	59 (C)	79 (B)	99 (B)
20 (C)	40 (B)	60 (C)	80 (C)	100 (C)

101 (D)	121 (D)	141 (B)	161 (C)	181 (D)
102 (C)	122 (B)	142 (D)	162 (B)	182 (C)
103 (D)	123 (A)	143 (D)	163 (C)	183 (B)
104 (A)	124 (C)	144 (B)	164 (D)	184 (C)
105 (B)	125 (B)	145 (D)	165 (B)	185 (C)
106 (B)	126 (A)	146 (A)	166 (A)	186 (C)
107 (C)	127 (C)	147 (D)	167 (C)	187 (A)
108 (D)	128 (B)	148 (C)	168 (B)	188 (A)
109 (C)	129 (B)	149 (D)	169 (C)	189 (D)
110 (B)	130 (A)	150 (C)	170 (D)	190 (C)
111 (B)	131 (B)	151 (B)	171 (C)	191 (B)
112 (A)	132 (B)	152 (C)	172 (B)	192 (C)
113 (C)	133 (C)	153 (A)	173 (C)	193 (C)
114 (C)	134 (D)	154 (D)	174 (A)	194 (A)
115 (D)	135 (C)	155 (C)	175 (C)	195 (C)
116 (D)	136 (D)	156 (C)	176 (A)	196 (C)
117 (C)	137 (C)	157 (B)	177 (B)	197 (D)
118 (C)	138 (C)	158 (D)	178 (B)	198 (A)
119 (B)	139 (A)	159 (B)	179 (D)	199 (C)
120 (B)	140 (C)	160 (D)	180 (D)	200 (C)

PART 1

1 1인 사진

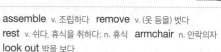

영국식

(A) She is assembling a cabinet.
(B) She is removing her eyeglasses.
(C) She is resting on an armchair.
(D) She is looking out a window.

> assemble v. 조립하다   remove v. (옷 등을) 벗다
> rest v. 쉬다, 휴식을 취하다; n. 휴식   armchair n. 안락의자
> look out 밖을 보다

해석 (A) 그녀는 캐비닛을 조립하고 있다.
    (B) 그녀는 안경을 벗고 있다.
    (C) 그녀는 안락의자에서 쉬고 있다.
    (D) 그녀는 창밖을 보고 있다.

해설 (A) [×] assembling(조립하고 있다)은 여자의 동작과 무관하므로 오답이다. 사진에 있는 캐비닛(cabinet)을 사용하여 혼동을 주었다.
    (B) [×] removing(벗고 있다)은 여자의 동작과 무관하므로 오답이다. 사진에 있는 안경(eyeglasses)을 사용하여 혼동을 주었다.
    (C) [○] 여자가 안락의자에서 쉬고 있는 모습을 가장 잘 묘사한 정답이다.
    (D) [×] looking out(밖을 보고 있다)은 여자의 동작과 무관하므로 오답이다. 사진에 있는 창문(window)을 사용하여 혼동을 주었다.

2 1인 사진

캐나다식

(A) He is kneeling to paint a wall.
(B) He is crouching to tie his shoelaces.
(C) He is inserting a plug into an outlet.
(D) He is cleaning the tiled floor with a mop.

> kneel v. 무릎을 꿇다   crouch v. 쪼그리고 앉다, 웅크리다
> tie v. 묶다, 매다   shoelace n. 신발 끈   insert v. 꽂다, 끼워 넣다
> outlet n. 콘센트   mop n. 대걸레; v. 대걸레로 닦다

해석 **(A) 그는 벽을 칠하기 위해 무릎을 꿇고 있다.**
    (B) 그는 신발 끈을 묶기 위해 쪼그리고 앉아 있다.
    (C) 그는 콘센트에 플러그를 꽂고 있다.
    (D) 그는 대걸레로 타일이 깔린 바닥을 청소하고 있다.

해설 (A) [○] 남자가 벽을 칠하기 위해 무릎을 꿇고 있는 모습을 가장 잘 묘사한 정답이다.
    (B) [×] 남자가 신발 끈을 묶기 위해서가 아니라 벽을 칠하기 위해 쪼그리고 앉아 있으므로 오답이다. He is crouching(그는 쪼그리고 앉아 있다)까지만 듣고 정답으로 선택하지 않도록 주의한다.

(C) [×] inserting(꽂고 있다)은 남자의 동작과 무관하므로 오답이다. 사진에 있는 콘센트(outlet)를 사용하여 혼동을 주었다.

(D) [×] 사진에 대걸레(mop)가 없고, 남자가 대걸레로 타일이 깔린 바닥을 청소하는 모습이 아니므로 오답이다.

최신토익경향

최근 Part 1에서는 목적이나 의도를 나타내는 to 부정사를 사용한 정답 보기들이 자주 출제되고 있다. to 부정사가 사용되면 문장이 길고 복잡해질 수 있어 까다롭다고 느끼기 쉽다. 예를 들어, 작업자가 크레인을 작동하고 있고, 크레인의 고리가 상자를 향하고 있는 모습의 사진이 출제되면, 정답으로 다음과 같은 것들이 나올 수 있다. 사진 속 상황을 자세히 보고 동작의 목적이나 의도까지 파악할 수 있어야 함을 명심하자.

• A crane is being used **to move a crate**.
크레인이 상자를 옮기기 위해 사용되고 있다.

• The worker is using a crane **to move a crate**.
작업자가 상자를 옮기기 위해 크레인을 사용하고 있다.

3 2인 이상 사진

 미국식

(A) The men are shoveling dirt into a truck.
(B) The men are wearing safety helmets at a worksite.
(C) One of the men is lifting a toolbox.
(D) One of the men is repairing a roof.

shovel v. ~을 삽으로 퍼내다; n. 삽 dirt n. 흙, 먼지
safety helmet 안전모 worksite n. 작업 현장 toolbox n. 공구함
roof n. 지붕

해석 (A) 남자들이 삽으로 흙을 트럭으로 퍼내고 있다.
(B) 남자들이 작업 현장에서 안전모를 착용하고 있다.
(C) 남자들 중 한 명이 공구함을 들어 올리고 있다.
(D) 남자들 중 한 명이 지붕을 수리하고 있다.

해설 (A) [×] shoveling dirt into a truck(삽으로 흙을 트럭으로 퍼내고 있다)은 남자들의 동작과 무관하므로 오답이다. 사진에 있는 dirt(흙)를 사용하여 혼동을 주었다.
(B) [○] 남자들이 작업 현장에서 안전모를 착용하고 있는 모습을 가장 잘 묘사한 정답이다.
(C) [×] 사진에 공구함을 들어 올리고 있는(lifting a toolbox) 남자가 없으므로 오답이다.
(D) [×] 사진에 지붕을 수리하고 있는(repairing a roof) 남자가 없으므로 오답이다.

최신토익경향

wear와 put on을 혼동하지 않도록 주의하자. wear는 이미 그것을 걸친 '상태'를 묘사하며, put on은 옷이나 장신구를 걸치는 '동작'을 묘사하는 표현임을 기억해 두자.

• She's **wearing** a long-sleeved shirt.
그녀는 긴 소매 셔츠를 입고 있다. (상태)

• She's **putting on** her shoes.
그녀는 신발을 신고 있는 중이다. (동작)

4 사물 및 풍경 사진

 호주식

(A) A picnic table has been positioned near a lamp post.
(B) A walkway is covered with leaves.
(C) Some bricks have been left in a pile.
(D) Some benches have been placed side by side.

lamp post 가로등 기둥 walkway n. 산책로, 보도 brick n. 벽돌
pile n. 더미, 무더기 side by side 나란히

해석 (A) 피크닉 테이블이 가로등 기둥 근처에 위치해 있다.
(B) 산책로가 나뭇잎으로 덮여 있다.
(C) 몇몇 벽돌들이 더미로 놓여 있다.
(D) 몇몇 벤치들이 나란히 놓여 있다.

해설 (A) [×] 사진에 피크닉 테이블(picnic table)이 없으므로 오답이다. 사진에 있는 가로등 기둥(lamp post)을 사용하여 혼동을 주었다.
(B) [×] 사진에서 산책로는 보이지만, 나뭇잎으로 덮여 있는(is covered with leaves) 모습은 아니므로 오답이다.
(C) [×] 사진에서 벽돌들은 보이지만, 더미로 놓여 있는(have been left in a pile) 모습은 아니므로 오답이다.
(D) [○] 몇몇 벤치들이 나란히 놓여 있는 모습을 가장 잘 묘사한 정답이다.

최신토익경향

side by side는 Part 1에서 사람이나 사물이 나란히 있는 모습을 묘사할 때 자주 사용되는 표현이다. 비슷한 뜻의 빈출 표현으로는 in a row(일렬로)와 next to each other(나란히) 등이 있으니 함께 알아두자.

• The men are walking **side by side**. 남자들이 나란히 걷고 있다.

• Vehicles are parked **in a row**. 자동차들이 일렬로 주차되어 있다.

• Two women are sitting **next to each other**.
두 여자가 나란히 앉아 있다.

5 2인 이상 사진

미국식

(A) One of the women is drinking from a coffee cup.
(B) An employee is cutting some bread into pieces.
(C) Some shelving units have been set up near an entranceway.
(D) Some light fixtures are suspended from the ceiling.

employee n. 종업원, 직원 shelving unit 선반
entranceway n. 출입구, 입구의 통로 light fixture 조명 기구
suspend v. 매달다, 걸다 ceiling n. 천장

해석 (A) 여자들 중 한 명이 커피잔으로 음료를 마시고 있다.
(B) 한 종업원이 빵을 조각으로 자르고 있다.
(C) 몇몇 선반들이 출입구 근처에 설치되어 있다.
(D) 몇몇 조명 기구들이 천장에 매달려 있다.

해설 (A) [×] 사진에 음료를 마시고 있는(drinking) 여자가 없으므로 오답이다. 사진에 있는 커피잔(coffee cup)을 사용하여 혼동을

주었다.
(B) [×] 사진에 빵을 조각으로 자르고 있는(cutting some bread into pieces) 종업원이 없으므로 오답이다. 사진에 있는 빵(bread)을 사용하여 혼동을 주었다.
(C) [×] 사진에서 선반들은 보이지만, 출입구(entranceway) 근처에 설치되어 있는 모습은 아니므로 오답이다.
(D) [○] 몇몇 조명 기구들이 천장에 매달려 있는 모습을 가장 잘 묘사한 정답이다.

6 사물 및 풍경 사진   ⟨3번⟩ 호주식

(A) Some trees are shading a pond in a park.
(B) A bicycle rack is situated next to a road.
(C) A fence separates a parking area from some trees.
(D) There is a basketball net attached to the side of a building.

pond n. 연못 bicycle rack 자전거 보관대
separate v. 구분하다, 분리하다

해석 (A) 몇몇 나무들이 공원에 있는 연못에 그늘을 드리우고 있다.
(B) 자전거 보관대가 도로 옆에 있다.
(C) 울타리가 주차 구역과 몇몇 나무들을 구분한다.
(D) 건물 옆면에 부착된 농구 그물망이 있다.

해설 (A) [×] 사진에 연못(pond)이 없으므로 오답이다. 사진에 있는 나무들(trees)을 사용하여 혼동을 주었다.
(B) [×] 사진에 자전거 보관대(bicycle rack)가 없으므로 오답이다.
(C) [○] 울타리가 주차 구역과 몇몇 나무들을 구분하는 모습을 가장 잘 묘사한 정답이다.
(D) [×] 사진에서 농구 그물망은 보이지만, 건물 옆면에 부착된 (attached to the side of a building) 모습은 아니므로 오답이다. 사진에 있는 건물(building)을 사용하여 혼동을 주었다.

PART 2

7 Where 의문문   ⟨3번⟩ 영국식 → 캐나다식

Where do we keep the extra plates?
(A) That costs extra.
(B) Look in the cupboard.
(C) A small bowl of salad.

extra adj. 여분의, 추가의; adv. 추가로 cupboard n. 찬장

해석 여분의 접시는 어디에 보관하나요?
(A) 그것은 비용이 추가로 들어요.
(B) 찬장을 확인해 보세요.
(C) 작은 샐러드 한 그릇이요.

해설 (A) [×] 질문의 extra(여분의)를 '추가로'라는 의미의 부사로 반복 사용하여 혼동을 준 오답이다.
(B) [○] 찬장을 확인해 보라는 말로, 여분의 접시를 보관하는 장소를

언급했으므로 정답이다.
(C) [×] 질문의 plates(접시)와 관련 있는 bowl(그릇)을 사용하여 혼동을 준 오답이다.

8 Who 의문문   ⟨3번⟩ 미국식 → 호주식

Who closed the store last night?
(A) That was our last chance.
(B) Around 10 P.M.
(C) It may have been Carter.

close v. (문을) 닫다 chance n. 기회

해석 어젯밤에 누가 가게 문을 닫았나요?
(A) 그게 우리의 마지막 기회였어요.
(B) 대략 오후 10시쯤이요.
(C) 아마 Carter였을 거예요.

해설 (A) [×] 질문의 last를 반복 사용하여 혼동을 준 오답이다.
(B) [×] 어젯밤에 가게 문을 닫은 사람이 누구인지 물었는데, 시점으로 응답했으므로 오답이다.
(C) [○] Carter였을 것이라며, 어젯밤에 가게 문을 닫은 사람을 전달했으므로 정답이다.

9 조동사 의문문   ⟨3번⟩ 캐나다식 → 영국식

Will you be using your laptop this weekend?
(A) An online reservation.
(B) Several innovative features.
(C) No, I won't need it.

reservation n. 예약 innovative adj. 혁신적인, 획기적인
feature n. 기능, 특징

해석 이번 주말에 당신의 노트북을 사용할 건가요?
(A) 온라인 예약이요.
(B) 몇 가지 혁신적인 기능이요.
(C) 아니요, 필요하지 않을 거예요.

해설 (A) [×] 질문의 laptop(노트북)과 관련 있는 online(온라인)을 사용하여 혼동을 준 오답이다.
(B) [×] 질문의 laptop(노트북)에서 연상할 수 있는 innovative features(혁신적인 기능)를 사용하여 혼동을 준 오답이다.
(C) [○] No로 이번 주말에 노트북을 사용하지 않을 것임을 전달한 후, 그것이 필요하지 않을 것이라는 부연 설명을 했으므로 정답이다.

10 What 의문문   ⟨3번⟩ 미국식 → 캐나다식

What should we prepare for the meeting with our client?
(A) Don't miss the meeting.
(B) Let's discuss that.
(C) Because the client arrived late.

miss v. 놓치다, 지나치다 discuss v. 논의하다, 의논하다

해석 고객과의 회의를 위해 무엇을 준비해야 하나요?

(A) 회의를 놓치지 마세요.

(B) 그것에 대해 논의해 봅시다.

(C) 고객이 늦게 도착했기 때문이에요.

해설 (A) [×] 질문의 meeting을 반복 사용하여 혼동을 준 오답이다.

(B) [○] 그것에 대해 논의해 보자는 말로, 고객과의 회의를 위해 무엇을 준비해야 하는지 모른다는 간접적인 응답을 했으므로 정답이다.

(C) [×] 질문의 client를 반복 사용하여 혼동을 준 오답이다.

11 Where 의문문

🎧 영국식 → 호주식

Where is the Pullman Engineering Conference being held?

(A) At the Hanami Hotel.

(B) A workshop on enhancing work efficiency.

(C) On May 13 and 14.

conference n. 학회, 회의 hold v. 열다, 개최하다
enhance v. 향상시키다, 높이다 efficiency n. 효율(성), 능률

해석 Pullman Engineering 학회는 어디에서 열리고 있나요?

(A) Hanami 호텔에서요.

(B) 업무 효율성 향상에 관한 워크숍이요.

(C) 5월 13일과 14일에요.

해설 (A) [○] Hanami 호텔에서라는 말로, 학회가 열리고 있는 장소를 언급했으므로 정답이다.

(B) [×] 질문의 Conference(학회)에서 연상할 수 있는 workshop (워크숍)을 사용하여 혼동을 준 오답이다.

(C) [×] 학회가 열리고 있는 장소를 물었는데, 날짜로 응답했으므로 오답이다. 질문의 Where를 When으로 혼동하여 이를 정답으로 선택하지 않도록 주의한다.

12 부정 의문문

🎧 호주식 → 미국식

Didn't you receive the memo about the schedule change?

(A) Here is your receipt.

(B) I was out of the office all day.

(C) In about two weeks.

receive v. 받다 receipt n. 영수증

해석 일정 변경에 대한 회람을 받지 못하셨나요?

(A) 여기 영수증이요.

(B) 저는 하루 종일 사무실에 없었어요.

(C) 약 2주 후에요.

해설 (A) [×] receive - receipt의 유사 발음 어휘를 사용하여 혼동을 준 오답이다.

(B) [○] 하루 종일 사무실에 없었다는 말로, 일정 변경에 대한 회람을 받았는지 모른다는 간접적인 응답을 했으므로 정답이다.

(C) [×] 질문의 schedule(일정)에서 연상할 수 있는 two weeks (2주)를 사용하여 혼동을 준 오답이다.

최신토익 경향

매회 1~3문제 출제되는 부정 의문문은 not을 포함한 조동사나 be동사로 시작하는 의문문이다. 부정 의문문은 상대방의 동의를 구하거나 사실 확인

또는 제안을 위한 의도로 주로 사용되며 긍정을 의미하는 Yes, 또는 부정을 의미하는 No로 응답할 수 있다. 최근에는 Yes/No를 생략한 응답이 자주 출제되고 있으니, 예문과 함께 실전에 대비하자.

Isn't this meeting room too small for our team?
이 회의실은 우리 팀에게 너무 작지 않나요?

<긍정> Maybe we should postpone the presentation.
발표를 연기해야 할 것 같아요.

<부정> Only three members will join us today.
오늘은 세 명만 참석할 거예요.

*<긍정> 발표를 연기해야 할 것 같다며 팀에게 회의실이 작다고 긍정하는 응답

<부정> 오늘은 세 명만 참석할 거라서 팀에게 회의실이 작지 않다고 부정하는 응답

13 Which 의문문

🎧 영국식 → 캐나다식

Which of the slides would you like me to replace?

(A) The ones about new market trends.

(B) The cost of replacement is low.

(C) They've recently been remodeled.

replacement n. 교체, 대체(품) remodel v. 개조하다

해석 제가 어느 슬라이드를 교체하길 원하시나요?

(A) 새로운 시장 동향에 관한 것들이요.

(B) 교체 비용이 저렴해요.

(D) 그것들은 최근에 개조되었어요.

해설 (A) [○] 새로운 시장 동향에 관한 것들이라는 말로, 교체하기를 원하는 슬라이드를 전달했으므로 정답이다.

(B) [×] replace - replacement의 유사 발음 어휘를 사용하여 혼동을 준 오답이다.

(C) [×] 질문의 replace(교체하다)에서 연상할 수 있는 remodeled (개조되었다)를 사용하여 혼동을 준 오답이다.

14 제공 의문문

🎧 미국식 → 호주식

Would you like me to help you move?

(A) Oh, you don't need to call her.

(B) My apartment number.

(C) I can do it myself.

move v. 이사하다, 움직이다 apartment n. 아파트

해석 이사하는 것을 도와드릴까요?

(A) 아, 그녀에게 전화하실 필요 없어요.

(B) 제 아파트 번호요.

(C) 혼자 할 수 있어요.

해설 (A) [×] 이사하는 것을 도와줄지를 물었는데, 이와 관련이 없는 그녀에게 전화할 필요 없다는 내용으로 응답했으므로 오답이다.

(B) [×] 질문의 move(이사하다)와 관련 있는 apartment(아파트)를 사용하여 혼동을 준 오답이다.

(C) [○] 혼자 할 수 있다는 말로, 이사하는 것을 도와주겠다는 제공을 거절한 정답이다. Would you like me to가 제공하는 표현임을 이해할 수 있어야 한다.

15 조동사 의문문

캐나다식 → 미국식

Have you visited the jazz festival?
(A) I don't like jazz.
(B) The concert hall on Main Street.
(C) We're glad you visited us.

해석 재즈 페스티벌에 가보셨나요?
(A) 저는 재즈를 좋아하지 않아요.
(B) 메인가에 있는 콘서트홀이요.
(C) 저희를 방문해 주셔서 기쁩니다.

해설 (A) [○] 재즈를 좋아하지 않는다며, 재즈 페스티벌에 가본 적이 없음을 간접적으로 전달했으므로 정답이다.
(B) [×] 질문의 jazz festival(재즈 페스티벌)과 관련 있는 concert hall(콘서트홀)을 사용하여 혼동을 준 오답이다.
(C) [×] 질문의 visited를 반복 사용하여 혼동을 준 오답이다.

16 부정 의문문

호주식 → 미국식

Shouldn't we repaint the exterior of our building?
(A) Thanks for painting my van.
(B) Yes. With brighter colors.
(C) An interior designer.

repaint v. 다시 칠하다 exterior n. 외관, 외부 van n. 승합차, 밴

해석 우리 건물 외관을 다시 칠해야 하지 않나요?
(A) 제 승합차를 칠해 주셔서 감사해요.
(B) 네. 더 밝은 색으로요.
(C) 인테리어 디자이너요.

해설 (A) [×] repaint - painting의 유사 발음 어휘를 사용하여 혼동을 준 오답이다.
(B) [○] Yes로 건물 외관을 다시 칠해야 함을 전달한 후, 더 밝은 색으로 해야 한다고 부연 설명을 했으므로 정답이다.
(C) [×] 질문의 exterior(외관)와 반대 의미인 interior(인테리어, 내부)를 사용하여 혼동을 준 오답이다.

17 Who 의문문

미국식 → 캐나다식

Who's taking over Ms. Richards's job?
(A) That would be Maya.
(B) You can place it right there.
(C) For the open secretary position.

take over 인계받다

해석 누가 Ms. Richards의 일을 인계받나요?
(A) Maya일 거예요.
(B) 그건 바로 거기에 두시면 돼요.
(C) 공석인 비서직에 대해서요.

해설 (A) [○] Maya일 거라며, Ms. Richards의 일을 인계받을 사람을 언급했으므로 정답이다.
(B) [×] 누가 Ms. Richards의 일을 인계받는지를 물었는데, 이와 관련이 없는 그것을 바로 거기에 두면 된다는 내용으로 응답했으므로 오답이다.

(C) [×] 질문의 job(일)과 관련 있는 position(직책)을 사용하여 혼동을 준 오답이다.

18 조동사 의문문

호주식 → 미국식

Has Jessica turned in the quarterly financial report yet?
(A) Where can I print this report?
(B) She's still working on it, I think.
(C) It cost a lot more to finance than expected.

turn in 제출하다 quarterly adj. 분기별의 financial adj. 재무의
cost v. 비용이 들다 finance v. 자금을 조달하다, 재원을 대다

해석 Jessica가 분기별 재무 보고서를 벌써 제출했나요?
(A) 이 보고서는 어디에서 인쇄할 수 있나요?
(B) 그녀는 아직 작업 중인 것 같아요.
(C) 자금 조달하는 데 예상보다 훨씬 더 큰 비용이 들었어요.

해설 (A) [×] 질문의 report를 반복 사용하여 혼동을 준 오답이다.
(B) [○] 그녀가 아직 작업 중인 것 같다며, Jessica가 분기별 재무 보고서를 아직 제출하지 않았음을 간접적으로 전달했으므로 정답이다.
(C) [×] financial - finance의 유사 발음 어휘를 사용하여 혼동을 준 오답이다.

19 선택 의문문

영국식 → 캐나다식

Do you prefer the leather sofa or the fabric one?
(A) They're not the same fabric.
(B) We need to choose a table first.
(C) Most people would agree.

prefer v. 선호하다 leather n. 가죽 fabric n. 천, 직물

해석 가죽 소파를 선호하시나요, 아니면 천 소파를 선호하시나요?
(A) 그것들은 같은 천이 아니에요.
(B) 우리는 탁자를 먼저 골라야 해요.
(C) 대부분의 사람이 동의할 거예요.

해설 (A) [×] 질문의 fabric을 반복 사용하여 혼동을 준 오답이다.
(B) [○] 탁자를 먼저 골라야 한다는 말로, 가죽 소파와 천 소파 둘 다 간접적으로 선택하지 않은 정답이다.
(C) [×] prefer - people의 유사 발음 어휘를 사용하여 혼동을 준 오답이다.

20 부가 의문문

호주식 → 미국식

This position requires some experience, doesn't it?
(A) Put your seat in an upright position.
(B) That's not where it goes.
(C) Yes, at least five years.

require v. 필요로 하다, 요구하다 experience n. 경력, 경험
upright adj. 똑바른, 꼿꼿한 at least 적어도

해석 이 일자리는 경력을 필요로 하죠, 그렇지 않나요?
(A) 좌석을 똑바른 상태로 둬주세요.
(B) 그건 거기에 두는 게 아니에요.

(C) 네, 적어도 5년이요.

해설 (A) [×] 질문의 position(일자리)을 '상태, 자세'라는 의미의 명사로 반복 사용하여 혼동을 준 오답이다.
(B) [×] 일자리에 경력이 필요한지 물었는데, 이와 관련이 없는 그곳에 두는 게 아니라는 내용으로 응답했으므로 오답이다.
(C) [○] Yes로 그 일자리가 경력을 필요로 함을 전달한 후, 적어도 5년이라는 부연 설명을 했으므로 정답이다.

21 평서문
🔊 캐나다식 → 영국식

Gas prices have been going up a lot recently.
(A) Travel is getting more expensive.
(B) The open spaces in the parking lot.
(C) Driving to work takes too much time.

space n. 자리, 공간 parking lot 주차장

해설 최근에 기름 가격이 많이 오르고 있어요.
(A) 이동하는 건 점점 더 돈이 많이 들고 있어요.
(B) 주차장에 있는 빈자리들이요.
(C) 직장까지 운전하는 것은 시간이 너무 오래 걸려요.

해설 (A) [○] 이동하는 건 점점 더 돈이 많이 들고 있다는 말로, 최근에 기름 가격이 많이 오르고 있다는 의견에 동의했으므로 정답이다.
(B) [×] 질문의 lot(많이)을 '부지'라는 의미의 명사로 반복 사용하여 혼동을 준 오답이다.
(C) [×] 질문의 Gas(기름)와 관련 있는 Driving(운전하는 것)을 사용하여 혼동을 준 오답이다.

22 Who 의문문
🔊 호주식 → 미국식

Who do you want to work on the prototype?
(A) Jae-min's team has done great work before.
(B) Photography skills.
(C) Various types of exercise equipment.

prototype n. 견본, 원형 photography n. 사진술
various adj. 다양한 equipment n. 기구, 장비

해설 견본 작업을 누가 하길 원하나요?
(A) Jae-min의 팀이 이전에 훌륭하게 해냈어요.
(B) 사진 기술이요.
(C) 다양한 종류의 운동 기구요.

해설 (A) [○] Jae-min의 팀이 이전에 훌륭하게 해냈다는 말로, 견본 작업을 하기를 원하는 사람을 간접적으로 전달했으므로 정답이다.
(B) [×] prototype - Photography의 유사 발음 어휘를 사용하여 혼동을 준 오답이다.
(C) [×] prototype - types의 유사 발음 어휘를 사용하여 혼동을 준 오답이다.

23 부가 의문문
🔊 영국식 → 캐나다식

Our clients are pleased with the new billing system, aren't they?
(A) We haven't had any complaints.   ○

(B) The bill is due next week.
(C) To update the system.

pleased adj. 만족한, 마음에 드는 billing n. 청구서 발송
complaint n. 불만 (사항), 항의 bill n. 청구서
due adj. 지급 기일이 된, 만기의

해설 우리 고객들은 새로운 청구서 발송 시스템에 만족하고 있어요, 그렇지 않나요?
(A) 우리는 어떠한 불만 사항도 받지 않았어요.
(B) 청구서는 다음 주가 지급 기일이에요.
(C) 시스템을 업데이트하기 위해서요.

해설 (A) [○] 어떠한 불만 사항도 받지 않았다며, 고객들이 새로운 청구서 발송 시스템에 만족하고 있음을 간접적으로 전달했으므로 정답이다.
(B) [×] billing - bill의 유사 발음 어휘를 사용하여 혼동을 준 오답이다.
(C) [×] 질문의 system을 반복 사용하여 혼동을 준 오답이다.

24 평서문
🔊 호주식 → 영국식

I heard you have a beautiful house near Bondi Beach.
(A) Clean the house carefully.
(B) I sold it last year.
(C) To get some beach towels.

carefully adv. 꼼꼼히, 주의 깊게

해설 당신이 Bondi 해변 근처에 아름다운 집을 소유하고 있다고 들었어요.
(A) 집을 꼼꼼하게 청소하세요.
(B) 작년에 그걸 팔았어요.
(C) 비치 타월을 사기 위해서요.

해설 (A) [×] 질문의 house를 반복 사용하여 혼동을 준 오답이다.
(B) [○] 작년에 그걸 팔았다는 말로, 지금은 Bondi 해변 근처에 집을 소유하고 있지 않음을 간접적으로 전달했으므로 정답이다.
(C) [×] 질문의 Beach를 반복 사용하여 혼동을 준 오답이다.

25 평서문
🔊 캐나다식 → 미국식

We should set up a conference call to discuss the contract.
(A) I'm available on Wednesday.
(B) The line was busy.
(C) The conference was informative.

conference call 전화 회의 contract n. 계약(서)
available adj. 시간이 있는, 이용할 수 있는 line n. 전화, 선
informative adj. 유익한

해설 우리는 계약에 대해 논의하기 위해 전화 회의를 준비해야 해요.
(A) 저는 수요일에 시간이 있어요.
(B) 전화는 통화 중이었어요.
(C) 그 회의는 유익했어요.

해설 (A) [○] 수요일에 시간이 있다는 말로, 전화 회의를 준비할 수 있는 시점을 전달했으므로 정답이다.
(B) [×] 질문의 conference call(전화 회의)과 관련 있는 line(전화)

을 사용하여 혼동을 준 오답이다.

(C) [×] 질문의 conference를 반복 사용하여 혼동을 준 오답이다.

최신토익경향

평서문은 매회 평균 3문제 정도 출제되며, 객관적인 사실이나 의견을 제시하거나 제안이나 요청을 전달하는데, 그 의도에 따라 답변이 다양하게 나올 수 있어 난도가 높다. 특히, 최근에는 제안이나 요청을 의도하는 평서문에 간접적으로 수락하거나 거절하는 응답이 출제되고 있으므로 예문과 함께 알아두자.

You need to organize these files.
이 파일들을 정리해 주셔야 해요.
<수락> I'll just submit this report.
　　　이 보고서만 제출할게요.
<거절> Cathy can manage that.
　　　Cathy가 그것을 할 수 있어요.
*<수락> 이 보고서만 제출하겠다는 말로, 보고서 제출 후에 파일 정리를 하겠다고 요청을 수락하는 응답
　<거절> 제3의 인물인 Cathy가 할 수 있다는 말로, 자신은 파일 정리를 못한다고 요청을 거절하는 응답

26 How 의문문

🔊 영국식 → 호주식

How can I sign up for the Spanish class?
(A) He followed the signs to the exit.
(B) I enjoy Spanish movies.
(C) Fill out this registration form.

sign up 등록하다, 가입하다　fill out ~을 작성하다
registration form 신청서

해석　스페인어 수업에 어떻게 등록할 수 있나요?
　　(A) 그는 표지판을 따라 출구로 갔어요.
　　(B) 저는 스페인 영화를 즐겨 봐요.
　　(C) 이 신청서를 작성하세요.

해설　(A) [×] 질문의 sign up(등록하다)의 sign을 '표지판'이라는 의미의 signs로 반복 사용하여 혼동을 준 오답이다.
　　(B) [×] 질문의 Spanish를 반복 사용하여 혼동을 준 오답이다.
　　(C) [○] 이 신청서를 작성하라는 말로, 스페인어 수업 등록 방법을 언급했으므로 정답이다.

27 제공 의문문

🔊 미국식 → 캐나다식

Would you like some tea while you wait?
(A) Could I have some water?
(B) The waiting room on the corner.
(C) No, a little lower.

waiting room 대기실, 대합실

해석　기다리는 동안 차 좀 드시겠어요?
　　(A) 물을 좀 마실 수 있을까요?
　　(B) 모퉁이에 있는 대기실이요.
　　(C) 아니요, 조금 더 낮게요.

해설　(A) [○] 물을 좀 마실 수 있을지를 되물어, 차를 마시라는 제공을 간접적으로 거절한 정답이다.

(B) [×] wait - waiting의 유사 발음 어휘를 사용하여 혼동을 준 오답이다.

(C) [×] 기다리는 동안 차를 마시겠는지를 물었는데, 이와 관련이 없는 조금 더 낮게라는 내용으로 응답했으므로 오답이다. 제공 의문문에 No로 응답했다고 해서 문장을 끝까지 듣지 않고 정답으로 선택하지 않도록 주의한다.

28 How 의문문

🔊 영국식 → 캐나다식

How much will it cost to fix the copier?
(A) The fax machine stopped working.
(B) The technician will let us know later.
(C) A couple of hours.

copier n. 복사기　fax machine 팩스기　technician n. 기술자

해석　복사기를 고치는 데 비용이 얼마나 들까요?
　　(A) 팩스기가 작동을 멈췄어요.
　　(B) 기술자가 나중에 알려줄 거예요.
　　(C) 몇 시간 정도요.

해설　(A) [×] 질문의 fix(고치다)와 관련 있는 stopped working(작동을 멈췄다)을 사용하여 혼동을 준 오답이다.
　　(B) [○] 기술자가 나중에 알려줄 것이라는 말로, 복사기를 고치는 데 드는 비용을 모른다는 것을 간접적으로 전달했으므로 정답이다.
　　(C) [×] 복사기를 고치는 데 드는 비용을 물었는데, 시간으로 응답했으므로 오답이다.

29 Why 의문문

🔊 호주식 → 영국식

Why do we have to provide a medical certificate when we take a sick day now?
(A) The hospital is across the street.
(B) Management has changed its policy.
(C) I hung my certificate on the wall.

medical certificate 진단서　sick day 병가
management n. 경영진, 운영진　policy n. 방침, 정책
certificate n. 자격증, 증명서

해석　우리는 왜 이제 병가를 낼 때 진단서를 제출해야 하나요?
　　(A) 병원은 길 건너편에 있어요.
　　(B) 경영진이 방침을 변경했어요.
　　(C) 저는 자격증을 벽에 걸어 두었어요.

해설　(A) [×] 질문의 medical certificate(진단서)와 관련 있는 hospital(병원)을 사용하여 혼동을 준 오답이다.
　　(B) [○] 경영진이 방침을 변경했다며, 병가를 낼 때 진단서를 제출해야 하는 이유를 언급했으므로 정답이다.
　　(C) [×] 질문의 certificate를 반복 사용하여 혼동을 준 오답이다.

최신토익경향

매회 1~2문제 출제되는 Why 의문문은 이유 또는 목적을 묻는 의문문으로 전치사 For나 Because of, 접속사 Because, 또는 To 부정사를 포함하여 답변하는 경우가 많다. 하지만 최근에는 이유 또는 목적을 나타내는 표현이 오답 보기에 포함되고, 정답에는 이러한 표현들이 생략된 채로 나와 오답률

이 높으니, 예문을 통해 최신 경향에 익숙해지자.

Why haven't you unpacked your belongings yet?
왜 당신의 소지품들을 아직 풀지 않았나요?

<답변> I was meeting with a colleague.
저는 동료와 만나고 있었어요.

* 소지품을 풀지 않은 이유가 동료와 만나고 있었기 때문이라고 답한 응답

30 평서문
3》 캐나다식 → 영국식

Please put the boxes in the warehouse after inspecting the products.
(A) When will they get here?
(B) On the loading dock.
(C) Yes. I mailed the packages.

warehouse n. 창고 inspect v. 검사하다, 점검하다
loading dock 하역장, 짐 싣는 곳 package n. 소포, 포장물

해석 제품들을 검사한 후 상자들을 창고 안에 넣어주세요.
(A) 그것들은 언제 여기에 도착할 건가요?
(B) 하역장에요.
(C) 네. 저는 소포들을 부쳤어요.

해설 (A) [○] 언제 상자들이 여기에 도착할 것인지 되물어, 상자들에 대한 추가 정보를 요구한 정답이다.
(B) [×] 질문의 warehouse(창고)에서 연상할 수 있는 loading dock(하역장)을 사용하여 혼동을 준 오답이다.
(C) [×] 질문의 boxes(상자들)와 관련된 packages(소포들)를 사용하여 혼동을 준 오답이다.

31 When 의문문
3》 영국식 → 호주식

When is Flight TW 907 scheduled to depart?
(A) Was your seat comfortable?
(B) It just took off a moment ago.
(C) To get to Dallas.

flight n. 항공편, 비행기 schedule v. 예정하다 depart v. 출발하다
comfortable adj. 편안한 take off 이륙하다

해석 TW 907 항공편은 언제 출발할 예정인가요?
(A) 좌석은 편안했나요?
(B) 조금 전에 이륙했어요.
(C) 댈러스로 가기 위해서요.

해설 (A) [×] 항공편 출발 예정 시간을 물었는데, 이와 관련이 없는 좌석이 편안했는지를 되묻는 내용으로 응답한 오답이다. 질문의 Flight(항공편)에서 연상할 수 있는 비행기 탑승과 관련된 seat(좌석)을 사용하여 혼동을 주었다.
(B) [○] 조금 전에 이륙했다는 말로, TW 907 항공편의 출발 시간이 이미 지났다는 간접적인 응답을 했으므로 정답이다.
(C) [×] 항공편 출발 예정 시간을 물었는데, 목적으로 응답했으므로 오답이다. 질문의 Flight(항공편)에서 연상할 수 있는 목적지와 관련된 Dallas(댈러스)를 사용하여 혼동을 주었다.

PART 3

[32-34]
3》 캐나다식 → 미국식

Questions 32-34 refer to the following conversation.

M: Amy, ³²**I was really impressed by the casserole and dessert you made for last night's dinner party**. Where do you get your recipes?
W: I sometimes use a site called MenuNow.com, which allows users to upload recipes. I also just invent my own.
M: ³³**Would you mind sending me some of your favorites?**
W: Of course. ³⁴**I would also recommend subscribing to the Chatty Chef's social media channel.** Her videos are easy to follow and include basic cooking tips and techniques for beginners.

casserole n. 캐서롤(오븐에 넣어서 천천히 익혀 만드는 요리)
recipe n. 요리법, 조리법 invent v. 개발하다, 발명하다
subscribe v. 구독하다, 가입하다 technique n. 기술, 기법
beginner n. 초보자, 초심자

해석
32-34번은 다음 대화에 관한 문제입니다.

남: Amy, ³²어젯밤 만찬회를 위해 당신이 만든 캐서롤과 디저트가 정말 인상적이었어요. 요리법은 어디서 얻으시나요?
여: 사용자들이 요리법을 업로드할 수 있는 MenuNow.com이라는 사이트를 가끔 이용해요. 저만의 것을 개발하기도 하고요.
남: ³³가장 좋아하는 것들 좀 보내주시겠어요?
여: 물론이죠. ³⁴Chatty Chef의 소셜 미디어 채널을 구독하는 것도 추천해 드리고 싶어요. 그녀의 영상은 따라 하기 쉽고 초보자들을 위한 기본적인 요리 조언과 기술이 포함되어 있어요.

32 특정 세부 사항 문제

해석 남자는 최근에 무엇을 했는가?
(A) 디저트를 준비했다.
(B) 모임에 참석했다.
(C) 요리 프로그램을 시청했다.
(D) 가전제품을 구입했다.

해설 남자가 최근에 한 일을 묻는 문제이므로, 질문의 핵심 어구(recently)와 관련된 내용을 주의 깊게 듣는다. 남자가 "I was really impressed by the casserole and dessert you made for last night's dinner party"라며 어젯밤 만찬회를 위해 여자가 만든 캐서롤과 디저트가 정말 인상적이었다고 한 것을 통해 남자가 최근에 모임에 참석했다는 것을 알 수 있다. 따라서 (B)가 정답이다.

어휘 gathering n. 모임 appliance n. 가전제품

Paraphrasing

dinner party 만찬회 → a gathering 모임

33 요청 문제

해석 남자는 여자에게 무엇을 하라고 요청하는가?
(A) 몇몇 주방용품을 제공한다.

TEST 4 PART 3 **149**

(B) 만찬회를 주최한다.
(C) 요리법을 공유한다.
(D) 새로운 요리를 맛본다.

해설 남자의 말에서 요청과 관련된 표현이 언급된 다음을 주의 깊게 듣는다. 남자가 여자에게 "Would you mind sending me some of your favorites[recipes]?"라며 가장 좋아하는 요리법을 좀 보내달라고 하였다. 따라서 (C)가 정답이다.

어휘 utensil n. (주방)용품, 도구   host v. 주최하다
taste v. 맛보다; n. 맛

34 제안 문제

해석 여자는 무엇을 제안하는가?
(A) 웹사이트에서 음식을 주문하기
(B) 몇몇 영상을 업로드하기
(C) 요리 학교에 등록하기
(D) 온라인에서 요리사를 보기

해설 여자의 말에서 제안과 관련된 표현이 언급된 다음을 주의 깊게 듣는다. 여자가 남자에게 "I would also recommend subscribing to the Chatty Chef's social media channel."이라며 Chatty Chef의 소셜 미디어 채널을 구독하는 것도 추천해 주고 싶다고 하였다. 따라서 (D)가 정답이다.

[35-37]   🎧 호주식 → 영국식

Questions 35-37 refer to the following conversation.

M: ³⁵**Can I see your ticket for tonight's basketball game?**
W: Here it is. But I have a question about parking. The main lot is full, so ³⁶**I parked near the side of the building. But now I'm worried that parking might not be allowed there.**
M: That area is for venue employees only. You need to move your car to the rear parking lot.
W: I understand. ³⁷**How much time until the game begins?**
M: I can hear the announcer now. That means ³⁷**the players are coming onto the court. You should hurry.**

allow v. 허용하다, 허락하다   venue n. 개최지, 장소   rear adj. 뒤쪽의
court n. 경기장

해석
35-37번은 다음 대화에 관한 문제입니다.
남: ³⁵오늘 밤 농구 경기 표를 보여주시겠어요?
여: 여기 있어요. 하지만 주차에 대해 질문이 있어요. 메인 주차장이 꽉 차서, ³⁶건물 옆쪽에 주차했어요. 그런데 지금 그곳에 주차하는 것이 허용되지 않을까 봐 걱정이에요.
남: 그 구역은 개최지 직원 전용이에요. 뒤쪽 주차장으로 차를 옮기셔야 해요.
여: 알겠습니다. ³⁷경기 시작까지 얼마나 남았나요?
남: 지금 아나운서 목소리가 들리네요. 그건 ³⁷선수들이 경기장으로 나오고 있다는 뜻이죠. ³⁷서두르셔야 해요.

35 장소 문제

해석 화자들은 어디에 있는 것 같은가?

(A) 공연장에
(B) 주민 센터에
(C) 스포츠 경기장에
(D) 영화관에

해설 화자들이 있는 장소를 묻는 문제이므로, 장소와 관련된 표현을 놓치지 않고 듣는다. 남자가 "Can I see your ticket for tonight's basketball game?"이라며 오늘 밤 농구 경기 표를 보여달라고 한 것을 통해 화자들이 스포츠 경기장에 있음을 알 수 있다. 따라서 (C)가 정답이다.

어휘 community center 주민 센터

36 문제점 문제

해석 여자는 무엇에 대해 걱정하는가?
(A) 장소 개장 시간
(B) 건물이 위치한 곳
(C) 주차 허용 시간
(D) 차량을 둔 곳

해설 여자의 말에서 부정적인 표현이 언급된 주변을 주의 깊게 듣는다. 여자가 "I parked near the side of the building. But now I'm worried that parking might not be allowed there."라며 건물 옆쪽에 주차했다고 한 후, 그곳에 주차하는 것이 허용되지 않을까 봐 걱정이라고 하였다. 따라서 (D)가 정답이다.

어휘 vehicle n. 차량

37 이유 문제

해석 남자는 왜 여자에게 서두르라고 말하는가?
(A) 행사가 막 시작되려고 한다.
(B) 표가 거의 매진되었다.
(C) 좌석이 예약될 수 없다.
(D) 서비스가 이용될 수 없을 것이다.

해설 질문의 핵심 어구(hurry)가 언급된 주변을 주의 깊게 듣는다. 여자가 "How much time until the game begins?"라며 경기 시작까지 얼마나 남았냐고 묻자, 남자가 "the players are coming onto the court. You should hurry."라며 선수들이 경기장으로 나오고 있다고 한 후, 서두르라고 하였다. 따라서 (A)가 정답이다.

어휘 be about to 막 ~하려 하다   sold out (표가) 매진된, 다 팔린
reserve v. 예약하다

[38-40]   🎧 미국식 → 캐나다식

Questions 38-40 refer to the following conversation.

W: Good afternoon. ³⁸**I am looking for the tea set you are advertising on your Web site. It'll be a birthday gift for my sister.**
M: Unfortunately, we are all sold out. And our other branches are out of that as well.
W: Do you know when you are getting more of it?
M: Probably next week.
W: Oh, no . . . ³⁹**Her birthday party is tonight.**
M: ⁴⁰**Why not get a gift card then?**

W: Good idea! I'll take one with a value of 50 dollars.

look for ~을 찾다 **advertise** v. 광고하다 **branch** n. 지점
out of 떨어져서, 동나서 **probably** adv. 아마 **gift card** 상품권
value n. 값어치, 가치

해석

38-40번은 다음 대화에 관한 문제입니다.

여: 안녕하세요. ³⁸저는 귀사의 웹사이트에서 광고하고 있는 차 세트를 찾고 있어요. 여동생의 생일 선물이 될 거예요.

남: 유감스럽게도, 모두 팔렸어요. 그리고 다른 지점들도 그것이 다 떨어졌어요.

여: 언제 그것이 더 들어오는지 아시나요?

남: 아마 다음 주예요.

여: 아, 안 돼요... ³⁹그녀의 생일 파티가 오늘 밤이에요.

남: ⁴⁰그럼 상품권을 구매하는 건 어떠세요?

여: 좋은 생각이에요! 50달러짜리로 살게요.

38 목적 문제

해석 여자는 왜 가게를 방문하고 있는가?
(A) 제품을 교환하기 위해
(B) 상품을 반품하기 위해
(C) 선물을 구매하기 위해
(D) 교환권을 상품으로 교환하기 위해

해설 대화의 목적을 묻는 문제이므로, 대화의 초반을 반드시 듣는다. 여자가 "I am looking for the tea set you are advertising on your Web site. It'll be a birthday gift for my sister."라며 웹사이트에서 광고하고 있는 차 세트를 찾고 있다고 한 후, 여동생의 생일 선물이 될 것이라고 하였다. 따라서 (C)가 정답이다.

어휘 **redeem** v. 상품으로 교환하다, 보완하다 **voucher** n. 교환권, 할인권

39 특정 세부 사항 문제

해석 오늘 밤에 무엇이 축하될 것인가?
(A) 졸업
(B) 생일
(C) 결혼
(D) 승진

해설 질문의 핵심 어구(tonight)가 언급된 주변을 주의 깊게 듣는다. 여자가 "Her[sister's] birthday party is tonight."이라며 여동생의 생일 파티가 오늘 밤이라고 하였다. 따라서 (B)가 정답이다.

어휘 **promotion** n. 승진

40 제안 문제

해석 남자는 무엇을 제안하는가?
(A) 다른 가게에 가기
(B) 상품권 구매하기
(C) 온라인 서비스 이용하기
(D) 멤버십 프로그램에 가입하기

해설 남자의 말에서 제안과 관련된 표현이 언급된 다음을 주의 깊게 듣는

다. 남자가 여자에게 "Why not get a gift card then?"이라며 상품권을 구매하는 게 어떤지를 물었다. 따라서 (B)가 정답이다.

어휘 **join** v. 가입하다

Paraphrasing

get 구매하다 → Buying 구매하기

[41-43] ⟨3회⟩ 영국식 → 캐나다식 → 호주식

Questions 41-43 refer to the following conversation with three speakers.

W: I'm glad you're both here. ⁴¹**Did you review the changes I intend to make to Ms. Hong's house?**

M1: Yeah. ⁴¹**I think the design is greatly improved.** The living room will seem much more spacious.

W: ⁴²**What about you, Kevin?**

M2: ⁴¹**I haven't had a chance to check them out.** ⁴²**I was really busy yesterday afternoon. I had to take some sample tiles to another client's home.**

W: I see. I actually have a copy of the revised floor plan on my desk. ⁴³**Could I bring it to you now to look over?**

M2: ⁴³**Sure.** I have some free time this afternoon.

review v. 검토하다 **intend to** ~하려고 하다 **greatly** adv. 크게, 대단히
spacious adj. 넓은, 널찍한 **revised** adj. 수정된, 변경한
floor plan 평면도 **look over** 살펴보다, 훑어보다

해석

41-43번은 다음 세 명의 대화에 관한 문제입니다.

여: 두 분 다 오시다니 좋네요. ⁴¹제가 Ms. Hong의 집에 변경하려고 하는 사항들을 검토해 보셨나요?

남1: 네. ⁴¹디자인이 크게 개선된 것 같아요. 거실이 훨씬 더 넓어 보일 거예요.

여: ⁴²당신은 어떤가요, Kevin?

남2: ⁴¹저는 그것들을 확인할 기회가 없었어요. ⁴²어제 오후에 정말 바빴어요. 다른 고객의 집에 견본 타일들을 가져가야 했거든요.

여: 그렇군요. 실은 제 책상 위에 수정된 평면도 사본이 있어요. ⁴³지금 살펴보게 가져다드릴까요?

남2: ⁴³물론이죠. 오늘 오후에 시간이 좀 있어요.

41 화자 문제

해석 화자들은 누구인 것 같은가?
(A) 안전 감독관들
(B) 투어 가이드들
(C) 인테리어 디자이너들
(D) 부동산 투자자들

해설 대화에서 신분 및 직업과 관련된 표현을 놓치지 않고 듣는다. 여자가 남자들에게 "Did you review the changes I intend to make to Ms. Hong's house?"라며 자신이 Ms. Hong의 집에 변경하려고 하는 사항들을 검토해 봤는지 묻자, 남자1이 "I think the design is greatly improved."라며 디자인이 크게 개선된 것 같다고 했고, 남자2가 "I haven't had a chance to check them out."이라며 그것들을 확인할 기회가 없었다고 한 것을 통해 화자들이 인테리어 디

자이너들임을 알 수 있다. 따라서 (C)가 정답이다.

어휘 inspector n. 감독관, 검사관 property n. 부동산, 재산
　　　investor n. 투자자

42 특정 세부 사항 문제

해석 Kevin은 어제 무엇을 했는가?
(A) 비품을 구매했다.
(B) 사본을 인쇄했다.
(C) 워크숍을 실시했다.
(D) 물품들을 배달했다.

해설 질문의 핵심 어구(Kevin ~ yesterday)가 언급된 주변을 주의 깊
게 듣는다. 여자가 "What about you, Kevin?"이라며 Kevin에
게 어떻게 생각하는지 묻자, 남자2[Kevin]가 "I was really busy
yesterday afternoon. I had to take some sample tiles to
another client's home."이라며 어제 오후에 정말 바빴다고 한 후,
다른 고객의 집에 견본 타일들을 가져가야 했다고 하였다. 따라서 (D)
가 정답이다.

어휘 conduct v. 실시하다, 이끌다 deliver v. 배달하다

Paraphrasing

take some sample tiles to ~로 견본 타일들을 가져가다 →
delivered some items 물품들을 배달했다

43 다음에 할 일 문제

해석 여자는 다음에 무엇을 할 것 같은가?
(A) 설계도를 검토한다.
(B) 회의에 참석한다.
(C) 서류를 가지고 온다.
(D) 고객에게 연락한다.

해설 대화의 마지막 부분을 주의 깊게 듣는다. 여자가 "Could I bring
it[copy of the revised floor plan] to you now to look over?"
라며 남자2에게 지금 살펴보게 수정된 평면도 사본을 가져다줄지 묻
자, 남자2가 "Sure."라며 좋다고 하였다. 따라서 (C)가 정답이다.

어휘 plan n. 설계도, 도면 retrieve v. 가지고 오다, 회수하다

Paraphrasing

bring 가져다주다 → Retrieve 가지고 오다

[44-46]

Questions 44-46 refer to the following conversation.　　3 호주식 → 미국식

M: ⁴⁴**Thanks for stopping in for this performance
evaluation. I'm pleased to say that during your first
six months, your work has been outstanding.**

W: That's good to hear. ⁴⁵**I really like the culture this
company has created. It is more relaxed and
welcoming than the last software firm I worked for.**

M: We're glad to hear that. ⁴⁶**The one complaint we have
is that you sometimes do not arrive at the office on
time in the morning.**　　　　　　　　　　　○

W: ⁴⁶**I'm sorry about that.** I have to take two trains to get
here from my home, and sometimes they are delayed.
I'm getting a car soon, though.

stop in for ~을 위해 들르다 performance n. 성과, 수행
evaluation n. 평가 outstanding adj. 뛰어난, 걸출한
welcoming adj. 친근한, 따뜻한 firm n. 회사
complaint n. 불만 (사항), 불평 on time 제시간에, 정각에

해석
44-46번은 다음 대화에 관한 문제입니다.

남: ⁴⁴성과 평가를 위해 들러주셔서 감사합니다. 첫 6개월 동안, 당신의 업무
가 뛰어났다고 말할 수 있어서 기쁩니다.

여: 다행이네요. ⁴⁵저는 이 회사가 조성한 문화가 정말 마음에 들어요. 제가
근무했던 이전의 소프트웨어 회사보다 더 편안하고 친근해요.

남: 그렇다니 다행이네요. ⁴⁶한 가지 불만 사항은 가끔 아침에 제시간에 사무
실에 도착하지 않으신다는 점입니다.

여: ⁴⁶죄송합니다. 집에서 여기까지 오려면 열차를 두 대 타야 하는데, 가끔
연착될 때가 있어요. 하지만 곧 차를 구입할 거예요.

44 주제 문제

해석 화자들은 주로 무엇에 대해 이야기하고 있는가?
(A) 직원의 성과
(B) 제품 후기
(C) 회사 규정
(D) 고객의 불만 사항

해설 대화의 주제를 묻는 문제이므로, 대화의 초반을 반드시 듣는다. 남자
가 "Thanks for stopping in for this performance evaluation.
I'm pleased to say that during your first six months, your
work has been outstanding."이라며 성과 평가를 위해 들러줘서
고맙다고 한 후, 첫 6개월 동안 여자의 업무가 뛰어났다고 말할 수 있
어서 기쁘다고 하였다. 따라서 (A)가 정답이다.

어휘 regulation n. 규정, 규제

45 특정 세부 사항 문제

해석 여자는 회사에 대해 무엇을 칭찬하는가?
(A) 좋은 분위기를 띤다.
(B) 많은 휴가를 제공한다.
(C) 유연한 일정 관리 체계를 갖추고 있다.
(D) 넉넉한 급여를 제공한다.

해설 질문의 핵심 어구(praise)와 관련된 내용을 주의 깊게 듣는다. 여자
가 "I really like the culture this company has created. It is
more relaxed and welcoming than the last software firm
I worked for."라며 이 회사가 조성한 문화가 정말 마음에 든다고 한
후, 근무했던 이전의 소프트웨어 회사보다 더 편안하고 친근하다고 하
였다. 따라서 (A)가 정답이다.

어휘 inviting adj. 좋은, 매력적인 atmosphere n. 분위기
flexible adj. 유연한, 융통성 있는 generous adj. 넉넉한, 관대한

46 특정 세부 사항 문제

해석 여자는 무엇에 대해 사과하는가?
(A) 보고서에 오류를 내는 것
(B) 마감일을 지키지 못하는 것
(C) **직장에 늦게 도착하는 것**
(D) 장비를 망가뜨리는 것

해설 질문의 핵심 어구(apologize)와 관련된 내용을 주의 깊게 듣는다. 남자가 "The one complaint we have is that you sometimes do not arrive at the office on time in the morning."이라며 한 가지 불만 사항은 가끔 아침에 제시간에 사무실에 도착하지 않는다는 점이라고 하자, 여자가 "I'm sorry about that."이라며 이에 대해 사과했다. 따라서 (C)가 정답이다.

어휘 deadline n. 마감일   equipment n. 장비

Paraphrasing

do not arrive at the office on time 제시간에 사무실에 도착하지 않는다 → Arriving late for work 직장에 늦게 도착하는 것

[47-49]

🎧 영국식 → 캐나다식

Questions 47-49 refer to the following conversation.

W: Hi, Tae-joon. ⁴⁷**Jess is in the hospital, so she won't be able to do her shift in the produce section of our store tomorrow.** Could you fill in for her?

M: Oh, but I'm really looking forward to my day off. ⁴⁸**I've been working extra hours lately because we're understaffed.**

W: I understand. ⁴⁸**But please reconsider. I'm planning to interview applicants soon. ⁴⁸So this won't happen again.**

M: OK. I can help out tomorrow.

W: Thanks. ⁴⁹**And in return, I'll give you an extra day off.**

produce n. 농산물   fill in ~을 대신하다, 채우다
look forward to ~을 기다리다, 고대하다   day off 휴일, 쉬는 날
understaffed adj. 인력이 부족한   reconsider v. 다시 생각하다
applicant n. 지원자   in return 대가로, 답례로

해석

47-49번은 다음 대화에 관한 문제입니다.

여: 안녕하세요, Tae-joon. ⁴⁷Jess가 병원에 있어서, 내일 우리 매장의 농산물 구역에서 근무할 수 없을 거예요. 당신이 그녀를 대신해 줄 수 있을까요?

남: 아, 하지만 저는 제 휴일을 너무나도 기다리고 있어요. ⁴⁸인력이 부족해서 저는 최근에 초과 근무를 해오고 있어요.

여: 이해해요. ⁴⁸그렇지만 다시 생각해 주세요. 곧 지원자들을 면접 볼 계획이에요. ⁴⁸그러니 다시는 이런 일이 없을 거예요.

남: 알겠어요. 내일 도와드릴 수 있어요.

여: 고마워요. ⁴⁹그리고 그 대가로, 휴일을 하루 더 드릴게요.

47 화자 문제

해석 화자들은 어디에서 일하는 것 같은가?

(A) 슈퍼마켓에서
(B) 식당에서
(C) 병원에서
(D) 출장 연회 업체에서

해설 대화에서 신분 및 직업과 관련된 표현을 놓치지 않고 듣는다. 여자가 "Jess is in the hospital, so she won't be able to do her shift in the produce section of our store tomorrow."라며 Jess가 병원에 있어서 내일 매장의 농산물 구역에서 근무할 수 없을 것이라고 한 것을 통해, 화자들이 슈퍼마켓에서 일한다는 것을 알 수 있다. 따라서 (A)가 정답이다.

어휘 medical clinic 병원   catering n. 출장 연회, 음식 공급

48 의도 파악 문제

해석 여자는 왜 "곧 지원자들을 면접 볼 계획이에요"라고 말하는가?
(A) **안심시키기 위해**
(B) 정보를 요청하기 위해
(C) 실수를 인정하기 위해
(D) 불확실성을 나타내기 위해

해설 질문의 인용어구(I'm planning to interview applicants soon)가 언급된 주변을 주의 깊게 듣는다. 남자가 "I've been working extra hours lately because we're understaffed."라며 인력이 부족해서 최근에 초과 근무를 해오고 있다고 하자, 여자가 "But please reconsider.", "So this won't happen again."이라며 다시 생각해 달라고 하면서 다시는 이런 일이 없을 것이라고 한 것을 통해 남자를 안심시키기 위함임을 알 수 있다. 따라서 (A)가 정답이다.

어휘 reassurance n. 안심(시키기)   admit v. 인정하다, 시인하다
indicate v. 나타내다, 내비치다   uncertainty n. 불확실성

49 제안 문제

해석 여자는 남자를 위해 무엇을 해주겠다고 제안하는가?
(A) 교육 자료를 준비한다.
(B) 매장 적립금을 준다.
(C) 전반적인 보수를 늘린다.
(D) **추가 휴가를 제공한다.**

해설 여자의 말에서 제안과 관련된 표현이 포함된 문장을 주의 깊게 듣는다. 여자가 남자에게 "And in return, I'll give you an extra day off."라며 그 대가로, 휴일을 하루 더 주겠다고 하였다. 따라서 (D)가 정답이다.

어휘 store credit 매장 적립금, 반환하는 물건값이 적힌 표
overall adj. 전반적인, 종합적인   compensation n. 보수, 보상(금)

Paraphrasing

give ~ an extra day off 휴일을 하루 더 주다 → Provide additional leave 추가 휴가를 제공하다

[50-52]

🎧 영국식 → 호주식

Questions 50-52 refer to the following conversation.

W: ⁵⁰**How are the preparations for the press conference next week going, Demir?**

M: Not well. Our CEO just asked me to include a presentation about the features of our upcoming smart TV, but I'm not very knowledgeable about it.

W: ⁵¹**Why don't you call Ms. Jameson, the head of product development?**

M: That's a good idea. ⁵²**Maybe she would also be willing to join me at next week's event** and take questions from reporters.

W: ⁵²**Ms. Jameson won't be available. She's been asked to speak at the annual shareholders' meeting in Dallas, so she'll be out of town for most of the week.**

preparation n. 준비 press conference 기자 회견
presentation n. 발표 feature n. 기능, 특징
knowledgeable adj. 아는 것이 많은 shareholder n. 주주
be out of town (출장 등으로) 도시를 떠나 있다

해석

50-52번은 다음 대화에 관한 문제입니다.

여: ⁵⁰다음 주 기자 회견 준비는 어떻게 되고 있나요, Demir?

남: 잘 안되고 있어요. 대표이사님이 방금 곧 출시될 스마트 TV의 기능에 대한 발표를 포함해 달라고 하셨는데, 제가 그것에 대해 아는 것이 많지 않아요.

여: ⁵¹제품 개발 책임자인 Ms. Jameson에게 전화해 보는 건 어때요?

남: 좋은 생각이네요. ⁵²아마 그녀도 흔쾌히 저와 함께 다음 주 행사에 참석해서 기자들의 질문을 받을 수도 있을 것 같아요.

여: ⁵²Ms. Jameson은 시간이 없을 거예요. 그녀는 댈러스에서 열리는 연례 주주총회에서 연설해 달라는 요청을 받았기 때문에, 그 주의 대부분은 출장으로 도시를 떠나 있을 거예요.

50 특정 세부 사항 문제

해석 남자는 어떤 행사를 계획하고 있는가?
(A) 회사 야유회
(B) 기자 회견
(C) 서비스 출시
(D) 직원 회의

해설 대화에서 질문의 핵심 어구(event ~ planning)와 관련된 내용을 주의 깊게 듣는다. 여자가 남자에게 "How are the preparations for the press conference next week going, Demir?"라며 다음 주 기자 회견 준비가 어떻게 되고 있는지 물었다. 따라서 (B)가 정답이다.

어휘 retreat n. 야유회

51 제안 문제

해석 여자는 무엇을 제안하는가?
(A) 관리자에게 연락하기
(B) 기능 목록 검토하기
(C) 모바일 기기 테스트하기
(D) 발표 참석하기

해설 여자의 말에서 제안과 관련된 표현이 언급된 다음을 주의 깊게 듣는다. 여자가 "Why don't you call Ms. Jameson, the head of product development?"라며 제품 개발 책임자인 Ms. Jameson에게 전화해 보라고 하였다. 따라서 (A)가 정답이다.

Paraphrasing

the head 책임자 → a manager 관리자

52 이유 문제

해석 Ms. Jameson은 왜 다음 주에 부재중일 것인가?
(A) 생산 시설을 점검할 것이다.
(B) 분석 보고서를 작성할 것이다.
(C) 잠재 고객을 만날 것이다.
(D) 출장을 갈 것이다.

해설 질문의 핵심 어구(unavailable next week)와 관련된 내용을 주의 깊게 듣는다. 남자가 "Maybe she[Ms. Jameson] would also be willing to join me at next week's event"라며 아마 Ms. Jameson도 흔쾌히 함께 다음 주 행사에 참석할 수도 있을 것 같다고 하자, 여자가 "Ms. Jameson won't be available. She's been asked to speak at the annual shareholders' meeting in Dallas, so she'll be out of town for most of the week." 이라며 Ms. Jameson은 시간이 없을 거라고 한 후, 그녀는 댈러스에서 열리는 연례 주주총회에서 연설해 달라는 요청을 받았기 때문에 그 주의 대부분은 출장으로 도시를 떠나 있을 것이라고 하였다. 따라서 (D)가 정답이다.

어휘 production facility 생산 시설 potential adj. 잠재적인 business trip 출장

Paraphrasing

be out of town 출장으로 도시를 떠나 있다 → go on a business trip 출장을 가다

[53-55] 🔊 미국식 → 캐나다식 → 영국식

Questions 53-55 refer to the following conversation with three speakers.

W1: Hello, Mr. Collins. ⁵³**As you requested, our mechanic inspected your car in preparation for your upcoming drive from LA to Chicago.** It just needed a little oil.

M: Were there any other issues?

W1: ⁵⁴**I'll let Penny answer that for you.** Here she is.

W2: ⁵⁴**I noticed that your tires are quite worn.**

M: Would it be dangerous to drive with them?

W2: I wouldn't risk it. You should probably replace them.

M: Hmm . . . ⁵⁵**Give me a few minutes to call my cousin.** She knows a lot about cars, so she can advise me about what to do.

request v. 요청하다 mechanic n. 정비사
in preparation for ~을 준비하기 위해 wear v. 닳다, 해지다
dangerous adj. 위험한 risk v. ~의 위험을 무릅쓰다; n. 위험
cousin n. 사촌 advise v. 조언하다

해석

53-55번은 다음 세 명의 대화에 관한 문제입니다.

여1: 안녕하세요, Mr. Collins. ⁵³요청하신 대로, 저희 정비사가 곧 LA에서 시카고까지 운전할 준비가 되도록 당신의 차량을 점검했어요. 기름만 조금 넣으면 됐어요.

남: 다른 문제는 없었나요?

여1: ⁵⁴그건 Penny가 대답해 드리도록 할게요. 여기 있네요.

여2: ⁵⁴타이어가 상당히 마모된 것을 발견했어요.

남: 그것들로 운전하면 위험할까요?

여2: 전 위험을 무릅쓰지 않겠어요. 그것들을 교체하셔야 할 것 같아요.

남: 흠... ⁵⁵제 사촌에게 전화할 시간을 좀 주세요. 그녀는 자동차에 대해 많이 알고 있어서, 어떻게 해야 할지 조언해 줄 수 있어요.

53 이유 문제

해석 남자는 왜 점검을 요청했는가?
(A) 자신의 차량을 판매하려고 한다.
(B) 장거리 자동차 여행을 갈 계획이다.
(C) 보험료를 덜 내길 바란다.
(D) 값비싼 수리를 피하길 원한다.

해설 질문의 핵심 어구(request an inspection)와 관련된 내용을 주의 깊게 듣는다. 여자1이 "As you requested, our mechanic inspected your car in preparation for your upcoming drive from LA to Chicago."라며 요청한 대로, 정비사가 곧 LA에서 시카고까지 운전할 준비가 되도록 차량을 점검했다고 하였다. 따라서 (B)가 정답이다.

어휘 road trip 장거리 자동차 여행 insurance n. 보험(료)

54 문제점 문제

해석 Penny는 무슨 문제를 발견했는가?
(A) 일부 타이어는 상태가 좋지 않다.
(B) 서비스 비용이 너무 비싸다.
(C) 엔진 부품이 손상되었다.
(D) 일부 부품은 재고가 없다.

해설 Penny의 말에서 부정적인 표현이 언급된 주변을 주의 깊게 듣는다. 여자1이 "I'll let Penny answer that for you."라며 Penny가 대답하도록 하겠다고 한 후, 여자2[Penny]가 "I noticed that your tires are quite worn."이라며 타이어가 상당히 마모된 것을 발견했다고 하였다. 따라서 (A)가 정답이다.

어휘 component n. 부품 out of stock 재고가 없는

Paraphrasing

tires are quite worn 타이어가 상당히 마모되어 있다 → Some tires are in poor condition 일부 타이어는 상태가 좋지 않다

55 다음에 할 일 문제

해석 남자는 다음에 무엇을 할 것인가?
(A) 약속을 잡는다.
(B) 친척에게 이야기한다.
(C) 웹사이트에 로그인한다.
(D) 지불을 확인한다.

해설 대화의 마지막 부분을 주의 깊게 듣는다. 남자가 "Give me a few minutes to call my cousin."이라며 사촌에게 전화할 시간을 좀 달라고 한 것을 통해 남자가 친척에게 이야기할 것임을 알 수 있다. 따라서 (B)가 정답이다.

어휘 make an appointment 약속을 하다 relative n. 친척
confirm v. 확인하다 payment n. 지불, 납부

Paraphrasing

cousin 사촌 → a relative 친척

[56-58]

🎧 호주식 → 미국식

Questions 56-58 refer to the following conversation.

M: Hello. ⁵⁶**I'm an architect, and I'm looking for some recycled glass for a project.**

W: You're in luck. We keep a large supply of recycled glass.

M: That's good to hear. Using recycled glass will significantly reduce my costs, right?

W: Unfortunately, no. ^{57/58}**Many are surprised that the process of transporting glass, separating it by color, and then recycling it is more expensive than producing new glass.**

M: Well, my clients prioritize sustainability. ⁵⁸**So I'd still like to buy some.**

architect n. 건축가 significantly adv. 상당히, 크게
process n. 과정 transport v. 운반하다, 수송하다
separate v. 분류하다, 나누다 produce v. 생산하다
prioritize v. 우선시하다 sustainability n. 지속 가능성

해석

56-58번은 다음 대화에 관한 문제입니다.

남: 안녕하세요. ⁵⁶저는 건축가이고, 프로젝트에 사용할 재활용 유리를 찾고 있어요.

여: 운이 좋으시네요. 저희는 재활용 유리를 대량으로 보유하고 있어요.

남: 다행이네요. 재활용 유리를 사용하는 건 비용을 상당히 절감할 거예요, 맞죠?

여: 유감스럽게도, 그렇지 않아요. ^{57/58}많은 사람들이 유리를 운반하고, 색상별로 분류한 다음, 재활용하는 과정이 새 유리를 생산하는 것보다 비용이 더 많이 든다는 사실에 놀라워해요.

남: 음, 제 고객들은 지속 가능성을 우선시해요. ⁵⁸그래서 저는 여전히 구매하고 싶어요.

56 화자 문제

해석 남자는 어떤 종류의 업체에서 일하는가?
(A) 부동산 중개소
(B) 환경 단체
(C) 건축 회사
(D) 재활용 센터

해설 대화에서 신분 및 직업과 관련된 표현을 놓치지 않고 듣는다. 남자가 "I'm an architect, and I'm looking for some recycled glass for a project."라며 자신은 건축가이고, 프로젝트에 사용할 재활용 유리를 찾고 있다고 한 것을 통해 남자가 건축 회사에서 일한다는 것을 알 수 있다. 따라서 (C)가 정답이다.

어휘 real estate 부동산 environmental adj. 환경의
architecture n. 건축(학)

57 특정 세부 사항 문제

해석 여자에 따르면, 많은 사람들이 제품에 대해 무엇이 놀랍다고 생각하는가?
(A) 가격
(B) 가용성
(C) 품질
(D) 공급원

해설 여자의 말에서 질문의 핵심 어구(surprising)가 언급된 주변을 주의 깊게 듣는다. 여자가 "Many are surprised that the process of transporting glass, separating it by color, and then recycling it is more expensive than producing new glass." 라며 많은 사람들이 유리를 운반하고, 색상별로 분류한 다음, 재활용하는 과정이 새 유리를 생산하는 것보다 비용이 더 많이 든다는 사실에 놀라워한다고 하였다. 따라서 (A)가 정답이다.

어휘 availability n. 가용성

58 의도 파악 문제

해석 남자는 왜 "제 고객들은 지속 가능성을 우선시해요"라고 말하는가?
(A) 결정을 정당화하기 위해
(B) 문제를 지적하기 위해
(C) 제안을 거절하기 위해
(D) 조언을 제공하기 위해

해설 질문의 인용어구(my clients prioritize sustainability)가 언급된 주변을 주의 깊게 듣는다. 여자가 "Many are surprised that the process of transporting glass, separating it by color, and then recycling it is more expensive than producing new glass."라며 많은 사람들이 유리를 운반하고, 색상별로 분류한 다음, 재활용하는 과정이 새 유리를 생산하는 것보다 비용이 더 많이 든다는 사실에 놀라워하자, 남자가 "So I'd still like to buy some."이라며 여전히 구매하고 싶다고 한 것을 통해 가격이 더 비싸도 재활용 유리를 구매하겠다는 자신의 결정을 정당화하기 위함임을 알 수 있다. 따라서 (A)가 정답이다.

어휘 justify v. 정당화하다   point out ~을 지적하다
reject v. 거절하다, 거부하다   proposal n. 제안, 제의

[59-61]

🎧 캐나다식 → 영국식

Questions 59-61 refer to the following conversation.

M: Good morning. ⁵⁹**I bought this sweater here yesterday, but I'd like to return it for a refund.**

W: ⁵⁹**Of course, sir. I'll just need to see the receipt.**

M: Sure. Hmm . . . ⁶⁰**I put it in my wallet before I left my home, but now it's gone. It must have fallen out somewhere.** Can I still get my money back?

W: I'm sorry, but I cannot process your request.

M: But the price tag is still attached. ⁶¹**Could I at least exchange it for something I like better?**

W: Hold on, please. ⁶¹**I need to ask my manager whether that is allowed.**

---

return v. 반품하다   refund n. 환불; v. 환불하다
fall out 떨어지다, 떨어져 나가다   process v. 처리하다

price tag 가격표   attach v. 붙이다, 첨부하다
at least 적어도, 최소한   exchange v. 교환하다

해석
59-61번은 다음 대화에 관한 문제입니다.
남: 좋은 아침입니다. ⁵⁹어제 여기서 이 스웨터를 구입했는데, 환불을 위해 반품하고 싶어요.
여: ⁵⁹물론이죠, 고객님. 영수증만 보여주시면 돼요.
남: 물론이죠. 흠... ⁶⁰집을 나서기 전에 그걸 지갑에 넣었는데, 지금은 없어졌어요. 어딘가에 떨어졌나 봐요. 그래도 돈을 돌려받을 수 있나요?
여: 죄송하지만, 고객님의 요청을 처리할 수 없어요.
남: 하지만 가격표는 아직 붙어 있잖아요. ⁶¹적어도 더 마음에 드는 무언가로 교환할 수 있을까요?
여: 잠시만 기다려주세요. ⁶¹관리자에게 그것이 허용되는지 물어봐야 해요.

59 화자 문제

해석 여자는 어디에서 일하는 것 같은가?
(A) 금융 기관에서
(B) 여행사에서
(C) 옷 가게에서
(D) 음식점에서

해설 대화에서 신분 및 직업과 관련된 표현을 놓치지 않고 듣는다. 남자가 "I bought this sweater here yesterday, but I'd like to return it for a refund."라며 어제 여기서 스웨터를 구입했는데 환불을 위해 반품하고 싶다고 하자, 여자가 "Of course, sir. I'll just need to see the receipt."이라며 영수증만 보여주면 된다고 한 것을 통해 여자가 옷 가게에서 일한다는 것을 알 수 있다. 따라서 (C)가 정답이다.

어휘 institution n. 기관   dining establishment 음식점

60 문제점 문제

해석 남자는 무슨 문제를 언급하는가?
(A) 잘못된 금액을 지불했다.
(B) 개인 물품을 손상시켰다.
(C) 거래 기록을 잃어버렸다.
(D) 홍보 행사에 불참했다.

해설 남자의 말에서 부정적인 표현이 언급된 주변을 주의 깊게 듣는다. 남자가 "I put it[receipt] in my wallet before I left my home, but now it's gone. It must have fallen out somewhere."라며 집을 나서기 전에 영수증을 지갑에 넣었는데 없어졌다고 하며, 어딘가에 떨어진 것 같다고 한 것을 통해 영수증, 즉 거래 기록을 잃어버렸음을 알 수 있다. 따라서 (C)가 정답이다.

어휘 transaction n. 거래, 처리

61 다음에 할 일 문제

해석 여자는 다음에 무엇을 할 것 같은가?
(A) 설문 조사를 진행한다.
(B) 가격을 확인한다.
(C) 할인을 요청한다.
(D) 규정을 확인한다.

해설 대화의 마지막 부분을 주의 깊게 듣는다. 남자가 "Could I at least exchange it for something I like better?"라며 적어도 더 마음에 드는 무언가로 교환할 수 있을지 묻자, 여자가 "I need to ask my manager whether that is allowed."라며 관리자에게 교환이 허용되는지 물어봐야 한다고 한 것을 통해 여자가 관리자에게 제품 교환 규정에 관해 확인할 것임을 알 수 있다. 따라서 (D)가 정답이다.

어휘 survey n. 설문 조사 policy n. 규정, 방침

[62-64]

3음 미국식 → 호주식

Questions 62-64 refer to the following conversation and price list.

W: I have some great news. ⁶²**Our company has been hired to replace the fence around Desmond Park.** The current one is quite old, and there is concern that it may fall down soon.

M: This is the third job we've gotten this week. ⁶³**The billboards we installed have been really effective at attracting customers.** Um, what type of wood should we use for the fence?

W: I was given a list of approved materials to choose from. As this project involves a public area, ⁶⁴**we should go with the most durable option even if it's the most expensive.** We should build something that the community will enjoy for a long time.

replace v. 교체하다 concern n. 우려, 걱정
billboard n. 광고판, 게시판 effective adj. 효과적인
attract v. 끌어들이다, 마음을 끌다 material n. 자재, 재료
durable adj. 내구성이 좋은, 튼튼한 community n. 지역 사회
oak n. 참나무, 오크(너도밤나뭇과 졸참나무속의 총칭) pine n. 소나무
spruce n. 가문비나무 cedar n. 삼나무, 향나무

해석

62-64번은 다음 대화와 가격표에 관한 문제입니다.

여: 좋은 소식이 있어요. ⁶²**우리 회사가 Desmond 공원 주변의 울타리를 교체하기 위해 고용되었어요.** 현재 울타리가 꽤 오래돼서, 곧 쓰러질 우려가 있어요.

남: 이건 이번 주에 우리가 받은 세 번째 일이에요. ⁶³**우리가 설치한 광고판이 고객들을 끌어들이는 데 정말 효과적이었어요.** 음, 울타리에는 어떤 종류의 목재를 사용해야 하나요?

여: 저는 고를 수 있는 승인된 자재 목록을 받았어요. 이 프로젝트는 공공장소와 관련 있기 때문에, ⁶⁴**가장 비싸더라도 가장 내구성이 좋은 옵션을 선택해야 해요.** 우리는 지역 사회가 오랫동안 즐길만한 것을 만들어야 해요.

자재	가격 (입방 피트당)
참나무	27달러
소나무	22달러
가문비나무	18달러
⁶⁴삼나무	34달러

62 주제 문제

해설 대화는 주로 무엇에 대한 것인가?
(A) 울타리를 세우는 것

(B) 다리를 건설하는 것
(C) 건물을 수리하는 것
(D) 출입문을 교체하는 것

해설 대화의 주제를 묻는 문제이므로, 대화의 초반을 반드시 듣는다. 여자가 "Our company has been hired to replace the fence around Desmond Park."라며 회사가 Desmond 공원 주변의 울타리를 교체하기 위해 고용되었다고 한 후, 울타리를 세우는 프로젝트에 대한 내용으로 대화가 이어지고 있다. 따라서 (A)가 정답이다.

어휘 construct v. 건설하다 gate n. 출입문, 정문

63 방법 문제

해설 남자에 따르면, 회사는 어떻게 광고해 오고 있는가?
(A) 이메일을 보냄으로써
(B) 표지판을 세움으로써
(C) 전단지를 나눠줌으로써
(D) 온라인에 게시함으로써

해설 질문의 핵심 어구(advertising)와 관련된 내용을 주의 깊게 듣는다. 남자가 "The billboards we installed have been really effective at attracting customers."라며 자신들이 설치한 광고판이 고객들을 끌어들이는 데 정말 효과적이었다고 하였다. 따라서 (B)가 정답이다.

어휘 put up 세우다, 내걸다 hand out 나눠주다, 배포하다
flyer n. 전단지

Paraphrasing

The billboards 광고판 → signs 표지판

64 시각 자료 문제

해설 시각 자료를 보아라. 여자가 선호하는 자재는 무엇인가?
(A) 참나무
(B) 소나무
(C) 가문비나무
(D) 삼나무

해설 제시된 가격표의 정보를 확인한 후 질문의 핵심 어구(material ~ prefer)와 관련된 내용을 주의 깊게 듣는다. 여자가 "we should go with the most durable option even if it's the most expensive"라며 가장 비싸더라도 가장 내구성이 좋은 옵션을 선택해야 한다고 하였으므로, 여자가 선호하는 자재는 삼나무임을 가격표에서 알 수 있다. 따라서 (D)가 정답이다.

[65-67]

3음 캐나다식 → 미국식

Questions 65-67 refer to the following conversation and list.

M: Thanks for calling Sky High Cable. How can I help you?

W: Hi. I'm unhappy with my current cable and Internet provider, and ⁶⁵**the person in the apartment above mine recommended that I try one of your company's packages.** Can I sign up over the phone?

M: Of course. Do you know which package you want?

W: I'm not sure, actually. ⁶⁶**I don't want to spend more** ◯

than 60 dollars per month, and I'm interested in your video-on-demand feature.

M: Then you should try our newest package. I'll just need to get some information from you, and then ⁶⁷I'll schedule a time for a technician to visit your home.

recommend v. 추천하다　sign up 가입하다, 등록하다
video-on-demand n. 주문형 비디오(VOD)　feature n. 기능, 특징
information n. 정보　technician n. 기술자

해석
65-67번은 다음 대화와 목록에 관한 문제입니다.

남: Sky High 케이블에 전화해 주셔서 감사합니다. 무엇을 도와드릴까요?

여: 안녕하세요. 저는 현재 케이블 및 인터넷 제공업체에 불만이 있는데, ⁶⁵제 아파트 위층에 있는 분이 귀사의 패키지 중 하나를 사용해 보라고 추천해 주셨어요. 전화로 가입할 수 있나요?

남: 물론이죠. 어떤 패키지를 원하는지 알고 계신가요?

여: 실은, 잘 모르겠어요. ⁶⁶저는 한 달에 60달러 넘게 지출하고 싶지 않고, 주문형 비디오 기능에 관심이 있어요.

남: 그럼 가장 최신 패키지를 이용해 보셔야겠네요. 고객님으로부터 몇 가지 정보만 받은 후에, ⁶⁷기술자가 댁에 방문할 시간을 잡아 드릴게요.

패키지	가격	주문형 비디오
기본	25달러	
일반	40달러	
⁶⁶프리미엄	55달러	V
고급	65달러	V

65 특정 세부 사항 문제

해석　여자에게 누가 Sky High 케이블을 써보라고 추천했는가?
(A) 동료
(B) 친구
(C) 이웃
(D) 친척

해설　여자의 말에서 질문의 핵심 어구(recommended ~ try Sky High Cable)와 관련된 내용을 주의 깊게 듣는다. 여자가 "the person in the apartment above mine recommended that I try one of your company[Sky High Cable]'s packages"라며 아파트 위층에 있는 사람이 Sky High 케이블의 패키지 중 하나를 사용해 보라고 추천해 주었다고 하였다. 따라서 (C)가 정답이다.

어휘　coworker n. 동료　neighbor n. 이웃

Paraphrasing

the person in the apartment above 아파트 위층에 있는 사람 → A neighbor 이웃

66 시각 자료 문제

해석　시각 자료를 보아라. 어느 패키지가 여자에게 가장 적합한가?
(A) 기본
(B) 일반
(C) 프리미엄

(D) 고급

해설　제시된 목록의 정보를 확인한 후 질문의 핵심 어구(package ~ most suitable)와 관련된 내용을 주의 깊게 듣는다. 여자가 "I don't want to spend more than 60 dollars per month, and I'm interested in your video-on-demand feature."라며 한 달에 60달러 넘게 지출하고 싶지 않고, 주문형 비디오 기능에 관심이 있다고 하였으므로, 여자에게 가장 적합한 패키지는 프리미엄 패키지임을 목록에서 알 수 있다. 따라서 (C)가 정답이다.

67 다음에 할 일 문제

해석　남자는 무엇을 할 것이라고 말하는가?
(A) 제품 설명서를 보낸다.
(B) 거래를 승인한다.
(C) 새로운 기능을 설명한다.
(D) 약속을 잡는다.

해설　대화의 마지막 부분을 주의 깊게 듣는다. 남자가 "I'll schedule a time for a technician to visit your home"이라며 기술자가 여자의 집에 방문할 시간을 잡아 주겠다고 하였다. 따라서 (D)가 정답이다.

어휘　product brochure 제품 설명서　authorize v. 승인하다
describe v. 설명하다, 묘사하다

Paraphrasing

schedule a time 시간을 잡다 → Arrange an appointment 약속을 잡다

[68-70]　🎧 영국식 → 호주식

Questions 68-70 refer to the following conversation and map.

W: Hi. ⁶⁸Could you tell me where to find the painting *Dutch Autumn*? I read an article about it in the newspaper yesterday, and I'm really interested in seeing it.

M: It's not on display yet. ⁶⁹It will be included in a temporary exhibit we're currently setting up in the Special Collections Room. It will open on May 21.

W: Oh, I am only in town for a few days.

M: Well, ⁷⁰you can still see other works by that painter, Nick Anderson. Just walk through the lobby into the Textiles and Ceramics Room. His works are in the room directly behind it.

on display 전시된　temporary adj. 임시의　exhibit n. 전시회
textile n. 직물, 옷감　ceramic n. 도자기　directly adv. 바로

해석
68-70번은 다음 대화와 지도에 관한 문제입니다.

여: 안녕하세요. ⁶⁸그림 *Dutch Autumn*을 어디에서 볼 수 있는지 알려주시겠어요? 어제 신문에서 그것에 대한 기사를 읽었는데, 정말 보고 싶어서요.

남: 아직 전시되지 않았어요. ⁶⁹그건 현재 특별 소장품실에 준비 중인 임시 전시회에 포함될 거예요. 5월 21일에 공개될 거예요.

여: 아, 전 며칠 동안만 이 동네에 있어요.

남: 음, ⁷⁰그래도 그 화가인 Nick Anderson의 다른 작품들은 보실 수 있어요. 로비를 지나 직물 및 도자기실로 걸어가세요. 그의 작품들은 그것 바로 뒤에 있는 전시실에 있어요.

68 언급 문제

해석 여자는 *Dutch Autumn*에 대해 무엇을 언급하는가?
(A) 다른 박물관에 의해 구입되었다.
(B) Mr. Anderson의 첫 번째 그림이다.
(C) 한 출판물에서 논해졌다.
(D) 많은 방문객을 끌어들이고 있다.

해설 여자들의 말에서 질문의 핵심 어구(*Dutch Autumn*)가 언급된 주변을 주의 깊게 듣는다. 여자가 "Could you tell me where to find the painting *Dutch Autumn*? I read an article about it in the newspaper yesterday"라며 그림 *Dutch Autumn*을 볼 수 있는 곳을 물으며, 어제 신문에서 그것에 대한 기사를 읽었다고 하였다. 따라서 (C)가 정답이다.

어휘 publication n. 출판물 attract v. 끌어들이다

Paraphrasing

the newspaper 신문 → a publication 출판물

69 다음에 할 일 문제

해석 남자에 따르면, 5월 21일에 무슨 일이 일어날 것인가?
(A) 컬렉션이 판매될 것이다.
(B) 전시회가 열릴 것이다.
(C) 한 예술가가 상을 받을 것이다.
(D) 박물관이 개관 시간을 변경할 것이다.

해설 질문의 핵심 어구(May 21)가 언급된 주변을 주의 깊게 듣는다. 남자가 "It[*Dutch Autumn*] will be included in a temporary exhibit we're currently setting up in the Special Collections Room. It will open on May 21."라며 *Dutch Autumn*은 현재 특별 소장품실에 준비 중인 임시 전시회에 포함될 것이며, 5월 21일에 공개될 것이라고 한 것을 통해 5월 21일에 전시회가 열릴 것임을 알 수 있다. 따라서 (B)가 정답이다.

70 시각 자료 문제

해석 시각 자료를 보아라. Mr. Anderson의 작품들은 어느 전시실에 있는가?
(A) 동아시아 미술

(B) 근대 유럽 미술
(C) 초기 유럽 미술
(D) 직물 및 도자기

해설 제시된 지도의 정보를 확인한 후 질문의 핵심 어구(works by Mr. Anderson located)와 관련된 내용을 주의 깊게 듣는다. 남자가 "you can still see other works by that painter, Nick Anderson. Just walk through the lobby into the Textiles and Ceramics Room. His works are in the room directly behind it."이라며 화가인 Nick Anderson의 다른 작품들은 볼 수 있다고 하면서, 로비를 지나 직물 및 도자기실로 걸어가라고 한 후, 그의 작품들은 그것 바로 뒤에 있는 전시실에 있다고 하였으므로, Mr. Anderson의 작품들이 있는 전시실은 직물 및 도자기실 뒤편에 있는 근대 유럽 미술 전시실임을 지도에서 알 수 있다. 따라서 (B)가 정답이다.

PART 4

[71-73]   3번 캐나다식

Questions 71-73 refer to the following talk.

Before everyone heads out for today's appointments, ⁷¹**I would like to discuss some recent feedback from customers. We continue to receive complaints about installers.** ⁷²**Please, when you are done installing a customer's appliance, check for anything that might have fallen on the floor. Also, be sure to wipe off any marks you made on floors or countertops.** I understand that it's easy to forget to do these things when you are rushing to complete a job. But ⁷³**it's important that we meet our customers' expectations so that they have a positive experience.** That way, they will recommend our services to others.

head out 출발하다, 향하다 complaint n. 불만, 불평
appliance n. 가전제품, 장치 wipe off ~을 닦아 내다 mark n. 자국
countertop n. (부엌의) 조리대 rush v. 서두르다
expectation n. 기대

해석
71-73번은 다음 담화에 관한 문제입니다.

오늘 약속을 위해 모두가 출발하기 전에, ⁷¹고객들로부터 받은 최근 의견에 관해 논의하고자 합니다. 우리는 설치 담당자들에 대한 불만을 계속 받고 있습니다. ⁷²고객의 가전제품 설치가 끝나면, 바닥에 떨어진 것이 있는지 확인하시기 바랍니다. 또한, 바닥이나 조리대에 남긴 자국은 반드시 닦아내 주세요. 작업을 완료하려고 서두르다 보면 이러한 것들을 하는 것을 잊어버리기 쉽다는 걸 잘 알고 있습니다. 하지만 ⁷³고객들이 긍정적인 경험을 할 수 있도록 우리가 그들의 기대에 부응하는 것이 중요합니다. 그래야, 그들이 다른 사람들에게 우리 서비스를 추천할 것입니다.

71 목적 문제

해석 담화의 주요 목적은 무엇인가?
(A) 회사의 계획을 발표하기 위해
(B) 최근의 고객 불만을 해결하기 위해

(C) 팀의 성과를 칭찬하기 위해
(D) 행사에 대해 상기시키기 위해

해설 담화의 목적을 묻는 문제이므로, 지문의 초반을 주의 깊게 듣는다. "I would like to discuss some recent feedback from customers. We continue to receive complaints about installers."라며 고객들로부터 받은 최근 의견에 관해 논의하고자 한다고 하며, 설치 담당자들에 대한 불만을 계속 받고 있다고 한 후, 해결 방안에 대한 내용으로 지문이 이어지고 있다. 따라서 (B)가 정답이다.

어휘 initiative n. 계획 performance n. 성과

72 특정 세부 사항 문제

해석 화자는 청자들에게 무엇을 하라고 지시하는가?
(A) 약속에 제시간에 도착한다.
(B) 측정값을 재확인한다.
(C) 모든 작업 후에 청소한다.
(D) 제품 테스트를 진행한다.

해설 화자가 청자들에게 하라고 지시하는 것을 묻는 문제이므로, 질문의 핵심어구(instruct)와 관련된 내용을 주의 깊게 듣는다. "Please, when you are done installing a customer's appliance, check for anything that might have fallen on the floor. Also, be sure to wipe off any marks you made on floors or countertops."라며 고객의 가전제품 설치가 끝나면 바닥에 떨어진 것이 있는지 확인하고, 바닥이나 조리대에 남긴 자국은 반드시 닦아내라고 하였다. 따라서 (C)가 정답이다.

어휘 double-check v. 재확인하다 measurement n. 측정(값)

Paraphrasing

wipe off 닦아 내다 → Clean up 청소하다

73 특정 세부 사항 문제

해석 화자는 무엇이 중요하다고 말하는가?
(A) 불필요한 지연 방지하기
(B) 적절한 안전장치 착용하기
(C) 교육에서 얻은 정보 기억하기
(D) 우수한 고객 서비스 제공하기

해설 질문의 핵심 어구(important)가 언급된 주변을 주의 깊게 듣는다. "it's important that we meet our customers' expectations so that they have a positive experience"라며 고객들이 긍정적인 경험을 할 수 있도록 그들의 기대에 부응하는 것이 중요하다고 하였다. 따라서 (D)가 정답이다.

어휘 unnecessary adj. 불필요한 safety gear 안전장치
recall v. 기억하다, 상기하다

[74-76]

Questions 74-76 refer to the following tour information.　　③ 영국식

Welcome to Wildon Castle. ⁷⁴**Before we begin, please put on your radio headset. Use of this device is included in the cost of this tour.** It will help you follow along with my ⊙

commentary. Also, I'll be waving this colored flag whenever we move to a new location, so watch for it if you get separated from the group. ⁷⁵**This happens sometimes when people stop to take pictures.** Lastly, ⁷⁶**please remember that consuming food or drink in the building is prohibited.** However, there are water fountains inside in case you get thirsty.

radio adj. 무선의, 무전의 device n. 기기, 장치
commentary n. 설명, 해설 wave v. 흔들다
separate v. (따로) 떨어지다, 헤어지다 consume v. 섭취하다, 소비하다
prohibited adj. 금지된 water fountain (분수식) 식수대
thirsty adj. 목이 마른

해석
74-76번은 다음 관광 안내에 관한 문제입니다.
Wildon 성에 오신 것을 환영합니다. ⁷⁴시작하기 전에, 무선 헤드셋을 착용해 주세요. 이 기기의 사용은 투어 비용에 포함되어 있습니다. 이것은 여러분이 제 설명을 따라오는 데 도움을 줄 것입니다. 또한, 저는 우리가 새로운 장소로 이동할 때마다 이 색이 칠해진 깃발을 흔들 것이므로, 만약 여러분이 무리에서 떨어지게 될 경우 이것을 잘 살펴봐 주세요. ⁷⁵이 일은 사람들이 사진을 찍기 위해 멈춰 섰을 때 가끔 발생합니다. 마지막으로, ⁷⁶건물 내에서 음식이나 음료를 섭취하는 것이 금지되어 있다는 것을 기억해 주세요. 하지만, 목이 마를 경우에 대비해서 내부에 식수대가 있습니다.

74 특정 세부 사항 문제

해석 투어 비용에 무엇이 포함되어 있는가?
(A) 건물의 지도
(B) 영화의 감상
(C) 기기의 사용
(C) 안내서의 사본

해설 질문의 핵심 어구(included in the price of the tour)와 관련된 내용을 주의 깊게 듣는다. "Before we begin, please put on your radio headset. Use of this device is included in the cost of this tour."라며 시작하기 전에 무선 헤드셋을 착용해달라고 한 후, 기기의 사용은 투어 비용에 포함되어 있다고 하였다. 따라서 (C)가 정답이다.

Paraphrasing

the price 비용 → the cost 비용

75 추론 문제

해석 화자는 Wildon 성에 대해 무엇을 암시하는가?
(A) 사람들이 사진을 찍는 것을 허용한다.
(B) 음료를 판매하는 부스를 포함하고 있다.
(C) 몇몇 방문객들에게 표 할인을 제공한다.
(D) 하루 중 특정 시간대에 붐빈다.

해설 질문의 핵심 어구(Wildon Castle)와 관련된 내용을 주의 깊게 듣는다. "This happens sometimes when people stop to take pictures."라며 이 일, 즉 무리에서 떨어지게 되는 경우는 사람들이 사진을 찍기 위해 멈춰 섰을 때 가끔 발생한다고 한 것을 통해 Wildon 성은 사람들이 사진을 찍는 것을 허용한다는 것을 알 수 있

다. 따라서 (A)가 정답이다.

어휘 permit v. 허용하다, 허락하다

Paraphrasing

take pictures 사진을 찍다 → take photographs 사진을 찍다

76 특정 세부 사항 문제

해석 청자들은 무엇을 하도록 상기되는가?
(A) 선물 가게를 둘러본다.
(B) 대여한 물품을 반납한다.
(C) 온라인 후기를 남긴다.
(D) 음식 먹는 것을 자제한다.

해설 질문의 핵심 어구(reminded to do)와 관련된 내용을 주의 깊게 듣는다. "please remember that consuming food or drink in the building is prohibited"라며 건물 내에서 음식이나 음료를 섭취하는 것이 금지되어 있다는 것을 기억하라고 하였다. 따라서 (D)가 정답이다.

어휘 browse v. 둘러보다

Paraphrasing

consuming food or drink 음식이나 음료를 섭취하는 것 → eating food 음식 먹는 것

[77-79]

🎧 호주식

Questions 77-79 refer to the following announcement.

Hello everyone, and thanks for coming to this press conference. ⁷⁷**I want to give you a quick update about the England Rowing Championships.** Due to reports of a storm on April 30 and the possibility of flooding, ⁷⁷/⁷⁸**we have decided to postpone our event to Thursday, May 5.** The event will take place on the Goldwater River, just west of Eaton. ⁷⁹**Anyone interested in attending should note that tickets are still available, but this won't last for long. We have limited space near the water.**

press conference 기자 회견 rowing n. 조정, 노 젓기
storm n. 폭풍 possibility n. 가능성 flooding n. 홍수, 범람
postpone v. 연기하다, 미루다 take place 개최되다, 일어나다
note v. 유의하다, 주목하다

해석
77-79번은 다음 공지에 관한 문제입니다.

안녕하세요 여러분, 그리고 이 기자 회견에 참석해 주셔서 감사합니다. ⁷⁷잉글랜드 조정 선수권 대회에 대한 간단한 업데이트를 알려드리고자 합니다. 4월 30일 폭풍에 대한 보도와 홍수 가능성으로 인해, ⁷⁷/⁷⁸행사를 5월 5일 목요일로 연기하기로 결정했습니다. 행사는 Eaton 서쪽의 Goldwater강에서 개최될 것입니다. ⁷⁹참석하는 것에 관심이 있으신 모든 분은 아직 표를 구매할 수 있지만, 이게 오래 남아있지는 않을 것이니 유의해 주십시오. 물가 근처에는 제한된 공간만 있습니다.

77 목적 문제

해석 공지의 목적은 무엇인가?

(A) 행사가 취소되었던 이유를 설명하기 위해
(B) 경주 코스에 대한 정보를 제공하기 위해
(C) 대회의 결승전 진출자들을 발표하기 위해
(D) 일정 변경에 대한 공지를 제공하기 위해

해설 공지의 목적을 묻는 문제이므로, 지문의 초반을 주의 깊게 듣는다. "I want to give you a quick update about the England Rowing Championships."라며 잉글랜드 조정 선수권 대회에 대한 간단한 업데이트를 알려주겠다고 한 후, "we have decided to postpone our event to Thursday, May 5"라며 행사를 5월 5일 목요일로 연기하기로 결정했다고 하였다. 따라서 (D)가 정답이다.

어휘 finalist n. 결승전 진출자 competition n. 대회, 경쟁

Paraphrasing

postpone ~ event 행사를 연기하다 → a schedule change 일정 변경

78 다음에 할 일 문제

해석 화자에 따르면, 5월 5일에 무슨 일이 일어날 것인가?
(A) 뇌우가 발생할 것이다.
(B) 대회가 열릴 것이다.
(C) 시상식이 열릴 것이다.
(D) 행사 등록이 마감될 것이다.

해설 질문의 핵심 어구(May 5)가 언급된 주변을 주의 깊게 듣는다. "we have decided to postpone our event[England Rowing Championships] to Thursday, May 5"라며 잉글랜드 조정 선수권 대회를 5월 5일 목요일로 연기하기로 결정했다고 하였다. 따라서 (B)가 정답이다.

어휘 thunderstorm n. 뇌우 awards ceremony 시상식
take place 열리다, 개최되다

79 의도 파악 문제

해석 화자는 "물가 근처에는 제한된 공간만 있습니다"라고 말할 때 무엇을 의도하는가?
(A) 관중들을 위한 더 많은 공간이 필요하다.
(B) 다른 장소가 선택될 것이다.
(C) 구역은 일반인에게 출입이 제한된다.
(D) 표가 곧 매진될 수도 있다.

해설 질문의 인용어구(We have limited space near the water)가 언급된 주변을 주의 깊게 듣는다. "Anyone interested in attending should note that tickets are still available, but this won't last for long."이라며 참석하는 것에 관심이 있는 모든 사람은 아직 표를 구매할 수 있지만, 이게 오래 남아있지 않을 것이니 유의하라고 한 것을 통해 표가 곧 매진될 수도 있음을 알 수 있다. 따라서 (D)가 정답이다.

어휘 spectator n. 관중 restricted adj. 출입이 제한되는

Questions 80-82 refer to the following telephone message. 〔3배〕 캐나다식

> ⁸⁰**This is Diego calling from the Royal Linen Service.** I was reviewing the account for your hotel, and I noticed something unexpected. ⁸⁰/⁸¹**The invoice for the last shipment of linens that we cleaned for your hotel has not yet been paid.** Please make the payment as soon as possible. ⁸²**Tomorrow's service is still on schedule,** but future services may be canceled if the payment is not received. If you think there has been an error, please call and discuss it with me. Thank you.
>
> account n. 계정, 계좌 invoice n. 청구서 shipment n. 배송, 수송
> linen n. 리넨 (제품) payment n. 결제

해석

80-82번은 다음 전화 메시지에 관한 문제입니다.

⁸⁰Royal Linen Service에서 전화드리는 Diego입니다. 고객님 호텔의 계정을 검토하고 있었는데, 예상치 못한 것을 발견했습니다. ⁸⁰/⁸¹저희들이 고객님의 호텔을 위해 세탁한 가장 최근의 리넨 제품들 배송에 대한 청구서가 아직 결제되지 않았습니다. 가능한 한 빨리 결제해 주시기 바랍니다. ⁸²내일 서비스는 여전히 예정대로 진행되지만, 결제가 완료되지 않으면 향후 서비스가 취소될 수 있습니다. 오류가 있다고 생각하시면, 전화주셔서 이에 대해 저와 논의해 주시기를 바랍니다. 감사합니다.

80 화자 문제

해석 화자는 어떤 종류의 업체에서 일하는가?
(A) 호텔 체인
(B) 회계 법인
(C) 세탁 서비스
(D) 배달 업체

해설 지문에서 신분 및 직업과 관련된 표현을 놓치지 않고 듣는다. "This is Diego calling from the Royal Linen Service."라며 Royal Linen Service에서 전화하는 Diego라고 자신을 소개한 후, "The invoice for the last shipment of linens that we cleaned for your hotel has not yet been paid."라며 자신들이 청자의 호텔을 위해 세탁한 가장 최근의 리넨 제품들 배송에 대한 청구서가 아직 결제되지 않았다고 한 것을 통해 화자가 세탁 서비스 업체에서 일한다는 것을 알 수 있다. 따라서 (C)가 정답이다.

어휘 accounting firm 회계 법인, 회계 사무소

81 특정 세부 사항 문제

해석 화자는 무슨 문제를 언급하는가?
(A) 청구서가 잘못되었다.
(B) 대금을 받지 못했다.
(C) 배송이 누락되었다.
(D) 이메일에 답장을 받지 못했다.

해설 질문의 핵심 어구(problem)와 관련된 내용을 주의 깊게 듣는다. "The invoice for the last shipment of linens that we cleaned for your hotel has not yet been paid."라며 자신들이 청자의 호텔을 위해 세탁한 가장 최근의 리넨 제품들 배송에 대한 청

구서가 아직 결제되지 않았다고 하였다. 따라서 (B)가 정답이다.

어휘 incorrect adj. 잘못된, 틀린

Paraphrasing

> The invoice ~ has not yet been paid 청구서가 아직 결제되지 않았다 → A payment was not received 대금을 받지 못했다

82 언급 문제

해석 화자는 내일 서비스에 대해 무엇을 말하는가?
(A) 평소보다 오래 걸릴 것이다.
(B) 예정대로 진행될 것이다.
(C) 일정이 변경되어야 한다.
(D) 사전 결제가 필요하다.

해설 질문의 핵심 어구(tomorrow's service)가 언급된 주변을 주의 깊게 듣는다. "Tomorrow's service is still on schedule"이라며 내일 서비스는 여전히 예정대로 진행된다고 하였다. 따라서 (B)가 정답이다.

어휘 in advance 사전에, 미리

Paraphrasing

> is ~ on schedule 예정대로 진행되다 → go on as planned 예정대로 진행되다

Questions 83-85 refer to the following introduction. 〔3배〕 미국식

> Thank you all for coming today. I would like to now introduce our first speaker, Nancy Beatty. ⁸³**She is the head researcher at Green Power Technologies, and she has received a patent for a new type of solar panel.** She will talk about the uses of this technology. ⁸⁴**I'm sure many of you have questions for her. However, she has a lot of material to cover.** And 20 minutes scheduled. ⁸⁴**So she asked that any inquiries be sent to her e-mail address,** which is on the screen behind me. ⁸⁵**When Ms. Beatty's talk ends at 2 P.M., we will watch a short documentary on nuclear power** that you are sure to find interesting.
>
> introduce v. 소개하다 head researcher 수석 연구원
> patent n. 특허 solar panel 태양 전지판 material n. 내용, 자료
> cover v. 다루다, 포함시키다 inquiry n. 문의, 질문
> nuclear power 원자력

해석

83-85번은 다음 소개에 관한 문제입니다.

오늘 참석해 주신 모든 분들께 감사드립니다. 이제 우리의 첫 번째 연사인 Nancy Beatty를 소개하겠습니다. ⁸³그녀는 Green Power Technologies 사의 수석 연구원이며, 새로운 유형의 태양 전지판에 대한 특허를 받았습니다. 그녀는 이 기술의 활용에 대해 이야기할 것입니다. ⁸⁴여러분 중 많은 분이 그녀에게 질문이 있을 것입니다. 하지만, 그녀는 다루어야 할 내용이 많습니다. 그리고 20분이 예정되어 있습니다. ⁸⁴그래서 그녀는 모든 문의를 그녀의 이메일 주소로 보내달라고 요청했는데, 그것은 제 뒤에 있는 화면에 있습니다. ⁸⁵오후 2시에 Ms. Beatty의 강연이 끝나면, 우리는 여러분이 분명 흥미롭다고 생각할 만한 ⁸⁵원자력에 관한 짧은 다큐멘터리를 시청할 것입니다.

83 특정 세부 사항 문제

해석 Ms. Beatty는 어떤 산업에서 일하는 것 같은가?
(A) 농업
(B) 운송
(C) 에너지
(D) 로봇 공학

해설 질문의 핵심 어구(Ms. Beatty ~ work in)와 관련된 내용을 주의 깊게 듣는다. "She[Ms. Beatty] is the head researcher at Green Power Technologies, and she has received a patent for a new type of solar panel."이라며 Ms. Beatty는 Green Power Technologies사의 수석 연구원이며, 새로운 유형의 태양 전지판에 대한 특허를 받았다고 하였다. 따라서 (C)가 정답이다.

어휘 agriculture n. 농업 robotics n. 로봇 공학

84 의도 파악 문제

해석 화자는 "그리고 20분이 예정되어 있습니다"라고 말할 때 무엇을 의도하는가?
(A) 행사가 추가되었다.
(B) Ms. Beatty가 시간에 대해 염려하고 있다.
(C) Ms. Beatty의 연설이 단축되었다.
(D) 계획이 변경되었다.

해설 질문의 인용어구(And 20 minutes scheduled)가 언급된 주변을 주의 깊게 듣는다. "I'm sure many of you have questions for her. However, she[Ms. Beatty] has a lot of material to cover."라며 청자들 중 많은 사람이 Ms. Beatty에게 질문이 있을 것이지만 그녀는 다루어야 할 내용이 많다고 한 후, "So she asked that any inquires be sent to her e-mail address"라며 그래서 그녀가 모든 문의를 이메일 주소로 보내달라고 요청했다고 한 것을 통해 Ms. Beatty가 시간에 대해 염려하고 있음을 알 수 있다. 따라서 (B)가 정답이다.

85 다음에 할 일 문제

해석 오후 2시에 무슨 일이 일어날 것인가?
(A) 영상이 재생될 것이다.
(B) 다과가 제공될 것이다.
(C) 질문이 답변될 것이다.
(D) 시연이 제공될 것이다.

해설 질문의 핵심 어구(2 P.M.)가 언급된 주변을 주의 깊게 듣는다. "When Ms. Beatty's talk ends at 2 P.M., we will watch a short documentary on nuclear power"라며 오후 2시에 Ms. Beatty의 강연이 끝나면, 원자력에 관한 짧은 다큐멘터리를 시청할 것이라고 한 것을 통해 오후 2시에 영상이 재생될 것임을 알 수 있다. 따라서 (A)가 정답이다.

어휘 refreshment n. 다과 demonstration n. 시연, 시범

Paraphrasing

a short documentary 짧은 다큐멘터리 → A video 영상

[86-88]

Questions 86-88 refer to the following excerpt from a meeting.

You may have heard that Starline Express plans to open a regional office in our city soon. Well, [86]**the company has expressed an interest in signing a multiyear contract with us**, and [87]**they want to lease 150 vans for their delivery fleet**. This could be a big contract, so I'd like our most experienced sales staff to handle the negotiations. A meeting with Starline's team has been set for Tuesday morning. Before then, [88]**someone will need to review our service contract to determine if changes need to be made for such a large client. I've asked Mr. Wallace to do this and then report any issues.**

regional adj. 지역의, 지방의 express v. 표하다, 나타내다
contract n. 계약(서) lease v. 임대하다 fleet n. (회사 소유의) 차량
experienced adj. 경험이 풍부한 handle v. 처리하다, 다루다
negotiation n. 협상 determine v. 결정하다

해석
86-88번은 다음 회의 발췌록에 관한 문제입니다.

Starline Express사가 조만간 우리 도시에 지역 사무소를 열 계획이라는 소식을 들으셨을 겁니다. 음, [86]그 회사에서 우리와 다년간의 계약을 체결하는 것에 관심을 표했고, [87]그들은 배송 차량으로 150대의 밴을 임대하고 싶어 합니다. 큰 계약이 될 수 있으니, 경험이 풍부한 영업 직원이 협상을 처리해 주었으면 합니다. Starline 팀과의 회의는 화요일 오전에 잡혀 있습니다. 그 전에, [88]누군가 서비스 계약서를 검토하여 대규모 고객을 위해 변경이 필요한지 결정해야 할 것입니다. 저는 Mr. Wallace에게 이것을 한 후에 문제가 있으면 보고해 달라고 요청했습니다.

86 주제 문제

해석 화자는 주로 무엇에 대해 이야기하고 있는가?
(A) 잠재 고객
(B) 임원 승진
(C) 장비 업그레이드
(D) 광고 캠페인

해설 회의의 주제를 묻는 문제이므로, 지문의 초반을 반드시 듣는다. "the company[Starline Express] has expressed an interest in signing a multiyear contract with us"라며 Starline Express사가 자신들과 다년간의 계약을 체결하는 것에 관심을 표했다고 한 후, 그 회사와의 계약에 대한 내용으로 지문이 이어지고 있다. 따라서 (A)가 정답이다.

어휘 potential adj. 잠재적인, 가능성이 있는 executive n. 임원
promotion n. 승진

87 청자 문제

해석 청자들은 어디에서 일하는 것 같은가?
(A) 기술 지원 센터에서
(B) 수리 시설에서
(C) 채용 대행사에서
(D) 차량 임대 회사에서

해설 지문에서 신분 및 직업과 관련된 표현을 놓치지 않고 듣는다.

"they[Starline Express] want to lease 150 vans for their delivery fleet"이라며 Starline Express사가 배송 차량으로 150대의 밴을 임대하고 싶어 한다고 한 것을 통해 청자들이 차량 임대 회사에서 일한다는 것을 알 수 있다. 따라서 (D)가 정답이다.

어휘 technical adj. 기술의, 기술적인 recruitment n. 채용, 신규 모집

88 특정 세부 사항 문제

해석 Mr. Wallace는 무엇을 확인할 것인가?
(A) 법적 계약서
(B) 판매 보고서
(C) 재무 기록
(D) 제품 설명서

해설 질문의 핵심 어구(Mr. Wallace)가 언급된 주변을 주의 깊게 듣는다. "someone will need to review our service contract to determine if changes need to be made for such a large client"라며 누군가 서비스 계약서를 검토하여 대규모 고객을 위해 변경이 필요한지 결정해야 한다고 한 후, "I've asked Mr. Wallace to do this and then report any issues."라며 Mr. Wallace에게 이것을 한 후에 문제가 있으면 보고해 달라고 요청했다고 하였다. 따라서 (A)가 정답이다.

어휘 description n. 설명서

Paraphrasing

check 확인하다 → review 검토하다
contract 계약서 → agreement 계약서

[89-91]

3» 영국식

Questions 89-91 refer to the following news report.

This is Jenna Thompson reporting live from Holton Falls. This morning, a Holton County Fire Brigade spokesperson announced that the massive forest fire north of the city has been put out. Although there were no injuries, over a dozen homes were lost. **[89]The fire was started by sparks from a malfunctioning power generator. [90]Holton Falls mayor Rick Hernandez** thanked the firefighters for extinguishing the flames. **[91]He also pointed out that instructions on what to do in the event of a future fire are posted on the municipal government's Web site. He encouraged all residents of Holton Falls to become familiar with them.**

county n. 자치주 fire brigade 소방대 spokesperson n. 대변인
massive adj. 대형의, 거대한 put out 진압하다, (불을) 끄다
injuries n. 부상자 malfunctioning adj. 오작동하는
power generator 발전기 extinguish v. 진압하다, (불을) 끄다
flame n. 불길, 불꽃 instruction n. 지침, 설명
municipal adj. 시의, 지방 자치제의
resident n. 주민, 거주자

해석
89-91번은 다음 뉴스 보도에 관한 문제입니다.
저는 Holton Falls에서 생방송으로 전해드리는 Jenna Thompson입니다.

오늘 아침, Holton 자치주 소방대 대변인은 도시 북쪽의 대형 산불이 진압되었다고 발표했습니다. 부상자는 없었지만, 12채가 넘는 주택이 소실되었습니다. [89]화재는 오작동한 발전기에서 발생한 불꽃에서 시작되었습니다. [90]Holton Falls 시장인 Rick Hernandez는 불길을 진압한 소방관들에게 감사를 표현했습니다. [91]그는 또한 향후 화재 발생 시 어떻게 해야 하는지에 대한 지침이 시 정부 웹사이트에 게시되어 있다고 언급했습니다. 그는 Holton Falls의 모든 주민이 그것들을 숙지할 것을 권장했습니다.

89 특정 세부 사항 문제

해석 화재의 원인은 무엇이었는가?
(A) 장비 결함
(B) 방치된 모닥불
(C) 극심한 날씨
(D) 차량 충돌

해설 질문의 핵심 어구(cause of the fire)와 관련된 내용을 주의 깊게 듣는다. "The fire was started by sparks from a malfunctioning power generator."라며 화재는 오작동한 발전기에서 발생한 불꽃에서 시작되었다고 하였다. 따라서 (A)가 정답이다.

어휘 unattended adj. 방치된, 지켜보는 사람이 없는
campfire n. 모닥불, 캠프파이어 collision n. 충돌

Paraphrasing

a malfunctioning power generator 오작동한 발전기 → Faulty equipment 장비 결함

90 특정 세부 사항 문제

해석 Mr. Hernandez는 누구인가?
(A) 회사 대변인
(B) 소방관
(C) 시 공무원
(D) 기자

해설 질문 대상(Mr. Hernandez)의 신분 및 직업과 관련된 표현을 놓치지 않고 듣는다. "Holton Falls mayor Rick Hernandez"라며 Rick Hernandez가 Holton Falls의 시장이라고 하였다. 따라서 (C)가 정답이다.

어휘 city official 시 공무원

Paraphrasing

mayor 시장 → A city official 시 공무원

91 제안 문제

해석 보도에 따르면, Holton Falls 주민들은 무엇을 하도록 권고받는가?
(A) 기부를 한다.
(B) 지침을 읽는다.
(C) 이미지를 게시한다.
(D) 수업에 참석한다.

해설 지문의 중후반에서 제안과 관련된 표현이 포함된 문장을 주의 깊게 듣는다. "He[Rick Hernandez] also pointed out that instructions on what to do in the event of a future fire are posted on the municipal government's Web site. He encouraged all residents of Holton Falls to become familiar with them."이라며 Rick Hernandez가 향후 화재 발생 시 어떻게 해야 하는지에 대한 지침이 시 정부 웹사이트에 게시되어 있다고 언급했고, Holton Falls의 모든 주민이 그것들을 숙지할 것을 권장했다고 하였다. 따라서 (B)가 정답이다.

어휘 donation n. 기부

Paraphrasing

instructions 지침 → guidelines 지침

[92-94]

미국식

Questions 92-94 refer to the following excerpt from a meeting.

Now, let's move on to the quarterly sales report. **92Unfortunately, our total revenue was much lower than it was during the same period last year.** It is not a major concern yet because **93we are still very competitive compared to other office chair manufacturers.** However, we must invest more in promotional efforts in order to expand our market share and improve our numbers. **94I would appreciate input from you. Please don't hesitate to send me any ideas you might have by the end of the week.** You all have my e-mail address. We will meet again on Monday to discuss everyone's proposals and decide on the approach we will take.

quarterly adj. 분기별의   revenue n. 수익   period n. 기간
competitive adj. 경쟁력 있는   manufacturer n. 제조업체
invest v. 투자하다   market share 시장 점유율
input n. 의견 (제공), 투입   hesitate v. 주저하다, 망설이다
proposal n. 제안, 제의   approach n. 접근 (방식)

해석
92-94번은 다음 회의 발췌록에 관한 문제입니다.

자, 분기별 매출 보고서로 넘어가겠습니다. 92유감스럽게도, 총수익이 작년 같은 기간에 비해 훨씬 적었습니다. 93우리는 여전히 다른 사무용 의자 제조 업체들에 비해 경쟁력이 매우 높기 때문에 아직 큰 우려 사항은 아닙니다. 하지만, 시장 점유율을 확대하고 수치를 개선하기 위해서는 홍보 활동에 더 많은 투자를 해야 합니다. 94여러분의 의견을 주시면 감사하겠습니다. 주말까지 어떤 아이디어든지 주저하지 말고 보내주세요. 여러분 모두 제 이메일 주소를 가지고 계십니다. 월요일에 다시 만나서 모두의 제안을 논의하고 우리가 취할 접근 방식을 결정하겠습니다.

92 주제 문제

해석 무엇이 주로 논의되고 있는가?
(A) 예산 변경
(B) 교육 방법
(C) 회사 확장
(D) 매출 감소

해설 회의의 주제를 묻는 문제이므로, 지문의 초반을 반드시 듣는다. "Unfortunately, our total revenue was much lower than it was during the same period last year."라며 유감스럽게도 총수익이 작년 같은 기간에 비해 훨씬 적었다고 한 후, 매출 감소를 해결

할 방안에 대해 제안해달라는 내용으로 지문이 이어지고 있다. 따라서 (D)가 정답이다.

어휘 budget n. 예산   expansion n. 확장, 확대

93 특정 세부 사항 문제

해석 화자의 회사는 무엇을 생산하는가?
(A) 가구
(B) 소프트웨어
(C) 여행 가방
(D) 신발

해설 질문의 핵심 어구(produce)와 관련된 내용을 주의 깊게 듣는다. "we are still very competitive compared to other office chair manufacturers"라며 여전히 다른 사무용 의자 제조업체들에 비해 경쟁력이 매우 높다고 하였다. 따라서 (A)가 정답이다.

어휘 furniture n. 가구   luggage n. 여행 가방
footwear n. 신발

Paraphrasing

office chair 사무용 의자 → Furniture 가구

94 의도 파악 문제

해석 화자는 왜 "여러분 모두 제 이메일 주소를 가지고 계십니다"라고 말하는가?
(A) 청자들에게 프로젝트에 대한 도움을 받는 방법을 상기시키기 위해
(B) 청자들에게 정기적인 상태 업데이트를 제출하도록 하기 위해
(C) 청자들에게 제안을 하도록 장려하기 위해
(D) 청자들에게 연락처 정보를 공유하도록 요청하기 위해

해설 질문의 인용어구(You all have my e-mail address)가 언급된 주변을 주의 깊게 듣는다. "I would appreciate input from you. Please don't hesitate to send me any ideas you might have by the end of the week."이라며 청자들에게 의견을 달라고 한 후, 주말까지 어떤 아이디어든지 주저하지 말고 보내달라고 한 것을 통해 화자가 청자들에게 제안을 하도록 장려하고 있음을 알 수 있다. 따라서 (C)가 정답이다.

어휘 regular adj. 정기적인   status n. 상태, 상황

[95-97]

영국식

Questions 95-97 refer to the following telephone message and list.

Hi, Mr. Kimura. This is Cheryl Ortega from the Wilson Public Library. I'm calling to remind you that you still have an overdue book. **95All the books you checked out on March 6 or later have been returned, but the one you checked out before then is still out.** You can return the book at the front desk when the library is open. Please note that **96we are closed on Sundays**, so you will have to use the drop-off box out front if you come then. You may also be interested to learn that **97we are now offering a selection of e-books through our Web site. Just log in with your username** ○

and password to read them online.

overdue adj. 연체된, 기한이 지난 check out (책을) 대출하다
drop-off box 반납함 a selection of 다양한

해석

95-97번은 다음 전화 메시지와 목록에 관한 문제입니다.

안녕하세요, Mr. Kimura. 저는 Wilson 공립 도서관의 Cheryl Ortega입니다. 아직 연체된 책이 한 권 있다는 것을 상기시키기 위해 전화드립니다. ⁹⁵**3월 6일과 이후에 대출하신 책은 모두 반납되었지만, 그전에 대출하신 것은 여전히 대출 중입니다.** 도서관이 열려 있을 때 안내 데스크에서 책을 반납하실 수 있습니다. ⁹⁶**일요일에는 휴관하므로,** 그때 방문하는 경우에는 앞에 있는 반납함을 이용해야 한다는 점을 유의해 주시기 바랍니다. 또한 ⁹⁷**저희가 현재 웹사이트를 통해 다양한 전자책을 제공하고 있다**는 사실에 관심이 있으실지도 모르겠네요. ⁹⁷**온라인으로 그것들을 읽으시려면 사용자 이름과 비밀번호로 로그인만 하시면 됩니다.**

책 제목	대출일
⁹⁵*Cross Channel: A Memoir*	3월 4일
Early Modern Germany	3월 6일
Ancient Greek Philosophy	3월 6일
Black Forest: A Novel	3월 8일

95 시각 자료 문제

해석 시각 자료를 보아라. 청자가 어느 책을 아직 반납하지 않았는가?
(A) *Cross Channel: A Memoir*
(B) *Early Modern Germany*
(C) *Ancient Greek Philosophy*
(D) *Black Forest: A Novel*

해설 제시된 목록의 정보를 확인한 후 질문의 핵심 어구(has ~ not yet returned)와 관련된 내용을 주의 깊게 듣는다. "All the books you checked out on March 6 or later have been returned, but the one you checked out before then is still out."이라며 3월 6일과 이후에 대출한 책은 모두 반납되었지만 그전에 대출한 것은 여전히 대출 중이라고 하였으므로, 청자가 아직 반납하지 않은 책은 *Cross Channel: A Memoir*임을 목록에서 알 수 있다. 따라서 (A)가 정답이다.

96 언급 문제

해석 화자는 도서관에 대해 무엇을 언급하는가?
(A) 일주일에 하루 문을 닫는다.
(B) 도서 연체 벌금을 인상했다.
(C) 안내 데스크를 이전했다.
(D) 반납함을 없앨 것이다.

해설 질문의 핵심 어구(library)와 관련된 내용을 주의 깊게 듣는다. "we are closed on Sundays"라며 일요일에는 휴관한다고 하였다. 따라서 (A)가 정답이다.

어휘 fine n. 벌금 relocate v. 이전하다

97 특정 세부 사항 문제

해석 화자에 따르면, 도서관 회원들은 무엇을 할 수 있는가?
(A) 무료 수업에 참여한다.
(B) 인기 있는 영화를 본다.
(C) 중고 출판물을 구입한다.
(D) 디지털 형태의 도서를 이용한다.

해설 질문의 핵심 어구(library members)와 관련된 내용을 주의 깊게 듣는다. "we are now offering a selection of e-books through our Web site. Just log in with your username and password to read them online."이라며 현재 웹사이트를 통해 다양한 전자책을 제공하고 있으며, 온라인으로 그것들을 읽으려면 사용자 이름과 비밀번호로 로그인만 하면 된다고 하였다. 따라서 (D)가 정답이다.

어휘 publication n. 출판물 access v. 이용하다 format n. 형태, 형식

Paraphrasing

e-books 전자책 → books in a digital format 디지털 형태의 도서

[98-100]   🎧 호주식

Questions 98-100 refer to the following announcement and flow chart.

Good morning, team. I have an important announcement. ⁹⁸**Our proposed design for a nonstick frying pan has been approved.** As it has the potential for high sales, management wants to get it into production as soon as possible. Therefore, ⁹⁹**we need to finish the testing stage by June 15 at the latest**. To ensure that this happens, ¹⁰⁰**I have requested that six additional staff members be assigned to our team. When they arrive tomorrow, please provide them with whatever help they need in figuring out their new duties.** The sooner they settle in, the sooner they can begin contributing to our project.

nonstick adj. 들러붙지 않는 management n. 경영(진)
production n. 생산 at the latest 늦어도 ensure v. 보장하다
additional adj. 추가의 assign v. 배정하다
figure out 파악하다, 이해하다 duty n. 업무, 일 settle in 적응하다
contribute v. 기여하다

해석

98-100번은 다음 공지와 업무 흐름도에 관한 문제입니다.

좋은 아침입니다, 팀원 여러분. 중요한 공지가 있습니다. ⁹⁸**우리가 제안한 들러붙지 않는 프라이팬 디자인이 승인되었습니다.** 판매량이 높을 가능성이 있기 때문에, 경영진은 가능한 한 빨리 생산에 돌입하기를 원합니다. 따라서, ⁹⁹**늦어도 6월 15일까지는 검사 단계를 마쳐야 합니다.** 이것이 가능하도록 보장하기 위해, ¹⁰⁰**우리 팀에 여섯 명의 추가 직원들이 배정되게 해달라고 요청했습니다. 내일 그들이 오면, 새로운 업무를 파악하는 데 필요한 모든 도움을 제공해 주시기 바랍니다.** 그들이 더 빨리 적응할수록, 우리 프로젝트에 더 빨리 기여하기 시작할 수 있습니다.

| 단계 1 디자인 승인 | ⁹⁹단계 2 검사 | 단계 3 생산 | 단계 4 제품 출시 |

98 화자 문제

해석 화자는 어떤 산업에서 일하는가?
(A) 전자제품
(B) 가정용품
(C) 건강
(D) 의류

해설 지문에서 신분 및 직업과 관련된 표현을 놓치지 않고 듣는다. "Our proposed design for a nonstick frying pan has been approved."라며 자신들이 제안한 들러붙지 않는 프라이팬 디자인이 승인되었다고 한 것을 통해 화자가 일하는 산업은 가정용품임을 알 수 있다. 따라서 (B)가 정답이다.

어휘 housewares n. 가정용품 fitness n. 건강

Paraphrasing

frying pan 프라이팬 → Housewares 가정용품

99 시각 자료 문제

해석 시각 자료를 보아라. 6월 15일까지 어느 단계가 완료되어야 하는가?
(A) 단계 1
(B) 단계 2
(C) 단계 3
(D) 단계 4

해설 제시된 업무 흐름도의 정보를 확인한 후 질문의 핵심 어구(June 15)가 언급된 주변을 주의 깊게 듣는다. "we need to finish the testing stage by June 15 at the latest"라며 늦어도 6월 15일까지는 검사 단계를 마쳐야 한다고 하였으므로 6월 15일까지 완료되어야 하는 단계는 단계 2임을 업무 흐름도에서 알 수 있다. 따라서 (B)가 정답이다.

100 요청 문제

해석 화자는 청자들에게 무엇을 하라고 요청하는가?
(A) 양식을 작성한다.
(B) 서비스를 추천한다.
(C) 동료들을 돕는다.
(D) 회의 일정을 변경한다.

해설 지문의 중후반에서 요청과 관련된 표현이 포함된 문장을 주의 깊게 듣는다. "I have requested that six additional staff members be assigned to our team. When they arrive tomorrow, please provide them with whatever help they need in figuring out their new duties."라며 팀에 여섯 명의 추가 직원들이 배정되게 해달라고 요청했으며, 내일 그들이 오면 새로운 업무를 파악하는 데 필요한 모든 도움을 제공해 주기 바란다고 하였다. 따라서 (C)가 정답이다.

어휘 fill out 작성하다, 기입하다 coworker n. 동료
reschedule v. 일정을 변경하다

Paraphrasing

provide ~ help 도움을 제공하다 → Assist 돕다
staff members 직원들 → coworkers 동료들

PART 5

101 명사 자리 채우기

해설 정관사(the)와 전치사(of) 사이에 올 수 있는 것은 명사이므로 명사 역할을 하는 동명사 (B)와 명사 (D)가 정답의 후보이다. '시내 주택 가격의 적정성에 관한 정치 토론'이라는 의미가 되어야 하므로 (D) affordability(적정성)가 정답이다. 동명사 (B)는 '시내 주택의 가격 여유가 되는 것에 관한 정치 토론'이라는 어색한 문맥을 만든다. 동사 (A)와 형용사 (C)는 명사 자리에 올 수 없다.

해석 시내 주택 가격의 적정성에 관한 정치 토론이 4월 11일에 PBS에서 방송될 것이다.

어휘 political adj. 정치의 debate n. 토론
broadcast v. 방송하다 afford v. 여유가 되다, 형편이 되다

102 격에 맞는 인칭대명사 채우기

해설 명사(machinery) 앞에서 형용사처럼 명사를 꾸밀 수 있는 인칭대명사는 소유격이므로 소유격 인칭대명사 (C) our가 정답이다. 소유대명사 (A), 목적격 인칭대명사 (B), 재귀대명사 (D)는 명사를 꾸밀 수 없다.

해석 우리의 기계에 대한 보증서는 소유주가 5년 동안 무료 점검을 받을 수 있다고 명시한다.

어휘 warranty n. (품질) 보증서 machinery n. 기계(류)
specify v. 명시하다 inspection n. 점검, 검토

103 동사 어휘 고르기

해설 '소비자 동향 보고서는 사람들이 전기 자동차에 매우 관심이 있다는 것을 시사한다'라는 문맥이므로 suggest(시사하다)의 3인칭 단수형 (D) suggests가 정답이다. (B)의 discover(발견하다, 깨닫다)도 해석상 그럴듯해 보이지만, 주어로 사람이 나와 새로운 정보를 발견하는 상황을 나타낼 때 쓰이므로 답이 될 수 없다. (A)의 persuade는 '설득하다', (C)의 recommend는 '추천하다, 권장하다'라는 의미이다.

해석 Meicum 자동차사에 의해 발행된 소비자 동향 보고서는 사람들이 전기 자동차에 매우 관심이 있다는 것을 시사한다.

어휘 issue v. 발행하다 highly adv. 매우, 단단히
electric car 전기 자동차

104 등위접속사 채우기

해설 빈칸은 절(The travel expense reimbursement requests ~ with receipts)과 절(the accounting department ~ reject them)을 연결할 수 있는 접속사 자리이므로 등위접속사인 (A), (C), (D)가 정답의 후보이다. '출장비 상환 요청서는 영수증과 함께 제출되어야 하고, 그렇지 않으면 회계 부서에서 거부할 수 있다'라는 의미가 되어야 하므로 등위접속사 (A) or(그렇지 않으면)가 정답이다. 전치사 (B) by(~에 의해; ~까지)는 절과 절을 연결할 수 없다.

해석 출장비 상환 요청서들은 영수증과 함께 제출되어야 하며, 그렇지 않으면 회계 부서에서 그것들을 거부할 수 있다.

어휘 reimbursement n. 상환, 변제   receipt n. 영수증
accounting n. 회계   reject v. 거부하다, 거절하다

105 부사 자리 채우기

해설 빈칸 앞의 동사(will be shipped)를 꾸밀 수 있는 것은 부사이므로 부사 (B) promptly(즉시)가 정답이다. 동사 또는 형용사 (A), 동사 또는 과거분사 (C), 동사 (D)는 동사를 꾸밀 수 없다.

해석 구매팀이 어제 주문한 주문품은 즉시 배송되어 이틀 내에 도착할 것이다.

어휘 prompt v. 촉발하다; adj. 즉각적인, 신속한

106 부사절 접속사 채우기

해설 이 문장은 주어가 없는 명령문으로 동사(use)와 목적어(the temporary ID card)를 갖춘 완전한 절이므로, ___ ~ the replacement는 수식어 거품으로 보아야 한다. 이 수식어 거품은 동사(get)가 있는 거품절이므로, 거품절을 이끌 수 있는 부사절 접속사 (B), (C)가 정답의 후보이다. '교체품을 받을 때까지 임시 사원증을 사용하세요'라는 의미가 되어야 하므로 (B) until(~할 때까지)이 정답이다. (C) since(~ 이후로, ~ 때문에)를 쓰면 어색한 문맥이 된다. 전치사 (A) during(~동안)은 거품절이 아닌 거품구를 이끈다. 부사 (D) also (또한)는 수식어 거품을 이끌 수 없다.

해석 교체품을 받을 때까지 인사팀에서 발급된 임시 사원증을 사용하세요.

어휘 temporary adj. 임시의   replacement n. 교체품, 대체품, 후임자

107 명사 관련 어구 완성하기

해설 '엄선된 가장 인기 있는 기사들이 발간될 것이다'라는 문맥이므로 빈칸 앞의 부정관사 A와 뒤의 전치사 of와 함께 '엄선된'이라는 의미의 어구인 A selection of를 만드는 명사 (C) selection(선택)이 정답이다. (A) model은 '모형, 모델', (B) type은 '유형, 종류', (D) member는 '구성원, 일원'이라는 의미이다.

해석 엄선된 *Bizlast* 잡지의 가장 인기 있는 기사들은 한정판 양장본으로 발간될 것이다.

어휘 release v. 발간하다, 공개하다

108 동명사 채우기

해설 빈칸은 전치사(to)의 목적어 자리이므로 명사 (A), (C)와 동명사 (D)가 정답의 후보이다. 빈칸 다음에 온 목적어(a convenient check-in ~ its flights)를 가질 수 있는 것은 동명사이므로 동사 provide(제공하다)의 동명사 (D) providing이 정답이다. 명사 (A)와 (C)는 목적어를 가질 수 없다. 동사 (B)는 명사 자리에 올 수 없다.

해석 Asia Pacific 항공사는 편리한 탑승 수속 경험과 비행기에서 높은 수준의 편안함을 제공하는 것에 전념한다.

어휘 be committed to ~에 전념하다   convenient adj. 편리한
comfort n. 편안함, 위로   provider n. 제공자, 부양자
provision n. 공급

109 부사 어휘 고르기

해설 'Ms. Jahidmal이 취업 제안을 수락할지 아직 결정하지 못하다'라는 문맥이므로 부사 (C) yet(아직)이 정답이다. 빈도 부사 (B) seldom (거의 ~하지 않는)도 해석상 그럴듯해 보이지만, 이미 부정의 의미를 담고 있어서 not과 같은 또 다른 부정어와 함께 올 수 없다. (A) once는 '예전에, 한 번', (D) shortly는 '곧, 얼마 안 되어'라는 의미이다.

해석 Ms. Jahidmal은 Pullman 화학 약품사로부터 받은 취업 제안을 수락할지 아직 결정하지 못했다.

어휘 accept v. 수락하다, 받아들이다   receive v. 받다, 얻다

110 짝을 이루는 표현

해설 빈칸 뒤의 weather(날씨)와 함께 '혹독한 날씨'라는 의미의 어구 severe weather를 만드는 형용사 (B) severe(혹독한)가 정답이다. (A) full은 '완전한', (C) precise는 '정확한', (D) scarce는 '부족한, 드문'이라는 의미이다.

해석 그 감독은 혹독한 날씨가 야외 장면의 촬영을 방해했기 때문에 그의 영화가 일정보다 뒤처졌다고 설명했다.

어휘 interfere v. 방해하다   outdoor adj. 야외의

> **최신토익경향**
>
> 빈칸 앞 또는 뒤의 단어와 어구를 이루는 단어를 골라야 하는 문제가 자주 나온다. 짝을 이루는 아래의 대표적인 어구들을 덩어리로 외워두자.
>
> • strictly prohibited 엄격히 금지된
> • cordially invited 정중하게 초대된
> • severe weather 혹독한 날씨
> • prestigious award 권위 있는 상
> • follow the instructions 설명을 따르다
> • conduct a survey 조사를 시행하다
> • fill the prescription 처방전대로 조제하다
> • meet the demand 수요를 충족시키다

111 전치사 채우기

해설 '약국의 세 번째 지점은 공원 맞은편에 위치해있다'라는 의미가 되어야 하므로 위치를 나타내는 전치사 (B) opposite(~의 맞은편에)이 정답이다. (A) besides는 '~에 더해서, ~뿐만 아니라'라는 의미이다. (C) into는 '~안으로'의 의미로 방향을 나타낸다. (D) against는 '~에 반하여, ~에 맞서, ~에 (접촉하여) 기대어'라는 의미이다.

해석 Wrightvita 약국의 세 번째 지점은 Greenwood 공원 맞은편에 위치해있다.

어휘 pharmacy n. 약국   locate v. ~에 위치하다, 위치를 찾다

112 부사절 접속사 채우기

해설 이 문장은 주어(The software of the N350 smartphone)와 동사(will update)를 갖춘 완전한 절이므로, ___ ~ prevent it은 수식어 거품으로 보아야 한다. 이 수식어 거품은 동사(are changed)가 있는 거품절이므로, 부사절 접속사인 (A), (B), (D)가 정답의 후보이다. '소프트웨어는 업데이트를 하지 못하도록 설정이 변경되지 않는다면 자동으로 업데이트된다'라는 의미가 되어야 하므로 (A) unless(~하지 않는다면)가 정답이다. (B) now that은 '~이기 때문

에', (D) whereas는 '~한 반면에'라는 의미이므로 어색한 문맥을 만든다. 부사 (C) almost(거의)는 거품절을 이끌 수 없다.

해석 N350 스마트폰의 소프트웨어는 그것을 하지 못하도록 설정이 변경되지 않는다면 자동으로 업데이트된다.

어휘 automatically adv. 자동으로 prevent v. ~하지 못하게 하다, 막다

113 to 부정사 채우기

해설 이 문장은 주어(Haskell Oil), 동사(hired), 목적어(a senior accountant)를 갖춘 완전한 절이므로, ____ ~ corporate value는 수식어 거품으로 보아야 한다. 이 수식어 거품은 동사가 없는 거품구이므로, 거품구를 이끌면서 '당사의 기업 가치를 평가하기 위해'라는 의미의 목적을 나타내는 to 부정사 (C) to evaluate가 정답이다. 동사 (A), (B)와 명사 (D)는 거품구를 이끌 수 없다.

해석 Haskell 정유사는 당사의 기업 가치를 평가하기 위해 Gold 회계 법인의 상급 회계사를 고용했다.

어휘 corporate value 기업 가치 evaluate v. 평가하다, 감정하다

114 부정대명사 채우기

해설 빈칸 앞의 동사(is)가 단수 동사이고 'Noah Moskovitz는 12명 중 한 명이다'라는 의미가 되어야 하므로 부정대명사 (C) one(하나)이 정답이다. (A) both(둘 다)와 (B) either(둘 중 하나)는 of 다음에 두 가지 대상이 와야 하므로 답이 될 수 없다. (D) all(모두)을 쓸 경우 'Noah Moskovitz는 인턴십 프로그램에 참가하도록 선발된 12명 중 모두이다'라는 어색한 문맥이 된다.

해석 Noah Moskovitz는 Verizon 그룹사의 하계 인턴십 프로그램에 참가하도록 선발된 12명 중 한 명이다.

어휘 select v. 선발하다, 뽑다 participate in ~에 참가하다

115 부사 어휘 고르기

해설 '객실들이 1박에 500달러에서 시작하기 때문에 휴가용 숙소를 다른 곳에서 찾아보았다'라는 문맥이므로 (D) elsewhere(다른 곳에서)가 정답이다. (A) anytime은 '언제나', (B) apart는 '따로, 떨어져', (C) likewise는 '마찬가지로'라는 의미이다.

해석 Coast 리조트의 객실들이 1박에 500달러에서 시작하기 때문에, Mr. Hervey는 자신의 휴가용 숙소를 다른 곳에서 찾아보았다.

어휘 per night 1박에, 하룻밤에 search for ~을 찾아보다
accommodation n. 숙소, 숙박 시설

116 명사 어휘 고르기

해설 '고객 송장에 반영된 수정은 가격 책정 오류의 결과였다'라는 문맥이므로 adjustment(수정, 조정)의 복수형 (D) adjustments가 정답이다. (B)의 setback(차질)도 해석상 그럴듯해 보이지만, setback은 주로 동사 receive나 experience 등과 짝을 이루어 '차질을 겪다'의 의미로 쓰이므로 빈칸 뒤의 made와는 어울리지 않는다. (A)의 role은 '역할, 임무', (C)의 clue는 '단서, 실마리'라는 의미이다.

해석 고객 송장에 반영된 수정은 매니저에 의해 발견된 가격 책정 오류의 결과였다.

어휘 pricing n. 가격 책정

117 수량 표현 채우기

해설 빈칸 뒤의 단수 가산 명사(sponsor)를 꾸밀 수 있는 수량 표현 (C) Each(각각의)가 정답이다. 수량 표현 (A) Several(여러)과 (D) Few(거의 ~없는)는 복수 가산 명사를 꾸며야 한다. (B) Those는 앞에 언급된 복수 명사를 대신하는 지시대명사로 쓰거나 'those + 수식어(관계절, 분사구, 전치사구)'의 형태로 '~한 사람들'이라는 의미로 쓰인다. Those가 지시형용사로 쓰일 경우 뒤에 복수 명사가 온다.

해석 세인트루이스 팝 뮤직 축제의 각 후원 업체는 행사 기간 동안 저마다의 지정된 스탠드를 갖는다.

어휘 sponsor n. 후원 업체 designate v. 지정하다
duration n. (지속) 기간

118 형용사 관련 어구 완성하기

해설 'Radford 진료소는 환자들의 진료 기록의 보안 및 무결성 유지에 대한 책임이 있다'라는 문맥이므로 빈칸 앞의 be동사 is와 뒤의 전치사 for와 함께 '~에 대한 책임이 있다'라는 의미의 어구 be accountable for를 만드는 형용사 (C) accountable이 정답이다. (A)의 eligible도 전치사 for와 함께 쓰일 수 있지만, '~에 자격이 있다'라는 의미로 어색한 문맥이 되므로 답이 될 수 없다. (B) interactive는 '상호적인'이라는 의미로 전치사 with와 함께 쓰이며, (D) subject는 '영향을 받기 쉬운'이라는 의미로 전치사 to와 함께 쓰인다.

해석 Radford 진료소는 환자들의 진료 기록의 보안 및 무결성 유지에 대한 책임이 있다.

어휘 integrity n. 무결성, 온전함 patient n. 환자

최신토익경향

빈칸 뒤의 전치사와 함께 어구를 이루는 형용사를 고르는 문제가 꾸준히 출제되고 있으므로 'be + 형용사 + 전치사' 표현을 알아두자.

- be responsible for ~에 대해 책임이 있다
- be accountable for ~에 대해 책임이 있다
- be eligible for ~의 자격이 있다
- be contrary to ~에 어긋나다, ~와 상반되다
- be subject to ~의 영향을 받기 쉽다
- be exempt from ~을 하지 않아도 된다
- be skeptical of ~에 회의적이다, ~을 의심하다

119 부사 자리 채우기

해설 동사(be addressed)를 꾸밀 수 있는 것은 부사이므로 부사 (B) effectively(효과적으로)가 정답이다. 형용사 (A), 동사 또는 과거분사 (C), 동사 또는 명사 (D)는 동사를 꾸밀 수 없다.

해석 생산 라인에서 발생하고 있는 잦은 문제들이 효과적으로 해결될 수 있도록 새로운 시스템이 도입되었다.

어휘 introduce v. 도입하다, 소개하다 frequent adj. 잦은, 빈번한
address v. 해결하다 effective adj. 효과적인
effect v. (결과를) 가져오다; n. 결과, 영향

120 전치사 채우기

해설 '구역을 떠나는 것을 삼가야 한다'라는 의미가 되어야 하므로 빈칸 앞의 동사 refrain과 함께 '~을 삼가다'라는 의미의 어구인 refrain from을 만드는 전치사 (B) from이 정답이다. (A) past는 '~을 지나 서'라는 의미로 위치를, (C) upon은 '~ 위에, ~ 후에'라는 의미로 위치 나 시점을, (D) onto는 '~ 위쪽으로'라는 의미로 방향을 나타낸다.

해석 Howell 섬으로 향하는 승객들은 여객선이 곧 탑승에 들어갈 예정이 므로 그 구역을 떠나는 것을 삼가야 한다.

어휘 passenger n. 승객 bound for ~로 향하는
refrain v. 삼가다, 자제하다

121 명사 자리 채우기

해설 소유격(Picton's)과 전치사(of) 사이에 올 수 있는 것은 명사이므로 명사 (D) acquisition(인수)이 정답이다. 동사 (A), (B), (C)는 명사 자 리에 올 수 없다.

해석 Picton사의 주요 경쟁사 인수에 대한 최신 소식은 *World Business* 팟캐스트에서 오늘 논의되었다.

어휘 competitor n. 경쟁사 acquire v. 인수하다

122 동사 관련 어구 완성하기

해설 'Evanston 공공도서관은 셀프 체크아웃 키오스크와 컴퓨터 실습실 을 갖추고 있다'라는 문맥에서 빈칸 앞의 be동사 is와 뒤의 전치사 with와 함께 '~을 갖추고 있다'라는 의미의 어구 be equipped with 를 만드는 equip(장비를 갖추다)의 p.p.형 (B) equipped가 정답이 다. (D)의 contain(포함하다, 함유하다)도 해석상 그럴듯해 보이지만, 전치사 in과 함께 '~안에 포함되어 있다'라는 의미로 쓰이므로 답이 될 수 없다. (A)의 present는 '주다, 제시하다', (C)의 examine은 '검토 하다, 조사하다'라는 의미이다.

해석 Evanston 공공도서관은 이제 5개의 셀프 체크아웃 키오스크와 컴퓨 터 실습실을 갖추고 있다.

어휘 laboratory n. 실습실, 실험실

123 전치사 채우기

해설 'Metlan사의 소프트웨어는 3대 운영 체제 중 하나이다'라는 의미가 되어야 하므로 셋 이상의 사람 또는 사물 사이에서 '~ 중에'라는 의미 를 나타내는 전치사 (A) among이 정답이다. (C) in between(~ 사 이에, ~ 중간에 끼여)도 해석상 그럴듯해 보이지만, 두 개의 대상 사이 에 있는 상태를 나타내는 전치사이므로 답이 될 수 없다. (B) prior to 는 '~ 전에'라는 의미로 시간을, (D) but for는 '~이 없다면'이라는 의 미로 가정을 나타낸다.

해석 Metlan사의 소프트웨어는 Neusoft사와 Adapta사의 소프트웨어 다 음으로 세계에서 가장 널리 사용되는 3대 운영 체제 중 하나이다.

어휘 widely adv. 널리, 크게 operating system 운영체제

124 형용사 어휘 고르기

해설 '좀체 사라지지 않는 우려를 해결하다'라는 문맥이므로 형용사 (C) lingering(좀체 사라지지 않는, 오래 가는)이 정답이다. (A) deliberate

은 '고의적인', (B) accurate은 '정확한', (D) versatile은 '다용도의, 다목적의'라는 의미이다.

해석 Cyon 의류사는 그 회사의 재정 건전성에 대한 좀체 사라지지 않는 우 려를 해결하기 위해 기자회견을 열 것이다.

어휘 press conference 기자회견 concern n. 우려, 걱정

125 형용사 자리 채우기

해설 빈칸 뒤의 명사(coverage)를 꾸밀 수 있는 것은 형용사이므로 형 용사 (B) exceptional(우수한, 뛰어난)이 정답이다. 동사 또는 전 치사 (A), 동명사 또는 전치사 (C), 명사 (D)는 형용사 자리에 올 수 없다. 빈칸을 앞에 나온 전치사(For)의 목적어 자리로 보고 동명사 (C) excepting을 쓸 경우, '불공정거래에 대한 보도를 제외하는 것으로 신문사에서 승진했다'라는 어색한 문맥을 만든다. 명사 (D) exception(제외)은 명사 coverage(보도)와 복합 명사를 이루지 못 하므로 답이 될 수 없다.

해석 불공정거래에 대한 우수한 보도로 Kassandra Parker는 *The Chicago Slate* 신문사에서 승진했다.

어휘 coverage n. 보도, 보상 범위 unfair adj. 불공정한
transaction n. 거래 receive a promotion 승진하다
except v. ~을 제외하다; prep. ~을 제외하고

126 현재분사와 과거분사 구별하여 채우기

해설 빈칸 뒤의 명사(healthcare technologies)를 꾸밀 수 있는 것은 형 용사이므로 형용사 역할을 하는 현재분사 (A)와 과거분사 (C)가 정답 의 후보이다. '유망한 건강 관리 기술들이 개발되었다'라는 의미가 되 어야 하므로 현재분사 (A) promising(유망한)이 정답이다. 과거분사 (C) promised는 '약속된 건강 관리 기술들이 개발됐다'라는 어색한 문맥을 만들기 때문에 답이 될 수 없다. to 부정사 (B)는 명사 앞에서 명사를 꾸밀 수 없다. 명사 또는 동사 (D) promise는 명사일 경우 명 사(healthcare technologies)와 복합 명사를 이루지 못하므로 답 이 될 수 없다. 동사일 경우 형용사 자리에 올 수 없으므로 답이 될 수 없다.

해석 유망한 건강 관리 기술들이 MedPlus사에 의해 개발되었다는 소문은 주식 시장 전체에 빠르게 퍼졌다.

어휘 spread v. 퍼지다 throughout prep. ~ 전체에, ~ 동안 내내
stock market 주식 시장

최신토익 경향

분사 문제는 평균 1~2문제 정도 꾸준히 출제된다. 특히, 의미로 구별해야 하는 현재분사와 과거분사는 정답을 고르기 까다로우니 분사 표현을 함께 출제된 명사와 함께 알아두자.

- troubling complaint 성가신 불만 사항 — troubled complaint (X)
- remaining work 남아 있는 일 — remained work (X)
- absorbing work 몰입하게 하는 작품 — absorbed work (X)
- secluded area 외딴 지역 — secluding area (X)
- advanced degree 석박사 학위 — advancing degree (X)
- dedicated employee 헌신적인 직원 — dedicating employee (X)
- experienced specialist 숙련된 전문가
  — experiencing specialist (X)

127 부정대명사 채우기

해설 동사(is expected) 앞에 주어가 없으므로 빈칸은 주어 자리이고, 빈칸 뒤의 형용사(exciting)의 꾸밈을 받아야 하므로 부정대명사 (B)와 (C)가 정답의 후보이다. 동사 is expected는 단수 동사이므로 단수 동사와 짝을 이루는 (C) Something(무언가)이 정답이다. (B) Many는 부정대명사로 쓰일 경우, '많은 사람들'이라는 의미로 복수 동사와 함께 쓰이므로 답이 될 수 없다. (A) Whatever는 복합관계대명사로 쓰일 경우 anything that(무엇이든 간에)의 의미로 문장에서 주어나 목적어로 쓰이기 때문에 뒤에 형용사(exciting)가 아니라 동사가 와야 한다. Whatever는 복합관계형용사로도 쓰일 수 있는데, 이 경우에는 뒤에 명사가 나와서 그 명사를 수식하는 역할을 하기 때문에 답이 될 수 없다. 부정형용사 (D) Other(다른)는 이미 언급한 것 이외의 것을 나타내며 복수 가산 명사 또는 불가산 명사와 함께 쓰인다. 참고로, -thing으로 끝나는 부정대명사는 형용사가 뒤에서 수식한다는 것을 알아둔다.

해석 9월에 게임 스타트업 회사인 Void One에 의해 흥미로운 무언가가 드러날 것으로 예상되지만, 그것이 무엇인지는 아무도 모른다.

어휘 exciting adj. 흥미로운, 신나는   reveal v. 드러내다, 밝히다

128 명사 어휘 고르기

해설 '가구가 조립을 필요로 하다'라는 문맥이므로 (B) assembly(조립)가 정답이다. (A) calculation은 '계산', (C) gravity는 '중력', (D) inventory는 '재고'라는 의미이다.

해석 Mados사의 가구는 조립을 필요로 하지만, 모든 제품은 필요한 도구들이 딸려온다.

어휘 tool n. 도구

129 태에 맞는 동사 채우기

해설 문장에 동사가 없으므로 모든 보기가 정답의 후보이다. 주어(All lawyers)와 동사(encourage)가 '모든 변호사들이 권고받다'라는 수동의 의미가 되어야 하므로 수동태 동사 (B) are encouraged가 정답이다. 참고로, 동사 encourage(권고하다)가 수동태로 쓰일 경우 뒤에 to 부정사와 함께 'be encouraged to 동사원형'의 형태로 쓰임을 알아둔다.

해석 Ross & Don 법률 사무소에 소속된 모든 변호사들은 국제법에 관한 그들의 지식을 지속적으로 향상시킬 것을 권고받는다.

어휘 affiliate v. 소속시키다, 제휴하다   continuously adv. 지속적으로

130 부사 어휘 고르기

해설 '소규모 기업 소유주들에게는 보통 어려운 과제이다'라는 문맥이므로 부사 (A) often(보통, 흔히)이 정답이다. (C) far(훨씬, 멀리)도 해석상 그럴듯해 보이지만, '훨씬'이라는 의미로 쓰일 경우 비교급과 함께 쓰여야 하므로 답이 될 수 없다. (B) well은 '잘', (D) hard는 '열심히, 힘들게'라는 의미이다.

해석 유능한 지원자들을 끌어모으고 숙련된 근로자들을 보유하는 것은 소규모 기업 소유주들에게는 보통 어려운 과제이다.

어휘 attract v. 끌어모으다   retain v. 보유하다, 간직하다   challenging adj. 어려운, 도전적인   owner n. 소유주, 주인

PART 6

131-134번은 다음 공고에 관한 문제입니다.

> 모든 영화 제작진 구성원들에게 알립니다.
>
> 이번 주말, 우리는 Dolly Sods 국립 공원에서 촬영할 것입니다. 촬영은 일정보다 2시간 일찍 시작될 것입니다. [131]**이는 여러분이 공원 입구에 일찍 와 있어야 한다는 것을 의미합니다.**
>
> 여러분이 도착하면, 제작 책임자를 찾으십시오. [132]**그가 여러분을 배정된 위치로 안내할 것입니다.** 우리는 계획된 장면들을 촬영하는 데 시간이 거의 없으므로, 모든 장비가 준비되어 오전 5시 정각까지 갈 준비가 되어있어야 합니다. [133]**촬영 감독님이 촬영 전에 리허설을 할 것입니다.** 모두가 대본의 관련 있는 부분들을 살펴보는 것이 현명할 것입니다.
>
> 우리는 이미 점심을 제공하기 위한 음식 출장 업체를 준비해 두었습니다. [134]**그것은 아침 촬영이 끝나는 대로 제공될 것입니다.**

ahead of 일찍, ~보다 빨리   assigned adj. 배정된, 할당된   sequence n. (연속된) 장면, 연속적인 사건들   equipment n. 장비   director n. 감독   relevant adj. 관련 있는, 연관된   portion n. 부분   arrange for 준비하다, 계획을 짜다   catering n. 음식 출장(업)

131 부사 어휘 고르기 주변 문맥 파악

해설 '이는 여러분이 공원 입구에 ____ 와 있어야 한다는 것을 의미한다'라는 문맥이므로 (A), (B), (D)가 정답의 후보이다. 빈칸이 있는 문장만으로 정답을 고를 수 없으므로 주변 문맥이나 전체 문맥을 파악한다. 앞 문장에서 '촬영은 예정보다 2시간 일찍 시작될 것이다(Shooting will start two hours ahead of schedule).'라고 했으므로 공원 입구에 일찍 와 있어야 함을 알 수 있다. 따라서 부사 (B) early(일찍)가 정답이다. (A) soon은 '곧', (C) briefly는 '짧게', (D) together는 '함께'라는 의미이다.

132 동사 어휘 고르기

해설 '그(제작 책임자)가 여러분을 배정된 위치로 ____ 할 것이다'라는 문맥이므로 (B) direct(안내하다)가 정답이다. (C) mention(말하다, 언급하다)도 해석상 그럴듯해 보이지만 목적어 자리에 듣는 대상(you)이 아닌, 말하는 대상(your assigned place)을 써야 하므로 답이 될 수 없다. (A) allow는 '허락하다', (D) resume은 '다시 시작하다'라는 의미이다.

133 올바른 시제의 동사 채우기 전체 문맥 파악

해설 '촬영 감독이 촬영 전에 리허설을 하다'라는 문맥인데, 이 경우 빈칸이 있는 문장만으로는 올바른 시제의 동사를 고를 수 없으므로 주변 문맥이나 전체 문맥을 파악하여 정답을 고른다. 앞부분에서 이번 주말에 Dolly Sods 국립 공원에서 촬영할 것이라고 했으므로, 촬영이 있는 시점이 미래임을 알 수 있다. 따라서 미래 시제 (C) will conduct가 정답이다. 과거진행 시제 (A), 과거 시제 (B)와 (D)는 미래의 일을 나타낼 수 없다.

어휘 conduct v. (특정 활동을) 하다

134 알맞은 문장 고르기

해석 (A) 지연으로 인해 야기된 불편에 대해 사과드립니다.
(B) 공원 입구 근처에는 주차 공간이 부족합니다.
(C) 이것은 영화에서 가장 중요한 장면입니다.
(D) 그것은 아침 촬영이 끝나는 대로 제공될 것입니다.

해설 앞 문장 'We've already arranged for a catering company to provide lunch.'에서 이미 점심을 제공하기 위한 음식 출장 업체를 준비해 두었다고 했으므로, 빈칸에는 점심 제공과 관련된 내용이 들어가야 함을 알 수 있다. 따라서 (D)가 정답이다.

어휘 shortage n. 부족, 결핍 serve v. 제공하다

135-138번은 다음 제품 설명에 관한 문제입니다.

> Slimline 컴퓨터 책상
>
> ¹³⁵Ferguson 가구사는 기능적인 가정용 및 사무용 가구를 생산하는 데 있어 큰 자부심을 가지고 있습니다. 저희는 이 접근법을 다양한 실용적인 기능을 갖춘 Slimline 컴퓨터 책상의 디자인에 적용했습니다.
>
> ¹³⁶Slimline 컴퓨터 책상을 차별화하는 것은 바로 입식 또는 좌식 책상의 역할을 할 수 있도록 조정될 수 있다는 것입니다. ¹³⁷두 모드 사이를 전환하기 위해 그저 레버를 당기기만 하세요. ¹³⁸당신이 그것을 어떻게 사용하는지와 상관없이, 그 인체공학적인 디자인은 확실히 당신이 목이나 허리 통증을 전혀 경험하지 않도록 해줄 것입니다. 그것은 또한 표준 소켓과 USB 소켓이 모두 내장된 전원 콘센트를 포함하고 있습니다.

take pride in ~에 자부심을 갖다 approach n. 접근법
practical adj. 실용적인 feature n. 특징, 특색
set apart 차별화하다, 눈에 띄게 하다 serve as ~의 역할을 하다
regardless of ~와 상관없이 ergonomic adj. 인체공학적인
outlet n. 콘센트, 전기 코드 구멍 socket n. 소켓, 꽂는 곳

135 형용사 어휘 고르기 주변 문맥 파악

해설 'Ferguson 가구사는 ____ 가정용 및 사무용 가구를 생산한다'라는 문맥이므로 (B), (C), (D)가 정답의 후보이다. 빈칸이 있는 문장만으로는 정답을 고를 수 없으므로 주변 문맥이나 전체 문맥을 파악한다. 뒤 문장에서 이 접근법을 다양한 실용적인 기능을 갖춘 Slimline 컴퓨터 책상의 디자인에 적용했다(We have applied this approach to the design ~, which has a wide variety of practical features).'라고 했으므로, 기능적인 가정용 및 사무용 가구를 생산한다는 것임을 알 수 있다. 따라서 형용사 (C) functional (기능적인, 실용적인)이 정답이다. (B) matching은 '어울리는', (D) customizable은 '주문에 따라 만들 수 있는'이라는 의미이다. (A) seasonal은 '계절에 따른'이라는 의미로 seasonal promotion(계절에 따른 판촉 활동)과 같은 표현으로 쓰인다는 것을 알아둔다.

136 태에 맞는 동사 채우기

해설 명사절 접속사(that) 뒤에 주어(it)만 있고 동사가 없으므로 동사 자리에 들어갈 수 있는 (A), (C), (D)가 정답의 후보이다. 주어(it)와 동사(adjust)가 '그것은 조정되다'라는 수동의 의미를 가지므로 수동태 동사 (D) can be adjusted가 정답이다. 과거진행 시제 능동태 (A)와 현재완료 시제 능동태 (C)는 뒤에 목적어가 와야 하므로 답이 될 수

없다. 전치사구 (B)는 동사 자리에 올 수 없다. 참고로, adjust는 '~에 적응하다'라는 의미의 자동사로 쓰일 수 있으며, 주로 뒤에 전치사 to와 함께 쓰인다.

어휘 adjust v. 조정하다, 조절하다

137 알맞은 문장 고르기

해석 (A) 저희는 매년 봄과 가을에 새로운 가구 라인을 출시합니다.
(B) 환불 및 교환은 구매 후 일주일 내로 가능합니다.
(C) 두 모드 사이를 전환하기 위해 그저 레버를 당기기만 하세요.
(D) 저희 경쟁업체들 중 어느 곳에서도 더 좋은 혜택을 받을 수 없을 것입니다.

해설 앞 문장 'What sets the Slimline computer desk apart is ~ serve as either a standing or sitting desk.'에서 Slimline 컴퓨터 책상을 차별화하는 것은 바로 입식 또는 좌식 책상의 역할을 할 수 있도록 조정될 수 있다는 것이라고 했으므로 빈칸에는 책상이 입식과 좌식 두 가지로 조정될 수 있는 것과 관련된 내용이 들어가야 함을 알 수 있다. 따라서 (C)가 정답이다.

어휘 release v. 출시하다 switch v. 전환하다, 바꾸다
competitor n. 경쟁업체, 경쟁자

138 명사절 접속사 채우기

해설 빈칸 이하(____ ~ use it)는 전치사 Regardless of의 목적어이므로 전치사의 목적어 자리에 올 수 있는 명사절을 이끄는 명사절 접속사인 모든 보기가 정답의 후보이다. 빈칸이 포함된 절이 주어(you), 동사(use), 목적어(it)를 갖춘 완전한 절이므로 뒤에 완전한 절이 오는 의문사 (A) how가 정답이다. 의문사 (B) which, 복합관계대명사 (C) whoever, 의문사 (D) whom은 뒤에 불완전한 절이 와야 하므로 답이 될 수 없다.

139-142번은 다음 광고에 관한 문제입니다.

> Blossom Haven: 꽃으로 둘러싸인 낙원이 기다리고 있습니다.
>
> 당신의 환상이 현실이 되는 저희 꽃 가게를 방문하세요! Blossom Haven에서, ¹³⁹여러분은 굉장히 아름다운 다수의 수입된 꽃들을 발견하실 수 있습니다. 특별한 행사를 계획하고 있든, 누군가의 하루를 반짝이게 해주기를 원하든, 저희의 플로리스트들이 도움을 주기 위해 여기 있습니다. ¹⁴⁰그들은 모두 3년 이상의 경력을 갖춘 전문가들입니다.
>
> 4주년을 기념하여, 저희는 귀중한 고객분들을 위한 특별한 선물을 준비했습니다. ¹⁴¹4월 1일부터 일주일 동안, 저희 가게에서 꽃을 구매하신 모든 고객분들은 금잔화와 라일락, 금어초로 만들어진 말린 꽃 액자를 받을 것입니다.
>
> ¹⁴²게다가, 4월 한 달 내내, 컴벌랜드 카운티 내 꽃 배달은 무료입니다. 저희의 모든 제품 사진을 확인하기 위해서는 www.blossomhaven.com을 방문하세요.

await v. 기다리다 stunning adj. 굉장히 아름다운, 깜짝 놀랄
an array of 다수의 valued adj. 귀중한, 소중한 receive v. 받다
frame n. 액자 entire adj. 내내, 전체의 complimentary adj. 무료의

139 현재분사와 과거분사 구별하여 채우기

해설 빈칸 뒤의 명사(flowers)를 꾸며줄 수 있는 것은 형용사이므로 형용사 역할을 하는 과거분사 (A)와 현재분사 (D)가 정답의 후보이다. 꾸밈을 받는 명사와 분사가 '꽃들이 수입되다'라는 수동의 의미이므로 과거분사 (A) imported(수입된)가 정답이다. 현재분사 (D) importing(수입하는)을 쓰면 '꽃들이 수입하다'라는 어색한 문맥이 된다. 동사 또는 명사 (B)는 명사를 꾸밀 수 없으며, 명사 (C)는 flowers와 복합명사를 만들 수 없으므로 답이 될 수 없다.

어휘 import v. 수입하다 importer n. 수입 업체, 수입국

140 알맞은 문장 고르기

해석 (A) 플로리스트들을 교육시키는 다양한 교육 기관이 있습니다.
(B) 꽃들을 수출할 때 엄격한 절차를 따라야 합니다.
(C) 그들은 모두 3년 이상의 경력을 갖춘 전문가들입니다.
(D) 모든 꽃 주문의 배송은 3일에서 5일을 잡으세요.

해설 앞 문장 'Whether you're planning a special event or simply want to brighten someone's day, our florists are here to assist.'에서 플로리스트들이 도움을 주기 위해 여기 있다고 했으므로, 빈칸에는 플로리스트의 전문성과 관련된 내용이 들어가야 함을 알 수 있다. 따라서 (C)가 정답이다.

어휘 various adj. 다양한, 여러 가지의 institution n. 기관
strict adj. 엄격한 professional n. 전문가; adj. 전문적인

141 동사 어휘 고르기

해설 '가게에서 꽃을 ____한 모든 고객들은 말린 꽃 액자를 받게 될 것이다'라는 문맥이므로 (B) purchase(구매하다)가 정답이다. (A) display는 '전시하다', (C) connect는 '연결하다', (D) fold는 '접다'라는 의미이다.

142 접속부사 채우기 전체 문맥 파악

해설 빈칸이 콤마와 함께 문장의 맨 앞에 온 접속부사 자리이므로, 앞 문장과 빈칸이 있는 문장의 의미 관계를 파악하여 정답을 선택한다. 앞 문장에서 4월 1일부터 일주일 동안, 가게에서 꽃을 구매하는 모든 고객들은 말린 꽃 액자를 받게 될 것이라고 했고, 빈칸이 있는 문장에서는 4월의 달 내내, 컴벌랜드 카운티 내 꽃 배달은 무료라고 했으므로, 앞에서 언급된 내용에 추가 정보를 덧붙일 때 사용되는 접속부사 (D) Additionally(게다가)가 정답이다.

어휘 instead adv. 대신에 if not 그렇지 않다면 after all 결국에는

143-146번은 다음 이메일에 관한 문제입니다.

수신: Hye-in Park <hipark@sabanbiz.com>
발신: Leonard Smithers <l.smithers@mcclureconsulting.com>
날짜: 6월 30일
제목: 후속 조치

Ms. Park께,

우리는 Millennium Center에서 열린 지난주 세미나에서 만난 바 있습니다. ¹⁴³기억하시겠지만, 우리는 귀하의 회사를 리브랜딩하는

것과 McClure 컨설팅사가 어떻게 도움을 줄 수 있는지에 관해 이야기했습니다. 저희 팀과 저는 보여드리고 싶은 제안을 가지고 있습니다. ¹⁴⁴무역 총회를 위해 7월 12일부터 16일까지 내내 귀하의 도시를 방문할 것입니다. 그 일정 즈음에 회의를 잡아보는 것이 어떨까요?

¹⁴⁵저희는 포괄적인 서비스를 제공합니다. 그 계획은 브랜드를 경쟁적으로 자리 잡게 하는 것부터 고객의 충성도를 이끌어내고 일관된 메시지 전달을 유지하는 것까지 모든 것을 포함하고 있습니다. 물론, 귀하의 의견 없이는 어떤 계획도 완전할 수 없을 것입니다. ¹⁴⁶이것이 바로 저희가 상세한 논의가 필요하다고 느끼는 이유입니다. 귀하의 답장을 기대하겠습니다.

Leonard Smithers 드림
McClure Consulting 부사장

---

present v. 보여 주다, 나타내다 convention n. 총회, 협약
position v. 자리 잡게 하다, 시장에 내놓다
competitively adv. 경쟁적으로 elicit v. 끌어내다
maintain v. 유지하다 consistent adj. 일관된
complete adj. 완전한; v. 완료하다

143 올바른 시제의 동사 채우기 전체 문맥 파악

해설 의문사(how) 뒤에 주어(McClure Consulting)만 있고 동사가 없으므로 동사인 (B), (C), (D)가 정답의 후보이다. 'McClure 컨설팅사가 도움을 주다'라는 문맥인데, 이 경우 빈칸이 있는 문장만으로 올바른 시제의 동사를 고를 수 없으므로 주변 문맥이나 전체 문맥을 파악하여 정답을 고른다. 뒷부분에서 이것과 관련하여 보여주고 싶은 제안이 있으니 회의를 잡자고 했으므로, 미래에 가능한 일임을 알 수 있다. 따라서 미래의 가능성을 나타낼 때 쓰는 조동사 could를 이용한 (D) could help가 정답이다. 관계절 (A)는 동사 자리에 들어갈 수 없다.

144 전치사 채우기

해설 '7월 12일부터 16일까지 내내 방문할 것이다'라는 의미가 되어야 하므로 기간을 나타내는 전치사 (B) through(~ 내내)가 정답이다. (A) along은 '~을 따라', (C) beside는 '~옆에', (D) toward는 '~을 향해'라는 의미이다.

145 형용사 어휘 고르기 주변 문맥 파악

해설 '____ 서비스를 제공한다'라는 문맥이므로 (A), (B), (D)가 정답의 후보이다. 빈칸이 있는 문장만으로 정답을 고를 수 없으므로 주변 문맥이나 전체 문맥을 파악한다. 뒤 문장에서 '그 계획은 브랜드를 경쟁적으로 자리 잡게 하는 것부터 고객의 충성도를 이끌어내고 일관된 메시지 전달을 유지하는 것까지 모든 것을 포함한다(The plan includes everything from positioning ~ and maintaining consistent messaging).'라고 했으므로 포괄적인 서비스를 보장하는 것에 전념한다는 것을 알 수 있다. 따라서 형용사 (D) comprehensive(포괄적인)가 정답이다. (A) arbitrary는 '임의의, 자의적인', (B) regional은 '지역의', (C) inflated는 '부풀린, 폭등한'이라는 의미이다.

146 알맞은 문장 고르기

해석 (A) 이것이 바로 저희가 상세한 논의가 필요하다고 느끼는 이유입니다.
(B) 인쇄 광고물은 한때 그랬던 것만큼 효과적이지는 않습니다.

(C) 고객들은 리브랜딩하는 것에 긍정적으로 반응했습니다.

(D) 매출은 지난해와 비교해서 이번 분기에 상승했습니다.

해설 앞 문장 'Of course, no plan will be complete without your feedback.'에서 귀하의 의견이 없다면 어떠한 계획도 완전하지 않을 것이라고 했으므로, 빈칸에는 의견을 얻는 것과 관련된 내용이 들어가야 함을 알 수 있다. 따라서 (A)가 정답이다.

어휘 effective adj. 효과적인 positively adv. 긍정적으로
quarter n. 분기, 4분의 1

PART 7

147-148번은 다음 제품 후기에 관한 문제입니다.

새 분쇄기에 만족해요!

몇 주 전에 저의 오래된 분쇄기가 작동을 멈췄습니다. 보증이 만료되었기 때문에, 새것을 구매하기로 결정했습니다. 처음에는, 제 여동생이 가지고 있는 모델을 고려하고 있었습니다. 하지만, 그것은 너무 비쌌습니다. 온라인으로 찾는 것은 모든 후기들이 편향된 것 같아 보였기 때문에 도움이 되지 않았습니다. ¹⁴⁷그런데 그때 한 동료가 Whirl Blade 234를 구입해 보라고 추천했고, 그의 말을 들어서 다행입니다. 그것을 이제 한 달간 사용하고 있는데 매우 인상 깊었습니다. 5단계의 속도 설정과 2리터짜리 용기로, 스무디부터 수프까지 모든 것을 만드는 데 그것을 사용할 수 있습니다. ¹⁴⁸유일한 문제는 받침대가 꽤 커서 제 조리대의 많은 공간을 차지한다는 것입니다. 하지만 이 단점은 그 분쇄기가 얼마나 조용한지에 의해 만회됩니다. 더할 나위 없이 추천하고 싶습니다.

- Sofia Vega

blender n. 분쇄기, 믹서기 warranty n. 보증
expire v. 만료되다, 만기가 되다 biased adj. 편향된, 선입견이 있는
colleague n. 동료 jug n. 용기, 물병 base n. 받침대, 맨 아랫부분
bulky adj. (부피가) 큰 take up (공간을) 차지하다
counter n. 조리대, 계산대 shortcoming n. 단점, 결함
make up for 만회하다, 보상하다

---

147 육하원칙 문제

해석 Ms. Vega는 왜 Whirl Blade 234를 선택했는가?

(A) 연장된 보증이 딸려 있다.

(B) 가장 비용이 적게 드는 선택이었다.

(C) 온라인에 많은 긍정적인 후기가 있었다.

(D) 동료에게 추천받았다.

해설 지문의 'But then a colleague suggested that I buy the Whirl Blade 234, and I'm glad I listened to him.'에서 한 동료가 Whirl Blade 234를 구입해 보라고 추천했고, 그의 말을 들어서 다행이라고 했으므로 (D)가 정답이다.

어휘 come with ~이 딸려 있다 extended adj. 연장된, 늘어난
costly adj. 비용이 많이 드는 coworker n. 동료

Paraphrasing

a colleague suggested 한 동료가 추천했다
→ was recommended by a coworker 동료에게 추천받았다

148 육하원칙 문제

해석 Ms. Vega가 Whirl Blade 234에 대해 마음에 들지 않는 한 가지는 무엇인가?

(A) 제한된 수의 속도

(B) 용기의 적은 용량

(C) 받침대의 큰 크기

(D) 극심한 소음 수준

해설 지문의 'The only problem is that the base is quite bulky and takes up a lot of space on my counter.'에서 유일한 문제는 받침대가 꽤 커서 조리대 공간을 많이 차지한다는 점이라고 했으므로 (C)가 정답이다.

어휘 capacity n. 용량, 능력 noise n. 소음, 잡음

Paraphrasing

bulky 큰 → large size 큰 크기

149-150번은 다음 문자 메시지 대화문에 관한 문제입니다.

Brett Adams [오전 10시 15분]

안녕하세요, Nancy. 저는 Garden City 공인중개사의 Brett입니다. 고객님께 딱 맞는 침실 2개짜리 집을 찾았어요. 금요일에 보실 수 있도록 일정을 잡을 수 있어요.

Nancy Lougheed [오전 10시 16분]

잘됐네요, Brett. 그 집을 빨리 보고 싶어요. 하지만 금요일 대신에 다음 주 월요일로 약속을 잡아 주실 수 있나요? ¹⁴⁹워크숍에 참석하기 위해 목요일에 시카고로 비행할 예정입니다. 일요일 저녁에나 돌아올 것 같아요.

Brett Adams [오전 10시 18분]

물론이죠. ¹⁵⁰하지만 그 전에 집주인이 제의를 받을 수도 있습니다. 이번 주 안에 볼 수 있도록 일정을 조정하는 게 좋을 수도 있어요.

Nancy Lougheed [오전 10시 20분]

알겠어요, Brett. ¹⁵⁰워크숍 주최자에게 이메일을 보내서 다른 날에 참석할 수 있는지 물어볼게요. 한 시간쯤 후에 다시 연락드릴게요.

Brett Adams [오전 10시 21분]

좋아요. 그럼 그때 얘기하죠.

realtor n. 공인중개사, 부동산 중개업자 view v. 보다, 여기다
property n. 집, 건물, 재산 appointment n. 약속, 임명
move things around 일정을 조정하다 organizer n. 주최자, 조직자

---

149 육하원칙 문제

해석 Ms. Lougheed는 왜 금요일에 만날 수 없는가?

(A) 진료 예약이 있다.

(B) 건물을 점검해야 한다.

(C) 점심을 먹기 위해 고객을 만날 것이다.

(D) 출장을 갈 예정이다.

해설 지문의 'I'll be flying to Chicago on Thursday to attend a workshop. I won't be back until Sunday evening.'에서 워크숍에 참석하기 위해 목요일에 시카고로 갔다가 일요일 저녁에나 돌아올 것 같다고 했으므로 (D)가 정답이다.

어휘 doctor's appointment 진료 예약 inspect v. 점검하다, 검사하다

150 의도 파악 문제

해석 오전 10시 20분에, Ms. Lougheed가 "Got it, Brett"이라고 썼을 때, 그녀가 의도한 것은?
(A) 집주인에게 연락하려고 한다.
(B) 이번 주에 이사할 계획이다.
(C) 그의 제안을 따르려고 할 것이다.
(D) 이미 그의 이메일을 받았다.

해설 지문의 'But the owner might get an offer before then. You might want to move things around so you can see it within this week.'에서 Brett이 이번 주 안에 집을 볼 수 있도록 일정을 조정하길 권유하자, Ms. Lougheed가 'Got it, Brett.'(알겠어요, Brett)이라고 한 후, 'Let me e-mail the workshop organizer and ask if I can attend another day.'에서 워크숍 주최자에게 이메일을 보내서 다른 날에 참석할 수 있는지 물어본다고 한 것을 통해, Ms. Lougheed가 Brett의 제안을 받아들여 자신의 일정을 변경하려고 할 것임을 알 수 있다. 따라서 (C)가 정답이다.

어휘 suggestion n. 제안 receive v. 받다, 받아들이다

151-152번은 다음 이메일에 관한 문제입니다.

수신: Mikhail Rozin <m.rozin@wavemail.com>
발신: Linda Newton <l.newton@aldertech.com>
날짜: 9월 3일
제목: 요청 #11708

Mr. Rozin께

Alder Tech에 연락해 주셔서 감사합니다. [151]9월 9일 목요일 오후 3시에서 오후 4시 사이에 저희 기술자 중 한 명이 세탁기를 고치기 위해 귀하의 주소지에 방문할 것입니다. 이 날짜가 곤란하시다면, 9월 7일까지 저희에게 연락하여 일정을 변경하세요.

[152]방문 당일에는, 기술자가 방해받지 않고 작업할 수 있도록, 반드시 세탁실에 장애물이 없도록 해 주시기 바랍니다. 특히, 세탁 바구니, 의류 및 세제 용기들은 다른 장소로 옮겨져야 합니다. 작업이 완료되면, 기술자는 그것이 정상적으로 작동하는지 확인시키기 위해 귀하께 세탁기를 검사하도록 할 것입니다. 물론, 귀하의 보증이 여전히 유효하기 때문에 어떠한 비용도 요구되지 않을 것입니다.

Linda Newton 드림
고객 담당자, Alder Tech

technician n. 기술자 fix v. 고치다, 수리하다
inconvenient adj. 곤란한, 불편한 obstruction n. 장애물
unimpeded adj. 방해받지 않는, 가로막는 것이 없는 detergent n. 세제
valid adj. 유효한, 타당한

151 추론 문제

해석 Mr. Rozin은 어떤 종류의 서비스를 요청한 것 같은가?
(A) 주택 개조
(B) 가전제품 수리
(C) 안전 점검
(D) 기기 설치

해설 지문의 'One of our technicians will visit your address on Thursday, September 9, ~ to fix your washing machine.'에서 기술자 중 한 명이 세탁기를 수리하기 위해 Mr. Rozin의 주소지에 방문할 것이라고 했으므로 Mr. Rozin이 가전제품 수리 서비스를 요청한 것임을 추론할 수 있다. 따라서 (B)가 정답이다.

어휘 renovation n. 개조, 보수 appliance n. 가전제품, (가정용) 기기
inspection n. 점검 installation n. 설치

Paraphrasing

washing machine 세탁기 → An appliance 가전제품
fix 고치다 → repair 수리

152 육하원칙 문제

해석 Mr. Rozin은 목요일에 무엇을 하라고 요청받았는가?
(A) 결제가 이루어졌는지 확인한다.
(B) 그의 집 주소를 보낸다.
(C) 공간에서 물품들을 치운다.
(D) 보증이 유효하다는 것을 입증한다.

해설 지문의 'On the day of the visit, please ensure that your laundry room is free of obstructions'에서 Mr. Rozin은 방문 당일에 반드시 세탁실에 장애물이 없도록 해 달라고 요청받았으므로 (C)가 정답이다.

어휘 remove v. 치우다, 제거하다 verify v. 입증하다, 확인하다

Paraphrasing

is free of obstructions 장애물이 없다 → Remove items 물품들을 치우다
laundry room 세탁실 → an area 공간

153-155번은 다음 기사에 관한 문제입니다.

올버니 (5월 25일)- Comfort Zone사에서 Fresh 370Z, Mist 405E, 그리고 Vapor 525X의 세 가지 모델을 포함한 신규 라인의 가습기를 공개했다. [153]Fresh 370Z가 가장 비싸며 와이파이 연결이 되는 유일한 제품이다. 소유자들은 자신의 스마트폰을 이용하여 그것을 켤 수 있고 설정을 조정할 수 있다. 용량의 측면에서, Vapor 525X는 가장 작은 물통을 가지고 있으며, 오직 1리터의 물만 수용한다. 그에 반해서, Mist 405E는 2.2리터의 물통을 가지고 있고, 이로 인해 셋 중 가장 크다. [154]이 세 가습기들을 이전 모델들에 비해 돋보이도록 돕는 한 가지 개선된 점은 그것들의 에너지 효율성이다. 그것들은 최대 레벨로 작동하는 경우에도 매우 적은 전기를 필요로 한다.

[155]누구든 새로운 가습기를 사려고 하는 사람이라면 이 모델들 중 한 개를 가지고 있는 사람들의 초반 의견을 살펴보기 위해 www.newproducts.com/comfortzone을 방문해야 한다. 이 가습기들은 모든 Comfort Zone 매장과 그 회사의 모바일 애플리케이션을 통해 구매 가능하다.

release v. 공개하다, 발매하다 humidifier n. 가습기
connectivity n. 연결 turn on ~을 켜다 tank n. 물통, 수조
hold v. 수용하다, 담다 improvement n. 개선 사항
stand out 돋보이다 previous adj. 이전의 operate v. 작동하다
in the market for ~을 사려고 하는

153 육하원칙 문제

해석 Fresh 370Z는 다른 모델들과 어떻게 다른가?
(A) 인터넷을 통해 제어할 수 있다.
(B) 다양한 부속품들이 딸려 있다.
(C) 자동으로 켜고 끄는 것이 가능하다.
(D) 진보된 안전 설정이 탑재되어 있다.

해설 지문의 'The Fresh 370Z is the most expensive and the only one with Wi-Fi connectivity. Owners can turn it on and adjust its settings using their smartphones.'에서 Fresh 370Z가 가장 비싸고 와이파이 연결이 되는 유일한 제품이며 소유자들은 자신의 스마트폰을 이용하여 그것을 켤 수 있고 설정을 조정할 수 있다고 했으므로, Fresh 370Z가 다른 모델들과 달리 인터넷을 통해 제어가 가능하다는 것을 알 수 있다. 따라서 (A)가 정답이다.

어휘 control v. 제어하다 a variety of 다양한
automatically adv. 자동으로 advanced adj. 진보된, 선진의

Paraphrasing

adjust its settings 설정을 조정하다 → is possible to control 제어할 수 있다
using ~ smartphones 스마트폰을 이용하여 → through the Internet 인터넷을 통해

154 육하원칙 문제

해석 세 개의 모든 가습기들이 공유하고 있는 개선점은 무엇인가?
(A) 간소화된 작동 방법
(B) 향상된 내구성
(C) 늘어난 용량
(D) 감소된 전기 사용

해설 지문의 'One improvement that helps these three humidifiers stand out from previous models is their energy efficiency. They require very little electricity even when operating at their maximum levels.'에서 이 가습기들을 이전 모델들에 비해 돋보이도록 돕는 한 가지 개선된 점은 에너지 효율성이라고 했고, 최대 레벨에서도 매우 적은 전기를 필요로 한다고 했다. 따라서 (D)가 정답이다.

어휘 simplified adj. 간소화된, 간략하게 한 durability n. 내구성

Paraphrasing

require very little electricity 매우 적은 전기를 필요로 하다
→ reduced power use 감소된 전기 사용

155 육하원칙 문제

해석 기사는 사람들에게 무엇을 하라고 제안하는가?
(A) 온라인 고객 설문조사를 완료한다.
(B) 제품 의견을 회사에 제출한다.
(C) 웹사이트에서 고객 후기를 읽는다.
(D) 서로 다른 모델들의 가격을 비교한다.

해설 지문의 'Anyone in the market for a new humidifier should visit www.newproducts.com/comfortzone to look over

early feedback from people who own one of these models.'에서 누구든 새로운 가습기를 사려고 하는 사람이라면 이 모델들 중 한 개를 가지고 있는 사람들의 초반 의견을 살펴보기 위해 웹사이트를 방문하라고 했으므로 (C)가 정답이다.

어휘 submit v. 제출하다 compare v. 비교하다

Paraphrasing

look over ~ feedback 의견을 살펴보다 → Read ~ reviews 후기를 읽는다

156-158번은 다음 이메일에 관한 문제입니다.

수신: Tobias Wu<t.wu@fastpost.com>
발신: Sarah Lewis<s.lewis@milfordcollege.com>
제목: 회신: 수업 등록
날짜: 8월 15일

Mr. Wu께

밀퍼드 대학교에서 관심 있는 강좌에 등록하지 못하셨다니 유감입니다. 처음 이메일에서 요청하신 대로, 컴퓨터 오류로 인한 것인지 확인하고자 기록을 확인했습니다. 그 경우는 아닌 것으로 보입니다. [156]수강하고자 하신 강좌인 거시경제학 202는 2학년 학생들에게만 열려 있습니다. 저희의 온라인 등록 시스템이 귀하께서 내년이 돼야 수강 신청할 수 있도록 할 것입니다.

하지만, [157]수강 요건을 충족하지 않은 특정 학생들을 위해 교수님들이 면제 양식을 제출할 수 있습니다. 면제를 요청하고 싶다면, Willis 교수님께 직접 연락하시기 바랍니다. [158-(A)]그녀는 현재 웨스턴 대학교에서 열리는 학술 세미나에 참석 중입니다. [158-(B)]그녀는 다음 주 초에 우리 교육기관으로 돌아올 예정이며 경제학과 홈페이지에 나와 있는 정규 근무 시간을 다시 시작할 예정입니다. 하지만 [158-(C)]그녀의 강의는 수요가 높아서 보통 최대 수강 인원이 빨리 채워진다는 점을 명심하세요. 그렇기에 그녀는 학생들에게 면제를 제공하는 것에 거의 동의하지 않습니다.

문의 사항이 있으시다면, 언제든 저에게 다시 연락하세요.

Sarah Lewis

학생 지원 서비스
밀퍼드 대학교

registration n. 등록 sign up for ~에 등록하다 waiver n. 면제, 제외
specific adj. 특정한, 구체적인 requirement n. 요건, 필요
resume v. 다시 시작하다, 재개하다 rarely adv. 거의 ~하지 않는, 드물게

156 추론 문제

해석 Tobias Wu에 대해 암시되는 것은?
(A) 강의 등록 마감 기한을 놓쳤다.
(B) 이전에 거시경제학 202를 수강한 적이 있다.
(C) 현재 대학교 1학년이다.
(D) 등록금 면제 신청을 취소했다.

해설 지문의 'The course you[Tobias Wu] are trying to take, Macroeconomics 202, is only open to second-year students. Our online registration system will not let you sign up for it until next year.'에서 거시경제학 202는 2학년 학생들에게만 열려

있고, 온라인 등록 시스템은 Tobias Wu가 내년이 돼야 그 강의를 수강할 수 있게 할 것이라고 했으므로 Tobias Wu는 현재 대학교 1학년이라는 것을 추론할 수 있다. 따라서 (C)가 정답이다.

어휘 deadline n. 마감 기한 withdraw v. 취소하다, 철회하다, 철수하다

157 동의어 찾기 문제

해석 2문단 첫 번째 줄의 단어 "meet"은 의미상 -와 가장 가깝다
(A) 주목하다
(B) 충족시키다
(C) 맞닥뜨리다
(D) 약속하다

해설 meet을 포함한 구절 'professors can submit a waiver form for specific students who do not meet the course requirements'에서 meet은 '충족시키다'의 뜻으로 사용되었다. 따라서 (B)가 정답이다.

158 Not/True 문제

해석 Willis 교수에 대해 언급되지 않은 것은?
(A) 다른 기관에서 열리는 회의에 참석 중이다.
(B) 다음 주에 평소의 업무 일정으로 돌아갈 것이다.
(C) 많은 학생들의 흥미를 끄는 강좌를 가르친다.
(D) 일 년이 안 되는 기간 동안 밀퍼드 대학교에서 학생들을 가르쳐왔다.

해설 (A)는 'She[Professor Willis] is currently attending an academic seminar at Western University.'에서 현재 웨스턴 대학교에서 열리는 학술 세미나에 참석 중이라고 했으므로 지문의 내용과 일치한다. (B)는 'She is expected to return ~ next week ~ will resume her regular office hours'에서 다음 주에 돌아와서 정규 근무 시간을 다시 시작할 예정이라고 했으므로, 지문의 내용과 일치한다. (C)는 'her courses ~ reach their maximum capacity quickly'에서 그녀의 강의는 최대 수강 인원이 빨리 채워진다고 했으므로 지문의 내용과 일치한다. (D)는 지문에 언급되지 않은 내용이다. 따라서 (D)가 정답이다.

어휘 usual adj. 평소의, 보통의 attract v. 흥미를 끌다, 매료시키다

originally adv. 원래, 본래 run v. 진행되다
electrical adj. 전기의, 전기를 이용하는 replace v. 교체하다, 대신하다
wiring n. 배선 (장치) light fixture 조명 기구 purchase v. 구매하다
refund n. 환불(금) process v. 처리하다

159 추론 문제

해석 공고는 어디에서 발견될 수 있을 것 같은가?
(A) 경기장에서
(B) 박물관에서
(C) 극장에서
(D) 기차역에서

해설 지문의 'We regret to announce that the special exhibit of ancient Roman and Greek artifacts has been postponed.'에서 고대 로마와 그리스 유물을 다룬 특별 전시회가 연기되었음을 알리게 되어 유감스럽게 생각한다고 했으므로 박물관에서 안내문을 발견할 수 있을 것임을 추론할 수 있다. 따라서 (B)가 정답이다.

어휘 theater n. 극장

160 Not/True 문제

해석 관람표에 대해 사실인 것은?
(A) 현장에서 구매될 수 있다.
(B) 3월 15일에 일어나는 행사를 위한 것이다.
(C) 몇몇 사람들에게 할인가로 판매된다.
(D) 전화로 환불될 수 있다.

해설 지문의 'People who have purchased tickets for the exhibit but cannot visit during the new dates should contact our customer service department at (302) 555-0393 by March 15. Please note that refund requests will not be processed after this.'에서 전시 관람표를 구매했지만 새로운 날짜에 방문할 수 없는 사람들은 3월 15일까지 (302) 555-0393으로 고객 서비스 부서에 연락하라고 했고, 이 이후에는 환불 요청이 처리되지 않는다고 했으므로 전화로 환불될 수 있음을 알 수 있다. 따라서 (D)가 정답이다.

어휘 venue n. 현장, 장소 occur v. 일어나다, 발생하다

159-160번은 다음 공고에 관한 문제입니다.

모든 방문객들은 주목해 주십시오.

[159]고대 로마와 그리스 유물을 다룬 특별 전시회가 연기되었음을 알려드리게 되어 유감스럽게 생각합니다. 원래 3월 마지막 2주 동안 진행될 예정이었던 해당 전시회는 이제 4월 1일에 시작하여 4월 12일에 종료될 것입니다. 지연 이유는 물품들이 전시될 홀의 전기 문제 때문입니다. 저희 기술자들이 모든 조명 기구들의 배선을 교체해야 할 것입니다.

[160]전시 관람표를 구매했지만 새로운 날짜에 방문할 수 없는 분들은 3월 15일까지 (302) 555-0393으로 고객 서비스 부서에 연락해 주셔야 합니다. 이 이후에는 환불 요청이 처리되지 않으니 참고해 주세요.

불편을 드려 죄송하며 양해해 주셔서 감사합니다.

---

artifact n. 유물, 공예품 postpone v. 연기하다, 미루다

161-163번은 다음 편지에 관한 문제입니다.

Dr. Lynn Butler
Gennexta사
샌프란시스코, 캘리포니아주

6월 12일

Dr. Butler께,

8월 15일부터 18일까지 연례 학회를 여는 텍사스 대학교 과학 센터를 대표하여 이 편지를 씁니다. — [1] —. [161]이 행사 조직 위원회의 일원으로서, 저는 적합한 초청 연사를 찾는 일을 담당하고 있습니다. 귀하께서 참가해 주시면 영광일 것 같습니다. — [2] —. [163]Gennexta사의 선임 연구원으로서, 귀하의 지식과 전문성은 참석자들에게 큰 관심을 불러일으킬 것입니다. — [3] —. 귀하의 교통비를 충당할 뿐만 아니라, 무료 숙박도 제공할 수 있습니다. [162]학회 참석자들이 이용할 수 있도록 기숙사가 보수 중이며, 7월 16일에 문을 열 것입니다.

— [4] —. 빠른 시일 내로 저희 사무실 직원이 전화로 연락을 드릴 것입니다.

Vincent Ortiz 드림
텍사스 대학교 과학 센터

on behalf of ~을 대표하여, 대신하여 senior adj. 선임의, 상급의
expertise n. 전문성, 전문 지식 attendee n. 참석자
cover v. 충당하다, 대다 dormitory n. 기숙사
be in touch with ~에게 연락하다

161 목적 찾기 문제

해석 편지의 목적은 무엇인가?
(A) 그룹의 신규 회원을 환영하기 위해
(B) 곧 있을 행사의 변경 사항을 알리기 위해
(C) 연사를 초대하기 위해
(D) 여행 일정의 세부 사항들을 확인하기 위해

해설 지문의 'As one of this event's organizers, I am responsible for finding suitable guest speakers. I was hoping you would do us the honor of participating.'에서 행사 조직 위원회의 일원으로서, 적합한 초청 연사를 찾는 일을 담당하고 있는데, 참가해 주시면 영광일 것 같다고 했으므로 (C)가 정답이다.

어휘 extend an invitation to ~를 초대하다, ~에게 초대장을 주다
itinerary n. (여행) 일정

162 육하원칙 문제

해석 7월에 무슨 일이 일어날 것인가?
(A) 과학 센터가 문을 열 것이다.
(B) 보수 작업이 완료될 것이다.
(C) 연구 계획안이 제출될 것이다.
(D) 재정 지원 요청이 승인될 것이다.

해설 지문의 'A dormitory is being renovated for the use of conference participants, and it will open on July 16.'에서 기숙사가 보수 중이며 7월 16일에 문을 열 것이라고 했으므로 7월에 기숙사 보수 작업이 완료될 것임을 알 수 있다. 따라서 (B)가 정답이다.

어휘 proposal n. 계획(안), 제안 funding n. 재정 지원, 자금 요청
approve v. 승인하다, 허가하다

163 문장 위치 찾기 문제

해석 [1], [2], [3], [4]로 표시된 위치 중, 다음 문장이 들어갈 곳으로 가장 적절한 것은?

"그들은 귀하께서 현재 진행하고 있는 프로젝트에 대한 이야기를 듣고 싶어 합니다."

(A) [1]
(B) [2]
(C) [3]
(D) [4]

해설 주어진 문장은 진행 중인 프로젝트에 대한 이야기를 듣는 참석자들과 관련된 내용 주변에 나와야 함을 예상할 수 있다. [3]의 앞 문장

인 'Given that you are a senior researcher at Gennexta Corporation, your knowledge and expertise would be of great interest to attendees.'에서 Gennexta사의 선임 연구원인 귀하의 지식과 전문성은 참석자들에게 큰 관심을 불러일으킬 것이라고 했으므로, [3]에 주어진 문장이 들어가면 귀하의 지식과 전문성은 참석자들에게 큰 관심을 불러일으킬 것이고, 그들(참석자들)이 프로젝트에 대한 이야기를 듣고 싶어 한다는 자연스러운 문맥이 된다는 것을 알 수 있다. 따라서 (C)가 정답이다.

어휘 currently adv. 현재

164-167번은 다음 안내문에 관한 문제입니다.

Webshow 구독 요금제

2월 1일부로, 164Webshow는 현행의 두 가지 요금제가 아닌 세 가지 요금제로 된 새로운 구독 모델을 시행할 것입니다. 165-(B)작년에 수행했던 전국적인 설문조사의 응답들을 반영하기 위해 이와 같은 결정을 내렸습니다. 그 메시지는 명확한데, 구독자들은 그들의 스트리밍 요구 사항을 충족하기 위해 더 많은 선택지가 필요하다고 느낍니다.

베이직 한 달에 10.99달러	스탠다드 한 달에 12.99달러	프리미엄 한 달에 17.99달러
• 166광고 포함	• 166광고 포함	• 166광고 없음
• 1개의 호환 기기	• 2개의 호환 기기	• 4개의 호환 기기
• 한 달에 5번의 다운로드	• 고화질의 모든 영상	• 고화질의 모든 영상
	• 무제한 다운로드	• 무제한 다운로드

구독자들에 대한 감사를 표하기 위해, 저희는 프리미엄 요금제의 3개월 무료 체험을 제공할 것입니다. 이 특별한 혜택에 대한 더 많은 정보를 원하신다면, www.webshow.com/upgrade를 방문해 주세요. 167-(C)2월 8일 이후로는 무료 체험을 신청할 수 없다는 점을 유의해 주시기 바랍니다.

subscription n. 구독(료), 가입 implement v. 시행하다, 실시하다
reflect v. 반영하다 response n. 응답, 반응
nationwide adj. 전국적인 high-definition n. 고화질
unlimited adj. 무제한의 free trial 무료 체험
sign up for ~을 신청하다

164 목적 찾기 문제

해석 안내문의 목적은 무엇인가?
(A) 회사 규정을 명확하게 하기 위해
(B) 기업 합병을 발표하기 위해
(C) 요금 인상에 대해 설명하기 위해
(D) 서비스 변경 사항을 기술하기 위해

해설 지문의 'Webshow will be implementing a new subscription model with three plans rather than the current two'에서 Webshow가 현행의 두 가지 요금제가 아닌 세 가지 요금제로 된 새로운 구독 모델을 시행할 것이라고 했으므로 (D)가 정답이다.

어휘 clarify v. 명확하게 하다, 분명히 말하다 regulation n. 규정, 규제
merger n. 합병 describe v. 기술하다, 묘사하다

165 Not/True 문제

해석 Webshow에 대해 언급된 것은?

(A) 웹사이트를 재설계했다.
(B) 고객들로부터 의견을 수렴했다.
(C) 최근에 다른 나라로 확장했다.
(D) 추가적인 콘텐츠를 스트리밍하기로 결정했다.

해설 지문의 'We made this decision to reflect the responses to a nationwide survey we conducted last year.'에서 작년에 수행했던 전국적인 설문조사의 응답을 반영하기 위해 이와 같은 결정을 내렸다고 했으므로 (B)는 지문의 내용과 일치한다. 따라서 (B)가 정답이다.

어휘 expand v. 확장하다, 넓히다   additional adj. 추가의

Paraphrasing

reflect the responses to a ~ survey 설문조사의 응답들을 반영하다 → gathered feedback from ~ customers 고객들로부터 의견을 수렴했다

166 육하원칙 문제

해석 프리미엄 요금제에서 특별한 것은 무엇인가?
(A) 홍보 자료가 시청자들에게 보이지 않는다.
(B) 여러 장치들이 하나의 계정에 등록될 수 있다.
(C) 고화질의 영상을 이용할 수 있다.
(D) 다운로드 횟수가 제한되지 않는다.

해설 지문의 'Includes advertisements'에서 베이직 요금제와 스탠다드 요금제에는 광고가 포함되어 있다는 것을 알 수 있고, 'No advertisements'에서 프리미엄 요금제에는 광고가 없다는 것을 알 수 있다. 따라서 (A)가 정답이다.

어휘 material n. 자료, 물질   multiple adj. 여럿의, 다양한
account n. 계정, 계좌   restricted adj. 제한된, 한정된

Paraphrasing

advertisements 광고 → Marketing materials 홍보 자료

167 Not/True 문제

해석 특별한 혜택에 대해 언급된 것은?
(A) 기업 고객들을 끌어모으기 위해 설계되었다.
(B) 프리미엄 요금제 구독을 필요로 한다.
(C) 제한된 기간 동안에만 유효하다.
(D) 2월 8일에 처음 시행될 것이다.

해설 지문의 'Please note that you will not be able to sign up for the free trial after February 8.'에서 2월 8일 이후로는 무료 체험을 신청할 수 없다는 것에 유의해 달라고 했으므로 (C)는 지문의 내용과 일치한다. 따라서 (C)가 정답이다.

어휘 design v. 설계하다, 고안하다   valid adj. 유효한
take effect 시행되다, 발효되다

Paraphrasing

not be able to ~ after February 8 2월 8일 이후로는 ~ 할 수 없다 → is only valid for a limited time period 제한된 기간 동안만 유효하다

168-171번은 다음 브로슈어에 관한 문제입니다.

Jolie 인테리어사
바닥재 설치

새로운 바닥재를 설치하는 것은 공간의 모습을 극적으로 변화시키고 여러분들의 집이나 사업체에 가치를 더할 수 있습니다. — [1] —. 그래서, **168저희는 여러분들이 Jolie 인테리어사의 전문가들의 안내를 요청할 것을 권합니다.**

168일단 저희에게 연락하시면, 169-(C)저희 회사의 상담원이 여러분들의 공간을 방문하여 몇몇 치수 측정을 진행할 것입니다. 방문 중에는 기록 용도와 프로젝트의 정확한 계획을 보장하기 위해 공간 사진이 촬영될 것입니다. 상담원은 또한 저희의 제품 목록을 보여드리고 여러분의 집에 가장 적합한 선택지를 결정하는 것을 도와드릴 것입니다. 저희의 전문적 직원들은 주거용 및 상업용 부동산에 적합한 바닥재를 알아보는 데 있어서 아주 많은 경험을 가지고 있습니다. — [2] —. 저희는 선택할 수 있는 매우 다양한 자재들을 보유하고 있습니다.

171선택을 완료하신 후에는, 상세히 적힌 송장을 제공받을 것입니다. — [3] —. 저희 창고에서 자재를 배송하기 전에 50퍼센트의 보증금이 요구될 것입니다. 예기치 못한 일이 없다면, 해당 주문은 2주 이내에 도착할 것이며, 그 시점에 **170설치가 시작될 것입니다.** — [4] —. **170작업의 규모에 따라 2일에서 5일까지 소요될 수 있습니다.** 저희 고객을 위한 추가된 편의로, 이전 바닥재의 제거 및 처분 비용은 청구하지 않습니다.

flooring n. 바닥재, 바닥   look n. 외관, 모양   guidance n. 안내, 지침   measurement n. (치수) 측정   deposit n. 보증금, 착수금   barring prep. ~이 없다면, ~을 제외하면   unforeseen adj. 예기치 못한   charge v. 청구하다, 부과하다   disposal n. 처분, 폐기

---

168 목적 찾기 문제

해석 브로슈어의 목적은 무엇인가?
(A) 몇몇 신제품을 홍보하기 위해
(B) 과정 개요를 제공하기 위해
(C) 정책 변경을 알리기 위해
(D) 몇 가지 주문 선택권을 제시하기 위해

해설 지문의 'we encourage you to request the guidance of the experts at Jolie Interiors. Once you contact us'에서 Jolie 인테리어사 전문가들의 안내를 요청할 것을 권하면서 연락하면 진행되는 바닥재 설치의 전반적인 과정에 대에 소개하고 있으므로 (B)가 정답이다.

어휘 promote v. 홍보하다, 촉진하다, 승진시키다   overview n. 개요

169 Not/True 문제

해석 Jolie 인테리어사에 대해 언급된 것은?
(A) 고객에게 사진을 찍을 것을 요구한다.
(B) 상업용 부동산을 개조하는 것을 전문으로 한다.
(C) 고객의 주거지로 직원들을 보낸다.
(D) 온라인에서 이용 가능한 목록을 발행한다.

해설 지문의 'a consultant from our company will visit your space'에서 상담원이 고객의 공간을 방문한다고 했으므로 (C)는 지문의 내용과 일치한다. 따라서 (C)가 정답이다.

어휘 specialize in ~을 전문으로 하다   residence n. 주거지, 주거

Paraphrasing

consultant from ~ company 회사의 상담원 → employees 직원
your space 여러분들의 공간 → residences 주거지

170 추론 문제

해석 설치에 대해 암시되는 것은?
(A) 대량 주문에 대해서는 무료로 진행된다.
(B) 전액 지불을 받은 후에 시작된다.
(C) 다른 회사에 의해 실시된다.
(D) 완료되는 데 일주일보다 적게 걸린다.

해설 지문의 'the installation process will commence ~ take from
two to five days'에서 설치가 2일에서 5일까지 소요된다고 했으므
로 설치가 완료되는 데 일주일보다 적게 걸린다는 것을 추론할 수 있
다. 따라서 (D)가 정답이다.

어휘 payment n. 지불, 납입   perform v. 실시하다, 수행하다

Paraphrasing

from two to five days 2일에서 5일까지 → less than a week
일주일보다 적게

171 문장 위치 찾기 문제

해석 [1], [2], [3], [4]로 표시된 위치 중, 다음 문장이 들어갈 곳으로 가장 적
절한 것은?

"그것은 적용되는 모든 세금뿐만 아니라 재료비와 인건비도 명시할
것입니다."

(A) [1]
(B) [2]
(C) [3]
(D) [4]

해설 주어진 문장은 세금 및 비용과 관련된 내용 주변에 나와야 함을
예상할 수 있다. [3]의 앞 문장인 'After you have made your
selections, you will be provided with a detailed invoice.'에
서 선택을 완료하면 상세하게 적힌 송장을 제공받을 것이라고 했으므
로, [3]에 주어진 문장이 들어가면 선택 완료 후에 상세하게 적힌 송
장을 받을 것이고, 그 송장에는 세금, 재료비, 인건비가 명시될 것이
라는 자연스러운 문맥이 된다는 것을 알 수 있다. 따라서 (C)가 정답
이다.

어휘 specify v. 명시하다, 상세히 말하다
applicable adj. 적용되는, 적용할 수 있는

172-175번은 다음 온라인 채팅 대화문에 관한 문제입니다.

Nicholas Yang (오전 11시 21분)
안녕하세요, 팀원 여러분. ¹⁷³다음 달 탈린에서 열리는 의료 기술 학회
에 대해 논의할 필요가 있어요. 현재 상황은 어떻습니까?

Maya Kowalczyk (오전 11시 22분)
¹⁷³모든 준비가 완료됐습니다. 오늘 아침 우리의 항공편과 호텔 예약
에 대해 확인받았어요.

Emily Maxwell (오전 11시 22분)
¹⁷²저는 우리 회사의 최신 소프트웨어 프로그램 시연을 아직 작업 중이
지만 곧 완료될 것입니다.

Nicholas Yang (오전 11시 23분)
좋아요! Maya, 우리의 호텔이 회의장 근처에 있나요, 아니면 교통편
을 마련해야 될까요?

Maya Kowalczyk (오전 11시 24분)
안타깝게도, 회의장 근처 호텔은 모두 예약되어 있어요. 매일 택시를
타야 할 거예요.

Nicholas Yang (오전 11시 25분)
비용이 많이 들 수 있겠네요. 하지만 ¹⁷⁴우리 중 아무도 그곳에 가본 적
이 없기 때문에, 다른 선택의 여지가 없는 것 같네요.

Emily Maxwell (오전 11시 26분)
저기, ¹⁷⁵Welcome to Tallinn 모바일 앱을 다운로드하는 건 어때요?
그것에 도시 가이드, 교통 체계 지도 등이 있어요. 현장까지 전차를 타
고 갈 수 있을지도 몰라요.

Nicholas Yang (오전 11시 26분)
고마워요, Emily! 그건 생각지도 못했어요. 그 앱에 틀림없이 다른 유
용한 정보들도 많이 있을 거예요.

----

confirmation n. 확인, 확정   demonstration n. 시연, 증명
arrange v. 마련하다, 준비하다   transportation n. 교통(편), 차량, 수송
transit n. 교통 체계   tram n. 전차, 트램

172 추론 문제

해석 작성자들은 어디에서 일할 것 같은가?
(A) 의료 서비스 제공업체에서
(B) 소프트웨어 개발 회사에서
(C) 휴대폰 회사에서
(D) 행사 기획사에서

해설 지문의 'I'm still working on the demonstration of our
company's latest software program'에서 Emily Maxwell이
자사의 최신 소프트웨어 프로그램 시연을 아직 작업 중이라고 했으
므로 작성자들이 소프트웨어 개발 회사에서 일한다는 것을 추론할 수
있다. 따라서 (B)가 정답이다.

어휘 development n. 개발

173 의도 파악 문제

해석 오전 11시 21분에, Mr. Yang이 "How are we looking"이라고 썼을
때, 그가 의도한 것 같은 것은?
(A) 기술의 가능한 용도에 대해 불확실하다.
(B) 서비스의 상황에 관심이 있다.
(C) 행사 준비에 관한 최신 정보를 원한다.
(D) 회사 방침에 대한 더 많은 설명이 필요하다.

해설 지문의 'We need to discuss the Medical Technology
Conference in Tallinn next month.'에서 Mr. Yang이 다음
달 탈린에서 열리는 의료 기술 학회에 대해 논의할 필요가 있다고 한
후, 'How are we looking'(우리 상황이 어떻게 되나요?)'이라
고 말한 다음, Maya Kowalczyk가 'We should be all set. I
received the confirmation this morning for our flight and

hotel bookings.'(모든 준비가 다 된 것 같아요. 오늘 아침 항공편과 호텔 예약에 대한 확인을 받았어요.)라고 대답한 것을 통해, Mr. Yang이 행사 준비에 관한 최신 정보를 원한다는 것을 알 수 있다. 따라서 (C)가 정답이다.

어휘 uncertain adj. 불확실한 status n. 상황, 상태

174 추론 문제

해석 작성자들에 대해 결론지을 수 있는 것은?
(A) 처음으로 탈린에 방문하게 될 것이다.
(B) 최근 새로운 회사와의 일을 받아들였다.
(C) 다른 나라의 지사로 전근 갈 것이다.
(D) 행사 기간 동안 무료 숙박을 제공받을 것이다.

해설 지문의 'none of us have ever been there'에서 Nicholas Yang이 우리 중 아무도 그곳에 가본 적이 없다고 했으므로 작성자들이 처음으로 탈린에 방문하는 것임을 추론할 수 있다. 따라서 (A)가 정답이다.

어휘 for the first time 처음으로 accept v. 받아들이다, 수락하다
transfer v. 전근 가다, 이동하다 lodging n. 숙박, 숙소

175 육하원칙 문제

해석 Ms. Maxwell은 왜 모바일 앱을 다운로드하는 것을 제안하는가?
(A) 사용자들이 셔틀버스 좌석을 예약할 수 있게 해 준다.
(B) 학회 일정을 제공한다.
(C) 교통수단 선택에 대한 자세한 정보를 포함한다.
(D) 다양한 현지 서비스에 대한 할인을 제공한다.

해설 지문의 'why don't we download the Welcome to Tallinn mobile app? It's got a city guide, transit maps, and more. It may be possible to take a tram to the venue'에서 Ms. Maxwell은 Welcome to Tallinn 모바일 앱을 다운로드할 것을 제안한 후, 그것에 도시 가이드, 교통 체계 지도 등이 있고, 현장까지 전차를 타고 갈 수도 있다고 했으므로 (C)가 정답이다.

어휘 seat n. 좌석 local adj. 현지의, 지역의

176-180번은 다음 공고와 이메일에 관한 문제입니다.

Harbor 공예품 시장
위치: 321번지 Oakridge로

¹⁷⁶Harbor 공예품 시장에는 많은 현지 상점들의 독특한 ¹⁷⁶핸드메이드 제품들을 특별히 포함합니다. 매주 주말 오전 10시부터 오후 7시까지 개장하는 그곳은 자신을 위해서 또는 당신이 아끼는 누군가를 위해서 특별한 것을 구입하기에 완벽한 장소입니다.

부스	매장	제품
101	Scented Light	꽃 향이 나는 양초
¹⁷⁶102	Colors of the Sea	¹⁷⁶아름다운 씨글라스로 만든 독특한 목걸이
¹⁷⁷103	The Pottery Wheel	¹⁷⁷특색이 있는 도자기 접시와 꽃병
¹⁷⁶104	Best Friends	¹⁷⁶다양한 스타일의 우정 팔찌
105	Cozy Corner	모든 사이즈의 패딩 이불과 담요

더 많은 정보를 위해서는, www.harbormarket.com을 방문하세요. ⊙

모든 문의사항은 customerservice@harbormarket.com으로 보내주세요.

craft n. 공예품, 수공업 feature v. 특별히 포함하다 pick up ~을 사다
fragrance n. 향, 향수 distinctive adj. 특색이 있는, 독특한

수신: customerservice@harbormarket.com
발신: Nina Reed <n.reed@zmail.com>
날짜: 5월 24일
제목: 시장

안녕하세요.

당신이 저를 도와주실 수 있기를 바랍니다. ¹⁷⁸지난 토요일에 Harbor 공예품 시장에서 구매한 것에 대해 제 돈을 돌려받는 방법을 알고 싶습니다. ¹⁷⁷저는 언니의 생일 선물로 큰 장식용 접시를 샀습니다. ¹⁷⁹딱 언니의 스타일이어서 저는 그것에 매우 만족했습니다. 하지만 집에 도착했을 때 바닥에 금이 간 것을 발견했습니다. 그리고 제가 상대했던 사람이 그날이 시장에 참여하는 마지막 날이라고 말했기 때문에 그것을 구매한 부스로 그냥 가져갈 수 없습니다. 누군가가 가능한 한 빨리 저에게 연락해 주시면 감사하겠습니다. ¹⁸⁰시장은 제 아파트 건물 옆에 있는 지하철역에서 두 정거장 밖에 떨어져 있지 않아서, 필요하다면 이번 주말에 들를 수 있습니다. 감사합니다.

Nina Reed

decorative adj. 장식용의 crack n. 금, 틈

176 육하원칙 문제

해석 부스 102와 부스 104의 유사점은 무엇인가?
(A) 손으로 만든 장신구를 판매한다.
(B) 재활용 유리로 만든 생활용품들을 특징으로 한다.
(C) 추가 비용을 내면 고객 맞춤 서비스를 제공한다.
(D) 바다를 주제로 한 다양한 제품들을 취급한다.

해설 공고의 'The Harbor Craft Market features unique, handmade products'에서 손으로 만든 독특한 제품들을 취급한다고 했고 부스 102는 목걸이, 부스 104는 팔찌를 판매하고 있음을 알 수 있다. 따라서 이 두 부스의 유사점은 손으로 만든 장신구를 판매한다는 것이므로 (A)가 정답이다.

어휘 similarity n. 유사점

Paraphrasing

handmade 손으로 만든 → crafted by hand 손으로 만든
necklaces / bracelets 목걸이 / 팔찌 → jewelry 보석

177 추론 문제 연계

해석 Ms. Reed는 어떤 부스에서 물건을 구매했을 것 같은가?
(A) 부스 101
(B) 부스 103
(C) 부스 104
(D) 부스 105

해설 Ms. Reed의 구입과 관련된 내용을 묻고 있으므로 Ms. Reed가 작성한 이메일을 먼저 확인한다.

단서 1 이메일의 'I bought a large, decorative plate for my sister as a birthday present.'에서 언니의 생일 선물로 큰 장식용 접시를 샀다고 했다. 그런데, 접시를 파는 부스가 어디였는지 제시되지 않았으므로 공고에서 관련 내용을 확인한다.

단서 2 공고의 'Booth 103', 'Distinctive ceramic dishes and vases'에서 부스 103에서 특색이 있는 도자기 접시들과 꽃병들을 판매하는 것을 알 수 있다.

두 단서를 종합할 때, Ms. Reed가 부스 103에서 접시를 구매한 것을 추론할 수 있다. 따라서 (B)가 정답이다.

178 목적 찾기 문제

해석 이메일의 목적은 무엇인가?
(A) 배달이 되었음을 확인하기 위해
(B) 환불 절차에 대해 문의하기 위해
(C) 몇몇 새로운 담료를 광고하기 위해
(D) 제품을 교환하는 방법을 알아내기 위해

해설 이메일의 'I would like to know how to get my money back for a purchase I made at the Harbor Craft Market last Saturday.'에서 지난 토요일에 시장에서 구매한 것에 대해 돈을 돌려받는 방법을 알고 싶다고 했으므로 (B)가 정답이다.

어휘 find out ~을 알아내다

Paraphrasing

how to get my money back for a purchase 구매에 대한 돈을 돌려받는 방법 → refund process 환불 절차

179 동의어 찾기 문제

해석 이메일에서, 1문단 세 번째 줄의 단어 "just"는 의미상 -와 가장 가깝다.
(A) 그저
(B) 최소로
(C) 그 너머에
(D) 꼭

해설 just를 포함한 문장 'It was just her style, so I was quite happy with it.'에서 just는 '딱, 꼭'이라는 뜻으로 사용되었다. 따라서 (D)가 정답이다.

180 Not/True 문제

해석 Ms. Reed에 대해 명시된 것은?
(A) 구매 건에 관하여 매장의 주인에게 연락할 것이다.
(B) 지역의 공예품 시장을 정기적으로 방문한다.
(C) 다음 달에 새 아파트로 이사 갈 것이다.
(D) 대중교통 시설 근처의 지역에 살고 있다.

해설 이메일의 'The market is only two stops away from the subway station next to my apartment building'에서 시장이 아파트 옆에 있는 지하철역에서 두 정거장 거리라고 했으므로 Ms. Reed가 지하철역 근처에 살고 있음을 알 수 있다. 따라서 (D)가 정답이다.

Paraphrasing

subway station 지하철역 → public transit facility 대중교통 시설

181-185번은 다음 구인 공고와 이메일에 관한 문제입니다.

181-(D) Blackstone 가전제품 회사는 녹스빌 지역에 배송 센터를 설립할 것입니다. 8월 14일에 운영을 시작할 예정이며, 미국 남동부 지역을 위한 회사의 주요 유통 중심지로서의 역할을 할 것입니다. 센터에 직원을 배치하기 위해, 현재 다음 직책에 대한 지원을 받고 있습니다:

직책	요건
창고 직원	• 건강한 신체 상태 • 관련 경력 1년
행정 보조원	• 학사 학위(경영학 또는 관련 전공) • 관련 경력 1년
182보안 요원	• 보안 교육 자격증 • **182**관련 경력 3년
배달 트럭 기사	• 상업용 운전면허 • 관련 경력 2년

합격자들은 경쟁력 있는 급여와 유급 병가를 받을 것입니다. **183**그들은 또한 근무 시간 동안 회사의 구내 카페테리아를 무료로 이용할 수 있습니다.

지원서를 받기 위해 여기를 클릭하고 작성된 양식을 humanresouces@blackstone.com으로 Denise Sawyer에게 보내십시오. 이력서나 자기소개서는 포함할 필요가 없습니다. 모든 직책의 마감일은 7월 1일입니다.

operation n. 운영 primary adj. 주요한 distribution n. 유통, 배분 staff v. ~에 직원을 배치하다 requirement n. 요건, 자격 warehouse n. 창고 relevant adj. 관련 있는 administrative adj. 행정의 assistant n. 보조원, 조수 undergraduate degree 학사 certificate n. 자격증, 면허증 commercial adj. 상업의 cover letter 자기소개서

수신: Denise Sawyer <humanresources@blackstone.com>
발신: Dale Uchida <d.uchida@waymail.com>
제목: 공석
날짜: 6월 27일
첨부: 지원서

Ms. Sawyer께,

저는 귀사의 웹사이트에 광고된 직책 중 하나에 대한 지원서를 첨부했습니다. **182**첫 번째 나열된 요건은 충족했지만, 명시된 3년이 아닌 2년의 경력만 가지고 있다는 점을 말씀드려야 할 것 같습니다. 하지만, 이전 고용주로부터 훌륭한 추천서를 받았고, **184**Blackstone에서 제가 맡을 모든 업무를 처리할 수 있을 것이라고 확신합니다.

질문이나 우려되는 점이 있으시면 제게 연락해 주세요. **185**제가 존슨 시티로 이사를 갈 절차를 밟고 있어서, 빨라도 7월 4일에야 면접이 가능할 것 같습니다.

Dale Uchida 드림

specified adj. 명시된 reference n. 추천서 employer n. 고용주 duty n. 업무, 임무 assign v. 맡기다, 배정하다 concern n. 우려, 걱정 at the earliest 빨라도

181 Not/True 문제

해석 Blackstone 가전제품 회사에 대해 사실인 것은?

(A) 새로운 인사부장을 고용했다.
(B) 본사를 녹스빌로 옮겼다.
(C) 지역 내에서 무료로 제품을 배송한다.
(D) 8월에 새로운 시설을 열 계획이다.

해설 구인 공고의 'Blackstone Appliances is establishing a shipping center in the Knoxville area. It is expected to begin operations on August 14'에서 Blackstone 가전제품 회사는 녹스빌 지역에 배송 센터를 설립하며, 8월 14일에 운영을 시작할 예정이라고 했으므로 (D)가 정답이다.

어휘 headquarters n. 본사 ship v. 배송하다 region n. 지역

Paraphrasing

establish 설립하다 → open 열다

182 추론 문제 연계

해석 Mr. Uchida는 어떤 직책에 관심 있는 것 같은가?
(A) 창고 직원
(B) 행정 보조원
(C) 보안 요원
(D) 배달 트럭 기사

해설 Mr. Uchida가 어떤 직책에 관심 있는 것 같은지를 묻고 있으므로 Mr. Uchida가 작성한 이메일을 먼저 확인한다.
단서 1 이메일의 'I should point out that while I have met the first listed requirement, I have only two years of experience rather than the specified three.'에서 첫 번째 나열된 요건은 충족했지만, 명시된 3년이 아닌 2년의 경력만 가지고 있다고 했다. 그런데 경력 3년이 명시된 직책이 무엇인지에 대해 제시되지 않았으므로 구인 공고에서 관련 내용을 확인한다.
단서 2 구인 공고의 'Requirements'에서 'Three years of relevant experience'가 제시된 직책은 'Security guard'임을 알 수 있다.
두 단서를 종합할 때, Mr. Uchida가 관심 있는 직책이 보안 요원임을 추론할 수 있다. 따라서 (C)가 정답이다.

183 육하원칙 문제

해석 구인 공고에 따르면, 합격자들은 무엇을 할 수 있을 것인가?
(A) 매주 근무 조를 선택한다.
(B) 회사에서 무료로 식사한다.
(C) 연간 성과 보너스를 받는다.
(D) 1년에 한 번 장기 휴가를 간다.

해설 구인 공고의 'They will also be able to take advantage of our on-site cafeteria at no charge during their shifts.'에서 합격자들은 근무 시간 동안 구내 카페테리아를 무료로 이용할 수 있을 것이라고 했으므로 (B)가 정답이다.

어휘 work shift 근무 조

Paraphrasing

at no charge 무료로 → for free 무료로

184 동의어 찾기 문제

해석 이메일에서, 1문단 네 번째 줄의 단어 "handle"은 의미상 -와 가장 가깝다.
(A) 허가하다
(B) 반영하다
(C) 처리하다
(D) 발견하다

해설 handle을 포함한 구절 'I am confident that I will be able to handle any duties I am assigned at Blackstone'에서 handle은 '처리하다'라는 뜻으로 사용되었다. 따라서 (C)가 정답이다.

185 Not/True 문제

해석 Mr. Uchida에 대해 명시된 것은?
(A) 지원서를 제출할 마감일을 놓쳤다.
(B) 전에 Blackstone에서 일한 적이 있다.
(C) 다른 도시로 이사 갈 것이다.
(D) 면접 일정을 추후로 변경할 것이다.

해설 이메일의 'I[Mr. Uchida] am in the process of moving to Johnson City'에서 Mr. Uchida가 존슨 시티로 이사 갈 예정이라고 했으므로 (C)가 정답이다.

어휘 relocate v. 이사 가다, 이전하다

Paraphrasing

in the process of moving to Johnson City 존슨 시티로 이사 가려는 절차를 밟고 있는 → is relocating to a different city 다른 도시로 이사 갈 것이다

186-190번은 다음 웹페이지, 광고, 후기에 관한 문제입니다.

				고객: Brandon Chang

Wilson 사무용품 - 프레즈노 지점

소개	쇼핑	**내 주문**	연락

주문번호: 08726
날짜: 9월 14일
주소: 121번지 Coleman가, 프레즈노, 캘리포니아주 93650

물품	수량	가격	합계
[187]Delta 컬러 프린터 잉크 카트리지	4	22.00달러	88.00달러
Brennan 편지지 크기의 백지 (500장 / 팩)	2	24.00달러	48.00달러
Mainline 금속 스테이플러	1	8.00달러	8.00달러
Acme 표준 스테이플러 침 (3,000 스테이플러 침 / 박스)	5	2.00달러	10.00달러
		[186]소계	[186]154.00달러
		세금	12.00달러
		총액	166.00달러

방문 수령 ○ 배송 ⊘

*186프레즈노 내 배송인 경우 10달러의 수수료가, 시 경계 외 지역으로의 배송인 경우 20달러의 수수료가 추가됩니다(150달러 이상 주문 시 면제됨).

quantity n. 수량 subtotal n. 소계 fee n. 수수료, 요금
limit n. 경계, 한계, 한도 waive v. 면제하다, 포기하다

Wilson 사무용품
당신이 필요로 하는 모든 것을 갖추고 있습니다!

어떠한 Wilson 사무용품 매장이라도 방문하셔서 가장 인기 있는 브랜드를 저렴한 가격에 만나보세요. 188매달, 새로운 종류의 제품들을 할인가에 제공합니다. 9월의 베스트 딜은 다음과 같습니다:

➢ 서류철 (15퍼센트 할인)
➢ 연필 및 볼펜 (10퍼센트 할인)
➢ 187프린터 잉크 (20퍼센트 할인)
➢ 색지 (10퍼센트 할인)

189이보다 더 큰 할인 금액을 원하시면, 오클랜드에 있는 저희의 신규 지점을 방문하세요. 개업을 기념하여 매장의 모든 제품이 40퍼센트 할인됩니다!

affordable adj. 저렴한, 적당한, 알맞은 savings n. 할인 금액
celebrate v. 기념하다, 축하하다

날짜: 9월 18일
평가: 별 4개

189지난 주말에 새 아파트로 이사한 후, 저는 홈 오피스를 위한 몇 가지 물건을 사기 위해 근처 Wilson 사무용품점에 들렀습니다. 이곳은 그 체인의 최신 지점이라, 모든 것이 매우 깨끗했습니다. 직원들이 매우 친절했던 것도 높이 평가했습니다. 다만, 190실제 가격이 더 눈에 띄게 표시되었다면 좋았을 것 같습니다. 일부 물건의 가격이 얼마인지 파악하느라 애를 먹었습니다. 예를 들어, Glide 230 사무용 의자의 스티커에는 200달러라고 적혀 있었습니다. 저는 이것이 판매 가격이고 원래 가격은 300달러가 넘는다고 생각했습니다. 하지만 스티커 가격에서 80달러가 할인된다는 것을 나중에 들었고, 이는 즉 120달러만 지불하면 된다는 말이었습니다. 그건 꽤나 당황스러웠습니다.

– Zita Laurent

move into ~로 이사하다 stop by ~에 들르다
appreciate v. 높이 평가하다, 고마워하다
polite adj. 친절한, 정중한 that being said 다만, 그렇지만
prominently adv. 눈에 띄게, 현저하게
assume v. 생각하다, 추정하다
confusing adj. 당황스러운, 혼란스러운

186 육하원칙 문제

해석 Mr. Chang의 총액에 왜 배송료가 추가되지 않았는가?
(A) 프레즈노시 경계 내에 거주한다.
(B) 매장에서 그의 물품을 수령하기로 선택했다.
(C) 주문품에 대해 요구되는 금액을 지불했다.
(D) 배달원에게 직접 지불하려고 한다.

해설 웹페이지의 'A fee of $10 will be added for deliveries within Fresno and $20 for deliveries to areas outside the city limits

---

(waived for orders over $150).'에서 150달러 이상 주문 시 배송료가 면제된다고 했고, 주문 내역표의 'Subtotal, $154.00'에서 주문 금액이 154달러인 것을 확인할 수 있으므로, 150달러 이상 주문하여 배송료가 면제되었음을 알 수 있다. 따라서 (C)가 정답이다.

어휘 intend to ~하려고 하다, 의도하다

187 육하원칙 문제 연계

해석 Mr. Chang은 어떤 제품을 할인을 받아 구매했는가?
(A) Delta 컬러 프린터 잉크 카트리지
(B) Brennan 편지지 크기의 백지
(C) Mainline 금속 스테이플러
(D) Acme 표준 스테이플러 침

해설 할인 품목에 대한 내용이 언급된 광고를 먼저 확인한다.
단서 1 광고에서 할인 중인 품목 4개를 확인한다. 이 중 Mr. Chang이 주문한 상품에 포함되는 것이 무엇인지를 확인해야 하므로, 주문 내역이 있는 웹페이지에서 관련 내용을 확인한다.
단서 2 웹페이지의 'Delta Color Printer Ink Cartridge'에서 Mr. Chang이 주문한 상품 중, 프린터 잉크 카트리지가 있음을 확인할 수 있다.
두 단서를 종합할 때, Mr. Chang이 할인을 받아 구매한 제품이 Delta 컬러 프린터 잉크 카트리지임을 알 수 있다. 따라서 (A)가 정답이다.

188 육하원칙 문제

해석 10월에 무슨 일이 일어날 것인가?
(A) 다른 품목들이 할인될 것이다.
(B) 추가적인 매장들이 개점할 것이다.
(C) 신제품 라인이 출시될 것이다.
(D) 인기 브랜드가 생산 중단될 것이다.

해설 광고의 'Each month, we offer new types of products at a discount.'에서 매달 새로운 종류의 제품들을 할인가에 제공한다고 했으므로 (A)가 정답이다.

어휘 discontinue v. (생산 등을) 중단하다, 그만두다

189 추론 문제 연계

해석 Ms. Laurent에 대해 암시되는 것은?
(A) 그녀의 구매품 중 하나를 반품하기로 결정했다.
(B) 곧 새 아파트로 이사할 것이다.
(C) Wilson 사무용품점에서 정기적으로 쇼핑한다.
(D) 현재 오클랜드의 주민이다.

해설 Ms. Laurent가 작성한 후기를 먼저 확인한다.
단서 1 후기의 'After moving into my new apartment last weekend, I stopped by a nearby Wilson Office Supplies to buy some things for my home office. This is the chain's newest branch'에서 Ms. Laurent는 지난 주말에 새 아파트로 이사한 후, 홈 오피스를 위한 몇 가지 물건을 사기 위해 Wilson 사무용품점에 들렀는데 그곳이 그 체인의 최신 지점이라고 했다. 그런데 Wilson 사무용품점의 최신 지점이 어디에 있는지 제시되지 않았으므로, 광고에서 관련 내용을 확인한다.
단서 2 광고의 'For even greater savings, visit our new

branch in Oakland.'에서 더 큰 할인 금액을 원하면 오클랜드에 있는 신규 지점을 방문하라고 했으므로, Wilson 사무용품점의 오클랜드 지점이 신규 지점임을 확인할 수 있다.

두 단서를 종합할 때, Ms. Laurent가 오클랜드에 있는 새 아파트로 이사해서 현재 그곳의 주민임을 추론할 수 있다. 따라서 (D)가 정답이다.

어휘 **regularly** adv. 정기적으로, 규칙적으로 **resident** n. 주민, 거주자

190 육하원칙 문제

해석 후기에 따르면, Ms. Laurent가 만족스러워하지 않았던 것은 무엇인가?
(A) 몇몇 직원들이 공손하지 않았다.
(B) 몇몇 사무용 가구가 너무 비쌌다.
(C) 몇몇 정보가 명확하게 제시되지 않았다.
(D) 몇몇 제품들은 찾기가 매우 어려웠다.

해설 후기의 'I wish the actual prices were displayed more prominently. I had a hard time figuring out how much some items cost'에서 실제 가격이 더 눈에 띄게 표시되었다면 좋았을 것 같다고 말하며, 일부 물품의 가격이 얼마인지 파악하느라 애를 먹었다고 언급했으므로, 가격 정보가 명확하게 제시되지 않은 것에 불만족스러워함을 알 수 있다. 따라서 (C)가 정답이다.

어휘 **well-mannered** adj. 공손한, 예의 바른
clearly adv. 명확하게, 분명하게 **present** v. 제시하다, 발표하다

191-195번은 다음 편지와 두 이메일에 관한 문제입니다.

Lucia Cruz
34번지 Packerston로
빅토리아, 브리티시컬럼비아주, V8T 3R2

Ms. Cruz께,

Better Beginnings 단체에 대한 귀하의 지난 지원에 감사드립니다. 귀하와 같은 관대한 기부자들의 도움으로, 저희는 400명이 넘는 저소득 가정의 초등학생들에게 학용품과 개인 교습 서비스를 제공할 수 있었습니다.

[191]저희의 최신 프로그램을 위해 기부하실 의향이 있는지 여쭤보고 싶습니다. 목표는 사회적으로 혜택을 받지 못한 환경의 학생들에게 인터넷 접속뿐만 아니라 태블릿 컴퓨터를 제공하는 것입니다. 어떠한 금액이라도 도움이 되겠지만, [192]1,000달러 이상 기부하신 분들은 5월 15일에 열리는 연례 모금 콘서트의 무료입장권을 선물로 제공받을 것입니다.

곧 소식을 들을 수 있기를 바랍니다.

Kevin Yang 드림

재정 지원 책임자
Better Beginnings사

assistance n. 도움 generous adj. 관대한, 너그러운
donor n. 기부자 school supplies 학용품 tutoring n. 개인 교습
low-income adj. 저소득의 make a donation 기부하다
disadvantaged adj. 사회적으로 혜택을 받지 못한
annual adj. 연례의 fundraising n. 모금

수신: Kevin Yang <k.yang@bb.com>
발신: Beth Meyers <b.meyers@bb.com>
제목: 새 프로그램
날짜: 4월 10일

안녕하세요 Kevin,

성공적인 모금 캠페인에 대해 축하드립니다! [192]Ms. Cruz로부터 받은 3,000달러의 기부금은 저희의 총액을 68,000달러에 이르게 했습니다. [193-(C)]이것은 저희의 원래 추정치를 크게 초과해서, 계획에 약간의 조정을 했습니다. 저희는 이제 75명이 아니라 100명의 학생들을 도울 수 있을 것입니다.

Redwood Communications사는 학생 한 명당 180달러만 내면 1년 동안 무제한 인터넷 접속을 제공할 것입니다. 그것은 평소 가격의 절반입니다. [194-(A)]Redwood Communications사를 설립한 지 1년도 채 되지 않은 사장이신 Sara Martinez는 이 프로그램을 훌륭한 마케팅 기회로 보고 있습니다.

기기와 관련하여, [195]저희는 태블릿당 최대 500달러를 쓸 수 있습니다. 선택권을 찾기 위해 여러 전자제품 공급업체에 연락했습니다. 기기를 고르면 알려드리겠습니다.

Beth Myers, 프로그램 담당자
Better Beginnings사

exceed v. 초과하다 estimate n. 추정(치) adjustment n. 조정

수신: Beth Meyers <b.meyers@bb.com>
발신: Amir Gupta <a.gupta@aspen.com>
제목: 선택권
날짜: 4월 21일

Ms. Myers께,

어제 귀사의 새 프로그램용 태블릿 컴퓨터에 대한 문의를 받았습니다. [195]The Edge 340은 Aspen 전자회사의 가장 많이 팔리는 모델 중 하나입니다. 그것은 10인치 화면과 32기가바이트의 저장 용량을 포함합니다. 또한 1년간 포괄적인 보증이 딸려 옵니다. [195]무엇보다도, 그러한 대량 주문에 대해 저희가 10퍼센트 할인을 제공할 수 있어서, 귀사에서는 개당 600달러만 지불하시면 될 것입니다.

태블릿이나 주문 과정에 대해 질문이 있으시면 알려주세요. 답변 기다리겠습니다.

Amir Gupta 드림
Aspen 전자회사

comprehensive adj. 포괄적인, 종합적인 warranty n. 보증

191 목적 찾기 문제

해석 편지의 목적은 무엇인가?
(A) 교육 자료의 전달을 확인하기 위해
(B) 재정적 기여를 요청하기 위해
(C) 학생 개인 교습에 도움을 요청하기 위해
(D) 온라인 행사의 세부 사항을 설명하기 위해

해설 편지의 'I would like to ask if you would be willing to make a donation for our latest program.'에서 최신 프로그램을 위해 기부할 의향이 있는지 물어보고 싶다고 했으므로 (B)가 정답이다.

어휘 educational adj. 교육의 contribution n. 기여, 공헌

Paraphrasing

> make a donation 기부를 하다 → financial contribution 재정적 기여

192 추론 문제 연계

해석 Ms. Cruz는 무엇을 받았을 것 같은가?
(A) 학교 교과서
(B) 상품권
(C) 공연 티켓
(D) 노트북 컴퓨터

해설 Ms. Cruz에게 보내진 편지를 먼저 확인한다.
단서 1 편지의 'those who give $1,000 or more will be provided with a complimentary pass to our annual fundraising concert'에서 1,000달러 이상 기부하는 사람들은 연례 모금 콘서트의 무료입장권을 제공받을 것이라고 했다. 그런데 Ms. Cruz가 얼마를 기부했는지에 대해 제시되지 않았으므로 첫 번째 이메일에서 관련 내용을 확인한다.
단서 2 첫 번째 이메일의 'The $3,000 donation from Ms. Cruz'에서 Ms. Cruz가 3,000달러를 기부했다는 것을 알 수 있다.
두 단서를 종합할 때, 3,000달러를 기부한 Ms. Cruz가 공연 티켓을 받았을 것임을 추론할 수 있다. 따라서 (C)가 정답이다.

Paraphrasing

> pass to ~ fundraising concert 연례 모금 콘서트의 입장권 → performance ticket 공연 티켓

193 Not/True 문제

해석 첫 번째 이메일에서 프로그램에 대해 언급된 것은?
(A) 예산 부족으로 인해 취소되었다.
(B) 많은 수의 학생 인턴들에게 일자리를 제공할 것이다.
(C) 원래 계획되었던 것보다 더 많은 참가자를 포함할 것이다.
(D) 공립학교의 강사에 의해 개설되었다.

해설 첫 번째 이메일의 'This greatly exceeds our original estimate, so I have made some adjustments to our plan. We will now be able to help 100 students rather than 75.'에서 모금액이 원래 추정치를 크게 초과해서 계획에 약간의 조정을 했고, 이제 75명이 아니라 100명의 학생들을 도울 수 있을 것이라고 했으므로 (C)가 정답이다.

어휘 shortfall n. 부족(량) participant n. 참가자
　　 establish v. 개설하다, 설립하다

194 Not/True 문제

해석 Redwood Communications사에 대해 사실인 것은?
(A) 1년이 안 되는 기간 동안 운영되어 왔다.
(B) 몇몇 무료 제품을 제공하는 것을 고려하고 있다.
(C) 일부 온라인 기능에 대한 학생의 접속을 제한한다.
(D) 멤버십 서비스를 시작했다.

해설 첫 번째 이메일의 'Company president Sara Martinez, who

founded Redwood Communications less than a year ago'에서 Redwood Communications사를 설립한 지 1년도 채 되지 않은 사장인 Sara Martinez라고 했으므로 (A)는 지문의 내용과 일치한다. 따라서 (A)가 정답이다.

어휘 feature n. 기능, 특징 launch v. 시작하다, 출시하다

195 추론 문제 연계

해석 Ms. Myers는 왜 Edge 340을 거절할 것 같은가?
(A) 화면 크기가 너무 작다.
(B) 저장 용량이 너무 부족하다.
(C) 구입 비용이 너무 높다.
(D) 보증 기간이 너무 짧다.

해설 Ms. Myers가 작성한 첫 번째 이메일을 먼저 확인한다.
단서 1 첫 번째 이메일의 'we can spend a maximum of $500 per tablet'에서 태블릿당 최대 500달러를 쓸 수 있다고 했다. 그런데 Edge 340이 얼마인지에 대해 제시되지 않았으므로 두 번째 이메일에서 관련 내용을 확인한다.
단서 2 두 번째 이메일의 'The Edge 340', 'Best of all, we can offer you a 10 percent discount for such a large order, so you will only have to pay $600 per unit.'에서 Edge 340이 대량 주문에 대한 10퍼센트 할인을 제공받아 개당 600달러라는 것을 알 수 있다.
두 단서를 종합할 때, 구입 비용으로 잡은 최대 500달러를 초과하므로 Edge 340을 거절할 것임을 추론할 수 있다. 따라서 (C)가 정답이다.

어휘 capacity n. 용량

196-200번은 다음 웹페이지, 이메일, 공고에 관한 문제입니다.

Double Stitch 중고품 가게

| 홈 | **소개** | 구매 | 판매 | 기증 | 연락 |

Double Stitch는 소렌토 지역에서 가장 인기 있는 위탁 판매 매장입니다. 저희는 매일 대량의 중고 상품을 판매하며 판매가의 15퍼센트만을 취득합니다. 저희는 의류, 보석, 핸드백, 벨트, 신발, 그리고 기타 액세서리를 받습니다. 196/199물품들은 양호한 상태여야 하며, 결함이 없어야 하고, 5년이 지나지 않아야 합니다. 모든 의류는 깨끗하게 세탁한 후 옷걸이에 걸린 채 들여와야 합니다. 웨딩드레스, 임부복, 또는 수영복은 받지 않습니다.

197-(D)매장에서 판매되는 모든 물품들은 최대 3개월 동안 진열되며, 그 이후에는 주인들에게 돌려보내질 것입니다.

---

thrift shop 중고품 가게 consignment store 위탁 판매점
secondhand adj. 중고의 merchandise n. 상품
retain v. 취득하다, 유지하다 condition n. 상태, 상황, 조건
defect n. 결함 maternity clothes 임부복

수신: Roman Butler<r.butler@doublestitchthrift.com>
발신: Cassie Robinson<c.robinson@olivemail.com>
제목: 문의
날짜: 4월 24일

Mr. Butler께,

안녕하세요, 저는 몇몇 물품들을 귀사의 매장을 통해 판매하는 것에 관심이 있습니다. ¹⁹⁸저희 가족이 최근에 더 작은 집으로 이사해서, 예전만큼 옷장 공간이 많지 않습니다. 그 물품들 중 일부는 더 이상 맞지 않는 것이지만, 다른 것들은 한 번도 입지 않았습니다. 모두 괜찮은 상태입니다. 여성용 코트, 핸드백 두 개, 그리고 귀걸이 몇 쌍으로 구성되어 있습니다. ¹⁹⁹남편의 10년 된 캐주얼 재킷 몇 벌도 있습니다. 그리고 마지막으로, 저의 딸의 운동화가 있습니다. 가능하다면, 매장에 들러서 물품들을 분류하고 가격을 책정하고 싶습니다. ²⁰⁰저는 화요일이나 수요일 오전 9시 또는 다른 날 오후 6시 이후에 시간이 됩니다. 제게 알려주세요.

Cassie Robinson 드림

----

decent adj. 괜찮은, 쓸만한   belong to ~의 것이다, ~에 속하다
athletic adj. 운동용의   sort through 분류하다, 자세히 살펴보다

Double Stitch 중고품 가게 운영 시간	
월요일	휴업
화요일	휴업
수요일	오전 10시 - 오후 6시
목요일	오전 10시 - 오후 6시
²⁰⁰금요일	오전 9시 - 오후 7시
토요일	오후 1시 - 오후 5시
일요일	오후 1시 - 오후 5시

공항로 55번 고속도로를 빠져나오세요. 저희는 Haven 쇼핑센터 건너편에 위치해 있습니다. 인근의 넓은 유료 주차장이 이용 가능합니다.

ample adj. 넓은, 넉넉한   paid adj. 유료의, 유급의

196 목적 찾기 문제

해석 웹페이지의 목적은 무엇인가?
(A) 몇몇 새로운 물품들을 알리기 위해
(B) 반품 절차를 설명하기 위해
(C) 몇몇 매장 정책에 대해 간략히 설명하기 위해
(D) 신규 이용객들을 환영하기 위해

해설 웹페이지의 'Items should be in good condition ~ We do not accept wedding gowns, maternity clothes, or swimsuits'에서 Double Stitch에서 어떠한 상태 및 조건들의 중고 의류를 받는지 설명하고 있다. 따라서 (C)가 정답이다.

어휘 outline v. 간략히 설명하다, 개요를 말하다

197 Not/True 문제

해석 Double Stitch에 대해 사실인 것은?
(A) 단순한 수선을 수행할 수 있다.
(B) 자체 의류 옷걸이를 제공한다.
(C) 주로 고급 상품을 받는다.
(D) 몇 달 후에 팔리지 않은 물품들을 돌려보낸다.

해설 웹페이지의 'All items sold through the store are displayed for a maximum of three months, after which they will be

sent back to the owners.'에서 판매되는 모든 물품들은 최대 3개월 동안 진열되며, 그 이후에는 주인들에게 돌려보낸다고 했으므로 (D)는 지문의 내용과 일치한다. 따라서 (D)가 정답이다.

어휘 minor adj. 단순한, 경미한   merchandise n. 상품, 물품
return v. 돌려보내다, 돌려주다

Paraphrasing

be sent back 돌려보내지다 → return 돌려보내다

198 Not/True 문제

해석 Ms. Robinson에 대해 이메일에 명시된 것은?
(A) 현재 살고 있는 집은 이전 집보다 넓지 않다.
(B) 매수할 부동산을 찾고 있다.
(C) 그녀의 가족은 운동하는 것을 즐긴다.
(D) 패션 업계에 종사하고 있다.

해설 이메일의 'My family recently moved into a smaller house'에서 가족이 최근 더 작은 집으로 이사했다고 했으므로 (A)는 지문에 명시되어 있다. 따라서 (A)가 정답이다.

어휘 property n. 부동산, 재산   industry n. (특정 분야의) 업, 산업

199 추론 문제 연계

해석 Ms. Robinson의 물품들 중 Double Stitch가 거절할 것 같은 것은?
(A) 여성용 코트
(B) 귀걸이
(C) 캐주얼 재킷
(D) 운동화

해설 Double Stitch가 거절할 것 같은 것을 묻고 있으므로 매장에서 취급하는 물품들에 대해 언급한 웹페이지를 먼저 확인한다.
[단서 1] 웹페이지의 'Items should be in good condition, ~ not more than five years old'에서 물품들이 양호한 상태여야 하고 5년이 지나지 않아야 한다고 했다. 그런데 Ms. Robinson이 팔고자 하는 물품들이 무엇인지 제시되지 않았으므로 이메일에서 관련 내용을 확인한다.
[단서 2] 이메일의 'I've also got a few of my husband's casual jackets, which are 10 years old.'에서 Ms. Robinson이 팔고자 하는 남편의 캐주얼 재킷이 10년 된 것이라는 내용을 확인할 수 있다.
두 단서를 종합할 때, Ms. Robinson의 물품들 중 10년이 된 남편의 캐주얼 재킷은 5년이 넘었으므로 Double Stitch에서 거절할 것임을 추론할 수 있다. 따라서 (C)가 정답이다.

어휘 reject v. 거절하다

200 육하원칙 문제 연계

해석 Ms. Robinson은 어느 요일에 그녀의 물품들을 가지고 갈 것인가?
(A) 수요일에
(B) 목요일에
(C) 금요일에
(D) 토요일에

해설 Ms. Robinson이 작성한 이메일에서 관련 내용을 먼저 확인한다.

단서 1 이메일의 'I[Ms. Robinson]'m free Tuesday or Wednesday at 9 A.M. or any other day after 6 P.M.'에서 Ms. Robinson이 화요일이나 수요일 오전 9시 또는 다른 날 오후 6시 이후에 시간이 된다고 했다. 그런데 물품들을 전달받는 Double Stitch의 운영 시간이 제시되지 않았으므로 공고에서 관련 내용을 확인한다.

단서 2 공고에서 'Friday: 9 A.M. - 7 P.M.'에서 Double Stitch가 화요일과 수요일을 제외한 다른 요일 중 오후 6시 이후에도 운영하는 요일은 금요일이라는 것을 알 수 있다.

두 단서를 종합할 때, Ms. Robinson은 금요일 오후 6시 이후에 물품을 가지고 갈 것임을 알 수 있다. 따라서 (C)가 정답이다.

TEST 5

LISTENING TEST
p.196

1 (B)	21 (B)	41 (D)	61 (B)	81 (B)
2 (C)	22 (A)	42 (B)	62 (D)	82 (D)
3 (C)	23 (B)	43 (C)	63 (A)	83 (B)
4 (D)	24 (C)	44 (C)	64 (C)	84 (D)
5 (A)	25 (B)	45 (A)	65 (B)	85 (A)
6 (D)	26 (A)	46 (B)	66 (C)	86 (C)
7 (B)	27 (B)	47 (A)	67 (D)	87 (A)
8 (C)	28 (C)	48 (A)	68 (D)	88 (D)
9 (A)	29 (A)	49 (C)	69 (B)	89 (B)
10 (A)	30 (A)	50 (A)	70 (D)	90 (C)
11 (B)	31 (C)	51 (B)	71 (A)	91 (D)
12 (A)	32 (C)	52 (D)	72 (C)	92 (B)
13 (B)	33 (B)	53 (D)	73 (D)	93 (C)
14 (A)	34 (C)	54 (A)	74 (B)	94 (C)
15 (B)	35 (B)	55 (B)	75 (D)	95 (B)
16 (C)	36 (D)	56 (D)	76 (C)	96 (A)
17 (A)	37 (A)	57 (A)	77 (A)	97 (D)
18 (B)	38 (B)	58 (D)	78 (D)	98 (B)
19 (A)	39 (A)	59 (B)	79 (B)	99 (D)
20 (B)	40 (B)	60 (C)	80 (C)	100 (A)

READING TEST
p.208

101 (B)	121 (D)	141 (B)	161 (D)	181 (B)
102 (B)	122 (C)	142 (C)	162 (C)	182 (B)
103 (C)	123 (B)	143 (B)	163 (D)	183 (C)
104 (D)	124 (C)	144 (C)	164 (D)	184 (A)
105 (B)	125 (B)	145 (C)	165 (B)	185 (D)
106 (C)	126 (A)	146 (A)	166 (B)	186 (B)
107 (B)	127 (A)	147 (B)	167 (D)	187 (C)
108 (D)	128 (B)	148 (C)	168 (C)	188 (B)
109 (B)	129 (D)	149 (C)	169 (A)	189 (D)
110 (B)	130 (C)	150 (D)	170 (C)	190 (C)
111 (A)	131 (D)	151 (B)	171 (C)	191 (D)
112 (A)	132 (A)	152 (D)	172 (D)	192 (D)
113 (C)	133 (B)	153 (A)	173 (C)	193 (B)
114 (B)	134 (C)	154 (C)	174 (A)	194 (A)
115 (A)	135 (B)	155 (D)	175 (B)	195 (C)
116 (A)	136 (B)	156 (B)	176 (C)	196 (B)
117 (A)	137 (A)	157 (D)	177 (D)	197 (B)
118 (D)	138 (C)	158 (C)	178 (D)	198 (A)
119 (C)	139 (A)	159 (B)	179 (A)	199 (C)
120 (D)	140 (B)	160 (A)	180 (D)	200 (C)

PART 1

1 1인 사진
🔊 호주식

(A) He's reaching for a wooden crate.
(B) He's climbing up a ladder.
(C) He's picking up some tools.
(D) He's sawing some wood.

crate n. 상자 ladder n. 사다리 tool n. 도구, 공구
saw v. 톱으로 자르다

해석 (A) 그는 나무로 된 상자를 향해 손을 뻗고 있다.
　　 (B) 그는 사다리를 오르고 있다.
　　 (C) 그는 몇몇 도구를 집어 들고 있다.
　　 (D) 그는 몇몇 목재를 톱으로 자르고 있다.

해설 (A) [x] 사진에 나무로 된 상자(wooden crate)가 없고, 남자가 상자
　　 를 향해 손을 뻗고 있는 모습이 아니므로 오답이다.
　　 (B) [o] 남자가 사다리를 오르고 있는 모습을 가장 잘 묘사한 정답
　　 이다.
　　 (C) [x] picking up some tools(몇몇 도구를 집어 들고 있다)는 남자
　　 의 동작과 무관하므로 오답이다.
　　 (D) [x] sawing some wood(몇몇 목재를 톱으로 자르고 있다)는 남
　　 자의 동작과 무관하므로 오답이다. 사진에 있는 목재(wood)
　　 를 사용하여 혼동을 주었다.

최신토익경향

최근 Part 1에서는 공사장 배경의 1인 또는 2인 이상 사진이 종종 출제되
고 있다. 공사장 배경 사진에서 인물의 동작을 묘사할 때 자주 사용되는 표
현들을 함께 알아두자.

• climb up a ladder 사다리를 오르다
• load a truck with tools 트럭에 도구들을 싣다
• shovel sand 삽으로 모래를 퍼내다

2 사물 및 풍경 사진
🔊 영국식

(A) A screen is being removed from a
stage.
(B) The guitars are leaning against some
chairs.
**(C) There are some musical
instruments on a stage.**
(D) Some microphones are being installed beside the
drums.

remove v. 제거하다 lean against ~에 기대다
musical instrument 악기 microphone n. 마이크
install v. 설치하다

해석 (A) 스크린이 무대에서 제거되고 있다.
(B) 기타들이 몇몇 의자들에 기대어 있다.
(C) 무대 위에 몇몇 악기들이 있다.
(D) 몇몇 마이크들이 드럼들 옆에 설치되고 있다.

해설 (A) [×] 사진에 스크린(screen)이 없으므로 오답이다. 사진에 있는 무대(stage)를 사용하여 혼동을 주었다.
(B) [×] 사진에 의자들(chairs)이 없으므로 오답이다. 사진에 있는 기타들(guitars)을 사용하여 혼동을 주었다.
(C) [○] 무대 위에 몇몇 악기들이 있는 모습을 정확히 묘사한 정답이다.
(D) [×] 사진에 마이크들은 보이지만 설치되고 있는(being installed) 모습은 아니므로 오답이다. 사진에 있는 드럼들(drums)을 사용하여 혼동을 주었다.

3 2인 이상 사진

🎧 캐나다식

(A) Objects in a display case are being replaced.
(B) Some clothes are being packed in shopping bags.
(C) One of the women is looking at a storefront window.
(D) One of the women is setting down her bag.

object n. 물건, 물체 display case 진열장, 진열대 pack v. 포장하다
storefront n. 가게의 앞쪽

해석 (A) 진열장에 있는 물건들이 교체되고 있다.
(B) 몇몇 옷이 쇼핑백에 포장되고 있다.
(C) 여자들 중 한 명이 가게 앞 진열창을 바라보고 있다.
(D) 여자들 중 한 명이 가방을 내려놓고 있다.

해설 (A) [×] 사진에 진열장에 있는 물건들은 보이지만, 교체되고 있는(being replaced) 모습은 아니므로 오답이다.
(B) [×] 사진에 옷과 쇼핑백은 보이지만, 옷이 포장되고 있는(being packed) 모습은 아니므로 오답이다.
(C) [○] 여자들 중 한 명이 가게 앞 진열창을 바라보고 있는 모습을 가장 잘 묘사한 정답이다.
(D) [×] 사진에 가방을 내려놓고 있는(setting down her bag) 여자가 없으므로 오답이다. 사진에 있는 가방(bag)을 사용하여 혼동을 주었다.

최신토익경향

최근 Part 1에서는 storefront(가게의 앞쪽)나 waterfront(물가)와 같이 명사 뒤에 front가 붙은 표현이 정답에 자주 등장하고 있다. 명사에 front가 붙을 경우, 위치에 대한 정보를 제공하는데, 문장에서 어떻게 쓰이는지 아래 예문을 통해 알아보자.

• The man is standing in front of the **storefront** window.
남자가 가게 앞 진열창 앞에 서 있다.
• They are sitting near the **waterfront**.
그들은 물가 근처에 앉아 있다.

4 2인 이상 사진

🎧 호주식

(A) A menu board has been hung on a wall.
(B) A street is being paved with bricks.
(C) An outdoor dining area is occupied.
(D) Some umbrellas have been closed.

menu board 메뉴판 hang v. 걸다, 매달다
pave v. (벽돌 등으로) 포장하다 brick n. 벽돌
occupy v. (공간을) 사용하다, 차지하다 umbrella n. 파라솔, 우산

해석 (A) 메뉴판이 벽에 걸려 있다.
(B) 거리가 벽돌들로 포장되고 있다.
(C) 야외 식사 공간이 사용 중이다.
(D) 몇몇 파라솔들이 접혀 있다.

해설 (A) [×] 사진에 메뉴판은 보이지만, 벽에 걸려 있는(has been hung on a wall) 모습은 아니므로 오답이다.
(B) [×] being paved(포장되고 있다)는 거리의 상태와 무관하므로 오답이다. 사진에 있는 거리(street)와 벽돌들(bricks)을 사용하여 혼동을 주었다.
(C) [×] 사진에 야외 식사 공간은 보이지만, 사용 중인(is occupied) 모습은 아니므로 오답이다.
(D) [○] 몇몇 파라솔들이 접혀 있는 모습을 가장 잘 묘사한 정답이다.

5 1인 사진

🎧 영국식

(A) The woman is holding a cooking utensil.
(B) The woman is grasping the handle of a drawer.
(C) The woman is pressing a button on a coffee machine.
(D) The woman is looking into a cupboard.

hold v. 들다, 잡다 cooking utensil 조리 도구
grasp v. (움켜)잡다, 꽉 쥐다 drawer n. 서랍 press v. 누르다
cupboard n. 찬장

해석 (A) 여자가 조리 도구를 들고 있다.
(B) 여자가 서랍의 손잡이를 잡고 있다.
(C) 여자가 커피 머신의 버튼을 누르고 있다.
(D) 여자가 찬장을 들여다보고 있다.

해설 (A) [○] 여자가 조리 도구를 들고 있는 모습을 가장 잘 묘사한 정답이다.
(B) [×] grasping the handle of a drawer(서랍의 손잡이를 잡고 있다)는 여자의 동작과 무관하므로 오답이다. The woman is grasping(여자가 잡고 있다)까지만 듣고 정답으로 선택하지 않도록 주의한다.
(C) [×] pressing a button(버튼을 누르고 있다)은 여자의 동작과 무관하므로 오답이다. 사진에 있는 커피 머신(coffee machine)을 사용하여 혼동을 주었다.
(D) [×] looking into a cupboard(찬장을 들여다보고 있다)는 여자의 동작과 무관하므로 오답이다.

최근 Part 1에서는 '들다, 잡다'라는 의미의 다양한 동사가 출제되고 있다. '들다, 잡다'를 의미하는 동사들을 예문과 함께 미리 학습해 두자.

- The woman is **holding** a tool. 여자가 도구를 들고 있다.
- He is **grasping** a spoon. 그가 숟가락을 움켜잡고 있다.
- The man's **gripping** a railing. 남자가 난간을 잡고 있다.

6 2인 이상 사진
[3l] 미국식

(A) A person is delivering plates of food.
(B) A person is pouring water from a bottle.
(C) Leaf images have been stitched on a tablecloth.
(D) Some people are sitting at a waterfront café.

deliver v. 전달하다, 배달하다   pour v. 따르다, 붓다
stitch v. 바느질하다, 꿰매다   tablecloth n. 식탁보
waterfront n. 물가, 해안가, 부둣가

해석 (A) 한 사람이 여러 접시의 음식을 전달하고 있다.
　　 (B) 한 사람이 병으로부터 물을 따르고 있다.
　　 (C) 나뭇잎 이미지가 식탁보에 바느질되어 있다.
　　 (D) 몇몇 사람들이 물가 카페에 앉아 있다.

해설 (A) [×] 사진에 여러 접시의 음식을 전달하고 있는(delivering plates of food) 사람이 없으므로 오답이다. 사진에 있는 접시들(plates)을 사용하여 혼동을 주었다.
　　 (B) [×] 사진에 물을 따르고 있는(pouring water) 사람이 없으므로 오답이다.
　　 (C) [×] 사진에 식탁보는 보이지만, 나뭇잎 이미지가 바느질되어 있는(have been stitched) 모습은 아니므로 오답이다. 사진에 있는 나뭇잎(Leaf)을 사용하여 혼동을 주었다.
　　 (D) [○] 물가 카페에 앉아 있는 사람들의 모습을 가장 잘 묘사한 정답이다.

PART 2

7 Who 의문문
[3l] 캐나다식 → 미국식

Who's playing the lead role in the play tonight?
(A) My seat is E3.
(B) An actor from Canada.
(C) The tickets are sold out.

play v. (역할을) 맡다, 연기하다; n. 연극   lead role 주연, 주역
seat n. 좌석, 자리   actor n. 배우   sold out 매진된, 다 팔린

해석 누가 오늘 밤 연극에서 주연을 맡나요?
　　 (A) 제 좌석은 E3이에요.
　　 (B) 캐나다 출신의 배우요.
　　 (C) 표가 매진되었어요.

해설 (A) [×] 질문의 play(연극)에서 연상할 수 있는 seat(좌석)을 사용하여 혼동을 준 오답이다.

(B) [○] 캐나다 출신의 배우라며, 오늘 밤 연극에서 주연을 맡을 사람을 언급했으므로 정답이다.
(C) [×] 질문의 play(연극)에서 연상할 수 있는 tickets(표)를 사용하여 혼동을 준 오답이다.

8 What 의문문
[3l] 영국식 → 호주식

What should we do about the broken window?
(A) A view of the ocean.
(B) Because I don't want to open it.
(C) Call a repair person.

broken adj. 깨진, 망가진   view n. 전망; v. 보다
repair person 수리공

해석 깨진 창문에 대해 우리가 무엇을 해야 하나요?
　　 (A) 바다 전망이요.
　　 (B) 제가 그것을 열고 싶지 않기 때문이에요.
　　 (C) 수리공에게 전화하세요.

해설 (A) [×] 질문의 window(창문)에서 연상할 수 있는 view(전망)를 사용하여 혼동을 준 오답이다.
　　 (B) [×] 질문의 window(창문)에서 연상할 수 있는 동작과 관련된 open(열다)을 사용하여 혼동을 준 오답이다.
　　 (C) [○] 수리공에게 전화하라는 말로, 깨진 창문에 대해 해야 할 행동을 언급했으므로 정답이다.

9 Be동사 의문문
[3l] 캐나다식 → 영국식

Are the boxes in the storage area unpacked?
(A) No. I'm on my way there now.
(B) In the storage room.
(C) To pack the suitcase.

storage area 창고 공간   unpack v. 열다, (포장을) 풀다
on one's way ~하는 중에   pack v. (짐을) 싸다, 포장하다
suitcase n. 여행 가방

해석 창고 공간에 있는 상자들이 열려 있나요?
　　 (A) 아니요. 제가 지금 그곳으로 가는 중이에요.
　　 (B) 창고 안에요.
　　 (C) 여행 가방을 싸기 위해서요.

해설 (A) [○] No로 창고 공간에 있는 상자들이 열려 있지 않다는 것을 전달한 후, 자신이 지금 그곳으로 가고 있다는 추가 정보를 제공했으므로 정답이다.
　　 (B) [×] 질문의 storage를 반복 사용하여 혼동을 준 오답이다.
　　 (C) [×] 질문의 unpacked(열다)와 반대 의미인 pack(싸다)을 사용하여 혼동을 준 오답이다.

10 제안 의문문
[3l] 미국식 → 캐나다식

Why don't we visit the new art gallery on Saturday morning?
(A) OK. I don't have any plans then.
(B) A famous artist's collection.
(C) Because the weekend is coming.

art gallery 미술관, 화랑 collection n. 모음집, 소장품

해석 우리 토요일 아침에 새로운 미술관에 가는 게 어때요?
(A) 네. 저는 그때 아무 계획이 없어요.
(B) 유명한 예술가의 모음집이에요.
(C) 주말이 다가오고 있기 때문이에요.

해설 (A) [○] OK로 토요일 아침에 새로운 미술관에 가자는 제안을 수락한 후, 그때 아무 계획이 없다는 부연 설명을 했으므로 정답이다.
(B) [×] art - artist's의 유사 발음 어휘를 사용하여 혼동을 준 오답이다.
(C) [×] 질문의 Saturday(토요일)와 관련 있는 weekend(주말)를 사용하여 혼동을 준 오답이다.

11 부가 의문문

영국식 → 호주식

You're going to drive Ms. Choi to the airport, aren't you?
(A) Show the driver your ticket.
(B) Her secretary will do it instead.
(C) The baggage claim area.

airport n. 공항 secretary n. 비서, 총무 instead adv. 대신(에)
baggage claim area (공항의) 수하물 찾는 곳

해석 당신이 Ms. Choi를 공항까지 태워다 줄 거죠, 그렇지 않나요?
(A) 당신의 표를 운전기사에게 보여주세요.
(B) 그녀의 비서가 대신 할 거예요.
(C) 수하물 찾는 곳이요.

해설 (A) [×] drive - driver의 유사 발음 어휘를 사용하여 혼동을 준 오답이다.
(B) [○] Ms. Choi의 비서가 대신 할 것이라는 말로, 자신이 Ms. Choi를 공항까지 태워다 줄 것이 아님을 간접적으로 전달했으므로 정답이다.
(C) [×] 질문의 airport(공항)와 관련 있는 baggage claim area(수하물 찾는 곳)를 사용하여 혼동을 준 오답이다.

12 평서문

캐나다식 → 영국식

Our company's new office will be located in the Baxter Building.
(A) I've never heard of it.
(B) The head of the legal department.
(C) The location of the party has changed.

locate v. 위치시키다, 두다 head n. 부장 legal department 법무팀
location n. 장소, 위치

해석 우리 회사의 새로운 사무실이 Baxter 건물 안에 위치할 거예요.
(A) 저는 그것에 대해 들어본 적이 없어요.
(B) 법무팀 부장이요.
(C) 파티의 장소는 변경됐어요.

해설 (A) [○] 자신은 Baxter 건물에 대해 들어본 적이 없다는 말로, 회사의 새로운 사무실이 위치할 장소가 어디인지 모른다는 것을 전달했으므로 정답이다.
(B) [×] 질문의 office(사무실)에서 연상할 수 있는 회사 부서와 관련 있는 legal department(법무팀)를 사용하여 혼동을 준 오답이다.
(C) [×] located - location의 유사 발음 어휘를 사용하여 혼동을 준 오답이다.

13 조동사 의문문

호주식 → 영국식

Has the training workshop been canceled?
(A) On the 23rd floor.
(B) It's been rescheduled for Thursday.
(C) The training materials.

training n. 교육, 훈련 cancel v. 취소하다, 정지하다
reschedule v. 일정을 변경하다 material n. 자료, 재료

해석 교육 워크숍이 취소되었나요?
(A) 23층에서요.
(B) 목요일로 일정이 변경됐어요.
(C) 교육 자료요.

해설 (A) [×] 질문의 training workshop(교육 워크숍)에서 연상할 수 있는 장소와 관련된 23rd floor(23층)를 사용하여 혼동을 준 오답이다.
(B) [○] 목요일로 일정이 변경됐다는 말로, 교육 워크숍이 취소되지 않았음을 간접적으로 전달했으므로 정답이다.
(C) [×] 질문의 training을 반복 사용하여 혼동을 준 오답이다.

14 How 의문문

미국식 → 호주식

How much were you charged for the hotel room?
(A) About 140 dollars per night.
(B) After only six days.
(C) With an online reservation.

charge v. 요금을 청구하다; n. 요금 reservation n. 예약

해석 그 호텔 객실에 얼마가 청구되었나요?
(A) 하룻밤에 약 140달러요.
(B) 불과 6일 만에요.
(C) 온라인 예약으로요.

해설 (A) [○] 하룻밤에 약 140달러라며, 호텔 객실에 청구된 금액을 언급했으므로 정답이다.
(B) [×] 호텔 객실에 얼마가 청구되었는지 물었는데, 기간으로 응답했으므로 오답이다.
(C) [×] 질문의 hotel room(호텔 객실)에서 연상할 수 있는 reservation(예약)을 사용하여 혼동을 준 오답이다.

15 When 의문문

호주식 → 캐나다식

When do the interviews for the editor position begin?
(A) In the conference room, I believe.
(B) Right after lunch today.
(C) Many qualified applicants.

interview n. 면접 qualified adj. 자격이 있는, 적격의
applicant n. 지원자

해석 편집자 직책의 면접은 언제 시작하나요?
(A) 제 생각에 회의실에서인 것 같아요.
(B) 오늘 점심 직후예요.
(C) 자격이 있는 많은 지원자들이요.

해설 (A) [×] 편집자 직책의 면접이 언제 시작하는지 물었는데, 장소로 응답했으므로 오답이다. interviews(면접)에서 연상할 수 있는 장소와 관련된 conference room(회의실)을 사용하여 혼동을 주었다. 질문의 When을 Where로 혼동하여 이를 정답으로 선택하지 않도록 주의한다.
(B) [○] 오늘 점심 직후라, 면접의 시작 시점을 언급했으므로 정답이다.
(C) [×] 질문의 interviews(면접)에서 연상할 수 있는 applicants(지원자들)를 사용하여 혼동을 준 오답이다.

16 조동사 의문문
[3에] 캐나다식 → 미국식

Does the new scheduling system work well?
(A) To enhance the security system.
(B) About the updated schedule.
(C) Yes. There's been no problems.

work v. 작동하다, 일하다   enhance v. 향상시키다, (가치를) 높이다
security adj. 보안의, 안전의

해석 새로운 일정 관리 시스템이 잘 작동하나요?
(A) 보안 시스템을 향상시키기 위해서요.
(B) 업데이트된 일정에 관해서요.
(C) 네. 아무 문제 없어요.

해설 (A) [×] 질문의 system을 반복 사용하여 혼동을 준 오답이다.
(B) [×] scheduling - schedule의 유사 발음 어휘를 사용하여 혼동을 준 오답이다.
(C) [○] Yes로 새로운 일정 관리 시스템이 잘 작동한다고 전달한 후, 아무 문제 없다는 부연 설명을 했으므로 정답이다.

17 How 의문문
[3에] 영국식 → 캐나다식

How often should I change my online account password?
(A) Once a month is recommended.
(B) It was easy to register.
(C) That Web site is well designed.

account n. 계정, 계좌   recommend v. 권장하다, 추천하다
register v. 등록하다, 기재하다   design v. 설계하다; n. 설계, 디자인

해석 제 온라인 계정 비밀번호를 얼마나 자주 변경해야 하나요?
(A) 한 달에 한 번이 권장돼요.
(B) 그건 등록하기 쉬웠어요.
(C) 그 웹사이트는 잘 설계되어 있어요.

해설 (A) [○] 한 달에 한 번이 권장된다는 말로, 온라인 계정 비밀번호를 얼마나 자주 변경해야 하는지를 전달했으므로 정답이다.
(B) [×] 질문의 account(계정)에서 연상할 수 있는 register(등록하다)를 사용하여 혼동을 준 오답이다.
(C) [×] 질문의 online(온라인)과 관련 있는 Web site(웹사이트)를 사용하여 혼동을 준 오답이다.

18 부정 의문문
[3에] 미국식 → 영국식

Aren't you going to stop by the bank this afternoon?
(A) Several large withdrawals.
(B) I already went earlier.
(C) No, he is a senior accountant.

stop by 들르다   withdrawal n. (계좌에서의) 인출
senior adj. 선임의, 상급의   accountant n. 회계사

해석 당신은 오늘 오후에 은행에 들르지 않나요?
(A) 몇몇 대규모 인출이요.
(B) 아까 이미 다녀왔어요.
(C) 아니요, 그는 선임 회계사예요.

해설 (A) [×] 질문의 bank(은행)와 관련 있는 withdrawals(인출)를 사용하여 혼동을 준 오답이다.
(B) [○] 아까 이미 다녀왔다는 말로, 오늘 오후에 은행에 들르지 않을 것임을 간접적으로 전달했으므로 정답이다.
(C) [×] 질문의 bank(은행)에서 연상할 수 있는 직업과 관련된 accountant(회계사)를 사용하여 혼동을 준 오답이다.

19 선택 의문문
[3에] 영국식 → 호주식

Do you want to take a bus or a taxi to the downtown branch?
(A) To pick up some coffee.
(B) They weren't too expensive.
(C) Xia will give us a ride.

downtown adj. 시내의   branch n. 지점
give ~ a ride ~를 태워다 주다

해석 시내 지점까지 버스를 타고 싶나요, 아니면 택시를 타고 싶나요?
(A) 커피를 가지러 가기 위해서요.
(B) 그것들은 너무 비싸지 않았어요.
(C) Xia가 우리를 태워다 줄 거예요.

해설 (A) [×] 시내 지점까지 버스를 타고 싶은지 택시를 타고 싶은지를 물었는데, 이유로 응답했으므로 오답이다.
(B) [×] 시내 지점까지 버스를 타고 싶은지 택시를 타고 싶은지를 물었는데, 이와 관련이 없는 그것들이 너무 비싸지 않았다는 내용으로 응답했으므로 오답이다.
(C) [○] Xia가 태워다 줄 것이라는 말로, 버스와 택시 둘 다 간접적으로 선택하지 않은 정답이다.

최신토익 경향

or로 연결된 두 가지 사항 중 하나를 선택하도록 요구하는 선택 의문문에서는 둘 중 하나를 직접적/간접적으로 선택하는 답변이 자주 출제되지만, 두 가지 중 아무것도 고르지 않는 간접적인 응답이 자주 나오고 있다. 주어진 선택 사항 중에 고르지 않는 경우, 고난도로 느껴질 수 있기 때문에 예문을 통해 미리 학습해 두자.

Would you like to meet with Dr. Lee today or tomorrow?
Dr. Lee와 오늘 만나고 싶으신가요, 아니면 내일 만나고 싶으신가요?

<답변> I usually see Dr. Yang.
저는 주로 Dr. Yang을 만나는데요.

* Dr. Lee와 만날 날을 오늘로 할지, 아니면 내일로 할지 선택하는 선택 의문문에 Dr. Yang과 주로 진찰을 본다며 둘 다 선택하지 않는 응답

20 평서문

I tried ordering lunch on this app, but it kept crashing.
(A) It's their most popular dish.
(B) Check if there is an update.
(C) Whichever restaurant you prefer.

crash v. (기능이) 멈추다, 충돌하다; n. 사고

해석 이 앱에서 점심을 주문하려고 했는데, 계속해서 기능이 멈췄어요.
(A) 그것은 그들의 가장 인기 있는 요리예요.
(B) 업데이트가 있는지 확인해 보세요.
(C) 어느 식당이든 당신이 선호하는 곳이요.

해설 (A) [×] 질문의 lunch(점심)에서 연상할 수 있는 dish(요리)를 사용하여 혼동을 준 오답이다.
(B) [○] 업데이트가 있는지 확인해 보라는 말로, 문제점에 대한 해결책을 제시했으므로 정답이다.
(C) [×] 질문의 ordering(주문하는 것)에서 연상할 수 있는 장소와 관련된 restaurant(식당)를 사용하여 혼동을 준 오답이다.

최신토익경향

평서문은 의문문과 달리 질문의 초점이 되는 부분이 없고 그 의도에 따라 다양한 응답이 가능하기 때문에 정답을 고르기 어려운 유형이다. 특히 최근에는 문제점을 언급하는 의도의 평서문에 해결책을 제시하는 응답이 자주 출제되고 있으니 다음 예문을 살펴보자.

It's always difficult to find a parking spot in our building.
우리 건물에서 주차 자리를 찾는 것은 항상 어려워요.

<답변> Here is a list of nearby public parking lots.
근처 공용 주차장 목록이에요.

* 주차 자리를 찾는 것이 어렵다는 문제점을 전달하는 의도의 평서문에 근처 공용 주차장 목록을 주면서 그곳을 이용해 보라는 해결책을 제시하는 의도의 응답

21 When 의문문

When is the awards ceremony planned for?
(A) For his excellent performance.
(B) In the first week of next month.
(C) That trophy is impressive!

awards ceremony 시상식 performance n. 성과, 공연
trophy n. 트로피, 전리품 impressive adj. 인상적인, 인상 깊은

해석 시상식은 언제로 예정되어 있나요?
(A) 그의 훌륭한 성과 때문이에요.
(B) 다음 달 첫째 주예요.
(C) 그 트로피는 인상적이에요!

해설 (A) [×] 질문의 awards ceremony(시상식)에서 연상할 수 있는 수상 이유와 관련된 performance(성과)를 사용하여 혼동을 준 오답이다.
(B) [○] 다음 달 첫째 주라며, 시상식이 개최될 시점을 언급했으므로 정답이다.
(C) [×] 질문의 awards ceremony(시상식)에서 연상할 수 있는 trophy(트로피)를 사용하여 혼동을 준 오답이다.

22 부가 의문문

This scanner needs to be replaced, right?
(A) We just bought it last year.
(B) There's extra paper here.
(C) Where did you set it up?

replace v. 교체하다, 대신하다 extra adj. 여분의, 추가의
set up ~을 설치하다

해석 이 스캐너는 교체돼야 해요, 그렇죠?
(A) 우리는 그것을 작년에 구매했어요.
(B) 여기 여분의 종이가 있어요.
(C) 당신은 그것을 어디에 설치하셨나요?

해설 (A) [○] 스캐너를 작년에 구매했다는 말로, 교체될 필요가 없음을 간접적으로 전달했으므로 정답이다.
(B) [×] 질문의 scanner(스캐너)에서 연상할 수 있는 사무용품과 관련된 paper(종이)를 사용하여 혼동을 준 오답이다.
(C) [×] 질문의 scanner(스캐너)에서 연상할 수 있는 기기와 관련된 set ~ up(설치하다)을 사용하여 혼동을 준 오답이다.

23 평서문

Let's ask Ms. Cho to analyze the sales figures.
(A) The analysis was accurate.
(B) She's not working until Monday.
(C) That one is currently on sale.

analyze v. 분석하다 sales figure 매출 수치, 매출액
analysis n. 분석 (내용) accurate adj. 정확한
on sale 할인 중인, 판매 중인

해석 Ms. Cho에게 매출 수치를 분석해 달라고 요청해 봅시다.
(A) 그 분석이 정확했어요.
(B) 그녀는 월요일이나 되어서야 근무해요.
(C) 그것은 현재 할인 중이에요.

해설 (A) [×] analyze - analysis의 유사 발음 어휘를 사용하여 혼동을 준 오답이다.
(B) [○] 그녀는 월요일이나 되어서야 근무한다는 말로, Ms. Cho에게 매출 수치를 분석해 달라고 요청해 보자는 제안을 간접적으로 거절한 정답이다.
(C) [×] 질문의 sales(매출)를 '할인 중'이라는 의미의 on sale로 반복 사용하여 혼동을 준 오답이다.

24 Which 의문문

Which store has an open assistant manager position?
(A) It is open until 10 P.M.
(B) I appreciate your assistance.
(C) The one in Collingwood.

해석 어느 매장에 부지점장 자리가 공석인가요?
(A) 그곳은 오후 10시까지 열어요.
(B) 도움을 주셔서 감사해요.
(C) Collingwood에 있는 곳이요.

해설 (A) [×] 질문의 open을 반복 사용하여 혼동을 준 오답이다.
(B) [×] assistant - assistance의 유사 발음 어휘를 사용하여 혼동을 준 오답이다.
(C) [○] Collingwood에 있는 곳이라는 말로, 부지점장 자리가 공석인 매장을 전달했으므로 정답이다.

25 Where 의문문

영국식 → 미국식

Where are we meeting with our clients?
(A) All of us found it interesting.
(B) Mr. Harris is arranging that.
(C) There will be five clients in total.

client n. 고객 arrange v. 처리하다, 정리하다

해석 우리는 고객들을 어디에서 만날 건가요?
(A) 우리 모두 그것이 흥미롭다고 생각했어요.
(B) Mr. Harris가 그 일을 처리하고 있어요.
(C) 총 다섯 명의 고객이 있을 거예요.

해설 (A) [×] 고객들을 어디에서 만날 것인지를 물었는데, 이와 관련이 없는 우리 모두 그것이 흥미롭다고 생각했다는 내용으로 응답했으므로 오답이다.
(B) [○] Mr. Harris가 그 일, 즉 고객들과 만날 장소를 정하는 일을 처리하고 있다는 말로, 고객들을 어디에서 만날 것인지 모른다는 간접적인 응답을 했으므로 정답이다.
(C) [×] 질문의 clients를 반복 사용하여 혼동을 준 오답이다.

26 Who 의문문

캐나다식 → 영국식

Who is going to show the visitors around our laboratory?
(A) Mindy will do it.
(B) The research is very promising.
(C) My favorite show.

show v. 안내하다, 보여 주다; n. 쇼, 프로그램 laboratory n. 실험실
promising adj. 유망한, 촉망되는

해석 누가 방문객들에게 우리 실험실을 안내할 건가요?
(A) Mindy가 할 거예요.
(B) 그 연구는 아주 유망해요.
(C) 제가 제일 좋아하는 쇼요.

해설 (A) [○] Mindy가 할 것이라는 말로, 방문객들에게 실험실을 안내할 사람을 언급했으므로 정답이다.
(B) [×] 질문의 laboratory(실험실)와 관련 있는 research(연구)를 사용하여 혼동을 준 오답이다.
(C) [×] 질문의 show(안내하다)를 '쇼'라는 의미의 명사로 반복 사용하여 혼동을 준 오답이다.

27 평서문

호주식 → 캐나다식

The construction project's deadline has been pushed back a week.
(A) The famous bridge in London.
(B) Why was that decision made?
(C) That project was a success.

deadline n. 마감일, 마감 기한 push back 미루다, 연기하다

해석 그 건설 프로젝트의 마감일이 일주일 미뤄졌어요.
(A) 런던에서 유명한 다리예요.
(B) 왜 그런 결정이 내려졌나요?
(C) 그 프로젝트는 성공적이었어요.

해설 (A) [×] 질문의 construction(건설)에서 연상할 수 있는 bridge(다리)를 사용하여 혼동을 준 오답이다.
(B) [○] 왜 그런 결정이 내려졌는지를 되물어, 건설 프로젝트에 대한 추가 정보를 요구하는 정답이다.
(C) [×] 질문의 project를 반복 사용하여 혼동을 준 오답이다.

28 Why 의문문

미국식 → 캐나다식

Why didn't we offer our loyal customers a discount this time?
(A) A successful promotion.
(B) From the customer service department.
(C) We gave gifts instead.

loyal customer 단골 고객 successful adj. 성공적인
promotion n. 판촉 활동, 홍보, 승진

해석 이번에는 왜 우리 단골 고객들에게 할인을 제공하지 않았나요?
(A) 성공적인 판촉 활동이요.
(B) 고객 서비스 부서에서요.
(C) 우리는 대신 선물을 제공했어요.

해설 (A) [×] 질문의 discount(할인)와 관련 있는 promotion(판촉 활동)을 사용하여 혼동을 준 오답이다.
(B) [×] 질문의 customers를 customer로 반복 사용하여 혼동을 준 오답이다.
(C) [○] 대신 선물을 제공했다는 말로, 이번에 단골 고객들에게 할인을 제공하지 않은 이유를 언급했으므로 정답이다.

29 Where 의문문

호주식 → 미국식

Where can I return this sweater I bought yesterday?
(A) I can take care of that.
(B) Don't put it in the washing machine.
(C) A refund was provided.

return v. 반품하다, 되돌려주다; n. 반납 washing machine 세탁기
refund n. 환불; v. 환불하다

해석 제가 어제 샀던 이 스웨터를 어디에서 반품할 수 있나요?
(A) 제가 그걸 처리해 드릴게요.
(B) 세탁기에 그것을 넣지 마세요.
(C) 환불이 제공되었어요.

해설 (A) [○] 자신이 처리해 주겠다는 말로, 스웨터를 어디에서 반품할 수 있는지를 간접적으로 전달했으므로 정답이다.
(B) [×] 질문의 sweater(스웨터)를 나타낼 수 있는 it을 사용하고, sweater(스웨터)에서 연상할 수 있는 의류와 관련된 washing machine(세탁기)을 사용하여 혼동을 준 오답이다.

(C) [×] return - refund의 유사 발음 어휘를 사용하여 혼동을 준 오답이다.

의문사 의문문 중에서 출제 빈도가 높은 편인 where 의문문에 대한 답변으로는 주로 특정 장소나 위치에 관한 정보가 나온다. 하지만, 최근 토익에서는 예측하기 어려운 답변이 정답으로 출제되고 있으니, 예문과 함께 가능한 답변을 미리 학습해 두자.

Where can I see last year's accounting records?
작년 회계 기록을 어디에서 볼 수 있나요?

<답변 1> You need to get permission first to see them.
그것들을 보기 위해서는 먼저 허가를 받아야 해요.

<답변 2> Kim knows where they are.
Kim은 그것들이 어디에 있는지 알고 있어요.

*<답변 1> 작년 회계 기록을 볼 수 있는 장소를 묻는 질문에 먼저 허가를 받아야 한다고 답변하는 예측하기 어려운 응답
<답변 2> 작년 회계 기록을 볼 수 있는 장소를 묻는 질문에 Kim이 알고 있으니 Kim에게 물어보라는 예측하기 어려운 응답

30 요청 의문문
영국식 → 캐나다식

Can you give me directions to the nearest subway station?
(A) I'm not familiar with this area.
(B) Public transportation is convenient.
(C) The express train to Westport.

direction n. 길, 방향 familiar adj. ~을 잘 아는, 익숙한
public transportation 대중교통 express adj. 급행의

해석 가장 가까운 지하철역으로 가는 길을 알려주시겠어요?
(A) 저는 이 지역을 잘 몰라요.
(B) 대중교통은 편리해요.
(C) Westport로 가는 급행열차요.

해설 (A) [○] 이 지역을 잘 모른다는 말로, 가장 가까운 지하철역으로 가는 길을 모른다는 간접적인 응답을 했으므로 정답이다.
(B) [×] 질문의 subway(지하철)와 관련 있는 Public transportation(대중교통)을 사용하여 혼동을 준 오답이다.
(C) [×] 질문의 subway(지하철)와 관련 있는 train(열차)을 사용하여 혼동을 준 오답이다.

31 How 의문문
호주식 → 미국식

How was the new logo the marketing team designed?
(A) About three weeks ago.
(B) A design degree.
(C) I wasn't in the meeting.

logo n. 로고, 상징 degree n. 학위, 정도

해석 마케팅팀이 디자인한 새로운 로고는 어땠나요?
(A) 3주쯤 전에요.
(B) 디자인 학위요.
(C) 저는 그 회의에 없었어요.

해설 (A) [×] 마케팅팀이 디자인한 새로운 로고가 어땠는지를 물었는데, 이와 관련이 없는 3주쯤 전이라는 내용으로 응답했으므로 오답이다.

(B) [×] 질문의 designed(디자인했다)를 '디자인'이라는 의미의 명사 design으로 반복 사용하여 혼동을 준 오답이다.
(C) [○] 자신은 그 회의에 없었다는 말로, 마케팅팀이 디자인한 새로운 로고가 어땠는지 모른다는 간접적인 응답을 했으므로 정답이다.

PART 3

[32-34]
미국식 → 호주식

Questions 32-34 refer to the following conversation.

W: ³²**What do you think of our department head's announcement yesterday about the new branch opening in Hong Kong? It'll be our company's first office in another country.**

M: It's pretty exciting. And ³³**I heard that the assistant branch manager hasn't been chosen yet. Why don't you submit an application?** You would be perfect for that role.

W: Hmm . . . I have always wanted to work abroad. ³⁴**Do you know who I should reach out to about this?**

M: ³⁴**Actually, Brenda Williams in human resources is in charge of the selection process.**

announcement n. 발표, 소식 exciting adj. 기대되는, 신나는
assistant branch manager 부지점장 submit v. 제출하다
application n. 지원서 abroad adv. 해외에서, 해외로
selection n. 선발

해석
32-34번은 다음 대화에 관한 문제입니다.

여: ³²홍콩에 새로운 지점을 개설한다는 어제 부서장님의 발표에 대해 어떻게 생각하세요? 그곳은 다른 나라에 있는 우리 회사의 첫 번째 지사가 될 거예요.
남: 정말 기대돼요. 그리고 ³³아직 부지점장이 뽑히지 않았다고 들었어요. 지원서를 제출하는 게 어때요? 당신이 그 역할에 제격일 것 같은데요.
여: 흠... 저는 항상 해외에서 일하고 싶었어요. ³⁴이것에 대해 누구에게 연락을 취해야 하는지 아세요?
남: ³⁴실은, 인사팀 Brenda Williams가 선발 과정을 담당하고 있어요.

32 특정 세부 사항 문제

해석 최근에 무엇이 발표되었는가?
(A) 부서 구조 조정
(B) 사업 협력
(C) 해외 진출
(D) 단합 행사

해설 질문의 핵심 어구(recently announced)와 관련된 내용을 주의 깊게 듣는다. 여자가 "What do you think of our department head's announcement yesterday about the new branch opening in Hong Kong? It'll be our company's first office in another country."라며 홍콩에 새로운 지점을 개설한다는 어제 부서장의 발표에 대해 어떻게 생각하는지 물은 후, 그곳은 다른 나라에 있는 첫 번째 지사가 될 거라고 하였다. 따라서 (C)가 정답이다.

어휘 restructuring n. 구조 조정, 기업 혁신 전략
partnership n. 협력, 동업 expansion n. 진출, 확장

33 제안 문제

해석 남자는 무엇을 제안하는가?
(A) 비서를 고용하기
(B) 직책에 지원하기
(C) 보고서를 제출하기
(D) 발표를 하기

해설 남자의 말에서 제안과 관련된 표현이 언급된 다음을 주의 깊게 듣는다. 남자가 "I heard that the assistant branch manager hasn't been chosen yet. Why don't you submit an application?" 이라며 아직 부지점장이 뽑히지 않았다고 들었다고 한 후, 여자에게 지원서를 제출할 것을 제안하였다. 따라서 (B)가 정답이다.

어휘 apply for ~에 지원하다 position n. 직책, 자리

Paraphrasing

submit an application 지원서를 제출하다 → Applying for ~에 지원하기

34 다음에 할 일 문제

해석 여자는 다음에 무엇을 할 것 같은가?
(A) 안내서를 읽는다.
(B) 지사를 방문한다.
(C) 동료와 이야기한다.
(D) 팀과 만난다.

해설 대화의 마지막 부분을 주의 깊게 듣는다. 여자가 "Do you know who I should reach out to about this?"라며 누구에게 연락을 취해야 하는지 묻자, 남자가 "Actually, Brenda Williams in human resources is in charge of the selection process."라며 인사팀 Brenda Williams가 선발 과정을 담당하고 있다고 한 것을 통해 여자가 동료인 Brenda Williams와 이야기할 것임을 알 수 있다. 따라서 (C)가 정답이다.

어휘 read through 읽다, 통독하다 guidebook n. 안내서

[35-37]   🎧 호주식 → 미국식 → 영국식

Questions 35-37 refer to the following conversation with three speakers.

M: ³⁵I'm glad you were both available to tour the space today. There's already a lot of interest in it because the rent is very reasonable.

W1: This is the perfect location for our new art gallery, and there's lots of parking. ³⁶What do you think, Cora?

W2: I like it. But ³⁶I'm a little worried that the lobby is too small.

M: Well, the building's owner might be willing to do some renovations if you agree to a long-term lease.

W2: That'd be fine with me.

W1: Me too. ³⁷Could you send us the lease agreement to review?

M: ³⁷I'll e-mail it this afternoon.

tour v. 둘러보다 space n. 공간 rent n. 임대료, 집세
reasonable adj. 가격이 저렴한, 합리적인 location n. 위치
renovation n. 개조, 보수 long-term adj. 장기의 lease n. 임대
agreement n. 계약서, 동의 review v. 검토하다; n. 검토

해석
35-37번은 다음 세 명의 대화에 관한 문제입니다.
남: ³⁵오늘 두 분 모두 공간을 둘러볼 수 있게 되어 다행입니다. 임대료가 매우 저렴해서 벌써부터 많은 관심을 받고 있어요.
여1: 저희의 새 화랑에 완벽한 위치이고, 주차 공간도 많네요. ³⁶어떻게 생각하세요, Cora?
여2: 마음에 들어요. 하지만 ³⁶로비가 너무 작아서 조금 걱정돼요.
남: 음, 장기 임대에 동의하신다면, 건물 주인이 일부 개조를 해줄 수도 있어요.
여2: 그러면 괜찮을 것 같아요.
여1: 저도요. ³⁷검토할 수 있도록 저희에게 임대 계약서를 보내주시겠어요?
남: ³⁷오늘 오후에 이메일로 보내드릴게요.

35 화자 문제

해석 남자는 누구인 것 같은가?
(A) 행사 주최자
(B) 부동산 중개인
(C) 안전 검사관
(D) 인테리어 디자이너

해설 대화에서 신분 및 직업과 관련된 표현을 놓치지 않고 듣는다. 남자가 "I'm glad you were both available to tour the space today. There's already a lot of interest in it because the rent is very reasonable."이라며 오늘 두 명 모두 공간을 둘러볼 수 있게 되어 다행이라고 한 후, 임대료가 매우 저렴해서 벌써부터 많은 관심을 받고 있다고 한 것을 통해 남자가 부동산 중개인임을 알 수 있다. 따라서 (B)가 정답이다.

어휘 organizer n. 주최자, 조직 위원 real estate 부동산
agent n. 중개인, 대리인 inspector n. 검사관, 감독관

36 문제점 문제

해석 Cora는 무엇에 대해 걱정하는가?
(A) 주차 공간 부족
(B) 개조 비용
(C) 건물 위치
(D) 공간 크기

해설 Cora의 말에서 부정적인 표현이 언급된 다음을 주의 깊게 듣는다. 여자1이 "What do you think, Cora?"라며 Cora에게 의견을 묻자, 여자2[Cora]가 "I'm a little worried that the lobby is too small"이라며 로비가 너무 작아서 조금 걱정된다고 하였다. 따라서 (D)가 정답이다.

어휘 lack n. 부족, 결핍

Paraphrasing

the lobby 로비 → an area 공간

37 특정 세부 사항 문제

해석 남자는 여자들에게 무엇을 보내겠다고 말하는가?

(A) 법적 계약서

(B) 재무 기록

(C) 명함

(D) 마케팅 책자

해설 질문의 핵심 어구(send)가 언급된 주변을 주의 깊게 듣는다. 여자1이 "Could you send us the lease agreement to review?"라며 검토할 수 있도록 자신들에게 임대 계약서를 보내 달라고 요청하자, 남자가 "I'll e-mail it this afternoon."이라며 오늘 오후에 이메일로 보내겠다고 하였다. 따라서 (A)가 정답이다.

어휘 financial adj. 재무의, 재정적인 record n. 기록
business card 명함 brochure n. (안내용) 책자, 설명서

Paraphrasing

the lease agreement 임대 계약서 → A legal agreement 법적 계약서

[38-40]

[3⅔] 캐나다식 → 미국식

Questions 38-40 refer to the following conversation.

M: Sandra, ³⁸I could use your help with this magazine advertisement I'm working on. It's a project for Northwest Bank, which is one of our firm's biggest clients.

W: Of course. What do you need?

M: ³⁹I can't figure out where to position this photograph of the bank's president.

W: Hmm . . . ³⁹Have you considered just taking it out? The ad would be more eye-catching without it.

M: But I was specifically instructed to include it. ⁴⁰Maybe I'll make two versions for the presentation I'll give during the meeting with the bank representatives tomorrow.

advertisement n. 광고 client n. 고객, 의뢰인
figure out 알다, 생각해 내다, 이해하다 position v. 배치하다, 두다
photograph n. 사진 president n. 회장 ad n. 광고
eye-catching adj. 눈길을 끄는 specifically adv. 특별히, 구체적으로
instruct v. 지시하다 representative n. 담당자, 대표

해석

38-40번은 다음 대화에 관한 문제입니다.

남: Sandra, ³⁸제가 작업 중인 잡지 광고에 도움이 필요해요. 그것은 Northwest 은행을 위한 프로젝트인데, 그 은행은 우리 회사의 가장 중요한 고객들 중 하나예요.

여: 물론이죠. 무엇이 필요한가요?

남: ³⁹이 은행장 사진을 어디에 배치해야 할지 모르겠어요.

여: 흠... ³⁹그냥 그걸 빼는 건 고려해 봤어요? 그게 없어야 광고가 더 눈길을 끌 것 같아요.

남: 하지만 저는 그것을 특별히 포함하라는 지시를 받았어요. ⁴⁰내일 은행 담당자들과의 회의 중에 제가 할 발표를 위해 두 가지 버전을 만들어야 겠어요.

38 화자 문제

해석 화자들은 어느 산업에서 일하는 것 같은가?

(A) 금융

(B) 마케팅

(C) 건강 관리

(D) 영화

해설 대화에서 신분 및 직업과 관련된 표현을 놓치지 않고 듣는다. 남자가 "I could use your help with this magazine advertisement I'm working on. It's a project for Northwest Bank, which is one of our firm's biggest clients."라며 작업 중인 잡지 광고에 여자의 도움이 필요하다고 한 후, 그것은 Northwest 은행을 위한 프로젝트인데 그 은행은 회사의 가장 중요한 고객들 중 하나라고 한 것을 통해 화자들이 마케팅 산업에서 일하는 것임을 알 수 있다. 따라서 (B)가 정답이다.

39 제안 문제

해석 여자는 남자에게 무엇을 하라고 제안하는가?

(A) 사진을 제거한다.

(B) 잡지를 구입한다.

(C) 사진을 찍는다.

(D) 프로젝트를 취소한다.

해설 대화에서 제안과 관련된 표현이 언급된 주변을 주의 깊게 듣는다. 남자가 "I can't figure out where to position this photograph of the bank's president."라며 은행장 사진을 어디에 배치해야 할지 모르겠다고 하자, 여자가 "Have you considered just taking it out?"이라며 은행장의 사진을 빼는 것을 고려해 보라고 하였다. 따라서 (A)가 정답이다.

어휘 remove v. 제거하다, 치우다 cancel v. 취소하다, 무효화하다

Paraphrasing

taking ~ out 빼는 것 → Remove 제거하다

photograph 사진 → a photo 사진

40 다음에 할 일 문제

해석 내일 무슨 일이 일어날 것 같은가?

(A) 담당자가 호출될 것이다.

(B) 발표가 진행될 것이다.

(C) 회의 일정이 변경될 것이다.

(D) 결제가 처리될 것이다.

해설 질문의 핵심 어구(tomorrow)가 언급된 주변을 주의 깊게 듣는다. 남자가 "Maybe I'll make two versions for the presentation I'll give during the meeting with the bank representatives tomorrow."라며 내일 은행 담당자들과의 회의 중에 할 발표를 위해 두 가지 버전을 만들겠다고 하였다. 따라서 (B)가 정답이다.

어휘 presentation n. 발표, 제출 reschedule v. 일정을 변경하다
payment n. 결제, 지불 process v. 처리하다

영국식 → 호주식

Questions 41-43 refer to the following conversation.

W: You look kind of stressed out, Elias. What's the matter?

M: ⁴¹**I was asked to locate a suitable restaurant for Mr. Romero's retirement party.** But I'm not having much luck.

W: What are you looking for?

M: Well, ⁴²**our manager said that the priority is booking a room separate from the main dining area for privacy.** But there will be 25 guests, and I can't find a restaurant with one that is big enough.

W: What about the Delmonico Steakhouse? Hold on . . . Um, ⁴³**look at this picture on its Web site.** The room can definitely accommodate that many people.

---

stressed out 스트레스 받는　locate v. (위치를) 찾다
suitable adj. 적합한, 알맞은　retirement n. 은퇴
priority n. 우선 (사항)　separate from ~과 분리된
privacy n. 프라이버시, 사생활　definitely adv. 확실히, 분명하게
accommodate v. 수용하다, 공간을 제공하다

해석

41-43번은 다음 대화에 관한 문제입니다.

여: 스트레스를 많이 받으신 것 같네요, Elias. 무슨 일이에요?

남: ⁴¹Mr. Romero의 은퇴 파티에 적합한 식당을 찾으라는 요청을 받았어요. 그런데 제가 운이 별로 없네요.

여: 무엇을 찾고 있나요?

남: 음, ⁴²관리자가 프라이버시를 위해서 주 식사 공간과 분리된 방을 예약하는 게 우선이라고 말했어요. 하지만 손님이 25명일 것인데, 충분히 큰 공간을 가지고 있는 식당을 찾을 수가 없어요.

여: Delmonico Steakhouse는 어때요? 잠시만요... 음, ⁴³웹사이트에 있는 이 사진을 보세요. 공간이 그 정도 많은 인원을 확실히 수용할 수 있어요.

41 주제 문제

해석　대화는 주로 무엇에 관한 것인가?
(A) 숙련된 작업자를 교체하는 것
(B) 고객 불만 사항을 해결하는 것
(C) 기업 행사에 참석하는 것
(D) 적절한 장소를 찾는 것

해설　대화의 주제를 묻는 문제이므로, 대화의 초반을 주의 깊게 들은 후 전체 맥락을 파악한다. 남자가 "I was asked to locate a suitable restaurant for Mr. Romero's retirement party."라며 Mr. Romero의 은퇴 파티에 적합한 식당을 찾으라는 요청을 받았다고 한 후, 적절한 장소를 찾는 내용으로 대화가 이어지고 있다. 따라서 (D)가 정답이다.

어휘　replace v. 교체하다, 대신하다
experienced adj. 숙련된, 경력이 있는
address v. 해결하다, 연설하다　complaint n. 불만 사항, 항의
corporate adj. 기업의, 회사의　venue n. 장소, 현장, 개최지

Paraphrasing

locate 찾다 → Finding 찾는 것

a suitable restaurant 적합한 식당 → an appropriate venue 적절한 장소

42 특정 세부 사항 문제

해석　관리자는 무엇을 우선 사항으로 명시했는가?
(A) 합리적인 예산
(B) 사적인 공간
(C) 유연한 일정
(D) 편리한 위치

해설　질문의 핵심 어구(priority)가 언급된 주변을 주의 깊게 듣는다. 남자가 "our manager said that the priority is booking a room separate from the main dining area for privacy"라며 관리자가 프라이버시를 위해서 주 식사 공간과 분리된 방을 예약하는 게 우선이라고 말했다고 하였다. 따라서 (B)가 정답이다.

어휘　reasonable adj. 합리적인, 가격이 저렴한　budget n. 예산, 비용
flexible adj. 유연한, 융통성 있는　convenient adj. 편리한, 가까운

43 특정 세부 사항 문제

해석　여자는 남자에게 무엇을 보여주는가?
(A) 지도
(B) 메뉴
(C) 이미지
(D) 이메일

해설　질문의 핵심 어구(show)와 관련된 내용을 주의 깊게 듣는다. 여자가 "look at this picture on its Web site"라며 웹사이트에 있는 이 사진을 보라고 하였다. 따라서 (C)가 정답이다.

Paraphrasing

picture 사진 → An image 이미지

캐나다식 → 영국식

Questions 44-46 refer to the following conversation.

M: Hello, Ms. Wallis. This is Jake Reed from Brandon Furniture.

W: Hi. ⁴⁴**Is this about the desk I ordered?**

M: ⁴⁴**Right. As you know, it's supposed to be delivered today. But it looks like it won't arrive until Thursday.** Our warehouse is short-staffed right now. I'm really sorry.

W: But ⁴⁵**I begin a new job on Wednesday.** It's fully remote, so I need my home office set up before then.

M: I see. ⁴⁶**I'll call our warehouse now and ask if one of the drivers is willing to work late today** so that we can get your desk to you. I'll let you know in about 10 minutes.

---

deliver v. 배달하다, 전달하다　warehouse n. 창고
short-staffed adj. 직원이 부족한　fully adv. 완전히, 충분히

TEST **5**

해커스 토익 실전 LC+RC 2

remote adj. 원격의
home office 홈 오피스(일할 수 있게 컴퓨터와 팩스 등을 갖추어 놓은 집)

해석
44-46번은 다음 대화에 관한 문제입니다.

남: 안녕하세요, Ms. Wallis. Brandon 가구의 Jake Reed입니다.

여: 안녕하세요. ⁴⁴제가 주문했던 책상에 관한 건가요?

남: ⁴⁴네. 아시다시피, 오늘 그것이 배달될 예정이었어요. 하지만 목요일이 되어서야 도착할 것 같아요. 지금 당장은 저희 창고에 직원이 부족한 상태예요. 정말 죄송합니다.

여: 하지만 ⁴⁵저는 수요일에 새로운 일을 시작해요. 완전히 원격이라, 그전에는 홈 오피스가 준비돼야 해요.

남: 알겠습니다. ⁴⁶지금 저희 창고에 전화해서 운전기사 중 한 명이 오늘 늦게까지 근무할 수 있는지 물어보고 고객님의 책상을 가져다드릴 수 있도록 하겠습니다. 약 10분 후에 알려드릴게요.

44 목적 문제

해석 남자는 왜 여자에게 전화하는가?
(A) 취소된 주문에 대해 문의하기 위해
(B) 소포 수령을 확인하기 위해
(C) 배달 지연을 알리기 위해
(D) 상품에 대한 결제를 요청하기 위해

해설 전화의 목적을 묻는 문제이므로, 대화의 초반을 반드시 듣는다. 여자가 "Is this about the desk I ordered?"라며 자신이 주문했던 책상에 관한 것이냐고 묻자, 남자가 "Right. As you know, it's supposed to be delivered today. But it looks like it won't arrive until Thursday."라며 그렇다고 한 후, 오늘 책상이 배달될 예정이었는데, 목요일이 되어서야 도착할 것 같다고 하였다. 따라서 (C)가 정답이다.

어휘 receipt n. 수령, 영수증 notify v. 알리다, 통지하다
request v. 요청하다, 신청하다; n. 요청, 요구

45 다음에 할 일 문제

해석 여자는 수요일에 무엇을 할 것이라고 말하는가?
(A) 새로운 일을 시작한다.
(B) 손상된 책상을 반납한다.
(C) 홈 오피스를 개조한다.
(D) 이전 고용주에게 전화한다.

해설 질문의 핵심 어구(Wednesday)가 언급된 주변을 주의 깊게 듣는다. 여자가 "I begin a new job on Wednesday"라며 자신이 수요일에 새로운 일을 시작한다고 하였다. 따라서 (A)가 정답이다.

어휘 return v. 반납하다, 돌려주다 damaged adj. 손상된
remodel v. 개조하다 former adj. 이전의, 전자의

Paraphrasing

begin a new job 새로운 일을 시작하다 → Start a new job 새로운 일을 시작하다

46 이유 문제

해석 남자는 왜 창고에 전화를 할 계획인가?
(A) 분실된 물건의 수색을 준비할 것이다.
(B) 직원에게 초과 근무를 요청할 것이다.
(C) 고객의 배송 주소를 확인할 것이다.
(D) 분실된 포장물에 대해 문의할 것이다.

해설 질문의 핵심 어구(call a warehouse)가 언급된 주변을 주의 깊게 듣는다. 남자가 "I'll call our warehouse now and ask if one of the drivers is willing to work late today"라며 지금 창고에 전화해서 운전기사 중 한 명이 오늘 늦게까지 근무할 수 있는지 물어보겠다고 하였다. 따라서 (B)가 정답이다.

어휘 verify v. 확인하다, 입증하다 inquire v. 문의하다, 묻다

Paraphrasing

one of the drivers 운전기사 중 한 명 → an employee 직원
work late 늦게까지 근무하다 → work overtime 초과 근무를 하다

[47-49]

🎧 미국식 → 캐나다식

Questions 47-49 refer to the following conversation.

W: ⁴⁷**Thanks for helping me set up the display case for this new novel, Greg.** Customers have been asking about this book for weeks now.

M: No problem. Oh, by the way . . . ⁴⁸**Did you see the notice in the break room?**

W: ⁴⁸**Do you mean the one about volunteering at the flea market to raise money for the animal shelter next Friday?**

M: Yeah. Our store is one of the event's sponsors.

W: I want to help out, but I'm scheduled to work here that day. Um . . . ⁴⁹**I'm going to go ask Mike to change shifts with me.**

set up 설치하다, 준비하다 display case 진열대, 진열 선반
novel n. 소설 by the way 그건 그렇고 notice n. 공지글, 공고문
volunteer v. 봉사활동 하다 flea market 벼룩시장
raise v. (기금을) 모으다, 들어 올리다 shelter n. 보호소
sponsor n. 후원 업체, 광고주; v. 후원하다 shift n. 교대 근무

해석
47-49번은 다음 대화에 관한 문제입니다.

여: ⁴⁷신규 소설의 진열대를 설치하는 데 도움을 주셔서 감사해요, Greg. 고객들이 지금까지 몇 주 동안 이 책에 대해 문의해 왔어요.

남: 문제없어요. 아, 그건 그렇고... ⁴⁸휴게실에 있는 공지글 보셨어요?

여: ⁴⁸다음 주 금요일에 동물 보호소를 위한 기금을 모으기 위해서 벼룩시장에서 봉사활동 하는 것에 관한 글 말인가요?

남: 네. 우리 가게가 그 행사의 후원 업체 중 하나예요.

여: 저도 돕고 싶은데, 그날 여기서 일할 예정이에요. 음... ⁴⁹Mike에게 교대 근무를 바꿔 달라고 부탁해야겠어요.

47 장소 문제

해석 대화는 어디에서 일어나는 것 같은가?

(A) 서점에서
(B) 슈퍼마켓에서
(C) 병원에서
(D) 자동차 대리점에서

해설 장소와 관련된 표현을 놓치지 않고 듣는다. 여자가 "Thanks for helping me set up the display case for this new novel, Greg."이라며 신규 소설의 진열대를 설치하는 데 도움을 주어서 고맙다고 한 것을 통해 서점에서 대화가 일어나고 있음을 알 수 있다. 따라서 (A)가 정답이다.

어휘 dealership n. 대리점, 판매 대리점

48 특정 세부 사항 문제

해석 직원들은 어떤 종류의 행사에 대해 공지 받았는가?
(A) 모금 행사
(B) 개업식
(C) 기자회견
(D) 워크숍

해설 질문의 핵심 어구(staff members notified about)와 관련된 내용을 주의 깊게 듣는다. 남자가 "Did you see the notice in the break room?"이라며 휴게실에 있는 공지글을 봤는지 묻자, 여자가 "Do you mean the one about volunteering at the flea market to raise money for the animal shelter next Friday?"라며 다음 주 금요일에 동물 보호소를 위한 기금을 모으기 위해서 벼룩시장에서 봉사활동 하는 것에 관한 글을 말하는 것인지 물었다. 따라서 (A)가 정답이다.

Paraphrasing

raise money 기금을 모으다 → A fundraiser 모금 행사

49 다음에 할 일 문제

해석 여자는 다음에 무엇을 할 것 같은가?
(A) 휴식을 취한다.
(B) 기부를 한다.
(C) 동료와 이야기한다.
(D) 진열대를 설치한다.

해설 대화의 마지막 부분을 주의 깊게 듣는다. 여자가 "I'm going to go ask Mike to change shifts with me."라며 Mike에게 교대 근무를 바꿔 달라고 부탁해야겠다고 한 것을 통해 여자가 동료와 이야기할 것임을 알 수 있다. 따라서 (C)가 정답이다.

어휘 donation n. 기부, 기증 coworker n. 동료, 협력자

[50-52] 3ᵢ 호주식 → 미국식

Questions 50-52 refer to the following conversation.

M: I'm a little worried. The tractor won't start. Hiring a mechanic will be expensive.
W: The warranty may still be valid. ⁵⁰Why don't you call the service center and check?
M: I'll do that now. ⁵¹Could you pass me my phone? It's on the counter right beside you.
W: Here you go . . . Do you need anything else?

M: No. You should talk to our workers, though. They are probably wondering what is going on.
W: Right. ⁵²I'll tell them that we won't be planting the crops today as planned.

tractor n. 트랙터, 견인차 mechanic n. 정비사
expensive adj. 비용이 많이 드는, 비싼 warranty n. (품질) 보증서
valid adj. 유효한, 타당한 plant v. 심다; n. 식물 crop n. 작물, 수확량

해석
50-52번은 다음 대화에 관한 문제입니다.
남: 저는 조금 걱정돼요. 트랙터가 시동이 걸리지 않아요. 정비사를 고용하는 것은 비용이 많이 들 거예요.
여: 보증서가 여전히 유효할 수도 있어요. ⁵⁰서비스 센터에 전화해서 확인해 보는 건 어때요?
남: 지금 그렇게 할게요. ⁵¹제 휴대전화 좀 건네주실래요? 당신 바로 옆에 있는 카운터 위에 있어요.
여: 여기요... 더 필요한 게 있으신가요?
남: 아니요. 하지만 저희 직원들에게 이야기해 주세요. 아마 무슨 일인지 궁금할 거예요.
여: 맞아요. ⁵²그들에게 오늘 계획했던 것처럼 작물을 심지 못할 거라고 말할게요.

50 의도 파악 문제

해석 여자는 왜 "보증서가 여전히 유효할 수도 있어요"라고 말하는가?
(A) 제안을 하기 위해
(B) 설명을 요청하기 위해
(C) 해명을 요구하기 위해
(D) 결정에 동의하기 위해

해설 질문의 인용어구(The warranty may still be valid)가 언급된 주변을 주의 깊게 듣는다. 여자가 "Why don't you call the service center and check?"라며 서비스 센터에 전화해서 확인해 보는 건 어떤지 물은 것을 통해 제안을 하기 위함을 알 수 있다. 따라서 (A)가 정답이다.

어휘 suggestion n. 제안 explanation n. 설명
clarification n. 해명, 설명

51 요청 문제

해석 남자는 여자에게 무엇을 요청하는가?
(A) 설명서
(B) 기기
(C) 음료
(D) 영수증

해설 남자의 말에서 요청과 관련된 표현이 언급된 다음을 주의 깊게 듣는다. 남자가 여자에게 "Could you pass me my phone?"이라며 자신의 휴대전화를 건네줄 수 있는지 물었다. 따라서 (B)가 정답이다.

어휘 beverage n. 음료, 마실 것

Paraphrasing

phone 휴대전화 → A device 기기

52 특정 세부 사항 문제

해석 여자는 직원들에게 무엇을 말할 것인가?
(A) 휴가가 허락될 것이다.
(B) 기계가 구매될 것이다.
(C) 센터가 방문될 것이다.
(D) 작업이 지연될 것이다.

해설 질문의 핵심 어구(tell some workers)와 관련된 내용을 주의 깊게 듣는다. 여자가 "I'll tell them[workers] that we won't be planting the crops today as planned."라며 직원들에게 오늘 계획했던 것처럼 작물을 심지 못할 것임을 말하겠다고 하였다. 따라서 (D)가 정답이다.

어휘 leave n. 휴가; v. 출발하다, 떠나다　grant v. 허락하다, 인정하다

[53-55]

[🔊] 미국식 → 캐나다식 → 호주식

Questions 53-55 refer to the following conversation with three speakers.

W: Good morning. My name is Beth Coyle, and I have an appointment at 2 P.M. I need shots taken for my modeling portfolio.
M1: Of course. **53You booked a two-hour session with our head photographer, Andy Amir, right?**
W: Yes. **54I saw his photographs on his social media account.** They were great.
M2: That's good to hear, Ms. Coyle. **53I'm Andy.** Are you ready to get started?
W: Yeah. But first, **55do you think this outfit is suitable?** If not, I brought some other options.
M2: It looks fine to me.

appointment n. 예약, 약속　outfit n. 의상, 옷

해석
53-55번은 다음 세 명의 대화에 관한 문제입니다.

여: 안녕하세요. 제 이름은 Beth Coyle이고, 오후 2시에 예약했어요. 제 모델직 포트폴리오를 위해 사진을 찍어야 해요.
남1: 물론이죠. 53저희 수석 사진작가인 Andy Amir와 두 시간 일정을 예약하셨어요, 그렇죠?
여: 네. 54그의 소셜 미디어 계정에서 사진들을 보았어요. 그것들은 정말 멋졌어요.
남2: 다행이네요, Ms. Coyle. 53제가 Andy입니다. 시작할 준비가 되셨나요?
여: 네. 하지만 먼저, 55이 의상이 적합하다고 생각하시나요? 그렇지 않다면, 저는 다른 옵션들을 좀 가져왔어요.
남2: 저에게는 괜찮아 보여요.

53 화자 문제

해석 남자들은 어디에서 일하는 것 같은가?
(A) 출판 회사에서
(B) 광고 대행사에서
(C) 미술관에서
(D) 사진 스튜디오에서

해설 대화에서 신분 및 직업과 관련된 표현을 놓치지 않고 듣는다. 남

자1이 "You booked a two-hour session with our head photographer, Andy Amir, right?"이라며 수석 사진작가인 Andy Amir와 두 시간 일정을 예약한 게 맞는지를 물은 후, 남자2가 "I'm Andy."라며 자신이 Andy라고 한 것을 통해, 남자들은 사진 스튜디오에서 일한다는 것을 알 수 있다. 따라서 (D)가 정답이다.

어휘 publishing n. 출판, 발행

54 이유 문제

해석 여자는 왜 Mr. Amir를 선택했는가?
(A) 온라인에서 그의 작품을 보았다.
(B) 그와 함께 프로젝트에 참여했었다.
(C) 회사로부터 그의 포트폴리오를 받았다.
(D) 광고에서 그를 발견했다.

해설 질문의 핵심어구(choose Mr. Amir)와 관련된 내용을 주의 깊게 듣는다. 여자가 "I saw his[Mr. Amir's] photographs on his social media account."라며 Mr. Amir의 소셜 미디어 계정에서 사진들을 보았다고 하였다. 따라서 (A)가 정답이다.

어휘 involve v. 참여시키다, 포함하다　notice v. 발견하다, 주목하다

Paraphrasing

saw ~ photographs 사진들을 보았다 → viewed ~ work 작품을 보았다

on ~ social media account 소셜 미디어 계정에서 → online 온라인에서

55 특정 세부 사항 문제

해석 여자는 무엇에 대해 묻는가?
(A) 장비 특징
(B) 복장 선택
(C) 계정 비밀번호
(D) 가격 옵션

해설 대화에서 여자의 말을 주의 깊게 듣는다. 여자가 남자에게 "do you think this outfit is suitable?"이라며 의상이 적합하다고 생각하는지를 물었다. 따라서 (B)가 정답이다.

어휘 equipment n. 장비, 용품　choice n. 선택(권)
account n. 계정, 계좌

Paraphrasing

outfit 의상 → clothing 복장

[56-58]

[🔊] 캐나다식 → 영국식

Questions 56-58 refer to the following conversation.

M: Now, **56I'll just need to weigh your luggage before I give you the boarding pass for your flight.** Please put it on the scale.
W: Sure. **57I think my bag is just under the limit. It's 20 kilograms, right?**
M: The limit is 18 kilograms. I'm afraid you're going to have to pay an additional fee.

W: Really? **58My carry-on bag is almost empty. I'll just move some stuff into it.**

weigh v. 무게를 측정하다   luggage n. 수하물, (여행용) 짐
boarding pass 탑승권   flight n. 항공편, 비행   scale n. 저울, 규모
limit n. 한도, 제한; v. 제한하다   fee n. 요금, 수수료
carry-on adj. 기내용의, 휴대용의   empty adj. 비어 있는; v. 비우다

해석
56-58번은 다음 대화에 관한 문제입니다.

남: 이제, 56항공편 탑승권을 드리기 전에 고객님의 수하물 무게를 측정해야 합니다. 저울에 올려주세요.

여: 물론이죠. 57제 가방이 한도에 조금 못 미치는 것 같아요. 20킬로그램이잖아요, 맞죠?

남: 한도는 18킬로그램이에요. 죄송합니다만 추가 요금을 내셔야 할 거예요.

여: 정말요? 58제 기내용 가방이 거의 비어 있어요. 물건을 그냥 거기에 옮길게요.

56 장소 문제

해석   화자들은 어디에 있는 것 같은가?
(A) 기차역에
(B) 버스 정류장에
(C) 페리 터미널에
(D) 공항에

해설   대화에서 장소와 관련된 표현을 놓치지 않고 듣는다. 남자가 여자에게 "I'll just need to weigh your luggage before I give you the boarding pass for your flight"라며 항공편 탑승권을 주기 전에 수하물 무게를 측정해야 한다고 한 것을 통해 화자들이 공항에 있음을 알 수 있다. 따라서 (D)가 정답이다.

어휘   railway station 기차역   ferry n. 페리, 배

57 의도 파악 문제

해석   남자는 왜 "한도는 18킬로그램이에요"라고 말하는가?
(A) 가정을 정정하기 위해
(B) 실수에 대해 사과하기 위해
(C) 변경 사항을 지적하기 위해
(D) 해결책을 제공하기 위해

해설   질문의 인용어구(The limit is 18 kilograms)가 언급된 주변을 주의 깊게 듣는다. 여자가 "I think my bag is just under the limit. It's 20 kilograms, right?"이라며 가방이 한도에 조금 못 미치는 것 같다며, 한도가 20킬로그램이 맞는지 묻자, 남자가 "The limit is 18 kilograms."라며 한도가 18킬로그램이라고 한 것을 통해 남자가 여자의 가정을 정정하고 있음을 알 수 있다. 따라서 (A)가 정답이다.

어휘   assumption n. 가정

58 다음에 할 일 문제

해석   여자는 다음에 무엇을 할 것인가?
(A) 옷을 구입한다.
(B) 신분증을 제시한다.

(C) 추가 요금을 지불한다.
(D) 물건들을 옮긴다.

해설   대화의 마지막 부분을 주의 깊게 듣는다. 여자가 "My carry-on bag is almost empty. I'll just move some stuff into it."이라며 기내용 가방이 거의 비어 있어서 물건을 그냥 거기에 옮기겠다고 하였다. 따라서 (D)가 정답이다.

어휘   identification card 신분증

Paraphrasing

some stuff 물건 → some items 물건들

[59-61]
③ 영국식 → 캐나다식

Questions 59-61 refer to the following conversation.

W: **59The Java Cup café chain just announced that it will begin selling sandwiches next month.** This really surprised me.

M: That's bad news for us. There's a Java Cup branch across the street from our deli. **60If our customers decide to get their lunches there while having coffee, our revenue will decline.**

W: Exactly. **61What about having daily specials? If people know they can get a different sandwich at a reduced price each day, they'll probably keep coming back.**

deli n. 조제 식품 판매점   revenue n. 매출, 수입
decline v. 줄어들다, 감소하다   special n. 특선 메뉴

해석
59-61번은 다음 대화에 관한 문제입니다.

여: 59Java Cup 카페 체인점이 다음 달부터 샌드위치 판매를 시작할 것이라고 방금 발표했어요. 이것은 저를 정말 놀라게 했어요.

남: 우리에겐 안 좋은 소식이네요. 우리 조제 식품 판매점 바로 건너편에 Java Cup 지점이 있잖아요. 60우리 고객들이 커피를 마시면서 그곳에서 점심을 먹기로 결정한다면, 우리 매출은 줄어들 거예요.

여: 맞아요. 61매일 특선 메뉴를 제공하는 것은 어떨까요? 사람들이 매일 다른 샌드위치를 할인된 가격에 구입할 수 있다는 사실을 알게 된다면, 아마 계속 찾아올 거예요.

59 특정 세부 사항 문제

해석   Java Cup 카페 체인점은 무엇을 발표했는가?
(A) 고객 클럽
(B) 제품군
(C) 상호 변경
(D) 가격 인상

해설   질문의 핵심 어구(Java Cup café chain announce)가 언급된 주변을 주의 깊게 듣는다. 여자가 "The Java Cup café chain just announced that it will begin selling sandwiches next month."라며 Java Cup 카페 체인점이 다음 달부터 샌드위치 판매를 시작할 것이라고 방금 발표했다고 하였다. 따라서 (B)가 정답이다.

어휘   product line 제품군

60 문제점 문제

해석 남자는 무슨 걱정을 표하는가?
(A) 판촉 행사가 곧 종료될 것이다.
(B) 도로가 차단될 것이다.
(C) 식당은 더 적은 돈을 벌 것이다.
(D) 점심 특선 메뉴가 인기가 없어질 것이다.

해설 남자의 말에서 부정적인 표현이 언급된 주변을 주의 깊게 듣는다. 남자가 "If our customers decide to get their lunches there[Java Cup branch] while having coffee, our revenue will decline."이라며 고객들이 커피를 마시면서 Java Cup 지점에서 점심을 먹기로 결정한다면 매출이 줄어들 것이라고 하였다. 따라서 (C)가 정답이다.

어휘 promotional adj. 판촉의, 홍보용의   earn v. 벌다, 얻다
unpopular adj. 인기가 없는

Paraphrasing

revenue ~ decline 매출이 줄다 → earn less money 더 적은 돈을 벌다

61 제안 문제

해석 여자는 무엇을 제안하는가?
(A) 자문가 만나기
(B) 정기 할인 제공하기
(C) 다른 지점 열기
(D) 재료 변경하기

해설 여자의 말에서 제안과 관련된 표현이 언급된 다음을 주의 깊게 듣는다. 여자가 남자에게 "What about having daily specials? If people know they can get a different sandwich at a reduced price each day, they'll probably keep coming back."이라며 매일 특선 메뉴를 제공하는 것은 어떤지 물은 후, 사람들이 매일 다른 샌드위치를 할인된 가격에 구입할 수 있다는 사실을 알게 된다면 아마 계속 찾아올 것이라고 하였다. 따라서 (B)가 정답이다.

어휘 regular adj. 정기적인   ingredient n. 재료

[62-64]

[3] 영국식 → 캐나다식

Questions 62-64 refer to the following conversation and map.

W: ⁶²**Did you hear that the underground parking area of our office building will be inaccessible from May 10 to 12?** Some workers will be repairing a water pipe.

M: But ⁶³**Ms. Sampson is coming here for a meeting on May 11.** She's a major client.

W: Don't worry. ⁶³**I've arranged to use the parking garage on the corner of Franklin Drive and 4th Avenue on those days.**

M: I'll call Ms. Sampson and give her directions.

W: When you do that, ⁶⁴**ask her for the license plate number of her vehicle.** I'll send it to the garage so that she won't be charged for parking.

underground adj. 지하의
inaccessible adj. 이용할 수 없는, 접근할 수 없는   water pipe 수도관 ○

parking garage 주차장   direction n. 길, 방향
license plate number (차량의) 등록 번호   vehicle n. 차량
charge v. 요금을 부과하다; n. 요금

해석
62-64번은 다음 대화와 지도에 관한 문제입니다.

여: ⁶²5월 10일부터 12일까지 사무실 건물의 지하 주차장을 이용할 수 없을 거라는 소식 들으셨어요? 몇몇 작업자들이 수도관을 수리할 거예요.

남: 하지만 ⁶³Ms. Sampson이 5월 11일에 회의를 위해서 이곳에 방문할 거예요. 그녀는 주된 고객이에요.

여: 걱정하지 마세요. ⁶³그날 Franklin로와 4번가 모퉁이에 있는 주차장을 이용하도록 준비해 놓았어요.

남: 제가 Ms. Sampson에게 전화해서 길을 알려드릴게요.

여: 그렇게 하실 때, ⁶⁴그녀에게 차량 등록 번호를 물어봐 주세요. 그녀에게 주차 요금이 부과되지 않도록 그것을 차고에 보내놓을게요.

62 문제점 문제

해석 여자는 무슨 문제를 언급하는가?
(A) 기술자가 늦을 것이다.
(B) 차량이 손상되었다.
(C) 도로가 막혔다.
(D) 시설이 닫힐 것이다.

해설 여자의 말에서 부정적인 표현이 언급된 주변을 주의 깊게 듣는다. 여자가 "Did you hear that the underground parking area of our office building will be inaccessible from May 10 to 12?"라며 5월 10일부터 12일까지 사무실 건물의 지하 주차장을 이용할 수 없을 거라는 소식을 들었는지 물었다. 따라서 (D)가 정답이다.

Paraphrasing

the underground parking area 지하 주차장 → A facility 시설
be inaccessible 이용할 수 없다 → be closed 닫히다

63 시각 자료 문제

해석 시각 자료를 보아라. Ms. Sampson은 어디에 주차할 것 같은가?
(A) 건물 A
(B) 건물 B
(C) 건물 C
(D) 건물 D

해설 제시된 지도의 정보를 확인한 후 질문의 핵심 어구(Ms. Sampson ~ park)와 관련된 내용을 주의 깊게 듣는다. 남자가 "Ms. Sampson is coming here for a meeting on May 11"라며 Ms. Sampson

이 5월 11일에 회의를 위해서 이곳에 방문할 것이라고 하자, 여자가 "I've arranged to use the parking garage on the corner of Franklin Drive and 4th Avenue on those days."라며 그날 Franklin로와 4번가 모퉁이에 있는 주차장을 이용하도록 준비해 놓았다고 하였으므로 Ms. Sampson이 주차할 곳은 건물 A임을 지도에서 알 수 있다. 따라서 (A)가 정답이다.

64 요청 문제

해석 여자는 남자에게 무엇을 하라고 요청하는가?
(A) 차고 주인에게 연락한다.
(B) 직원에게 길 안내를 제공한다.
(C) 고객에게 정보를 요청한다.
(D) 주차권을 구입한다.

해설 여자의 말에서 요청과 관련된 표현이 언급된 다음을 주의 깊게 듣는다. 여자가 남자에게 "ask her[Ms. Sampson] for the license plate number of her vehicle"이라며 Ms. Sampson에게 차량 등록 번호를 물어보라고 하였다. 따라서 (C)가 정답이다.

어휘 parking pass 주차권

Paraphrasing

the license plate number of ~ vehicle 차량 등록 번호 → information 정보

[65-67]

③ 호주식 → 미국식

Questions 65-67 refer to the following conversation and directory.

M: Belmont Department Store. How may I help you?
W: Good morning. ⁶⁵**Your Web site shows that you do not currently have the Wave Z10 Dishwasher in stock. When will you get more?**
M: Actually, a shipment just arrived this morning.
W: ⁶⁶**I'll stop by the store tomorrow, then. I want to compare that dishwasher with a few other ones.**
M: Sure. Our sales staff will be happy to assist you.
W: Oh, and ⁶⁷**I heard that you were offering all loyalty club members a 10 percent discount. Is that sale still on?**
M: ⁶⁷**Yes.** Just show your card to the cashier when you pay.

dishwasher n. 식기 세척기   in stock 재고가 있는
shipment n. 배송, 수송품   stop by ~에 들르다
compare v. 비교하다, 비유하다   assist v. 돕다, 보조하다
cashier n. 계산원   appliance n. 가전제품, (가정용) 기기
goods n. 용품, 제품

해석
남: Belmont 백화점입니다. 무엇을 도와드릴까요?
여: 안녕하세요. ⁶⁵웹사이트에 현재 Wave Z10 식기 세척기의 재고가 없는 것으로 보여요. 언제 더 입고되나요?
남: 사실, 오늘 아침에 배송이 막 도착했습니다.
여: ⁶⁶그러면 제가 내일 매장에 들를게요. 그 식기세척기를 다른 몇 가지 제품들과 비교해 보고 싶어요.

남: 물론이죠. 저희 영업 직원이 기꺼이 도와드릴 것입니다.
여: 아, 그리고 ⁶⁷모든 고객 클럽 회원들에게 10퍼센트 할인을 제공하고 있었다고 들었어요. 그 할인이 아직 진행 중인가요?
남: ⁶⁷네. 결제할 때 계산원에게 카드를 제시하기만 하면 됩니다.

Belmont 백화점	
층	매장
1	의류
⁶⁵2	가전제품
3	스포츠용품
4	가구

65 시각 자료 문제

해석 시각 자료를 보아라. 여자가 문의한 제품은 어느 층에 있는가?
(A) 1층
(B) 2층
(C) 3층
(D) 4층

해설 제시된 안내판의 정보를 확인한 후 질문의 핵심 어구(product ~ asked about)와 관련된 내용을 주의 깊게 듣는다. 여자가 "Your Web site shows that you do not currently have the Wave Z10 Dishwasher in stock. When will you get more?"라며 웹 사이트에 현재 Wave Z10 식기 세척기의 재고가 없는 것으로 보이는데 언제 더 입고되는지를 문의하였으므로 여자가 문의한 제품이 있는 층은 2층임을 안내판에서 알 수 있다. 따라서 (B)가 정답이다.

Paraphrasing

Dishwasher 식기 세척기 → Appliances 가전제품

66 이유 문제

해석 여자는 왜 내일 매장을 방문할 것인가?
(A) 이전 구매품을 교환하기 위해
(B) 쿠폰을 사용하기 위해
(C) 몇몇 모델들을 비교하기 위해
(D) 상품권을 구매하기 위해

해설 질문의 핵심 어구(visit the store tomorrow)와 관련된 내용을 주의 깊게 듣는다. 여자가 "I'll stop by the store tomorrow, then. I want to compare that dishwasher with a few other ones."라며 내일 매장에 들러 식기 세척기를 다른 몇 가지 제품들과 비교해 보고 싶다고 하였다. 따라서 (C)가 정답이다.

어휘 make use of ~을 사용하다   gift certificate 상품권

Paraphrasing

visit 방문하다 → stop by 들르다

67 특정 세부 사항 문제

해석 남자는 여자에게 무엇에 대해 보장하는가?
(A) 멤버십 카드가 유효하다.
(B) 소포가 오늘 배달될 것이다.

(C) 담당자가 전화를 할 것이다.

(D) 판촉 행사가 아직 진행 중이다.

해설 질문의 핵심 어구(assure)와 관련된 내용을 주의 깊게 듣는다. 여자가 "I heard that you were offering all loyalty club members a 10 percent discount. Is that sale still on?"이라며 모든 고객 클럽 회원들에게 10퍼센트 할인을 제공하고 있었다고 들었는데 아직 할인이 진행 중인지 묻자, 남자가 "Yes."라며 맞다고 하였다. 따라서 (D)가 정답이다.

어휘 valid adj. 유효한, 타당한 available adj. 진행 중인, 이용할 수 있는

Paraphrasing

sale 할인 → A promotion 판촉 행사

Is ~ on 진행 중이다 → is ~ available 진행 중이다

[68-70]

3세 캐나다식 → 영국식

Questions 68-70 refer to the following conversation and calendar.

M: ⁶⁸**Do we have enough employees at our vegetable market, or do we need to hire more?**

W: We are going to need new staff members for the summer, I think.

M: I guess you're right. ⁶⁹**Our region is famous for cucumbers, so the month in which they are harvested is always the busiest for us.**

W: I'll put a sign in our window saying we are looking for help, then.

M: We probably won't get many applicants if we just do that. ⁷⁰**I'll post a job advertisement on an employment Web site as well.**

vegetable n. 야채, 채소 region n. 지역 cucumber n. 오이 harvest v. 수확하다 sign n. 팻말, 신호 as well 또한, 역시

해석

68-70번은 다음 대화와 달력에 관한 문제입니다.

남: ⁶⁸우리 야채 시장에 충분한 직원들이 있나요, 아니면 더 고용해야 할까요?

여: 여름에는 신입 직원들이 필요할 것 같아요.

남: 당신 말이 맞을 것 같네요. ⁶⁹우리 지역은 오이가 유명해서, 그것들이 수확되는 달이 항상 가장 바빠요.

여: 그러면, 제가 우리 가게 창문에 일손을 구하고 있다는 팻말을 붙여 둘게요.

남: 그렇게만 해서는 많은 지원자들을 얻지 못할 거예요. ⁷⁰제가 구인 웹사이트에도 구인 광고를 게시할게요.

수확 달력				
	6월	⁶⁹7월	8월	9월
비트	√			
호박			√	
오이		√		
감자				√

68 특정 세부 사항 문제

해석 남자는 무엇에 대해 문의하는가?

(A) 신선한 야채를 보관하는 것

(B) 더 많은 고객을 유치하는 것

(C) 영업시간을 변경하는 것

(D) 추가 직원들을 고용하는 것

해설 대화에서 남자의 말을 주의 깊게 듣는다. 남자가 여자에게 "Do we have enough employees at our vegetable market, or do we need to hire more?"라며 야채 시장에 충분한 직원들이 있는지, 아니면 더 고용해야 할지 물었다. 따라서 (D)가 정답이다.

어휘 store v. 보관하다, 저장하다; n. 가게 attract v. 유치하다, 끌어모으다 operating adj. 영업의, 운영상의

Paraphrasing

more 더 → additional 추가의

employees 직원들 → workers 직원들

69 시각 자료 문제

해석 시각 자료를 보아라. 시장에서 가장 바쁜 달은 어느 달인가?

(A) 6월

(B) 7월

(C) 8월

(D) 9월

해설 제시된 달력의 정보를 확인한 후 질문의 핵심 어구(busiest month at the market)와 관련된 내용을 주의 깊게 듣는다. 남자가 "Our region is famous for cucumbers, so the month in which they are harvested is always the busiest for us."라며 화자들이 있는 지역은 오이가 유명해서 그것들이 수확되는 달이 항상 가장 바쁘다고 하였으므로 시장에서 가장 바쁜 달은 7월임을 달력에서 알 수 있다. 따라서 (B)가 정답이다.

70 제안 문제

해석 남자는 무엇을 해주겠다고 제안하는가?

(A) 매장 진열대를 다시 채운다.

(B) 농산물 공급업체에 연락한다.

(C) 마케팅 자료를 디자인한다.

(D) 온라인 게시글을 쓴다.

해설 남자의 말에서 제안과 관련된 표현이 언급된 다음을 주의 깊게 듣는다. 남자가 "I'll post a job advertisement on an employment Web site as well."이라며 구인 웹사이트에도 구인 광고를 게시하겠다고 하였다. 따라서 (D)가 정답이다.

어휘 restock v. 다시 채우다, 보충하다 supplier n. 공급업체 material n. 자료, 재료

Paraphrasing

post ~ advertisement on ~ Web site 웹사이트에 광고를 게시하다 → Make an online post 온라인 게시글을 쓰다

PART 4

[71-73]

Questions 71-73 refer to the following telephone message.

Ms. Martins, this is Leslie Sparks calling. ⁷¹**After considering my options, I have decided to go with the rental unit you showed me last week.** I like the location in the Castro neighborhood. And a one-bedroom unit should be sufficient during my stay from March 1 to June 30. ⁷²**One thing that is still unclear is if the fitness center on the second floor can be used free of charge.** Regardless, ⁷³**please set up a time with the owner for me to sign the contract**. You can reach me at 555-3984. Have a nice morning.

rental n. 임대, 대여   unit n. 숙소, 단위
neighborhood n. 지역, 이웃, 인근   sufficient adj. 충분한
unclear adj. 불확실한, 잘 모르는   free of charge 무료로
owner n. 주인, 소유주   contract n. 계약(서)
reach v. 연락하다, 도달하다

해석
71-73번은 다음 전화 메시지에 관한 문제입니다.

Ms. Martins, 저는 Leslie Sparks입니다. ⁷¹선택지들을 고려해 본 후에, 저는 지난주에 보여주셨던 임대 숙소로 결정했습니다. Castro 지역의 위치가 마음에 들어요. 그리고 3월 1일부터 6월 30일까지 제가 머무는 동안 침실이 하나인 곳이면 충분할 것 같아서요. ⁷²한 가지 아직 불확실한 것은 2층에 있는 헬스클럽이 무료로 이용 가능한지 여부입니다. 어쨌든, ⁷³제가 계약서에 서명할 수 있도록 집주인과 시간을 잡아주세요. 555-3984로 연락해 주시면 됩니다. 좋은 아침 되세요.

71 목적 문제

해석   화자는 왜 전화를 하고 있는가?
(A) 청자에게 결정을 알리기 위해
(B) 방이 이용 가능한지 확인하기 위해
(C) 청자에게 제안을 고려할 것을 요청하기 위해
(D) 아파트를 볼 것을 요청하기 위해

해설   전화의 목적을 묻는 문제이므로, 지문의 초반을 반드시 듣는다. "After considering my options, I have decided to go with the rental unit you showed me last week."이라며 선택지들을 고려해 본 후에, 지난주에 보여 줬던 임대 숙소로 결정했다고 한 후, 계약을 위해 시간을 잡아달라는 내용으로 지문이 이어지고 있다. 따라서 (A)가 정답이다.

어휘   notify v. 알리다, 통지하다   decision n. 결정, 판단

72 특정 세부 사항 문제

해석   화자는 무엇에 대해 확신이 없는가?
(A) 계약서를 어디로 보내야 하는지
(B) 지역에서 무엇을 해야 하는지
(C) 시설을 사용하는 게 무료인지
(D) 임대 기간이 언제 종료될지

해설   질문의 핵심 어구(unsure about)와 관련된 내용을 주의 깊게 듣는

다. "One thing that is still unclear is if the fitness center on the second floor can be used free of charge."라며 한 가지 아직 불확실한 것은 2층에 있는 헬스클럽이 무료로 이용 가능한지 여부라고 하였다. 따라서 (C)가 정답이다.

어휘   facility n. 시설, 기능   period n. 기간, 시기

Paraphrasing

unsure 확신이 없는 → unclear 불확실한
free of charge 무료로 → free 무료인

73 요청 문제

해석   화자는 청자에게 무엇을 하라고 요청하는가?
(A) 신청을 취소한다.
(B) 보증금 결제를 처리한다.
(C) 계약서를 수정한다.
(D) 약속을 정한다.

해설   지문의 중후반에서 요청과 관련된 표현이 포함된 문장을 주의 깊게 듣는다. "please set up a time with the owner for me to sign the contract"라며 계약서에 서명할 수 있도록 집주인과 시간을 잡아달라고 하였다. 따라서 (D)가 정답이다.

어휘   deposit n. 보증금, 착수금   revise v. 수정하다, 개정하다

Paraphrasing

set up a time 시간을 잡다 → Arrange an appointment 약속을 정하다

[74-76]

Questions 74-76 refer to the following talk.

⁷⁴**Next Tuesday, we will need to replace all of the winter clothing on our sales floor with spring clothing.** And we will do this after the store has closed so as not to inconvenience our customers. I estimate that the task will take about three hours if enough of you are involved. ⁷⁵**Please let me know by the end of the day whether you are available to help out.** ⁷⁶**Those of you who decide to participate will receive a list of the products we need to take out that day from Mr. Parker, the store's assistant manager.**

sales floor 매장   inconvenience v. 불편하게 하다; n. 불편
estimate v. 예상하다, 추산하다; n. 견적서
involve v. 참여시키다, 관련시키다   participate v. 참여하다, 참석하다
assistant manager 부관리자, 부팀장

해석
74-76번은 다음 담화에 관한 문제입니다.

⁷⁴다음 주 화요일에, 우리는 매장에 있는 모든 겨울 의류를 봄 의류로 교체해야 할 것입니다. 그리고 고객들을 불편하게 하지 않도록 하기 위해 매장 영업이 끝난 후에 이 작업을 할 것입니다. 저는 충분한 인원이 참여한다면 그 일이 약 세 시간 소요될 것이라고 예상합니다. ⁷⁵여러분들이 도와줄 수 있는지 여부를 오늘까지 저에게 알려주시기 바랍니다. ⁷⁶참여하기로 결정하신 분들은 매장 부관리자인 Mr. Parker로부터 그날 반출해야 할 제품 목록을 받

을 것입니다.

74 다음에 할 일 문제

해석 다음 주 화요일에 무슨 일이 일어날 것인가?
(A) 상점이 평소보다 더 일찍 문을 닫을 것이다.
(B) 새로운 상품들이 진열될 것이다.
(C) 옷이 할인가에 제공될 것이다.
(D) 관리자가 작업 공간을 점검할 것이다.

해설 질문의 핵심 어구(next Tuesday)가 언급된 주변을 주의 깊게 듣는다. "Next Tuesday, we will need to replace all of the winter clothing on our sales floor with spring clothing."이라며 다음 주 화요일에 매장에 있는 모든 겨울 의류를 봄 의류로 교체해야 할 것이라고 하였다. 따라서 (B)가 정답이다.

어휘 inspect v. 점검하다, 검사하다   workspace n. 작업 공간

75 요청 문제

해석 화자는 청자들에게 무엇을 하라고 요청하는가?
(A) 매주 초과 근무를 한다.
(B) 자신의 근무 가능 여부를 알린다.
(C) 오래된 옷을 보관 창고에 둔다.
(D) 문을 닫은 후 매장을 청소한다.

해설 지문의 중후반에서 요청과 관련된 표현이 포함된 문장을 주의 깊게 듣는다. "Please let me know by the end of the day whether you are available to help out."이라며 청자들이 도와줄 수 있는지 여부를 오늘까지 알려달라고 하였다. 따라서 (B)가 정답이다.

어휘 on a weekly basis 매주, 주 단위로
storage area 보관 창고, 저장소

76 특정 세부 사항 문제

해석 화자에 따르면, Mr. Parker는 무엇을 제공할 것인가?
(A) 안전 장비
(B) 신청서
(C) 제품 목록
(D) 청소용품

해설 질문의 핵심 어구(Mr. Parker provide)와 관련된 내용을 주의 깊게 듣는다. "Those of you who decide to participate will receive a list of the products we need to take out that day from Mr. Parker, the store's assistant manager."라며 참여하기로 결정한 사람들은 매장 부관리자인 Mr. Parker로부터 그날 반출해야 할 제품 목록을 받을 것이라고 하였다. 따라서 (C)가 정답이다.

어휘 gear n. 장비, 복장   registration n. 신청, 등록
supply n. 용품, 보급품; v. 공급하다

[77-79]   3배 미국식
Questions 77-79 refer to the following excerpt from a meeting.

Before we end today's meeting, ⁷⁷**I want to provide an update on the Norton Public Library landscaping project**. We will begin work next Wednesday. ⁷⁸**Note that the parking lot next to the library only allows one hour** ○

---

of parking without a special permit. I will provide these to everyone on the first day of the project. One more thing . . . As you know, we will be planting several trees in front of the building, as well as bushes along the walkways. ⁷⁹**The city government has decided not to use exotic plant species and to go with local ones. It makes sense.** They will be easy to maintain.

landscaping n. 조경   parking lot 주차장
permit n. 허가(증); v. 허락하다   plant v. (식물을) 심다; n. 식물
bush n. 덤불   walkway n. 산책로   exotic adj. 외래의, 이국적인
make sense 이해하다, 말이 되다   maintain v. 유지 관리하다

해석
77-79번은 다음 회의 발췌록에 관한 문제입니다.
오늘 회의를 마치기 전에, ⁷⁷Norton 공공 도서관 조경 프로젝트에 대한 최신 정보를 전달하고자 합니다. 우리는 다음 주 수요일에 작업을 시작할 것입니다. ⁷⁸도서관 옆 주차장은 특별 허가증 없이는 한 시간만 주차를 허용한다는 점에 유의하세요. 제가 프로젝트 첫날에 모든 분들께 이것들을 드릴 것입니다. 한 가지 더... 아시다시피, 우리는 건물 앞에 여러 그루의 나무를 심고, 산책로를 따라 덤불도 심을 것입니다. ⁷⁹시 정부는 외래종을 사용하지 않고 현지 식물을 사용하기로 결정했습니다. 이해가 됩니다. 그것들은 유지 관리가 쉬울 테니까요.

77 화자 문제

해석 화자는 어떤 산업에서 일하는가?
(A) 조경
(B) 접객
(C) 언론 매체
(D) 배송

해설 지문에서 신분 및 직업과 관련된 표현을 놓치지 않고 듣는다. "I want to provide an update on the Norton Public Library landscaping project"라며 Norton 공공 도서관 조경 프로젝트에 대한 최신 정보를 전달하고자 한다고 한 것을 통해 화자는 조경 산업에서 일한다는 것을 알 수 있다. 따라서 (A)가 정답이다.

어휘 hospitality n. 접객(업), 환대

78 특정 세부 사항 문제

해석 화자는 청자들에게 무엇을 줄 것인가?
(A) 사용 설명서
(B) 신청서
(C) 신분증명서
(D) 주차권

해설 질문의 핵심 어구(give the listeners)와 관련된 내용을 주의 깊게 듣는다. "Note that the parking lot next to the library only allows one hour of parking without a special permit. I will provide these to everyone on the first day of the project."라며 도서관 옆 주차장은 특별 허가증 없이는 한 시간만 주차를 허용한다는 점에 유의하라고 한 후, 프로젝트 첫날 청자들에게 이것들을 줄 것이라고 하였다. 따라서 (D)가 정답이다.

Paraphrasing

a special permit 특별 허가증 → Parking passes 주차권

79 의도 파악 문제

해석 화자는 "그것들은 유지 관리가 쉬울 테니까요"라고 말할 때 무엇을 의도하는가?
(A) 현지 시설들은 충분하다.
(B) 그녀는 선택에 동의한다.
(C) 그녀는 다른 선택안을 선호한다.
(D) 건축 자재는 내구성이 뛰어나다.

해설 질문의 인용어구(They will be easy to maintain)가 언급된 주변을 주의 깊게 듣는다. "The city government has decided not to use exotic plant species and to go with local ones. It makes sense."라며 시 정부는 외래종을 사용하지 않고 현지 식물을 사용하기로 결정했다고 한 후, 이것이 이해가 된다고 한 것을 통해 시 정부의 선택에 동의하는 것임을 알 수 있다. 따라서 (B)가 정답이다.

어휘 adequate adj. 충분한, 적절한 durable adj. 내구성이 뛰어난

[80-82]
[호주식]
Questions 80-82 refer to the following announcement.

Attention, all passengers. In approximately 15 minutes, 80the train will be arriving at Tahoma Station. For those of you attending the national baseball championship game this afternoon, 80the stadium is on Parker Avenue, just one block from the station. 81Travelers who require a taxi can catch one at the stand next to Exit 3. If you are continuing on with us, 82please note that there will be a 30-minute delay before we depart for the next station. There is a problem with the doors of one of the cars, and a technician will need to replace a damaged part. We apologize for the inconvenience.

passenger n. 승객 approximately adv. 약, 대략
stadium n. 경기장
stand n. (택시·버스 등이 승객을 기다리는) 승차장, 정류소
delay n. 지연, 지체; v. 미루다 depart v. 출발하다, 떠나다
technician n. 기술자, 기사 damaged adj. 손상된
apologize for ~하여 죄송하다, ~에 사과하다

해석

80-82번은 다음 공지에 관한 문제입니다.

주목해 주십시오, 모든 승객 여러분. 약 15분 후, 80열차가 Tahoma 역에 도착합니다. 오늘 오후에 열리는 전국 야구 선수권 대회 경기에 참석하시는 분들의 경우, 80경기장은 역에서 한 블록 떨어진 Parker가에 있습니다. 81택시가 필요한 여행객들은 3번 출구 옆 승차장에서 택시를 잡으세요. 계속 저희와 함께하신다면, 82다음 역을 향해 출발하기까지 30분 정도 지연될 수 있음을 유의해주시기 바랍니다. 열차 중 한 칸의 문에 문제가 있어, 기술자가 손상된 부품을 교체할 것입니다. 불편을 드려 죄송합니다.

80 특정 세부 사항 문제

해석 화자는 Tahoma역 근처에 무엇이 있다고 말하는가?

(A) 관공서
(B) 국립 박물관
(C) 스포츠 시설
(D) 공공 공원

해설 질문의 핵심 어구(Tahoma Station)가 언급된 주변을 주의 깊게 듣는다. "the train will be arriving at Tahoma Station"이라며 열차가 Tahoma역에 도착할 것이라고 한 후, "the stadium is on Parker Avenue, just one block from the station"이라며 경기장이 역에서 한 블록 떨어진 Parker가에 있다고 하였다. 따라서 (C)가 정답이다.

어휘 national adj. 국립의

Paraphrasing

the stadium 경기장 → A sports facility 스포츠 시설

81 언급 문제

해석 3번 출구에 대해 무엇이 언급되는가?
(A) 중앙 출입구이다.
(B) 택시 승차장 근처에 있다.
(C) 수리를 위해 폐쇄되었다.
(D) 큰 호텔 옆에 있다.

해설 질문의 핵심 어구(Exit 3)가 언급된 주변을 주의 깊게 듣는다. "Travelers who require a taxi can catch one at the stand next to Exit 3."라며 택시가 필요한 여행객들은 3번 출구 옆 승차장에서 택시를 잡으라고 하였다. 따라서 (B)가 정답이다.

82 이유 문제

해석 화자에 따르면, 왜 지연이 있을 것인가?
(A) 승무원이 교체될 것이다.
(B) 역이 청소될 것이다.
(C) 차량에 연료가 공급될 것이다.
(D) 수리가 될 것이다.

해설 질문의 핵심 어구(delay)가 언급된 주변을 주의 깊게 듣는다. "please note that there will be a 30-minute delay before we depart for the next station. There is a problem with the doors of one of the cars, and a technician will need to replace a damaged part."라며 다음 역을 향해 출발하기까지 30분 정도 지연될 수 있음을 유의해달라고 한 후, 열차 중 한 칸의 문에 문제가 있어서 기술자가 손상된 부품을 교체할 것이라고 하였다. 따라서 (D)가 정답이다.

어휘 crew n. 승무원, 선원 fuel v. 연료를 공급하다; n. 연료

Paraphrasing

will ~ replace a damaged part 손상된 부품을 교체할 것이다
→ A repair will be made 수리가 될 것이다

Questions 83-85 refer to the following news report.

> [3] 캐나다식

> **83This is Dale Sanchez reporting live from Harrison Park. Preparations are underway here for the final concert by the jazz musician Sonny Wallace,** who recently announced his intention to retire. The free outdoor show is expected to attract over 2,000 fans to the park this afternoon. While the organizers are pleased, **84some people living in the area worry about being inconvenienced by traffic congestion.** The nearby streets are very narrow. Therefore, the city government is encouraging attendees to use public transportation. **85Stay tuned for more about this news story following a short commercial break.**

report v. 보도하다, 보고하다; n. 보도 preparation n. 준비, 대비
underway adj. 진행 중인 intention n. 의사, 의도 retire v. 은퇴하다
attract v. 끌어모으다 organizer n. 주최자, 조직 위원
pleased adj. 반기는, 기쁜 congestion n. 혼잡 narrow adj. 좁은
encourage v. 권장하다, 격려하다 attendee n. 참석자
following prep. ~ 후에 commercial break 광고

해석
83-85번은 다음 뉴스 보도에 관한 문제입니다.

83Harrison 공원에서 생방송으로 보도하고 있는 Dale Sanchez입니다. 여기서 재즈 음악가 Sonny Wallace의 마지막 콘서트를 위한 준비가 한창 진행 중인데, 그는 최근 은퇴 의사를 밝혔습니다. 그 무료 야외 공연은 오늘 오후 2,000명이 넘는 팬들을 끌어모을 것으로 예상됩니다. 주최자들은 반기지만, 84그 지역에 거주하는 일부 사람들은 교통 혼잡으로 인해 불편을 겪게 되는 것을 우려합니다. 인근 도로가 매우 좁습니다. 따라서, 시 정부는 참석자들에게 대중교통을 이용할 것을 권장하고 있습니다. 85짧은 광고 후에 이 보도 기사에 대한 자세한 내용을 계속 들어주세요.

83 특정 세부 사항 문제

해석 Harrison 공원에서 어떤 종류의 행사가 열릴 것인가?
(A) 스포츠 대회
(B) 음악 공연
(C) 불꽃놀이
(D) 미술 전시회

해설 질문의 핵심 어구(Harrison Park)가 언급된 주변을 주의 깊게 듣는다. "This is Dale Sanchez reporting live from Harrison Park. Preparations are underway here for the final concert by the jazz musician ~"이라며 Harrison 공원에서 생방송으로 보도하고 있는 Dale Sanchez라고 한 후, 여기서 재즈 음악가의 마지막 콘서트를 위한 준비가 한창 진행 중이라고 하였다. 따라서 (B)가 정답이다.

어휘 competition n. 대회, 경연 performance n. 공연, 업무

Paraphrasing

concert 콘서트 → A musical performance 음악 공연

84 의도 파악 문제

해석 화자는 "인근 도로가 매우 좁습니다"라고 말할 때 무엇을 의도하는가?

(A) 제안이 수용 가능하다.
(B) 계획이 비현실적이다.
(C) 위치가 알맞지 않다.
(D) 걱정이 당연하다.

해설 질문의 인용어구(The nearby streets are very narrow)가 언급된 주변을 주의 깊게 듣는다. "some people living in the area worry about being inconvenienced by traffic congestion"이라며 그 지역에 거주하는 일부 사람들이 교통 혼잡으로 인해 불편을 겪게 되는 것을 우려한다고 한 것을 통해 도로가 좁아서 사람들의 걱정이 당연함을 알 수 있다. 따라서 (D)가 정답이다.

어휘 acceptable adj. 수용 가능한 impractical adj. 비현실적인
unsuitable adj. 알맞지 않은 legitimate adj. 당연한, 합법적인

85 특정 세부 사항 문제

해설 청자들은 다음에 무엇을 들을 것인가?
(A) 광고
(B) 교통 최신 정보
(C) 일기 예보
(D) 인터뷰

해설 질문의 핵심 어구(hear next)와 관련된 내용을 주의 깊게 듣는다. "Stay tuned for more about this news story following a short commercial break."라며 짧은 광고 후에 이 보도 기사에 대한 자세한 내용을 계속 들어달라고 하였다. 따라서 (A)가 정답이다.

어휘 forecast n. 예보, 예측; v. 예측하다

Paraphrasing

commercial break 광고 → An advertisement 광고

Questions 86-88 refer to the following advertisement.

> [3] 영국식

> **86Do you want your glasses to reflect your unique personality? If so, Vision Masters has what you need!** **87What makes us stand out from our competitors is that we help our customers create personalized frames.** Our professional designers will consult with you to fully understand your idea. Then, we will use our advanced software to create exactly what you want. Once the design is finalized, your frames will be ready for pickup within a week. Still not convinced? **88Go to our Web site, and look through the many glowing reviews from our customers.** You will see that we never disappoint!

reflect v. 반영하다 unique adj. 독특한, 개별적인
personality n. 개성, 성격 stand out 눈에 띄다
competitor n. 경쟁사, 경쟁자 personalized adj. 개인 맞춤형의
frame n. (안경)테, (액자)틀 professional adj. 전문적인; n. 전문가
consult v. 상담하다 advanced adj. 고급의 exactly adv. 정확하게
finalize v. 완성하다, 마치다 pickup n. 수령
convinced adj. 확신하고 있는 look through ~을 살펴보다, 훑어보다
glowing adj. 생생한, 빛나는 disappoint v. 실망시키다, 낙담시키다

해석
86-88번은 다음 광고에 관한 문제입니다.

⁸⁶당신의 안경에 자신만의 독특한 개성을 반영하기를 원하시나요? 그렇다면, Vision Masters가 당신이 필요한 것을 가지고 있습니다! ⁸⁷저희를 경쟁사들로부터 눈에 띄게 만드는 점은 고객님들이 개인 맞춤형 안경테를 만들 수 있도록 도와드린다는 점입니다. 저희 전문적인 디자이너들이 고객님의 생각을 완벽하게 이해하기 위해서 상담을 진행할 것입니다. 그리고 나서, 저희는 고객님이 원하는 것을 정확하게 제작해 내기 위해 고급 소프트웨어를 사용할 것입니다. 일단 디자인이 완성되면, 안경테는 일주일 이내에 수령이 준비될 것입니다. 아직 확신이 없으시다고요? ⁸⁸저희 웹사이트를 방문하시어, 고객님들의 많은 생생한 후기를 살펴보세요. 저희가 절대 실망시키지 않는다는 것을 알게 될 것입니다!

86 주제 문제

해석 무엇이 광고되고 있는가?
(A) 가정용품 가게
(B) 의류 양품점
(C) 안경점
(D) 공예품 시장

해설 광고의 주제를 묻는 문제이므로, 지문의 초반을 반드시 듣는다. "Do you want your glasses to reflect your unique personality? If so, Vision Masters has what you need!"라며 안경에 자신만의 독특한 개성을 반영하기를 원한다면, Vision Masters가 필요한 것을 가지고 있다고 하였다. 따라서 (C)가 정답이다.

어휘 boutique n. 양품점, 값비싼 옷을 파는 가게   eyewear n. 안경류
craft n. (수)공예, 기술; v. 공예품을 만들다

Paraphrasing

glasses 안경 → eyewear 안경

87 특정 세부 사항 문제

해석 화자는 업체에 대해 무엇이 특별하다고 말하는가?
(A) 맞춤형 제품을 만든다.
(B) 무료 수리를 제공한다.
(C) 천연 재료를 사용한다.
(D) 배송 서비스를 제공한다.

해설 질문의 핵심 어구(special about the business)와 관련된 내용을 주의 깊게 듣는다. "What makes us stand out from our competitors is that we help our customers create personalized frames."라며 경쟁사들로부터 눈에 띄게 만드는 점은 고객들이 개인 맞춤형 안경테를 만들 수 있도록 도와준다는 점이라고 하였다. 따라서 (A)가 정답이다.

어휘 custom adj. 맞춤형의   complimentary adj. 무료의

Paraphrasing

special 특별한 → stand out from ~ competitors 경쟁사들로부터 눈에 띄다

personalized 개인 맞춤형의 → custom 맞춤형의

88 제안 문제

해석 화자는 청자들에게 무엇을 하라고 권하는가?

(A) 회원권을 신청한다.
(B) 추첨에 참여한다.
(C) 온라인 주문을 한다.
(D) 몇몇 의견을 읽는다.

해설 지문의 중후반에서 제안과 관련된 표현이 포함된 문장을 주의 깊게 듣는다. "Go to our Web site, and look through the many glowing reviews from our customers."라며 웹사이트를 방문하여 고객들의 많은 생생한 후기를 살펴보라고 하였다. 따라서 (D)가 정답이다.

어휘 sign up for ~을 신청하다   raffle n. 추첨, 복권 판매
feedback n. 의견

Paraphrasing

look through ~을 살펴보다 → Read 읽다

reviews 후기 → feedback 의견

[89-91]

Questions 89-91 refer to the following podcast.

Welcome to this week's episode of *Open World*. ⁸⁹**Today, I want to talk about White Sands Beach, a hidden gem of a travel destination located in California.** To get to it by car, follow Highway 101 north from San Francisco until you reach the small town of Greenwood. This community is famous for its scenic beach and delicious seafood. However, visitors should note that ⁹⁰**the Coast Lodge is the only hotel in Greenwood, and it has a small number of rooms.** Bookings must be made well in advance. ⁹¹**There is also a company called Ocean Experience that can arrange everything from snorkeling to fishing trips.** I'll provide details about its prices at the end of this podcast.

hidden adj. 숨겨진   gem n. 명소, 보석   get to ~에 도착하다
community n. 마을, 지역 사회   be famous for ~으로 유명하다
scenic adj. 아름다운, 경치가 좋은   seafood n. 해산물
note v. 유의하다, 기록하다   booking n. 예약, 계약
in advance 미리, 앞서   arrange v. 준비하다, 마련하다
detail n. 자세한 정보, 세부 사항

해석
89-91번은 다음 팟캐스트에 관한 문제입니다.

이번 주 *Open World* 에피소드에 오신 것을 환영합니다. ⁸⁹오늘, 캘리포니아에 위치한 숨겨진 관광 명소인 White Sands 해변에 대해 이야기하려고 합니다. 자동차로 도착하시려면, 작은 마을인 Greenwood에 도착할 때까지 샌프란시스코에서 101번 고속도로를 따라 북쪽으로 가시면 됩니다. 이 마을은 아름다운 해변과 맛있는 해산물로 유명해요. 하지만, ⁹⁰Greenwood에는 Coast Lodge가 유일한 호텔이며, 적은 수의 객실을 보유하고 있다는 점에 유의하셔야 합니다. 예약이 꼭 미리 되어야 해요. ⁹¹스노클링부터 낚시 여행까지 모든 것을 준비할 수 있는 Ocean Experience라는 회사도 있습니다. 제가 이 팟캐스트의 마지막에 그곳의 가격에 대한 자세한 정보를 알려드릴게요.

89 청자 문제

해석 팟캐스트는 누구를 위한 것인가?
(A) 호텔 소유주들
(B) 여행가들
(C) 자동차 애호가들
(D) 예술가들

해설 지문에서 신분 및 직업과 관련된 표현을 놓치지 않고 듣는다. "Today, I want to talk about White Sands Beach, a hidden gem of a travel destination located in California."라며 오늘 캘리포니아에 위치한 숨겨진 관광 명소인 White Sands 해변에 대해 이야기하려고 한다고 한 것을 통해 팟캐스트가 여행가들을 위한 것임을 알 수 있다. 따라서 (B)가 정답이다.

어휘 enthusiast n. 애호가, 열렬한 지지자

90 언급 문제

해석 화자는 Coast Lodge에 대해 무엇을 말하는가?
(A) 두 번째 지점을 열었다.
(B) 객실들을 곧 개조할 수도 있다.
(C) 소수의 손님들을 수용할 수 있다.
(D) 방문객들에게 가이드 투어를 제공한다.

해설 질문의 핵심 어구(Coast Lodge)가 언급된 주변을 주의 깊게 듣는다. "the Coast Lodge is the only hotel in Greenwood, and it has a small number of rooms"라며 Greenwood에는 Coast Lodge가 유일한 호텔이고 적은 수의 객실을 보유하고 있다고 하였다. 따라서 (C)가 정답이다.

어휘 accommodate v. 수용하다, 공간을 제공하다

Paraphrasing

has a small number of rooms 적은 수의 객실을 보유하고 있다 → accommodate few guests 소수의 손님들을 수용하다

91 특정 세부 사항 문제

해석 화자는 무슨 정보를 공유할 것인가?
(A) 행사 일정
(B) 행사장 위치
(C) 업체 이름
(D) 활동 비용

해설 질문의 핵심 어구(information ~ share)와 관련된 내용을 주의 깊게 듣는다. "There is also a company called Ocean Experience that can arrange everything from snorkeling to fishing trips. I'll provide details about its prices at the end of this podcast."라며 스노클링부터 낚시 여행까지 모든 것을 준비할 수 있는 Ocean Experience라는 회사도 있다고 한 후, 이 팟캐스트의 마지막에 그곳의 가격에 대한 자세한 정보를 알려주겠다고 하였다. 따라서 (D)가 정답이다.

어휘 activity n. 활동

Paraphrasing

information 정보 → details 자세한 정보

prices 가격 → costs 비용

[92-94]
🎧 미국식

Questions 92-94 refer to the following talk.

Good morning. As you know, **⁹²we've decided to hold cooking classes as a way to get more customers to come to the store and buy our kitchen appliances.** Today is the first day. **⁹³A group of beginners arrives this morning at 11.** And it's almost 10 already. **⁹³We still have a lot to do in preparation.** I'll go to the supermarket now to get the remaining ingredients we need for the class. While I'm gone, **⁹⁴I'd like the rest of you to arrange some chairs for the students in the area where our instructor will be demonstrating cooking techniques.** We will need 15 in total.

appliance n. (가정용) 기기, 가전 beginner n. 초보자, 초심자
preparation n. 준비, 대비 remaining adj. 나머지의, 남아 있는
ingredient n. 재료 rest n. 나머지 instructor n. 강사
demonstrate v. 시연하다, 설명하다 technique n. 기법, 기술
in total 총, 통틀어

해석

92-94번은 다음 담화에 관한 문제입니다.

좋은 아침입니다. 아시다시피, **⁹²우리는 더 많은 고객이 매장에 와서 우리 주방 기기를 구매하도록 할 방법의 일환으로 요리 수업을 열기로 결정했습니다.** 오늘이 첫날이에요. **⁹³초보자 무리가 오늘 아침 11시에 도착합니다.** 그리고 벌써 10시가 다 되어갑니다. **⁹³우리는 아직 준비할 게 많습니다.** 제가 지금 수업에 필요한 나머지 재료들을 사러 슈퍼마켓에 갈게요. 제가 없는 동안, **⁹⁴나머지 분들은 강사님이 요리 기법을 시연할 공간에 학생들을 위한 의자 몇 개를 준비해 주세요.** 총 15개가 필요합니다.

92 화자 문제

해석 화자의 회사는 무엇을 판매하는 것 같은가?
(A) 교육 자료
(B) 요리 도구
(C) 사무용품
(D) 스포츠 장비

해설 대화에서 신분 및 직업과 관련된 표현을 놓치지 않고 듣는다. "we've decided to hold cooking classes as a way to get more customers to come to the store and buy our kitchen appliances"라며 더 많은 고객이 매장에 와서 주방 기기를 구매하도록 할 방법의 일환으로 요리 수업을 열기로 결정했다고 하였다. 따라서 (B)가 정답이다.

어휘 educational adj. 교육의, 교육적인 gear n. 장비

Paraphrasing

kitchen appliances 주방 기기 → Cooking equipment 요리 도구

93 의도 파악 문제

해석 화자가 "그리고 벌써 10시가 다 되어갑니다"라고 말할 때 무엇을 의도하는가?

(A) 몇몇 직원들이 늦게 도착했다.
(B) 매장이 정규 시간에 문을 닫을 것이다.
(C) 몇몇 작업들이 빨리 되어야 한다.
(D) 마감일이 변경될 것 같다.

해설 질문의 인용어구(And it's almost 10 already)가 언급된 주변을 주의 깊게 듣는다. "A group of beginners arrives this morning at 11."이라며 초보자 무리가 오늘 아침 11시에 도착한다고 한 후, "We still have a lot to do in preparation."이라며 아직 준비할 게 많다고 한 것을 통해 몇몇 작업들이 빨리 완료되어야 함을 알 수 있다. 따라서 (C)가 정답이다.

어휘 regular adj. 정규의, 정기적인

94 다음에 할 일 문제

해석 청자들은 다음에 무엇을 할 것인가?

(A) 강사와 만난다.
(B) 교통편을 마련한다.
(C) 가구를 준비한다.
(D) 시연을 제공한다.

해설 지문의 후반부를 주의 깊게 듣는다. "I'd like the rest of you to arrange some chairs for the students ~"라며 나머지 사람들은 학생들을 위한 의자 몇 개를 준비해 달라고 하였다. 따라서 (C)가 정답이다.

Paraphrasing

arrange some chairs 의자 몇 개를 준비하다 → Set up some furniture 가구를 준비하다

[95-97]

3ᵈ 영국식

Questions 95-97 refer to the following excerpt from a meeting and schedule.

I'd like to inform everyone that Maya won't be able to come in today due to a family emergency. So ⁹⁵/⁹⁶**Brian will be taking over Maya's cut and coloring appointment today.** The client has already been informed and is comfortable with the change. However, please allow me to remind you that ⁹⁶/⁹⁷**a customer complained yesterday about a treatment drying out her hair.** Nothing is more important to us than our clients' satisfaction. Please don't get distracted while working.

inform v. 알리다, 통지하다 take over ~을 대신하다, 인계받다
appointment n. 예약, 약속
be comfortable with ~을 이해하다, ~을 편하게 여기다
remind v. 상기시키다, 다시 한번 얘기하다 satisfaction n. 만족
distracted adj. 주의가 산만한, 집중하지 못하는

해석

95-97번은 다음 회의 발췌록과 일정표에 관한 문제입니다.

Maya가 급한 가족 일로 인해 오늘 오지 못한다는 것을 모두에게 알려드리고자 합니다. 그래서 ⁹⁵/⁹⁶Brian이 오늘 Maya의 커트 및 염색 예약을 대신할 것입니다. 그 고객님은 이미 알고 계시며 변동에 대해 이해하셨습니다. 하지만, ⁹⁶/⁹⁷어제 한 고객님이 자신의 머리를 건조하게 만들었다고 시술에 대해 불평하셨다는 사실을 상기시켜 드리고자 합니다. 저희에게는 고객님들의 만족보다 더 중요한 것은 없습니다. 일하는 동안 주의가 산만해지지 않도록 해주세요.

예약 일정		
		1월 18일
시간	고객	직원
오전 10시	Barbara Lloyd	Lydia Parker
오전 11시 30분	⁹⁵Steven Jeffrey	Maya Jimenez
오후 2시 15분	Simone Meyer	Connor Abramovich
오후 6시	Kenichi Isaki	Dillon Smith

95 시각 자료 문제

해석 시각 자료를 보아라. Brian은 어떤 고객에게 서비스를 제공할 것 같은가?

(A) Barbara Lloyd
(B) Steven Jeffrey
(C) Simone Meyer
(D) Kenichi Isaki

해설 제시된 일정표의 정보를 확인한 후 질문의 핵심 어구(Brian)가 언급된 주변을 주의 깊게 듣는다. "Brian will be taking over Maya's cut and coloring appointment today"라며 Brian이 오늘 Maya의 커트 및 염색 예약을 대신할 것이라고 하였으므로 Brian이 서비스를 제공할 고객은 Steven Jeffrey임을 일정표에서 알 수 있다. 따라서 (B)가 정답이다.

96 청자 문제

해석 청자들은 누구인 것 같은가?

(A) 미용사들
(B) 치과 의사들
(C) 재정 고문들
(D) 기술자들

해설 지문에서 신분 및 직업과 관련된 표현을 놓치지 않고 듣는다. "Brian will be taking over Maya's cut and coloring appointment today"라며 Brian이 오늘 Maya의 커트 및 염색 예약을 대신할 것이라고 한 후, "a customer complained yesterday about a treatment drying out her hair"라며 어제 한 고객이 자신의 머리를 건조하게 만들었다고 시술에 대해 불평했다고 한 것을 통해 청자들이 미용사들임을 알 수 있다. 따라서 (A)가 정답이다.

어휘 financial adj. 재정의, 금융의 advisor n. 고문, 조언자

97 특정 세부 사항 문제

해석 화자에 따르면, 어제 무슨 일이 일어났는가?

(A) 한 직원이 휴가를 요청했다.
(B) 정책 변경이 시행되었다.
(C) 프로젝트 마감일이 지켜지지 않았다.
(D) 한 고객이 불만을 제기했다.

해설 질문의 핵심 어구(yesterday)가 언급된 주변을 주의 깊게 듣는다. "a customer complained yesterday about a treatment drying out her hair"라며 어제 한 고객이 자신의 머리를 건조하게 만들었다고 시술에 대해 불평했다고 하였다. 따라서 (D)가 정답이다.

어휘 implement v. 시행하다, 실시하다 complaint n. 불만, 불평

Paraphrasing

a customer 고객 → A client 고객

complained 불평했다 → made a complaint 불만을 제기했다

[98-100]

③ 호주식

Questions 98-100 refer to the following talk and pie chart.

⁹⁸**Our company has experienced a significant drop in sales due to increased competition.** We are actually losing a lot of money right now. ⁹⁸**This means we're going to have to cut down on some departmental expenses.** I've prepared this chart showing each department's share of our budget. Most of our funds are going to manufacturing, and I don't think we should cut back in that department. However, ⁹⁹**spending in the department that uses 20 percent of our budget can be reduced without severely impacting operations.** ¹⁰⁰**I'll be passing out this chart so you all can get a closer look at these figures.**

cut down on ~을 줄이다 departmental adj. 부서의, 부문의
expense n. 비용, 경비 fund n. 자금, 돈 manufacturing n. 제조(업)
severely adv. 심하게, 혹독하게 impact v. 영향을 미치다
operation n. 운영 figure n. 수치 lawn mower 잔디 깎는 기계

해석

98-100번은 다음 담화와 원그래프에 관한 문제입니다.

⁹⁸우리 회사는 심화된 경쟁으로 인해 상당한 매출 감소를 겪었습니다. 실제로 현재 많은 손실을 보고 있습니다. ⁹⁸이는 우리가 일부 부서의 비용을 줄여야 한다는 뜻입니다. 저는 각 부서의 예산 비중을 보여주는 이 그래프를 준비했습니다. 대부분의 자금이 제조에 투입되고 있는데, 그 부서의 비용을 줄여서는 안 된다고 생각합니다. 하지만, ⁹⁹예산의 20퍼센트를 사용하는 부서의 지출은 운영에 심하게 영향을 미치지 않으면서 줄일 수 있습니다. ¹⁰⁰여러분 모두가 이 수치를 자세히 살펴볼 수 있도록 이 그래프를 나눠드리겠습니다.

Turner 잔디 깎는 기계:
총지출 비율

마케팅 18%
제조 35%
영업 27%
회계 20%

98 목적 문제

해석 담화의 목적은 무엇인가?
(A) 예산 증가를 발표하기 위해
(B) 문제를 해결하기 위한 방법을 설명하기 위해
(C) 계획의 실행을 비판하기 위해
(D) 팀의 성과를 칭찬하기 위해

해설 담화의 목적을 묻는 문제이므로, 지문의 초반을 주의 깊게 들은 후 전체 맥락을 파악한다. "Our company has experienced a significant drop in sales due to increased competition.", "This means we're going to have to cut down on some departmental expenses."라며 회사가 심화된 경쟁으로 인해 상당한 매출 감소를 겪었으며, 이는 일부 부서의 비용을 줄여야 한다는 뜻이라고 한 후, 비용을 줄이는 방법에 대한 내용으로 지문이 이어지고 있다. 따라서 (B)가 정답이다.

99 시각 자료 문제

해석 시각 자료를 보아라. 화자는 어느 부서의 지출을 삭감할 것을 제안하는가?
(A) 제조
(B) 마케팅
(C) 영업
(D) 회계

해설 제시된 원그래프의 정보를 확인한 후 질문의 핵심 어구(department ~ recommend cutting spending on)와 관련된 내용을 주의 깊게 듣는다. "spending in the department that uses 20 percent of our budget can be reduced without severely impacting operations"라며 예산의 20퍼센트를 사용하는 부서의 지출은 운영에 심하게 영향을 미치지 않으면서 줄일 수 있다고 하였으므로 지출을 삭감할 것을 제안하는 부서는 회계 부서임을 원그래프에서 알 수 있다. 따라서 (D)가 정답이다.

100 다음에 할 일 문제

해석 화자는 다음에 무엇을 할 것 같은가?
(A) 자료를 배포한다.
(B) 몇 가지 수정을 한다.
(C) 그룹 발표를 본다.
(D) 새로운 발표자를 소개한다.

해설 지문의 마지막 부분을 주의 깊게 듣는다. "I'll be passing out this chart so you all can get a closer look at these figures."라며 청자들 모두가 수치를 자세히 살펴볼 수 있도록 그래프를 나눠주겠다고 하였다. 따라서 (A)가 정답이다.

어휘 distribute v. 배포하다, 나눠주다 correction n. 수정, 정정
presentation n. 발표, 제출 introduce v. 소개하다

Paraphrasing

be passing out 나눠주다 → Distribute 배포하다

PART 5

101 주어와 수일치하는 동사 채우기

해설 문장에 동사가 없으므로 동사 (A)와 (B)가 정답의 후보이다. 주어(The organizers)가 복수 명사이므로 동사 report(전하다, 보고하다)의 과거형 (B) reported가 정답이다. 3인칭 단수형 (A)는 단수 주어와 함께 써야 한다. 명사 (C)와 동명사 또는 현재분사 (D)는 동사 자리에 올 수 없다.

해석 주최자들은 기술 학회가 기록적인 참석자 수를 가졌다고 전했다.

어휘 organizer n. 주최자, 조직자 record-breaking adj. 기록적인

102 명사 자리 채우기

해설 전치사(of) 뒤에 올 수 있는 것은 명사이므로 (A), (B), (C)가 정답의 후보이다. '제품 라인을 선보일 것이다'라는 의미가 되어야 하므로 명사 product(제품)의 복수형 (B) products가 정답이다. (A) produce (농작물, 생산물)를 쓰면 어색한 문맥이 되고 (C) production(생산)은 생산 과정이나 생산량을 의미하므로 이 문맥에는 적절하지 않다. 참고로 (A)의 produce는 동사일 때 '생산하다'라는 의미로 쓰임을 알아둔다. 동사 또는 과거분사 (D)는 명사 자리에 올 수 없다.

해석 XinZu 안경사는 유행을 타지 않는 안경테 스타일을 특징으로 삼는 제품 라인을 선보일 것이다.

어휘 present v. 선보이다, 제시하다 feature v. 특징으로 삼다
timeless adj. 유행을 타지 않는 frame n. 안경테, 틀

103 부사 자리 채우기

해설 동사구(go over)를 꾸밀 수 있는 것은 부사이므로 부사 (C) carefully(주의 깊게)가 정답이다. 형용사 (A)와 명사 (B), 형용사의 비교급 (D)는 동사를 꾸밀 수 없다.

해석 만약 당신의 계약서가 수정된다면, 그것을 주의 깊게 검토하여 당신이 변경된 사항들에 동의하는 것을 확실하게 하세요.

어휘 go over ~을 검토하다 ensure v. 확실하게 하다, 보장하다
agree with ~에 동의하다

104 부사 어휘 고르기

해설 '직원들을 동기부여할 방법들을 찾기 위해 세미나에 주기적으로 참석하게 하다'라는 문맥이므로 (D) periodically(주기적으로)가 정답이다. (A) artificially는 '인공적으로', (B) loosely는 '느슨하게', (C) overly는 '너무, 몹시'라는 의미이다.

해석 Renfrew 소프트웨어사는 당사의 관리자들이 그들의 직원들을 동기부여할 방법들을 찾는 것을 돕기 위해 리더십 세미나에 주기적으로 참여하도록 한다.

어휘 motivate v. 동기부여하다

105 현재분사와 과거분사 구별하여 채우기

해설 이 문장은 주어(Our keynote speaker), 동사(delivered), 목적어(a speech)를 갖춘 완전한 절이므로, ___ ~ allotted는 수식어 거품으로 보아야 한다. 보기 중 수식어 거품이 될 수 있는 것은 현재분사 (B)와 과거분사 (D)이고, 빈칸 앞의 명사(speech)를 '지속하는 연설'이라는 능동의 의미로 수식하고 있으므로 현재분사 (B) lasting(지속하는)이 정답이다. 동사 last가 '지속하다'라는 의미로 쓰일 경우 자동사이므로 수동형인 과거분사 (D)는 답이 될 수 없다. 동사 또는 부사 (A)와 부사 (C)는 수식어 거품을 이끌 수 없다.

해석 올해 우리의 기조연설자는 할당된 시간보다 20분 더 오래 지속하는 연설을 했다.

어휘 keynote speaker 기조연설자 deliver a speech 연설을 하다

allot v. 할당하다 last v. 지속하다; adv. 마지막에
lastly adv. 마지막으로

106 명사 어휘 고르기

해설 '새 쇼핑센터 개점식에 모든 근로자들의 참석을 요청했다'라는 문맥이므로 (C) presence(참석)가 정답이다. (A) reason은 '이유, 이성', (B) companion은 '동행, 동반자', (D) method는 '방법'이라는 의미이다.

해석 Alba 할인 마트는 당사의 새 쇼핑센터 개점식에 모든 근로자들의 참석을 요청했다.

어휘 request v. 요청하다 opening n. 개점(식), 공석

107 형용사 자리 채우기

해설 빈칸 뒤의 명사(fine)를 꾸밀 수 있는 것은 형용사이므로 형용사 (B)와 형용사 역할을 하는 현재분사 (D)가 정답의 후보이다. '상당한 벌금을 지불하다'라는 의미가 되어야 하므로 형용사 (B) considerable(상당한)이 정답이다. 현재분사 (D) considering을 쓸 경우, '숙고하는 세금'이라는 어색한 문맥을 만든다. 동사 (A)는 형용사 자리에 올 수 없고, 명사 (C) consideration(고려)은 fine(벌금)과 함께 복합 명사를 이루지 못하므로 답이 될 수 없다.

해석 Slansea사는 명시된 기한까지 요구받은 세금 신고서를 제출하지 않아서 상당한 벌금을 지불해야 했다.

어휘 fine n. 벌금 failure n. ~하지 않음, 실패 specified adj. 명시된

최신토익 경향

최근에는 명사를 수식하는 자리에 형용사와 분사를 구별하는 문제가 자주 출제되는데, 형태와 의미가 유사하여 오답률이 높은 편이다. 정확한 의미와 함께 알아두자.

- creative 창의적인 - created 창작된
- acceptable 만족스러운 - accepting 흔쾌히 받아들이는
- understandable 이해할 만한 - understanding 이해심 있는
- disruptive 지장을 주는 - disrupted 방해를 받은
- persuasive 설득력 있는 - persuaded 확신하는
- exhaustive 철저한 - exhausted 기진맥진한, 탈진한

108 전치사 채우기

해설 이 문장은 주어(management), 동사(will be introducing), 목적어(some changes)를 갖춘 완전한 절이므로, ___ determinations by the board는 수식어 거품으로 보아야 한다. 이 수식어 거품은 동사가 없는 거품구이므로, 거품구를 이끌 수 있는 전치사 (A)와 (D)가 정답의 후보이다. '이사회에 의한 결정의 결과로 변화를 도입하다'라는 의미가 되어야 하므로 (D) As a result of(~의 결과로)가 정답이다. (A) Throughout(~내내, ~도처에)을 쓰면 '이사회에 의한 결정 내내 변화를 도입하다'라는 어색한 의미가 된다. 접속부사 (B) Thereafter(그 후에)와 (C) Meanwhile(한편, 그동안에)은 수식어 거품을 이끌 수 없다.

해석 이사회에 의한 결정의 결과로, 경영진은 직원 복리 후생 제도에 몇 가지 변화를 도입할 것이다.

어휘 determination n. 결정 board n. 이사회, 위원회

introduce v. 도입하다, 소개하다   benefits package 복리 후생 제도

109 동사 어휘 고르기

해설 '기사가 다양한 방식들을 다루다'라는 문맥이므로 cover(다루다)의 3인칭 단수형 (B) covers가 정답이다. (A)의 transport는 '이동시키다, 운송하다', (C)의 distribute는 '배부하다, 유통시키다', (D)의 implement는 '시행하다'라는 의미이다.

해석 *Business Weekly*에서 발행된 그 기사는 새 노동법이 고용주들에게 영향을 미칠 다양한 방식들을 다룬다.

어휘 publish v. 발행하다, 출판하다   labor law n. 노동법
employer n. 고용주

110 태에 맞는 동사 채우기

해설 문장에 동사가 없으므로, 동사 (A)와 (B)가 정답의 후보이다. 주어(The Wiltshire Convention Center)와 동사(host)가 'Wiltshire 컨벤션 센터가 개최하다'라는 능동의 의미이므로 능동태 동사인 (B) has been hosting이 정답이다. 참고로, 현재완료진행 시제는 과거부터 현재까지 계속되는 일을 나타내는 시간 표현(for more than 10 years)과 주로 함께 쓰인다. 빈칸 뒤에 목적어(the region's ~ events)가 나왔으므로 과거형 수동태 (A)는 답이 될 수 없다. to 부정사 (C)와 관계사절 (D)는 동사 자리에 올 수 없다.

해석 Wiltshire 컨벤션 센터는 10년 넘게 그 지역의 가장 유명한 행사들을 개최해 오고 있다.

어휘 region n. 지역   prestigious adj. 유명한, 명성이 있는

111 명사 자리 채우기

해설 정관사(the)와 전치사(of) 사이에 올 수 있는 것은 명사이므로 명사 (A) intention이 정답이다. 동사 (B)와 (D), 동사 또는 과거분사 (C)는 명사 자리에 올 수 없다. 참고로, with the intention of를 '~할 목적으로'라는 의미의 숙어 표현으로 알아둔다.

해석 관광객들에게 도시의 명소들로의 용이한 접근을 제공할 목적으로 보스턴에 정기 왕복 버스 서비스가 시작되었다.

어휘 access n. 접근   attraction n. 명소   intend v. 의도하다

112 부사절 접속사 채우기

해설 이 문장은 필수성분(All tenants ~ recyclable materials)을 갖춘 완전한 절이므로 _____ ~ their trash는 수식어 거품으로 보아야 한다. 이 수식어 거품은 주어(they), 동사(dispose of), 목적어(their trash)를 갖춘 완전한 절이므로 부사절 접속사 (A) when(~하는 경우, ~할 때)이 정답이다. 관계대명사 또는 명사절 접속사 (B) that은 관계대명사로 쓰일 경우 뒤에 불완전한 절이 오고, 명사절 접속사로 쓰일 경우 뒤에 완전한 절이 올 수 있지만 이때 명사절은 문장에서 주어, 동사의 목적어, 또는 보어 역할을 하므로 답이 될 수 없다. 전치사 또는 부사 (C), 관계대명사 또는 의문사 (D)는 완전한 절을 이끌 수 없다.

해석 모든 세입자들은 그들이 쓰레기를 버릴 때 모든 재활용품들을 분리하도록 상기된다.

어휘 tenant n. 세입자   remind v. 상기시키다   separate v. 분리하다
dispose of ~을 버리다, 처분하다

113 형용사 어휘 고르기

해설 '관리 직책은 채용을 포함한 많은 책임이 따른다'라는 문맥이므로 (C) supervisory(관리의, 감독의)가 정답이다. (A) hesitant는 '주저하는, 망설이는', (B) apparent는 '분명한, 명백한', (D) obedient는 '말을 잘 듣는, 순종적인'이라는 의미이다.

해석 Strachan 서점의 관리 직책은 채용을 포함한 많은 책임이 따른다.

어휘 position n. 직책, 지위   come with ~이 따르다, 함께 가다
responsibility n. 책임   recruitment n. 채용

114 동사 어휘 고르기

해설 '기술적 문제들로 인해, 어쩔 수 없이 6월 15일로 음악회 일정을 변경했다'라는 문맥이므로 (B) reschedule(일정을 변경하다)이 정답이다. (D) cancel(취소하다)도 해석상 그럴듯해 보이지만, '음악회가 6월 15일로 취소됐다'라는 어색한 문맥을 만들기 때문에 답이 될 수 없다. (A) bother는 '성가시게 하다', (C) associate은 '연상하다, 연관짓다'라는 의미이다.

해석 끊임없는 기술적 문제들로 인해, 행사장 관리자는 어쩔 수 없이 6월 15일로 음악회 일정을 변경했다.

어휘 persistent adj. 끊임없는, 계속되는
force v. (어쩔 수 없이) ~하게 만들다   venue n. 행사장, 장소

최신토익경향

최근, 동사 어휘 문제에서 의미가 비슷한 동사들이 보기에 2개 이상 제시되어 난이도가 높은 경우가 있다. 의미를 정확하게 구별하여 알아두자.

• promote 홍보하다 — support 지지하다, 지원하다
• possess (자산·능력을) 보유하다 — contain ~이 들어있다
• expire (유효 기간이) 만기가 되다 — invalidate (계약을) 무효화하다
• evaluate 평가하다 — estimate 예측하다, 추산하다
• decrease (수량을) 줄이다 — minimize 최소화하다

115 다른 명사를 수식하는 명사 채우기

해설 빈칸은 관계대명사절(that ~ selected)의 꾸밈을 받는 명사 자리이므로 빈칸 앞의 명사 chip(칩)과 함께 쓰여 '칩 제조업체'라는 의미의 복합 명사 chip manufacturer를 만드는 명사 (A) manufacturer(제조업체)가 정답이다. (D) manufacturing(제조업)을 쓸 경우 어색한 문맥을 만들기 때문에 답이 될 수 없다. 동사 또는 명사 (B)와 (C)는 동사로 쓰일 경우 명사 자리에 들어갈 수 없고, 명사로 쓰일 경우 각각 '제조(업)', '제품'이라는 의미로 어색한 문맥을 만든다.

해석 Dunbar사는 Kayline 컴퓨터사가 향후 5년간 자사의 공급업체로 선정한 칩 제조업체이다.

어휘 select v. 선택하다   supplier n. 공급업체

116 격에 맞는 인칭대명사 채우기

해설 빈칸은 명사절 접속사(that)가 생략된 명사절의 주어 자리이므로 주어 자리에 들어갈 수 있는 주격 인칭대명사 (A)와 소유대명사 (C)가 정답의 후보이다. '그녀가 그 직위에 관심이 있다'라는 의미가 되어야 하므로 (A) she가 정답이다. 소유대명사 (C) hers는 '그녀의 것이 그 직위에 관심이 있다'라는 어색한 문맥을 만들기 때문에 답이 될 수 없

다. 소유격 인칭 대명사 (B)와 재귀대명사 (D)는 주어 자리에 올 수 없다.

해석 부서장의 사임 소식을 듣자마자, Ms. Flint는 그 직위에 관심이 있다는 것을 내비쳤다.

어휘 department head 부서장 resignation n. 사임, 사직
indicate v. 내비치다, 나타내다

117 수량 표현 채우기

해설 빈칸 뒤의 복수 명사(cans)를 꾸밀 수 있는 수량 표현인 (A)와 (B)가 정답의 후보이다. '남아 있는 흰색 페인트 통이 없었다'라는 의미가 되어야 하므로 수량 표현 (A) no(~이 없는)가 정답이다. (B) every는 복수 명사를 꾸밀 경우 '~마다'라는 의미로 쓰이므로 답이 될 수 없다. 참고로, every가 '모든'이라는 의미로 쓰일 경우에는 단수 가산 명사를 꾸민다. 부정대명사 (C) anyone(아무나, 누구든지)은 명사를 꾸밀 수 없고, 부정대명사 또는 부정형용사 (D) another(또 다른 하나; 또 다른 하나의)는 이미 언급한 것 이외의 또 다른 하나를 가리킬 때 사용되어 형용사로 쓰일 경우 뒤에 단수 가산 명사가 온다.

해석 Main가에 있는 페인트 용품점과 Blackwell가에 있는 페인트 용품점 둘 다 남아 있는 흰색 페인트 통이 없었다.

어휘 supply store 용품점, 물품 창고

118 전치사 채우기

해설 이 문장은 주어(people), 동사(continue), 목적어(to order food)를 갖춘 완전한 절이므로, ___ ~ in delivery fees는 수식어 거품으로 보아야 한다. 이 수식어 거품은 동사가 없는 거품구이므로, 거품구를 이끌 수 있는 비교급 표현 (A)와 전치사 (C), (D)가 정답의 후보이다. '배달 요금 인상에도 불구하고, 사람들은 계속 주문한다'라는 의미가 되어야 하므로 전치사 (D) Despite(~에도 불구하고)가 정답이다. 비교급 표현 (A) Rather than(~라기보다)과 (C) Instead of(~ 대신에)는 각각 어색한 문맥을 만든다. 부사절 접속사 (B) Even though(비록 ~이지만)는 거품절을 이끌어야 하므로 답이 될 수 없다.

해석 배달 요금 인상에도 불구하고, 사람들은 모바일 플랫폼에서 음식을 계속 주문한다.

어휘 fee n. 요금, 수수료

119 부사 어휘 고르기

해설 '환자들은 약속을 못 지킬 것으로 예상된다면 적어도 하루 일찍 알려야 한다'라는 문맥이므로 (C) at least(적어도, 최소한)가 정답이다. (A) evenly는 '균등하게, 고르게', (B) jointly는 '공동으로', (D) too much는 '지나치게'라는 의미이다.

해석 환자들은 만약 그들이 약속을 지킬 것으로 예상된다면 적어도 하루 일찍 병원에 알려야 한다.

어휘 notify v. 알리다, 통지하다 in advance 일찍, 미리
appointment n. 약속, 예약

120 명사 관련 어구 완성하기

해설 '우편 라벨이 찢어졌기 때문에 소포가 예정대로 운송될 수 없었다'라는 문맥이므로 빈칸 앞의 명사(mailing)와 함께 '우편 라벨'이라

는 의미의 어구 mailing label을 만드는 명사 (D) label(라벨, 표)이 정답이다. (A) program(프로그램)도 명사 mailing과 함께 mailing program(우편 프로그램)으로 쓰일 수 있지만 '우편 프로그램이 부분적으로 찢어지다'라는 어색한 문맥을 만들기 때문에 답이 될 수 없다. (B) term은 '용어', (C) sector는 '(산업 등의) 부문, 분야'라는 의미이다.

해석 우편 라벨이 부분적으로 찢어졌기 때문에 소포가 예정대로 수령인에게 운송될 수 없었다.

어휘 partially adv. 부분적으로 torn adj. 찢어진 recipient n. 수령인

121 to 부정사 채우기

해설 빈칸 앞에 to 부정사를 목적격 보어로 취하는 동사 ask가 있으므로 to 부정사 (D) to bring이 정답이다. 참고로, 이 문장은 목적어와 목적격 보어를 취하는 5형식 동사 ask(요구하다, 필요하다)가 수동태로 쓰이면서 목적어(Applicants for the graphic designer position)가 주어 자리에 오고 목적격 보어(to bring)가 동사 뒤에 남은 형태임을 알아둔다. 동사 (A), 동명사 또는 현재분사 (B), 동사 (C)는 ask의 목적격 보어 자리, 즉 to 부정사 자리에 올 수 없다.

해석 Westwood 언론사의 그래픽 디자이너 직책의 지원자들은 면접에 그들의 포트폴리오를 가져올 것을 요청받는다.

어휘 applicant n. 지원자 bring v. 가져오다

122 명사 어휘 고르기

해설 '더 많은 양의 음식을 더 빨리 배분하기 위해서, 무료 급식소에 자원봉사자를 추가하는 것은 불가피했다'라는 문맥이므로 (C) addition(추가)이 정답이다. (A) submission은 '제출', (B) compliance는 '준수', (D) formation은 '형성(물)'이라는 의미이다.

해석 더 많은 양의 음식을 더 빨리 배분하기 위해서, Clover 무료 급식소에 자원봉사자를 추가하는 것은 불가피했다.

어휘 distribution n. 배분, 유통 quantity n. 양
volunteer n. 자원봉사자 inevitable adj. 불가피한, 필연적인

123 형용사 자리 채우기

해설 빈칸 뒤의 명사(damage)를 꾸밀 수 있는 것은 형용사이므로 형용사 역할을 하는 현재분사 (A)와 형용사 (B)가 정답의 후보이다. '그 지진은 구조상의 파손을 야기할 만큼 강력하지는 않았다'라는 의미가 되어야 하므로 형용사 (B) structural(구조상의, 구조적인)이 정답이다. 현재분사 (A)는 '그 지진은 구조화시키는 파손을 야기할 만큼 강력하지는 않았다'라는 어색한 문맥을 만든다. 부사 (C)와 명사 또는 동사 (D)는 형용사 자리에 올 수 없다. 명사 (D)를 써서 structures damage를 복합 명사로 본다 해도, 복합 명사를 복수형으로 만들 때는 뒤의 명사에 -e(s)를 붙여야 하므로 답이 될 수 없다.

해석 그 지진은 그 지역에 있는 건물들에 어느 중대한 구조상의 파손을 야기할 만큼 강력하지는 않았다.

어휘 earthquake n. 지진 produce v. 야기하다, 생산하다
major adj. 중대한, 주요한 structurally adv. 구조상으로

124 부사 자리 채우기

해설 동사(has urged)를 꾸밀 수 있는 것은 부사이므로 부사 (C) rigorously(엄격하게)가 정답이다. 형용사 (A), 명사 (B), 형용사의 비교급 (D)는 동사를 꾸밀 수 없다.

해석 Fox 연구소는 자료가 정확한지 확실히 하기 위해 과학자들이 그들의 실험 자료를 검토할 것을 엄격하게 권고해 왔다.

어휘 urge v. 권고하다, 촉구하다 examine v. 검토하다, 살펴보다
experimental adj. 실험의 accurate adj. 정확한
rigorous adj. 엄격한 rigorousness n. 엄격함, 혹독함

125 동사 어휘 고르기

해설 '게임 이용자들은 최신판을 다운로드하는 데 문제를 겪어 오고 있다'라는 문맥이므로 experience(겪다)의 현재분사형 (B) experiencing이 정답이다. (A)의 pass는 '지나가다', (C)의 relate는 '관련시키다', (D)의 establish는 '설정하다, (관계를) 수립하다'라는 의미이다.

해석 Dazzle 엔터테인먼트사의 인기 있는 온라인 게임 이용자들은 최신판을 다운로드하는 데 문제를 겪어 오고 있다.

어휘 latest adj. 최신의

126 부사절 접속사 채우기

해설 이 문장은 주어(Mr. Gresley), 동사(created), 목적어(a ~ spreadsheet)를 갖춘 완전한 절이므로 _____ ~ be easily tracked는 수식어 거품으로 보아야 한다. 이 수식어 거품은 동사(can be tracked)가 있는 거품절이므로, 거품절을 이끌 수 있는 부사절 접속사 (A)와 (C)가 정답의 후보이다. '비용이 쉽게 추적될 수 있도록 하기 위해서 예산 스프레드시트를 만들어냈다'라는 의미가 되어야 하므로 목적을 나타내는 부사절 접속사 (A) so that(~ 하도록 하기 위해서)이 정답이다. (C) given that은 '~을 고려하면'이라는 의미이다. 분사구 (B) based on(~에 근거하여)과 전치사 (D) according to(~에 따라)는 거품절을 이끌 수 없다.

해석 Mr. Gresley는 비용이 쉽게 추적될 수 있도록 하기 위해서 포괄적인 예산 스프레드시트를 만들어냈다.

어휘 comprehensive adj. 포괄적인 expense n. 비용
track v. 추적하다

127 형용사 어휘 고르기

해설 '신중한 투자자들은 2년 안에 생산 능력을 두 배로 늘리겠다는 계획에 너무 야심적이라고 생각한다'라는 문맥이므로 형용사 (A) ambitious (야심적인, 야심 있는)가 정답이다. (B) compliant는 '순응하는, (법을) 준수하는', (C) reputable은 '평판이 좋은', (D) prevalent는 '널리 퍼져 있는'이라는 의미이다.

해석 몇몇 신중한 투자자들은 Beaumont 기업이 2년 안에 당사의 생산 능력을 두 배로 늘리겠다는 계획에 너무 야심적이라고 생각한다.

어휘 cautious adj. 신중한, 조심스러운 investor n. 투자자
double v. 두 배로 만들다 capacity n. 능력, 역량

128 명사 자리 채우기

해설 allow(허용하다, 허락하다)의 수동태 be allowed 뒤에는 명사 또는 to 부정사가 올 수 있으므로 명사 (B) entry(입장, 출입)가 정답이다. 참고로, 이 문장은 타동사 allow가 2개의 목적어, 즉 간접 목적어 (Visitors to Nova Medical Supplies)와 직접 목적어(entry)를 갖는 4형식 동사로 쓰였고, 주어 자리에 간접 목적어가 오면서 수동태(are allowed) 뒤에 직접 목적어가 남은 형태임을 알아둔다.

해석 Nova 의료 용품사 방문객들은 유효한 손님용 출입증을 소지하고 있는 한 입장이 허용된다.

어휘 valid adj. 유효한 guest pass 손님용 출입증

최신토익경향

최근, 4형식 또는 5형식 동사의 수동태 뒤 빈칸에 명사를 정답으로 고르는 문제들이 난이도 높은 문제로 출제되고 있으며, 오답률도 높은 편이다. 뒤에 명사를 취할 수 있는 4형식/5형식 동사의 수동태 표현을 알아두자.

- be allowed + 명사 ~을 허락받다
- be awarded + 명사 ~을 받다
- be granted + 명사 ~을 받다
- be elected + 명사 ~으로 선출되다
- be named + 명사 ~으로 임명되다
- be considered + 명사 ~으로 여겨지다

129 접속부사 채우기

해설 빈칸은 접속사 but과 함께 절(City council member ~ efficient)과 절(she cares ~ populations)을 연결하고 있으므로, 절과 절을 연결하는 접속부사인 모든 보기가 정답의 후보이다. '시 의회 구성원인 Ariak Miller는 똑똑하고 유능하지만, 그보다 더 중요하게도 복지에 깊은 관심을 갖고 있다'라는 의미가 되어야 하므로 (D) more importantly(그보다 더 중요하게도)가 정답이다. (A) in contrast는 '그에 반해서', (B) until now는 '지금까지', (C) to that end는 '그러기 위해서'라는 의미이다.

해석 시 의회 구성원인 Ariak Miller는 똑똑하고 유능하지만, 그보다 더 중요하게도 취약 계층의 복지에 깊은 관심을 갖고 있다.

어휘 efficient adj. 유능한, 효율적인 welfare n. 복지
vulnerable adj. 취약한

130 명사 어휘 고르기

해설 '위생을 개선하기 위해 해충 방제 전문가와 계약을 체결하다'라는 문맥이므로 (C) practitioner(전문가)가 정답이다. (A) identifier는 '식별자', (B) composer는 '작곡가', (D) designer는 '디자이너'라는 의미이다.

해석 Lyon 유제품 회사는 당사의 공장 위생을 개선하기 위해 해충 방제 전문가와 계약을 체결했다.

어휘 contract n. 계약(서) improve v. 개선하다 hygiene n. 위생

PART 6

131-134번은 다음 공고에 관한 문제입니다.

> 8월 5일 오후 2시에, 기술자들이 전기 수리 작업을 수행할 수 있도록 하기 위해 저희 사무실의 3층 전기가 차단될 것입니다. ¹³¹그 작업은 30분 이상 지속되지는 않을 것으로 예상됩니다. ¹³²그 전에 여러분이 작업 중인 모든 파일을 저장한 후 컴퓨터를 꺼주세요. ¹³³15분 전에 미리 스피커를 통해 이에 대해 알리는 안내 방송이 나올 것입니다. 언제 컴퓨터를 다시 켤 수 있는지는 나중에 알려드리겠습니다. ¹³⁴불편을 드려 죄송합니다. 질문이 있다면, 직속 상사에게 보내시기 바랍니다.

electricity n. 전기   shut down (기계 등을) 정지시키다   turn off 끄다
beforehand adv. ~전에 미리, 사전에
direct v. 보내다, ~로 향하다   immediate supervisor 직속 상사

131 알맞은 문장 고르기

해석 (A) 그들은 저희에게 설치 과정이 성공적이었다고 확실히 말했습니다.
(B) 기술자들이 수리를 할 날짜는 정해지지 않았습니다.
(C) 일정 관리 시스템은 실시간 알림을 보냅니다.
(D) 그 작업은 30분 이상 지속되지는 않을 것으로 예상됩니다.

해설 앞 문장 'the electricity on the third floor of our office will be shut down to let technicians conduct some electrical repairs'에서 기술자들이 전기 수리 작업을 수행할 수 있도록 전기가 차단될 거라고 했으므로, 빈칸에는 전기 수리 작업과 관련된 내용이 들어가야 함을 알 수 있다. 따라서 (D)가 정답이다.

어휘 assure v. 확실히 말하다, 보장하다   installation n. 설치
real-time adj. 실시간의   last v. 지속하다

132 관계대명사 채우기

해설 이 문장은 주어가 없는 명령문이고 동사(save)와 목적어(any files)를 갖춘 완전한 절이므로, ___ ~ working on은 수식어 거품으로 보아야 한다. 이 수식어 거품은 빈칸 앞의 명사(any files)를 선행사로 갖는 관계절이므로 (A)와 (C)가 정답의 후보이다. 관계절(~ working on) 내에 목적어가 없으므로 목적격 관계대명사 (A) which가 정답이다. 소유격 관계대명사 (C) whose는 뒤에 꾸밈을 받는 명사가 와야 하므로 답이 될 수 없다. 전치사 (B) among(~ 사이에)과 (D) from (~로부터)은 관계절을 이끌 수 없다.

133 올바른 시제의 동사 채우기 전체 문맥 파악

해설 문장에 주어(An announcement)만 있고 동사가 없으므로 (B)와 (D)가 정답의 후보이다. '스피커를 통해 이에 대해 알리는 안내 방송이 나오다'라는 문맥인데, 이 경우 빈칸이 있는 문장만으로는 올바른 시제의 동사를 고를 수 없으므로 주변 문맥이나 전체 문맥을 파악하여 정답을 고른다. 앞부분에서 '3층 전기가 차단될 것이다 (the electricity on the third floor of our office will be shut down)'라고 했으므로 안내 방송이 나오는 시점은 미래임을 알 수 있다. 따라서 미래 시제 (B) will be made가 정답이다. 과거완료 시제 (D)는 과거의 특정 시점 이전에 발생한 일을 표현하므로 답이 될 수 없다. to 부정사구 (A)와 관계사절 (C)는 동사 자리에 올 수 없다.

134 명사 어휘 고르기 전체 문맥 파악

해설 '___에 대해 사과하다'라는 문맥이므로 모든 보기가 정답의 후보이다. 빈칸이 있는 문장만으로 정답을 고를 수 없으므로 주변 문맥이나 전체 문맥을 파악한다. 앞부분에서 '그 전에 여러분이 작업 중인 모든 파일을 저장한 후 컴퓨터를 꺼주세요(Please save any files you are working on and turn off your computers before that time).'라고 했으므로 불편한 상황에 대해 사과하고 있음을 알 수 있다. 따라서 (C) inconvenience(불편)이 정답이다. (A) cancellation은 '취소, 무효화', (B) resistance는 '반대, 저항', (D) breakage는 '파손'이라는 의미이다.

135-138번은 다음 광고에 관한 문제입니다.

> 당신에게 꼭 맞는 인터넷 요금제를 선택하세요.
>
> QuikLink로, 당신은 가장 저렴한 가격으로 가장 빠른 인터넷 속도를 얻게 될 것입니다. ¹³⁵범위가 기본부터 프리미엄까지 다양한 5개의 여러 가정용 인터넷 요금제 중에서 선택하십시오. ¹³⁶각 요금제는 안정적이고 속도가 빠른 연결이 특징입니다. 저희의 요금제에 대해 자세히 알아보려면, ¹³⁷그저 www.quicklink.com에 방문하기만 하세요. ¹³⁸당신의 필요에 맞는 요금제를 찾은 다음 등록할 옵션을 선택하세요. 그 절차는 빠르고 쉬우며, 당신은 곧바로 가입될 것입니다. 자, 무엇을 기다리시나요? 오늘 QuikLink의 회원이 되세요!

affordable adj. 저렴한, 감당할 수 있는   match v. (서로) 맞다, 일치하다
process n. 과정, 절차

135 현재분사와 과거분사 구별하여 채우기

해설 빈칸 앞의 명사(plans)를 꾸며줄 수 있는 것은 형용사이므로 형용사 역할을 하는 현재분사 (B)와 과거분사 (C)가 정답의 후보이다. 꾸밈을 받는 명사와 분사가 '범위가 기본부터 프리미엄까지 다양한 요금제'라는 능동의 의미이므로 현재분사 (B) ranging이 정답이다. 과거분사 (C) ranged를 쓸 경우 해석상 그럴듯해 보이지만, 동사 range (범위가 ~이다)는 자동사이므로 수동형인 과거분사로 쓸 수 없다. 명사 또는 동사 (A)와 (D)는 명사를 꾸밀 수 없다. 참고로, range from A to B는 '(범위가) A에서 B까지 다양하다'라는 의미의 관용 표현이다.

136 알맞은 문장 고르기

해석 (A) 둘 다 주거용 또는 기업용 고객에게 적합합니다.
(B) 각 요금제는 안정적이고 속도가 빠른 연결이 특징입니다.
(C) 장기 회원 전용 프로그램을 마련했습니다.
(D) 그것들은 연말에 출시될 것입니다.

해설 앞부분에서 5개의 다양한 가정용 인터넷 요금제 중에서 선택하라고 했으므로 빈칸에는 요금제의 특징과 관련된 내용이 들어가야 함을 알 수 있다. 따라서 (B)가 정답이다.

어휘 residential adj. 주거의, 거주에 알맞은   stable adj. 안정적인
exclusive adj. 전용의, 독점적인

137 부사 자리 채우기

해설 빈칸 뒤의 동사(visit)를 꾸밀 수 있는 것은 부사이므로 부사 (A)

simply(그저, 단순히)가 정답이다. 형용사 (B), 동사 (C), 형용사의 비교급 (D)는 동사를 꾸밀 수 없다.

138 동사 어휘 고르기 주변 문맥 파악

해설 '____할 옵션을 선택하다'라는 문맥이므로 모든 보기가 정답의 후보이다. 빈칸이 있는 문장만으로 정답을 고를 수 없으므로 주변 문맥이나 전체 문맥을 파악한다. 뒤 문장에서 '그 절차는 빠르고 쉬우며, 당신은 곧바로 가입될 것이다(The process is quick and easy, and you'll be signed up in no time).'라고 했으므로 등록할 옵션을 선택하는 것임을 알 수 있다. 따라서 (C) register(등록하다)가 정답이다. (A) expand는 '확장하다', (B) advance는 '진보하다, 나아가다', (D) search는 '찾다, 검색하다'라는 의미이다.

139-142번은 다음 웹페이지 정보에 관한 문제입니다.

Eco-Trail 배낭에 대하여

[139]Chester 산악용 장비 회사는 자연에서 시간을 보내는 모두가 자연을 보호하고 싶어 한다는 것을 잘 알고 있습니다. [140]쓰레기를 줄이기 위해, 저희는 100퍼센트 재활용된 소재로 만든 친환경 배낭을 개발했습니다. Eco-Trail 배낭의 원단은 버려진 음료수병에서 나온 플라스틱 섬유로 전부 이루어졌습니다. [141]틀은 오로지 재활용된 알루미늄으로 만들어졌습니다. 이러한 소재들의 튼튼함은 매우 내구성 있는 배낭을 만드는 것을 가능하게 합니다. [142]그래서 소유자들은 조만간 교체품이 필요하지는 않을 것입니다. 최종 결과는 바로 사용자의 환경발자국을 크게 줄여주는 배낭입니다.

equipment n. 장비 recognize v. 잘 알다, 깨닫다 fabric n. 원단
entirely adv. 전부, 완전히 discard v. 버리다, 처분하다
durable adj. 내구성이 뛰어난, 견고한 end result 최종 결과
environmental footprint 환경발자국, 환경에 미치는 악영향

---

139 부정대명사 채우기

해설 빈칸은 명사절 접속사(that)가 이끄는 절의 주어 자리이므로 주어 자리에 올 수 있는 대명사 (A), (B), (D)가 정답의 후보이다. 빈칸 뒤에 주격 관계대명사절의 동사(spends)가 단수 동사이고 명사절의 동사(wants) 역시 단수 동사이므로 단수 취급하는 부정대명사 (A) everyone(모두)이 정답이다. 지시대명사 (B) those(~한 사람들)와 부정대명사 (D) others(다른 사람들)는 복수 취급하므로 답이 될 수 없다. 재귀대명사 (C) ourselves(우리 스스로)는 목적어 자리 또는 부사 자리에 온다.

140 올바른 시제의 동사 채우기 전체 문맥 파악

해설 문장에 동사가 없고 빈칸 뒤에 목적어(an eco-friendly backpack)가 있으므로 능동형 동사 보기 (A), (B), (C)가 정답의 후보이다. '쓰레기를 줄이기 위해 친환경 배낭을 개발하다'라는 문맥인데, 이 경우 빈칸이 있는 문장만으로는 올바른 시제의 동사를 고를 수 없으므로 주변 문맥이나 전체 문맥을 파악한다. 앞 문장에서 Chester 산악용 장비 회사는 자연에서 시간을 보내는 모두가 자연을 보호하고 싶어 한다는 것을 잘 알고 있다고 했고, 뒷부분에서 Eco-Trail 배낭의 원단에 대해 상세히 설명하고 있으므로, Chester 산악용 장비 회사가 친환경 배낭을 개발한 결과를 나타내야 한다. 따라서 현재완료 시제 (B) have created가 정답이다. 과거진행 시제 (A)는 특정한 과거 시점

에 진행되고 있던 일을, 미래 시제 (C)는 미래에 일어날 일, 미래 상황에 대한 추측이나 의지를 나타낸다. 수동태 (D)는 뒤에 목적어를 취할 수 없다.

141 알맞은 문장 고르기

해석 (A) 이 배낭은 좁은 공간에 쉽게 보관할 수 있습니다.
(B) 틀은 오로지 재활용된 알루미늄으로 만들어졌습니다.
(C) 이 제품은 미리 주문해야 할 것입니다.
(D) 다양한 부속품들이 별도로 판매됩니다.

해설 앞 문장 'The fabric of the Eco-Trail Backpack is composed entirely of plastic fibers from discarded beverage bottles.'에서 Eco-Trail 배낭의 원단은 버려진 음료수병에서 추출한 플라스틱 섬유로 전부 이루어졌다고 했고, 뒤 문장 'The strength of these materials makes it possible to craft a very durable backpack.'에서 이러한 소재들의 튼튼함은 매우 내구성 있는 배낭을 만드는 것을 가능하게 한다고 했으므로 배낭의 소재와 관련된 내용이 들어가야 함을 알 수 있다. 따라서 (B)가 정답이다.

어휘 store v. 보관하다 solely adv. 오로지

142 명사 어휘 고르기 주변 문맥 파악

해설 '그래서 소유자들은 조만간 ____이 필요지는 않을 것이다'라는 문맥이므로 모든 보기가 정답의 후보이다. 빈칸이 있는 문장만으로는 정답을 고를 수 없으므로 주변 문맥이나 전체 문맥을 파악한다. 앞 문장에서 소재들이 튼튼하여 매우 내구성 있는 배낭을 만드는 것을 가능하게 한다고 했으므로 배낭 소유자들은 조만간 새 배낭, 즉 교체품이 필요하지 않을 것임을 알 수 있다. 따라서 명사 (C) replacement(교체품)가 정답이다. (A) modification은 '수정, 변경', (B) confirmation은 '확인', (D) demonstration은 '제품 시연, 설명'이라는 의미이다.

143-146번은 다음 설명서에 관한 문제입니다.

Welting G5B 전동 칫솔을 구입해 주셔서 감사합니다. [143]강력한 회전 브러쉬로, 이 기기는 당신의 구강 건강뿐만 아니라 치아의 모습을 개선시킬 것입니다. 이 세척 지침을 따르세요.

일주일에 한 번 정도, 칫솔모를 분리하여 따뜻한 물에 헹구어야 합니다. [144]그다음에, 홈이나 융기 부분에 닿을 수 있도록 하면서, 젖은 천으로 손잡이를 닦아주세요. 절대로 손잡이를 물에 담그지 마십시오. [145]손상될 수도 있는 전기 부품들이 있습니다. 마지막으로, 칫솔이나 충전기에 박테리아가 형성되는 것을 방지하기 위해 순한 소독제로 충전기를 닦으세요. [146]당신의 안전을 위해, 세척하기 전에 플러그를 뽑을 것이 권고됩니다.

rotate v. 회전하다 oral adj. 구강의, 입의 remove v. 제거하다, 없애다
damp adj. 젖은 groove n. 홈 ridge n. 융기, 솟은 부분
submerge v. (물에) 담그다 disinfectant n. 살균제, 소독약
form v. 형성되다 unplug v. 플러그를 뽑다

---

143 명사 자리 채우기

해설 정관사(the)와 전치사(of) 사이에 올 수 있는 것은 명사이므로 명사 (B) appearance(모습)가 정답이다. 동사 (A), 동사 또는 과거분사 (C)는 명사 자리에 올 수 없다. 동명사 또는 현재분사 (D)는 동명사일

경우 '나타나는 것, 출현'이라는 의미로 어색한 문맥을 만들고, 현재분사일 경우 명사 자리에 올 수 없다.

어휘 appear v. 나타나다, ~처럼 보이다

144 접속부사 채우기 주변 문맥 파악

해설 빈칸이 콤마와 함께 문장의 맨 앞에 온 접속부사 자리이므로, 앞 문장과 빈칸이 있는 문장의 의미 관계를 파악하여 정답을 선택한다. 앞 문장에서 칫솔모를 분리하여 따뜻한 물에 헹구라고 했고, 빈칸이 있는 문장에서는 젖은 천으로 손잡이를 닦으라고 했으므로 앞에서 말한 내용과 다음 단계로 이어지는 내용의 문장에서 사용되는 접속부사 (C) Next(그다음에)가 정답이다.

어휘 in that case 그런 경우에는, 그렇다면
similarly adv. 마찬가지로, 유사하게 and yet 그렇다 하더라도

145 알맞은 문장 고르기

해설 (A) 각 구성품은 매일 세척돼야 합니다.
(B) 그것은 완전히 방수가 가능하도록 설계되었습니다.
(C) 손상될 수도 있는 전기 부품들이 있습니다.
(D) 울퉁불퉁한 표면이 그것을 움켜잡기 훨씬 쉽게 만듭니다.

해설 앞 문장 'Never submerge the handle in water.'에서 절대로 손잡이를 물에 담그지 말라고 했으므로, 빈칸에는 손잡이 부분을 물에 담그면 안 되는 이유와 관련된 내용이 들어가야 함을 알 수 있다. 따라서 (C)가 정답이다. (A)는 앞부분에서 '일주일에 한 번 정도'라고 했으므로 답이 될 수 없다.

어휘 component n. 구성품, 부품, 요소 electrical adj. 전기의
uneven adj. 울퉁불퉁한, 평평하지 않은 grip v. 움켜잡다; n. 움켜쥠

146 동사 어휘 고르기

해설 '당신의 안전을 위해, 세척하기 전에 플러그를 뽑을 것이 권고됩니다'라는 문맥이므로 동사 advise(권고하다, 조언하다)의 과거분사 (A) advised가 정답이다. (B)의 affect는 '영향을 미치다', (C)의 evaluate는 '평가하다', (D)의 provide는 '제공하다'라는 의미이다.

PART 7

147-148번은 다음 구인 공고에 관한 문제입니다.

종업원 자리

Broadview 식당은 손님들에게 기억에 남을 만한 식사 경험을 만들어 주는 것을 도울 종업원을 찾고 있습니다. **147-(B)합격자는 주간 또는 야간 근무 중에서 선택할 수 있지만**, 약간의 주말 근무가 필요할 것입니다.

식당 종업원으로서의 이전 경험이 선호되지만 필수는 아닙니다. 그러나, 저희는 지원자들이 음식을 나르는 종업원 자격 프로그램을 마칠 것을 요구합니다. 더불어, 뛰어난 의사소통 능력뿐만 아니라, **148스트레스를 많이 받는 환경에서 여러 작업을 동시에 수행할 수 있는 능력도 보여줘야 합니다.**

그 자리에 지원하려면, 이력서를 Joshua Williams에게 j.williams ⟳

@broadviewdiner.com으로 보내주십시오.

server n. 종업원, 서빙하는 사람 diner n. (작은) 식당
memorable adj. 기억에 남을 만한 successful applicant 합격자
mandatory adj. 필수의, 의무적인 certificate n. 자격
demonstrate v. 보여주다, 입증하다 capacity n. 능력
perform v. 수행하다 simultaneously adv. 동시에

147 Not/True 문제

해석 Broadview 식당에 대해 명시된 것은?
(A) 시골 지역에 위치해 있다.
(B) 직원들에게 교대 근무 유연성을 제공한다.
(C) 주말에는 늦게까지 영업한다.
(D) 수상 경력이 있는 요리사가 이끈다.

해설 지문의 'The successful applicant can choose between working days or evenings'에서 합격자는 주간 또는 야간 근무 중에서 선택할 수 있다고 했으므로 (B)는 지문의 내용과 일치한다. 따라서 (B)가 정답이다. (A), (C), (D)는 지문에 언급되지 않은 내용이다.

어휘 rural adj. 시골의, 지방의 shift n. 교대 근무 flexibility n. 유연성

Paraphrasing

> can choose between working days or evenings 주간 또는 야간 근무 중에서 선택할 수 있다 → offers shift flexibility 교대 근무 유연성을 제공한다

148 육하원칙 문제

해석 직책에 대한 요건으로 무엇이 열거되어 있는가?
(A) 유사한 직무에 대한 이전 경험
(B) 요리 학교 졸업
(C) 압박감 속에서 동시에 여러 가지 일을 할 수 있는 능력
(D) 여러 언어에 대한 유창함

해설 지문의 'they must demonstrate a capacity to perform multiple tasks simultaneously in a high-stress environment'에서 스트레스를 많이 받는 환경에서 여러 작업을 동시에 수행할 수 있는 능력을 보여줘야 한다고 했으므로 (C)가 정답이다.

어휘 graduation n. 졸업 culinary adj. 요리의, 조리의
institute n. 학교, 협회 ability n. 능력
multitask v. 동시에 여러 가지 일을 하다 fluency n. 유창성

Paraphrasing

> a capacity to perform multiple tasks simultaneously 여러 작업을 동시에 수행할 수 있는 능력 → Ability to multitask 여러 가지 일을 할 수 있는 능력
> in a high-stress environment 스트레스를 많이 받는 환경에서 → under pressure 압박감 속에서

149-150번은 다음 웹페이지 내 정보에 관한 문제입니다.

임대용 상업 공간

149만약 여러분 상점의 현 위치가 불만이시라면, Sommerville의 The Village Square에 있는 최근에 비워진 이 상업 공간을 임대하는 것 ⟳

을 고려해 보세요. 그것은 깨끗하고, 현대적인 디자인을 가지고 있으며 매일 상당한 양의 유동 인구가 유입됩니다.

세부 사항:
- 100평방미터
- 뒤쪽 출입이 가능한 보관 창고
- 직원과 고객을 위한 충분한 주차 공간
- 장기 계약에 유리한 조건의 최소 1년 계약

¹⁵⁰⁻⁽ᴮ⁾20년 전에 설립된 The Village Square는 대규모 주거 지역 사회의 구미에 맞춘 인기 많은 지역 명소입니다. ¹⁵⁰⁻⁽ᴰ⁾그곳은 많은 버스 정류장과 Rosedale 지하철역 근처에 위치해 있습니다. 도움을 받기 위해서는, 517-555-0429로 Riggson 부동산에 문의하시거나 여기를 클릭하십시오.

commercial adj. 상업의 lease n. 임대 rent v. 임대하다
vacate v. 비우다 substantial adj. 상당한 foot traffic 유동 인구
storage n. 보관, 저장 rear adj. 뒤쪽의 ample adj. 충분한
favorable adj. 유리한 terms n. 조건 establish v. 설립하다
beloved adj. 인기 많은 cater to ~의 구미에 맞추다, ~를 만족시키다
landmark n. 명소, 랜드마크 residential adj. 주거의
situate v. 위치시키다

149 육하원칙 문제

해석 정보는 누구를 대상으로 하는가?
(A) 신규 주택 매수자
(B) 취업 지원자
(C) 소기업 소유주
(D) 주거용 임차인

해설 지문의 'If you are unhappy with the current location of your shop, consider renting this recently vacated commercial space'에서 만약 상점의 현 위치가 불만이라면, 최근에 비워진 상업 공간을 임대하는 것을 고려해 보라고 했으므로 (C)가 정답이다.

어휘 purchaser n. 매수자, 구매자 tenant n. 임차인, 세입자

150 Not/True 문제

해석 The Village Square에 대해 사실인 것은?
(A) 현재 여러 개의 비어 있는 공간이 있다.
(B) 최근에야 건설되었다.
(C) 지역 문화 회관을 포함한다.
(D) 대중교통으로 접근할 수 있다.

해설 지문의 'It is situated close to the Rosedale Subway Station and many bus stops.'에서 Rosedale 지하철역과 여러 버스 정류장 근처에 위치해 있다고 했으므로 (D)는 지문의 내용과 일치한다. 따라서 (D)가 정답이다. 'Established 20 years ago, The Village Square ~'에서 20년 전에 설립되었다고 했으므로 (B)는 지문의 내용과 일치하지 않는다. (A)와 (C)는 지문에 언급되지 않은 내용이다.

어휘 vacancy n. 비어 있는 공간, 빈방 construct v. 건설하다
accessible adj. 접근할 수 있는

151-152번은 다음 후기에 관한 문제입니다.

청소의 필요성을 위해 Sanitaria를 선택해 주셔서 감사합니다. 다음의 표를 완성해 주세요. 1에서 5까지 하나의 숫자를 선택하여 각 서비스에 대한 귀하의 만족도를 표시해 주시는데, 5가 가장 높은 수준의 만족도를 의미합니다. ¹⁵¹적용되지 않는 구역에 대해서는 N/A를 선택해 주세요.

구역	1	2	3	4	5	N/A
¹⁵¹침실					✓	
¹⁵¹거실				✓		
¹⁵¹식사실				✓		
¹⁵¹욕실					✓	
회의실						✓
로비						✓

추가 의견: ¹⁵²⁻⁽ᴬ⁾/⁽ᴮ⁾저는 직원들이 예정대로 도착하여 작업을 매우 빨리 완료한 것에 감사했습니다. ¹⁵²⁻⁽ᴰ⁾그들은 또한 전문적이고 친절한 태도로 행동했습니다. ¹⁵²⁻⁽ᶜ⁾제가 가진 유일한 불만은 웹사이트에서 시간을 예약하기가 매우 어려웠다는 것입니다. 그것이 계속 멈추어서, 저는 어쩔 수 없이 수차례에 걸쳐 로그인을 할 수밖에 없었습니다.

Jared Louis의 후기

indicate v. 표시하다, 나타내다 satisfaction n. 만족도, 충족
additional adj. 추가의 behave v. 행동하다
professional adj. 전문적인, 전문가의 courteous adj. 공손한, 정중한
manner n. 태도, 방식 book v. 예약하다 freeze v. (작동을) 멈추다
repeatedly adv. 수차례에 걸쳐, 반복적으로

151 추론 문제

해석 서비스는 어디에서 수행된 것 같은가?
(A) 사무실에서
(B) 주택에서
(C) 컨벤션 센터에서
(D) 의료 시설에서

해설 지문의 'Select N/A for any areas that do not apply'에서 적용되지 않는 구역은 N/A를 선택해 달라고 했고, 표의 'Bedroom', 'Living room', 'Dining room', 'Bathroom'의 경우 N/A가 아닌 점수가 선택되어 있으므로, 서비스가 침실, 거실, 식사실, 욕실을 갖추고 있는 장소인 주택에서 수행되었다는 것을 추론할 수 있다. 따라서 (B)가 정답이다.

어휘 medical adj. 의료의 facility n. 시설

152 Not/True문제

해석 Mr. Louis는 어떤 문제를 언급하는가?
(A) 시작 시간이 예기치 않게 미뤄졌다.
(B) 청소가 계획된 것보다 완료되는 데 더 오래 걸렸다.
(C) 직원이 비전문적인 태도로 행동했다.
(D) 온라인으로 예약 일정을 잡기가 어려웠다.

해설 지문의 'The only complaint I have is that it was very hard to book a time through your Web site.'에서 웹사이트에서

시간을 예약하기가 매우 어려웠다고 했으므로 (D)는 지문의 내용과 일치한다. 따라서 (D)가 정답이다. (A)와 (B)는 'I appreciated that the workers arrived on schedule and completed the work very quickly.'에서 직원들이 일정에 따라 도착하여 일을 매우 빠르게 완료했다고 했으므로 지문의 내용과 일치하지 않는다. (C)는 'They also behaved in a professional and courteous manner.'에서 직원들이 전문적이고 공손한 태도로 행동했다고 했으므로 지문의 내용과 일치하지 않는다.

어휘 push back 미루다 unexpectedly adv. 예기치 않게, 예상외로

Paraphrasing

to book a time 시간 예약하기
→ An appointment ~ to schedule 예약 일정 잡기
through your Web site 웹사이트에서 → online 온라인으로

153-154번은 다음 문자 메시지 대화문에 관한 문제입니다.

Lily Ramirez (오전 8시 54분)
안녕하세요, Conrad. 당신이 주문했던 상품을 방금 받았어요. 지금 그 상자들을 분류할 거예요. **153그 물품들 중 진열대 위에 올려야 할 것이 있나요, 아니면 전부 뒤쪽에 보관해 둬야 할까요?**

Conrad Cho (오전 8시 57분)
고마워요, Lily. 수량이 맞는지 확인해 주시면 좋겠어요. 지금 당장은 뒤쪽에 다 넣어주세요. 제가 들어가서 한번 볼게요.

Lily Ramirez (오전 9시 1분)
알겠어요. 수량은 송장과 일치하지만, 커피 머그잔 하나에 손상이 있는 것을 확인했어요.

Lily Ramirez (오전 9시 4분)
154몇 개 더 찾아서 사진을 몇 장 찍었어요. 이것들에 대해 공급업체에 연락해야 할까요?

Conrad Cho (오전 9시 6분)
큰일은 아니에요. 154목록만 작성해서 별도의 상자에 모두 함께 포장해 주세요. 제가 오늘 늦게 공급업체에 그것들을 교체해 달라고 요청할게요.

product n. 상품, 제품 sort v. 분류하다 quantity n. 수량
invoice n. 송장 damage n. 손상 supplier n. 공급업체
separate adj. 별도의

---

153 육하원칙 문제

해석 Ms. Ramirez는 무엇에 대해 질문하는가?
(A) 주문한 물품들을 어디에 둘지
(B) 배송이 몇 시에 이루어질지
(C) 동료가 출근하는지 아닌지
(D) 커피 머그잔을 어떻게 포장하는지

해설 지문의 'Do any of the items have to go up on display, or should I store everything in the back?'에서 Ms. Ramirez가 그 물품들 중 진열대 위에 올려야 할 것이 있는지, 아니면 전부 뒤쪽에 보관해야 할지 묻고 있으므로 (A)가 정답이다.

어휘 place v. 두다, 배치하다 package v. 포장하다

---

154 의도 파악 문제

해석 오전 9시 6분에, Mr. Cho가 "It's not a big deal"이라고 쓸 때, 그가 의도한 것 같은 것은?
(A) Ms. Ramirez는 그가 도착할 때까지 기다릴 것이다.
(B) Ms. Ramirez는 물품들을 쉽게 수리할 수 있다.
(C) Ms. Ramirez는 공급업체에 전화할 필요가 없다.
(D) Ms. Ramirez는 회의에 참석하지 않을 것이다.

해설 지문의 'I found a couple more and took some photos. Should I contact the supplier about these?'에서 Ms. Ramirez가 손상된 머그잔을 몇 개 더 찾아서 사진을 찍었다며 이것들에 대해 공급업체에 연락해야 할지 묻자, Mr. Cho가 'It's not a big deal'(큰일은 아니에요)이라고 한 후, 'Just make a list and pack them all together in a separate box. I'll ask the supplier later today to replace them.'에서 목록만 작성해서 별도의 상자에 모두 함께 포장해 달라며, 자신이 공급업체에 그것들을 교체해 달라고 요청하겠다고 한 것을 통해, Ms. Ramirez는 공급업체에 전화할 필요가 없다는 것을 알 수 있다. 따라서 (C)가 정답이다.

어휘 repair v. 수리하다 attend v. 참석하다

155-157번은 다음 이메일에 관한 문제입니다.

수신: Nina Breyer <n.breyer@kbc_law.com>
발신: Stefan Randolph <s.randolph@artkolekt.com>
날짜: 7월 14일
제목: 회신: 물품 9199번

Ms. Breyer께,

문의해 주셔서 감사합니다. ─ [1] ─. 유감스럽지만 저희 카탈로그의 9199번인 Adam Wynn의 *Desert Landscape 1*이 판매되었음을 알려드립니다. 아시다시피, **155그는 꽤 인기 있는 예술가입니다.** 그렇긴 하지만, 저희는 권해드릴 수 있는 다른 그림들도 있습니다. ─ [2] ─. 하나는 Mr. Wynn의 약간 더 작은 작품입니다. **155또 다른 그림은 Lena O'Lear라는 새로 발견된 화가의 작품입니다.** 두 작품 모두 귀하께서 구입하고자 했던 그림과 비슷한 따뜻한 색조들을 가지고 있어서, **156귀하의 새 사무실 색과 잘 어울릴 것입니다.** ─ [3] ─. Ms. O'Lear의 그림은 또한 훨씬 더 저렴할 것입니다.

157그 그림들을 온라인으로 보시려면 여기를 클릭하시면 됩니다. ─ [4] ─. **157두 그림 모두 아직 대중에 공개되지 않았기 때문에, 현재 접근이 제한되어 있습니다.** 언제나처럼, 제가 도와드릴 수 있는 게 있다면 주저하지 마시고 저에게 연락해 주세요.

Stefan Randolph 드림
고객 영업, Art Kolekt

inquiry n. 문의, 질문 regret to 유감스럽지만 ~하다, 후회하다
slightly adv. 약간, 조금 significantly adv. 훨씬, 상당히
access n. 접근 restrict v. 제한하다, 한정하다 assist v. 돕다

---

155 추론 문제

해석 Ms. O'Lear에 대해 사실일 것 같은 것은?
(A) 최근에 미술 전시회에 참가했다.
(B) Mr. Wynn과 함께 미술을 공부했다.
(C) 그녀의 그림을 세 가지 다른 사이즈로 판매한다.

(D) Mr. Wynn만큼 잘 알려져 있지 않다.

해설 지문의 'he[Mr. Wynn] is quite a popular artist'에서 Mr. Wynn은 꽤 유명한 예술가라고 한 뒤, 'Another is from a newly discovered painter named Lena O'Lear.'에서 또 다른 그림은 Lena O'Lear라는 새로 발견된 화가의 작품이라고 했으므로 Ms. O'Lear가 Mr. Wynn만큼 잘 알려져 있지 않다는 것을 추론할 수 있다. 따라서 (D)가 정답이다.

어휘 exhibit n. 전시회 well-known adj. 잘 알려진

156 육하원칙 문제

해석 Ms. Breyer는 왜 그림을 구입하려고 하는가?
(A) 개인 소장품을 완성하기 위해
(B) 새 사무실 공간을 꾸미기 위해
(C) 친구에게 선물로 주기 위해
(D) 판매된 예술품을 대신하기 위해

해설 지문의 'they should match the colors of your new office'에서 새로운 사무실의 색과 잘 어울릴 것이라고 했으므로 Ms. Breyer가 새 사무실을 꾸미기 위해 그림을 구입한다는 것을 알 수 있다. 따라서 (B)가 정답이다.

어휘 complete v. 완성하다 personal collection 개인 소장품
decorate v. 꾸미다, 장식하다 replace v. 대신하다

157 문장 위치 찾기 문제

해석 [1], [2], [3], [4]로 표시된 위치 중, 다음 문장이 들어갈 곳으로 가장 적절한 것은?

"등록된 사용자 이름과 비밀번호로 로그인할 준비를 하시길 바랍니다."

(A) [1]
(B) [2]
(C) [3]
(D) [4]

해설 주어진 문장은 로그인과 관련된 내용 주변에 나와야 함을 예상할 수 있다. [4]의 앞 문장인 'You may click here to view the paintings online.'에서 그 그림들을 온라인으로 보려면 여기를 클릭하라고 했고, 뒤 문장인 'Neither painting has been made available to the public yet, so access is currently restricted.'에서 두 그림 모두 아직 대중에 공개되지 않았기 때문에 현재 접근이 제한되어 있다고 했으므로, [4]에 주어진 문장이 들어가면 두 그림 모두 아직 대중에 공개되지 않아 접근이 제한되어 있으므로 그림을 온라인으로 보려면 등록된 사용자 이름과 비밀번호로 로그인할 준비를 하라는 자연스러운 문맥이 된다는 것을 알 수 있다. 따라서 (D)가 정답이다.

어휘 sign in 로그인하다, 등록하다 registered adj. 등록된

158-160번은 다음 편지에 관한 문제입니다.

Kalina Winnicka
Winnicka 패션 회사
302번 해안 진입로
로스앤젤레스, 캘리포니아, 90015

9월 9일

Ms. Winnicka께,

158저희 회사는 귀하의 의류 브랜드를 남미 전역에 판매하기 위한 독점 라이선스 계약에 관심이 있습니다. 저희는 그러한 모험이 성공으로 가는 큰 잠재력을 가지고 있다고 믿습니다. 159그 지역 내에서는 전 세계적으로 알려진 패션 브랜드에 대한 강한 수요가 존재하며, 특히 158귀하가 목표로 하는 12세에서 16세의 소비자 인구 통계 집단 사이에서는 더욱 그러합니다.

160-(B)/(C)수십년 동안 이 시장에 서비스를 제공한 경험과 현지 상황에 대한 조예 깊은 지식은 저희 회사를 이러한 수요를 충족시키는 것에 있어 특별한 위치에 놓이게 합니다. 게다가, 160-(D)지역 내 소매업체와의 기존 파트너십이 귀하의 의류를 널리 유통되도록 보장할 것입니다.

저희 측 담당자가 제안에 대해 자세히 논의할 수 있도록 곧 귀하에게 연락을 드려 화상 회의 약속을 잡을 것입니다. 귀하의 시간과 배려에 미리 감사드립니다.

Andrew Kigame 드림
Crosstown 패션 회사 사장

---

exclusive adj. 독점의, 독점적인 venture n. 모험, 투기적 사업
potential n. 잠재력, 가능성 deep adj. 강한, 깊은 demand n. 수요
recognized adj. 알려진, 인정된 particularly adv. 특히
demographic n. 인구 통계 집단 intimate adj. 조예 깊은, 친밀한
position v. (위치에) 놓다, 두다 existing adj. 기존의, 존재하는
retailer n. 소매업체, 소매업자 ensure v. 보장하다
proposal n. 제안 in detail 자세히, 상세하게 in advance 미리
consideration n. 배려

158 추론 문제

해석 Ms. Winnicka의 회사에 대해 암시되는 것은?
(A) 남미에 공장을 열었다.
(B) 파트너십에 대해 Mr. Kigame에게 연락했다.
(C) 어린 소비자들을 위한 의류를 만든다.
(D) 공석에 지원자를 찾고 있다.

해설 지문의 'Our[Mr. Kigame's] company is interested in an exclusive licensing deal to sell your[Ms. Winnicka's] clothing brands throughout South America.'에서 Ms. Winnicka의 회사에서 의류를 만든다는 것을 알 수 있고, 'your[Ms. Winnicka's] target demographic of consumers aged 12 to 16'에서 Ms. Winnicka의 회사가 목표로 하는 소비자 인구 통계 집단이 12세에서 16세 사이의 소비자들이라고 했으므로 Ms. Winnicka의 회사는 어린 소비자들을 위한 의류를 만든다는 것을 추론할 수 있다. 따라서 (C)가 정답이다.

어휘 applicant n. 지원자 open position 공석

159 동의어 찾기 문제

해석 1문단 두 번째 줄의 단어 "deep"은 의미상 -와 가장 가깝다.
(A) 고정된
(B) 강렬한
(C) 다양한
(D) 적절한

해설 deep을 포함한 문장 'There is deep demand within the region

for globally recognized fashion brands'에서 deep은 '강한'이라는 뜻으로 사용되었다. 따라서 (B)가 정답이다.

160 Not/True 문제

해석 Crosstown 패션 회사의 장점으로 언급되지 않은 것은?
(A) 세계적인 대표성
(B) 광범위한 경험
(C) 현지 지식
(D) 지역 파트너십

해설 지문의 'Decades of experience serving this market and an intimate knowledge of local conditions'에서 수십 년 동안 이 시장에 서비스를 제공한 경험과 현지 상황에 대한 조예 깊은 지식이라고 했으므로 (B)와 (C)는 지문에 언급된 내용이다. 'our existing partnerships with retailers in the region'에서 지역 내 소매업체와의 기존 파트너십이라고 했으므로 (D)는 지문에 언급된 내용이다. (A)는 지문에 언급되지 않은 내용이다. 따라서 (A)가 정답이다.

어휘 representation n. 대표(성) extensive adj. 광범위한
regional adj. 지역의

Paraphrasing

in the region 그 지역 내에서 → Regional 지역의

161-163번은 다음 광고에 관한 문제입니다.

Royal Oak 출판사

Royal Oak 출판사는 신인 작가들을 지원하는 데 자부심을 가지고 있습니다. ¹⁶¹따라서 여름 컬렉션에 신인 소설가들의 작품 네 편을 포함하게 되어 매우 기쁩니다. 6월 1일부터 전국 서점에서 구입할 수 있으니 꼭 읽어보시기 바랍니다!

Pauline Mao의 *Complications*
이민자들이 직면한 어려움을 탐구하는 이 이야기는 영국 생활에 적응하기 위한 Ms. Mao의 어린 시절 노력들을 따라갑니다. 11.99파운드

Yolanda Wilcox의 *Dark Reflection*
한 귀족의 살인 사건을 다룬 흥미로운 역사 소설로 15세기 런던의 세계를 독자들에게 생생하게 전달합니다. 10.99파운드

David Bach의 *A Path Forward*
¹⁶²1990년대에 음악 회사에서의 Mr. Bach의 경험을 바탕으로 한 이 소설은 큰 성공을 꿈꾸는 젊은 팝스타의 이야기를 담고 있습니다. 12.99파운드

Colin Sanders의 *Conflict Zone*
Mr. Sanders는 14년간의 군 생활에서 끌어낸 ¹⁶³당시의 상세한 지도와 장비들의 사진으로 완성된 스릴 넘치는 2차 세계대전 이야기를 만들어 냈습니다. 14.99파운드

이 책들에 대한 더 많은 정보를 위해서는
www.royaloak.co.uk를 방문하세요.

---

take pride in ~에 자부심을 갖다 novelist n. 소설가
exploration n. 탐험 face v. 직면하다 immigrant n. 이민자
struggle n. 노력, 분투 adapt v. 적응하다 intriguing adj. 흥미로운
tale n. 이야기, 소설

161 목적 찾기 문제

해석 광고의 목적은 무엇인가?
(A) 회사의 특별한 할인을 광고하기 위해
(B) 여름 프로그램에 참여를 장려하기 위해
(C) 서점의 개점식을 홍보하기 위해
(D) 다가오는 제품 출시를 알리기 위해

해설 지문의 'We are therefore excited to include four works by first-time novelists in our summer collection. They will be available in bookstores across the country on 1 June, and we encourage you to check them out!'에서 신인 소설가들의 작품 네 편이 6월 1일에 서점에 출시되니 확인해 보라고 했고, 이어서 각 작품을 소개하고 있으므로 (D)가 정답이다.

어휘 publicize v. 광고하다, 알리다 promote v. 홍보하다
release n. 출시

162 Not/True 문제

해석 Mr. Bach에 대해 명시된 것은?
(A) 다른 나라로 영구히 이전했다.
(B) 대학생 때 역사를 공부했다.
(C) 엔터테인먼트 업계에서 일했다.
(D) 10년 넘게 군에서 복무했다.

해설 지문의 'Based on Mr. Bach's experience in the music business during the 1990s, ~'에서 Mr. Bach가 1990년대에 음악 회사에서 일한 경험이 있다고 했으므로 (C)가 정답이다.

어휘 permanently adv. 영구히, 영구적으로

Paraphrasing

music business 음악 회사 → entertainment industry 엔터테인먼트 업계

163 육하원칙 문제

해석 어떤 책이 다양한 설명용 그림들을 포함하는가?
(A) *Complications*
(B) *Dark Reflection*
(C) *A Path Forward*
(D) *Conflict Zone*

해설 지문의 '*Conflict Zone* by Colin Sanders', 'Mr. Sanders draws on ~ tale, complete with detailed maps and photographs of equipment from the period'에서 Mr. Sanders의 *Conflict Zone*에 상세한 지도와 장비들의 사진이 담겨 있다고 했으므로 (D)가 정답이다.

어휘 graphic n. 설명용의 그림, 삽화

164-167번은 다음 공고에 관한 문제입니다.

¹⁶⁴Gladstone 문화 센터에서 다큐멘터리 *The Depths Below*의 특별 상영을 주최할 것입니다. ─ [1] ─. ¹⁶⁹⁻⁽ᴬ⁾그것은 호주의 Great Barrier Reef를 탐험하며, 이 복잡한 생태계에 거주하는 다양한 생명체들과 그것들이 직면하는 많은 환경적인 위험에 초점을 맞추고 있습니다. ○

— [2] —. ^{165-(B)}지난달 국립예술위원회에 의해 최우수 신작 다큐멘터리 부문에서 수상작으로 선정된 The Depths Below는 놀라운 시각 자료와 시사하는 바가 많은 내용으로 ^{165-(D)}비평가들에게 높이 평가받아 왔습니다.

그 행사는 4월 5일 저녁 6시부터 9시까지 진행될 것입니다. 그 다큐멘터리의 상영 시간은 2시간이며, 감독인 Peter Warren의 이야기가 뒤따를 것입니다. — [3] —. 유명한 해양 생물학자이기도 한 Mr. Warren은 우리의 바다를 지키기 위해 행해져야 하는 것들뿐만 아니라 다큐멘터리를 제작하는 것의 어려움에 대해서도 이야기할 것입니다. ¹⁶⁶이후, 그는 관객들의 질문에 답할 예정입니다.

이 다큐멘터리 상영은 Gladstone 문화 센터에서 진행 중인 환경 인식 시리즈의 일환입니다. ¹⁶⁷일반 입장권의 가격은 23달러이고 온라인으로 구매될 수 있습니다. — [4] —. 이 놀라운 기회를 놓치지 않으시려면 지금 움직이세요!

host v. 주최하다, 열다 explore v. 탐험하다, 탐구하다
focus on ~에 초점을 맞추다 diverse adj. 다양한
organism n. 생명체, 유기체 inhabit v. 거주하다, 살다
complex adj. 복잡한 ecosystem n. 생태계
environmental adj. 환경의 face v. 직면하다, 마주하다
praise v. 높이 평가하다, 칭찬하다 critic n. 비평가
stunning adj. 놀라운, 굉장히 아름다운 visual n. 시각 자료
thought-provoking adj. 시사하는 바가 많은
be followed by ~이 뒤따르다 renowned adj. 유명한
biologist n. 생물학자 respond to ~에 답하다, 응답하다

164 주제 찾기 문제

해석 무엇이 공고되고 있는가?
(A) 연극 제작
(B) 미술 전시회
(C) 책 서명회
(D) 영화 상영

해설 지문의 'The Gladstone Cultural Hub will be hosting a special showing of the documentary~.'에서 Gladstone 문화 센터에서 다큐멘터리의 특별 상영을 주최할 것이라고 했으므로, 영화 상영에 대해 공고되고 있음을 알 수 있다. 따라서 (D)가 정답이다.

어휘 production n. 제작 exhibit n. 전시회, 전시품

165 Not/True 문제

해석 The Depths Below에 대해 명시된 것은?
(A) 허구의 상황에 대한 설명을 제시한다.
(B) 국가의 상을 받은 작품이다.
(C) 한 달 전에 극장에서 개봉되었다.
(D) 대중에게 광범위한 비판을 받았다.

해설 지문의 'Selected as the winner in the Best New Documentary category by the National Arts Council last month'에서 지난달 국립예술위원회에 의해 최우수 신작 다큐멘터리 부문에서 수상작으로 선정됐다고 했으므로 (B)는 지문의 내용과 일치한다. 따라서 (B)가 정답이다. (A)는 'It explores the Great Barrier Reef in Australia, focusing on the diverse

organisms inhabiting this complex ecosystem and the many environmental risks they face.'에서 The Depths Below는 호주의 Great Barrier Reef를 탐험하며, 이 복잡한 생태계에 거주하는 다양한 생명체들과 그것들이 직면하는 많은 환경적인 위험에 초점을 맞추고 있다고 했으므로 지문의 내용과 일치하지 않는다. (D)는 'The Depths Below has been praised by critics for its stunning visuals and thought-provoking content.'에서 놀라운 시각 자료와 시사하는 바가 많은 내용으로 비평가들에게 높이 평가받았다고 했으므로 지문의 내용과 일치하지 않는다. (C)는 지문에 언급되지 않은 내용이다.

어휘 present v. 제시하다 fictional adj. 허구의
recipient n. 받는 대상, 수령인 release v. 개봉하다, 공개하다
widespread adj. 광범위한 criticism n. 비판

166 추론 문제

해석 행사의 마지막 부분 동안 무슨 일이 일어날 것 같은가?
(A) 새로운 촬영 일정이 공개될 것이다.
(B) 참가자들이 감독에게 몇 가지 질문을 할 것이다.
(C) 자선 단체를 위한 기부가 요청될 것이다.
(D) 참석자들에게 유인물이 배포될 것이다.

해설 지문의 'Afterwards, he[Mr. Warren] will respond to inquiries from audience members.'에서 상영 후 감독의 이야기가 있고 그 후에 관객들의 질문에 답할 것이라고 했으므로, 행사의 마지막 부분 동안 참가자들이 감독에게 질문을 할 것임을 추론할 수 있다. 따라서 (B)가 정답이다.

어휘 participant n. 참가자 donation n. 기부 handout n. 유인물
distribute v. 배포하다, 나눠주다

167 문장 위치 찾기 문제

해석 [1], [2], [3], [4]로 표시된 위치 중, 다음 문장이 들어갈 곳으로 가장 적절한 것은?

"티켓 판매액의 일부는 해양 보호 활동에 사용될 것입니다."

(A) [1]
(B) [2]
(C) [3]
(D) [4]

해설 주어진 문장은 티켓과 관련된 내용 주변에 나와야 함을 예상할 수 있다. [4]의 앞 문장인 'Regular admission costs $23 and can be purchased online.'에서 일반 입장권의 가격은 23달러이고 온라인으로 구매할 수 있다고 했으므로, [4]에 주어진 문장이 들어가면 일반 입장권은 23달러이고 온라인으로 구매할 수 있으며, 티켓 판매액의 일부는 해양 보호 활동에 사용될 것이라는 자연스러운 문맥이 된다는 것을 알 수 있다. 따라서 (D)가 정답이다.

168-171번은 다음 기사에 관한 문제입니다.

> Indus Group의 새로운 방향
>
> 7월 14일—Indus Group은 인도의 구자라트 지역에 대규모 풍력-태양열 발전 시설에 대한 계획을 발표했다. 그 새로운 하이브리드 시 ○

설의 부지는 이미 선정되었으며, [168]착공식은 10월 1일에 열릴 예정이다. 미달러로 4천만 달러 이상의 예산과 18개월의 일정으로, 그 회사는 건축 단계 동안 문제가 없을 것이라고 확신한다.

Indus Group의 최고 경영자인 Alia Basu는 인도 정부의 지원에 감사를 표했다. "[169]에너지부에 의해 제공된 다양한 세금 혜택과 보조금이 없었다면, 이 프로젝트는 결코 고려되지 않았을 것입니다,"라고 그녀가 말했다. "그 시설은 오염을 일으키거나 기후 변화의 원인이 되지 않으면서 수천 명의 주민들에게 전기를 공급할 것입니다." [170]이것은 3개월 전 최고 경영자로 승진한 이후 Ms. Basu의 첫 번째 계획이며, Indus Group을 친환경 기술의 주요 기업으로 만들고자 하는 그녀의 바람을 나타낸다.

Indus Group의 최근 프로젝트의 환경적 이점을 둘러싼 집중적 홍보에도 불구하고, 이에 대한 일부 반발이 남아 있다. [171]구체적으로 말하자면, 하이브리드 발전소가 수익성이 없을 것이고 회사의 주가에 부정적으로 영향을 미칠 것이라는 우려가 있다. 이에 대응하여, Indus Group은 다음 달에 특별 주주총회를 개최할 계획이다. 프로젝트에 대한 추가적인 재정 및 기술 관련 세부 사항은 그때 제공될 것이다.

direction n. 방향 massive adj. 대규모의 site n. 부지
plant n. 시설, 공장 groundbreaking ceremony 착공식, 기공식
phase n. 단계 assistance n. 지원, 도움 grant n. 보조금
supply v. 공급하다 contribute to ~의 원인이 되다, ~에 기여하다
climate n. 기후, 날씨 initiative n. 계획, 진취성
move up into ~로 승진하다 represent v. 나타내다
desire n. 바람, 욕구
green technology (환경 보존을 위한) 친환경 기술
media hype 집중적 홍보, 미디어 동원 홍보 surround v. 둘러싸다
benefit n. 이점, 혜택, 이익 opposition n. 반발, 반대
profitable adj. 수익성이 있는 stock price 주가
shareholders meeting 주주총회

168 육하원칙 문제

해석 10월 1일에 무슨 일이 일어날 것으로 예상되는가?
(A) 발전소 부지가 최종적으로 선정될 것이다.
(B) 에너지 회사가 경쟁업체와 합병할 것이다.
(C) 건설 프로젝트가 공식적으로 시작할 것이다.
(D) 시설의 운영 예산이 승인될 것이다.

해설 지문의 'the groundbreaking ceremony is scheduled to take place on October 1'에서 착공식이 10월 1일에 열릴 예정이라고 했으므로 (C)가 정답이다.

어휘 competitor n. 경쟁업체, 경쟁자 officially adv. 공식적으로
commence v. 시작하다 approve v. 승인하다

Paraphrasing

the groundbreaking ceremony is scheduled to take place 착공식이 열릴 예정이다 → A construction project will officially commence 건설 프로젝트가 공식적으로 시작할 것이다

169 추론 문제

해석 에너지부에 대해 암시되는 것은?
(A) 회사에 재정적 지원을 제공했다.
(B) 에너지 기업에 대한 세금을 인상했다.

(C) 오염에 대한 규제를 강화했다.
(D) 많은 주민들로부터 항의를 받았다.

해설 지문의 'the various tax incentives and grants offered by the Ministry of Energy'에서 에너지부에 의해 제공된 다양한 세금 혜택과 보조금이라고 했으므로 에너지부가 회사에 재정적 지원을 제공했다는 것을 추론할 수 있다. 따라서 (A)가 정답이다.

어휘 corporation n. 기업 strengthen v. 강화하다
regulation n. 규제

Paraphrasing

various tax incentives and grants 세금 혜택과 보조금
→ financial support 재정적 지원

170 Not/True 문제

해석 Ms. Basu에 대해 명시된 것은?
(A) 기후 변화에 맞서 싸우는 단체들에 기금을 기부한다.
(B) Indus Group과 관련된 여러 계획에 착수했다.
(C) 최근에 고위 관리직으로 승진했다.
(D) 친환경 기술을 사용하는 것에 대한 의심을 내비쳤다.

해설 지문의 'This is Ms. Basu's first initiative since being moved up into the CEO position three months ago'에서 이것은 3개월 전 최고 경영자로 승진한 이후 Ms. Basu의 첫 번째 계획이라고 했으므로, Ms. Basu가 최근에 고위 관리직으로 승진했다는 것을 알 수 있다. 따라서 (C)가 정답이다.

어휘 senior management 고위 관리직, 간부직
uncertainty n. 의심, 불확실성

Paraphrasing

being moved up into ~로 승진한 → was promoted to ~로 승진했다
the CEO position 최고 경영자 → a senior management position 고위 관리직

171 육하원칙 문제

해석 Indus Group은 왜 다음 달에 회의를 열 것인가?
(A) 기자들에게 정보를 제공하기 위해
(B) 새로운 회사 임원을 소개하기 위해
(C) 투자자들의 걱정을 해결하기 위해
(D) 기술 혁신을 보여주기 위해

해설 지문의 'Specifically, there are concerns that the hybrid power plant will not be profitable and will negatively affect the company's stock price. In response, the Indus Group plans to hold a special shareholders meeting next month.'에서 하이브리드 발전소가 수익성이 없을 것이고 회사의 주가에 부정적으로 영향을 미칠 것이라는 우려가 있는데, 이에 대응하여 다음 달에 특별 주주총회를 개최할 계획이라고 했으므로 (C)가 정답이다.

어휘 journalist n. 기자 executive n. 임원, 경영자
address v. 해결하다, 다루다 investor n. 투자자
reveal v. 보여주다, 드러내다 innovation n. 혁신

172-175번은 다음 온라인 채팅 대화문에 관한 문제입니다.

Carlos Ortega [오전 10시 20분]
Nathan 씨, Tara 씨, 좋은 아침입니다. 여러분께 공유드릴 것이 있어요. 우리 CEO가 방금 제게 ¹⁷²브랜트퍼드시가 Tyler 강 위에 새 대교를 설계하고 건설하는 일에 우리 회사를 선택했다고 알려주셨습니다. 우리 세 사람이 이 일을 이끌어 갈 거예요.

Nathan Boyle [오전 10시 22분]
와, 중요한 프로젝트가 되겠네요. 긴장은 되지만, 그것에 참여하게 되어 기쁩니다.

Tara Hong [오전 10시 23분]
저도 그래요. 그 프로젝트의 예산에 관한 어떤 세부 사항이 있을까요?

Carlos Ortega [오전 10시 24분]
그것은 600만 달러로 정해졌습니다. ¹⁷³작년에 브랜트퍼드시 의회가 개인 및 기업 기부자로부터 기금을 모으기 위해 특별 행사를 개최한 것으로 알고 있어요. 큰 성공을 거두었죠.

Nathan Boyle [오전 10시 26분]
대교 자체에 관한 것인요? 어떤 유형을 설계할 것인지, 그리고 우리가 알고 있어야 하는 어떤 특별한 요구 사항이 있을까요?

Carlos Ortega [오전 10시 28분]
그린빌에 작년에 세워진 것과 비슷한 현수교를 강력히 선호해요. 하지만 문제는 ¹⁷⁴Tyler 강을 가로지르는 대교가 화물선이 그 아래로 통과할 수 있도록 들어 올려질 수 있는 부분을 포함해야 한다는 거예요.

Tara Hong [오전 10시 30분]
진심인가요? 그건 정말 복잡할 텐데요. 그리고 비용 또한 많이 들 거예요. ¹⁷⁴예산을 초과하지 않고 그것을 해낼 수 있을지 모르겠어요.

Nathan Boyle [오전 10시 32분]
Carlos 씨, 저는 그게 문제가 되지 않을 것 같아요. 이전 회사에서 비슷한 대교 프로젝트를 진행했던 적이 있거든요. 원하신다면, 비용을 줄이기 위해 제 팀이 취했던 조치들에 대한 발표를 준비할 수 있습니다. 아마도 수요일 오후까지는 준비할 수 있을 것 같네요.

Carlos Ortega [오전 10시 34분]
Nathan 씨, 고마워요. ¹⁷⁵지금 행정 보조원에게 연락해서 주 회의실을 그날 사용할 수 있도록 해둘게요.

---

share v. 공유하다, 나누다 take the lead 이끌어 가다, 앞장을 서다
undertaking n. 프로젝트, (힘든) 일 nervous adj. 긴장된, 초조해하는
budget n. 예산 council n. 의회 requirement n. 요구 사항, 요건
preference n. 선호, 선호되는 것 suspension bridge 현수교
catch n. 문제(점), 걸림돌 raise v. 들어 올리다 ship traffic 화물선
previous adj. 이전의 put together (한데 모아) 준비하다, 만들다
administrative adj. 행정의 assistant n. 보조원, 조수

172 추론 문제

해석 글쓴이들은 어떤 분야에서 일하는 것 같은가?
(A) 채용
(B) 회계
(C) 수송
(D) 건설

해설 지문의 'the city of Brantford has chosen our company to design and build a new bridge over the Tyler River'에서 브

랜트퍼드시가 Tyler 강에 새로운 대교를 설계하고 건설하는 일에 글쓴이들의 회사를 선택했다고 했으므로, 그들이 대교 설계 및 건설 작업과 관련 있는 건설 분야에서 일한다는 사실을 추론할 수 있다. 따라서 (D)가 정답이다.

173 Not/True 문제

해석 브랜트퍼드시 의회에 대해 언급된 것은?
(A) 여러 기업을 고용했다.
(B) 새로운 부동산을 매입했다.
(C) 작년에 모금 행사를 개최했다.
(D) 대규모 대출을 신청했다.

해설 지문의 'I guess the Brantford city council organized a special event last year to collect funds from private and corporate donors.'에서 브랜트퍼드시 의회가 개인 및 기업 기부자로부터 기금을 모으기 위해 작년에 특별 행사를 개최했다고 했으므로 (C)는 지문의 내용과 일치한다. 따라서 (C)가 정답이다. (A), (B), (D)는 지문에 언급되지 않은 내용이다.

어휘 hire v. 고용하다 multiple adj. 여러, 다수의
purchase v. 매입하다, 구매하다 property n. 부동산
apply for ~을 신청하다

Paraphrasing

a special event ~ to collect funds 기금을 모으기 위한 특별한 행사 → fundraiser 모금 행사

174 의도 파악 문제

해석 오전 10시 30분에, Ms. Hong이 "Are you serious"라고 썼을 때, 그녀가 의도한 것은?
(A) 프로젝트의 실현 가능성에 관해 우려한다.
(B) 예산이 늘어난 것에 기뻐한다.
(C) 제안에 대한 Mr. Ortega의 거절에 놀랐다.
(D) 업무를 시작하기를 열망한다.

해설 지문의 'the bridge over the Tyler River has to include a section that can be raised to allow ship traffic to pass underneath'에서 Mr. Ortega가 Tyler 강을 가로지르는 대교는 화물선이 그 아래로 통과할 수 있도록 들어 올려질 수 있는 부분을 포함해야 한다고 하자, Ms. Hong이 'Are you serious?'(진심인가요?)라고 한 뒤, 'I'm not sure we can pull it off without going over budget.'이라며 예산을 초과하지 않고 그것을 해낼 수 있을지 모르겠다고 한 것을 통해 Ms. Hong이 프로젝트의 실현 가능성에 관해 우려한다는 것을 알 수 있다. 따라서 (A)가 정답이다.

어휘 feasibility n. 실현 가능성 rejection n. 거절
be eager to ~하기를 열망하다

175 추론 문제

해석 Mr. Ortega는 다음에 무엇을 할 것 같은가?
(A) 그룹 발표를 준비한다.
(B) 시설을 이용하기 위해 예약한다.
(C) 새로운 팀 구성원을 선정한다.
(D) 건물 관리자에게 연락한다.

해설 지문의 'I'll contact our administrative assistant now and ensure that we can use the main conference room on that day.'에서 행정 보조원에게 연락해서 주 회의실을 그날 사용할 수 있도록 해두겠다고 했으므로, Mr. Ortega가 시설을 이용하기 위해 예약할 것임을 추론할 수 있다. 따라서 (B)가 정답이다.

어휘 reservation n. 예약

Paraphrasing

the main conference room 주 회의실 → a facility 시설

176-180번은 다음 보고서와 기사에 관한 문제입니다.

Wheelz 자동차 대여 고객 만족도 조사 요약 (6월)		
분류	고객 만족도	전월 대비 변화
차량의 청결도	93퍼센트	+8퍼센트
모델의 다양성	56퍼센트	-7퍼센트
직원의 친절도	78퍼센트	+10퍼센트
176요금의 적정성	17616퍼센트	-3퍼센트
전반적인 고객 만족도 변화: +8퍼센트		
177이 분석은 마케팅 이사인 Sandra Sharpe에 의해 수행되었습니다. 질문은 s.sharpe@wzauto.com으로 보내져야 합니다. 관련 보고서는 권한이 부여된 직원에 의해 www.wzauto.com/archives에서 이용될 수 있습니다.		

summary n. 요약 cleanliness n. 청결(도) variety n. 다양성
helpfulness n. 친절도, 유익성
affordability n. 적정성, 적당한 가격으로 구입할 수 있는 것
analysis n. 분석 authorized adj. 권한이 부여된
personnel n. 직원

마이애미 (9월 12일)—어제 오후 기자 회견에서, 178Wheelz 자동차 대여사는 플로리다, 텍사스, 켄터키에 있는 8개 도시로 추가 확장할 계획을 밝혔다. 177이번 달 Sandra Sharpe의 은퇴 결정에 따라 그녀의 자리를 인계받은 Adam Willis는 기자들에게 회사의 현재 시장 점유율을 지키고 수익을 유지하기 위해 확장이 필요하다고 말했다. "저희는 다른 자동차 대여 체인점으로부터 받는 압박감이 커지고 있습니다,"라고 그는 말했다. "앞으로 나아가지 않는다면, 뒤처질 것입니다."

179Willis는 또한 회사의 최고경영자가 1월 2일까지 모든 새로운 지점들이 반드시 완전한 준비를 갖출 수 있도록 하기 위해 직접 해당 프로젝트를 총괄하고 있다고 설명했다. 180회사는 11월 15일에 입사 지원서 접수를 시작할 것이다. "저희는 어떤 지연도 예상하지 않으며, 저희의 자동차 대여 서비스가 훨씬 더 많은 사람들에게 이용 가능할 수 있기를 기대합니다,"라며 Willis가 마지막으로 덧붙였다.

press conference 기자 회견 take over 인계받다
expansion n. 확장 profit n. 수익, 이득 pressure n. 압박(감), 압력
forward adv. 앞으로 personally adv. 직접, 개인적으로
operational adj. 준비를 갖춘, 운영상의
anticipate v. 예상하다, 기대하다

176 추론 문제

해석 보고서에서 Wheelz 자동차 대여사에 대해 암시되는 것은?

(A) 더 많은 자동차 모델을 제공할 계획을 세웠다.
(B) 차량들이 좀처럼 청소되지 않는다.
(C) 요금이 다수의 고객들에게 비싸다고 여겨진다.
(D) 고객 만족도에서 전반적인 하락을 보였다.

해설 보고서의 'Affordability of rates'와 '16%'에서 요금의 적정성에 대한 고객 만족도가 16퍼센트라고 했으므로 Wheelz 자동차 대여사의 요금이 다수의 고객들에게 비싸다고 여겨진다는 것을 추론할 수 있다. 따라서 (C)가 정답이다.

어휘 rarely adv. 좀처럼 ~하지 않는 drop n. 하락, 감소

177 Not/True 문제 연계

해석 Mr. Willis에 대해 사실인 것은?
(A) 6월에 요약 보고서를 작성했다.
(B) 은퇴할 의사를 밝혔다.
(C) 플로리다 지점으로 전근 갈 것이다.
(D) 마케팅 부서에서 일한다.

해설 Mr. Willis가 언급된 기사를 먼저 확인한다.
단서 1 기사의 'Adam Willis, who took over Sandra Sharpe's position this month following her decision to retire'에서 이번 달 Sandra Sharpe의 은퇴 결정에 따라 Adam Willis가 그녀의 자리를 인계받았다고 했다. 그런데 인계받은 자리에 대한 정보가 제시되지 않았으므로 보고서에서 관련 내용을 확인한다.
단서 2 보고서의 'This analysis was conducted by Sandra Sharpe, Director of Marketing.'에서 Sandra Sharpe가 마케팅 이사였다는 것을 확인할 수 있다.
두 단서를 종합할 때 Mr. Willis가 마케팅 이사였던 Sandra Sharpe의 자리를 인계받았으므로 마케팅 부서에서 일한다는 것을 알 수 있다. 따라서 (D)가 정답이다.

어휘 retire v. 은퇴하다 transfer v. 전근 가다, 옮기다

178 목적 찾기 문제

해석 기사의 목적은 무엇인가?
(A) 최근 시장 동향을 분석하기 위해
(B) 새로운 기업 임원을 소개하기 위해
(C) 회사의 이전을 발표하기 위해
(D) 회사의 확장 계획을 설명하기 위해

해설 기사의 'Wheelz Auto Rental laid out its plans to expand into eight more cities ~'에서 Wheelz 자동차 대여사는 8개 도시로 추가 확장할 계획을 밝혔다고 알리고 있으므로 (D)가 정답이다.

어휘 trend n. 동향, 추세 relocation n. 이전, 이동

179 동의어 찾기 문제

해석 기사에서, 2문단 첫 번째 줄의 단어 "directing"은 의미상 -와 가장 가깝다.
(A) 이끄는
(B) 다루는
(C) 보내는
(D) 제한하는

해설 directing을 포함한 구절 'Willis also explained that the CEO

of the company is directing the project personally to ensure that all of the new branches are fully operational by January 2.'에서 directing은 '총괄하는'이라는 뜻으로 사용되었다. 따라서 (A)가 정답이다.

180 육하원칙 문제

해석 기사에 따르면, 11월 15일에 무슨 일이 일어날 것인가?
(A) 지점이 문을 열 것이다.
(B) 프로젝트 팀이 구성될 것이다.
(C) 사업 부지가 선정될 것이다.
(D) 채용 절차가 시작될 것이다.

해설 기사의 'The company will start accepting job applications on November 15'에서 회사가 11월 15일에 입사 지원서를 받기 시작할 것이라고 했으므로, 11월 15일에 채용 절차가 시작될 것임을 알 수 있다. 따라서 (D)가 정답이다.

Paraphrasing

start accepting job applications 입사 지원서를 받기 시작하다
→ A hiring process ~ begin 채용 절차가 시작되다

181-185번은 다음 웹페이지들에 관한 문제입니다.

| **소개** | 위치 | 후기 | 연락 |

Nuestra Casa로 여러분을 초대합니다!
정통 멕시코 요리를 즐기세요.

Nuestra Casa는 샌디에이고에서 멕시코 음식으로 가장 인기 있는 곳입니다. 181-(B)주인인 Miguel Gomez가 Harris가 위치에 이 식당을 처음 열었을 때, 그의 목표는 그 도시의 주민들에게 고국의 요리를 소개하는 것이었습니다. 그 후로 30년이 넘었지만, 181-(B)그는 여전히 그 도시에서 최고의 멕시코 음식을 요리하고 있습니다!

잠시 들르셔서 저희의 일일 특선 요리를 이용해 보세요:

월요일 & 수요일 & 금요일: 모든 애피타이저가 반값에 제공됩니다.
화요일 & 목요일: 부리토 하나를 구매하고, 두 번째 부리토를 무료로 받으세요.
토요일: 모든 주요 요리와 함께 무료 디저트를 받으세요.
184일요일: 단돈 12.99달러에 무제한 생선 타코를 즐기세요.

우리의 182-(A)9인조 마리아치 밴드인 Los Músicos는 182-(B)평일에는 오후 8시까지, 그리고 주말에는 오후 10시까지 연주합니다. 만약 여러분이 182-(C)이 음악가들이 연주하는 전통 민속 음악을 즐기신다면, 182-(D)그들의 노래를 스트리밍하기 위해 www.losmusicos.com을 방문하세요.

여러분은 무엇을 기다리고 있나요? 오늘 밤 Nuestra Casa를 방문하세요!

authentic adj. 정통의, 진짜의   goal n. 목표   resident n. 주민
dish n. 요리, 접시   homeland n. 고국
take advantage of ~을 이용하다   appetizer n. 애피타이저, 전채
entrée n. 주요 요리   unlimited adj. 무제한의   piece n. 구성원
mariachi n. 마리아치(멕시코 전통 악단)   folk adj. 민속의

| 소개 | 위치 | **후기** | 연락 |

직장 동료들과 가족들로부터 이 식당에 대해 많은 긍정적인 이야기를 들은 후, 저는 마침내 이 식당에서 먹어 볼 수 있게 되어 기뻤습니다. 183대학교 때 동창이 고객을 만나기 위해 시내에 있어서, 183/184지난 일요일에 그곳에 저녁 식사를 예약했습니다. 184일일 특선 요리는 합리적인 가격이었고 재료는 매우 신선했습니다. 분위기도 정말 인상 깊었습니다. 모든 직원들이 친절했고, 메인 식사 공간의 장식은 밝고 쾌적했습니다. 185이 식당에 대해 제가 겪은 유일한 문제점은 제가 도착했을 때 협소한 주차장이 완전히 차 있었다는 것입니다. 저는 약 세 블록 떨어진 주차장에 제 차를 두고 가야 해서 불편했습니다. 이 문제를 해결하면 결과적으로 손님들에게 더 나은 경험을 제공하게 될 것입니다.

Astrid Larsson 게시, 4월 20일

coworker n. 직장 동료   classmate n. 동창   reservation n. 예약
reasonably adv. 합리적으로   ingredient n. 재료
atmosphere n. 분위기   decoration n. 장식   bright adj. 밝은
cheerful adj. 쾌적한, 발랄한   completely adv. 완전히
garage n. 주차장, 차고   inconvenient adj. 불편한
deal with ~을 해결하다, 다루다

181 Not/True 문제

해석 Nuestra Casa에 대해 언급된 것은?
(A) 여러 나라의 요리를 특징으로 한다.
(B) 주인이 손님들을 위해 음식을 준비한다.
(C) 위치가 여러 번 바뀌었다.
(D) 4월에 다시 문을 열 예정이다.

해설 첫 번째 웹페이지의 'Over three decades later, he[Miguel Gomez] is still cooking the best Mexican food in the city!'에서 Miguel Gomez는 여전히 그 도시에서 최고의 멕시코 음식을 요리하고 있다고 했으므로 (B)는 지문의 내용과 일치한다. 따라서 (B)가 정답이다.

어휘 cuisine n. 요리

Paraphrasing

is ~ cooking 요리하고 있다 → prepares food 음식을 준비한다

182 Not/True 문제

해석 Los Músicos에 대해 사실이 아닌 것은?
(A) 총 9명의 음악가를 포함한다.
(B) 매주 토요일에는 오후 8시까지 공연한다.
(C) 전통적인 스타일의 민속 음악을 연주한다.
(D) 사람들이 온라인으로 노래를 이용할 수 있게 한다.

해설 Los Músicos가 언급된 첫 번째 웹페이지를 확인한다. (A)는 'nine-piece mariachi band'에서 9인조 마리아치 밴드라고 했으므로 지문의 내용과 일치한다. (B)는 'plays until 8 P.M. on weekdays and 10 P.M. on weekends'에서 평일에는 오후 8시까지 그리고 주말에는 오후 10시까지 연주한다고 했으므로 지문의 내용과 일치하지 않는다. 따라서 (B)가 정답이다. (C)는 'traditional folk music these musicians perform'에서 이 음악가들이 연주하는 전통 민속 음악이라고 했으므로 지문의 내용과 일치한다. (D)는 'visit www.

losmusicos.com to stream their songs'에서 그들의 노래를 스트리밍하려면 www.losmusicos.com을 방문하라고 했으므로 지문의 내용과 일치한다.

어휘 include v. 포함하다 perform v. 공연하다

183 육하원칙 문제

해석 Ms. Larsson은 누구와 저녁을 먹었는가?
(A) 새로운 직장 동료
(B) 가족 구성원
(C) 과거 동창
(D) 비즈니스 고객

해설 Ms. Larsson이 작성한 후기가 있는 두 번째 웹페이지에서 관련 내용을 확인한다. 'A classmate from my university days was in town to meet a client, so I made a reservation for dinner there last Sunday.'에서 대학교 때 동창이 고객을 만나기 위해 시내에 있어서, 지난 일요일에 그곳에 저녁 식사를 예약했다고 했으므로 (C)가 정답이다.

Paraphrasing

a classmate from my university days 대학교 때 동창 → former classmate 과거 동창

184 추론 문제 연계

해석 Ms. Larsson에 대해 암시되는 것은?
(A) 저녁으로 해산물 요리를 주문했다.
(B) 밴드가 너무 시끄럽다고 생각했다.
(C) 전에 Nuestra Casa를 방문한 적이 있다.
(D) 예약 날짜를 변경했다.

해설 질문의 핵심 어구인 Ms. Larsson이 작성한 후기가 있는 두 번째 웹페이지를 먼저 확인한다.
단서 1 두 번째 웹페이지의 'I made a reservation for dinner there last Sunday', 'The daily special was reasonably priced and the ingredients were very fresh.'에서 지난 일요일에 저녁 식사를 예약했고, 일일 특선 요리를 먹었다고 했다. 그런데 일요일의 일일 특선 요리가 무엇인지에 대해 제시되지 않았으므로 첫 번째 지문에서 관련 내용을 확인한다.
단서 2 첫 번째 웹페이지의 'Sundays: Enjoy unlimited fish tacos for only $12.99.'에서 일요일의 일일 특선 요리가 생선 타코라는 것을 알 수 있다.
두 단서를 종합할 때, Ms. Larsson이 저녁으로 해산물 요리를 주문했음을 추론할 수 있다. 따라서 (A)가 정답이다.

185 육하원칙 문제

해석 두 번째 웹페이지에 따르면, Nuestra Casa는 어떻게 고객들에게 더 나은 경험을 제공할 수 있는가?
(A) 몇몇 요리의 가격을 낮춤으로써
(B) 직원들에게 더 많은 교육을 제공함으로써
(C) 메인 식사 공간을 다시 장식함으로써
(D) 추가 주차 공간을 확보함으로써

해설 두 번째 웹페이지의 'The only issue I have with this restaurant

---

is that the small parking lot was completely full when I arrived. I had to leave my car in a garage about three blocks away, which was inconvenient. Dealing with this issue would result in a better experience for customers.'에서 이 식당에 대해 자신이 겪은 유일한 문제점은 자신이 도착했을 때 협소한 주차장이 완전히 차 있었다는 것이고 약 세 블록 떨어진 주차장에 차를 두고 가야 해서 불편했다고 하면서, 이 문제를 해결하면 결과적으로 손님들에게 더 나은 경험을 제공하게 될 것이라고 했으므로 (D)가 정답이다.

어휘 redecorate v. 다시 장식하다 secure v. 확보하다

186-190번은 다음 두 이메일과 회람에 관한 문제입니다.

수신: Neil Shannon <n.shannon@mexigo.com>
발신: Rebecca Tan <r.tan@postouchsolutions.com>
날짜: 4월 12일
제목: 합의한 조건

Mr. Shannon께,

앞서 저희와 만나 주셔서 감사합니다. 합의 조건을 요약하기 위해 이 메일을 쓰게 되었습니다.

합의된 바에 따라, POS Touch Solutions사는 우드베리에 있는 Mexigo 식당마다 하나씩 총 네 대의 셀프 주문 키오스크를 설치할 것입니다. 첫 설치 비용은 한 대당 1,800달러입니다. [186-(B)]저희는 또한 결함이 있는 하드웨어의 무상 수리와 주기적인 소프트웨어 업데이트를 제공할 것입니다. 저희 키오스크는 가동 시간 비율이 99.9퍼센트에 달하기 때문에 잦은 수리가 필요할 것으로 예상하지 않는다는 점을 주목하세요.

[187]기술자의 방문을 필요로 하는 다른 서비스는 방문당 450달러의 비용이 별도로 청구될 것이지만, 저희가 원격으로 해결할 수 있는 기술적 문제들에 대해서는 150달러만 청구할 것입니다. 저희 기술자들은 24시간 내내 키오스크를 점검할 수 있습니다.

오류가 있다면 제게 연락해 주세요. 그렇지 않으면, 주말 전에 최종 계약서를 보내드리겠습니다.

Rebecca Tan 드림
지역 영업 부사장, POS Touch Solutions사

---

agreed adj. 합의된 terms n. 조건 summarize v. 요약하다
agreement n. 합의 initial adj. 초기의, 처음의 installation n. 설치
repair n. 수리 defective adj. 결함이 있는 periodic adj. 주기적인
anticipate v. 예상하다 frequent adj. 잦은 uptime n. 가동 시간
separately adv. 별도로 remotely adv. 원격으로, 멀리서
around the clock 24시간 내내 regional adj. 지역의, 지방의

수신: Rebecca Tan <r.tan@postouchsolutions.com>
발신: Neil Shannon <n.shannon@mexigo.com>
[188]날짜: 8월 19일
제목: 장비 철거 및 재설치

Ms. Tan께,

[189]Goldfinch가에 있는 저희 식당이 이달 말 수리를 위해 임시로 문을 닫을 예정임을 알려드립니다. 저희는 8월 31일까지 Poplar가에 있는 저희 창고로 모든 장비를 옮기는 것을 목표로 하고 있습니다. ⟳

따라서 그 날짜 전에 셀프 주문 키오스크를 제거하고 나중에 다시 설치하고 싶습니다.

[188]현재로서는, 언제쯤 수리가 끝날지 확실치 않습니다. 다음 달 초까지는 확실한 답변을 드릴 수 있습니다. [187]일단은, 위 장소로 기술자를 보내 철거 작업을 진행해 주시길 바랍니다.

Neil Shannon 드림
지역 운영 관리자, Mexigo 식당

---

equipment n. 장비 removal n. 철거, 제거
reinstallation n. 재설치 temporarily adv. 임시로
aim v. 목표로 하다 warehouse n. 창고

[회람]

수신: Mexigo 전 직원 (Goldfinch 지점)
발신: Sarah Martinez, 지점 관리자
날짜: 10월 4일
주제: 신속한 업데이트

[189]새로 수리된 곳이 곧 문을 열 준비가 될 것임을 확정할 수 있습니다. 여러분이 기억하다시피, 키오스크에서 주문하기 위해 줄을 서있는 사람들이 정문을 종종 막았습니다. 따라서, 우리는 키오스크를 직원 휴게실 옆으로 옮기고 그 자리에 더 많은 테이블을 들일 예정입니다. 저희는 다시 문을 열기 전에 공급업체로부터 새 테이블 판이 배송되기를 기다리고 있을 뿐입니다.

많은 분들께서 다른 지점으로 새로 발령을 받은 후 다시 돌아오고 싶어 하셨을 것입니다. 여러분의 인내심과 협조에 감사를 표하기 위해, 회사는 이번 주 토요일에 Hellman 공원에서의 야유회를 준비했습니다. [190]일정이 겹치는 것을 피하기 위해 여러분의 교대 근무 시간을 옮기는 것과 관련하여 이미 다른 지점 관리자들에게 연락했습니다.

---

block v. 막다 tabletop n. 테이블 판 reassign v. 새로 발령내다
patience n. 인내심 cooperation n. 협조
arrange for ~을 준비하다

---

186 Not/True 문제

해석 첫 번째 이메일에서, POS Touch Solutions사에 대해 언급된 것은?
(A) 한 달에 한 번 소프트웨어를 업데이트한다.
(B) 몇몇 무료 서비스를 제공한다.
(C) 곧 자사 키오스크를 재설계할 계획이다.
(D) 우드베리에 본사가 있다.

해설 첫 번째 이메일의 'We will also provide free repairs of defective hardware and periodic software updates.'에서 결함이 있는 하드웨어의 무상 수리와 주기적인 소프트웨어 업데이트도 제공한다고 했으므로 지문의 내용과 일치한다. 따라서 (B)가 정답이다.

어휘 complimentary adj. 무료의 redesign v. 재설계하다
main office 본사

Paraphrasing

free repairs 무상 수리 → complimentary services 무료 서비스

---

187 육하원칙 문제 연계

해석 Mexigo 식당은 8월에 POS Touch Solutions에게 얼마의 비용을 청구받을 것인가?
(A) 0달러
(B) 150달러
(C) 450달러
(D) 1,800달러

해설 Mexigo 식당의 지역 운영 관리자 Mr. Shannon이 작성한 두 번째 이메일을 먼저 확인한다.
단서 1 두 번째 이메일의 'For now, please send a technician to the above location to carry out the removal.'에서 기술자를 보내 셀프 주문 키오스크 철거 작업을 진행해 달라고 했다. 그런데 셀프 주문 키오스크 철거 비용이 얼마인지 제시되지 않았으므로 첫 번째 이메일에서 관련 내용을 확인한다.
단서 2 첫 번째 이메일의 'Other services that require a visit from a technician will be charged separately at a cost of $450 per visit'에서 기술자의 방문이 필요한 서비스는 방문당 450달러의 비용이 별도로 청구될 것이라는 것을 확인할 수 있다.
두 단서를 종합할 때, 기술자의 방문이 필요한 Mexigo 식당의 셀프 주문 키오스크 철거 서비스에 450달러의 비용이 청구될 것임을 알 수 있다. 따라서 (C)가 정답이다.

---

188 추론 문제

해석 Mr. Shannon은 언제 Ms. Tan과 설치 날짜를 확정했겠는가?
(A) 8월에
(B) 9월에
(C) 10월에
(D) 11월에

해설 두 번째 이메일의 'Date: August 19'과 'At this time, I[Mr. Shannon]'m not sure when the renovations will be done. I can give you[Ms. Tan] a firm answer by early next month.'에서 이메일이 작성된 8월 19일 현재로서는 언제쯤 수리가 끝날지 잘 모르겠으며, 다음 달 초까지는 확실한 답변을 줄 수 있다고 했으므로 Mr. Shannon이 9월에 Ms. Tan과 설치 날짜를 확정했다는 것을 추론할 수 있다. 따라서 (B)가 정답이다.

---

189 추론 문제 연계

해석 Goldfinch가에 있는 식당에 대해 암시되는 것은?
(A) 곧 한 대 이상의 키오스크를 보유하게 될 것이다.
(B) 우드베리 소재지 네 곳 중 가장 오래된 곳이다.
(C) Poplar가에 있는 창고와 가깝다.
(D) 고객들로 붐비는 주문 구역이 있었다.

해설 Goldfinch Street이 언급된 두 번째 이메일을 먼저 확인한다.
단서 1 두 번째 이메일의 'I need to inform you that our restaurant on Goldfinch Street will be temporarily closing at the end of the month for renovations.'에서 Goldfinch가에 있는 식당이 수리를 위해 이번 달 말에 임시로 문을 닫을 예정이라고 했다. 그런데 Goldfinch가에 있는 식당에 대한 정보가 제시되지 않았으므로 회람에서 관련 내용을 확인한다.
단서 2 회람의 'I can confirm that the newly renovated

location ~ people standing in line to order at the kiosk often blocked the main entrance.'에서 새로 수리된 곳이 이전에는 키오스크에서 주문하기 위해 줄을 서 있는 사람들이 정문을 종종 막았다고 했다.

두 단서를 종합할 때, Goldfinch가 있는 식당은 이전에 주문 구역이 붐볐다는 것을 추론할 수 있다. 따라서 (D)가 정답이다.

어휘 close adj. 가까운 crowded with ~로 붐비는

190 육하원칙 문제

해석 회람에 따르면, Ms. Martinez는 왜 다른 지점 관리자들에게 연락했는가?
(A) 고용 계획에 대해 문의하기 위해
(B) 그들을 개관식에 초대하기 위해
(C) 일부 업무 시간을 재편성하기 위해
(D) 이전에 대한 도움을 요청하기 위해

해설 회람의 'I[Ms. Martinez]'ve already contacted the other branch managers about moving your shifts around to avoid any scheduling conflicts.'에서 Ms. Martinez가 교대 근무 시간을 옮기는 것에 대해 이미 다른 지점 관리자들에게 연락했다고 했으므로 일부 업무 시간을 재편성하기 위해 다른 지점 관리자들에게 연락했음을 알 수 있다. 따라서 (C)가 정답이다.

어휘 assistance n. 도움, 지원

Paraphrasing

moving your shifts around 교대 근무 시간을 옮기다
→ reorganize ~ work hours 업무 시간을 재편성하다

191-195번은 다음 두 이메일과 청구서에 관한 문제입니다.

수신: 모든 프리랜서 여행 가이드
발신: Brett Owen <b.owen@voyagertours.com>
제목: 수수료
날짜: 5월 10일

관광 시즌이 다가옴에 따라, ¹⁹¹저는 업데이트된 수수료 목록을 제공하고자 합니다. 이것은 지난여름에 여러분 중 다수에게 받았던 대금이 충분하지 않았다는 의견을 반영하고 있습니다. 바라건대, 여러분 모두 이 변화에 만족하셨으면 합니다.

관광 유형	설명	수수료
¹⁹⁴개인 반나절 관광	한 명의 고객에게 4곳의 도시 명소 관광 제공	¹⁹⁴100달러
개인 하루 관광	한 명의 고객에게 8곳의 도시 명소 관광 제공	175달러
단체 반나절 관광	최대 6명의 고객에게 4곳의 도시 명소 관광 제공	140달러
단체 하루 관광	최대 6명의 고객에게 8곳의 도시 명소 관광 제공	220달러
¹⁹³추가 요금	¹⁹³예정된 것보다 더 오래 걸린 관광에 대해서는, 시간당 요금이 추가 시간에 적용될 것입니다.	¹⁹³시간당 25달러

이 업데이트된 수수료를 여러분의 청구서에 꼭 반영해 주십시오. ¹⁹²저희 회계 장부 담당자가 7월에 휴가를 갈 예정이니, 평소 하던 대로 Mr. Parsons에게 청구서를 보내지 말고 이 기간 동안은 제게 바로 이메일을 보내 주셔야 합니다.

Brett Owen 드림, Voyager 투어사

approach n. 다가옴; v. 다가오다 reflect v. 반영하다
insufficient adj. 불충분한 surcharge n. 추가 요금
hourly adj. 시간당, 1시간마다의 rate n. 요금
apply v. 적용하다, 지원하다 bookkeeper n. 회계 장부 담당자

Voyager 투어사

송장 번호: 0112
여행 가이드: Madeline Terrence
이메일: m.terrence@speedmail.com
날짜: 6월 29일

날짜	세부 사항	수수료
6월 11일	개인 반나절 투어(오전)	100달러
6월 23일	단체 하루 관광	220달러
¹⁹³6월 23일	¹⁹³추가 요금	¹⁹³25달러
	총합	345달러

수신: Madeline Terrence <m.terrence@speedmail.com>
발신: Brett Owen <b.owen@voyagertours.com>
제목: 6월 청구서
날짜: 7월 4일

안녕하세요 Madeline,

당신의 6월 청구서에 오류가 있어 보입니다. ¹⁹⁴당신은 6월 15일에 다른 관광 가이드인 James Sand가 아팠을 때 그를 대신해 주셨습니다. 하지만, 그날 진행하신 개인 반나절 관광이 포함되어 있지 않습니다. 가능한 한 빨리 업데이트된 청구서를 저에게 보내주세요. 그것을 받는 대로, 당신의 계좌에 대금을 이체하겠습니다.

¹⁹⁵또한, 남부 캘리포니아의 주요 관광 명소에 대한 3일짜리 단체 관광을 계획하고 싶어 하는 여행사로부터 연락을 받았습니다. 당신이 항상 고객들로부터 긍정적인 후기를 받는 점을 감안하여, 저는 당신이 이 일에 딱 맞을 거라고 생각합니다. 수수료에 대해 논의하시려면 555-0398로 저에게 전화 주십시오.

Brett Owen 드림, Voyager 투어사

fill in for ~를 대신하다 conduct v. 하다, 수행하다
transfer v. 이체하다, 옮기다 payment n. 지불 금액, 지불
account n. 계좌

191 목적 찾기 문제

해석 첫 번째 이메일의 목적은 무엇인가?
(A) 몇몇 투어의 일정을 조정해줄 것을 요청하기 위해
(B) 추가 가이드들을 고용할 것임을 설명하기 위해
(C) 직원들에게 의견을 요청하기 위해
(D) 지불 금액 변경을 알리기 위해

해설 첫 번째 이메일의 'I want to provide an updated list of fees'에

서 업데이트된 수수료 목록을 제공하고자 한다고 했으므로 (D)가 정답이다.

어휘 additional adj. 추가의

Paraphrasing

an updated list of fees 업데이트된 수수료 목록 → a payment change 지불 금액 변경

192 추론 문제

해석 Mr. Parsons는 누구일 것 같은가?
(A) 판매원
(B) 여행사 직원
(C) 여행 가이드
(D) 회계사

해설 Mr. Parsons가 언급된 첫 번째 이메일의 'Please note that our bookkeeper will be on leave in July, so you should e-mail the invoices directly to me during this period rather than to Mr. Parsons as you usually do.'에서 회계 장부 담당자가 7월에 휴가를 갈 예정이니, Mr. Parsons에게 청구서를 보내지 말고 이 기간 동안은 자신에게 바로 이메일을 보내라고 했으므로 Mr. Parsons가 회계사라는 것을 추론할 수 있다. 따라서 (D)가 정답이다.

어휘 agent n. 직원, 대리인

Paraphrasing

bookkeeper 회계 장부 담당자 → An accountant 회계사

193 추론 문제 연계

해석 Ms. Terrence에 대해 결론지을 수 있는 것은?
(A) 6월에 다른 달보다 더 많은 관광을 했다.
(B) 예정된 것보다 더 오래 걸리는 관광을 이끌었다.
(C) 한 달 전에 Voyager 투어사에 입사했다.
(D) 관광 날짜를 변경해 달라고 요청했다.

해설 Ms. Terrence가 언급된 청구서를 먼저 확인한다.
단서 1 청구서의 'June 23', 'Surcharge', '$25'에서 6월 23일에 추가 요금이 25달러 있는 것을 알 수 있다. 그런데 어떤 경우에 25달러가 지급되는지에 대해 제시되지 않았으므로 첫 번째 이메일에서 관련 내용을 확인한다.
단서 2 첫 번째 이메일의 'Surcharge', 'For longer-than-scheduled tours, an hourly rate will be applied to the extra time.', '$25/hour'에서 예정된 것보다 더 오래 걸린 관광은 시간당 25달러의 추가 요금이 적용될 것이라는 것을 알 수 있다.
두 단서를 종합할 때, Ms. Terrence는 예정된 것보다 더 오래 걸리는 관광을 이끌었음을 추론할 수 있다. 따라서 (B)가 정답이다.

어휘 lead v. 이끌다, 지도하다

194 육하원칙 문제 연계

해석 Ms. Terrence가 Voyager 투어사에 청구할 것을 잊어버린 금액은 얼마인가?
(A) 100달러

(B) 175달러
(C) 140달러
(D) 220달러

해설 Ms. Terrence에게 보내진 두 번째 이메일을 먼저 확인한다.
단서 1 두 번째 이메일의 'You[Ms. Terrence] filled in for another tour guide, James Sand, when he became ill on June 15. However, the individual half-day tour you conducted that day is not included.'에서 Ms. Terrence가 6월 15일에 다른 관광 가이드인 James Sand를 대신했는데, 그날 진행한 개인 반나절 관광이 포함되어 있지 않다고 했다. 그런데 개인 반나절 관광에 대한 청구 금액이 제시되지 않았으므로 첫 번째 이메일에서 관련 내용을 확인한다.
단서 2 첫 번째 이메일의 'Individual Half-Day Tour'와 '$100'에서 개인 반나절 관광이 100달러인 것을 확인할 수 있다.
두 단서를 종합할 때, Ms. Terrence가 Voyager 투어사에 청구할 것을 잊어버린 금액은 개인 반나절 관광의 수수료인 100달러인 것을 알 수 있다. 따라서 (A)가 정답이다.

어휘 bill v. 청구하다, 청구서를 보내다

195 육하원칙 문제

해석 두 번째 이메일에 따르면, Mr. Owen은 왜 Ms. Terrence에게 그에게 전화하라고 하는가?
(A) 출장비 상환을 확인하기 위해
(B) 고객들의 후기에 대해 논의하기 위해
(C) 특별 근무 비용을 협상하기 위해
(D) 인기 있는 관광지에 대한 제안을 받기 위해

해설 두 번째 이메일의 'Also, I[Mr. Owen] have been contacted by a travel agent that wishes to arrange a three-day group tour ~ I think you[Ms. Terrence] would be perfect for this. Please call me at 555-0398 to discuss your fee.'에서 Mr. Owen이 3일짜리 단체 관광을 계획하고 싶어 하는 여행사로부터 연락을 받았는데, Ms. Terrence가 이 일에 딱 맞을 거라고 생각한다며, 수수료에 대해 논의하려면 555-0398로 자신에게 전화하라고 했으므로 특별 근무에 대한 비용을 협상하기 위해 전화하라는 것을 알 수 있다. 따라서 (C)가 정답이다.

어휘 reimbursement n. 상환, 변제 negotiate v. 협상하다

Paraphrasing

discuss ~ fee 수수료에 대해 논의하다 → negotiate the price 비용을 협상하다

196-200번은 다음 브로슈어, 기사, 이메일에 관한 문제입니다.

Skilled Builders 교육 기관
www.skilledbuilders.au

호주 남동부에서 40년 이상 서비스를 제공해 온 Skilled Builders 교육 기관은 높은 역량을 갖춘 졸업생들을 배출하며, 196-(B)쓸모 있는 기술을 개발하는 데 초점을 맞춘 실무 교육을 제공합니다. 다음 프로그램에 등록할 수 있습니다: ◉

프로그램	설명
자격증 I	견습 기간 준비를 위한 기본적인 기술 학습
자격증 II	목공업의 실용적이고 이론적인 측면 학습
199자격증 III	199면허를 받은 배관공이나 전기기사로서 자격 취득 준비를 위한 전문 기술 획득
자격증 IV	건설 프로젝트를 관리하거나 건설 사업체를 운영하기 위한 기술과 지식 습득

재정 지원이 필요하시다면 문의해 주시기 바랍니다. 호주 정부와의 제휴를 통해 수업료 보조금을 받을 수 있습니다.

serve v. (서비스를) 제공하다 graduate n. 졸업생
calibre n. 역량, 자질 hands-on adj. 실무의, 직접 해보는
usable adj. 쓸모 있는, 사용 가능한 enrolment n. 등록
certificate n. 자격증 apprenticeship n. 견습 기간, 수습 기간
practical adj. 실용적인 theoretical adj. 이론적인
carpentry n. 목공 qualify v. 자격을 취득하다
plumber n. 배관공 electrician n. 전기기사 knowledge n. 지식
tuition n. 수업료, 등록금 subsidy n. 보조금, 장려금
partnership n. 제휴 government n. 정부

The Perth Standard

Skilled Builders 교육 기관
퍼스에 캠퍼스를 열다
Ewan Reynolds 작성

퍼스 (11월 18일)—브리즈번, 캔버라, 애들레이드에 캠퍼스를 둔 유명한 교육 아카데미인 Skilled Builders 교육 기관이 퍼스에 네 번째 분점을 열 것이다. 198학생들은 이미 1월 22일에 시작하는 이 캠퍼스에서의 첫 수업들에 등록하고 있다.

기자 회견에서, Skilled Builders 교육 기관의 최고 경영자 Leslie Mitchell은 나라에 건설 붐이 일면서 등록자 수가 늘어날 것으로 예상한다고 말했다. "제 목표는 저희가 국내 최고의 훈련된 인력 공급업체가 되는 것입니다. 197내년에는, 모든 건설 업종을 충족시킬 더 많은 수업을 만들고 싶습니다,"라고 그녀는 말했다.

관심 있는 독자는 info@skilledbuilders.au에 연락하여 수업 일정, 수업료 및 다른 세부 사항들에 대해 자세히 알 수 있다.

undergo v. 일어나다, 겪다, 경험하다 aim n. 목표
supplier n. 공급업체 personnel n. 인력

수신: Skilled Builders <info@skilledbuilders.au>
발신: Tony Ayoub <t.ayoub@peoplemail.com>
제목: 긴급한 문의
198날짜: 11월 21일

관계자분께,

제 이름은 Tony Ayoub이고 귀사의 새로운 캠퍼스에서 수업을 듣는 것에 관심이 있습니다. 198저는 빨리 마칠 수 있도록 다음 가능한 날짜에 수강하고 싶습니다. 저의 지역에는 많은 취업 기회가 있습니다.

199저는 자격증 시험을 준비하는 수업을 듣고 싶습니다. 이곳 호주로 이주해 오기 전에 저는 고국에서 수년간 전기기사로 근무했습니다. 하지만, 저는 문제가 있습니다. 몇 달 동안 일이 없었기 때문에, 200제가 수업료를 낼 수 있을지 모르겠습니다. 그래서, 저는 지원을 신청하 ○

고 싶습니다. 어떤 필요조건이 있는지 알려주실 수 있나요?

감사합니다.

Tony Ayoub 드림

urgent adj. 긴급한, 시급한 immigrate v. 이주해 오다
requirement n. 필요조건, 요건

196 Not/True 문제

해석 브로슈어에서 Skilled Builders 교육 기관에 대해 명시된 것은?
(A) 수업 시작 날짜를 옮겼다.
(B) 실습을 통해 학생들을 가르친다.
(C) 졸업생을 위한 직업 소개 서비스를 제공한다.
(D) 학생들이 원격으로 수업에 참여할 수 있도록 한다.

해설 브로슈어의 'offering hands-on instruction with a focus on developing usable skills'에서 쓸모 있는 기술을 개발하는 데 초점을 맞춘 실무 교육을 제공한다고 했으므로 Skilled Builders 교육 기관은 실습을 통해 학생들을 가르친다는 것을 알 수 있다. 따라서 (B)가 정답이다.

어휘 job placement 직업 소개 remotely adv. 원격으로

Paraphrasing

> hands-on instruction 실무 교육 → practical training 실습

197 육하원칙 문제

해석 기사에 따르면, Ms. Mitchell은 무엇을 하고 싶어 하는가?
(A) 건설업에 들어간다.
(B) 더 다양한 수업을 도입한다.
(C) 더 많은 국제 학생들을 받아들인다.
(D) 다른 업계를 위한 수업을 제공한다.

해설 기사의 'Next year, I[Leslie Mitchell] want to create more courses that cater to all of the building trades'에서 내년에 모든 건설 업종을 충족시킬 더 많은 수업을 만들고 싶다고 했으므로 Ms. Mitchell이 더 다양한 수업을 도입하고 싶어 한다는 것을 알 수 있다. 따라서 (B)가 정답이다.

어휘 enter v. (새 직업 등에) 들어가다 a variety of 다양한

Paraphrasing

> more 더 많은 → a larger variety of 더 다양한

198 추론 문제 연계

해석 Mr. Ayoub에 대해 사실일 것 같은 것은?
(A) 1월에 수업을 시작하길 원한다.
(B) 해외로 이주하는 것을 준비하고 있다.
(C) 공무원에 지원했다.
(D) 퍼스에서 새로운 사업을 시작했다.

해설 Mr. Ayoub이 작성한 이메일을 먼저 확인한다.
단서 1 이메일의 'Date: 21 November'와 'I[Mr. Ayoub] hope to take it at the next available date so that I can finish soon.'에서 Mr. Ayoub이 11월 21일에 보낸 이메일에서 다음 가능

한 날짜에 수강하고 싶다고 했다. 그런데 다음 가능한 수강 날짜가 언제인지에 대해 제시되지 않았으므로 기사에서 관련 내용을 확인한다.

단서 2 기사의 'Students are already signing up for the first classes at this campus, which begin on 22 January.'에서 학생들이 이미 1월 22일에 시작하는 이 캠퍼스에서의 첫 수업들에 등록하고 있다고 했으므로, 다음 가능한 수강 날짜가 1월 22일인 것을 알 수 있다.

두 단서를 종합할 때, Mr. Ayoub은 1월에 과정을 시작하길 원한다는 것을 추론할 수 있다. 따라서 (A)가 정답이다.

어휘 overseas adv. 해외로 government job 공무원

199 추론 문제 연계

해석 어떤 수업이 Mr. Ayoub의 요구를 가장 잘 충족할 것인가?
(A) 자격증 I
(B) 자격증 II
(C) 자격증 III
(D) 자격증 IV

해설 Mr. Ayoub이 작성한 이메일을 먼저 확인한다.

단서 1 이메일의 'I[Mr. Ayoub] want to take a course in preparation for a licensure exam. I was working as an electrician in my home country for many years before immigrating here to Australia.'에서 Mr. Ayoub이 자격증 시험을 준비하는 수업을 듣고 싶다고 하면서, 고국에서 수년간 전기기사로 일했다고 했다. 그런데 전기기사 자격증 시험과 관련된 과정이 어떤 것인지 제시되지 않았으므로 브로슈어에서 관련 내용을 확인한다.

단서 2 브로슈어의 'Certificate III'와 'Gain specialist skills in preparation for qualifying as a licensed plumber or electrician'에서 자격증 III 과정에서 배관공 또는 전기기사 자격 취득 준비를 위한 전문 기술을 익힐 수 있다는 것을 확인할 수 있다.

두 단서를 종합할 때, Mr. Ayoub의 요구를 가장 잘 충족해 줄 수업은 '자격증 III' 과정임을 추론할 수 있다. 따라서 (C)가 정답이다.

200 육하원칙 문제

해석 Mr. Ayoub은 무엇에 대해 문의하는가?
(A) 웹사이트에 가입하는 것
(B) 온라인으로 일부 수업을 듣는 것
(C) 수업료 보조금을 획득하는 것
(D) 캠퍼스 위치를 찾는 것

해설 이메일의 'I[Mr. Ayoub] am not sure that I can pay the tuition for a course. So I would like to apply for assistance. Could you tell me what the requirements are?'에서 자신이 수업료를 지불할 수 있을지 모르겠다며 지원을 신청하고 싶다고 했고, 어떤 필요조건이 있는지 알려달라고 했으므로 Mr. Ayoub이 수업료 보조금을 획득하는 것에 대해 문의하는 것을 알 수 있다. 따라서 (C)가 정답이다.

어휘 secure v. 획득하다, 확보하다

5천 개가 넘는
해커스토익 무료 자료!

대한민국에서 공짜로 토익 공부하고 싶으면

| 해커스영어 Hackers.co.kr ▾ | 검색 |

RC 정수진   RC 이상길

토익 강의

베스트셀러 1위 토익 강의 150강 무료 서비스,
누적 시청 1,900만 돌파!

Q1

토익 실전 문제

토익 RC/LC 풀기, 모의토익 등
실전토익 대비 문제 제공!

LC 한승태   RC 김동영

최신 특강

2,400만뷰 스타강사의
압도적 적중예상특강 매달 업데이트!

고득점 달성 비법 무료

토익 고득점 달성팁, 파트별 비법,
점수대별 공부법 무료 확인

전원
무료
*미션 달성 시

가장 빠른 정답까지!

615만이 선택한 해커스 토익 정답!
시험 직후 가장 빠른 정답 확인

더 많은
토익 무료자료 보기 ▶